Current Biography
Yearbook
1979

CURRENT BIOGRAPHY

YEARBOOK

1979

EDITOR

Charles Moritz

ASSOCIATE EDITORS

Evelyn Lohr

Henry Sloan

Kieran Dugan

Judith Graham

THE H. W. WILSON COMPANY

NEW YORK

PHOTO CREDITS

FORTIETH ANNUAL CUMULATION—1979

PRINTED IN THE UNITED STATES OF AMERICA

International Standard Serial No. (0084-9499)

Library of Congress Catalog Card No. (40-27432)

PREFACE

The aim of CURRENT BIOGRAPHY YEARBOOK 1979, like that of the preceding volumes in this series of annual dictionaries of contemporary biography, now in its fourth decade of publication, is to provide the reference librarian, the student, or any researcher with brief, objective, accurate, and and well-documented biographical articles about living leaders in all fields of human accomplishment the world over.

CURRENT BIOGRAPHY YEARBOOK 1979 carries on the policy of including new and updated biographical sketches that supersede earlier, outdated articles. Sketches have been made as accurate and objective as possible through careful researching by CURRENT BIOGRAPHY writers in newspapers, magazines, authoritative reference books, and news releases of both government and private agencies. Immediately after they are published in the eleven monthly issues, articles are submitted to biographees to give them an opportunity to suggest corrections in time for CURRENT BIOGRAPHY YEARBOOK. To take account of major changes in the careers of biographees, sketches have also been revised before they are included in the yearbook. With the exception of occasional interviews, the questionnaire filled out by the biographee remains the main source of direct information.

In the back of the volume under *Organizations* can be found the names of those who head organizations. Some persons who are not professional authors but who have written books are included under *Literature* in addition to their vocational fields. The pages immediately following contain: *Explanations; Key to Reference Abbreviations; Key to Pronunciation;* and *Key to Abbreviations.* The indexes at the end of the volume are *Biographical References; Periodicals and Newspapers Consulted; Classification by Profession;* and *Cumulated Index—1971-1979.* The 1940-1950 index can be found in the 1950 yearbook; the 1951-1960 index, in the 1960 yearbook, and the 1961-1970 index in the 1970 yearbook. The three decennial indexes are cumulated in CURRENT BIOGRAPHY CUMULATED INDEX 1940-1970.

For their assistance in preparing CURRENT BIOGRAPHY YEARBOOK 1979, I should again like to thank the associate editors.

Charles Moritz

Explanations

Authorities for biographees' full names, with some exceptions, are the bibliographical publications of The Wilson Company. When a biographee prefers a certain name form, that is indicated in the heading of the article: for example, Niemöller, (Friedrich Gustav Emil) Martin means that he is usually referred to as Martin Niemöller. When a professional name is used in the heading, as, for example, Anne Bancroft, the real name (in this case Annemarie Italiano) appears in the article itself.

The heading of each article includes the pronunciation of the name if it is unusual, date of birth (if obtainable), and occupation. The article is supplemented by a list of references to sources of biographical information, in two alphabets: (1) newspapers and periodicals and (2) books. (See the section *Biographical References*, found in the rear of this volume.)

Key to Reference Abbreviations

References to some newspapers and periodicals are listed in abbreviated form; for example, "Sat Eve Post 217:14 S 30 '44 por" means *Saturday Evening Post*, volume 217, page 14, September 30, 1944, with portrait. (For full names, see the section *Periodicals and Newspapers Consulted*, found in the rear of this volume.)

January—Ja	July—Jl	Journal—J
February—F	August—Ag	Magazine—Mag
March—Mr	September—S	Monthly—Mo
April—Ap	October—O	Portrait—por
May—My	November—N	Weekly—W
June—Je	December—D	Review—R

Key To Pronunciation

ā	āle	ō	ōld	ü	Pronounced approximately as ē, with rounded lips: French u, as in *menu* (mə-nü); German ü, as in *grün*
â	câre	ô	ôrb		
a	add	o	odd		
ä	ärm	oi	oil		
		o͞o	o͞oze		
ē	ēve	o͝o	fo͝ot	ə	the schwa, an unstressed vowel representing the sound that is spelled a as in sofa e as in fitted i as in edible o as in melon u as in circus
e	end	ou	out		
g	go				
ī	īce	th	then		
i	ill	th	thin		
x	German ch as in *ich* (ix)	ū	cūbe	zh	azure
		û	ûrn; French eu, as in *jeu* (zhû), German ö, oe, as in *schön* (shûn), *Goethe* (gû'te)	′	= main accent
N	Not pronounced, but indicates the nasal tone of the preceding vowel, as in the French *bon* (bôN).			″	= secondary accent
		u	tub		

Key To Abbreviations

AAAA	Amateur Athletic Association of America
A.A.U.	Amateur Athletic Union
ABA	American Bar Association
ABC	American Broadcasting Company
ACA	Americans for Constitutional Action
A.C.L.U.	American Civil Liberties Union
ADA	Americans for Democratic Action
AEC	Atomic Energy Commission
AEF	American Expeditionary Force
AFL	American Federation of Labor
AFL-CIO	American Federation of Labor and Congress of Industrial Organizations
ALA	American Library Association
AMA	American Medical Association
A.P.	Associated Press
ASCAP	American Society of Composers, Authors and Publishers
ASNE	American Society of Newspaper Editors
B.A.	Bachelor of Arts
BBC	British Broadcasting Corporation
B.D.	Bachelor of Divinity
B.L.S.	Bachelor of Library Science
B.S.	Bachelor of Science
CAA	Civil Aeronautics Administration
CAB	Civil Aeronautics Board
C.B.	Companion of the Bath
C.B.E.	Commander of (the Order of) the British Empire
CBS	Columbia Broadcasting System
C.E.	Civil Engineer
CEA	Council of Economic Advisers
C.E.D.	Committee for Economic Development
CENTO	Central Treaty Organization
CIA	Central Intelligence Agency
CIO	Congress of Industrial Organizations
C.M.G.	Companion of (the Order of) St. Michael and St. George
Com.	Commodore
CORE	Congress of Racial Equality
D.A.R.	Daughters of the American Revolution
D.C.L.	Doctor of Civil Law
D.D.	Doctor of Divinity
D.Eng.	Doctor of Engineering
DEW	Distant Early Warning Line
D.F.C.	Distinguished Flying Cross
D.J.	Doctor of Jurisprudence
D.Litt.	Doctor of Literature
D.Mus.	Doctor of Music
DP	Displaced Person
D.Pol.Sc.	Doctor of Political Science
D.Sc.	Doctor of Science
D.S.C.	Distinguished Service Cross
D.S.M.	Distinguished Service Medal
D.S.O.	Distinguished Service Order

ECA	Economic Cooperation Administration
ECOSOC	Economic and Social Council
EDC	Economic Defense Community
EEC	European Economic Community
ERA	Equal Rights Amendment
ERP	European Recovery Program
ESA	Economic Stabilization Administration
FAO	Food and Agriculture Organization
FBI	Federal Bureau of Investigation
FCC	Federal Communications Commission
FEPC	Fair Employment Practice Committee
FHA	Federal Housing Administration
FOA	Foreign Operations Administration
FPC	Federal Power Commission
FSA	Federal Security Agency
FTC	Federal Trade Commission
GATT	General Agreement on Tariffs and Trade
G.B.E.	Knight or Dame, Grand Cross Order of the British Empire
G.C.B.	Knight Grand Cross of the Bath
G.O.P.	Grand Old Party
H.M.	His Majesty; Her Majesty
HUD	Housing and Urban Development
IBM	International Business Machine Corporation
ICBM	Intercontinental Ballistic Missile
ICC	Interstate Commerce Commission
I.C.F.T.U.	International Confederation of Free Trade Unions
IGY	International Geophysical Year
I.L.A.	International Longshoremen's Association
I.L.G.W.U.	International Ladies' Garment Workers' Union
I.L.O.	International Labor Organization
INS	International News Service
IRA	Irish Republican Army
IRO	International Refugee Organization
J.D.	Doctor of Jurisprudence
K.B.E.	Knight of (the Order of) the British Empire
K.C.	King's Counsel
K.C.B.	Knight Commander of the Bath
L.H.D.	Doctor of Humanities
Litt.D.	Doctor of Letters
LL.B.	Bachelor of Laws
LL.D.	Doctor of Laws
M.A.	Master of Arts
M.B.A.	Master of Business Administration
MBS	Mutual Broadcasting System

M.C.E.	Master of Civil Engineering		REA	Rural Electrification Administration
M.D.	Doctor of Medicine		RFC	Reconstruction Finance Corporation
M.E.	Master of Engineering		RKO	Radio-Keith-Orpheum
METO	Middle East Treaty Organization		ROTC	Reserve Officers' Training Corps
MGM	Metro-Goldwyn-Mayer			
M.Lit.	Master of Literature			
M.P.	Member of Parliament		SAC	Strategic Air Command
M.P.P.D.A.	Motion Picture Producers and		SALT	Strategic Arms Limitation Talks
	Distributors of America		S.J.	Society of Jesus
MRP	Mouvement Républicain Populaire		SCAP	Supreme Command for the Allied
MSA	Mutual Security Agency			Powers
M.Sc.	Master of Science		SEATO	Southeast Asia Treaty Organization
Msgr.	Monsignor, Monseigneur		SEC	Securities and Exchange Commission
			SHAEF	Supreme Headquarters, Allied
NAACP	National Association for the			Expeditionary Force
	Advancement of Colored People		SHAPE	Supreme Headquarters, Allied
NAB	National Association of			Powers Europe
	Broadcasters		S.J.D.	Doctor of Juridical Science
NAM	National Association of		SLA	Special Libraries Association
	Manufacturers		S.T.B.	Bachelor of Sacred Theology
NASA	National Aeronautics and Space		S.T.D.	Doctor of Sacred Theology
	Administration			
NATO	North Atlantic Treaty Organization		TVA	Tennessee Valley Authority
NBC	National Broadcasting Company		T.W.U.A.	Textile Workers Union of America
NEA	National Education Association			
NLRB	National Labor Relations Board		UAR	United Arab Repubic
N.M.U.	National Maritime Union		U.A.W.	United Automobile, Aircraft, and
NOW	National Organization for Women			Agricultural Implement Workers
NRA	National Recovery Administration			of America
NRPB	National Resources Planning Board		UMT	Universal Military Training
NYA	National Youth Administration		U.M.W.A.	United Mine Workers of America
			U.N.	United Nations
O.A.S.	Organization of American States		UNESCO	United Nations Educational, Scientific, and Cultural Organization
O.B.E.	Officer of (the Order of) the British Empire		UNICEF	United Nations Children's Fund
OCD	Office of Civilian Defense		UNRRA	United Nations Relief and Rehabilitation Administration
OEEC	Organization for European Economic Cooperation		U.P.I.	United Press and International News Service
OMB	Office of Management and Budget		USO	United Service Organizations
OPA	Office of Price Administration		U.S.S.R.	Union of Soviet Socialist Republics
OPEC	Organization of Petroleum Exporting Countries		U.S.W.A.	United Steel Workers of America
OPM	Office of Production Management			
OWI	Office of War Information		VA	Veterans Administration
			V.F.W.	Veterans of Foreign Wars
PBS	Public Broadcasting Service			
P.E.N.	Poets, Playwrights, Editors, Essayists and Novelists (International Association)		W.F.T.U.	World Federation of Trade Unions
			WHO	World Health Organization
Ph.B.	Bachelor of Philosophy		WMC	War Manpower Commission
Ph.D.	Doctor of Philosophy		WPA	Work Projects Administration
PLO	Palestine Liberation Organization		WPB	War Production Board
PWA	Public Works Administration			
			YMCA	Young Men's Christian Association
Q.C.	Queen's Counsel		YMHA	Young Men's Hebrew Association
			YWCA	Young Women's Christian Association
RAF	Royal Air Force			
RCA	Radio Corporation of America			

Current Biography Yearbook 1979

Adler, Kurt Herbert

Apr. 2, 1905- Conductor; opera director.
Address: b. c/o San Francisco Opera
Association, War Memorial Opera House, 301
Van Ness Ave., San Francisco, Calif. 94102;
h. 2058 Vallejo Street, San Francisco, Calif.
94123

The year 1978 marked a double jubilee for Viennese-born Kurt Adler, the hard-driving general director of the San Francisco Opera Company: his golden anniversary in opera, and his silver anniversary as head of the company. The celebration, culminating in a gala concert on November 19, focused worldwide attention on a man uncomfortable with publicity, a rare kind of celebrity who once told Anthony Boucher in an interview for *Opera News* (September 30, 1961): "All the biography about me they write too much already. If people want to know, they'll find it all in *Who's Who*. We talk about the opera company."

The San Francisco Opera is now regarded as the number two company in the United States, second only to the Metropolitan, although its quarters, orchestra, and stage are considerably smaller than those of the New York house, and its season is considerably shorter. It also labors under the handicap of being tied to the schedules of the San Francisco Symphony, which serves as its orchestra. Nevertheless, Kurt Herbert Adler, who took over the directorship of the house after the death of its founder, Gaetano Merola, in 1953, has transformed what was once a regional and ultraconservative company into an operatic center famous for its American premieres, boldness in repertory, and debut appearances of now internationally famous singers. He currently presides over a twelve-week fall season, a shorter spring season, a touring group, and other flourishing projects.

Kurt Herbert Adler was born in what he has described as a "dark, heavily carpeted, typical Victorian house" in Vienna, Austria, to Ernst and Ida (Bauer) Adler, on April 2, 1905. His father, a music-loving engineer, encouraged the musical education of his talented son, who at thirteen could sightread the piano score of Wagner's *Die Walküre*. The Vienna State Opera, under Franz Schalk and Richard Strauss, where Kurt Herbert Adler was a regular standee in the famous fourth gallery during his youth, supplemented his studies at the Academy of Music, the Conservatory, and the University of Vienna's Music-Historical Institute. From 1925 to 1928 he gained his first professional experience as a conductor at the Max Reinhardt Theater, where the famous stage director once gave him some advice that he has acted on ever since: "Remember, young man, in the theater nothing is impossible." During the next decade he served as assistant director of the Civic Opera in Kaiserslautern, Germany, and conducted in Austria, Czechoslovakia, and Italy as well. A brief stint as one of several assistants to Arturo Toscanini during the 1936 Salzburg Festival and another of teaching as an instructor at Salzburg's Mozarteum rounded out his musical apprenticeship.

Because of the imminent threat of the Anschluss, Adler moved early in 1938 to the United States, where he joined the Chicago Grand Opera Company as conductor and chorus master. Two years later, he moved on to the San Francisco Opera, where he quickly entered the ranks of Gaetano Merola's "prompt, orderly, reliable Germans." It is said that in trying to lure Adler to San Francisco, Merola asked him: "How can anyone live in Chicago? Chicago is merely a place to change trains." The excellence of Adler's performance as chorus master, conductor, and chief deputy made him the logical choice to succeed Merola on the latter's death in 1953. He became artistic director immediately, and three years later was named general director. "You don't have a job," conductor Bruno Walter told him at the time. "You have a mission."

As part of that mission, Adler inherited a modest regional company whose drawbacks included its elegant but outmoded quarters, the San Francisco War Memorial Opera House, and a short season hemmed in by summer, on the one hand, and the scheduling requirements of its musicians, the San Francisco Symphony Orchestra, on the other. Long reputed for its fine casts, the San Francisco Opera had become by the early 1950's, as Adler explained to Barry Hyams in an interview for *Saturday Review* (June 10, 1978), mainly a vehicle for "presenting singers—predominantly stars and the star system." "Some operas were staged," he conceded, "but they were the exception." He therefore launched a master plan to introduce fresh, and at the time, radically modern staging, lighting, and decor, and to enliven the tired and standardized repertory, which served as a stable for the usual war horses.

During Adler's inaugural season, which lasted from September 17 through October 21, 1954, the San Francisco Opera, which in its first thirty-one years had never attempted an important premiere, presented two daring novelties: the first American stage production of Cherubini's one-act comedy, *The Portuguese Inn*, and the first West Coast staged performance of Honegger's *Joan of Arc at the Stake*. Assessing them in the New York *Times* (October 24, 1954), critic Alfred Frankenstein pronounced the season "the most interesting in local operatic history." "This new regime," he concluded, "promised much and it fulfilled every one of its commitments, often more brilliantly than anyone expected."

With the support of a city devoted to opera, Kurt Herbert Adler shaped the San Francisco Opera over the years into an international company whose recent seasons have averaged sixty-six performances during a twelve-week period. His artistic and box-office successes quelled the discontent of conservative board members and opera patrons who at first objected to his policy of supplementing so-called "bread and butter" operas with rarely performed works. By 1978 the company had chalked up the impressive score of two world and eighteen American premieres. Among them were Walton's *Troilus and Cressida* (1955), Poulenc's *Dialogues of the Carmelites* (1957), Strauss's *Die Frau ohne Schatten* (1959), Britten's *A Midsummer's Night's Dream* (1961), Dello Joio's *Blood Moon* (1961), Janacek's *The Makropulos Case* (1966), Berlioz's *Les Troyens* (1966), and Von Einem's *The Visit of the Old Lady* (1972). When asked about his stress on twentieth-century works, Adler told *Newsweek*'s Hubert Saal (Novem-

ber 28, 1966): "Few composers take time now to compose operas. We must show interest. I am fully aware of the survival chance, but opera is always a gamble. There is a big cemetery of operas. But on the way to the cemetery, the cortège can at least be seen— and, who knows, even stopped." Adler is justifiably proud of the receptiveness and openmindedness of his subscription audience who, as he explained to Speight Jenkins in an interview for *Opera News* (October 1972), "no longer come just for entertainment but to experience a real art form."

Dependent in its early days on New York's Metropolitan Opera for most of its artistic personnel, the San Francisco Opera under Adler assiduously wooed internationally established singers and promising newcomers alike. His discernment was responsible for introducing to the American opera stage such first-rank foreign artists as Birgit Nilsson, Elisabeth Schwarzkopf, Geraint Evans, Leonie Rysanek, Boris Christoff, Gabriella Tucci, and —one token engagement in Miami excepted —both Joan Sutherland and Luciano Pavarotti. Striking a balance between imported and native talent, Adler brought out from relative obscurity such stellar Americans as Mary Costa, James McCracken, Marilyn Horne, Beverly Sills, Jess Thomas, Thomas Stewart, and George Shirley. Leontyne Price, who made her opera debut at San Francisco in 1957 as Madame Lidoine in Poulenc's *Dialogues of the Carmelites*, once commented: "I sort of grew up in San Francisco vocally and professionally." She still looks upon Adler as the "guiding figure" in her operatic career.

Since taking over the helm, Kurt Herbert Adler has launched several highly inventive programs. Viewed as a unit, they foster the artistic development of gifted young singers, conductors, stage directors, and designers through workshops, repertory experience, and engagements with the main company. As early as 1954 he established the annual San Francisco Opera Auditions, in which some 400 contestants living west of Illinois compete for cash prizes and a summer concert appearance under Adler's baton at San Francisco's Stern Grove. In the Merola Opera Program, inaugurated in 1957, as many as twenty-one regional finalists study vocal and acting techniques during a ten-week summer training session whose highlights include three-hour seminars with Adler and participation in full-scale opera productions. The Spring Opera Theater (or SPOT), founded in 1961 to complement the major fall season, draws on talented beginners for popularly priced performances, primarily in English, of contemporary works or of experimentally staged staples from the standard repertoire.

In 1967 Adler fathered the Western Opera Theater, featuring a touring group of fledgling singers—"my little ones, my babies" he calls them—who present quality opera to outlying communities. Through the Brown Bag Opera, established in 1974, corporations and community groups sponsor performances for office and factory workers in parks and public buildings. In the spring of 1977 Adler introduced a joint pilot program with Affiliate Artists to guarantee six promising singers and a conductor a two-or-three-year full-time professional engagement with either the San Francisco Opera or its other units.

Adler's unremitting quest for perfection at the San Francisco Opera has elicited comments about his *Obergruppenführer* complex, combining, as one critic expressed it, Bismarckianism with Viennese courtliness. No aspect of the company's operations from lighting to guest lists and program notes escapes his sharp surveillance. "Just when you think Adler is finally holed up in his office," Leontyne Price once recalled as quoted in *Time* (September 25, 1972), "he will turn up in the chorus or pop out from behind a bush to tell you your train is a foot too long." With a stamina that belies his age he puts in fourteen-hour days during the season and forages for new talent in Europe and New York. He once attended forty-two operas in twenty-five cities in forty-four days. His vacations are more often than not "48-hour jokes."

From his nearly 800 employees Adler demands similar loyalty, dedication, and long hours. "A secretary shouldn't be just a typist," he told Hubert Saal. "Opera must be important to her. Everyone must be willing." Although one interviewer sardonically observed that secretaries flow through his outer office like water over Niagara Falls, the end result, according to the German-born stage director Paul Hager who has worked with Adler a great deal, is a company that runs "so smoothly you can play on it like an instrument."

Adler's obsessive attention to detail helps keep the budget of the San Francisco Opera shipshape. "We still count dimes," he assured Barry Hyams. "Maybe we don't count nickels anymore, and I cut out pennies from our budget figures only a year or two ago." Attendance, which generally runs about ninety-eight percent of capacity, pays for approximately sixty percent of running expenses. An annual carry-over deficit of under one percent attests to Adler's fund-raising skills with foundations, private underwriters, and county, city, and federal officials.

For several years he confronted the urgent choice of an heir-apparent for his multifaceted role. "I wish I would know someone," he told Barry Hyams. "We are working with extremely limited means, and not everybody would want to do it this way. . . . I hope it would be an amicable turnover so that my work, a lifetime's work, was not in vain— that it doesn't shake the company." The board of directors finally found a suitable successor for Adler in the person of Terry McEwen, an executive vice-president of London Records.

He is scheduled to take over the direction of the San Francisco Opera on Adler's projected retirement, to be effective in 1982.

In 1973 Beverly Sills helped persuade Kurt Herbert Adler to return to the podium of the San Francisco War Memorial Opera House after absenting himself from it for more than a decade. "I didn't want to conduct because I don't know if you can conduct bars and dollars at the same time," he quipped to Speight Jenkins. Adler conducts at least one opera production yearly, in addition to the summer festivals at San Francisco's Stern Grove and Golden Gate Park. He has led the Los Angeles Philharmonic at Hollywood Bowl and has served as guest conductor at the Teatro San Carlo in Naples, Italy. His fairly recent entry into recordings has already brought him acclaim as a conductor on recital albums, notably London Records' *O Holy Night* and *Verismo Arias* featuring Luciano Pavarotti and Maria Chiara respectively.

A writer for *Time* (September 25, 1972) once profiled Adler as "a short man with an advancing paunch, soft, silver-gray hair over the collar, and kind, blue, bespectacled eyes." Although he formerly dressed conservatively, his casual working dress often consists these days of a wildly checkered sports coat, blue jeans, and sneakers. He married his third wife, Nancy Miller, who is almost forty years his junior, on August 23, 1965. By his second wife, the former Diantha Warfel, whom he divorced in 1963 after a twenty-three-year marriage, he has two children: a son, Ronald Huntington, a stage director, and a daughter, Kristin Diantha, who is married to the former football star tackle Charles ("Chuck") Krueger. In his rare spare time he enjoys tennis and swimming.

A trustee of the National Opera Institute and a founder and board member of OPERA America, Adler is also active on the music advisory panel of the National Endowment for the Arts and in the International Association of Opera Directors. He has received honorary doctorates of music from the University of the Pacific and the University of San Francisco and holds many awards including the University of California Berkeley Citation and the St. Francis of Assisi Award. The Italian, West German, and Austrian governments have honored him with decorations. In 1972 Adler became the first American to receive the U.S.S.R.'s Bolshoi Theatre Medal.

In celebration of his twenty-five years as general director of the San Francisco Opera and his fifty years in opera, Adler received in 1978 the honorary title of Dean of American Opera Producers from OPERA America and the National Opera Institute's Repertory Award. The celebrations culminated on November 19, 1978 with an anniversary gala at the San Francisco War Memorial Opera House, for which some persons paid up to $500 for admission. Among the operatic celebrities who gathered to honor the longest-reigning operatic director in opera today were Elisabeth Schwarzkopf, Dorothy Kirsten, Bidú Sayão, and Licia Albanese. In commemoration of the occasion, he received the San Francisco Opera Medal, made of Tiffany gold.

References: HiFi 12:42+ Ja '62 por, 25:MA6+ Ap '75 pors; Newsweek 68:66+ N 28 '66; N Y Times p68 N 9 '75, II p17 S 28 '75 por; Opera News 26:20+ S 30 '61 pors, 32:18+ S 23 '67 pors, 38:14+ O '73 pors; Sat R 5:22+ Je 10 '78 pors; Time 82:64 S 27 '63 por, 100:90 S 25 '72; International Who's Who, 1977-1978; Who's Who in America, 1977-1978; Who's Who in Opera, 1976

Allen, Woody

Dec. 1, 1935- Comedian; motion picture director; actor; writer. Address: c/o Rollins & Joffe, 130 W. 57th St., New York City, N.Y. 10019

NOTE: This biography supersedes the article that appeared in Current Biography in 1966.

Urban America's favorite worrywart, the brilliant actor-filmmaker Woody Allen, began developing his public persona as a stand-up comic in the early 1960's. Writing his own material then, as he does now (with collaboration on screenplays from Marshall Brickman), Allen presented himself in the beginning as a self-deprecatory, gag-spouting nebbish from Brooklyn, an image he carried over to the screen and gradually refined in his early motion pictures, beginning with Take the

Money and Run (1969). The cynicism hidden in Love and Death (1975) went largely unnoticed, but Allen's basic seriousness (his key personal metaphor for life is a concentration camp from which no one escapes alive) was unmistakable in Annie Hall (1977), the bittersweet comedy about the failed love affair of Alvy Singer (Allen), an anxiety-ridden comedian from Brooklyn, and the title character (Diane Keaton), a "shiksa" from the Midwest, and it became overpowering in the Bergmanesque Interiors (1978).

Annie Hall swept the Academy Awards for 1977, and in the opinion of most critics Manhattan (1979) was an even greater triumph— a masterfully crafted, technically stunning but artistically subdued seriocomedy in which Allen came of age both as auteur and actor. In addition to his work in cinema, Allen has written for the theatre and recorded his stand-up routines on three albums; he contributes humorous pieces to the New Yorker and other magazines; and he collaborates on a syndicated "Woody Allen" comic strip.

Woody Allen was born Allen (Alan in some sources) Stewart Konigsberg in Brooklyn, New York on December 1, 1935 to Martin and Nettie Konigsberg, both of whom were Orthodox Jews. His father, Allen says, worked at "a million little short-lived jobs," and his mother kept the account books in a flower shop. Many of the gags in his early stand-up monologues were facetious gibes at his parents. "Their values," he would joke, "are God and carpeting." Or: "I was in analysis for years because of a traumatic childhood. I was breast-fed through falsies."

With his one sibling, a sister, Allen was raised in the Flatbush section of Brooklyn. He "hated every second" of Hebrew school, he told Ken Kelley in an interview for Rolling Stone (July 1, 1976), and his attitude toward public school was just as negative. "I loathed every day and regret every day I spent in school. I like to be taught to read and write and add and then be left alone." The only school subject that interested him was English composition. "Even while I was reading nothing but Donald Duck and Batman [he did not become interested in literature until he was eighteen] I could write real prose in school compositions. There was never a week when the composition I wrote was not the one that was read to the class."

Outside of baseball and basketball, Allen's favorite activities in childhood were those of a loner: reading comic books, for example, or listening to Duffy's Tavern, The Great Gildersleeve, and Fibber McGee and Molly on the radio, or following the fortunes of the New York Giants. "I never ever ate with the family," he told Frank Rich when Rich interviewed him for an article in Esquire (May 1977). "And I never ever did any extracurricular activities at school. [At home] I'd go right into my bedroom and shut the door—immediately. Consequently, I was able to get some things done. I could learn an instrument. I became adept at sleight of hand, which took me endless hours and which I can still do."

Allen regularly attended stage shows at the Flatbush Theatre, observing the tricks of the magicians and jotting down the jokes of the comedians. At fifteen he began writing quips and sending them to Earl Wilson and other newspaper gossip columnists under the name Woody Allen. The mention of his name in a Wilson column led to a $25-a-week job with a press agent, writing one-liners for attribution to the agent's clients. Later he was hired to turn out material for Peter Lind Hayes, Herb Shriner, and other NBC radio and television performers, and after graduating from Midwood High School in Brooklyn (with a 71 average) he joined the staff of Sid Caesar's television show. At the same time, in keeping with the wishes of his parents, he enrolled successively at New York University and the City College of New York. He considered it "a blessing" to be expelled from both within a few months for low marks and poor attendance.

In 1961 Allen left a $1,700-a-week job writing for the Garry Moore Show to venture into the precarious career of a performer. He became a stand-up comic with the encouragement of business associates and friends, who literally had to push the stage-frightened neophyte onstage in many of his early engagements in Greenwich Village clubs. Within a year or so he had mustered enough confidence in his act to handle national exposure on the Tonight Show and other television shows. Allen's chief models in the beginning were Mort Sahl and Bob Hope, insofar as they were "standup monologists who talk as themselves" in "this great monologue style," with "great phrasing." The stage persona he chose as his own was, he has said, a "schlemiel image" that "never did describe me. I've never been that. It's an appellation for the unimaginative to hang on me. The things I did on nightclub stages were fantasies or exaggerations from my own life—school, women, parents—which I set out in an amusing way. But you look up after a year and the press has created you: 'Well, he's a small man at odds with mechanical objects who can't cope with relationships with women.' But all I was doing was what was funny."

Allen's jokes about not coping with relationships with women ranged from exaggerations of the positive ("On my wedding night my wife stopped in the middle of everything to give me a standing ovation") to surreal negativisms ("Someday they're gonna give me a birthday party and wheel out a tremendous birthday cake, and a giant naked woman will leap out of the cake and hurt me and leap back in"). One of his most imaginative club routines was a piece of literal gallows humor in which he saw his life pass before his eyes as he was about to be lynched by the Ku Klux Klan: "I saw myself as a kid again. Goin' to school. Swimmin' at the swimmin' hole. Fryin' up a mess o' catfish. Goin' down to the general store. Gettin' a piece of gingham for Emmy Lou. And I realize . . . it's not my life. They're gonna hang me in two minutes and the wrong life is passing before my eyes."

A landmark date in Allen's career was the night in 1964 when the motion picture producer Charles K. Feldman and the actress Shirley MacLaine caught his act at the Blue Angel nightclub in New York City. Allen's routines cracked Miss MacLaine up, and Feldman gave Allen his first movie job—writing the screenplay for and playing a supporting role in What's New, Pussycat? (United Artists, 1965), a slapstick bedroom farce directed by Clive Donner and starring Peter O'Toole as a womanizer frantically trying to avoid monogamy. The film was a huge commercial success, grossing $17,000,000, but Allen, whose artistic control of the material was limited, was unhappy with it. "I never considered that one mine," he has said. "I hated it, hated making it, and it was the reason I became a director."

As a warmup to becoming a director, Allen took a straight Japanese grade-B spy thriller (the rights to which were purchased from Toho Films) and turned it into an inexpensive comedy by inserting himself as narrator and dubbing in inappropriate dialogue. The result was What's Up, Tiger Lily? (American International, 1966). In the James Bond spoof Casino Royale (Columbia, 1967), he played Bond's (David Niven's) nutty, girl-crazy nephew.

On Broadway, Allen's comedy Don't Drink the Water, about a Newark caterer (Lou Jacobi) on vacation with his wife and daughter in an Iron Curtain country, was the surprise hit of the 1966-67 season. His second play, Play It Again, Sam—about a neurotic film critic who seeks a new love, with the help of the ghost of Humphrey Bogart, after his wife leaves him—ran on Broadway from February 12, 1969 to March 14, 1970. Allen played the lead through most of the Broadway run, and he starred in his film adaptation of the play, which was directed by Herbert Ross and released by Paramount in 1972.

The first unadulterated "Woody" movie was Take the Money and Run (Cinerama, 1969), a mock documentary written by Allen in collaboration with Mickey Rose and starring Allen as a young man who aspires to become public enemy number one and fails even to make the ten-most-wanted list. In fact, Virgil Starkwell (Allen) cannot even rob a bank without the tellers and bank officials arguing with him over the illiterate wording of his holdup note. "The nicest surprise of Take the Money and Run," Vincent Canby wrote in the New York Times (August 19, 1969), "is that it shows [Allen] has been able to complement visually the word-oriented humor of the writer-performer."

The scattershot style of humor in *Take the Money and Run* was carried over into *Bananas* (1971), the first of Allen's films released by United Artists. In that wacky parody, written by Allen and Mickey Rose, Fielding Mellish (Allen) finds himself the leader of a Latin American revolution, involved in such tasks as requisitioning from a countryside delicatessen an order of sandwiches for the troops "to go" ("200 tuna on whole wheat; 300 BLT on toast; and 400 grilled cheese—360 on rye, thirty-five on whole wheat, four on white, and one on a roll"). "The movie," Martin Knelman wrote in the Toronto *Globe and Mail* (March 15, 1971), "is held together only by Allen's personality and his bizarre and unique sense of comedy, which seems to be connected more to the golden age of radio comedy than to any movie tradition."

Everything You Always Wanted to Know About Sex But Were Afraid to Ask (United Artists, 1972) was Allen's wild parody of Dr. David Reuben's then popular sex manual, a film in which he played, among other roles, a sperm pale with trepidation as it waits to be ejaculated, backed up by a crew looking like NASA preparing a space launching. "The remarkable thing," William Wolf wrote in *Cue* (August 12, 1972), "is that Allen isn't obscene, just cleverly risqué, as he masterfully satirizes movies, TV, and literature while having fun with sex."

Allen's first collaboration with his screenplay-writing partner Marshall Brickman was *Sleeper* (1973), in which he played Miles Monroe, a Greenwich Village health-food restaurant owner who checks into a hospital for a minor ulcer operation and wakes up in a defrosting lab 200 years later. Among the enthusiastic reviews was that written for the New York *Times* (December 18, 1973) by Vincent Canby, who observed, "The fine madness of *Take the Money and Run* and *Bananas,* which were largely extensions of his nightclub routines, is now apparent in the kind of slapstick comedy that can only be done in films." In a change of pace from the flow of movies of which he was the auteur-actor, Allen starred in the McCarthy-era seriocomedy *The Front* (Columbia, 1976), written by Walter Bernstein and directed by Martin Ritt, as a small-time bookmaker who begins a lucrative second career lending his name to the scripts of blacklisted playwrights.

"The first two [films] that I made," Allen recounted in an interview with Ira Halberstadt for an article in *Take One* (November 1978), "I was thrilled just to make them funny and that's all I cared about. I just wanted to survive and to make them. I didn't care about anything else, everything was coordinated with the joke, everything. Then with *Everything You Always Wanted to Know About Sex* I was trying very hard to develop as a filmmaker. I pushed that further in *Sleeper*. By the time I did *Love and Death* I was very concerned with the filmmaking aspect, and with wanting to do darker things, not deal with a lot of conventional stuff."

Set in the Czarist Russia of the early nineteenth century, *Love and Death* (1975) was a mock epic, on the scale of *War and Peace,* starring Woody Allen as a self-professed "militant coward" in the Napoleonic wars and Diane Keaton as the reluctant bride, who admonishes him as he begins to touch her in the nuptial bed, "Don't. Not here." As Judith Crist observed in *New York* (June 16, 1975), in *Love and Death* "Allen goes for the character rather than the cartoon, the situation rather than the set-up, the underlying madness rather than the surface craziness." She wished that "Tolstoy, Turgenev, Chekhov, [and] Dostoevski [could] be living at this hour, if only to see themselves as Woody Allen does in his new film *Love and Death,* a wonderfully funny and eclectic distillation of the Russian literary soul and style."

But Allen was disappointed, as he told Natalie Gittelson when she interviewed him for an article in the New York *Times Magazine* (April 22, 1979), that "the serious intent underlying the humor [in *Love and Death*] was not very apparent to most audiences. "Laughter submerges everything else. That's why I felt that, with *Annie Hall,* I would have to reduce some of the laughter. I didn't want to destroy the credibility for the sake of the laugh."

"Anhedonia"—a psychiatric term meaning the opposite of hedonism, the inability to experience pleasure—was the title Allen originally wanted to give to *Annie Hall,* until the people at United Artists dissuaded him. A tender, introspective, semi-confessional story of failed relationships, *Annie Hall* (United Artists, 1977) alternated between the comic and the bittersweet, with the latter prevailing. Judith Crist, writing in the *Saturday Review* (May 14, 1977), spoke for a wide consensus in hailing it as "Allen's most satisfying creation and our most gratifying comedic experience in recent years." The film received Academy Awards for best picture, best director (Allen), best screenplay (Allen and Marshall Brickman), and best actress (Diane Keaton).

"If *Annie Hall* was this era's 'nervous romance,' *Interiors* is its genteel nightmare, Janet Maslin wrote in reviewing the stark, stylized *Interiors* (United Artists, 1978). Allen wrote and directed but did not appear in *Interiors,* a somber psychological drama, devoid of the slightest hint of comic relief, about the breakdown of a middle-aged wife (Geraldine Page), a compulsively perfectionist interior decorator whose husband (E. G. Marshall) is leaving her for another woman (Maureen Stapleton), and about the related disintegration of her family (notably daughters played by Diane Keaton, Marybeth Hurt, and Kristin Griffith). Allen thought that *Interiors* would probably be "a catastrophe" at the box office and was surprised when it turned a modest profit. As for critics, they were divided in their ability to accept the "new," suddenly grim Allen.

The charm and humor of *Annie Hall* and the drama and serious themes of *Interiors* were blended in *Manhattan* (United Artists, 1979), a black-and-white paean to Allen's beloved home city. In Manhattan, love problems were tied in with soul-searching about "selling out" personally and artistically. Allen played Isaac Davis, a television writer who quits his job and seeks consolation in relationships with two women (Mariel Hemingway and Diane Keaton) after his wife (Meryl Streep) leaves him and writes a book exposing the failure of their marriage in embarrassing detail.

Typical of the raves received by *Manhattan* was Jack Kroll's notice in *Newsweek* (April 30, 1979): "Allen's growth in every department is lovely to behold. . . . The increasing visual beauty of his films is part of their grace and sweetness, their balance between Allen's yearning romanticism and his tough eye for the fatuous and sentimental—a balance also expressed in his best screenplay yet, co-authored with the estimable Marshall Brickman. Allen's own acting, his incarnation of his own persona, gets better and better. His specialty—the stumbling, bumbling speech that expresses witty befuddlement—reaches eloquent heights in *Manhattan*."

Allen himself has said of *Manhattan*: "It's my own feelings—my subjective, romantic view—of contemporary life in Manhattan. I like to think that a hundred years from now, if people see the picture, they will learn something about what life in the city was like in the 1970's. They'll get some sense of what it looked like and an accurate feeling about how some people lived, what they cared about." Short humorous pieces by Allen, many of them first published in the *New Yorker*, have been collected in *Getting Even* (Random House, 1971) and *Without Feathers* (Hamilton, 1976).

Woody Allen is a short man of serious mien who reportedly is never "on" in private life. His typical attire consists of a plaid shirt, corduroy trousers, and an Ivy League tweed jacket, except on the street, when he disguises himself in long coats, large hats, and other outlandish costumes. He insists that he is "not reclusive"—just "not gregarious." His favorite hangouts, when he does hang out, are Elaine's, the Manhattan restaurant, and Michael's Pub, also in Manhattan, where he plays the clarinet with a semipro New Orleans-style jazz band once a week. But his favorite activity is work, especially writing, which he says he can do anywhere (a knack he acquired in the hubbub of television writing) but which he prefers to do in his bedroom. He finds writing therapeutic, along with psychoanalysis, which he has undergone for twenty-three years. Among his recreations is following the fortunes of the New York Knicks basketball team.

Allen has been married twice, to Harlene Rosen, a teacher, for five years beginning in 1954, and to Louise Lasser, the actress, who was in several of his early films, also for five years beginning in 1966. Both marriages ended in divorce. For a period of time he had a third close relationship, with Diane Keaton, his frequent costar. Allen now lives in a duplex penthouse overlooking Fifth Avenue in Manhattan.

The comedian does not drink or smoke, abhors drugs, and eats moderately. Among the humorists and comedians of the past who most influenced him, he says, were George S. Kaufman, Groucho Marx, Robert Benchley, and S. J. Perelman. Although he has been reported to be an atheist, he retains what he describes as "the urban Jewish mentality" of "feeling one step ahead of trouble and anxiety." He believes in "anarchy," in the sense of "individual responsibility for choice of behavior." That philosophy fits in with his view of life as a concentration camp, as he explained to Frank Rich in the *Esquire* interview: "The concentration camp is the real test: There are those who make moral decisions and betray their best friends . . . and there are others who behave with unbelievable courage. That's exactly what happens in life—some respond terribly and some beautifully. I've never been well tested, and I have the greatest fears and doubts about how I'd respond under real pressure."

References: Cue 48:31+ Je 8 '79 pors; Esquire 87:72+ My '77; New Yorker 49:39+ F 4 '74 por; Times 1113:62+ Ap 30 '79 pors; Rolling Stone p34+ Jl 1 '76 pors; Lax, Eric. On Being Funny: Woody Allen and Comedy (1975)

Anderson, John B(ayard)

Feb. 15, 1922- United States Representative from Illinois. Address: b. 1101 Longworth Office Building, Washington, D.C. 20515; h. 2720 35th Pl., NW Washington, D.C. 20007

"I don't care whether you call me a conservative or a liberal, so long as you give me credit for having ideas," Congressman John B. Anderson said shortly after declaring his candidacy for the 1980 Republican Presidential nomination. In his ten terms in office, Anderson has shifted from orthodox conservatism to middle-of-the-road pragmatism, tending toward moderation in fiscal policy and liberalism on social issues. Regarded by many of his colleagues as one of the ablest Representatives, he is a skillful legislator, an adroit politician, and perhaps the best extemporaneous speaker on Capitol Hill. In June 1979 he resigned as chairman of the House Republican Conference, a powerful and prestigious post he had held for a decade, in order to pursue the American Presidency, with an "issues" campaign de-

John B. Anderson

signed to attract moderate and liberal Republicans into his fold.

John Bayard Anderson was born on February 15, 1922 in Rockford, Illinois, one of the six children of E. Albin Anderson, a Swedish immigrant, and his wife, Martha Edna (Ring) Anderson. (Three of his siblings died in early childhood.) The Andersons operated a small grocery store in the predominantly Scandinavian section of Rockford, where John often helped out after school and on Saturdays. The closely knit family was devoutly religious and often attended evangelical tent meetings in the vicinity. At one such meeting, when he was about nine, John Anderson was, as he put it years later, "so moved by the message being preached that I made a public confession of my desire to accept the Lord Jesus Christ as my personal savior."

At Rockford Central High School, Anderson acquired a reputation as a skilled debater, won "a loving cup or two" for extemporaneous speaking, and was the valedictorian of his 1939 graduating class. Three years later, he graduated from the University of Illinois with an A.B. degree in political science and with membership in Phi Beta Kappa. He immediately enrolled in the university's graduate law school, but his legal education was interrupted by two-and-one-half years of service as a field artilleryman in the United States Army. During his ten-month tour of duty in Europe, Anderson took part in four major campaigns and won four battle stars.

Returning to the University of Illinois College of Law after the war's end, Anderson took his J.D. degree in 1946. He spent the next two years working in an apprentice position with a Rockford law firm, then, in search of

"some larger satisfaction," accepted a graduate fellowship to Harvard University Law School. While at Harvard, he supported himself by teaching part-time at Northeastern University School of Law, in Boston. After receiving his LL.M. degree from Harvard in 1949, Anderson practised law in Rockford until he entered the foreign service in July 1952 as a staff adviser to the United States High Commissioner for Germany in West Berlin. Despite his objections to the foreign service's "paramilitary organization and structure," he found life overseas to be, in his words, "both stimulating and exciting." Nevertheless, he resigned in 1955 to return to private law practice in his hometown.

The following year, a group of local Republican leaders asked Anderson to seek the party's nomination in the upcoming race for state's attorney of Winnebago County. He survived the hard-fought primary contest and easily won the general election in the heavily Republican county. While serving the third year of his term as state's attorney, Anderson decided to run for the Congressional seat being vacated by Representative Leo Allen. A relatively unfamiliar figure in the crowded five-man field that included a well-known state senator, he campaigned extensively, concentrating his effort in his home county, the most populous in the Sixteenth Congressional District. His attractive, highly personal campaign style, combined with overwhelming support from the large Swedish-American community, gave him a decisive victory in the April 1960 Republican primary, virtually assuring him of election in November.

In his voting during his first few years in Congress, John B. Anderson consistently hewed to the traditional Old Guard Republican line. He opposed, for example, President John F. Kennedy's plan to create a new department for housing and urban development and fought all Democratic proposals to expand federal welfare programs and increase assistance to the cities. In 1964, moreover, he campaigned strenuously for the election of the ultraconservative Republican Presidential nominee, Senator Barry M. Goldwater, as a member of the so-called "Paul Revere team" that crisscrossed the country to publicize the Republican platform. Recognizing his contributions to the conservative cause, Americans for Constitutional Action gave him an 88 percent rating over his first six years in office.

In the mid-1960's, however, Anderson began to moderate his stance, supporting such measures as increased federal aid to education, expanded food stamp programs, consumer protection, gun licensing, and federally guaranteed housing loans. Some observers attributed his shift toward the center at least partly to the demographic changes in Anderson's district as Chicago-based industries moved into the Rockford area, bringing with them the traditionally more liberal blue-collar voters. Anderson himself explained his drift away from Republican orthodoxy to Paul Duke in an interview for the *New Republic* (February 1, 1968): "There are not many members who have the apocalyptic vision of Paul, who suddenly switch course overnight, declaring henceforth I will be a conservative no more. You acquire more knowledge, you study new ideas, you recognize change, so you grow."

Anderson's most dramatic break with the conservative wing of his party came during the House Rules Committee debate on open housing legislation in the spring of 1968. The bill in question, already passed by the Senate, made it illegal for an individual to refuse to rent or sell property on the basis of race, color, or creed. Two years earlier, Anderson had joined other committee Republicans in opposing a similar bill, primarily because he felt that it infringed upon the rights of property owners to dispose of their holdings as they saw fit. This time, however, Anderson voted with the committee's seven Democrats, and his was the determining vote in the 8-7 decision to send the bill directly to the House floor, thus bypassing a Senate-House conference that would have watered it down considerably. Anderson had at first wanted to send the bill to conference, but he changed his mind after reading the recently published report of the National Advisory Commission on Civil Disorders, which found, among other things, that poor housing was an important factor in the total discontent of the black community.

At the time of the House debate, Washington was torn by the racial violence that followed in the wake of the assassination of Dr. Martin Luther King Jr., the civil rights leader. Opponents of the open housing bill contended that its passage would amount to capitulation to the rioters, but Anderson disagreed. "We are not simply knuckling under to pressure or listening to the voices of unreasoning fear and hysteria if we seek to do that which we believe in our hearts is right and just," he said on the House floor. "I legislate today not out of fear, but out of a deep concern for the America I love. We do stand at a crossroad. We can continue the slide into an endless cycle of riot and disorder, or we can begin the slow and painful ascent toward the yet distant goal of equality of opportunity for all Americans, regardless of race or color." As Anderson took his seat, his colleagues burst into spontaneous applause. Many veteran Capitol Hill observers credited the Congressman's inspiring speech with turning sentiment in favor of the legislation, which passed the House by a 250-172 vote.

Late in 1968 President-elect Richard Nixon chose Melvin R. Laird, the chairman of the House Republican Conference, to be the Secretary of Defense in his new Administration. Encouraged by friends and colleagues, Anderson mounted a vigorous campaign to succeed Laird as conference chairman, the third most influential post in the House Republican hierarchy and, at a party caucus on January 2, 1969, he handily defeated his two rivals for the job, Jackson E. Betts of Ohio and Albert H. Quie of Minnesota. When the Ninety-first Congress convened later that month, Anderson assumed his new leadership responsibilities, intent on mobilizing support for President Nixon's programs in the House and on building up public confidence in Republican leadership. "The only way we can regain supremacy in Congress is to convince the country there is a new spirit of creativity in the Republican party," he explained to Paul Duke. "We've got to prove that we don't want to retreat to some backwater, that we, too, are concerned and have consciences, that we are bothered because people are ill-housed and ill-fed."

Anderson endorsed Nixon's "New Federalism," an ambitious plan to strengthen and reinvigorate state and municipal governments. He was especially impressed by the President's revenue-sharing program, which would, in his words, bring the government "a little closer to the people whom it is designed to serve" by putting the money in the hands of those best able to judge local needs. "If we can replace the image in the average citizen's mind of an anonymous and faceless bureaucracy, with a feeling that many people at all levels of government are working together in a cooperative effort to cure the ills of our society, we will have given new meaning and new stature to representative democracy," he wrote in his book *Between Two Worlds: A Congressman's Choice* (Zondervan, 1970). Although Anderson occasionally clashed with the White House, criticizing, for example, Nixon's record on civil rights, he generally supported both the domestic and the foreign policies of the Republican President.

In Anderson's opinion, American involvement in the Indochina war was "the most tragic error in diplomatic and military policy" in the nation's history. At first, he defended President Nixon's program of negotiation, Vietnamization, and phased troop withdrawal as the only "honorable, moderate course," but as the war dragged on into the 1970's, he grew increasingly critical. He publicly condemned the Cambodian incursion and, on the House floor, voted to override a Presidential veto of a bill that severely limited the Chief Executive's war-making powers. To avoid a similar catastrophic entanglement in the future, he recommended that the United States refrain from playing "policeman to the world" and adopt instead a "more restrained policy." As a substitute for unilateral American assistance, he suggested strengthening the United Nations' peace-keeping functions "as a vital aim of our own foreign policy" and fostering "the kind of development that will preserve a nation's independence and promote its self-reliance."

Anderson has always favored a strong defensive posture, but during the Vietnam war he began to question the economic burden of the escalating arms race. Convinced that the government could trim billions of dollars from the defense budget simply by eliminating waste, duplication, and inefficiency, he proposed to funnel the money saved into urban renewal, aid to education, health care, and other social services. "It will do us little good to be armed to the teeth to deter external threats if we are not able to cope with the internal threats posed by pressing domestic problems," he reasoned. "When we talk about the security of the United States, we must consider internal as well as external conditions. And the internal conditions today are such that they do pose a real threat to the continued security of our country."

Appalled by the unimaginable horror of nuclear war, Anderson was the first Republican Congressional leader to complain publicly about Nixon's postponements of the strategic arms limitation negotiations with the Soviet Union. "The time has come," he said on the House floor in June 1969, "to call a halt to this insane nuclear version of keeping up with the Joneses." Once the talks were under way, Anderson urged the Administration to suspend tests of the MIRV ballistic missile for the duration of the SALT meetings and proposed a joint Soviet-American moratorium on MIRV deployment. More recently he voted against additional appropriations for the B-1 bomber and large, nuclear-powered aircraft carriers.

Anderson's independence cost him the backing of the sixty to seventy hard-line conservative Republicans, known as "the Sam Devine Group," after their unofficial leader, Congressman Samuel L. Devine of Ohio. Arguing that Anderson did not represent orthodox Republican views, Devine tried to oust him from the chairmanship of the House Republican Conference in January 1971. Anderson's narrow margin of victory, 89-81, indicated the extent of the schism between moderate Republicans and Nixon loyalists. Anderson dutifully denounced the economic proposals of Senator George S. McGovern, the Democratic candidate in the 1972 Presidential contest, but just a few months after Nixon's reelection, he spoke out against the Administration's handling of the Watergate affair. In May 1973, he was one of eighteen House Republicans who cosponsored a resolution calling for the naming of a special prosecutor to investigate the scandal. Twelve months later, he asked the President to "spare the nation one last agony" by resigning from office. Anderson was vindicated by Nixon's resignation and, after the Democratic landslide in the 1974 off-year Congressional election thinned the ranks of his conservative critics, he never again faced a serious challange to his chairmanship of the House Republican Conference.

Regularly returned to Congress by respectable pluralities, Anderson came up against his toughest opponent in the 1978 primary. With heavy backing from such national conservative groups as the Gun Owners of America and the National Conservative Political Action Committee, the Reverend Don Lyon, an evangelical minister, attacked Anderson as a representative of "the Republican left." Thanks to a large Democratic crossover vote, Anderson won the primary and went on to take the general election by a comfortable margin.

In recent years Anderson has continued to confound political lobbyists by voting liberal on most social welfare issues and conservative on economic issues. To cite one example, he recommended a more investment-oriented approach to control inflation and offered taxation and spending alternatives. On other domestic issues he was a vocal supporter of civil rights measures, including the Equal Rights Amendment, government-funded abortions for the poor and other progressive social legislation, campaign financing reform, and rational energy policy. A decade after he pushed the groundbreaking legislation through the House, Anderson was still fighting for an end to racial segregation in housing, which he has described as "an American brand . . . of apartheid." In foreign affairs he approved the new Panama Canal treaties and the normalization of diplomatic relations with the People's Republic of China as important elements in a policy of "constructive and creative internationalism." In 1978 the liberal Americans for Democratic Action rated Anderson's performance at 55 percent while the conservative Americans for Constitutional Action put it at 44 percent.

Frustrated in Congress, where the average member, in his words, "feels like he is the object of a taffy pull," Anderson tested the Presidential political waters in the spring of 1979 and on June 8 formally announced his candidacy for his party's nomination. He was the seventh announced Republican candidate. Pledging to "rebuild the Republican party on as broad a base as possible," he proposed "to arouse an appeal to the conscience and reason of Americans" and added, "I believe I know and share the aims and aspirations of the average American." He outlined to reporters his "Midwest strategy" for establishing a credible candidacy in the early "snowbelt" primaries, and for later racking up substantial gains in Illinois, Michigan, Wisconsin, and Iowa, where he is better known. To underline his serious intent as a Presidential candidate, Anderson cut himself off from possible political alternatives by announcing that he would not seek reelection to the House nor run for the United States Senate.

Tall and lean, John B. Anderson has thick white hair and the handsome, regular features of an aging matinee idol. He and the former Keke Machakos were married on January 4, 1953. They have five children: Eleanora, John Bayard Jr., Diane, Karen Beth, and Susan Kimberly. The family maintains homes in Washington and in Rockford, where Anderson is an active member of the First Evangelical Free Church. In 1964 he was named Outstanding Layman of the Year by the National Association of Evangelicals. In addition to *Between*

Two Worlds, Anderson has written *Vision and Betrayal in America* (World Books, 1975), edited *Congress and Conscience* (Lippincott, 1970), a collection of essays by his legislative colleagues, and contributed chapters to *We Propose: A Modern Congress* (1966), *Republican Papers* (1968), *Baker's Dictionary of Christian Ethics* (1973), and *The Future of the American Presidency* (1975).

References: N Y Times p12 Ja 3 '69 por; New Repub 160:22+ F 1 '69; Almanac of American Politics, 1978; Congressional Directory 1978; Who's Who in America, 1978-79; Who's Who in American Politics, 1977-78

Ashley, Thomas (William) Ludlow

Jan. 11, 1923- United States Representative from Ohio. Address: b. 2406 Rayburn Office Building, Washington, D.C. 20515

For a quarter of a century Thomas Ludlow Ashley has represented Ohio's Ninth Congressional District on Capitol Hill, but he seldom attracted national attention until he was named chairman of the House of Representatives' newly created Ad Hoc Committee on Energy in 1977. An old-style liberal with considerable legislative skill, Ashley tackled the national energy crisis with the same vigor and political know-how he used to formulate the innovative housing and community development legislation of the 1960's and early 1970's, including what was the then revolutionary concept of urban homesteading. Widely admired for his ability to

move stalled bills out of committee, Ashley pledged that there would be "no dawdling" on his energy committee. "If it's do-able, I think we'll be able to do it," he assured reporters shortly after he accepted the appointment. "I have some confidence in the House. It can rise above parochialism—and it has—and can act in the national interest."

Thomas William Ludlow Ashley was born in Toledo, Ohio on January 11, 1923 to William Meredith Ashley, an attorney and businessman, and Mary Alida (Ludlow) Ashley. Ashley, who numbers among his forebears some early English settlers of Virginia, is the great-grandson of James M. Ashley, the radical Republican Congressman who introduced the resolution to impeach President Andrew Johnson in 1867 and later served as the territorial governor of Montana. Raised in a fashionable suburb on Toledo's west side, Lud Ashley, as he prefers to be known, attended neighborhood elementary schools before transferring to the Kent School, a preparatory school in Kent, Connecticut.

Immediately after his high school graduation in 1942, Ashley enlisted in the United States Army and served in the Pacific theatre until the end of World War II. Discharged in 1946, he resumed his education at Yale University. He received his A.B. degree two years later, and his LL.D. degree from Ohio State University in 1951. He practised law in Whitehouse, Ohio and in his hometown for about a year and then accepted a position in New York City as assistant director of special projects for Radio Free Europe.

As the 1954 primary election approached, Democratic party leaders in the traditionally Democratic Ninth Congressional District in northwest Ohio caucused to choose a candidate to challenge two-term incumbent Representative Frazier Reams, an independent. Their first choice, Michael V. DiSalle, a former governor of the state, declined to run, but suggested Lud Ashley as an attractive alternative. "In Toledo we don't ordinarily find a good young Democrat in that social set," DiSalle explained years later to an interviewer for Ralph Nader's Congress Project. "I wanted to get someone with a diverse background. We had to find someone who could replenish the Democratic voters in that area. . . . Lud was just that kind of young fellow at that time. I felt he would develop into a fine public official." With the politically astute DiSalle managing his campaign, Ashley easily won the primary and took 35 percent of the vote in the three-way general election in November to defeat his opponents by a narrow margin.

Because he felt that his work for Radio Free Europe gave him special qualifications, Ashley sought a place on the House Committee on Foreign Affairs, but was assigned instead to the Banking and Currency Committee, now known as the Banking, Finance, and Urban Affairs Committee. Recognizing that housing was, in his words, "a really virgin area where you wouldn't be hamstrung by development," he managed to get appointed to the housing subcommittee. Over the next few years Ashley emerged as the most outspoken critic of the federal government's housing program which, in his view, lacked a coherent growth policy. To give housing and community development some direction he pushed for a reexamination of existing programs and in 1968 persuaded Wright Patman, his committee chairman, to authorize hearings on national urban growth. Those hearings provided the impetus for the passage of the Housing and Urban Development Act of 1970, which amounted to a legislative mandate for the President to formulate a national urban growth strategy.

He first unveiled the plan at the annual meeting of the National Service to Regional Councils in New Orleans on March 10, 1971. Contending that adequate living standards depended on sound and orderly development in all parts of the nation, he argued that it was the federal government's responsibility to devise a national urban policy incorporating social, economic, and other appropriate factors to serve as a guide in making specific decisions that not only affect the pattern of urban growth but also provide a framework for the development of interstate, state, and local growth and stabilization policy.

Ashley himself wrote substantial portions of the aid program for new communities. That program called for the establishment of the Community Development Corporation within the Department of Housing and Urban Development to assist eligible developers in planning and executing community construction programs and to administer the distribution of the loans, grants, and guarantees that were the backbone of the plan. The protracted floor debate on the bill occasionally became acrimonious, with some Congressmen criticizing its scope, complexity, and "dubious features." In defense of the measure, Ashley maintained that "with planning and with ingenuity, both public and private, it is possible to achieve through new community development a far more suitable living environment than we presently enjoy."

To counter the intensive lobbying of the housing special interest groups, Ashley commissioned papers from city planners, architects, social scientists, and large-scale housing developers, organized field trips to blighted sections of inner cities and to new towns under construction, and deliberately exposed the more conservative members of the housing subcommittee to progressive ideas. One of those ideas was to convert existing housing into pleasant, low-cost living quarters for the poor. To that end, Ashley recommended the creation of an urban homestead loan program to help the residents of viable

neighborhoods obtain loans to improve their homes and apartment buildings. He also suggested awarding local governments federal grants to pay for programs aimed at upgrading public facilities in designated preservation areas.

In an effort to disperse the poor into suburban areas where the chance for upward mobility was far greater than in the inner cities, Ashley proposed that HUD funds be given not to the home builders, but to housing agencies in the form of block grants. That proposal was strenuously opposed by the National Association of Real Estate Boards, the Mortgage Bankers Association, the National Association of Home Builders and other groups who claimed that it created more bureaucratic red tape and reduced the flexibility of home builders. After much discussion, the concept was tabled in the subcommittee, and the final bill, considerably watered down, contained only a mild incentive for cities to draw up housing assistance plans.

Many of Ashley's constituents benefited directly from his efforts on the housing subcommittee. The urban renewal measures that he supported in committee and on the House floor provided much of the funding for the revitalization of Toledo's central business district and decaying residential neighborhoods and for the construction of Oak Openings, a new development in a rural area near Toledo's airport. Grateful voters have regularly returned Ashley to Congress by impressive majorities that have reached as high as 71 percent. His only serious challenge in thirteen general elections came in 1974, after his arrest on a drunk-driving charge. He won that election by slightly under 7,000 votes.

Ashley's promotion of local efforts in urban renewal often brought him into close contact with local bankers who helped finance the housing projects. That working relationship developed into a tendency on Ashley's part to view bank consolidations, mergers, and expansion into nonbanking fields more favorably and to defend the Federal Reserve System's independence from elected officials. "I listen to [the bankers] and I think they have some strong arguments," Ashley told the interviewer for the Nader Congress Project. "We do depend on our commercial banking system for a substantial amount of credit for the growth we're interested in. I'm interested unashamedly in a strong banking industry. . . . We need them."

His outspoken support of the banking industry often put him at odds with Wright Patman. The conflict between the two men came to a head in 1965, when Patman repeatedly postponed committee action on a Senate revision of the 1960 Bank Merger Act that had been prompted by a recent Supreme Court decision overturning several controversial bank mergers. Ashley and other so-called "Ivy League liberals" who served as a counterweight to Patman's conservatism convened a rump session of the Banking Committee in Patman's absence to approve the measure for a floor vote. Although their effort failed, it forced Patman to accept a compromise restricting the application of the Clayton and Sherman antitrust laws in bank merger cases. Drafted by Ashley and Representative Henry S. Reuss, the compromise bill authorized approval of bank mergers if the anticompetitive effects were clearly outweighed by the benefits to the community, and it exempted from pending antitrust litigation three banks merged before the Supreme Court ruling.

Over the years Ashley has voted with his party on most domestic, social, and bread-and-butter issues. He has been particularly consistent in voting for civil rights, federal aid to education, health care, consumer protection, tax reform, and environmental safeguards. Although he was numbered among the staunchest supporters of the Vietnam war during the 1960's, he eventually revised his opinion and in October 1973 voted with the majority to limit the President's war-making powers. Since that time he has regularly approved reductions in the defense budget, including proposed cuts in the appropriations for nuclear-powered aircraft carriers and for the development of the controversial B-1 bomber.

Despite his proclivity for agreeing with the Democratic majority, Ashley retains a fiercely independent streak. In 1959, for instance, he and a colleague voted against a House resolution opposing the admission of the People's Republic of China to the United Nations. He later explained his vote by saying that the resolution was "undesirable and unnecessary" and that it limited the President's "flexibility" in conducting foreign policy. Two years later he was one of only six Congressmen to approve a cutoff in funds for the House Un-American Activities Committee. Moderately liberal, he has most recently been rated at 55 percent by the liberal Americans for Democratic Action and at 15 percent by the Americans for Constitutional Action, a conservative group.

Increasingly critical of Richard Nixon's imperial Presidency, Ashley lashed out at the President in 1973 over the Administration's "new federalism." While conceding that the concept itself was "as American as apple pie," Ashley contended that its key element —general revenue sharing—lost its potential impact because of the accompanying cuts in federal urban renewal and model cities programs. In a speech that he made to the National League of Cities in San Juan, Puerto Rico on December 3, 1973, he belittled the plan as "a mandate from the White House to accept its definition of a more orderly process of government" and denounced the "aggrandizement of power in the White House at the expense of Congress" as "a trade-off which many of us find unwise and dangerous, to put it mildly." The following month he promised that if the House Judiciary Committee failed to ask for Nixon's impeachment, he would do it himself on a personal-privilege motion. "He [Nixon] violated the law through conspiracy and obstruction of justice," Ashley told newsmen on January 17, 1974. "I'm saying he's guilty of misdemeanors. I'll construe the Constitution very narrowly and just go on the basis of the criminal code of the United States."

When President Jimmy Carter formulated a national energy policy in the spring of 1977, Thomas P. ("Tip") O'Neill Jr., the Speaker of the House, chose Lud Ashley, a neutral in the energy debate, to head the forty-member Ad Hoc Committee on Energy, which had been set up to oversee and coordinate the energy-related proposals of other House committees and thus sidestep potential jurisdictional tangles. Because Toledo's leading industries depended on reliable energy sources, there was some concern that Ashley would be swayed by pressures from home, but he insisted that he would act in the "larger national interest." "[The energy program] is going to be very tough medicine, which means that there are going to be strong reactions," he explained to Martin Tolchin in an interview for the New York Times (March 29, 1977).

Among the twenty-odd recommendations made by Ashley's committee at its first meeting in July 1977 were proposals to ease restrictions on interlocking utility directorates, raise the taxes on industrial users of oil and natural gas, and double the four-cents-per-gallon excise tax on gasoline. The extra tax revenue would be used to aid urban mass transit systems and to pay for the research and development of alternative energy sources. In Ashley's opinion, the biggest problem to be solved by the government was public apathy. "It would have helped if instead of the blackout of New York, there had been a blackout of the country," he said, as quoted in the New York Times (July 24, 1977). "We would be somewhat more crisis-oriented than we are at the present time."

Lud Ashley is a lean man of medium height with thinning brown hair and what one reporter has described as "sad" eyes. He and his wife, the former Kathleen Marie Lucey, an attorney, were married in August 1967. They have two sons, William Meredith Ludlow and Mark Michael. An earlier marriage ended in divorce.

References: N Y Times B p8 My 4 '77; Newsweek 89:24 My 9 '77 por; Almanac of American Politics, 1978; Congressional Directory, 1977; Who's Who in America, 1978-79

Bakshi, Ralph

*Oct. 26, 1938(?)- Filmmaker. Address: b.
Bakshi Productions, 6430 W. Sunset Blvd.,
Los Angeles, Calif. 90028*

Both in content and form the films of Ralph
Bakshi have greatly extended the boundaries
of screen animation, transforming that art
radically from the kiddie image of the Walt
Disney trademark. Charles Champlin, arts
editor of the Los Angeles *Times*, suggested
the boldness of his pioneering effort in the
onomatopoeic assertion that Bakshi "zoomed,
zonked, slammed, bammed, whammed, splash-
ed, slashed, and smashed his way into the
blinking, blanking public eye" as the creator
of three disquieting adult urban studies that
were "hard-spoken, raunchy and dazzling in
about equal doses." *Fritz the Cat* (1972) became the film industry's first X-rated feature-
length cartoon; *Heavy Traffic* (1973) distinguished itself as the first animated cartoon
with material drawn from the artists's personal observations and inner life; and *Coonskin* (1975) was the first full-length cartoon
devoted to the black experience in America.

When he had offended nearly everyone, at
times even some of the many moviegoers who
rejoiced in his work, and had raised the question of whether his films are satire or pornography, Bakshi turned from explicit social
comment to *Wizards* (1977), a futuristic antiwar fable that may be regarded as a prelude
to his adaptation of J.R.R. Tolkien's *The Lord
of the Rings* (1978), his most ambitious movie.
Having earlier developed new ways of fusing
live action with cartoon footage, Bakshi made
cartoon history by shooting *The Lord of the
Rings* entirely in live action and then tracing

the film frame by frame for animation. He
has referred to the realistic motion he thus
achieved to enhance his storytelling as "moving paintings."

Ralph Bakshi was born on or about October
26, 1938, the son of Russian Jews who had
immigrated to Haifa, Palestine and then moved
to the United States with their one-year-old
son and their older daughter. The father found
work as a low-paid sheet-metal laborer, and
the family settled in the Brownsville section
of Brooklyn, a neighborhood of Jews, Italians,
and blacks where eight-year-old Ralph, playing in the streets, once found himself splat-
tered with the blood of a Mafia leader who
had his head blown off nearby. Memories of
his childhood no doubt helped to generate
the anger seething in *Heavy Traffic*, which he
has said shows the frustration and anguish of
"vulgar people trapped in a vulgar environment."

In an interview, however, with Gregg Kil-
day of the Los Angeles *Times* (August 23,
1973), Bakshi denied that *Heavy Traffic* is as
autobiographical as some viewers supposed
or that his own parents resembled the hate-
filled parents of the film's young hero, Michael.
"There was a total vibrancy in my family,"
he recalled; "there was a do-or-die situation
which you love when you look back on it;
there was growing up free of any social commitments, which I think is very important to
an artist. . . . My parents were the best thing
I can say about my life. In the jungle I grew
up in, they were the only thing that really
held my head together."

To avoid involvement in street fights, Ralph
Bakshi spent much of the idle time of his boyhood on the roof watching the pigeons and
daydreaming. In an intellectually unstimulating
community that, he once complained, lacked
even a Jewish theatre, he resorted to cutting
out comic-book figures like Superman and making up stories for them to act out. As a teenager he expressed his fantasies in drawing—
doodling tirelessly. A guidance counselor at
Thomas Jefferson High School in Brooklyn
steered Bakshi to art courses there, and, after
an incident of some minor "street trouble,"
as he put it, she had him transferred to the
High School of Industrial Arts (now the High
School of Art and Design) in Manhattan. In
1956 he graduated with the top award in
cartooning.

Although reportedly he would have preferred
to draw a newspaper comic strip, on leaving
high school Ralph Bakshi began a $400-a-week
job as an opaquer or cel painter for CBS
Terrytoons in New Rochelle, New York. ("Cels"
are the celluloid sheets on which the animator's drawings are made.) Soon afterward
a change in management enabled him to advance to the position of animator without the
customary years of preparation. Bakshi explained to Martin Kasindorf who interviewed
him for an article in the New York *Times
Magazine* (October 14, 1973), "I followed the

ethic of art school—be a good boy, draw pretty pictures, make lots of money and shut up." In 1964 he moved ahead as a director, and a year and a half later he became creative director for all of Terrytoon's cartoons. After eight months Bakshi took over the direction of Paramount's cartoon department in Manhattan. That costly studio was shut down six months later, in November 1967.

The two crows Hekyll and Jekyll and other products, however successful commercially, seemed to Bakshi a debasement of the medium of animation. "I was bored, starting to drink," he said of that period of his life, as Hollis Alpert quoted him in the Saturday Review (March 9, 1974). "I wasn't quite clear what I wanted to do or say, but I knew it had to be my own kind of thing. At night, while working at studios by day, I began secretly creating the kind of characters that eventually turned up in Heavy Traffic." Bakshi has stated that the brutally realistic novel Last Exit to Brooklyn (1964) by Hubert Selby, who had been a teenage friend, helped release him from his inhibitions in his search for creative freedom. At the same time, his interest in the work of George Grosz, David Levine, and Jules Feiffer turned him in a satirical direction.

Bakshi's partner in launching a new age of animation was Steve Krantz, the film producer and promoter responsible for such Saturday morning TV cartoon fare as Spiderman and Rocket Robinhood, as well as for educational films. In return for Bakshi's promise to reorganize a Toronto studio for Krantz and set up a new one in New York, Krantz agreed to help in the production of the adult cartoons that Bakshi longed to undertake. Rather than gamble on an original idea, Krantz chose the popular Zap Comix' randy comic strip Fritz the Cat as the basis of their venture. Financed mainly by a small distribution company called Cinemation Industries, work was begun in the fall of 1969. As a film, Fritz the Cat took off from the original to such an extent that Robert Crumb, the comic strip's creator, disassociated himself from the project. Bakshi, moreover, had problems with prudish or indignant animators.

Fritz the Cat, the world's first full-length X-rated cartoon, was unreeled at the Cannes Film Festival of 1972 to "glee and catcalls," echoing the response of American moviegoers and critics. The protagonist Fritz, variously described in reviews as "a collegiate Candide with WASP hangups" and "a sort of Henry Miller feline character," is a swinging New York University dropout and hip revolutionary, fatuous yet "rather endearing." The other human stereotypes also have animal counterparts: cops are pigs and blacks are crows. In her ecstatic review in New York (April 17, 1972) Judith Crist praised the film as "more than a multi-level milestone movie: it's a gloriously funny, brilliantly pointed and superbly executed entertainment, right on target —and its target is, at long-awaited last, the muddle-headed radical chicks and slicks of the sixties." Champlin of the Los Angeles Times (May 13, 1972) summed up Fritz: "Whatever its failings, [it] is richly graphic and uncommonly bold and ambitious social commentary." But the film seemed a "counterfeit item" to Paul D. Zimmerman, who censured it in Newsweek (May 15, 1972) as "a harmless, mindless, pro-youth saga calculated to shake up only the box office." It did, in fact, shake up the box office to a total of $30,000,000. Comparing his work to the Ashcan School of American painting, Bakshi countered criticism of his film as lamentable and offensive in taste with the observation: "Reality isn't in good taste."

The novel means by which Bakshi had achieved Fritz's reality included a soundtrack of voices taped on location, such as those of Black Panthers in a Harlem bar, and backgrounds drawn by animators from actual photographs of New York scenes. He declined to develop his animation techniques through additional pornographic animal cartoons, but instead, with the backing of American International, he told the story of a young New York cartoonist in a new form, Heavy Traffic (1973), another X-rated film. Krantz produced Heavy Traffic, but split with Bakshi in 1973 and alone brought out the inadequate Nine Lives of Fritz the Cat in 1975.

"An impressionistic study of a young man's imaginings—self-dramatizing, overstated, grotesque, part dreamlike, more often nightmarish" was Champlin's description of Heavy Traffic in the Los Angeles Times (August 9, 1973). He also called attention to the film's redeeming "strains of compassion and wistful innocence." To support an artist's right of free expression, the Museum of Modern Art in New York offered a showing of the controversial film on August 7, 1973, and on that occasion the director of the museum's film department, Willard Van Dyke, wrote in the program notes, "If you are not offended by some part of Heavy Traffic, perhaps you are not offendable. Make no mistake, however, it is a brilliantly executed, very important film."

Some critics delighted in the "corruscating cascades of images" in Heavy Traffic—the "mind-spinning mix" of live sequences with animation and of figures drawn against photographed backdrops or well-known paintings such as Edward Hopper's Night Hawks (1942). Bakshi's use of the language of twentieth-century art, as Mike Barrier pointed out in Print (March 1974), often reflects his appreciation of the Expressionistic and surrealistic idioms. Barrier recognized the mastery with which Bakshi uses the resources of animation to place an aesthetic distance between the viewer and episodes of violence, but found him less effective in handling storyline exposition.

Shortly before dissolving his partnership with Krantz, Bakshi wrote the screenplay for Coonskin, in a highly concentrated effort of three twenty-hour days, and sold it to Albert

S. Ruddy, the producer of *The Godfather*. The film that Bakshi intended to be his "homage to the black man" again combines animation with live-action photography, this time in a corrosive version of Joel Chandler Harris' Uncle Remus animal stories—featuring animated Br'er Rabbit, Br'er Bear, and Br'er Fox as Southern Blacks who take over the Harlem rackets from the Mafia—enclosed in a jailbreak plot with live performers. Denounced as racist by CORE and others, Bakshi was roughed up at a preview showing at the Museum of Modern Art in November 1974. After some month's delay Ruddy found a small, independent firm, Bryanston Films, to take over distribution from Paramount.

Among its defenders, Joyce Gould Boyum of the *Wall Street Journal* (August 11, 1975) appraised *Coonskin* as Bakshi's "richest and most mature work." She found charges of racism unjustified: "For sending a strange undercurrent of sadness through his brash humor and grotesque and gaudy imagery, Bakshi creates a mood more suggestive of sympathy than hatred." In his comments for the New York *Times* (August 21, 1975) Richard Eder wrote admiringly of Bakshi's success in conveying "the hallucinatory violence and frustration of American life, specifically black city life," and he argued for *Coonskin* as "a rarity in contemporary American filmmaking: a picture that is lyrically violent, yet in no way exploits violence."

With *Coonskin* in limbo after Bryanston went bankrupt, Bakshi completed what he called a "New York version of *American Graffiti,*" *Hey Good Lookin'*, which deals with interracial gang warfare in the 1950's. As its director explained, it remains unreleased because Warner Brothers feared that the dispute over *Coonskin* made it "too hot to handle." Bakshi then wrote, produced, and directed a comic-book film that he intended to be wholly inoffensive, *Wizards* (Twentieth Century-Fox, 1977), a PG-rated antiwar fantasy set in the distant future where elves and fairies pit their magic against the wicked forces of the science-technology of human mutants. The technically brilliant cartoon, which cost $1,500,000 to make and grossed $20,000,000, was described in the Los Angeles *Times* (March 2, 1977) as "a feast for the eyes, a nonstop succession of imaginings and imageries that are beautiful, startling, funny, powerfully ominous, classically cartoonish, visions of heaven and hellfire." An allegory of the conflict between good and evil, *Wizards* laid the groundwork in theme and execution for *The Lord of the Rings* (United Artists, 1978).

"The first realistic painting in motion"—a distinction that Bakshi claims for *The Lord of the Rings*—has as its subject matter, perhaps ironically, the fantastic domain and denizens of Middle Earth, with which Bakshi had fallen in love when he read Tolkien at eighteen. Several producers, including Walt Disney, had considered a screen treatment of Tolkien's mythology, but apparently had foreseen the risks and had regarded its problems as defeating. With the backing of Paul Zaentz, head of Fantasy Films, Bakshi obtained the rights to the book, then held by MGM, in the fall of 1976. The screenplay that he engaged Chris Conkling and Peter S. Beagle to write displeased some reviewers for being too reverential toward the source, including so much highly condensed material that relationships are incomprehensible to viewers unfamiliar with the epic, and for ending abruptly, midway through the trilogy.

The visual achievement of *Lord of the Rings* was more impressive. In refining the old rotoscope technique, Bakshi filmed costumed actors against stark backgrounds on location in Spain and Hollywood and then traced the images in each frame with artistic alterations to effect nuances of expression, shadowing, and slow motion. The result, wrote Joseph Gelmis in *Newsday* (November 11, 1978) is "a fantasy overlay imposed upon absolutely natural movements and figures." Spectacular backgrounds were painted in diverse styles suggestive of Brueghel, Goya, Turner, Wyeth, and other artists. Bakshi employed some 600 artists, animators, and technicians to trace, sketch, and develop characters. "I assigned artists to characters like actors," he remarked. In spite of his pains, Bakshi was faced with such critical comments as Vincent Canby's in the New York *Times* (November 15, 1978): "His hobbits look very much like Disney dwarfs, though somewhat more introspective." Many Tolkien devotees, however, very likely agreed with the conclusion of William Carlton of the New York *Daily News* (November 19, 1978): "No movie could ever do full justice to a work like *Lord of the Rings*, but this one comes as close as humanly possible; it's a fantastic visual translation of a great literary tapestry."

Before he goes much beyond preliminary discussions of a possible sequel to the *Rings*, Bakshi is reportedly scheduled to work on a film, "American Pop," for release by Columbia Pictures. His new venture in animation is expected to use seventeen musical numbers in tracing the development of American music from 1910 to 1980. According to *Take One* (November 1978), in late 1978 he also began filming a live-action comedy for Warner Brothers to be called "If I Catch Her, I'll Kill Her."

Ralph Bakshi is a well-built man who stands six feet two inches tall, weighs 210 pounds, and has shaggy black hair, dark-brown eyes, a broad smile, and an open manner. He speaks with a Brooklyn accent. When just out of high school, Bakshi married a Brownsville girl, and he has a son by that marriage, which ended in divorce after five years. He lives with his second wife, Elizabeth Bakshi, and their son and daughter in a fifteen-room house in the Hancock Park section of Los Angeles. In moments of relaxation at his office studio he listens to medieval music on his portable stereo. He has a large collection of illustrated children's books, including Arthur Rackham's work, and he names *Pinocchio* as his favorite children's film. As for adult films, he replied to a question from Scott Eyman, who interviewed him for *Take One:* "I could watch *Lawrence of Arabia* forever, *Mean Streets*, almost all of Scorsese. For form and structure Eisenstein." He went on to tell Eyman what he hoped ultimately to accomplish: "I want to make an animated film that is perfect in satire, in humour, in story, in structure, in motion, and in color. I've done it in bits and pieces, but never as a whole entity."

References: Los Angeles Times IV p1+ Ag 23 '73 por, IV p1+ Ag 24 '78 por; N Y Times p22 Ag 14 '73 por, II p19 N 10 '74 por; N Y Times Mag p40+ O 14 '73 por; Newsweek 82:87 Ag 27 '73 por, 89:110+ My 9 '77; Print 28:51+ Mr '74 por; Sat R/World 1:40+ Mr 9 '74 por; Take One 6:34+ N '78 por; Time 102:50 Ag 27 '73

Balthus

Feb. 29, 1908- French artist.
Address: b. c/o Pierre Matisse Gallery, 41 E. 57th St., New York City, N.Y. 10022

"The best way to begin is to say: 'Balthus is a painter of whom *nothing is known*. And now let us have a look at the paintings.'" So ran the advice that the artist volunteered to John Russell, who was organizing a catalogue of his works for an exhibit at the Tate Gallery in London in 1968. That admonition clearly reflects the artist's inviolable sense of privacy and individuality. Not one to follow trends, Balthus has assiduously avoided new movements in modern art and has instead followed a path of realism that is congenial to his own private vision. Picasso, who owned his "The Children," painted in 1937, once said of him: "Balthus is so much better than all these young artists who do nothing but copy me. He is a real painter." Like his close friend, the late Alberto Giacometti, Balthus renders the human figure in an existential isolation. But while Giacometti's studies are isolated, stark, and gaunt, Balthus' figures are characterized by a dreamy, inner preoccupation and sensual fullness.

Balthus, whose full name is Comte Balthazar Klossowski de Rola, was born in Paris, France on February 29, 1908 to Eric and Baladine Klossowski. His father was a painter associated with the impressionist school and a renowned art critic whose monograph on Honoré Daumier became a standard text. Balthus' mother was also a painter. Descended, on his father's side, from Polish aristocrats who immigrated to France in the mid-nineteenth century, Balthus is also related to the Gordons of Scotland, the most prominent member of whom was Lord Byron. After spending his early childhood in Paris, in 1914 Balthus moved with his family to Switzerland, where he lived in Berne and Geneva and made frequent visits to England.

His precocious talent was encouraged by such visitors to his parents' home as the artists Pierre Bonnard, André Derain, and Edouard Vuillard, and in particular, the poet Rainer Maria Rilke. Among the literary and artistic influences of his formative years were *Images d'Epinal* (1830), a popular collection of illustrations of life in a French town in the Vosges; the German children's books of Dr. Heinrich Hoffmann, especially his didactic and occasionally gruesome *Struwwelpeter*; and Lewis Carroll's *Alice's Adventures in Wonderland* and *Through the Looking Glass*, illustrated by John Tenniel. The last named may have inspired the images of young girls gazing into mirrors and of mysterious cats that became recurrent themes in Balthus' work. He was also inspired by English literature, especially the works of Emily Brontë, and by the writings of such Americans as Thoreau, Melville, Hawthorne, Poe, and Faulkner. Artistically, while acknowledging his debt to the nineteenth-century French realist painter Gustave Courbet, he also drew some inspiration from the surrealists' probings into the unconscious mind. The panoramic views of the Lake of Thuns and the peaks of the Bernese Oberland, which he visited on holidays during his years in Switzerland made a profound impression on him and later inspired the landscapes he painted in the 1930's.

At eleven Balthus drew a series of sketches for a picture book about his lost cat and showed them to Rilke. Charmed by them, the poet wrote the accompanying text in French and had the book published in Zurich in 1921 under the title *Mitsou*. Rilke then invited the boy to his home in the Valais region of the Swiss Alps and, noticing his fascination with Chinese and Japanese art, introduced him to the Chinese novels of the French author Victor Segalen, which Balthus chose to illustrate years later.

In 1924, the year he returned to Paris, the sixteen-year-old Balthus decided to make his career in art. Avoiding the academies, he followed the age-old tradition of copying old masters, especially the major Italian Renaissance painter Piero della Francesca. Accompanied by the writer André Gide, he traveled in Italy, working and studying in Florence, Arezzo, and Piero's hometown of Borgo San Sepolcro. In 1928 he painted frescoes for a church in the town of Beatenburg in the Bernese Oberland. Balthus' military service in the French army in Morocco from 1929 to 1933 inspired, among other works, his 1949 painting "The Spahi and His Horse." In 1933 he drew a series of illustrations for an edition of Emily Brontë's *Wuthering Heights*, and later he turned one of them into a painting depicting himself as Heathcliff.

The Galerie Pierre in Paris, a focal point for surrealism, presented Balthus' first one-man show in 1934. Although he had been markedly influenced by the impressionists, on his return from Morocco he had changed and now seemed more affected by Piero della Francesca and Georges Seurat. Antonin Artaud, in his review of the show, pointed to Balthus' organic realism, knowledge of forms and light, power of creating sphinx-like figures, and a Davidian technique adapted to modern sensibilities.

The most enthusiastically greeted work in the show was *The Street*, painted in 1933. (Balthus had worked on an earlier version in 1929, before his service in Morocco.) Executed in sharp contrasts, with a dynamic interplay of figures, it has the formal pictorial structure that characterizes most of Balthus' work, combined with a strange, dream-like mood. The figures are frozen in their inner world, immobilized in a state of inner contemplation. Albert Camus likened the experience of looking at *The Street* to that "of gazing through glass at people petrified by some kind of enchantment, not for ever, but for a split second, after which they will resume their movements." The painting was bought by the American collector and museum director James Thrall Soby, who helped to popularize Balthus in the United States, before his 1938 show at the Pierre Matisse Gallery, in New York City. Another early Balthus painting that created something of a sensation was his erotic *The Guitar Lesson* (1934).

Fascinated by the theatre, Balthus designed costumes and sets for Jules Supervielle's French adaptation of Shakespeare's *As You Like It* and Antonin Artaud's production of Shelley's *The Cenci*, presented in Paris in 1935. The poet Pierre-Jean Jouve, a friend of Balthus, reviewed a performance of the Shelley tragedy in an article for the *Nouvelle Revue Française* that could be aptly applied to much of Balthus' other work. "For *The Cenci*," he wrote, "Balthus has invented, designed, constructed a prodigious space, a decor at once inward, symbolic and Italian in which everything joins up with an extreme simplicity and force." During rehearsals of *The Cenci* Balthus drew a portrait of Artaud at a table in the Café du Dôme, which the poet published in the May 1935 issue of *La Bête Noire*, edited by Jériade and Maurice Raynal.

On his return to Switzerland in 1935, Balthus painted the beloved landscape of his boyhood. *The Mountain*, which he created between 1935 and 1937, and reworked in 1939, was an outstanding example of that period. A rustic scene with three figures predominating, it excavated childhood memories and included a young friend who had died in his youth. Although the painting emulates Courbet, it has a slightly surreal quality of its own. *The Children*, painted in 1937, presents the dramatic juxtaposition of two girls, one crouched on the floor, reading, the other directly behind her straddling a chair, while facing in the opposite direction. In it the restlessness and curiosity of youth are dramatically illustrated. Purchased by Picasso in 1941, it is slated to go to the Louvre as part of the Picasso donation. Also dating from that period are two well-known Balthus portraits of fellow artists. His *Portrait of André Derain* (1936) depicts an ebullient Derain, with the dream-like figure of a young model in the background, while his *Joan Miró and His Daughter Dolores* (1937-38) is a tender study of father and child.

Called up for World War II military service but demobilized after a month because of poor health, Balthus moved in 1940 to the department of Savoie, where he painted *The Cherry Tree*, a lovely, richly colored pastoral scene with a figure reaching into a tree in the foreground. Reminiscent of oriental art, with its delicate rendering of the tree, it has the richness of color common to many of his landscapes. *Landscape of Oxen*, painted from the same location, reveals an entirely different feeling. Depicting a peasant pulling oxen in front of a forbidding landscape, it was rendered during the Nazi occupation of France and reflects the grim mood of the time. Expanding on his 1937 painting, *The Children*, Balthus rendered a sharper delineation of his subjects and a more detailed interior in his *The Living Room*, painted in 1942.

In 1943 Balthus moved to Berne, where he executed his *Gotteron Landscape* and the now famous *Golden Days*, a sensuous study of a

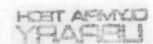

young girl languishing on a chaise longue as she gazes into a mirror. Her knee is raised as her dress falls back, and her bodice is in disarray. In the background a young man stokes a fire. Although the figure is dressed, Balthus presented his subjects in similar poses in such nude works as his 1954 paintings *The Room* and *Nude with Cat*. In a not untypical reaction to his work, Emily Genauer speculated about his adolescent subjects in the New York *Herald Tribune* magazine (December 1, 1963): "What are the figures really doing? . . . Why do they seem to have some terrifying knowledge of corruption, while their face and demeanor remain innocent?" Referring to his bizarre world of children and adolescents, Balthus said, as quoted in *Life* (January 28, 1957): "Some say my paintings are sinister and abnormal. But I have had the same vision since I was four. Perhaps that is abnormal." Later, jokingly referring to the fact that he was born on February 29 during a leap year, he observed, as quoted in *Time* (May 12, 1961): "Having had only twelve birthdays, I may consider myself only twelve years old."

Back in Paris, Balthus designed the sets for Albert Camus' dramas *La Peste* and *L'Etat de Siège* in 1948 and for a production of *Cosi fan Tutte*, presented at Aix-en-Provence in 1950. In compliance with a request by the owner of La Méditerranée, a seafood restaurant on the Place de L'Odéon, where he hobnobbed with writers, artists, and actors, Balthus agreed to paint a shop sign. *The Méditerranée's Cat* depicts a smiling cat, seated at a terrace dining table, dressed in striped shirt and slacks, with fork and knife poised in his paws. A line of startled mullets are carried over a rainbow into his plate, as a young woman pulls away in a skiff. A lovely orange lobster sits on a platter to his left, waiting to be eaten. Totally unlike his other works, *The Méditerranée's Cat* has a light, whimsical air.

Returning to Italy, in 1951 Balthus painted his muted green landscape of Sermoneta, which was acquired by Camus. From 1952 to 1954 he worked on *Le Passage du Commerce Saint-André*, also known as *La Cour*. Apparently an outgrowth of his 1933 work *The Street*, it presents a subtle scene that has figures moving deeply into the picture plane rather than remaining in a frontal position. The sharpness of detail in *The Street* has given way to more ambiguity and illusion in the later painting. The mood is quiet, the light almost dawnlike.

Another of his monumental and somewhat enigmatic works is *The Room*, completed in 1954. To the left, a nude girl lies sleeping on a chaise longue. On the right, a sinister female figure pulls back a drape, as a cat looks at her questioningly from the side. The flesh of the nude dazzles the viewer against the muted background of the room. It reminds one of the stage settings done by Balthus, with light falling upon the principal performer.

From 1954 to 1961 Balthus lived at the Chateau de Chassy, near Autun, while his wife and children remained in Switzerland, and during that period he produced sixty-one paintings. His *Colette in Profile* and *Girl in White*— a portrait of his cousin, Frédérique Tison, whom he occasionally used as a model—were among his outstanding paintings of that period. James Thrall Soby commented, after examining *Girl in White*, that it "confirms Balthus' place in the exalted portrait tradition which a hundred years ago included Corot, Courbet, and Millet at his infrequent best."

Balthus' *Big Landscape with Trees*, painted from an aerial view in rich pinks and greens, and his *Bouquet of Roses on a Window Sill*, an opulently colored landscape enhanced by a yellow pitcher with pink and orange flowers, reveal his remarkable versatility. Equally interesting is his *Fruit on the Window Sill*. Based on two earlier water colors, it conveys the distinct quality of a Cézanne, with its careful modeling of the fruit and its almost cubistic background. *The Window*, painted in 1955, updates an earlier work of the same title. In the original study the interior of the room is emphasized, but in the later painting the window is enlarged, and the viewer is taken directly to the landscape beyond. According to critics, the painting is reminiscent of Pierre Bonnard's work, with its muted blues, violets, and pinks. Using a more decorative background motif, Balthus painted *Cup of Coffee* intermittently between 1956 and 1961. Reminiscent of Matisse, it retains the soft, subtle colors of Balthus' palette. That theme was carried further in *The Turkish Room*, painted between 1963 and 1966.

Returning to a simpler theme, Balthus painted *Nude in Front of the Mantle*, depicting the childlike figure of a young girl in profile gazing into a mirror as her arms hold up her long hair, as if imagining herself as a woman. *The Dream*, painted about the same time, is a sharply rendered work reminiscent of his earlier *The Children*. In it a dream messenger brings a sleeping young woman a bright red poppy.

In 1961 André Malraux, as President Charles de Gaulle's Minister of State responsible for culture, asked his friend Balthus to become director of the Académie de France in Rome, at the Villa Médicis, explaining that he wanted "a second ambassador in Italy," an ambassador of French culture. Balthus accepted and directed the school until his retirement in 1977. During his tenure he made extensive renovations in the interior and gardens of the old villa, restored old frescoes, established new galleries, and mounted outstanding exhibits. Although he completed only six paintings during that period, he considered his tenure at the Villa Médicis a highlight of his career.

Taking time out to visit Japan and explore its art treasures and folk traditions, Balthus learned colloquial Japanese and the rudiments of calligraphy. *The Turkish Room*, completed after his return, was the first of his works to enter the French national museums. Between 1967 and 1970 he completed two other large works, *Japanese Figure with Black Mirror* and *Japanese Figure with Red Table*, both reflecting his long-standing affinity with oriental art and his exquisite sense of color. When shown at the Pierre Matisse Gallery in New York City in 1977, they brought wide acclaim to the artist. Thomas Hess, reviewing the exhibit, wrote in *New York* magazine (November 21, 1977): "Looking at herself in a mirror, the 'Japanese Figure' examines her face and body; she watches herself become a vessel of generation. She doesn't sense the oncoming of maturity, as do the nymphets of Balthus' famous earlier paintings; she observes the beginning of a new life. Which suggests mortality."

From 1967 to 1973 Balthus worked on *The Card Game* with its sinister and mysterious interchange between the male and female players. An earlier version of that painting was executed between 1948 and 1950. In the first version the man is pensive, the woman calculating, but both are young and possess a poignant innocence. In the later work the mood has hardened. The man is menacingly reaching toward the woman as she sits resolutely, still holding the last card. In place of vulnerability there seems to be coldness and hate, and some critics have suggested that Balthus saw this as the natural development between male and female.

Since 1938 Balthus has had frequent exhibitions at New York City's Pierre Matisse Gallery, and in 1956 a retrospective show of his work was mounted at the Museum of Modern Art. Other locations where his work has been shown include Chicago's Art Club, the Tate Gallery and Lefevre Gallery in London, the Galerie Moos in Geneva, the Civica Galleria d'Arte Moderna in Turin, and the Musée Cantini in Marseilles. In Paris his work has been exhibited at the Musée des Arts Decoratifs, the Galerie Wildenstein, the Galerie Henriette Gomes, and the Galerie Claude Bernard.

Relatively little is known of the private life of Balthus, who is considered something of an eccentric recluse. From his first marriage, which took place in 1937, he has two sons. During his visit to Japan in the 1960's he met a young woman named Setsuko, who became his model and, later, his second wife. She bore him two children, of whom the elder died in infancy. Described in *Time* (May 12, 1961) as "every inch the worldly aristocrat," Balthus can converse in French, English, German, and Italian. A painstaking artist, he sometimes requires as many as forty sittings for a single portrait. According to James Thrall Soby, "There is a strong Byronic cast to Balthus' own temperament; he shares to the full the English poet's aristocracy of spirit, contempt for convention, and essential solitude of creative mind."

References: Contemporary Artists (1977); Leymarie, Jean. Balthus (1979); McGraw-Hill Dictionary of Art (1969); Phaidon Dictionary of Twentieth Century Art (1973); Praeger Encyclopedia of Art (1971)

Barthes, Roland (bart rô-läɴ')

Nov. 12, 1915- French critic; writer. Address: b. c/o Georges Borchardt Inc., 136 E. 57th St., New York City, N.Y. 10022; h. 11 rue Sevandoni, Paris, France 75006

The heir apparent to Jean-Paul Sartre's pre-eminent position in French intellectual life is the brilliant and wide-ranging "high critic" Roland Barthes, the chief exponent of *la nouvelle critique* and especially of semiology. The "tentative" science of semiology adapts Saussurean linguistics and the ahistorical method of Claude Lévi-Strauss and Roman Jakobson for the purpose of making a structural analysis of language in literature and other "sign systems," including those of "ritual, convention, or public entertainment." Barthes addressed himself to "the mythology of literary language" in his first book, his literary manifesto, *Writing Degree Zero* (1953), and went on to demythologize the language of mass culture in *Mythologies* (1957). In those and later studies, including highly sophisticated literary criticism revealing the unifying metaphors in the work of Jean

Racine and others, his consistent theme has been the artificiality of all human communications systems, and his expressed aim has been "to attack and destroy the idea that signs are natural," especially when those signs reinforce "the essential enemy—the bourgeois norm."

Barthes is the stellar contributor to the journals *Tel Quel, Communications,* and *La quinzaine Littéraire,* and he lectures on "the sociology of signs, symbols, and representations" in the sixth division of the École Pratique des Hautes Études in Paris. Through all his changing allegiances, from quasi-Marxism to the neo-Freudianism of Jacques Lacan, and despite his deliberately difficult, often aphoristic, sometimes elliptical style, Barthes is, in the words of Susan Sontag, "the most consistently intelligent" as well as "the most important and useful critic—stretching that term—to have emerged anywhere" in the last quarter century. With rare exceptions, Barthes's books have been published in France by Éditions du Seuil and in English translation by Jonathan Cape in England and by the Hill and Wang division of Farrar, Strauss and Giroux in the United States.

Roland Barthes was born in Cherbourg, France on November 12, 1915, one of two sons of Henriette (Binger) and Louis Barthes. Following the death of their father, a naval officer, in a World War I battle in the North Sea in 1916, Roland and his brother were raised by their mother in the Protestant home of their grandparents in Bayonne, France, in conditions of genteel poverty. Their aunt Alice Barthes was a piano teacher, and the Barthes's home was the center of musical life in Bayonne. Roland himself learned to play the piano and to compose music even before he learned to read.

Citing an interview with his biographee in *Gulliver* (March 1973), Philip Thody in *Roland Barthes: A Conservative Estimate* (1977) noted Barthes's acknowledgment of the dominating mother figure in his life and of his frustration, as Thody paraphrased, "at not being able to live a Freudian childhood to the full." "He also made a remark which confirmed what critical readers of his work had long suspected: that an Oedipus with no Laius to kill will invent one; and that in Barthes's case his Laius was what he calls the *doxa,* the stifling set of received and ready-made opinions, of stereotypes and fixed ideas, that he sees as characterizing the bourgeoisie. Indeed his attack on what is not, after all, so very unusual a target is so violent and unreasoning that it cannot have wholly conscious origins. Significantly enough, he makes a point of saying that his mother cut herself free from her original bourgeois milieu by learning a manual trade, and he also bears no personal grudge against Bayonne itself. Like all good middle-class Parisians, he spends his holidays with his provincial relatives." Barthes has also attacked, increasingly with the years, the "doxa" of the Left.

Having learned to support herself and her sons by bookbinding, Henriette Barthes in 1924 moved her ménage to Paris, where Roland attended the Lycée Montaigne and the Lycée Louis-le-Grand and took *baccalauréat* degrees in 1933 and 1934. With his outstanding academic record in literature and philosophy, he would have gone on to the Ecole Normale Superiéure and the competitive examination for the *agrégation*—the traditional requisite for university teaching in France —had not serious health problems intervened. As Thody suggests in his book on Barthes, "The slightly ironic tone in Barthes's later remark about how natural it was in France to be 'Catholique, marié et bien diplômé' is thus perhaps explicable by the fact that he was almost fifty before he secured a permanent teaching appointment."

In May 1934, when he was eighteen, Barthes suffered the first of a series of attacks of pulmonary tuberculosis that would recur intermittently until he was thirty. After recovering from an initial lesion in his left lung, he spent four years reading French, Latin, and Greek at the University of Paris, where he was a founder of the Groupe de Théâtre Antique, a student dramatic company. Later, as a mythologist, he would make the motto of the classical Roman actor his own: *Latatus prodeo*—"I come forward pointing at my mask."

Barthes took his *licence* in classical letters in 1939 and, exempted from military service, taught at a lycée in Biarritz in 1939-40 and at the Lycée Voltaire and the Lycée Carnot in Paris in 1940-41. In 1941, after taking a *diplôme d'études supérieures* in Greek tragedy, he suffered a relapse of tuberculosis, and during the following five years he was confined to a series of sanitoria, hospitals, and convalescent homes. In the midst of that period of illness, in 1943, he took his final *licence* in grammar and philology, and while undergoing treatment at the Sanatorium des Etudiants de France at Saint-Hilaire-du-Touvet in the Isère he did several months of premedical study with the abortive idea that he might go into psychiatric medicine.

Following a final convalescent period in Paris, in 1946 and 1947, Barthes held a succession of posts, including teacher at the French Institute in Bucharest, Romania, reader in French at the University of Alexandria, Egypt, and literary adviser to Éditions de l'Arche. At the Centre National de Recherche Scientifique he was a teaching fellow in lexicology from 1952 to 1954 and a research fellow in sociology from 1955 to 1959. In 1960 he joined the faculty of the École Pratique des Hautes Études.

Barthes's first book was the compact literary manifesto and polemic *Le Degré zéro de l'écriture* (1953; *Writing Degree Zero,* 1967), an implicit refinement of and departure from the position taken by Jean-Paul Sartre in *Qu'est-ce que la littérature?* (What is Literature, 1947). Barthes took an essentially Marxist position in agreeing with Sartre that, with the definitive disintegration of the "bourgeois consensus" in the nineteenth century, French literature had "become dissociated from the society consuming it," with the result that, while a common literary language remained, there was an increasing fragmentation of personal styles in writing. But whereas Sartre tended to view much modernist experimentation as an elitist enemy of "revolutionary consciousness," Barthes took a subtler position, on the side of "those neutral modes of writing, here called 'the zero degree of writing,'" exemplified in "colorless writing like Camus', Blanchot's or Cayrol's for example, or conversational writing like Cayrol's." (Shortly afterward he would insert, at the head of the list, antinovelists like Natalie Sarraute and Alain Robbe-Grillet.) Conversely, he considered "realist" writing "more artificial" than any other mode, because it made no attempt to recognize the network of preconceptions through which it filtered events while claiming to give "the closest account of nature."

Later Barthes gave the gist of his argument in semiological terms, thereby explaining, incidentally, why, in theory as well as in practice, in his own writing, he does not consider clarity, or at least easy "accessibility" of meaning, desirable: *"Writing Degree Zero* . . . was, all told, nothing but a mythology of literary language. There I defined writing as the signifier of the literary myth, that is, as a form which is already filled with meaning and which receives from the concept of Literature a new signification. I suggested that history, in modifying the writer's consciousness, had provoked, a hundred years or so ago, a moral crisis of literary language: writing was revealed as signifier, Literature as signification; rejecting the false nature of traditional literary language, the writer violently shifted his position in the direction of an anti-nature of language. The subversion of writing was the radical act by which a number of writers have attempted to reject Literature as a mythical system. Each revolt of this kind has been a murder of Literature as signification: all have postulated the reduction of literary discourse to a simple semiological system, or even, in the case of poetry, to a pre-semiological system. . . . Some went as far as the . . . scuttling of the discourse, silence—whether real or transposed—appearing as the only possible weapon against the major power of myth: its recurrence."

As Susan Sontag wrote in her preface to the American edition of *Writing Degree Zero,* "Barthes's myths about literature are extremely talented, even masterful, and do satisfy the need for intellectual cohesion, comparable to the way myths in the more ordinary sense, according to Lévi-Strauss, produce social cohesion." For Lévi-Strauss, myths, whether primitive or civilized, are models for description, logical techniques for resolving basic antinomies or explaining fundamental conditions in thought and society.

In *Michelet par lui-même* (Michelet by Himself, 1954), Barthes, typically, paid less attention to the nineteenth-century romantic historian's ideology than his "existential thematics," and in Michelet's physical obsessions he found the factors contributing to his richness of language and giving a saving unity to his "petty bourgeois" world view. Such statements as, "For Michelet, Blood is the cardinal substance of History," were considered scandalous in some quarters, but generally the book was well received. It contributed, to Barthes's reputation as a leader of the new school of criticism engaged in analyzing literary work in the light of physical, emotional, and psychological categories.

In reading the Swiss linguist Ferdinand de Saussure's *Cours de linguistique générale* (Course in General Linguistics, 1916), Barthes became convinced that "by treating 'collective representations' as sign-systems, one might hope to go further than the pious show of unmasking them and account in detail for the mystification which transforms petit-bourgeois culture into a universal nature." His first attempt to study the "language" of mass culture and to analyze that language semiologically was in monthly contributions to *Les Lettres nouvelles* between 1954 and 1956. As Susan Sontag observes, those "brilliant essay-epiphanies" on advertising campaigns, commercial products, the cinema, items in the tabloid press, and other mass-cultural phenomena disclosed "the witty concreteness of Barthes's sensibility, his talent for sensuous phenomenological description." Barthes later explained: "The starting point of these reflections was usually a feeling of impatience at the sight of the naturalness with which newspapers, art, and common sense constantly dress up a reality which, even though it is the one we live in, is undoubtedly determined by history. In short, in the account given of our contemporary circumstances, I resented seeing Nature and History confused at every turn."

His monthly contributions to *Les Lettres nouvelles,* along with two additional essays, were brought together in *Mythologies* (1957; *Mythologies,* 1972). The most positive of the essays was the first, "The World of Wrestling," in which he expressed admiration for that frankly "staged" sport: "The public is completely uninterested in knowing whether the contest is rigged or not, and rightly so: it abandons itself to the primary virtue of the spectacle, which is to abolish all motives and consequences: what matters is not what it thinks but what it sees. . . . Wrestling presents man's suffering with all the amplification of tragic masks." *Mythologies* ends with the long essay "Myth Today," considered a landmark in the structuralist movement. In it Barthes describes myth as a semiological system that is defined not "by the object of its message but by the way in which it utters this message" and that has "the task of giving an historical intention a natural justification, and making contingency appear eternal. Now this process is exactly that of bourgeois ideology. . . . Yes, myth exists on the Left, but it does not have there the same qualities as bourgeois myth. Left-wing myth is inessential."

Barthes's name did not become a household word in France until the controversy generated by his book *Sur Racine* (1963; *On Racine*, 1964), in which he approached the tragic poet as "the empty center around which his plays can be read" and saw the essence of his plays to be "the use of force within a situation that is generally erotic." In a rebuttal in *Le Monde* Raymond Picard charged Barthes with "dogmatic impressionism," with over-generalizing, and with indulging in pseudoscientific neologisms, and the prolonged Barthes-Picard quarrel became a *cause celèbre*. In his book *Structural Poetics* (1975) Jonathan Culler described *On Racine* as an exploration of "the common structures that may be derived from a writer's works using a systematic theory based on a linguistic model." The rationale for that method was set forth by Barthes in *Critique et vérité* (Criticism and Truth, 1966).

In *Eléments de sémiologie* (1965; *Elements of Semiology*, 1967) Barthes provided an introductory guide to the science of semiology, which "aims to take in any system of signs, whatever their substance and limits; images, gestures, musical sounds, objects, and the complex association of all these, which form the content of ritual, convention or public entertainment: these constitute, if not languages, at least systems of signification." The difficult theoretical book has come into wide use as a textbook.

In *Système de la mode* (The Fashion System, 1967) Barthes explored the social implications of fashion through the classificatory systems reflected in the language used in women's magazines. *S/Z* (1970; *S/Z*, 1975) was a meticulous, line-by-line analysis of Balzac's novella *Sarrasine* disclosing, or decoding, five codes, or voices, operating within the story, forming its structure and providing its meaning.

In essays on Saint Ignatius of Loyola, the Marquis de Sade, and Charles Fourier, Barthes concentrated on the personal, secondary language systems of those men and on the pleasure or "passion" involved in writing. The essays were brought together in *Sade, Fourier, Loyola* (1971), a book that was, as Philip Thody remarks, "a further application

of the truism running through the whole of Barthes's thinking on literature, and which he has had the talent to present as one of the most provocative ideas of twentieth-century French literary criticism: the idea that books are made of words, not things."

Barthes's mobility and range were evident in *Essais critiques* (*Critical Essays*, 1972), containing essays written between 1953 and 1963. Among them were the three pieces that established him as the champion of the anti-novels of Alain Robbe-Grillet and the one on Bertolt Brecht in which theatre is conceived as an arena for spectacle (as in wrestling) rather than for vicarious emotion. Later essays were collected in *Image/Music/Text*, published by Hill and Wang in 1978. Another collection of essays, *La Tour Eiffel*, was translated into English as *The Eiffel Tower* (1978).

The title of literary critic is accepted by Barthes only with the utmost reluctance, because, contrary to the traditional connotation of that appellation, he is more interested in sharing delight than in passing judgment. An unabashed hedonist, he recorded with enthusiasm in *L'Empire des signes* (Empire of Signs, 1970) his observations as a visitor to Japan, where he found a culture and civilization in which he felt more at home than he had ever felt anywhere before. In literature itself, he followed up his discussion of pleasure in *Sade, Fourier, Loyola* with *Le Plaisir du texte* (1973; *The Pleasure of the Text*, 1976), in which he examined the pleasure, sensual as well as mental, experienced in reading. His hedonism was implicit in his witty, laconic but elegant antiautobiography *Roland Barthes par Roland Barthes* (1975; *Roland Barthes*, 1977) and explicit in *Fragments d'un discours amoureux* (1977; *A Lover's Discourse*, 1978), a fragmented discourse on the language of love "from a unisex point of view." In the *Saturday Review* (September 2, 1978), Stephen Koch described *A Lover's Discourse* as "a desperate and rather solemn collection of personal meditations" in which "one sometimes glimpses the affair that provokes them (an affair with an indeterminate abstraction named X, the relationship obviously homosexual)." But Koch conceded that the book made Barthes's "rise to intellectual stardom complete," and other critics found it "brilliantly inventive," "triumphant," "vivid," and "delightful." In France, where it drew raves even from left-wing critics usually inimical or indifferent to Barthes, it sold 60,000 copies within months. "Barthes's only mistake may be that *A Lover's Discourse* argues its case with too much grace and charm," Douglas Davis wrote in *Newsweek* (December 18, 1978). "Whereas he was once the aloof prophet of semiology . . . , he is now the new voice of warmth, of sentiment. The shift is not likely to help him preserve his cherished isolation."

Roland Barthes "talks like a soft-spoken vicar and lives like an ascetic church mouse," Douglas Davis reported after visiting him in his "bland, barely furnished" apartment on rue Sevandoni in Paris. "He apologizes at the door for his notorius aversion to socializing. 'I find it hard to bear seeing several people at a time,' he says." In addition to maintaining his Paris flat, Barthes shares a home with his mother in the country, near Bayonne. For recreation, he plays the piano, paints watercolors, watches television, or takes a book to bed with him. As might be deduced from his writing, his favorite authors include Proust, Goethe (especially *The Sorrows of Young Werther)*, and Nietzsche (whom he quotes: "I fear we are not getting rid of God because we still have grammar"). In his enjoyment of the freedom that money can bring, he is glad to have escaped the mammon-hating systems of Marxism, Christianity, and orthodox Freudianism. He suffers, he says, from migraine headaches and attacks of "panic boredom," but his chief malady is linguistic—he *sees* language: "J'ai une maladie, moi: je vois le langage."

Contrary to the "old myth" that the work, or ritual, of writing is "a simple mechanical technique" at the service of thought, Barthes believes that "trivialized actions, like writing, are in fact heavily charged with meaning." Regarding the "protocols" of his own "ceremony" of work, he told Jean-Louis de Rambures in a *Le Monde* interview published in translation in the *Guardian* (March 2, 1974)

that he is highly organized and cannot work in hotel rooms or even in libraries but only in his "customary environment." That environment is a work space in his Paris apartment that is divided into "microspaces" for typewriter, work table, materials, card file, and so forth—an arrangement of space that is exactly reproduced in his country residence. Working daily from 9:30 in the morning until 1:00 in the afternoon, he first writes out an entire manuscript with a "good fountain pen" that facilitates "smooth penmanship." (Although he is naturally left-handed, he appears in photographs to be writing with his right hand.) "Then I do it over from beginning to end on a typewriter, using two fingers, since I don't know how to type." He said he had just bought an electric typewriter in the hope that he "can change over to a more dactylographic way of writing." Barthes, who foresees semiology as ultimately destroying itself in a "semioclasm," compares his system of analysis to the ship Argo, "each piece of which the Argonauts gradually replaced, so that they ended with an entirely new ship, . . . an object with no other cause than its name, with no other identity than its form."

References: Guardian p16 Mr 2 '74 por; *Who's Who in France, 1971-72; World Authors: 1950-1970* (1975)

Belli, Melvin M(ouron)

July 29, 1907- Lawyer; writer. Address: b. Belli Building, 722 Montgomery St., San Francisco, Calif. 94133; 6330 Wilshire Blvd., Beverly Hills, Calif. 90048

Silver-haired, silver-tongued Melvin M. Belli, the headline-making San Francisco trial lawyer with a flair for showmanship, whose name appears on the doors of legal offices in Los Angeles, Washington, D.C., New York City, Munich, and Tokyo, has spent nearly half a century devotedly and energetically practising criminal and civil law. Best known as a tort lawyer specializing in malpractice and negligence litigations, Belli pioneered in the use of "demonstrative evidence" in civil cases. With his uncommon blend of legal and medical knowledge, he has earned millions of dollars in damages for his clients. His trailblazing work in the application of warranty law in the 1940's and 1950's set the stage for the consumer and environmental class-action suits of the 1970's. Among his criminal cases, he is best remembered for his defense of Jack Ruby, the man who shot and killed Lee Harvey Oswald while millions watched on television.

Melvin Mouron Belli, the son of Caesar Arthur Belli, a banker, and Leonie (Mouron)

Belli was born on July 29, 1907 in Sonora, California, where his Swiss grandfather had settled in 1880's. An only child in what he has since described as a "usually silent household," Belli credits his maternal grandmother, Anna

Mouron, "a salty, earthy woman" who was the first female pharmacist in California, with instilling in him, as he put it, "what free spirit I have." As a boy, he haunted her Rexall Union drugstore, fascinated by her collection of porcelain apothecary jars with mysterious names and even more mysterious contents, by the surgical instruments that had belonged to his grandfather, a physician and surgeon, and especially by the human skeleton ensconced beneath the stairs. He was bored by his school lessons, but he enjoyed reading encyclopedias, like *The Book of Knowledge,* Edgar Rice Burroughs' Martian stories, and the novels of Robert Louis Stevenson.

When Belli was a teenager, he moved with his family to the outskirts of Stockton, California, where his father had purchased a fruit farm. It was in a Stockton High School public-speaking class that he discovered his oratorical talents. After addressing his fellow students for the first time—a delightful experience he later likened to "swimming in a pool of warm oil"—Belli joined the debating team. His other extracurricular activities included serving as sports editor of *The Guard and Tackle,* the school newspaper, and taking the role of the flashy movie director in the senior class production of the John Emerson-Anita Loos play, *The Whole Town's Talking.*

Suspended from school just two weeks short of graduation after having been caught at a boisterous beer party in the school newspaper office, Belli had his "first personal experience with The Law" when his father decided to sue the school principal for the boy's diploma. Belli described the incident in his no-holds-barred autobiography *Melvin Belli; My Life On Trial* (Morrow, 1976). "[Judge Rutherford] hauled out [of his rolltop desk] a couple of writs, a replevin, a bench warrant, a subpoena duces tecum, a habeas corpus, a habeas diplomam, and a handful of old bail bonds. He stuck them all together with notary public seals and a red ribbon, put on his W. C. Fields top hat . . . and served the whole thing on the principal. I got my diploma on the spot." Although he still recalls the episode as "the most majestic legal encounter in my entire life," Belli insists that it was not the reason he decided to become a lawyer. "I can remember, even as a child, that I already knew I'd be a lawyer someday," he wrote in his autobiography. "There was no particular trial lawyer or trial that inspired me, just the profession of lawyering itself."

Following his unorthodox graduation from high school in 1925, Belli enrolled at the University of California at Berkeley, where he led a "carefree, floating-in-the-stream existence." To earn extra money, he took a variety of odd jobs, and even went so far as to perform outrageous stunts, such as eating moths and "streaking," to entertain prospective fraternity pledges. He received his B. A. degree in June 1929, then, eager for adventure, worked his way to Europe on a freighter. Returning to California several months later, he took a job as a board marker in a San Francisco brokerage office, where he stayed until the stock market crash in October. Since it was too late in the semester to enter law school, Belli took a job as an ordinary seaman with the Dollar Steamship Lines and shipped out for the Orient

In the fall of 1930 Belli enrolled at Boalt Hall, the University of California's prestigious law school. He had been only an average student as an undergraduate, but he worked hard at Boalt and graduated thirteenth in his class of 150. He received his LL.B. degree in the spring of 1933, in the depths of the Depression, when few law firms were hiring. Taken on as an undercover investigator for the federal government's National Recovery Administration, Belli posed as a hobo and rode the rails for the next several months. "Moving out and about then [with the Okies], riding in and on and underneath freight cars, 'bumming,' standing in soup lines, sleeping in skid-row 'jungles,' I don't know how many times I got thrown out of different towns in the Southwest," Belli told Alex Haley, who interviewed him for *Playboy* magazine, "but I know that's when I developed my deep strong sympathy for the underdog and the outcast." His shocking report served as the basis for a migrant worker relief program.

As a tyro in search of a practice, Belli went to great lengths to attract attention. He held his first press conference in 1936, sitting on a campstool behind an orange-crate desk in a makeshift San Francisco office rented from the California Racing Board. He had just persuaded British Foreign Secretary Anthony Eden to make a trans-Atlantic phone call in behalf of his client, a British subject involved in a San Quentin prison break. The man was convicted and executed, nonetheless, and, as Belli, who had been advising condemned prisoners free of charge at the urging of the Catholic chaplain, Father George O'Meara, later remarked wryly, "I had my *whole* practice wiped out." He had a bit more success when he convinced prosecutors to halve the sentence of Frank Avilez, the infamous "Black-Gloved Rapist," from 440 to 220 years.

Before turning his attention to civil law, however, Belli discovered by chance an effective new way to use demonstrative evidence. In the midst of a criminal case in which he was trying to prove that Ernie Smith, a black inmate of San Quentin who was accused of murdering another prisoner, had acted in self-defense, he accidentally dropped a drawer full of knives and assorted weapons confiscated from the other convicts on the floor. Shocked, the jury acquitted Smith. "I had learned," Belli said later, "that jurors learn through *all* their senses, and if you can tell them and show them, too, let them see and feel and even taste or smell the evidence, then you will reach the jury."

With the vivid impacts of his often startling exhibits, Belli brought more drama into the courtroom in civil actions, particularly those involving personal injury, than any other lawyer. For example, in the case of an injured cablecar motorman, not only did Belli haul into the courtroom a huge mockup of the Powell and O'Farrell Streets intersection, cable cars included, but he also set up a blackboard to help the jury compute the damages. The $31,883.25 award to the victim was, in Belli's words, "a big award" for 1938. Two years later, in court in behalf of Katherine Jeffers, a young woman who had lost her leg in a street-car accident, he studiously ignored for days a tantalizing package wrapped in butcher's paper, then slowly unwrapped it, and dropped his client's artificial leg into a surprised juror's lap. Miss Jeffers was awarded $100,000. A giant six-by-eight-foot aerial photograph, on which each of thirty-five witnesses pinpointed his precise location when he heard the siren supposedly unheard by the truck driver who rammed into the fire engine, severely injuring several firemen, was the potent device that caused the jury to vote the largest award in a personal-injury suit to that date—$225,000—to one of the firemen.

Belli, whose fees were customarily one-third of the award, and nothing at all if he lost, exulted in his victories, many of which were based on precedents he had himself created. "It was like hitting a seven at the crap tables in Harrah's Club in Reno and letting my winnings ride while I threw another seven," he declared. "And I felt good because I had elevated the injured little guy to the economic level of stocks and bonds, a prize Hereford, a yacht, old paintings and prized violins." He ducked the occasional brickbats hurled his way by disgruntled insurance companies and decided "to enjoy the love and affection the world bestows on winners." In trying to "look the part," he hired tailors to do "variations on the standard lawyer's charcoal gray. They made me suits with a slightly rakish Western cut, all the jackets lined in red silk, high slash pockets on the trousers, no pleats and spare all the way down to my . . . calf-high black boots molded from a plaster cast of my foot by Peal's of London."

As his reputation grew, Belli zealously spread his gospel of "adequate" awards based on demonstrative evidence in lectures, seminars, journal articles, and books. A 1951 lecture tour that imparted his strategies to some thirty-five bar associations and law schools was followed by the first of the annual one-day Belli seminars. Those popular seminars were an outgrowth of the rap sessions at the annual conventions of the antiestablishment National Association of Claimants Compensation Attorneys, over which Belli presided for several years.

A prolific writer, Belli edited the series Trial and Tort Trends (1951-1966), wrote Modern Trials (Bobbs, 1954), a study of personal injury cases, the three-volume Modern Damages (1959-63), and Ready for the Plaintiff! A Story of Personal Injury Law (Holt, 1956), a handbook for the general public. Combining his love of travel and the law, he published Belli Looks at Life and Law in Japan (Bobbs, 1961) and Belli Looks at Life and Law in Russia (Bobbs, 1964).

Belli was crowned the "King of Torts" by journalist Robert Wallace for a Life magazine profile in 1954, but he drew even more press attention when, in 1955, he successfully sued on behalf of seventy-nine persons who had contracted polio from a defective batch of polio vaccine produced by Cutter Laboratories. In that and other pilot cases in the 1950's, Belli broadened the principle of absolute liability that he had first demonstrated in the Escola v. Coca-Cola case in 1944. In that precedent-setting decision, the California Supreme Court ruled that the plaintiff need not prove negligence because of the res ipsa loquitur doctrine (literally, the thing speaks for itself). Thus, the long-standing doctrine of privity—that is, the assumption of an implied contract between industry and the consumer—was overturned. "If there is one legal decision upon which Ralph Nader built, this is it!" he boasted in his autobiography, not without some justification. Since the 1960's Belli has been trying, in many litigations, to apply the warranty principle, which holds that manufacturers must stand behind their products, to cigarettes and cancer. Belli charted the growing legal trend to change social policy by litigation in The Law Revolt; A Summary of Trends in Modern Criminal and Civil Law, published in 1968 by the Trial Lawyers Service Company.

At the crest of his career, Belli agreed to defend Jack Ruby for the murder, before live television cameras, of Lee Harvey Oswald, President John F. Kennedy's suspected assassin, in the basement of the Dallas, Texas city jail on November 24, 1963. After an unsuccessful attempt for a change of venue, Belli built his defense on the contention that Ruby had shot Oswald during "some kind of blackout" caused by psychomotor epilepsy and was, therefore, not guilty by reason of temporary insanity. Harold Scarlett described Belli's summation to the jury in an article for the Houston Post: "[Belli] ranged over a lifetime of learning. Like a mountain goat, he leaped unerringly from Pasteur to the hunchback of Notre Dame, to Anatole France and 'Penguin Island,' to Humpty Dumpty, to President Kennedy. . . . Gifted by nature with a velvety, hypnotic voice that could charm cobras out of their baskets . . . , he played that voice like a symphony. It was by turns a Stradivarius, a bugle, an oboe, a snare-drum racing at breakneck speed through the key pages of the trial testimony."

When the jury returned a guilty verdict, an angry Belli told reporters that the decision represented "a victory for bigotry." He added that Judge Joe B. Brown, in presiding over that "kangaroo court," had committed "thirty errors" and had gone "down the line for every motion the district attorney made." Belli made a strong case for the violation of Jack Ruby's rights under Texas law in *Dallas Justice; The Real Story of Jack Ruby and His Trial* (McKay, 1964), which he wrote with Maurice C. Carroll, a reporter who covered the trial for the New York *Herald Tribune*.

The enormous national publicity accorded Belli for his part in the sensational Ruby trial made him a full-fledged celebrity. He appeared as himself in the motion picture *Wild in the Streets* (American International, 1968), a satirical melodrama about a youth takeover of the United States, and he had a cameo role in *Gimme Shelter* (Cinema V, 1970), a film record of the Rolling Stones' American tour. He and his young son, Caesar, appeared in an episode of *Star Trek*, the popular science fiction television series, and he played a big-time defense lawyer on the short-lived CBS-TV series, *Arnie*.

In the courtroom Belli continued to star in colorful or bizarre civil and criminal cases. He defended the civil rights of topless waitresses, the Berkeley "free-speech" demonstrators, racketeer Mickey Cohen, avant-garde comedian Lenny Bruce, and Winnie Ruth Judd, the convicted trunk murderess who had disappeared from the Arizona State Hospital after having served some thirty years of her term. (He got her sentence commuted to time served.) In a corollary to the long drawn-out case of the so-called "Soledad Brothers," he filed a civil suit on behalf of the relatives and fellow inmates of three black convicts who had been shot to death by a white prison guard in 1970. The favorable decision by an all-white jury marked the first time that a guard had been successfully sued for violating a prisoner's constitutional rights.

Belli has always welcomed medical malpractice litigations as a way of "[putting] the fear of God in some of the unqualified men in medicine." He has, over the years, represented a victim of a botched sex-change operation, a fourteen-year-old girl permanently blinded during her hospital stay, and two teen-aged black girls who were sterilized without authorization. He recently filed a $2 million suit against thirteen insurance companies for allegedly threatening and intimidating doctors who had been called to testify in malpractice trials. "I didn't personally invent malpractice," he reminded Digby Diehl in an interview reprinted in Diehl's book, *Supertalk* (1974). "It is the result of irresponsible bums practising medicine who really don't know what they're doing and leave human wrecks around. . . . Juries are beginning to realize that there's no limit on the value of human life. Maybe doctors will begin to respect the same principle."

In an epilogue to *My Life on Trial*, Belli advocated prepaid legal care in order "to make due process available to *everyone*." He comments: "Increasingly, I see good law and good lawyering working to the benefit of all the people, thus protecting the people from the lawlessness of big business and big government. . . . For every injury and injustice, there is a remedy in the law. Or ought to be." Belli has occasionally resorted to such a remedy in his own highly publicized run-ins with the legal establishment. He has been feuding with the American Bar Association for years and in 1972 filed a $2 million class-action suit against the publishers of the Martindale-Hubbard *Law Directory* on behalf of the non-rated lawyers listed in the directory. Himself non-rated, Belli contended that the directory's ratings system created "a self-perpetuating trust" that favored "a small, silk-stocking, knickerbocker, split-fee club of inept commercial lawyers" and discriminated against "far more capable young lawyers who are not yet involved with the Establishment."

Among the honors that Belli has received are the J.D. degree from New England School of Law and the decoration of the St. Brigidian Order. He belongs to many professional organizations, including the International Academy of Trial Lawyers, of which he is a fellow, director, and former dean.

Melvin M. Belli has changed little since Jack Smith of the Los Angeles *Times* described him in 1963 as "handsome, tending slightly to portliness, with wavy, silver-gray hair and gray eyes that seem gentle but can bear down on a hostile witness like Gatling guns." Energetic and ebullient, he thrives on work and puts in long hours at his opulent Victorian office, which some visitors have compared to "a gold-rush whorehouse," but which Belli describes as "a museum of my life and travels." When he does take time off, he is most likely to be found puttering in the garden of his home in the Pacific Heights section of San Francisco, California.

In his autobiography, Belli, whose annual income is in six figures, admits to "a penchant for all good things bright and beautiful, kinky and flawed, for good wines, great tables, wide travels and beautiful women." He and his fifth wife, the former Lia Triff, were married on June 3, 1972. They have one daughter, Melia. He has five children—Richard R., Melvin Mouron, Jean, Susan, and Caesar Melvin—from his earlier marriages.

References: L A Times F p1+ Jl 28 '63 por; Life 37:71+ O 18 '54 pors; Sat Eve Post 237:28+ F 8 '64 pors; Times 73:23 Ja 26 '59 por, 82:48 D 20 '63 pors; Washington Post K p7 N 7 '76 pors; Playboy. Playboy Interviews (1967); Sheresky, Norman. On Trial (1977); Wallace, Robert. Life and Limb (1955); Who's Who in America, 1978-79

Berganza, Teresa (ber-gän'thä)

Mar. 16, 1935- Singer. Address: b. c/o
Vitoria/F. Keller, Alcalá 30-5 o, Madrid 14,
Spain; h. Gaztambide 26, Madrid 15, Spain

The beguiling Spanish opera and concert singer Teresa Berganza is a soprano after Rossini's heart, a shining example of that rare species, the mezzo-coloratura. With her magnetic presence, her combination of warm, velvety tone with cool, impeccable technique, and her buoyant, seemingly effortless delivery, Miss Berganza has been captivating international audiences since 1957. As a recitalist she has a repertory ranging from Spanish arias to German *lieder* and French and Italian art songs, and as an opera diva she is best known for her ability to sing such florid roles as Rosina in the *The Barber of Seville* and Cinderella in *La Cenerentola* as Rossini wrote them, in the mezzo register, midway between ordinary soprano and contralto. "This is a voice of haunting timbre," the critic Louis Biancolli wrote when Miss Berganza made her New York City debut in 1962, "pliant and mellow . . . resonant and carrying, even on the slightest breath," and Eric Salzman once tried to sum up her artistry in eleven words: "Overwhelming perfection that is intelligent [and] pure, yet rich, warm, and expressive."

Teresa Berganza was born on March 16, 1935 in Madrid, Spain to Guillermo Berganza, an accountant, and Ascensión (Vargas) Berganza. She has a brother and a sister, namesakes of their parents. Miss Berganza was musically inclined from childhood, but her original aspiration was to become a nun, and with that in mind she entered the Conservatory of Music in Madrid to study piano and organ, instruments that might be useful to a religious schoolteacher or a church or convent choir leader. Three factors made her change her mind about her vocation: her voice teacher at the conservatory, Lola Rodríguez Aragón, among others, encouraged her to pursue a singing career; the encouragement was reinforced by her winning first prize in voice at the conservatory as well as the Premio Grande de Lucrezia Arana; and she met Félix Lavilla, a fellow student of piano at the conservatory, who became her husband and accompanist.

Miss Berganza made her professional debut at the Athenaeum in Madrid in 1955. Reluctant to travel abroad, she might never have embarked on her international career were it not for the persistence of Gabriel Dussurget, the director of the Aix-en-Provence (France) Festival, who finally offered to arrange her air passage to Paris for an audition. As she later told an interviewer for the French review *Musica* (July-August 1965): "The airplane ticket was the magic word. I had never flown, and I wanted like crazy to see what it was like: that was what decided me."

After her successful audition with Dussurget in Paris, Miss Berganza sang at the Maggio Musicale in Florence, Italy, in June 1957, and the following month she made her Aix debut as Dorabella in *Così fan tutte*. In 1958 she made her first appearance at the Teatro alla Scala in Milan, Italy, singing Isolier in Rossini's *Le Comte Ory*, and in Glyndebourne, England, singing Cherubino in Mozart's *The Marriage of Figaro*.

Also in 1958 Miss Berganza made her American debut with the Dallas Civic Opera as Neris in Cherubini's *Medea* and as Isabella in Rossini's *L'Italiana in Algeri*. Reviewing the latter in the Dallas *Morning News* (November 5, 1958), John Rosenfield described Miss Berganza as "a pint-sized soubrette with legitimate claims to piquancy and grace [and] a spontaneous and coquettish humor."

When Miss Berganza returned to Glyndebourne in 1959 in the title role of Rossini's *La Cenerentola*, Noel Goodwin, the music critic of the London *Daily Express*, serving as correspondent for the New York *Herald Tribune* (August 16, 1959), recalled seeing her the year before, "a slim, small figure with features that Goya or Velásquez might have painted [singing] 'Non si più' with dazzling artistry." Goodwin went on to say of her Cinderella: "Her voice is flawlessly right and vivid throughout a wide range, with that dark-hued southern bite so characteristic of her race and an amazing agility."

In 1960 Miss Berganza made her first appearance at the Royal Opera House in Covent Garden, London as Rosina in a production of *The Barber of Seville* directed by Carlo Maria Giulini, and the next year she performed at La Piccola Scala as the Queen in *Orontea*. The singer, who was pregnant at the time of her performance in Milan, was quoted in *Time* (June 23, 1961): "I have much less stage fright with baby in me, because I think of him and not the audience. I took care not to push my high notes, because too much diaphragm might bump him on the head. He was quiet while I was singing, but as soon as I stopped he started to applaud with his feet."

"She is of the operatic elect . . . ," Louis Biancolli wrote in the New York *World-Telegram and Sun* (April 11, 1962) after witnessing Miss Berganza's New York debut with the American Opera Society in a concert performance of *La Cenerentola* at Carnegie Hall. "Her warm, limpid singing was like a jewel embedded in the gold of a surrounding performance that was brilliant from every point of view." What impressed Biancolli even more than "the soft beauty of the voice and the miracle of skill that coped with the sternest florid hurdles with ease" was "the absolute naturalness" of her performance. "For all the rigors of the music and the throng hanging on every note, she might have been in her own home, so relaxed was she at every moment. She is both a born singer and a made artist."

In the New York *Times* of the same day, Harold C. Schonberg compared Miss Berganza to the immortal mezzo Conchita Supervia: "If she does not have Supervia's temperament, she brings several other things —musicianship, care in phrase, sensitivity, and taste. She is an artist, and a modest one. She is also a most handsome woman, who carried herself with grace and dignity. Her voice has an attractive, slightly husky timbre, and she handles it like a first-class technician."

Later in 1962 Miss Berganza made her New York recital debut in a program of French, Italian, and Spanish songs at the Metropolitan Museum of Art with her husband, Félix Lavilla, at the piano. On that occasion John Gruen wrote in the New York *Herald Tribune* (November 19, 1962): "Miss Berganza's recital was of such staggering beauty and refinement, of such incredible accomplishment that one's objectivity dims before the dazzling impact of her artistry. To start with, she confronts her audience with that typically Spanish blend of pride, modesty, dignity, and reserve, beneath which flows an intense and fiery passion. In singing she can move from moments of the most intimate tenderness to a most fearful hatred and rage. . . . Technically, she works miracles in phrasing. . . . Each [song was] approached from within, each unfolded with the subtlety of implication rather than the more tempting lures of overstatement." Gruen likened her voice, with its "sinuous, reed-like flexibility," to a woodwind instrument. "It need not be employed with extroverted bravura because it is so well placed and so well focused that everything carries through a minimum of effort."

The reception given Miss Berganza when she made her first professional appearance in Washington, D.C. was "tumultuous," as Paul Hume reported in the Washington *Post* (January 4, 1965). Of the program of songs by Debussy, Milhaud, Poulenc, and others that she gave at Constitution Hall, Hume wrote: "No recording or broadcast can suggest the quiet beauty that flows from the circle in which she stands. And how can anything but her actual presence convey the true ring of the unending nuances that constantly color her voice in mezzo-tints of iridescent hues."

Later in 1965 Miss Berganza gave a recital consisting of Italian arias, Mussorgsky's "Nursery Songs," and Spanish art songs at the Metropolitan Museum. Eric Salzman of the New York *Herald Tribune* (November 29, 1965) was swept off his feet but forced himself, he said, to eschew a "love letter" and stick to a catalog of the "hard facts": "purity of tone; a light, crystalline beauty of mezzo sound; total, dead-center accuracy. . . ; light, firm vocal agility and extraordinary control; [a] long, overwhelming, breath-taking pianissimo [which] suddenly opened out to a glorious full sound; absolute equality of tone color and dynamic in every register." Following that catalog of Miss Berganza's virtues, Salzman wrote: "Miss Berganza demonstrated that it is possible to have enormous personality, presence, and projection without a wink, a sob, or a shout. . . . Without a single wring or tear, our hearts were broken."

New York City music lovers, already enamored of Miss Berganza as a concert singer and recitalist, took her more than ever to their hearts when she made her debut with the Metropolitan Opera as Cherubino on October 11, 1967. When she sang Rosina with the Met the following year, Raymond Ericson observed in the New York *Times* (November 8, 1968): "She is certainly the most charming Rosina at the Met since her compatriot Victoria de los Angeles. Like her, she sings the music in a low key, which makes it much more appealing to the ear than the constant chirping of coloratura sopranos one is usually subjected to." Reviewing a Carnegie Hall recital by Miss Berganza for the same newspaper three days later, Donal Henahan noted that "hers is a basically small voice that loses beauty when pushed" but "her artistry is not to be denied, and was at its glorious best in her first encore, Montsalvatge's 'Lullaby to a Negrito,' which she crooned as only she knows how."

A devoted mother who begrudged the time spent away from her growing family, Miss Berganza in the early 1970's reduced her international schedule, seldom venturing beyond Great Britain, where she performed at the Edinburgh Festival, at Harrogate, and at Covent Garden. Listening to her in a recital at Covent Garden, Stephen Walsh of the London *Observer* (February 9, 1975) noticed that while the extreme ends of her voice are "of exquisite quality and perfectly controlled," she uses them rather sparingly, and he concluded that most of the important nineteenth century mezzo parts would be physically and stylistically taxing for her. "All the same," he wrote, "a technique sturdy enough to sing Fauré's 'Après un rêve' without any flaw in lyrical continuity isn't to be underrated, while for sheer fusion of method, sensibility, and intelligence Berganza's singing of songs from the Mörike Lieder and *Spanisches Liederbuch* of Wolf was an object lesson."

For many years Miss Berganza turned down all invitations to sing the title role in *Carmen*. When she finally essayed *Carmen* at the 1977 Edinburgh Festival, Andrew Porter in his review in the *New Yorker* (September 26, 1977) observed that "her timbre is not passionate" and while her voice was "exquisitely supple, seductive, and intelligent," it "lacked the power to give full dramatic value to such fortissimo outbursts as 'Jamais Carmen ne cédera!'"

Miss Berganza's recordings on the London label include Isabella in Rossini's *L'Italiana in Algeri*, Ruggiero in Handel's *Alcina*, Jesús Arambarri's *Eight Basque Songs*, and Gerardo Gombau's *Seven Airs of Aragón*. She has made several recordings of the Spanish zarzuela, including Chapí's *La Bruja* (London) and *Zarzuela Arias* (Zambra). The latter, a winner of the Grand Prix du Disque, contained arias by Chueca, Luna, Chapí, and Giménez.

Teresa Berganza is a short, handsome, dark-haired woman described by reporters as having a "Murillo face," a beauty that seems to radiate from within, and a modest, charming manner. She and Félix Lavilla were married on November 30, 1957 and have three children: Teresa, Javier, and Cecilia. They live in Madrid and have a country house in El Escorial, where the singer likes to fish and hunt. She also enjoys going to bullfights, and she reportedly never misses Sunday Mass. Her honors include the title Dame of the Most Noble Order of Isabella the Catholic, conferred on her by the Spanish government.

References: Music and Musicians 8:7 My '60 por; Musical Events 23:10+ My '68 por; Opera 18:192+ Mr '67 por; Opera N 31:16 F 25 '67 por; International Who's Who in Music (1977); Rosenthal, Harold. Great Singers of Today (1966); Rosenthal, Harold, and Warrack, John. Concise Oxford Dictionary of Opera (1972); Who's Who, 1978-79; Who's Who in Opera, 1976

Bilandic, Michael A(nthony)

Feb. 13, 1923- Former Mayor of Chicago.
Address: b. c/o Democratic Party of Cook County, 10 N. La Salle St., Chicago, Ill. 60602

A product of the Cook County Democratic organization that has controlled Chicago's city hall for nearly half a century, Michael A. Bilandic was an unassuming corporate lawyer until Mayor Richard J. Daley persuaded him to run for alderman in 1969. As Daley's confidant and protégé, he accepted increasingly responsible and powerful positions in the City Council over the next few years. In December 1976 Bilandic succeeded to the mayoralty on Daley's death and in the following June was elected to the post in his own right. Bilandic's soft-spoken and low-key political style prompted Mike Royko, an irreverent Chicago newspaper columnist, to dub him "Mayor Bland," but even Royko conceded that Bilandic seemed to be doing "a reasonably good job." Discontent among Chicago's voters, however, surfaced in the February 1979 primary, when Bilandic

was defeated by Jane Byrne, who went on to win the general election against a Republican mayoral candidate in April.

Michael Anthony Bilandic was born on February 13, 1923 in Chicago, Illinois, the son of Matthew and Domenica (Lebedina) Bilandic, Croatian immigrants. He was raised in Bridgeport, an insulated community of white working-class families in southwest Chicago, popularly called "Back of the Yards" because of its proximity to the sprawling stockyards that once were the economic backbone of the area. The Bridgeport district is at the heart of the eleventh ward, the power base of the Irish-American Democratic politicians who have governed Chicago since the early 1930's.

After graduating from Chicago's De La Salle High School, Bilandic went on to college, but his undergraduate education was interrupted in 1942 by World War II. He spent the next four years with the United States Marine Corps in the South Pacific. Discharged with the rank of first lieutenant in 1946, he completed his education, earning a B.S. degree from the University of Notre Dame in 1947 and a J.D. degree from De Paul University in 1948. He was ad-

Michael A. Bilandic

mitted to the bar the following year. For the next twenty-eight years, Bilandic, a corporate law specialist, worked for the same Chicago law firm, most recently known as Anixter, Delaney, Bilandic & Piggott, where he rose from a $25-a-week law clerk to senior partner. From 1964 to 1967 he was a master in chancery for the Cook County Circuit Court, a post roughly equivalent to that of administrative assistant, and from 1965 to 1968 he also served as a special assistant to the Illinois state attorney general.

Bilandic first got involved in local politics because he felt that a lawyer "ought to know what was going on." He canvassed the eleventh ward for his Bridgeport neighbor, Richard J. Daley, then running for his first term as mayor of Chicago, in 1955, and for the next decade, he was an active, if inconspicuous figure in eleventh ward politics. In 1969, at Mayor Daley's invitation, Bilandic declared his candidacy for the post of eleventh ward alderman, and with Daley's unqualified support, easily won the election. He took his seat on the Chicago City Council, and in the following year was named to the Council's powerful finance committee.

As one of the more articulate members of Daley's inner circle, Bilandic was occasionally called upon to speak for the mayor. For instance, at the Democratic National Convention in July 1972, Bilandic stood in for Daley in denouncing the convention's seating of a group of anti-Daley delegates led by William S. Singer, a maverick alderman, and the Reverend

Jesse Jackson. A few weeks later he presented to the public a report outlining the major ordinances enacted during the first sixteen months of Daley's fifth term as proof that the Chicago City Council was, in his words, "the best and most effective legislative body in the country." When some of the mayor's critics complained that the Council acted only at Daley's instigation, Bilandic conceded that most of the important legislation had indeed been suggested by the mayor, but argued that it was part of Daley's "innovative genius that [he] doesn't introduce things unless they are plausible, beneficial, and workable."

In 1974 Bilandic acquired even more power and influence when he was chosen to chair the City Council's committee on environmental control, and in May of that year, Daley himself selected him to succeed Alderman Thomas E. Keane—who had been indicted by a federal grand jury for conspiracy and mail fraud—as chairman of the finance committee. During the four months of relative inactivity that followed his mild stroke in mid-1974, Daley often asked Bilandic to accompany him to political functions and public appearances. Taking a more active role in Council proceedings, Bilandic acted as floor leader for Daley's legislative program and steered a number of the mayor's proposals through the complicated enactment process.

On December 20, 1976 Mayor Daley died of a heart attack, leaving the Cook County Democratic machine in disarray and Chicago's municipal authorities in confusion over the city's vague laws of succession. After a week of backroom political maneuvering, Bilandic emerged as the ideal compromise candidate for the interim post of acting mayor. Preferred by the late mayor's family and staff and by Daley loyalists, Bilandic eventually won the support of Wilson Frost, the black president pro tem of the City Council who withdrew his own name from contention after he failed to receive the expected endorsement of fellow black councilmen. Bilandic's pledge to refrain from entering the then unscheduled special mayoral election to fill the remaining two years of Daley's unexpired term brought him additional backing from moderate political and ethnic groups and on December 28, 1976, Michael Bilandic was chosen acting mayor of Chicago by an almost unanimous vote of the City Council.

On January 31, 1978, in a move that generated considerable controversy, the Chicago Democratic Central Committee voted forty-seven to two to slate Bilandic as the organization's candidate in the upcoming special mayoral election. In accepting the committee's designation, Bilandic explained that although he had promised not to become a contender for the mayoralty when he assumed the post of acting mayor, he had decided to enter the race because, as he put it, "every segment of our city has urged me to present myself as a candidate." To the surprise of many veteran political observers, Democratic minority and ethnic leaders abandoned their own candidates to throw their support behind Bilandic, and both business and labor backed his candidacy. Milton Rakove, a professor of political science at the Chicago campus of the University of Illinois and the author of a book about the Daley machine, analyzed Bilandic's peculiar appeal for the *Christian Science Monitor* (February 2, 1977): "He's a workhorse, like Daley. He loves those sixteen-, seventeen-, eighteen-hour workdays. He knows the budget, the business leaders. People forget, only in his later years did Daley acquire charisma. The organization will carry the vote for Bilandic, too."

During the primary campaign Bilandic played up his friendship with Daley and made frequent sentimental references to the departed mayor. He closed one rally by saying, "We're going to show them we're all together and *he'll* be smiling down on each and every one of us." Some of Bilandic's critics protested that he overemphasized the association, even going so far as to imitate Daley's distinctive speech patterns. Concentrating his efforts on the ward heelers and precinct workers who traditionally turn out the Democratic vote in Chicago, Bilandic avoided questioning by reporters and refused to debate any of his five challengers. Like his predecessor, he generally restricted his public appearances to party functions and ethnic gatherings, where he capitalized on his position as an incumbent by pledging to "pursue programs [his] administration [had] already begun—revitalization of Midway Airport, expansion of employment opportunities, and development of the Southwest Economic Corridor."

As expected, Bilandic won the April 19 election, polling 50.4 percent of the some 600,000 votes cast in an unusually light turnout for Chicago, while his nearest competitor, Alderman Roman Pucinski, took a surprising 32 percent. Bilandic did especially well in black areas, where he garnered nearly twice as many votes as Harold Washington, a black state senator, but his relatively weak showing citywide indicated to some political analysts, among them Len O'Connor, that a sizable proportion of Democratic voters was ready to split from the machine's choice. Bilandic's final vote tally was about 9 percentage points less than the total he amassed in the usually accurate pre-election straw poll conducted by the Chicago *Sun-Times*. According to its results, 72 percent of the voters and 82 percent of the Democrats preferred Bilandic to the other candidates because he offered continuity.

During the ensuing general election campaign against Dennis H. Block, the only Republican on the fifty-member Chicago City Council, Bilandic stressed the importance of that continuity in the management of the city's affairs. More open-minded and flexible than Daley, he persuaded the City Council to hire more minority policemen and to create more public service jobs for unemployed Hispanic youths. Moreover, in the first few months of his term as acting mayor, he helped to mediate separate labor disputes involving gravediggers, butchers, and musicians from the orchestra of the Chicago Lyric Opera. But perhaps his biggest coup was the compromise decision on the controversial crosstown expressway that brought to an end fifteen years of haggling and released $1.5 billion of federal money earmarked for highways and mass transit facilities throughout the state. Bilandic and James R. Thompson, Illinois' Republican governor, negotiated an agreement providing funds for the construction of a new downtown subway system as well as for the crosstown expressway and for a statewide rebuilding of roads.

The transportation agreement was an obvious triumph for Bilandic, but on the eve of the election he was faced with the first crisis of his young administration. On June 4, 1977 rioting broke out during Puerto Rican Day festivities in Humboldt Park on the city's northwest side. The fighting, burning, and looting raged for two days. By the time order was restored, three people were dead, 100 more were injured, and 154 were under arrest. After conferring with influential Democrats, Bilandic met at city hall on June 6 with leaders of the local Puerto Rican community to devise methods for dealing with such problems as joblessness, dilapidated housing, inadequate educational facilities, and alleged police harassment in Chicago's rapidly growing Hispanic-American neighborhoods.

The next day, Bilandic easily defeated his Republican opponent, 475,169 to 130,945. His overwhelming victory was muted by the lowest voter turnout in sixty-six years, a fact that prompted Paul Delaney of the New York *Times* (June 9, 1977) to suggest that Bilandic might have to assert himself and possibly change his style in order to be the Democratic nominee for mayor at the next regularly scheduled election in 1979. "I've never been a table pounder, a shouter, or a screamer," Bilandic said, as quoted in the *Guardian* (October 2, 1977). "I've basically been an achiever. . . . In order to do that you don't need to be boisterous."

Eager to attract businessmen and industrial developers to Chicago, Mayor Bilandic supported the newly established Economic Development Commission's repeated attempts to persuade the Ford Motor Company to build a proposed $500,000,000 plant in Chicago. Ford eventually decided to locate in Cincinnati, Ohio, but business leaders interpreted Bilandic's efforts as evidence of his sincere desire to build up the job market in Chicago. To stimulate the local real estate market and entice moderate-income families back into the city, the new mayor approved an innovative plan to sell $100,000,000 in tax-free municipal bonds and use the proceeds to make loans to prospective home buyers at 8 percent interest, thus undercutting conventional loans by 20 percent. Businessmen praised his sophisticated grasp of financial affairs, his decisiveness, and his willingness to seek the advice of specialists.

From Mayor Daley, Bilandic inherited a potentially explosive school desegregation program that took effect in September 1977. Most neighborhoods accepted the limited voluntary plan, which involved the busing of black children from overcrowded inner city schools to underutilized white schools, without incident, but in Bogan Park, a white enclave on the southwest side, angry pickets greeted the arriving black students. Contending that his chief function was "to provide for the safety of all the people involved and not to interfere with the Board of Education's policy-making role," Bilandic steered a cautious middle course. When both sides accused him of a failure of leadership, the mayor publicly defended his refusal to take a personal stand on the issue. "My personal opinion isn't of any great significance," he said, as quoted in the New York *Times* (September 19, 1977). "You get all sorts of opinions on busing. The question is: Does it improve education? Does it help anybody other than the bus companies? It's not a simplistic situation. The educators are studying and analyzing these problems and trying to make a determination. There is not a unanimity of opinion."

Bilandic's fledgling administration weathered the storm of protests over busing only to be faced with allegations of impropriety in the awarding of airport concession contracts. Mike Royko disclosed in the Chicago *Daily News* that two of Daley's former law partners had owned large blocks of stock in Airline Canteen Service, Inc., which had controlled the newsstands and lucrative novelty shop concessions at Chicago's busy O'Hare International Airport since 1962. Despite O'Hare's enormous volume of traffic, Airline Canteen annually reported profits that were substantially lower than those of similar concessions at smaller American airports. Outraged, Bilandic ordered an immediate investigation and an audit of the company's books to discover if Chicago was being illegally deprived of revenues to which it was entitled under the terms of the original concession agreement. When the inquiry was sidetracked by the theft of Airline Canteen's books, Bilandic ended the contract and set up a blue-ribbon panel to choose new concessionaires.

At the same time, Bilandic came under fire from Jane Byrne, the city's commissioner for consumer sales, for allegedly conspiring to raise taxi fares. In an eight-page notarized memorandum to herself written in July 1977 and made public by Walter Jacobson, a WBBM-TV news commentator, the following November, Mrs. Byrne charged that Bilandic, in a "fraudulent and conspiratorial action," had "greased" the way for the 11.86 percent hike in the fare. In a televised interview with Jacobson, Bilandic explained that the increase had been approved after appropriate City Council hearings on the subject and that he had only tried to avert a crippling taxi strike. Both Bilandic and Mrs. Byrne submitted to highly publicized polygraph tests. Bilandic passed easily, but the results of Mrs. Byrne's test, in the words of the examiner, showed an "unexplained emotional response" to one of the questions. The mayor immediately fired Mrs. Byrne and ordered an exhaustive investigation of the affair by a special committee of the City Council. When the committee eventually exonerated Bilandic from any wrongdoing, Mrs. Byrne publicly denounced its verdict as "a whitewash and a coverup" and vowed to challenge Bilandic in the 1979 primary. On February 27 she defeated the incumbent mayor by a margin of 15,000 votes. Her victory was attributed in part to the severity of the winter weather, which triggered an expression of long-standing dissatisfaction with the city's services.

A man of average height and trim build, Michael Bilandic maintains his youthful appearance by working out regularly at a police training gymnasium and by swimming and playing tennis. A serious runner, he jogs daily and in September 1977 took part in the first annual Mayor Daley Marathon. On July 15, 1977 Bilandic married Heather Morgan, then the executive director of the Chicago Council on Fine Arts. Bilandic and his wife live in Bridgeport, next door to his childhood home. They have one son, Michael Morgan Bilandic.

References: Fortune 98:74+ S 1 '78 pors; Guardian p9 O 2 '77; N Y Times A p18 Je 9 '77 por; Who's Who in America, 1978-79

Bliss, Anthony A(ddison)

Apr. 19, 1913- Executive director of the Metropolitan Opera; lawyer. Address: b. Metropolitan City Opera, Lincoln Center, New York City, N.Y. 10023

Plagued by financial problems in an era of soaring costs and the drying up of supplementary funds from private philanthropists and public sources, the Metropolitan Opera of New York, America's premier operatic company, has found fiscal crisis to be a chronic state of existence in recent years. In the hope of alleviating that situation, the directors of the Met, in 1974, appointed Anthony A. Bliss to the newly created post of its executive director. A Wall Street lawyer who has been associated with the Met for nearly thirty years as a board member and as president of the Metropolitan Opera Association during the time

Anthony A. Bliss

when it moved to its present home in Lincoln Center, Bliss seems the perfect choice for the demanding position. He combines a solid understanding of business and financial matters with a genuine love for opera and a personal dedication to the Met that is rooted in his family's history.

Born on April 19, 1913 in New York City, Anthony Addison Bliss is the son of financier Cornelius Newton Bliss, a one-time business partner of J. P. Morgan, and of Zaidee (Cobb) Bliss. He has one brother, Cornelius Newton Bliss Jr., and one sister, Eliza Bliss Parkinson.

As a scion of one of New York's elite old families, long listed in the Social Register and noted for its benefactions in the world of the arts, Anthony Bliss grew up in an ambiance that drew upon a heritage of noblesse oblige in the cultural sphere. His aunt, Lillie P. Bliss, for example, was one of the organizers of the Museum of Modern Art, but the family's paramount concern, for social as well as artistic reasons, was the Metropolitan Opera. Cornelius Bliss had been a Met stockholder and the owner of a box in the fabled Grand Tier, known popularly as the "Diamond Horseshoe," ever since the reorganization following the Opera House fire in 1892. He served as chairman of the Met's board of directors from 1938 to 1946, and was a member of the board from 1932 until his death in 1949.

Raised on the family's Long Island estate, Anthony Bliss attended the Met for the first time at the age of six to hear Caruso. He graduated from the Groton School in Groton, Connecticut in 1932 and then entered Harvard College. After receiving his B.A. degree in 1936, he attended Columbia University Law School for two years and then transferred

to the University of Virginia Law School, from which he received his LL.B. degree in 1940. In 1943 he was admitted to the New York State bar. Meanwhile, in January 1941 he entered the United States Naval Reserve as an ensign, winning an air medal and rising to the rank of lieutenant commander before his discharge in January 1946. He then joined, and ever since has been associated with, the Wall Street law firm of Milbank, Tweed, Hadley, & McCloy.

Because Cornelius Bliss disapproved of father-and-son teams on the board of the Metropolitan Opera Association, Anthony Bliss did not become one of the Met's directors until several months after his father's death in 1949. Thereafter, despite his continuing full-time involvement in his law practice, Bliss spent two or three evenings a week at the Opera House, and often some of his afternoons as well. Immersing himself in even the most mundane details of setting up a production, he proved so apt a pupil that on one occasion in 1954, during a ten-hour union walkout, he was able to fill in as a stagehand for a dress rehearsal of Bellini's Norma.

Like virtually every other reasonably objective appraiser of the old Metropolitan Opera House, constructed in the 1880's, Bliss discovered that the building at 1423 Broadway, occupying most of the block between Thirty-ninth and Fortieth Streets, was irremediably inadequate. To quote Irving Kolodin in The Metropolitan Opera (Knopf 1967), it was "a relic of another day's thinking, no longer suitable for the purpose it served, and vastly more costly to maintain for that reason." Bliss became convinced that the survival of the Met depended upon its finding and moving to a new home, a goal that became the guiding principle of his activities on the board for many years to come.

With a new opera house still only a dream, Bliss and his fellow directors had to concentrate on a matter of much more immediate interest, the Met's persistent money problem, punctuated almost annually by a substantial budgetary deficit. The financial distress of the Met was soon set in high relief as a result of the appointment of Rudolph Bing as general manager in 1950, for the strong-willed Bing, a center of controversy almost from the day of his assuming the post, had a penchant for mounting expensive productions that strained the Met's resources to the limits, while his dealings with performers and theatrical unions, both financial and otherwise, were often abrasive.

During the early years of Bing's tenure the board of directors began to split into pro- and anti-Bing factions, not so much on artistic grounds as over the question of whether the Met could afford to follow the path laid out by its general manager. Bliss was staunchly affiliated with the group, headed by Mrs. August Belmont, that gave Bing the firm backing he required, both by raising ticket prices and by devising new methods of raising funds for the Met. Around 1951, recognizing that he had become the chief spokesman for the new ideas and approaches emanating from its younger members, the board appointed Bliss to its executive committee. Soon after he also became chairman of the Met's television committee and a member of its labor committee.

During the next few years, Bliss and his associates among the board's "young guard" succeeded in convincing the other directors that economic necessity required the Met to find a new home as soon as possible. Various sites and solutions were discussed, none of them satisfactory, and the overall problem became more grave when the New York Philharmonic Orchestra, faced with the proposed (but subsequently not effected) demolition of its base of operations at Carnegie Hall, also found itself in need of a new home.

From the efforts to deal with the combined needs of those two major New York City musical institutions evolved the plan to build a gigantic new cultural center at Lincoln Square on Manhattan's Upper West Side as part of a federally and state-backed urban renewal program. Once proposed, the Lincoln Center idea was endorsed as unquestionably the best solution, and in October 1955, thanks largely to Bliss's efforts, the Met's board of directors voted unanimously to move to the new locale. With that decision made, a sense of anticipatory excitement gripped everyone connected with the Met, especially after Bliss became president of the Metropolitan Opera Association in January 1956. Involving himself wholeheartedly in the task of planning and financing the new house, Bliss went to Europe that spring to study the latest developments in opera construction and design.

Meanwhile, the exigencies of day-to-day operations in the old house remained a primary concern. Exacerbated by Bing's often highhanded manner, strikes and the threat of strikes became an ever-present feature of the Met's daily life, reaching a crescendo, perhaps in August 1961, when Bing, in a confrontation with the union representing the Met orchestra's musicians, arbitrarily canceled the forthcoming season. The season took place after all, however, when the dispute was settled through the intervention of Secretary of Labor Arthur J. Goldberg.

As the chief officer of a group of businessmen primarily concerned with the Met's business affairs, Bliss backed Bing during the labor embroilments. The basis for discord always existed, however, for while the board granted Bing the artistic autonomy he demanded, and willingly limited its role to money matters, the distinction between "artistic" and "financial" was often more apparent than real.

Those sources of potential conflict festered throughout the Bing regime. The Met in that same period, according to Clive Barnes (Opera News, October 1975), was characterized by a "comparatively mediocre" artistic reputation, "both nationally and particularly internationally." It was therefore perhaps inevitable that relations between Bliss and Bing would begin to deteriorate. Other factors contributed as well, among them, according to Harriett Johnson, writing in the New York Post (November 22, 1974), Bing's unresponsiveness to Bliss's ideas for backstage improvements in the new Opera House under construction at Lincoln Center. Some sources also indicate that Bliss and Bing disagreed about the operations of the Met's ballet company and its national operatic company, both of which Bliss had strongly supported as means of earning additional income and building wider interest in the opera's activities.

The published accounts, including both Harriett Johnson's in the Post and Bob Micklin's in Newsday (March 9, 1975), agree that a series of bitter disputes took place between Bliss and Bing, but none of the news reports offered any details. The conflict between the two men was camouflaged for a time by the joy attendant upon the completion of the new opera house and its gala opening on September 16, 1966, but following that event "the feud," in Harriett Johnson's words, "became an open rupture, and Bing was responsible, so the story went, for Bliss's being removed as president of the Met board." Other sources indicate that Bliss's colleagues on the board were dissatisfied with his failure to solve the Met's financial headaches, a view that may be substantiated by the fact that he was replaced as president by George Moore, a banker who previously had served as the Metropolitan's treasurer.

Whatever the reason, Bliss left the presidency of the Metropolitan Opera Association in April 1967, although he remained a member of the board and of the executive committee, and returned to his legal career. His interest in music persisted, however, and in 1970 he became chairman of the board of the Foundation for American Dance, sponsoring organization of the ailing Joffrey Ballet, which he restored to a position of preeminence and economic health through careful fiscal management and such commonsense expedients as reducing the length of its two annual seasons.

The Met's financial and other problems, however, not only persisted in Lincoln Center but became even more serious, and after Bing's departure in the summer of 1972, followed by the premature death in an automobile accident of his successor, Goeran Gentele, it suffered from what was widely regarded as well-meaning but ineffective direction under its new general manager, Schuyler G. Chapin. While the operating costs of the Met increased by quantum leaps during the inflationary 1970's, bringing its annual budget to about $24 million by 1975, income from ticket sales and fund-raising lagged behind. By the mid-1970's the Met had an annual deficit of about $8-9 million each year before contributions. In fact, according to published estimates, it was losing $15,000 on each performance in the new opera house.

On November 21, 1974 the board of directors appointed Bliss to the newly created post of executive director of the Metropolitan Opera, a move that Harold C. Schonberg, in the New York *Times* (December 11, 1974), interpreted as "clearly . . . a vote of no confidence in . . . Chapin." Unlike Bliss's former associations with the Met, all of which were voluntary, the new post was a permanent full-time position, paying a substantial salary. In order to accept it, Bliss became a consulting, rather than a regular, member of his law firm and, in addition, resigned his chairmanship of the board of the Joffrey Ballet.

The new post of executive director, although designed to make it possible to devise and implement solutions to the Met's perennial problems, seemed poorly defined, if not somewhat nebulous, to many observers. That seemed especially the case since Chapin was to remain on as general manager, charged with day-to-day administration of the Met and with responsibility for making "artistic" decisions. Bliss himself insisted that he had no intention of interfering in artistic matters, maintaining that he was unqualified, but he added: "There will be no artistic overrule —unless we can't afford it." The widespread concern, moreover, was not alleviated by the explanation tendered by William Rockefeller, the president of the Metropolitan Opera Association: "To use a business analogy, Mr. Bliss is the operating officer. Mr. Chapin reports to Mr. Bliss. Mr. Bliss reports to me."

Distressed by the Bliss appointment, Hubert Saal wrote in *Newsweek* (December 2, 1974): "Like it or not, Bliss represents a take-over . . . by a highhanded board of directors whose 50 members consist mostly of Wall Street bankers and businessmen with not a single artist among them. . . . Despite Bliss's impressive credentials, this new appointment can't help but be troubling to many who are concerned for the health of America's most prestigious cultural institution." Saal conceded, however, that "Bliss is his own man, and there is no one more devoted to the Met." Saal voiced the hope that Bliss might "yet persuade the board that in the world of art, unlike Wall Street, Mammon is the servant of the muses."

More positive appraisals were forthcoming from many other quarters, however. The general opinion was perhaps best summed up by Clive Barnes in *Opera News* (October 1975): "[Bliss] does know his opera. He is also a good judge of both men and occasion. The board felt that Bliss, with his varied experience and commitments, was just the man to get the company out of its present and varied mess, home and dry, while being dragged— cheerfully, one hopes—into the twentieth century. He was the man not necessarily to inspire but to supervise a new artistic era for the Met, using a velvet hand in a steel glove. Personally, I think the board may just have made the right choice. There were few alternatives."

Some of the uncertainty resulting from Bliss's appointment diminished in 1975, following Chapin's dismissal. For the first time in its history, the Met decided to dispense with a general manager, and artistic direction was vested in James Levine, the principal conductor, with whom Bliss has a good and highly productive working relationship.

Since Bliss shoulders the responsibility for the fiscal well-being of the Metropolitan Opera, he will inevitably be involved in making decisions that have a direct or indirect impact on its artistic policies. But as Clive Barnes pointed out in *Opera News* (October 1975), while he may keep his eye on the ledger in the short term, Bliss knows that the Met's survival in the long run depends on its becoming "the major opera company in the world . . . an artistic treasure that no responsible agency could possibly let die."

A former member of the National Council on the Arts, the National Endowment for the Arts, and the National Opera Institute, Anthony A. Bliss is chairman of the National Corporate Fund for Dance, treasurer of the Allie L. Sylvester Fund, a member of the board of the American Arts Alliance, and a trustee of both the United States Trust Company of New York and the Portledge School in Locust Valley, New York. He belongs to the Association of the Bar of New York City as well as to the American, International, New York State, and Nassau County bar associations. His clubs include the Century Association, the River Club, the Wall Street Club, the Creek Club, the Chesapeake Dog Club, and the Beaver Dam Winter Sports Club.

Anthony Bliss was married for the first time on December 22, 1937 to Barbara Field, the great-granddaughter of the department-store magnate Marshall Field. Following their divorce on December 11, 1941 he married, on June 9, 1942, the actress Mimi Lilygren, better known by her stage name, Jo Ann Sayers, who starred in the original Broadway production of *My Sister Eileen* as well as in such films as *Young Doctor Kildare* and *The Man with Nine Lives*. His second marriage ended in divorce on July 12, 1967, and on July 24, 1967 he married his third wife, Sally Brayley, a former leading dancer with the National Ballet of Canada, the Metropolitan Opera Ballet, the American Ballet Theatre, and the Joffrey Ballet, who is currently the director of Joffrey II. Bliss has a daughter, Barbara Mestre, from his first marriage; a daughter, Eileen (Mrs. Eileen Bliss Andahazy), and two sons, Anthony Addison Jr. and John Wheeler, by the second; and two sons, Mark Brayley and Newton, from his present marriage.

Anthony Bliss, who is almost six feet tall, weighs about 160 pounds, and has brown hair and brown eyes, impressed Clive Barnes as being "lean, elegant, and patrician," and as having "an air of firmness and confidence about him." Tennis, swimming, and observing wildlife are among his favorite recreations. His favorite operas are *Otello*, *Boris Godounov*, and *Tristan and Isolde*.

References: N Y Times p36 O 29 '57 por; Opera News 40:13+ O '75 por; Biographical Encyclopedia and Who's Who of the American Theatre, 1966; Martindale-Hubbell Law Directory, 1977; Who's Who in America, 1978-79

Bolger, William F(rederick Leonard)

Mar. 13, 1923- Postmaster General of the United States. Address: b. United States Postal Service, 475 L'Enfant Plaza S.W., Washington, D.C. 20260

William F. Bolger, who went to work for the United States Post Office as a clerk way back in 1940, rose up the ranks to become Postmaster General in 1978. As head of the Postal Service—the quasi-private corporation that replaced the United States Post Office Department in 1971, pursuant to the Postal Reorganization Act of 1970—Bolger directs 30,000 post offices and 650,000 employees delivering 92 billion pieces of mail each year. His first year and a half in office was marked by labor disputes, attempts to eliminate large operating deficits, and a growing debate about the proper role of the Postal Service in American society. On the positive side, Bolger has announced that in the fiscal year ending September 30, 1979, the service came up with its first surplus in thirty-two years.

William Frederick Bolger, who is of Irish descent, was born on March 13, 1923 in Waterbury, Connecticut, the son of George Bolger, a mill foreman, and Catherine (Leary) Bolger. He has three brothers and one sister. Orphaned by the age of seventeen, he left home and went to Washington, D.C. after graduating from the Wilby School in Waterbury. "It was 1940 and there just weren't any jobs in Waterbury," he told Jack Severson of the Philadelphia Inquirer (August 31, 1978). "But I knew the government was hiring people."

After a few months clerking at the Federal Bureau of Investigation, Bolger became a finance clerk in the United States Post Office Department, as the mail service was then known. During World War II he was a bombardier with the Eighth Air Force, and after the war he returned to the Post Office Department. He took night courses in accounting at George Washington University until 1949, when he dropped out just a few credit hours short of a degree.

Bolger worked in a variety of clerical and administrative positions at Post Office Department headquarters until 1955, when he became administrative assistant to the district manager for Maine, an assignment in which he gained invaluable experience with small post office and rural delivery activities. From June 1956 to August 1957 he was assistant district manager for the state of New Hampshire. At the New England regional headquarters in Boston from 1957 to 1971, Bolger held a series of posts of increasing responsibility, culminating in the position of regional director.

In 1970 Congress passed the Postal Reorganization Act, which abolished the Post Office Department and established the Postal Service, an independent agency run by an eleven-person board of governors appointed by the President. The reorganization was designed to depoliticize postal operations and put them on a business-like basis. The act called for a gradual annual decrease in the federal subsidy for the mail service, with the eventual goal of putting the Postal Service on a self-supporting basis.

When the reorganization went into effect, on July 1, 1971, Bolger became manager of the Boston metropolitan area. In August 1972 he was transferred to Philadelphia as acting assistant Postmaster General for mail processing for the Eastern Region, and six months later he went to New York to become Regional Postmaster General, Eastern Region. In July 1973 he became the founding Regional Postmaster General of the Northeast Region, with offices in New York City.

In September 1975 the board of governors of the Postal Service named Bolger deputy Postmaster General, and two and a half years later it elected him to succeed Postmaster General

Benjamin F. Bailar. In announcing the election on March 1, 1978, board chairman M. A. Wright praised Bolger as "truly outstanding" in his day-to-day management of postal operations. Bolger himself held a press conference in which he set forth his agenda. His first priority, he said, was to end high operating deficits by raising the price of postage and cutting costs through tighter management, greater mechanization, and elimination of some services. He promised to be cautious, however, in considering such economy proposals as closing rural post offices and doing away with Saturday deliveries. Regarding the latter proposal, he said he would try "to give the public the facts and let citizens decide if they can forego the sixth day of service."

When Bolger assumed his $66,000-a-year post on March 16, 1978, he became the sixty-fifth Postmaster General of the United States in a line of succession stretching back to Benjamin Franklin in 1775. Two of his predecessors had risen from the postal ranks—the last was Jesse M. Donaldson of the Kansas City Post Office, appointed by President Truman in 1947 —but Bolger's appointment was the first to be made outside the political patronage system.

From the beginning, there was Congressional opposition to Bolger's determination to keep the Postal Service on a course free of political ties and in the direction of financial independence as well. In an attempt to regain the authority over the mail service that it relinquished with the Postal Reorganization Act of 1970, the House of Representatives in April 1978 overwhelmingly passed HR 384-11, a bill that would return to the President the power to appoint the Postmaster General and to Congress the authority to set postal rates and to veto proposed changes in the level of service provided. The sentiment of the House as expressed in HR 384-11 was to eliminate the goal of self-supporting mail operations, to hold rates down and provide still larger federal subsidies to finance the postal deficit, which was already $920,000,000 annually. The House-passed bill failed to win approval in the Senate.

The debate over postal rates and service was spurred by proposals to raise again the cost of a first-class stamp, which had risen from five cents in 1968 to thirteen in 1978. The Postal Service and the Carter Administration proposed retaining the thirteen-cent rate for private letters and raising the fee for first-class business mail to sixteen cents. That proposal was rejected in May 1978 by the independent Postal Rate Commission, which sets rates subject to judicial appeal by the Postal Service. Instead, the commission established a uniform fifteen-cent rate for all first-class letters. It also raised the rates for priority mail and parcel post—a move that threatened to weaken the Postal Service's ability to compete with private carriers. Although unhappy with the decision, the board of governors of the Postal Service accepted the new rates without protest following discussions with Bolger.

Worse trouble loomed on the labor front. When bargaining opened in April 1978 for a new contract for 570,000 postal workers in four major unions, Bolger and his management colleagues sought to remove a clause in the old contract prohibiting layoffs, and, under anti-inflationary pressure from the White House, they also sought to hold any wage increase down to 5.5 percent a year. For their part, the unions demanded job security and wage increases of 7 percent in the first year of the contract and 5 percent in the second, in addition to cost-of-living payments to offset 65 percent of the prevailing inflation rate.

In a tentative agreement reached in July, the no-layoff clause was retained and annual pay and cost-of-living increases totaled 19.5 percent, spread over three years—a very venial breach of the White House anti-inflationary wage-price guidelines. Most union leaders predicted ratification, but the rank and file refused to go along. In defiance of the federal law forbidding strikes by postal employees, several hundred staged wildcat walkouts, and in August the three major postal unions threatened to strike if the Postal Service refused to re-open negotiations. A contingency plan for the delivery of priority mail by federal troops was readied, but the crisis was defused on August 28, when Bolger and the union leaders agreed to a compromise: negotiations would resume under mediation and go into binding arbitration if not settled within fifteen days. When the negotiators failed to come to an agreement, mediator James J. Healy announced on September 13 that he would settle the issues himself. Three days later Healy awarded the postal workers an augmented, automatic cost-of-living increase, balanced by a concession to management—the no-layoff clause would not apply to employees hired in the future. The new settlement was ratified by all postal unions by the end of October. In keeping with the cost-of-living clause, workers are twice a year given pay raises equal to 65 percent of the increase in the consumer price index.

Bolger recognized that the new pact could have serious implications for his efforts to make postal operations self-supporting. In a speech on September 28 he observed that while the wage increase was "definitely not inflationary," the uncapped cost-of-living provision in the settlement opened "a whole new dimension" in Postal Service finances. "If inflation takes off the way it did from 1973 to 1975," he said, "then Katie bar the door." He predicted, however, that postal rates would not go up for two and a half years in the absence of a dramatic increase in the rate of inflation.

Bolger elaborated on the prediction in an interview published in U.S. News and World Report (June 25, 1979): "In spite of inflation, the Postal Service is going to come up with its first surplus in thirty-two years. In the year that ends September 30, we expect to have a 180-million-dollar surplus. We will have a deficit in fiscal 1980 of about a half billion dollars. But even that won't force us to ask for higher rates any sooner than the summer of 1980." It usually takes about ten months to get a decision on a rate hike from the Postal Rate Commission.

In an attempt to recover lost business (parcel post, lost to United Parcel Service and Federal Express) and to prevent further losses, Bolger is trying to streamline the Postal Service to make it more competitive with private firms. The service has expanded its express mail service and offers next-day service in more than 1,000 cities and same-day service at fifty-one airports. It would like to expand its use of electronic mail to include computer-originated and satellite-beamed mail, but public policy questions about competition with the private sector must first be resolved.

The Postal Service has successfully fought competition from private courier services by invoking its legal monopoly on letter mail delivery. Bolger has defended the Postal Service's monopoly on letter mail by pointing to its recently introduced Express Mail Metro Service and noting that the Service must use some of its routes and services to subsidize others. "If private enterprise would provide universal service, I think we *ought* to get out," he told Phyllis Berman of *Forbes* (June 11, 1979). "If anyone had the ability or desire to set up 160,000 routes and 40,000 retail outlets, I'd recommend to Congress that we lock the door to this building [the Postal Service's new headquarters]."

William F. Bolger and Marjorie Tilton, then a postal clerk, were married on December 17, 1949. They have two grown daughters, Catherine and Margaret. A lean man, five feet eleven inches tall and weighing 160 pounds, Bolger has silver hair and bushy eyebrows. "I think he has excellent rapport with all people," a former colleague told Jack Severson of the *Philadelphia Inquirer*. "He has the reputation of being honest in his dealings with everyone." Bolger often arrives at his office at 7:30 A.M. and works late into the evening. For recreation, he reads, swims, plays golf, skis, and does outdoor cooking for small groups of friends. Every summer he vacations on Cape Cod. "I was born in New England," he said when interviewed for the "Man in the News" profile in the New York *Times*, "and I will return there. I like to get up there and get out on that beach. You just prop yourself up and read a good book; there's nothing like it."

References: N Y Daily News p14 Mr 2 '78 por; N Y Times A p16 Mr 2 '78 por; Philadelphia Inquirer C p2 Ag 31 '78 por; Congressional Directory, 1979

Bombeck, Erma

Feb. 21, 1927- Writer. Address: b. c/o Field Newspaper Syndicate, 401 N. Wabash Ave., Chicago, Ill. 00011

For Erma Bombeck, the champion of the suburban housewife and probably America's most popular woman comic writer, humor arises from such mundane matters of everyday life as dealing with housework ("My second favorite household chore is ironing. My first being hitting my head on the top bunk bed until I faint"), teen-agers ("Don't ever say you understand them. It breaks down the hostile relationship between you that it takes to understand one another"), and such deadly contemporary perils as "car-pool crouch" disease. "My type of humor is almost pure identification," Mrs. Bombeck once told a reporter. "A housewife reads my column and says, 'But that's happened to ME! I know just what she's talking about!'" A newspaper reporter before she quit work to care for a husband and three children, Mrs. Bombeck started writing a humor column for beleaguered housewives to exorcise her own case of the suburban torpors in 1964. In 1965 it became syndicated and is today carried in 800 newspapers. She also lectures, appears regularly on the ABC-TV show *Good Morning, America*, and is the author of six books, including *The Grass is Always Greener Over the Septic Tank*, *If Life is a Bowl of Cherries—What Am I Doing in the Pits?*, and *Aunt Erma's Cope Book; How to Get from Monday to Friday . . . in 12 Days*.

The only child of Erma (Haines) and Cassius Fiste, Erma Bombeck was born Erma Louise Fiste on February 21, 1927 in Dayton, Ohio. After the death of her father, who worked as a laborer for the city of Dayton, when Erma was nine years old, her mother went to work at a General Motors factory in Dayton. Mrs. Fiste later was remarried to Tom Harris, also an employee at General Motors. Erma Bombeck has one older half-sister, Thelma Cimprich, who lives in Dayton.

"I knew what I wanted to do from the eighth grade on," Mrs. Bombeck wrote on a questionnaire for Current Biography. "I wanted to write light stuff and read every humorist I could get my hands on." Among the authors that she read were James Thurber, Robert Benchley, H. Allen Smith, and Max Schulman. While attending Patterson Vocational High School in Dayton, she wrote a humor column for the school newspaper. The school program required students to alternate classes with work experience, and Erma Bombeck worked part-time as a secretary for a daily newspaper, the Dayton Journal-Herald. After graduating from high school in 1944, she went to work full-time for the Journal-Herald as a copy girl, but left after a year to attend college. At the University of Dayton she wrote humor for the student newspaper and magazine and majored in English. During her college years she worked at various jobs, including doing public relations work for the local YMCA, editing a shoppers' newspaper, writing a column for a department store house organ, and handling a termite control account for an advertising agency. In 1949 she graduated from college with a B.A. degree.

After college Erma Fiske went back to work for the Dayton Journal-Herald as a reporter. At first she was relegated to writing obituaries and preparing the radio listings, but later she became a feature writer for the women's page. She also wrote a housekeeping column, which she described to Marilyn Goldstein (Newsday, June 5, 1969) as "sort of a sick Heloise." "I told people to clean their johns, lock them up, and send the kids to the gas station at the corner." Meanwhile, on August 13, 1949, Erma Fiske married William Lawrence Bombeck, a former sportswriter for the Journal-Herald. When her first child, Betsy, was born in 1953, Mrs. Bombeck quit work to become a full-time housewife and mother.

"I didn't do anything except blow up sterilizers for ten or eleven years," Mrs. Bombeck has said of the decade she spent at home with her daughter and the two sons that followed, Andrew and Matthew. Finally, in 1964, she had to find out if she could do anything besides take stains out of bibs. "I was thirty-seven," she has recalled, "too old for a paper route, too young for social security, and too tired for an affair." She persuaded a small weekly newspaper outside Dayton, the Kettering-Oakwood Times, to pay her $3.00 a week to write a

humor column on what she calls the "utility-room beat." In 1965 the Dayton Journal-Herald hired her to produce two columns a week, and within a few weeks she was being syndicated by Newsday Specials. In 1970 she moved her thrice-weekly column to the Publishers-Hall Syndicate and later that same year to the Field Newspaper Syndicate.

From the beginning Erma Bombeck's columns have dealt with such prosaic realities of the housewife's world as dirty ovens ("If it won't catch fire today, clean it tomorrow"); daytime naps; sibling rivalry ("Who gets the fruit cocktail with the lone cherry on top"), gardening; and parent-teacher conferences. Like Phyllis Diller's, much of her humor is self-deprecatory ("When I say I'm tense [in a bathing suit] that's the greatest understatement since Noah reported the weather to be a little overcast with light showers"), and most of it is elaborated by exaggeration or, as she put it to Betty Dunn of Life (October 1, 1971), getting "carried away with the absurdity of a situation." "My son came home from a basketball game one night last winter," Mrs. Bombeck told the reporter as an example of how her humor works. "I had made him wear boots and when I asked him if he'd had a good time, he said, 'I was humiliated. Nobody was wearing boots!' I could picture the whole scene: the gymnasium, the screaming crowd, the hush that fell when he walked in. Then a spotlight following him to his seat. Then everybody chanting: 'He is darling, he is cute; he is wearing baby boots!' Then you get carried away even farther—to downtown, going by a store window full of boots, and you think: 'Are you crazy? You'll starve to death! No one will buy them!' I like to get into a little subject like that and just run with it."

In 1967 Mrs. Bombeck published her first book, a selection of her newspaper columns entitled, like the columns themselves, At Wit's End (Doubleday). By the late 1960's she was syndicated in 200 newspapers and in demand for lectures around the country, but she limited the number of engagements she filled so that she could be with her family. Or, as she more picturesquely phrased it, "I can't be gone more than two days because that's all the underwear we have."

In collaboration with cartoonist Bil Keane, Erma Bombeck in 1971 wrote a book about the trials and traumas of living with adolescents entitled Just Wait Till You Have Children of Your Own! (Doubleday). In her next book, I Lost Everything in the Post-Natal Depression (Doubleday, 1973), Mrs. Bombeck introduced chapters with titles like "Put Down Your Brother, You Don't Know Where He's Been," "She Has a Cold. Shoot Her," and "We Have Measles... It Must Be Christmas." "This is no Class A Number 1 out-of-control housewife we have here," wrote Pamela Marsh of the Christian Science Monitor (August 8, 1973), "but a deliberate comic who doesn't place a foot or a word wrong without deliberate intent."

In *The Grass is Always Greener Over the Septic Tank* (McGraw-Hill, 1976), Mrs. Bombeck revealed the truth about the suburbs, a place "where," as her publisher noted, "they planted trees and crabgrass came up, they planted schools and taxes came up, where they died of old age trying to merge onto the freeway, and where they finally got sex out of the schools and back into the gutter." She also introduced her readers to such typical suburban characters as Wanda the school-bus driver, Ralph the Little League coach who played to lose, and the Ten Most Unwanted Women in the Shopping Center Parking Lot. Although her previous books had enjoyed brisk sales, *The Grass is Always Greener Over the Septic Tank* was the first really to take off in a spectacular way. It remained on the best-seller lists for nearly a year and sold over half a million copies in hardcover. "Bombeck's humor is aimed at pointing up the absurdities of the suburban American, middle-class lifestyle, with its trivia, its real or imagined 'necessities,'" wrote J. W. Powell of the *Library Journal* (November 15, 1976), who went on to complain that the author's humor had become diluted by overexposure in newspapers and on television. But H. T. Anderson of *Best Sellers* (January 1977) was rapturous in his praise. "She manages with the deftness of a trapeze artist to come up with a smile on her face in the midst of unaccountable maneuvers," he wrote. "She takes her joy and strength from the things she satirizes—we need more of that!"

With Carol Burnett struggling valiantly as the harried heroine and Charles Grodin trying to do his best as her husband, a made-for-television movie version of *The Grass is Always Greener Over the Septic Tank* was shown in prime time over the CBS network on October 25, 1978. Carol Burnett was Mrs. Bombeck's personal choice for the role of Dorothy Benson, the "very down-to-earth, sane," and "concerned mother" who is the cinematic persona of Erma Bombeck. After watching that two-hour-long, abortive tryout for a possible situation comedy series, the television critic for *Time* (October 30, 1978) expressed the hope that "someone at CBS has the good sense to mow *Grass* down at this early stage."

Erma Bombeck's next book, *If Life is a Bowl of Cherries—What Am I Doing in the Pits?* (McGraw-Hill, 1978), hit the best-seller lists shortly after its publication in the spring of 1978 and remained there throughout the year. Mrs. Bombeck has recently become something of a fixture on television, especially on ABC's *Good Morning, America* where she has been a twice-weekly regular since November 1976. Her column is currently syndicated in 800 newspapers, even more than those that carry the veteran humor columnist Art Buchwald. From 1969 to 1974 Mrs. Bombeck con-

tributed a column to *Good Housekeeping*, and she has written free-lance pieces for such mass circulation magazines as *Reader's Digest*, *Family Circle*, *Redbook*, and *McCall's*. Her solitary record album is characteristically entitled *The Family that Plays Together... Gets on Each Other's Nerves.*

Although she has her own opinions on politics and world affairs, "they're not for the column or the books," Mrs. Bombeck assured Herbert Mitgang of the New York *Times Book Review* (April 23, 1978). "Lots of subjects can't be handled humorously. I stick close to home —I'm still exploiting my children, husband, and family life. I know what my domain is." Yet there are moments when the humorist lapses into seriousness. "We scream censorship when there is murder committed before our children's eyes on the tube," she wrote in *I Lost Everything in the Post-Natal Depression*. "We can endure it when it appears on the six o'clock news with a dateline: Vietnam. My children in their short span on earth have seen Watts in flames, mothers with clubs and rocks protesting schools, college students slain by national guardsmen, mass slaughter in California, and political conventions that defy anything they have seen on a movie screen. . . . I challenge you to protect a generation from violence that has seen the horrors of Kent, Dallas, and Attica."

"Art Buchwald and I are wonderful friends," Erma Bombeck told a reporter for *People* (May 22, 1978). "He founded a mythical group called the American Academy of Humor Columnists. It's like the Academy Awards. There are just five of us in it and we're going to meet once a year and give each other ten awards each." Mrs. Bombeck's real-life awards have included the National Headliner prize of Theta Sigma Phi, the professional society for women in journalism and communications, in 1969, and the Mark Twain award for humor. She has received honorary doctorates from Scholastica College in Duluth, Minnesota, Rosary College in Chicago, and Bowling Green University in Ohio. Mrs. Bombeck is a member of Theta Sigma Phi, Sigma Delta Xi, and Women in Communications, and in 1978 she was appointed to the President's National Advisory Committee for Women.

When Erma Bombeck first began writing her column, she worked in the morning, tapping out her copy on a typewriter that was propped on the edge of a bed in her Dayton home. Now she works from 9 until 3 each day in an office that was once the garage of her nine-room ranch-style house in a suburb of Phoenix, Arizona, where the Bombecks moved in 1971. A twenty-minute nap each afternoon helps Mrs. Bombeck to keep up with her busy schedule. For many years an administrator in the Dayton public school system, her husband is now a high school principal in Phoenix. Her two older children, Betsy and Andy, live in Phoenix, while Matt is going to college in California.

Mrs. Bombeck, who is a Roman Catholic and a Democrat, has green eyes and hair that she described for *Current Biography* as "light brown (subject to change)." She is five feet two inches tall and weighs 125 pounds. "Erma Bombeck looks the way she writes: short, good-humored, somehow expectant—as if she's waiting for a pot to boil over," reported Diane K. Shah in *Newsweek* (January 2, 1978). "And for all her success [she now earns $500,000 a year]—and an occasional ultrasuede dress—Bombeck still prides herself on being Justa Housewife, who really still does her own laundry." These days, however, she is helped out by a cleaning woman who comes in twice a week. She also employs a part-time secretary for twelve hours a week to handle her correspondence.

Although she supports the women's movement and the Equal Rights Amendment, Mrs. Bombeck disapproves of the way feminists, in her opinion, have neglected housewives. "When did a woman selling orange slices in the dime store become more impressive than a woman who did a darned good job raising three kids for twenty years?" she asked in a recent column. In her spare time she plays tennis and devotes time to several charities, including serving on the boards of the Arizona Kidney Foundation and Esperanza. In response to a request for miscellaneous biographical facts, Erma Bombeck wrote for *Current Biography*: "I was against the war... all of them. I was a Girl Scout Captain in the 1960's, but have since retired. Also home room mother, chairman of pillow case bingo, and Dust Anonymous."

References: Biog N 2:489 My/Je '75 pors; Life 71:66+ O 1 '71 pors; N Y Times Bk R p42 A p23 '78 por; Newsday A p2 Mr 20 '69 por, A p 2 Je 5 '69 por; Newsweek 91:60 Ja 2 '78 pors; People 9:30+ My 22 '78 pors; Washington Post D p6 O 19 '66 por; Contemporary Authors 1st rev vols 21-24 (1977); Who's Who in America, 1978-79

Botha, P(ieter) W(illem) (bō'tä)

*Jan. 12, 1916- Prime Minister of South Africa.
Address: b. Office of the Prime Minister,
Pretoria, South Africa; h. P.O. Box 47,
Cape Town, South Africa*

On September 28, 1978 P. W. Botha, a career politician, was elected South Africa's eighth Prime Minister, succeeding John Vorster, after a three-way contest within the ruling National party. As Defense Minister, a post he had occupied since 1966, Botha developed a hard-line military style that conditioned his tough responses to guerrilla attacks in neighboring South West Africa and United Nations proposals for bringing peace to the area. On the other hand, he has taken a decidedly conciliatory approach in the question of race relations, surpassing his predecessors in his willingness to modify South Africa's strict policy of racial separation known as apartheid.

Pieter Willem Botha was born on January 12, 1916 on a farm in the Paul Roux District of the Orange Free State, one of South Africa's four provinces. His father was also named Pieter Willem, and his mother's maiden name was de Wet. Botha graduated from the Voortrekker High School in Bethlehem, near his birthplace, and joined the National party in his teens. He studied law at the University of the Orange Free State at Bloemfontein from 1932 to 1935 but dropped out without graduating, to devote himself to party affairs. At twenty he moved to Cape Province to become a full-time political organizer for the National party. Although his native Orange Free State was considered a stronghold of racial conservatism, Botha seems to have been more influenced by "Cape liberalism," involving a flexible attitude toward the Cape province's substantial "Colored" minority of persons of mixed racial heritage.

During his ten years as a National party organizer, Botha reportedly at times resorted to strong-arm tactics but refrained from the kind of pro-Nazi subversive activity that led to the internment of other Nationalist leaders, including John Vorster, during World War II. His success in the Cape Province led to his appointment in 1946 as public information officer of the National party, responsible for publicity campaigns in all four provinces of South Africa, and in the same year he became first secretary of the Nasionale Jeugbond (National Youth League). In May 1948 Botha was elected to the Parliamentary seat for George, Cape Province, which he still represents, and he played a key role in the defeat of Jan Christiaan Smuts's United party by the Nationalists, who have dominated South African politics ever since. As chief secretary of the National party in the Cape Province from 1948 to 1958, Botha gained a detailed knowledge of politics on the grassroots level.

Botha was appointed deputy minister of the interior by Prime Minister H. F. Verwoerd in October 1958 and attained Cabinet status when he was named Minister of Colored Affairs and Minister of Community Development and Housing in August 1961. In 1964 he became Minister of Public Works as well. His proposals for direct involvement in the central government by Colored South Africans and those of Asian ancestry, under a formula similar to the Swiss canton system, earned him popularity among those minorities, who, unlike members of the black majority, did not have semi-autonomous tribal homelands.

Bypassing several senior ministers, Prime Minister H. F. Verwoerd gave Botha the important position of Defense Minister in April 1966. After Verwoerd was assassinated in September of that year by a white South African whose motives remain obscure, Botha, was considered one of several possible successors to the Prime Ministership. But the post went to the more experienced John Vorster, who had been Minister of Justice in the Verwoerd Cabinet.

Continuing to serve as Defense Minister in the Vorster Cabinet, Botha was also unanimously elected leader of the National party in the Cape Province in November 1966 and became leader of the House of Assembly in the national Parliament in January 1975. As Defense Minister, he instituted voluntary military service for blacks, Coloreds, Asians, and women. He established the Civil Defense College for women and organized the Cape Corps, a crack military unit of Colored South Africans. Botha's toughminded determination to attain military independence for South Africa earned him the nickname "Piet Wapen," or "Pete the Weapon." Aware that national self-reliance was a necessary goal in view of United Nations attempts to alter South Africa's apartheid policy by means of sanctions, Botha increased the defense budget within a decade from about $100,000,000 to nearly $2 billion. In the process, he obtained for South Africa a wide range of sophisticated armaments and instituted a crash program of counterinsurgency training in preparation for possible future attacks from black African nations and the Soviet Union. When, in June 1975, the British government abrogated the 1955 Simonstown naval agreement with South Africa in an effort to repudiate apartheid, Botha called

the cancellation "a challenge rather than a tragedy" and invited friendly nations to use South Africa's naval base facilities.

In August 1975 Botha supervised South Africa's clandestine dispatching of troops to intervene in the civil war in Angola, then in the process of achieving independence from Portugal. The action was originally aimed at protecting the multimillion-dollar Cunene River hydroelectric project, in which South Africa had a major interest. Toward the end of the year South Africa expanded its involvement in Angola by committing its troops to aid pro-Western forces in their efforts to prevent a takeover by leftist guerrillas who were backed by the Soviet Union and Cuba. But, having failed to enlist international support from Western nations, Botha was compelled to withdraw South African forces from Angola in March 1976.

The South African government was especially concerned with maintaining its control over mineral-rich South West Africa, or Namibia, and keeping it out of the hands of the independence-seeking leftist South West Africa People's Organization (SWAPO), which had been staging periodic guerrilla raids on the territory from Angola and neighboring Zambia. A former German colony, South West Africa had been occupied by South Africa during World War I and administered by it under a 1920 League of Nations mandate. Although that mandate was nullified by the United Nations in 1966, South Africa refused to surrender control and extended its security and apartheid laws to the territory in defiance of the United Nations. Responding to continued guerrilla incursions into South West Africa, Botha declared in November 1976 that his government would not allow "murder, chaos, and disorder" to extend into the territory, and that South Africa would "hit back hard" if SWAPO and the newly independent leftist government of Angola were to try to "liberate" the area.

In early 1978 the United States, Great Britain, France, West Germany, and Canada proposed a plan to the United Nations Security Council for bridging the transition from South West Africa to independent Namibia by means of U.N.-supervised one-man, one-vote elections, and the South African government indicated a willingness to go along with the U.N. plan. But in May, Botha ordered what he called a "limited military operation" into Angola in response to alleged SWAPO guerrilla activity, and efforts to resolve the South West Africa problem became stalemated. Botha declared his opposition to the U.N. plan at a congress of the Transvaal National party later that year, charging its proponents with seeking to "establish a Marxist state on the banks of the Orange River" and asserting that the government was not prepared to hand South West Africa over to "Marxist terrorists." Nevertheless, the acceptance of a modified U.N. plan by the

SWAPO leadership in early September seemed to indicate that there was reason to hope for an ultimate solution to the Namibia problem.

On September 20, 1978 Prime Minister Vorster suddenly announced his retirement for reasons of poor health. At the same time he revealed that South Africa would withdraw its earlier assent to the U.N.-supervised independence plan for Namibia. Instead it would hold its own elections in the territory in December, several months ahead of schedule, before SWAPO and the U.N. supervisory force could be ready. The decision, which had reportedly been formulated by Botha, was motivated, according to Vorster, by a fear that the U.N.'s postponement of elections would endanger Namibia's security and by the fact that the details of U.N. supervision during the transition period had been worked out without consulting the South African government. But most Western observers were convinced that South Africa was determined not to relinquish its hold on Namibia and to prevent SWAPO from coming to power.

Following the resignation of Vorster, who then assumed the ceremonial post of national President, the contest for the Prime Ministership became a three-way race between P. W. Botha, Foreign Relations Minister Roelof F. ("Pik") Botha (not a relative), and Minister of Plural Relations Cornelius Petrus ("Connie") Mulder. Although Mulder was the early frontrunner, his reputation had been tarnished by allegations earlier in the year about financial irregularities in the dismantled Department of Information, which he formerly headed. "Pik" Botha, relatively young and a moderate liberal, was the choice of over 80 percent of white South Africans, according to an opinion poll. But the deeply conservative and hierarchy-conscious National party's 172-member caucus on September 28, 1978 selected the most senior Cabinet member, P. W. Botha, who received seventy-eight votes to Mulder's seventy-two after "Pik" Botha withdrew from the race.

In accepting the Prime Ministership, Botha indicated that he would remain Defense Minister within his own Cabinet and promised to "continue the great work" of his predecessor and devote his "life to the achievement of peace." Although he ruled out any abandonment of apartheid, he promised to work toward improvement in race relations, and he asserted that under his administration South Africa would maintain its "strategic position on the Cape sea route." Botha affirmed his government's determination to hold elections in South West Africa in December in defiance of the U.N., but he left the door open for future discussion of the Namibian problem.

In the December 1978 elections in South West Africa, boycotted by SWAPO because they lacked international supervision, the Democratic Turnhalle Alliance (DTA), a conservative multiracial party created and dominated by South Africa, won 82 percent of the popular vote and forty-one of the fifty seats in the new assembly. Although the elections were not internationally recognized, the Botha government's vague promise to consider the U.N. plan for Namibia at some future date averted a confrontation at the same time that it maintained South African control over South West Africa for the time being.

Within the spectrum of National party politics, Botha stands somewhere between the *verkrampte* (ultraconservative) and *verligte* (enlightened) tendencies. His long-standing reputation as a hard-liner, applies more to his views on national defense than on race relations. In the past Botha supported changes in apartheid policy, including desegregation of parks, selected restaurants, and public transportation. In 1974, as head of the Cape Province branch of the National party, he forcefully opposed ultraconservatives in their efforts to prevent integration of a Cape Town theatre complex. Botha also served as chairman of a constitutional committee that in 1977 formulated a plan incorporating some of his earlier recommendations for multiracial government. A constitutional provision along those lines is scheduled to take effect in 1980.

Botha's openness to change is reflected in his November 1978 appointment of Dr. Pieter G. Koornhof, one of the most reform-minded members of the government, as Minister of Plural Relations and Development, following Mulder's resignation. Previously responsible for eliminating racial segregation from most major sports in South Africa, Koornhof won further praise from liberals when shortly after joining the Botha Cabinet he rescinded a government order for demolition of the Crossroads squatters' camp near Cape Town, illegally occupied by some 20,000 blacks. In the spring of 1979 he began to institute multiracial regional advisory commissions to counsel the government on problems faced by black people in urban areas. Botha has also indicated a willingness to consider revisions in the 1936 Land Act, which is the basis of land allocation along racial lines in South Africa. The act, which has always been a fundamental tenet of the National party, allots only 15.4 percent of all land in South Africa to blacks, who make up about 70 percent of the country's population. After holding a series of private meetings with Botha on that and other issues in January 1979, eight of South Africa's elected black "homeland" leaders described the Prime Minister as "open, honest, receptive, flexible," and "a breath of fresh air."

The Prime Minister's reform efforts have at times been inhibited by conservatives within his party. The strongest opposition comes from Andries P. Treurnicht, representing the National party's *verkrampte* faction, who as party leader in the populous Transvaal Province holds a power base in Parliament almost as large as that of the three other provinces combined. Fearing the end of white supremacy,

Treurnicht opposes all concessions to blacks. In deference to Treurnicht's stature within the party, Botha was obliged to appoint him to a Cabinet post when he reshuffled his government in June 1979, but to the dismay of conservative Transvaal Nationalists he presented him with the least sensitive portfolio, that of Public Works, Statistics, and Tourism. As part of his Cabinet reorganization, Botha also ousted the strongly rightwing Minister of Prisons, Police, and Justice, James Kruger, who had been responsible for the government's bloody suppression of the Soweto riots of 1976-77.

Botha's ability to make the changes he desires has also been hampered by allegations of a massive misuse of public funds on the part of top government officials. In late 1978 press reports revealed a secret multimillion-dollar influence-peddling campaign aimed at winning support at home and abroad for South Africa's racial policies. Government funds were reportedly used to establish the Citizen, a pro-apartheid newspaper, and there were indications of secret international operations by South African officials, as well as efforts to cover up the activity. But when Judge Anton Mostert, who had been appointed to conduct an official public inquiry, published documents in early November confirming the reports, Botha dismissed him and created a secret three-man commission headed by Justice R. P. Erasmus.

In its report of April 2, 1979 the Erasmus commission disclosed that several high-ranking members of the Vorster administration had been involved in the scandal, but it cleared Botha, who had declared earlier that he would resign if he or any other member of his Cabinet were implicated. To prevent further public exposures that might prove embarrassing, Botha introduced legislation requiring the government's consent before allegations of official corruption could be published, but strong criticism in the press compelled him to drop it. Nevertheless, despite such problems as unemployment and a housing shortage, especially for blacks, as well as industrial strife, a lack of investment capital, continued skirmishes with SWAPO guerrillas over Namibia, and South Africa's growing isolation on the world scene, Botha appeared to many observers to be firmly in control of his country as of late 1979.

P. W. Botha and Elize Rossouw were married on March 13, 1943. The couple has three daughters, Elanza Maritz, Amelia Paschke, and Rozanne, and two sons, Pieter and Rossouw. Familiarly known by the Afrikaans pronunciation of his first initials, "Peevee" Botha is a tall, bald, and bespectacled man whose mild appearance belies his reputation for hot-tempered emotional outbursts. His honors include the Portuguese Grand Cross of the Military Order of Christ, the State President's Decoration for Meritorious Service, a decoration from

Paraguay, and an honorary doctorate in military science from the University of Stellenbosch. His hobbies include horseback riding, hiking, gardening, and hunting, but according to his wife, "he really hasn't time for anything but politics." Botha tries to live up to the dictum of his favorite historical figure, American Confederate General Thomas J. ("Stonewall") Jackson: "Do your duty and leave the rest to God."

References: Guardian Weekly 117:7 O 8 '78 por; N Y Times A p3 D 12 '78 por; Newsweek 92:58+ O 9 '78 pors; U S News 35:44 O 9 '78 por; International Who's Who, 1978-79; Who's Who of Southern Africa, 1979

Bradshaw, Terry

Sept. 2, 1948- Professional football player. Address: b. c/o Pittsburgh Steelers, 300 Stadium Circle, Pittsburgh, Pa. 15212

The first National Football League quarterback to lead his team to three NFL championships is Terry Bradshaw of the Pittsburgh Steelers, whose most recent Super Bowl victory was over Dallas in January 1979. When the unassuming Bradshaw, former star quarterback at Louisiana Tech, went to Pittsburgh as the number one pro draft choice in 1970, he was, as he recalls, "scared" and "trying too hard." For several years, when he shared quarterbacking duties successively with Terry Hanratty and Joe Gilliam, Bradshaw had the reputation of being "dumb," but in 1974, when he passed Pittsburgh to its first championship season, that reputation began to change, and he is now generally ranked among pro football's top tacticians, especially good at "audibles," or changing plays at scrimmage. He is also one of the NFL's most feared scramblers, and in passing, always his forte, he now ranks near 100 in league ratings, as compared with 55.1 five years ago. Bradshaw and receiver Lynn Swann constitute the league's best passing combination.

Terry Bradshaw was born in Shreveport, Louisiana on September 2, 1948 to William and Novis Bradshaw, God-fearing Southern Baptists who raised their sons accordingly. William Bradshaw, a runaway from a broken home in the Tennessee hills, learned the value of discipline in his rise from odd jobs to plant manager. He therefore ran a strict household, with curfew, regular Bible readings, and prohibitions against smoking and drinking.

With the exception of three years when the Bradshaws lived in Camanche, Iowa, Terry and his older brother, Gary, and younger brother, Craig, grew up in Cedar Grove and Woodlawn, in the Shreveport area. Taken to revival meetings by his mother, Terry was "witnessing" from the age of fifteen. He considered becoming a minister but decided that as a football player he "could reach more people than a preacher because young people look up to and listen to football players."

Bradshaw laughs at the idea that his talent as a passer is "natural," pointing out that he spent years of his boyhood throwing footballs at tires and buckets in his backyard before perfecting his eye and his arm. During his sophomore and junior years at Woodlawn High School he spent most of his time on the bench. Finally becoming starting quarterback in his senior year, he led the Woodlawn team to an 8-1-1 record and the semifinals of the Louisiana high school championship playoffs, in which he passed for 176 yards and two touchdowns and made two more touchdowns on the ground. In high school he also pitched for the baseball team, but it was in track that he was most accomplished, throwing the javelin 244 feet eleven inches, an American high school record.

Many colleges and universities sought Bradshaw for track, but Terry preferred quarterbacking and accepted a football scholarship at Louisiana Tech. In his freshman and sophomore years there he was number two quarterback, behind Phil Robertson. Moving into the starting position in his junior year, he threw for 2,890 yards and twenty-two touchdowns, leading his team to the Gulf States Conference championship and the Grantland Rice Bowl, where it defeated Akron University for the position of best small-college team in the country. In his senior year he passed for more than 2,000 yards, bringing his college totals to 463 completions in 879 attempts for 7,149

yards and forty-two touchdowns. He finished his college career in the Senior Bowl, where he passed for 267 yards and two touchdowns and won the game's Most Valuable Player award.

Chuck Noll, the Pittsburgh Steelers' coach, first saw Bradshaw in live action in practice for the Senior Bowl. "I was really startled," Noll has recounted. "I knew from the films that he had a strong arm, but film doesn't measure intensity. He really winged it in there." According to Pete Retzlaff, the general manager of the Philadelphia Eagles, Noll's reaction was a common one among professionals, even though Bradshaw, as a small-college player ignored in the All-America listings, was little known among lay football fans. "O. J. Simpson might have gotten more publicity last year," Retzlaff said at the time, "but internally, within the league, there's much more talk about Bradshaw."

The Steelers, having finished last in the National Football League with only one win in fourteen starts in 1969, had first choice in the 1970 pro draft, and they chose Bradshaw. Extraordinary feats were expected of him when he arrived in Pittsburgh, and he was too green at the time to handle even the ordinary failures. At first touted as the savior who overnight would turn the perennially losing Steelers into winners, he soon found himself the victim of a less flattering stereotype, that of "Li'l Abner," a big, handsome, slow-witted country bumpkin. "I wanted so bad to make the Steelers a winner," he later said, "so they'd be proud of me. Maybe I wanted it too much, put too much pressure on myself. I made mistakes, plenty of mistakes, and some of them were stupid mistakes. From stupid I went to dumb, and that's the image I've been stuck with."

In his professional debut, Bradshaw replaced Terry Hanratty as quarterback at the beginning of the second half of an exhibition game in Jacksonville, Florida. The curious crowd had been shouting for his appearance, and Bradshaw was so unnerved by the experience that in the initial huddle, after stuttering out the signals, he reportedly vomited on tight end Bob Adams. But he overcame his nervousness sufficiently to lead the team to victory in that game and four subsequent preseason games.

In the 1970 season itself Bradshaw acquitted himself less well, completing only eighty-three of 218 passes for 1,410 yards and a miserable completion percentage of 38.1. "That first year was horrible," he has recounted, as quoted by Phil Musick in Sport (February 1979). "I was so embarrassed, so ashamed. . . . But we won five games and I got some understanding of what was going on, the hardships, the cold truth, the bitterness about this game. I learned that it wasn't rah-rah college anymore. . . . 'If you lose, doggone . . . tough. We'll win next week.' Now it was, 'Hey, you S.O.B., I lost two bucks on you.' "

Bradshaw's quarterbacking was much improved in 1971, when he completed 203 of 373 passes for 2,259 yards and a percentage of 54.4 The Steelers also improved, but only slightly, finishing the season 6-8. The following season, when Bradshaw completed 147 passes out of 308 for 1,887 yards and a percentage of 47.7, the Steelers finally rolled into the winning column with an 11-3 record and their first American Football Conference title.

In 1973 the Steelers again reached the NFL playoffs, but Bradshaw's share in their glory was diminished by a separated shoulder that kept him out of four games and by increasing problems in his first marriage, to Melissa Babish, Miss Teen Age America of 1969. That marriage ended after eighteen months, in 1974. The demoralization Bradshaw felt in his personal life was exacerbated when, in training camp, he was displaced as starting quarterback by Joe Gilliam.

Looking back at his situation in 1974, Bradshaw told Ron Fimrite for *Sports Illustrated* (December 18, 1978): "I'm a Baptist, a Christian. I pulled away from it that year. I felt a lot of guilt over the divorce, and I'd lost my job. I'd failed. I didn't become an alcoholic or a whoremonger, but I was moody and depressed and I drank and hustled women in bars—a total jerk having a ball. I have never enjoyed those things. I'd been a devout Christian for so long, getting away from it affected me mentally. The ton of guilt brought me to my knees. I guess you could say God blitzed me and gave me a shot to the head, and no one threw me a flag."

A rededicated Bradshaw was back in the starting lineup by midseason 1974. His performance was only fair until, following a mediocre game against Houston, the twelfth of the season, he was surprised to be told by Chuck Noll that he would be the starting quarterback from then on, no matter what happened. Responding to the coach's confidence in him, he began playing as he never had before, and the Steelers rallied around him, sweeping the last two games of the season and the playoffs and capturing their first NFL championship with a 16-6 victory over the Minnesota Vikings in Super Bowl IX. The clinching touchdown against Minnesota was accomplished with a four-yard pass by Bradshaw.

"It was as if he had hit rock bottom right before our eyes and pulled himself back up without anybody having to give him a hand," defensive tackle Joe Greene observed. "He convinced us all that he was a man who could accept a man's challenges, a man's ups and downs. When a person changes like that, you just have to have confidence in him." Running back Franco Harris said: "When he matured, we matured. Some people find success right away, others struggle. He struggled and we struggled with him."

Bradshaw and the Steelers maintained their superb level of play throughout the following season, when the team won twelve out of fourteen games as their quarterback completed 165 of 286 throws for 2,055 yards and eighteen touchdowns. Bradshaw was chosen All-Pro for the first time and the Steelers were again victorious in the Super Bowl, over the Dallas Cowboys.

The decisive touchdown in the 21-17 victory over the Cowboys in Super Bowl X came as a result of Bradshaw's alertly anticipating a Dallas safety blitz. At the line of scrimmage he called for a pass to Lynn Swann; he released the ball before the Cowboy line piled on him; and Swann caught the sixty-four-yard pass in open air. Sportswriters observed that it was play-calling as smart as any "intellectual" quarterback, such as Fran Tarkenton or Bob Griese, ever displayed.

The change in Bradshaw was not from "dumb" to "smart," as many viewed it, but from anxious to confident, as Bradshaw saw it. "The secret to playing well, to reading defenses well and calling a good game," he told one reporter, "is simple . . . be relaxed. You have to have confidence in yourself so you can use your ability to its fullest." Coach Noll pointed out that Bradshaw was one of only seven quarterbacks in the NFL who called his own plays. "It's easier for a coach to call all the plays and have the guys react like robots. But we prefer to give the players—and particularly the quarterback—all the information possible and then let them make the difficult decisions," he said. "This takes a long time, and, unfairly, it can lead to a bad rap like the one Terry got."

In 1976, when the Steelers won ten and lost four, Bradshaw was sidelined half the season with injuries. In the games he played, he completed ninety-two out of 192 passes for 1,117 yards and ten touchdowns. Contributing to the respect he was earning from his teammates was his bravery in transcending his painful injuries, including dislocated fingers, a fractured nose, a broken collarbone and ribs, and a torn hip muscle. With his knee so badly sprained that he could barely walk, he gave the best performance of his career up to that time in a divisional playoff victory over Baltimore in December 1976, completing fourteen out of eighteen passes for 264 yards and three touchdowns. "That's the day he finally destroyed all that crap that was written about him," defensive tackle Joe Greene later commented. Another Steeler observed: "We always knew he was tough, but what he did that day went beyond being tough. It was heart."

Playing almost the entire 1977 season with a fractured bone in his left wrist, Bradshaw completed 162 passes out of 314 for 2,523 yards and seventeen touchdowns. Through 1977 his pro career totals in passing were 1,008 completions in 2,019 attempts for a 49.9 percentage, 13,279 yards, ninety-three touchdowns, and 118 interceptions in the regular seasons and 136 completions in 257 attempts for a 52.9 percentage, 1,960 yards, fifteen TD's, and sixteen interceptions in postseason play. Rushing, he gained 1,795 yards in 308 attempts, and scored twenty-seven touchdowns in the regular season and 214 yards in thirty-four attempts and two touchdowns in postseason play.

In leading Pittsburgh to its third championship in 1978, Bradshaw had a brilliant season, completing 207 out of 368 passes for a 56.3 percentage, 2,995 yards, and twenty-eight touchdowns. In the Super Bowl he gave the finest performance of his career, passing for 318 yards and four TD's—both Bowl records—as the Steelers defeated the Cowboys 35-31. Already chosen in the Associated Press poll as NFL Player of the Year, he was the unanimous choice for Most Valuable Player in the championship game.

The burliest quarterback in the National Football League, blond-haired Terry Bradshaw is six feet three inches tall, weighs 215 pounds, and has the sturdy legs of a running back. Indeed, were he not so good at passing, he might be known for rushing; in practice with the Steelers he still leads the pack in the mile run. Bradshaw is a shy man who speaks with a soft drawl. Because he is going bald prematurely, he often wears hairpieces, supplied to him by a wig company for which he does endorsements. His other activities outside of football include raising cattle on his 440-acre ranch in Grand Cane, Louisiana and singing country and Western music (he recorded the album *I'm So Lonesome I Could Cry* on the Mercury label in 1976). Also, he had a one-line cameo motion picture role, in a fight scene in *Hooper* (Warner, 1978) with Burt Reynolds. Bradshaw's only apparent vice is chewing tobacco.

On June 6, 1976, two years after his first marriage ended in divorce, Bradshaw married Alicia Jo ("Jo Jo") Starbuck, the professional ice skater, who shares his Christian faith and prays with him daily on the telephone when they are apart. His current happy marriage probably contributes to his equanimity as a quarterback. He told John Jeansonne of *Newsday* (January 22, 1979) that he is "mentally prepared" for the inevitable times when he is "absolutely horrible" on the football field because he now has "experience" and "a lot of faith" and believes that "football is not the most important thing in the world." Unspoiled by success, Bradshaw humbly rates himself as a "good" quarterback but not a "great" one of the "consistent" calibre of a Bob Griese, Roger Staubach (his would-be nemesis in Super Bowl XIII), Ken Stabler, or Bert Jones. Many knowledgeable observers would not agree. "Watching Bradshaw play quarterback," ex-Steeler Bob Adams has said, "is like watching a rose bloom in slow motion."

References: Newsweek 93:58+ Ja 22 '79 pors; People 11:26 Ja 22 '79 pors; Sporting News 186:21 N 25 '78 pors; Time 113:80+ Ja 22 '79 pors; Bradshaw, Terry, and Diles, Dave L. Terry Bradshaw (1979); Devaney, John. The Picture Story of Terry Brawshaw (1977); Hasegawa, Sam. Terry Bradshaw (1977)

Brewster, Kingman, Jr.

June 17, 1919- United States Ambassador to the United Kingdom of Great Britain and Northern Ireland. Address: b. United States Embassy, 24/31 Grosvenor Square, London W1, England; h. "Winfield House," Regent's Park, London N1, England

NOTE: This biography supersedes the article that appeared in Current Biography in 1964.

After serving for fourteen years as president of Yale University, Kingman Brewster Jr. was appointed by President Jimmy Carter in April 1977 to succeed Anne Armstrong as United States Ambassador to the United Kingdom of Great Britain and Northern Ireland. He brought to his new post diplomatic skills honed in successfully dealing with the explosive campus crises of the late 1960's, when he maintained peace at Yale but angered some conservatives with his unorthodox positions. As Ambassador to the Court of St. James's he has maintained a low profile, considering his role as primarily that of advising Washington on British attitudes and concerns.

Kingman Brewster Jr.—a direct descendant of Elder William Brewster, who came from

Nottingham, England to Massachusetts on the *Mayflower* in 1620—was born in Longmeadow, Massachusetts, on June 17, 1919, one of the three children, and the only son, of Kingman Brewster Sr. and the former Florence Foster Besse. His surviving sister, Mary, is Mrs. Robert W. Kennedy of Cambridge, Massachusetts. Brewster's father, a Harvard-trained lawyer who practised for many years with a law firm in Washington, D.C., was a McKinley Republican. His mother, an alumna of Wellesley and Radcliffe, was a liberal Democrat who was described by her son in an interview for the *New Yorker* (January 11, 1964) as a "marvellously speculative and philosophical type of person." Their marriage ended in divorce when Brewster was six.

After his mother's remarriage, Brewster lived in the Cambridge, Massachusetts home of his stepfather, Edward Ballantine, a professor of music at Harvard University. Their house, which contained two grand pianos, was "filled with stimulating people," such as jurist Felix Frankfurter and pianist Rudolf Serkin. The family spent their summers on Martha's Vineyard, where Brewster developed his lifelong love for sailing.

Brewster obtained his secondary education at the Belmont Hill School near Boston, where his extracurricular activities included debating, working on the school newspaper, and taking part in theatrical productions. Precociously interested in politics, he worked on the 1936 reelection campaign of the independent Republican Senator George W. Norris of Nebraska, who was both an isolationist and a supporter of New Deal policies. Allowed to skip his senior year by taking special tutoring, Brewster joined his family for the remainder of his stepfather's sabbatical year in England and Austria. His visit to Europe at a time when momentous events were taking place that led up to the outbreak of World War II "made things meaningful" for him when he entered Yale College in 1937.

At Yale, Brewster won the freshman debating prize, served on the community council and the junior prom committee, and belonged to the Aurelian Honor Society, the Pundits, the Political Union, and the Elizabethan Club. Something of an iconoclast, he resigned from Zeta Psi fraternity because of the "mumbojumbo" prevailing in its rites and declined membership in the prestigious Skull and Bones Society. In 1940-41 he served as chairman of the *Yale Daily News*.

Brewster's most active extracurricular involvement as an undergraduate was with the America First Committee, devoted to keeping the United States out of the looming European conflict. He founded an American First chapter at Yale, caused a stir by inviting Charles A. Lindbergh to expound his isolationist doctrine on campus, defended his views before a Congressional committee in 1940 and, in collaboration with *Harvard Crimson* editor Spencer

Klaw, stated his case in the article "We Stand Here" in the *Atlantic Monthly* (September 1940). But after Congress ratified President Franklin D. Roosevelt's interventionist policies by passing the lend-lease bill in the fall of 1941, Brewster resigned from the America First Committee.

Graduating in 1941, Brewster obtained his B.A. degree in the humanities *cum laude*, won the Andrew D. White Prize for his senior thesis in European history, and was chosen by his classmates as the graduate who had done the most for Yale. He then went to Washington, D.C. where he worked for Carl Spaeth as special assistant coordinator for economics in the Office of Inter-American Affairs, headed by Nelson A. Rockefeller. After the United States entered World War II, Brewster joined the United States Naval Reserve and served as an aviator on anti-submarine patrols in the North and South Atlantic. He was discharged in 1945 with the rank of lieutenant.

Prodded by his continuing interest in public affairs, Brewster decided to study law after the war. "I had no intention of practising," he explained to the *New Yorker* interviewer. "I wanted to save the world, and I knew that if you go into politics and public affairs, you always have to deal with lawyers, and you don't want them to pull the wool over your eyes, so, in self-defense, you become a lawyer too." He enrolled in Harvard Law School, where he served as treasurer and note editor with the *Harvard Law Review*. After obtaining his LL.B. degree *magna cum laude* in 1948 he went to Paris to work as assistant general counsel for Milton Katz, one of his former professors, who was then the United States Special Representative in Europe for the Economic Cooperation Administration, which administered the Marshall Plan. Kingman Brewster later remembered his Paris experience as "a marvellous year" and recalled that "working for the reconstruction of Europe had a great lift to it."

On Katz's advice, Brewster returned to the United States in 1949 to become a research associate in the department of economics and social science at the Massachusetts Institute of Technology (MIT) in Cambridge. In 1950 he joined the Harvard Law School faculty as an assistant professor, and three years later he was promoted to full professor. According to a colleague who was quoted in *Newsweek* (October 21, 1963) he "quickly permeated all phases of the university's life." Brewster served on Harvard committees and lectured occasionally for the university's economics department. He was also affiliated with the Harvard Graduate School of Public Administration, the Harvard Center for International Affairs, and the Center for International Studies at MIT. In addition, he served in the 1950's as a consultant to the State Department, the International Cooperation Administration, the

President's Materials Policy Commission, and the Mutual Security Agency.

A specialist in antitrust and international economic problems, Brewster wrote *Antitrust and American Business Abroad* (McGraw, 1958) and collaborated with Milton Katz on *The Law of International Transactions and Relations; Cases and Materials* (Stevens, 1960). His teaching skills elicited mixed reactions, with some students finding him more effective in small seminars than in large lecture classes. Looking back on his years as a professor, Brewster told an interviewer for *Time* (October 21, 1963): "I worked harder than I ever have before or since. Because of the caliber of the students, you find yourself spending most of your time on the ropes."

Brewster had known A. Whitney Griswold, the president of Yale University, since his undergraduate days, when Griswold was a junior faculty member in New Haven, and their friendship deepened during summers spent at neighboring vacation homes on Martha's Vineyard. In 1960 Griswold persuaded him to become Yale's provost, the university's second-ranking officer. After spending a year as provost-designate, Brewster succeeded Norman S. Buck as provost in the fall of 1961. In addition to undertaking his administrative duties, he conducted seminars at Yale Law School, where he held the rank of professor.

As provost, Brewster was responsible for supervising all faculty members and reviewing educational budgets. Since Griswold was not a gregarious man, Brewster served as his liaison with the faculty. Their mutual confidence helped to smooth the transfer of power that occurred in 1962, when Griswold, terminally ill with cancer, was forced to turn over more and more of his responsibilities to Brewster.

When Griswold died on April 19, 1963, Brewster became acting president of Yale. Although he was reportedly the near unanimous choice of faculty and students, the Yale Corporation debated for six months before it formally agreed on October 12 to name him president. Sworn in on April 11, 1964 as Yale's seventeenth president, Brewster became the first lawyer to occupy the post and the first since 1900 without a Ph.D. degree. At his inauguration, Brewster promised that the university would not remain aloof from the outside world but added: "The nation needs to preserve safe havens where ruthless examination of realities will not be distorted by the aim to please or inhibited by the risk of displeasure."

Brewster inherited a university that had tripled its endowment during Griswold's administration but had begun to suffer serious budget deficits and to face competition from the major West Coast universities for faculty and students. While maintaining Yale's traditional excellence in liberal arts, the new president moved to upgrade the graduate science and medical faculties. Committees of outside scholars were formed to advise on curriculum changes. Key positions were filled by younger, more activist personalities, such as novelist John Hersey, who became master of Pierson College, one of Yale's twelve undergraduate colleges, and Charles Taylor Jr., who was appointed provost at the age of thirty-five.

Even more significant reforms came in Yale's admission policies. Less emphasis was placed upon the traditional preference for sons of alumni, with the result that the percentage of "legacies" in the undergraduate student body dropped from 30 to 15 percent. In 1960 the ratio of private to public school graduates in Yale College was two to one; by 1970 those figures were reversed. Furthermore, university enrollment of blacks increased from 2 percent in 1963 to 12 percent in 1977. The crowning blow for some conservative alumni was the admission of undergraduate women in 1969.

While introducing those reforms, Brewster maintained a high public profile, which led Harold Howe, the United States Commissioner of Education, to refer to him in 1967 as "one of the most lively voices in higher education today." After taking office, Brewster had criticized administrators who "shrink like prunes in happy ideological anonymity." He did not hesitate to speak out publicly against United States involvement in Vietnam and against flagrant inequities in the military draft. His public image was further shaped by the comic strip *Doonesbury*, drawn by Yale graduate Garry Trudeau, which sometimes features a phlegmatic but sympathetic university administrator named "President King" who bears a striking resemblance to Kingman Brewster. Apart from fulfilling his academic duties, Brewster served on the President's Commission on Law Enforcement and Administration of Justice from 1965 to 1967 and on the national advisory commission on Selective Service in 1966-67, and he was chairman of the National Policy Panel of the U.N. in 1968.

In the spring of 1970 Brewster was confronted by a major challenge when some 15,000 demonstrators converged on New Haven in support of eight members of the Black Panther party on trial for murder and kidnapping. Offering Yale's hospitality to the crowd, Brewster said: "I am appalled and ashamed that things should have come to such a pass that I am skeptical of the ability of black revolutionaries to achieve a fair trial anywhere in the United States." Many conservatives felt that the remark showed a serious lack of judgment, and Vice-President Spiro T. Agnew called on Yale alumni to demand "a more mature and responsible person to head the university." But the Yale community rallied to Brewster's defense with a petition signed by 3,000 students.

While other major American universities were suffering disruptions and riots in the late 1960's and early 1970's, Brewster managed to keep the peace at Yale through what was described in *Newsweek* (April 18, 1977) as "a shrewd blend of diplomacy and discipline." But despite that achievement and his success in increasing the university's academic strength, a substantial number of alumni reduced their financial support in reaction to Brewster's policies. By 1977 that lack of support had manifested itself in continuing budget deficits and a stalled fundraising campaign.

On April 7, 1977 President Jimmy Carter announced that he had chosen Brewster—whom he had first met in 1971—to succeed Texas Republican Anne Armstrong as Ambassador to Great Britain. The nomination was one of ten recommended by Carter's newly established advisory board on ambassadorial appointments. Brewster quipped that his departure from New Haven might be worth $100,000,000 to Yale fundraisers, but he later explained that after he had served fourteen years as president the time had come for a change. Honored with an LL.D. degree, a standing ovation, and student chants of "Long live the King!" he remarked in his farewell address at Yale's 1977 commencement: "I will miss opportunities like this because I am about to enter a profession whose public utterances, as someone said, are halfway between a cliché and a falsehood. This may be the last chance to say what I mean and mean what I say."

Confirmed by the United States Senate on April 29, Brewster was sworn in by his old friend Secretary of State Cyrus Vance on May 16, 1977 as United States Ambassador to Great Britain—the fifty-fourth to occupy the post since John Adams arrived in London in 1785. His public profile in the United Kingdom has been uncharacteristically low—by his own standards and even by those of his predecessors—since he has eschewed high-visibility ceremonial events in favor of involvement with substantive issues. In connection with his ambassadorial duties, Brewster has traveled extensively throughout the British Isles—to Scotland, Wales, Northern Ireland, the West Country, the Midlands, and Yorkshire. He has cultivated British political leaders of all parties and has engaged in informal give-and-take discussion with bankers, businessmen, trade union leaders, and others. Brewster believes that the United States and Great Britain have a "special relationship" conditioned by a mutual tradition of common law.

In an interview with R. W. Apple Jr., of the New York *Times* (March 19, 1979), Brewster pointed out that he did not see himself as a walking advertisement for "the American way of life," as a party giver, or even as the chief channel of communication between London and Washington, D.C. "My role is to advise my government on British attitudes and concerns in the fullest way possible," he explained. "I therefore try to see as many people as possible. I hope I have managed to heighten Washington's sensibilities to British problems and prejudices on major questions like Rhodesia, the neutron bomb, and the European monetary system." In the view of a leading British political journalist, Brewster has "a broader and deeper knowledge of the leaders of this country than anyone Washington has sent over here since David Bruce in the 1960's."

Brewster is a member of the corporation of the Belmont Hill School, president of the board of directors of the Buckingham Society, a past director of National Educational Television, a trustee of the Urban Institute and of the Carnegie Endowment for International Peace, a consultant to the National Endowment for the Humanities and to the commission on higher education of the Department of Health, Education and Welfare, and a director of the American Council of Learned Societies, the Kaiser Family Foundation, and the Salzburg Seminar in American Studies. He has served on the policy review board of the Public Agenda Foundation and the international advisory council of the Population Institute.

Other organizations with which Brewster has been affiliated include the American Council on Education, the American Academy of Arts and Sciences, the Council on Foreign Relations, the New England Association of Schools and Colleges, the Connecticut Council on Higher Education, and the Connecticut Conference of Independent Colleges. The Ambassador, who holds a number of honorary degrees, was presented with an "award for excellence in human relations" by the Society for the Family of Man of the New York Council of Churches in 1970 and was awarded membership in the French Legion of Honor in 1975.

On November 30, 1942 Kingman Brewster Jr. married Mary Louise Phillips, a Vassar alumna whom he had met at a post-football party at Yale. They have five grown children: Constance, Kingman 3d, Deborah, Alden, and Riley, and several grandchildren. Brewster is a sturdily built man with graying hair and lively brown eyes. According to John Bainbridge, he has "a fine laugh, quick and strong." A skilled yachtsman, he has won a number of sailing competitions along the Eastern Seaboard, but his ambassadorial duties have left him little time to pursue his favorite sport in Britain. Brewster is, in his own words, "a would-be Republican" who "can't find enough good ones to vote for," and he admits that he gets "more stimulation by talking to people than by retreating to the library."

References: N Y Times A p9 Mr 17 '77 por; N Y Times Mag p30+ F 12 '67 pors; New Yorker 53:141+ D 12 '77; Newsweek 89:63 Ap 18 '77 por; Time 89:78+ Je 23 '67 pors; Directory of American Scholars (1974); International Who's Who, 1978-79; Leaders in Education (1974); Who's Who, 1979-80; Who's Who in America, 1978-79; Who's Who in American Politics, 1979-80

Brown, Dee

Feb. 28, 1908- Writer. Address: b. c/o Harold Matson Company, Inc., 22 E. 40th St., New York City, N. Y. 10016

"The story of the American West has all the elements of the *Iliad* and *Odyssey*," Dee Brown wrote in his introduction to *The Westerners* (Holt, 1974), his popular coffee-table history of the Old West. "It is a heroic world of quests and wars, of journeys into remote lands, of daring hunts, last stands, and legendary exploits." A librarian by profession and a historian of that "heroic world" by inclination, Brown has written more than twenty books, the most famous being *Bury My Heart At Wounded Knee,* his best-selling account of the wholesale destruction of the American Indian's ancient civilization. Enriched by the odd bits of information he gleans from official records, diaries, memoirs, unpublished letters and papers, nineteenth-century newspapers, and other unusual sources, Brown's scrupulously detailed books are both scholarly and entertaining. His most recent book is *Teepee Tales of the American Indian* (Holt, 1979), an illustrated collection of Indian tales and legends retold for modern youngsters.

One of the four children of Daniel Alexander and Lula (Cranford) Brown, Dee Alexander Brown was born in Alberta, Louisiana on February 28, 1908. After the death of his father, a timberman, five years later, he moved with his mother and his brother and sisters to Ouachita County, Arkansas, where Lula Brown worked as a store clerk while her mother took care of the children. Grandmother Cranford, whose father had known Davy Crockett, regaled Dee Brown with tales about the legendary fron-

tiersman and recollections of the hardships she and her husband had endured during the Civil War as first one army, then the other, occupied the county. Many Indians worked on the oil rigs in the area, and most of Brown's childhood friends were Indians. "We would go to the western movies together and it was then that I had my first real revelation about Indians," he told Lila P. Freilicher, who interviewed him for *Publishers Weekly* (April 19, 1971). "My buddy said to me, 'You know, those aren't real Indians.' I started reading about Indians as soon as I learned to read."

When he was about fifteen, and a student at Little Rock (Arkansas) High School, Brown and his cousin scraped together enough money to buy a small hand press. The two fledgling journalists turned out a neighborhood tabloid, to which Brown contributed articles and editorials, one of which condemned the booming oil business that had "assassinated" the Arkansas countryside. Following his graduation from high school in 1927, Brown moved to Harrison, Arkansas, where he worked as a printer and occasional reporter for the Harrison *Times* for a few years before entering Arkansas State Teachers College as a history major. He defrayed his educational expenses by working as a student assistant in the college library.

At the nadir of the Great Depression, Brown traveled to Washington, D. C. in search of employment. By his own count, he worked at about fifty different jobs before he took a "bottom-of-the-ladder" civil service position as an assistant in the United States Department of Agriculture library in 1934. Having decided on a career in librarianship because of the "ready accessibility of books," he enrolled at George Washington University and obtained his B. L. S. degree in 1935. Four years later, he was named librarian of the federal government's Beltsville Research Center in Beltsville, Maryland and he remained in that position until he was drafted into the United States Army in 1942.

Brown was assigned to the Eightieth Infantry Division, but he spent most of the next three years in special services—mainly library-related tasks in the Washington, D. C. area. Discharged with the rank of sergeant in 1945, he moved on to a post as librarian in the technical information library at the Army's Aberdeen (Maryland) Proving Ground. Returning to the Midwest in 1948, he joined the staff of the University of Illinois Library as the librarian for the College of Agriculture. He took his M. L. S. degree at the university's Graduate School of Library Science in 1951 and advanced steadily up the academic ladder. He was promoted to the rank of professor in 1962, a post he held until his retirement in 1972.

To earn extra money, Brown began writing magazine stories in the 1930's. One of his efforts took third prize in a short story contest late in the decade and attracted the attention of New York literary agents. Encouraged by their interest, he wrote a satiric novel about the Washington bureaucracy. Macrae-Smith Company agreed to publish it, but abruptly withdrew its offer after the United States entered World War II, on the ground that it was reluctant to print anything derogatory to the government in a time of national crisis. As a substitute, Brown offered his still incomplete "patriotic" novel based on the life of Davy Crockett. By working feverishly, he finished the book in just two months, and about six weeks later, in mid-1942, Macrae-Smith published *Wave High the Banner.*

To beguile the time on slow days at the Army library, Brown and a colleague, Martin F. Schmitt, collected and annotated the faded photographs of the West that they had encountered while combing the files of the National Archives in search of military photographs. Within months, the two men had in their hands a unique and astonishingly complete pictorial record of American westward expansion. Eager to share their treasure trove, they sounded out several publishers. Eventually they signed a contract with Charles Scribner's Sons, which agreed to publish, over the next several years, three profusely illustrated volumes of frontier history.

The first volume, *Fighting Indians of the West,* described by Dee Brown as the "story of the advancing frontier and the retreating Indian," appeared in 1948. It was followed in 1952 by *Trail Driving Days,* a dispassionate history of the annual cattle drives, and in 1955 by *The Settlers' West,* a remarkable account of the pleasures and perils of life in the Old West, as told in the pioneers' own words. All three books were widely praised as "fascinating" and "valuable" histories that at long last "[took] the Old West away from the spurious westerns," as one reviewer put it.

In 1954 the University of Illinois Press published Brown's *Grierson's Raid,* a day-by-day narrative of the daring 600-mile Union foray through Confederate territory in 1863 that was led by Benjamin Henry Grierson, an Illinois music teacher who hated horses and, as Brown put it, "would have much preferred leading an orchestra instead of a brigade of wild-riding cavalrymen." As the foundation for his book, Brown used Grierson's unpublished autobiography and family journals, papers, and letters. Writing in the *American Historical Review* (April 1955), R. H. Woody commended him for making "skillful use of unusually interesting source materials" and for dexterously turning them into a "graphic story of military adventure" that was "a minor classic of its kind." Similar praise greeted *Bold Cavaliers; Morgan's 2nd Kentucky Cavalry Raiders* (Lippincott, 1959), Brown's colorful chronicle of the hard-fighting Confederate band of "alligator horses" under the command of John Hunt Morgan.

Seeking to dispel what he called the "sunbonnet myth" of the stoic pioneer woman, Brown relied largely on personal diaries for his *The Gentle Tamers: Women of the Old Wild West* (Putnam, 1958). Among the two dozen women he followed across the plains were Lola Montez, Carrie Nation, Belle Starr, Calamity Jane, Elizabeth Custer, and such less familiar figures as Frances Grumman, the sheltered young Army wife widowed by the Fetterman Massacre in 1866; Janette Riker, who survived a Montana winter alone in a covered wagon; and Loreta Janeta Velasquez, who fought through the Civil War disguised as a man, and then went West "dressed in frilly furbelows to catch herself a husband."

Although some reviewers quibbled about omissions, citing Sacagewea, Lewis and Clark's Indian guide, and Jessie Frémont, the wife of explorer John Charles Frémont, as the most glaring examples, most agreed that the book was, on the whole, a well-researched, wittily written "contribution to Americana." One of Brown's most durable works, *The Gentle Tamers* proved particularly popular in Western Europe, and a handsome edition published in West Germany by Hoffman and Campe remained on the bestseller lists for months.

Brown turned his hand to fiction when he discovered in the mid-1950's that publishers paid writers advances for novels, as a matter of routine. "In those days, I just could not get enough money together to buy a new car . . . ," he explained to Anne Courtmanche-Ellis in an interview for the *Wilson Library Bulletin* (March 1978). "So you could tell when I bought cars. It was when I'd just sold another western." Brown's westerns include *Yellowhorse* (Houghton Mifflin, 1956), *Cavalry Scout* (Permabooks, 1958), *The Girl From Fort Wicked* (Doubleday, 1964), and *Action at Beecher Island* (Doubleday, 1967). He also wrote a humorous novel, *They Went Thataway* (Putnam, 1960), and several books for children: *Showdown at Little Big Horn* (Putnam, 1964), an unvarnished account of Custer's Last Stand; *Andrew Jackson and the Battle of New Orleans* (Putnam, 1972); and *Tales of the Warrior Ants* (Putnam, 1973), a description of the behavior of warrior ants based on the observations of scientists and explorers.

In his *Fort Phil Kearny, an American Saga* (Putnam, 1962), Brown recreated in meticulous detail the daily life at that Dakota Territory outpost in the months leading up to the Fetterman Massacre on December 21, 1866. Lured on that day by the taunts of Crazy Horse and a handful of braves, Brevet-Colonel William Judd Fetterman led his eighty men into an ambush by massed Sioux, Cheyenne, and Arapaho warriors. There were no survivors. Brown's dramatic reconstruction of the incident brought home to one reviewer not only "the personal tragedy of this blunder" but also those "of all the Indian Wars of the West." The book owes much of its immediacy to official government records, published journals of officers and their wives, and recollections of Indian participants.

Since his youth, Brown had been fascinated by the so-called "galvanized Yankees"—those Confederate prisoners enlisted from Union prisons for frontier duty in the United States Volunteers. (He suspected that his maternal grandfather, who came home from the Civil War "with a tall tale about why he was wearing Union pants," had been a reluctant Volunteer.) He outlined the history of that long neglected group in The Galvanized Yankees (Univ. of Illinois Press, 1963). Historians generally welcomed the carefully documented book, which represented the first full treatment of the subject, although one or two of them chastised the author for his "pedestrian" narration and attention to "superfluous" details.

Throughout his career Brown has occasionally been criticized by historians for ignoring the canons of historiography. Edwin H. Cady, a professor of history at Indiana University, summarized his colleagues' complaints in a review of Brown's The Year of the Century: 1876 (Scribner, 1966) for the Journal of American History (November 1966): "The difficulties attendant on his methods are those endemic to 'popular history.' Temptations to facile irony and other razzmatazz rob his style of precision. His perspective is largely interior and intimate, therefore his canvas is very broad, he resorts to poster strokes and colors, and one is comfortable with his history in a ratio inverse to one's independent knowledge of the materials."

Reviewers for popular periodicals, however, seldom found fault with Brown's books. Like thousands of readers, they were enchanted by The Year of the Century, his sprightly examination of Americans and American institutions at the time of the country's centennial. Brown evoked the confident and exuberant spirit of 1876 in his gallery of portraits of, among others, Presidential candidates Rutherford B. Hayes and Samuel J. Tilden; showman Phineas T. Barnum, who capitalized on "the peculiar gullibility of the times," as did novelists Horatio Alger Jr. and Mrs. E. D. E. N. Southworth; and Dwight L. Moody, the "former Chicago shoe salesman whose principal aim in life was to "reduce the population of hell by one million souls."

In the late 1960's Dee Brown spent most of his spare time reviewing the records of treaty meetings, the Indian tribal histories, and the "sources of almost forgotten oral history" he had gathered over the previous twenty-five years. Appalled by the realization that the West had been won by genocide, he decided to retell "the conquest of the American West as the victims experienced it, using their own words whenever possible." "What surprised and hurt me most was how much the Indians believed the white man over and over again," he told Roberta Brandes Gratz in an interview

for a New York Post profile (April 22, 1971). "Their trust in authority was amazing. They just never seemed to believe anyone could lie." (He is fond of quoting Red Cloud, the great chieftain of the Oglala Teton Sioux, who once said: "The white man made us many promises, more than I can ever remember, but they never kept but one: they promised to take our land, and they took it.") Writing at night, it took Brown two years to complete Bury My Heart at Wounded Knee; an Indian History of the American West (Holt, 1970). To maintain his Indian viewpoint over the months, he told himself each evening, as he sat down to write, "I'm an old Indian. . . . I'm a very, very old Indian, and I'm remembering the past. And I'm looking toward the Atlantic Ocean."

No one, least of all Dee Brown, expected his unsparing indictment of the federal government's savage treatment of Indians in the last half of the nineteenth century to become a best seller, but aided by overwhelmingly enthusiastic reviews, Bury My Heart at Wounded Knee reached the number one spot on the national best-seller list and eventually sold more than 1,000,000 copies in the United States alone. But as he told Martin Walker of the Guardian (September 21, 1974), he treasures most the opinion of a "great big ole heavy-set Indian" from California: " 'You didn't write that book. Only an Indian could have written that book!' He said, 'Every time I read a page, I think: "That's the way I feel." ' "

An indefatigable researcher, Brown is convinced that he would never have unearthed certain materials if he had not been a trained librarian. Still, he cheerfully admits that he often stumbles across the most useful sources in the library stacks through serendipity. "Other writers . . . may know exactly what they want and where they're going," he has explained. "I don't. I've got to have surprises. It's almost uncanny how they come swimming into my hands when least expected."

Denied access to the Union Pacific Railroad's extensive archives, Brown used standard nineteenth-century historical sources, published railroad company histories, contemporary newspaper and magazine articles, and travelers' accounts for Hear That Lonesome Whistle Blow; Railroads in the West (Holt, 1977). Focusing on the Union Pacific-Central Pacific route, the first of the transcontinental links, he described the construction of the railroad network and its immeasurable impact on the national economy. His conclusion that the railroads "were built mainly for the purpose of financial exploitation" angered the railroad industry. Union Pacific executives were especially upset by what they felt was a "sensationalized" and "intentionally distorted" account. Brown countered, as quoted in the New York Times (December 3, 1976), that it was "pretty late in American history to rewrite and cover up what the railroads did."

The critics generally sided with Brown, applauding *Hear That Lonesome Whistle Blow* as a "careful, candid appraisal" and as a welcome antidote to "prewar westerns like [Cecil B. DeMille's] *Union Pacific*" and "old-fashioned school histories." Although conceding that Brown told his story "passably well within the limits of the muckraking tradition," Philip French spoke for several dissenters when he rebuked the author for overemphasizing the "shoddy deeds." "An understanding of American nineteenth-century history is impossible without appreciating the pervasive corruption and the railroad companies' contribution to it," French wrote in the *New Statesman* (September 30, 1977), "[but] . . . to make them the central issue . . . is to abuse history and forge a false link to the past."

"There is something in his manner that reminds you of John Wayne," Martin Walker observed after meeting Dee Brown in 1974, "[He has] a relaxed assurance, a sense of the West that hates government of any kind, that does not believe in the rights of states, that stems from the Jeffersonian, the anarchic American tradition." A hefty six-footer with brown eyes and graying brown hair, Brown keeps in trim by gardening and bicycling around his Little Rock, Arkansas neighborhood. He and his wife, Sally B. (Stroud) Brown, whom he married in 1934, have two children, Mitchell and Linda. In addition to being named Illinoisian of the Year by the Illinois News Broadcasters Association in 1972, Brown has been honored with the ALA's Clarence Day Award, the New York Westerners' Buffalo Award, and a Christopher Award. He is a member of American Historians, Western Writers of America, Westerners Corral, the Authors Guild, and Beta Phi Mu, the honorary fraternity for librarians.

References: *Guardian* p9 S 21 '74 por; *N Y Post* Ap 22 '71 por; *Wilson Lib Bul* 52:553+ Mr '78 pors; *Contemporary Authors* vols 15-16 (1966); *Who's Who in America, 1978-79*

Bumpers, Dale (Leon)

Aug. 12, 1925- United States Senator from Arkansas. Address: b. 6243 Dirksen Senate Office Building, Washington, D.C. 20510

Dubbed a "giant killer" for defeating formidable opponents on his way to becoming governor of Arkansas and later a United States Senator, Dale Bumpers is one of that new generation of moderate and liberal Southern politicians who have cast off the albatross of race to enter the mainstream of American politics. An effective campaigner who won his elections with the help of his appealing personality, he turned his attention to issues of substance after taking office. As governor of Arkansas, Bumpers helped to bring his state into the twentieth century through executive reorganization, graduation of the income tax, and the creation and expansion of government services. In the United States Senate he has proved to be a dedicated and effective legislator who is concerned with increasing the efficiency of the upper chamber, protecting the environment, and formulating a viable energy policy.

Dale Leon Bumpers, the youngest of William Rufus and Lattie (Jones) Bumpers' three children, was born on August 12, 1925 in Charleston, Arkansas, a farming community of 1,500 inhabitants in the Ozark foothills near the Oklahoma border. His father served a term in the state legislature before opening a hardware store in Charleston and transmitted to his children his love for American history and politics. Dale's sister Elizabeth recalled in an interview with Anthony Mancini of the New York *Post* (June 1, 1974) that the Bumpers children had "a very close-knit family with a very fine Christian father and mother. . . . We were brought up with the work ethic, encouraged to get an education, and told we could do anything we wanted." From a young age Dale, his brother, and his sister were leaders in school and church activities.

After serving in the United States Marines as a sergeant during World War II, Bumpers earned a bachelor's degree at the University of Arkansas in 1948 and a law degree from

Northwestern University in 1951. Meanwhile, he took over his father's hardware store after his parents were killed in a car crash in 1949. Returning home from Northwestern, he established a profitable law practice, began breeding Angus cattle on a 350-acre farm, and became a pillar of the community as a choirmaster and Sunday school teacher at the local Methodist church, as president of the local school board, and as city attorney. In 1962 Bumpers ran unsuccessfully for the state legislature.

Although unknown beyond his native Franklin County, Bumpers decided to enter the 1970 Democratic gubernatorial primary and sold his herd of Angus cattle for $95,000 to finance a highly effective television campaign. That medium showed his good looks to advantage and contrasted his genial, relaxed, and low-key style with the overheated racial rhetoric of his major opponent, the segregationist former governor Orval Faubus. As Bumpers later told Tom Wicker of the New York Times (May 9, 1971), "I tried to appeal to the best in people in my campaign." Coming from the mountains rather than the lowland delta region of Arkansas, he spoke with more of a Western twang than a Southern drawl and made clear that he was a racial moderate and populist. Bumpers pledged to unify divergent groups and urged prison reforms, higher teacher salaries, more vocational training, tax reform, and better programs for the poor. He also alluded indirectly to the scandals that had besmirched the Faubus era of 1955-66.

In the August 1970 preferential primary Faubus, with 36 percent of the vote and Bumpers with 20 percent, led the eight-man field to compete head-to-head in the primary runoff. During the two-week runoff campaign Bumpers continued to adopt his non-abrasive campaign approach, refusing to debate his opponent. Although Faubus launched a series of personal attacks against the Charleston lawyer, as a writer for Time (September 21, 1970) reported, they "merely rebounded off Bumpers' wholesome persona." Furthermore, the enemies Faubus had made during his controversial tenure put him under a major disadvantage. On September 8, 1970 Bumpers won the runoff with 58 percent of the vote.

In the general election the Democratic nominee faced incumbent liberal Republican Governor Winthrop Rockefeller, who was seeking his third two-year term. Bumpers again stressed the personal appeal generated by his smoothly earnest style rather than his stands on issues, discreetly avoided controversial subjects, and eloquently contrasted his own modest origins with the wealth and power of the Rockefeller family. Although reportedly outspent by over $1,000,000, he received 62 percent of the vote.

Confounding those critics who complained that he was all personality and no substance, Bumpers proved to be one of the most forceful governors in Arkansas history, modernizing the antiquated and stagnant state government through administrative and tax reform and expansion of social services. During the 1971 session of the state legislature he achieved the first reorganization of the government in memory. By consolidating about sixty separate executive agencies into thirteen superdepartments, the reorganization established a cabinet system at a saving of $235,000,000 to taxpayers.

In 1971 Governor Bumpers also persuaded the legislature to enact a $30,000,000 tax increase, the largest in the history of Arkansas. His tax package featured an income tax reform that increased the top bracket of the state income tax from 5 percent to 7 percent, the first graduation in the tax since its establishment in 1929. Further highlighting his commitment to progressive taxation, he eliminated income tax liability for the lowest income groups and resisted proposals to increase the sales tax from 3 percent to 4 percent.

As a result of the Governor's tax program, Arkansas had a surplus of $135,000,000 at the end of 1972. When the biennial legislature convened again in January 1973, many representatives favored tax cuts, but Bumpers called for a vast array of programs to modernize government services, and the majority of his measures were passed, especially in the area of education. The legislature adopted his proposals for a statewide system of kindergartens; free high school textbooks; an average salary increase for teachers of $1,100; increased general aid to school districts; a sevenfold increase in assistance to schools for special education and a requirement of full services to the handicapped by 1979; a special appropriation to the fifty poorest school districts; a more than threefold boost in funds for high school vocational programs; and an extension of educational television to the entire state.

For higher education Bumpers secured bills liberalizing the terms of state grants for community colleges, increasing operating funds for Arkansas' colleges and universities, and launching the largest construction program in state history. In other fields he obtained decentralization of health education facilities to make medical care available throughout the state; expansion of Medicaid to help those on welfare obtain prescription drugs; greater state funding for community mental health and mental retardation programs; enough money to enable the prisons to replace the trustee system with paid employees; and state aid for prison schools. By executive action he raised the proportion of black state employees from 10 percent to 19 percent.

Bumpers owed his success in large measure to the fact that his softpedaled and affable approach to politics proved as persuasive to Arkansas legislators as it had been to the state's voters in 1970. A state representative observed that "he can veto your bill and make you like it." Remaining popular with the electorate, he refused to become the tool of any power group or to deal with Arkansas' courthouse politicians. He ran a scandal-free administration and gained a reputation for integrity. Even as he pushed for progressive programs he retained his image as a small-town lawyer and Sunday school teacher, thereby pleasing conservatives as well as liberals. In his 1972 bid for a second term Bumpers took 75.4 percent of the vote against three opponents in the Democratic primary, and a survey taken early in 1974 gave him a 90 percent approval rating for job efficiency.

Meanwhile, Bumpers was gaining recognition as one of an attractive new breed of moderate Southern Democratic governors that also included Reuben Askew of Florida and Jimmy Carter of Georgia. Having abandoned their region's traditional racial politics, such men could deal with the real problems of their states and hope to become leading figures in the national Democratic party. In 1972 Bumpers moved toward national stature, when, after the McGovern debacle, he became the acknowledged leader of the Democratic Governors' Conference in its efforts to rebuild the party. In 1972 he also began accepting speaking engagements that over the next two years took him to all fifty states to discuss American problems.

With his political stock constantly rising, it was not entirely surprising that on March 11, 1974 Bumpers announced that he would enter the May 28, 1974 Democratic senatorial primary against incumbent J. William Fulbright, a veteran of the United States Senate for almost three decades and perhaps the most famous member of that august body. Although chairman of the Senate Foreign Relations Committee and a world-renowned critic of American foreign policy, Fulbright had antagonized many Arkansans over the years by his cerebral and aristocratic style, the infrequency of his visits back home to the state, his preoccupation with foreign affairs to the seeming exclusion of the state's problems, and his opposition to the Vietnam war.

Since early polls gave Bumpers a substantial lead, he adopted the strategy of avoiding blunders and, as in 1970, sought to project his personal appeal instead of looking for confrontations with his opponent on controversial issues. According to Bill Terry in the Washington Post (June 1, 1974), he asserted, "I am not running against Senator Fulbright but for the U.S. Senate." Acknowledging that he and the Senator agreed on most issues, Bumpers rejected the incumbent's challenge to three one-hour debates. Although he cited the need for national goals in such areas as energy policy, health care, and tax reform, he avoided taking a stand on many key national problems.

Bumpers urged the need for new leadership in the face of what he claimed was a lack of public confidence in government. "The people," Roy Reed of the New York Times (March 12, 1974) quoted him as saying, "are pleading for

leadership that will restore their faith." Instead of attacking his opponent directly, Bumpers implicitly linked Fulbright to Watergate by contending that all Washington was a mess and that only new legislators could clean it up. Again Bumpers proved to be a successful campaigner, routing his rival by 65.2 percent to 34.8 percent and carrying 71 out of 75 counties. In November 1974 he defeated his token Republican opponent with 85 percent of the vote.

Immediately after his triumph observers speculated that Bumpers might be the 1976 Democratic Vice-Presidential nominee or a Presidential candidate at a later date. The success of his fellow Southerner Jimmy Carter in the 1976 Presidential primaries ruled out the immediate possibility of a place on the national ticket for Bumpers, but meanwhile he was building up a solid record of achievement in the Senate, just as he had done in the Arkansas statehouse.

Soon after coming to Washington, Bumpers voiced some concern over what he felt was the inefficiency of the Senate's operations. He commissioned a Library of Congress study, which in 1976 revealed that almost half of that body's subcommittees had met four times or less in 1975. Bumpers accordingly argued that some of the subcommittees were unnecessary and should be abolished or consolidated. Noting that three-quarters of the subcommittees that had met ten times or less the previous year were chaired either by the chairman of the full committee or by a Senator who chaired two or more other subcommittees, he called for a wider distribution of subcommittee chairmanships. His efforts led to a major revamping of the committee system to eliminate duplication and give every majority party senator at least one subcommittee chairmanship.

Environment and energy policy became two of Bumpers' major interests. In 1975 he chaired the Aeronautical and Space Science Committee's ad hoc subcommittee on the upper atmosphere, which held hearings on whether the fluorocarbon gases used for aerosol spray can propellants were harming the earth's ozone layer. He stood at the forefront of the drive that led to a federal ban on fluorocarbons for aerosol sprays. The following year he took part in an unsuccessful effort to bar supersonic airplanes in the United States, maintaining that they violated the federal government's noise standards.

A persistent proponent of mandatory gas rationing, in 1977 Bumpers offered an amendment to President Jimmy Carter's energy bill that would have required the chief executive to declare a mandatory rationing plan. According to the 1977 Congressional Quarterly Almanac, Bumpers argued on the Senate floor that "we are not going to conserve any significant amount of oil or gasoline in this country on a voluntary basis," but his proposal received only 15 votes. Two years later he was still pressing for mandatory rationing from his seat on the Senate Energy Committee.

A critic of nuclear power, in 1975 Bumpers offered an amendment requiring the President to report in full detail on nuclear power accidents to the senators and representatives from affected states and districts. The amendment was defeated, but in the ensuing years he met with some success in transferring federal research funds from nuclear energy to studies of alternate energy sources such as solar and wind power.

One of the most liberal Southern Democrats in the Senate, from 1975 through 1977 Bumpers, of all Southern Democratic senators, voted least frequently with the majority of his regional party colleagues when aligned against a majority of Northern Democrats. In 1975 he was among six out of seventeen Southern senators who voted for aid to New York City. Two years later, he opposed production and development of the neutron bomb and helped to thwart plans to build a $1.6 billion atomic aircraft carrier. In 1978 he

enthusiastically endorsed an unsuccessful Administration bill that would have provided substantial funds for promoting prepaid medical practices to be known as health maintenance organizations.

On September 4, 1949 Dale Leon Bumpers married Betty Lou Flanagan, a former schoolmate. With their two sons and one daughter, they constitute a closely knit family. Bumpers stands six feet tall and has broad shoulders and handsome, granitic features. Concerned about his public image, he does not smoke, drink, or indulge in profanity in public. In private, however, he has been known to smoke cigars, quaff an occasional gin and tonic, and relish a racy story. For recreation he plays tennis, hunts quail, plays the trumpet, and sings in what has been described as a pleasing baritone.

References: N Y Post p22 Je 1 '74 pors; N Y Times p26 My 30 '74 por; N Y Times Mag My p26+ '74 pors; Newsweek 83:25+ Je 10 '74 por; Who's Who in America, 1978-79

Caddell, Patrick H(ayward)

May 19, 1950- Public opinion analyst.
Address: b. Cambridge Survey Research, Inc.,
10 Moulton St., Cambridge, Mass. 02138

At an age when most young men are taking their first tentative career steps, Patrick H. Caddell has reached the height of his profession as a public opinion pollster. While working for Democratic Presidential aspirants

George S. McGovern in 1972 and Jimmy Carter in 1976, Caddell established a reputation as an expert in analyzing public opinion in the United States. As president of Cambridge Survey Research, one of the most respected organizations of its kind, he conducts public opinion research and analysis for political candidates, business firms, and other clients. Caddell publishes the quarterly Cambridge Reports, which provide subscribers with in-depth surveys on various subjects. Since Jimmy Carter took office as President in 1977, he has continued to serve as a close confidant and adviser within Carter's inner circle.

Patrick Hayward Caddell was born in Rock Hill, South Carolina on May 19, 1950, the son of Newton P. Caddell, a now retired United States Coast Guard chief warrant officer, and of the former Janie Burns. He grew up at Coast Guard stations in various parts of the United States, including Falmouth, Massachusetts, Charleston, South Carolina, and Jacksonville, Florida. At an early age, Caddell became fascinated with the process of political polling, which—apart from a passion for baseball—has remained his chief interest. When he was only in the fifth grade in Charleston, he conducted a poll of his classmates and predicted that Richard Nixon would carry that city in the 1960 election. At sixteen, as a precocious junior at Bishop Kenny High School, a Roman Catholic parochial school in Jacksonville, he set up a "voter election model" of the Jacksonville area based on election predictions from early returns. By 1968 he was conducting polls for Fred Shultz, the speaker of the Florida House of Representatives. Out of the $200 he received for a poll he paid fellow students to gather vote counts for his election-night predictions on station WJXT-TV in Jacksonville.

At Harvard College, where he majored in history and government and wrote a senior thesis on "the changing South," Caddell was, according to one professor, "not outstanding" as a student. As he later told Charles Mohr of the New York Times (August 1, 1976), he regarded Harvard as a sort of intellectual "smorgasbord" and sampled courses without working "overly hard." Despite his continued interest in polling, he did not specialize in courses in statistics and mathematics—the tools of the polltaking craft. "I went to one statistics class and lasted five minutes," he informed Mohr. "I discovered that whatever they were doing and I was doing had nothing in common."

Continuing his polling activity as a Harvard undergraduate, Caddell helped to compile some 2,000 pages of public opinion research for the successful 1970 gubernatorial campaign of John J. Gilligan of Ohio, but his income from that work averaged only eighteen cents per hour. Not long after that, he and two Harvard classmates, John Gorman and the late Daniel Porter, established their own company, Cambridge Survey Research, Inc., and conducted surveys in Massachusetts, Florida, Illinois, and elsewhere.

In the fall of 1971, as the 1972 Presidential campaign drew near, Caddell offered his services to Senator Edmund S. Muskie of Maine. Later he was approached in Miami by Senator George S. McGovern's campaign manager Gary Hart (now United States Senator from Colorado), who was impressed by his "sense of moods and attitudes." For the modest fee of $500, Caddell conducted a poll for McGovern in New Hampshire that brought him national recognition because he "was dealing more in themes than in simple statistics." Still an undergraduate when he took up his first assignment for McGovern, he briefly left the campaign during the California primary to take a swimming test required for his 1972 graduation from Harvard.

McGovern was impressed with the young pollster's analysis of American public opinion, in which he concluded that there was much popular dissatisfaction with the entire American political process, and that Americans were becoming alienated from their political institutions. He contended that both McGovern and Alabama Governor George C. Wallace were deriving support from alienated Americans and that McGovern could gain votes from Wallace's constituency. McGovern therefore tried to broaden his support by focusing his campaign not only on anti-Vietnam war feeling but also on populist themes. That assessment of the transferability of Wallace voters to McGovern proved to be mistaken, however, when McGovern was trounced by Richard Nixon in the 1972 Presidential election.

Nevertheless, the publicity he received helped Caddell to expand his polling business. In 1972, in addition to playing a role in the McGovern campaign, he worked for several Senate and House candidates. Then as now in electoral contests, he worked only for Democrats, usually liberals. His polling operations continued to grow in the 1974 elections when he increased the number of his political clients.

In 1974 Caddell and his associates set up an additional corporation, Cambridge Reports, Inc., which produces major in-depth surveys of American public opinion on economic, political, and social questions. Its quarterly report, for which subscribers pay $20,000 per year, includes over 300 pages of text, tables, and appendices, based on random opinion surveys of 1,500 persons and the continued monitoring of views of a panel of 700 respondents. In addition to the Democratic National Committee, Cambridge Reports numbers among its clients such major corporations as Exxon, Westinghouse Electric, Aetna Life & Casualty, Amoco, and Sears Roebuck. It has maintained about twenty to thirty clients per year since 1974. For an additional fee the clients can request data on "proprietary" questions of particular interest to them.

While expanding his polling activities to the private sector, Caddell trained his sights on the 1976 election. Convinced that McGovern would have little chance of regaining the Democratic Presidential nomination, he switched his allegiance to Jimmy Carter in 1975. When Caddell first met Carter in June 1972, during a McGovern campaign trip through the South, he found him "very intelligent, bright, and stimulating" and was favorably impressed by "his value system and his passion to do right." Some observers have suggested that his switch, at a time when McGovern was still in the running, was motivated by opportunism, but Caddell has explained that his political views had changed since 1972, and that his emphasis had shifted from preoccupation with the Vietnam war to concern with the broader issue of the erosion of public confidence in basic American institutions.

Working closely with Carter, Caddell was the only non-Georgian admitted to the intimate circle of Carter advisers. A principal adviser on campaign strategy, he again stressed the need for the candidate to win over alienated voters. Early in the contest he urged Carter not to conduct a traditional issue-oriented campaign, since voters were becoming increasingly skeptical as to whether candidates would translate their promises on issues into effective action. Noting the affinity between Carter and Caddell, one political journalist has remarked, as quoted by Mohr: "Jimmy would cut the cards if he was playing poker with his mother. But he trusts Caddell."

Caddell made some errors in his campaign strategy, such as wrongly predicting Carter victories in Nebraska and Maryland and advising Carter to enter the Massachusetts primary in which the Georgian came in a poor fourth. He also was responsible for recommending Robert Shrum as a Carter speechwriter. But Shrum resigned after only nine days, denouncing Carter for being "manipulative and deceptive."

Unlike other close Carter advisers, such as Hamilton Jordan and Jody Powell, Caddell never formally entered government service, choosing instead to remain a private citizen engaged in public opinion research. Despite his nongovernmental status, however, he wields considerable political influence and is regarded as an insider at the White House. "Jimmy Carter is the most important relationship I have," he told Charles Mohr. Caddell, who has a pass to the White House, meets regularly with Carter's staff aides and has easy access to the President, who continues to rely heavily upon his polls and his advice. He is reimbursed for his work for Carter by the Democratic National Committee from a special White House political fund.

Caddell encountered sharp criticism when a fifty-six-page memorandum he had submitted to President-elect Carter in December 1976 was uncovered by the news media in May 1977. It recommended popular symbolic gestures such as fireside chats, town hall meetings, and reduction in staff limousines for top government executive officials. According to Henry Fairlie, writing in the New Republic (June 11, 1977), the main theme of the memorandum was that "Carter had won only because in the final stages of the campaign, he pulled in his liberal horns, and projected a conservative image." The memo provoked negative reactions, particularly among liberals.

When Carter's popularity among voters reached an all-time low in mid-1979, Caddell furnished the President with polling analyses revealing the basic pessimism of the American people about their government and their future, and urged him to deal with the popular "mood." The major problems in the United States, he contended, were cultural, not political, and he recommended that the President concentrate less on running the government and more on leading the country.

What Carter needed, Caddell asserted in a lengthy memo issued in the summer of 1979, was to exercise a new style of leadership by taking bold, "breakthrough" actions that would reveal his courage and creativeness. Caddell contends that since the Watergate crisis the public view of the Presidency has changed, and that Americans now distinguish between Carter's job rating and his personal rating. Thus he has expressed hope that in the 1980 election the President's positive attributes, like his honesty and sincerity, would override the negative reactions to such issues as his controversial handling of the energy crisis. Some members of the Administration, including Vice-President Walter F. Mondale, challenged Caddell's analyses and argued that the President should focus directly on such substantive problems as energy, inflation, and unemployment.

Caddell has encountered occasional criticism for alleged conflict of interest. For example,

New York Times columnist William Safire criticized Caddell's firm for accepting an $80,-000-a-year contract with the Saudi Arabian government, charging that such a business undertaking by one of Carter's closest advisers was improper. Caddell also came under criticism for his work in behalf of Westinghouse Electric, to which he offered a memorandum in March 1976 proposing that the corporation engage in a campaign to promote public acceptance of nuclear energy. When representatives of the Scientist Institute for Public Information, an environmentalist public interest group, learned of that memorandum, it canceled its contract for a poll with Caddell's firm.

In his own defense Caddell maintains that he supplies nothing more than a service to his clients, that his Cambridge Reports are "purely a research product," and that his company plays "no advocacy or representational role." Stephen Chapman observed in the New Republic (November 25, 1978): "No one has turned up any evidence that [Caddell] has ever intervened with Carter on behalf of a client; no doubt if he did, the President would quickly put him in his place." And David Broder noted in the Washington Post (May 29, 1977) that Caddell's practice of taking on both political and private clients "is generally backed in the polling profession, where it is customary for firms to handle both political and business or interest-group clients at the same time."

Some observers have questioned Caddell's professional standing as a pollster and have criticized him for lack of methodological rigor in conducting his public opinion surveys. According to Stephen Chapman, "many experts and pollsters say Caddell's surveys are poorly conceived and sloppily worded." Chapman adds, however, that Caddell's eminence is in his skills at interpreting the results of the data, and that according to his admirers "he has unrivalled insights into public opinion."

In addition to serving the Carter Administration and his business clients, Caddell continues to conduct polls and compile surveys for other Democratic candidates. In 1978 he was involved in some twenty political campaigns, including those of Connecticut Governor Ella T. Grasso and Florida Governor Bob Graham. He also worked for the unsuccessful Presidential candidate, Diego Arria, in the Venezuelan election of 1978. In addition, Caddell and Gerald Rafshoon, President Carter's media consultant, have handled publicity and marketing research for director Francis Ford Coppola's ambitious Vietnam war film Apocalypse Now (1979).

Patrick H. Caddell, a bachelor, maintains an apartment on Boston's Beacon Hill as well as a rented house in the Georgetown section of Washington that he shares with Presidenial campaign manager Tim Kraft, and he drives a Mercedes-Benz. In addition to the Cambridge office that serves as his organization's headquarters Caddell also has an office in Washington, near the White House. Formerly corpulent, Caddell shed some sixty pounds from his six-foot frame between 1976 and 1979. He once more wears a beard, as he did during his Harvard days, and appears much older than his years. His practice of setting his watch fifteen minutes fast has still not kept him from being chronically late for appointments. Because of his busy schedule he is not able to lead as active a social life as he would like. "I'm at my peak," he told Clare Crawford of *People* magazine (November 21, 1977). "But I've paid a price for it. When I was younger I gave up a lot of activities, especially in terms of my peer group. I haven't traveled. I don't own much. And it's been a while since . . . I've had a relationship with a woman for any period of time." *Time* magazine has designated "Pat" Caddell as one of the 200 "future leaders of America."

References: N Y Times p28 Ag 1 '76 por; A p10 Ag 2 '76; A p14 Ag 14 '79 por; Nation p778+ Je 25 '77; New Repub 179:12+ N 25 '78; New Yorker 55:45+ Ag 27 '79; Newsweek 80:31+ O 9 '72; People 8:44+ N 21 '77 pors; Washington Post A p3 My 29 '77 por; Stroud, Kandy. How Jimmy Won (1977)

Carreras, José

Dec. 5, 1946- Spanish singer. Address: b. c/o CAMI, 165 W. 57th St., New York City, N.Y. 10019; c/o Carlos Caballé, Via Augusta 59, Barcelona 6, Spain

Four years after Spanish opera lovers applauded José Carreras at Barcelona's Teatro del Liceo in his brief appearance in 1970 as Flavio in *Norma*, the young tenor won over audiences at London's Covent Garden as Alfredo in *La Traviata* and then at New York's Metropolitan Opera when, in the fall of 1974, he sang Cavaradossi in *Tosca*. In his exceptionally rapid rise to international popularity he has been recognized as an exponent of the remarkable new school of Spanish tenors that includes Placido Domingo, Giacomo Aragall, Alfredo Kraus, and others. The New York *Times* critic John Gruen, who has compared him also to the Italian Luciano Pavarotti, hailed Carreras as "a singer possessed of a superior voice of lyric verging on dramatic quality [and of] romantic good looks which invariably enhance any role he undertakes, producing the aura of immediacy and theatrical credibility."

The youngest of three children, José María Carreras Coll was born in Barcelona, Spain on December 5, 1946 to José María and María Antonia (Coll) Carreras. He has a brother, Alberto, and a sister María Antonia, both chemists. His father was a teacher before the Spanish Civil War and afterward a policeman; he ultimately joined the cosmetics business begun by his two older children and now owns a small chemical plant. Mrs. Carreras was a hairdresser by profession. Except for José Carreras Coll's grandfather, who had been passionately fond of opera, no one in the family displayed any particular interest in music, but at the age of about seven the boy was taken by his mother to see the Mario Lanza film *The Great Caruso*. When they returned home, José staged his own performance of everything he could remember hearing and seeing on the screen. Thereafter, he often organized make-believe recitals and operas in his room, singing any and all arias he happened to hear on records or over the radio.

Recognizing the potential talent of their younger son, the Carreras parents enrolled José in the Barcelona Conservatory when he was seven, to begin eight years of musical studies, including piano and solfeggio, in addition to a regular curriculum. Carreras has recalled that he tried singing the role of Otello at the age of eight. His father and mother meanwhile bought subscriptions for him and his brother to Barcelona's opera season at the historic Gran Teatro del Liceo. José Carreras' first appearance of consequence, and his first paying part, came when he was eleven, as the boy soprano in the role of the Trujamán in Manuel de Falla's *El Retablo de Maese Pedro* under the direction of José

Iturbi at the Liceo. In his late teens Carreras entered the University of Barcelona to study chemistry, but also began vocal training with Jaime Francisco Puig, the voice teacher of his friend the Catalan tenor Giacomo Aragall. Soon concluding that his future lay not in chemistry but in singing, Carreras decided to return to the conservatory while continuing with private voice classes. "It was the best thing I ever did," he told John Gruen of the New York *Times* (February 26, 1978). "I realized that while I may not have been the best of singers, I would definitely not have been the best of chemists."

In his first mature operatic appearance, in January 1970 in Barcelona's Liceo, José Carreras sang the minor part of Flavio in Montserrat Caballé's first performance of the Bellini opera *Norma,* which he followed in February with the role of Ismaele in *Nabucco.* He made what he considers his "real debut" at the Liceo in late December 1971 as Gennaro to Miss Caballé's Lucrezia in Donizetti's *Lucrezia Borgia.* Impressed by Carreras' ability, the Barcelona-born soprano recommended him to her brother and manager, Carlos Caballé, who then gave much attention to the young tenor's career. Carreras has said that the Caballés became his virtual "family," helping him to become both an artist and a more complete human being. "Madame Caballé set a standard for all my future endeavors," Carreras told Gruen in the New York *Times* interview.

With guidance from the Caballés, José Carreras prepared for what was quickly to become an important international career. He made his Italian debut in 1971 as Rodolfo in *La Bohème* in Parma, where favorable notices led to his London appearance in a concert version of the Donizetti opera *Maria Stuarda* with Miss Caballé. Carreras returned to Parma later in the year to enter the Verdi competition, which he won. That success in turn brought an offer from Julius Rudel of the New York City Opera for an American debut as Pinkerton in Puccini's *Madama Butterfly,* a role that Carreras sang in March 1972 to Nancy Shade's Cio-Cio San.

Briefly reviewing that first, unheralded Carreras performance in New York, music critic Allen Hughes noted in the New York *Times* (March 17, 1972) that the City Opera has found "a new tenor who could be a valuable addition to the company if his singing is as pleasing in other works." Among the Catalan's virtues, he reported, were "a fine-grained voice that is on the light side but carries well," pleasant looks, and good comportment. A two-year contract with the New York City Opera resulted from what the *Times* review called that "solid debut," enabling Carreras to acquire experience and enlarge his repertory in such roles as Edgardo in *Lucia di Lammermoor,* the Duke in *Rigoletto,* Rodolfo in *La Bohème,* Cavaradossi in *Tosca,* and Alfredo in *La Traviata.*

José Carreras' skill as a quick study was used to advantage in July 1972 when Aragall became ill two days before a concert version of Donizetti's seldom-performed *Caterina Cornaro* in London at the Royal Festival Hall, with the title role to be sung by Caballé. In the part of Gerardo, which he was given thirty-two hours to learn, Carreras impressed *Opera* editor Harold Rosenthal with his "bright, young sound and virile tenor voice which he uses to thrilling effect." In 1972 Carreras also made his first appearance with the Staatsoper in Vienna, and when he returned to the United States later that year, he sang in a concert performance of *Rigoletto* conducted by James Levine at the Hollywood Bowl. During the fall of 1972 he appeared not only in three productions of the New York City Opera, but also in a single performance of Rossini's *Pietra del Paragone* as Giocondo; that Clarion Concert presentation at Alice Tully Hall of Lincoln Center was also his first recording, on the Vanguard label. Back again in New York in December 1972, for the third visit that year, he made his Carnegie Hall debut as Arvino in a concert version of Verdi's opera *I Lombardi* under the baton of Eve Queler.

Besides appearing for the first time with the San Francisco Opera, as Rodolfo in *La Bohème,* and with other American opera companies, during the following seasons Carreras sang in such widely separated countries as Japan, Germany, and Argentina. London audiences applauded his singing Alfredo in *La Traviata* in March 1974 in his Royal Opera House debut at Covent Garden and during a later season welcomed him back in the roles of Pinkerton in *Butterfly* and Nemorino in *L'Elisir d'Amore.*

When Carreras led off the 1974-75 season of the New York City Opera opposite Beverly Sills in *Lucia di Lammermoor,* he proved to Harold C. Schonberg of the New York *Times* (August 29, 1974) that he was ready to sing "against Miss Sills or anyone else." Calling Carreras "good news for any opera company," Schonberg reported, "He is a lyric tenor with plenty in reserve, dead center on pitch, youthful in timbre, firm in production. In short, he is a prize, and is by far the best tenor the City Opera has had since the young Placido Domingo." In his New York *Times* interview with Gruen, Carreras looked back on his three seasons with the New York City Opera company: "It was a fabulous experience, and I can assure you that singing at the New York City Opera is the best thing that can happen to a young artist. It opens the window to the future." In gratitude he sang a benefit performance for the City Opera in March 1978 at a musical soirée in Manhattan.

Included in the future that the New York City Opera opened to Carreras was his November 18, 1974 debut at the Metropolitan Opera as Cavaradossi in *Tosca*. Enthusiastic fans hailed him as a star that night, awarding him with prolonged applause after his first aria and stopping the show for about a minute with a roar of approval after his "E lucevan le stelle" in the final act. Concurring in the audience's delight, Robert Sherman of the New York *Times* (November 20, 1974) pronounced Carreras' performance "a resounding success" and went on to report, "His tone was clear, bright, totally without strain, his singing fluid and highly expressive. Harriett Johnson agreed in the New York *Post* (November 19, 1974) that Carreras belonged at the Met: "His lyric voice is a remarkable one, full enough to do some lyric-dramatic roles like the one at his debut. His production is positive and allows him to pour out tones with ease no matter what the register."

Shortly after his Met triumph as Cavaradossi, José Carreras made his debut opposite Montserrat Caballó at La Scala in Milan as Riccardo in *Un Ballo in Maschera*, thereby confirming his entry into the top echelons of the international operatic world. Later, having demonstrated his versatility in a joint recital with the Italian soprano Katia Ricciarelli for a 1975 Columbia Artists "Series of Stars" program at Carnegie Hall in New York, he returned to the role of Riccardo in his first appearance at Chicago's Lyric Opera in 1976.

During the 1976 Salzburg Festival, José Carreras was heard under the direction of Herbert von Karajan in the title role of Verdi's *Don Carlos*, a highly appealing performance that he repeated at that festival in 1977 and at the 1979 Easter Festival in Salzburg. He is slated to appear in a Vienna production as Don Carlos and in Karajan's film version of the work. Also at Salzburg, Carreras sang in the Verdi Requiem for Karajan and during the 1978 summer festival he appeared in a Karajan presentation of *Il Trovatore* given worldwide television coverage. Disclosing in *Opera News* (February 11, 1978) that Karajan had persuaded Carreras to sing the role of Radames in *Aïda* at the 1979 Salzburg Festival, Stephanie von Buchau quoted the lyric tenor as explaining, "It is *only* for Karajan that I will sing this role, for at least five years. We have discussed it, and he plans a very lyrical approach."

The Royal Opera's 1977 revival of the Franco Zeffirelli production of *Tosca* at Covent Garden brought Carreras one of many welcomed opportunities to sing with Montserrat Caballé. Max Loppert told readers of the *Financial Times* (September 28, 1977) of his gratitude for beautiful singing, but also of his disappointment that both stars failed to fulfill the dramatic possibilities of their roles. "The figure José Carreras cut as painter and revolutionary was strangely anonymous," he wrote, "—though vocally, after a husky start, he rose bravely to the climaxes, both the voice and the stance wanted boldness, fierce conviction." When, however, Carreras undertook the same role, singing opposite Teresa Kubiak, at the Metropolitan Opera toward the close of the 1977-78 season, Allen Hughes praised him in the New York *Times* (March 31, 1978) as being "about as nearly an ideal Cavaradossi as one could realistically hope for." To support his appraisal, Hughes observed, "His tenor voice seemed in absolutely first-class condition, and his singing had just the right combination of suppleness and authority to make him a vocally commanding personality from beginning to end. And his acting had the ease and naturalness an assured young man can bring to the role."

Before giving that sterling performance at the Met, Carreras had sung in a production of *Don Carlos* with Katia Ricciarelli and Nicolai Ghiaurov at Covent Garden during the fall of 1977. He joined an all-star cast for the opening of the La Scala season in another presentation of *Don Carlos*, conducted by Claudio Abbado in December. Returning to La Scala the following May, he costarred with Montserrat Caballé in performances that Zubin Mehta conducted of *La Forza del Destino*.

José Carreras' schedule for the 1978-79 season included appearances in Massenet's *Werther* at the San Francisco Opera, later in London, and then with Teresa Berganza in Zurich. For reasons of health he had to cancel his first scheduled performances during the fall of 1978 in a revival of Verdi's *Luisa Miller* at the Metropolitan Opera, but when he stepped into the part of Rodolfo in December, he was warmly welcomed by audiences and critics. Referring to Carreras as one of the production's "most valuable ornaments," Raymond Ericson assured opera fans in his review for the New York *Times* (December 6, 1978), "If the tenor is not a subtle artist or a communicative actor, he is a full-throated, exciting singer. If there are minor flaws in his vocalism—scooping up to notes, for example—he remains a first-rate operatic artist." Like Ericson, Speight Jenkins, music critic for the New York *Post*, made special mention of Carreras' rendition of "Quando le sere al placido," his major aria, which, Jenkins wrote, "he sang poetically and with superb control." Jenkins found, moreover, that Carreras as Rodolfo had "more stage presence and dramatic intensity than he has sometimes shown here."

The growing Carreras discography includes recordings of *Tosca* and *Lucia di Lammermoor*; of such Verdi operas as *Il Corsaro*, *I Due Foscari*, *Un Giorno di Regno*, *La Battaglia di Legnano*, *Macbeth*, and *Simon Boccanegra*; the Richard Strauss opera *Der Rosenkavalier*; and the first complete recording of *Elisabetta, Regina d'Inghilterra*; as well as several aria recordings. Among the new recordings to which Carreras is committed are those of *Un Ballo in Maschera* and *La Bohème*, both with Caballé for Philips; *Aïda* in Vienna with

Mirella Freni for the EMI/Angel label; and Verdi's *Stiffelio* for Philips.

In the spring of 1971 José Carreras married his fiancée of five years, a former student of economics at the University of Barcelona whom he met while attending a performance of *La Forza del Destino* at the Teatro del Liceo. His wife, Mercedes Carreras, lives in Barcelona with their son, Alberto, whom Carreras visits whenever he is in Europe with even twenty-four hours to spare. In his conversation with Gruen he acknowledged that "one of the hazards of building a career" involves the strain that absence from home puts upon a marriage. His recreations include playing tennis and pelota, the fast national game of Spain, as well as listening to opera and other music, both live and on record.

When studying a new role, he finds it helpful to listen to other tenors' recordings. As he admitted to Gruen, "The point is, I need to know how Bjoerling or Di Stefano or Caruso dealt with a role. And I can learn from Corelli and Bergonzi and most certainly from my great contemporaries." Of those contemporaries, Luciano Pavarotti, Giacomo Aragall, and Placido Domingo are especially good friends of his. Among José Carreras' goals is singing Mozart and Wagner at some future date.

References: Hi Fi 27:MA-2+ S '77 por; N Y Times II p19 F 26 '78 pors; Opera N 37:17 D 9 '72 por, 42:13 F 11 '78 pors; N Y Post p45 D 1 '78 por, p20 Mr 18 '78; Who's Who in Opera, 1976

Cartland, Barbara

July 9, 1901- British writer. Address: c/o Bantam Books, 666 Fifth Ave., New York City, N.Y. 10019; h. "Camfield Place," Hatfield, Hertfordshire, England

The world's all-time best-selling author of romantic fiction is Barbara Cartland, whose books number more than 230 and whose sales have passed the hundred million mark. Miss Cartland dictates to her amanuenses, at the rate of two a month, Regency-style historical novels of unconsummated love, in which virgins are wooed by raffish aristocrats who remain fully and resplendently clothed at all times. The glamorous seventy-eight year-old Briton, who has been churning out her period

pieces for more than half a century, attributes the recent great surge in her popularity to a readership that is surfeited with pornography. "I never specifically describe the sex act because it's such a bore laid bare," she has explained. "My readers wonder if they're normal if they don't have sex upside-down, swinging from a chandelier. So I'm their escape, their fairy tale. I give them the glamour and the beautiful clothes and the marvelous attentive men they are starved of."

Barbara Cartland's chief publisher in her native England is Hutchinson. In the United States, Bantam Books publishes two new paperbacks by her a month; Jove Publications brings out one, either old or new, approximately every month; and Dutton issues several new Cartland titles in hardcover each year. In addition to historical fiction Miss Cartland writes books of autobiography, biography, history, personal philosophy, health, charm, etiquette, cookery, and verse, and for Bantam Books she edits the "Barbara Cartland Library of Love" and the "Barbara Cartland Novels of Ancient Wisdom" series.

A direct descendant of the Dukes of Hamilton and the Scobells, an old Saxon family, Barbara (Hamilton) Cartland was born in England on July 9, 1901 to Bertram and Polly (Scobell) Cartland. About her mother, who died at age ninety-eight in 1976, she has written *Polly, My Wonderful Mother* (Jenkins, 1956). Winston Churchill wrote the introduction to *Ronald Cartland* (Collins, 1942), a biography of her brother, a Tory Member of Parliament who was killed at Dunkirk in World War II. She told Nina King of *Newsday* (June 23, 1979) that her brother was "a great visionary" and that *Ronald Cartland* was "literally dictated" to her. "I didn't have to think. It just came out." Another brother, Tony, also died at Dunkirk.

Miss Cartland was educated at home (by a governess who doubled as a tutor), at the Malvern Girls' College, and at Abbey House,

Netley Abbey, Hampshire. As she recalled in one of her autobiographical works, *We Danced All Night* (Hutchinson, 1971), by her late teens she was reading as many as three lending-library novels a day, escapist works "in the grand way" by such writers as Elinor Glyn, Edith Maude Hull, Baroness Orczy, and Ethel M. Dell. She decided to try her own hand at such writing after her father's death in Flanders in 1918 left the family with a reduced income. Her mother wanted her to get a job, but she "was dancing all night with beautiful young men" and "didn't wish to have a job at all."

In 1922 she began contributing items to a gossip column in the London *Daily Express* at five shillings an item. "I did that for a bit and I wrote one or two little mimsy articles for the *Express*—sort of "Youth Speaks Out," she recalled in the *Newsday* interview with Nina King, "and Lord Beaverbrook sent for me and he said, 'I like the way you write,' and then he taught me to write. And the reason my books are so readable is they're journalese." She quoted the historian Sir Arthur Bryant as considering her "a very good writer because she never uses a superfluous word." "Don't you see?" she added. "That's journalism."

Barbara Cartland's first novel, *Jigsaw*, was published by Duckworth in 1925. "It wasn't very good," she acknowledged to an interviewer for "Talk of the Town" in the *New Yorker* (August 9, 1976), "but it was a huge success simply because I was a debutante—a girl who was supposed to be a lady and had soiled her lily-white hands with work." In 1924 she wrote *The Mayfair Revue*, performed for charity by some of her young high-society peers. The costumes for the revue were designed by Norman Hartnell, who later became couturier to Queen Elizabeth II and who has designed wardrobes for Miss Cartland (including that for her 1979 American promotional tour). For the London stage she also wrote the play *Blood Money*, which had its premiere in 1925. Her extra-literary activities during her debutante days ranged from a series of radio self-improvement talks to carrying the first airplane-towed mail in a glider from Manston Aerodrome to Reading.

"So that's how it all started," Miss Cartland said in recounting to Nina King of *Newsday* how she came to write her first novel. "Then I wrote two or three other books in my own hand, then I started to dictate, then I got bitten by the bug and now I can't stop." *Sawdust* (1926) and *If a Tree Is Saved* (1929) were published by Duckworth, and with *For What?* (1930), Hutchinson became the major publisher of her novels.

Dangerous Experiment, published by Hutchinson in 1937, was for many years the only one of her books issued in the United States, where the title was changed to *Search for Love* (Greenberg, 1937). In a review in the *Springfield Republican* (September 13, 1937), the story was described as "a light type of popular romance, with an obviously romantic way of solving moral problems." The moral problem was that of a wife who feels neglected when her explorer husband goes off to Tibet; the solution was for her to give vent to her defiance by going on a cruise with an admirer.

Miss Cartland's first nonfiction effort, *Touch the Stars: A Clue to Happiness,* was published by Rider & Company in 1935. During the 1930's Hutchinson published fifteen of her novels, including *Virgin in Mayfair* (1932) and *Passionate Attainment* (1935). An additional novel, *The Black Panther* (1939), was published by Rich & Cowan, which also issued five of the score of novels she wrote in the 1940's, including *No Heart Is Free* (1948) and *A Duel of Hearts* (1949). Hutchinson published the others, except one, *Sleeping Swords* (R. Hale, 1942), a political novel that she wrote under her married name, Barbara McCorquodale. Hutchinson also published two volumes of her autobiography: *The Isthmus Years: Reminiscences of the Years 1919-1939* (1943) and *The Years of Opportunity 1929-45* (1948).

During World War II Miss Cartland served as chief services welfare officer and librarian for Bedfordshire, where she was also a member of the St. John Ambulance Brigade. Sharing her late brother's ideal of service to others through political office, she successfully campaigned as a Conservative for the Socialist-held seat of Hatfield on the Hertfordshire County Council in 1956. During her nine years as a county councillor she was instrumental in securing better conditions in homes for the aged, stationary camps and education for gypsies, and higher financial and professional status for midwives, and she campaigned against the fluoridation of drinking water.

Meanwhile her literary output was growing at an accelerating pace. Twenty-eight new novels saw print in the 1950's, ten of them under her married name, and during the same decade she wrote several historical biographies and such other works of nonfiction as *Marriage for Moderns* (Jenkins, 1955), *Look Lovely, Be Lovely* (Jenkins, 1958), and *Vitamins for Vitality* (Foyle, 1959). Her hundredth book, the novel *The Fire of Love,* was published by Hutchinson in 1964.

In the United States the 1949 novel *A Hazard of Hearts* was reprinted by Pyramid in 1969; four years later Bantam began publishing new Cartland titles at the rate of one a month; and on the strength of mass market demand a new Bantam contract was signed in October 1975 calling for two new titles monthly. On June 25, 1976 Miss Cartland occupied the number one and number two spots simultaneously on the B. Dalton paperback bestseller list with *The Slaves of Love* and *An Angel in Hell.*

Also published in 1976 was *Passions in the Sand,* a good example of the typical Cartland plot. An upper-class English virgin in a fit of pique bolts her engagement to an aging peer and heads for North Africa, to join an adventurous cousin; en route she falls in love with a dashing, aggressive "sheikh," who turns out to be a Spanish duke in disguise and therefore of proper class for marrying her. The story ends with the hero lifting the heroine up in his arms and carrying her "away into the shadows." Venturing into a new professional field in 1978 Miss Cartland, backed by the Royal Philharmonic Orchestra, recorded Barbara Cartland's *Album of Love Songs,* an LP on which she sings a selection of such songs as "A Nightingale Sang in Berkeley Square" and "Always."

The total sales of Miss Cartland's books passed the 100,000,000 mark in the spring of 1979. In explaining her popularity, Miss Cartland notes two main factors: the inevitable cyclical swing away from pornography to romance, which she dates from 1975, and the revulsion that women in particular feel toward pornography. In the new edition of the autobiographical volume *I Search for Rainbows* (Hutchinson, 1967; Bantam, 1977) she wrote: "When the [romantic] boom came and pornography began to fade in Sweden and Denmark and all the other countries, the one person who had '150 virgins' lying about was me." In an essay published in the London *Times* and reprinted in the New York *Times* (April 15, 1977), she quoted Walt Disney as saying, "Every time they make a pornographic film I make money," and she added, "I am convinced that every time women look at vulgar, filthy, degrading pornography they buy a 'Barbara Cartland.' " She told Wendy Thomas in an interview for the New York *Sunday News* (September 26, 1976): "All women crave beauty, and that's one of the reasons why I think my books do so extraordinarily well."

Barbara Cartland's attitude toward pornography ties in with her stand on feminism and her interest in health. "Liberation for women," she has said, "really means they can sleep with whoever they want to, but what women forget is that they cannot have sex without getting emotionally involved, which means they get upset. People who allow themselves to get emotionally upset get sick, and no one can have great love affairs unless they're healthy. Pornography is in such demand today because so many people are unhealthy." Everyday, Miss Cartland takes some ninety vitamin pills and other dietary supplements, and she distributes her health discoveries and concoctions (such as a pill combining ginseng and vitamin B-15) through her Health and Happiness Club. She is a founder and the president of the National Association of Health in England.

Barbara Cartland married Alexander George McCorquodale in 1927 and divorced him in 1933. Three years after the divorce, on December 28, 1936, she married her first husband's cousin, Hugh McCorquodale, who died in 1963.

Miss Cartland has a daughter, Raine, by her first husband and two sons, Ian and Glen, by her second. She lives in grand style in a twenty-seven-room mansion on her 400-acre estate near Hatfield in Hertfordshire. There is a "dog ghost" on the estate, if Miss Cartland is correct, and there is certainly a large human retinue: a chauffeur to drive her in her Rolls-Royce, a cook, upstairs and downstairs maids, a butler, and the pool of ten secretaries and typists that constitutes her literary factory. She "writes" for a couple of hours every afternoon, dictating upwards of 6,000 words. Often she does so while reclining on a pink-cushioned sofa in her library, a white rug over her, a hot-water bottle at her feet, and her Pekingese, Tai-Tai, at her side.

She gathers background inspiration and material for her stories by reading history and by traveling. In her autobiographical "esoteric" chronicle *I Seek the Miraculous* (Dutton, 1978), she wrote of a trip to Greece during which "we climbed down to the sanctuary of Athene [and] the plot for a new book was there, waiting only for me to dictate it. I even knew the title—*Kiss the Moonlight.*" Her "esoteric experiences" are of great importance to her. "I believe very much in an afterlife," she told Nina King of *Newsday.* "I believe in reincarnation."

When Wendy Thomas interviewed Miss Cartland for the *New York Sunday News,* she was, Miss Thomas wrote, "all dolled up and in a beaded and embroidered hot-pink chiffon dress, looking as if she's two decades late for some formal cocktail party." The *New Yorker* interviewer described her as "rather tall, stylishly stout, with very slender legs, blond-rinsed hair, and blue eyes accented by bluish-green eye shadow and dark false eye-lashes." In the *Newsday* interview the author said that she did not overly miss "the grand society" in which she mingled in her youth, and while she did deplore the loss of "the good manners," she thought they "will come back." What she did think "a terrible mistake" was the erosion of "law and order" through the publicizing of political scandals. "They all say, 'There's the aristocracy for you' [or] 'Oh, look at the White House—all corrupt,' pushing them all in together. You know that doesn't do any good. People have got to have heroes of some sort."

References: 50 Plus 19:40+ Ap '79 por; Macleans 91:114+ D 11 '78 por; N Y Sunday News mag p14+ S 26 '76 por; New York 11:48+ F 13 '78 por; New Yorker 52:17+ Ag 9 '76; Newsday mag p19+ Je 3 '79 por; People 8:93+ S 19 '77 pors; Pub W 209:46+ Je 7 '76; Sat Eve Post 250:58+ Mr '78 por; Wall St J p1+ S 1 '76; Writers Digest 59:22+ Je '79 pors; Contemporary Authors 1st rev vols 9-12 (1974); Who's Who, 1979; Who's Who in America, 1978-79; World Who's Who of Women, 1974-75

Chaikin, Sol C.

*Jan. 9, 1918- Labor union official. Address: b.
International Ladies Garment Workers Union,
1710 Broadway, New York City, N.Y. 10019;*

As president of the International Ladies Garment Workers Union, Sol C. Chaikin heads an
organization famous in the annals of American
labor history, but also one that is being increasingly battered and threatened in the
marketplace by the invasion of inexpensive
goods of foreign or domestic nonunion manufacture. Chaikin, who was elected to the
presidency in 1975 to finish out the term
of Louis Stulberg and reelected in his own
right two years later, relied on his training as a lawyer and on his more than thirty
years of experience as a labor organizer
to return the ILGWU to its preeminent position
in the labor movement. In just three years he
overhauled the union's creaking internal machinery, initiated mutually supportive alliances
with rival unions, and negotiated a precedent-
shattering contract that completely revised the
decades-old piecework payment system. Chaikin has been so successful that he is often
mentioned in the trade press as a likely third-
force candidate to succeed George Meany as
president of the AFL-CIO.

Born in New York City, New York on January 9, 1918, Sol C. Chaikin is the only one
of the three offspring of Sam and Beckie
(Schechtman) Chaikin to live past early childhood. His parents, Russian Jews who had
immigrated to the United States around 1910,
worked in the garment industry, his father as
a cloakmaker and his mother as a dressmaker,
and, throughout their working lives, both were
active members of the ILGWU. The Chaikins

lived for a time in Harlem and in the Brownsville section of Brooklyn, before settling permanently in the East Bronx. Each summer, Sol
Chaikin escaped from the city's oppressive
heat to his uncle's chicken farm, where he
acquired his longtime nickname "Chick." After
attending public elementary school, he commuted by subway to Townsend Harris Hall
High School, a special school for academically
gifted students, from which he graduated in
1934.

Following four years at the City College of
New York, Chaikin enrolled at St. Lawrence
Law School. The period of the late 1930's was
a time of great expansion and promise for
American labor unions, punctuated by the passage of the National Labor Relations Act and
the Fair Labor Standards Act and by the formation of the CIO. Caught up in the fervor of
the burgeoning labor movement, Chaikin decided that he was more interested in working
for the ILGWU than in a career as a lawyer,
but he nevertheless completed his course of
study, received his LL.B. degree in June 1940,
and passed the New York bar exam the following August. A few days later he was hired
by David Dubinsky, the president of the
ILGWU, as an organizer for Local 178 in Fall
River, Massachusetts.

After spending a few months on the job,
Chaikin became the business agent for Local
281 in Boston and Lowell, Massachusetts, a
post he held until he entered the United States
Air Force in 1943. He spent the next several
years in the South Pacific and earned several
battle stars for his service in China, Burma,
and India. Discharged with the rank of sergeant in 1946, he returned to New England to
manage ILGWU Local 226 in Springfield, Massachusetts.

An extremely able negotiator who could
obtain major concessions from employers even
when bargaining from a weak position, Chaikin advanced to the post of manager of the
Western Massachusetts District of the ILGWU's
Northeast Department in 1948 and to director
of its Lower Southwest Region, comprising
Texas, Arkansas, Oklahoma, and Louisiana, in
1955. He returned to New York in 1959 as
assistant director of the Northeast Department,
the union's largest single unit, encompassing
the nine-state New England-New York-Penn-
sylvania area. At the ILGWU's triennial convention in Miami, Florida in May 1965, Chaikin
was elected an international vice-president of
the union. That same year he became associate
director of the Northeast Department, which
at that time had about 95,000 members. From
November 1968 to November 1973 he was also
the chairman of the American Trade Union
Council for Histadrut, the Israeli labor federation.

In the meantime, the ailing Louis Stulberg,
who had succeeded David Dubinsky as president and general secretary-treasurer of the
ILGWU in 1966, decided to separate the two
top union management posts to indicate the

preferred line of succession. There was some talk that the job of secretary-treasurer might go to Shelley Appleton, the manager of Sportswear Local 23-25 and former President Dubinsky's son-in-law, but in February 1973, at a meeting in Bal Harbour, Florida, the union's twenty-six-member executive board chose Chaikin to become the number-two man in the national hierarchy. They were motivated, at least in part, by Chaikin's enormous popularity with the rank and file. When Stulberg announced his retirement in May 1975, the executive board unanimously named Chaikin to complete his unexpired term, beginning on the following September 1. The next month, at a national convention of the AFL-CIO in San Francisco, California, Chaikin was elected a vice-president of the organization and a member of its executive council.

At the time of Chaikin's election to the presidency, the ILGWU, once a pacesetter in American labor relations, had long since been left behind by larger and more powerful unions, such as the U.A.W. and the United Steel Workers of America. By the mid-1970's the average hourly wage of a garment worker was just two-thirds of the average amount paid other manufacturing employees. Moreover, union membership was down dramatically, having dropped from more than 457,000 in 1970 to under 405,000 in 1975. Because of the resulting decline in dues revenues, the union was forced to draw upon its investment income to maintain a level of pensions and other benefits and services that was already significantly lower than that of many other industries.

Several factors contributed to the ILGWU's difficulties. In its early years the union was dominated by immigrant Jewish and Italian workers, most of them male. By the 1970's it had large numbers of blacks and Hispanics, and about 80 percent of its members were women, many of them heads of families. That shift in membership was not reflected commensurately at the management level and, as a result, the degree of understanding between the union's leaders and the rank and file was lessened. The structure of the garment industry itself complicated contract bargaining procedures. Instead of having to deal with only a handful of corporate employers, as is the case in most industries, the ILGWU had to negotiate with thousands of small independent companies. Another drawback to progressive contract agreements was the union's traditional acceptance of the piecework rate of payment for its members. Because garment workers were paid by the finished piece, profit-minded employers were reluctant to invest in labor-saving, assembly-line production equipment, knowing that increased production would mean increased labor costs.

The resulting inefficiency and high production costs in union shops led directly to the ILGWU's most urgent problem: the production of inexpensive clothing by nonunion workers in the Southern and sunbelt states that have right-to-work laws prohibiting the closed union shop and in Asia, Latin America, and Eastern Europe. To keep production costs down, American garment manufacturers increasingly tapped the vast pools of cheap labor in the Far East. In 1961 foreign-made apparel accounted for only 4 percent of the women's and children's clothing market in the United States. Fifteen years later, one of every four garments sold was manufactured abroad. "Hong Kong is like Seventh Avenue East, the place is so crowded with American buyers and manufacturers ... [placing] orders to flood this country with garments made by workers who earn sixteen to twenty-six cents an hour," Sol Chaikin warned, as quoted in the New York Times (April 13, 1977). "Unless there is active government intervention now to make needed changes in the multi-fiber trade agreement regulating textile and apparel imports, the domestic industry will be demoralized in a few years and hundreds of thousands of our workers will be dumped on welfare." He estimated that 250,000 jobs had already been lost to foreign workers.

Plagued from the outset of his presidency by an annoyingly widespread feeling that the ILGWU was "sluggish and lacked spirit," Chaikin started a series of sweeping reforms to demonstrate to union members and to the garment industry that he represented a new and different kind of leadership. Among other things, he restructured the union's internal machinery and introduced modern managerial techniques ranging from computerized data processing to radio and television advertising. To strengthen the union's leadership group, he recommended the election of two able and popular officers, Shelley Appleton as general secretary treasurer and Frederick R. Siems as an additional executive vice-president, at the ILGWU's 1977 convention. Moreover, recognizing that his workers and those who produce apparel for men and boys face the same problems, Chaikin established a friendly working relationship with Murray H. Finley, his counterpart in the Amalgamated Clothing and Textile Workers Union. The ILGWU had been at odds with that union since the 1930's because of the sharp personal and political differences between Dubinsky and Amalgamated's president, Sidney Hillman.

Perhaps more importantly, Chaikin inaugurated a new era of cooperation between labor and management, ending decades of squabbling. Over the past several years the union's management-engineering department has held regular seminars to teach employers how to modernize operations and cut costs. In mid-1976 Chaikin himself gave a productivity seminar for more than 200 industry executives. Of even greater long-term significance, however, was Chaikin's radical departure from the entrenched piece-work rate system in the contract agreement reached with women's dress manufacturers in February 1977. That contract tied piece rates to the overall production efficiency of the plant and to the workers' income and, for the first time, offered employers an incentive to modernize their plants.

Under the new contract all piece workers were guaranteed an hourly minimum wage, but piece rates, set to yield an average of 25 percent above the minimum, were related to each individual plant's work cycle. The rates would be adjusted lower when the output was high and vice versa. Although Chaikin concedes that many unforeseen wrinkles will have to be ironed out, he hopes that the new system will eventually extend to all branches of the garment industry. "We have begun to ameliorate the distress of the last fifteen years and particularly of the last five," he told Lee Dembart, in an interview for the New York Times (February 3, 1976). "We're not sure that this is going to work, but we're damn sure that the system we've had hasn't worked for the last fifteen years." His long-term goal, which depends on general acceptance of a single standard for setting piece rates, is one industry-wide contract.

Enlisting the support of the national labor movement, Chaikin enlarged the ILGWU's campaign to unionize the South. He increased the number of field organizers to recruit new members and lobbied for a higher federal minimum wage to undercut the advantage of nonunion manufacturers. To stem the rising tide of cheap imported garments, he approved a massive $4,000,000 advertising campaign designed to attract consumers to union-made goods. But the catchy tune urging buyers to "look for the union label" has had only a negligible impact on the bargain-hunting public. As Chaikin explained on NBC TV's Today in January 1978, the import issue is "primarily and essentially one of economic and foreign policy, not consumer choice." "What we in the ILGWU and the labor movement are attempting to educate the American people on is the simple fact that when the consumer buys imported goods at a cheaper price, they must pay extra taxes for higher American unemployment and welfare as more industries leave this country," he said. "What we are stressing is the fact that in the apparel industry, which uses rather simple, primary machinery the world over, there is a vast difference between the wage scales of American workers and Asian workers, who work for an an average of one-tenth less than their American counterparts; that's the crux of the import problem—namely, that U.S. workers are being displaced from their jobs by competition from low-wage goods from overseas."

Chaikin has been pushing for a change in the tariff schedule, which now requires an American firm to pay import duty only on the increase in value represented by the work done abroad. (In most cases, the garments are made from domestic fabric cut in the United States, then shipped abroad for sewing.) "We're not altogether unfeeling," Chaikin told Joyce Purnick, who interviewed him for a New York Post (June 7, 1975) profile. "We don't want to close out all imports. But if we do away with one-and-one-third million jobs in this country, we're doing away with opportunities. This union is a point of entry into the working force for so many who might otherwise be marginally employed." In alliance with Murray Finley, George Meany, the president of the AFL-CIO, and such strange bedfellows as the nonunion manufacturers with whom he is in conflict on other issues, Chaikin asked President Jimmy Carter to negotiate new agreements between the United States and the exporting countries restricting the annual growth in imports to 3 percent.

As Carter's labor representative to the Commission for Security and Cooperation in Europe, meeting in Belgrade, Yugoslavia in September 1977 to review the 1975 Helsinki Agreement, Chaikin raised some diplomatic hackles by roundly condemning the Soviet Union for its repression of dissidents. He was also a delegate to the International Labor Organization's World Employment Conference in Geneva, Switzerland in 1976 and has represented the AFL-CIO and kindred organizations at conferences to strengthen the cause of trade unionism in Argentina, Brazil, Chile, Egypt, Israel, and Japan, among other places. Chaikin was recently named to a special committee of the AFL-CIO executive council established to consult with President Carter's new labor-management panel, chaired by the Secretary of Labor, Ray Marshall.

Sol Chaikin is or has been associated with a variety of civic and social policy organizations, including the National Urban Coalition, the Atlantic Council of the United States, the Trilateral Commission, the Brookings Institution Round Table Center, Freedom House, the American Veterans Committee, the National Committee for Labor Israel, the Workmen's Circle, the Jewish Labor Committee, and the Long Island Jewish-Hillside Medical Center. He chairs a special committee of the Economic Policy Council of the United Nations Association of the United States of America. In 1977 Chaikin was the recipient of the Histadrut Humanitarian Award.

A curly-haired, chunky, energetic man, Sol Chaikin looks a decade younger than his sixty-one years. He is good-humored and gregarious and enjoys spinning folksy tales and writing poetry. He and his wife, Rosalind (Bryon) Chaikin, a special education teacher whom he married on August 31, 1940, divide their time between their house in Great Neck, New York and their vacation home in Ft. Lauderdale, Florida. They have four children —Robert Evan, Eric Bryon, David Reed, and Karen—and several grandchildren.

References: Forbes 121:32+ Ja 23 '78 por; N Y Post p20 Je 7 '75 pors; N Y Times p71 My 29 '75 por; Who's Who in America, 1978-79; Who's Who in Labor, 1976

Chaplin, Geraldine

July 31, 1944- Actress. Address: b. c/o Paul Kohner Inc., 9169 Sunset Blvd., Los Angeles, Calif. 90069

As the daughter of the late British-born Hollywood comedian Charlie Chaplin and the granddaughter of the late American playwright Eugene O'Neill, Geraldine Chaplin made a relatively easy entrance into the acting profession, but without her own talent and offbeat photogenic looks she would not have been able to establish the reputation she now enjoys as an international actress. With one or two exceptions, all of her credits have been in the cinema. Since 1965, when the British director David Lean cast her as the wife of the title character in *Doctor Zhivago*, she has accumulated more than thirty screen credits, including many of the Buñuelesque films of the Spanish director Carlos Saura, her close personal as well as professional collaborator; of Robert Altman, the American creator of omnibus plots; and of Altman's protégé, Alan Rudolph. Altman has described Miss Chaplin as "a remarkable actress who has as wide a range as anyone performing today. She's like a racehorse you pick for its breeding."

The first of the eight children of British-born Sir Charles Spencer Chaplin and Oona (O'Neill) Chaplin, Geraldine Chaplin was born in St. John's Hospital in Santa Monica, California on July 31, 1944. Because her mother had been disinherited by Eugene O'Neill, who disapproved of her marriage to Chaplin, Geraldine never met her maternal grandfather. During the first eight years of her life she was raised in the Chaplin mansion in Beverly Hills, California. When she was seven years old she had a walk-on role in her father's film *Limelight* (United Artists, 1952), in which she recited one line ("Mrs. Alsop is out").

On September 17, 1952 the Chaplins sailed from New York City on a six-month world cruise on the *Queen Elizabeth*. Two days later United States Attorney General James P. McGranery ordered immigration officials to bar the reentry into the United States of Charlie Chaplin (who had never become an American citizen) pending an investigation. There was no hint as to the purpose of the investigation, but it was generally assumed that it would have something to do with the uproar in the American press over Chaplin's "leftist" sympathies, which were anathema in that time of McCarthyism. Tired of harassment, Chaplin moved to Switzerland, where he settled on a twenty-acre estate overlooking Vevey, with his family and a menagerie that eventually included wolves, badgers, mice, a fox, crocodiles, a crow, and an eagle. "In Hollywood," Geraldine Chaplin has recalled, "we had millions of cats. We started with a lot of cats in Switzerland, but they all managed to get on the road and be killed."

Miss Chaplin attended the village school in Corsier, near Vevey, and, for seven years beginning at age ten, the convent boarding school of Mont Olivet, a little farther away, where she ranked third in her class academically. When Rex Reed interviewed her for the New York *Times* (December 19, 1965), she recalled that her schooling was French but "at home everything remained American." "It was a strange life, and the Europeans thought we were all crazy. The crazy Chaplins in the big house on the hill, they called us. We had no friends, only our animals." There was, however, a steady stream of visiting celebrities—including Picasso, Casals, Braque, Stravinsky, and Chou En-lai—that she regretted having been too "babyish" to appreciate.

Her first aspiration was to the ballet, which she studied in Switzerland for four years as a teenager and subsequently for two years at the Royal Ballet School in London before deciding that she had not begun training early enough to attain excellence in dance. She had only one professional engagement as a dancer, in the chorus of a production of *Cinderella* in Paris in December 1963. Her performance on that occasion received publicity out of all proportion to its importance, as Miss Chaplin recounted to Rex Reed: "I was terrible but I ended up on the front pages. Only one of twenty little dancers in the chorus of *Cinderella*, but you'd have thought I was Pavlova. Sure, they were exploiting me. My father was furious!"

In Paris, Miss Chaplin stayed with her halfbrother Sydney and his wife, Noëlle Adam. They introduced her to the agent Claude Briac, who helped her land a part in the film *Par un beau matin d'été* (On A Beautiful Summer Morning), of which she later said: "It was one of the worst movies ever made, and if David Lean or anyone else had ever seen it I never would have gotten a job in *Doctor Zhivago* or anything else."

As Tonya in *Doctor Zhivago* (MGM, 1965) Miss Chaplin received mixed notices, ranging from "shiny but vapid" to "ingratiating, warm, and gentle." In the middle was William Wolf, who observed in *Cue* (January 8, 1966) that "if pretty Miss Chaplin can act, this isn't a fair test; here all she has to do is smile a lot as the stiff-upper-lip wife." Among the most positive appraisals were those of Kenneth Tynan in the *London Observer* (May 1, 1966), who thought that Tonya was played "with growing confidence by the bright-eyed Geraldine Chaplin," and Judith Crist in the New York *Herald Tribune* (December 23, 1965), who found Miss Chaplin "pert and probable" in the midst of the "cardboard characters" whom Lean "shuffled through a ridiculous plot."

Following *Doctor Zhivago*, Miss Chaplin was cast as Princess Golovine in the French motion picture *J'ai tué Rasputine* (I Killed Rasputin, 1966), directed by Robert Hossein. She also had roles in the British mystery *Stranger in the House* (Rank, 1966) and the Italian film *Andremo in Città* (We Will Go to the City, 1966), directed by Nello Risi, among other films.

During the filming of *Doctor Zhivago* in Spain, Miss Chaplin met the young director Carlos Saura, a protégé of Louis Buñuel who provided the spark that ignited her talent and with whom she later set up a *ménage*. Their first professional collaboration was *Peppermint Frappé*, (1967), released, like most of Saura's films, by Elias Querejeta. It was the *outré* story of the obsessions of an aging introverted Spanish provincial physician named Julian, who falls in love with Elena (Miss Chaplin), the young bride of his playboy brother, Pablo. Rebuffed by her, he, in his twisted mind, converts his peasant nurse, Ana (also played by Miss Chaplin), into her *doppelgänger*. The nurse accepts the role and she and the doctor end the movie in a wild dance after he pushes the car in which Pablo and Elena are sitting off a cliff, killing them. "Miss Chaplin is excellent in the dual role, demonstrating great range," William Lyon wrote in his dispatch from Madrid to *Variety* (September 6, 1976). "As sophisticated Elena she is alternately innocent and childlike or cruel and calculating. As the nurse she is at first shy, later seductive."

As Alexandra in a revival of *The Little Foxes* at the Ethel Barrymore Theatre in New York City from December 19, 1967 to January 20, 1968, Miss Chaplin drew a nomination for "most promising new Broadway actress" in *Variety*'s poll of New York drama critics. Back in Spain, she was cast as the wife involved in a morbid, tragic love triangle in *Stres es tres, tres* (Stress is Three, Three, 1968), and when the film was shown at the Venice Film Festival she was described in *Variety* (September 18, 1968) as a "lovingly lensed" actress who "fits the bill as the gamine wife."

The actress collaborated with Saura and Rafael Azcona on the script of *La Madriguera* (1969), in which she and Per Oscarsson portray a married couple who indulge in psychodramatic games that become their reality and lead to homicide. When the film was released under the title *Honeycomb* in the United States in November 1972, the New York critics generally panned it. In the New York *Post* (November 24, 1972), Frances Herridge suggested that only the fact that Miss Chaplin was a coauthor could explain "why she would play so insufferable a role in so irritating a film." Roger Greenspun, writing in the New York *Times* (November 23, 1972), thought that Oscarsson "has no relation to his part" and that Miss Chaplin "is better, but not good enough." But Judith Crist of *New York* (December 4, 1972) considered the picture "a bothersome quality film" in which Miss Chaplin was "excellent in performance."

In *The Hawaiians* (United Artists, 1970), the sequel to *Hawaii*, based on James Michener's sprawling historical novel, Miss Chaplin played Purity, the quietly psychotic wife of Whip Hoxworth (Charlton Heston). Archer Winsten of the New York *Post* (June 19, 1970) thought she did so "nicely," and if other reviewers disagreed, most of them were too busy faulting the cluttered epic itself to say so.

According to Derek Malcolm of the *Guardian* (May 25, 1972), Miss Chaplin was "lovely, but wasted" in the science-fiction film *Zero Population Growth*, (Sagittarius, 1971), in which she and Oliver Reed starred as a twenty-first-century couple defying a law forbidding childbirth under pain of death. The reviewer for *Variety* (January 10, 1973) described as "well-enacted" her role as a hostage held by a secret agent in the espionage thriller *Innocent Bystander* (Paramount, 1972).

Richard Lester cast Miss Chaplin as Anne of Austria in his cinematic burlesque of Alexander Dumas's *The Three Musketeers*, released as two films, *The Three Musketeers* (Twentieth Century-Fox, 1974) and *The Four Musketeers* (Twentieth Century-Fox, 1975). Critics called her "lovely" and "stunning" in the role, and Rex Reed, writing in the New York *Sunday News* (April 21, 1974), declared, "Geraldine's performance in this heavily star-encrusted spectacle is like a luminescent natural pearl in a washtub of noisy and nacreous oyster shells."

Carlos Saura's metaphorical *Ana y los lobos* (Ana and the Wolves), made in 1971 and released the following year, starred Miss Chaplin as Anar, a young governess hired by three brothers, representing various Spanish taboos and other hang-ups, to work in their decaying mansion, which apparently symbolizes Spain itself. In Saura's *Cría Cuervos* (1975), she was cast as a pianist who gives up her career for her family only to die of uterine cancer soon afterward—a role that brought her some of the best notices of her career when the film was released in the United States as *Cría!* in 1977. In 1976 Saura directed her in *Elisa, vida mia* (Elisa, Darling), and two years later in *Los Ojos vendados* (Blindfolded) which represented Spain at the 1978 Cannes Festival.

One of Miss Chaplin's most memorable performances, for many Americans at least, was that as Opal, the dizzy BBC reporter in Altman's *Nashville* (Paramount, 1975), a brilliant, kaleidoscopic musical melodrama about a political campaign set in the country-and-western capital of the United States. In Altman's *Buffalo Bill and the Indians* (United Artists, 1976), she was cast as Annie Oakley. Among others, William Wolf of *Cue* (September 29, 1978) thought she was a "standout" as the wedding coordinator undaunted by a disastrous nuptial day in Altman's subversive, controversial black-comedy attack on the American nuclear family, *A Wedding* (Twentieth Century-Fox, 1978).

Altman produced Alan Rudolph's *Welcome to L.A.* (United Artists, 1976) and *Remember My Name* (United Artists, 1979). In the first— a film whose several vignettes fit its theme song, "City of One-Night Stands"—Miss Chaplin was cast in the role of a neglected housewife who fantasizes herself to be Garbo's Camille; in the second she is again a woman scorned, one who reacts to the unfaithfulness of her husband (Anthony Perkins) with murderous fury. Reviewing *Remember My Name* in the London *Financial Times* (February 9, 1979), Nigel Andrews contrasted Miss Chaplin —"a scarecrow sylph in shirt and jeans"—with the Barbara Stanwycks and Joan Crawfords of yore: "Times have changed and so have movie heroines. Miss Chaplin is a cinematic Medea for the 1970's: gawky, oddball, in manner simultaneously mad and matter-of-fact. Rudolph gives the scenes between her and Anthony Perkins . . . a spring-heeled tragicomic tension more vibrant and precise than anything in *Welcome to L.A.*" Later in 1979 Miss Chaplin portrayed Lily Bart in a television production of Edith Wharton's novel *The House of Mirth.*

Geraldine Chaplin is a slim, petite woman, barely five feet tall, who has a distinctive freckle birthmark under each of her long-lashed gray-green eyes. Among her favorite composers and writers are, respectively, J. S. Bach and Katherine Mansfield. In approaching a role, she reads the script several times, takes notes as she does so, and tries to construct a complete family and personal history for the character. She and Carlos Saura live quietly in a spacious Madrid penthouse apartment with their son Shane Saura Chaplin O'Neill.

References: N Y Post p19 D 26 '65 por, p42 Je 11 '77 pors; N Y Times II p7 D 19 '65 por; Look 29:57+ Ap 20 '65 pors; Parade p4+ Ja 1 '78 pors; Who's Who in America, 1978-79

Chase, Chevy

Oct. 8, 1943- Comedian; actor; writer.
Address: b. Rm. 200, KTLA Studios, 5800 Sunset Blvd., Los Angeles, Calif. 90028

When NBC's irreverent weekly comedy show *Saturday Night* first invaded the small screen, in October 1975, one member of that live late-night program's subversively funny troupe in residence, the Not Ready for Prime Time Players, stood out from the rest—Chevy Chase, a master of clumsy pratfalls and deadpan outrage. Originally and still basically a writer, Chase either wrote or ad-libbed most of his own material on *Saturday Night,* the high point of which was his "Weekend Update," a spoof of newscasts. Looking disarmingly like everybody's favorite stripe-tied anchorman, the clean-cut Chase would intone in a resonant, sincere voice, "Good evening. I'm Chevy Chase, and you're not," and then launch into what were probably the most hilariously controversial topical comments on television. Chase, who left *Saturday Night* at the beginning of the 1976-77 season, has since done several television specials and starred in the motion picture *Foul Play.* His long-term plans lie chiefly in the direction of writing combined with producing.

Chevy Chase described his family background to Tom Burke of *Rolling Stone* (July 15, 1976) as "upper middle-class, WASPish." He was born Cornelius Crane Chase in New York City on October 8, 1943 to Edward Tinsley Chase, a writer and editor now an executive at G. P. Putnam's Sons, the book publishers, and Cathalene (Crane) Chase, the plumbing heiress. When he was a newborn, his paternal grandmother began calling him

Chevy—perhaps in facetious allusion to the Washington, D.C. suburb—and the name stuck. Chase has an older brother, Ned, now a Legal Aid lawyer in New York, and several half siblings from subsequent marriages of his parents, who separated when he was four.

Growing up on Manhattan's Upper East Side, Chase lived with his mother and visited regularly with his father. Summers, he went to live with his paternal grandparents in Woodstock, New York or, during a brief period, to visit his rich maternal grandfather, Cornelius Crane, in Ipswich, Massachusetts. "I've experienced what seems to be all sides of this country," he told Mitchell Glazer, the executive editor of Crawdaddy (September 1978). "When I was six or seven I used to spend holidays at Castle Hill with Cornelius, sailing on his 200-foot yacht, watching all the servants work all over the mansion. At an early age I was taught how to deal with the very wealthy. I guess I was the very wealthy, in a sense." But he inherited either none or very little of the Crane wealth, because Grandfather Crane divorced Chase's grandmother to marry a Zen Buddhist and reportedly ended up leaving most of his money to a Buddhist temple.

As Chase has told various interviewers, while he "always wrote" he "was not drawn to academia" and was "too wired up" to concentrate on school work. His schoolmates remember him as the class cutup. His checkered academic itinerary began at P.S. 6 and the Dalton School, both on Manhattan's Upper East Side, and proceeded through the Riverdale Country School in Riverdale, New York, and the Stockbridge School in Stockbridge, Massachusetts. After a year at Haverford College in Haverford, Pennsylvania, he transferred to Bard College in Annandale-on-Hudson, New York. At Bard, where he majored in English and played soccer, he took a B.A. degree in 1967. Later he completed a course in audio engineering at the Institute of Audio Research in Manhattan.

Chase began experimenting with television technique in association with two fellow students at Bard, Ken Shapiro, a former child TV actor and the owner of a small home Sony video recording system, and Lane Sarasohn. In 1967 Shapiro and Sarasohn, with the help of Chase and others, formed Channel One, an Off-Off-Broadway production company, in a storefront theatre in Manhattan's East Village, where they presented videotaped lampoons of commercials, newscasts, kiddie shows, documentaries, and other TV fare. Seventy-five minutes' worth of their best sketches were later brought together in the motion picture Groove Tube, released by the Levitt-Pickman Corporation in 1974.

Meanwhile, Chase also played piano with the short-lived rock group Chamaeleon Church, which cut the album Chamaeleon Church on the MGM label in 1968; worked at sundry other jobs, including tennis pro, truck driver, and bartender; wrote a parody for the young people's satirical comic magazine Mad (April 1970) titled "A TV Scene We'd Like to See: The Impossible Mission Force"; and, with Ken Shapiro, appeared as a white-faced mime in a segment of the public television comedy omnibus The Great American Dream Machine in 1971.

Chase made his theatrical debut in National Lampoon's Lemmings, a musical revue, spun off from the adult satirical magazine National Lampoon, which brutally satirized the drug scene and other self-destructive fads and foibles of rock 'n' roll culture. The show opened at the Village Gate cabaret theatre in Greenwich Village, New York City in January 1973 with Chase in two featured appearances: as a rabid motorcycle gang member and as a John Denver type singing about a family freezing to death in the glorious Rockies of Colorado. Chase remained in the cast of Lemmings through the revue's eleven-month run Off Broadway and the show's subsequent national tour.

In 1974 Chase contributed as a writer and performer to two other National Lampoon productions: the album White House Tapes and the weekly syndicated National Lampoon Radio Hour. That same year he moved to Los Angeles, where he wrote television material for comedians Alan King and the Smothers Brothers. His script for a King network special in 1974 brought him a Writers Guild of America award.

Lining up to see Monty Python and the Holy Grail at a movie theatre in Los Angeles in February 1975, Chase met and struck up a conversation with the young Canadian-born television producer Lorne Michaels, who was soon to start work on Saturday Night for NBC. Struck by Chase's gift for repartee, Michaels asked him to write for the prospective show, which was conceived as a late-night format in which audacious young comic talent might express itself without the straitjacket inhibitions of prime time. After doing summer stock with Paul Lynde and Alice Ghostley, Chase accepted Michaels' offer and signed on with Saturday Night as a writer. He wanted to double as a performer, and when he was given the opportunity to do so he clicked immediately. Among the sixteen other creative crew members enlisted by Michaels were several more alumni of National Lampoon magazine or its spinoffs, including writers Michael O'Donoghue and Anne Beatts and the multitalented John Belushi. Others, including Dan Aykroyd and Gilda Radner, had worked with Michaels on Canadian television.

Saturday Night entered the NBC schedule as a live replacement for reruns of the Tonight Show Starring Johnny Carson at 11:30 P.M. on October 18, 1975. (It was originally called Saturday Night Live, but the name was changed to avoid conflict with a sports show of the same name.) The show quickly surpassed the Carson reruns in the ratings and went on to become NBC's sole smash hit of 1975-76, with an estimated viewership of 10,000,000, especially heavy among college students and other young adults. "Our show," Lorne Michaels pointed out to Gerry Nadel when Nadel interviewed him for *New Times* (May 28, 1976), "is the first by and for the generation that came of age in the sixties."

The ninety-minute show, presented live from New York City three out of four Saturdays a month, had guest hosts ranging from comedians Richard Pryor and George Carlin to actress Raquel Welch and President Gerald Ford's press secretary Ron Nessen and such musical guests as Simon and Garfunkel and the rock band the Rolling Stones. The announcer was veteran Don Pardo, doing a travesty of his familiar game-show pitch.

The *pièce de résistance* was the humor provided by *Saturday Night*'s Not Ready for Prime Time Players: Chevy Chase, Gilda Radner, Jane Curtin, Laraine Newman, Don Aykroyd, John Belushi, and Garrett Morris. Each of the players was featured in two or more sketches in each program. Among Chase's specialties were regular pratfalls, slow, artful, acrobatic feats many of which were done in mimicry of an allegedly accident-prone President Ford.

One of the most popular segments of the show was "Weekend Update," the parodic newscast conceived, written, and performed by Chase. ("I set it up," he once explained, "for the preppie side of me to get shredded") "President Ford pierced his left hand with a salad fork at a luncheon celebrating Tuna Salad Day at the White House today," Chase would intone. "Alert Secret Service agents seized the fork and wrestled it to the ground. . . . The United Nations General Assembly passed a resolution equating Zionism with racism. Sammy Davis Jr., a convert to Judaism, was quoted as saying, 'What a breakthrough! Now, finally, I can hate myself.' And finally, Generalissimo Francisco Franco is still dead." When Dan Aykroyd would appear on the newscast as an earnest citizen reading an editorial reply, Chase would do cockeyed mugging behind him. Commercials read by Chase included one for "Purina Rat Chow." The comedian won two Emmys for his work on *Saturday Night*, one for writing and the other for performing. Later, in 1978, he won another Emmy for cowriting a script for a television special which had starred Paul Simon.

After leaving *Saturday Night*, in October 1976, Chase did specials for pay television's Home Box Office and for NBC. His NBC assignments included hosting chores on Academy Award and Emmy presentations and the *Chevy Chase Show*. The latter program—in which Chase was supported by comedian Tim Conway, the band Stuff, and the singing Shapiro Sisters—was aired on May 5, 1977. When the show was in preparation, William Murray, a writer for *TV Guide* (May 5, 1977), witnessed several of the comedy routines in progress, in-

cluding "Dog Disco," a rock program for canines, and a telephone commercial in which a feeble old woman never managed to get to the phone before it stopped ringing. "What some of these sketches may lack in taste," Murray observed, "they will obviously make up for in daring, a commodity scarce on prime time."

In other sketches on the *Chevy Chase Show*, Chase spoofed the Emergency Broadcasting System tests and played a physician offering facetious health and sex advice to teenagers, a game show host who has a spinal tap waiting as the prize behind the secret door, and a Jack LaLanne type with a physical fitness program for the dead. While noting that "the Chase repertory is curiously fixated on disease, medicine, and even death," John J. O'Connor of the New York *Times* (May 5, 1977) noted that Chase came across as "a Nader Raider with a sense of humor," who "still manages to use his good looks brilliantly in the service of deadpan comedy."

In his review of the *Chevy Chase Show* in the same day's Washington *Post*, Tom Shales wrote: "The *Chevy Chase Show* is by turns funny, very funny, not very funny, acrobatic, shamelessly violent, slightly refreshing, at times too cute and largely lacking in human warmth. . . . There is something precious and preppy about [Chase]. But it's this obnoxious part of his personality that makes him so much fun to watch and sometimes fascinating; he's almost as irresistible in his smugness as Jack Paar was in his emotionalism. They are blood brothers of the tube."

When Chase returned to *Saturday Night* as guest host in February 1978, the show received the highest rating in its history— 12.6 and a 38 percent share of the television audience. According to NBC researchers, 25,000,000 viewers watched all or part of the telecast. Chase fans were treated to a rerun of many of their favorite *Saturday Night* segments when NBC aired *The Best of Saturday Night Live* on January 10, 1979.

As a motion-picture star, Chase made his debut in the romantic comedy thriller *Foul Play* (Paramount, 1978), in which he was cast as a San Francisco police investigator who comes to the aid of Gloria Mundy (Goldie Hawn), a librarian whose life is threatened when she inadvertently gains knowledge of an assassination plot. Many critics, accustomed to Chase's special brand of zaniness on television, felt deprived in seeing his humor reduced to cool wit on the big screen. Typical was Richard Schickel of *Time* (July 31, 1978), who wrote: "It is hard to remember when a talented comic had fewer moments of risibility. He should thank his genes for the natural ease and charm he has to fall back upon. They allow him to sink bemusedly into the scenery without recourse to the desperation moves a lesser man might try. As a result, Chase will doubtless live to fight upon the silver screen at least one more day." With Michael O'Donoghue,

Chase has been working on what he calls his "first linear work," a motion picture comedy drama tentatively titled "Saturday Matinee," a parody of movies of the 1940's and 1950's. The project is the first under a contract with producer Marty Erlichman that calls for three films, to be released by United Artists.

Chevy Chase recognizes that the key element in his instant success on *Saturday Night* was the incongruity between his bright, reassuring appearance and his bad-boy antics. "I guess I just look so straight and normal," he has said, "nobody expects me to pick my nose and fall." His forte is physical comedy. "I very rarely write cerebrally," he once pointed out, in his *Saturday Night* days. "I don't read a lot of satire. So while a writer like O'Donoghue, who is very literary, goes in one direction, I go in another." In answer to those who called Chase's type of comedy "sophomoric," especially when it bordered on the cruel (as when he represented America's "droolers" in a takeoff on help-the-handicapped television appeals), O'Donoghue said on one occasion: " 'Sophomoric' is the liberal code for funny."

Chevy Chase, a handsome, neatly groomed man, six feet four inches tall, with a disarming smile and an affable manner, has been described by interviewers as having a "country club face" and coming across as "Joe College" or "a nice young banker fresh from triumphs on some Ivy League campus." Typical of his everyday apparel are Brooks Brothers shirts open at the neck, corduroy pants, and canvas boots or sneakers.

Mitchell Glazer of *Crawdaddy*, interviewing Chase in his Beverly Hills home, noted a photograph of the comedian at age seven on the fireplace mantel: "It is a telling shot. All the ingredients—the wide smile offset by slightly closed, doubting eyes; the innocence, and, unbelievably, the cynicism—shine from little Chevy. He is coyly poised, with his left hand cradling the tilted, not quite angelic face. Any instant you expect the index finger to creep up his cheek and bury itself vigorously in his ear." Chase has been married twice, most recently to the actress Jacqueline Carlin, from December 1976 until May 1978, when divorce proceedings were begun.

Chase has found it difficult adapting to life in Los Angeles. "New York does provide you with enough anxiety to produce comedy," he observed in the *TV Guide* interview. "L.A. is a cow town and after a while your brain begins to atrophy out here. That's why the TV it produces is such junk. It doesn't deal with anything except the medium itself." Chase keeps in mind the threat that stardom poses to "perspective," because, as he told Tom Burke in the *Rolling Stone* interview, he does not want to lose his "base," which is "to make fun of bullshit." But he accepts success gladly: "We've all got that one thing in common: We are all surely going to die. So, hey, while we're on our way, why not try and go out a star?"

References: Crawdaddy p42+ S '78 pors; N Y Post p20 Ap 3 '76 por; N Y Times II p25+ My 1 '77 por; New York 8:34+ D 22 '75 pors; People 5:79+ Ap 12 '76 pors; Rolling Stone p32+ Jl 15 '76; Seventeen 154:174 S '76; International Television Almanac, 1979; Who's Who in America, 1978-79

Clayburgh, Jill

Apr. 30, 1944- Actress. Address: b. c/o Paramount Pictures Corp., 1 Gulf and Western Plaza, New York City, N.Y. 10023

When directing Jill Clayburgh in her recent *Luna*, the Italian filmmaker Bernardo Bertolucci became aware of "a very strange and mysterious quality she has," which he described, as quoted in *American Film*, as the ability "to move from one extreme to the other in the same shot, be funny and dramatic within the same scene." The emotional range and contrasting expressions that she displays in a single portrayal, such as that of Erica in *An Unmarried Woman* (1978), are paralleled in the ups and downs and the diversified and sometimes antithetical achievements of her career as a whole. In Broadway musicals and other stage productions, in TV dramas like *Hustling*, and in an assortment of motion pictures, she has created her characters through an "acting technique that results in winsome naturalness," as William Wolf pointed out in *Cue* (March 31, 1978), ". . . quick movements, glances, shrugs, half-smiles, and pensive, revealing expressions that make her . . . effervescent, original, and convincing."

Jill Clayburgh was born in New York City on April 30, 1944 to Albert Henry and Julia (Door) Clayburgh. The family included a younger brother and an older half-brother. Her mother had been production secretary to the producer David Merrick before her marriage. Although she was Jewish, the Clayburgh household in which Jill was reared, in a fashionable neighborhood on Manhattan's Upper East side, has been described by the writer Julie Baumgold, who was a childhood friend of Jill, as "haute Wasp." The vice-president of the Bancroft Bookcloth Company, her father is a well-to-do urbanite who frequents Manhattan art galleries and attends Broadway openings. He is also a lover of opera, as was his mother, the opera singer and New York socialite Alma Clayburgh.

In several press interviews Jill Clayburgh has recalled the difficulties for her of growing up in Manhattan. She was an overly sensitive, willful, and self-destructive child whose worried parents took her to a psychiatrist when she was eight or nine. She has a happy memory, however, of her early ventures in acting. "I loved the fantasy of movies and theatre," she told Helen Dorsey, who interviewed her for the New York Sunday News (August 24, 1975). "My friend, Julie Baumgold, and I used to perform every day at home in something we called 'Shooting Star and Silver Star.'" Her favorite play was Peter Pan, and her favorite actress was Jean Arthur, who starred on Broadway as Barrie's perennial boy. Julie Baumgold, a classmate of Jill at Town School, wrote of her young friend in New York (December 15, 1975), "She was an elegant, tall little girl with a summer house in Greenwich, classes at Mr. Barclay's dancing school, and a big smile."

Later, at Manhattan's exclusive Brearley School, Jill Clayburgh studied hard and competitively. Her serious-mindedness became further apparent in her choice of philosophy, religion, and literature as her subjects of special concentration at Sarah Lawrence College. Although she also had a few courses in the theatre arts, she would perhaps not have been attracted to the stage at that time if her roommate, Andra Ankers, an aspiring actress, had not persuaded her to spend a vacation as an apprentice in summer stock at the Williamstown Theater Festival in Massachusetts. Besides painting scenery, she played a one-line part in Shaw's Man and Superman, an experience that steered her toward the discovery of the emotional release she would find in acting.

While still in college, Jill Clayburgh co-starred with her friends Robert De Niro and Jennifer Salt in her first film, The Wedding Party, an independently financed production that another friend, Brian De Palma, helped to direct. After she had obtained her B.A. degree from Sarah Lawrence in 1966, she studied acting in Manhattan with Uta Hagen.

Another of her teachers, John Lehne, who favored a modified form of the Method acting, also served intermittently as her coach for several years. Through the influence of her mother, who had kept an interest in the theatre, she became a member of the Charles Playhouse in Boston, where she worked in both the children's and the adult companies.

One of the Boston repertory productions in which Miss Clayburgh appeared, along with The Balcony and Love for Love, among others, was Jean-Claude van Itallie's America Hurrah, whose cast included Al Pacino. They formed a romantic attachment, and after moving to New York together, they acted in a double bill of playlets by Israel Horovitz that opened in January 1968 at the Off-Broadway Astor Place Theater—Jill Clayburgh in the curtain raiser, It's Called the Sugar Plum, and Al Pacino in the more highly regarded The Indian Wants the Bronx. Later in 1968 they repeated their roles at the Spoleto Festival of Two Worlds in Italy.

Off-Broadway audiences also saw Jill Clayburgh in the fall of 1969 in Henry Bloomstein's satiric Calling in Crazy as a half-hearted nonconformist who becomes a militant rebel and in the spring of 1970 in Tina Howe's comedy The Nest. Clive Barnes of the New York Times (April 10, 1970), who added The Nest to his worst-plays list, described the scene in which Jill Clayburgh was featured: "The dramatic highlight comes when one girl naked to the waist gets caught up with the sugar icing of a gigantic cake. One of the men licks the icing off her bare breasts." Years later she recalled the incident with amusement when explaining in an interview that it was nothing new for her to play roles that called for appearing in scanty clothing or in the buff.

Although Jill Clayburgh's career had not yet begun its ascent, it became more diversified. She performed in episodes of the television programs N.Y.P.D. (ABC, 1968) and On Stage (NBC, 1969); portrayed Grace Bolton for about a year on the TV soap opera Search for Tomorrow; made TV commercials for Camay Soap; and appeared as Judith in a production of Shaw's The Devil's Disciple presented by the American Shakespeare Festival at Stratford, Connecticut during the summer of 1970. Miss Clayburgh then made her debut on Broadway, in October 1970, as the beautiful, spirited Hannah Cohen of The Rothschilds, a musical about the Jewish family that moved up from the Frankfurt ghetto in the late eighteenth century to become the wealthiest bankers of Europe. Haskel Frankel, in his review for the National Observer (October 26, 1970), singled out for special mention her performance in the courtship episode with Nathan, one of the five Rothschild sons: "With only one scene in which to establish herself, Miss Clayburgh offers just the right combination of British fire and ice that would make any man knock himself out to get her."

The Rothschilds ran for over a year at the Lunt-Fontanne Theater, but Jill Clayburgh left the cast well before the close of the musical to go to Los Angeles to play what proved to be a critically disastrous Desdemona to James Earl Jones's Othello at the Mark Taper Forum in 1971. While on the West Coast, she accepted the role of Naomi in Ernest Lehman's screen adaptation of Philip Roth's novel *Portnoy's Complaint* (Warner Brothers, 1972), portraying the Sabra with whom Portnoy seeks sexual adventure in Israel.

Bob Fosse brought Jill Clayburgh back to Broadway, via the Kennedy Center in Washington, in October 1972 in another long-running musical, his sparkling, lavishly produced *Pippin*, whose title character is the son of Charlemagne. As Catherine, in that fusion of American experimental theatre, morality play, and *commedia dell'arte*, she played a conniving young widow determined to persuade Pippin that in marriage to her he would find the happiness he sought. Winning him over in one of the show's "blockbusters," to use Walter Kerr's term, Miss Clayburgh proved, as she had in the musical The Rothschilds, that she is endowed with a highly creditable singing voice.

The role on the New York stage that Jill Clayburgh desperately coveted, as she has repeatedly admitted, was Chrissy, the go-go dancer in David Rabe's *Boom Boom Room* (later titled *In the Boom Boom Room*). But in the tryouts in 1973 for Joseph Papp's production of that play at Lincoln Center, she lost to Madeline Kahn. Theatregoers, therefore, next saw Miss Clayburgh, in 1974, not as Chrissy but as Dottie Moore in Tom Stoppard's intellectually acrobatic *Jumpers*, in which Diana Rigg had scored a hit when the play was performed in London two years earlier. At the Washington premiere of *Jumpers* Jill Clayburgh had the disadvantage not only of comparison by some critics between her style of acting and that of the British star, but also of opening night mishaps that gave the impression of insufficient preparation in production.

Covering the first night of *Jumpers* on Broadway at the Billy Rose Theater, Allan Wallach maintained in *Newsday* (April 23, 1974), "When this production originated in Washington two months ago, some critics felt Jill Clayburgh was miscast as Dottie. If so, she has overcome the mistake, mastering the complexities involved in playing a woman who is playfully sensuous yet fully aware of the currents of thought flowing around her." John Simon in *New York* (May 13, 1974) blamed the playwright more than the actress for the "no character" of Dottie.

Because of her failure to win the role of Chrissy, Miss Clayburgh had become convinced that she would improve her chances on the New York stage if she had "a Hollywood name," such as Madeline Kahn enjoyed.

Her part in *The Thief Who Came to Dinner* (Warner Brothers, 1973) had not been prominent enough to earn her recognition, nor was that in *The Terminal Man* (Warner Brothers, 1974). The turning point in her career came when she was cast as a prostitute, Wanda, in the made-for-television movie *Hustling*, Fay Kanin's adaptation of Gail Sheehy's investigative study of prostitution in New York City. In an interview with Bernard Drew for *American Film* (April 1979), Jill Clayburgh explained why her interpretation of the character was so convincing: "I played this whore as funny, sensitive, childlike, and quite mad, a girl who just doesn't know how to make it, a state I know something about." For her performance in *Hustling*, which was presented on ABC-TV on February 22, 1975, she won an Emmy nomination. She costarred with Peter Falk in another notable TV movie, a story of cancer-stricken lovers titled *Griffin and Phoenix* (ABC, 1976). In nondramatic appearances on television she has been seen as guest hostess on NBC's popular *Saturday Night Live*.

On the strength of her acting in *Hustling*, the director Sidney J. Furie chose Jill Clayburgh to portray the movie star of the 1930's and early 1940's Carole Lombard in *Gable and Lombard* (Universal, 1976). Generally panned as offensively vulgar, the film was further described by Pauline Kael in the *New Yorker* (February 23, 1976) as "the most raunchy, meaningless movie about Hollywood yet." More generous than most critics, who felt that despite her talent Miss Clayburgh could not overcome the clumsy script, William Wolf wrote in *Cue* (February 21, 1976), "She is extremely likeable, has the salty lines, and succeeds in creating a personality while all elements work against her."

Aboard the luxury passenger train from which her next movie took its name, *Silver Streak* (Twentieth Century-Fox, 1976), Miss Clayburgh was the secretary who speedily seduces the mild-mannered editor, played by Gene Wilder, in a romantic interlude of that detective spoof. "Clayburgh urgently needs to find a suitable movie to showcase her talents," Joseph Gelmis observed in his review of the film for *Newsday* (December 10, 1976). *Silver Streak*, however, did offer her a few moments to display her considerable gifts as a comedienne, as did *Semi-Tough* (United Artists, 1977), Michael Ritchie's satire on professional football and est-type self-improvement fads. In the role of Barbara Jane Bookman, the lovely, rich, profanity-spouting girlfriend of two football players, "she expresses a range of emotions from hysterical tears to a longshoreman's temper," Robert Martin informed readers of the Toronto *Globe and Mail* (November 18, 1977). He furthermore asserted, "She is also that rare commodity among young American film stars, an actress who is sexy without being merely a sex object."

One filmmaker who recognized that particular asset of Jill Clayburgh was Paul Mazursky, who explained, as quoted in *American Film* (April 1979), why he cast her as the heroine of *An Unmarried Woman* (Twentieth Century-Fox, 1978): "I was looking for three qualities: vulnerability, intelligence, and a sexuality that wasn't brazen." As Erica Benton, she played a woman traumatized by the desertion of her husband, a stockbroker, for a younger woman after seventeen years of marriage. With few exceptions, among them Stanley Kauffmann of the *New Republic*, critics agreed that Jill Clayburgh attained a virtually flawless performance. In his evaluation for the *National Review* (April 14, 1978), John Simon found her Erica to be "a woman rendered in all the complex interplay of antithetical impulses, ranging from subservience and vulnerability to angry or hopeful resilience. The actress exudes a wealth of inner activity and an ample repertoire of fascinatingly changing expressions, better than any kind of static, conventional prettiness." Miss Clayburgh's creation of Erica brought her an Oscar nomination for best actress, the best-actress award (shared with Isabelle Huppert of France) of the Cannes Film Festival, and New York's Golden Apple as best film actress.

Having found that roles for actresses as rewarding as Erica are rare in today's movie industry, Jill Clayburgh turned down scripts for almost a year before she accepted the part of an opera singer in Bernardo Bertolucci's *Luna* (Twentieth Century-Fox) and soon afterward that of a nursery schoolteacher in Alan J. Pakula's *Starting Over* (Paramount). The release of both pictures about the same time in 1979 offered moviegoers a startling contrast in characterization. In the former she played a self-centered mother whose relationship with her son stops only slightly short of incest, and in the latter, an unglamorous, but appealing divorcée whom Joseph Gelmis admired in *Newsday* (October 14, 1979) as being "recognizable as a person, amusing and sad and big-hearted."

Neither film had yet been released when Miss Clayburgh portrayed the character whose humorous and tragic qualities had long attracted her—the morally wounded but gallant go-go dancer in the Long Beach (California) Theater Festival presentation of *In the Boom Boom Room* in April 1979. While seeing little merit in Peter Flood's direction, Sylvie Drake wrote in the Los Angeles *Times* (April 19, 1979) that the production "benefits from a lucid and immensely vulnerable central performance by Jill Clayburgh."

During the preceding month, in March 1979, Jill Clayburgh had married the author of the play, David Rabe. As reported in *Us* (May 29, 1979), the couple moved into a West Side Manhattan apartment and decided upon a country house in Pennsylvania as a second home. According to *Us* moreover, "Not interested in chic clothes or social events, Clayburgh admits, 'My biggest extravagance is where I live.'"

Jill Clayburgh has natural brown hair, blue-green eyes, a slightly uptilted nose, and a face that she had described as "sweet-looking" almost to her own disbelief. She stands five feet eight and a half inches tall, weighs 120 pounds, and, like Erica of *An Unmarried Woman*, she jogs regularly to maintain a willowy figure and physical fitness. At the age of twenty-six she began to take psychotherapy seriously. "It has helped me more than anything else," she was quoted in the New York *Times* (December 15, 1976) as saying, ". . . I support it so wholly that I would never think not to talk about it. It's so wonderful." Inclined to be introspective and worrisome, she does not rejoice in giving interviews and is reluctant to appear on TV game or talk shows. Although she seeks professional recognition, she shuns the celebrity treatment, insisting, "I want to be an actress, not a personality."

References: *American Film* 4:19+ Ap '79 pors; *Los Angeles Times Calendar* p50 Ap 15 '79 por; *N Y Sunday News* III pl Ag 24 '75 por; *N Y Times* C p16 D 15 '76 por, C p8 Ja 20 '78 por; *Newsday* mag p21 Je 18 '78 por; *Rolling Stone* p26+ S 7 '78 pors

Claytor, W(illiam) Graham, Jr.

Mar. 14, 1912- United States Deputy Secretary of Defense. Address: b. Department of Defense, Pentagon Bldg., Washington, D.C. 20350; h. 2912 N St., NW, Washington, D.C. 20007

In the wake of a Cabinet reshuffle by President Jimmy Carter in July 1979, W. Graham Clayor Jr. replaced Charles W. Duncan Jr. as Deputy Secretary of Defense. When Claytor had earlier been appointed to succeed J. William Middendorf 2d as head of the Department of the Navy, in February 1977, he became the first Secretary of the Navy ever to have commanded commissioned ships. Claytor is a railroad buff who had practised law as an associate and partner of the topflight Washington firm of Covington & Burling for nearly thirty years before being elected president of the Southern Railway Company in 1967. In the Carter Administration he had the weighty responsibility of managing the business aspects of the United States sea force at a time when defense planners were critically examining the Navy's budget and its role in future wars. Urging flexibility in planning for the next century, he endorsed as a guideline the recent Naval Force Planning Study, popularly known

W. Graham Claytor Jr.

as "Seaplan 2000," which calls for a fleet large enough to maintain world stability, contain major crises, and deter the outbreak of a major war.

William Graham Claytor Jr. was born on March 14, 1912 in Roanoke, Virginia to William Graham and Gertrude Harris (Boatwright) Claytor. He has a younger brother, Robert Buckner Claytor, who also became a railroad executive. Their father was an electrical engineer who attained prominence as a utilities executive. Graham Claytor acquired his early education at the Haverford School in Pennsylvania and the Riverdale Country School in New York City. Later as a Phi Beta Kappa student at the University of Virginia, he specialized in mathematics and physics. When he graduated with the B.A. degree in 1933, however, he realized that the Depression had reduced job opportunities in his chosen field, electrical engineering, and he enrolled in the Harvard Law School for graduate work. After serving as president of the Harvard Law Review, he was awarded the J.D. degree summa cum laude in 1936.

Before he was admitted to the New York bar in 1937 and to the District of Columbia bar in 1938, Claytor worked as a law clerk for Judge Learned Hand of the United States Court of Appeals for the Second Circuit in 1936-37 and for Associate Justice Louis D. Brandeis of the United States Supreme Court in 1937-38. The two justices, who were among the nation's top jurists, differed in temperament and in the jobs they assigned the clerks, but Claytor credits both with teaching him how to make decisions and present a case. "I learned what kind of arguments to make and what kind not to make in a court brief," he explained in an interview

for Nation's Business (October 1976), ". . . to get rid of all the secondary points and concentrate on the essentials."

In 1938 Dean Acheson, who later became Secretary of State, and his partners in the Washington law firm of Covington, Burling, Rublee, Acheson & Shorn hired Claytor as an associate. But even before the United States entered World War II, he took a leave of absence for Naval service. Commissioned an ensign in the Navy in September 1940, Claytor went on active duty the following January. He was stationed first at the Washington Navy Yard and then aboard the USS Opal. He commanded the submarine chaser USS SC-516 in 1942-43, the destroyer escort Lee Fox in 1943-44, and the destroyer escort Cecil J. Doyle in 1944-45. His most memorable experience occurred near the end of the war when the Doyle became the first vessel to reach the survivors of the 1,199-man crew of the USS Indianapolis, sunk by Japanese torpedoes on July 30, 1945. Claytor's quick action contributed to the rescue of more than 300 men who had spent four days in shark-infested waters.

By the time he was released from active duty in the Navy, in 1946, Claytor had attained the rank of lieutenant commander. He returned to Covington & Burling, becoming a partner in 1947. The private practice of law proved so congenial to Claytor that when, in September 1963, he was offered the post of vice-president for law of the Southern Railway Company, he accepted only on the condition that he could divide his time between Covington & Burling and Southern, which has its headquarters in Washington. Gradually becoming more deeply involved in the railway, he left the law firm in September 1967, after being selected to succeed D. William Brosnan, who was retiring as president of the Southern. In an interview for the New York Times (February 4, 1968), Bronson said that he had recommended the lawyer's promotion because he had shown "an aptitude for operations and a ready understanding of the greatest challenge which the railroads face, which is to innovate services, equipment and pricing which will attract new business, hold existing business and recoup lost business."

Under the leadership of Claytor, an exponent of the team approach in management, Southern, which is the eighth largest railway in the United States, maintained its position as the most profitable line in the nation. The president admitted that historical circumstance accounted for part of the Southern's success. "The South stayed depressed after the Civil War, so our system didn't overbuild like the Northeast," he noted in statements quoted in the press. "We're benefiting in the South from losing the Civil War." He recognized, moreover, that Southern's 10,545 miles of track, connecting St. Louis, New Orleans, Jacksonville, and Washington, serve "the fastest-growing industrial area in the country." But Claytor also pointed out that Southern poured profits back into the business, analyzed customers' needs with better understanding, and led the way in technological innovations that increased productivity "not by forcing men to work harder, but by giving them better tools to work with."

As president of Southern, Claytor became confident that America's railroads could regain their former prominence in the nation's transport system. "The railroads have the technical capability of moving the freight more efficiently than any other mode of transportation," he told Robert E. Bedingfield of the New York Times (May 24, 1970). Although Claytor accepted the necessity of regulation for common carriers, he pinpointed dealing with the government as the industry's major problem. "I think we've got to have more government assistance," he argued, "comparable to the kind of government support that is given to competing modes." He pointed out that railroads devoted 20 percent of their revenues to the upkeep of their tracks, while the federal government assumed almost all the expenses of maintaining the highways and waterways used by trucks and barges. In particular, Claytor advocated that the government provide for loans that would enable financially weak lines to purchase new equipment and for compensation to railroads required by law to operate unprofitable runs.

While at Southern, Claytor resisted being drawn into mergers that offered greater size and prestige but no more efficiency, and he opposed railroad involvement outside the transportation industry. "I don't have an expertise in manufacturing textiles or bottling soft drinks and I don't think my team does," he once remarked. "I think we can run a better operation by sticking to what we know." Claytor, however, favored diversification within the transportation field and charged that the national policy prohibiting the common ownership of railroads and other carriers brought about "unnecessary inefficiency and needless costs for all modes." He argued that the Interstate Commerce Commission should permit mergers among its regulated industries, including trains, trucks, barges, and buses, and recommended that those businesses eventually join with ones offering air and ocean transport services. "If a transportation company could sell just that—transportation—and then perform it by whatever modes or combination of modes produced the required service at the cheapest cost, everyone would be ahead," Claytor explained, as quoted in the Washington Post (December 21, 1969). "Competition would remain, but it would be more effective competition between true transportation companies."

Claytor advanced to the chairmanship of Southern Railway on February 24, 1976, but resigned from that position within a year, when President Jimmy Carter named him Secretary of the Navy in the new Democratic Administration. Formally announced on February 7, 1977, the nomination won Senate confirmation on February 11. In an exception to his conflict-of-interest policy, Carter did not require Claytor to sell all his stocks. To protect the Claytors from a "serious and unreasonable financial loss" from capital gains taxes, Carter allowed the Secretary to put his railroad stocks in a blind trust and ordered him to abstain from taking part in decisions affecting the Southern line.

Partly because of his wartime experience aboard combat ships, Claytor's appointment was cheered in the Navy. "This is a Secretary who understands the Navy," a retired vice-admiral was quoted as saying. "He's already one of us and he doesn't even know where his office is, yet." Carter's efforts to deal with skyrocketing shipbuilding costs soon brought Secretary Claytor into controversy with planners at the Defense Department and at the Office of Management and Budget who wanted to modify the Navy's strategic role and cut $21 billion from its shipbuilding budget over the next five years. He reacted sharply to proposals to focus the Navy's attention on keeping open the sea lanes vital to the defense of the Central European land mass. Members of Secretary of Defense Harold Brown's staff who urged that approach were using "systems analysis as a cover for what is really subjective judgment," he argued, and warned that diminution of the Navy would jeopardize American interests in the western Pacific, the Indian Ocean, the Persian Gulf, and the eastern Mediterranean.

At the 1978 Current Strategy Forum of the Naval War College in Newport, Rhode Island, Claytor expressed concern that America "not create the Naval equivalent of the Maginot Line—in effect sizing our Naval strength against a single scenario without regard for the uncertainty of the world in the years ahead." Calling for greater military expenditures, he warned that "we cannot be the 'now' generation or the 'me' generation. We must, as Americans did in the past, make some tough decisions and some sacrifices to benefit those who follow us." On another occasion he compared defense spending to insurance premiums: they "won't increase your productivity or your standard of living, but they must be paid to protect against disaster."

Since budgetary restrictions required that a choice be made between types of aircraft carriers in the current shipbuilding program, Claytor, differing with Chief of Naval Operations James Holloway, expressed a preference for smaller, conventionally powered vessels over large, nuclear ones like Nimitz-class aircraft carriers. "One $2 billion carrier," he once observed, "soaks up a lot of money that could be spent on other ships" to bring the Navy closer to its goal of a 600-ship fleet. Claytor has also ironed out a number of problems with shipbuilders. On June 9, 1978, after long negotiations, he announced that the General Dynamics Corporation would absorb $359,000,000 out of an $843,000,000 overrun in the construction of eighteen nuclear-powered Los Angeles-class attack submarines. Eleven days later the Secretary revealed that Litton Industries would accept $200,000,000 out of a $647,000,000 loss in the building of five assault ships and thirty Spruance-class destroyers.

"We must plan as Lewis and Clark did— to take along whatever we might need for a whole range of unforeseen contingencies," Secretary Claytor contended in his continuing debate with Defense Department planners. "We can't do otherwise because we just don't understand the wars we haven't fought yet, especially the ones in the twenty-first century." Insisting that the key to the future will be "maximum flexibility," he reasoned that the ships delivered to the Navy in the 1980's must be capable of a full range of operations. Claytor urged the quick development of Vertical/Short Takeoff and Landing (V/STOL) planes, which, he predicted, "will become the backbone of the fleet air wing of the future." V/STOL aircraft will allow the Navy to triple or quadruple its carrier force by reducing the size requirements for the ships and will enable it to equip even small frigates and transports with their own air support. Although confident that the United States retains a "wide quantitative advantage" over the growing Soviet navy in the critical area of antisubmarine warfare, he pointed out that the proposed Seafarer communications network, which can free American submarines from having to surface daily for messages, is necessary to increase the nation's offensive capability under the sea. He also called for developing ships with more effective air defense systems and weapons for close-in fighting.

Shortly after he had taken office as Secretary of the Navy, Claytor declared in his first interview for Navy Times (April 25, 1977), "People are the most important thing in the Navy." One way he suggested to encourage competent officers to prolong their service in the Navy was to make officers' pensions "vested," like those of businessmen, so that even men and women who leave after ten years will have claim to some later compensation. That benefit may enable the Navy to retain for a longer period young officers who are willing to serve more than a single tour of duty but who do not want a full career in the service. He also wanted to provide greater rewards for petty officers by restricting sea pay to those enlisted personnel who have achieved petty officer status and have spent three years at sea; at present, the money is divided in very small amounts among all the noncommissioned sailors aboard ships. Claytor's position on the issue of unions in the military was that trade unionism would be incompatible with the kind of undivided leadership needed in the Navy.

As Secretary, Claytor took relatively liberal, yet restrained, stands on two of the most controversial personnel matters affecting the Navy. He was not willing to remove the bar against homosexuals in the Navy, but in April 1977 he upgraded from "other than honorable" to "honorable" the discharge of a young Annapolis graduate ousted from the Navy because of his unorthodox sexual preferences. The Secretary committed himself to changing the statute barring women from sea duty. He was quoted in Navy News as saying that "there are just one hell of a lot of things that women can do and ought to do" on permanent assignments to noncombat vessels and in temporary berths on combat ships in peacetime. To the dismay of some women, however, Claytor opposed assigning women full time on combat ships that may be required to operate in wartime for months without stops for liberty or recreation. "Let's get the women assimilated in other ships first," he advised; "let's get some experience."

As part of his Cabinet shake-up in the summer of 1979, Carter named Claytor Acting Secretary of Transportation, following the departure of Brock Adams. Soon afterward, on July 20, Carter submitted to the Senate Armed Services Committee the nomination of Claytor as Deputy Secretary of Defense, succeeding Charles W. Duncan Jr., who became head of the Department of Energy. Claytor's appointment was approved unanimously on July 26.

Throughout his career Claytor has been active in business, professional, and civic organizations. In addition to the Southern Railway and its affiliates, he had been a director of the Florida East Coast Railway Company; the Richmond, Fredericksburg and Potomac Railroad Company; the Richmond-Washington Company; J.P. Morgan and Company; the Morgan Guaranty Trust Company; and the Penn Virginia Corporation. He has also served on the board of directors of the Association of American Railroads and is a member of the American Bar Association, the American Judicature Society, the American Law Institute, the American Society of Corporate Executives, and the National Railway Historical Society. His clubs include the City Tavern Association, the International, and the Metropolitan in Washington; the Broad Street in New York; the Boston in New Orleans; the Shenandoah in Roanoke; the Commonwealth in Richmond; and the Chevy Chase and the Gibson Island in Maryland. He belongs to the Protestant Episcopal Foundation of the District of Columbia and was a trustee of the Episcopal Home for Children in Washington from 1960 to 1965.

W. Graham Claytor Jr. married Frances Murray Hammond of Roanoke on August 14, 1948, when both were lieutenant commanders in the Naval Reserve. During World War II, after graduating with the first class of WAVES from the training school at Smith College in 1942, Mrs. Claytor served in New York City on the staff of the commander, Eastern Sea Frontier, keeping track of ships and convoys crossing the Atlantic. The Claytors have a daughter, Frances Murray, and a son, William Graham

3d. For recreation Claytor turns to hunting, fishing, and sailing. His favorite hobby, one that he shares with his wife, is maintaining a model railroad, which runs through the garden of his Georgetown home.

References: Duns 104:46+ D 74 por; Forbes 117:32 Ja 15 '76 por; N Y Times III p3 F 4 '68 por; National Cyclopedia of American Biography current vol L (1972); Nations Bsns 60:102+ F '72 por; Navy Times p1+ Ap 25 '77 por; Congressional Directory, 1978; Who's Who in America, 1978-79

Cowley, Malcolm

Aug. 24, 1898- Writer. Address: b. Viking Press, 625 Madison Ave., New York City, N.Y. 10022; h. Church Rd., Sherman, Conn. 06784

In his reminiscent account of writers and writing in America over the past sixty years, —And I Worked at the Writer's Trade (1978), Malcolm Cowley identified himself as a literary historian and proposed a generational method in studying the waves of changes in style and outlook that occur in the flow of literature. He himself belongs to that luminous group of post-World War I writers whom Gertrude Stein called the Lost Generation. And while his broad literary interests include many diverse writers of the past and present, it is his own generation that he celebrated in his famous work, Exile's Return (1934), and other books. One of the cen-

tury's most influential critics, Cowley has kept his humanistic judgments free of dogma and pedantry in hundreds of book reviews and literary essays—many of them for the New Republic, of which he was literary editor from 1929 to 1944—and in introductions to books he has edited.

Malcolm Cowley was born on August 24, 1898 in the Allegheny hills village of Belsano, Pennsylvania to William Cowley, a homeopathic physician, and Josephine (Hutmacher) Cowley. His father practised in Pittsburgh, which was for the most part Cowley's early home, but his preference for the country made him feel that he belonged in Belsano, where the family spent the summers. He has recalled, nevertheless, that as a student at Peabody High School in Pittsburgh, he had the time of his life. One of his friends from early childhood was Kenneth Burke, also a student of Peabody High School, with whom in adolescence he began to exchange a long series of letters that included discussions of the books they were reading.

In 1915 Cowley enrolled in Harvard University, but like many other young men of his generation, he was distracted from study by an urge to serve in World War I. Leaving college in the spring of 1917, he joined the American Ambulance Service in France, where he drove a munitions truck for the French army for several months. He returned to Harvard in February 1918 and shortly afterward was elected president of the Harvard Advocate, a distinction that he has attributed not to brilliance, but rather to his availability as a member of the editorial board not planning immediate enlistment in the Army. But in the autumn he, also, was in uniform and had completed a week's instruction in artillery officers' training school before the signing of the Armistice.

When Cowley was eventually awarded his B.A. degree cum laude from Harvard, in the winter of 1920, he had actually attended classes for a total of less than three years. On his release from the Army and before his return to college, he had lived for several months in Manhattan's Greenwich Village, so impoverished and hungry that writing for him necessarily became a trade, a means of paying the rent. Through his girlfriend Peggy, later his wife, he met Clarence Britten, the literary editor of the Dial, a fortnightly little magazine, who assigned him books to be reviewed in a hundred words at a penny a word. While awaiting payment for the reviews upon publication, he sold the books to secondhand bookstores to help make ends meet. During the summer of 1919 he began contributing book reviews also to the New Republic.

Although he would have preferred to spend his time working on his poetry, even after his graduation from Harvard Cowley had to take free-lance assignments from various magazines to support himself during his literary apprenticeship in New York. He also held a regular job as a copy writer for about a year with *Sweet's Architectural Catalogue*. His attitude in his early twenties toward writing was what he has called "anti-careerist." As he explained in—*And I Worked at the Writer's Trade; Chapters of Literary History, 1918-1978* (Viking, 1978), "I wanted to be a writer, but not a celebrated writer appearing in glossy magazines. I wanted to live obscurely, limit my needs, and preserve my freedom to write something new and perfect at some moment in the future; that was the dream of producing a masterpiece that obsessed the young writers of my age group." In his hackwork, meanwhile, he tried to give more than he was paid for. His clean, logical prose delighted editors, who were spared the ordeal of revising.

An American Field Service Fellowship enabled Cowley to study French literature and history in France during 1921-22 at the Université de Montpellier. When the fellowship was renewed for a second year, he moved to Giverny, near Paris. Besides hobnobbing with many young American expatriate writers, with whose little magazines *Broom* and *Secession* he was editorially involved, he made friends with Tristan Tzara, Louis Aragon, and other leaders of the Dada and Surrealist movements.

Back home again in New York in the summer of 1923, Cowley resumed his association with *Sweet's Architectural Catalogue* as well as free-lance book reviewing for journals. He added to his income by translating several books from the French, including Pierre MacOrlan's *On Board the Morning Star* (Boni, 1924), Joseph Delteil's *Joan of Arc* (Minton, 1926), and Paul Valéry's *Variety* (Harcourt, 1927). Toward the end of the decade he yielded to the encouragement of the poet Hart Crane, a close friend, that he make a book of the poems he had written for magazines during the past ten years. Cowley devoted considerable time to revising and arranging the autobiographical sequence of the fifty-six poems that make up *Blue Juniata*, whose publication by Jonathan Cape and Harrison Smith in 1929 he regards as marking the end of his literary apprenticeship.

The enthusiastic reception that the critics gave *Blue Juniata* included several warm tributes to Cowley's lyrical gifts, but some reviewers valued it most of all as an account of the development of the poet and of his fellow writers involved in the literary revival of the 1920's. Allen Tate wrote of the collection in the *New Republic* (August 28, 1929), "As a document of the first post-war generation, it is unique. Cowley's generation appeared after the war had given the 'genteel tradition' and the provincial ways of life in America a staggering blow. This volume is the record kept by a member of this genera-tion who broke with his past, witnessed the moral collapse of Europe, and returned to make the best of the confused intellectual life of post-war New York." Seventeen of Cowley's other poems, also concerned with the alienated of his generation, were collected in *The Dry Season* (New Directions, 1941) and later included with the poems of his first volume and nineteen additional poems in *Blue Juniata: Collected Poems* (Viking, 1968).

Cowley became literary editor of the *New Republic* in 1929, succeeding Edmund Wilson. Among the many beginners in literature that he encouraged was the teen-age John Cheever, whose first short story, "Expelled," he published in the *New Republic* in 1930. He refused to give books to Erskine Caldwell for review because he feared that reviewing would interfere with what he recognized as Caldwell's gift for storytelling. But he helped many free-lance book reviewers, including Alfred Kazin, who wrote in *Starting Out in the Thirties* (1965), "The lead review in the *New Republic*, a single page usually written by Cowley himself, brought the week to focus for people to whom this page, breathing intellectual fight in its sharp black title and solid double-columned lines of argument, represented the most dramatically satisfying confrontation of a new book by a gifted, uncompromising critical intelligence."

While applying his wide-ranging appreciation of literature to his job at the *New Republic* until 1944, Cowley continued to be preoccupied with the themes he had explored in his poetry In 1934 he published the book for which he is best known, *Exile's Return; A Narrative of Ideas* (Norton). The ideas were those of the writers of the 1920's who could not resume their old patterns of behavior and, with a somewhat naïve exhilaration, tried to pursue art as a way of life in Paris or in Greenwich Village, outside the mainstream of American culture. Their exile ended late in the decade with the Wall Street crash, when they began to become absorbed into society as a whole through involvement in various group efforts.

A revised edition of *Exile's Return*, which Viking published in 1951, had as its subtitle *A Literary Odyssey of the 1920's*, to underscore the ordeal of wandering, of estrangement and reconciliation, of departure and return that Cowley shared with his contemporaries after World War I. His sympathy stemmed not only from similar experiences, but also from his friendships with Hart Crane, Ernest Hemingway, F. Scott Fitzgerald, Ezra Pound, and other major literary figures of the time. Although his text, aside from additions, remained substantially unchanged from the earlier edition, by 1951 Cowley had been able to introduce a new perspective on the writings of the 1920's.

Later, from the vantage point of two more decades, Cowley reexamined his favorite subject in *A Second Flowering; Works and Days of the Lost Generation* (Viking, 1973). Choosing eight representative writers—Fitzgerald, Hemingway, Crane, John Dos Passos, E. E. Cummings, Thornton Wilder, William Faulkner, and Thomas Wolfe—he "dealt with their early dream of literary life," as he explained in his Foreword, "their subsequent careers at home and abroad, and the works they produced during a period that now seems to have been a second flowering of American literature." The literary giants of an earlier generation, such as Longfellow, Hawthorne, and Thoreau, had been the subject of Van Wyck Brooks's *The Flowering of New England, 1815-1865* (1936). Cowley's memoir of life and literature in the early 1930's, "The Dream of the Golden Mountains," is scheduled for publication by Viking in 1980.

Among the first to recognize the potential of some of the brilliant writers of his own age, Cowley continued to champion their work with appraisals that for the most part time has proved to be remarkably sound. Some scholars consider one of his most valuable contributions to American literature to be his rescue of William Faulkner from obscurity in the mid-1940's with his editing of *The Portable Faulkner* (Viking, 1945). Cowley's long introductory essay on the unity of Faulkner's work, which was included in *A Second Flowering*, has been praised by William Styron, writing in the New York Times Book Review (May 6, 1973), as "a lucid jewel of exegesis." To the delight of literary historians and readers of Faulkner, Cowley published his eighteen-year correspondence with the novelist in *The Faulkner-Cowley File: Letters and Memories, 1944-1962* (Viking, 1966), which tells how *The Portable Faulkner* was put together and what effect the book and its critical reception had on Faulkner's reputation.

At the time that Cowley began his correspondence with Faulkner, he no longer had editorial responsibility at the *New Republic*, but he continued to write for that magazine. A collection of his essays and reviews that had appeared in the *New Republic* from 1929 to 1941, with a few pieces from other periodicals, were published in *Think Back on Us; A Contemporary Chronicle of the 1930's* (Southern Illinois Univ. Press, 1967). Although Cowley characteristically mixes his reflections on social and literary matters, Henry Dan Piper, who edited the book, arranged the articles chronologically in two parts, "The Social Record" and "The Literary Record."

Many of Cowley's articles convey a sense of the burning concern of writers of the Depression years with political issues and their readiness for moral involvement in social causes. His own leftist sympathies brought

him a storm of abusive criticism after the Hitler-Stalin pact of August 1939 and made him the target of the Dies Committee when he went to work in late 1941 for the Office of Facts and Figures, a newly formed wartime government agency headed by the poet Archibald MacLeish. After resigning from his Washington job in the spring of 1942, as he recalled in —*And I Worked at the Writer's Trade,* he resolved "not to join anything in the future. Not to write statements. . . . Not to attend meetings. . . . I felt politically amputated, emasculated, but then I had never been happy among politicians. Now, with a sense of release and opportunity, I could get back to my proper field of interest."

How happy Cowley was among writers he demonstrated again in *The Literary Situation* (Viking, 1954), a group of previously published essays emended and meshed into a sociological study of the occupation of writing in present-day America. Many of the book's shrewd perceptions derive from the author's own experiences in literary journalism. In the more extended and reflective chapters of *A Many-Windowed House; Collected Essays on American Writers and American Writing* (Southern Illinois Univ. Press, 1971), Cowley offers interpretations and appraisals of Hawthorne, Walt Whitman, Horatio Alger, Lafcadio Hearn, Henry James, and other writers as well as observations on various literary subjects such as criticism.

Besides promoting the values of literature in book reviews and essays, over the years Cowley has edited, with introductions, many books, some of which, like *The Portable Faulkner,* have made the work of a writer more easily available, by spurring a demand for reprints, and have increased readers' appreciation of the text. His editions of works by a single author include Brantz Mayer's *Adventures of an African Slaver* (Routledge, 1928); *The Portable Hemingway* (Viking, 1944); with Hannah Josephson, *Aragon: Poet of the French Resistance* (Duell, 1945); *The Portable Hawthorne* (Viking, 1948); *The Complete Poetry and Prose of Walt Whitman* (Pellegrini, 1948) and *Leaves of Grass: The First (1855) Edition* (Viking, 1959); and F. Scott Fitzgerald's *Stories* (Scribner, 1951).

Among the books Cowley has edited that concern more than one writer are *After the Genteel Tradition: American Writers Since 1910* (Norton, 1937; Southern Illinois Univ. Press, 1964) and, in collaboration with Howard E. Hugo, *The Lessons of the Masters: An Anthology of the Novel from Cervantes to Hemingway* (Scribner, 1971). He also edited and wrote the introduction to *Writers at Work: The Paris Review Interviews* (Viking, 1958), which became the first volume in a distinguished series and has been recognized as a model for literary interviewing.

"Being a literary historian is a rewarding but not a lucrative profession," Cowley observed in —*And I Worked at the Writer's Trade.* "After 1948 I supplemented my income by doing a good deal of knockabout teaching and lecturing at various universities." He was visiting professor at the University of Washington in Seattle in 1950; Stanford University in 1956, 1959, 1960-61, and 1965; University of Michigan in 1957; University of California at Berkeley in 1962; Cornell University in 1964; University of Minnesota in 1971; and University of Warwick in England in 1973.

Since 1948 Cowley has been literary adviser of the Viking Press in New York City and is currently serving as general editor of a school series, the Viking Classical Library. He is also a director of the Corporation of Yaddo, the arts foundation in Saratoga Springs, New York, which provides a retreat for writers; a member of the National Institute of Arts and Letters, of which he was president from 1956 to 1959 and from 1962 to 1965; and a member of the American Academy of Arts and Letters, of which he was chancellor from 1967 to 1977. Cowley's awards include the Levinson Prize in 1927, the Harriet Monroe Memorial Prize in 1939 for verse published in *Poetry* magazine, a grant from the National Institute of Arts and Letters in 1946, and a $10,000 award from the National Endowment for the Arts in 1967. He is also the recipient of honorary doctorates from Franklin and Marshall College, Colby College, the University of Warwick, and the University of New Haven.

During his bohemian days, in 1919, Malcolm Cowley married Marguerite Frances Baird, who was also known in Greenwich Village literary circles as Peggy Johns, because she had been married to the poet Orrick Johns. After his divorce from his first wife in 1932, Cowley married Muriel Maurer, on June 18, 1932. By that marriage he has a son, Robert William, who became an editor of Random House. Malcolm Cowley collaborated with his son on *Fitzgerald and the Jazz Age* (Scribner, 1966), one of several books he edited involving the work of F. Scott Fitzgerald.

Recounting a recent conversation with Cowley at the Harvard Club in New York, George Plimpton, publisher of the *Paris Review,* wrote of his friend in the New York *Times Book Review* (April 30, 1978), "His manner is brisk, his voice hearty. He wears a hearing aid, but this is the only visible concession to his years." Cowley keeps a trim figure and has blue eyes, a clipped mustache, and a full head of gray hair. A countryman at heart, in the late 1920's he used part of a $100 prize for his poetry for a down payment on a bucolic haven near Patterson, New York. Later he moved to a converted barn in rural Sherman, Connecticut, where he has spent as much time as he can in reading, reminiscing, writing, gardening, and cultivating pine trees.

References: Contemporary Authors 1st rev vols 5-8 (1969); Contemporary Literary Critics (1975); Twentieth Century Authors (1947), First Supplement (1955); Who's Who in America, 1978-79

Crespin, Régine

Feb. 23, 1927. French singer Address: b. c/o Herbert H. Breslin, Inc., 119 W. 57th St., New York City, N.Y. 10019; h. 3 Avenue Frochot, 75009 Paris, France

The dramatic soprano Régine Crespin, who is known as much for her acting ability and commanding presence as for her resplendent vocal powers, is one of the few French opera singers of our day who enjoys international star status. Something of a rarity in that she feels as much at home in the German and Italian repertoires as she does in the French, Miss Crespin has sung at such shrines of German opera as Bayreuth and Salzburg, at Italy's La Scala, and at major operatic houses in Europe and the Americas. In the course of her long career she has been equally busy as a recitalist, as a recording artist with some five companies in the United States and abroad, and as a soloist with leading symphony orchestras throughout the world. Viewing her, not without justification, as a kind of national resource, French enthusiasts have called her "la Régine nationale."

Régine Crespin was born on February 23, 1927 in Marseilles, France to a French father, Henri Crespin and an Italian mother, Marguerite (Di Meirone) Crespin. She grew up in

Nîmes, in the South of France, and although her parents wanted her to study pharmacy, she turned to singing at seventeen after having taken piano lessons for about ten years. Her early teachers included Georges Jouatte, a tenor, Madame Louis Fourestier, a pupil of Lilli Lehmann, and a soprano named Kossa whose career predated World War I. Although at first her voice was small and high, with use it eventually developed a mezzo-like lower register with a loss of high notes, and finally developed into a powerful dramatic soprano. Miss Crespin obtained her baccalauréat, along with three first prizes, from the Paris Conservatoire. She made her operatic debut in 1951 at Mulhouse, France, where she sang Elsa in Wagner's *Lohengrin;* that same year she made her Paris Opéra debut in the same role. In the next few years the Parisian public heard her in *Tosca, Il Trovatore, Otello, Die Walküre, Oberon, Fidelio, Der Rosenkavalier,* and *Le Nozze di Figaro.*

In the mid-1950's the French composer Francis Poulenc heard Miss Crespin sing the role of Desdemona in Verdi's *Otello* at the Paris Opéra. Backstage he complimented her on her performance and confided his plan to set to music *Les Dialogues des Carmélites,* Georges Bernanos' drama about the "psychology of fear" operating among a group of Carmelite nuns sentenced to death during the French Revolution. Familiar with the play, Miss Crespin at first scoffed at the possibility of turning it into an opera. Surprisingly, Poulenc was not rebuffed by her audacity, but invited her to visit him. When he played her the music she would sing as the new prioress, Madame Lidoine, as the nuns await their execution she was forced to change her mind. "Then and there," she says, "I knew this was going to be a beautiful opera." On June 21, 1957 Régine Crespin appeared in the world premiere of *Les Dialogues des Carmélites* at the Paris Opéra. Later Miss Crespin and the rest of the original cast recorded the entire opera for Angel Records, under the baton of André Cluytens.

In the summer of 1958 Régine Crespin made her debut at the Bayreuth Festival in Germany as Kundry in *Parsifal* after being coached in the role by the late Wieland Wagner, the composer's grandson, to whom she had been referred by André Cluytens. That same year the Paris Opéra staged a new production of Verdi's *Un Ballo in Maschera* for her. On May 28, 1959 England's Glyndebourne Festival celebrated its twenty-fifth anniversary by producing for the first time Richard Strauss's *Der Rosenkavalier* with Régine Crespin as the Marschallin. The opera received thirteen performances and was repeated again at the 1960 festival with Miss Crespin sharing the role with another soprano. That same year witnessed her debut at La Scala in the title role of Ildebrando Pizzetti's 1915 opera *Fedra,* and her debut at the Vienna State Opera as

Sieglinde in Wagner's *Die Walküre.* Her Marschallin served as the vehicle for her Berlin State Opera debut in 1960 and for her debut at Covent Garden in London in 1961.

Régine Crespin's American debut had originally been scheduled to take place at the Metropolitan Opera House in a revival of *Der Rosenkavalier,* but because of an emergency at the Chicago Lyric Opera it took place instead in Chicago, with the blessing of the Met, on October 26, 1962, in a production of Puccini's *Tosca.* Two more Chicago performances followed before a Met audience finally heard her Marschallin on November 19, in a cast that included Otto Edelmann, Hertha Töpper, and Anneliese Rothenberger. Harold C. Schonberg spoke for all of his colleagues when he wrote in the New York *Times* (November 20, 1962): "In Miss Crespin, the Metropolitan and *Der Rosenkavalier* have a singer worthy of the great tradition of house and opera. She gave a simply beautiful performance." That splendid tradition included the legendary Lotte Lehmann who sang the role many times at the Metropolitan during her career, and who shared the standing ovation as codirector of the production. The *New Yorker* critic Winthrop Sargeant (December 1, 1962) hailed Crespin as "quite a phenomenon." "She has a large voice," he wrote, "which she handles with enormous intelligence and an exquisite feeling for nuance. She sings German, even the Viennese dialect of it that appears here and there in the role, as if she had been born on the Danube instead of on the Mediterranean." That season Miss Crespin sang the Marschallin six more times, in addition to appearing in a performance of *Un Ballo in Maschera.*

In music more off the beaten track, in January 1963 Régine Crespin sang the role of Julia in a concert version of Spontini's rarely performed *La Vestale,* which was given by the Concert Opera Association in Philharmonic Hall at Lincoln Center, dominating the evening, according to Miles Kastendieck of the *Christian Science Monitor* (January 16, 1963) with her "distinctive stage presence and her notable sense of style." The following season she appeared in *Fidelio, Tannhaüser,* and *Un Ballo in Maschera* at the Chicago Lyric Opera before going to Carnegie Hall for another assignment in a concert version of a seldom encountered opera. As Salomé in Massenet's *Hérodiade* (last heard in New York City around 1905), she prompted Alan Rich to report in the New York *Herald Tribune* (December 11, 1963) that she "raised the word 'magnificent' to some new and unexplored level of meaning. Vocally, even histrionically . . . she was overwhelming."

Her first Met appearance as Elsa in *Lohengrin* at a Saturday matinee was generally well received by the critics, with Louis Biancolli observing in the New York *World Telegram and Sun* (February 3, 1964) that "once in a while this sounds like a voice divided against itself—

now smooth and ravishing, now strident and pinched," but "when the music was comfortable for her, she sang with great beauty and expressiveness; indeed, at times there was no living Elsa to surpass her." Miss Crespin sang six more performances of the work in New York that winter, and the following season she was back in Chicago for performances of *Tosca* and *Ariadne auf Naxos*.

At her first appearance as soloist with the New York Philharmonic, Régine Crespin sang Ravel's *Shéhérazade,* a setting for voice and orchestra of three poems by Tristan Klingsor, and "Ah, Perfido," a concert aria with Italian text, by Beethoven. Among the viewers who preferred her Beethoven were John Gruen of the New York *Herald-Tribune* (February 5, 1965), who heard in her Ravel a disconcerting "iciness" and Harriett Johnson of the New York *Post* (February 5, 1965), who complained that her "personal involvement with these songs . . . left something to be desired." That incongruity can perhaps best be explained by Régine Crespin's own comments on her native tongue, as reported by John Kraglund of the Toronto *Globe and Mail* (November 5, 1963): "I sing in three languages—German, Italian, and French, and my preference for them is in that order. French is too difficult a language to sing. There are too many nasal sounds."

As if to belie that statement, Miss Crespin excited an enthusiastic audience at her first New York recital six weeks later at Hunter College with a dozen French songs and arias by Gounod, Poulenc, Ravel, Saint-Saëns, Roussel, Fauré, and Debussy, among other selections. In March 1965 she sang Sieglinde in *Die Walküre* for the first time at the Met, and in April a capacity house heard her for the first time as Tosca when she took over the role from the departing Maria Callas. The rest of her year was both marred by a backstage dispute with tenor Giuseppe di Stefano at the Teatro Colón in Buenos Aires in July that left her in tears, and gladdened by her return to the Paris Opéra in October, after a two year absence, where she triumphed in the title role in a new production of Gluck's *Iphigénie en Tauride*. In March 1966 she returned to the Metropolitan Opera for the close of the company's valedictory season at the rundown old house on Thirty-ninth Street, and at the Gala Farewell on April 16 she joined mezzo-soprano Biserka Cvejic for the duet "L'amo come il fulgor del crato" from Ponchielli's *La Gioconda*. In between her Met operatic performances that season in *Parsifal, Tosca,* and *Un Ballo in Maschera*, Miss Crespin found time for a recital at the Metropolitan Museum of Art that featured German lieder and French art songs.

During the 1967-68 season New Yorkers heard Régine Crespin undertake both of the leading soprano roles in Wagner's *Die Walküre*. In December she sang Sieglinde twice, at the Met, stepping in for an ailing colleague, and on February 21 she sang her first Met Brünnhilde.

Noting that she had sung both roles in Europe and had recorded them as well, Allen Hughes observed in the New York *Times* (February 23, 1968): "There was no doubt about her ability to cope with either one . . . it goes almost without saying that she was impressive as Brünnhilde. Her voice was full-bodied and pliant . . . and her experience in the repertory has given her Wagnerian poise and presence. The chances are, however, that she is more suited temperamentally to the softer human role of Sieglinde. There is a natural warmth in her singing and stage manner that asserts itself almost as soon as she has sung 'Hojotoho' and keeps her Brünnhilde from being as supernatural and as heroic as one would expect."

In the course of the following season Miss Crespin again performed both of the *Die Walküre* soprano roles and appeared in a Carnegie Hall recital of songs by Schumann, Berg, Poulenc, and Duparc. She gave her regal interpretation of the Marschallin not only at Lincoln Center but also during the Met's spring tour in Boston, Cleveland, Atlanta, Memphis, and Detroit. Her next four seasons at the Metropolitan included portrayals of Giulietta in Offenbach's *The Tales of Hoffman*, Charlotte in Massenet's *Werther*, Santuzza in Mascagni's *Cavalleria Rusticana*, and the Marschallin in *Der Rosenkavalier*.

In 1970, as a result of the breakup of her marriage and emotional problems dating back to childhood, Régine Crespin suffered a vocal crisis. As she told Stephen Wadsworth of *Opera News* (January 13, 1979): "When I felt bad, I was lazy and did not work again. . . . I went one, maybe two years without vocalizing, maintaining. Soon I was not able to do some little thing. . . . So you lose half a tone, you lose a pianissimo. You lose some quality you never even consciously knew you had. . . . I decided either I really correctly and properly face myself and what I'm doing, or I stop." After her agent found her a new vocal teacher, she dropped certain roles no longer suitable for her voice: Tosca, Elsa, all the Verdi heroines. She is now singing mezzo roles "but as a soprano." When she returned to the Met after an absence of two seasons it was in a role she had never done on the stage before—Bizet's *Carmen*—although she had sung two concert performances in preparation for an Erato recording with conductor Alain Lombard. Formerly convinced that Carmen is a role strictly for mezzo-sopranos, she now counts it as one of her favorites along with Sieglinde, the Marschallin, and Dido in Berlioz' *Les Troyens*.

Writing of her first Met performance in *Carmen* in the New York *Post* (October 31, 1975), Speight Jenkins noted: "Miss Crespin made Carmen in every gesture more a French woman than a gypsy, and her sexiness engulfed everyone in the audience capable of comprehending it. At first she was almost too lightly coquettish with her hair too styled, but then it became clear that hers was a Carmen who commanded her man with female-ness, not bitchiness. . . . Who there will ever forget the seductiveness of her Seguidilla? Or the delightful, really funny byplay with José in Act IJ? . . . Vocally, she has returned to the good health of a decade ago." That season she also took part, with resounding success, in the American premiere of another nineteenth-century French work, Jules Massenet's oratorio, *Marie Magdeleine*, in a performance by the Sacred Music Society at Lincoln Center.

Once characterized as a "dignified Wagnerian body wedded to the soul of a soubrette," Régine Crespin has turned in recent years to lighter music. She has taken part in complete recordings for Angel Records of three Offenbach operettas, *La Grande-Duchesse de Gérolstein*, *La Périchole*, and *La Vie Parisienne*, and in a Carnegie Hall recital she sang what critic Allen Hughes, writing in the New York *Times* (April 25, 1975) described as "the most peculiar assortment of French songs and arias this listener has ever encountered . . . more reminiscent of the French chanson tradition . . . than the French mélodie, or art song."

When, in the mid-1970's, Régine Crespin was approached by Met officials who wanted to cast her as the old prioress in the company's first production of Poulenc's *Dialogues of the Carmelites*, she expressed reluctance for several reasons. For one thing, the tessitura of the heavily dramatic role was, in her opinion, too low for her, and for another, she hesitated because the production was to be sung in English. Not only had she never sung in that language before, but she would also be the only foreigner in the cast. But a new look at the score assured her that the music was not, after all, outside her range, and although she experienced some difficulty with a few English sounds when the production had its Met premiere in February 1977, the majority of critics in attendance felt her diction was clearer than any other singer in the cast. And her much acclaimed performance as the old prioress, especially in the harrowing twenty-minute death scene, fulfilled Poulenc's prophesy, made years earlier when she had spoken to him enviously of the dramatic possibilities of the role, that she would sing it someday.

After a season's absence from the Met, Régine Crespin returned with her distinctive interpretation of Carmen, late in November 1978. Later that season she appeared as Charlotte in Massenet's *Werther*, a role she had sung while still a student. The part, according to Allen Hughes of the New York *Times* (January 20, 1979) "is so right for her, or she for it, that her singing seems like natural speech and her acting the expected movements and responses of a woman in Charlotte's milieu and predicament."

Régine Crespin is a Chevalier de l'Ordre National du Mérite, a Chevalier de la Légion d'Honneur, and a Commandeur de l'Ordre des Arts et des Lettres. Her marriage, in 1962, to the French novelist, critic, poet, and translator Lou Bruder ended in divorce. With an eye to eventual retirement, Miss Crespin has begun to teach part-time at the Paris Conservatory. Apart from her annual two-month vacation at her villa on Majorca, her chief diversions are reading, listening to pop music, and going out on an occasional night on the town with friends, when she dances in discos and indulges in the singer's cardinal sins—smoking and drinking.

References: Hi Fi 27:86+ S '77 por; N Y Times II p11 Ap '65 por; Opera N 27:15 D 22 '62 por, 43:9+ Ja 13 '79 por; International Who's Who, 1978-79; Thompson, O., ed. International Cyclopedia of Music and Musicians, 1964; Who's Who, 1979-80; Who's Who in Opera, 1976; Who's Who In the World, 1978-79

Culver, John C.

Aug. 8, 1932- United States Senator from Iowa. Address: Room 344, Russell Senate Office Building, Washington, D.C. 20510

Democrat John C. Culver, the senior United States Senator from Iowa, is among the most effective legislators on Capitol Hill. The eloquent Culver, who might be described as a Kennedy liberal, entered politics as an assistant to Senator Edward M. Kennedy and continued his governmental career in the House of Representatives, where he served from 1965 to 1975 and rose to leadership of the liberal caucus. In the Senate, where his current six-year team started in 1975, he serves on the

Judiciary Committee, the Armed Services Committee, The Environment and Public Works Committee, and the Small Business Committee, and he chairs four subcommittees. From those forums, and as a brilliant floor manager, he has worked for reform of the legislative process; continuation of social-welfare and other programs threatened by the current backlash against big-spending liberalism; environmental protection; "cost-effective defense" and strategic arms limitation; the maintenance of foreign aid; and amicable relations, where possible, with Communist and non-aligned countries.

As the 1980 elections approach, Culver's position is considered vulnerable, given Iowa's long-term voting history, conservative Roger William Jepsen's capture of its junior Senate seat in 1978, and President Carter's weakness in some recent public-opinion polls. The Republicans have marked Culver as one of their special targets for 1980, and conservative fund-raisers have begun a major effort to collect money for the campaign against him.

The son of Republican parents, John C. Culver was born in Rochester, Minnesota on August 8, 1932, and he grew up in Cedar Rapids, Iowa. After graduating from Franklin High School in Cedar Rapids, Culver enrolled at Harvard University, where he became a close friend of another Harvard freshman, Edward M. Kennedy. At Harvard, Culver majored in American government and played fullback on the football team. He took his B.A. degree cum laude in 1954.

A professional draft choice, Culver passed up the opportunity for a career in football to accept the Lionel de Jersey Harvard Scholarship at Cambridge University in England. After a year (1954-55) at Cambridge's Emmanuel College, he did a three-year tour of duty with the United States Marine Corps, in which he rose to the rank of captain, and he then studied law at Harvard, where he received his LL.B. degree in 1962.

Culver worked in Edward M. Kennedy's successful campaign for the Senate in 1962, and during the following year he served as a legislative assistant to Senator Kennedy in Washington. Returning to Iowa, he practised law briefly before entering politics, as the Democratic contender in the 1964 Congressional contest in the state's Second District. In that traditionally Republican district Culver won election to the 89th Congress in the Democratic sweep of November 3, 1964, and, as he was reelected by ever-increasing margins to the 90th, 91st, 92nd, and 93rd Congresses.

In the House, Culver was a farm bloc Congressman who generally aligned himself with Northern urban liberals. In the late 1960's, as controversy over the war in Vietnam became acrimonious, he opposed punitive measures directed against the antiwar movement and such related proposals as the one making "desecration of the flag" a federal offense. As the war wore on, he became increasingly dovish.

As a Congressman, Culver consistently voted in favor of civil rights legislation, poverty programs, and assistance for cities. In keeping with his role as the spokesman for an urbanized region of an agricultural state, he fostered a program that encouraged Congressmen from urban and rural districts to exchange visits in order to learn more about each other's problems. Culver's vote against a $250,000,000 loan guarantee for the Lockheed Aircraft Corporation, which subcontracted with Collins Radio of Cedar Rapids, risked the wrath of his constituency. On the other hand, he courted its favor by supporting measures for rural and small town development, resisting high tariffs that might hurt the substantial export trade in machinery and processed farm products from his district, and advocating imposts to protect Iowa's farmers and livestock men.

As the lone liberal on the Communist-hunting House Un-American Activities Committee (HUAC), Culver appended to bills approved by HUAC dissenting reports stressing the measures' threats to civil liberties. After a ringing speech by Culver culminating a floor fight against a HUAC attempt to breathe life back into the Subversive Activities Control Board, Representative Thomas L. Ashley of Ohio led the tribute to Culver with the words: "This is one of the most courageous statements I have ever heard on the floor of this House during the thirteen years I have served in this body. Our colleague from Iowa . . . represents a district which is anything but secure politically. Nevertheless, he has chosen to speak out forcefully on an issue and to take a position which can easily be misconstrued, misrepresented, and misunderstood. This is an act of statesmanship and courage."

Culver also helped reinvigorate the House Foreign Affairs Committee (which had become a rubber stamp for administration policies), and as chairman of its Foreign Economic Policy Subcommittee he held important meetings in 1971 on America's relations with Britain, the Common Market, Canada, and Japan. As a member of the Select Committee on Committees, he took part in a year-and-a-half-long study of ways to modernize the structure of the House. Overall, Culver's liberal stance earned him ratings of 88, 92, and 100 by the Americans for Democratic Action in, respectively, 1972, 1973, and 1974, and it won him the chairmanship of the Democratic Study Group, a caucus of liberal Representatives, in the 93rd Congress.

With strong support from organized labor and an assist from the onus of Watergate on the Republicans, Culver captured 52 percent of the vote in his race against David M. Stanley, a wealthy conservative attorney, for the United States Senate in 1974. As a Senator, Culver proceeded to build up one of the most consistent records for voting in agreement with the Democratic majority and against the conservative coalition.

During his first two years in the Senate Culver's ADA ratings were 100 and 94. In key votes during those years he went on record for no-fault auto insurance, cuts in defense spending, sanctions against Rhodesia, repeal of the Hatch Act, protection of wetlands, federal subsidization of abortions, split-up of oil companies, common situs picketing, and disclosure of "redlining" (discriminating against urban ghettos in dispensing real-estate loans and mortgages) by banks, and he voted against nuclear breeder reactors, the B-1 bomber, and the sale of arms to Chile.

At Culver's suggestion, the Senate in 1975 established a panel of nine outside observers and two Senate employees to study the operation of the upper house. The group, known as the Culver Commission and headed by his predecessor in office, Harold Hughes, made its final report on March 1, 1977. Its conclusions strongly reflected Culver's opinions that an independent legislature requires its own sources of information and that an effective one anticipates rather than responds to crises. Culver's ideas were reflected in the commission's recommendations that a professional manager administer Senate services, that the use of office space be coordinated and rationalized, that the Senate develop its own information system and make better use of computers, and that major committees assume responsibility for long-range analyses of national problems.

Culver's fight against the B-1 bomber was waged in a series of battles that included one in which he delayed the spending of money for the bomber until February 1977—when a new Administration might have an opportunity to review the matter. In her book on Culver, *Senator* (1979), which first appeared as a series of articles in the *New Yorker,* Elizabeth Drew observed: "This procedural approach to a substantive issue—making something seem a matter of process, and therefore more reasonable than a frontal attack—is . . . characteristic of Culver's legislative style. . . . When President Carter [who took office in January 1977] was making up his mind on whether to go ahead with the bomber, Culver, on behalf of and at the behest of its Congressional opponents, made the case to Carter against it. Carter eventually canceled the plane."

In 1977 Culver unsuccessfully fought the Carter Administration's proposal to sell the sophisticated Airborne Warning and Control System (AWACS) to Iran. During the first half of 1978 he voted against severing all diplomatic and economic relations with Cuba, against the prohibition of aid or trade with Vietnam, Cambodia, Uganda, and Cuba, against a 5 percent cut in foreign assistance, against an across-the-board cut in appropriations for the Treasury, and against an amendment to delete funds to be used by the Treasury for monitoring firearms.

In mid-1978, as Culver was in the process of successfully attaching to a military appropriations bill an amendment against any big Navy aircraft carriers in the future, he explained to Elizabeth Drew: "I have to decide . . . how to pick my shots, how to remain credible, not be irrelevant. It's hard enough to make these fights and still stay viable. The fights are very emotional; strong interests are involved. I try to approach it in a constructively critical way —to fight for a cost-effective defense. So I challenge where I don't think the military is doing enough to provide us with the proper readiness, and I challenge on excessive expenditures." At a time when inflation is the most serious problem facing the nation, he pointed out that "the Pentagon dollar is the most inflationary you can spend."

Later in 1978 Culver successfully managed the anti-noise Quiet Communities Act of 1978 through to passage in the Senate. Still later in the year, as head of the Resource Protection Subcommittee of the Environment and Public Works Committee, he successfully mediated between the environmentalists, who wanted to strengthen the Endangered Species Act, and the builders (including business interests) who wanted to weaken the act in the interest of "progress." His solution was an amendment calling for the arbitration of disputes by an Endangered Species Committee, composed of six federal agency heads and the governor of the affected state. The committee could, by a vote of at least five to two, authorize the continuation of challenged projects. Adopted by a margin of 94 to three, Culver's measure maintained adequate conservation safeguards while depriving anti-ecology conservatives of an excuse to prevent the renewal of the Endangered Species Act.

Among his other Senate stands, Culver has opposed tax credits for tuition and retaliating against Soviet newsmen for their government's harassment of American correspondents, and he has supported the volunteer Army, the Panama Canal treaties, and the gradual withdrawal of American troops from Korea. As the chairman of the Juvenile Delinquency Subcommittee of the Judiciary Committee, he has worked for programs to keep troubled and troublesome youths in detention facilities separate from those that house hardened criminals.

Above all, Culver has rejected the thesis that nuclear war can be a rational policy alternative. Looking to "arms control by mutual agreement" as humanity's only realistic hope, he is among the Senators most intensely interested in the ratification of the Strategic Arms Limitation Treaty. He has been unable to convince the United States government to undertake a full-scale study that would indicate in horrifying detail what a nuclear war would actually entail, but a study of the Soviet civil defense system done at his request by the Library of Congress refutes the argument of those alarmists who say that the Soviet system would embolden the Soviets to undertake a nuclear war. "The study indicates that the Soviet civil-defense system, while representing a significant national effort, is by no means sufficiently effective to encourage the Soviets to risk starting a nuclear war . . . ," he has pointed out. "Even under the 'worst case' assumptions of this study, nuclear war would be a disaster for the Soviet Union. . . . The bottom line in all this is that . . . the casualties would be awesome. . . . Soldiers in every country . . . are trained with the can-do spirit, and the can-do spirit can lead to nuclear war—holocaust, believe it or not."

Although the Senator says that he has been "relatively comfortable" with President Jimmy Carter, he has opposed the President on many important occasions. He was one of five Democrats to vote against confirming Griffin Bell as Attorney General, he has clashed with the White House on American arms sales several times; and before the fall of the Shah in Iran he charged the White House with keeping up "the Nixon Administration's fundamental policy of giving the Shah just about anything he could afford." Senator Culver's main complaint, however, is with Carter's general leadership. He has chided the President for not establishing a rational set of policy goals and for failing to make the compromises necessary to build an effective coalition. "In the Presidency," he says, "you have to realize you're going to make some people happy and some people mad, and you have to decide how that's going to be sliced." Culver rejects efforts to be "above" politics, pointing out that "an astute and enlightened exercise of political power is what enables a democratic society to achieve its best potential."

"There's a compassionate side," Culver says of his constituency, "and there's even an internationalist side, through the state's interest in world trade. . . . All this gives the state a sophistication and vital strains that, properly appealed to, will support very progressive purposes." In any case, Culver believes that a Senator must lead and teach his constituents as well as mirror their views. Whether he is dealing with his constituents or colleagues, Culver knows the importance of personal contact. He spends about one working weekend a month in Iowa and his office handles a steady stream of communications from the voters back home. In Washington, Culver takes time to visit the few places where Senators have a chance to relax together in the Capitol —the cloakroom, gymnasium, dining room, and the office of the Secretary of the Senate. He is especially close to Senators Kennedy, Gaylord Nelson of Wisconsin, and William Hathaway of Maine, and he maintains ties with a number of old friends in the House. "To really make it work," he argues, "you have to know an awful lot of people." At the same time, however, he rejects the philosophy of "getting along by

going along." According to one observer, Culver "cultivates the powers that be by his company and good fellowship but not by his vote."

John C. Culver is a big man of imposing presence, standing six feet two inches tall and weighing about 250 pounds. His strong voice enables him to dispense with the lapel microphone used by most Senators, and his sharp sense of humor and matching temper enliven his speeches, which he prefers to deliver extemporaneously, after careful preparation. The Senator no longer drinks alcoholic beverages (which mixed badly with his temper), but he continues to enjoy an occasional cigar. His church is the Presbyterian.

Senator Culver is married to the former Ann Cooper, who was once a diving and skating champion. The Culvers have four children, Christina, Rebecca, Catherine, and Chester John. The Senator, whose net worth was estimated at $100,000 to $200,000 at the time of his election to the Senate, supplements his income by public speaking and some investments. The Culvers maintain a home overlooking the Mississippi River in McGregor, Iowa.

References: New Yorker 54:40+ S 11 '78; 54:45+ S 18 '78; Congressional Directory, 1979; Drew, Elizabeth. Senator (1979); Who's Who in America, 1978-79; Who's Who in American Politics, 1979-80

Curry, John

Sept. 9, 1949- Skater. Address: b. c/o Kirk Singer, 1841 Broadway, New York City, N.Y. 10023

Moving with the elegance, grace, and purity of line of a premier danseur, John Curry uses virtuoso ice skating stunts—split flips, spread eagles, double axels, and flying camels—to create what dance critic Walter Terry has called "a legitimate new art form": ice dancing. Ever since he won his first major national competition in 1970, the British-born Curry, who has studied dance with Robert Christopher, Joyce Graeme, Martha Graham and Alvin Ailey, has been remarkable for his exemplary technique, his assured balance, his seemingly weightless jumps, and his extraordinary sensitivity to music. Following his sweep of the Olympic, European, and World men's figure skating titles in 1976, Curry astounded skating enthusiasts when he spurned lucrative offers from internationally renowned ice shows to produce *IceDancing*, an original ice revue distinguished by the imaginative "ballets" of some of the world's best contemporary choreographers, including Kenneth MacMillan, Twyla Tharp, and John Butler, and by his own distinctive ice choreography.

John Curry

John Anthony Curry was born in Birmingham, England on September 9, 1949, the youngest of three sons of Joseph Henry Curry, the owner of a small precision instrument factory, and Rita Agnes (Pritchard) Curry. Even as a very young child, John Curry was entranced by drama and dance. His parents often took him to see the traveling musical comedy and ballet companies that played in Birmingham and afterwards, he staged miniature versions of those productions, as well as imaginary plays and ballets, in a model theatre that he had built himself.

"I wanted to be a dancer before I even knew ice skating existed," Curry told Joan Pikula, who interviewed him for *After Dark* (December 1976). "But my family decided that it wasn't a good thing for me to do. Boys in ballet . . . wasn't a particularly common idea." After seeing *Aladdin,* a televised ice show, he asked to take skating lessons, and his father, hoping to deflect the boy's interest from ballet, readily agreed. But Curry only thought of skating as dancing on the ice. "It never occurred to me to consider it a sport," he admitted to Miss Pikula, "until much later."

Working with Ken Vickers, an instructor at the Summerhill Ice Rink, Curry quickly mastered the basic gliding techniques and, when he was eight years old, won his first competition—the Hop, Skip and Jump. He subsequently won many children's competitions and collected armloads of tiny trophies that, to him, "looked like fancy egg-cups." For years his skating lessons were sandwiched in between his classes at the Solihull School and his other athletic pursuits, but after his father's death in the mid-1960's, he decided to concentrate on skating.

Curry studied briefly with the Swiss coach Armand Perrin in Solihull, then moved to Richmond to take lessons from Arnold Gerschwiler, an expert in school figures. To support himself, he worked part-time in a small supermarket in Richmond, then at the London office of the National Cash Register Company. He skated daily and, despite his tight schedule and his even tighter budget, he always found enough spare time and money to take a regular ballet class. His diligence paid off when he won the Junior British Championship in 1967, the Jennings Trophy for free skating at the Nottingham Ice Stadium in 1968, and the British National Championship in 1970.

In the early 1970's, after spending a summer in the United States training under Peter Dunfield, Curry returned to Richmond to study with Alison Smith, a former pupil of Gerschwiler's. Under her guidance, he came in sixth in compulsory figures and eleventh in free skating at his first Olympic Games in Sapporo, Japan in 1972 and, later that year, finished fourth in the World Championships at Bratislava, Czechoslovakia. Impressed by Curry's prodigious technique and uncommon style, Ed Mosler, a sports enthusiast and the chairman of the fund-raising section of the United States Olympic Committee, offered to finance his training. Elated, Curry threw himself into his training with renewed dedication and the next year, he finished third in the European Championships. But, by his own account, he skated "abysmally" at the following World Championships meet in Munich, Germany and, as a result, dropped to seventh place.

Disappointed and discouraged, he briefly considered giving up skating to become a professional dancer. Instead, he approached Slavka Kahout, the trainer of Janet Lynn, the American Olympic medalist. Miss Kahout referred him to Gus Lussi, who specialized in jumps, and Carlo Fassi, a respected teacher of compulsory figures. At Lussi's school in Lake Placid, New York, Curry, while practising his jumps on a twenty-by-thirty-foot rectangle of ice, fell on the average of thirty or forty times a day. "All that anybody saw of me was an endless series of slides across the ice, ending—all too soon in that confined space—in a heap crumpled against the barrier," he recalled in Keith Money's *John Curry* (Knopf, 1978). But within three weeks he had learned to achieve elevation by muscular coordination rather than by speed and had immeasurably improved his jump. Moving on to Denver, Colorado for his classes with Fassi, Curry worked doggedly on his compulsory figures until, as he put it, "skating could not have seemed easier."

At the 1975 European Championships in Copenhagen, Denmark, Curry did especially well in the school figures competition and placed second in the final points tally. A few weeks later, he finished third in the World

Championships in Colorado. Realizing that an Olympic gold medal was within his reach, Curry purposefully set out to win it. Because judges had frequently complained that his free-skating programs were "too balletic," he deliberately eliminated the artistic elements from his programs and, in his words, "packaged" the prescribed stunts and technical figures "in an obvious manner, with simple music, basic manner, basic steps." Remembering that he had lost points in Copenhagen when some judges objected to the unorthodox, form-fitting costume he had designed for his *Rite of Spring* free-skating program, Curry began wearing plain dark trousers and a matching turtleneck sweater. Finally, to learn how to control the nervousness that plagued him during competitions, he attended est seminars.

Despite a bad fall in his free-skating program, Curry won the British Championships in December 1975 by a wide margin. The following month, at the European Championships in Geneva, Switzerland, he came up against Vladimir Kovalev, the reigning European champion, and Sergei Volkov, the reigning World Champion. He finished second in the execution of school figures and in the two-minute short program and first in free skating to capture the title. Buoyed by his win, he went to Innsbruck, Austria for the Winter Olympic Games confident of victory. "Of all the competitions I had ever been in . . . , I had never been more sure of winning anything than I was of winning that gold medal," he said later. "I had so programmed myself that I was going to win that I went through the whole thing in a very calm and collected manner."

After coming in second in the Olympics school figures contest, Curry took top marks for his short program and for his spectacular, but disarmingly graceful free-skating program to music from Minkus' *Don Quixote* grand pas de deux. The latter program was highlighted by a perfectly executed triple toe loop followed by a triple salchow and triple loop and three triple jumps. His gold medal was the first won by a Briton since 1964. After a few days' rest, Curry flew to Göteburg, Sweden, where he competed for the World Champion title. He was not at his best in the initial two sections of the competition and fell behind Kovalev and Jan Hoffman, but with a superlative performance in the pressure-packed free-skating event, which accounts for 50 percent of the total marks, he overtook both men and, to thunderous applause, accepted his third international championship medal in three months.

Deluged with million-dollar-plus contracts from all the major ice shows, Curry, after much agonizing, decided to go it alone. "I didn't want to be just another Olympic champion who got a potfull of money and ran," he said, as quoted in the *Christian Science Monitor* (October 1, 1976). "I always have felt that ice shows are presented like a circus, all tinsel and feathers. . . . My ambition always has been to present figure skating as an art form." To that end, he hired Norman Maen, the choreographer, to create several skating numbers for his BBC-TV special, *John Curry Ice Spectacular*, to be telecast on Christmas Day, 1976. Maen choreographed a bluesy solo for Curry to "I Got It Bad and That Ain't Good" and a sensuous, languid pas de deux, *L'Après-midi d'un Faune*, for Curry and Peggy Fleming.

Based on the celebrated Nijinsky ballet for the Ballets Russes de Diaghilev, Maen's *L'Après-midi d'un Faune* underscores the sustained sound of the Debussy music with long, slow, sinuous phrases interspersed with glides in the familiar angled crouch of Nijinsky's faun. Taking advantage of the skater's seamless movement, Maen, at one point, required Curry, as the faun, to move slowly forward in arabesque, stop, rise on "point," then travel backward. When the work had its premiere in New York City in November 1978, dance critics were stunned. Although a handful thought it was a pretentious imitation, most agreed with Walter Terry of the *Saturday Review* that it was "ravishingly beautiful."

Curry asked the iconoclastic choreographer Twyla Tharp to create a solo for him to perform at *Superskates III*, a benefit for the United States Olympic Fund at New York City's Madison Square Garden in November 1976. Set to Tommaso Albinoni's Concerto for Trumpet in B Flat, *After All* is a variation on school figures enlivened by the addition of typically Tharpian slouches, off-center balances, coiling turns, and abrupt shifts in speed and direction. In her review of a later performance of the piece for *New York* (December 11, 1978) magazine, Marcia B. Siegel commended Miss Tharp for rethinking the whole problem of performance from a skater's point of view. "[She] has given Curry a real dance that makes use of the *skater's* possibilities . . . ," Miss Siegel said. "She lets Curry travel quietly, motionlessly. . . . She even lets him stop sometimes, and in arresting that rhythmic, nearly monotonous motion, she clarifies and crystallizes him after all as not merely a technician, not merely a star, but an artist."

With the help of Larry Parnes, the theatre impresario, and Peter Darrell, the director of the Scottish Ballet, Curry organized a small company of like-minded skater-dancers and put together his own ice show, *Theatre of Skating*, which opened at the Cambridge Theatre in London, England on December 27, 1976. The program included, in addition to other works, *L'Après-midi d'un Faune*, which has become Curry's signature piece; Maen's *Jazz Suite*, featuring a soft-shoe shuffle by Curry; Peter Darrell's subdued and lyrical *Scenes of Childhood*; and Kenneth MacMillan's *Feux Follets*, a solo of fast-moving spirals and flying camels designed specifically for Curry.

After performing for eleven weeks on the constricting rink at the Cambridge Theatre, the production moved to larger quarters at the

London Palladium for a twelve-week, sold-out engagement. For that run, Curry added two examples of his own choreography; *Valse Glace and Winter 1895,* two new works by Ronald Hynd; and *Icarus,* a dramatic narrative ballet by John Butler. *Icarus* was enthusiastically received by audience and critics alike at its premiere, with Curry's sensitive, powerful portrayal of Icarus coming in for the most laurels.

According to the critical consensus, Curry himself may be the best of the ice choreographers because he knows the advantages of skating—the speed, the blurringly fast spins, the seemingly interminable glides—as well as the disadvantages. "Skating is its own worst enemy, because it's so easy to be lyrical and because it's so easy to travel on endless curves," he explained to Alan M. Kriegsman, in an interview for the Washington *Post* (January 7, 1979). "One gets lost in it all, and it can all become a big mish-mash." Curry integrates such crowd-pleasing technical stunts as the triple jump into his choreography, cleverly camouflaging the preparation for those feats with glides in balletic attitudes. But he is quick to remind interviewers that he always starts with skating. "If there is a movement or sequence of movement that doesn't require ice, there is no need to try it on ice," he told Walter Terry of the *Saturday Review* (March 3, 1979). "What I try to achieve is something that cannot be done in any other medium."

For many in the audience, Curry's *Moon Dances,* a series of divertissements for six commedia dell'arte figures, and *Anything Goes,* a flashy solo for Jo Jo Starbuck, were the highlights of his *IceDancing,* which began its American tour at the Shubert Theatre in Philadelphia, Pennsylvania on November 13, 1978. More balletic than his *Theatre of Skating,* the show also included Tharp's *After All;* MacMillan's *Feux Follets;* Butler's *Icarus;* Maen's *Faune;* Douglas Norwick's jokey *Scoop;* Donald Saddler's *Palais de Glace,* a lively Edwardian ensemble piece reminiscent of Sir Frederick Ashton's famous ballet, *Les Patineurs;* and two new works by principal dancers of the New York City Ballet—Jean-Pierre Bonnefous' neo-Romantic *IceMoves* and Peter Martins' *Tango-Tango,* a witty, seductive pas de deux for Curry and Miss Starbuck.

IceDancing proved so popular that it moved to Broadway's Minskoff Theatre on December 19, 1978, following its scheduled run at the Felt Forum, before continuing its national tour. On seeing the production for the first time, most American critics echoed the accolades of their British counterparts. There were, however, a few dissenters, among them M. Anatole Gurewitsch, who complained in the *New Republic* (February 17, 1979) that the program was largely "ennobled and refined . . . ice-revue material."

Although Arlene Croce, the influential dance critic for the *New Yorker,* thought *IceDancing*

was "aesthetically confusing" and an "uninteresting compromise" that was "neither skating nor dancing," she nevertheless conceded that the show "worked," principally because of Curry's dance-trained bearing. "Curry's greatest distinction, to me—greater even than his long, perfectly balanced line—is that he always looks lifted out of his skates, as if he were riding a stream of air," she wrote in her column of December 18, 1978. "His contact with the ice is resilient: he's able to go up or down, to stretch or contract at will. And the freedom of his style is what the ice dancers of the future should be training for."

In 1978 Curry set up a school of skating in New York City to teach his ice-dancing techniques to competitive skaters and to aspiring skater-dancers. Curry himself conducts the eight-week sessions, emphasizing in his instruction style, phrasing, line, carriage, and musicality. The off-the-ice kinesthetic warm-up routine and special exercises that he has devised for his students are derived partially from traditional ballet barre exercises and include training in *port de bras.* "Skating is a dance form," he emphasized to Joan Pikula in the *After Dark* interview. "Where skating has probably gone *so* wrong is in training skaters to jump and nothing else. . . . I feel those efforts should be much more balanced, that skating should be a more complete picture, like anything else. If you are exceptionally good at jumps, but can't skate or express yourself or use the music properly, it doesn't mean anything."

A strikingly handsome man whose physical resemblance to Anthony Dowell, the Royal Ballet's premier danseur, has been noted by more than one dance critic, John Curry is of average height and slim, muscular build, with wavy brown hair and brown eyes. Interviewers have found him to be charming, open, and infectiously enthusiastic. He lives alone in a three-room apartment in New York City's Greenwich Village, where he occasionally cooks dinner for his friends, many of whom are dancers. For relaxation, he paints and attends movies, plays, and most frequently, ballets.

Admittedly a "frustrated dancer," Curry still takes ballet class daily and he recently began dancing in public without his skates. In late 1978 he and Anthony Dowell danced an excerpt from Ashton's *Façade* at a London benefit for the Royal Ballet and, on April 30, 1979, at a gala fund-raiser for American Ballet Theatre at the Metropolitan Opera House in New York City, the two delighted balletomanes with a top-hat-and-tails routine created for them by Peter Gennaro, the jazz choreographer. "I suppose had I become a dancer, my life would probably have been easier," he told John Gruen in an interview for the New York *Times* (November 19, 1978). "I may have landed in the Royal Ballet and I might have been fairly good. . . . But I actually adore skating. I love the sensation, it's incredibly exhilarating. The fact is, skating, like dancing, is extremely difficult and it *can* be extremely beautiful."

References: *After Dark* 9:76+ D '76 pors; *N Y Times* II p18 N 19 '78 por; *People* 11:68+ Ja 15 '79 pors; Money, Keith. *John Curry* (1978); *Who's Who*, 1979-80

Dale, Clamma

July 4, 1948- Singer. Address: b. c/o ICM Artists, Ltd., 40 W. 57th St., New York City, N.Y. 10019

The soprano Clamma Dale is a performer in the tradition of her idol, the late Maria Callas—a singer with theatrical flair and a commanding stage presence to match her golden voice. Miss Dale first won acclaim for her sensuous portrayal of the Catfish Row siren in the Houston Grand Opera Company's 1976-77 Broadway revival of *Porgy and Bess*, and with the New York City Opera and other companies she has developed a repertoire that includes Antonia and Giulietta in *The Tales of Hoffman*, Nedda in *I Pagliacci*, Countess Almaviva in *The Marriage of Figaro*, the title role in *Tosca*, Pamina in *The Magic Flute*, Mistress Ford in *Falstaff*, and Saint Teresa I in *Four Saints in Three Acts*.

Beyond her opera, recital, and concert work, the striking Miss Dale looks forward to other ventures, including, possibly, straight acting in various media. "I'm a new breed," she

has said, "I can do it all." "Clamma Dale . . . is a star in every sense of the word," Alan Rich wrote when she was singing Bess on Broadway, "—a beautiful young woman who apparently knows everything there is to know about using her body to create a character, a singer with an impeccable command of tone and line to make her music breathe and surge and mean what it was intended to mean."

Clamma Churita Dale—whose first name is a variation of Clement, her maternal grandmother's last name—was born in the Philadelphia suburb of Chester, Pennsylvania on July 4, 1948 to Clara V. Dale and the late Granville Dale, an oil refinery worker and part-time jazz musician. Miss Dale has told interviewers that her father was her first music mentor, the "rock" on which her success was built, and that both of her parents were "terribly reinforcing," imbuing her with the attitude that, as a black, "you not only had to be good—you had to be the best."

"In grade school, I was a clarinetist," Miss Dale has recalled, "and I kept playing until I was about sixteen. I used to sing around the house for my parents and friends. In the eighth-grade chorus, my teacher assigned us a song, and somehow one voice kept sticking out. She made us sing individually until she found that voice. After that I was made a soloist with the chorus."

Miss Dale received her formal music training in public school in Chester and in the Settlement Music School in Philadelphia, where she studied on a scholarship while in high school. By the time her voice lessons began at the Settlement Music School, when she was about fourteen, she could play the piano, the cello, and the saxophone in addition to the clarinet. "I decided when I was eighteen," she told Anna Quindlen of the New York *Post* (September 25, 1976), "that all other instruments were just imitations of the human voice."

After graduating from high school, Miss Dale majored in voice at the Juilliard School in New York City on a series of partial scholarships. While a student, she worked in the complaint department at Hertz Rent-A-Car in Manhattan and at several other jobs, including Christmas gift wrapper at Weinberg's department store in Chester. Following her graduation from Juilliard, in 1970, she began building her operatic repertoire in productions of the Bronx Opera Company, the Brooklyn Opera Theatre, and the Metropolitan Opera's Mini-Met as well as in productions staged at the Mannes College of Music and the Manhattan School of Music. Meanwhile, she supported herself by singing in churches, synagogues, and the like and by teaching music at an elementary school in Brooklyn and a course in music, art, and poetry appreciation to prison inmates on Rikers Island.

In 1974 Miss Dale spent six months on the West Coast, three of them in the role of Bess in a musical-comedy version of *Porgy and Bess* at the Los Angeles Civic Light Opera. Although she found the role unsatisfying, because she felt that the production reduced Bess and the other characters to caricatures, she almost stayed in California, as she told Anna Quindlen: "I'd had success there, and I enjoyed the climate. [But] when I found out there was nothing [for me at that time] in California I came back [to New York]. I started thinking about films, and that's dangerous, because with all the black exploitation films—that's not my head. I'm an artist. I didn't hustle this long to go off and do *Blacula*."

Returning to the Juilliard School of Music for her master's degree, Miss Dale studied voice with Alice Howland and Hans Heinz. During her graduate year at Juilliard she reassessed her capabilities and her goals, as she recounted in an interview with Bob Micklin for *Newsday* (February 20, 1977): "I spent a whole bloody year pulling myself looking for every personal and professional flaw I could find. It was a very difficult year. It's not a simple move to decide to immerse yourself completely in a career. I knew I had to give it serious thought, and I had the opportunity to question everything before I really went ahead."

In May 1975 Miss Dale took her master's degree, and the following month she signed a three-year contract with the New York City Opera. When she made her debut with the Manhattan company as Antonia in Offenbach's *The Tales of Hoffman,* she received a standing ovation, and Allen Hughes in his review in the New York *Times* (October 5, 1975) remarked on her "considerable style," her "compelling stage presence," and her "vital and communicative" singing. Five days later she switched to the role of Giulietta in the same production, and still later she sang the roles of Nedda and Musetta.

As the first-prize winner in the fiftieth annual Walter W. Naumberg voice competition, Miss Dale gave a recital in Alice Tully Hall at Lincoln Center of works by Purcell, Schubert, Fauré, Barber, Copland, Dello Joio, Diamond, and Ginastera. Reviewing the recital in the New York *Times* (May 5, 1976), Donal Henahan said that he was above all impressed with the "intelligence and instinct that guided her control over the music's internal drama" and her knowing "how to create a magical hush and how to prolong it to exactly the right degree."

After tryouts in Houston, Washington, D.C., Philadelphia, Toronto, and Ottawa, the Houston Grand Opera brought its production of *Porgy and Bess* to New York City's Uris Theater in September 1976. This was the third Broadway revival of the work since the initial production of 1935-36, but it was the first to treat it as a grand opera in folk style, as composer George Gershwin and librettist DuBose Hey-

ward had intended. Included, for example, were parts of the original score rarely heard by audiences anywhere, such as the orchestrally accompanied recitatives. Because the demands on the singers of the principal roles were strenuous, there were alternating casts, with Esther Hinds and Irene Oliver backing up the first-night Bess, Clamma Dale.

Robert Jones, writing in the New York *Sunday News* (October 3, 1976), described the Houston Opera production as a "masterpiece," adding: "Towering in the center of all this excellence . . . is the Bess herself, a young woman with the improbable name of Clamma Dale. Tall, lanky, arrogant, her every move a lascivious taunt to the audience, Dale drapes impure sex over the stage of the Uris as generously as she pours out floods of rich, strong, wide-ranging soprano sound. Dale is a star, and no one who has seen her is going to dispute that point." The reviewer for *Time* (November 1, 1976) enumerated her contributions to the characterization as "high musical polish and dramatic intelligence, a voice of molten gold, and the fierce grace of a stalking leopard."

When *Cue's* Golden Apple for best Broadway actress was awarded to Miss Dale, Nancy McKeon wrote in that magazine (November 27-December 10, 1976): "Dale's voice is an instrument rare to the Broadway stage; her acting is powerful and moving. . . . As distinguished producer Otto Preminger, who presented Dale with her award, pointed out, if one adds her beauty and sensuality to her vocal and acting gifts, one has a Broadway Bess of incomparable magnitude."

Following the close of *Porgy and Bess,* in January 1977 after 128 performances, Miss Dale took part in a performance of Licinio Refice's choral symphonic poem *Sacra rappresentazione di S. Cecilia* with the Sacred Music Society at Avery Fisher Hall and then went to Washington, D.C. to sing at a gala and an inaugural ball for President Jimmy Carter. In succeeding months with the New York City Opera Clamma Dale sang the Countess in the *Marriage of Figaro* and Nedda in *I Pagliacci,* both to mixed notices. Bill Zakariasen, reviewing *The Marriage of Figaro* in the New York *Daily News* (March 1, 1977), reported that she had "initial trouble focusing tone and holding pitch," but "once she opened up, her purple voice was a treat to hear." John Rockwell of the New York *Times* (March 17, 1977), while noting that "Miss Dale has not been quite as rapturously received on her return to opera after her triumph as Bess," found her Nedda "the most exciting portrayal of the night." "At the climaxes her voice rang out thrillingly," Rockwell wrote, "and her command of the stage was always exciting."

In the second of her Naumberg award recitals at Alice Tully Hall, Miss Dale's selections ranged from songs by Alban Berg and Benjamin Britten through French and German works to the New York premiere of Ryan Edwards' "Creole Girl" and the Gospel song "Amazing Grace." Speight Jenkins of the New York *Post* (May 6, 1977) thought her rendition of Poulenc's "Les Chemins de l'Amour" was "simply marvelous," done in a "light, easy style with plenty of grace." Raymond Ericson of the New York *Times* (May 7, 1977) disagreed, asserting that her treatment of the Poulenc song "didn't work." But he thought her a "different artist when she could cut loose in a lively or dramatic song—Falla's 'Seguidilla,' the fast portions of the "Air de Lia" from Debussy's 'L'Enfant Prodigue.'"

Venturing into popular song, Miss Dale had an eight-night engagement at the Manhattan Theatre Club in June 1977, singing numbers by such composers as Duke Ellington, Paul Williams, and Rodgers and Hart. "She showed that she can sing popular song," John S. Wilson of the New York *Times* (June 3, 1977) wrote, "with results that are so stunning that those who do it on a full-time basis might pick up a few pointers from her. . . . Miss Dale concentrated on the soft, warm colors of her voice. Her singing was sometimes intimate and relaxed, sometimes tightly controlled; but it never spilled over into the large vocal qualities that would overwhelm the songs."

When Leonard Bernstein conducted the New York Philharmonic in the New York City premiere of his *Songfest*, a cycle of American poems for six singers and orchestra, at Avery Fisher Hall in December 1977, Clamma Dale was one of the soloists. "Miss Dale's full, free, luscious soprano was outstanding whatever she did," Harriett Johnson wrote in the New York *Post* (December 16, 1977), and in the long Julia de Burgos poem, sung in the original Spanish, both she and Bernstein were stupendous."

Clamma Dale is a statuesque woman, five feet ten and a half inches tall. According to Bob Micklin in his *Newsday* article, she dresses like "a top fashion model" and seems "in constant motion." "Physically," Jack Hiemenz wrote in *High Fidelity/Musical America* (December 1977), "her impact is one of imperial sensuousness; the face is typecast to play passionate princesses. She talks a mile a minute [and] the recurring theme in a Clamma Dale conversation isn't music, it's drama." Hiemenz quoted her as saying that she was a singer who was also "a dramatic actress" and that she was interested in the possibilities offered by television: "We have never before been so heavily *visual* an audience. Thanks to Maria Callas, we now know what kind of dramatic experience can happen on the operatic stage. . . . Opera is moving into an area where mass media is a necessity. Using mass media and being part of it—and using it intelligently—can help shape many people's ideas and change a lot of stereotype thinking about what opera and operatic artists are all about."

Miss Dale's residence is a comfortable but hardly luxurious floor-through brownstone apartment on Manhattan's Upper West side, an entire wall of which is lined with makeshift raw wood bookshelves. The singer is a vegetarian, a teetotaler, and a practitioner of yoga. Regarding marriage, she has said: "It would take a very strong person to marry me. . . . I'm much softer than people think. But I am also very much in control of what I do.'" Miss Dale's voice teacher, of long standing, is Cornelius Reed. She still plays the clarinet, albeit not professionally.

References: Ebony 32:137 Ag '77 por; N Y Times II p15 My 2 '76 por, p28 S 29 '76 por; People p44+ N 22 '76 por

Della Femina, Jerry (fə-mēˊnə)

July 22, 1936- Advertising executive. Address: b. Della Femina, Travisano & Partners Inc., 625 Madison Ave., New York City, N.Y. 10022

Without the conventional background of the man in the gray flannel suit but with a flair for pungent one-liners, Jerry Della Femina secured a place in American advertising during the height of Madison Avenue's "creative revolution" of the 1960's as a much-publicized, highly paid copywriter. Such provocative headlines as "Before Hitler Could Kill 6 Million Jews, He Had to Burn 6 Million Books" for McGraw-Hill Book Company and "What's the ugliest part of your body?" for Pretty Feet often shocked with their brashness while winning coveted advertising awards and selling the client's product. As Della Femina himself realizes, they reflected the world view of a street-wise kid out of a working-class Brooklyn neighborhood. They gained him recognition, money, and power—all before he was thirty—in an industry that had long been dominated by well-connected WASP businessmen.

Staking his reputation and talent on an agency of his own, Della Femina survived the more stringent business atmosphere of the 1970's as chief executive officer of one of Madison Avenue's most successful agencies. Della Femina, Travisano & Partners, which he spawned with no accounts in 1967, has billings twelve years later of over $100,000,000 and ranks thirty-sixth in the country in gross income, according to Advertising Age. His renown within the industry was eclipsed by the wide public recognition he attained with the publication in 1970 of his book From Those Wonderful Folks Who Gave You Pearl Harbor; Front-Line Dispatches from the Advertising War, which has become an advertising classic. In 1978 he was named one of the nation's top three advertising copywriters at the annual meeting of the American Association of Advertising Agencies.

Jerry Della Femina was born in Brooklyn, New York on July 22, 1936, the older of two sons of Michael and Concetta (Corsaro) Della Femina. His father was a native American, having been born to newly arrived Italian immigrants. His mother had been brought to the United States at the age of four. During a thirty-year period that began in 1909, all the members of the large Della Femina family left their village near Naples to settle in the forty-square-block area of Brooklyn known as Gravesend. In Jerry's childhood his grandparents, who never learned the language of their adopted country, lived with him and his parents. Because Italian was spoken exclusively in the home, he could not speak English when he began attending school at six.

Like other teenagers in a neighborhood where gambling was a way of life, he became an accomplished crapshooter. Demonstrations of his skill with dice in the halls of Lafayette High School led to his expulsion on two occasions. While growing up in what he has called "an Italian semi-ghetto," he also acquired a drive for success equated with respect. "I could say that success/respect was the theme of the neighborhood," he explained to Ross Firestone, who interviewed him for The Success Trip (1976). "And more than anyone else, I wanted it and I wouldn't stop until I got it."

On graduation from high school in 1954, Della Femina began working as an advertising messenger for the New York Times, where his father was employed as a paper cutter and where his brother, Joseph, later took a job in classified ads. "I used to deliver proofs of ads to department stores on Fifth Avenue," Della Femina recalled irreverently in From Those Wonderful Folks Who Gave You Pearl

Harbor (Simon & Schuster, 1970). "Wherever I went . . . I used to see guys sitting around with their feet propped up on desks. I liked that and used to ask people who these cats were with their feet up. They were the department-store copywriters. That's when I made up my mind that copywriting was for me." He enrolled in Brooklyn College to take night courses for a year in advertising.

From 1954 to 1961 Della Femina earned meager wages in a succession of odd jobs while looking for a position as a copywriter. He sold toys in Macy's and bathrobes in Gimbel's, worked as a shipping clerk for a shirt company, and carried sixty-pound bags of checks for National City Bank. His worried family often urged him to forsake his ambitions in advertising for the more secure route of civil service. Except for turning out a few truss ads for the advertising Exchange, the closest he came to a copywriter's desk during those years was as a mail boy in the now defunct ad agency Ruthrauff & Ryan.

Unemployed for several months, Della Femina singled out Daniel & Charles for pursuit in 1961 and sent that agency a series of unsolicited sample ads, signed only J.D.F., that eventually landed him his first full-time job in advertising. "After that it was the easiest thing in the world," he has related, as quoted in The Success Trip. "I was a copywriter. . . . I liked it. It liked me. I saw I could do almost anything I touched." At Daniel & Charles he wrote ads for Kayser-Roth, the apparel firm, and began to develop a reputation in the advertising industry for both eccentricity and talent.

By 1963, when Della Femina moved to Fuller & Smith & Ross, an agency then specializing in industrial accounts, he had more than tripled his beginning salary at Daniel & Charles of $100 a week. After six months or so he was offered a job as copy chief and a vice-presidency at Ashe & Englemore. He turned down the vice-presidency, reasoning that if he were to be promoted to that office a few months later, people would say he must be doing a sensational job.

With his appointment in 1964 as creative director of Delehanty, Kurnit & Geller, Della Femina had the opportunity for major advancement in his career. As Charles Sopkin reported in the New York Times Magazine (January 26, 1969), DKG "had a good reputation for its creative output and for its tolerance of eccentricity." It was during his two and a half years at that agency that Della Femina produced his award-winning ads for Pretty Feet and for Talon Zippers, in which a baseball catcher informs a pitcher, "Your fly is open." The two Gold Keys awarded to him by the Advertising Writer's Association of New York and the two ANDYs from the Advertising Club of New York, each reportedly adding $5,000 to $10,000 a year to a copywriter's salary, confirmed Della Femina's recognition in the industry for creative work, quite aside from the attention he gained by his offbeat antics.

In one of his many disagreements with Shep Kurnit, head of the DKG agency, Della Femina called a strike of the entire creative department that tied up operations for two days. The issue concerned where to run an ad, and when Della Femina won the argument, the ad drew the overwhelming response of more than 300,000 inquiries, even though it did not offer a coupon. Of Della Femina, Kurnit has since said, as quoted in *Advertising Age* (April 24, 1978), "His whole life-style is to be a provocateur."

While at DKG, Della Femina decided to open an agency of his own. But before he could do so, he felt the need of package goods experience to complete his advertising education. His desire, moreover, to learn about "Big Agency Style," to use his phrase, led him to move in 1966 to one of the largest and more conservative of the old-line agencies, Ted Bates, where, in the words of one Bates' executive he quickly stood out as a "natural rebel."

As a thirty-year-old, $50,000-a-year creative supervisor, Della Femina demanded and got one of the first contracts in the history of Bates' creative department. An agency known for its hard sell and cautiously executed advertising, Bates hired Della Femina to flesh out its creative department with the expectation that he would brighten the agency's image among prospective clients and serve as a magnet to draw talented people to Bates from other agencies The relationship proved discordant almost from the beginning.

Within six months at Bates, Della Femina made what the press described as a "prickly" speech in North Carolina about federal intervention in advertising that almost caused him to be fired. Referring to "nincompoops in Washington" who imposed "ridiculous" and "harebrained" restrictions on advertising, the speech was widely reported in the media, largely as a result of Della Femina's efforts in circulating it. The reaction of the chairman of the board at Bates was an immediate ruling that henceforth all speeches by personnel had to be properly cleared. His letter to the New York *Times* disavowing Della Femina's opinions as the agency's views was excerpted in the advertising column the following day. Della Femina again went against the grain of senior agency executives when he became the first to be called before Bates' newly instituted creative review board. Bristling at the idea of being reviewed, he took a tape recorder to the session—a maneuver that resulted in two hours of awkward babble and small talk because of the board members' fear of putting their ideas about advertising on record.

At Bates, Della Femina further consolidated his reputation in the industry for attention-getting, controversial advertising. For example, he persuaded Yogi Berra to appear in Ozone Hair Spray commercials alongside copy that read, "Yogi Berra is one of those sissies who uses his wife's hair spray." He also spread word through friends at other agencies of his iconoclastic creations that were deemed too controversial to run.

The best known of Della Femina's gambits was one that flabbergasted some of his coworkers and delighted others during his first day at Bates. At a meeting to discuss the headline for the account of the Japanese electronics company Panasonic, he exclaimed: "I see it all now. I see an entire campaign built around this headline." Having gained attention and aroused suspense, he told his listeners, "The headline is, the headline is: 'From Those Wonderful Folks Who Gave You Pearl Harbor.'" Nevertheless, Della Femina and his team turned the faltering Panasonic account around within a year.

At a time when a new kind of advertising agency, known as the "boutique," was proliferating at the abnormally high rate of over thirty a year, Della Femina hatched one of his own. In September 1967, inspired by the success of the legendary Mary Wells, he gambled on setting up his own agency with an $80,000 loan provided by partner Ron Travisano. Two others from the Panasonic creative team at Bates also signed on as partners of Jerry Della Femina & Partners. The agency's name was later changed to Della Femina, Travisano & Partners.

Today, when few of the so-called "hot shops" of the 1960's remain, having disappeared with the boom years of the last decade, Della Femina sits as chairman of the board of a $100,000,000 agency with offices in New York and Los Angeles. Della Femina, Travisano & Partners has consistently produced award-winning advertising for such clients as Emory Air Freight, Blue Nun, WABC-TV, H & R Block, Teacher's Scotch, and Kretschmer's Wheat Germ. During the last few years the agency has been one of three to dominate the awards in the category of radio advertising.

Soon after Della Femina opened his office on Madison Avenue, he acquired as his first clients Squire for Men, the Montego Beach Hotel, and the Jamaica Inn Hotel. For Squire, a hairpiece manufacturer, he wrote the line, "Are you still combing your memories?" as part of a campaign that won him another Gold Key and two more ANDYs. The three accounts were not enough to keep the agency solvent, and by December two partners had bailed out. Travisano decided to stay on and if necessary to sell his house to keep the agency afloat. With expenses of $2,000 a week and only $11,000 in the bank, Della Femina risked $3,000 on the year's biggest Madison Avenue Christmas party, inviting friends as well as enemies, the trade press, and potential new business. His idea was to look successful and sell the "success" of the agency. The next day new accounts started to arrive, and in a little over a year the burgeoning agency was billing $8,000,000.

Della Femina, who had been getting write-ups in the trade press before founding his own agency, greatly profited from an article in the New York Times Magazine on January 26, 1969. The Times, wanting to profile one of the new creative boutiques, chose his shop reportedly quite by chance. The morning after the article appeared, the agency received the Blue Nun account, for which it produced white wine commercials that contributed much to its reputation for creativity. Acknowledging his uncanny ability to attract publicity, Philip H. Dougherty wrote in his daily advertising column in the New York Times (May 17, 1978), "From his earliest days as an agency leader, Mr. Della Femina has understood the kind of story that the advertising press was looking for and has been able most of the time to deliver it. It is a skill that most major ad agency executives lack and the one that professional public relations people strive for, not always successfully." Characteristically, Della Femina has said, "I love p.r. It's the only thing that's free in America."

By Della Femina's own estimates his agency reaped $5,000,000 to $8,000,000 in new billings from the publication of From Those Wonderful Folks Who Gave You Pearl Harbor, which was edited by Charles Sopkin, who had written the New York Times Magazine article about his work. The tales-told-out-of-school character of the book angered many within the industry. But it was, at least in part, a shrewd pitch for business. By identifying himself with the successful newer agencies of the era such as Carl Ally or Leber, Katz, Paccione and the somewhat older but creatively eminent Doyle, Dane, Bernbach, as well as by dropping names and disclosing big business intrigue, he established himself as a seasoned insider. Stuart W. Little praised the book in the Saturday Review (May 9, 1979) as "funny, hard-boiled, knowledgeable, and brilliant in analyzing the pervasive insecurities of the business." Della Femina's projected sequel to From Those Wonderful Folks is tentatively titled "They're Killing Us With Slower Bullets." In collaboration with Sopkin he is also the author of the autobiographical An Italian Grows in Brooklyn (Little, Brown, 1978).

In April 1978 Della Femina was named one of the nation's top three copywriters at the annual meeting of the American Association of Advertising Agencies, although he had not written an ad in three years. He regards his demise as a copywriter as being in the long-term interest of his agency, because he feels that agencies are hurt by principals who continue to dominate creative output. In recent years he has been aggressively running the new-business team along with vice-president of new-business development, James D. Michelson. In addition to winning many copywriting awards for "creative excellence," Della Femina has been recognized for his wider role as an industry leader. He was named Advertising Executive of the Year in 1970, and in 1978 advertising columnist Dougherty of the New York Times picked Della Femina, Travisano & Partners as "the hottest agency in town."

Jerry Della Femina and Barbara Rizzi were married in 1956 and have three children, Donna, Michael, and Jodi. The Della Feminas live in a large apartment on fashionable Beekman Place in New York City. In a blistering discussion in his autobiography of the role of the Roman Catholic church in the Italian-American enclave in which he was raised, Della Femina wrote, "When I was sixteen, I packed all organized religion in." With his six-foot frame, rusty complexion, shaved head, wiry mustache, and chin beard, Della Femina presents a striking appearance. These days, advertising's veteran of self-promotion believes that it is in the best interests of his company to maintain an uncharacteristic low profile. Clients, he feels, should knock on his door for the agency itself, not for him. "The cult of personality is dead," is the way he put it during an Advertising Age interview. "Or anyway, in labored breathing."

References: Advertising Age p66 Ap 24 '78 por, N Y Times Mag p32+ Ja 26 '69 pors; New York p79+ O 23 '78 por; Time 95:78 Je 22 '70 por; Della Femina, Jerry. From Those Wonderful Folks Who Gave You Pearl Harbor (1970), An Italian Grows in Brooklyn (1978); Who's Who in America, 1978-79

Di Suvero, Mark (sōō'vər-ō)

Sept. 18, 1933- Sculptor. Address: b. c/o Richard Bellamy, 333 Park Ave. So., New York City, N.Y. 10010

Distinctly the sculpture of its own time in its celebration of industrial images and materials, Mark di Suvero's work nevertheless embraces many classical influences as well as idioms of twentieth-century art—cubism, constructivism, surrealism, and abstract expressionism, among others. The immediacy of its appeal as public sculpture owes much to the personal exuberance and idealism of an artist who commands attention by gigantic scale and combines solidity and mobility and soaring elegance with an endearing playfulness. Although some of his most interesting work may be seen in a gallery or on a large tabletop, di Suvero best fulfills his intentions of enhancing life and increasing his viewers' awareness of today's environment in monumental sculptures whose bold reaching out into space becomes a metaphor of human aspiration. He demonstrated

Mark di Suvero

the appropriateness of his work to bustling outdoor urban settings in a magnificent exhibition throughout Greater New York City given during 1975 in connection with his major retrospective at the Whitney Museum.

Born of Italian parents in Shanghai, China on September 18, 1933, Mark di Suvero was the third child of Vittorio di Suvero, a Venetian of Sephardic Jewish descent, and Matilde (Millo) di Suvero, who is of French as well as northern Italian stock. The two older children in the family were Victor and Marie Louise; a fourth child, Henry, was born three years after Mark. In 1930 Vittorio di Suvero, a former naval officer, had moved to China, where he served as an agent of the Italian government in business interests in Shanghai and Tientsin. After the outbreak of World War II, the father, whose sympathies were pro-British, left China with his family for the United States, arriving in California in 1941.

"Marco Polo," the name di Suvero's parents had given him, seemed unsuitable for a boy growing up in San Francisco; so he called himself Mark Shawn. "After school, when he was a little boy, a Mrs. [Malo] Lowell from Boston taught him art," his mother recalled years later in talking with a reporter for the Washington Post (November 15, 1977), "and she started him as a sculptor. He did small things then." Mrs. di Suvero, herself, taught school in San Francisco, while her husband, who had been trained in naval architecture, was employed in a shipyard. Shortly before his expected graduation from high school, Mark di Suvero dropped out to work at odd jobs.

Resuming his education in 1953, di Suvero took courses for a year at San Francisco City College before enrolling in the University of California at Santa Barbara. "I became depressed with the fact that [at Santa Barbara] I couldn't make an original contribution in my major, philosophy," he once told James Monte, who wrote the introduction for the catalogue of the 1975 Whitney exhibition. As if in compensation, he found an outlet for his creative drive in a sculpture course given by Robert Thomas. When he transferred in 1955 to the Berkeley campus of the University of California, where he earned his degree in philosophy in 1957, he continued to work in sculpture, with Stephen Novak as his teacher.

Later in 1957 di Suvero and his friend Charles Ginnever, also a sculptor, drove from California to New York. Their arrival in Manhattan proved to be a turning point in the careers of both Californians because of the impact on their work made by contact with artists of the New York School, exponents of the gestural style of abstract expressionist painting. While absorbing new aesthetic influences—along with the industrial imagery of the city's docks, bridges, and skyscrapers—di Suvero supported himself through an assortment of jobs, including carpentry. In March 1960, as he was delivering a load of lumber, an elevator accident crushed his spine. Despite a prognosis that he would never walk again, within two years he was able to abandon his wheelchair. Regardless of the lasting impairment to his legs and back, moreover, he has insisted upon expressing himself in a type of sculpture that often involves hazard and strenuous physical effort—a determination that represents, as Anthony Haden-Guest wrote in New York (November 17, 1975), "a triumph over chance and risk, which is also a leitmotif of his work."

Seven months after his accident, Mark di Suvero had his first one-man exhibition in New York, at Richard Bellamy's Green Gallery. The show was hailed as an event of historic importance by the sculptor and critic Sidney Geist, who argued in Arts Magazine (December 1960), "The real stuff of history is made of those moments of which one can say: From now on nothing will be the same. One felt this at di Suvero's show. Here was a body of work at once so ambitious and intelligent, so raw and clean, so noble and accessible that it must permanently alter our standards of artistic effort."

One of the impressive sculptures of the Green show, Hankchampion (1960) was named after di Suvero's younger brother, who helped in assembling its various components. Like Che Faró senza Eurydice (1959) and Barrel (1959), also on view in that first show, Hankchampion consisted of found objects that evoked associations with their original functions. The "junk" materials that di Suvero incorporated in his sculptures included wood, rope, chains, bolts, and nails. With his penetration of space by weathered beams he achieved a vigor and spontaneity suggestive of effects attained by the paintbrush thrusts of the gestural artists Franz Kline and Willem de Kooning. Di Suvero's work was recognized, moreover, as belonging in the cubist-constructivist tradition. Besides using industrial materials, he follows the constructivist technique of joining separate elements of a work so that instead of being displaced by a solid mass, space is enclosed and becomes part of an abstract structural design. The desire that di Suvero has shown for making art relevant to life in the workaday world is reminiscent also of the concern of constructivists of early Soviet art and of the Bauhaus in Germany in the 1920's with idealistic programs of social rebuilding.

Because of his injuries from the elevator shaft accident, for several years di Suvero was unable to work on sculpture of the aggressive scale of *Hankchampion,* which measured about six by twelve by nine feet and was unusually large for a creation of 1960, though modest in size compared to his later monumental pieces. During the early months of his recuperation he fashioned rather small configurations, sitting in his wheelchair and wearing an asbestos apron so that he could weld pieces on his lap or on a low bench. For the first time he used steel in combination with wood, in *Attic* (1961) and in *Eatherly's Lamp* (1961), which refers to the American bombardier at the time of Hiroshima's devastation by the atomic bomb. *Attic,* with its springy bounce, also provides an early example of the motion that di Suvero likes to introduce into his sculpture—a mobility echoing that of Alexander Calder, who had mastered the principles of delicate balance and tension that make kinetic sculpture possible.

While striving to regain his strength, di Suvero also resumed work on a series of bronze hands, which he had begun in 1958 and which has continued to engage him over the years. The palm of the hand in *Hand Pierced* (1959) is skewered by a spike, and in *Raft* (1963) a hand desperately clutches a fragment of hefty timber. "These Rodin-like images of survival and defiance are full of expressionist anguish," Robert Hughes wrote in *Time* (December 1, 1975). "As autobiography they are corny but moving."

Together with his friends and fellow gestural sculptors Tom Doyle and Peter Forakis and with other artists, in 1963 di Suvero founded the Park Place Gallery in Manhattan. By early 1966 he was able to exhibit in that cooperative galley several new works expressive of his joy in his return to large scale. Discussing two giant mobiles of urban vitality, *The A Train* and *New York Dawn (For Lorca),* Hilton Kramer pointed out in the New York Times (January 30, 1966) that like the English artist Anthony Caro, di Suvero has given sculpture "an almost architectural range." He perceived "something Whitmanesque in the gesture and sweep of Mr. di Suvero's sculptural imagination" and also credited him with "a Whitmanesque ambition" in his intention of "making

sculpture what it once was: a glorious public art, capable of sustaining the scrutiny of the crowd, robust enough to stand its ground amid the tumult of modern life."

Among di Suvero's other important large mobiles of the 1960's is *Pre Columbian* (1965), which offers the viewer a ride on an automobile tire, as do *Love Makes the World Go 'Round* (1963), *Laurie's Love Seat* (1964), and *Nova Albion* (1964-65). Other found objects that he now used in his sculpture, often along with new materials, included chairs, as in *Homage to Brancusi* (1962) and *Amerigo for My Father* (1963). The former is one of several works—*Homage to Stuart Davis* is another—in which di Suvero pays tribute to artists to whom he may feel indebted. On the question of the sculptor's eclecticism, Thomas B. Hess observed in *New York* (December 15, 1975), "It's important to consider di Suvero's hero-worshiping character—it sets him apart from so many trivially original (i.e. gimmicky) artists."

In addition to massive outdoor pieces, di Suvero continued to produce modestly scaled sculptures. At a group show in 1968 at the Noah Goldowsky Gallery in New York, of which Bellamy was an associate, he exhibited a group of so-called "tabletop" works that included *Vietnam Piece.* Because of his opposition to American escalation of the fighting in Vietnam, he had been chosen in 1966 to design the fifty-five-foot-high Los Angeles Peace Tower, to which artists throughout the world were invited to contribute panels protesting the war. In 1971 he restated his opposition to the war in his steel sculpture *Homage to the Viet Cong.*

The intensity of his antiwar feeling drove di Suvero, also in 1971, to leave the United States for Europe, where he intended to remain for the duration of the war. While living for a time in Venice, he collaborated with engineers on a lock system designed to cope with the flooding problems of that city of canals. In the Netherlands, di Suvero, whose sculpture reflects his affinity with places where things are made and repaired, such as machine shops and garages, worked and lived in a factory in Eindhoven. Invited to Chalon-sur-Saône in France, he took part in a civic program to "establish a relation between the works, the labor, and the daily life of an artist with the population." With the help of the townspeople and the owners of a local steel company and a shipyard, he constructed several large sculptures from which the citizens chose the one they wanted permanently installed in Chalon.

During his four years of self-imposed exile, di Suvero had one-man exhibitions at the Stedelijk vanabbemuseum in Eindhoven and the Wilhelm-Lehmbrück-Museum in Duisberg, West Germany, both in 1972, and in the Jardin des Tuileries in Paris in 1975. The show in the Tuileries, accorded di Suvero by the French Minister of Culture, Michel Guy, was an unprecedented honor, since no contemporary artist and no American had ever before had his work displayed at that national shrine.

Some of the five large outdoor sculptures that Parisians saw in the gardens were shipped to New York City in midsummer for installation in the borough-wide exhibition sponsored by the city and cultural organizations as an extension of a retrospective of di Suvero's work at the Whitney Museum of American Art. The long-planned Whitney show had been delayed several years because of the sculptor's reluctance to exhibit in the United States during the Vietnam War and then had been postponed from the spring to the fall of 1975 so that di Suvero could accept the Tuileries invitation. Fifty pieces of fourteen feet and under were shown at the Whitney Museum itself, while a dozen or more enormous sculptures were on view at open-air sites in the five boroughs.

"Nothing like this one-man sculptural blitz has ever before occurred in New York—or, indeed, in any other city as far as one knows," Kramer wrote in the New York Times Magazine (January 25, 1976). No show of matching extravagance had ever been devoted, for example, to the work of David Smith or Alexander Calder, sculptors of perhaps more secure reputation than di Suvero. Critics attributed much of the success of the artistic event to collective effort and public involvement, including the assistance from Seatrain Shipbuilding Yards in Brooklyn, which provided working space for the sculptor, and Tishman Realty and Construction Company and Con Edison, which lent their trucks and cranes.

Crowds gathered at various sites throughout the city to watch di Suvero operate the huge cranes that he has said he uses as a painter would use his paintbrushes. The first work of the show to be installed, in early September 1975 in Manhattan's Battery Park, was the black steel For Lady Day (1968-69), named for the blues singer Billie Holiday. Two weeks later in the Seagram Building Plaza in Manhattan, di Suvero erected Praise for Elohim Adonai (1966), an important wood and steel work whose top section rotates around a central axis. He chose Prospect Park in Brooklyn for his bright red Are Years What? (For Marianne Moore) (1967) and Cadman Plaza Park in Brooklyn for Mother Peace (1970), which is also painted red.

Among other sculptures included in the New York show were Ik Ook (Me Too), which di Suvero had created in Eindhoven in 1971-72, and La Petit Clef, one of the several pieces he had made and installed in Chalon-sur-Saône in 1973. Another Chalon piece, the red Ave (1973), installed at Flushing Meadow Park for the exhibition, is considered by James Monte to be one of di Suvero's finest works. Like much of his recent sculpture, Ave shows a development toward spareness, a decrease in the number of parts and in part-to-part interplay. In small mobiles, however, such as the "spinners, tumble pieces, and puzzles," exhibited at the Janie C. Lee Gallery in Houston in early 1978, he indulged his fascination with intricately engineered configurations.

Di Suvero's turn toward reductivism in large-scale work is, moreover, less apparent in his monumental thirty-five ton Isis, a forty-three-by sixty-five-by thirty-three-foot sculpture that has as its primary element a sizable section of a ship's bow. Commissioned by the Institute of Scrap Iron and Steel, Inc., Isis was donated to the Hirshhorn Museum and Sculpture Garden in Washington, D.C. and dedicated in July 1978. Abram Lerner, the director of Hirshhorn, has explained, as quoted in Art News (July 1978), that di Suvero was chosen by the institute not only because of his earlier use of scrap metal, but also "because of his ability to transform this metal into something exciting, ecstatic, adventurous, contemporary." A television film about di Suvero, North Star, named after one of his sculptures and coproduced by François de Menil and the art critic Barbara Rose, was presented on the Public Broadcasting System about the time of the dedication of Isis.

Although colossal in size and weight and strength, di Suvero's work is not forbidding. He delights in having viewers, many of whom are children, contribute to his sculptures by rocking, swinging, sleeping, or climbing on them. Some spectators find that his structures invite graffiti, like the Muhlenberg College students who wrote "For Sale" on a di Suvero piece, but then changed their minds about wanting to part with it. When making a sculpture in 1976-77 for a federal building in Grand Rapids, he decided that because of what he discerned to be the gregariousness of the citizens, he would include a suspended rubber "gondola" to accommodate five or more passengers. The gondola, which was not in the original design, and other alleged irregularities aroused the opposition of the General Services Administration in Washington, but a public outcry in support of di Suvero saved the sculpture for the city.

In critical comments relevant to Mark di Suvero's show at ConStruct in Chicago in 1979, Jim Fuhr discussed ways in which the sculptor "reduces the physical and psychological distance between the audience and the work of art." The beds, seats, and platforms of some of his larger sculptures invite the spectator to become "one of their working parts." In certain smaller pieces, like tumblers and puzzles, di Suvero engages the spectator in rearranging interconnected parts in a variety of ways.

Mark di Suvero put together Isis and other fairly recent sculptures in his outdoor studio in Petaluma, California, but in 1978 he was reported to have moved back to New York City to be closer to Baltimore, where he had accepted a commission for the waterfront area.

When he installs a sculpture, he works with speed and fierce intensity, usually wearing a hard hat and sometimes a welder's mask. According to the New York *Times* critic John Russell, he is a man of "spectacular good looks." He has gray eyes and long, flowing red hair. Kramer described him in the New York *Times Magazine* article as "a bearded patriarch with an ungainly walk and a generous, open smile, noisy and even rude to those he deemed the uptown enemies of art but gentle to his friends and associates." To Hess, writing in *New York,* "Di Suvero is an artist-hero in the noble lineage of Delacroix and Courbet—lion-maned, ox-eyed or fox-eyed (depending on the occasion), given to temperamental gestures and Delphic utterance."

References: Art in Am 66:100+ Mr/Ap '78; N Y Times II p25 Ja 30 '66, p29 My 17 '75 por, p50 N 13 '75, II p1+ N 23 '75; N Y Times Mag p10+ Ja 25 '76 por; New York 8:90+ N 17 '75 por, 8:94+ D 15 '75; Time 106:50+ D 1 '75 por; Washington Post N 15 '77 por; Contemporary Artists (1977); Phaidon's Encyclopedia of Art and Artists (1978); Who's Who in American Art (1978)

Donleavy, J(ames) P(atrick) (don-lē'vē)

Apr. 23, 1926- Writer. Address: b. c/o Delacorte Press/Seymour Lawrence, 1 Dag Hammarskjold Plaza, 245 E. 47th St., New York City, N.Y. 10017; h. Levington Park, Mullingar, County Westmeath, Ireland

The American-born Irish novelist and dramatist J. P. Donleavy created a genuinely original comic character in Sebastian Dangerfield, the wastrel who is the protagonist of Donleavy's rollicking first novel, *The Ginger Man,* set in the Dublin of the 1940's. When that classic of the contemporary picaresque was first published, in France in 1955, it was considered pornographic by the standards of the time, and in its unexpurgated form it was banned in the major English-speaking countries until the mid-1960's. Largely by word of mouth, it slowly attracted a cult following, chiefly among college-age readers, which grew into a world readership that has purchased more than 5,000,000 copies. Donleavy's subsequent works include a volume of short stories, six novels, and several plays based on his fiction. The additional novels include *A Singular Man* (1963) and *The Destinies of Darcy Dancer, Gentleman* (1977).

Donleavy's antiheroes tend to be alienated, dislocated, desperate men, usually either impoverished or very rich, who ease the pain of the human condition and the existential horror of death by their sense of the absurd and their priapic and other outrageous misadventures. Richard Gilman has ranked Donleavy as "one of the true forerunners and legitimizers of the hurtfully comic sensibility" and, along with John Barth, John Hawkes, and Donald Barthelme, one of the handful of contemporary American-born fiction writers "who continue to make it new but also good."

James Patrick Donleavy was born on April 23, 1926 in a small townhouse that still stands (New York City is preserving it as an example of eighteenth century architecture) at 8 Willow Street, Brooklyn, New York. His father, James Patrick Donleavy Sr., an ex-seminarian who had emigrated from Ireland, worked as a florist at the Ritz Carlton Hotel before becoming a building inspector with the New York City Fire Department. His mother, Margaret Donleavy, was also an immigrant, as he related to Phil Casey of the Washington *Post* (October 28, 1973): "My mother came from Ireland, and all the food in our house was canned and preserved. I felt highly deprived that I couldn't have Coca Cola. My life was totally different from that of my friends and other people I knew."

With his younger brother, Timothy, Donleavy was raised in the Bronx, in a white frame house that his father bought at 233 East 238th Street, near Van Cortlandt Park. In his essay "An Expatriate Looks at America," published in the *Atlantic* in December 1976, Donleavy evoked scenes of a serene and peaceful childhood, in the fragmented-sentence style typical of him: "Playing marbles on the dusty hard ground. Along summer shady streets of the uttermost northern Bronx. Or wandering woods shooting chipmunks with slingshots carved from the forked branches of the dogwood tree. Folk would give you an apple and a quarter if you mowed their lawn. Fights could be mean but were mostly fair."

By temperament a scrapper, Donleavy has never been known to back away from a fight. In secondary school he excelled at boxing as well as track—and apparently at little else. At Fordham Prep School, a Jesuit institution in the Bronx that is affiliated with Fordham University, he was expelled in his junior year because, as he recounted to Phil Casey, "They seemed to think I had revolutionary tendencies and that I was a bad influence on the student body." He finished out the year at Roosevelt High School, a public school in the Bronx, and then matriculated at Manhattan Prep, the Roman Catholic high school at that time affiliated with Manhattan College. He graduated from Manhattan Prep "narrowly," he told Casey—in June 1944.

For their vacations, the Donleavys usually motored across the United States or went to a summer house on Long Island. When working at a summer job clipping grass in Woodlawn Cemetery in the Bronx, Donleavy has recalled, he "was constantly imagining the lives of the people who were buried there." When Charles Monaghan, interviewing him for the Sunday supplement Book Week (December 15, 1968), asked whether he recalled any books from his childhood, he replied, "I can't remember anything that I picked up myself. I was a bit of a backward child. The comic strip 'The Katzenjammer Kids.' That, I think, must have been my major reading for many years."

During the final year of World War II Donleavy served in the United States Navy, which appointed him to the Naval Academy Preparatory School in Port Deposit, Maryland, where he specialized in mathematics but began to develop an interest in literature. "There was a professor there who asked me about my reading and if I had ever read James Joyce," he told Charles Monaghan in the Book Week interview. "I hadn't. But about that time, I read Thomas Wolfe." (He read some of Joyce later.)

Donleavy went on to say that for three and a half years beginning in 1946 he studied at Trinity College in Dublin on the GI Bill. "I did bacteriology there. I had always wanted to be a doctor. Another early interest of mine was composing. I spent a lot of time studying music and it is still one of my greatest interests. [Also] I got my literary education at Trinity. The people one associated with were people of great literary education and I picked up a lot about books through talking with my friends." But he said that he "never read a word" of any of the established Irish literary figures, such as William Butler Yeats, A.E., or Lady Gregory.

His bent was more toward Henry Miller and Franz Kafka. Regarding Kafka, he told Monaghan: "It's not his style that interests me, but his position, what he was writing about. For instance, every young man wants certain things: money, position. But things stand between you and them. Kafka had a keen sense of how intimidating those things are, [things such as] office routine, let's say. In this, he was one of the forerunners of the modern world. The world now is one of total intimidation and terror. You know, some people think Sebastian Dangerfield in The Ginger Man is an iconoclast and rogue but that's the opposite of what he is. He's intimidated."

Leaving Trinity College without taking a degree, Donleavy lived for several years on a farm in County Wicklow, Ireland, and then for several more years in England, where he married his first wife, Valerie Heron, and began raising a family. According to some accounts, at the beginning of his career he was a painter, and his first writing for public consumption was for catalog introductions to exhibitions of his paintings in Dublin. His first professional writing consisted of "backpagers," stories and short sketches, for the Manchester Guardian.

Donleavy completed the first draft of The Ginger Man during a year's visit to his native land, when he lived on eleven dollars a week in various locations, including Bridgeport, Connecticut, Boston, Massachusetts, and his parents' house in the Bronx. When he returned to Ireland, the late Brendan Behan, the writer, who was then still a house painter and an old pub-crawling crony of Donleavy's, read the manuscript and told Donleavy that he considered it, with its lilting garrulity, an "act of love for Ireland."

The title character of The Ginger Man is Sebastian Dangerfield, a boozing, womanizing, sponging expatriate American living in Dublin with his English wife and their child. The cunning, charming Dangerfield is a life-loving man of sensitivity run amuck, an ostensible student of law at Trinity College whose energies are totally diverted into a desperate defense against the forces threatening him, from creditors and the burden of family responsibility through repressive religion to sheer existential terror.

After rejection by some dozen other publishers, The Ginger Man was finally published by Maurice Girodias' Olympia Press, in the internationally notorious Traveler's Companion series, in 1955. Expurgated editions were issued in England in 1956 and in the United States in 1958, and complete editions were published in those countries by, respectively, Corgi Books Ltd., in 1963 and the Delacorte Press in 1965.

Critical reception of The Ginger Man was sharply divided, especially early on. Among those who hailed it were Dorothy Parker, who called it "a rigadoon of rascality, a bawled-out comic song of sex," and Vivian Mercier, who ranked it "an Irish comic masterpiece in the tradition of the twelfth-century Vision of the MacGongline" (*Nation*, May 24, 1958). Critics at the other end of the spectrum were indignant or disgusted by what they considered the novel's obscenity and blasphemy.

Over the years, the polarization diminished, so that by 1975 the entry on Donleavy in *World Authors 1950-1970* could read: "It has been generally agreed that Dangerfield, whatever makes him run, is a major comic creation, and that Donleavy has developed a unique prose voice in which to describe him. His rapid, telegraphic, alliterative style accommodates windy rhetoric and pure lyricism as readily as bawdry and bathos, savors of Mr. Jingle as well of Joyce and Henry Miller. Dangerfield describes his actions in the third person, his thought in the first person—a narrative device much admired by critics, which enables him to speak both as a sufferer and observer."

"This same idiosyncratic and marvelously flexible voice has been heard in all of Donleavy's subsequent novels, but none of them so far has equaled the success of *The Ginger Man*. They have seemed to most critics variously interesting but variously inferior approaches to the same theme. This theme, Donleavy says, is Donleavy himself, inasmuch as all his work draws on his 'dreams and inner desires . . . is all a kind of emotional autobiography.' "

The subsequent novels were *A Singular Man* (Little, 1963; Bodley Head, 1964), about George Smith, a Sebastian Dangerfield grown rich, but, mysteriously, more desperate; *The Saddest Summer of Samuel S* (Delacorte, 1966; Eyre and Spottiswoode, 1967), about a writer undergoing psychoanalysis in Vienna; *The Beastly Beatitudes of Balthazar B* (Delacorte, 1968; Eyre and Spottiswoode, 1969), the picaresque story, set mainly in Dublin, of another moneyed eccentric; and *The Onion Eaters* (Delacorte, 1971; Eyre and Spottiswoode, 1971), an account of the kinkiness, sexual and otherwise, of Clementine Clayton Claw Cleaver Clementine, a landed gentleman with three testicles, and his weird companions at Charnel Castle.

The comprehensive critical view has perhaps best been summed up by Charles Masinton in *J. P. Donleavy: The Style of His Sadness and Humor* (1975): "*A Singular Man* and *The Saddest Summer of Samuel S* sustain a generally high level of literary craftsmanship. . . . And the three novels that come after . . . especially *The Beastly Beatitudes of Balthazar B*, have passages of crisp humor or great lyrical beauty. But . . . the books following *The Ginger Man* do not have the inventive force, the raw energy, or the inspiration that make it a superior piece of fiction."

Several of the short stories eventually collected in *Meet My Maker, the Mad Molecule* (Little, 1964; Bodley Head, 1965) provided the inspiration for Donleavy's play *Fairy Tales of New York*, a play that follows the expatriate Cornelius Treacle Christian back to America, sees him through the burial of his wife, his employment in a funeral parlor, and his entrance into the American business world. As John Elsom observed in his essay on Donleavy in *Contemporary Dramatists* (1977), the flexibility of the theatrical form gave added scope to Donleavy's "great gifts for caricature, witty dialogue, and buoyant fun." After noting the emphasis that Donleavy placed on the contrast between the Democratic ideals professed by American society and the snobbish attitudes (such as the adulation of European "breeding"), Elsom wrote: "The spurious emotionalism of the funeral parlor is related to Christian's moving grief; and the sheer falseness of an overcommercialized society is exposed with a delicate skill that only Evelyn Waugh and Edward Albee have matched." Most critics agreed that the novel about Cornelius Christian, *A Fairy Tale of New York* (Delacorte, 1973; Eyre, Methuen, 1973) was less successful than the play.

The production of *Fairy Tales of New York* in London in 1961 was a commercial success and brought Donleavy an award from the London *Evening Standard*. The censorship of the play when it was produced in Dublin in November 1971 is the subject of Donleavy's satirical essay "What They Did in Dublin." The stage adaptation of *The Ginger Man*, produced on Broadway during the 1963-64 season, brought Donleavy a Brandeis University Creative Arts Award. All of his plays, including the theatrical versions of *A Singular Man* and *The Saddest Summer of Samuel S*, were published in *The Plays of J. P. Donleavy* (Delacorte, 1972).

Donleavy's *The Unexpurgated Code: A Complete Manual of Survival and Manners* (Delacorte, 1975) is a satirical manual of etiquette, with drawings by the author, covering such topics as throwing a party, improving one's accent, social climbing, bad breath, enemas, and pimple squeezing. Critics found it an affront or a delight, depending on their level of tolerance. One who took the book in stride was John Leonard of the New York *Times* (December 7, 1975), who wrote. "It comes right out of [his novels] in its preoccupation with class, anatomy, forgery, rudeness, the love of money, and the fear of death. . . . The only analogies around are in the works of Jonathan Swift, . . . especially his scatological poems."

Reviewing Donleavy's seventh novel, *The Destinies of Darcy Dancer, Gentleman* (Delacorte, 1977), Thomas LeClair wrote in the New York *Times* (November 6, 1977): "*The Destinies of Darcy Dancer, Gentleman* is not very different in quality from [Donleavy's] first novel, when it is re-read and not just fondly remembered. While sensibility is stronger in *The Ginger Man,* it and *Darcy Dancer,* along with Donleavy's five other novels, are essentially literate entertainments, unpretentious picaresques with flaws that shouldn't be taken any more seriously than their pleasures. Repetition, simple-mindedness, even sentimentality, are evident in Donleavy's previous works and in *The Destinies of Darcy Dancer, Gentleman,* too; they are part of the deal we have to make for the comedy and the stutter-step prose. Like an ice show or circus, it's a good deal every two or three years (*The Onion Eaters* excepted)." Donleavy's eighth novel, *Schultz,* about the frantic sexual escapades of an American impresario in London's West End, was issued by Delacorte in 1979.

In his book on Donleavy, Charles G. Masinton likened him to several other post-World War II American-born novelists, including Joseph Heller and Thomas Pynchon, in his "desire to project a private vision of experience rather than depict the manners of a certain social group or render in accurate detail the surfaces of the public world, as the older realists do." Masinton observed: "He does use various realistic techniques whenever they suit his purposes (he has a precise ear for dialogue and in *The Ginger Man* describes parts of Dublin with great fidelity, for instance); but he approaches fiction primarily as an expressive art and not as a means of faithfully recording his observations of the common everyday world." Masinton felt that *The Ginger Man* was a vigorous, confident "paean to joy, a celebration of life over death," but that subsequently "a pervasive gloominess" began to settle over Donleavy's fiction. "The wonder is . . . that his comic sense has persisted in the midst of it and that he has continued to write superb comic dialogue and to invent absurdly funny predicaments for his protagonists."

J. P. Donleavy, known to his close friends as Mike but to his mother as Junior, is five feet eight inches tall, weighs about 155 pounds, and has green eyes, a bearded, ascetic-looking face, and a shy manner. He speaks in a soft, well-modulated, halting voice with a clipped cosmopolitan accent and a British idiom, including the use of "one" for "I." By his first wife, Donleavy has two grown children, Karen and Philip. He was divorced in 1969, and in the following year he married Mary Wilson Price, an American actress he met during the rehearsals for a stage production of *A Singular Man.* The Donleavys live in a mansion on a 180-acre estate and cattle farm on the shores of Lough Owel in Ireland.

An Irish citizen since 1967, Donleavy enjoys tax-exempt status in accordance with a 1969 Irish law favorable to writers and other artists. In an interview televised on the CBS program *60 Minutes* on April 1, 1979 he said he considered his tax-free status "at least as important as winning the Nobel Prize." Years before he told an audience, "One day, while innocently looking into the window of an old established cheese shop in London, the definition of what writing is all about hit me. Writing is turning one's worst moments into money. . . . It is a victory to remain a writer, to reach the age of forty, be solvent, and still love your trade." During the same speech he described his long and finally successful legal battle to wrest control of the rights to *The Ginger Man* from Maurice Girodias. Donleavy now owns the Olympia Press, in his wife's name.

The author, who does not smoke and now drinks only occasionally, keeps in shape by jogging, playing soccer, and haymaking on his farm. Seven days a week, from eight in the morning until three in the afternoon, without fail, he writes. "I might spend three months on the first three pages of a novel," he has said. "I work hard on every sentence and every word. I work on the sound of the word and the look of the word, trying to extract every possible thing the word has for conveying meaning."

Donleavy's reading ranges from technical books and biographies to popular magazines and newspapers but seldom takes in novels, outside of an occasional bestseller. "I dislike 'writing' . . . ," he once said. "I dislike 'writers,' especially American writers. They're constantly on the outlook for grants, so they can avoid working for a living. Grants and fellowships are established to destroy writers and they succeed. My business is to put out some work and make a living at it."

References: Guardian p10 Ja 26 '73 por; *N Y Times* p50 D 7 '75 por; *N Y Times B* pl My 13 '77 pors; *Newsday* W p3 F 10 '68 por; *Washington Post* L p5 O 28 '73 por; *Contemporary Authors* vols 9-12 (1974); Vinson, Jane, ed. *Contemporary Dramatists* (1977); *World Authors: 1950-1970* (1975)

Drew, Elizabeth (Brenner)

Nov. 16, 1935- Journalist; author. Address: b. Suite 722A, 1028 Connecticut Ave., NW, Washington, D.C. 20036; h. 3112 Woodley Rd., NW, Washington, D.C. 20008

One of the few correspondents to win major awards in both print and broadcast journalism, Elizabeth Drew has been observing the Washington political scene with a detached, perceptive eye since the early 1960's. In her articles for the *Atlantic* and, later, for the *New Yorker,* and in the books spun off from those articles, she concentrated on the "hows"

Elizabeth Drew

and "whys" of the political process or, in her words, the "intersection of human relationships with institutions." She used the same unbiased investigative approach that distinguished her writing in questioning her guests on PBS's *Thirty Minutes With . . .*, an award-winning weekly political interview show broadcast in the early 1970's. Unusually successful in the tightly-knit, male-dominated field of political journalism, Mrs. Drew has won the respect of her colleagues for her accuracy, fairness, and sense of responsibility. "Every place I've been, everything I've done has been . . . serious journalism," she said once. "That's my line of work."

Of German-Jewish descent, Elizabeth Brenner Drew was born on November 16, 1935 in Cincinnati, Ohio, the younger child and only daughter of William J. Brenner, a furniture manufacturer, and his wife, the former Estelle Jacobs. Miss Brenner had, as she puts it, "a very conventional Midwestern growing up." She attended the local elementary school, joined the Girl Scouts, and spent her summers at Camp Walden in Maine. In an interview with Judith Michaelson of the New York *Post* (September 20, 1975), she explained her peculiarly Midwestern heritage: "Cincinnati is a *nice*, Midwestern, not too small, not too large, funny combination of being in the North with a strong Southern influence, so it's German and Southern and hillbilly . . . with a strong cultural streak, symphonies, spring festivals, theatre in the park, even opera at the zoo. . . . It's deep in your roots and you run into someone from the Midwest, and it's a very strong contact." Following her graduation from Cincinnati's Walnut Hills High School in 1953, she enrolled at Wellesley College in Wellesley,

Massachusetts. A Durant scholar, she majored in political science, with minors in history and English, and spent the summer after her junior year in Washington, working as an intern for the Democratic Senate Campaign Committee. She received her B.A. degree, Phi Beta Kappa, in 1957.

A few weeks later, Miss Brenner moved to Boston, Massachusetts where, after taking a crash secretarial course, she found work as a secretary in a small architectural firm. Eager to break into publishing, she eventually landed a job as an associate editor for the *Writer*. She remained with that magazine until 1959, when she returned to Washington. Hired as a temporary office assistant by *Congressional Quarterly*, Miss Brenner quickly learned, in her words, "how to take complex legislation and try to explain it, how to read a defense bill and a budget." Applying her newly acquired expertise, she gradually worked her way up to senior editor, a post she continued to hold after her marriage on April 11, 1964 to J. Patterson Drew, a lawyer then with the Agency for International Development. She left the staff of *Congressional Quarterly* in January 1975.

For the next three years Elizabeth Drew wrote free-lance articles on such varied subjects as gun control, civil rights, public housing, the cigarette lobby, civil defense, automobile safety regulations, education, and the Congressional legislative process for several magazines, including the *Reporter*, the *New Republic*, the New York *Times Magazine*, and the *Atlantic*. Impressed by her unsparing reports on the federal bureaucracy, the *Atlantic* hired her as its Washington editor in November 1967. In that observation post, Mrs. Drew continued to turn out thoughtful, carefully crafted pieces on governmental commissions, hunger in America, and the United States Army Corps of Engineers, among other topics. One much discussed article, "The Health Syndicate: Washington's Noble Conspirators," told how Mary Lasker, the philanthropist, and a group of celebrity physicians persuaded Congressmen to vote huge sums for medical research.

One morning in September 1970, just a few minutes after he and his wife had set off for their respective offices, J. Patterson Drew committed suicide by jumping off a bridge. Mrs. Drew described the shattering experience to Megan Rosenfeld in an interview for the Washington *Post* (May 16, 1979): "You had to pick yourself off the floor and piece yourself back together. When bad things happen to you, you do not feel. You have to feel, so that you can heal and come out the other side, whole and healthy." Characteristically, Mrs. Drew immersed herself in her work. Casting about for still something else to do, she explored with TV executives the possibility of a weekly, prime-time political interview show. Taken by the idea, WETA-TV producers set to work. In January 1971 *Thirty Minutes With . . . ,* hosted by Elizabeth Drew, was added to the

Public Broadcasting Service's program roster. It was eventually picked up by 150 of the 210 public television stations then in operation.

Thirty Minutes With . . . brought back the lengthy, in-depth, one-to-one interview that had virtually disappeared from television since the heyday of Edward R. Murrow. As Mrs. Drew interviewed, over the months, such national and international figures as Senators Edmund S. Muskie, George S. McGovern, and Edward M. Kennedy, Indian Prime Minister Indira Gandhi, King Hussein of Jordan, California Governor Ronald Reagan, and the Cabinet officers and White House staffers of President Richard Nixon, Washington correspondents trooped to her tapings, knowing they were certain to pick up a newsworthy item or two. A soft-spoken, persistent, but disarming interrogator, Mrs. Drew managed to charm her guests into answering the most probing questions. John Chancellor, the coanchorman of NBC-TV's nightly network news program, once admiringly remarked of his colleague: "Liz can slip in the knife in the nicest possible way."

Mrs. Drew repeatedly emphasized to journalists who interviewed her that she was deliberately "low-key" and "noncombative" to avoid putting her guests on the defensive. "I try to strike a balance where I am not so aggressive or antagonistic that my subject ends up issuing verbal press releases," she said, as quoted in *Newsweek* (December 13, 1971). "The more relaxed a guest is, the more revealing his answers. The panel show's primary purpose is to make news, and the questioning becomes a contest between the guest and the panel."

Although she was unfailingly respectful, even when some guests, among them Patrick Buchanan, one of Nixon's speechwriters, took advantage of the opportunity to expound Administration policy, Mrs. Drew never side-stepped controversial issues or toned down provocative questions. "The people I interview may be powerful and important, but they work for the public. We pay their salaries," she explained to Lucia Johnson Leith, who interviewed her for the *Christian Science Monitor* (October 6, 1972). "They all deserve respect, but they are accountable. That's what democracy is about." For her "informed and incisive" interrogations, Mrs. Drew won, in 1973, an Alfred I. duPont-Columbia University Award, one of broadcasting's top honors.

In June 1973, after two and one-half years of broadcasts, *Thirty Minutes With . . .* was discontinued. Later that month Mrs. Drew signed on with WTOP-TV, the *Post*-Newsweek station in the capital, as a political commentator and special assignment reporter. That same year she left the *Atlantic* to become a regular contributing editor for the *New Yorker*.

As a working journalist in Washington during the summer of 1973, a position she has since described as "like being at the battle-front," Mrs. Drew watched with increasing trepidation as the Watergate scandal mushroomed into a constitutional crisis. With the encouragement of William Shawn, the editor of the *New Yorker*, she began to keep a journal of that unparalleled period in American history. She started her journal on September 4, the day she knew "instinctively" that President Nixon would not complete his second term. "It was an extraordinary assignment, and I kind of invented it as it went along," she told Judith Michaelson. "One of the reasons I did it as a journal is that I wanted to show what life was *really* like then. Retrospective accounts tend to make it all seem neater, more inevitable, like there was a logical progression of events. But it was hardly that way. It was a mess. I also wanted the public to remember . . . how shocked and stunned and enraged and amused we were."

Over the next eleven months Mrs. Drew filled more than three dozen notebooks, carefully recording the daily revelations of the extent of the Watergate conspiracy, commenting on the changing moods of government and political leaders and of the people, illuminating the incredibly complicated impeachment proceedings, delineating the strains on the Constitution, and occasionally adding her own considered judgments. She closed her journal on August 9, 1974, the day Richard Nixon resigned from the Presidency, marveling at "what a close call we had."

"It is already coming into fashion to say that 'the institutions' have performed, that 'the system' has worked, but this is not really so clear," Mrs. Drew observed in her entry for August 7. "The ending of the Nixon Administration . . . was not as certain . . . as history may make [it] seem. The 'institutions' and the 'system' are not self-implementing. They can work only if there are enough people who are sufficiently concerned and wise—as well as in a position—to make them work. . . . Our safety lay in those who saw what the issue was, and who, when it wasn't easy to do so, pressed on. Now we know what real danger is. Perhaps we actually needed some people to come to power who would test the limits. . . . Nixon may have been . . . our greatest reformer. He showed us the possible consequences of our acquiescence, inattention, cynicism."

Excerpts from Mrs. Drew's journal appeared in issues of the *New Yorker* in 1973 and 1974. In 1975 Random House, Inc., published the entire diary as *Washington Journal: The Events of 1973-1974*. From her colleagues Mrs. Drew earned unanimous praise for her shrewd judgment, her uncanny sense of perspective, and her sober, thorough reporting. "The book's distinctive value lies in its careful rendering of the whole scene and of each event," William V. Shannon observed in the New York *Times Book Review* (September 14, 1975). "[Mrs. Drew's] journal can be compared in wine connoisseur's language to a good, young vintage. It is drinkable now, but lay it away on your library shelf for five or ten years and then you will really appreciate its fullness and character."

At William Shawn's suggestion, Elizabeth Drew kept a second journal, beginning on January 1, 1976, as she followed *"Homo candidatus"* along the bicentennial campaign trail. She proceeded, as she noted in her introduction to *American Journal: The Events of 1976* (Random, 1977), on the assumption that 1976 would be a significant year because, among other things, "the country would be electing a President against the background of a particularly large number of great questions, national and international." Some of those questions were about "the strange and brutal process" of Presidential politics itself.

During the course of the campaign, Mrs. Drew interviewed campaign staffers, party regulars, trade union leaders, economists, historians, politicians, and all the major candidates. Interwoven into her meticulous record of that unusual political season were lucid discussions of such transcendent issues as nuclear proliferation, energy, and environmental protection, but the book remains essentially a chronicle of, in her words, "the grand strategies, the tactics, the fumbling and confusions, [and] the absurd details" of a uniquely American electoral process.

American Journal, which was serialized in the *New Yorker,* received mixed reviews upon its publication in book form. Writing in the *Christian Science Monitor* (September 9, 1977), Mark Stevens thought Mrs. Drew's writing was "more wry than ever" and left the reader "as entertained as any good novel." Other critics, among them Richard Reeves, found the book to be "marked by a clear intelligence," but "cool." "[It] suffers from the eccentricities of [the *New Yorker*]," Reeves complained in the New York *Times Book Review* (September 11, 1977). He especially objected to the editing—which sometimes reduced copy "to a style reminiscent of 'see Spot run' "—to the "long, self-serving interviews," and to the "cautious-newspaper phrasing."

But the detached and unadorned prose that annoyed Reeves delighted Nelson W. Polsby, a political science professor at the University of California at Berkeley. "[Mrs. Drew's] not afraid to be boring," he said, as quoted in the Washington *Post* (May 16, 1979). "Her main insight is that process and routine matter. . . . She's willing to get it right, which sometimes means taking a long time and a lot of details that some people can't get through. But for [scholars] who really should be getting first-hand exposure to the material, her writing is the purest and finest ore we can get."

In her next book, *Senator* (Simon & Schuster, 1979), Mrs. Drew turned her attention to the "process" of Congressional legislation and to the "routine" of a United States Senator. She chose for her profile John Culver of Iowa because he was a moderate Democrat, well-respected by his colleagues, and because he was "reflective." For ten days, she dogged Culver's footsteps as he plotted legislative strategy, attended committee meetings, led a Senate floor fight, engaged in behind-the-scenes political horse-trading, and mingled with constituents on a weekend visit to his home state.

"I thought it was important to make the point that there are effective people who care about the country . . . because of the widespread and largely justified disillusionment with politics and because politicians are all we've got," Mrs. Drew explained to Megan Rosenfeld. "If we give up on them, I don't know what we've got—we've got a choice between a dictatorship, shooting it out or letting politicians mediate." Less widely reviewed than her earlier books, *Senator* was, as the *Christian Science Monitor*'s reviewer, Curtis J. Sitomer, put it, "something of an enigma . . . neither scintillating nor dull" to most of the critics. The general consensus was that the "admirable realism" of Mrs. Drew's "efficient" recreation of the Senate's atmosphere overshadowed her "rather plastic portrait" of Senator Culver.

Mrs. Drew contributes articles, from time to time, to the Washington *Post,* the *New Republic,* the New York *Times Magazine,* and other publications. She is a frequent guest on *Agronsky & Company* (PBS) and occasionally appears as a panelist on *Meet the Press* (NBC) and *Face the Nation* (CBS). Despite some initial misgivings, she served as one of the three questioners at the first debate between Presidential candidates Carter and Ford in September 1976. Mrs. Drew is the recipient of the 1970 Award for Excellence from the Society of Magazine Writers and the 1973 Wellesley Alumnae Achievement Award. In 1977 she was named Woman of the Year in Communications by the *Ladies Home Journal.* She holds honorary doctorates in humane letters from Hood College, Yale University, Trinity College, and Reed College.

Slim and petite, Elizabeth Drew stands five feet two and one-half inches tall and weighs 105 pounds. She has chin-length, reddish-brown hair, usually worn in a pageboy style, and large brown eyes. She lives alone in the red brick house in the Cleveland Park section of Washington that has been her home since the mid-1960's. For relaxation, she plays tennis, gardens, listens to classical music, and reads. She is especially fond of the novels of Anthony Trollope. "I want to get away from print, sometimes, and noise," she confessed to Louise Sweeney. "You need what in the computer world they call 'down time,' when you're not *at* something . . . poles of calm and quiet. Peace."

References: *Christian Sci Mon* p10 O 6 '72 por, p14 D 19 '77 por; *N Y Post* p19 S 20 '75 por; *Newsweek* 78:74+ D 13 '71 por; *Washington Post* B p1+ My 16 '79 por; *Who's Who in America,* 1978-79

Eanes, António (dos Santos) Ramalho
(yä'nēsh)

Jan. 25, 1935- President of Portugal. Address:
b. Oficina do Presidente, Palácio do Belém,
Lisbon 3, Portugal

General António Ramalho Eanes, commander in chief of the armed forces, took his oath of office on July 14, 1976 as Portugal's first freely elected President in half a century. With the support of the country's three largest parties —the Socialists, the Popular Democrats (now Social Democrats), and the Center Democrats —Eanes had won a landslide victory after campaigning on a pledge to bring law and order to an economically distressed nation that had been plagued by political confusion since its revolution of April 1974. Although he is reported to favor a secure place for free enterprise in the Portuguese economy, he also pledged to support the constitution of 1976, which is committed to a Socialist goal. President Eanes' term of office is five years.

António dos Santos Ramalho Eanes was born in Alcains, a village in central Portugal near the Spanish border, on January 25, 1935, the son of Manuel dos Santos Eanes, a building contractor, and Maria do Rosario Ramalho. As reported in the Christian Science Monitor (July 13, 1976), he was born in "a whitewashed farm cottage," and "his mother, who dresses in the traditional black and still works hard in her vegetable garden, said that as a child her son loved to ride the neighbor's donkey, then graduated to horses and eventually chose the army, partly because it was one way to continue his favorite pastime." But also, like many youths from families of modest means in Portugal and other nations, Eanes viewed enlistment in the army as an avenue to upward mobility. After completing his high school education in Castelo Branco, near his home village, in 1953 he entered the Escola da Guerra, the national military academy, from which he graduated in 1956. Apparently to advance his army career, he attended classes at the Higher Institute of Applied Psychology and at the Lisbon Faculty of Law.

Posted overseas at a time when Portugal was losing control over its far-flung colonial empire, Second Lieutenant Eanes served in Portuguese India from 1958 to 1960, Macao in 1962, and Mozambique in 1964 and from 1966 to 1968. Briefly during 1968, having returned to Lisbon, he taught physical education at the national military academy. When he resumed service abroad, Captain Eanes helped to lead the military opposition to anti-Portuguese guerrilla activity in Portuguese Guinea, from 1969 to 1973, and in Angola, where he served in the rank of major in 1073 74. Before being transferred to Angola, he had enjoyed a brief respite from the colonial wars as director of the department of cultural and recreational affairs at the military academy in Lisbon.

His disillusionment with the hopelessness of Portugal's continued presence in Africa led Major Eanes to join the Movimento das Forças Armadas (Armed Forces Movement), a group of young army officers who were seeking to overthrow the right-wing fascist dictatorship of António de Oliveira Salazar. Since Eanes was in Angola at the time, he could not take part in the bloodless coup d'état of April 25, 1974, which brought António de Spínola to power. When Spínola shortly afterward became provisional President, he summoned Eanes, his former aide in Guinea, to Lisbon to take charge eventually of Portuguese television. Eanes became a member of the ad hoc committee for mass media in June 1974, later director of television programming, and in September chairman of the board of directors of the Portuguese television company.

In his administration of national television operations, Major Eanes earned a reputation for scrupulous objectivity in reporting and found himself in frequent conflict with Portugal's hardline Communist party. Less than a year after his appointment he was forced to resign in the face of Communist accusations of "incomprehensible neutrality" and "probable implication" because he permitted impartial reporting of the March 11, 1975 attempt by rightist supporters of former President Spínola to take power.

An inquiry that Eanes himself demanded cleared him of complicity in the abortive coup and enabled him to resume his rapid rise from the middle ranks. Promoted to lieutenant colonel and attached to the general staff of the armed forces, he was sent to test the solidity of moderate support in military units throughout the country. He also became associated with a group of officers, known as "The Nine," whose political activities intensified the politicization within the army and may have precipitated a leftist uprising in November 1975. Eanes was credited with organizing the resistance to the attempted military coup and with crushing it with a minimum of violence.

Eanes' role in blocking the far-left grab for control earned him elevation to the exalted rank of four-star general and appointment to army chief of staff in December 1975. He quickly asserted his power by reorganizing the military and by tightening discipline, which he regards as "the principal factor of cohesion in the forces." Although he himself is a product of the army, he said that he wanted the army to play a lesser role in national affairs. Within two years, by December 1977, General Eanes had reduced the armed forces from a colonial peak of over 200,000 to 36,000. His December orders forbade partisan activities by soldiers, in accordance with his belief that the army exists "to defend national interests, and to guarantee the institutions established by the freely expressed will of the people through their votes."

Nevertheless, after he had declared his intention, on May 14, 1976, to campaign for the office of President, General Eanes seemed eager to claim the backing of most of the Portuguese armed forces for his candidacy. The country's three largest, non-Communist parties, which had won more than 80 percent of the vote in the legislative elections the preceding April, urged him to run, as did three groups on the left. Except for being recognized as a firm anti-Communist and as a supporter of the newly enacted Portuguese constitution, General Eanes was a largely unknown political figure. In his campaign he pledged to promote democratic socialism and to bring law and order to the strife-torn postrevolutionary nation. He also promised to strengthen the economy, install democratic institutions, and re-establish liberty. Responding to his ambitious and appealing program, on June 27, 1976 large numbers of voters gave General António Ramalho Eanes 61.54 percent of their votes, and on July 14, 1976 he was sworn in as the first Portuguese President to be elected by free, universal suffrage. Two days later he fulfilled a campaign pledge by naming Socialist leader Mário Soares as Premier.

When General Ramalho Eanes succeeded General Francisco da Costa Gomes, who had presided over the country's chaotic first two postrevolutionary years, he inherited, as his predecessor had, serious economic and social problems from the Salazar years of dictatorship. Not only was Portugal suffering from a generally backward and inefficient industrial sector, but it had a stagnant agricultural production and a perennially high trade deficit. Half the country's defense budget had gone toward the debilitating colonial wars, and political instability after the 1974 revolution prevented the development of a clear economic policy. Furthermore, while the 1974 revolution broke up industrial monopolies, wiped out large family landholdings, and nationalized the banks, insurance companies, and basic industries, the country's agricultural and industrial productivity continued to decline, labor demanded higher wages and produced less, and dollar reserves declined to the point where Portugal had to begin selling its gold. Emigrant workers no longer sent their earnings to families back home, and tourists avoided the country. Exacerbating the domestic economic disorganization was the return to Portugal of over 600,000 refugees and military personnel from the former African colonies. Inflation and unemployment remained high.

During President Eanes's first year in office the country's economic situation continued to deteriorate. The trade deficit reached about $1 billion; real wages fell to 1974 levels; both inflation and unemployment rose to above 25 percent. By October 1977, however, some signs of recovery had appeared, as tourists began to return, as Portuguese workers abroad again sent money home, and as the returned Portuguese colonial settlers and demobilized soldiers began to adjust to the country's lower standard of living. During the last months of 1977 Portugal negotiated with the International Monetary Fund for a $750,000,000 loan so that the government could carry out a program of reform to strengthen its economic structure. With the loan, however, came stiff conditions: the International Monetary Fund insisted on a comprehensive austerity program to check inflation and reduce trade deficits. The inability of Portuguese officials to deal with those exacting terms contributed to a prolonged major political crisis.

The political stalemate developed with the fall of Premier Mário Soares' government in December 1977 following a unanimous vote of no confidence in his Socialist party's efforts to resolve the country's economic difficulties. Portugal's system of government provides for the appointment of the Premier by the President after he has consulted with the Council of the Revolution, of which he is chairman, and with the parties represented in the Legislative Assembly. Despite his reported impatience with Soares' failure to make social and economic progress, President Eanes did not name a new Premier in December, but encouraged the efforts of the leaders of the Socialist and conservative Center Democratic parties to assemble a coalition. The alliance that they formed, however, lasted for only six months. In July 1978 the Center Democrats walked out of the coalition, complaining that Socialist policies in agriculture and farming and socialized health care were too far to the left. The Center Democrats objected to the Socialists' unequal distribution of agricultural credits, to the delay in returning illegally seized estates in the Alentejo region to the original owners, and to government's support of collective farms in the southern part of the country. The conservatives have blamed the collective farms for the disastrous fall in agricultural production that caused Portugal to import more than 40 percent of its food in 1978.

President Eanes expected that Soares would keep his pledge to resign if the Socialist-led coalition again collapsed, as it did in July. When the Premier yielded to his party's insistence that he stay in office, Eanes, who is said to have "felt his military sense of honor outraged," dismissed him. On August 10, 1978, after Portugal's badly polarized four-party system proved unable to organize another coalition, Eanes resorted to appointing a nonpartisan technocrat to the post of Premier. The industrial executive Alfredo Jorge Nobre da Costa, who had been Minister of Industry and Technology under Soares, was sworn in on August 28. Seventeen days later his government was toppled by the combined votes of the Socialist and Center Democratic parties.

To many political observers in Lisbon, as well as to Eanes, the arguments for the National Assembly's rejection of da Costa seemed untenable, particularly since the appointment was an interim one, to last only until another coalition government could be formed or until elections could be held. Neither politicians nor the electorate, however, desired the expense and disruption of elections called before those regularly scheduled for 1980. The editor of Lisbon's prestigious weekly newspaper Expresso found the reasons for the fall of da Costa's government "emotional in tone, stubborn in content, and weak in argument." President Eanes responded to the latest political impasse by refusing to consult with any politicians for a week. He explained in a press interview that "everybody needed to reflect calmly, to de-dramatize things, and to have a little silence for a few days."

After a two-month delay, during which the politicians failed to agree on a coalition, President Eanes again initiated the formation of a new government. This time he took the precaution of seeking the opinions of Socialist and Center Democratic leaders, with the result that the Legislative Assembly ratified his choice of Carlos Mota Pinto as Premier. Mota Pinto is a law professor and a moderate progressive who had once served in Soares' Cabinet as Minister of Commerce and Tourism. In June 1979, however, as political conflict worsened, Mota Pinto resigned, and the following month Eanes dissolved parliament and called for new elections in the fall.

The continual bickering among Portugal's political parties has led to increasing public impatience with the snail's pace of the promised transition to Socialism and, according to James M. Markham of the New York Times (January 21, 1979), has even tended to discredit the idea of democratic government. Another Western reporter, Ronald Koven, wrote in the Washington Post (September 24, 1978), "General Eanes seems to be working out a direct relationship with the electorate that reaches over the heads of the politicians." In January 1979 some of the President's advisers suggested that he deal with the institutional contest between chief of state and legislature by creating a strong Presidency "in the style of Charles de Gaulle of France." Although Eanes' political intentions have remained unclear, Koven quoted him as saying in September 1978, "Democracy shouldn't be a game in Lisbon between the parties and the President, but something involving the whole population.... It is my historical responsibility first to consolidate democracy, and second to act so that the constitution works fully to let the Portuguese people see both its defects and its good points." The voters would then be able to decide what "kind of Presidency they want in the future."

President Eanes' preoccupations with tensions on the domestic front have overshadowed his efforts in foreign policy. During 1976 he reestablished diplomatic relations with India after a break of twenty years and signed treaties of cooperation and an oil agreement with Venezuela. Under his administration Portugal has furthered its integration into Western Europe by gaining admission to the Council of Europe, working toward full membership in the Common Market, and taking a stronger role in NATO. Eanes signed a treaty of friendship and cooperation with Spain in May 1978, when King Juan Carlos and Queen Sophia made a state visit to Lisbon. Said to be convinced that his country "can be a Western bridge to the key nations of Africa," he met with Angolan President Agostinho Neto in June 1978 and has been encouraging the survival of the Portuguese language in the former colonies.

In 1970 António Ramalho Eanes married Maria Manuela Duarte Neto Portugal, a lawyer in the Ministry of Social Affairs who accompanied her husband throughout his political campaign and who is credited with reinforcing his growing political confidence. They have two sons, Manuel António and Miguel. The President enjoys horseback riding, reading, and collecting antique clocks. Among his many military decorations are the War Cross Second Class, the Silver Medal for Distinguished Services with Palm Leaf, the Silver Medal for Exemplary Behaviour, the Commemorative Medal of the Portuguese Armed Forces, and the Degree of Knight of the Military Order of Aviz.

Before running for public office, Eanes seemed to conform easily to the stereotype of a cold, stern, unbending army officer. To increase his appeal to voters during the campaign, he tried to cultivate a more friendly manner, wore untinted glasses instead of his customary dark ones, and occasionally dressed somewhat casually. He remains, however, a quiet, shy, intensely hardworking man who rarely smiles in public. Helen Gibson, Lisbon correspondent for the Christian Science Monitor (May 25, 1976), quoted a Western diplomat as telling her, "Eanes is one of the most honest and upright men I have ever met in any military. If he seems taciturn, it is perhaps because he carries out his own idea of discipline on himself."

References: Economist 263:7+ My 28 '77 por; N Y Times p3 Je 29 '76 por, IV p4 D 25 '77 por, A p2 Ja 22 '79 por; Washington Post S 24 '78 por; Britannica Book of the Year, 1977; International Who's Who, 1978-79; International Year Book and Statesmen's Who's Who, 1978-79

Ehrlichman, John D(aniel)

Mar. 20, 1925- Author; former government official. Address: b. c/o Simon & Schuster, The Simon & Schuster Building, 1230 Avenue of the Americas, New York City, N.Y. 10020

From January 1969 until he resigned under pressure in April 1973, John D. Ehrlichman, President Richard Nixon's pugnacious domestic affairs adviser, was second only to chief of staff H. R. Haldeman in the insular White House staff hierarchy. As one of those closest to the President, he took part in the cover-up, or attempted cover-up, of the Watergate scandal. Disgraced and imprisoned for his role in that political conspiracy, he emerged from jail, after serving eighteen months of his sentence, a seemingly changed man and began a new life as a writer of cynical "inside" political novels and as a syndicated radio news commentator.

"Ehrlichman came in [to the White House] as an arrogant man who had the appearance of a good man, and left as a better man with the appearance of an arrogant man," William Safire, a former Nixon speechwriter, observed in his personal history of the Nixon Administration, Before the Fall (1975). "More than any of the men in close, he was a product of Nixon's."

John Daniel Ehrlichman, the only child of Rudolph I. and Lillian C. (Danielson) Ehrlichman, was born on March 20, 1925 in Tacoma, Washington. His father, who had been a pilot for the United States Army during World War I, enlisted in the Royal Canadian Air Force in the early years of World War II and was killed in a plane crash in 1941. Raised in Washington state and California, Ehrlichman worked as a milk truck driver, a store clerk, and a mailman before he entered the United States Army Air Corps as an aviation cadet in 1943. As the lead navigator in a "pathfinder" squadron of the Eighth Air Force, he flew twenty-six bombing missions over Germany, for which he was awarded the Distinguished Flying Cross and the Air Medal with clusters.

Discharged from the service with the rank of first lieutenant in 1945, Ehrlichman enrolled on the G.I. Bill at the University of California at Los Angeles where he met H. R. ("Bob") Haldeman, forming a long-lasting friendship that would eventually lead him into the White House. After taking his A.B. degree in 1948, Ehrlichman went on to the Stanford University School of Law. He received his LL.B. degree in 1951 and was admitted to the California bar a few months later. Settling in Seattle, Washington the following year, he soon passed that state's bar and, with several colleagues, established his own law firm, Hullin, Ehrlichman, Roberts and Hodge. He remained a partner in that firm until 1968. Ehrlichman gradually acquired a reputation locally for his expertise in real estate law, and in 1967 he was hired as an instructor in law at the University of Washington.

Because he often had to deal with government officials of both parties on matters pertaining to zoning regulations and land use, Ehrlichman usually avoided partisan political involvement. He had followed Vice-President Richard Nixon's career with interest, however, and when his old friend Bob Haldeman, then a top advertising executive and a longtime Nixon campaign aide, invited him to work in Nixon's 1960 Presidential drive, he readily agreed. As a member of Haldeman's "advance" team, Ehrlichman was primarily concerned with logistics and public relations, but he occasionally indulged in the kind of unethical, "dirty tricks" politicking that was later to characterize Nixon's 1972 reelection campaign. According to Barry Sussman's The Great Cover-up: Nixon and the Scandal of Watergate (1974), Ehrlichman, on "something of an intelligence-gathering mission," infiltrated the camp of Nelson A. Rockefeller, Nixon's principal opponent, and even acted as Rockefeller's chauffeur during the North Dakota primary campaign. He later worked in Nixon's disastrous 1962 California gubernatorial race against Edmund G. Brown.

Six years later, when Nixon announced that he was again a candidate for the Presidency, Ehrlichman rejoined his political team as the national tour director. An efficient, no-nonsense organizer, he effectively managed the candidate's 50,000-mile campaign schedule, but Ehrlichman was more than an ordinary advance man. Nixon especially prized his loyalty, efficiency, and willingness to follow orders. Following his victory in the November 1968 general election, the new President-elect persuaded his trusted aide to accept an appointment as Presidential counsel. A year later, Ehrlichman moved up a notch to Presidential assistant for domestic affairs. In 1970 he took on, in addition, the duties of executive director of the Domestic Council and in 1971 he became a member of the Property Review Board and the Council on International Economic Policy.

Despite his lack of previous governmental experience, Ehrlichman appeared uncommonly well suited to his job as coordinator of the Administration's domestic programs. "He was one of those indispensable individuals who could translate policy, once set, into programs and action," Theodore H. White wrote in his 1973 book The Making of the President 1972. "His shop was one of the few at the White House where ideas were seriously entertained —good ideas, too, on energy, on land-use policy, on urbanization, on preservation of the American environment." Moreover, White added, Ehrlichman, unlike most of his colleagues in the White House inner circle, had "a sense of history" and "a true appreciation for the long-range shape of American problems."

The White House's "closet liberal," in William Safire's judgment, Ehrlichman argued forcefully for manpower retraining and other antipoverty programs, liberalized abortion laws, welfare reform, a national energy policy, and governmental reorganization. He was convinced that "we have lived too long with the consequences of attempting to gather all power and responsibility in Washington." As a corrective, he proposed a "six-pointed Presidency" made up of the President, four "elevated" Cabinet officers—for economic affairs, human resources, natural resources, and community development—and the head of the Office of Intergovernmental Relations, an outgrowth of his own Domestic Council that would work directly with mayors and governors. He contended that such a decentralization of the federal bureaucracy would not only permit the President to concentrate on policy, but also cause "a revolution in local government" by giving state and municipal authorities "the resources to decide on their own local priorities."

Like Haldeman, Nixon's iron-handed chief of staff, Ehrlichman met daily with the President and, over the months, the two Nixon intimates assumed considerable indirect and extraconstitutional power. Along with Attorney General John N. Mitchell and a few other trusted aides, they became the secretive Nixon's sounding board and planning committee. Utterly devoted to furthering Nixon's interests, they were the filter through which the vast apparatus of government, both formal and informal, reported to him and the means through which he exercised his executive and political authority.

Although Ehrlichman's authority within the White House was hardly comparable to Haldeman's, the two men were indistinguishable to the American public. Known in the press as "Herdleman and Erdleman" or "the Berlin wall," they constituted a kind of palace guard that shielded the increasingly reclusive and insecure President from uncongenial intrusion. As early as March 1969, just two months after Nixon took office, Ehrlichman asked one of his subordinates to develop a political "intelligence capability" to provide "investigative support" for the White House. In September 1971 he authorized a "covert operation" in an attempt to unearth incriminating information about Daniel Ellsberg, who had leaked the "Pentagon Papers" to the newspapers earlier that year. Acting on those instructions, the White House "plumbers" unit, so-called because of its assignment to fix leaks, burglarized the office of Ellsberg's psychiatrist. Ehrlichman was so dismayed by the group's tactics that he officially disbanded the unit, but it continued to operate undercover, stockpiling political gossip for use in the 1972 election.

In June 1972 five of the so-called "plumbers" were arrested while breaking into the headquarters of the Democratic National Committee in the Watergate complex in downtown Washington, setting in motion a course of events that developed into the worst political scandal in the nation's history. At first the Administration tried to fob off the break-in as a "third-rate burglary," but the dogged investigative reporting of the Washington Post's Bob Woodward and Carl Bernstein and other journalists gradually uncovered the extent of the conspiracy and the degree of White House complicity. Ehrlichman initially favored what Theodore H. White has called "the hangout, tell-all story," but he eventually not only went along with the cover-up but even suggested which of those officials involved was dispensable. It was Ehrlichman who advised Nixon to leave L. Patrick Gray 3d, the acting director of the FBI who had been tied to the Watergate defendants, "twisting slowly, slowly in the wind."

After two Administration officials, John W. Dean 3d and Jeb Stuart Magruder, implicated them in the cover-up, Haldeman and Ehrlichman resigned, at the President's request, on April 30, 1973. The following July, Ehrlichman testified before the seven-member, bipartisan Senate Select Committee on Presidential Campaign Activities, better known as the Ervin Committee. Combative and not yet disillusioned, he haughtily defended himself and the President. His parting words to the committee were words of warning to would-be government office seekers: "Be prepared to defend your sense of values when you come here. You'll encounter a local culture which scoffs at patriotism and family and morality just as it adulates the opposite."

In August, Ehrlichman moved back to Seattle with his family. Because he had been suspended from the bar, he could not practise law, but he did work occasionally as a legal consultant while preparing for his upcoming trial on conspiracy charges. Listening to the White House tapes for the first time, hearing Nixon "working both sides of the street," as he put it, hardened him and, when he took the stand at his trial in Washington, D.C. in December 1974, he was the first of the alleged conspirators to turn on Nixon. He contended that the President had deliberately misled and deceived him and, at one point, remembering the day he had been dismissed, he broke into tears. The evidence against him, however, proved overwhelming, and on January 1, 1975 Ehrlichman was convicted of conspiracy, obstruction of justice, and two counts of perjury. "I was impacted more by those trials than anything that has ever happened to me," he told Nick Thimmesch in an interview for the Washington Post's Potomac Magazine (January 2, 1976). "That experience brought forth in me an aspect of vanity and of personal pride. It was very much an attack on my veracity, and a lot of my own image of myself at that time. It was a hard thing to let go."

Disbarred, deeply in debt, and emotionally shattered, Ehrlichman left his wife and family shortly after the trial and moved to Sante Fe, New Mexico to make, in his words, "a disconnection." Adopting a relaxed and reflective lifestyle, he spent much of his time writing and sketching, but he also worked with local Indian and Chicano church and community groups as a volunteer counselor because it made him "feel useful." He tried to persuade Judge John J. Sirica, the presiding Watergate judge, to accept his volunteer work as alternative service. "While prison might knock out of me a lot of my pride and self-will, I truly would like to be able to do that rehabilitation myself," he told the judge, but to no avail.

While awaiting a decision on his appeal, Ehrlichman completed work on The Company, a roman à clef quarried from his Washington experiences. Published by Simon & Schuster in 1976, the book was an immediate best seller, less for its literary merits than for its author's presumed insights into government operations and thinly disguised portraits of familiar political figures, from the profane, suspicious, and self-doubting President Richard Monckton to the egomaniacal Teutonic national security

adviser. A highly rated twelve-hour television adaptation of the book, Washington: Behind Closed Doors, which was broadcast by ABC in September 1977, boosted sales of the paperback tie-in even higher.

The Company was "as square as a Sherlock Holmes story and as fascinating," Arnold Beichman wrote in his review for the Christian Science Monitor (July 26, 1976). "What makes [it] fun to read is that you can tell the players without a score-card." Although he conceded that the narrative was deftly written, Richard Todd, in an appraisal for the Atlantic (July 1976), complained that Ehrlichman had been "recklessly coy in his choice of form if he has something of historical importance to say." "If we are to read this novel as history," he wrote, "it raises some intriguing issues. At a minimum Ehrlichman is saying that intramural warfare in the executive branch of the government and its intelligence agencies was worse than we know even now, after three years of damaging revelations about the Nixon Administration, the FBI, and the CIA. Is he also saying something more exact?"

Having decided to abandon his appeal effort, Ehrlichman reported to the federal minimum-security prison camp at Safford, Arizona on October 28, 1976 to begin serving his thirty-month to five-year term. Prison life was onerous, "like the army," he said afterwards, but he encountered little of the brutality and violence he had anticipated. Most of his fellow inmates were Mexican illegal aliens and after leaving Safford in April 1978, he published in Esquire magazine a lengthy article about the treatment they received in American jails. Assigned to a relatively easy job in the prison's boiler room, he used his free time to write a second political novel.

Although Ehrlichman insisted it was "all fiction," The Whole Truth (Simon & Schuster, 1979), in which an idealistic young lawyer stumbles upon a high-level cover-up of a CIA-instigated coup in South America, bore more than a passing resemblance to recent events in the capital and, like its predecessor, it was chockablock with easily recognizable Washington figures: a folksy Southern Senator, a cruel chief of staff, a crafty attorney general and his loud-mouthed, alcoholic wife, among others. "The message of this entertaining political pop novel by one of the more thoughtful members of the Nixon gang," wrote Richard Lipez in Newsday (May 20, 1979), "seems to be that a President can get away with attempted murder if he's cunning enough to go on TV and tell the truth about it. It's an interesting notion, though my guess is that, if it ever happened, a sizable portion of the electorate would then ask, 'What is he really covering up?'"

Other reviewers were equally cynical. Steve Neal writing in the Chicago Tribune (May 6, 1979), observed that "Ehrlichman's 'fictional' portrait of his onetime boss is far less of a caricature than Nixon's own version." And

Robert Sherrill, in his review for the Washington *Post* (April 29, 1979), deplored the commercial exploitation of Ehrlichman's supposed inside information: "An -advance blurb says the book contains 'sensational revelations that will make headline news.' Well, only if the reader risks translating innuendo into fact, or is willing to conclude that the acts of bribery, chicanery, press manipulations and conflicts of interests . . . are based on actual events that Ehrlichman participated in or knew of. . . . But before Ehrlichman and his promoters start asking for headline space, he should step out from behind the devious protection of a very ordinary novel and talk straight for once."

Perhaps goaded by such remarks, Ehrlichman is currently working on a nonfiction book about the Watergate scandal. He regularly contributes articles to magazines and newspaper opinion columns. Among his recent articles is "Mexican Aliens Aren't a Problem . . . They're a Solution," which appeared in *Esquire* in August 1979. He is also the author of an essay, "The Effect of Elections on Doing the Business of Government," for *The American Electoral Process*. In addition, he tapes a daily two-minute news commentary, "The View from Here," which is syndicated to 125 radio stations by the Mutual Network and occasionally roams the lecture circuit, reportedly for $3,000 a speech.

Ehrlichman has mellowed considerably since his days in the White House. Always affable and good-humored, he has become, according to one interviewer, "nearly as laid-back as the old town [of Santa Fe] itself." Burly and healthy-looking, he has brown eyes, a well-tanned face, and a neatly trimmed salt-and-pepper beard. When he is not writing, Ehrlichman can usually be found sketching, gardening, or reading. He also enjoys trout fishing and playing tennis. A devout Christian Scientist, he does not smoke or drink. Ehrlichman and the former Jeanne Fisher, a UCLA classmate, were married on August 21, 1949. They have five children: Peter, Jan, Thomas, Jody, and Robert. That marriage ended in divorce. On November 3, 1978 he married Christine Peacock McLaurine, an interior designer with a young son by a previous marriage, whom he met while shopping in a Manhattan furniture store. The Ehrlichmans live in a 160-year-old, wall-enclosed adobe house on a hilltop in Santa Fe, New Mexico.

References: Bsns W p54+ Mr 3 '73 por; Esquire 86:64+ Jl '76; Newsday II p4+ Ap 30 '79 pors; Newsweek 84:20+ D 23 '74 por, 88:35 D 13 '76, 90:40+ O 17 '77; Time 95:15+ Je 8 '70 por; Washington Post mag p16+ Ap 29 '79 pors; B pl+ My 8 '79 pors; Contemporary Authors vols 65-68 (1977); International Who's Who, 1978-79; Who's Who in America, 1978-79; Who's Who in American Politics, 1973-74

Estes, E(lliott) M(arantette)

Jan. 7, 1916- Corporation executive; automotive engineer. Address: b. General Motors Corporation, 3044 W. Grand Blvd., Detroit, Mich. 48202

Described as "innovative, energetic, hard-driving, enthusiastic and fiercely competitive," E. M. ("Pete") Estes rose steadily through the ranks before succeeding Edward N. Cole as president and chief operating officer of General Motors, now the world's largest corporation, in the fall of 1974. Beginning as a student engineer in the 1930's, Estes served his apprenticeship under such legendary GM figures as Charles F. Kettering and Semon E. Knudsen before heading the Pontiac and then the Chevrolet motor division in the 1960's. In both posts he revitalized his products, breaking sales records in the process. Estes became GM's fifteenth president in 1974, at a time when the corporation was at its nadir, reeling from the combined effects of the Arab oil embargo and business recession. He is credited with major responsibility for the downsizing and fuel economy policies that bolstered GM's market dominance and precipitated a dramatic turnabout in its fortunes.

Elliott Marantette Estes was born in the Wakeman Hotel, owned by his maternal grandparents, in the tiny town of Mendon, Michigan on January 7, 1916. His mother Jesse Isabelle (Marantette) Estes, helped her parents run the hotel, and his father, Ernest Louis Estes, worked as a clerk in the local bank.

When Estes was nine or ten he moved with his parents and younger sister to the nearby town of Constantine, where his father soon became chief cashier in the bank. Reflecting on his boyhood, Estes told Desmond Wilcox, author of *The Americans* (Delacorte Press, 1978): "We had an automobile in those days . . . and we had plumbing in the house after I was about ten years old; prior to that we just went out into the backyard. I wouldn't say we were rich, but we were middle class in a small town. I had a strict moral upbringing, my mother was a Catholic, my father was a Protestant, and so they joined a church somewhere in between those two and we went every Sunday."

Estes' lifelong fascination with machines began at an early age. At fourteen he learned to drive and repair his parents' Flying Cloud automobile, an experience he recalled as the "beginning of my infatuation with moving things." He was also interested in the steam engines and threshing machines he discovered on an uncle's farm; and once he attached a one-cylinder engine to his coaster wagon so that it would move under its own power. At Constantine High School Estes took as many mathematics and physics courses as he could. Because the small school "could only get together about eleven fellows for football and six or so for basketball," he was able to play on both teams.

On graduating from high school, Estes got a job at the local creamery, where he did manual labor for a dollar a day. Then, after the New Deal's minimum wage law went into effect, his daily pay abruptly jumped to $3.20. Although for a time he considered a career as a dairyman, he eventually grew restless. Remembering a high school aptitude test that indicated a talent for engineering, he quit his job in 1934 after a year during which he had saved $1,000. He was about to enter Michigan State University when a providential letter from a cousin, who was employed at General Motors Truck and Coach in Pontiac, persuaded him to enter the General Motors Institute at Flint, Michigan instead. A prime factor in the Institute's favor was the fact that its graduates were virtually assured of a job at General Motors—an important consideration during the Depression, which had hit the Estes family hard.

It was at GMI that Estes earned his nickname. On his first day in the school machine shop, a supervisor in the tool crib arbitrarily dubbed him "Pete," and the name stuck. By end of his first semester, Pete Estes ranked second in his class and was rewarded by being transferred to the GM Research Laboratories. There he worked under the watchful eye of the renowned engineer-inventor Charles F. Kettering on diesel injectors and radial aircraft engines, among other projects. In addition to shouldering his work-study load, Estes washed dishes, did janitor

duty, and worked in the school machine shop to earn tuition and living expenses.

After qualifying for a graduation certificate at GMI in 1938, Estes was urged to work for a degree in order to be "in the swim" at General Motors. He therefore went for two years to the University of Cincinnati, where he studied hydraulics and business administration and obtained a B.S. degree in mechanical engineering in 1940. He then returned to the GM Research Laboratories for a full-time position as a research engineer. For the next six years he worked on a variety of Kettering projects, some of them important to the United States defense effort during World War II. They included prototype high-compression engines and a remote-control robot plane that has been described as "probably the world's first guided missile."

Estes received what he considers his "first big break" in 1946, when he was transferred from the GM Research Laboratories—where he was a senior research engineer—to the Oldsmobile Division. There he worked as a motor development engineer on the team engaged in producing the high-performance rocket V-8, the world's first high-compression automobile engine. Its successful completion in 1949 "put Oldsmobile on the map," according to Estes. By 1954 he was assistant chief engineer at Oldsmobile.

When Semon E. Knudsen was appointed general manager of the Pontiac Division in 1956 he invited Estes to join his division as chief engineer. Pontiac, then known as an "old lady's" car, was mired in sixth place among American car companies, and Knudsen and Estes, working as a team, were determined to change its image. They aggressively upgraded Pontiac's engineering and design staffs. According to *Motor Trend* magazine (February 1965), "Estes . . . bought, borrowed and stole some of the best engineering brains in Detroit." Among his recruits was John Z. DeLorean, the maverick automotive genius who later became a top GM executive before resigning in 1973 to establish his own automobile manufacturing company. With Knudsen concentrating on restyling and Estes on "under-the-skin" engineering and performance, Pontiac was transformed almost overnight into a sleek, powerful, medium-priced car that caught the imagination of the auto-buying public. It leaped from sixth to third place, surpassed only by Chevrolet and Ford in overall sales. Some of the changes for which Estes was most directly responsible as chief engineer included a 225-horsepower economy engine, the perimeter frame, the four-cylinder Tempest engine, and, most important of all, the "wide-track" principle of expanding the wheelbase to improve stability and safety, so far as the design permits. The wide track was soon copied by virtually all United States automakers.

When Knudsen left Pontiac for Chevrolet in November 1961 he chose Estes to succeed him as general manager. Elected at the same time to a GM vice-presidency, Estes became, at forty-five, the youngest general manager ever to head any of GM's five car divisions. At Pontiac he continued Knudsen's policy of continually improving mechanical performance and updating styling. He also added some new touches of his own, such as placing inspectors at intervals along the assembly line to catch mistakes early, instead of waiting for them to show up in the finished product, and personally test-driving a different model home from work each night. He was also responsible for introducing the sporty GTO. But his greatest accomplishment was in lifting Pontiac sales to new heights. In just three and a half years he succeeded in doubling sales, increasing Pontiac's third-place lead over Oldsmobile by 173,000 units, and expanding the company's market penetration to a record 9 percent. According to Joseph C. Ingraham of the New York *Times* (September 14, 1963), Estes was automotive management's 1962 "rookie of the year" and a frontrunner for car-makers' "man-of-the-year" honors for 1963. And a profile in *Motor Trend* (February 1965) noted that Estes' tenure as chief engineer and general manager of Pontiac marked "a success era unequaled in recent automotive history."

When Knudsen was placed in charge of Canadian and overseas operations in June 1965, Estes succeeded him as general manager of the Chevrolet motor division. As the leading producer of automobiles in the United States, Chevrolet accounted for nearly 60 percent of GM car sales, and ranked as one of the country's top five companies. The year he took over, Chevrolet manufactured 3,000,000 cars and trucks, a world record for a single company. But Estes also inherited some major problems, including Ralph Nader's scathing attack on the Chevrolet Corvair in his book *Unsafe at Any Speed* (1965). In response to that attack, GM executives hired detectives to pry into Nader's private life. Estes has never revealed the extent of his personal involvement with that affair, but he later told Desmond Wilcox: "I don't know that, even now, I would regard that as a mistake. Perhaps the mistake was to apologize at the Senate investigation for having done it." Nader eventually sued GM and was awarded $425,000 in damages.

But Estes' most difficult task at Chevrolet was to hold off Ford's strong bid for sales leadership. Spurred by the success of the Mustang, the fastest-selling new car in history, Ford in 1966 came close to unseating Chevrolet as the nation's number one auto maker. Estes, however, quickly countered by introducing the Camaro. In 1968 he supervised the most sweeping model change in Chevrolet history, making significant altera-

tions in the Corvair, Camaro, and regular Chevrolet lines, in addition to totally redesigning the Corvette, Chevy II, and Chevelle. By 1969 Chevrolet was again outselling Ford by a hefty margin.

In one of a series of management shuffles Estes left Chevrolet for GM's corporate headquarters in February 1969 to succeed Donald L. Boyes as group executive of the car and truck group. In March 1970 Estes—who had never traveled farther from the United States than Bermuda—was named vice-president for overseas operations. That post, which made him "heir apparent" for the GM presidency, was seen by Estes as the high point of his "learning curve" as a corporation executive. Reversing a policy that overseas operations must be completely GM-owned, Estes played a key role in initiating a program that enabled the corporation to engage in joint ventures with foreign companies and to acquire equity interests in them. During his tenure GM negotiated agreements with automakers in Japan, Korea, the Philippines, Singapore, Zaire, and other countries. Estes left overseas operations in 1972, when he was named executive vice-president of the operations staff and elected to the GM board of directors.

On September 30, 1974 GM announced that Estes had been elected to replace Edward N. Cole, who was retiring at sixty-five, as GM's president and chief operating officer. Unexpectedly, he was granted overall responsibility for GM's fast-growing overseas business in addition to domestic operations, a dramatic expansion of the president's role, and the corporation bylaws had to be modified to permit the change. Estes took over the presidency at a crucial moment in GM's history. Sales had plummeted to their lowest point in thirty years, GM stock was at a record low, and a sharp rise in fuel prices in 1974 had rendered many of the company's admittedly poor-mileage cars undesirable. As a result, GM's share of the auto market had shrunk alarmingly. The corporation's response to demands for antipollution and safety legislation failed to satisfy environmentalists and consumer advocates; its relations with organized labor had deteriorated; and according to some observers it had not kept up with the times.

Refuting the contention of its critics that GM had lost its leadership, Estes and board chairman Thomas A. Murphy took drastic measures to revitalize the corporation. Estes had once commented, as quoted in *Motor Trend* (July 1970): "General Motors is a heavy machine, but we are much more flexible than people generally think." As president, he set out to prove his point. His first step was to scale down GM's complete line of full-size and intermediate-size cars, drastically cutting weight and raising fuel efficiency. That required not merely a facelift but total redesign—an enormously risky and expensive undertaking. Nevertheless, GM committed $15 billion toward shrinking the size and weight of its entire product line, a move that was described in *Duns Review* (December 1977) as "the greatest gamble in the history of American business." To help finance the move, GM in 1975 offered $600,000,000 worth of notes and debentures, the largest single borrowing undertaken by any company in industrial history.

The second phase of the changeover involved an attack on the subcompact market with the introduction in 1976 of the Chevette, Detroit's first minicar, which had been developed as a result of Estes' efforts. By 1978 Chevette led the entire subcompact field in sales, trailed by Toyota's Corolla and Ford's Pinto. That same year GM led the industry in fuel efficiency, although only four years earlier it had ranked last. GM has announced plans to further lighten its cars by substituting such materials as aluminum and fiber glass for heavier steel parts, and it has been experimenting with alternatives to the gasoline engine. For 1979, GM announced three completely redesigned personal luxury cars: the Cadillac Eldorado, the Buick Riviera, and the Oldsmobile Toronado. Among the standard features of those cars are front-wheel drive, independent front and rear suspension, and electronic leveling control. As a result of such bold innovations, GM is once again a prosperous, dynamic corporation. In 1977 it edged out Exxon to recapture the number one spot on *Fortune* magazine's list of America's 500 largest corporations, with 797,000 employees, sales totaling $55 billion, and earnings of $11.62 per share. *Dun's Review* in December 1977 designated GM one of the five best-managed companies of the year.

Estes has also borne the brunt of some controversy. In 1977 it was discovered that GM had been installing Chevrolet engines in its higher-priced Buick, Pontiac, and Oldsmobile cars. In announcing GM's offer in April 1977 to exchange the affected cars for new ones or give customers free mechanical performance insurance, Estes remarked: "Interchange of engines across a number of our product lines is not new to GM or the auto industry. And it will continue and even grow." Later that same year Estes was exposed to more criticism when two lawsuits charged GM with favoritism toward two of Estes' sons who have connections with the corporation. Estes' biggest headache, however, has been what he considers "unreasonable" requirements imposed on the industry by federal agencies and Congress. "We're going flat out, and spending as much money as there is, and we still cannot design . . . what they want," Estes told Desmond Wilcox. He called government interference "one of the major problems facing the motor industry today."

In a speech in California in January 1979 Estes appealed to the government to ease its standards for fuel economy in the 1980's, arguing that the increase in car prices would be excessive. But in August he told University of Michigan students that with its 1985 models General Motors fully expected to exceed the government standard of 27.5 miles per gallon as a fleet average. He indicated that the consumer shift to more fuel-efficient cars provided incentive to move ahead.

The president of General Motors rises at six A.M. or earlier, begins the day with a dip in his backyard pool, and is driven to work by an armed bodyguard-chauffeur. A wiry six-footer with jet-black hair and a mustache, he is warm, friendly and outgoing. Accessible to customers and employees alike, he frequently visits the assembly line, shaking hands with workers. He remains highly competitive. "I've been sixth, fifth, fourth, third and first, but I've never been second —and don't intend to be," he has said. Estes works ten to twelve hours a day and often on weekends, and he displays a singleminded devotion to his job and family. In rare leisure hours he is an avid gardener and enjoys golf, tennis, hunting, fishing, and gin rummy. An ardent fan of the Detroit Lions football team, he attends every home game he can. He smokes very little and takes only an occasional drink. Estes holds honorary doctorates from the University of Cincinnati, Kalamazoo College, and Northern Michigan University.

E. M. Estes and his first wife, Cathryn, a graduate nurse whom he met as a student, were married about 1938; she died in 1965. They had three sons: Thomas, now a sales executive with the GM supplier Display Corporation International of Milwaukee; Edward, a Georgia Cadillac dealer; and William, who runs a Chevrolet dealership in Indiana. Estes also has seven grandchildren. With his present wife, Constance, formerly his secretary, whom he married in 1967, he lives in the affluent Detroit suburb of Bloomfield Hills, in a long, white, single-story house with three acres of lawn and a garden that stretches to the bank of a small stream. He retains a reputation for knowing more about his product than many of his mechanics and engineers. It is not unusual to see his driveway cluttered with exotic turbine, electric, or other experimental cars on a Sunday morning, or to catch him whirling around the block in one on a test run. "I love automobiles," he affirms, "driving them, fooling around with them, selling them."

References: Biog N p1260+ N '74 por; Car and Driver 21:38+ Ja '76 por; Life 61:131+ O 14 '66 pors; Motor Trend 17:76+ F '65 por; N Y Times III p14 Mr 24 '74; International Who's Who, 1978-79; Wilcox, Desmond. The Americans (1978)

Fahd, Crown Prince of Saudi Arabia
(fäd)

1922 (?)-. Address: Council of Ministers, Jidda, Saudi Arabia

The crown prince and first deputy premier of Saudi Arabia, Fahd Ibn Abdul Aziz is technically second in command to his half-brother, King Khalid, but most commentators agree that he dominates the Saudi government. The prince's policies, backed by approximately $40 billion in annual oil revenues, affect the course not only of his nation, but also of a host of other Middle Eastern countries that depend on Saudi largess. An energetic and astute administrator with more than twenty years of experience in the ministries of education and the interior, Fahd is perhaps the most progressive member of the royal family. In recent years, he has pressed for economic diversification that will reduce Saudi Arabia's total reliance on oil. Prince Fahd chairs the Council of Ministers and is a member of several important executive bodies, including the National Security Council and the Council of Senior Princes.

Born in Riyadh in 1922, Fahd Ibn Abdul Aziz is one of the forty-odd sons of Abdul Aziz Ibn Saud, the powerful heir of the sultan of the Nejd district of central Arabia who unified the warring desert tribes and, in 1932, founded the kingdom of Saudi Arabia. To strengthen his position, King Ibn Saud married the daughters of both allied and rival chieftains. Prince Fahd's mother, Hassa Bint Ahmad al-Sudeiri—reportedly the favorite of Ibn Saud's scores of wives—was a member of the influential Sudeiri clan. Educated at home in the traditional manner of desert princes, Fahd acquired a general education as well as religious training in the teachings of the Koran and in the purist principles of the Wahabi sect from his Islamic tutors; from his father he learned falconry, camel racing, and other Arab sports. After he reached adulthood, the prince studied at universities in Europe and in the United States.

Leadership in Saudi Arabia, a nation without a constitution, a parliament, or popular elections, is the responsibility of the descendants of Ibn Saud. Of the approximately 3,000 adult princes who trace their parentage to him or to his five brothers, about fifty wield real power. The sons of Ibn Saud, from whose ranks the nation's monarchs have come since the founder's death in 1953, are at the heart of Saudi affairs. Numbering thirty at present, they are divided into factions of full-blood brothers. As the eldest of Hassa's seven sons, Fahd is the leader of the so-called "Sudeiri Seven," who constitute the strongest force in the economic and political life of the country.

After being appointed Minister of Education in 1953, Prince Fahd introduced to the nation a system of public elementary and secondary education that was eventually expanded to include girls' schools. During a reorganization of the government in 1962, in which most of the actual power was delegated to Crown Prince Faisal because of King Saud's ineptness, Fahd was named Minister of the Interior. Five years later, he assumed the additional responsibilities of second deputy premier. The dual role gave Fahd substantial power both at home and abroad. He controlled the national guard, the so-called "White Army" of loyal tribesmen that Faisal used as a counterbalance to the regular army, helped formulate the nation's oil and investment policies, and represented the king at international meetings. Convinced that economic diversification was essential for Saudi Arabia's survival, he established a corps of Western-trained Saudi technicians to oversee the development and operations of new industries. Perhaps his most important accomplishment in the area of foreign affairs was his negotiation in 1974 of a far-reaching economic and military accord with the United States.

At a royal reception on March 25, 1975 King Faisal was shot to death by a nephew, Prince Faisal Ibn Musad Abdul Aziz. Immediately after the assassination, the five senior Saudi princes caucused and, within an hour, announced the succession of Khalid Ibn Abdul Aziz, Fahd's older half-brother, to the throne. The new king quickly named Fahd crown prince. Because of his administrative experience and his knowledge of foreign affairs and of the oil industry, some Western observers had expected that Fahd would be chosen King instead of Khalid, a quiet, retiring man who had suffered several heart attacks. Even after Khalid's enthronement, there was widespread speculation about the permanence of his monarchy.

Over the next few weeks most foreign commentators came to believe that while the King reigned, the crown prince actually ruled. Indeed it was Prince Fahd who on March 31, 1975 issued the new government's first policy statement. Speaking for his monarch, Fahd promised to continue the modernization programs and social reforms begun by Faisal and to strengthen and expand the government by setting up a consultative assembly. He emphasized that while the new regime strongly supported all efforts to achieve disarmament, political self-determination, and the peaceful settlement of international disputes, it was prepared to "employ all its resources" to "regain the lost rights of the Palestinian people and get back the occupied Arab territories" from Israel. At the same time he pledged to beef up the country's military capability so that Saudi Arabia would become "a force in the defense of the Arabian nation and of the Arab cause."

In the months that followed, Khalid proved to be more than a figurehead, but Fahd, in his post as first deputy premier, continued to play a vital role in the management of the kingdom's day-to-day domestic affairs and in the formulation of foreign policy. Employing skills honed through years of negotiating with Bedouin tribal chiefs while Minister of the Interior, Fahd tried to bring some measure of stability to the turbulent Middle East. In the interest of Arab unity, he stepped in to resolve several simmering regional controversies that threatened to boil over into armed conflicts. Largely through his efforts, a long-standing argument between Syria and Iraq, which are controlled by opposing factions of the Baath political party, over the sharing of the waters of the Euphrates River and a territorial dispute between leftist Algeria and royalist Morocco were settled amicably.

Alarmed by the growing Communist presence in the Middle East, Fahd used a variety of tactics to undercut Soviet influence. Among other things, he approved substantial loans to Syria and offered economic assistance and other forms of aid and support to Somalia, Eritrea, and Djibouti to help them withstand pressure from Soviet-backed Ethiopia. Closer to home, he negotiated a new border agreement with Iraq, Saudi Arabia's radical neighbor to the north, that included an Iraqi promise to end anti-Saudi broadcasts. Worried about a possible partition of Lebanon between warring Moslems and Christians, he warned right-wing Christian militiamen that the establishment of a Christian state "on the debris of the present coexistence" among the nation's religious groups would have "the most serious consequences" for Saudi-Lebanese relations. But he remained in contact

with leaders from both sides and, in October 1976, engineered a conference of Arab League nations that drew up the guidelines for a negotiated peace under the watchful eye of an Arab League peacekeeping force. Throughout the thirty years of its existence, Israel has been the sorest point of Saudi foreign policy. Neither Fahd nor Khalid is as anti-Jewish as Faisal was, and the prince has even gone so far as to suggest that Saudi Arabia might officially recognize Israel after a comprehensive peace agreement has been signed. As recently as October 1978, however, Fahd advised the Israelis "either to take advantage of the opportunity for a just and lasting peace—an opportunity which does not always crop up—or to take the other option, whose consequences only God can know."

As the price of a settlement, Fahd demanded the return of all Arab lands occupied by Israel since the Six-Day War in June 1967 and the establishment of a Palestinian state. Arguing that the comparatively moderate Palestine Liberation Organization offered a much better hope for a negotiated peace than the radical Popular Front for the Liberation of Palestine, the prince openly supported Yasir Arafat, the PLO chairman. Behind the scenes, he tried to persuade Arafat to renounce terrorism in favor of negotiation, but the private talks collapsed when Egyptian President Anwar Sadat met Israeli Prime Minister Menahem Begin in Jerusalem in November 1977.

At first Saudi Arabia took a cautious wait-and-see position on the Sadat-Begin negotiations, although many Western observers interpreted Fahd's decision to televise the two leaders' joint news conference as a tacit endorsement of their efforts. When, after months of fruitless bargaining, Begin, Sadat, and President Jimmy Carter constructed a framework for a bilateral peace accord at a United States-sponsored summit meeting at Camp David, Maryland in September 1978, Fahd tried to protect Egypt from the wrath of the Arab League. While recognizing that it would be "suicide" for Saudi Arabia to side completely with Sadat, Fahd blocked attempts by the Arab hard-liners to blacklist Egypt and impose other punitive sanctions.

In an interview with Arnaud de Borchgrave for *Newsweek* (March 26, 1979), Fahd predicted that the separate Egyptian-Israeli peace treaty would "trigger convulsions in the region . . . by making the people at the center of the whole problem [the Palestinians] more desperate than they already are." The prince, who had canceled a scheduled visit to Washington, D.C. in mid-March because he did not want to appear to be endorsing the bilateral agreement, proposed the establishment of a pan-Islamic committee to work with the United States on a comprehensive peace settlement involving all the confrontation states that included provisions for a Palestinian homeland and the return of East Jerusalem to Arab control. Immediately after the peace treaty was signed on March 26, 1979, Arab foreign and finance ministers gathered in Baghdad, Iraq to consider diplomatic and economic sanctions against Egypt and also against the United States, for its sponsorship of the treaty.

In Fahd's opinion, the limited Egyptian-Israeli treaty not only further fragmented the Middle East, but also strengthened the hand of Soviet-backed radicals. Since the overthrow in January 1979 of the Shah of Iran by Islamic revolutionaries led by Ayatollah Ruhollah Khomeini, Saudi leaders, including Prince Fahd, have felt increasingly threatened by Soviet gains in the countries encircling the Arabian peninsula. Their worries were borne out in late February, when Marxist South Yemen invaded North Yemen, a pro-Western Saudi ally. In response to the crisis, Fahd put the Saudi armed forces on full alert and called an emergency meeting of the Arab League. At that meeting, held in Kuwait on March 6, the Arab foreign ministers negotiated a ceasefire and adopted a peace plan, proving, in Fahd's words, that "cooperation among ourselves is the best approach to solving regional crises."

To safeguard their territorial integrity in the wake of the collapse of the American-backed regime in Iran, the Saudi rulers have, in recent weeks, edged away from the United States toward a more neutral position. The Saudi Foreign Minister, Prince Saud al Faisal, went so far as to thank the Soviet Union, with whom Saudi Arabia has no diplomatic relations, for its "positive stands" in supporting the Arabs' position in a comprehensive peace settlement. But Prince Fahd is quick to point out that the gesture does not reflect a reassessment of Saudi-American relations. "These are turbulent times," he explained to Arnaud de Borchgrave, "and Saudi Arabia, like the United States, must respond to regional and global changes in terms of its own national interest. . . . A special relationship, which our two countries enjoy, is certain to involve 'special differences.'"

Expressing a sense of "responsibility toward world society," Prince Fahd has, in general, used the Saudi Arabian oil weapon with restraint. Shortly after he became crown prince, he agreed to American requests to expand Saudi oil-producing capacity to avert an anticipated worldwide energy shortage. He did so despite dire financial predictions from his young economic advisers, who argued that Saudi oil was worth more in the ground awaiting future sale than in barrels purchased with inflated Western currency. "My country, which possesses the world's largest oil reserves, won't be the cause for weakening mankind's ability to live in stability and prosperity," Fahd said, as quoted in the *Wall Street Journal* (March 31, 1975). "I am among those who don't believe in threaten-

ing and bargaining on principles. I am also not the sort of person to use negative pressure." Under his orders, the government approved an $11 billion plan to boost production from the 1978 level of about 10,000,000 barrels a day to 14,000,000 barrels a day by the early 1980's.

Because he believes that sharp increases in petroleum costs jeopardize the international economy, Prince Fahd has tried to hold the line on world oil prices. His obstinacy has occasionally caused some dissension within OPEC's ranks, as it did in April 1977, when Saudi Arabia refused to raise its prices to conform with those of other OPEC members. Unwilling to risk an open break with OPEC during the Iranian crisis in late 1978, he went along with a four-step 14.5 percent boost for 1979. Fahd blamed the unusually steep rise on the West's inability to control inflation and advised the industrial powers to stabilize their currencies to prevent future increases.

Ignoring pleas for moderation by Sheik Ahmed Zaki Yamani, the Saudi Minister of Petroleum and Mineral Resources, OPEC voted on March 27, 1979 an additional 9 percent hike in the basic price of crude oil and authorized individual members to impose discretionary surcharges. According to some reports, the Saudis—the West's chief oil supplier—agreed to cut back production in exchange for pricing concessions from OPEC hard-liners, many of whom had demanded increases of up to 35 percent in retaliation against the Egyptian-Israeli peace treaty.

While continuing to honor long-standing Saudi-American ties, Fahd has brought Arabia into closer contact with Europe, the best customer for Middle Eastern oil. Within months of becoming crown prince, Fahd negotiated major economic agreements with President Valéry Giscard d'Estaing of France and Prime Minister Harold Wilson of Great Britain. He also gave more consideration to European firms in competition for lucrative Saudi business contracts. For example, in January 1978 a consortium headed by the Philips Group, a Dutch company that employed one of Fahd's sons as its agent, won a major contract to modernize the Saudi telecommunications system. The decision, which promises to gross more than $3 billion for Philips and its partners, L. M. Ericsson of Sweden and Bell Canada International, was a severe blow to two American firms, Western Electric and International Telephone and Telegraph.

Within Saudi Arabia's boundaries, Fahd pressed for government assumption of the nation's oil reserves from the Arabian-American Oil Company. "Oil is unique," he reasoned. "It is a natural resource and our livelihood depends on it. We, not outsiders, should control our oil." The driving force behind Saudi Arabia's current $142 billion five-year development plan, the prince strongly supports the concept of a welfare state.

Among other things, the Saudi government provides the people with free medical care and free education through the university level and turns over to employees its investments in new factories. Although he personally favors modernization, Fahd is careful not to offend Islamic conservatives. "Our approach is exactly opposite to that of Atatürk of Turkey," he explained, as quoted in *Time* (April 7, 1975). "Atatürk imposed changes on his people from the top. We try to act as a catalyst, giving the people a glimpse of change and letting them decide to accept it."

On behalf of Khalid, Fahd has encouraged the distribution of power to provincial authorities "so as to form another stone in the towering structure of our country," but he does not intend to introduce American style democracy, believing that open elections would undermine the position of the Western-trained technocrats who run the Saudi bureaucracy. "We have invested heavily in educating these young men," he told a reporter for *Time* (May 22, 1978), "and now we want to collect a dividend on our investment. But if we were to have elections, these young men would not be elected. The winners would be rich businessmen who could buy the votes. Our real talent would not be used."

Fahd esteems "Bedouin democracy," and on five days each week he holds a "majlis," or informal hearing, at which citizens present petitions or air their grievances. Afterwards, by custom, all are invited to join the prince for dinner. "Anyone in the kingdom is welcome to this table, no matter what his status," Fahd explained. "If they were all bankers or army generals, it would be assumed they were invited because of their position. But these are simple people. Anyone, anyone can come here, and that gives them confidence in their government."

A heavy-set, bearded man with a rolling gait, Prince Fahd is, by all accounts, amiable, good-humored, talkative, self-confident, and a consummate diplomat. "He makes you think he agrees with you, no matter what you discuss," one long-time friend remarked and an unnamed Western official told Joseph Kraft, "Being with him is like taking a hot bath. You glow all over." The prince speaks and reads English, but he regularly uses an interpreter for international affairs. The prince is fond of soccer and camel racing, but his favorite recreation is camping in the desert with his brothers. Fahd, who lives in a marble palace in Riyadh, is married and has several children. His sons have attended European and American schools.

References: Cur World Leaders 21:7 N '78; N Y Times p11 Mr 26 '75; N Y Times Mag p8+ Jl 6 '75 por; New Yorker 51:111+ O 20 '75; Time 91:34+ My 22 '78 por; International Who's Who, 1978-79

Fauntroy, Walter E(dward)

Feb. 6, 1933- United States Representative from the District of Columbia. Address: b. 2441 Rayburn House Office Building, Washington, D.C. 20515

The preeminent figure in Washington city politics is the Reverend Walter E. Fauntroy, a civil rights activist of the 1960's who has been elected four times since 1971 as the District of Columbia's nonvoting delegate to the House of Representatives. In 1973 he helped to secure a limited form of home rule for the federal city, which has a black majority, and in 1978 a Constitutional amendment granting the District the same representation on Capitol Hill that it would receive as a state. A Democrat, Fauntroy is a leading member of the House Black Caucus and heads a subcommittee probe of the 1968 assassination of the Reverend Dr. Martin Luther King Jr.

Walter Edward Fauntroy, the fourth of William T. and Ethel (Vine) Fauntroy's seven children, was born in Washington, D.C. on February 6, 1933. His father was a clerk in the United States Patent Office; his mother, a part-time seamstress. Raised in the blighted Shaw ghetto on the northwest side of the city, Walter was a sickly but pugnacious child who earned the respect of his peers by boxing and by playing baseball, basketball, and football for the local Police Boys Club. He also built soapbox racers. "I was always smaller, and I guess that helps to make you try harder," he explained to one interviewer.

Even as a boy, Fauntroy was drawn to the New Bethel Baptist Church, just down the street from his home. "I didn't understand then that we were living on a plantation," he told Vincent Peka of the Washington *Post* (April 6, 1969), "but I sensed it—the dope, the bootleg liquor, the payoffs to the cops, the general fear of the white man." The church was, for him, "a light in the wilderness in those days." He spent much of his free time helping the church to raise money and, while in junior high school, decided on a career in the ministry. When he graduated second in his class from Dunbar High School in 1952, the church reciprocated by giving him the money to pay for his freshman year at the Virginia Union University in Richmond, Virginia. Fauntroy received his B.A. degree, *cum laude*, in 1955, and went on to attend Yale University's Divinity School on a Bess and Charles Woodward scholarship. There he so distinguished himself that Kingman Brewster Jr., the president of Yale, offered him the deanship of the divinity school upon the completion of his B.D. degree in 1958, but he declined the offer to accept the pastorate of the New Bethel Baptist Church.

Believing that religion was more than "something you preach up from the pulpit, sing up from the choir, shout up from the pews and then lock up in the church building on Sunday morning," Fauntroy took part in the demonstrations, sit-ins, marches, and negotiations of the civil rights movement in the 1960's. "The gospel which we preach is not simply good history," he said, as quoted in *Ebony* (June 1978), "it is good news. You see, it is good history that the Master fed 5000 people some 2000 years ago. But it is 'good news' when his followers of today act in the living present to feed the hungry, clothe the naked, and set at liberty those that are captive."

A friend since 1954 of the Reverend Dr. Martin Luther King Jr., Fauntroy was named director of the Washington, D.C. bureau of Dr. King's Southern Christian Leadership Conference (SCLC), the largest and most influential of the civil rights groups, in 1960 and, as such, acted as its chief lobbyist for the passage of the Civil Rights Act of 1964 and the Voting Rights Act of 1965.

As one of the SCLC's key strategists, he also coordinated its campaign against segregation on a national level. Among other achievements, he helped to arrange the freedom rides in 1961, the protest marches on Albany, Georgia in 1962 and on Birmingham, Alabama in 1963, the massive March on Washington in August 1963 in which 200,000 people peacefully demanded jobs and freedom, and the march on Selma, Alabama in 1965. In recognition of his efforts, President Lyndon B. Johnson appointed Fauntroy vice-chairman of the White House Conference to Fulfill These Rights, which was created in 1966 to advise the President on the implementation of the new civil rights

legislation. After Dr. King's assassination in April 1968, Fauntroy worked closely with the slain leader's successors to map out strategy for a Poor People's Campaign. That drive climaxed in a mass demonstration in Washington, D.C. in May 1968 that put pressure on Congress to enact national antipoverty legislation.

At the local level, the Reverend Mr. Fauntroy opposed those urban renewal programs that displaced thousands of blacks, using as his rallying cry the slogan "Urban renewal is Negro removal." In 1965, to help those forced out of their homes, he cofounded the Coalition of Conscience, which pushed for additional welfare assistance. In the following year he and other local clergymen set up the Model Inner City Community Organization (MICCO), a neighborhood planning agency dedicated, in Fauntroy's words, to making urban renewal "work for black people instead of against them."

As MICCO's unpaid executive director, a post he held until 1971, Fauntroy drew up a program to insure that the 45,000 residents of the Shaw ghetto were involved in the planning and rebuilding of their neighborhood. With $2,800,000 in federal urban renewal funds, he hired black architects, city planners, and construction engineers and recruited and trained unemployed blacks to work on the project, which included blueprints for homes, schools, shops, libraries, and recreational facilities.

Although many of the new apartment complexes were built by neighborhood sponsors, Fauntroy constantly lobbied for additional federal money. He had been named vice-chairman of the Presidentially-appointed nine-member Washington city council in 1967 and had many contacts on Capitol Hill, but some Republican Congressmen strenuously objected to his association with the Black United Front, a coalition of moderate and militant leaders of black nationalist groups. Fauntroy repeatedly rejected Congressional demands that he resign from the city council, but when President Richard Nixon directed the Department of Housing and Urban Development to allocate some $30,000,000 to MICCO in January 1969, Fauntroy left his municipal post to devote all his time to the implementation of the MICCO program. It was the largest single inner city renewal project in the country and the first to be wholly planned and administered by the residents of the affected area.

On September 9, 1970 President Nixon signed a bill giving the District of Columbia a nonvoting delegate in the House of Representatives. The following month, Fauntroy announced his candidacy for the Democratic nomination to that post. His two chief opponents, both prominent members of the black community, outspent him two-to-one and one of them had won the endorsement of the local Democratic central committee, but Fauntroy had the support of Washington's black pastors, who exercised considerable influence over their congregations, and of such civil rights leaders as Coretta Scott King, the revered widow of Dr. Martin Luther King, and Hosea Williams, a high-level SCLC official. On January 12, 1971 he scored an upset victory in the primary election with 44 percent of the vote, beating his nearest competitor by 13 percent.

Fauntroy's major opponent in the March 23 general election was Republican John A. Nevius, a white lawyer. Because 71 percent of the city's 756,000 residents were black and Democrats outnumbered Republicans six-to-one, Fauntroy emerged as the strong favorite in the six-man contest. A charismatic and colorful campaigner with a lively, street-smart style, Fauntroy shunned party conclaves and fundraisers in favor of walking tours of the city, during which he met personally with the voters on a one-to-one basis. Campaigning on the theme "He's going to get us all together," he emphasized his record as a civil rights strategist and pledged to forge a progressive national coalition of black "nation power" and white "forces of goodwill." To illustrate that proposed alliance, he concluded his stump speeches with his arms raised high above his head, one hand clenched in the black power salute, the other in the two-finger "V" sign of the antiwar movement.

Fauntroy's liberal platform called for among other things, federally funded day-care centers, improved higher education facilities, mass transit subsidies, and "a guaranteed annual income at levels of decent support for those who work and are underpaid, those who are seasonally unemployed, and those in need." His main plank, however, was home rule and full Congressional representation for the District of Columbia. Capturing 59 percent of the vote to Nevius' 25 percent, Fauntroy easily won the seven black wards with a four-and-a-half-to-one majority over his Republican opponent, while losing the single white ward, including Georgetown and its affluent surroundings, by a two-to-one margin. Sworn into the House on April 19, 1971, he was soon seated as a voting member of the House District of Columbia Committee, which along with its Senate counterpart, initiated legislation for the city. Fauntroy also became the thirteenth member of the House Black Caucus.

Using a strategy reminiscent of the civil rights movement, Fauntroy immediately set out to push a home rule bill through the House District of Columbia Committee by developing a citizens' constituency for it. During the spring of 1971 he organized meetings throughout the city to drum up support for the proposal and the following July, he and Massachusetts Senator Edward W. Brooke formed a national nonpartisan coalition of twenty-six organizations backing self-rule for Washington. But the conservative House panel, which had long been the chief obstacle to the passage of home rule legislation, was then dominated by Chairman John L. McMillan of South Carolina and other diehard Southern Republicans. Despite Fauntroy's relentless lobbying efforts, the committee turned down the self-government bill passed by the Senate in 1971.

Fauntroy was more successful in other areas of domestic legislation directly affecting the lives of his constituents. It was his vote, for example, that killed in committee a proposal doubling the city's grocery tax and he single-handedly persuaded his colleagues to vote against a bill denying overtime pay to employees of municipal hospitals unless they had put in more than eighty hours in two weeks. Although he is prevented by law from voting on the House floor, Fauntroy can introduce legislation. Among those bills he submitted during his first term were proposals to establish a national sickle cell anemia program, impose sanctions on foreign countries that produce heroin, and make the land on the Bolling-Anacostia military reservation available for the construction of civilian housing projects and hospitals.

Intending to use his fifteen-member delegate slate as a bargaining chip on such national issues as equal economic opportunities for minorities as well as on wholly local issues like home rule, Fauntroy entered the May 1972 Democratic Presidential primary as a favorite son candidate. Urging his fellow Washingtonians to vote "not so much for a man, but a plan, not so much for a rap as a map," he promised to deliver the District of Columbia delegation and other uncommitted minority delegates to the Democratic aspirant who was most sympathetic to home rule and to black political demands. "We must learn to use our power and stop relying on simple benevolence," he explained, as quoted in the New York Times (December 8, 1971). "I have no illusions about my being a candidate with a serious chance for the Presidency. My purpose is limited only to securing the best possible deal for the District of Columbia."

Heeding his wishes, the major contenders stayed out of the Washington contest and the Fauntroy slate won easily. As promised, when one of the Democratic Presidential hopefuls, Senator George S. McGovern, endorsed most of Fauntroy's "Washington agenda," Fauntroy rounded up more than forty uncommitted votes, which helped McGovern score a first ballot victory at the Democratic National Convention the following month. In appreciation, the senator asked Fauntroy to make a seconding speech at the convention, thus giving him his first national exposure. Fauntroy himself was easily reelected to a second term in 1972 and has been returned to the House by sizable majorities, reaching as high as 85 percent, in the subsequent biennial elections.

In January 1973 the House Democratic Committee on Committees awarded Fauntroy seniority on legislative committees despite his status as a non-voting delegate. The increase in rank was enough to make him chairman of the District of Columbia's judiciary subcommittee. He also secured a seat on the powerful Banking and Currency Committee, which gave him new bargaining power in working for home rule. More importantly, the 1972 electoral defeat of Congressman McMillan, brought about, in part, by Fauntroy's skillful organization of South Carolina's black voters, and other personnel changes resulted in a pro-home rule majority on the District of Columbia Committee.

Now in a better position to promote home rule, Fauntroy adopted a more subdued, traditional political style. "When you carry a big stick, you can afford to work quietly," he explained to Martha Hamilton in an interview for the Washington *Post* (July 15, 1973). Because compromise was essential to the prompt passage of any home rule bill, Fauntroy agreed to back a measure providing for the direct election of a mayor and a thirteen-member council but retaining Congressional control over expenditures. The limited home rule bill, with an added Senate stipulation giving Congress a veto over all council legislation, was signed into law by President Nixon on December 24, 1973.

Fauntroy briefly considered running for the office of mayor against Walter E. Washington, a moderate black who had held that post by Presidential appointment since 1967, but decided instead to remain in the House. Over the next two years, he and Washington fought for control of the local Democratic party organization. Fauntroy won at least temporary control in May 1976 when his uncommitted delegate slate, unofficially for the Presidential candidacy of Senator Hubert H. Humphrey, overwhelmingly outpolled Washington's pro-Humphrey slate. Fauntroy's supporters also captured almost all of the contested seats on the District of Columbia Democratic central committee.

Describing his action as an effort to end "the tyranny of taxation without representation," Fauntroy announced in May 1975 an all-out drive for a Constitutional amendment to give the District of Columbia full representation in Congress. The following year he approved a compromise amendment that gave Washington one voting delegate in the House of Representatives, leaving further representation to the determination of law. That measure fell forty-five votes short of the two-thirds majority required for passage. Two years later, with the blessing of President Jimmy Carter, Fauntroy submitted for consideration a bill giving the District of Columbia the status of a state in the election of Congressional representatives, the allocation of Presidential electors, and the ratification of Constitutional amendments. When the House passed that amendment in March 1978 by a vote of 287 to 127, Jim Wright, the House majority leader, gave much of the credit for

its passage to Fauntroy, who had organized a coalition of fifty-three local and national organizations called "Self-Determination for D.C." to generate support for equal representation. The Senate followed suit five months later.

Standing five feet nine inches tall, Walter E. Fauntroy has the compact, tightly muscled body of a disciplined athlete. He excells at most sports and regularly takes first place in several events in the annual "King of Capitol Hill" track and field competition. An especially good sprinter, he recently ran the sixty-yard dash in 6.5 seconds, just six-tenths of a second off the world record. Gifted with an excellent tenor voice, he often concludes political rallies with a moving interpretation of "The Impossible Dream," from the Broadway musical *Man of La Mancha*. In 1975 he recorded an album of sacred and secular songs. He has asked that the proceeds from the sales of the LP be equally divided between the New Bethel Baptist Church and the Martin Luther King Jr. Center for Social Change in Atlanta, Georgia. Walter E. Fauntroy married Dorothy Simms, whom he met at Virginia Union University, on August 3, 1957. They have one son, Marvin.

References: Ebony 33:31+ Je '78 pors; N Y Times p24 Ja 14 '71 por; Washington Post C p1 Ap 8 '69 pors, C p1 Mr 10 '71 por, A p1+ Ap 20 '71 pors, B p1+ Mr 26 '72 por; Who's Who in America, 1978-79; Who's Who in American Politics, 1979-80; Who's Who in the East, 1978-79

Feinstein, Dianne

June 22, 1933- Mayor of San Francisco.
Address: Office of the Mayor, City Hall, San Francisco, Calif. 94102

Most Americans were unaware of Dianne Feinstein until that dramatic moment on November 27, 1978 when, as acting Mayor of San Francisco, she announced at a hastily organized press conference that Mayor George R. Moscone had been assassinated, along with her colleague on the Board of Supervisors, Harvey Milk. A week later the board, of which Mrs. Feinstein was president, elected her to fill out the remainder of Moscone's term, which runs through 1979. In the mayoral election on November 7, 1979 Mayor Feinstein claimed more votes than any other candidate, but neither she nor her chief challenger, Supervisor Quentin Kopp, also a Democrat, drew the necessary 50 percent of the returns. A runoff was scheduled for December 11, 1979.

The San Francisco mayoralty is a nonpartisan office, but Mayor Feinstein's identity

Dianne Feinstein

as a Democrat is well known. Early in her career she was considered a liberal, especially in such matters as ecology and environment, but over the years she moderated her position and developed strong ties with business interests and a reputation for fiscal conservatism. As mayor, she has tried to bridge the diverse interest groups in her highly cosmopolitan domain and to restore a sense of order and peace to a city that in recent years has had more than its share of tragedies and traumas, from the Symbionese Liberation Army's "war" to the Zebra murderers' grisly reign of terror. The assassinations of Moscone and Milk came just nine days after the city had been shaken by news of the suicide-murder in a jungle commune in Guyana of hundreds of members of the Reverend Jim Jones's San Francisco-based People's Temple.

Dianne Feinstein was born Dianne Goldman in San Francisco, California on June 22, 1933 to Dr. Leon Goldman, a Jewish physician who still practises and teaches medicine, and Betty (Rosenburg) Goldman, a Catholic Russian-American who modeled clothes in one of San Francisco's exclusive salons. "I was brought up supposedly with some Catholic religion and some Jewish, and I was to choose," Mrs. Feinstein told Steven V. Roberts when Roberts interviewed her for the New York Times in 1971. "I went to a convent [school] and I went to a temple at the same time, but I don't think that works very well. You are what you are. But the experience did give me a deep respect for both religions."

"When I was sixteen years old," Dianne Feinstein recounted in a 1971 interview with John Peterson for the National Observer, "I knew this [government service] was what I

wanted to do." The initial vocational catalyst was an uncle in the garment business for whom she sometimes modeled new lines; that uncle used to take her to meetings of the Board of Supervisors, which he called the "Board of Stupidvisors," telling her, "Dianne, you get an education and do a better job."

After graduating from the Convent of the Sacred Heart High School in San Francisco, Dianne Feinstein matriculated at Stanford University, where she majored in history and political science and, in 1954-55, served as vice-president of the student body. "There wasn't much of a social conscience on campuses in the '50's," she recalled in the Times interview with Steven V. Roberts, "but the people from our generation survived; we weren't burned out early; we had the reprieve of our college years to generate strength." She received her B.S. degree in 1955.

The springboard of Mrs. Feinstein's career in politics and government was her expertise in criminal justice. She began to familiarize herself with that field in 1955 and 1956, when, as a Coro Foundation public affairs intern, she worked in various government agencies and helped prepare a study of the administration of justice in California. "For women to be effective in political life they've got to have an area of expertise in which they can speak with authority," she said in the interview with Steven V. Roberts. "Women often become so divided they don't zero in on any one thing and their efforts aren't as meaningful."

In 1956 and 1957 Mrs. Feinstein worked as an administrative assistant with the California Industrial Welfare Commission, which oversees the implementation of the state minimum wage law. With the birth of her daughter, she went into temporary retirement, from which she emerged in 1962, when Governor Edmund G. Brown appointed her to the California Women's Board of Terms and Paroles. For four years she met with the other board members three times a month in Los Angeles, making decisions regarding the sentences and paroles of women in the state prison system.

Following another hiatus in her career, when her first marriage ended in divorce, Mrs. Feinstein served on the San Francisco City and County Advisory Commission for Adult Detention and the Mayor's Commission on Crime for two years, until she won election to the Board of Supervisors. She joined the board in 1969 and was its president from 1970 to 1972 and again from 1974 to 1976.

Being a San Francisco supervisor is normally a part-time job, but Mrs. Feinstein worked at it full time, with a calculated sacrifice of time at home. "I can't participate in the running of the house," she told a reporter at the time. "I have a housekeeper who does everything—the marketing, the preparing and serving of meals. But I've always felt that the important thing was the kind of time you spend with your family, not the amount. I like to spend

Class A time with them, when I'm fresh and interesting and fun for the family."

Responding to the strong, repeated pleas of San Francisco liberals, Mrs. Feinstein challenged Democratic Mayor Joseph Alioto in the 1971 mayoralty race. She explained to a reporter at the time that among her reasons for seeking municipal rather than state or national office were family exigencies and the fact that "this is where the salvation of America's problems lies. As the cities go, so goes the whole nation."

In some of the campaign rhetoric directed against her, Mrs. Feinstein was called "Mrs. Clean," a sobriquet she proudly accepted as an allusion to her fight against hard-core pornography and the more egregious of the North Beach nightclub sex shows. But the key issues of the campaign were high-rise construction in downtown San Francisco and busing for the purpose of public school integration. While she did not go so far as to endorse a referendum—rejected by the voters —that would have prohibited the construction of any building over six stories high without voter approval, she did profess to "offer the alternative to Mayor Alioto's philosophy." "San Francisco doesn't need the developers," she declared. "They need us and should be allowed to come in only on our terms." All of the principal candidates encouraged resistance to court-ordered busing, except Mrs. Feinstein, who told parents they were obliged to comply. Seeing their opportunity to offset her wide popularity, her opponents capitalized on the fact that she was sending her own daughter to a private school; the effect was evident at the polls on November 2, 1971, when she finished third, with 55,175 votes, behind Mayor Alioto, with 97,252, and Republican Harold S. Dobbs, with 69,786.

Mrs. Feinstein again finished third in the mayoral election of November 1975, when none of the eleven candidates received the majority vote necessary for election. (Alioto was not among the eleven because a mayor of San Francisco is limited by law to two terms.) In the runoff election the following month, George R. Moscone, a liberal Democrat, defeated the conservative Republican John Barbagelata.

On November 27, 1978 Mayor Moscone and Harvey Milk, a supervisor who happened to be the first avowed homosexual ever elected to office in San Francisco, were shot to death in City Hall and Daniel White, a disgruntled former supervisor, was charged with the double assassination. White had resigned as a supervisor seventeen days before for family and financial reasons but had been trying to reclaim the post. Moscone was apparently amenable until dissuaded by the protests of Milk, among others. Police said that there was no ostensible connection between the City Hall murders and the mass ritualized tragedy in the People's Temple commune in Guyana earlier in the month.

As if born and bred for the task, Mrs. Feinstein assumed mayoral power without hesitation and with firm authority immediately following Moscone's assassination. On December 4, 1978 her colleagues on the board of supervisors elected her to fill out the rest of Moscone's term and she was sworn in by Chief Justice Rose Bird. Committing herself to the "emotional reconstruction" of the city and the forging of a government "as just and as good as our people," she stated: "One of the things we need to do is reestablish priorities in this city of what is acceptable behavior and how we generate a community [in which the diverse elements] get along with each other, a community where violence is not condoned. I feel a very great need to heal and bind."

In retrospect, Mayor Feinstein has said of the time of the assassinations: "The situation was so stark, so unreal, so terrible that everybody [had] a great sense of shock. What really had to be done was, one, reassure people, two, put the bricks back together, and three, do what's best, because sometimes what happens is violence begets violence."

One of Mayor Feinstein's first official acts was to carry out her predecessor's intention of appointing Don Horanzy to the supervisor's seat vacated by Dan White and to name Louise Renne as her own successor on the Board of Supervisors. Recognizing that the late Harvey Milk's election was tantamount to the creation of a "gay seat" on the board, she was careful to choose a homosexual Harvey Britt for that seat, albeit a homosexual more moderate than the lesbian activist Anne Kronenberg, Milk's administrative assistant, whom gay leaders preferred. In a statement to the members of the homosexual community, she asked them to try to avoid public behavior that might offend the sensibilities of the heterosexual majority. That request fit in with her general efforts to reduce friction between diverse ethnic and cultural groups and to dispel the image that had intensified over the years of San Francisco as a haven for eccentrics.

The biggest problem facing Mayor Feinstein during her first months in office was financial: how to fund city agencies in the wake of Proposition Thirteen, the property tax-reducing measure voted into law by the California electorate in 1978. Her most manifest success was in working closely with Police Chief Charles Gain to reduce crime by beefing up law enforcement and making it more visible, especially along Market Street and in the Tenderloin district. In general, she recognized that she was serving out Mayor Moscone's mandate, not her own, and therefore she tried to implement policy initiated by him. Because he had been elected by a motley coalition of activists, liberals, homosexuals, and other minorities, that policy tended to be liberal where members of minority groups were concerned.

Dianne Feinstein is a black-haired woman, striking in appearance, charming in manner, well-modulated and eloquent in speech, and impeccable in dress. Typical of her wardrobe is a three-piece black wool suit and a white blouse tied at the neck with what fashion writers in San Francisco call a "Dianne bow." The mayor's only child, her daughter Katherine Anne, is from her first marriage, to Jack Berman, a lawyer. That marriage ended in divorce, and in 1962 she was married a second time, to Bertram Feinstein, a neurosurgeon, who died in June 1978. Recently she announced plans to marry Richard Blum, a San Francisco investment banker. The mayor lives in San Francisco's exclusive Pacific Heights neighborhood.

References: *Christian Sci Mon* p6 D 6 '78 por; *Los Angeles Times* p19 Mr 6 '79 por; *N Y Times* p42 O 20 '71 por; A p20 D 5 '78 por; p6 F 10 '79 por; *Nat Observer* p1+ O 30 '71; *Newsweek* 92:26+ D 11 '78 por; *Washington Post* B p1+ Mr 14 '79 por; *Who's Who of American Women,* 1979-80

Feld, Irvin

May, 9, 1918- Circus producer. Address: b. Ringling Bros. and Barnum & Bailey Circus, Suite 1100, 1015 18th St., NW, Washington, D.C. 20036

In 1967, after undergoing a ten-year apprenticeship as manager and booking agent of "The Greatest Show on Earth," Irvin Feld bought the Ringling Bros. and Barnum & Bailey Circus, then deeply mired in debt. Capitalizing on his experience as a musical entrepreneur and theatrical promoter, Feld turned the operation around in a little more than a decade and, in so doing, salvaged a venerable American institution. "I have found that if you give the public more than their money's worth while maintaining a high standard of quality they will respond fully with their support," he has said. "I have always insisted on giving the paying public more than they expect." In 1977 the circus' two traveling units played to more than 7,000,000 people in eighty cities, taking in more than $40,000-000. In November 1978 Feld announced that the circus would tour a third unit, beginning in February 1979, the one-ring Monte Carlo Cirque International.

Irvin Feld was born on May 9, 1918 in Hagerstown, Maryland, one of the six children of Isaac and Jennie (Mansh) Feld. His father, a Russian-Jewish immigrant, operated a small clothing and home-furnishing store. Even as a small boy, Feld spent his summer vacations working at odd jobs to supplement the family's slender income. When he was thirteen, he joined his older brother Israel on the carnival circuit in Maryland and Pennsylvania, peddling half-ounce bottles of snake oil from a colorful collapsible stand he had designed himself. "I looked about nine," he told Jacquin Sanders in an interview for the New York *Sunday News* magazine (May 14, 1972), "but that helped my spiel. People were sorry for me." Eventually, the two boys sold imitation vanilla and lemon extracts in addition to their popular cure-all. During the school year, the Feld brothers and two of their sisters sold toothpaste, aspirin, rubbing alcohol, and other products door-to-door. They were arrested several times for peddling without a license, but always managed to talk their way out of it.

After graduating from Park Forest High School, Feld became a full-time salesman for the supply house that had furnished his all-purpose remedy. He so impressed his employers with his skill as a salesman that they soon advanced him the money to open a drugstore in a predominantly black neighborhood in Washington, D.C. There he sold sundries, patent medicines, and "lookalikes"— inexpensive substitutes for popular brand-name items. Well-liked in the black community, Feld prospered and, within a few years, added a soda fountain and a record department to his store. There were relatively few record outlets in the city at the time, and Feld cashed in on the growing demand for popular music by opening three Super Music City record shops in as many years.

In the late 1940's Feld branched out into the record producing business, when he formed his own private company to record such local artists as Erroll Garner, the jazz pianist, and Arthur Smith, a country singer whose single, "Guitar Boogie," sold more than 1,000,000 copies. After being introduced to gospel music by his black customers, Feld organized and promoted live gospel shows in the Washington area. Those productions became more and more ambitious, progressing from hired halls to movie theatres to large arenas and culminating in an all-star outdoor concert featuring Sister Rosetta Tharpe on July 3, 1949 at Griffith Stadium, the home of the Washington Senators baseball team. "I sold 28,000 seats, and the police let me sell another 2,000 standing room," Feld told Jacquin Saunders. "We also sold close to 15,000 souvenir postage stamp Bibles, which I'd picked up specially for the event. They were one inch by one inch and cost a dollar." The following year Feld sponsored a "wedding concert" at the Stadium, during the course of which Sister Rosetta was publicly married.

Anticipating the rock 'n' roll craze, Feld, in conjunction with the Gale Agency, organized national tours for the "Biggest Show of Stars" in the early 1950's. His road company, which he regularly visited on tour, included such relatively unknown performers as Chubby Checker, Bill Haley and the Comets, Fats Domino, Frankie Avalon, Clyde McPhatter and the Drifters, and the Everly Brothers. The shows played eighty cities in eighty days and earned handsome profits for their forward-looking producer. During one visit to Montreal in the mid-1950's Feld met Paul Anka, then only fifteen, but after listening to his demonstration record, he put Anka on the tour and became his personal manager. Under his guidance, Anka's career skyrocketed with a succession of Top Ten hits, beginning with "Diana." By the 1960's Feld was arranging personal appearances for some of the highest-priced entertainers in the business, including Harry Belafonte, Andy Williams, Frank Sinatra, and Nat King Cole. He even produced the Washington, D.C. debut of the Beatles on their first American tour in 1964.

In the mid-1950's, concurrent with his career as a musical entrepreneur, Feld became the manager and booking agent of the financially troubled Ringling Bros. and Barnum & Bailey Circus. Having at first refused Feld's offer to assume complete operational and financial responsibility for the circus, John Ringling North, the nephew of the founding Ringling brothers and the circus' major stockholder, put Feld in charge of virtually everything but the show itself in 1956. Feld's first move was to phase out the traditional "big top" tent and book the circus into the municipal indoor sports arenas that were springing up around the country. Because it took about 1,500 roustabouts and eighty work elephants several days to put up and take down the huge tent in each city on the circuit, the big top added considerably to the circus' general operating expenses. Furthermore, the tent was vulnerable to the caprices of the weather, and its seating capacity was limited. By booking the circus in indoor amphitheatres, Feld cut operating costs by more than $50,000 a week and, at the same time, extended the length of the annual national tour to ten and one-half months.

Despite Feld's astute fiscal management, the circus continued on its downhill slide. Plagued by problems of aging personnel (the average age of the company members was forty-six, and seven of its fourteen clowns were over seventy), of absentee ownership after John Ringling North moved to Europe in 1962, and of competition from television, "The Greatest Show on Earth" degenerated into a flashy Las Vegas floor show. Finally, in 1967, with the circus $1,700,000 in debt, Feld persuaded North to sell the show for about $8,000,000 to a triumvirate he headed that included his brother Israel, a partner in all his previous business ventures, and Judge Roy N. Hofheinz, the operator of the Houston Astrodome. The official ceremony deeding the circus to Feld and his group took place at the Colosseum in Rome, with a lion cub in attendance and every photographer that Feld could find. "I wanted to make sure the whole world knew the circus had changed hands," Feld told reporters. "It was the happiest moment of my life."

As president and chief executive officer of the Ringling Bros. and Barnum & Bailey Circus, Feld instituted a series of drastic and lasting changes. To restore the faith of the American public in "The Greatest Show on Earth," he insisted that tank towns see the same production as the New York critics. The Las Vegas tawdriness disappeared, and along with it, the aging showgirls, who were replaced by wholesome, acrobatic youngsters who brought back the traditional circus routines. Distressed by the imminent retirement of such world-renowned Ringling clowns as Lou Jacobs and Otto Griebling, in September 1968 Feld established the world's first "Clown College," in Venice, Florida, a tuition-free, eight-week school where the oldtimers taught their craft to promising newcomers. Because they were, in his words, "making fun of people and sickening to me," Feld eliminated the freak sideshows. Perhaps most importantly, he more than doubled the size of the circus by establishing a second unit, equal in size and quality to the original. The so-called Red and Blue Units, each with original acts, toured the country simultaneously so that audiences would never see the same production two years in a row.

To recruit the talent he needed to expand his circus, Feld turned to European circuses. "I saw twenty-four circuses to get fifteen acts acceptable to us," he said, as quoted in the New York *Times* (March 31, 1969). "I wanted to get Gunther Gebel-Williams, [the wild animal trainer] of the Circus Williams, a show that's been touring Europe for 150 years, but European circuses are terribly competitive and they guard their routes the way Detroit guards new car models." Feld finally purchased the entire circus for $2,000,000 in order to obtain the animal trainer's services. "Gebel-Williams is really a superstar," he continued. "I hate to use the word. We never use a name in our advertising or in our billing. The show is really the star."

Feld still scouts European circuses annually, always searching for new and exciting acts to introduce to American audiences. At one point, he reviewed forty-six Continental circuses in thirty-five days. "Once in a while, after a couple of weeks on dusty lots in the midst of a blazing Italian summer, you get the feeling you've seen everything," he told an interviewer for *Time* magazine (May 4, 1970). "Then out of the blue comes an act so spectacular that you get shivers up your spine." At any given time, Ringling Bros. and Barnum & Bailey has on its roster performers from about twenty countries, including aerialists from Mexico and South America, animal trainers from West Germany and Spain, teeterboard acrobats from several Eastern European countries, and unicyclists from the streets of Harlem in New York City. To keep the acts fresh and thrilling, Feld refuses to renew the contracts of those performers who do not substantially revise and improve their routines for each new production by, in his words, "going one degree past the limit of how far they can go."

In its first decade under Feld's stewardship, the circus received glowing reviews from critics and reestablished itself as a financially profitable enterprise. The centennial edition of "The Greatest Show on Earth" won warm praise from New York *Times* critic Howard Thompson when it opened in New York City's Madison Square Garden in March 1970: "[It] is what anyone young and young-spirited might expect or even demand—a huge-glittery cavalcade of artists and animals spilling into the Garden's cavernous maw and performing their heads off amid some bright, glistening birthday trimmings." Two years later, Joe Cohen wrote in *Variety* (May 5, 1972) that the new show had "more vitality and color" than many earlier productions. "Its Blue Unit is bright and imaginative [and] has a springy feeling," he said, "but seems to be invested with the wisdom of age to balance its youthful mien. . . . This is the

fourth year in which Irvin Feld has been its top man. He seems to have taken the circus farther along in his brief tenure. He has penetrated the Iron Curtain countries for talent and has assembled a set of acts capable of top entertainment." Cohen singled out for special praise the Spanish lion-tamer Pablo Noel, tiger-tamer Charley Baumann, and Mendez & Seitz and the Flying Gaonas, the trapeze artists.

In the late 1960's Feld founded five subsidiary companies to produce records and television programs, publish sheet music, and operate and franchise fast-food restaurants and motels, all under the name Ringling Bros. and Barnum & Bailey. He also entered into merchandising agreements with the manufacturers of a variety of consumer products, ranging from bed linens to vitamins, allowing them to market more than 200 items under the circus' trademark. In addition, he formed the Klowns, a circus-oriented pop vocal group. Although the Klowns never achieved stardom, they appeared on their own television special on ABC-TV in November 1970 and recorded a single and an album for RCA that same year. Feld sold his chain of record stores in 1967, but he continued to operate the outdoor Carter Barron Amphitheater in Washington, D.C. on a twenty-five-year lease from the federal government and the municipally owned Baltimore Civic Center.

In 1971 Feld sold the circus to Mattel, Inc., the toymakers, for an estimated $50,000,000 in stock. The new owners retained his services as president, producer, and chief executive officer under a long-term contract. Feld immediately began collaborating with Jim Fowler, the designer of NBC-TV's *Wild Kingdom*, on a proposed 600-acre amusement park and entertainment complex in Orlando, Florida. Four years later, Ringling Bros. and Barnum & Bailey's Circus World, which included a dozen separate show attractions, rides, shops, restaurants, a hotel, and a permanent "big top" with deliberate gaps in the canvas so visitors could indulge their childhood fantasies by "sneaking" inside for the show, opened to the public. "I have great respect for the Disney organization," Feld told one interviewer, "but it's all animation. It's not real. We're live, real people, real animals performing, and you know they're real because there's a guy with a bucket and broom following them." An enormous success, Circus World was expanded in 1978.

In 1974 Kenneth Feld joined his father as coproducer of the circus. Together they orchestrated a lavish extravaganza of traditional acts, aerial ballets, and parades, climaxing in a spectacular finale in which children from the audience are invited to participate. Feld makes the final decisions on almost all aspects of the production—costumes, lighting, music, sound, running order and timing, publicity, and ticket pricing. Determined to keep prices reasonable, he takes pride in the fact that a family of four can see the circus for less than the price of a single orchestra ticket to a Broadway show. "I would like to be remembered for having made a contribution to the continuance of the circus," he said recently. "It's practically all we have left of good, wholesome, clean entertainment that the whole family can enjoy."

When, in March 1979, Ringling Bros. and Barnum & Bailey Circus acquired "Ice Follies" and "Holiday on Ice" from Arthur and William Wirtz, Irvin and Kenneth Feld could lay claim to the distinction of being the leading impresarios of touring shows in the entire world. A few months later, discussing the bright future of their arena, Kenneth Feld wrote in Variety (July 18, 1979): "Right now we're getting down to the serious business of bringing about the dawn of a new Ice Age—not one that is going to freeze everything over, but an epoch that will see a revival of this genre of entertainment."

Irvin Feld married the former Adele Schwartz on March 5, 1946. A widower for many years, he shared a large apartment in Washington, D.C. with Israel Feld's widow, who helped raise his two children, Kenneth and Karen, a publicity agent for the circus. Described as a "bland-looking but endlessly energetic" man, Feld is totally devoted to the circus and regularly puts in eighteen-hour days, seven days a week. "When I believe in something, I can do it," he once said. "From the time I was a kid, I always wanted to do things that had never been done. I've been doing them, and I don't want to quit. I'm having too much fun. The days are seldom long enough for all I want to do."

References: Bsns W p76+ Ap 13 '68; N Y Sunday News Mag p38+ My 14 '72; N Y Times p28 Mr 3 '69, p38 Mr 25 '70; Nations Bsns 66:53+ O '78 pors; Time 95:74+ My '70; Who's Who in America, 1978-79

Field, Sally

Nov. 6, 1946- Actress. Address: c/o Twentieth Century-Fox Film Corp., 1345 Avenue of the Americas, New York City, N.Y. 10019

Once the symbol of innocent but flighty adolescence, the pert and vivacious television and motion picture actress Sally Field has emerged as a serious and multitalented performer. Typecast at the beginning of her career as the winsome teenage surf bunny in the television comedy series Gidget (1965-66), and then as the perky, often airborne Sister Bertrille in the series The Flying Nun (1967-70), Miss Field devoted herself to refining her acting skills during the early 1970's. She returned in 1976 with critically acclaimed performances in director Bob Rafelson's film Stay Hungry and in the made-for-television movie Sybil, for which she won an Emmy award.

Her most successful performance has been her portrayal of the earthy, Southern textile worker turned union activist in Norma Rae (1979), for which she was named best actress at the 1979 Cannes Film Festival. In addition to varied motion picture and television work, Miss Field has appeared in a successful series of action comedies opposite Burt Reynolds, including Smokey and the Bandit (1977). With reference to her metamorphosis from fluffy television personality to serious actress, Miss Field has commented: "I grew and didn't buckle under when they wanted me to remain cute forever."

Sally Field was born in Pasadena, California on November 6, 1946, the daughter of Richard Field, now the owner of a drugstore, and Margaret Field, a Paramount starlet of the 1950's. When Sally was about four her parents were divorced, and her mother married Jock Mahoney, a former stuntman and one of the many actors who played Tarzan in the movies. The Mahoneys moved to the San Fernando Valley, where Sally grew up. She has an older brother, Richard Jr., now a nuclear physicist, and a younger half-sister, Princess, who has begun a career as an actress.

"There was never a time when I didn't want to be an actress," Miss Field told Guy Flatley of Newsday (March 2, 1979). She distinctly remembers being carried on her mother's hip as the latter—who became known professionally as Maggie Mahoney—recited passages from Chekhov and Shakespeare during acting classes with Charles Laughton. By the age of seven Sally was writing plays and casting them with neighborhood children. She also performed pantomime, wearing her mother's clothes and cosmetics, and acted out scenes from movies in front of a mirror. "I was very reclusive and always highly emotional," she told Lois Armstrong of People (April 25, 1977). "I didn't feel I was allowed to express it, so I would cry and scream in front of the mirror and be very sexy. Acting was the place where I could be me."

As a student in junior high school, and later at Birmingham High School, in the San Fernando Valley, Sally Field took part in a variety of extracurricular activities, including cheerleading and drama. In the tenth grade she performed a scene from Suddenly Last Summer. "Suddenly everybody at school knew who I was. . . . I got to be a sort of coach to other students," she reminisced in an article in Seventeen (January 1966). Among her admiring fellow students was Cindy Williams, later of Laverne & Shirley fame. Miss Field also had leading roles in school productions of The Miracle Worker and The Man Who Came to Dinner.

Immediately after graduating from high school in 1964 Miss Field enrolled in the Columbia Pictures Workshop, which tried to develop new talent for the studio. One evening, while she was waiting for her brother to pick her up, Screen Gems casting director Eddie Foy 3d, a friend of the Mahoneys, spotted Sally and asked her to test for the title role in Gidget, a new ABC-TV series. After six months of testing, in competition with more than 150 girls, she was awarded the role, at a salary of $450 a week. The comedy, which survived only one season, related the adventures of a teenage nymphet—portrayed earlier by Sandra Dee in a series of innocuous beach movies—who spent much of her time ogling surfers. Although Gidget was panned as trivial and coy, reviewers described Miss Field as "fresh," "sparkling," "wholesome," "natural," and "refreshing." She received thousands of letters from teenage fans each week, and the show's cancellation, effective September 1966, triggered an avalanche of protest mail.

Offered the lead in The Flying Nun, a new situation comedy, Miss Field at first turned it down, hoping for more serious work, but finally was persuaded to accept it. The show, which, according to its producer, Harry Ackerman, combined elements from Mary Poppins and The Sound of Music, was launched as a prime-time series by ABC on September 7, 1967. As the slightly irreverent young novice who continually shook up the staid convent of San Tanco in Puerto Rico, Miss Field made that frothy comedy eminently endurable. The ninety-pound Sister Bertrille's most distinctive characteristic was an ability to fly: whenever a heavy gust of wind caught her starched cornette, she was whisked into the air.

Joan Walker observed in Cue (September 23, 1967): "The Flying Nun is enchanting and Miss Field is enchanting. She is beautiful without being Hollywood-beautiful; she is hoydenish without being tough; she is sunny without being sticky about it." But at least one perceptive critic regarded the show as a squandering of her abilities. "It was long ago obvious," he wrote in Variety (September 13, 1967), "that Miss Field has talent, but she is so busy being the cutesy comedienne that she has overlooked being the actress."

The Flying Nun made Sally Field a star at twenty-one and brought her an income of $4,000 a week. Later, in an interview with David Sterritt of the Christian Science Monitor (April 14, 1976), she said regarding her early success: "I sometimes wish it hadn't happened to me so young. It happened before I had time to stop and think, 'Is this what I really want to do?' " But she is equally quick to acknowledge a debt to television. "I was getting paid for learning . . . ." she admitted, "so I'm thankful to TV—it's a tremendous learning ground, a workshop."

For her final foray into television situation comedy, Miss Field appeared as Sally Burton, a newlywed endowed with extrasensory perception, in NBC's short-lived The Girl With Something Extra (1973-74), costarring John Davidson. Although Sally's ability to read minds resulted in some predictably amusing, if tasteless, situations, the show was flayed by most critics and folded after seven months. Earlier she had made guest appearances on episodes of the NBC-TV shows Occasional Wife (1966), Hey Landlord (1967), Bracken's World (1970), and Night Gallery (1971), and in ABC-TV's Marcus Welby, M.D. (1971). She also appeared occasionally, from 1971 to 1973, as Clementine Hale in the ABC western comedy series Alias Smith and Jones. In 1974 she presided over the Miss Teenage America Pageant, presented on CBS-TV.

Miss Field made her motion picture debut in 1967, in the film version of A.B. Guthrie Jr.'s Pulitzer Prize-winning novel The Way West (United Artists), after its director, Andrew V. McLaglen, saw her in an episode of Gidget. In it she played saucy Mercy McBee, a sixteen-year-old passenger on a wagon train traveling along the Oregon Trail in 1843. Television movies in which Sally Field starred include Marriage: Year One (NBC, 1971), about the problems faced by two newlyweds; Hitched (NBC, 1971), a western comedy; Home for the Holidays (ABC, 1972), about four daughters protecting their father from a homicidal maniac; and Bridger (ABC, 1976), about the legendary nineteenth-century mountain man Jim Bridger. She received special praise for her performances in the television films Maybe I'll Come Home in the Spring (ABC, 1970), in which she sensitively played a young woman who trades family life for a commune existence and drug trips, and *Mongo's Back in Town* (CBS, 1971), a grim crime drama adapted from a story by a convict about a hired killer returning to his hometown.

Despite such varied assignments, Miss Field became disillusioned with her career and image. "There were plenty of offers to do 'The Sally Field Show' and lots of other junk," she told Guy Flatley, "but I said 'no thanks.' The truth was that nobody around me had any respect for me; to them, I was a joke. So I took the plunge and changed everything at once—I got rid of my agent, my business manager, my house, and my husband. For three years I dropped out and studied and did summer stock."

Miss Field first joined the Actors Studio in New York City between her first and second season as *The Flying Nun*, and during that period she gave a starring performance in a production of Jean-Paul Sartre's *The Respectful Prostitute* that was singled out as brilliant by the studio's director, Lee Strasberg. From 1973 to 1975 she devoted herself to the Actors Studio almost full time. She also toured with the Kenley Players in Ohio and studied under the theatrical coach David Craig, Nancy Walker's husband. "I was totally addicted to his class for almost two years," she told Judy Klemesrud of the New York *Times* (December 27, 1977). "His class just glowed, it illuminated."

Finally she was offered a role she liked, that of the free-spirited health spa receptionist in director Bob Rafelson's quirky look at bodybuilding, *Stay Hungry* (United Artists, 1976). Although the movie, like such previous Rafelson efforts as *Five Easy Pieces* and *The King of Marvin Gardens*, evoked mixed reactions, Miss Field and her costars Jeff Bridges and Arnold Schwarzenegger reaped virtually uniformly favorable notices. Frank Rich wrote in his New York *Post* review (April 26, 1976): "The diminutive Miss Field . . . is a particular revelation. While not movie-star gorgeous, this actress is a powerfully sexy comedienne."

Almost on the heels of *Stay Hungry* came another choice role for Miss Field, in the television film *Sybil*. Broadcast in two segments on November 12 and 13, 1976 as "The Big Event/NBC World Premiere Movie," the film told the true story of a woman who, because of childhood traumas, developed sixteen different personalities. Some of the scenes in that disturbing drama were copied verbatim from tapes of sessions between the real Sybil and her psychiatrist—played in the film by Joanne Woodward. In his review in the New York *Times* (November 12, 1976), John J. O'Connor observed: "In perhaps the most surprising revelation of the season, Sally Field is incredibly riveting as Sybil. The former star of *The Flying Nun* . . . moves from Sybil through the various personalities in a dazzling tour de force." On September 11, 1977 the Academy of Television Arts and Sciences awarded her an Emmy in the category "outstanding lead actress in a drama or comedy special." Joanne Woodward, who in 1958 won an Oscar for a similar role in *The Three Faces of Eve*, has said of Miss Field: "Sally's amazing—the best under-thirty actress I ever worked with."

Portraying Sybil was an emotionally draining experience for Sally Field. Three weeks after filming was completed, she accepted an offer to appear as Burt Reynolds' girlfriend in the good-old-boy chase caper, *Smokey and the Bandit* (Universal, 1977) about bootleggers and rednecks in the Deep South. "I . . . had had it with intensity," she said in the *People* interview. "I really wanted to go off and laugh and have a good time." Commenting on Miss Field's performance, the critic for *Variety* (May 18, 1977) found "her good sense of humor and foxy-funny lady role . . . a total delight," while Joy Gould Boyum of the *Wall Street Journal* (June 13, 1977) felt that she was "really much too good for this movie." *Smokey and the Bandit* became the second-biggest box-office draw of 1977, after *Star Wars*. Miss Field had smaller roles in two additional Burt Reynolds comedy hits, *The End* (United Artists, 1978) and *Hooper* (Warner, 1978).

Miss Field's next starring role was that of a girl who befriends a disturbed Vietnam war veteran, played by Henry Winkler, during the course of a cross-country odyssey in the comedy-drama *Heroes* (Universal, 1977), which was far from a critical success. She made an even less auspicious appearance as Michael Caine's love interest in Irwin Allen's *Beyond the Poseidon Adventure* (Warner, 1979). Referring to her part in the film, she told Elizabeth Kaye of *Look* (August 1979): "It was God's way of giving me one final kick in the behind. I'll never do anything like it again."

A surprise hit of 1979 was *Norma Rae* (Twentieth Century-Fox), director Martin Ritt's unflinching examination of labor strife in an unorganized textile factory in the Deep South. After Jane Fonda turned down the title role, Ritt persuaded Sally Field to accept it, telling her that he needed the kind of actress who "submerges herself and doesn't come up for air." Based on the life of the textile worker and labor activist Crystal Lee Sutton, the partly fictionalized movie details the struggles of Norma Rae Webster, a dirt-poor, feisty young woman, who joins forces with Reuben Warshawsky, a liberal Jewish labor organizer from New York, in a fight to bring unionism to a small Southern company town, and at the same time validates her claim to personal dignity. A subplot relates the courtship and eventual marriage of Norma Rae to a decent but untutored gas station attendant, played by Beau Bridges.

Both the film and Miss Field drew high praise from audiences and also from the critics, who saluted her performance as "high-spirited," "beautifully conceived," "spectacular," and her best to date. The critic for *Variety* (February 28, 1979) ranked her among "the finest contemporary actresses"; Gene Siskel wrote in the

Chicago *Tribune* (March 2, 1979): "Sally Field, one of our most underrated actresses, gives a thoroughly winning performance . . . [and] makes her character's enormous transformation believable"; and Stanley Kauffmann rhapsodized in the *New Republic* (March 17, 1979): "Cheers—cheers from the heart—for Sally Field." Not long after the release of *Norma Rae* early in 1979, Miss Field's name was being mentioned as an Academy Award contender. In May she was named best actress at the Cannes Film Festival and received a standing ovation when *Norma Rae* was screened. The film was a commercial as well as critical success; in the first six weeks it grossed $8,000,000.

Although Miss Field was scheduled to costar with Burt Reynolds in a sequel to *Smokey and the Bandit*, Reynolds announced in June 1979 that he would not hold her to it. "She'd probably do it if I asked her to," he said, as quoted in *People* (June 11, 1979), "but after *Norma Rae* she should only do important things." Since 1977 the names of Miss Field and Reynolds have been romantically linked. Shortly before the release of *Norma Rae* she appeared in *Vanities* at the Burt Reynolds Dinner Theatre in the actor's hometown of Jupiter, Florida and costarred with Reynolds in its production of *The Rainmaker*.

Sally Field married Steve Craig, her high school sweetheart, in Las Vegas, Nevada on September 16, 1968. From their marriage, which ended in divorce five years later, she has two sons, Peter, born in 1969, and Elijah, born in 1972. She and Burt Reynolds divide their time between her house in Studio City, California and his home in the Bel-Air section of Los Angeles, and they share a condominium in Florida. The petite, dark-haired, brown-eyed actress stands five feet two inches tall and weighs 100 pounds. Although she is not especially politically minded, she campaigned for George S. McGovern in 1972 because, she said, "I had two sons and [there was] a war going on." A self-described "hermit" and "old-fashioned girl," and a nonpractising Roman Catholic, Miss Field keeps a journal and enjoys reading, playing the piano, and making quilts

References: Look 2:38 Ag '79 pors; N Y Post p44 My 8 '76 por; N Y Sunday News mag p4 Je 4 '67 por; p8+ O 2 '77 pors; N Y Times p54 D 27 '77 por; Redbook p33+ Je 79 por; TV Guide 14:16+ My 28 '66 por

Firkusny, Rudolf (fir'kŌŌsh-nē)

Feb. 11, 1912- Pianist. Address: b. c/o Columbia Artists Management, 165 W. 57 St., New York City, N.Y. 10019; h. Staatsburg, N.Y. 12580

Rudolf Firkusny, the Czech-born pianist who has made his home in the United States for the past forty years, has built an enduring reputation in his own decidedly low-keyed fashion. Perhaps best summed up by the New York *Times* critic Donal Henahan as "an Old-World craftsman of a pianist," Firkusny is noted for the substance and seriousness of his programming, and for a style that shuns empty virtuosity, even though his keyboard technique can meet any exacting test. Although renowned as an exponent and promoter of the music of his native land in concerts and in recordings, he has managed to avoid being labeled as a Czech specialist. Yet much of that music would have remained unheard in the United States were it not for him. Invited regularly to play with major orchestras of Europe and the United States, Firkusny has performed more than fifty times with the New York Philharmonic alone, and as performer and teacher, he has long been associated with the music festivals of Aspen, Colorado and Lucerne, Switzerland. Some virtuosi may command higher fees, but for Rudolf Firkusny "the great satisfaction" is that "after all these years," he is "still in.'

The youngest of the three children of Rudolf and Karla (Sindelarova) Firkusny, Rudolf Firkusny was born on February 11, 1912 in Napajedla, Moravia, now Czechoslovakia. Three years later, following the death of the father, a lawyer, Rudolf, his brother, Leos, and his sister, Marie, were taken to the city of Brno by the mother. Soon young Ruda, as he was then called, was discovered picking out tunes on the piano, and after a year of music lessons his extraordinary ability to improvise at the piano marked him as a true child prodigy. At that point his mother took the daring step of taking him to the citys most eminent musician, Leos Janacek. The irascible composer, in spite of his contempt for prodigies whom he viewed as "trained monkeys," agreed to instruct the boy in composition but insisted that he look elsewhere for a piano teacher. Together they studied such "moderns" as Debussy and Stravinsky, and left the "classics" to Ruda's other teachers. He took the boy to all the premieres of his operas. In speaking of Janacek to Stephen E. Rubin of the New York *Times* (April 8, 1973), Firkusny recalled: "Even at the age of 5, I was terribly impressed by him as a person and as a composer. I was with him during the years of his greatest output, from 1918 until his death in 1928. He was like a dynamo, and I felt it. I was also able to hear all his works, which came one after another." In another interview he said that Janacek opened "the gates of music" for him.

Apart from studying with Janacek, Firkusny attended secondary school and the Conservatory of Music in Brno, where he studied piano, first with Mrs. Kurzova, then with her husband, Vilem Kurz. He made his debut, which he recalls as "great fun," in 1922, at the age of ten, at the Smetana Hall in Prague when he performed Mozart's Concerto No. 26 in D ("Coronation"). Later he studied with Rudolf Karel and Josef Suk in Prague, took courses at its Piano Master Academy, studied composition with Rudolf Karel, and attended the Masaryk University in Brno. Although Janacek felt that his pupil possessed a genuine creative gift, Firkusny eventually gave up composition and improvisation, and his final effort was a piano concerto that he wrote and performed "for the first and last time" in Prague. Firkusny has explained: "I wanted to continue, but if you compose, I think you have to do it more or less the way you study an instrument. You have to really work. You have to write, I don't know, maybe five or six piano sonatas which are good for nothing, and finally you may hit something with the seventh. I just didn't have this much time. I had to study repertory and make a living playing."

When Firkusny was eighteen his teachers sent him to test the waters with recitals in Vienna, Berlin and Paris, and as the reports that came back turned out to be favorable he went on a tour of Italy, finally returning to his "bachelor's life in a lovely apartment in Prague." In spite of having been told by the celebrated French pianist Alfred Cortot, "You don't need a teacher, you need a public," Firkusny continued studying as well as fulfilling concert engagements. He made his London debut in 1933 and worked with the great Artur Schnabel, beginning that same year, in Germany, Italy, and the United States.

In 1938 Firkusny, who vividly remembered the celebrations marking the proclamation of the birth of the Czech Republic in 1918 that he witnessed as a small boy, observed its twentieth anniversary by giving three recitals of Czech music in Prague. But then came the Munich Pact that paved the way for the German occupation of Czechoslovakia in 1939. When he refused an official suggestion that he play in Germany, he was told that he would be forced to perform there, whether he wanted to or not. Firkusny fled to Paris by way of Switzerland, where he joined the Czech Army in Exile, performing for the troops, and when the Germans overran France he moved again, this time to Portugal. By giving concerts in Lisbon and Oporto he accumulated enough money to come to the United States, as he had been advised to do by the Czech government in exile in London. Firkusny had made his New York City debut during an American tour the year before at Town Hall in a recital that featured Liszt's Sonata in B-minor, a Chopin group, two chorale preludes by Bach as arranged by Busoni, and works by the Czech composers Smetana, Martinu, and Suk. A reviewer for the New York *Herald Tribune* (January 14, 1938) found the almost twenty-six-year-old pianist to be "an experienced artist," who "showed an unusually expert technique which effectively served well matured and individual ideas." Firkusny, however, plays down the significance of that early period and dates his "real debut" in New York City from a later Town Hall appearance that he made in 1941. In 1943 he undertook a concert tour of South America.

When Rudolf Firkusny arrived in the United States he complained that the only Czech music he heard performed was Dvorak's Symphony No. 9 ("New World") and Smetana's overplayed symphonic poem *Moldau* from *My Fatherland*. To remedy that lack, in the early 1940's he gave the first performance in New York in sixty-five years of Dvorak's Piano Concerto in G-minor, with the New York Philharmonic. In 1945 he gave the world premiere performance in Dallas, Texas of a work dedicated to him by its composer, the Third Piano Concerto of his fellow-exile Bohuslav Martinu, whose Second Piano Concerto he had premiered in Prague in 1935. In 1946 he returned to Prague and played with the Czech Philharmonic during his country's first postwar music festival. On March 15, 1947 at Carnegie Hall, in addition to interpreting works by Mozart, Schumann, and Debussy, Firkusny gave the first American performance of *April Preludes*, the Opus 13 of Vitezslava Kapralova, a Czech composer and the first Czech woman conductor. On that occasion, according to Olin Downes of the New York *Times* (March 16, 1947), the pianist's style was "more sensitive and varied, his tonal palette considerably richer than it used to be." In 1948, after the Communist takeover of Czechoslovakia, Firkusny became an American citizen and did not play with a Czech orchestra again for seventeen years.

In 1959 Firkusny toured Australia and New Zealand, and in the fall of that year he gave a recital at Carnegie Hall that displayed all of his imaginative programming virtues and challenged all of his musical gifts. First, in recognition of the often overlooked fact that all composers are not dead, he programmed the premiere of Carlisle Floyd's Piano Sonata, dedicated to the pianist. There followed some Czech pieces, including a "Scene" from Martinu's opera *Julietta* and Smetana's Concert Etude in C-major; the four Impromptus of Schubert's Opus 90; four Preludes, and the imposing C-major Fantasy of Schumann. One of his steadfast admirers among the critics, Harold C. Schonberg wrote the next day in the New York *Times* (October 14, 1959): "He is not a passionate pianist; his art is sane, lyric and balanced, always under superb control, and capable of imaginative flights. It is entirely satisfying; and with just a shade less inhibition it would be staggering." A little over a year later, Schonberg received a new impression of Firkusny's stature during his performance of the Brahms First Piano Concerto with the New York Philharmonic. He noted in the New York *Times* (December 3, 1960): "There seemed to be a new dimension. . . . He piled into the chords and octaves of the first movement with tremendous sonority, yet without losing tonal control, and he shaped the melodic elements with more surety than before."

After almost two decades of estrangement, Rudolf Firkusny was reunited with the musicians of the Czech Philharmonic in August 1963 at the Salzburg Festival in Austria, where they performed Beethoven's Piano Concerto No. 3 in C-Minor under the direction of another Czech-born musician, George Szell, the famed conductor of the Cleveland Orchestra. A large audience obliged both soloist and conductor to take six bows, and the appreciative members of the string section rapped their bows noisily on their music stands. It was Firkusny's fourth appearance at the world-renowned festival, but the first for the Czech Philharmonic, which seldom performs in the West.

After completing a 1967 concert tour of the Far East, Rudolf Firkusny appeared in Lincoln Center's "Great Performers Series" at Philharmonic Hall on January 17, 1968, almost thirty years to the day of his American debut, with a program containing Beethoven's Sonata in C-minor, Opus 10, No. 1; Schubert's Sonata in A-minor, Opus 52; Chopin's Sonata in B-minor, Opus 58; and Janacek's *In the Mist*. Writing in the New York *Times* (January 18, 1968), Allen Hughes remarked that although Firkusny underplayed a bit more than usual, in the slow movements of the Beethoven and Chopin sonatas "the balances between melody and accompaniment, the beautifully turned phrases and the absolute poise of the lyricism were such that the listener could wish for nothing finer."

Later, on October 22, 1968, what was to have been a hopeful celebration of the fiftieth anniversary of the birth of the Czechoslovak Republic turned out to be a benefit for Czech refugees fleeing foreign occupation, this time by troops of the Warsaw Pact nations who invaded the country that autumn. Along with many other well-known musicians, Firkusny signed a protest declaring that they would not perform in any country that had taken part in the invasion. Then he played his all-Czech recital in Carnegie Hall, covering music from the late eighteenth century and into the twentieth, beginning with Benda and Dussek, going on to Tomaschek and Vorischek, through Smetana and Dvorak, and ending with Vitezslav Novak's Sonata Eroica, written in 1900, and Janacek's sonata subtitled *Street Scene, October 1, 1905*. The last named composition was inspired by the bayoneting of a Czech youth by Germans during a nationalist demonstration in Brno. Reporting on the concert in the New York *Times* (October 23, 1968), Harold C. Schonberg wrote: "This was a very difficult program, but he went through it with accuracy, making everything sound simple."

In 1969 Firkusny commissioned a piano piece from the composer Paul Reif. The result, *Pentagram*, a work in five movements, received its premiere in 1971 at a recital at Hunter College in New York City. In 1972 his interpretations of the complete piano works of Janacek were issued by Deutsche Grammophon Gesellschaft, including the Capriccio for piano, left hand, and wind instruments, and the Concertino for piano, two violins, viola, clarinet, horn and bassoon. Although primarily a solo artist, Firkusny occasionally ventures into the chamber music field. In January, for example, he performed the Dvorak Piano Quartet in E-flat with the Guarneri Quartet in New York's Avery Fisher Hall, and four years later joined David Soyer, the cellist of that group, in a recital of sonatas by Chopin, Mendelssohn, and Richard Strauss at the Metropolitan Museum of Art's Grace Rainey Rogers auditorium.

When, in the stifling summer of 1979, the townsfolk of Spillville, Iowa (population 350) held a three-day music festival honoring the seventy-fifth anniversary of the death of its most famous visitor, Antonin Dvorak, Firkusny was on hand to perform the Czech composer's Piano Concerto in G Minor. "I always wanted to visit this little place—it's very dear to the Czech people," Firkusny said. His performance set off an ovation that lasted for fully three minutes.

Rudolf Firkusny, a Roman Catholic, is five feet eleven and half inches tall, and has gray eyes and short gray hair. His friendly but reserved and gentlemanly manner betrays his "Old World" background. The words most often used to describe his playing—"elegant" and "patrician"—apply equally to his person. In 1965, after many years of what seemed to be confirmed bachelorhood, Firkusny married the young and attractive Tatiana Nevole, whom he met while visiting his family in Czechoslovakia, in the same year that he began teaching at the Juilliard School in New York. He continues to teach there, on a part-time basis. The Firkusnys and their two small children, Veronique and Igor, live near Lincoln Center in an apartment described by Robert Jones of the New York *Daily News* (August 21, 1977) as "a skyhigh aerie . . . spotless and spare, handsome and homey." On its walls hang framed manuscripts of Leos Janacek. They also have a country home in Staatsburg, New York. "Sometimes I play a little better, sometimes a little worse," Firkusny told Stephen E. Rubin during their New York *Times* interview. "I'm very human. I know it; and I know it has its advantages and disadvantages. But that's how I am and I can't change it. I'm not one of those pianists who always plays like a machine."

References: N Y Post p39 O 21 '68 por; Thompson, Oscar. International Cyclopedia of Music and Musicians 1975; Who's Who in America, 1978-79; International Who's Who, 1978-79

Freud, Anna

Dec. 3, 1895- Psychoanalyst. Address: 20 Maresfield Gardens, London NW3 5SX, England

"True daughter of an immortal sire," as Ernest Jones, Sigmund Freud's biographer, once called her, Anna Freud has dedicated her career of nearly six decades to advancing the theory and practice of the science founded by her father. Her several books and over one hundred papers, published more or less steadily since 1922 and now collected in the United States in the seven-volume *The Writings of Anna Freud* (International Universities Press), have earned her great respect among colleagues, who consider her the ranking psychoanalyst of today. Through her clinical experience, mainly with children, she has helped to broaden the scope of psychoanalytic technique, and her theoretical contributions have been applied to adults as well. She has been influential in education and allied fields and has made psychoanalytic concepts relevant to legal issues as they affect children. Many of her writings, in the limpid, graceful prose for which she is noted, are as accessible to the lay public as to the trained analyst. Although she has lived since 1938 in London, an emigrée from Vienna, her greatest influence has been in the United States, where her followers and coworkers have brought her work to the forefront of psychoanalytical developmental psychology.

On December 3, 1895, Martha (Bernays) Freud gave birth to a "nice, complete little woman," as Sigmund Freud wrote to his friend, the physician Wilhelm Fliess. If the child had been a boy, Freud intended that he would be Fliess's namesake, but, he told his friends, "if he turns out to be a daughter, she will be called Anna." The last of Freud's six children, and his third daughter, she was named after Anna (Hammerschlag) Lichtheim, whose father had been a teacher of Freud's and later a personal friend. Anna Lichtheim was also one of Freud's favorite patients, but is not to be confused with the patient in the well-known case of "Anna O."

Anna Freud attended the Cottage Lyceum in Vienna while growing up at Freud's famous address, Berggasse 19, where she was to live until the Nazi occupation forced the family to flee in 1938. Little information—apart from fictionalized or dubious accounts—exists concerning Anna Freud before her identification with the psychoanalytic movement in the 1920's. During her childhood, in 1900, however, Freud used one of her dreams to illustrate his theory of wish-fulfillment in *The Interpretation of Dreams*. At nineteen months old Anna had a vomiting attack and was subsequently put to bed hungry. That night, apparently dreaming, she cried out in her sleep for wild strawberries and other treats to eat.

In a rare autobiographical glimpse, Anna Freud has said that as a young child she was interested only in stories and tales that "might be true." She has recalled, "In the face of any unrealistic or supernatural element—my attention flagged and disappeared." And that quality, she added, she retained throughout her life. Her father wrote her, when she was an adolescent, that her plans for school could wait until she had learned to take her duties less seriously. In fact, Anna Freud left school early, ending her formal education without completing the Gymnasium, or secondary school. For several years thereafter she taught elementary school, before focusing her interest on psychoanalysis.

As early as 1913, when Anna Freud was eighteen and her father fifty-seven, the latter wrote to a colleague: "My closest companion will be my little daughter, who is developing very well at the moment." Freud recognized Anna, moreover, as an unconscious source (as Cordelia, King Lear's youngest daughter) for a paper he wrote on "The Theme of the Three Caskets"—concerning a motif used by Shakespeare. He also referred to Anna as his Antigone, Oedipus' daughter and his caretaker in old age.

Her father's companion, secretary, and student, Anna Freud began to attend meetings of the Vienna Psycho-Analytical Society in November 1918. Her first paper, "Beating Phantasies and Day Dreams," was published in 1922 and was the basis for her formal admission to the Vienna society. In 1925 she became secretary of the newly established Vienna Training Institute, headed by Helene Deutsch. Having been psychoanalyzed by her father, Anna Freud herself began to practise in 1923, during a period when Freud's theories were still provoking bitter opposition from medical specialists and the more academic psychologists.

In the mid-1920's psychoanalysts made their first systematic attempts to observe normal childhood behavior through detailed scrutiny of all aspects of behavior and to treat young neurotic children. Anna Freud gave a series of lectures in 1926 and 1927 that led to the establishment of a *Kinderseminar*, a seminar that helped to train such prominent child analysts as Berta Bornstein, Dorothy Burlingham, Erik Erikson, and Margaret Mahler, among others. According to Robert Sussman Stewart, writing in the New York *Times Book Review* (January 23, 1972), Anna Freud in her early thirties had some of her father's "commanding presence—'a certain lilt of the head and a fire in the eyes,' as one coworker described it. She also had her father's ability, though on a smaller scale, to rally others or, more to the point, to generate disciples when she needed them."

Divergent thinking within broad psychoanalytic circles quickly led to the establishment of two "brands" of child analysis. One —the "Continental"—was associated with Anna Freud and her colleagues, mostly in Vienna; and the other—"British"—was headed by Melanie Klein, an Austrian-born analyst who had settled in London. Melanie Klein suggested that basic concepts of psychoanalytic technique could be applied directly to child analysis, and she developed a theory and a vocabulary of her own, based on speculations concerning the first year of life. Anna Freud proposed a modified version of adult analysis; for specific theoretical reasons she did not believe that the usual techniques of analysis were applicable to children. At issue were fundamental concepts of analysis, such as the nature of the ego and the possibility of transference, as well as questions of methodology relating to the integrity of observation of, and inference from, the behavior of infants. Although some of the conflicts have moved toward rapprochement in recent years, the Klein-Freud controversies have evolved and persisted to the present day, resulting in factionalism, strife, and, lately, a certain amount of intellectual interpenetration of the opposing camps.

On another front, Anna Freud helped to change the focus of classical Freudian psychoanalysis with the publication in 1936 of *The Ego and the Mechanisms of Defense.* The early years of psychoanalysis had been given to what became known as "id analysis," which centered on the patient's unconscious wishes and on aspects of libidinal development, regression, and fixation. With the advent of the so-called "structural theory" in the mid-1920's—that is, the tripartite view of the mind as ego, id, and superego—the stage was set for a technical shift of interest. An initial impetus came from Wilhelm Reich's influential *Character Analysis* (1933), but Anna Freud's book dealt in an orthodox and systematic way with how the ego develops and ministers to the disparate demands of the id, the superego, and the outside world. Analysts, accordingly, began to concern themselves with the defensive aspects of their patients' personalities, in addition to the interpretation of unconscious wishes and instinctual strivings. The ego was to be seen not only as the conscious "self," but as the largely silent, defensive mediator that could be opened to change and development through analysis. Furthermore, Anna Freud extended her father's discussion of anxiety in his *Inhibitions, Symptoms, and Anxiety* (1926). Late in his career Freud had clarified his view that anxiety is a signal indicating danger, of which the ego must somehow be relieved. Anna Freud discussed the choice of defense—repression, denial, rationalization, and other mechanisms—in terms of the source of danger. That line of thinking, which emphasized the role of reality and the ego's adaptational abilities, has had immense significance for the development of what came to be known as "ego psychology."

After the Nazi invasion of Austria in March 1938, the Freuds could no longer work in Vienna. To escape the persecution that other Jews were suffering, in June 1938 the family left for London, where they made their home at Maresfield Gardens the following September. Of her relationship with her father in his last years, Ernest Jones wrote, "Both were very adverse to . . . sentimentality. . . . It was a deep silent understanding and sympathy that reigned between them. The mutual understanding must have been . . . extraordinary, a silent communication. . . . The daughter's devotion was as absolute as the father's appreciation of it." Sigmund Freud died at the age of eighty-three, on September 23, 1939.

During World War II, in collaboration with Dorothy Burlingham, Anna Freud directed the Hampstead War Nursery, a residential center for some eighty children, many of whom had been separated from their parents and had lost their homes in the bombings. Characteristically, Miss Freud conducted the nursery also as a laboratory of child development and, with Dorothy Burlingham, recorded its course in *Infants without Families, Reports on the Hampstead Nurseries, 1939-1945*, which was published in 1973 as the third volume of her collected writings. Also with Dorothy Burlingham she wrote *War and Children* (Medical War Books, 1943; Greenwood Press, 1973).

Since 1952 Anna Freud has served as director of the Hampstead Child-Therapy Course and Clinic, which she founded after the war, in 1947, to replace the Hampstead War Nursery. The study and research, clinical practice, and training at Hampstead, the largest center of its kind in the world, have contributed to the burgeoning of what Anna Freud prefers to consider as a subspecialty of psychoanalysis—psychoanalytic child psychology. To some extent she has remained independent of, and occasionally removed from, the mainstream of psychoanalytic thought as it has developed over the past four decades, some times passing cautionary judgment on reigning views and withholding opinions on issues while awaiting further clinical and theoretical developments. The esteem in which she is held can hardly be overestimated: in one 1970 poll she was regarded by both psychoanalysts and psychiatrists as the most outstanding living psychoanalyst.

Like other pioneering psychoanalysts, nevertheless, Anna Freud has seen her theories subjected from time to time to distortion and misrepresentation. Although, for example, she has argued for the middle way between extremes of restraint and license, she has repeatedly been charged with advocating total permissiveness for all children. She has consistently refused to disregard the complexity of child development and was originally cautious of direct observation of children as a research instrumentality, which she feared might lead to behaviorism. Initial successes in that research approach led her to experiment with, and establish, a careful methodology for just such a purpose. With colleagues at Hampstead she has created a diagnostic tool, the developmental profile, which assesses systematically and in detail the lines of childhood development and the possibilities of their arrest leading to pathology. She has attempted research comparing neurosis as it appears in the child and later in the adolescent and the adult. Critical of laying too much stress on the obscure, very early periods of childhood, she regards preverbal behavior as a difficult basis upon which to draw other than speculative conclusions.

Practical and realistic, Anna Freud has open-mindedly evaluated the various rules and regimens of psychoanalysis as "tools of the trade" that are flexible givens, subject to modification. In exposition of "luminous coherence," as Robert Coles described her writing in the *New Yorker* (September 23, 1972), she has discussed her work since the end of World War II in *Indications of Child Analysis and Other Papers, 1945-1956; Research at the Hampstead Child-Therapy Clinic and Other Papers, 1956-1965; Normality and Pathology in Childhood: Assessments of Development* (1965); and *Problems of Psychoanalytic Training, Diagnosis, and the Technique of Therapy, 1966-1970*—the four concluding volumes of her collected work.

One area in which Anna Freud has been especially interested in applying concepts of analytic child psychology involves issues in family law, such as child custody. She worked for brief periods during the 1960's at the Yale Law School and the Yale Child-Study Center. Later she collaborated with two Yale professors, Joseph Goldstein and Albert Solnit, on *Beyond the Best Interests of the Child* (Free Press, 1973). The authors of that study stress the importance of the psychological parent to the child, often apart from the biological parent, who has generally been given legal precedence. To safeguard the child's interests and provide particularly for the continuity of the parental relationship, they suggest that the child be represented by counsel and they offer new guidelines for divorce proceedings and cases concerning custody, foster care, and adoption.

For the first time since the Nazi Anschluss, Anna Freud returned to Vienna, in June 1971, and although she is known to shun public attention, received an ovation at the opening of the twenty-seventh International Psychoanalytical Congress. Revisiting the city the following year, she was awarded an honorary M.D. degree from the University of Vienna. She also holds the Grand Decoration of Honor in Gold of Austria, bestowed in 1975, and honorary degrees from Clark University, the University of Chicago, Yale University, and other universities. She is a member of the British Psycho-Analytic Society and Institute of Psycho-Analysis and is an editor of the prestigious annual *Psychoanalytic Study of the Child*.

Anna Freud has never married. In younger years she was a pretty, much-sought-after woman, with strong, regular features enhanced by short, cropped hair and dark, deep-set eyes. More recently described as frail-looking and white-haired, she has nevertheless maintained unflagging professional involvement, writing, lecturing, and conducting seminars. In an address before the New York Psychoanalytic Society in 1968, she commented on the youth of the 1960's: "Young people now are not interested in man's struggle against himself, but in man's struggle against society. They see that what psychoanalysis may lead to is adaptation to society. That's the last thing they have in mind." She assured her audience, however, "Psychoanalysis will grow, and it will take us deeper and deeper into life."

References: N Y Times Bk R p1+ Ja 23 '72 por; International Who's Who, 1978-79; Roazen, Paul. Freud and His Followers (1975); Who's Who, 1978-79

Gerulaitis, Vitas (gâr-ōō-lī'təs vē'täs)

July 26, 1954- Tennis player. Address: b. c/o United States Tennis Association Inc., 51 E. 42d St., New York City, N.Y. 10017

In the words of sportswriter Mike Lupica, Vitas Gerulaitis has brought "a great youthful flamboyance to a men's field suffering from terminal All-American boyism." Gerulaitis, an exciting player known for his speed, exceptional range, and gymnastic ability, has quickly advanced through the ranks of world-class professionals since joining the circuit five years ago and he has won three of the seven major international tournaments. Although he was ranked fourth in the world in 1978 and fifth in 1979, he must yet win the Wimbledon or United States Open title to gain entrance into what he has called "the two-mile high club" of Bjorn Borg, Jimmy

Connors, and Guillermo Vilas. Gerulaitis' flashy game and on-court comic antics for the Pittsburgh Triangles, the Indiana Loves, and, most recently, the New York Apples, have proved to be especially popular with team tennis fans. He also regularly plays for the United States Davis Cup team as a matter of "national pride."

The only son of Vitas and Aldona Gerulaitis, Lithuanian immigrants who came to the United States in 1949, Vitas Kevin Gerulaitis was born in Brooklyn, New York on July 26, 1954. His father worked as a packer and truck driver during his first few years in this country and then as a researcher for a pharmaceutical house; he now operates a travel and insurance agency. In the late 1930's Vitas Gerulaitis Sr. was Lithuania's top tennis player and a member of its Davis Cup squad. Mrs. Gerulaitis shared her husband's interest in sports and paired with him to win the German mixed doubles table tennis championship in the late 1940's.

As a child, Vitas Gerulaitis was more interested in playing soccer, basketball, and Little League baseball than in playing tennis, but he and his younger sister Ruta, now a nationally ranked professional tennis player, learned the rudiments of the game from their father on the public courts in Howard Beach, Queens. Recognizing the boy's natural quickness and coordination, the elder Gerulaitis encouraged his son to focus his physical energy on tennis and obtained for him a prized junior membership in the exclusive West Side Tennis Club in Forest Hills, Queens, then the home of the United States Open. As his interest in the sport grew, young Gerulaitis volunteered to work extra hours on the grounds crew just to be near the action on the courts.

When he was fifteen years old, Gerulaitis won the greater New York parochial schools' championship, and the following year he surprised Columbia University's top male player, 6-0, 6-0, in an exhibition match. Impressed by Gerulaitis' talent, the owner of the Port Washington (New York) Tennis Academy let him practise for nothing and Harry Hopman, the captain of Australia's invincible Davis Cup team in the 1950's and the academy's resident pro, agreed to coach him. Under Hopkins' guidance, Gerulaitis won all but two of the major junior tournaments in 1972. The sixth-ranked junior in the country, he was picked by *World Tennis* magazine to compete in the annual Shepparton (Australia) Lawn Tennis Club Easter weekend tournament and in exhibitions in Sydney and Melbourne. To the astonishment of his Australian hosts, Gerulaitis, who had expected to play only in the junior events, won both the men's open and the men's "A" singles tournaments.

After graduating from Archbishop Molloy High School in 1972, Gerulaitis chose from among his many scholarship offers to enroll at Columbia University as a John Jay scholar. For several months he tried to combine academic pursuits and a heavy tournament schedule, but he finally dropped out of school in April 1973. Turning his full attention to tennis, he made it to the semifinals of the Louisville Classic on the grueling World Championship Tennis (WCT) pro tour and teamed up with Brian Teacher to take the United States Clay Court Amateur doubles championship. In 1974, his first full year on the circuit, he grossed over $80,000 from WCT tournaments and World Team Tennis (WTT) play for the Pittsburgh Triangles. During that year he picked up invaluable tips and immeasurably improved his game in frequent two-to-three-hour practice sessions with Ken Rosewall, the veteran coach of the Triangles.

Gerulaitis demonstrated just how much his game had improved at the United States Pro Indoor tournament in January 1975. In a dazzling display of shot-making he mowed down Ove Bengtson, Tom Okker, Raul Ramirez, Paul Gerken, and John Alexander, in straight sets, before falling to seventh-seeded Marty Riessen, 6-7, 7-5, 2-6, 7-6, 3-6, in the final. The following month, at the National Indoor tennis tournament in Salisbury, Maryland, he took Jimmy Connors, the two-time defending champion, to five sets before running out of steam, 7-5, 5-7, 1-6, 6-3, 0-6. When an injured Connors withdrew from their next scheduled meeting, in the final of the Independent Players Association tourney at the Felt Forum in New York City in March, Gerulaitis topped his replacement, Wojtek Fibak, 0-3, 7-5, then took on all comers in a free-for-all match with the spectators.

Gerulaitis was eliminated in the first round of singles competition at Wimbledon in June 1975, but he and Sandy Mayer unexpectedly whipped pair after pair of more experienced players to take the men's doubles title, beating the team of Colin Dowdeswell and Allan Stone, 7-5, 8-6, 6-4. Two months later, at the United States Open in Forest Hills, Gerulaitis was the first seeded player to fall by the wayside as he dropped a hard-fought, second-round match to François Jauffret, the six-time French national champion, 6-7, 5-7, 5-7. He fared better in the mixed doubles competition, where he and his sister Ruta made it as far as the quarterfinals. Although he failed to capture a major men's singles title, Gerulaitis compiled an enviable record on the WCT circuit, winning nineteen matches while losing only five, and when the Pittsburgh Triangles won the WTT league championship, he was voted the most valuable player in the playoffs. Named the "most improved player" of 1975 by *Tennis* magazine, he moved up to fourth place in the national rankings.

In 1976 WCT play, Gerulaitis frequently reached the finals only to lose close matches to more experienced players. Even so, he came within one match of making the top eight for the WCT Championship. Unseeded at Wimbledon, he fought his way through the crowd and, in the fourth round, upset Arthur Ashe, the defending champion and number-one seed, 4-6, 8-9, 6-4, 6-3, 6-4. "I never thought I could win the match until the first game of the fifth set, and I choked like crazy," Gerulaitis confessed to Mike Lupica in a post-game interview for the New York *Post* (June 28, 1976). "But it was only that one game. . . . I thought I had a win like this coming. I've beaten all the best players in the world and it was about time I did it at a big tournament." Possibly because he was fatigued by his physically and emotionally exhausting match against Ashe, Gerulaitis lost in the quarterfinals to Raul Ramirez. On the slow clay surface of Forest Hills two months later, he breezed through the early rounds of play to reach the round of sixteen before losing to top-seeded Jimmy Connors in straight sets.

In the spring of 1977 Gerulaitis' pro career took a turn for the better as he piled up a string of WCT victories and continued to dazzle the team tennis fans. But even Gerulaitis was somewhat surprised by his victory in the Italian Open—one of the most difficult international tournaments because of the highly partisan crowds. A serve-and-volley player, he was not expected to do well on the slow clay court, but he overcame occasional fits of erratic serving to defeat Adriano Panatta, Brian Gottfried and, in the final, Antonio Zugarelli, by a score of 6-2, 7-6, 3-6, 7-6. He was the first American to win the Italian Open since 1960.

Before and during the 1977 Wimbledon competition, Gerulaitis practised daily with Bjorn Borg, who perhaps best matches his speed and agility, to perfect his grass court game. Gerulaitis' extra practice sessions paid off as he subdued Tom Gorman, Sandy Mayer, Stan Smith, Dick Stockton, and Billy Martin to reach the semifinals, where he took on Borg in an epic contest that sportswriters described as the most memorable match of the centenary championships. Trading lobs and drop shots, the two played remarkably even tennis for five sets, with Borg eventually coming out on top, 6-4, 3-6, 6-3, 3-6, 8-6. Afterwards, Gerulaitis regaled reporters with a side-splitting monologue about some of Wimbledon's stuffier traditions. When asked how he could be so cheerful after such a heartbreaking loss, he replied, "This was my winning speech, and I didn't want to waste the good material."

Boosted to ninth place in the world rankings by his vastly improved game, Gerulaitis was seeded eighth at Forest Hills in August 1977. He won rather easily in the early rounds, then fell victim to Harold Solomon's consistent ground strokes and effective passing shots, 6-7, 3-6. Blaming the loss on his failure to adapt his aggressive, attacking style to the slow, composition surface, he vowed to "find the holes" in his game and "patch them up."

Having built his game around speed, range, and agility (he is fast enough to run down opponents' shots until they commit fatal errors), he concentrated on perfecting his occasionally tentative forehand and his admittedly weak second serve. He used his more authoritative second serve, clean ground strokes, and stinging passing shots to good advantage on the Australian grass circuit in October 1977, winning the Brisbane and Perth championships and coming in second in the Sydney and New South Wales competitions. Two months later he overcame the debilitating effects of blistering heat and ignored an attack of severe leg cramps in the fourth set to defeat Great Britain's John Lloyd, 6-3, 7-6, 5-7, 3-6, 6-2, in the final of the Australian Open.

Coming on the heels of a scandal that could have ruined his professional career, the Australian victories were especially sweet. On October 12, 1977, while Gerulaitis was playing in the Brisbane tournament, the New York *Post* published in "Newk's Tennis World" —a syndicated column ostensibly written by John Newcombe, a former Wimbledon champion, but actually ghostwritten by John Thirsk, an Australian sportswriter—an interview in which Gerulaitis revealed that he had smoked "a little grass" and experimented with cocaine.

Stunned, Gerulaitis agreed to be questioned by the *Post*'s Jim O'Brien to set the record straight. In that interview, published on November 15, 1977, he admitted that he had tried "a lot of drugs" as a teenager because it was "the cool thing to do," but emphasized that he was now "100 percent against the use of drugs." "There's only one way to be a great athlete," he told O'Brien. "You've got to work as hard as you can, and keep your body in the best possible shape. . . . I decided that the best possible way to kill the idea that I was deep into drugs, or anything of that kind, was to show everyone the kind of tennis I could play."

For the first few months of the WCT circuit in 1978, Gerulaitis played his usual competent game, but invariably lost the championships by close scores, most frequently to Bjorn Borg. At the all-star meet for the top eight WCT finishers in Dallas, Texas in May 1978, he beat Raul Ramirez and advanced to the final when Borg withdrew from the tournament because of an infected thumb. Gerulaitis' adversary in the final was "Fast" Eddie Dibbs, who had beaten him—although not decisively—in all four of their previous meetings. Gerulaitis jumped to an early lead by intercepting Dibbs's usually lethal passing shots with volleys and by forcing him to attack. Increasingly confident as the match wore on, he varied the pace, direction, and

angle of his approach shots, mixed in a few precisely placed drop shots and lobs, and eventually overwhelmed Dibbs, 6-3, 6-2, 6-1, to take his third major title in twelve months. "There have been some funny decisions over the last year in the United States rankings," he said after the match, as quoted in the Toronto *Globe and Mail* (May 15, 1978), "but this makes me the top American player. I'm ready to challenge the big three. I'm going after Connors, Borg, and Vilas."

Fourth ranked in the world as the 1978 Wimbledon contest got under way, Gerulaitis, playing with a strep throat infection, lost to Connors in the semifinals, 7-9, 2-6, 1-6. A few days later he was on the court again at the Forest Hills Invitation Tournament, a twelve-man round-robin event he could barely squeeze into his crowded schedule. During the course of this tournament he also carried the New York Apples to a 28-22 win over the Phoenix Racquets in a team tennis meet and played in a WTT all-star match in Las Vegas, Nevada. Nevertheless, he breezed into the final undefeated and trounced Ilie Nastase, 6-2, 6-0, in just fifty-nine minutes to take the $100,000 first prize.

Seeded fourth at the United States Open, Vitas Gerulaitis was widely considered to be the principal challenger to Borg because both Connors and defending champion Vilas were having mediocre years. Before play began, he analyzed his chances for *Cue* magazine (August 19, 1978): "The serve is still the part of my game that needs the most work if I'm going to be number one. . . . I can stay with [Borg] on groundstrokes. . . , I volley better and I'm a little more aggressive around the net. My whole attitude has changed, too. Before, I used to play for the fun a little more. Now I go out there to win and get off the court as fast as possible." Unaccustomed to the hard and fast composition surface at the new National Tennis Center in Flushing Meadows, Queens, he was tested in the early rounds by lesser seeded players, but he settled down sufficiently by the quarterfinals to defeat Johan Krick in a one-sided match, 6-1, 6-2, 6-2. Borg, fresh from his third consecutive Wimbledon singles title, downed Gerulaitis in the semifinals, 6-3, 6-2, 7-6. In 1979 Gerulaitis won the Italian Open and the Austrian Grand Prix, among other competitions, but again failed to win the United States Open.

Vitas Gerulaitis is a lean, rangy six-footer who usually weighs in at about 160 pounds. He has an angular face with prominent cheekbones, pale blue eyes, shaggy, shoulder-length blond hair and, according to one interviewer, a smile that is "at once smart-alecky and endearing." Reporters say he is unfailingly polite, congenial, ingenuous, and accessible. Admittedly "a little flakier" than most of the touring pros, he cheerfully confesses to spending virtually all his earnings, which amounted to over $700,000 in winnings and endorsements in 1978, on clothes and cars. As of September 1978, he owned two Rolls-Royces (a Corniche and a Silver Cloud), a Mercedes, a Porsche, and a Ferrari. "They're like my children," he told the Washington *Post's* Barry Lorge. "I baby them. My Corniche gets treatment that some of my girlfriends would like to have. If Dom Perignon made motor oil, that's what they would get."

Because of his weakness for fashionable nightclubs, stylish clothes, and expensive cars, Gerulaitis was christened "Broadway Vitas" by the popular press, and magazines are as likely to feature photographs of him dancing at Studio 54, Infinity, or other "in" Manhattan discos as playing tennis. He jokes that all the publicity has occasionally helped him "to get a table in a restaurant," but insists that his playboy image is exaggerated. "If I did 10 percent of what I'm supposed to be doing, according to articles written about my off-the-court activities, I'd be a cripple," he told one interviewer. "Or they'd have to bury me in the family plot." Belying that image, he neither smokes nor drinks, practises up to six hours a day, and often checks in to a tennis academy to prepare for an important tournament. Although he keeps an apartment in New York City "for emergencies," Gerulaitis continues to live with his family in the $250,000 Kings Point, Long Island house he bought several years ago. In the backyard is a regulation-size tennis court that he recently had resurfaced to match the court in Flushing Meadows.

Two years ago, Gerulaitis established the Vitas Gerulaitis Foundation to teach tennis to underprivileged inner-city children. Acting on his own initiative, he organized benefit parties at his favorite discos to raise money for equipment and for a scholarship fund to send promising young players to tennis camps for intensive training and devised a program of free clinics at local parks and playgrounds. Taught by Billie Jean King, Arthur Ashe, Bjorn Borg, Fred Stolle, Ray Ruffels, and Gerulaitis himself, the clinics drew huge crowds throughout the summer of 1978. "I like to feel that I can put something back into the game, not just keep taking from it," Gerulaitis wrote in a New York *Times* (August 28, 1978) article explaining his idea. "Tennis has been very good to me and we're all making a lot of money out of it . : ., but the players must be able to give something back to the community." A sportswriter for *Today* (August 27, 1979) acknowledged, "The inspiration he provides could blossom in some better-motivated lives and even some future world-class players."

References: *People* 9:32+ Jl 3 '78 pors; *Sport* 65:96+ S 1 '77 pors; *Sports Illus* 47:24+ Ag 15 '77 pors; *Tennis* 13:61 S '77 por; *World Tennis* 25:23+ N '77 por

Giannini, Giancarlo (jän-nē′nē jän-kär′lō)

Aug. 1, 1942- Italian actor. Address: b. Via Mercalli 6, Rome, Italy

Giancarlo Giannini, the popular Italian actor with the luminous, wonderfully agile eyes, attained international stardom through the witty, cynical films of the scenarist-director Lina Wertmuller. The first of those black comedies was *The Seduction of Mimi* (1972), in which Giannini plays a Sicilian rustic turned factory worker done in by the preposterous feudal code of manhood he is expected to live by; the most acclaimed was *Seven Beauties* (1976), about a contemptible, strutting Neapolitan *macho* who is driven to crawling for survival. Outside of his half dozen collaborations with Miss Wertmuller, Giannini has worked in more than fifty motion pictures, under numerous directors, from Visconti to Antonioni. As Clarke Taylor observed in the *Soho Weekly News* (January 29, 1976), he is "a chameleon actor, with a completely different physicality in each role," and he "utterly beguiles his audience, no matter what the role- or the subject of the film."

The son of an electrical engineer, Giancarlo Giannini was born on August 1, 1942 in La Spezia in northwest Italy, and he grew up there, in Naples, and in Rome. Following in his father's footsteps, he studied engineering, but on the way to earning his diploma he was drawn to acting, as he recalled when Clarke Taylor interviewed him for the *Soho Weekly News*: "On the stage I saw people having a good time pretending to be other people, and they had a need to talk to other people. Perhaps because of my own timidity,

I could see myself in this situation. A man needs to explode with other people, and acting allows one to explode."

Giannini studied at the Academy of Theatre in Rome, and he began essaying Shakespearean roles in 1963. The most memorable of his early credits was Romeo in Franco Zeffirelli's production of *Romeo and Juliet*, which won first prize at the Festival of Nations in Paris in 1964. The first of Giannini's many starring roles on Italian television was that of David Copperfield in a twelve-episode dramatization of the novel by Charles Dickens. His early film vehicles included *Stasera mi butto* and *Le Sorelle*, and among his later film credits were Cellini in *Anzio* (Columbia, 1968), Saverio in *Arabella* (Universal, 1969), Lieutenant Hans Ruppert in *Fraulein Doktor* (Paramount, 1969), and Inspector Tellini in *The Black Belly of the Tarantula* (MGM, 1972).

As Judith Crist noted in *New York* (November 3, 1969), Giannini and Patrizia Valturri were "charming" in the supporting roles of the young lovers in Stanley Kramer's *The Secret of Santa Vittoria* (United Artists, 1969). While Marcello Mastroianni and Monica Vitti drew most of the critical attention, Giannini, as the young pizza baker, contributed his full share of hilarity to *The Pizza Triangle* (Warner Brothers, 1970), a slapstick farce about a tragic love triangle.

Meanwhile, Lina Wertmuller and Giannini had met in 1963, when Miss Wertmuller saw the young actor play Puck in a production of *A Midsummer Night's Dream*. As he gained influence as a matinee idol, Giannini put Miss Wertmuller in contact with people able to boost her career as a filmmaker. Her husband, the sculptor Enrico Job, once testified that without Giannini's championing of her career Miss Wertmuller might "still be waiting for a chance."

The first cinematic collaboration of Wertmuller and Giannini was *Rita la zanzara* (Rita the Mosquito, 1966), and their initial theatrical venture together was the premiere production of Miss Wertmuller's play "Two Plus Two No Longer Make Four," in 1968. In 1971 and 1972 Miss Wertmuller filmed a screenplay of her own, a practice she would pursue from then on. The 1971-72 production was *Mimi metallurgico ferito nell'onore* (Mimi the Metal Worker, His Honor Betrayed), the boisterous story of a simple Sicilian, played by Giannini, who becomes the comic victim of the social codes represented by Mafia and *machismo*.

Mimi metallurgico ferito nell'onore brought Miss Wertmuller the best director award at the 1972 Cannes Film Festival. Two years later a truncated version of the film was distributed in the United States under the title *The Seduction of Mimi* by New Line Cinema. "One suspects that the filmmaker's political and social comments have been given short shrift in the translation, or lost in the episodic plotting and cutting," Judith Crist wrote on that occasion in *New York* (June 24, 1974). "But thanks to Giannini's artistry, which includes an almost Chaplinesque gift for mime and near-camp, you get a cheery taste of gander-goose relations."

Giannini won the best actor award at the 1973 Cannes Film Festival for his performance as Tunin, the crazed peasant anarchist sheltered by prostitutes in a Roman bordello as he plots the assassination of Mussolini in Miss Wertmuller's *Love and Anarchy* (Steinman-Baxter). When that bitterly humorous study in the irreconcilability of politics and passion was released in the United States by Peppercorn-Wormser Film Enterprises, Paul D. Zimmerman of *Newsweek* (April 29, 1974) described the performances of Giannini and Mariangela Melato as "breathtaking."

Miss Melato again starred opposite Giannini in Miss Wertmuller's *Swept Away (By an Unusual Destiny in the Blue Sea of August)*, distributed by Medusa Films in Europe beginning in 1974 and released in the United States under the auspices of Cinema V in 1975. In that film Giannini plays Gennarino, a Communist seaman working as a deckhand on the yacht of Raffaela, a haughty capitalist (Miss Melato); when they become marooned on a Mediterranean island, Gennarino passionately, violently subjugates his employer; when they are rescued, she reverts to class and abruptly terminates her submissive love.

Vincent Canby's review of *Swept Away* in the New York *Times* (September 18, 1975) attributed the "enormous appeal of the comedy" to the way the two stars "tear into their roles with a single-minded intensity that manages to be both hugely comic and believable. . . . They are the best things to happen to Italian comedy since Marcello Mastroianni and Sophia Loren." Jay Cocks of *Time* (October 6, 1975) observed that Giannini and Miss Melato brought "an awkward poignancy, a true but misplaced tenderness to Wertmuller's ruthless and unruly romance."

In Wertmuller's *Settebellezze* (Medusa, 1976), or *Seven Beauties*, set in the years before and during World War II, Giannini plays Pasqualino, a petty Neapolitan hoodlum with a twisted male-chauvinist concept of honor and an instinct for survival at any price, including his own degradation. Few scenes in the history of cinema equal in grotesque impact the one in which Giannini, as Pasqualino, determined to survive a Nazi death camp, pretends to love the repulsive, obese female camp commandant. Critics described Giannini as portraying Pasqualino with "sulfurous splendor" and inspiring "some new physiological reaction, between laughter and tears." In 1977 *Seven Beauties* was nominated for an Academy Award for best foreign-language film and Giannini was nominated for an Oscar for best actor.

Miss Wertmuller and Giannini formed a temporary partnership, called Liberty Films, to produce Miss Wertmuller's first English-language film, *The End of the World in Our Usual Bed in a Night Full of Rain*, (Warner Brothers, 1978), the story of the disintegrating marriage of a Communist journalist (Giannini) and his American wife (Candice Bergen), a photographer and a feminist. The film was widely panned, with critics referring to it as a "banal" execution in "self parody" that was "all concept with no center." In his review in the *New Republic* (February 18, 1978), Stanley Kauffmann wrote, "Wertmuller's best work to date . . . had superb vigor, the zest of real assurance and real skill, and a rococco filigree that she had learned from Fellini. . . . All these strengths she used in her loving struggle with her Italy, with what Italians do to their lives and to their country. . . . Here [in *A Night Full of Rain*] we get little more than the energies. . . . The best features of the film are the performances of the pair [Giannini and Bergen], acting that has body despite the malnutrition of the script. Giannini . . . growls as humorously and lunges as balletically as ever, and his English . . . has most of the pleasant roller-coaster music of his Italian."

Mixed reviews greeted *Sesso Matto* (Dean Films and Cineterrena, 1976), distributed in the United States by In-Frame Films under the title *How Funny Can Sex Be?* In that set of eight Rabelaisian sketches written by Dino Risi and Ruggero Maccari and directed by Risi, Giannini, in the opinion of Vincent Canby of the New York *Times* (September 20, 1976), could only display "remnants" of worthier performances, "in the Groucho-like walk" and "the dainty pursuit of lust."

Laura Antonelli, Giannini's costar in *How Funny Can Sex Be?*, teamed up with him again in the late Luchino Visconti's last film, *The Innocent* (Analysis Film Releasing Corporation, 1978), based on Gabriele D'Annunzio's novel of manners about a nineteenth-century Tuscan aristocratic cad. After Visconti's death, Giannini assumed responsibility for the editing of the film, and he fought successfully for the restoration of footage excised in the British and American versions.

After seeing *The Innocent*, Cynthia Heimel, commenting in the *Soho Weekly News* (January 18, 1979), called the movie "rotten." "By the end of the movie you hate them all [the characters] and want everyone who is not dead already immediately run over by a truck," Miss Heimel wrote. "But Giannini is uncanny. He can stand mutely for five minutes and you know every thought that's going through his brain. He doesn't even twitch a lot. I have never seen an actor who oozes so much energy and emotion. Al Pacino came close, yelling 'Attica, Attica.' "

American audiences can look forward to seeing Giannini in Mario Monicelli's *Travels With Anita*, Michelangelo Antonioni's "Patire o Morire" (To Suffer Or To Die), and Miss Wertmuller's "Between Two Men Because of a Widow." In addition to acting, Giannini works as a dubber of voices for Italian versions of the motion pictures of such actors as Dustin Hoffman, Al Pacino, and Jack Nicholson, because he finds he is thus able "to draw out their secrets." He researches his roles carefully, using a tape recorder to capture regional accents; works at his own make-up; and uses yoga for muscular control. When making a film, he tries to be involved in every aspect of the production, from camera angles to daily rushes. Not surprisingly, he is looking forward to trying his hand at directing.

Giancarlo Giannini has two sons, Lorenzo and Adriano, from his marriage to Livia Giampalmo, which ended in divorce several years ago. Giannini is high-strung but much more controlled than his personae on the screen would suggest. Physically, he is slight, standing five feet nine inches tall and weighing 145 pounds, and his movements have been described as "cat-like." His recreations include photography, painting, and cooking.

According to interviewers, Giannini has a warmer personality and is better looking and better dressed (in a casual way) than any of his characters. His face is wan; his green eyes are marvelous professional tools, able to change from soulful orbs to sinister slits in a twinkling and to register a range of emotions from despair to rage, desire, or cynicism. "To make people laugh is a very difficult art," Giannini has said. "To make people laugh and cry simultaneously is almost impossible. It's what fascinates me the most.".

References: N Y *Sunday News* III p11 F 16 '75 por; N Y *Times* II p1+ N 16 '75 pors; *Time* 107:58+ F 16 '76 pors; *Village Voice* p79+ F 2 '76 pors; *Women's Wear Daily* p6 Ja 9 '79 pors; *Annuario del Cinema Italiano, 1976-1977, International Motion Picture Almanac, 1978*

Grade, Lew

Dec. 25, 1906- British motion picture and television producer. Address: b. Associated Communications Corporation, Ltd., 17 Great Cumberland Place, London W1A 1AG, England

"I am Mr. Average," Lew Grade is fond of saying. "My tastes are the tastes of the average person throughout the world." Grade is chairman and chief executive officer of Associated Communications Corporation, Ltd., the single largest supplier for Great Britain's commercial television system and a major producer of

Lew **Grade**

motion pictures for worldwide consumption. ACC subsidiaries produce and distribute television programs and feature films to more than 100 countries and do especially well in the insatiable American market, where Grade's numerous TV hits have included *The Avengers*, *The Saint*, and *The Muppet Show*. ACC also runs one of the most lucrative commercial television franchises in England, operates more than a dozen legitimate theatres in London and in other British cities, manages Britain's third largest chain of film theatres, produces and sells records, tapes, and cassettes, publishes comic books and sheet music, makes theatrical costumes, and even holds the Muzak franchise for the United Kingdom. In the company's 1977-1978 fiscal year, gross income from those diverse enterprises exceeded $200,000,000.

Lew Grade was born Lewis (Louis, according to some sources) Winogradsky on December 25, 1906 in Tokmak, a town in southeastern Russia, the first of the three sons of Isaac Winogradsky, a tailor's assistant, and his wife Olga. In 1912 the family immigrated to London, England, where Isaac Winogradsky worked as a tailor's presser and operated a small embroidery factory in London's impoverished East End. Grade attended the Rochelle Street School until he was fourteen, but then dropped out to help his father run the family business.

Not too long after that, Isaac Winogradsky died, and Lew and his brother Bernard (now Lord Delfont, Baron of Stepney and chairman and chief executive officer of EMI Film and Theatre Corporation) entered Charleston contests to earn extra money, taking turns at wearing their one presentable suit. Lew's

energetic dancing brought him several first prizes, and in 1927, at the age of twenty, he changed his surname to Grade and went into vaudeville. Billing himself as the "World's Champion Charleston Dancer," he successfully played the vaudeville circuit in Great Britain and on the Continent for several years.

Having learned from experience that there was more money to be made in representing performers than in being one, Lew Grade, in partnership with his younger brother Leslie, set up a talent agency—Lew and Leslie Grade, Ltd.—and gradually built it into the largest in Europe. Even while fulfilling his military obligation during World War II, Lew Grade was essentially a talent agent. Unfit for active duty because of water on the knee, he organized traveling shows to entertain the troops. After the war, his agency booked popular American stars, including Bob Hope, Jack Benny, and Danny Kaye into the London Palladium and, beginning in 1947, introduced such European headliners as Edith Piaf to audiences in the United States. When, in 1967, he sold the agency to EMI, the musical and theatrical conglomerate, for a reported $22,000,000 in EMI stock, it numbered among its clients dozens of international stars, among them, Vanessa Redgrave and Sir Laurence Olivier.

Meanwhile, in the mid-1950's, Lew Grade got in on the ground floor of British commercial television when he and a group of business associates formed Associated Television Corporation (ATV) and put up £500,000 to purchase the commercial franchises for the Midlands during the week and for London on weekends. Under the British commercial television system, established by an act of Parliament in 1954, only one commercial network, operating as a franchiser of the Independent Broadcasting Authority, may broadcast in a given geographic area at any one time. In a series of franchise shifts effective in 1968, ATV lost its London weekend franchise and got in its place the weekend franchise for the Midlands.

In an action typical of his style of intuitive decision-making, Grade, who was deputy managing director of ATV in the late 1950's, risked almost 80 percent of that young company's capital on the production of an untested action-adventure series based on the Robin Hood legend. Disregarding the lack of interest on the part of a potential sponsor, he approved the completion of a full season of episodes and then sold the series not only in Britain, but in the United States and in other countries as well. Ultimately 143 episodes of *Robin Hood* were made. Some twenty years after the series first went on the air it was still being broadcast in countries as diverse as Poland and Kuwait, and in the United States alone, it earned more than $20,000,000.

Grade's television exports to the United States over the years have included the costume adventure series *Ivanhoe* and *Lancelot*;

Secret Agent, a fast-paced spy thriller starring Patrick McGoohan; The Avengers, a slick spoof of the James Bond genre that made Diana Rigg and Patrick Macnee international stars; the variety series This is Tom Jones and The Julie Andrews Hour; and such popular crime dramas as The Protectors, The Baron, and The Saint. Nevertheless, American networks have viewed many of ATV's productions with considerable skepticism. The Saint, for example, was turned down by all three major networks. Undeterred, Grade sold the show directly to ninety-odd local stations. After it had demonstrated its drawing power, NBC picked it up in 1967 as a summer replacement. Still in syndication, The Saint has proved to be one of Grade's most durable series.

By the late 1970's Lew Grade's productions accounted for slightly more than 25 percent of all programming broadcast on British commercial television, and his sales to networks and individual television stations in the United States exceeded $100,000,000 annually. The international audience for ATV series and special programs, distributed worldwide by its subsidiaries, ITC Entertainment, Ltd. and ITC Entertainment, Inc., is numbered in the hundreds of millions. At the end of 1978 Grade's most popular series, The Muppet Show, featuring Jim Henson's lovable puppet characters, had a global audience of an estimated 235,-000,000 viewers in 100 countries.

Mass entertainment in the form of variety shows and universally appreciated action-adventure series for international distribution became Grade's formula for success in television, but his catering to such a common denominator of taste rankled some highbrow British television critics, who nicknamed him "Low Grade." But Grade defended his escapist entertainment, repeatedly reminding reporters during interviews that "People come home after a hard day's work, and all they want to do is relax." He contended that all of his programs, regardless of subject matter, were made with taste and discretion. "I'm against sex and bad language on the television screen," he assured Alan Bunce of the Christian Science Monitor (October 16, 1972). "And I'm against the kind of violence where someone takes a knife and rips someone. But what is wrong with a punch up? The hero always wins. What are you going to do, kiss the fellow on the cheek and say, 'Give me back the gold'?"

Grade delighted in pointing out to his critics that ATV produced about one-third of all the documentaries televised in Great Britain and that it had, in recent years, contributed significantly to the development of what he calls the "quality special" with such programs as the National Theatre's production of Eugene O'Neill's Long Day's Journey Into Night, starring Sir Laurence Olivier as James Tyrone. That special program was eventually broadcast in the United States by ABC-TV. Convinced that the American public was "ready for a higher quality of television," Lew Grade went over the heads of apathetic network executives to sell a clutch of critically praised miniseries, including The Strauss Family and Edward VII, to independent stations and to network affiliates eager for alternative programming under the prime time access rule.

After spending twenty-five years in the business, Grade still selects series proposals as quickly and instinctively as he did Robin Hood. "I go by intuition. Not by research," he told John Berendt in an interview for Esquire (September 1976). "Its my first reaction that counts. . . . Give me an idea typed on one page, and if I like it, I can make someone a very rich man." His reputation for correctly gauging popular taste is so well established within the industry that he can sell most series pilots with a one-minute transatlantic telephone call or a quick stopover during one of his frequent overseas business trips. A rare failure was Shirley's World, a short-lived series tailor-made for Shirley MacLaine that he had presold to ABC-TV in 1972. "I did everything in my power to make that show a hit," he said, as quoted in the New York Daily News (October 22, 1972), "[but] Shirley wanted to get some kind of message across, an impossibility in an entertainment program. . . . By the time I got a look at that first episode, twelve had already been shot. I couldn't believe it." Although he canceled production immediately, he still lost $1,500,000.

Grade's most ambitious television project to date was Jesus of Nazareth, an $18,000,000 two-part biography that was shown on British, American, and Italian television during the Easter season of 1977. A coproduction of ATV and Radiotelevisione Italiana, Jesus of Nazareth withstood the critical scrutiny of Catholic, Protestant, Jewish, Muslim, and Mormon religious leaders, only to be attacked by American evangelical groups who excoriated it, in the words of the fundamentalist leader Bob Jones, as "wicked" and "a blasphemy." Yielding to pressure from several Bible-thumping groups, General Motors Corporation withdrew its sponsorship, although it had invested $3,000,000 in the initial expenses of production. Procter & Gamble immediately picked up the program, and it was telecast, as planned, on Palm and Easter Sundays in 1977, to generally hospitable reviews. More than 91,000,000 Americans and 21,000,000 Britons watched the two programs, and in Italy an estimated 84 percent of the viewing public tuned it in. Jesus of Nazareth won for Grade the first Royal Television Society Cyril Bennett Award for an "outstanding original contribution to television programming."

By the mid-1970's the income from television productions accounted for just over one-third of ATV's pretax profits, with the remainder coming from its diversified interests, including a string of eleven of London's theatres, and from the production and worldwide distribution of feature films. Lew Grade's first film venture was *Desperate Characters* (1971), a scathing indictment of disintegrating upper-middle-class life in New York City, starring Shirley MacLaine and Kenneth Mars, that pleased even such an often disgruntled critic as Stanley Kauffmann. Since then, most of his films have been, in his words, "action-adventure, with a love interest": *The Tamarind Seed* (1974), with Julie Andrews as a vacationing widow and Omar Sharif as a philandering Russian military attaché; *The Eagle Has Landed* (1976), in which Michael Caine and Donald Sutherland play German undercover agents plotting to assassinate Winston Churchill; *The Domino Principle* (1977), Stanley Kramer's film of Adam Kennedy's stylish thriller about political assassination starring Gene Hackman, Candice Bergen, and Richard Widmark; *March or Die* (1977), with Catherine Deneuve as the elegant camp follower of French Foreign Legionnaires Gene Hackman and Terence Hill; and *The Boys From Brazil* (1978), in which a relentless tracker of Nazi war criminals (Sir Laurence Olivier) finally corners his archenemy (Gregory Peck).

Like his television series, Grade's motion pictures are intended for the international market. "I'm making pictures I can sell in Timbuktu, Finland, and the United States," he once told a reporter. To guarantee worldwide box-office appeal, Grade fills his movies with big-name stars. He recently agreed to produce Lina Wertmuller's *Vengeance* only after she promised to hire Sophia Loren and Marcello Mastroianni for the leading roles. "I told her that she could continue to make films that the critics liked, but the public didn't pay to see or she could hire great actors, have my backing, and get both good reviews and a big audience," he explained to Patrick McCarthy, who interviewed him for the Fairchild Syndicate in November 1978. As his support for *Vengeance* demonstrates, not every Lew Grade film is an adventure story. He produced Ingmar Bergman's psychodrama, *Autumn Sonata* (1978) and a handful of profitable comedies, including *The Return of the Pink Panther* (1975), *The Pink Panther Strikes Again* (1976), and the satiric *Movie Movie* (1978).

Grade usually has a dozen or more high-budget, star-studded films—"monster movies," as he puts it—in production at a time. Cashing in on his reputation for delivering mass-market winners, he frequently sells a film to a theatre chain even before shooting has begun, thereby cutting both his initial financial outlay and his distribution risk. In 1975 Grade joined the executives of the Boston-based General Cinema Corporation, the owner of the largest movie theatre chain in the United States, to form a new motion picture production company, Associated General Films. Three years later, he set up Marble Arch Productions, an American subsidiary, to make television series and feature films and, with Lord Delfont, established Associated Film Distributors, Inc., to act as the sole distributor of his films in the United States and Canada. Tightening his hold on the British film industry, Grade acquired in early 1979 Intereuropean Property Holdings, the owner of the third-largest chain of movie theatres in the United Kingdom.

Lew Grade looks like a cartoon of the stereotyped Hollywood mogul—short, heavy-set, a hard-driving, compulsive worker who makes multimillion-dollar deals between puffs on oversized Havana cigars. But he tempers that image with his gregariousness, ready wit, and contagious enthusiasm. "I don't work for the money," he told a reporter for *Broadcasting* (October 23, 1972). "I do it for the pleasure of the work. . . . Work is my hobby." At his desk by 6:00 A.M., he regularly puts in a twelve-to-fourteen-hour day, spending much of that day burrowing through heaps of manuscripts. As with his television ventures, he has occasionally misjudged the public's response, having turned down *The Exorcist* because it was "horrible," and *Jesus Christ Superstar* because it was "wrong to make light of a subject as important as that."

In August 1978 Grade's annual salary was raised from £59,500 (about $128,000) to £210,428 (about $452,000), a jump of 250 percent. The size of the increase prompted protests in Parliament and an official government inquiry, even though the raise, because it was paid by an American subsidiary of ACC, was technically not in violation of the government's strict wage guidelines. Coming to Grade's defense, James Bartholomew of the London *Financial Times* argued that Grade was virtually the only successful producer in an otherwise moribund British film industry. Grade himself said simply, "I'm worth the money, and if I were in America, I'd get much more for much less work."

Among the show business figures who have worked with him, Grade is both liked and respected for his integrity in business dealings, his sharp eye for a potential hit, and his general affability. "Lew and I have never had a contract," the New York talent agent Sam Cohn told *Esquire's* John Berendt. "Our arrangement is he'll be fair." Given to grand gestures, Grade once impulsively invited the eighty guests at a dinner party in Los Angeles, California to visit him in London, then hired a jumbo jet and flew them to England for an all-expenses-paid, four-day holiday. When he is not globe-trotting on business, Grade enjoys spending quiet evenings at home with his wife, the former Kathleen Sheila Moody, whom he married in 1942. They have one son, Paul Nicholas.

In recognition of his achievements, Lew Grade was knighted in 1969 and created a baron, Lord Grade of Elstree, in 1976. (Elstree is the site of one of his biggest film studios.) He takes his responsibilities as a life peer seriously and tries to attend the House of Lords at least once a month. Grade has received three Queen's Awards to Industry for Export Achievements and orders of merit from the Tunisian and Italian governments. In 1975 he was the guest of honor at a testimonial dinner given by the leaders of the American television industry, part of which was subsequently broadcast by ABC as *A Salute to Lew Grade*. On January 17, 1979, Pope John Paul II presented to Grade, a Jew, the Order of Knight Commander of St. Silvester with Star, the highest Vatican honor that can be given to a non-Catholic.

References: Christian Sci Mon p8 O 16 '72 por; Esquire 86:84+ S '76; Forbes 119:42+ My 1 '77 por; N Y Sunday News III p15 O 22 '72 por; N Y Times p79 Ap 5 '66 por; Time 98:80 O 4 '71 por; Today (Westchester) B pl N 6 '78 por; International Who's Who, 1978-79; Who's Who, 1979; Zec, Donald. Some Enchanted Egos (1973)

Gray, Hanna Holborn

Oct. 25, 1930- President of the University of Chicago. Address: b. Office of the President, University of Chicago, Chicago, Ill. 60637

As president of the University of Chicago, Hanna Holborn Gray is the first woman to serve as chief executive officer of a major American coeducational institution of higher learning. Throughout her career, Mrs. Gray has compiled an impressive series of "first woman" milestones, and by any standard, she is an outstanding scholar and a resourceful administrator. A professor of Renaissance and Reformation history by training, she was dean of the College of Arts and Sciences at Northwestern University and provost, then acting president of Yale University before taking on the presidency of the University of Chicago in July 1978. In keeping with that university's long-standing policy that all its faculty members teach at all levels, Mrs. Gray also teaches an undergraduate course in European history.

Hanna Holborn Gray was born into a distinguished academic family in Heidelberg, Germany on October 25, 1930. Her mother, Annemarie (Bettmann) Holborn, the daughter of a professor of medicine at Heidelberg University, took a doctorate in classical philology at Friedrich Wilhelm University, now the Humboldt University at Berlin. Her paternal grandfather, a physical chemist, was the director of a scientific research institute in Berlin and her father, the respected European historian Hajo Holborn, taught at both Heidelberg University and the Berlin Hochschule für Politik. She has one older brother, Frederick, who served as an administrative assistant to President John F. Kennedy before joining the political science faculty at the School of Advanced International Studies at Johns Hopkins University.

In the year 1934 Professor Hajo Holborn was dismissed from his academic posts because of his opposition to the Nazi party and, not long after that, the Holborns immigrated to the United States. They settled in New Haven, Connecticut because Professor Holborn, thanks to the intercession of the Carnegie Foundation, which had endowed his Berlin chair, had been offered a post on the Yale University faculty. The Holborns became naturalized American citizens in 1940.

By her own account, Hanna Holborn was "a brat," an "ill-behaved, tomboyish, independent, stubborn, and bad-tempered" child who was strictly disciplined by her parents. Among other restrictions, the Holborns monitored their children's movie-going and limited their radio listening to two programs a week in addition to news broadcasts and classical music concerts. "We were brought up under all kinds of German theories," Mrs. Gray told Giovanna Breu in an interview for *People* magazine (October 30, 1978). "We weren't allowed to use pillows, and we had to eat rye bread. White American bread was some kind of unhealthy thing." She especially resented having to wear dirndl skirts. "I wanted to look like the other American children, with plaid skirts, knee socks, and saddle shoes," she said.

Her parents were more liberal in their approach to her intellectual development and need for self-reliance. From an early age, they encouraged Hanna to explore the neighborhood on her own, to read widely, and to make her own choices, "so long as they were serious." She attended the Foote School, a private institution favored by faculty families. During World War II, the school's student body and teaching staff were enriched by an influx of foreigners who had sought refuge in the United States, and Hanna was, as she put it years later, "stretched" by her extraordinary teachers and by "those English children." During school vacations she often lied about her age to get summer jobs that she thought would help prepare her for a hoped-for career in journalism or publishing.

When she was fifteen, Hanna Holborn enrolled at Bryn Mawr College in Bryn Mawr, Pennsylvania. Because most of her classmates were older, wealthier, and more mature socially, her freshman adjustment was difficult. She soon settled in, however, and in a short time, she was writing editorials, sometimes critical of the school administration, for the Bryn Mawr College News. After taking her A.B. degree summa cum laude in 1950, Hanna Holborn continued her education as a Fulbright scholar at St. Anne's College, Oxford University. On her return to the United States in 1952, she enrolled in the doctoral program in Renaissance intellectual history at Radcliffe College in Cambridge, Massachusetts, but interrupted her work the following academic year—1953-54—to teach history at Bryn Mawr. On June 19, 1954 Miss Holborn married Charles Montgomery Gray, a Harvard graduate student she had met in a seminar on Erasmus. That autumn she resumed her graduate studies on an American Association of University Women fellowship. From 1955 to 1957, while completing her dissertation, "History and Rhetoric in Quattrocento Humanism," she was a teaching fellow in Harvard University's history department.

On receiving her Ph.D. degree in 1957, Hanna Gray joined the Harvard faculty as an instructor in history. Two years later she advanced to the rank of assistant professor. Her lectures were unusually well-attended and her students reportedly applauded at the conclusion of many sessions. In 1960 Mrs. Gray moved with her husband to Chicago, where he was an associate professor at the University of Chicago. After spending a year as a research fellow at the Newberry Library, she too joined the university faculty as an assistant professor of history. In 1964 she was granted tenure and promoted to associate professor. During the latter half of the 1960's Hanna Holborn Gray headed the undergraduate history faculty and, with her husband, edited the Journal of Modern History. Respected by faculty and students alike, Mrs. Gray defused one potentially explosive situation when she chaired a committee reviewing the denial of tenure to Marlene Dixon, a sociologist and militant feminist. The students, who had staged a sit-in to protest Professor Dixon's dismissal, accepted the committee's conclusion upholding the original decision.

During that period Hanna Gray was a visiting lecturer at Harvard (1963-64); a research fellow (1966-67) and visiting scholar (1970-71) at Stanford University's Center for Advanced Study in the Behavioral Sciences; a visiting associate professor of history at the University of California at Berkeley (1970-71); and a Phi Beta Kappa visiting scholar (1971-72). Her scholarly research bore fruit in several well-received essays, including "Valla's Encomium of St. Thomas Aquinas and the Humanist Conception of Christian Antiquity," published in Essays in History and Literature (Newberry Library, 1965), and "Machiavelli: The Art of Politics and the Paradox of Power," which appeared in The Responsibility of Power (Doubleday, 1967), a festschrift volume of historical essays in honor of her father, written by his students and friends, and edited by Leonard Krieger.

In 1972 Hanna Gray became the first woman to be named dean of arts and sciences at Northwestern University in Evanston, Illinois, heading the undergraduate college, with an enrollment of 3,000 and 550-member faculty. Serving in addition as professor of history, she remained at Northwestern until July 1974, when she returned to New Haven, her old hometown, to become the provost of Yale University. The Yale appointment was a double distinction since the post had never before been held by a woman and only rarely by a non-Yale graduate, but Mrs. Gray, who had served as a Yale trustee since 1971, was well acquainted with the university and its staggering fiscal deficit. Responsible for the overall planning of the operating budget and the academic curriculum, she struck a balance between retrenchment and the maintenance of vital programs and educational excellence. She judiciously pared nonessential programs, settled a crippling eighty-day strike by Yale's 1,400 service employees and, at the risk of losing some popularity on campus, closed the Faculty Club, thus saving the university some $85,000 annually.

Since the provostship has often served as a steppingstone to the presidency of Yale, there was widespread speculation, almost from the outset of her tenure, that Hanna Gray was the chosen successor of the incumbent president, Kingman Brewster Jr. When Brewster resigned in May 1977 to become United States Ambassador to Great Britain, Mrs. Gray automatically became Yale's acting president. Continuing her policy of fiscal toughness, she tightened requirements for tenure, instituted a hiring freeze, and raised undergraduate tuition by $350 a year. To aid students caught in the financial crunch, Mrs. Gray came out in favor of a program of direct federal aid to students.

Despite many indications that Yale's rather traditionalist alumni, on whom it depends for financial contributions, would have resented the appointment of a woman to the university's top post, Hanna Gray was one of the search committee's prime candidates for the presidency. In December 1977, however, she unexpectedly and dramatically removed herself from contention when she agreed to succeed John T. Wilson as the tenth president of the University of Chicago. Although she candidly admitted to having had some qualms about her decision, Mrs. Gray told reporters that she had decided to accept the "irresistible invitation" because "Chicago is an absolutely first-rate institution where we have the momentum to make a difference in the world of education." "What I am bringing [to the job] is a very high regard for the institution and for the city in which the institution is situated," she said at a news conference on January 9, 1978. "What I am bringing is some experience with the institution."

When she officially took office on July 1, 1978 at a salary reported to be in the mid-$40,000 range, Hanna Gray assumed responsibility for one of America's most prominent universities. Founded in 1891 by John D. Rockefeller, the so-called "Harvard of the Midwest," occupies more than 140 buildings in the Hyde Park district on Chicago's south side, as well as other facilities, such as the Yerkes Observatory in Williams Bay, Wisconsin. Its undergraduate college, four graduate divisions, and six professional schools have a total enrollment of nearly 8,000 students and a faculty of 1,050, giving it an almost unequaled 1:8 faculty-student ratio. Because about 40 percent of its 90,000 living alumni work in the field of higher education the University of Chicago is also known as the "teacher of teachers." Of its former students and faculty, 140 are currently college presidents, and forty-two are Nobel laureates.

Hanna Holborn Gray's chief concern as president is to maintain the university's academic quality in the face of inevitable financial constraints, for Chicago, like most other American universities, has been seriously afflicted by the recession-inflation cycle of the 1970's. Its problem is compounded, however, by its deliberate policy of keeping undergraduate tuition nearly $1,000 below that of comparable Ivy League universities, and by its reluctance to use graduate teaching assistants, resulting in higher instructional costs.

Although its most recent four-year fund-raising drive, which ended in June 1978, fell $105 million short of its announced goal of $280 million, the university currently has a balanced budget. But Mrs. Gray makes a distinction between a balanced budget and "fundamental financial health." Because of soaring costs, inflationary pressures, and the declining value of endowments, she believes that Chicago, too, must rigorously tighten its belt and carefully plan for the future. "We have to accept the fact that the go-go period of growth is over," Mrs. Gray told Paul Galloway in an interview for the Chicago Sun-Times (July 16, 1978). "We know that the college-age population is not growing,

and we know that public support for education isn't something that is going to grow indefinitely, so we've got to learn to live in a situation of limitations without thinking that limitations are necessarily negatives. We must learn to make the right choices for change. . . . The major priority is to learn to develop, to innovate, to adapt, to produce fresh ideas, and to support the best of what is new in the disciplines without necessarily growing."

To keep liberal education alive in an institution that has for decades concentrated on graduate study and professional training, Mrs. Gray plans to make the undergraduate college "more visible," "a little larger," and "a little more fun." To offset planned tuition increases and attract more freshmen from the middle class, she has proposed a revision of the student loan program, allowing students to repay their loans over a longer period of time. She also favors active recruitment of minority students and, although she flatly rejects quota systems as "immoral," she supports flexible affirmative action programs. A self-described "old-fashioned Bryn Mawr feminist," she is especially interested in increasing teaching and administrative opportunities for women. "I'm interested in the goals of equal opportunity in general," she explained to Paul Galloway. "That includes equal opportunity for women. I'm interested in being sure that people are able, through their own competence, to develop their own independence. These are goals for women, but they are also goals for people. I find it hard to make the distinction."

Mrs. Gray is a former member of the National Council on the Humanities, the Carnegie Institution of Washington, and the Institute for Advanced Study at Princeton University. She is a fellow of the American Academy of Arts and Sciences, a member of the Senate of Phi Beta Kappa, the American Historical Association, and the Renaissance Society of America, and a trustee of Bryn Mawr College, the Center for Advanced study in the Behavioral Sciences, and the Mayo Foundation. Named a director of J. P. Morgan & Co. and its subsidiary, the Morgan Guaranty Trust Co., in 1976, she is also a director of the Cummins Engine Company. Lawrence University, Grinnell College, St. Mary's College, Denison University, Wheaton College, and Oxford University, among others, have awarded her honorary degrees.

Since moving to Chicago, the Grays have made their home in the fifteen-room President's House on campus. The couple also has a nineteenth-century farmhouse in Vermont. Charles Gray, the author or coauthor of several scholarly works, including Renaissance and Reformation England, 1509-1714 (Harcourt, 1973) and The History of the Common Law in England (University of Chicago Press, 1971), is a professor of history at the University of Chicago. Although her husband plays squash or tennis daily, Mrs. Gray, in her words, "just sits." She is, however, an avid baseball and football fan and often attends the home games of the Chicago Bears as well as most of the university's sports contests.

In her New York *Post* (September 25, 1976) profile, Hope MacLeod described Hanna Holborn Gray as a "pleasant-faced woman with graying hair, alert blue eyes, sensible attire, and unpretentious manner." Mrs. Gray's friends and colleagues say she is warm and unfailingly cheerful, an amusing raconteur, and an accomplished mimic, especially of Dr. Henry A. Kissinger, the former Secretary of State. "I really like what I'm doing," she told Hope MacLeod. "I'm almost never bored. There are obviously things one enjoys less and there are aspects of work that are tedious, but that doesn't necessarily make them boring. Real work, after all, involves tough stuff and tedious stuff as well as the interesting stuff."

References: Intellect 102:209 Ja '74; N Y Post p23 S 25 '76 por; N Y Times p23 D 11 '77 por; People 10:86+ O 30 '78 pors; Directory of American Scholars, 1974; Who's Who in America, 1978-79; Who's Who of American Women, 1977-78

Guidry, Ron (gid'rē)

Aug. 28, 1950- Baseball player. Address: b. New York Yankees, Yankee Stadium, 161st St. and River Ave., Bronx, N.Y. 10451

The New York Yankees years ago built their reputation as the "Bronx Bombers" on the power hitting of such legendary sluggers as Babe Ruth, Lou Gehrig, Joe DiMaggio, and Mickey Mantle; in 1978 it was Ron Guidry, the tobacco-chewing, flame-throwing pitcher who captured the headlines as he helped the revived Yankees win their third straight American League pennant with his shotgun left arm. A product of the Yankee farm system, Guidry spent six years in the minor leagues before making the Yankee squad in 1977. Relying almost exclusively on his smoking fastball, "Louisiana Lightnin'" Guidry won twenty-five games during the 1978 regular season while losing only three, and his earned-run average was an awe-inspiring 1.74. In the modern era only Sandy Koufax has had a comparable year.

Perhaps most importantly for the Yankees, Guidry has developed into a dependable "stopper." Fifteen of his victories, including the 1978 division title playoff win over the Boston Red Sox, came after Yankee losses. Although he was the unanimous choice for the 1978 American League Cy Young Award, Guidry insists he still has a lot to learn about pitching. "I still need a lot of polishing," he said in a recent interview. "I still don't put myself in the same league as [Jim] Palmer or [Tom] Seaver or [Jim ("Catfish")] Hunter." In 1979, when the Yankees finished fourth in the American League East, Guidry won eighteen and lost eight in thirty-three appearances, and his earned-run average was 2.78.

The descendant of French exiles from Nova Scotia who settled in the Mississippi River bayous in the mid-eighteenth century, Ronald Ames Guidry was born in Lafayette, Louisiana on August 28, 1950 to Roland Guidry, a railroad conductor, and his wife Grace. He has one brother, Travis, who is eighteen years his junior. An impudent, prankish youngster —a *canaille*, or "little rascal" in the Cajun dialect of his family—Ron Guidry spent much of his childhood playing practical jokes. Because his mother feared he would get in trouble, Guidry was not allowed to join the other neighborhood boys in sports, but he often watched pickup baseball games at the local playground. One afternoon, a Little League coach saw him retrieve a ball that had rolled foul in the outfield and fire it back toward the mound. Recognizing the boy's natural ability, the coach persuaded the Guidrys to let their son join the Little League team.

Since Lafayette's Northside High School, which Guidry attended in the mid-1960's, did not have a baseball team, he played outfield and pitched for the local American Legion team. Meanwhile, he tested his exceptional speed on Northside's track squad and quarterbacked a Teener League touch football team to two consecutive citywide championships. After graduating from high school in 1968, Guidry enrolled at the University of Southwestern Louisiana to study architecture on an American Legion scholarship. Inevitably he went out for extramural baseball and quickly earned a spot on the team's pitching staff, even though he was, by his own modest account, "not very good." His college career totals, however, include one no-hitter, several one-hitters, and a very respectable 2.37 earned-run average—a record good enough to attract the attention of major league scouts, among them Atley Donald, a former pitcher for the New York Yankees. On Donald's recommendation, the Yankees selected Guidry as their third choice in the free-agent draft in June 1971.

For the next four years Guidry shuttled between Yankee farm clubs in Tennessee, Florida, North Carolina, and Connecticut, compiling an undistinguished 13-16 record with an overall ERA of 3.60. But coaches were quick to point out to the skeptical Yankee management the young pitcher's high strikeout percentage, his strong, whiplike delivery, and his quick reflexes. Converted to a short reliever, Guidry gave up twenty-four runs on forty-six hits and fanned seventy-six men in sixty-three innings for Syracuse in 1975. Although he won just one more game than he lost, his ERA dropped dramatically from 5.62 in 1974 to 2.86. Called up to the Yankees later that year, he was the pitcher of record in only one of the ten games in which he appeared (he lost), but he still managed to give a fairly good account of himself, allowing six earned runs in fifteen innings.

In spring training in 1976 Guidry pitched exceptionally well and was promised the backup slot in the bullpen, behind Sparky Lyle, the Yankees' ace "fireman." Instead he was shunted to Syracuse to make room for more experienced, high-priced hands on the tight pitching roster. A few weeks later, however, he was back in Yankee Stadium pitching against the Yankees' archrival, the Boston Red Sox, in a hard-fought contest marked by a bench-emptying brawl. In a relief role, a rattled Guidry gave up four earned runs on four hits, including a towering two-run blast by Carl Yastrzemski, in just one-third of an inning. He spent the next forty-six games in the bullpen, without throwing a single pitch.

On July 6 the Yankees optioned Guidry to Syracuse. Frustrated, discouraged, and tired of being "yanked up and down like a yo-yo," Guidry packed his car and, with his wife Bonnie, headed south to Louisiana. "Bonnie talked me into giving it one more chance," he told Steve Jacobson in an interview for Newsday (April 23, 1978). "I made a U-turn and reported to Syracuse. If I hadn't it would

have bothered me all my life, wondering if I was really that bad that they couldn't use me or if I was really good enough."

In his first time out with Syracuse, Guidry was summoned from the bullpen in the eighth inning to preserve a slim one-run lead. With the bases loaded and only one out, he calmly struck out the first two men to face him, and in the ninth inning he retired the side with three more strikeouts. As the club's top short relief man, Guidry quickly grew accustomed to pitching himself out of trouble. In the forty innings he pitched for Syracuse, he struck out fifty batters, walked thirteen, and gave up only four runs on fifteen hits for an astounding ERA of 0.68. Impressed, the Yankees added Guidry to their pitching roster for the pennant playoffs against the Kansas City Royals, but his sole appearance was as a pinch runner. He did not play in the World Series, which the Yankees dropped to the Cincinnati Reds in four straight games.

Admittedly out of practice, Guidry was repeatedly "shelled" in spring training exhibition games in 1977. "It seems to me the reason you have spring training is to get in shape," he explained to Sam Moses, in an interview for a Sports Illustrated (January 22, 1979) profile. "The way I get in shape is by just throwing fastballs, fastballs, fastballs, right down the middle. Let them hit it. . . . In spring training, nothing counts." But when Guidry's ERA mushroomed to 10.24, George M. Steinbrenner, the Yankees' owner, began casting around for a trade. Gabe Paul, then the Yankees' general manager and now the president of the Cleveland Indians, jumped to Guidry's defense. "When you see a fellow perform the way Guidry did in Syracuse, see the native talent, the strength of his arm, his ability to get out of a jam, his attitude, you have to pay attention to a pitcher like that," Paul told Sam Moses. "If George had offered him up for a trade, they'd have stood in line for him."

After making a handful of strong appearances in relief, Guidry was pressed into service as a starting pitcher on April 29, 1977. Facing the Seattle Mariners on just one hour's notice, Guidry nervously loaded the bases in the first inning before he settled down to retire the side. With his blinding fastball and a deceptive slider learned from Sparky Lyle, he kept batters guessing for eight and one-third innings before handing over the ball to Lyle, who saved the 3-0 shutout for Guidry's first major league victory.

As the Yankees tried to make do with a pitching staff crippled by injuries, Guidry was shifted back and forth from starting assignments to stints in the bullpen. Accustomed to brief relief appearances, he seemed to be physically incapable of pitching a complete game. In five of his six starts, he left the mound after eight and one-third innings. Finally, in a game against Kansas City on

June 16, Guidry went the distance to win, 7-0, with a three-hitter. By the midseason All-Star break, Guidry, with his record of six wins and five losses, had won a regular slot in the pitching rotation.

When, from the beginning of August to the middle of September, the Yankees won twenty-eight out of thirty-four games and climbed from third place to first in the American League East standings, their phenomenal surge was largely due to Ron Guidry's dependable pitching. The most reliable of the Yankee starters, he won eight straight games down the stretch, including two consecutive walk-less shutouts. In one astonishing display of control against the second-place Red Sox on September 13, he struck out the side with ten pitches and went on to win, 4-2. Guidry finished out the regular season with a 16-7 record and an ERA of 2.82. His 176 strikeout total was high for the team and second only to Nolan Ryan's in the American League.

Down by one game to Kansas City in the American League playoffs in October 1977, Billy Martin, the Yankee manager, looked to his star pitcher to even the score. Turning in a superlative performance, Guidry systematically mowed down the Royals, allowing just three scattered hits and two runs as the Yankees won, 6-2. With the playoffs tied at two games apiece, Guidry took to the mound again after only two days' rest—he normally requires four—in the fifth and deciding game. Obviously tired and admittedly "a little leery," he gave up three runs before he was relieved by Mike Torrez in the third inning. In the fourth game of the World Series, Guidry held the power-hitting Los Angeles Dodgers to four hits and lowered their team batting average against Yankee pitching to a dismal .190. The Yankees took the series, four games to two.

With Catfish Hunter injured and Don Gullett and Andy Messersmith on the disabled list, Guidry turned out to be the mainstay of the starting pitching staff during the first half of the 1978 season. By mid-June, despite occasional bouts of what he called the "seventh-inning blues," he had chalked up ten straight victories and his 1.57 ERA was by far the best in the major leagues. His most spectacular win—his eleventh—came on June 17 when he struck out eighteen California Angels before a stomping, screaming crowd in Yankee Stadium. Guidry admitted later that he "got away with a lot" because the cheering made the batters "a little nervous." "That game established me in the hitters' minds," he told Steve Jacobson of Newsday (November 1, 1978). "Guys started being defensive after that." The eighteen strikeouts shattered Bob Shawkey's sixty-year-old club record. Before he was finally stopped at thirteen wins by the Milwaukee Brewers on July 7, Guidry broke another club record—that for consecutive victories, which had been jointly held at twelve games by Tom Zachary and Atley Donald.

As the Yankees scrambled to make up a fourteen-game deficit in the last half of the season, Guidry continued to baffle opposing teams with his consistently superlative pitching. A self-described "power pitcher," he has no use for what he calls "trickery" and relies almost entirely on his fastball, usually hurled at about ninety miles per hour, and his wicked, offspeed slider, which he throws with a motion he has compared to "pulling down a windowshade." Working quickly and rhythmically, with no wasted motion, he uses his entire body to give the ball an extra push. Supremely confident and self-assured on the mound, he fears no hitter in the league, with the possible exception of Rod Carew. "When I'm strong and throwing hard, the hitters aren't going to hit me very much," he told one reporter. "I don't care if they bring a telephone pole up there." Moreover, Guidry is an excellent fielder and routinely turns bunts and dribblers into easy outs.

In September the Yankee pennant drive accelerated, and Guidry contributed to that effort with two successive shutouts over the Red Sox. But the Sox fought back and the division title rested on the outcome of a single playoff game. With the pennant at stake, Bob Lemon, who had taken over as manager in late July, called on Guidry. Pitching just three days after his last victory, Guidry gave up two runs on six hits before entrusting the game to Rich "Goose" Gossage in the sixth inning. The Yankees erupted for five runs in the late innings to capture the division title and preserve Guidry's twenty-fifth victory.

In the league playoffs against Kansas City, Guidry held the Royals to one run on seven hits and, with the help of Gossage, won the deciding fourth game. Following two humiliating defeats in Dodger Stadium, the Yankees returned to New York and sent their "stopper" to the mound in the third game of the World Series. Exhausted from the long, pressure-packed season, Guidry had trouble controlling his slider, and his fastball, the most effective weapon in his arsenal, did not have "that extra pop." In nine innings he threw 160 pitches, an unusually high number for him, walked seven men while striking out only three, and gave up one run on eight hits. The game was saved for him by the fielding of third baseman Graig Nettles, who made three sensational plays—two with the bases loaded—to rob the Dodgers of at least five runs. Rallying behind their pitcher, the Yankees scraped together five runs to take the first of four straight games and also to capture their second consecutive world championship.

Guidry's statistics for the regular season were awesome. He led the majors in wins (twenty-five), shutouts (nine), winning percentage (.893) and ERA (1.74). His ERA was the second lowest by a lefthander in American League history and his winning percentage was the best ever by a twenty-game winner. Opposing teams batted just .193 against him, and his 248 strikeouts, the second-best total in the league, established a new club record, breaking the previous mark of 239 set by Jack Chesbro in 1904 (when the Yankees were still known as the Highlanders).

With those totals, Guidry clinched the Cy Young award, and in the eyes of many baseball aficionados he deserved the American League's Most Valuable Player Award as well. His chief competitor for the MVP was Jim Rice, the Boston slugger who led the majors in hits, triples, homers, RBI's, and total bases. Some sportswriters contended that Rice deserved the award because he, unlike Guidry, played every day; others, among them *Newsweek's* Pete Axthelm, reasoned that "while the Red Sox might be a respectable team without Rice, the Yanks would be nowhere at all without Guidry." Inevitably drawn into the controversy, Guidry reminded reporters that Rice had gotten only two hits off him all year. "If they [the Baseball Writers Association of America, the organization that bestowes the award] don't want to give the MVP to a pitcher, they should put an asterisk next to it," he said. When Rice won the balloting, 352 votes to Guidry's 291, Guidry issued a public statement congratulating the outfielder, adding that it gave him "something to gun for in 1979." Guidry won the Seagram Seven Crowns of Sport Award and shared the Joe Cronin Award for Distinguished Achievement with Rice. Named to the All-Star teams selected by the *Sporting News, Baseball Bulletin,* the Associated Press, and United Press International, he was also chosen as the Major League Player of the Year and Man of the Year by the *Sporting News,* Major League Player of the Year by *Baseball Digest,* Performer of the Year by *Baseball Quarterly,* and Male Athlete of the Year by the Associated Press.

Compared to such players as Pete Rose, Rod Carew, and Reggie Jackson, whose astronomical salaries have altered the economics of professional baseball, Ron Guidry is a bargain. His salary in 1978 was $38,000 and his current contract, which runs through 1981. carries a salary of about $200,000 annually. Guidry has turned down more than $200,000 in endorsement offers and steadfastly refuses to lend his name to any product he does not use. He recently agreed to appear in commercials for Burger King, the fast-food chain that sponsors baseball's pitch, hit, and run contest, "because that's working with kids." Guidry has also volunteered his services for the Special Olympics, a program of athletic training and competition for mentally retarded youngsters. With his younger brother, who is mentally retarded, Guidry spends as much time in the off season as possible, and he has taught him how to play football, basketball, and baseball.

A lean and sinewy five feet eleven inches tall, Guidry never weighs more than 160 pounds. He has a handsome, finely chiseled face, wavy blue-black hair, what have been described as "root-beer colored" eyes, and a riverboat cardshark's mustache. His long, thin legs are deceptively strong, and he works out regularly on a Nautilus machine to give himself the power to "drive off the mound" even harder. A soft-spoken and unassuming man with a wry sense of humor, he is well-liked by his often contentious teammates, and sportswriters say he is uncommonly cooperative and genuinely grateful for the attention showered on him.

On September 23, 1972 Guidry married Bonnie Rutledge. During the season the Guidrys and their daughter Jamie live in a rented apartment in Hackensack, New Jersey. They make their winter home outside Lafayette, Louisiana in a three-bedroom cedar house with a cathedral ceiling that Guidry himself designed. There, accompanied by his grandfather, boyhood friends, and, occasionally, by Catfish Hunter, he hunts ducks and small game almost daily. He still enjoys a game of touch football and recently took up golf. When forced indoors by the weather, he plays chess and ping-pong or reads histories of the Civil War. In an interview in February 1979 Guidry conceded that it would be difficult to live up to his league-leading performance. "There is no reason to expect it will happen again soon," he said. "To tell the truth, I'll be just as happy not winning twenty if I could win the one game that gives up another pennant."

References: Esquire 91:78+ Ja 2 '79 pors; Sport 67:39+ O '78 por, 68:14+ F '79 pors; Sporting News p24 Je 17 '78 por, p3+ Ja 6 '79 por; Sports Illus 50:62+ Ja 22 '79 pors; Linn, Ed. Inside the Yankees: the Championship Year (1978)

Hamilton, Margaret

Dec. 9, 1902- Actress. Address: c/o Michael Thomas Agency, 22 E. 60th St., New York City, N.Y. 10022

For over half a century Margaret Hamilton's performances in some seventy-five movies, in at least as many stage plays throughout the United States, and in more radio and television dramas than she can remember, have given audiences the impression that

Margaret Hamilton

virtually all the characters she portrays have been tailored especially for her. In the two roles, however, for which she is instantly recognized, the Wicked Witch of the West of *The Wizard of Oz* and Cora of the Maxwell House Coffee television ads, she created nontypecast personalities in different media. Both are genuine, as are her contrasting portrayals for the theatre of Mrs. Malaprop and Grandma of *The American Dream*, because she combines sincerity and imagination with a sharp and sure technical proficiency. Appropriately for an actress who had once set her heart on a career as a kindergarten teacher, Margaret Hamilton is likely to owe a place in Americana to the witch that she has enacted a dozen times in musical versions of *Oz* on the stage while enthralling new generations of youngsters as the 1939 film continues to be shown periodically on TV.

Margaret Hamilton Meserve was born in Cleveland, Ohio on December 9, 1902, the youngest of the four children (three girls and one boy) of Walter Jones Hamilton, an attorney, and Jennie (Adams) Hamilton. Her musically accomplished mother had given up her career as a pianist and organist after her marriage. One of Margaret Hamilton's assets as a character actress has been her distinctive nose, whose bump she inherited from her father. At school she was so fond of her kindergarten and first-grade teachers that she wanted to follow their example. Accounting further for her early desire to be a schoolteacher, she has said, "I was born loving devotedly—first my dolls, then babies and children (little ones)."

When she was twelve, Margaret Hamilton helped in the kindergarten at Hathaway

Brown School, a private school now in Shaker Heights. As a student there she later enjoyed being cheerleader for the basketball team, which was the only team that competed with teams from other girls' schools, and, more significantly, she gloried in performing in the senior play. In her first taste of acting she portrayed an elderly Englishman, Sir Peter Antrobus, in *Pomander Walk*. Encouraged by the enthusiastic applause of her friends and some of her relatives, she suggested to her parents that she ought to train for the stage—a course that seemed all the more imperative because she had been studying voice with Miss Grace Probert for the past four years. "You'll do no such thing," her mother replied. "You'll go to Wheelock, as you've always wanted to, and when you know how to earn your living, you can fool around with the theatre all you want to."

Wheelock Kindergarten Training School (now Wheelock College) in Boston, in which she enrolled in 1921, gave Miss Hamilton no cause for regret. Rather, she feels, her better understanding of children has enriched her life. At the school she served as president of the senior class and played Jo in a student production of *Little Women*. When she had obtained her teaching certificate in 1923, she returned to Cleveland to work for a year in the Hough neighborhood as an assistant kindergarten teacher. During the next three years she ran her own nursery school, before going to New York to teach kindergarten in the Rye Country Day School. But with the death of her mother the following year, she became needed at home.

Again Miss Hamilton opened her own private nursery school in Cleveland. The Broadway plays she had seen while living fairly near Manhattan, however, had rekindled her desire for an acting career, and in 1927 she became a member of the Cleveland Play House, where she had earlier, in 1923, appeared for the first time on the professional stage in *The Man Who Ate the Popomack*. During her three-year apprenticeship at the Play House she performed in twenty-five roles, including Prossy in *Candida* and Miss Prism in *The Importance of Being Earnest*. "At last I experienced the indescribable joy of doing what I longed to do," she has recalled, as quoted in the *Wheelock Alumnae Quarterly* (Winter 1971). ". . . I think this is the greatest joy of all—to be able to do the thing you truly, deeply want to do. In other words, to express your particular gift."

Guided by another aspiring actress, with whom she had appeared in a revue one summer at the Dennis Playhouse in Massachusetts, Miss Hamilton made the rounds of Broadway casting agents through a long, desperate year that nevertheless left her enthusiasm for the theatre undiminished. During the summer of 1931 she met the producer Arthur Beckhard, who gave her a part in one of several new plays he was trying out in Greenwich, Connecticut. As Helen in Rose Franken's *The Hallams,* she portrayed a warmhearted, though acerbic, wife whose victimization by a possessive mother-in-law takes the form, in part, of being required to help herself to grapes whenever they are passed. In that role Margaret Hamilton made her Broadway debut when the play, retitled *Another Language,* opened at the Booth Theatre in April 1932.

A surprise hit that ran for nearly a year on Broadway, *Another Language* also became Miss Hamilton's passport to Hollywood. She repeated the role of Helen Hallam in MGM's 1933 release of Rose Franken's film adaptation of the play, matching the effectiveness of her stage performance. From then on she divided her time between the theatre and the screen with apparently easy adjustment of her talents to different media demands. After appearing in the short-lived melodrama *The Dark Tower* on the New York stage in the fall of 1933 and in five movies of 1934, including *Broadway Bill* (Columbia), she played Lucy Gurget, the redoubtable cook on an Erie Canal barge, in *The Farmer Takes a Wife,* which opened on Broadway in October 1934. Because of the authenticity of her characterization, she was cast in the same role in Fox's 1935 film version of the play.

The star of *The Farmer Takes a Wife,* both on the stage and screen was Henry Fonda, with whom Margaret Hamilton again appeared in *Way Down East* (Fox). In that 1935 remake of D. W. Griffith's silent classic, she portrayed the prissy, trouble-making town gossip. Her other roles of the 1930's included a boardinghouse landlady in *Chatterbox* (RKO), the housekeeper of a mountain lodge in *The Moon's Our Home* (Paramount); the outraged woman who slaps the villainous schoolgirl in *These Three* (Goldwyn-United Artists), a movie based on Lillian Hellman's *The Children's Hour;* a fiancée of twenty years in *Mountain Justice* (Warner Brothers); a teacher in a reform school in *A Slight Case of Murder* (Warner Brothers); and a five-time widow in *Stablemates* (MGM).

In all, Margaret Hamilton played in some twenty-five films before being cast as the detestable Mrs. Gulch and the Wicked Witch of the West in MGM's 1939 masterpiece, *The Wizard of Oz*—a dual role for which she tried out in competition with, among others, Gale Sondergaard, who had a knack for sinister characterization. Because of her fondness for children, Miss Hamilton enjoyed creating the crackle-voiced, green-skinned, broom-wielding personification of evil, the nemesis of the young heroine, Dorothy, played by Judy Garland. The witch, however, is not Margaret Hamilton's favorite role. "I don't look on it as any great shakes of acting," she explained to Al Cohn in an interview for *Newsday* (March 19, 1978). "It's not subtle or restrained. It isn't any of the things you like to think might apply to your acting."

To extend its appeal to adults, *The Wizard of Oz* combines a certain sophistication with its broad characterization. Children, nevertheless, no doubt account for the high Nielsen ratings that the film has regularly received since it was first telecast in 1956. Its popularity on TV annually generates hundreds of letters to Miss Hamilton, mainly from children. She repeatedly advises parents that children under seven may be upset by a witch that older children find delightfully scary.

Despite her identification with the witch in the minds of audiences, Miss Hamilton was able to dispel that image in a great many, if not so diversified, character roles. "I've done some hard-bitten parts," she once said in summing up the Hollywood phase of her career, "but most of the time I've been the cantankerous cook or the acidulous aunt with a corset of steel and a heart of gold." In one of her more memorable movies, the Mae West-W. C. Fields farcical western, *My Little Chickadee* (Universal, 1940), she was the gossipy Mrs. Gideon, whose malicious tattling threatens the efforts of Miss West's Flower Bell Lee to redeem her reputation.

Moviegoers saw Miss Hamilton only briefly in another classic, *The Ox-Bow Incident* (Twentieth Century-Fox, 1943), in which she was scarcely more than a face in the crowd. But as the housekeeper Hilda in the psychological thriller *Guest in the House* (United Artists, 1945), she effected "some acute character delineation," in the words of Howard Barnes of the New York *Herald Tribune* (February 11, 1945). Her other roles include the stern spinster in *George White's Scandals* (RKO, 1945); the maid of a political boss in Frank Capra's *State of the Union* (MGM, 1948); the unsympathetic schoolteacher in *The Red Pony* (Republic, 1949); the judge's wife in the antic western *The Beautiful Blonde from Bashful Bend* (Twentieth Century-Fox, 1949); and the threatening, witch-like housekeeper, Elaine Zacharides, in *13 Ghosts* (Columbia, 1960).

Recreating character types by now long familiar to her, Miss Hamilton was Mrs. Klopplebobbler, the harridan of *The Daydreamer* (Embassy, 1966), based on Hans Christian Andersen's stories, and the maid, Mae, in the excellent supporting cast of the domestic drama-comedy *Rosie* (Universal, 1967). In Robert Altman's satiric fantasy *Brewster McCloud* (MGM, 1970) she played Daphne Heap, the nasty-tempered dowager who in exchange for subsidizing the Houston Astrodome is privileged to sing the National Anthem at its sports and civic events and who dies wearing the ruby slippers that the witch coveted in *The Wizard of Oz*. She had a minor role in the convoluted crime melodrama *The Anderson Tapes* (Columbia, 1971).

For some fifteen years Margaret Hamilton lived in Los Angeles before establishing permanent residence in New York City in 1951.

Wherever her home has been, she has traveled back and forth from coast to coast to perform in both the movies and the theatre and later also in television. Discussing her preference for the stage in an article that she wrote for *Junior League News* several years ago, she spoke of the importance to her of the response of the audience and went on to say, "Only in the theatre do you have the opportunity to experiment, to change, to grow, to better each performance."

On an early excursion from Hollywood, during the summer of 1941, Margaret Hamilton played in stock at the Lakewood Theatre in Skowhegan, Maine. Among the seventeen plays in which she appeared were *Major Barbara*, *Old Acquaintance*, and *Ladies in Retirement*. After an absence of almost a decade she returned to Broadway in the fall of 1943 as Gertrude in *Outrageous Fortune*. She later won good notices from New York critics for her portrayals of Mrs. Zero in *The Adding Machine* (1956) and Clara in the two-character *Save Me a Place at Forest Lawn* (1963), among others. Dolly Tate of *Annie Get Your Gun*, Aunt Eller of *Oklahoma!*, and Parthy Ann Hawks of *Show Boat* were her roles in musicals in which she performed in both New York and regional productions.

Los Angeles theatregoers meanwhile saw Miss Hamilton as the aunt in *On Borrowed Time* (1946) and as Grandma, one of her favorite roles, in Edward Albee's *The American Dream* (1962). Another of her many roles on the West Coast was the holier-than-thou Mrs. Dudgeon in a 1978 production of *The Devil's Disciple*, a play in which she had toured in the summer of 1958. At the Seattle Repertory Theatre she appeared as the dotty spiritualist Madame Arcati in *Blithe Spirit* (1966) and in various classical roles, including Mrs. Malaprop in *The Rivals* (1967-68). For fifty-one weeks during 1974-75 she toured as Madame Armfeldt in Stephen Sondheim's *A Little Night Music*, stealing the show with ease, some critics thought, by her performance as the retired high society courtesan.

During the premiere season of the BAM Theater Company of the Brooklyn Academy of Music, Margaret Hamilton shared in the warm praise that greeted Langdon Mitchell's comedy of manners *The New York Idea* (March 1977), in which she played the crabbed aunt, Miss Heneage, and Chekhov's *The Three Sisters* (May 1977), which provided one of the roles she has most enjoyed, the nurse. Over the years audiences at the Cleveland Play House have joyfully welcomed Margaret Hamilton back several times, most recently to open the 1978-79 season as the odious hypochondriac, Mrs. Bramson, in Emlyn Williams' thriller *Night Must Fall*.

When television was young and "live," Margaret Hamilton, whose voice had long been well known to radio listeners, performed in dozens of dramatic productions, including *The Man Who Came to Dinner* (CBS, 1954),

The Devil's Disciple (NBC, 1955), *The Trial of Lizzie Borden* (ABC, 1957), and *The Silver Whistle* (1959). She has had running parts in *Secret Storm*, *As the World Turns*, and other continuing dramas; has played in episodes of *The Patty Duke Show*, *The Addams Family*, and *The Partridge Family*, among similar series; and has made scores of guest appearances on comedy and variety programs such as *This Is the Week That Was* and the Johnny Carson, David Frost, Dick Cavett, and Paul Lynde shows.

On television commercials Miss Hamilton has been seen as the harassed woman trying to cope with an excessively busy day for Jell-O and has been heard as the voice of Emily Tipp, an amusing cartoon character of popular ads for Tip-Top Bread. Since 1972 she has delighted millions as Cora, the New England storekeeper who sells only one brand of coffee—Maxwell House. As Jo-Ann Balzarini pointed out in the New York *Daily News* (May 28, 1978), "Cora is a high visibility role . . . and Hamilton is a consummate pro and knows how to milk a part for all its worth." Reviewing *The New York Idea* for *New York* (April 11, 1978), Alan Rich wrote that one of the stars he fell in love with was "Margaret Hamilton officiating at the teapot with the same mastery as when she dispenses Maxwell House in the TV ads."

Margaret Hamilton is an honorary trustee of the Cleveland Play House and was the recipient in 1977 of the Governor's Award of the State of Ohio. Her other tributes include the Award of Excellence of the John F. Kennedy Center for the Performing Arts's American College Theatre Festival of 1974. Wheelock College awarded her an honorary degree of Doctor of Science in Education degree in 1970 with an accompanying citation that recognized her humanitarian, as well as her professional, accomplishments.

As a member of the Veterans Hospital Radio & TV Guild, Miss Hamilton visits hospitals to work with disabled veterans interested in the theatre and broadcasting. She is also active in the efforts of Bedside Network to entertain hospital patients. In 1969 she helped to found AMAS, a repertory school and theatre in New York City, of which she is a director and a former vice-president. She serves on the council of Actors Equity Association and belongs to Zeta Phi Eta, the professional speech communication fraternity. She has said she is pleased to be a member, moreover, of the Detroit Dancing Cuckoos, a branch of the International Sons of the Desert, an organization dedicated to the perpetuation of the memory of Laurel and Hardy. The slogan is "Two minds with but a single thought." Her political party is the Republican.

At the outset of her career, on June 13, 1931, Margaret Hamilton married Paul Boynton Meserve, a landscape architect. She is the mother of a son, Hamilton Wadsworth

Meserve, now a banking executive, and has three grandchildren. After her marriage had ended in divorce in 1938, she raised her son alone in California, where she was active in the PTA, served for a time as president of the Beverly Hills board of education, and was a member of the Los Angeles Junior League. She also taught Sunday school at the Community Presbyterian Church in Beverly Hills.

Margaret Hamilton is one of those exceptional actresses whose stage presence has little to do with physical stature. She stands five feet tall and weighs 115 pounds. Her eyes are brown and her hair is graying brown. Press interviewers have commented on her vibrancy, her lively sense of humor, and her considerate, pleasant manner, which is also somewhat brisk and down-to-earth. An articulate woman, she enjoys conversation and is the author of the introduction to Aljean Harmetz' *The Making of the Wizard of Oz* (1977). At her apartment in the Gramercy Park section of Manhattan, she has a grand piano that she plays for her own amusement.

References: *After Dark* 11:48+ *Mr* '70 pors; *Biog N* p761+ *Jl* '74 pors; *Cleveland Plain Dealer* mag p1+ *O* 13 '78 pors; *Films in R* 28:403+ *Ag* '77 pors; *Newsday* mag p18+ *Mr* 19 '78 pors; *People* 7:57 *Ap* 25 '77 pors; *Wheelock Alumnae Q* p8+ *winter* '71 pors; *Notable Names in the American Theatre* (1976); *Who's Who in the Theatre, 1977*

Hammond, John (Henry, Jr.)

Dec. 15, 1910- Former recording company executive; jazz impresario; writer; social activist. Address: b. c/o Columbia Records, 51 W. 52d St., New York City, N.Y. 10019; h. 444 E. 57th St., New York City, N.Y. 10022

Few individuals have had more impact on popular music in the United States than John Hammond, one of the greatest talent scouts in American musical history and a leading catalytic agent in the development of jazz. During a career spanning nearly half a century he discovered, or started on the road to fame, scores of superstars, including Billie Holiday, Benny Goodman, Count Basie, Lionel Hampton, Aretha Franklin, and Bob Dylan. Over the years Hammond has also made his mark as a writer on jazz, produced hundreds of recordings, and promoted such historic jazz events as the *Spirituals to Swing* concerts of the late 1930's. Since his retirement as a vice-president of Columbia Records in 1975 he has continued to work as a free-lance consultant. Closely related to Hammond's interest in jazz has been his lifelong passion for social justice and racial equality for the blacks who virtually created that American art form.

John Henry Hammond Jr., the youngest of the five children, and only son, of John Henry and Emily Vanderbilt (Sloane) Hammond, was born in New York City on December 15, 1910. On his mother's side, he was a great-great-grandson of Commodore Cornelius Vanderbilt and a grandson of William Douglas Sloane of the W. & J. Sloane furniture stores. His father, a banker, railroad executive, and lawyer, was the son of a Civil War general. With his four older sisters—Emily (Mrs. Jack Franklin), Adele (Mrs. John Olyphant), Alice (Mrs. Benny Goodman), and Rachel (Mrs. Jack Speiden)—John Hammond grew up in the family's six-story mansion on East 91st Street and spent summers at Dellwood, the Hammonds' estate at Mount Kisco, New York.

During his childhood, Hammond was exposed to the narrow social attitudes and hidebound Republicanism endemic among White Anglo-Saxon Protestant members of his class. For a time he was influenced by the Christian Science faith of his mother. "I shared her religious fervor, her prejudices, and her saintly resolve to set an example for others," he recalled in his autobiography, *John Hammond On Record* (Summit Books, 1977). "Like her, I was already the reformer, . . . an inheritor of the guilt and therefore the obligations of wealth." Later he was inspired by the liberal Protestantism and pacifism of his first cousin, the Reverend Henry Sloane Coffin, and considered entering the ministry. Hammond received his early education in a succession of private institutions on Manhattan's Upper East Side—the Froebel

League, St. Bernard's School, and the Browning School. At fourteen he entered the exclusive Hotchkiss School, a preparatory school in Lakeville, Connecticut.

Passionately fond of music from his earliest childhood, Hammond developed an eclectic taste, ranging from Rachmaninoff to the Original Dixieland Jazz Band, and by the time he was twelve he had become an avid collector of records. "All music fascinated me," he has recalled, "but the simple honesty and convincing lyrics of the early blues singers, the rhythm and creative ingenuity of the jazz players, excited me the most. It was not long before I discovered that most of them—certainly all those I liked best—were black." His interest in show business was further stimulated by his discovery of its bible, *Variety*, of which he became a dedicated reader.

As a student at Hotchkiss, Hammond took advantage of his weekly visits to New York City for violin lessons, for attending shows at Harlem's Alhambra Theatre featuring such artists as Bessie Smith, or for listening to Fletcher Henderson's orchestra at the old Roseland Ballroom. He broadened his intellectual range, adding the *Nation*, the *New Republic*, and the *New Masses* to his regular reading, and attending Sunday philosophy classes given by John McChesney, a freethinking English teacher whom he admired.

In the summer of 1929, following his graduation from Hotchkiss, John Hammond was hired as an apprentice newspaperman by Ernest Gruening, then the crusading editor of the Portland (Maine) *Evening News*, who later became Governor of Alaska and Senator from Alaska. "I learned more than I can ever acknowledge about journalism, the civil rights movement, and trade unionism from . . . Gruening," he told John McDonough of *High Fidelity* (June 1976). Hired again the next summer as a reporter, Hammond covered the state gubernatorial campaign and exposed the hardships suffered by Maine's Indians. Meanwhile, in the fall of 1929, he entered Yale University, his father's alma mater. Indifference to his studies, and a recurring bout with hepatitis led him to drop out of Yale in early 1931, much to his father's dismay.

At twenty-one, Hammond moved into a modest Greenwich Village apartment and had his name removed from the Social Register. "I did not revolt against the system," he has explained. "I simply refused to be part of it." Meanwhile he had made his entrance on the jazz scene as a writer. During the 1930's he was a correspondent for three British publications: *Gramophone* (1931 to 1933), *Melody Maker* (1933 to 1937), and *Rhythm* (1937 to 1939). He was music critic for the Brooklyn *Daily Eagle* (1933 to 1935), associate editor of publisher Irving Mills' *Melody News* (1934 to 35), a columnist for *Down Beat* (1934 to 1941), and copublisher and coeditor of *Music and Rhythm* (1942-43).

With an annual income of about $12,000 a year from family trust funds, Hammond began in the early 1930's to subsidize the recording and promotion of jazz artists. In 1931-32 he recorded pianist Garland Wilson and produced the first recordings of Fletcher Henderson's orchestra, for the Columbia label. Having acquired ownership of the Public Theatre on Manhattan's Lower East Side in the spring of 1932, Hammond staged jazz concerts there, featuring Fletcher Henderson, Luis Russell, and others. For about six months in 1932 he also worked for New York radio station WEVD as an announcer, disc jockey, and producer of jazz programs, using racially mixed bands, a practice uncommon at the time.

From 1933 to 1936 Hammond was American recording representative for the English Columbia and Parlophone Company Ltd., which prospered at a time when in the United States many recording companies, including American Columbia, went bankrupt. Shortly after his return from England in the spring of 1933 he made friends with Benny Goodman, a promising but as yet relatively unknown young clarinetist from Chicago. Hammond took Goodman along on his nightly excursions to Harlem and persuaded him to recruit a group of musicians for recording sessions. It was to the accompaniment of Goodman and others that Hammond produced the final recordings of the legendary "Empress of the Blues," Bessie Smith, in late 1933. About that time, Hammond also supervised the first recordings of the then unknown, eighteen-year-old Billie Holiday with accompaniment by Goodman's ensemble. Hammond had discovered Miss Holiday the previous year in a Harlem speakeasy and considered her the best jazz singer he had ever heard.

Encouraged by Hammond, Goodman organized his first permanent band, which in 1934 scored a hit on the NBC radio showcase *Let's Dance*. Hammond recruited for the Goodman group such pristine talent as drummer Gene Krupa, and he persuaded Fletcher Henderson to write its arrangements. After he discovered Teddy Wilson, a young black pianist, sitting in for Earl ("Fatha") Hines in a Chicago nightclub, Hammond organized the Benny Goodman Trio—consisting of Goodman, Krupa, and Wilson—which in early 1936 became the first racially integrated jazz group to perform publicly before a paying audience. Not long after that, the trio became a quartet with vibraharpist Lionel Hampton, whom Hammond had discovered playing in a skid row club in downtown Los Angeles. By 1937 Goodman was being heralded as the "King of Swing," a distinction that he owed largely to Hammond.

One of Hammond's happiest serendipities was his discovery of Count Basie. One evening, in Chicago, while listening to an experimental station on his car radio, he heard Basie and his nine-member band, including saxophonist Lester Young, on one of their nightly broadcasts from the Reno Club in Kansas City. Impressed by Basie's "extraordinary economy of style," Hammond went to Kansas City and talked him into coming to New York. Basie's immensely successful first recordings, produced by Hammond in October 1936, helped bring black music into the mainstream.

Other discoveries made by Hammond during the 1930's included Helen Humes, who became vocalist for the Basie band after Hammond had arranged for her to enter an amateur contest at the Apollo Theatre; guitarist Charlie Christian, whom he sought out in an Oklahoma City honky-tonk on recommendation of pianist-composer Mary Lou Williams and brought into the Goodman ensemble; and pianist Meade Lux Lewis, who was washing cars in a Chicago garage where Hammond had traced him after hearing an obscure recording of his "Honky-Tonk Train Blues." It was Lewis who, under Hammond's sponsorship, triggered the "boogie-woogie" piano craze of the late 1930's.

In addition to working for English Columbia, Hammond was recording director for Irving Mills in 1934; supervised recording sessions for Vocalion-Brunswick (1935 to 1938); and served as sales manager for Columbia Masterworks in 1937. Through Henry Hammond Inc., which he formed with Joseph Losey and Irving Jacoby, Hammond helped to produce Albert Bein's reform-school drama Little Ol' Boy, starring Burgess Meredith, at the Playhouse Theatre on Broadway in 1933 and produced the Civil War comedy-drama Jayhawker, by Sinclair Lewis and Lloyd Lewis, starring Fred Stone, at the Cort Theatre in late 1934. But despite favorable reviews, neither production lasted more than a few weeks. In 1938 Hammond helped to finance and organize talent for Barney Josephson's Café Society Downtown in Greenwich Village, which attracted the first integrated nightclub audiences outside of Harlem.

Meanwhile, Hammond devoted much time and effort to social causes. In the early 1930's he accompanied John Dos Passos, Edmund Wilson, and others to Pineville, Kentucky to support striking coal miners. In 1933, at the request of Ernest Gruening, then editor of the Nation, he went to Alabama to report on the second trial in the Scottsboro case, a cause célèbre among civil rights champions, involving nine young black men accused of rape. Two years later he covered its further proceedings for the New Republic. He joined the board of directors of the National Association for the Advancement of Colored People in 1935 and remained with it for over thirty years, finally resigning as a vice-president in 1967 in protest against its refusal, under executive director Roy Wilkins, to take a stand against United States involvement in Vietnam.

Although Hammond had misgivings about the Communist party, viewing its protean policies on racial matters as opportunist, he used its publication New Masses as a platform for some of his crusades, including an attack on race discrimination in labor unions. In 1937 he published a series of articles charging unfair practices in the recording industry. Unable to find another sponsor for the landmark Spirituals to Swing concert he was planning to present in 1938 at Carnegie Hall, he accepted sponsorship by Eric Bernay of New Masses on the condition that it not be used as a vehicle for political propaganda.

For some years, Hammond had been planning that concert, which would bring together the elements of American black music from its early beginnings to contemporary jazz. With the help of Goddard Lieberson, who later became a Columbia Records executive, Hammond rounded up some spectacular talents. Presented at Carnegie Hall on December 23, 1938, From Spirituals to Swing was opened by boogie-woogie pianists Meade Lux Lewis, Albert Ammons, and Pete Johnson. In addition to the Goodman and Basie ensembles and such veteran musicians as saxophonist Sidney Bechet and pianist James P. Johnson, the concert featured a number of newcomers, including gospel singer Sister Rosetta Tharpe, Mitchell's Christian Singers, primitive blues singer Big Bill Broonzy, and harmonica player Sonny Terry. The resulting critical acclaim prompted Hammond to stage a second Spirituals to Swing concert on Christmas Eve 1939. Sponsored by the Theatre Arts Committee, and featuring Goodman, Basie, Ida Cox, Charlie Christian, the boogie-woogie pianists, and the Golden Gate Quartet, the concert was, according to Hammond, "very professional and not half as exciting" as the first. Strangely enough, two decades elapsed before recordings of the Spirituals to Swing concerts were released by Vanguard in 1959.

In 1939 Columbia Records, which had come under the ownership of CBS, hired Hammond as its assistant recording director, a position he occupied until 1943. Among the artists he recorded during that period, on the Columbia and other labels, were Charlie Christian, Red Norvo, Mildred Bailey, Ida Cox, Joe Sullivan, Eddy Howard, and Paul Robeson. He also presided over the only American recording session of pianist Walter Gieseking and helped to arrange for the company to record the Budapest String Quartet. In 1940 he supervised Benny Goodman and violinist Joseph Szigeti in the recording of Contrasts, which Goodman had commissioned from Béla Bartók. During the spring and summer of 1943 he toured the United States at the behest of Billy Rose and Oscar Hammerstein 2d to find a cast for the Broadway production of the all-black musical Carmen Jones.

Drafted into the United States Army in the fall of 1943, Hammond served as an enlisted man with Information & Education in several camps in the South, including Fort Benning, Georgia. He helped to mount camp shows with such artists as Ella Fitzgerald, Dizzy Gillespie, and Billy Eckstine, and took part in the production of an Office of War Information documentary featuring jazz. Wherever he went, he tried to combat racial discrimination, with only occasional success.

Discharged in January 1946, Hammond returned briefly to Columbia Records but resigned a few months later, after he joined the board of directors of Keynote Records, a small company specializing in jazz and folk music. In mid-1946, while still on the Keystone board, he became recording director for Majestic Records, but disagreements with its executives caused him to leave that post after seven months. In early 1947 he was named president of Keystone Records, where in collaboration with Mitch Miller, a young oboist whom he placed in charge of its new classics department, he produced, among other recordings, one of Igor Stravinsky conducting his *Dumbarton Oaks Concerto*. When Mercury Records took over Keystone later that year, Hammond became vice-president of the combined company, serving until 1952. Under the Mercury label he released recordings by such artists as David Oistrakh, Ralph Kirkpatrick, Alexander Schneider, and Mitch Miller.

Continuing his journalistic activities in the 1950's, Hammond wrote for the New York *Daily Compass* from 1950 to 1952, for the New York *Times* in 1953-54, for the *Herald Tribune* in 1955-56, and for the *Saturday Review* in 1958-59. He was music editor of *Gentry* in 1956-57 and a contributor to *Hi-Fi Music at Home* in 1958. From 1953 to 1956 he also served as a lecturer at New York University. During the McCarthy witch-hunts of the 1950's he came under scrutiny, but no evidence of "subversive activity" was found against him.

As director of popular music for Vanguard Records from 1953 to 1958, Hammond produced a series of high-quality jazz recordings featuring such artists as Mel Powell, Buck Clayton, Vic Dickenson, Sir Charles Thompson, Jo Jones, Ruby Braff, Jimmy Rushing, and Brother John Sellers. Invited by Goddard Lieberson, he returned to Columbia Records as a staff producer in 1959. He remained with Columbia for sixteen years, becoming director of talent acquisition in May 1963 and vice-president in charge of talent acquisition in July 1973.

Soon after rejoining Columbia Records, Hammond signed up pianist Ray Bryant and the controversial folk singer Pete Seeger, then still blacklisted by CBS. In early 1960, after hearing a demonstration record sung by Aretha Franklin, a minister's daughter from Detroit, Hammond hailed her as "the most dynamic jazz voice" since Billie Holiday and obtained a Columbia contract for her. But later he complained that efforts by other producers to make her a "pop star" spoiled the purity of her style. In the summer of 1961 Hammond discovered twenty-year-old Bob Dylan as a back-up guitarist and harmonica player for folk singer Carolyn Hester. Although neither Dylan's voice nor his performance on the instruments seemed impressive at the time, Hammond saw in him a "superlative artist" with an "acuity of vision of American life." Dylan's subsequent success proved that those who had referred to him as "Hammond's folly" were mistaken.

Other notable performers brought by Hammond to Columbia Records included the Canadian poet and singer Leonard Cohen, whom he signed up in 1962; rock singer and composer Bruce Springsteen, who joined the roster in 1973; and trombonist-bandleader Bill Watrous, who came in 1975. In addition, Hammond helped to promote comebacks for the long-retired veteran jazz stars Eubie Blake and Alberta Hunter.

On reaching sixty-five, the mandatory retirement age for CBS employees, in December 1975, Hammond was honored in a gala two-part program entitled "The World of John Hammond" presented by *Soundstage* over PBS-TV, featuring a cross section of his protégés, from Benny Goodman to Bob Dylan. Hammond was offered a contract to continue to produce records for Columbia as an independent, and he and his wife formed the Snum Music Corporation. Among his most recent discoveries is the young Polish jazz pianist Adam Makowicz, who began to record for Columbia in mid-1977.

Hammond is a past president of the East Coast chapter of the National Academy of Recording Arts and Sciences and a vice-president of the Newport Jazz Festival. He has served on the boards of directors of Rutgers University's Institute of Jazz Studies, Horizon Press, Crisis Publishing Company, and the Professional Children's School and Northside Center for Child Development in New York City. In 1971 he received a special Grammy award for his work on the reissue by Columbia of the Bessie Smith library, and the Yale University school of music honored him in 1973 with its certificate of merit. In 1979 he was named to head a commission to make selections for the White House record library.

John Hammond was first married on March 13, 1941 to Jemison McBride. They had three sons: John Paul ("Jeep"), a blues singer and guitarist; Douglas, who died in infancy; and Jason, who runs a farm in Massachusetts. After his divorce in 1948, Hammond was married on September 8, 1949 to Esmé O'Brien Sarnoff, formerly the wife of Robert Sarnoff and daughter-in-law of RCA board chairman General David Sarnoff. Hammond is trim and youthful in appearance and ebullient in manner and, according to Leonard Feather, has "intense opinions on almost every subject." Indifferent to fashion, he has worn his now graying hair in a bristly crew cut since he was seventeen. Although several heart attacks forced him to curtail his physical activities, Hammond is still an early riser with a "compulsion to see, to read, to hear everything as soon as possible." An accomplished violist, he enjoys playing in informal concerts, and his personal collection of recordings numbers in the tens of thousands.

References: Hi Fi 26:59+ Je '76 pors; New Yorker 53:60+ Ja 9 '78; Newsweek 77:92 Mr 29 '71 por; Washington Post K p1+ F 1 '70 por, C p1+ N 14 '77 por; Feather, Leonard. Encyclopedia of Jazz (1960); Hammond, John and Townsend, Irving. John Hammond On Record (1977); Who's Who in America (1978-79)

Helms, Jesse A.

Oct. 18, 1921- United States Senator from North Carolina. Address: b. Rm. 4104, Dirksen Senate Office Bldg., Washington, D.C. 20510; Federal Bldg., Raleigh, N.C. 27601; Box 2944, Hickory, N.C. 28601

The staunchest of the members of the conservative coalition in the United States Senate is Jesse Helms, the first Republican in this century to represent North Carolina in the upper chamber of the Congress, to which he was elected in 1972 and reelected in 1978. "Unless and until we can get back to the faith of our fathers," Helms believes, "and learn how to be honest with ourselves in terms of economics and politics and government and all the rest, we don't have a chance to solve the other problems down the line." Among the problems of most concern to him are crime, drug abuse, taxes, and deficit spending, but he has emerged, in the opinion of the conservative commentator M. Stanton Evans, "a conservative leader in almost every

sector of political combat." In 1977 Evans wrote in the National Review: "Whether the subject up for discussion is the right to life, the excesses of big government, the snub of Solzhenitsyn, or the Reagan bid for President, Helms has ridden to the sound of the cannon."

Jesse A. Helms was born in Monroe, North Carolina on October 18, 1921 to Alexander and Ethel Mae Helms. After studying at Wingate (North Carolina) Junior College and Wake Forest College, he worked as city editor of the Raleigh (North Carolina) Times, in 1941 and 1942. During World War II he served in the United States Navy.

Helms was news and program director at radio station WRAL in Raleigh from 1948 until 1951, when he went to Washington as administrative assistant to Senator Willis Smith. In Washington he also served as administrative assistant to Senator Alton Lennon, in 1953. He was executive director of the North Carolina Bankers Association from 1953 to 1960 and chairman of the board of Specialized Agricultural Publications Inc., in Raleigh from 1964 to 1972. The first elective office he held was on the Raleigh City Council, where he served from 1957 to 1961 and whose committee on law and finance he chaired from 1959 to 1960.

For twelve years, from 1960 until 1972, Helms was executive vice-president of the Capital Broadcasting Company, which operates WRAL-TV, radio station WRAL, and the Tobacco Radio Network, a regional news network. During that time he wrote and broadcast daily editorials which were at variance with what he called the "consistent bias in national television network news programs."

That bias was particularly evident, in his view, in the reporting of "the civil rights uproar" in the South during the 1960's. He called that reportage "absolutely contrived— this wasn't news, this was a little one-act play," consisting of "staged" events. During his tenure with the Capital Broadcasting Company, which at one time or another was affiliated with each of the three major networks, he filed some 500 protests with the networks against "instances of deliberate bias." "Of course," he said later, "it amounted to absolutely nothing."

One of his favorite targets as a television and radio commentator was academic freedom, which he felt went too far in some instances. One such instance was reported to him by a student in the freshman English class of Michael Paull at the University of North Carolina at Chapel Hill. Paull assigned the class to rephrase Andrew Marvell's poem "To His Coy Mistress," and some of the results, read aloud in class, were blunt to the point of obscenity. "No doubt," Helms complained in one of his editorials, "the boys enjoyed the vicarious frolic of talking about erotic matters in the presence of girl students." The matter became a cause célèbre and the chancellor of the university relieved Paull of his duties pending a "full investigation."

On the subject of busing and education, Helms on one occasion said: "One can only conclude that in the view of the federal courts education no longer counts for anything. Only integration. It is time that reasonableness and logic be reintroduced into solving the problems of education." Regarding race relations, he asserted, "Blacks and whites can together learn that there is no cause for hostility simply because rabble-rousers preach it, or because social activists claim it exists."

Other common themes in his editorials were the danger of Communism and the need for a strong national defense posture within the world community. "National defense is indeed expensive—and so is an adequate police," he is still fond of pointing out. "Surely any rational citizen can understand that it is better to have it and not need it than to need it and not have it. The difference is a matter of survival itself."

His other targets included the waste and extravagance involved in misconceived, mismanaged, or irresponsible government programs; the plight of the "farmers who produce our food, fibers, tobacco, and other products . . . who labor to feed and clothe all the rest of us"; lax criminal justice, "the kind of powder-puff, by-your-leave pats on the wrist that return criminals to the street an hour or so after they have been arrested"; inadequate compensation for the police and firemen who break "up mobs and put . . . out the fires set by arsonists"; and a welfare system that is, in its present form, a "tragic outrage" with which the American public is "fed up—and has every right to be."

Originally a Democrat, Helms turned Republican in 1970 despite his disappointment with the pragmatism of President Nixon. "Richard Nixon," he said in an editorial broadcast on November 5, 1971, "the man who won his spurs in politics as an anti-Communist, is now—well, you know about his appeasement of the Chinese Communists in Peking and the warm embrace he has given the Communist dictator from Yugoslavia, Marshal Tito."

In the 1972 North Carolina Senate race, Helms upset the favorite, Democrat Nick Galifianakis, by a 120,000-ballot margin, with 56 percent of the vote. After taking office in January 1973, he was assigned to the Senate's Agriculture and Forestry Committee and its Banking, Housing, and Urban Affairs Committee. During his first term he introduced an amendment calculated to circumvent the Supreme Court rulings against prayer in the public schools; he voted in favor of the death penalty, the resumption of aid to Turkey, and "no knock" legislation; and he voted against school busing, the approval of Presi-

dent Gerald R. Ford's nomination of Nelson A. Rockefeller as Vice-President, government subsidization of abortions, licensing of handguns, reduction in the number of American armed forces abroad, the creation of a consumer protection agency, the Panama Canal treaties, federal loans to New York City, and food stamps for strikers. Americans for Constitutional Action, which stands against "the current movement of our Nation to Socialism and a regimented society," gave him ratings of 100 percent in 1973 and 1974. The liberal Americans for Democratic action rated him at 0 and 5 percent; the AFL-CIO's Committee on Political Education, 18 and 10 percent; the progressive Republican Ripon Society, 33 and 23 percent; the Consumer Federation of America, 8 and 0 percent; the League of Women Voters, 0 and 30 percent. The National Security Index of the American Security Council, which advocates the maintenance and development of large weapons systems and is viewed by its critics as the lobby for the military-industrial complex, did not rate him in 1973, but gave him a rating of 100 percent in 1974.

At the Republican National Convention in Kansas City, Missouri in August 1976 Helms supported Ronald Reagan, and although he was not a delegate he played an important behind-the-scenes role in the shaping of the party's platform. At that time William Rusher, the publisher of the *National Review* magazine, and Richard A. Viguerie, the publisher of the *Conservative Digest* and a conservative activist, announced that Helms was the prospective choice for Presidential candidate of the third party that they and other conservative leaders were trying to form.

Viguerie became Helms's fund raiser, and in Helms's 1978 Senatorial reelection campaign he raised a phenomenal $6,200,000, most of it through a nationwide direct-mail drive. Two-thirds of the contributions came from outside North Carolina, and the contributors ranged from the National Rifle Association to oil interests. At the polls in November 1978 Helms defeated the Democratic candidate, John R. Ingram, with 54 percent of the vote. During the first months of his new six-year term in the Senate, Helms introduced legislation to end sanctions against Rhodesia and to repeal the Credit Control Act, which he described as "little more than a means of providing total federal control of the financial system of this country."

Helms expounded his political philosophy in the book *When Free Men Shall Stand* (Zondervan, 1976). In his review of that book in the *National Review* (January 7, 1977) M. Stanton Evans wrote: "Senator Helms does not approach the issues on an ad hoc basis, but sees them all in terms of an overarching strategic vision. He understands that the fundamental problem of our time is a religious one, stemming from a loss of faith and values, and that all the particular ills that we complain of derive from this initial failure."

Jesse A. Helms and Dorothy Coble were married on October 31, 1942. They have two daughters, Jane (Mrs. Charles R. Knox) and Nancy (Mrs. John C. Stuart), and a son, Charles. Helms is a deacon and Sunday school teacher at the Hayes Barton Baptist Church in Raleigh, a Grand Orator of the Grand Lodge of Masons of North Carolina, and a trustee of the board of directors of Camp Willow Run, a "youth camp for Christ" at Littleton, North Carolina. He is also a trustee of Meredith College, John F. Kennedy College, and the Delaware Law School. He is a very active member of the advisory council of Americans Against Union Control of Government.

The soft-spoken, bespectacled Helms is a past president of the Raleigh Rotary Club and is on the board of directors of the North Carolina Cerebral Palsy Hospital in Durham, North Carolina, North Carolina United Cerebral Palsy Inc., and the Wake County Cerebral Palsy Rehabilitation Center in Raleigh. His honors include the Southern Baptist National Award for Service to Humanity, two Freedoms Foundation awards for his television and radio editorials, the Richard Lee Award, the Order of Lafayette Freedom Award, citizenship awards from the North Carolina American Legion and the North Carolina Veterans of Foreign Wars, and the Outstanding Service Award of the Council Against Communist Aggression. Also, he is the first Republican to win the Golden Gavel Award, for presiding over the Senate for at least 100 hours. "Somewhere, somehow, the public must learn that it's of small importance whether a candidate has charisma or glamour," Helms has observed. "The paramount thing is whether a man believes in the principles of America and whether he is willing to stand up for them, win or lose."

References: N Y Sunday News p27 Ag 15 '76 por; Washington Post A p22 N 9 '72 por; Almanac of American Politics, 1978; Congressional Directory, 1978; Douth, George. Leaders in Profile (1975); Who's Who in America, 1978-79; Who's Who in American Politics, 1977-78

Howard, Ron

Mar. 1, 1954- Actor; director. Address: b. c/o William Schuller Agency, 9110 Sunset Blvd., Los Angeles, Calif. 90069

At twenty-four, Ron Howard already has behind him an acting career of some twenty years and is, in addition, the youngest director in Hollywood. Despite the many strong roles that he has played outside of stereotype, such as the emotionally shattered World War II pilot in the television movie Locusts (1974), Howard is probably implanted in the consciousness of millions of Americans as a kind of Norman Rockwell freckle-faced boy next door, everybody's favorite soda jerk. They remember him when he was a cute little moppet growing to puberty on the television situation comedy The Andy Griffith Show (1960-68); they saw him as the clean-cut high school graduate, president of his class, in the hit nostalgia film American Graffiti (1973); and every week they witness the prolongation of his straight-arrow adolescence in American Graffiti's sanitized cousin, ABC's long-running situation comedy Happy Days, another beneficiary of the nostalgia boom. Howard's first directing effort was the film Grand Theft Auto (1977), a car chase comedy in which he also starred, and his second was the made-for-TV movie Cotton Candy (1978). Howard and many others from the cast of American Graffiti were reunited in its much less successful sequel, More American Graffiti, which was released by Universal Pictures in 1979.

Ron Howard was born on March 1, 1954 in Duncan, Oklahoma to Rance Howard, an actor, director, and writer, and Jean Howard, who was an actress until Ron's birth. His younger brother, Clint, is also an actor, a veteran of two seasons on the television series Gentle Ben. Ronny, as he was then known, was first seen on screen in *Frontier Woman* (TOP, 1956) when he was eighteen months old, and he made his first appearance on stage in a summer stock production of *The Seven Year Itch*, directed by his father at the Hilltop Theatre in Baltimore, when he was two.

In an interview with Edwin Miller for *Seventeen* (March 1975), Howard recalled how, as a toddler, he would watch rehearsals of the plays his father was directing: "Once, when they were doing *Mister Roberts*, I started picking up on the dialogue. We developed this game where my dad played Mr. Roberts and I played Pulver. Then we started other scenes and my dad got a big kick out of it, . . . which gave him the idea of my acting. But acting was never pressed on me. It was something I did with my dad, so when I started doing it with other people it was just a matter of playing the game with them, something I did for fun. The fun has remained, because otherwise I would have gotten out. And my dad always made sure I was totally prepared. Now I blow lines in a scene once in a while, but then I never did. By the time I knew what I was doing, the fear was gone."

The young actor's television credits go back to 1956, when he was seen on the *Kraft Theatre* and the *Red Skelton Show*, but he dates his career as a full-fledged actor from 1959, when, at five, he was cast in two teleplays on CBS: *Black December* on *Playhouse 90* and *Barnaby and Mr. O'Malley* on the *General Electric Theatre*. In the latter he played the little loner with the frolicsome fairy godfather (Bert Lahr) created by cartoonist Crockett Johnson. His later television credits included appearances on *The Danny Kaye Show* and roles in episodes of *Dennis the Menace*, *The Many Loves of Dobie Gillis*, *The Danny Thomas Show*, *Gomer Pyle*, *Dr. Kildare*, *The Fugitive*, *The Monroes*, *The FBI*, and *The Big Valley*. On the large screen, he played Billy Rhinelander, one of the children of an American tourist couple (E. G. Marshall and Anne Jackson) who are part of an international group fleeing from Budapest at the time of the abortive 1956 Hungarian revolt in Anatole Litvak's *The Journey* (MGM, 1959), which boasted a splendid cast that included Yul Brynner and Deborah Kerr.

After seeing Howard as Barnaby on the *General Electric Theatre*, producer Sheldon Leonard cast him as Opie on *The Andy Griffith Show*, which began its eight-year run on CBS on October 3, 1960. That bucolic situation comedy, set in a small town in North Carolina, dealt with the daily problems of the widower sheriff Andy Taylor (Griffith), his son (Howard), and his friends. "Dad and I would write a lot of Opie's lines," Howard told Paul Rosenfield of the Los Angeles *Times* (August 19, 1977). "Rusty Hamer on Danny Thomas' show was always putting down adults. We figured Opie got respect by commanding it. In the later years, Andy Griffith admitted the show was based on my relationship with my dad." He described that relationship in the *Seventeen*

interview with Edwin Miller: "As an actor and growing up as a kid, I think I've had the best of both worlds because of my father [who] was pretty apprehensive about my getting into all this [and] made sure I kept things in perspective. Once, in my first year on the Griffith show, when I got cranky about doing a scene or something, he picked me up and spanked me right there on the set. He explained that I had to be responsible, that people were trying to work."

Conversely, Howard recounted, his father would intervene to stop adults on the set from teasing him. "It's tough for a little kid—he's playing, having a terrific time joking around, then suddenly he's supposed to work. And kids have a natural tendency to mimic adults. The first few times everybody thinks it's cute, then suddenly the kid's a brat. My father didn't want that to happen either, so I was very fortunate."

To keep Ron's childhood as normal as possible, his parents insisted that his contract include a clause exempting him from promotional tours, and when he was not working they enrolled him in public schools. "In school I was always a novelty at first," he told Edwin Miller. "People got very jazzed up about the idea of having a kid actor in class. That would blow over in a couple of weeks and then I was able to blend right in. By the time I was in high school, I was a big sports nut. I even turned down jobs when I made the basketball team—not the varsity, but the B team—and wanted to stick with it when we went on the road to play other schools. I didn't work for nine months, and that's when I learned I missed acting."

In between his assignments for *The Andy Griffith Show* Ron Howard was cast in four motion pictures. In *Five Minutes to Live* (American International Pictures, 1961), re-released as *Door-to-Door Maniac* (1966), starring Johnny Cash, he played the precocious child of a bank executive (Donald Woods) who is under pressure from criminals demanding $70,000. As the introspective small brother of Marian the librarian (Shirley Jones) in the musical *The Music Man* (Warner Brothers, 1962), starring Robert Preston, he was "an appealing conductor of sentiment," as Bosley Crowther noted in the New York *Times* (August 24, 1962). Critics found him "wholly likable" and "thoroughly disarming" as the son choosing a stepmother in *The Courtship of Eddie's Father* (MGM, 1963), in which he costarred with Glenn Ford, Shirley Jones, Stella Stevens, and Dina Merrill. A decade later, in her *TV Guide to the Movies* (1974), Judith Crist still found *The Courtship of Eddie's Father* "worth watching because of Ronny Howard," who "manages to turn sentiment into tenderness and giggles into belly laughs and win over the hardest hearts in the process." In *Village of the Giants* (Embassy Pictures, 1965), a science-fiction venture based on *The Food of the Gods* by H. G. Wells, he played the young character named Genius, who discovers a substance that produces enormous growth in those who eat it.

Howard's additional work on television during the run of the The Andy Griffith Show included a role in the musical Tippy Top on CBS's General Electric Theatre, in December 1961, and the lead in A Boy Called Nuthin' on NBC's The World of Disney, in December 1967. In 1969, after the Griffith show had run its course, he played in episodes of Judd for the Defense (ABC), Land of the Giants (ABC), Daniel Boone (NBC), Lancer (CBS), and Gunsmoke (CBS). His second World of Disney two-part feature, Smoke, aired on NBC in February 1970, and later in the same year he was seen in an episode of Lassie on CBS. In his second series venture, Howard costarred with Henry Fonda in The Smith Family, about the home life of a policeman. That show, introduced on ABC in January 1971, was cancelled in 1972. In the Disney big-screen production The Wild Country (Buena Vista, 1971), the members of a pioneer Western family were portrayed by Howard, Steve Forrest, Vera Miles, and Howard's brother Clint—"all winning folk of estimable character and grit," as the reviewer for the New York Times (February 11, 1971) observed.

The surprise screen hit of 1973 was the low-budgeted American Graffiti (Universal, 1973), a slice of nostalgia evoking the adolescence and coming of age in a small city in northern California of its auteur, George Lucas. That gentle backward look at youthful lifestyles in the pre-Vietnam decade was shot on location in what Lucas described as "jukebox" color, amid the choreographed cruising of cars with radios emitting a collage of period pop songs. Set on one restless night in the waning summer of 1962, the plot interwove the story lines of four recent high school graduates, with the emphasis on moments of decision for the introspective class intellectual, Curt Henderson (Richard Dreyfuss), who opts to go East to college, and for the class president, Steve Bollinger (Howard), who settles for the safe local junior college route in order to remain near his cheerleader girlfriend, Laurie (Cindy Williams).

Snaring the hearts of critics and public alike, American Graffiti rang up dizzying grosses, received five Oscar nominations, including that for Best Picture of 1973, and drew raves for its "lovely and persuasive" rendering of past innocence, for catching "not only the charm and tribal energy of the teen-age 1950's but also the listlessness and the resignation that underscored it," and for a "definitive, remarkably resonant portrait of adolescence [that] transcends all generation gaps."

A lagniappe of American Graffiti's success was the contribution it made to the marketability on network television of Happy Days, a situation comedy about the emotional growing pains of Richie Cunningham, the adolescent middle son in a family living in a fictional suburb of Milwaukee in 1955. With Howard in the ingenuous role of Richie, the pilot for it was televised as a segment of ABC's Love American Style three years earlier. The real-life schoolboy experiences Howard was undergoing at that time made it easy for him to invest Richie with credibility. As he related in the Seventeen interview, "I never participated very much in the social scene as far as going to parties and that sort of thing [was concerned], although when I look back I realize that girls were a little standoffish. They didn't throw themselves in my direction. Either they were nervous about someone in my position or they didn't care. I was going through the same kind of nervous anxiety that Richie goes through all the time on Happy Days."

Launched by ABC as a prime-time series on January 15, 1974, Happy Days immediately edged past its competition on NBC and CBS in the ratings and within a month it was firmly established, with more than a 30 percent share of the viewing audience. "The early indications, then, are that Happy Days will be around for a while," Laurence Laurent wrote in the Washington Post (February 24, 1974), "and the biggest reason for its survival is not the hokey format but the skill of the oldest young professional performer in television, Ron Howard."

Benjamin Stein, who reviewed Happy Days for the Wall Street Journal (March 26, 1974), found its Cunningham family to be "preternaturally wholesome, but stop[ping] just short of being emetic." The "central appeal," Stein wrote, was "the state of constant cheerful anticipation . . . a characteristic of teenage youth" exuded by Richie in the midst of the challenges facing him weekly on the road to adulthood. "Although he never succeeds, he never stops trying. His gullibility is his salvation [as] every time, a friend comes running in with some new plan that is going to revolutionize his life. Richie believes it and is excited."

Chief among Richie's mentors was Arthur Fonzarelli, better known as Fonzie or The Fonz, a street-wise, swaggering, leather-jacketed automobile mechanic and biker. Fonzarelli, played by Henry Winkler, was absent from the pilot for Happy Days, and when the series began he was just one of several featured characters. But gradually he surpassed Richie in popularity and from the beginning of the 1975-76 season the producers made him the central character. The shift in emphasis left Howard feeling "awkward" at first but, ultimately, not threatened, as he told Judy Klemesrud in an interview for the New York Times (June 22, 1977): "Maybe if Henry Winkler and I hadn't liked each other, and if we were two different people, there would be problems. But we're all on the series to make it as successful as possible, and it benefits us all that Fonzie is tremendously popular." In the 1977-78 season, Happy Days had an estimated audience of 34,000,000 in 22,000,000 homes.

As a harried young fruit picker determined to escape from poverty in the CBS drama *The Migrants*, Howard gave an "outstanding" performance, "more than effective enough to erase any resentment about his talents being wasted in the new *Happy Days* series," as John J. O'Connor observed in the New York Times (February 1, 1974). The strength of that role won him another powerful assignment, in *Locusts*, originally titled *Black Harvest*, an ABC *Movie of the Week* (October 9, 1974) in which he convincingly portrayed a combat flier who goes to pieces after seeing his best friend blown up in a plane. The entire Howard family was in the cast of the ABC television movie *Huckleberry Finn* (March 25, 1975), in which Ron played the title role.

On the big screen, Ron Howard shared credits with Cloris Leachman in *Happy Mother's Day . . . Love, George* (Cinema V, 1973), a psychological melodrama; played an impressionable Texas farm boy in *The Spikes Gang* (United Artists, 1974), starring Lee Marvin; and as the boy who idolizes the dying cowboy (John Wayne) in the elegiac western *The Shootist* (Paramount, 1976), showed "surprising depth," as Rex Reed wrote in *Vogue* (September 9, 1976).

Meanwhile, Ron Howard was aiming at becoming a director. At fifteen he began experimenting with a Super 8 camera—later he won a national Kodak film contest with a Super 8 short—and after graduating from Burroughs High School in Burbank, California, in 1972, he studied cinema arts in the Department of Communications at the University of Southern California. He starred in one of producer Roger Corman's money-making grade B thrillers, *Eat My Dust!* (New World, 1976), a car chase comedy, with the understanding that Corman would later give him the opportunity to direct. That opportunity came with *Grand Theft Auto* (New World, 1977), another film in the same genre, a slapstick orgy of bloodless automobile wrecks. Howard and his father cowrote the screenplay for *Grand Theft Auto*, and both were in the film, Ron in the starring role, as a youth who elopes with a heiress against her father's wishes and Rance as a detective involved in chasing the couple. Reviewers described that first directing effort as "creditable," done with a "broad" but "amiable" and "well-disciplined" touch, and people in the industry were impressed with the production statistics: *Grand Theft Auto* set a Corman company record for camera setups (ninety-one in a single day); it was completed in four weeks on a budget of $602,000; and it grossed $15,000,000.

Among those impressed was Deanne Barkley, a vice-president of NBC, who asked Howard to come up with a movie for the network. The result was *Cotton Candy*, cowritten with his brother Clint, a high school story of first love and of student misfits who form their own rock band. The cast starred Clint Howard, Charles Martin Smith (who played Terry the

Toad in *American Graffiti*), and Brenda Matthews, and included his father, as the principal, and his mother and wife in cameo roles. It was first televised on NBC on October 26, 1978.

"Ron can't make a decision about where to go for dinner, but he had an answer for everybody on the set," Charles Martin Smith told a reporter after the making of *Cotton Candy*. "It was amazing. He was totally in control." As a director, Howard is planning six more movies for NBC, two for Paramount Pictures (*Happy Days* is a Paramount production), and one more for Roger Corman. With his father and brother he has formed a film production company, Major H Productions.

Blue-eyed, redheaded Ron Howard and Cheryl Alley, his high school sweetheart, were married on June 7, 1975. They live in an unpretentious three-bedroom home in Laurel Canyon in California, from which Howard commutes to Studio City in a Volkswagen van. Neither of them smokes or drinks hard liquor, and their wildest recreation is watching the Dodgers or old movies on television, a pastime during which Howard enjoys washing down junk food or a hamburger with beer. A modest, easygoing, friendly person, he hopes "never to let business take full control" of his lifestyle. "Acting is what I do for a living, and I love it," he has said. "But it's not my whole life. I hope to always have something else that I can turn to. I hope to have a family that really means something to me. Because when you've got that, you can handle almost anything."

References: People p72+ S 6 '76 pors, p90+ Je 12 '78 pors; Seventeen 34:100+ Mr '75 pors; TV Guide 25:9+ D 24 '77 pors; Who's Who in America, 1978-79

Hughes, Ted

Aug. 17, 1930- British poet. Address b. c/o Faber & Faber Ltd., 3 Queens Square, London WC1N 3AU, England

With the publication of *The Hawk in the Rain* in 1957 and *Lupercal* in 1960, Ted Hughes was acclaimed as the most significant English poet to have emerged since World War II. Those critics who questioned that assessment objected mainly to the pessimistic tone, the raw language, and the Lawrencian ferocity of his poems about the animals and birds of his native Yorkshire. Drawing on his training as an anthropologist for the powerful mythic images in the macabre *Wodwo* and the nihilistic *Crow*, Hughes created a black vision of a meaningless world. Later works, especially *Gaudete*, seemed to offer at least a glimmer of hope.

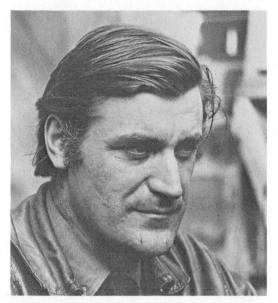

Ted Hughes

Keith Sagar, the literary critic and Hughes scholar, believes Hughes to be "a great poet" because his is "the purest poetry, charged poetry, visionary, revelatory poetry that sees into the life of things, that takes over where all other modes of apprehending reality falter." Sagar contends that in his poetry Hughes is attempting to recover "the lost sense of the sacredness of Nature." In addition to his impersonal poems examining the paradoxical nature of man, Hughes has written drama, illuminating literary criticism, and plays and short stories for children. He received the Premio Internazionale Taormina in 1973, the Queen's Medal for Poetry in 1974, and the O.B.E. in 1977.

The youngest of the three children of William Henry Hughes, a carpenter, and Edith (Farrar) Hughes, Edward James Hughes was born on August 17, 1930 in Mytholmroyd, a small mill town in West Yorkshire that was surrounded by bleak, windswept moors where, in Hughes's words, he could "never escape the impression that the whole region [was] in mourning for the First World War." William Hughes survived the Dardanelles campaign in World War I and his recollections of that catastrophic ordeal fired his son's imagination with vivid scenes of violence, courage, suffering, and death—scenes that came to life daily as he watched the predatory birds, beasts, and human hunters stalking their prey on the moors. In spite of the seemingly senseless slaughter, the spirit of the moorland was to him ultimately "exultant."

When Ted Hughes was seven years old, he moved with his family to Mexborough, Yorkshire, where his parents opened a stationery and tobacco shop. While a student at Mexborough Grammar School, he began to write poetry, mostly bloodthirsty narratives about Zulus and cowboys. Hughes's work matured rapidly under the guidance of interested teachers and, in 1948, he won an open exhibition to Pembroke College, Cambridge University. Before he could take up the scholarship, however, he served two years in the Royal Air Force. He spent much of that period working as a radio mechanic on an isolated three-man station in eastern Yorkshire, with "nothing to do but read and reread Shakespeare and watch the grass grow."

Upon his discharge in 1951, Hughes entered Cambridge intending to read English literature but, finding the curriculum not to his liking, he switched to archaeology and anthropology. His study and research in those subjects, as well as his intensive reading of folklore and poetry—especially that of William Butler Yeats—had a profound influence on his work. Otherwise, Hughes found Cambridge to be "a most deadly institution unless you're aiming to be either a scholar or a gentleman."

Following his graduation in 1954, Hughes took an assortment of jobs, working variously as a gardener, a night watchman, a zoo attendant, a schoolteacher, and a script reader. He published an occasional poem in the Cambridge University poetry magazines and, early in 1956, he and a few friends launched St. Botolph's Review, a highbrow literary magazine that survived only one issue. At its inaugural party, Hughes met Sylvia Plath, the young American poet who was then studying at Newnham College, Cambridge, on a Fulbright Fellowship. They were married on June 16, 1956. The couple settled in Cambridge, where Ted Hughes taught English and drama at a nearby high school while his wife completed her studies. They both got up at dawn to write poetry. "We would write poetry every day," Hughes said years later. "It was all we were interested in, all we ever did. We were like two feet, each one using everything the other did."

In 1956 the Poetry Center of the Young Men's and Young Women's Hebrew Association of New York held a competition for unpublished poets. First prize was the simultaneous British and American publication of the winning poems. Sylvia Plath typed up the best of her husband's poems and entered them in the competition. Out of nearly 300 entries, W. H. Auden, Stephen Spender, and Marianne Moore, the competition's judges, chose Hughes's poems. Collected under the title The Hawk in the Rain, they were published in September 1957 by Harper & Row in the United States and Faber & Faber in England.

The Hawk in the Rain includes love poems, some war poems, and a number of extraordinary poems, including the title poem, "The Jaguar," and "Wind," that celebrate the awesome power and beauty of nature. Keith Sagar, in his exhaustive analysis of Hughes's work, *The Art of Ted Hughes* (1975), maintains that the central theme of all these poems is man in relation to the elements, to the earth, to animals, to time, and to his own mortality. Using rhythms and rhymes with a raw power reminiscent of Gerard Manley Hopkins, Hughes was, in Sagar's words, "able to cope with the biggest things; [his language] can generate energies equal to the great primal energies of the world." It was the primitive forcefulness of that language, particularly in the unsentimental descriptions of animals, that so impressed many critics. Although some complained that Hughes's poems were overly derivative of such poets as Yeats, D. H. Lawrence, Dylan Thomas, and Wilfred Owen, and others disliked his "sex-and-violence imagery" and his "melodramatic and slapdash hyperbole," most agreed that *The Hawk in the Rain* was one of the most important first volumes of verse to be published in English since World War II. The collection won first prize in the 1958 Guinness Poetry Awards.

At the time of *The Hawk in the Rain's* publication, Ted Hughes was living in the United States, where he was a member of the English department at the University of Massachusetts. He resigned after a year to devote all his attention to writing poetry. Supported by a Guggenheim Foundation grant that he had received in the spring of 1959, he and his wife spent a few months at Yaddo, the artists' colony at Saratoga Springs, New York, where each of them completed a collection of poems—Sylvia Plath, *The Colossus* and Ted Hughes, *Lupercal.*

Like its predecessor, *Lupercal* (Faber, 1960; Harper, 1960) reveals an uncommon awareness of the untamed beauty and gross brutality of the natural world and its parallels in human society. In "Hawk Roosting," the most anthologized of all Hughes's poems, the hawk flies "direct/Through the bones of the living," parrots "shriek as if they were on fire," and even the thrushes are "terrifying." Taking his inspiration not only from the remembered violence of the birds and beasts of his Yorkshire childhood, but also from a variety of folk tales, legends, and myths, Hughes created a brutal, chaotic world populated by bloodlusting beasts and animalistic men.

Defending *The Hawk in the Rain* against accusations of morbidity and sadism, the poet insisted that his work was "not about violence but vitality." In his view, men attain an animal level of energy only "when they've gone mad." The majority of critics, however, concurred with a reviewer for the *Times Literary Supplement* who, in a critique for the April 15, 1960 issue, complimented the technical virtuosity that made a "narrow, vivid, rather obsessive range of images . . .

seem so generally relevant to our contemporary world." *Lupercal* won for Hughes the Somerset Maugham Award in 1960 and the Hawthornden Prize in 1961 and confirmed his standing as a poet of the first rank.

Returning to England in December 1959, the Hugheses settled in London and then, in 1961, moved to the Devonshire countryside. While Sylvia Plath put the finishing touches on her celebrated novel *The Bell Jar,* Ted Hughes wrote poems, radio plays, short stories, book reviews, and an oratorio. The couple separated shortly before Miss Plath committed suicide in February 1963. For the next few years, Hughes wrote no adult verse, although he did publish several volumes of prose and poetry for children, including *The Earth-Owl and Other Moon People* (Faber, 1963), published by Viking in the United States thirteen years later as *Moon Whales,* and *Nessie the Mannerless Monster* (Faber, 1964), which was retitled *Nessie the Monster* (Bobbs-Merrill, 1974) for American readers.

Recklings, a limited edition of rather opaque poems in a variety of styles published by Turret Books in 1966, was in many ways the progenitor of *Wodwo,* Hughes's next major work. Taking its title from the ambiguous creature encountered by Sir Gawain in the medieval romance *Sir Gawain and the Green Knight, Wodwo* (Faber, 1967; Harper, 1967) includes forty poems, five short stories, and a surrealistic radio play whose images recall Robert Graves's monumental study in myth, *The White Goddess.* Although the animal and nature poems in *Wodwo* are as vivid as anything in Hughes's earlier collections, their tone is generally bleaker and their concerns are more obviously metaphysical. Hughes's growing fascination with mythology, especially the mythology of the pagan White Goddess of the seasons who is identified with the poetic Muse, is especially evident in a number of these poems.

Hughes saw traces of both the wodwo and the hawk in Leonard Baskin's engravings of oddly anthropoid crows. These solitary, omnivorous, and seemingly indestructible birds, which are figures of ill omen in folklore all over the world, captured Hughes's imagination and he immediately set to work on an epic tale interspersed with harsh, grating "crow songs." He never finished the epic, but in 1970 Faber published sixty-six of the "songs" as *Crow: From the Life and Songs of the Crow.* An American edition was released by Harper in 1971. *Crow* followed the career of a mythical quasi-human bird who, like "a sort of cosmic Kilroy," in Christopher Porterfield's words, was "in on everything from the creation to the ultimate nuclear holocaust," either as a demon, a witness, or a victim. "He is minced, dismembered, rendered cataleptic, but always he bobs back," Porterfield wrote in his review for *Time* (April 5, 1971). "In his graceless, ignoble way.

he is the lowest common denominator of the universal forces that obsess Hughes. He is a symbol of the essential survivor, of whatever endures, however battered."

In "Lineage," a parody of Biblical "begats," Crow's heritage is traced back to God "Who begat Nothing/Who begat Never/Never Never Never/Who begat Crow/Screaming for blood/ Grubs, crusts/Anything/Trembling featherless elbows in the nest's filth." A ravenous predator, Crow recognized that violence is natural and guilt universal—"Everything took the blame"—in God's new world. Turning aside divine attempts to rehabilitate him, Crow gradually usurped God's role and, in general, interfered with His designs.

For Irvin Ehrenpreis, writing in the *New York Review of Books* (August 17, 1978), *Crow* was "perhaps a more plausible explanation for the present condition of the world than the Christian sequence." Peter Porter, who reviewed *Crow* for the *Guardian* (October 15, 1970), also commended Hughes for taking "legendary material as old as Gilgamesh or Eden" and making it apply to everything from "modern genocides" to the "smaller disasters of individual human lives." Commenting on the poems for *Newsweek* (April 12, 1971), Jack Kroll wrote: "Crow is the blackness of all of us, including the whiteness that was. In these poems that hit like rocks and bite like beaks, Hughes speaks the ultimate prophecy: life will survive in a terrain and continuum of destruction." Crow has turned out to be even more tenacious than his creator realized. Hughes recently completed a number of new Crow poems that will be incorporated in an expanded edition of the original work.

In 1971 Hughes accompanied Peter Brook, the director, and his International Center for Theatre Research to Iran for the Fifth Shiraz Festival. While there, he wrote *Orghast*, a play in which much of the dialogue is in an invented language—also called Orghast—he devised on the theory that the human voice can project very complex mental states by sound alone. The Prometheus legend, on which *Orghast* is based, is also the subject of twenty-one poems collected in *Prometheus on His Crag* (Rainbow Press, 1973). Keith Sagar saw in both of these works evidence that Hughes had arrived at a "final reconciliation" of man and his suffering—a sense that we are fortunate to be human, "not simply in spite of pain and death but in a mysterious way because of them."

Another collection of poems inspired by Baskin drawings was published as *Cave Birds* by Scolar Press in 1975 and, in an enlarged edition, by Faber in 1978. It is one of several approaches to a theme that has increasingly preoccupied Hughes in recent years. This is the Gravesian idea that modern man has sinned by denying "the White Goddess"— the primordial, natural part of himself—and

embracing instead a sterile, intellectual humanism. Made aware of his psychic guilt, the protagonist of *Cave Birds* embarks on a quest of sorts and, after various ordeals and transmutations, suffers an "ego death" and at length achieves a kind of rebirth.

This theme is central in *Gaudete* (Faber, 1977; Harper, 1977). In this long, complicated, and cryptic tale, an Anglican clergyman, the Reverend Nicholas Lumb, is carried away by elemental spirits, who have work for him in the supernatural world. To take his place in the real world, the spirits carve a spurious Lumb out of an oak log. As might be expected of a figure created from an oak tree —an ancient fertility spirit—the new Lumb organizes the women of the parish into a seraglio for his own use, announcing that one of them will bear a new Messiah. The results are tragicomic and ultimately disastrous, since the desacralized modern world cannot control the primordial forces thus released. Eventually, the spirits "cancel" the bogus Lumb, the cuckolded husbands raid the parish hall, where an orgy is in progress, and hunt the false Lumb to his death. It is the false Lumb's last day that is the subject of *Gaudete*. In a lyrical epilogue, the real Lumb reappears on the west coast of Ireland, performs a small miracle, and "roams about composing hymns and psalms to a nameless female deity."

Gaudete was originally conceived as a film and the story is told, as Irvin Ehrenpreis wrote in the New York *Review of Books* (August 17, 1978), "in cinematic, detached episodes, using the present tense and mixing descriptive prose with hyperbolic free verse." Ehrenpreis recognized that the story embodied elements from Christianity and from various pagan myths, including those of Dionysus and the White Goddess, and was itself "a myth of death and resurrection." Many critics confessed that they were mystified by the poem and some complained about its "hyperbolic shrillness" and verbal "overkill." But Keith Sagar, who is perhaps Hughes's most perceptive critic, regards *Gaudete* as "the most important poetic work in English in our time."

Sagar explains *Gaudete* as a psychological analogue. In his interpretation, there is only one Lumb, a civilized, voluntary celibate who, having denied his natural instincts for too long, is for a time possessed by the demonic forces he has tried to stifle. They drive him mad and destroy his ego, but in the end he recovers, transformed, as a kind of shaman— the possessor of psychic gifts of great importance to mankind. The reborn Lumb's "hymns and psalms," Sagar writes, describe "a highly refined course of moral self-development. . . . The basic image of the whole work has been that of the split, the split psyche, the split between men and women, man and nature, the profane and the sacred. This split is the wound to be healed. What is sought is an adjustment in consciousness and feeling which will enable us to recognize these 'opposites' as . . . parts or phases of a single whole."

In *Remains of Elmet* (Faber, 1979), a book of poems about his native Calder Valley in West Yorkshire, Hughes continued his myth-making, but with a relaxation of the tension that had marked some of his earlier work. Equaled in their eloquence by the accompanying photographs of Fay Godwin, the poems trace the history of the "last British kingdom to fall to the Angles" from paleolithic times, through the development of nonconformism and industrialism, to the desuetude of the present.

In addition to his adult verse, Hughes has written a powerful adaptation of Seneca's *Oedipus* (Faber, 1969; Doubleday, 1972), which was first produced by Britain's National Theatre Company in 1968; librettos for two operas by Gordon Crosse, *The Demon of Adachigahara* (Oxford Univ. Press, 1969) and *The Story of Vasco* (Oxford Univ. Press, 1974); several collections of poems, including *Moon-Bells and other Poems* (Chatto, 1978) and *Season Songs* (Faber, 1976; Viking, 1975), intended primarily, but not solely, for young readers; delightful plays for children, some of which were published in *The Coming of the Kings* (Faber, 1970) and in *The Tiger's Bones* (Viking, 1974); and a number of prose stories for children, the most notable being *The Iron Man* (Faber,

1968), a fanciful tale that was published as *The Iron Giant* (Harper, 1968) in the United States. He drew on his much-admired BBC radio programs that explained the mechanics of poetry to children for *Poetry in the Making* (Faber, 1967), which was later released in an American edition by Doubleday as *Poetry Is*. Hughes has also edited books of poems by Emily Dickinson, Keith Douglas, Shakespeare, and Sylvia Plath, and has translated poems by Vasko Popa, János Pilinszky, and Yehuda Amichai.

Ted Hughes is a tall, dark man with a hawk-like profile and a penetrating gaze. He and his present wife, the former Carol Orchard, whom he married in 1970, live in the thatched cottage in Devon that has been his home since 1961. He has two children, Frieda and Nicholas, from his earlier marriage to Sylvia Plath. In an interview in the *London Magazine* (January 1971), Hughes said: "We go on writing poems because one poem never gets the whole account right. There is always something missed. . . . In the end, one's poems are ragged, dirty, undated letters from remote battles and weddings and one thing and another."

References: Commonweal 94:483+ S 17 '71; *Mlle* 48:34+ Ja '59 por; *Nation* 226:53+ Ja 21 '78; *Newsweek* 77:114+ Ap 12 '71; *Sat R* 40:43 N 9 '57, 54:39 O 2 '71; Sagar, Keith. *Ted Hughes* (1975), *The Art of Ted Hughes* (1975); *Who's Who*, 1978

Hunter, Alberta

Apr. 1, 1895- Singer; songwriter. Address: b. c/o The Cookery, 21 University Pl., New York City, N.Y. 10003

"There's plenty of good tunes, Honey, left in an old violin," insist the lyrics of the blues song "Workin' Man," written some years ago by Alberta Hunter, one of the great ladies of the golden age of jazz. The sentiment expressed seems eminently appropriate to Miss Hunter herself. A contemporary of Bessie Smith, Sophie Tucker, Josephine Baker, and Louis Armstrong, she came from the slums of Memphis to triumph as a leading blues singer in Chicago and New York during the 1920's and as the toast of four continents in the 1930's and 1940's. After working for two decades in virtual obscurity as a nurse in a New York City hospital, she was persuaded in 1977, at the age of eighty-two, to make a comeback. Her recent performances before capacity audiences at the Cookery in New York's Greenwich Village demonstrate that Alberta Hunter has lost none of her evergreen vitality and that her popularity is not just based on nostalgia.

A native of legendary Beale Street in Memphis, Tennessee, Alberta Hunter was born on April 1, 1895. (Some sources give 1897

as the year of her birth.) She had an older sister, called La Tosca, and a younger half-sister, Josephine Beatty. "My mother worked as a chambermaid for Miss Myrtle and Miss Emma in a sporting house on Gayoso Street," she told Whitney Balliett in an interview for the *New Yorker* (October 31, 1977). "My father, Charles Hunter, was a Pullman porter, but he died before I ever knew him. We girls stayed most of the time with my grandmother, Nancy Peterson, who also looked after all my cousins." A sickly youngster, Alberta was known by the childhood nickname "Pig" —because, as she recalls, "I was quite messy at that age." She remembers her grandmother's advice: "Keep busy, be a lady, keep your clothes clean even if they're raggedy, stay away from whiskey, and never put a cigarette in your mouth. And do your work the best you can." Her budding talent for singing was encouraged by her music teacher who persuaded her to perform in school concerts.

When she was about eleven—having heard that singers could earn as much as $10 a week in the Windy City—Alberta Hunter decided to go north to Chicago on the invitation of one of her teachers, who happened to have a child's pass for the railroad. There she looked up a friend who got her a job as second cook in a boardinghouse, peeling potatoes and performing other kitchen chores for room and board plus $6 a week, $2 of which she sent to her mother. Dressing up to appear older, Alberta soon began to sneak into bars, looking for a chance to sing. "I'd get kicked out of joints and go right back in," she has recalled in one of her press interviews.

Eventually she was hired to sing four hours a day for $5 a week at Dago Frank's, a favorite hangout for pimps and their "sportin' gals," who took the frail twelve-year-old under their protective wing. She remained there for a year and ten months, developing her musical talent and learning such songs as "All Night Long," "Where the River Shannon Flows," and "Melancholy Baby" from the piano player. After Dago Frank's was closed down, Alberta Hunter went to work at another Chicago jazz club, Hugh Hoskins'. "The dangerous element, like Give-a-Damn Jones, hung out there, but so did the pickpocket women, and they did everything in their power to show me how to live a clean life," she told Whitney Balliett. "When I wrote 'Reap What You Sow,' I was thinking of some of those rough types." While performing at Hugh Hoskins' she achieved some local popularity as a jazz singer, and the club had to be enlarged to accommodate the crowds that came to hear her sing the blues. By that time, according to Robert Palmer of the New York *Times* (October 14, 1977), she had "developed a sophisticated blues style, using her velvety contralto like a sweet C-melody saxophone. She did not belt the blues, she insinuated them."

After performing for about three years at Hugh Hoskins', Alberta Hunter was hired for $12 a week to sing at the Panama Café, where her fellow entertainers included Cora Green, Florence Mills, and Bricktop—later the owner of a world-renowned Paris nightclub. It was at the Panama that Miss Hunter introduced "St. Louis Blues" to Chicago audiences. For a while she also sang next door, at the De Luxe Café, before moving across the street to Bill Bottoms' famous Dreamland Café, then Chicago's leading showcase for New Orleans-style jazz.

Starting at the Dreamland shortly after the end of World War I at a salary of $17.50 a week, Alberta Hunter sang with the resident ensemble, King Oliver's Creole Jazz Band, which also featured clarinetist Sidney Bechet, pianist Lil Hardin, drummer Minor Hall and, later on, cornetist Louis Armstrong. "That Dreamland was some place," Miss Hunter reminisced, as quoted by Martin Williams in *Jazz Masters of New Orleans* (Macmillan, 1967). "It was *big* and always packed. And you *had* to be a singer then—there were no microphones and those bands were marvelous. . . . Singers then would go around from table to table . . . hustlin' dollars in tips. . . . I made a lot of money that way." The audiences at the Dreamland included pickpockets, politicians, and gamblers, future musicians like Eddie Condon and Benny Goodman, and such celebrities as Al Jolson and Sophie Tucker. After hearing her interpretations of "Someday Sweetheart" and "A Good Man Is Hard to Find," Miss Tucker sent her maid to Alberta Hunter, asking her to come to her dressing room and teach her the songs. "I would never go, so her piano player would come over and listen and get everything down," Miss Hunter told Whitney Balliett. "But I was crazy about her as a singer, and she influenced me."

In 1921 Miss Hunter began to record such songs as "Bring Back the Joys" and "He's a Darn Good Man," with piano accompaniment by Fletcher Henderson, for Black Swan, the first black-owned recording studio in the United States. Later she recorded for Paramount and other labels, backed up by such topflight instrumentalists as Armstrong, Bechet, Fats Waller, Zutty Singleton, Perry Bradford, and Eubie Blake, and she became the first black vocalist to record with a white band—the Original Memphis Five. She also recorded some songs, including "Nobody Knows the Way I Feel," for the Gennet label under the name of her sister Josephine Beatty. Her "Downhearted Blues," which she wrote in collaboration with Lovie Austin and recorded for Paramount in 1922 was turned into a major hit by Bessie Smith, whose 1923 Columbia recording sold 780,000 copies within six months. "I'm still collecting the royalties," Miss Hunter said in a recent interview. "I'm too slick to let 'em cheat me outta that!"

Convinced that she had gone as far as she could in Chicago, Alberta Hunter went to New York City in 1923. A few days after her arrival she was chosen to replace Bessie Smith in the Broadway production of Eddie Hunter's all-black musical comedy *How Come?* at the Apollo Theatre, where her first performance brought her a standing ovation. She remained with the show for about a year and also went on national tour with it. Later she obtained a part in another musical, *Change Your Luck*, at the George M. Cohan Theatre. She was also for a time at the Club Basha in Harlem as vocalist for the Red Onion Jazz Babies, which included Sidney Bechet and Louis Armstrong among others and made a number of recordings. Then she went back to Chicago, working at the Royal Garden and the Phoenix and appearing with Earl Hines at the Sunset Cafe. She is credited with having originated the "Black Bottom" at about that time, a dance made popular by Ann Pennington in *George White's Scandals of 1926*.

During an engagement at Michaelson's nightclub in Cincinnati, Alberta Hunter met Willard Saxbe Townsend, a waiter and army veteran. They were married and went to Chicago, but the marriage lasted only about two months. "He was so nice and I know he deserved a good wife, so I left him and went to Europe," Miss Hunter told Holly Hill in an interview published in the *East Side Express* (February 9, 1978). "He remarried, got a college degree, became head of the redcaps' union in Chicago, and was the only Negro on the executive board of the C.I.O. We remained good friends [until his death a few years ago], but I never gave marriage another thought."

Like many black American artists in the 1920's and 1930's, Alberta Hunter went to Europe, partly to escape the trammels of racial discrimination in her own country. After an engagement in Monte Carlo she went to London, where she stayed near Regent's Park in a house in which Marian Anderson was a fellow resident. She performed with Noble Sissle and took part in a benefit at the London Palladium that included Oscar Hammerstein II, Jerome Kern, and Florenz Ziegfeld among the audience. An audition for the 1928 production of *Show Boat* at London's Drury Lane Theatre won her the part of Queenie in a cast that featured Paul Robeson—whom she greatly admired—as Joe, Sir Cedric Hardwicke as Cap'n Andy, and Mabel Mercer as a member of the chorus. Her renditions of "Can't Help Lovin' Dat Man" earned her ovations, and she considers her eleven months with the show—which King George V and Queen Mary once attended —a highlight of her career.

About 1930 Alberta Hunter went to Paris where, after taking a Berlitz course in French, she appeared in a show called *Vive Paris*, sang at the Chez Florence, and succeeded Josephine Baker at the Casino de Paris. Then she went on the road, performing at clubs in Copenhagen, Alexandria, Cairo, Athens, Istanbul, and "the place in Vienna where Hitler used to drink beer." In the fall of 1934, after a brief return to the United States, she turned up once more in London, appearing at the Dorchester Hotel with Jack Jackson, with whom she made several recordings, including "Stars Fell on Alabama," and taking part in BBC Dance Orchestra broadcasts. Among her audiences at the Dorchester was the Prince of Wales (the future King Edward VIII and Duke of Windsor), who was entranced by her performance, and Noël Coward, who wrote the song "I Travel Alone" especially for her.

Back in the United States, Miss Hunter performed in nightclubs and vaudeville, sang on the New York radio stations WEAF and WJZ, and was featured, along with Maxine Sullivan, on the NBC radio show *Chamber Music Society of Lower Basin Street*. She appeared as Dolly in DuBose Heyward's musical drama *Mamba's Daughters*, starring Ethel Waters, which opened at Broadway's Empire Theatre on January 3, 1939 and ran for 162 performances.

During World War II, Alberta Hunter joined the U.S.O. and took its first black rhythm and blues unit overseas to entertain the troops. She gave special performances for Generals Dwight D. Eisenhower and Douglas MacArthur, and by the end of the war she had flown six times around the world and made twenty-five visits to Europe, Asia, and the South Pacific. After the war she resumed her nightclub work, but in the early 1950's she was again active in the U.S.O., entertaining American troops in Korea. She visited Europe with Snub Mosley in 1952 and then toured Canada and spent some time performing in Chicago nightclubs before returning to New York.

The death, in early 1954, of Alberta Hunter's mother, to whom she had been very close, made her decide to give up her singing career eventually and do something to "help humanity." Over the objections of friends, she enrolled in the school for practical nursing at the Harlem YWCA. Meanwhile she continued to sing at the Bon Soir nightclub, and in 1954-55 she understudied three major roles for the show *Mrs. Patterson*, starring Eartha Kitt, at Broadway's National Theatre.

After graduating from nursing school in 1957, Alberta Hunter obtained a job as a scrub nurse at Goldwater Memorial Hospital on New York City's Roosevelt Island. During the next twenty years she never missed a day's work, and her past remained a well-kept secret. Except for doing some recording—including an LP album that she made with Lovie Austin and Her Blues Serenaders for the Riverside label in 1961—she remained aloof from show business. Finally, in April 1977, the hospital administrators, believing that she had reached the mandatory retirement age of seventy (she was actually eighty-two), forced her to retire and gave her "a beautiful farewell party and a pin." Miss Hunter admits that she would have remained at her nursing duties indefinitely if permitted to do so. "It's so gratifying to be a nurse," she told Bruce Cook of the Washington Post (October 22, 1978). "Even those you know will never get well you can help because you know you can comfort them. Yes, it was worth it. All twenty years of it."

"Bored to tears" by her enforced retirement, Alberta Hunter could not remain inactive. During the summer of 1977 she attended a party given by Bobby Short for her old friend Mabel Mercer. Among the guests was Charlie Bourgeois, an official of the Newport Jazz Festival, who after hearing her sing put her in touch with jazz impresario Barney Josephson, the owner of the Cookery, a Greenwich Village nightclub-restaurant. During her initial six-week stint at the Cookery, beginning on October 10, 1977, she created such a sensation that her engagement was extended indefinitely by Josephson, who became her manager. "To witness one of her performances is to forget yourself completely," Iris Schneider wrote in the New York Daily News (April 9, 1978). "Hands clap, fingers snap, the laughter is loud, and . . . each musical phrase is punctuated by cries of 'Oh Yeah' and 'Ding it, baby' from the audience. It is truly a mutual love affair. And . . . her blues, laments, and sexy double entendres are as vampy and believable as ever." As of the spring of 1979, Alberta Hunter was still performing regularly at the Cookery, giving two shows each weekday and three on Saturdays.

Unable to honor more than a few of the offers that flooded in after her comeback, Alberta Hunter accepted a commission from the Hollywood director Robert Altman to record the soundtrack for his film Remember My Name. To fit the mood of the movie, she composed two new blues numbers, including the title song, which, in a display of improvisatory talent, she made up as she recorded. Neither the music nor the lyrics required editing. She also updated eight of her earlier compositions, among them "Downhearted Blues" and "Workin' Man." Invited to the film's premiere in Memphis in October 1978, Miss Hunter was honored by the city fathers and the Beale Street Heritage Foundation, and Tennessee Governor Ray Blanton proclaimed a statewide "Alberta Hunter Day." The Remember My Name soundtrack was issued as an LP on the Columbia Records label in 1978.

In June 1978 Alberta Hunter was featured, along with the nonagenarian jazz pianist Eubie Blake, in a concert of "jazz for the young and the young at heart," which was presented at New York University's Loeb Student Center as part of the Newport Jazz Festival. In January 1979 she sang to a sold-out house at the Baird Auditorium of the Smithsonian Institution's Museum of Natural History in Washington, D.C. She has performed at the White House, where she won plaudits from President Jimmy Carter. Much in demand for television appearances, she has been seen on the Today Show, 60 Minutes, and the Dick Cavett Show, and she has made nonsinging commercials.

Although the blues remain her forte, Miss Hunter considers herself a "variety artist" rather than a blues singer. Her repertoire includes gospel numbers, show tunes, standards like "Pennies From Heaven" and "The Best Things in Life Are Free," and material in French, Italian, German, Yiddish, and Danish. She often glosses the lyrics she sings with a witty commentary of her own. Unable to read or write a note of music, she composes tunes in her head and then has someone transcribe them for her. Among her recent compositions is the blues number "I Want a Two-Fisted, Double-Jointed, Rough and Ready Man." Artists who have recorded her works include Eddy Arnold, Dinah Washington, Ella Fitzgerald, and Mildred Bailey.

Alberta Hunter makes her home in a two-room cooperative apartment on Manhattan's 139th Street and maintains a studio on Roosevelt Island. Small and fragile, she "seems to grow in size and strength the moment she starts singing," in the words of Bob Micklin of Newsday (March 5, 1978), who sums her up as "an easy woman to love." Geraldine Chaplin, who stars in Remember My Name, has said that Miss Hunter reminds her of her father, Charlie Chaplin. According to Whitney Balliett, "Head on, Alberta Hunter is egg-shaped, and sideways she is Egyptian. Her face is lean and tight and handsome, and her gray-black hair is swept back into finger-size braids. Her brown eyes are clear, and she talks in a staccato. . . . Her voice is steady and rich and her vibrato betrays none of the quaveriness that often besets older singers." She usually wears a simple skirt and blouse, and her heavy gold earrings have become one of her trademarks.

A lover of all music, except "that loud, electronic stuff," Alberta Hunter listens to recordings of Ray Charles or Mahalia Jackson, and also to opera, especially Carmen, I Pagliacci, and Madama Butterfly. She likes to shop in New York City department stores and to ride in city buses, and she still visits some of her former hospital patients. Although not a churchgoer, she is devoutly religious. "I don't read the Bible because I don't understand it," she has said, "but I understand

God." Exulting in her belated celebrity, she considers herself "the happiest woman in the world."

References: N Y Times C p26 O 14 '77, p12 N 25 '78 por; New Yorker 53:100+ O 31 '77 por; Newsweek 90:101 O 31 '77 pors; Rolling Stone p18 Ag 24 '78 por; Balliett, Whitney. American Singers (1979); Chilton, John. Who's Who of Jazz (1970); Kinkle, Roger D. Complete Encyclopedia of Popular Music and Jazz 1900-1950 (1974)

Irving, John (Winslow)

Mar. 2, 1942- Writer. Address: b. c/o Peter Matson, Harold Matson Co., Inc., 22 E. 40th St., New York City, N.Y. 10016; h. RFD 3, 216A, Putney, Vt. 05346

With the publication in 1978 of the The World According to Garp, an extravagant novel full of grotesquerie, John Irving was elevated to a status enjoyed by just a handful of contemporary novelists—Joan Didion, Joseph Heller, and Kurt Vonnegut Jr., to name a few—whose works bridge the gap between popular and serious American fiction. Garp, which was nominated for the National Book Award for fiction, became Irving's first best seller, although his three earlier entries had generated a warm critical response. Freed from the ecomic necessity of college teaching by Garp's phenomenal success, Irving is currently working on his fifth novel. "I'm a novelist, and all I want to write right now is another novel," he said recently. "And then another and

another, for the time remaining."

Of Scottish descent, John Winslow Irving was born on March 2, 1942, in the old Colonial town of Exeter, New Hampshire to Colin F. N. and Frances (Winslow) Irving. His father was a teacher of Russian history at and treasurer of Phillips Exeter Academy, the famous boys' prep school. One of three children, Irving laconically, and perhaps facetiously, described his family in an article for Esquire (March 27, 1979): "My father the schoolteacher and treasurer; my mother, the mother and hospital volunteer; my sister the forklift driver and artist; my brother the nightclub performer and paramedic." His childhood was, as he told one reporter, so happy and "peaceful" that "as a story, [it] would put you to sleep before I got out of grammar school." His only suffering occurred in his mid-teens, when he realized he wanted to become a writer. "How lonely that was!" he told Thomas Williams in an interview for the New York Times Book Review (April 23, 1978). "There was nothing like majoring in French or going to law school or medical school to look forward to; I had a terrible sense of how different I was from all my friends, and I didn't want to be different at all."

After graduating from Exeter Academy, Irving studied at the University of Pittsburgh (1961-62) and at the University of Vienna (1963-64) before enrolling at the University of New Hampshire, where he received his B.A. degree, cum laude, in 1965. He continued his education at the University of Iowa and took his M.F.A. degree in 1967. Returning to New England later that year, he accepted an assistant professorship in the English department at Mount Holyoke College in South Hadley, Massachusetts.

In 1969, at the age of twenty-seven, John Irving published his first novel, Setting Free the Bears (Random House). Drawing on his experiences as a college student in Europe, Irving told the picaresque tale of two aimless young Austrians, Siegfried ("Siggy") Javotnik and Hannes Graff, who meet by chance and impulsively take off on a motorcycle journey that ends abruptly when Siggy is killed by a swarm of angry bees. During their spree the two play several relatively harmless pranks and conceive an elaborate plan to free the animals in Vienna's Hietzinger Zoo as a protest against a return of fascism. After Siggy's death, Hannes decides to go ahead with the "zoo bust" on his own. Guided by Siggy's detailed notes describing the daily routine at the zoo, he overpowers the night watchman and releases most of the animals from their cages. On the surface, Setting Free the Bears is a typical American rite de passage novel about adolescent escape and revolt, but it also touches on the universal themes of freedom and responsibility, rebellion and restraint. "All men," Hannes observes at the end of the book, have names, and specific places where they're "allowed to go."

For a first novel, *Setting Free the Bears* received considerable critical attention and most of the reviews were, with some reservations, favorable. Writing in the *Saturday Review* (February 8, 1969), H. S. Resnik was somewhat mystified by Irving's apparent failure to find his "American identity and sensibility." Still, he was greatly impressed by the author's "uncommon imaginative power." A reviewer for *Time* magazine (February 14, 1969) singled out for special praise Irving's sensitive characterizations and unusually perceptive descriptive passages: "[He] describes all immediate and sensual events with poetic grace—even such prosaic occurrences as the starting of a motorcycle." But Martin Levin, in his review of what he called a "mixture of Till Eulenspiegel and Ken Kesey" for the New York *Times Book Review* (February 9, 1969), wondered why, "as mile after mile of souped-up prose speeds by, is the author telling us all this?" He concluded that Irving had "dumped some of the material of experience" into his novel, which is "less than the sum of its parts."

In 1969 and 1970 Irving worked with Irvin Kershner, the motion picture director, an experience on which he drew in writing his second novel, *The Water-Method Man* (Random, 1972), for which he received a grant from the Rockefeller Foundation. Fred ("Bogus") Trumper, the "water-method man," is a sound editor for an underground filmmaker. (The book takes its title from the treatment prescribed for Trumper's urinary problem.) In that long and complex novel, which jumps from first to third person, from past to present tense, and from one literary form to another, the major themes and devices of Irving's subsequent fiction begin to emerge. His concern with love and sex is particularly apparent in *The Water-Method Man,* and although he does not depend so heavily on the melodramatic episodes that would characterize his later work, his penchant for exaggeration and his ability to weave the bizarre into the ordinary fabric of daily life are obvious. "People do go to extremes, after all," he has explained. "It's in the extremes that we often recognize how we truly are."

The Water-Method Man also offers the first instance of the idiosyncratic use of autobiographical detail that has marked all of Irving's fiction since *Setting Free the Bears.* Irving and the book's protagonist, "Bogus" Trumper, graduated from Exeter, attended the same universities, and played the same collegiate sports. They even share the same birthday and wedding anniversary. But those elements in common, as the author has pointed out, do not make him an autobiographical novelist. "I use as ruthlessly as I can anything I know as 'landmarks'—places such as postwar Vienna, the familiar habits of people, my own love of wrestling, which features in my novels—but I am very thankful I am not in any way an autobiographical writer," he told Barbara A. Bannon in an interview for *Publishers Weekly*

(April 24, 1978). "I've led a very ordinary, uninteresting life. I've never been tempted to think that anything that happened to me personally was fascinating or interesting to other people. If you do not have a personal axe to grind, you are free to imagine a story as best you can—you can purge your own worst fears by exaggerating them thoroughly."

Critical reaction to *The Water-Method Man* was mixed. Topsy Smalley, who reviewed the book for the *Library Journal* (June 15, 1972), was one of the book's more enthusiastic supporters. In her opinion, Irving wrote "with sensitivity" and "rare humor" and meshed his hero's "quest for 'where he's at' with fundamental emotional touchstones." Paul Majkut, who assessed it for *Best Sellers* (July 1, 1972), disagreed. He found the book to be "light" and "even risqué," but "not exceptionally funny." Moreover, he said, it "[avoided] every real human issue present throughout the land, throughout the world. . . . [The author and his book] are the product of academic 'creative writing'; both are stylistically and thematically . . . rooted in the Writer's Workshop at the University of Iowa; both are natural corn."

Irving did, in fact, spend the three years following the publication of *The Water-Method Man* as writer-in-residence at the University of Iowa, and he was a visiting lecturer at its workshop. It was during that period that he began contributing short stories, among them "Lost in New York" and "Almost in Iowa," and occasional pieces, such as "Gorgeous Dan," a profile of Olympic wrestling champion Dan Gable, to *Esquire, Playboy,* and other magazines. Wrestling, Irving's favorite sport, is a consistent metaphor in his work and figured in the title of his third novel, *The 158-Pound Marriage* (Random, 1974).

In *The 158-Pound Marriage* an unnamed introspective narrator analyzes and evaluates his wife's affair with Severin Winter, a German professor and wrestling coach, and his own liaison with Severin's wife, Edith. Irving was consciously indebted to Ford Maddox Ford's *The Good Soldier* for that novel about two couples who exchange partners, but the extended wrestling metaphor emphasized the tense, combative relationships of the principal characters and gave the rather melodramatic story an added dimension.

Except for occasional objections to the gratuitous violence of some scenes and the inclusion of "left-over pieces of writing from works-in-progress," the reviews of *The 158-Pound Marriage* were the most favorable Irving had yet received. A typical appraisal was that by Martin Levin, who had disliked Irving's first book, for the New York *Times Book Review* (November 3, 1974): "Mr. Irving develops [his] theme in a deft, hard-hitting style, breaking cleanly at the clinches. His lean prose is perfectly attuned to the subject matter, which might easily have sunk into the ooze of a sloppier rhetoric. . . . What he demonstrates beautifully is that a one-to-one relationship is more demanding than a free-for-all."

In 1975 Irving returned from Iowa to resume teaching at Mount Holyoke. The following year he also taught on the staff of the Bread Loaf Writer's Conference in Middlebury, Vermont. "I'm one of those people who can teach and write at the same time," he told Jerry Tallmer in an interview for the New York Post (July 1, 1978). "I can do it almost painlessly and well, with my left hand." Irving remained on the faculty at Mount Holyoke, blocking out future novels in his spare time, until the financial success of The World According to Garp, published by E. P. Dutton in 1978, liberated him to pursue his writing career full time.

"I really began with a very simple idea," Irving told Barbara Bannon, in explaining the genesis of Garp. "I wanted to write a novel about a mother and son, a very individual woman and a very individual son." An eccentric radical feminist, Jenny Fields, Garp's mother, deliberately conceives her child by a dying lobotomized soldier during World War II. Raised in the New England boarding school where his mother works as a nurse, Garp becomes a writer. Some of his work, such as "The Pension Grillparzer," a short story, is incorporated into the novel. He marries Helen Holm, a literature teacher who is the daughter of a wrestling coach, and they have two children.

Into that rather simple structure, Irving injected large doses of sex and violence, gallows humor, and social satire. For example, in the bizarre automobile accident that is the book's central tragedy, one of Garp's beloved children is killed, another loses an eye to a gearshift, and his wife's lover is sexually mutilated. Broadly conceived and executed, The World According to Garp is high melodrama. Irving himself has described it as "artfully disguised soap opera." "I mean to make you laugh, to make you cry; these are soap-opera intentions, all the way," he told one reporter.

Although Irving has repeatedly insisted that he "[made] up all the important things," autobiographical details abound in The World According to Garp, and Garp's life, at many crucial points, exactly parallels that of the author. Detecting those similarities, one critic suggested that the novel was, on one level, "a sort of treatise on how reality is processed by fiction." "It takes a sophisticated view of the relations in art between the imaginary and the actual," Julian Moynahan wrote in the New York Times Book Review (April 23, 1978). Garp was, above all, a "demonstration of how fiction, in creating a world of its own, remains tied by the lifeline of the writer's experience to the world we all share."

Compared by appreciative reviewers to the novels of Joseph Heller and Vladimir Nabokov, The World According to Garp was variously described as "an X-rated soap opera with grandeur," a "self-indulgent fantasy," and a "comic scourge, terminally funny." For more than one reviewer, however, the novel was essentially a brilliant, insightful exploration of the "imperfect, often puzzling, but enduring relationships" between people and between "memory and imagination, life and art: all the fragile networks men and women erect against the hazards of the world," as William McPherson observed in the Washington Post.

The charge of excessive violence sounded virtually the only sour note in the chorus of otherwise almost unanimously laudatory reviews. Margaret Drabble and Thomas Williams, the novelists, were among those who commented on the unusual juxtaposition of outrageous comedy and gothic violence. But to Irving, the combination of "so much joy and comedy with so much violence and pain" was "truthful exaggeration." "I don't see comedy and tragedy as contradictions—in the same way I believe something can be simultaneously funny and sad—I don't see that unhappy endings undermine rich and energetic lives," he explained in an interview for the New York Times Book Review (April 23, 1978). "There are no happy endings; death is horrible, final, and frequently premature. But that's not cause for some sort of blanket cynicism or sophomoric despair; that's just a strong incentive to live purposefully, to be determined about living well."

The World According to Garp hit the hardcover best seller lists within weeks of its publication and remained there for six months, selling more than 115,000 copies. When Pocket Books released the paperback reprint in January 1979 with a splashy nationwide advertising campaign based on the slogan "I Believe in Garp," Irving became an instant celebrity. "I'm enough of an ex-jock to like the applause —and even more, the butterflies, knowing people are now waiting for my next novel," he acknowledged to an interviewer for People magazine (June 19, 1978). By the midsummer of 1979 he had completed six chapters of The Hotel New Hampshire, which is scheduled for publication in 1980. "I don't know how far away the end is—only what it is," he said. "I know the last sentence, but I am very much in the dark concerning how to get to it."

John Irving is slightly under average height and has a muscular physique, the product of his years of amateur, Olympic free-style wrestling and long-distance running. He has regular features, dark hair, and an olive complexion. To keep in shape, he runs daily, wrestles twice a week, and occasionally skis. Although he admires the work of some of his contemporaries, including John Cheever, Joseph Heller, Kurt Vonnegut Jr., and Günter Grass, he usually restricts his reading to earlier writers, such as Charles Dickens, Joseph Conrad, Virginia Woolf, and Thomas Hardy, whom he especially admires for "his stern judgments and his crankiness." "I missed so many books when I was being educated," he explained to one reporter. "I keep going back to read those writers I never got around to reading. And I do a lot of rereading of the books I greatly admire." On August 20, 1964 Irving married Shyla Leary, an abstract painter and photographer whose works hang on the walls of their home, a converted barn,- in Putney, Vermont. The Irvings have two sons, Colin and Brendan.

References: N Y Post p16 Jl 1 '78 por; N Y Times Book R p26 Ap 23 '78 por; People 10:108+ Ja 1 '79 pors; Pub W 213:6+ Ap 24 '78; Washington Post Ep1+ Ap 30 '78 por; Contemporary Authors 1st rev vols 25-28 (1977)

Jackson, Henry M(artin)

May 31, 1912- United States Senator from Washington. Address: b. 137 Russell Senate Office Building, Washington, D.C. 20510; h. Everett, Washington 08201

NOTE: This biography supersedes the article that appeared in *Current Biography* in 1953.

Political know-how, experience, and the authority born of key committee assignments make Henry M. ("Scoop") Jackson one of the most influential Senators in the United States. The Democrat from the state of Washington has represented his constituency for more than a quarter of a century in the Senate, where he ranks fifth in seniority. In 1972 and 1976 Jackson made determined but unsuccessful bids for his party's Presidential nomination. A liberal on domestic matters but a "hawk" on issues of foreign policy and national security, Jackson is known to some as "the last of the red-hot cold warriors." He staunchly supported United States involvement in Vietnam and has continued to advocate a strong American military establishment vis-à-vis the Soviet Union. At the same time he has been a consistent champion of Israel and of Soviet Jewry.

Henry Martin Jackson was born on May 31, 1912 in the milltown of Everett, Washington, the youngest of the four children of Peter and Marine (Anderson) Jackson, who had both emigrated from Norway before they met and married. His father, who had changed the family name from Gresseth, was a laborer, and later an independent contractor, and he also served as secretary of Local 190 of the Plasterers and Cement Masons Union. His mother was a strong-willed, religious woman who chose her son's middle name in honor of Martin Luther. When Henry Jackson was four, his sister Gertrude gave him the nickname "Scoop," because she thought that he resembled a comic-strip cub reporter of that name who managed to maneuver others into doing his work.

While attending local public schools, Jackson established a reputation for hard work and business acumen as a paperboy for the Everett *Daily Herald*. In his teens he also worked for a time in a local sawmill and became a union member. After graduating in 1930 from Everett High School, where he delivered a commencement address on "law and order," he briefly attended Stanford University in California but returned home when he learned of the dismal career prospects in his chosen field, the foreign service. Supported by savings from summer jobs and earnings as a waiter and dishwasher, Jackson then studied at the University of Washington in Seattle, where he graduated with a B.A. degree and also found time to manage the basketball team. On obtaining his LL.B degree from its law school in 1935 he worked briefly at the Everett office of the Federal Emergency Relief Agency, and after passing the state bar examination later that year he joined the local law firm of Black & Rucker, with which he remained until 1938.

Bitten by the political bug, Jackson set his sights on becoming prosecuting attorney of his native Snohomish County. He trounced the lackadaisical incumbent in the Democratic primary and easily defeated the Republican candidate in the general election. During his term of office, from 1938 to 1940, Jackson crusaded against bordellos, gambling houses, and speakeasies, earning for himself the nickname "Soda Pop." Soon not only law-abiding citizens but also those who pined for the days of laxer enforcement and wanted to get rid of him were touting Jackson for higher office. His opportunity came in 1940 when the second Washington district's Representative in Congress decided to run for the Senate. Jackson defeated five other Democrats in the primary, and rode President Franklin D. Roosevelt's coattails to victory in November.

Entering the United States House of Representatives at the opening of the Seventy-seventh Congress in January 1941, Jackson served for six consecutive terms. He enlisted in the United States Army in 1943 but retained his House seat and returned to Washington, D.C. in early 1944, after Roosevelt recalled all uniformed Congressmen to the Capitol. Although Jackson, along with other West Coast officials, condoned the restrictions placed on the freedom of Japanese-Americans during World War II, his record was for the most part liberal, and it included a vote in 1945 against establishment of a permanent House Un-American Activities Committee.

Defeating Payson Peterson for the fourth consecutive time, Jackson was the only Democratic Congressman from the Northwest to survive the Republican landslide of 1946. He voted in vain against overriding President Harry S. Truman's veto of the 1947 Taft-Hartley Labor-Management Relations Act, a measure restricting the rights of unions that was unpopular in his district, where the killing of members of the Industrial Workers of the World in the Everett Massacre of 1916 was still bitterly remembered. With greater success, Jackson promoted the development of defense industry and hydroelectric resources of his region and, as a member of the Joint Committee on Atomic Energy, the expansion of nuclear power.

Campaigning as a champion of public power and atomic energy development, and supported by organized labor and farmers' groups, Jackson ran for the United States Senate in 1952 and was one of only two Democrats to unseat Republican Senators in the face of General Dwight D. Eisenhower's stunning victory in the Presidential race. He defeated the incumbent, Harry P. Cain, an archconservative, by a vote of 595,675 to 460,884, after a bitter contest in which each candidate accused the other of being "soft on Communism."

Taking his seat in the United States Senate in January 1953, Jackson was assigned to Senator Joseph R. McCarthy's permanent investigations subcommittee of the Committee on Government Operations. Eventually he began to question the Wisconsin Republican's far-reaching allegations of Communist subversion in the State Department and the armed forces, and in July 1953 he joined his fellow Democrats, John L. McClellan of Arkansas and Stuart Symington in withdrawing from the panel until McCarthy allowed them to hire their own staff assistant, Robert F. Kennedy, as minority counsel. Later, during the televised Army-McCarthy hearings, Jackson, by his methodical questioning of the committee chairman and his assistants, played a key role in the process that eventually led to McCarthy's censure. In recognition of his role in the hearings, the Democratic leadership rewarded him with key assignments on the Committee on Interior and Insular Affairs, the Armed Services Committee, and the Joint Committee on Atomic Energy.

A leading exponent of the controversial view that a "missile gap" existed between the United States and the U.S.S.R., Jackson criticized the Eisenhower Administration for defense policies that in his view were causing the United States to lose its lead in weapons technology. In 1960 Jackson, by that time a close friend of John F. Kennedy, was a leading contender for the Democratic Vice-Presidential nomination. But at the Los Angeles convention the Senator failed the test of delivering a united Washington state delegation to Kennedy, who then decided that he needed Lyndon B. Johnson's help in the South more than Jackson's in the West. Jackson became the chairman of the Democratic National Committee and campaigned effectively in behalf of Kennedy, but after the election, he resigned the post and apparently broke with the Kennedys.

Although his allegiance to the party never wavered, Jackson came increasingly into conflict with fellow Democrats in the 1960's. He opposed President Kennedy's creation of the Arms Control and Disarmament Agency in 1961 and voted only with reluctance for the Soviet-American ban on above-ground nuclear testing two years later. In 1963 he also led an investigation of Secretary of Defense Robert S. McNamara's decision to award the contract for the TFX fighter-bomber to the General Dynamics Corporation of Texas rather than to the Boeing Company of Washington state.

Jackson's main clash with many of his fellow Democrats came over the Vietnam conflict. A firm subscriber to the "domino theory," the Senator had suggested the possibility of American intervention in Indochina even before the defeat of the French at Dienbienphu in 1954, as a means of preventing Soviet and Chinese domination of Southeast Asia. Jackson urged the vigorous prosecution of the war and was an early advocate of the bombing of North Vietnamese military targets and the mining of Haiphong harbor. "I've opposed the war of attrition," Jackson told Christopher S. Wren of Look (September 21, 1971). "I felt the logical thing to do was to wind up, get the men out, and give the South Vietnamese a chance to survive by themselves."

By the end of the 1960's Jackson found himself being embraced by old foes and spurned by old friends. In 1968 President-elect Richard Nixon offered him the post of Secretary of Defense. The Senator declined, apparently fearing that, as a Democrat in a Republican Administration, he could become the scapegoat in the Vietnamese debacle. Although Jackson voted for the Cooper-Church amendment of 1970 to curtail United States involvement in Cambodia, he generally went along with President Nixon's Indochina policies and endorsed the Administration's defense program. It was largely as a result of his efforts that an attempt to bar deployment of the antiballistic missile (ABM) was defeated by a two-vote margin in the Senate in August 1969.

In his home state, antiwar Democrats mounted an effort to prevent Jackson's reelection to the Senate in 1970, and the King County Democratic Convention, based in Seattle and its suburbs, backed Carl Maxey, a black attorney from Spokane, for his Senate seat. Nevertheless, Jackson won the Democratic primary with 84 percent of the vote and, endorsed by the Nixon Administration, went on to defeat Republican Charles Elicker in November, again receiving 84 percent in the year's most lopsided Senate race.

Within the broad spectrum of American politics, Jackson defies classification as either a liberal or a conservative. The liberal Americans for Democratic Action reduced its rating of him from 100 percent in 1961 to 40 percent in 1972. By 1974 his ADA rating had risen to 62 percent, but he scored higher with the League of Conservative Voters, which gave him a rating of 71 percent for that year. On issues involving labor, Jackson received consistently high ratings from the Committee on Political Education (COPE) of the AFL-CIO.

Jackson, who has sent his children to an integrated public school in the District of Columbia, takes pride in his strong voting record on civil rights and was praised for his work in behalf of American Indians after he became chairman of the Interior and Insular Affairs Committee in 1963. On the other hand, he drew fire from liberals for proposing a Constitutional amendment against the use of busing as a means of achieving school integration. Notwithstanding his strong position on defense, Jackson denies that he is a tool of the Pentagon and bristles at the charge that he is "the Senator from Boeing." He justifies his support of the B-1 bomber, the C5A transport plane, the Trident submarine, and other expensive military hardware, arguing that too much is preferable to too little in matters of security, and he maintains that "the true test of a man is where he stands on national defense."

A self-styled "Truman Democrat," Jackson sees as his natural constituency the broad political center examined in The Real Majority (1970) by Richard M. Scammon and Ben J. Wattenberg. From that base he made two serious attempts to capture the White House. In 1972 he thought he could surpass President Nixon on bread-and-butter issues while matching him on law and order and on national defense. With Wattenberg as his speechwriter and strategist, Jackson concentrated on the effort to defeat Senator George S. McGovern for the Democratic nomination and, according to McGovern's campaign workers, popularized the charge that McGovern was the candidate of "amnesty, abortion, and acid." But he encountered a formidable rival in Alabama Governor George C. Wallace, and his best performance in the primaries was a third-place finish in Florida, with 13.5 percent of the vote.

Four years later the mood of the nation augured better for a Jackson candidacy. The Senator tossed his hat into the ring as early as February 1975 and entered carefully chosen primaries, soliciting the support of organized labor by means of a strong economic program. In March 1976 Jackson got off to a good start in Massachusetts, with a 23 percent plurality in a nine-way race. But although he received a plurality of 38 percent in the New York primary in April, he failed to achieve his predicted landslide. When Jimmy Carter soon defeated him in the labor stronghold of Pennsylvania, Jackson withdrew from active pursuit of the nomination, and in June 1976 he announced his endorsement of Carter.

Despite the foundering of Jackson's Presidential hopes, voters in the state of Washington have continued to support the man who helped to bring a nuclear reactor to Hanford, shipyards to Bremerton, a navy base to Oak Harbor, the only Trident submarine base to Bangor, irrigation and reclamation projects to the eastern part of the state, and defense contracts to the western cities. In 1976 he won reelection to the Senate, defeating Republican George M. Brown with 71.8 percent of the vote.

Within the Senate, Jackson has held on to his positions of authority. When the Interior Committee was reconstituted in the mid-1970's into the Committee on Energy and Natural Resources, he was named its chairman. He continues to sit on the Armed Services and Governmental Affairs committees and chairs the Armed Services subcommittee on arms control. Jackson also is a member of the Select Committee on Intelligence.

Concerned with the environment before it came to the fore as a major national issue, in 1969 Jackson became the only elected official to win the Sierra Club's John Muir award for conservation. That same year he won the Bernard Baruch Foundation conservation award, and in 1970 he received the National Wildlife Federation's legislator of the year award. As chairman of the Interior Committee, he was the driving force behind the National Environmental Quality Act of 1969, which required federal agencies, before undertaking new projects, to submit environmental impact statements. He was also responsible for the creation, in 1968, of Washington State's North Cascades National Park, and he was behind the effort to win passage of a land use policy and planning assistance bill to help the states formulate master plans to control development. On some issues, however, Jackson has clashed with environmentalists; for example, he angered some by supporting the proposed construction of the supersonic transport plane (SST). Jackson insists that economic and environmental concerns must be kept in balance. "It's fine for the people who have made it to say we won't have any more economic growth," he has asserted. "How about the six million at the poverty level? We have an obligation to them."

Senator Jackson's concern with the economy has been intensified by the energy crisis, beginning in 1973. To make Americans more independent of foreign fuel suppliers he called for the development of solar and thermal power as well as nuclear energy. An advocate of the Alaska pipeline, he has also supported offshore oil drilling with adequate environmental controls. At the same time, Jackson has been a harsh critic of the energy industry. As chairman of the Senate's National Fuels and Energy Policy Study, he obtained a report from the Federal Trade Commission in 1973, indicating that federal programs had benefited the big oil producers at the expense of consumers. In January 1974, as chairman of the Senate's Permanent Subcommittee on Investigations, he criticized executives of seven major oil companies for high profits collected by their firms during the 1973 crisis. In recent years Jackson has played a key role in the formulation of energy legislation in the Senate and has been in the forefront of the effort to limit windfall gains by oil companies.

Since 1970, when he modified the Defense Procurement Act with an amendment guaranteeing Israel enough aircraft for its protection, Jackson has been the most outspoken Democrat on matters of concern to the Jewish state. The Senator attributes his sensitivity to Jewish issues to his mother's aversion to anti-Semitism, and to his pilgrimage, shortly after World War II, to the Buchenwald concentration camp. In 1974 he was named "man of the year" by the Judaic Heritage Society, and he has received substantial financial contributions from Jews during his Presidential campaigns. Jackson regards Israel as a bastion against Soviet expansion in the Middle East, and he interprets the plight of Soviet Jews as proof of the U.S.S.R.'s lack of commitment to human rights. To underscore his concern for Soviet Jewry, between 1972 and 1974 Jackson almost singlehandedly held up a treaty granting trade credits and the commercial status of "most favored nation" to the Soviet Union. He relented when Secretary of State Henry Kissinger assured him, in October 1974, that Moscow would relax its restrictions on Jewish emigration, but in January 1975 the Soviet Union withdrew from the agreement, partly out of displeasure with the so-called "Jackson Amendment."

Although distrust of the Soviet Union remains the linchpin of Jackson's foreign policy, he has tempered his cold war philosophy and no longer regards the Communist world as a monolith. An early supporter of fostering ties with the Chinese Communists, he called for diplomatic recognition of the People's Republic of China following a visit to Peking in July 1974. Jackson continues to have deep reservations about détente with the U.S.S.R. a view in which he is supported by two key members of his staff, Richard Perle and Dr. Dorothy Fosdick. He called the 1972 sale of wheat to the Soviet Union the "great grain robbery" and criticized the low interest loans extended to the U.S.S.R. by the Export-Import Bank in 1974. As chairman of the Senate subcommittee on arms control, Jackson has been especially critical of American concessions in the Stra-

tegic Arms Limitation Talks. As the price for his support of the SALT I ABM Treaty and Offensive Weapons Agreement of 1972, which allowed the Soviet Union an advantage in the number and payload of land-based missiles, he secured an amendment that guaranteed parity to the United States in future dealings with the U.S.S.R. Jackson was even more critical of the SALT II treaty, signed by Carter and Soviet President Leonid I. Brezhnev at Vienna in June 1979. Convinced that the agreement clearly favored the U.S.S.R., Jackson denounced the Carter Administration's assent to it as "appeasement in its purest form" and called for its renegotiation.

Henry M. "Scoop" Jackson is five feet nine and one-half inches tall and of stocky build. He dresses conservatively, is serious in his demeanor, and is said to lack charisma. A man of simple tastes, he does not smoke, seldom drinks, and finds relaxation in swimming, playing ping-pong, and going on bicycle tours with his family. Since 1952 he has placed his additional income from writing and speaking into a scholarship fund for needy Everett students. He has been a Presbyterian since his mother's conversion from Lutheranism to that religious denomination during his childhood. Jackson is a member of the board of regents of the Smithsonian Institution, the board of overseers of Whitman College in his home state, and the board of advisers of the John F. Kennedy Institute of Politics at Harvard University.

Previously "too busy" to marry, Jackson ended a lengthy bachelorhood on December 16, 1961, when he married Helen Eugenia Hardin, a divorcée twenty-one years his junior, who had been the secretary of Senator Clinton P. Anderson of New Mexico. The Jacksons live with their teenage children, Anna Marie and Peter Hardin, in a four-bedroom house in the Spring Valley section of Washington, D.C. They also own a large house in Everett that was once the home of the archconservative millionaire banker, William Butler. In 1970 Jackson annexed the title "father of the year" to his other distinctions.

References: Atlan 233:76+ Je '74 por; Biog N 2:569+ My/Je '75 por; Esquire 84:88+ S '75 por; Fortune p123+ Je '74 pors; N Y Times Mag p13+ O 3 '71 pors, p27+ N 23 '75 pors; Almanac of American Politics, 1978; Congressional Directory, 1979; Douth, George. Leaders in Profile (1975); Nader, Ralph, ed. Citizens Look at Congress: Henry Jackson (1972); Ognibene, Peter J. Scoop: The Life and Politics of Henry M. Jackson (1975); Political Profiles: The Eisenhower Years (1977), The Kennedy Years (1976), The Johnson Years (1976); Prochnau, William W. and Larsen, Richard W. A Certain Democrat; Senator Henry M. Jackson (1972); Who's Who in America, 1978-79; Who's Who in American Politics, 1979-80

Jarvis, Howard (Arnold)

*Sept. 22, 1902- Social activist. Address: b. c/o
William Morris Agency, 151 El Camino Dr.,
Beverly Hills, Calif. 90212*

The driving force behind a spreading American
tax revolt of possibly radical repercussions is
Howard Jarvis, a retired wealthy businessman
and the principal author of the initiative by
which in June 1978 California voters reduced
their property taxes by 57 percent. Their
approval of his proposed amendment, known
as Proposition 13, transformed Jarvis from a
perennial crank in West Coast politics into
an influential figure whose endorsement has
been sought by many of the nation's leaders
in Washington. In his appearances on network
TV shows, his address before the National
Press Club, his many speeches at political
meetings, and his radio and television broadcasts in several European countries, he has
targeted what he regards as profligate government spending, which he has argued would
necessarily be decreased if voters refused to
make revenues available. Exhorting taxpayers
throughout the United States to take up the
cudgels against federal spending and levies,
Jarvis has tried to cap his Proposition 13
victory by forming the American Tax Reduction Movement.

Howard Arnold Jarvis was born on September 22, 1902 in the copper-mining town of
Magna, Utah, where he grew up with strict
Mormon nurturing. His father, John Ransome
Jarvis, was a state supreme court judge who
hoped that his son would also make law his
profession. Because of the suddenness of his
emergence upon the national scene, information in the press about Jarvis' early years
tends to be uncertain. He is reported to have
earned straight "A's" at the University of
Utah and to have graduated from its law
school, but he decided to become a journalist
rather than an attorney. With $15,000 borrowed
from a local bank, he bought the Magna *Times*,
an expiring weekly that he turned into a
flourishing newspaper. At thirty he owned a
chain of eleven papers estimated to be worth
more than $100,000. One reflection of his civic-
mindedness was his service in the late 1920's
on a commission that added sales and copper-
mining levies to Utah's tax laws. He ran unsuccessfully as a Republican for the state
legislature at the same time that he managed
his father's winning campaign as a Democratic candidate for a seat in that body.

Attending the Republican National Convention in 1932 meant a turning point in Jarvis'
life. As a press officer in President Herbert
Hoover's entourage, he shared a Chicago hotel
suite with the California delegate Earl Warren, who eventually became Chief Justice of
the Supreme Court and was at that time the
district attorney of Alameda County. Warren's
enthusiasm over his state aroused Jarvis'
interest, and in 1934, after the death of his
wife, he sold his newspapers and moved with
his eight-year-old daughter to Oakland. "When
I arrived there, I was wet behind the ears,"
Jarvis has recalled, as quoted in *Time* (June
19, 1978). "All I had was money." He invested
in a small chemical factory and later in an
aluminum foundry and a factory that manufactured noise-prevention pads made of latex.

As soon as the Japanese attacked Pearl
Harbor, the federal government commandeered
his supply of latex, thereby closing the factory. That takeover may well have helped to
convince Jarvis of the wasteful practices of
big government, because, he has maintained,
the latex was later discovered unused in
storage. He nevertheless prospered as the
owner of the Femco Corporation, which employed some 13,000 people after World War II
in the production of aircraft and missile parts
and a variety of home appliances, including
garbage disposal units, electric irons, and gas
heaters. In politics, at the same time, he was
the Midwest regional manager for Dwight D.
Eisenhower's Presidential campaigns in 1952
and 1956 and the Western states manager for
Richard Nixon's 1960 race for the White House.

In 1962 Jarvis retired from business to safeguard his health. At the urging of his neighbors, including elderly homeowners hard
pressed to meet rising property taxes, he
accepted the chairmanship of the United Organization of Taxpayers. "Lower taxes and
less government became my holy grail," he
told reporters of *Newsweek* (June 19, 1978).
Combative and irrepressible, he was soon a

familiar figure at tax meetings in the Los Angeles City Hall, shouting down his opponents and sometimes alienating more taxpayers than he persuaded. As reported in *Time* (June 19, 1978), one observer summed up the reaction to him: "We never knew whether he was a messiah or a maniac." According to his own count, he thwarted thirty-three local bond issues in fifteen years. In his crusade for cuts in both taxes and government spending, he turned to elective politics, running on antitax platforms for the Republican nomination to the United States Senate in 1962, for a seat on the State Board of Equalization, which supervises tax rates, in 1970, and for mayor of Los Angeles in 1977. He lost all three contests, but gained larger audiences and gradually added to his following.

Probably the greatest boost to Jarvis' cause came from voter alarm over California's accelerated increase in property taxes, which during the year 1976 rose between 48 percent and 120 percent. Protecting homeowners, whom he has called "the most important people in this country," from bearing an unfair share of the tax burden became Jarvis' special mission. He outlined his arguments in an interview with Arthur Zich for *New Times* (June 12, 1978): "Property taxes should pay for property-related services only. They should not be made to pay for schools and nursing homes and what not. These things should be paid for by everybody. Everybody uses the sewer system. Everybody should pay for it." A self-described constitutionalist, Jarvis moreover told his audiences at hundreds of meetings as he canvassed the entire state, "The Constitution talks about the rights of life, liberty, and property, not food stamps, illegal aliens, and welfare."

Determined to put his ideas before the voters, Jarvis tried in 1976 to collect the 500,000 signatures required to place an amendment on the ballot, but lacked slightly more than 1,000. In May 1977 he formed a partnership with Paul Gann, a retired real estate salesman and president of People's Advocate, a taxpayers' association. Within the prescribed period of 150 days they gathered 1,264,000 signatures to assure the inclusion on the June 1978 ballot of a 389-word constitutional amendment known as "Proposition 13."

The Jarvis-Gann initiative proposed to limit the tax allowed on a piece of real estate to 1 percent of its full cash value as determined by the 1975-76 assessment. It provided for holding annual increments in assessments to 2 percent, with the condition that the full market value would be reestablished whenever a piece of property was sold. Proposition 13 also increased to a two-thirds majority the margin needed in the California legislature to enact new state taxes and mandated a two-thirds favorable vote by the "qualified electors" before new local taxes could be imposed. "I wrote the initiative myself," Jarvis informed

Arthur Zich, "and took it to the finest legal minds I could find, including the California Legislative Council."

California's Governor Edmund G. Brown Jr. and most political leaders opposed Jarvis-Gann, as did the League of Women Voters, the AFL-CIO, and a host of other organizations. State Senator Peter Behr, a liberal Republican, described Proposition 13, which aimed to cut taxes by about $7 billion, as "a shot of fiscal heroin bringing on a very brief high followed by a deep and lasting depression." Only one major California newspaper, the Los Angeles *Herald Examiner*, endorsed Jarvis-Gann. Even Pacific Telephone, which, as the state's largest property owner, stood to gain $1.3 million annually, opposed it. "The initiative has grown out of legitimate frustrations of California taxpayers," Pacific Telephone's president Ted Saenger commented, as quoted in *New Times*. "But we fear that it might well create a different set of problems entirely."

Foes of Jarvis-Gann questioned the proposition's legality and equity, arguing that the multipart amendment violated California's constitutional requirement that an initiative deal with only one subject. They charged that the measure violated the "equal protection" clause of the Fourteenth Amendment to the United States Constitution by taxing current owners of properties at lower rates than persons who buy them subsequent to its adoption. While Jarvis said that "qualified electors" meant all registered voters, his opponents pointed out, Gann maintained that it meant only those who cast ballots. Finally, critics contended that Proposition 13 would primarily benefit commercial owners, who pay 65 percent of the California property taxes, and that homeowners would come to carry an ever-increasing share of the property tax burden because private dwellings are more frequently sold than commerical properties.

Jarvis called his adversaries "liars" and "popcorn balls," described their arguments as "a crock of manure," and labeled the League of Women Voters "a bunch of nosy broads who front for the big spenders." He accused business foes of Proposition 13 of "cowardice" and complained that they "support the status quo and give money to both parties." Responding to the charge that landlords would reap windfall profits, Jarvis, who is paid $20,400 a year to be the director of the Apartment Association of Los Angeles County, a lobbying group for landlords, promised that his clients would translate their tax savings into reduced rents. He assured the skeptical that if rents were not reduced, he would press for rent controls.

Jarvis' campaign had the support of Milton Friedman, the conservative Nobel Prize-winning economist from the Hoover Institution of Stanford University, and the assistance of Butcher-Forde, a Newport Beach consultant firm. Polls showed that his arguments appealed to many Californians adversely affected by inflation as well as by rising taxes on increasing property values. Some citizens thought that the amendment would be a blow to the welfare system, though it is almost exclusively supported by state and federal taxes, rather than the local taxes, which Proposition 13 affects. Further incited by news that forthcoming property assessments had tripled in some cases, 65 percent of the Californians who voted on June 6 cast their ballots in favor of Proposition 13. "Now we know how it felt when they dumped English tea in Boston harbor," Jarvis told victory celebrants, proclaiming "a new revolution."

No one could forecast with certainty the long-range effects of Proposition 13. To Jarvis' embarrassment, it did not lead to general rent reductions later in the year; on the contrary, some landlords raised rents. But the amendment did not cause massive social dislocations either. When it was passed, Governor Brown, who had supported a less drastic tax-reduction proposal, called the state legislature into special session. Although he had earlier said that the state would not come to the rescue if the Jarvis-Gann proposition were approved, Brown persuaded the lawmakers to allocate $5 billion of the almost $6 billion state budget surplus in direct loans and aids to local governments. His action minimized the impact of Proposition 13 for the time being. But state posts were left vacant when their occupants resigned or retired, state employees and welfare mothers were denied cost-of-living increases, and other projects were curtailed or canceled. Drastic cuts in local educational and recreational budgets necessitated the closing of some libraries and the reduction or suspension of some programs in the visual arts and the performing arts.

Although Proposition 13 still faced a court test to resolve constitutional issues raised by the California Teachers Association, its shock waves quickly crossed the nation. A Gallup poll conducted for Newsweek showed that 57 percent of the American public wanted a major tax cut in their states. "This is just the beginning," Jarvis forecast. "We're sending a message to the rest of the country. The dominos are beginning to fall. The tax revolt has begun." Several states, including Michigan, Nevada, Ohio, and Oregon, put antitax amendments on the ballot for November 1978, and Jarvis visited other states to encourage residents to demand similar measures.

Soon after California voters approved Proposition 13, Jarvis took his message to Washington. He met Congressional leaders from both parties, but he did not receive an invitation to the White House from President Jimmy Carter, whom he has described as "badly mixed up" on taxes. Standing on the steps of the Internal Revenue Service Building on June 19, 1978, Jarvis announced the formation of the American Tax Reduction Movement, whose goal is to slash federal spending by $100 billion and to cut federal income taxes by 10 percent each year for the next four years. He has preferred to "let the elected officials decide" what programs should have their funds axed. On September 26, 1978 some 6,000,000 viewers watched a half-hour television show on which Jarvis urged Americans to fight against federal spending and to help his movement financially. He came into conflict, however, with some of his chief Republican allies for his refusal to endorse tax-cut packages that lacked an accompanying limit on disbursements, calling such proposals "a bucket of steam." Although Jarvis has branded most politicians as "frauds, thieves, crooks, and opportunists," the American Tax Reduction Movement contributed to the 1978 Congressional campaigns of 138 candidates, mainly Republicans, who indicated support for his tax-cutting plan.

"I've been called a right-wing extremist, a gadfly, a tax advocate, a demagogue, an anarchist, and a populist," Jarvis enumerated in an interview with Sally Quinn of the Washington Post (June 20, 1978). "They're all true in a way." Among his various controversial views are his beliefs that Richard Nixon was no more guilty in his deeds than certain other contemporary occupants of the White House and that "political ethics and character are different from private ethics and character." He has dismissed the American press as "the general ally of big government and big labor," has criticized welfare as a "narcotic" that "will eventually destroy the country," and has equated the "new morality" with the old morality that supposedly brought the fall of the Roman Empire. In his opinion, women have "emotional and physical handicaps" that make it difficult for them to lead; he has said, "I'd rather have a gal on the pedestal, m'self."

The furor over Proposition 13 brought Jarvis into the limelight even for such personal matters as his trial in July 1978 on charges of having been driving while intoxicated in March of that year. The drunk driving charge was dropped when the jury voted eleven to one for acquittal, but Jarvis was fined $40 for driving with an expired license. Jack Anderson, the syndicated columnist, made the more serious allegation that Jarvis was linked to three fund-raising rackets. Anderson reported that Businessmen for Goldwater in 1964, the National Freedom to Work Committee in 1965, and the Friends for Hayakawa Committee in 1976 improperly withheld funds from their alleged beneficiaries and were eventually forced by the authorities to stop collecting money. In his defense, Jarvis maintained that his involvement was minimal and that he did not personally profit from the ventures in any way.

In his interview with Sally Quinn, the twice-widowed Howard Jarvis said of his third wife,

Estelle Jarvis, "For 15 years she's been worth 10 carloads of platinum." They, and her sister, live in a modest West Los Angeles house that has been assessed at $80,000. According to a *Time* (June 19, 1978) cover story on Jarvis, "The face is bulldoggish, the figure dumpy, the voice a throaty croak. There are no silken buzz words in Jarvis' earthy speeches." Backsliding from his Mormon upbringing, he enjoys drinking vodka and smoking a pipe. He also delights in his celebrity—his appeal to newsmen and his advance bookings on the lecture circuit. In collaboration with Robert Pack, he told the inside story of Proposition 13 in a book, *I'm Mad as Hell*, published in October 1979 by Times Books.

References: Harpers 257:18+ N '78 por; N Y Times A p25 Je 8 '78 por; New Times 10:44+ Je 12 '78 por; Newsweek 91:20+ Je 19 '79 pors; Time 111:21 Je 19 '78 por, 112:15 Jl 3 '78 por; Today A p19 N 6 '78 por; Washington Post B p1+ Je 20 '78 pors

Jewison, Norman

July 21, 1926- Canadian film producer; director.
Address: b. c/o United Artists Corp.,
729 7th Ave., New York City, N.Y.
10019

One of the growing number of filmmakers who have rejected the Hollywood studio system to produce and direct their own films, Norman Jewison has created a string of movies that are at the same time intellectually provocative and commercially successful. The Canadian filmmaker's pictures include *The Russians Are Coming, The Russians Are Coming*, a comedy pointing out the absurdities of the Cold War; *In the Heat of the Night*, an Academy award-winning detective melodrama; *Fiddler on the Roof*, an adaptation of the celebrated Broadway musical; and *Rollerball*, a nightmare vision of a corporate-run society in the twenty-first century.

While all his films have scored at the box office, some have been the targets of critical brickbats. That dichotomy has perhaps been best explained by a critic for *Variety*, who wrote: "Jewison often has a way of taking esoteric concepts and making them play in Peoria, as it were, which doesn't go down too well with heavy thinkers. However, it goes down very smoothly with the mass audience, whose members have their bread and circus while being exposed to some ideas." Before turning to independent production in the mid-1960's, Jewison learned his craft as a director of variety specials for Canadian and American television and as a director under contract to Universal Pictures, for which he made what he has called "innocuous Hollywood comedies."

Of Protestant Irish stock, Norman F. Jewison, the son of Percy Joseph and Irene (Weaver) Jewison, was born on July 21, 1926 in Toronto, Canada, where his father ran a small dry-goods store in the city's East End. Ever since he had first learned to recite all eleven verses of *The Shooting of Dan McGrew* at the age of six, Jewison wanted to be an entertainer. He was a willing and eager performer at Masonic social functions and in school theatrical and musical productions, and he was always prepared to regale his parents' guests with recitations and humorous monologues.

Following his graduation from Malvern Collegiate Institute in 1944, he joined the Royal Canadian Navy as an ordinary seaman. Navy credits subsequently helped to finance his education at Victoria College, University of Toronto, from which he received a B.A. degree in 1950. During his college years, Jewison worked at a variety of jobs, including waiting on tables and driving a cab, and he invariably spent his summer holidays hitchhiking around the United States.

After his graduation from college, Jewison tried to get a production job in Canadian television, but he was advised by Stuart Griffith, a Canadian Broadcasting Corporation (CBC) executive, that he would have a better chance for an entry level position in London. Taking Griffith's advice, he withdrew his entire savings of $140 and booked passage on a Greek freighter bound for London. There, he lived from hand to mouth for two years, supporting himself with odd jobs and occasional employment at the BBC as a script writer of children's shows and as an actor in bit parts requiring an American accent.

When, in 1952, Griffith offered him a job in the CBC's training program, Jewison returned to Canada.

Jewison's rise at the CBC was swift. Within a few years he was directing and producing its top variety shows, including *The Big Revue*, *Wayne and Shuster*, *Showtime*, and the short-lived *Barris Beat*. Impressed by his refreshing approach to variety programming, Larry Auerbach, a talent representative for the William Morris Agency, invited the young director to come to New York City for job interviews. On the basis of those interviews and videotapes of his Canadian broadcasts, CBS signed Jewison to a three-year contract in 1958. His first task was to resuscitate *Your Hit Parade*, a former top-rated favorite that had fallen on evil days. By restaging the entire production, Jewison improved the show to such an extent that it once again soared in the ratings and reached the top spot in its time period.

Following a season with *Your Hit Parade*, Jewison directed the *Andy Williams Show*, a twelve-week summer replacement series. His next assignment for the network was *The Big Party*, a lavishly produced variety show sponsored by Revlon, Inc., the cosmetics manufacturer. Angered by what he considered to be undue and unwarranted sponsor interference in program production, Jewison resigned before the first *Big Party* show was aired, an advantageous decision since the show turned out to be a costly flop. Because it was too late in the season to take up another series, Jewison arranged to direct several specials. His first, a showcase for Harry Belafonte called *Tonight with Belafonte*, was such a success that it led to a string of similar variety specials for such performers as Danny Kaye, Judy Garland, Andy Williams, and Jackie Gleason, as well as the elaborately staged musical tributes *The Fabulous Fifties* and *The Broadway of Lerner and Loewe*. Jewison's productions earned several Emmy Award nominations, and in 1960 he won the award for best single variety program with *The Fabulous Fifties*.

Disillusioned by the effects of the ratings wars on television programming, Jewison moved to Hollywood, California in 1961. Two years later he made his motion picture directorial debut in *40 Pounds of Trouble* (Universal), a standard sentimental comedy starring Tony Curtis that was enlivened by a climactic chase through Disneyland. The film fared so well at the box office that Universal signed him to a seven-picture contract. His next film, *The Thrill of It All* (1963), a frothy matrimonial farce written by Carl Reiner for Doris Day, then the biggest female box-office draw, and James Garner, became one of the all-time big money-makers for the studio. Miss Day also starred in the domestic comedy *Send Me No Flowers* (1964), and Garner played the leading role in *The Art of Love* (1965), a lushly produced black comedy with a Parisian

setting. Meanwhile, Jewison kept his hand in television by serving as executive producer of *The Judy Garland Show*, a weekly variety program that premiered on CBS in September 1963.

Longing for more artistic control over his films, Jewison got out of his contract with Universal on a technicality after completing *The Art of Love*. At the request of MGM, he immediately took over the direction of *The Cincinnati Kid* (1965) from Sam Peckinpah. A taut, spare reworking of Robert Rossen's award-winning 1961 film *The Hustler*, *The Cincinnati Kid* pitted Steve McQueen as the young, brash, amateur poker player who overplays his luck against Edward G. Robinson, a wily professional gambler.

With *The Russians Are Coming, The Russians Are Coming* (United Artists, 1966), which he both directed and produced, Jewison at last achieved complete artistic control. The film, a cold war comedy that he once described as "[his] version of *War and Peace*," relates the interactions of the townsfolk of a small New England island with the Russian seamen who have accidentally run their submarine aground. The film not only charmed moviegoers and reviewers, but also won applause from the United States Senate and from *Pravda*, the Soviet Communist party newspaper. "By personalizing a dangerous confrontation between Russians and Americans," wrote Robert Alden in a typical review (New York *Times*, May 26, 1966), "[the film] reveals, through broad farce, the good and bad in both, the strengths and weaknesses of people under stress and the fundamental fact that, after all, Russians and Americans are basically human beings and, therefore, share basic human qualities. And not one whit of this lesson is accomplished by preaching, but rather by a hilarious troupe of actors telling a hilarious tale in a hilarious way."

As Jewison used broad comedy to plea for peaceful coexistence in *The Russians Are Coming*, so in his next feature, *In the Heat of the Night* (United Artists, 1967), he used the thriller genre to condemn racial intolerance. In this highly praised film, Virgil Tibbs, a big-city detective played by Sidney Poitier, is called in to help solve a murder in a small, insular Mississippi town. Baffled by the case, the local sheriff, a pompous bigot portrayed by Rod Steiger, grudgingly admits his dependence on the black detective. Although several critics felt the plot was mediocre, most agreed with Bosley Crowther, who wrote in his review for the New York *Times* (August 3, 1967), "The fascination of [the film] is in the crackling confrontations between the arrogant small-town white policeman, with all his layers of ignorance and prejudice, and the sophisticated Negro detective with his steely armor of contempt and mistrust." Contributing to the tension were Jewison's tightly controlled direction and Haskell Wexler's photography, which effectively captured the stifling heat and oppressive atmosphere of the Deep South.

Nominated for seven Academy Awards, *In the Heat of the Night* won the Oscar for best picture and best screenplay, and for its costar, Rod Steiger, the Oscar as best actor. It also received the New York Film Critics Award as the best picture of 1967. Notwithstanding its honors, some film historians contend that *In the Heat of the Night* was never accorded the eminence it deserved because of the phenomenal popular and critical success of *Bonnie and Clyde*, Arthur Penn's technically brilliant gangster film, which was released at the same time.

The Thomas Crown Affair (United Artists, 1968), a big-heist adventure with a twist, starred Steve McQueen as the handsome young business tycoon who masterminds a bank robbery to outwit the Establishment and Faye Dunaway as the glamorous, single-minded insurance investigator who is determined to prove his guilt. Shot mainly on location in Boston, Massachusetts, the film illustrated Jewison's mastery of the latest visual tricks, such as multiple images. A handful of reviewers thought the film worked as a slick, stylish cat-and-mouse thriller; the majority considered it to be little more than "an animated color supplement" that was, as *Time's* Stefan Kanter noted, "stunning on the surface," but "undernourished" in terms of plot and character development.

Loosely based on the early life of Ben Hecht, the novelist and playwright who began his career as a yellow journalist in the rough-and-tumble world of turn-of-the-century Chicago, *Gaily, Gaily* (United Artists, 1969) is a bumptious, farcical comedy about a young man's loss of innocence that Jewison described as "an American *Tom Jones*." While most critics appreciated its "cinematic wit," "exuberant charm," and rich, nostalgic detail, a few faulted Jewison's "heavy-handed" direction, which, as Gary Arnold commented in his Washington *Post* (February 24, 1970) review, failed to capture "the uninhibited but poignant elegy to youth and recreation of a vanished era that Hecht had in mind."

Jewison's most ambitious project up to that time was his $9,000,000 film version of the long-running Broadway musical *Fiddler on the Roof*, which had been adapted from Sholom Aleichem's story about Tevye, a poor Jewish milkman, and his five daughters in pre-Revolutionary Russia. In order to make his film as realistic as possible, Jewison spent months studying Jewish history, talking with Hassidic rabbis in Israel, and learning everything he could about nineteenth-century *shtetl* life. For added verisimilitude, he chose a cast of relatively unknown performers, headed by Topol, the Israeli actor, and shot much of the film on location in Yugoslavia.

When *Fiddler on the Roof* was released by United Artists in 1971, it quickly became a box-office hit, but many critics were less enthusiastic than the moviegoing public. Their main objection was outlined by Paul Zimmerman in *Newsweek* (November 12, 1971): "With a few notable exceptions, musicals rarely travel well from stage to screen. They tend to straddle the artificial conventions of the Broadway musical and the implicit realism of location shooting without finding a new style—and flop. It is with a sizable thud that *Fiddler on the Roof* reaches the screen, a great Goliath of a musical toppled by its own size and weight." Judith Crist, however, thought that Jewison had not only surmounted many of the inevitable problems of stage-to-screen transitions, but had also enhanced "this universal story" with inherently cinematic details.

Jewison again brought a Broadway musical to the screen with *Jesus Christ Superstar* (Universal, 1973), the rock opera in which young tourists on a visit to Israel reenact the last seven days of Christ's life. During its Broadway run, the play was widely denounced by Jewish groups for its alleged anti-Semitism in portraying the Jews as responsible for Jesus' death, and Jewison's screen adaptation, which he coproduced and cowrote as well as directed, was similarly criticized. Despite the deluge of negative reviews, *Jesus Christ Superstar* was a big commercial success in the United States and abroad.

In the early 1970's, Jewison became increasingly involved in motion picture production for United Artists. He produced *The Landlord* (1970), a satirical comedy about interracial relationships directed by Hal Ashby, his former film editor; *Billy Two-Hats* (1973), Ted Kotcheff's offbeat western and, in 1975, his own *Rollerball*. For *Rollerball*, Jewison created an Orwellian world controlled by giant corporations that have crushed individual freedom and organized as the sole outlet for mass expression a bloodthirsty, lethal game called rollerball. The most remarkable aspect of the film, which drew few favorable reviews, was the game itself—a bloody mixture of roller derby, motorcycle race, and gladitorial combat. To Jewison's horror, several sports promoters, hoping to cash in on the film's popularity with the public, briefly considered presenting actual rollerball contests.

Jewison explored another form of organizational power in *F.I.S.T.* (United Artists, 1978), an examination of corruption in the American labor movement, as exemplified by the fictional Federation of Interstate Truckers, a Teamster-style union, and its tough, ruthless leader, Johnny Kovak (Sylvester Stallone), whose rise through the ranks bears more than a passing resemblance to the career of James R. ("Jimmy") Hoffa, the Teamsters' former president. (Jewison has repeatedly denied that the film is based on Hoffa's life.) The sophisticated photography, painstaking period detail and "finely individualized flashes" that so impressed some critics were seen as drawbacks by others and most reviewers dismissed this ambitious effort as "slick, predictable agitprop," a "misfired would-be proletarian epic," or a "long-winded" soap opera.

On July 11, 1953, Norman Jewison married Margaret Ann Dixon, a former fashion model. The Jewisons and their three children, Kevin, Michael, and Jennifer, have lived in London, England since 1970, but they make regular trips to their eighty-acre farm outside Toronto. Jewison is short and lean with a broad face, brown eyes, and dark hair tinged with gray. In his spare time he enjoys outdoor activities like gardening, skiing, and sailing. Those who know him say he is ebullient, self-confident, and unfailingly enthusiastic about his profession. "All my life I have wanted simply to express myself in the best way I know how as an individual," he told Dennis Barker of the Guardian (November 30, 1974). "I have always fought against ever having to work for someone else."

References: Coronet 4:82+ Ag '66 pors; Guardian p8 N 30 '74 por; Macleans 76:21+ Ja 5 '63 pors, 81:30+ O '68 pors; Toronto Globe and Mail p16 My 2 '78 por; Canadian Who's Who, 1973-75; Who's Who in America, 1976-77

Joel, Billy

May 9, 1949- Singer; songwriter; musician. Address: b. c/o Columbia Records, 6121 W. Sunset Blvd., Los Angeles, Calif. 90028

New York's bravura "piano man," the energetic, street-wise singer and songwriter Billy Joel, is the current most popular American male pop recording artist. With *Piano Man* (1973), his second album, Joel went "gold" (million dollar-earning), and his two most recent LP's, his fifth and his sixth, *The Stranger* and *52nd Street*, have gone "platinum" (million copy-selling) several times over. Joel's songs—ranging from the sentimental ballads "New York State of Mind" and "Just the Way You Are" to the aggressively upbeat "My Life" and "Big Shot"—while influenced by the driving rhythms and raucousness of rock music, are more reminiscent of some of the better Tin Pan Alley songs of decades past, with their rich melodies and memorable lyrics.

The ease with which Joel absorbs and makes his own a wide range of musical styles has led some concert and record reviewers to view him as being eclectic and imitative. But even as severe a critic as Stephen Holden has been forced to concede that Joel is a "consummate showman" with "plenty of heart." In February 1070 the Academy of Recording Arts and Sciences presented Joel with two Grammys for "Just the Way You Are"—best record of 1978 and best song of 1978.

William Martin Joel was born in the Bronx. New York City on May 9, 1949 to Howard Joel, an Alsatian Jew who worked as a General Electric engineer, and Rosalind (Nyman) Joel, who was of English and Russian-Jewish ancestry. After the father returned to Europe, Mrs. Joel raised Billy and his sister on her meager salary as a secretary. Joel credits his immersion in music and reading as a child partly to the fact that his mother never had the money to repair their broken television set, with the result that Joel had to find other ways of amusing himself.

Another positive formative influence was his maternal grandfather, Philip Nyman, as Joel recounted to Tony Schwartz of *Newsweek* (December 11, 1978): "He was a total education freak who read everything—algebra books, books about paleontology. He turned me into a reader. I think I got a lot of my romantic notions reading Fitzgerald and Hemingway and Twain. He'd also take us to the Brooklyn Academy of Music to see Nureyev or the Prague Chamber Orchestra."

Joel grew up in Hicksville, Long Island and nearby Levittown, the first tract housing development in the United States, which he characterizes as "the Brooklyn of the suburbs." Living in a heavily Italian-American neighborhood, he says, he became "Italian by assimilation," and his songs would certainly suggest a gentile more than a Jewish background. Joel began banging away at the family piano when he was two. "When we saw that he loved Mozart at four," Carl Arrington quoted his mother as saying in *Us* (April 4, 1978), "I took him by the scruff of the neck and dashed off to find him piano lessons." He took lessons for twelve years, eventually receiving classical training under Morton Estrin, a Hicksville teacher who was a member of the faculty at Hofstra University. Somehow he also found time to hang out with a street gang, play handball, and do some bantam-weight boxing.

In the early 1960's Joel began to be influenced by popular music, notably that of such soul-based American singers as James Brown and such British groups as the Beatles, with their melodic invention. "When they [the Beatles] came along, I was ripe for the plucking," he recalled in the interview with Tony Schwartz of *Newsweek*. "Basically, I'm a melody freak and they were the masters." In another interview, with John Rockwell of the *New York Times* (December 10, 1978), he said, "If there's anybody I've modeled myself on, it's Paul McCartney. And it's never been picked up on. I see critics compare me to Elton John, I see Harry Chapin, and I go, 'No, no, it's *McCartney*.'"

Other strong influences were the type of British rock popularized by Stevie Winwood and Traffic and the rhythm-and-blues of Ray Charles and various Motown artists. Of his songwriting approach, Joel told Dave Marsh in an interview for an article in *Rolling Stone* (December 14, 1978): "Maybe it's English [filtered] through an original American classical sense. There has to be a sense of form, structure, efficiency. If you do something for a while, get the hell out of it and do something different. I mean, I'm a Jimi Hendrix freak. To me, he was a genius. And I don't throw genius around. To me there's only a few of them. Jimi Hendrix was a genius like Mozart was a genius, George Gershwin, Aaron Copland, Bach."

When Joel was fourteen he and some friends formed a combo that played at teen parties, with Joel on the electric organ, and two years later he became the pianist with the Hassles, a popular local bar band. His late-night work helped meet the mortgage payments on the Joels' Levittown home, but it wrought havoc with his school work, and he never received his high school diploma.

Joel supplemented his income as a musician by painting houses, dredging oysters, and, briefly, writing rock music criticism for *Changes* magazine. The Hassles recorded two albums, and after they disbanded Joel and Hassles' drummer Jon Small formed a short-lived duo called Attila, which cut an album in 1970.

At twenty-one Joel fell into a state of depression. "I'd just broken up with a girl, nothing seemed to be happening musically, and I was feeling kinda isolated," he has recalled. "I began to think I was suicidal, so I checked into a psychiatric observation ward. It was horrible. You're literally helpless and everyone around you is literally crazy—guys with Napoleonic complexes, homicidal maniacs, paranoids, heavy alcoholics, all shoved together. I wanted to get out after the first day. Alongside those other people, I realized what a jerk I was to feel sorry for myself, how OK I really was." He was released after three weeks.

Joel's first solo album, *Cold Spring Harbor* (Paramount, 1972), recorded under a contract with Family Productions, was a fiasco. Against his wishes, the back-up sound was cluttered with strings and horns, and in the mastering the speed was incorrectly accelerated from 33⅓ rpm to 33⅔ rpm, giving Joel's voice a tremulous near-soprano quality. In addition, there was a bitter legal wrangle over publishing and tour profits. "I was under a five-year contract [with Family Productions]," he later explained. "They owned my music publishing and even cross-collateralized my writing royalties. I was on the road with a band for six months in 1972 and nobody got paid."

While his lawyer was trying to extricate him from the Family Productions imbroglio, Joel went incognito to Los Angeles, where he played piano and sang in a cocktail lounge for a year and a half under the name Bill Martin. Meanwhile, back East a tape that Joel had made of "Captain Jack," his song about the wasted life of a young suburban heroin addict, had become an underground hit with FM listeners, prompting Clive Davis to approach Joel in one of his last talent-discovering coups for Columbia Records. After reaching a compromise with Paramount, Joel signed with Columbia, which issued the single "Piano Man" on November 2, 1973 and the album of the same name a week later. The other tracks on the album included "Captain Jack," "Travelin' Prayer," and "The Ballad of Billy the Kid." The success of the album, and especially of the title cut, was a mixed blessing, causing Joel to be typed for some time as a Harry Chapin-like storyteller.

Reviewing an appearance by Joel at Max's Kansas City, the Manhattan nightclub, John Rockwell wrote in the *New York Times* (February 23, 1974): "He plays it [the piano] both versatilely and virtuosically. His backup quartet is similarly proficient: tight and subtle. But what is important is Mr. Joel's songs and the way he sings them. There is an overt theatricality in his work. The texts are deliberately rhetorical in their language—even the frequent bits of rather grubby, day-to-day detail are used theatrically. The tunes and arrangements court the bombastic. . . . Words are inflected melodramatically; his voice—an orotund, high baritone—has a melodramatic, throbbing vibrato."

Later in 1974 Columbia Records released Joel's third album, *Streetlife Serenade*. "Joel's

Piano Man album was so uniformly excellent that it's almost unnatural that he could follow it up with a second that would be just as good, but *Streetlife Serenade* actually meets the standards set by its predecessor," Steven Gaynes wrote in the New York *Sunday News* (September 29, 1974). "There's no fat on the LP, just solid cuts of rocking, foot-thumping songs—many of them heavily stocked with those stinging lyrics Joel is so brilliant at. You won't be able to escape a song called 'The Entertainer,' which [when performed] at a SRO concert at Carnegie Hall last spring . . . brought down the house. [It] is easily the best song written about the modern music business, its meat-rack marketing techniques, and the fickleness of the public." The trade publication *Cashbox* magazine named Joel the Best New Male Vocalist of 1974.

After spending three years in Los Angeles, Joel decided to move back to New York. "I didn't go out there with the intention of staying," he explained in the *Rolling Stone* interview with Dave Marsh. "I just went out there to try to get my business affairs straightened out. When the New York financial crisis started happening, there was a lot of anti-New York sentiment in L.A. from former New Yorkers and I got pissed off. I woke up one day and just said, 'I'm going back.'"

Joel did not move directly to New York City; he first spent several months upstate, in Highland Falls, New York. There he wrote the music for his fourth album, *Turnstiles*—the music, not the words, because as he later explained, "all there was around me were birds and trees, so I kept writing birds and trees lyrics." The words were written after he took up residence in Manhattan, in October 1975. *Turnstiles*, produced by Joel himself, was recorded at the Ultra-Sonic Studios in Hempstead, Long Island with local veterans backing him up: Liberty DeVitto on drums, Doug Stegmeyer on bass, Russell Javors on guitar, and Richie Cannata on saxophone. The standout cuts on *Turnstiles* (Columbia, 1976) were "Summer, Highland Falls," "Say Goodbye to San Francisco," and "New York State of Mind." The last-named was intended by Joel to be "a standard for Manhattan."

Joel's business and production problems remained only partly solved until 1977, when his wife Elizabeth, the ex-wife of his erstwhile colleague drummer Jon Small, became his manager and arranged for Phil Ramone to be his producer. Ramone was just the collaborator Joel needed. With his help, Joel took a fresh approach toward his music, building arrangements not around the piano but around the whole band, including the guitar of Steve Khan and the saxophone of Richie Cannata, who had appeared on the *Turnstiles* album.

The first of Joel's albums produced by Ramone was *The Stranger* (Columbia Records, 1977), which sold upwards of 4,000,000 albums, more than any previous Columbia LP with the exception of Simon and Garfunkel's *Bridge Over Troubled Waters*, which had been released in 1970. No fewer than four hit singles were generated by *The Stranger*: "Just the Way You Are," "Movin' Out," "She's Always a Woman," and "Only the Good Die Young."

"Only the Good Die Young," about a young man giving his Roman Catholic girlfriend a variation of the old gather-ye-rosebuds argument, drew protests from Roman Catholic quarters and was banned on some radio stations. Joel explained to Eve Zibart of the Washington *Post* (October 8, 1978) that the song was not anti-Catholic: "The point is not Catholicism, the point is lust. When you're young and sexually crazed, you'll tell anybody anything. The image is of some kid throwing pebbles at his girlfriend's window: *Don't listen to your parents, don't listen to your religious upbringing. . . .*"

Even more successful commercially than *The Stranger* was *52nd Street* (Columbia, 1978), and it was at least as successful artistically, in its own quite different way. "Whereas *The Stranger*—particularly in its centerpiece, 'Scenes from an Italian Restaurant'—captured the texture of urban neighborhood life in an Edward Hopper-like light, *52nd Street* evokes the carnivalesque neon glare of nighttime Manhattan, using painterly strokes of jazz here and there to terrific effect," Stephen Holden wrote in his review in *Rolling Stone*. "The characters in Joel's new compositions—a Puerto Rican street punk ('Half a Mile Away'), a social climber ('Big Shot'), a sexual bitch ('Stiletto'), a barfly sports fan ('Zanzibar'), and a Cuban guitarist ('Rosalind's Eyes')—comprise a sidewalk portrait gallery of midtown hustlers and dreamers."

The *pièce de résistance* of *52nd Street* was a song about teenage sex in the big city, "Until the Night," an admiring caricature of Phil Spector and the "blue-eyed soul" of the Righteous Brothers. "Billy Joel and Phil Ramone are the first artist/producer combination to capture the precarious balance between the ludicrous and the monumental in Phil Spector . . . ," Holden observed, "and Joel's lyric—simultaneously nonsensical, self-parodying, and romantic—is as charming as it is bogus." Reviewing *52nd Street* in the New York *Times* (December 10, 1978), John Rockwell wrote: "The trouble with Mr. Joel's stance, as far as his critics are concerned, is that he combines bantam cock aggression—normally an attribute prized in rock and rollers—with a penchant for middle-of-the-road balladeering. To this writer's taste, while there are undeniable moments of the bathetic in Mr. Joel's work (e.g. 'Just the Way You Are,' with its sexism and sentimentality), and while some of his songs noodle on a bit facelessly in a jazz-rocking idiom, he has a lot of strong pop appeal and an attractive blend of rock energy and jazzish sophistication."

A two-and-a-half-month, forty-six-city tour by Joel wound up with a three-night stand in the 19,500-seat Madison Square Garden in New York City, beginning on December 14, 1978. Of the first night's performance, Daphne Davis wrote in *Cue* (January 19, 1979): "Perched above the stage at one of three pianos in some imaginary cocktail lounge of the soul, he delivered his marvelous Tin Pan Alley rock love ballads and penetrating stories and mood narratives about Rosalinda, Billy the Kid, Virginia, and other characters whose lives and adventures flood radio stations. Though some find Joel's flashy, sophisticated lyrics and crackling pop piano playing that mimic the rhythms of city and suburban life too mainstream, I am a sucker for them as well as Joel's assault on alienation and his call for people to get closer. Like New Jersey's Bruce Springsteen, another urban/suburban rocker, Billy Joel exhibits love rather than contempt for his audiences and they, in turn, respond to his attractively raspy edge and view of life."

In March 1979 Joel was the most fervently received of the contingent of American musicians—the others included Stan Getz, Kris Kristofferson, Rita Coolidge, the Fania All-Stars, and Stephen Stills—who went to Havana, Cuba to take part in the historic "Havana Jam '79," the first cultural interchange between the United States and Cuba since 1959. As Jim Jerome reported in *People* (March 19, 1979), "Over the past twenty years the only other living person who has moved an audience with such charismatic intensity in this same venue (to use the rock term) has been Fidel Castro."

Billy Joel is a short man, five feet eight inches tall, who wears old blue jeans and beat-up sneakers, with jacket and loosened tie added when he is on stage. He and his wife live on an estate overlooking the sound near Oyster Bay, Long Island, and they also maintain their Manhattan apartment. The house on the estate has twelve rooms, including a gym and a combination studio-library containing one of his two pianos and a sound-mixing machine. For recreation, Joel reads, works out or spars a few rounds in his gym, and follows the fortunes of the New York Yankees.

In his article in the New York *Sunday News* Steven Gaines described Joel as looking "a bit rumpled." "His hair was uncombed and in shock...," Gaines wrote. "His deep-set brooding eyes add to his appearance of a street punk. He tries to be hard and tough, but he only looks vulnerable and cute. He has what people call 'street smarts,' backed by an uncanny ability to cut through hype and pretense." When Maureen Early interviewed him for *Newsday* (January 9, 1979), she found him to be "quiet and soft-spoken, not at all the dynamic personality he is on stage." And John Rockwell of the New York *Times* (December 10, 1978) observed that "he seems to come by his boyish, street-wise personality naturally" and that "while his overt populism

sometimes turns sentimental both in his songs and his conversation, it's a philosophy that seems to be deeply rooted in him." Joel told Rockwell: "I have a real cynicism about this whole star thing. I don't think I'm so special. I just do what I do."

References: ASCAP in Action p16+ Fall '79; N Y Sunday News II p9 S 29 '74; N Y Times II p16+ D 10 '78; Newsday II p3+ Mr 31 '74, II p3+ Je 6 '76 por, II p4+ Ja 9 '79 pors; Newsweek 92:67+ D 11 '78 pors; Rolling Stone p71+ D 14 '78 pors

John Paul II, Pope

May 18, 1920- Supreme Pontiff of the Roman Catholic Church. Address: Vatican City

In a time of crisis and controversy in the Roman Catholic Church and of need for the championing of human rights in the world, a strong moral leader, widely and enormously respected, has emerged in the person of the "Pilgrim Pope," John Paul II, the former Karol Cardinal Wojtyla of Poland, the first non-Italian Pontiff in 455 years and the first Slavic pope ever. In March 1979, five months after his election, John Paul issued the encyclical *Redemptor Hominis*—which begins with the sentence, "The redeemer of mankind, Jesus Christ, is the center of the universe and of history"—but in general he departs from papal tradition in preferring to do his work as universal pastor directly, in personal contact with his worldwide flock.

Pope John Paul is a complex man. A warm, earthy father figure, whose very presence wins the hearts of the millions who cheer him at every turn in his international pilgrimages, he is also a formidable philosopher, experienced in dialogue with Marxism, and a cagey religious statesman, steeled in the crucible of totalitarianism. Coming as he does from a country where the church is under siege, where faith is not to be questioned but to be asserted against the demands of an atheistic state, John Paul approaches the spiritual disarray of Catholicism in the West with an urgent sense that the permissiveness in faith and discipline rampant since Vatican Council II has gone far enough. While espousing the ecclesiastical renewal set in motion by the council, he reaffirms such traditional doctrines as the permanence of clerical vows (he has not consented to the laicization of a single priest, as contrasted with the 2,000 a year who were dispensed by Pope Paul VI), an exclusively male priesthood, and the centuries-old stands against divorce, artificial means of birth control, sex outside of marriage, homosexual acts (as distinguished from homosexuality), and abortion. While conservative theologically, he is liberal in his work for "the construction of a just world," a goal that includes peace, disarmament, and the conquering of world hunger, and his constant reiteration of the inalienable, irreducible value of the individual human person.

The second of two children in a strict Catholic family, Pope John Paul II was born Karol Jozef Wojtyla in Wadowice, Poland on May 18, 1920. His mother Emilia (Kaczorowska) Wojtyla, who was of Lithuanian descent, died when he was nine, and his much older brother, Edmund, a physician, died four years later. His father, Karol Wojtyla Sr., a pensioned army sergeant, died in 1942.

As a schoolboy, Karol Wojtyla excelled in athletics and dramatics as well as academic work. In 1938 he enrolled as a student of literature at Jagiellonian University in Krakow, where he acted with an amateur theatrical troupe and participated in poetry readings and literary discussion groups. During the Nazi occupation of Poland, he began his seminary studies clandestinely, while earning his living as a manual laborer in a quarry and a chemical factory.

Wojtyla was ordained in Krakow on November 1, 1946. Following his ordination, he first did pastoral work with French working-class youth as well as with Polish refugees in France and then engaged in further study at the Pontifical Angelicum University in Rome. At the university he studied under the eminent French Dominican Reginald Garrigou-Lagrange, an uncompromising traditionalist who contributed to his theological conservatism. His doctoral dissertation in theology was on the sixteenth-century Spanish poet and mystic St. John of the Cross, and his postdoctoral thesis in philosophy (required for university status in Poland) was a study relating the phenomenological thought of Max Scheler to the treatment of ethics in the works of St. Thomas Aquinas.

Back in Poland, Wojtyla did parish work for several years before becoming a professor of ethics at the Catholic University of Lublin. In 1958 he was consecrated Auxiliary Bishop of Krakow, under Archbishop Eugeniusz Baziak. Four years later, after the death of Archbishop Baziak, he was named Vicar Capitular, in charge of the Archdiocese of Krakow, and he became Archbishop in name as well as in fact in 1964. Pope Paul VI elevated him to the Cardinalate on May 29, 1967.

Meanwhile, at Vatican Council II (1962-65), Wojtyla addressed the Council fathers on several occasions, most memorably on the subject of religious liberty—which, he pointed out, the Church could not claim for itself without conceding it to others. As a Cardinal, Wojtyla made several international journeys, including two trips to the United States, one in 1969 and the other in 1976.

At the time of his elevation to the Cardinalate, Wojtyla was regarded by the Communist regime in Poland as "moderately reformist," "tough but flexible," by contrast with the Primate of Poland, Cardinal Wyszynski, who was then considered a hard-line anti-Communist of the old school. (Recently, Wyszynski, in a step advantageous to the Church, began cooperating with the government in developing nonideological social and economic programs). But from the beginning, the people, and especially the young and the workers, knew him to be a resilient enemy of Communism and champion of human rights, a powerful preacher and sophisticated intellectual able to defeat Marxists in their own line of dialogue.

The Communist authorities feared Wojtyla for his wit but respected him for his statesmanship, as George Blazynski noted in *Pope John Paul II* (1979): "Wojtyla recognized the importance of giving expression to Polish national feeling—of which the Church is the most important embodiment—without allowing it to take an explosive form that would provoke a brutal reaction by forces within and perhaps without the country."

Blazynski went on to say that Wojtyla, like Wyszynski, became a symbol of the Church as the alternative repository of a universal doctrine based on Christian rather than Marxist values. "Cardinal Wojtyla is identified in Poland as the chief advocate of still greater concessions by the State toward the Church and the people. The main issue is that of respect for all human rights, but in particular he has been concerned about education, access to the mass media, the elimination of censorship, the abandonment of atheistic propaganda and pressure, the building of churches, and freedom of religious instruction."

Following the deaths of Pope Paul VI, in August 1978, and Pope John Paul I, in September 1978, the College of Cardinals met, on October 15, 1978, in secret conclave in the Vatican to elect the 263rd (or 262nd, according to some historians) successor to St. Peter as Bishop of Rome. In the eighth round of voting, on October 16, the Cardinals chose Karol Cardinal Wojtyla, who accepted the election (with tears in his eyes) and chose the name John Paul. Shortly after his election was announced, the new Pope appeared on a balcony overlooking St. Peter's Square and addressed the crowd in his powerful voice in Italian. "I was afraid to receive this nomination," he said, "but I did it in the spirit of obedience to Our Lord and in the total confidence in his mother, the most holy Madonna." Like John Paul I, he declined coronation and was simply installed as Pope during a pontifical Mass in St. Peter's Square on October 22, 1978.

The day following John Paul's election, the Polish Episcopate issued this statement: "The servant of the Church of Krakow and of all Poland, the Deputy Chairman of the Conference of the Polish Episcopate, has been elected servant of the servants of God. We believe that it is the achievement not only of the Holy Spirit, but also of Holy Mary, the Mother of the Church, and our Lady of Jasna Gora, whom the newly elected Pope loves so much, and we believe that it is the result of the prayers of the entire Polish people who have received this reward for their faith and the vitality of their religion."

A month later Andrew M. Greeley could write in his journal, as he recounts in his book The Making of the Popes 1978 (1979): "Karol Wojtyla, Papa Jan Pawel, owns this city [Rome] backwards and forwards, up and down, every which way. . . . His moves, his presence, his smile, his friendliness, his gesture have . . . pleased everyone. He has won the Romans. Indeed, wherever he goes there are tens of thousands of them. . . . He is great with crowds —shaking hands, smiling, talking, kissing babies."

Greeley noted a "poster one sees on the pillars and walls of the Via della Conciliazone, put up by the Communist mayor of Rome welcoming the Polish pope as a hero of the resistance against the Nazis during the war." He further observed, "The protocol types are still trying to close in on him, but without success. He just dismisses them. The more serious problem is with the security types, who are worried silly . . . as is the Italian government, which has to worry about traffic jams whenever he moves out of the Vatican."

The Pope's electrifying impact on the populace in Rome was duplicated—indeed exceeded—time and again as he traveled beyond the borders of Italy. For his first trip abroad, in January 1979, he chose Latin America, home of almost half of the world's 720,000,000 Roman Catholics and a major focal point of those priests and prelates committed to the controversial "liberation theology," which is viewed by some of its critics as a call for leftist—perhaps even revolutionary—activism.

Throngs of sizes estimated variously between 1,000,000 and 3,000,000 people greeted John Paul in the Dominican Republic and later in Mexico. Striking a careful balance between concern for the poor and oppressed and a repudiation of "politicized theology," he told a conference of Latin American bishops in Puebla, Mexico on January 28 that while "the Church must work in favor of a more just and equitable distribution of goods, not only within each nation but also in the world in general," it cannot accept "this idea of Christ as a political figure, a revolutionary." The Pope elaborated: "If the Church makes herself present in the defense of or in the advancement of man, she does so in line with her mission [which] is religious and not social or political. . . . The Church wishes to stay free with regard to the competing [political] systems."

John Paul's return to his native Poland for nine remarkable days in June 1979 was a major breakthrough that gave new hope to the subject peoples of Eastern Europe. The thunderous outpouring of religious and patriotic affection he elicited throughout the officially atheistic country came at a time when the government was already embarrassed over food shortages because of an unexpected failure of its most recent agricultural plan. "But it was the Pope's appeal to the young that frightened the Communist party most," Paul Martin wrote in a dispatch to Newsweek (August 2, 1979). Martin quoted a Polish academic: "It's one thing to have the party soul-searching about flunking a growth target. But admitting you've lost the youth is another."

On September 30 the Pontiff flew to Ireland, where he celebrated Mass for 1,200,000 people (the largest number to attend a Mass any time, anywhere) in Dublin. Moving on to Drogheda, near the border of strife-torn Ulster, he begged Catholics and Protestants alike, and especially the militant provisional wing of the Irish Republican Army, "to turn away from the paths of violence and return to the ways of peace."

After praying at the Shrine of Our Lady of Ireland at Knock on October 1, John Paul flew on to the United States. During his six-day whirlwind American tour, the six American cities he visited—Boston, New York, Philadelphia, Des Moines, Chicago, and Washington, D.C.—declared virtual holiday, and public officials outdid each other in providing him with a reception that was, in toto, of staggering, unprecedented magnitude. Similarly, private citizens, Catholic and non-Catholic alike, flocked by the millions to glimpse the Pope. It was only a few short years ago that such mass forgetfulness of sectarian difference would have been unthinkable (and, politically, suicidal) in the United States.

Among the highlights of the Pope's American tour were his address on world problems, especially peace and disarmament, at the United Nations, his playful give-and-take with an audience of Catholic high school students at Madison Square Garden in New York City, and his meeting with Jimmy Carter in the White House (a papal "first," among the numerous firsts being accumulated by John Paul).

During the Pope's visit to the United States he warned members of the "consumer" society to beware of the dangers of secularism, materialism, and selfishness, and admonished them to accept a lowering of their living standards to help the have-nots in their own country and in the Third World. On several occasions he pointed out that human life is a "precious gift of God" and called on Catholics to "stand up every time life is threatened" by abortion, lax marital standards, and the limiting of family size for the sake of material comfort. There were protests; the most dramatic occurred during the last day of Pope John Paul's visit, when Sister Theresa Kane, president of the Leadership Conference of Women Religious, introducing John Paul to an audience of women religious at the Shrine of the Immaculate Conception in Washington, surprised him by stating, "The Church must regard the possibility of women being included in all the ministries of the Church."

Next the Pope reportedly planned to visit the Philippines and Brazil; and China, Israel, and Russia were on his prospective itinerary. At an unprecedented four-day session of the College of Cardinals in Rome in November 1979 John Paul reported to and consulted with the prelates on church finances and other matters. He also planned to call the Netherlands' bishops to a special meeting in Rome in an effort to settle the serious rift between Dutch conservatives and liberals. Father James Davern, the president of Donnelly College in Kansas City, observed that the Pope sensed "a drifting in the church and he is trying to get in touch with all groups to get his house in order." The Jesuit theologian Avery Dulles suspected that John Paul "feels a certain era is coming to an end and he wants to get us into a phase where people will come together. He is trying to mobilize the worldwide church."

Among the books written by Pope John Paul are Miłość i odpowiedzialność (1962), a statement on sex, marriage, and birth control that has been translated into English as Fruitful and Responsible Love (Seabury, 1979); the phenomenological treatise Osoba i czyn (1969), published in English as The Acting Person (Raidal, 1969); Znaki sprzeczności (1976), a spiritual testament, translated into English as Sign of Contradiction (Seabury, 1979); and his study of the directives of Vatican II and their implementation, translated into English as The Future of the Church (Harper, 1979). He has also written poetry and

some drama under the pseudonym Andrej Jawien. A collection of free verse was published under the title Wielkanocne czuwanie (Easter Vigil and Other Poems, Random, 1979).

In his book on the papal elections, Andrew M. Greeley writes: "Wojtyla the poet is a deep, complicated, anguished, hopeful, and affectionate man. Wojtyla the playwright is even more interesting. His The Goldsmith Shop, which appeared in Znak in 1960, was written (again under the pseudonym of Andrej Jawien) for an attempt in the late 1950's to revive the Rhapsody Theatre of his good friend Mieczyslaw Kotarczyk. The Rhapsody Theatre, if one is to judge from The Goldsmith Shop, tended toward symbolic, metaphysical, and poetic presentation and was very 'modern' in its approach to stagecraft. . . . The author of the play has a profound insight into the dynamics of human relationships and, in particular, a very sensitive grasp of the things that can go wrong in a marriage."

On record, the Pope can be heard singing in his rich baritone voice on Pope John Paul II Sings at the Festival of Sacrosong (Infinity Records, 1979). Sacrosong is an ecumenical music festival that the Pope founded when he was Archbishop of Krakow. Among the cuts on the LP is the Pope's own composition, "The Moment of the Entire Life."

Burly and vigorous, Pope John Paul is five feet ten and a half inches tall and weighs 175 pounds. Two serious accidents in his youth—he was struck on one occasion by a tram and on another by a truck—have left him with a slight stoop in the shoulders, which becomes more pronounced when he is tired. He was once the complete athlete and outdoorsman, regularly skiing, backpacking, and boating in his kayak, but he must now usually content himself with putting a jog into his walks in the Vatican Gardens. He does not smoke, and his drinking is generally confined to a glass of wine with his meals.

The Pontiff speaks fluent Italian and flawless Latin in addition to his native Polish, and he can jump from English to French, German, and Spanish with relative ease. He writes his speeches and other pronouncements himself, in longhand, using the pronoun "I" instead of the traditional papal "We." But he refuses to let himself become so bogged down in the day-to-day business of his office as to deprive himself of the pleasure of going out among his "alleluia people." His joy in his vocation is never more evident than when he is moving—at his characteristic deliberate, confident pace—through a crowd, stopping to chat, to shake a hand, to crack a joke, and, above all, to take a child lovingly in his arms.

References: N Y Daily News p1+ S 30 '79 pors; Hebblethwaite, Peter, and Kaufmann, Ludwig S.J. John Paul II (1979); Malinski, Mieczyslaw. Pope John Paul II (1979); Orman, James. The People's Pope (1979)

Kahn, Alfred E(dward)

Oct. 17, 1917- United States government
official. Address: b. 200 Old Executive Office
Building, Washington, D.C. 20500; h. 910
Independence Ave. S.E., Washington, D.C.
20003

Political commentators have called the task
of stemming inflation one of the most thank-
less jobs in government. Since October 25,
1978 that job has belonged to Alfred E. Kahn,
President Jimmy Carter's choice to direct
Phase II of the Administration's anti-inflation effort as chairman of the interagency
Council on Wage and Price Stability, succeeding Charles L. Schultze. A former professor of economics, Kahn brought to his
new post a healthy respect for and understanding of free-market incentives. As chairman of New York's Public Service Commission and, later, of the federal Civil Aeronautics Board, he initiated tough consumer-
oriented policies and, in the latter post, masterminded the deregulation of the airlines.
Kahn is known for his quick wit, his independence, and his candor. In a short speech
accepting the Presidential appointment, he
assured his fellow citizens that Carter's program of voluntary wage-price guidelines had
to succeed. "We either demonstrate that we
are an American people," he said, "or that
we are just 200,000,000 people at war with
one another."

Alfred Edward Kahn was born in Pater-
son, New Jersey on October 17, 1917, one
of the three children of Jacob Kahn, a Russian-Jewish immigrant who was employed
as a silk mill worker, and Bertha (Orlean)
Kahn. He attended Evander Childs High

School in New York City, graduating in 1933.
Just three years later, at the age of eighteen,
Kahn received his A.B. degree in economics,
summa cum laude and Phi Beta Kappa, from
New York University. After earning his M.A.
degree from NYU in 1937, he did further
postgraduate work at the University of Missouri. He then went on to Yale University,
which granted him a Ph.D. degree in 1942
on submission of his doctoral thesis on Great
Britain's role in the world economy. While
writing his thesis, Kahn worked in Washington, D.C. as a research economist for
the Brookings Institution, the Justice Department's antitrust division, and the international economics unit of the Department of
Commerce.

Following a brief stint as a private in the
United States Army from June to September
1943, Kahn moved to New York City, where
he worked as an economist for the Commission on Palestine Surveys and then, briefly,
for the Twentieth Century Fund. In the fall
of 1945 he moved to Ripon, Wisconsin to
take a post as assistant professor and chairman of the economics department at Ripon
College. Two years later, he joined the faculty
of Cornell University in Ithaca, New York,
where he quickly advanced through the academic ranks to a full professorship in 1955.
Highly regarded by students and faculty, he
chaired the university's department of economics from 1958 to 1963, sat on its board
of trustees from 1964 to 1969, and served
as dean of its College of Arts and Sciences
from 1969 until he took a leave of absence
to enter public service in 1974. Since 1967
he has been Cornell's Robert Julius Thorne
Professor of Economics.

While at Cornell, Kahn was coauthor of
two books, *Fair Competition; the Law and
Economics of Antitrust Policy* (Cornell Univ.
Pr., 1954) and *Integration and Competition
in the Petroleum Industry* (Yale Univ. Pr.,
1959), and wrote scores of articles on regulatory and antitrust policies. His *The Economics of Regulation: Principles and Institutions* (Wiley, 1970), a massive two-volume
work, has become the standard textbook on
government regulation of business and industry. In all his works, Kahn has argued
in favor of an economy controlled by free
market forces rather than by governmental
regulations. At various times during his tenure
at Cornell, he was a senior staffer for President Dwight D. Eisenhower's Council of Economic Advisers; an economic adviser of the
American Telephone and Telegraph Company;
a special consultant to the Department of
Justice, the Federal Trade Commission, the
Ford Foundation, and National Economic Research Associates; and a member of the
National Academy of Sciences' review committee on sulfur dioxide emissions and the
Federal Energy Administration's environmental advisory committee.

Kahn's expertise in the field of utilities regulation brought him to the attention of New York Governor Malcolm Wilson who, on April 29, 1974, appointed the professor chairman of the Public Service Commission, the agency that regulates the operations of utilities in the state. In an effort to cut consumers' costs, Kahn immediately set out to revise the utilities' rate structures, erase management inefficiencies, and spur competition. Among other innovations, he introduced lower electric rates in off-peak hours, permitted customers to hook up their own equipment to the New York Telephone Company's system, and required the telephone company to charge customers for directory assistance and credit the accounts of those users who did not make such calls.

Impressed by Kahn's record as chairman of the Public Service Commission, President Jimmy Carter, who shared Kahn's views on reducing government regulation and increasing competition, appointed him in May 1977 to succeed John Robson as chairman of the Civil Aeronautics Board. At the time of his appointment, few industries were as tightly regulated as the airlines. Since its creation in 1938, the CAB had not certified a single new domestic carrier. Moreover, it closely controlled air routes, kept fares high, and consistently discouraged applications for special rates on fare reductions.

Taking office a few hours after his Senate confirmation on June 10, 1977, Kahn began a series of sweeping revisions that amounted to de facto deregulation. He allowed airlines to sell seats at discounts of up to 70 percent in some cases and encouraged such innovations as Laker Airways' Skytrain, a no-frills, no-reservations shuttle service between New York and London that cost about $100 less than the cheapest roundtrip fare. He even permitted domestic carriers to slash fares by up to 50 percent without prior approval of the CAB. In another marked departure from previous practice, Kahn began letting the national airlines choose their own routes. To reduce the resulting congestion at major airports, he ordered the reopening of smaller, subsidiary airports, such as Midway Airport in Chicago, to commercial traffic.

On the international front, Kahn granted "fill-up" rights to international airlines, giving them the opportunity to carry domestic passengers between points in the United States on international flights, opened up Pan American's overseas market to domestic carriers, and more than doubled the number of transatlantic gateways by approving direct air service to Europe from eleven more American cities. In ratifying the plan for expanding transatlantic service, President Carter overruled the CAB's recommendation and awarded the Dallas-to-London route to Braniff instead of to Pan American. Kahn immediately called a news conference to denounce the Chief Executive's decision. "He is the President and he has the right to make a judgement, and I have the right to disagree with it, and I do," Kahn said, adding that Carter's notion of competition struck him as "naïve."

During interviews Kahn emphasized that the CAB's job was to "protect competition, not protect companies." Although he conceded that a competitively structured industry is more vulnerable to depression, he argued that competition forces businesses to become, in his words, "leaner, more efficient, more careful." "They're not free to overacquire, to enter markets that might not be logical for them to enter, secure in the knowledge that the government will bail them out," he explained, as quoted in Forbes magazine (October 16, 1978). "There are already signs that price competition is eliminating a lot of slovenliness in route planning, in system operations, and in . . . efficiency."

But Kahn was careful to point out to reporters that he did not advocate absolute free enterprise. "I am not an 'abolish government' man," he told one interviewer. "We've had forty-five years of government interventions and in many cases they've been important and they've worked. But there are areas in which government is trying to protect existing interests, and airlines are an outstanding example. That is where government intervention should disappear." Kahn had repeatedly recommended the abolition of his agency and strongly supported the Carter Administration's airline deregulation bill providing for the phasing out of the CAB. The bill was signed into law in October 1978.

Unaccustomed to so much freedom and competition, American airline executives feared the worst when Kahn started his systematic deregulation of their industry. But a little more than a year later, when all but a few carriers were enjoying record profits, most of them came around to his side. Carter's inflation fighters were similarly pleased. Although most retail prices were rising at an annual rate of about 10 percent as of October 1978, the cost of an airline ticket was considerably lower than it had been a year earlier. Hoping that Kahn could work his magic on the economy as a whole, Carter appointed him on October 25, 1978 to direct Phase II of the Administration's anti-inflation program. At first reluctant to accept the post because the chances for "demonstrable success" were slim, Kahn agreed only after Carter had promised him a free hand.

The main points of Phase II were voluntary guidelines on wages and prices designed to hold increases in wages and fringe benefits to 7 percent annually and to keep price increases under 5.75 percent. The plan also set limits on the growth of federal spending and called for a cut of at least $10 billion in the budget deficit. The President's goal was a modest cut in the inflation rate to between 6 and 6.5 percent per year. "If the job were merely one of administering those standards, I certainly wouldn't have taken it," Kahn told John Walcott, who interviewed him for *Newsweek* magazine (November 6, 1978). "The fight against inflation requires an attack on all sources of government-induced inefficiency in the economy. I become not Mr. Wage and Price Regulator, but Mr. Efficiency in Government, Mr. Deregulator, or Mr. Minimizer of Coercion."

The initial reaction to Phase II was distressing. The stock market dropped sharply and the value of the dollar declined even further abroad. The nation's most powerful labor leader, AFL-CIO President George Meany, denounced the voluntary program as "inequitable and unfair" and demanded that Congress replace it with mandatory wage and price controls, a measure both Kahn and the President strongly opposed. While many business leaders publicly supported Phase II, they criticized it privately as a weak and ineffectual plan, leading inevitably to mandatory controls, a recession, or both. Kahn himself, in a speech to the American Retail Federation on November 15, 1978, warned, "If the inflation accelerates—is permitted to accelerate—sooner or later we will have such a tightening, such a total breakdown of the organization and morale of our economy that we will have a deep, deep depression." President Carter dismissed Kahn's gloomy prediction as "idle talk," and cautioned his outspoken adviser to tone down his public statements. Kahn protested that he could not "weigh every word," but he eventually agreed to temper his remarks. In a concession of sorts, he substituted the word "banana" for "depression." "I am using 'bananas' very freely these days," he told one reporter.

Because so many other factors were involved, Kahn conceded shortly after taking office that it could be a year or more before the voluntary wage and price guidelines perceptibly slowed the inflation rate, but he promised a few "small victories" along the way. His first two months on the job brought few victories of any kind. Top labor leaders ignored his telephone calls and businessmen expressed confusion about the guidelines, some of which were revised after seven weeks. The consumer price index for October 1978, made public a month after Kahn took office, showed inflation running at an annual rate of almost 10 percent and, for the first time, it went over the 200 mark—meaning that the dollar bought only half of what it had purchased in 1967. The October figures, Kahn admitted, were "God awful." Commenting on the anti-inflation program's shaky start, an economic analyst for the *Wall Street Journal* (November 21, 1978) raised doubts about its ultimate success. "The Carter Ad-

ministration inflation fighters are overwhelmed by it," he wrote. "They are unequal, at least so far, to the huge task of organizing, explaining and running the program."

Perhaps the worst blow to the Administration's anti-inflation program came on December 17, 1978, when the Organization of Petroleum Exporting Countries announced price raises for 1979 totaling 14.5 percent, far more than expected. Saying he was "profoundly unhappy and terribly disappointed," Kahn warned that OPEC's decision would adversely affect the fight against inflation by increasing the cost of gasoline, fuel oil, and petroleum products. Two days later, government economists conceded that the 1979 inflation rate would exceed 7 percent, well over the President's Phase II goal. "Inflation is a situation in which we, all of us, are demanding—in rents, profits, tax rebates —real pieces of a pie that adds up to more than the pie," Kahn told Ralph Blumenthal in an interview for a New York *Times Magazine* profile (January 14, 1979). "Inflation is not like deregulation. It's a social disease. It's not susceptible to crash programs."

The challenge, as Kahn sees it, is to find what is "economically rational in an irrational world and how to get from here to there." Because he believes that inflation is, in part, a byproduct of overregulation, Kahn is working on plans for deregulating railroads and trucking to bring down freight costs. He is also looking into ways to cut housing and health-care costs, modify federal farm policy, remove antitrust immunity from ocean shipping and insurance, and promote competition among public utilities. So that he can concentrate on streamlining the federal bureaucracy, he leaves the jawboning to Robert S. Strauss, President Carter's special representative for trade negotiations, and the day-to-day management of the wage-price standards program to Barry Bosworth, the director of the Council on Wage and Price Stability.

Known for his drolleries, Kahn resents reporters' attempts to make him, as he puts it, "a character . . . like Earl Butz or a callous Henny Youngman." On more than one occasion his off-the-cuff remarks have wound up as front-page headlines. For example, a reference to Arab oil sheiks as "poor schnooks" (he later explained that by "schnooks" he meant "impotent cartelists") was widely quoted. Kahn's devotion to candor is, in his words, "almost pathological." "If I have to choose between being forthright and candid and intellectually honest and keeping this job, I will select the former," he told Ralph Blumenthal. "I just can't appear as a faceless bureaucrat." Kahn's aversion to bureaucracy extends to the obfuscations and circumlocutions of bureaucratese, or "gobbledygook." While at the CAB, he circulated a memorandum in which he asked his staff "to try very hard to write . . . in straightforward, quasi-conversational prose—as though you were talking to real people."

Alfred E. Kahn has been described by reporters as looking like "a slightly manic professor" and "a small, furious bookkeeper." He is a slight, wiry man, standing five feet nine and one-half inches tall and weighing 163 pounds, with thinning brown hair and brown eyes. To keep fit, he jogs and swims daily, plays tennis and, during the winter, takes brief skiing holidays. A self-described "sandlot singer," he is passionately fond of Gilbert and Sullivan operettas and played leading roles in Cornell Savoyard producions of *Iolanthe*, *Yeoman of the Guard*, and *Ruddigore*. He once confessed to an interviewer that he would have traded his career for the role of the lawyer in the hit Broadway musical, *A Little Night Music*. Kahn and his wife, Mary (Simmons) Kahn, whom he married on October 10, 1943, have three children: Joel, an anthropologist; Rachel, a teacher; and Hannah, a dancer. They also act as guardians of their nephew, Peter Boone. The Kahns have a town house on Capitol Hill in Washington, D.C. and a second home near Lake Cayuga in New York.

*References: N Y Times III p1+ Ap 23 '78,
III p1+ N 12 '78; Newsweek 92:32 N 6 '78 por;
People 10:71+ O 2 '78 pors; Time 111:63
My 8 '78 por; Who's Who in America, 1978-79*

Kenton, Stan

*Feb. 19, 1912- Musician; recording artist.
Address: b. The Creative World of Stan
Kenton, P.O. Box 35216, Los Angeles,
Calif. 90035; h. 1012 S. Robertson Blvd.,
Los Angeles, Calif. 90035*

BULLETIN: Stan Kenton died in a Hollywood hospital on August 25, 1979. *Obituary: N Y Times D p7 Ag 27 '79*

Flamboyant, controversial, and relentlessly dedicated to his music, Stan Kenton has been defining and enlarging the scope of American jazz and modern music since 1941 when he shook the floorboards of the Rendezvous Ballroom in Balboa, California with his first big band. During the 1940's and 1950's Kenton, who is a pianist, arranger, and composer as well as a bandleader, attracted enthusiastic audiences with his artistry in rhythm and progressive jazz bands and his innovations orchestra, which featured a large string section and played a blend of jazz and classical music. In the 1960's and 1970's—otherwise lean years for jazz musicians and big bands—Kenton presented some of his most impressive experiments, including his mellophonium band and his ambitious neophonic orchestra with which he presented a landmark series of jazz/modern music concerts at the Los Angeles Music Center from 1965 to 1967. His band has also conducted jazz clinics at schools and colleges.

Although he was elected to the *Downbeat* Music Hall of Fame in 1954, Kenton has never been wholeheartedly accepted by the jazz establishment. Nevertheless, he has been widely admired for his training, nurturing, and showcasing of the talents of a generation of jazz soloists. Kenton is considered to be a pioneer in the development of what is often called the "Third Stream"—the blending of American jazz and European classical music traditions. Typically, his music features a shattering brass section, intricate harmonies, polytonality, and a wide variation in tempi. Between 1943 and 1970 Kenton recorded nearly fifty albums on the Capitol label. Since 1970, he has released his works on his private label, The Creative World of Stan Kenton.

Stanley Newcombe Kenton was born in Wichita, Kansas on February 19, 1912 to Stella (Newcombe) and Thomas Floyd Kenton. He has two younger sisters, Beulah Kenton Jordan, a psychologist, and Irma Mae Kenton Hopkins. The Kenton children were brought up mostly by their mother, since their father spent long periods away from home on various business ventures, and eventually the Kentons divorced. When Stan Kenton was five years old, his family moved to California and two years later settled in the Los Angeles suburb of Huntington Park. His mother took a job in a factory there and was soon able to buy an old, upright piano. She began giving piano lessons, but was unable to interest her son in playing the instrument, even though he enjoyed music. It was not until a few years later, when he first heard jazz played by his musician cousins, Billy and Arthur Kenton, that he decided to dedicate his life to music. "From the time I was fourteen years old, I was all music," Kenton told Carol Easton, the author of his biography, *Straight Ahead* (1973). "Nothing else ever entered my head."

Kenton threw himself into his studies with enthusiasm, taking lessons in jazz piano from the organist at a local theatre and practising up to ten hours a day. When he was not playing, he listened to records by his new idols, among them George Gershwin, Earl "Fatha" Hines, Benny Carter, and Louis Armstrong. By then a resident of Bell, another Los Angeles suburb, and a student at Bell High School, Kenton formed a musical group called the Belltones, which played at school dances and parties. Then he began picking up individual gigs at local nightspots. After graduating from Bell in 1930, he was able, despite the Depression, to eke out a living for himself as a $5-a-night musician.

Later that year Kenton went to San Diego, where he played at a speakeasy with a six-piece combo, then moved on to Las Vegas, Nevada, playing at speakeasies, gambling joints, and whorehouses. During the next few years Kenton played piano with a number of bands, the most important being Everett Hoagland's, which was at that time the only real jazz ensemble in Southern California. Hoagland nourished and encouraged Kenton's talent by using some of his arrangements and by allowing him to rehearse the band. In between tours Kenton got studio jobs in Hollywood and around 1937 took a year off to study music theory with Charles Dalmores. In 1939 Kenton was hired as the piano player and assistant conductor of the pit band at Earl Carroll's Vanities theatre on Sunset Boulevard. It was a good job, but Kenton was restless and, in August 1940, he quit to form his own band.

After nearly a year of countless auditions and occasional financial problems, Stanley Kenton and his Orchestra opened at the Rendezvous Ballroom in Balboa, California, a beachfront community south of Los Angeles, on June 6, 1941. The dance band was an instant success and packed the 3,000-person ballroom nightly throughout the summer. The band members, all unknown and mostly very young, were as enthusiastic as the crowd. They included Pee Wee George on drums, Howard Rumsey on bass, and Bob Gioga on saxophone. A triumphant five-week engagement at the Hollywood Palladium followed and, every night, the distinctive Kenton sound was broadcast nationwide by remote hookup on one or more radio networks.

But the Kenton band's ascendancy soon met with some setbacks, as jazz critics began to voice the complaints that were to become familiar over the years. The band was too stiff; it did not "swing" and it was too loud, without any contrasts or shadings. When the band went East to perform at the Roseland Ballroom in New York early in 1942, it met with a disastrous reception. Unlike Californians who danced the jitterbug and reveled in the band's fast, noisy beat, New Yorkers found the music totally undanceable. Over the war years, the band struggled as sidemen came and went, responding to the call of draft notices. By 1943, there were few holdovers from the original band, but that year Kenton hired a dazzling sixteen-year-old tenor saxophonist named Stan Getz, and arranged a thirty-nine-week tour with Bob Hope, the comedian.

After cutting a few unheralded singles on the Decca label, Kenton signed with Columbia Records in 1943. Several hit records followed, including "Eager Beaver"; "Artistry in Rhythm," the band's theme song based on a theme from Ravel's *Daphnis and Chloe;* "And Her Tears Flowed Like Wine," featuring Anita O'Day, the band's female vocalist; and "Tampico," sung by Miss O'Day's successor, June Christy. In 1945 Kenton acquired the talents of several established soloists, including trombonist Kai Winding, trumpeter Ray Wetzel, and bassist Eddie Safranski, and the troupe played to sold-out audiences from coast to coast. By the time this first band, which he had come to call his "artistry in rhythm" band, disbanded in April 1947, Kenton was recognized as one of the country's top big band leaders.

Kenton went back on the road later that same year with his new "progressive jazz" band, which he envisioned as an ensemble that would be more devoted to developing modern jazz than to playing popular dance music. He wanted to play only concert dates, but economic realities forced him to accept dance hall engagements as well. This band, which featured the arrangements of Pete Rugolo, was one of Kenton's most renowned groups, winning the 1947 and 1948 *Downbeat* magazine awards as the best big band. After a year and a half of grueling tours, Kenton dissolved the progressive jazz ensemble in December 1948.

Intrigued by the idea of merging jazz and classical music, Stan Kenton next organized his forty-piece "innovations in modern music" orchestra, which resembled a miniature symphony orchestra, complete with a sixteen-piece string section. An early forerunner of "Third Stream" music, Kenton's orchestra fired the imaginations of jazz musicians. Prominent among the outstanding musicians to join the band were Bud Shank on flute and saxophone, Art Pepper on alto sax, and trumpeters Shorty Rogers, Chico Alvarez, Buddy Childers, and Maynard Ferguson. Probably more than any of his other aggregations, Kenton's innovations orchestra became known for its militantly modern dissonance, especially when it played the works of avant-garde composer Bob Graettinger. Graettinger's major work, the nerve-jangling four-part suite, *City of Glass,* first performed by the progressive jazz band in 1948, was rescored for strings and became an important part of the innovations repertory.

In between the innovations orchestra tours, Kenton played dance gigs with a smaller band and, in 1952, bowed to economic necessity by organizing his "new concepts in artistry in rhythm" band, a nineteen-piece ensemble more oriented to ballroom engagements. After touring the United States with singers Nat "King" Cole and Sarah Vaughn, Kenton set out on his first European tour in 1953. It was a phenomenal success and in 1956 he returned to the Continent, that time adding Great Britain to his itinerary.

Early in 1954 Kenton put together a package billed as "A Festival of Modern American Jazz" and featuring the Kenton ensemble with such all-stars as Charlie Parker, Billie Holliday, and Dizzy Gillespie for a cross-country tour of the United States. It was so successful that he repeated the formula later in the year with the "Second American Festival of Modern Jazz." Kenton briefly hosted an ambitious CBS-TV show in 1955 entitled *Music '55,* but it was considered too "high-brow" and was soon cancelled for lack of a sponsor. Important recordings from the mid-1950's include *The Kenton Era* (1954), an expensive four-record sum-up of his career to that point, and *Cuban Fire* (1956), an engaging collection of Afro-Cuban pieces arranged by Johnny Richards.

Wearying of life on the road, Kenton purchased the Rendezvous Ballroom in Balboa in 1957 as a permanent home for his band. They opened in December, but it soon became apparent that his music was not popular enough to draw consistently large crowds. After just three months, he shuttered the ballroom and went back on tour, playing the major theatres, dance halls, and jazz festivals. When the growing popularity of rock 'n' roll eroded his box office draw, Kenton organized in 1961 yet another band. Billed with typically high-sounding language as "A New Era in Modern American Music," the band became known as the mellophonium band, so named for the hybrid instrument that Kenton added to the brass section. (The mellophonium is a cross between a trumpet and a trombone and sounds rather like a French horn.) The mellophonium band toured the country to critical accolades and recorded eleven albums, including the Grammy award-winning discs *West Side Story* (1961) and *Adventures in Time* (1962).

After a disappointing tour of England late in 1963, Kenton disbanded the mellophonium ensemble and remained in seclusion for nearly a year. During that time he cut one record with studio musicians, *Wagner/Kenton,* which featured his own piano solos and arrangements. Most critics dismissed the album as a pretentious and bombastic treatment of Wagner's themes, but Kenton was undaunted and his next venture—a "neophonic" orchestra —was widely acclaimed. A "jazz arranger's dream band," with fourteen brasses, five saxophones, and a large percussion section, the orchestra attracted the cream of Hollywood studio musicians, former Kenton sidemen, and jazz-oriented composers, many of whom performed with the orchestra as soloists.

The neophonic orchestra gave its first performance at the Pavillion of the Los Angeles Music Center in January 1965, and went on to play an annual series of concerts there for three seasons. Among the guest artists were George Shearing, Miles Davis, Dizzy Gillespie, Gerry Mulligan, and the Modern Jazz Quartet. Typical of the critical response to the concerts was that of the music critic for the *Christian Science Monitor* (April 22, 1966), who wrote: "One gets the feeling that this is what Stan Kenton has been working up to all his musical life . . . . , music that has integrity, individuality, and modernity, without bogging down in atonality, electronic gimmicks, and self-conscious abstractions."

Although it was artistically successful, the neophonic orchestra lost money, and Kenton was forced to supplement his income by playing with a pickup band, cutting records, and doing occasional guest spots on television. From 1965 to 1969 Kenton stayed largely in the Los Angeles area, but in 1970 he went on the road again with a new band. He has continued to tour regularly since then and has recently added to his crowded schedule a number of "jazz clinics" at high schools and colleges around the country.

An articulate man, Kenton enjoys talking about his music and he has always been unusually accessible to the press. In 1960 he set up his own promotional organization, The Creative World of Stan Kenton. Dissatisfied with the promotion he was getting from Columbia, which had only a few of his nearly fifty albums in print, Kenton began marketing his own records on the Creative World label in 1970. Leasing the masters from Columbia, he reissued many of his older recordings and he continues to cut new ones. Creative World also distributes LP's by other jazz artists and publishes sheet music. Kenton merchandises these records through his *Creative World Magazine.*

Stan Kenton has been able to maintain the grueling pace of touring over the years despite periodic bouts with alcoholism and depression. Once, in 1949, while undergoing psychoanalysis, he considered abandoning his musical career to become a psychiatrist. More recently, Kenton has been sidelined by illness, first in 1972 when he was hospitalized for an aneurysm, and then in 1977 when he suffered a cerebral hemorrhage. When he is not touring, Kenton resides in Los Angeles. He has been married three times and has three children, Leslie, Dana, and Lance, and several grandchildren.

Kenton is a lanky six feet, four inches tall and has blue eyes and wavy white hair. Charismatic on stage and off, he is said to have inspired unusual loyalty among the many musicians who have worked with him over the years. Always outspoken, Kenton has dismissed rock as "children's music" and country music as "a national disgrace," but he is philosophical about the popularity of those genres. "I don't feel that the masses have any taste," he told Thomas Lyles in an interview for the Washington *Star* (July 5, 1975). "Sophistication only exists in one or two percent of the masses. And that two percent is the two percent that has to support jazz, classical music and the arts. The masses can't communicate with art."

References: N Y Sun News mag p4 Ap 15 '62 pors; Easton, Carol. Straight Ahead (1973); Simon, George T. The Big Bands (1974); Who's Who in America, 1978-79

Kertész, André (kâr′tēs)

July 2, 1894- Photographer. Address:
h. 2 5th Ave., New York City,
N.Y. 10011

In choosing André Kertész the winner of the 1973 Paris Prix Nadar for *André Kertész: Sixty Years of Photography* (1972), a comprehensive assemblage of his pictures, the jury argued that he was entitled to the award on four counts: "as a humorist, as a photographer, as a painter, and as a poet." That decision suggests the richness and complexity of the work of the pioneering, self-taught photographer who is credited with having led the way in photojournalism for Henri Cartier-Bresson and other prominent European photographers, but of whom Gene Thornton, impressed by a dreamlike element in his pictures, wrote in the New York *Times*, "He is no more a photo reporter than Watteau was." Throughout a career that has now reached sixty-seven years, Kertész has celebrated three cities—his native Budapest, Paris, and New York—in photographs of formal excellence that search out the warmer, more gentle aspects of human relationship through symbolic and anecdotal details and offer a fresh and exhilarated perception of daily life.

The son of Leopold and Ernestine (Hoffman) Kertész, André Kertész was born in Budapest, Hungary on July 2, 1894 into a family of booksellers and landowners. He grew up on a farm where he had some instruction in beekeeping, and having "learned everything in the stable," as he told Dorothy S. Gelatt in an interview for *Popular Photography* (November 1974), he had an early knowledge of the ways of domestic animals like those that were to abound in his pictures—work horses, sheep, cows, pigs, and goats. At the urging of his mother he once considered remaining on the land and becoming what he has called "a gourmet farmer." For a time he also tried to follow his uncle's advice that he make banking his lifework.

In adolescence, however, when he bought his first camera, Kertész discovered that what he wanted to do most of all was to take pictures. After he had received his baccalaureate from the Hungarian Academy of Commerce in 1912 and had begun working as a clerk on the Budapest Stock Exchange, he spent most of his free time photographing street scenes and genre subjects. With his small ICA box camera he tried to capture realistically and candidly what he felt to be distinctive instances or moments of life that "said everything." "For a youngster, his instincts and insights were profound, and his composition strikingly simple and original," Dorothy S. Gelatt wrote in *Popular Photography*. ". . . His earliest glass-plate-camera pictures anticipated the instantaneous freedom that other photographers discovered decades later with the first 35-mm still cameras."

When Kertész was twenty, his older brother gave him a Voigtländer camera, which he carried with him on hikes to photograph scenes of nature and rural life. But because the camera was heavy and its glass plates were cumbersome, he learned to take pictures only of what was significant to him. The lessons he taught himself in selectivity remained with him afterward in using small cameras, such as the Leica, which he preferred for the ease in handling and freedom of movement they allowed.

Some of the photographs that Kertész made during World War I with the relatively small glass plates of a Goërz Tenax camera are solemn and poignant, rather than obviously dramatic, documents of everyday life disrupted by mobilization and the breaking up of families and similar ordeals of war. Others reflect the innocence of an earlier time, such as those depicting the play of children untouched by violence. While serving in the Austro-Hungarian army, he was wounded in 1915, and although he eventually resumed his work as a photo reporter, many of his pictures were lost in Béla Kun's Bolshevik revolution that followed the war. His extant prewar and later Hungarian pictures show his eagerness to explore the possibilities of his medium under varying conditions of angle, weather, and light.

Recognition in the form of a prize for a satiric self-portrait from *Borsszem Janko* magazine in 1917, as well as publication of his photographs in *Erdekes Ujsag* and other illustrated magazines, strengthened Kertész' confidence in his untutored skill with the camera. Aware that postwar Hungary offered little encouragement for his artistic development, in 1925 he left for Paris with his Voigtländer and Goërz Tenax cameras. He spent his first night in an inexpensive *pension* on the Rue Vavin, where from his window the next morning in the excitement of discovery he took the classic picture that launched the most productive period of his career—a composition of windows and shutters on the building across the way.

Other photographs that Kertész made during his first year in Paris include those of the Seine from Pont Saint Michel, fishermen behind Notre Dame, Boulevard Malesherbes at midday, the fountain in the Place de la Concorde, Place Furstenberg, chairs near the Medici Fountain, Notre Dame at night, the Eiffel Tower, and dozens of other landmarks. Those and scores of later street scenes, landscapes, portraits, and animal studies record a joyous, appreciative exploration of the city. Experimenting with vantage point, he photographed a neighborhood carnival from the top-floor apartment of an obliging stranger. He took a picture of Paris rooftops and Sacré Coeur from the top of the Great Mosque of Paris in 1929, when he became the first person allowed to photograph in the minaret. With the permission also of the director of the Académie Française, he photographed scenes behind its huge clock and through the clock's glass face he took a picture of the Louvre. In 1928 he had bought his first Leica camera, which proved to be particularly well suited to his adventurous versatility and flexibility as a photographer.

In the exchange of ideas among French and emigré artists in Paris' cafés, Kertész found the supportive creative climate he had lacked in Budapest. His friends included the painters Maurice de Vlaminck, Pieter Mondrian, Fernand Léger, and Marc Chagall; the sculptors Ossip Zadkine and Alexander Calder; Colette and many other avant-garde writers; and filmmakers. The photographs that he made of many of them, sometimes also of their studios and families, constitute "a picture history of artistic Paris in the '20s and early '30s that has no counterpart," Dorothy S. Gelatt wrote in *Popular Photography*.

Occasionally, for the purpose of conveying a mood or impression, Kertész experimented with his lens to achieve a soft focus, such as in his 1925 picture of the stairs of Montmartre, but from the beginning of his work in photography he declined to use his camera to duplicate the effects of painting or to follow stylistic fashions in art. His increasing interest in form, stimulated by his association with artists, was expressed generally in the subtlety of his pictures' composition and specifically in his work during the early 1930's on a series of nude distortions, some of them witty and satirical, that he had begun in Budapest. Commenting on the surrealist qualities of the more than 150 photographs in that group, Carole Kismaric wrote in her introduction to *André Kertész* (1977) in the Aperture History of Photography series, "Even more than in his street pictures, there was a sense of life as a dream. The surrealist concept of transforming reality into fantasy made its way into Kertész' technique. His work came to influence his friends' paintings."

As photographic reportage, moreover, Kertész' unposed pictures had a marked influence on the French photographers Brassaï and Henri Cartier-Bresson. The latter, who also searched with his camera for what he called "the decisive moment," has been quoted as acknowledging, "Ah, Kertész. We all owe him a great deal." In her survey of Kertész' accomplishments in the *Saturday Review* (December 26, 1964), Margaret R. Weiss pointed out, "His distinctive brand of reporting set the pattern for European photography of the period."

Kertész' influence, beyond the impact he had on his immediate friends, was notably extended by his one-man show in 1927 at the gallery Sacre du Printemps in Paris. The Dadaist poet Paul Dermeé prefaced the show's catalogue with a poem in which he compared Kertész to a thirteenth-century monk who had been the only sighted man in a home for the blind: ". . . No rearranging, no posing, no gimmicks, nor fakery./Your technique is as honest, as incorruptible, as your vision./In our home for the blind,/Kertész is Brother Seeing-Eye." His show drew such enthusiastic attention that he was invited to exhibit his photographs the following year in the First Independent Salon of Photography.

Soon after his arrival in Paris, Kertész had begun supporting himself through free-lance photography for the *Frankfurter illustrierte,* *UHU* magazine, *Berliner illustrierte, Strasberger illustrierte, Le Nazionale de Fiorenze,* and other top-flight European periodicals. He became a major contributor to the French magazines *Vu,* which began publication in 1928, and *Art et Médecine,* which first appeared in 1930. During the 1930's Éditions d'Histoire et d'Art published three collections of his photographs: *Enfants* (1933), sixty prints of children; *Paris vu par André Kertész* (1934); and *Nos amies les bêtes par André Kertész* (1936). A fourth book, *Les cathédrales du vin,* was published by Établissements Sainrapt et Brice in 1937.

Kertész had, therefore, become regarded as an illustrious member of the School of Paris when, in 1936, he was offered a one-year contract to work in New York for Keystone Studios, a leading commercial picture agency. He arrived in the United States in October of that year, and eight months later, after he had terminated his contract, he was unable to return to Paris because of the imminence of war. Thirty-five of Kertész' photographs had been included in the exhibition of modern European photography at the Julien Levy Gallery in New York in 1932, and his reputation as a photo reporter had also preceded him to the United States. But for reasons that may be simplistically summed up as a clash between Kertész' European sensibilities and the objectives of American journalism, he could not work in New York in the same individually creative manner that he had in Paris.

An editor for *Life,* America's most popular illustrated magazine, criticized Kertész wtih the protest: "Your pictures *say* too much." His work, as Carole Kismaric explained, made words unnecessary: "It was profoundly symbolic, whereas *Life* wanted to pinpoint the world clearly in its readers' minds almost as though it were a newspaper." He free-lanced for other magazines, however—including *Harper's Bazaar, Vogue, Town & Country, Collier's,* and *Coronet*—from 1937 to 1949, when he signed an exclusive contract with Condé Nast Publications. During the next thirteen years he engaged in commercial photography—fashions, interiors, portraits—much of it in color, for *House & Garden* and other Condé Nast magazines.

According to Dorothy S. Gelatt, Kertész "tragically regrets" his first twenty-five years in the United States. His name and effort, however, were not confined to commercial illustration. In 1945 he published his delightful *Day of Paris* (J. J. Augustin), and in 1946 he had a one-man show at the Art Institute in Chicago. From time to time, between magazine assignments, he roamed Manhattan with his Leica to satisfy his creative impulses. In 1962 he ended his contract with Condé Nast to work entirely for himself in his own earlier, personal idiom.

Although Kertész was given a one-man show at Long Island University in New York in

1962, the actual discovery in the United States of his photographic mastery may be said to have begun in 1964, when the director of photography, John Szarkowski, mounted a retrospective of his work at the Museum of Modern Art. Reviewing a later major one-man show in New York, "André Kertész: Themes and Variations," at the Hallmark Gallery in 1973, Hilton Kramer of the New York *Times* (January 17, 1973) called attention to "the appeal of a vision that finds its revelations in the small detail, the unexpected aside, the marginal glimpse, and yet confers on this 'minor' material a formal rigor of the highest order." Kramer went on to say that during his earlier years in the United States, Kertész' style had few admirers: "He was a kind of casualty of our inability to appreciate his subtlety and humor and great refinement." A less gratified critic, Martin Levine of *Newsday* (January 29, 1973), objected to some pictures that he thought had "trivial" messages or "rather facile juxtapositions" or were "insipidly pretty." But he found much to praise in the Hallmark show, including an engaging series about people reading, the theme of Kertész' collection *On Reading* (Grossman, 1971). Another group of his related photographs was published in *Distortions* (Knopf, 1976)

The photographs in Kertész' two Manhattan shows and in *André Kertész: Sixty Years of Photography, 1912-1972* (Grossman, 1972) attest that whatever his locale—Budapest, Paris, or New York—his abiding preoccupation has been with expressions of the human comedy. Kramer's observation in the New York *Times* (March 3, 1974) that "Kertész brings a lover's eye to his encounters with the world," applies especially to his photographs of Paris. He prefaced his collection of over 200 pictures, *J'aime Paris: Photographs Since the Twenties* (Grossman, 1974), with the declaration: "I write with light/and the light of Paris/helped me express what I felt/and what I feel: *J'aime Paris.*" In 1976 the French Cultural Services in New York presented a fifty-print exhibition of Kertész' tribute to Paris.

Kertész, who became an American citizen in 1944, has lived for more than twenty-five years in a twelfth-floor apartment overlooking Washington Square in Manhattan. In his cityscapes of New York, like those of Budapest and Paris, he delights in the perseverance of nature—birds, trees, flowers—amid steel, glass, and concrete, and for that reason he often focuses his lens on parks and squares. Brendan Gill wrote in the introduction of one collection of Kertész' New York pictures, *Washington Square* (Grossman, 1975), "Kertész on his balcony arms himself with camera and bulky zoom lens to shoot the many lives of the Square, of the narrow streets that bound it, and of the nearby roof gardens and terraces. Now and again he descends to encounter his fellow creatures—men, women, dogs, cats, and birds—on *terra firma*, eye to eye." A selection of his New York photographs has also been published in *Of New York*, which was released by Alfred A. Knopf, Inc. in 1976.

Twenty of Kertész' more recent pictures were shown at the Light Gallery in Manhattan in 1978. Made during the period from the spring of 1976 to the summer of 1978, the photographs of birds in flight and a bird paperweight on the photographer's desk and other domestic still lifes reflect the feelings of Kertész at the time of the illness and death of his wife, the former Elizabeth Sali, whom he had married on June 17, 1933. Ben Lifson commented in the *Village Voice* (September 25, 1978), "At the same time, [the photographs] continue in genres that we have long associated with Kertész, ... and although his style has not changed radically since the 30s, they paradoxically seem the most contemporary and explorative work being shown in New York today." André Kertész' honors include the silver medal at the Exposition Coloniale, Paris in 1930; gold medal at the IVth Mostra Biennale Internazionale della Fotografia, Venice in 1962; Commander of the Order of Arts and Letters, awarded by the French government in 1976; and the City of New York Mayor's Award of Honor for Arts and Culture, conferred in 1977.

References: Art in Am 64:103+ Jl/Ag '76; N Y Times p41 Ja 17 '73 por; Pop Photo 75:136+ N '74 por; Sat R 47:28+ D 26 '64; Kismaric, Carole. André Kertész (1977); Who's Who in America, 1978-79

Khomeini, Ayatollah Ruholla (Mussavi)
(kō-mā′nē)

May 17, 1900(?)- Iranian religious leader.
Address: b. Madresseh Faizieh, Qom, Iran;
h. 61 Kuche Yakhchal Ghazi, Qom, Iran

Entering the Iranian scene like a long-heralded messiah, the Ayatollah Ruholla Khomeini returned to his native country on February 1, 1979, after more than fourteen years in exile, to direct the revolution that had driven the Shah Mohammed Riza Pahlevi from his throne sixteen days earlier. Khomeini, who first gained prominence as an opponent of the Shah in 1963, holds no formal political office but derives his authority from his position as leader of the Shi'ite Muslims, who comprise some 92 percent of Iran's 36,000,000 people. In the beginning, the Ayatollah seemed to have a substantial majority of the Iranian population behind him. But it soon became evident that the increasingly oppressive Khomeini regime, with its large-scale executions, xenophobia, censorship of the media, imposition of rigidly puritanical moral standards, and failure to resolve the country's grave economic and social problems, confirmed the worst fears of its critics.

Ayatollah Ruholla ("soul of God") Mussavi Khomeini—whose name according to some accounts was originally Ruholla Hendi—was born in the small city of Khomein, some 180 miles south of Teheran, in what was then known as Persia, the youngest of the six children of Sayed Mustafa Mussavi and his wife, Hajar Saghafi. According to *Time* (July 16, 1979), "one plausible date" for his birth is May 17, 1900; other sources give the year as 1901 or 1902. Around 1930 he took on the surname of Khomeini, referring to his birthplace. The honorific title "ayatollah" ("reflection of God") was added to his name in the late 1950's, when he had won enough of a following to be recognized as one of the several hundred Shi'ite leaders in Iran who bear that designation. By the early 1960's he had become one of a half dozen men known by the title "Ayatollah al-Ozma," or "grand ayatollah," who stand out above the rest.

Khomeini's maternal grandfather was an ayatollah, as was his father and one of his brothers. Another brother became a lawyer. When Ruholla was five months old, his father, then the head of the local community, was killed while embarking on a religious pilgrimage to Iraq. Some sources contend that he was shot to death by government agents because he opposed the oppressive Qajar dynasty; others suggest he was killed by bandits, by henchmen of a local feudal baron, in a personal dispute with the provincial governor, or in a conflict with a rival landowner over water rights. In what was then considered a bold act for a Persian woman, Ruholla's mother testified in court against her husband's killer, who was convicted and executed.

Brought up by his mother and a paternal aunt—a strong-willed woman who instilled in him the obligation to take up the struggle against Islam's opponents—Ruholla attended Koranic school in his hometown and was apparently an apt student as well as an enthusiastic soccer player. When he was fifteen, following the death of both his mother and his aunt, Ruholla's education came under the supervision of his eldest brother. At nineteen he moved to Arak to undertake advanced studies and came under the tutelage of the Ayatollah Abdul Karim Haeri, one of the leading Islamic theologians of his time. When Haeri moved to Qom about 1922, to transform that city into a new center of Muslim culture and to found the Madresseh Faizieh, a leading institution of Islamic learning, Ruholla accompanied him. Except for the years he spent in exile, he has lived and taught at that institution ever since.

Completing his formal education at Qom, Ruholla became an authority on Islamic law and jurisprudence and studied Islamic mysticism. He also took an interest in the works of Aristotle and Plato, and it was Plato's *Republic* that later served as a model for his concept of an Islamic republic. During his early years at Qom he also wrote lyric poetry. At twenty-seven he began to teach philosophy, and about a year later he went on the obligatory pilgrimage to Mecca.

Khomeini soon made his mark as a *ulema*, or religious scholar. Over the years he wrote twenty-one books, mainly on Islamic theology, of which eleven were published, and he has been credited with having trained some 1,200 leaders who became the religious elite of Iran. Although his interpretive teaching of Shi'ite philosophy evoked some criticism from older scholars, he was venerated by students who emulated his practice of strict self-discipline and intense spiritual activity. In the lengthy discussions of ethics and morals that he conducted after his classes he encouraged his students to challenge his ideas. In keeping with Shi'ite tradition, which held that all Muslim rulers since the death, in the seventh century, of Ali—the son-in-law of the prophet Mohammed—were usurpers, but that the true Imam, or leader of Islam, would someday emerge, Khomeini linked the legitimacy of Muslim leadership with the national identity of Iran and stressed the inseparability of religion and politics.

Khomeini first gained public attention with his book *Kasf' ol-Assraar* (Unveiling the Mysteries), published in 1941—the year that Riza Shah Pahlevi was forced out by British and Soviet authorities because of his pro-Nazi sympathies and was succeeded by his son, Mohammed Riza Shah. In it he attacked the old Shah for his dictatorial rule, his persecution of the Muslim clergy, his systematic destruction of Islamic culture, and his subservience to foreign powers.

During the short-lived National Front government of Dr. Mohammed Mossadegh, who came to power in 1951, Khomeini sympathized with his opposition to the Shah but remained aloof because he regarded the Prime Minister as being too secular. When Mohammed Riza Shah visited Qom in 1953, Khomeini was the only one of some forty clerics to refuse to rise. Influenced by the militant Arab nationalism of Egyptian President Abdel Gamal Nasser in the 1950's, he became increasingly outspoken in his denunciations of the Shah and his ties to the United States and Israel. In public statements he condemned the Jewish state and fulminated against the "Washington-Tel Aviv-Teheran Axis."

Although other ayatollahs were judged more learned, by 1962 Khomeini was recognized as leader of the Shi'ite community because of his outspokenness against the Shah. In November of that year he led the clergy in a successful general strike against a government ruling that witnesses in court were no longer required to swear by the Koran. When in early 1963 the Shah launched his "White Revolution," Khomeini inveighed against proposed agrarian reforms that were to deprive the Shi'ite clergy of much of its landed property, and against provisions for women's rights which, he maintained, would result in exploitation and corruption of women, rather than their liberation. At issue, according to Khomeini and his supporters, was the erosion of the clergy's dominant voice in such matters as marriage, education, and morals, and destruction of the constitutional checks and balances designed to keep legislation in harmony with Islamic law.

When in the spring of 1963 the Shah's forces broke into the Madresseh Faizieh in Qom, killing about twenty young mullahs, Khomeini won massive support among students at Teheran University, who distributed as many as 200,000 copies of his invectives against the government. In the weeks that followed, many of Khomeini's supporters were killed in riots against the Shah's regime, and martial law was imposed in Teheran.

In June 1963, after the Shah had tried in vain to persuade him through an emissary to drop his opposition, Khomeini was arrested. He spent several months in detention and was under house arrest for almost a year, becoming a martyr in the eyes of many of his countrymen. His final arrest came in November 1964, after he had denounced parliamentary approval of a status-of-forces agreement exempting United States military forces in Iran from jurisdiction of Iranian courts, a measure that he saw as undue submission to foreign domination. He was sent into exile in Turkey, but when Iranian students there organized large-scale demonstrations in his behalf the Turkish authorities were anxious to get rid of him. In 1965 he settled in the Shi'ite holy city of An Najaf, in the desert of southern Iraq, not far from the tomb of the Imam Ali.

At An Najaf, Khomeini headed a theological school and maintained contact with his disciples in his own country through Iranian pilgrims. Continuing his relentless opposition to the Shah in his lectures, he called for political action to weed out corruption and Western influence in Iran, and for the replacement of the Shah's regime with his concept of an Islamic republic. Using modern technology to advance his age-old principles, he sent tape-recorded lectures back to Iran, where they were heard clandestinely at mosques throughout the country.

In the late 1960's and early 1970's, Khomeini's influence among his countrymen seemed to wane, as Iranians tried to cope with their oil boom and the resulting economic development. He provoked some controversy with his volume of lectures published about 1970 under the title "Islamic Government," in which he said at one point: "We want a leader who would cut off the hand of his own son if he caught him stealing, or stone a member of his own family who had indulged in fornication." In the same work he maintained that "the Jews and their foreign masters" were preparing "to rule over the entire planet." When Yasir Arafat, the head of the Palestine Liberation Organization, visited him in Iraq in the early 1970s, Khomeini welcomed his pledges of moral and material support.

In 1971, when the Shah held a grandiose celebration to commemorate the 2,500th anniversary of the Persian monarchy, Khomeini denounced the "imperial feast" as "megalomaniacal and extravagant." He expressed himself in a similar vein on the occasion of the Shah's 1976 celebration marking the fiftieth anniversary of the Pahlevi dynasty, but his pronouncements seemed to have gone largely unnoticed. The Shah reportedly said in 1976: "Khomeini? No one refers to him in Iran except the terrorists."

Meanwhile, growing numbers of Iranians realized that they had derived little benefit from the economic boom, that their country was coming increasingly under Western influence, and that the Shah's government was more repressive than ever. The Shi'ite religious establishment—the only major institution that the Shah had been unable to suppress or shape to his liking—thus became the logical vehicle for mounting revolutionary sentiment. As the exiled Ayatollah came more and more to symbolize opposition to the Shah, Iranians looked to him for leadership.

When in the fall of 1977 Khomeini's oldest son, Mustafa, died at An Najaf under mysterious circumstances, it was widely believed (but never proved) that SAVAK, the Shah's secret police, had been responsible. Shortly thereafter, Khomeini sent an open letter to the Iranian people, of which hundreds of thousands of copies were distributed, denouncing the "absurdities of this incompetent agent"— the Shah—and called on the armed forces to "liberate their country." To discredit Khomeini, the Shah's ministry of information planted an article in the Teheran newspaper Ettela'at in January 1978, questioning his piety and linking him to the outlawed Communist Tudeh party. It also hinted that the Ayatollah was not of pure Iranian but of partly Indian ancestry by alluding to the fact that his paternal grandfather had once lived in India. But the article backfired, giving Khomeini nationwide publicity and touching off mass demonstrations throughout Iran by his supporters, who brandished posters bearing his portrait as their battle flag.

Under pressure from the Shah, the government of Iraq expelled Khomeini in October 1978, and he flew to France, where he was granted a temporary residence permit. Establishing his headquarters in the village of Neauphle-le-Château, some twenty-five miles west of Paris, Khomeini for the first time had access to the international press through the steady stream of journalists and other callers. Direct-dial telephone connections enabled him to remain in contact with Teheran, and his calls for strikes, mass demonstrations, days of mourning, and civil disobedience met with instant response in his homeland. Commanding a network of some 180,000 mullahs, and supported financially by the wealthy bazaar merchants, the Ayatollah increased his influence in Iran by remote control.

Meanwhile, as conditions deteriorated, the Shah vacillated between last-ditch efforts at liberalization and increased martial law. On December 29, 1978, with the economy virtually at a standstill, largely as a result of oil workers' strikes inspired by Khomeini, the Shah designated Dr. Shahpur Bakhtiar, a leader of the Union of National Front Forces, to form a new civilian government, effective January 6, 1979. As the Shah left Iran for Egypt on January 16, ostensibly to go on vacation, Bakhtiar assumed power with a nine-member regency council. Meanwhile, in preparation for his imminent return to Iran, Khomeini announced formation of a Council of the Islamic Revolution. As millions demonstrated in his support in Teheran and provincial cities, the Ayatollah indignantly dismissed President Jimmy Carter's plea that he give the new government a chance. Calling the Bakhtiar government "illegal," he demanded the immediate resignation of the Prime Minister and his council.

On February 1, 1979, after last-minute efforts by Bakhtiar to block or delay his return, Khomeini triumphantly entered Teheran, while cheering millions lined the city's streets. Addressing them, the Ayatollah threatened to arrest Bakhtiar and his aides if they refused to step aside and promised that he would not "let the United States bring the Shah back." On February 11, after several days of fighting between Khomeini supporters and the armed forces, Bakhtiar resigned, and the Council of the Islamic Revolution named a provisional government, with Mehdi Bazargan, a respected liberal and the leader of the religiously oriented National Liberation Movement of Iran, as Prime Minister. At the same time, army commanders withdrew their troops to the barracks and declared their neutrality, thereby averting a threatened military coup. One of the first moves of the Khomeini regime was to sever relations with Israel and to extend recognition to Yasir Arafat's PLO. On the other hand, Iran's 80,000 Jews were assured that their rights would be safeguarded.

Taking up residence in Qom on March 1, Khomeini declared that he would devote "the remaining one or two years" of his life to rebuilding Iran "in the image of Mohammed" and to purging every vestige of Western culture. When on March 30 and 31 an estimated 97 percent of the Iranian electorate in a referendum approved the establishment of an Islamic republic, the Ayatollah hailed the new regime as a "government of God." In May he formed a special militia, the Guardians of the Islamic Revolution. A draft constitution based on the tenets of Islam was released by the government in June. As of the fall of 1979 the constitution, including a clause formally giving Khomeini supreme power over public and military affairs, awaited final approval by an assembly of experts and ratification by the electorate.

Meanwhile, it became evident that Bazargan's government in Teheran was a façade, while the real power resided in the Ayatollah. What particularly dismayed Bazargan was the practice of Khomeini's revolutionary tribunals to hold summary trials and order executions without consulting his government. Among the 600 or more sentenced to death by November 1979, there were not only functionaries of the Shah's regime—such as former Prime Minister Amir Abbas Hoveyda—but also homosexuals, brothel keepers, adulterers, and persons found guilty of such charges as "waging war on God and his emissaries' and "insulting the Imam [Khomeini]."

The Ayatollah's rigid standards on manners and morals also evoked much controversy. His edicts, issued in March, abrogating the family protection law and mandating that women be clothed in the traditional *chador*, touched off mass demonstrations by women in Teheran. Other prohibitions included bans on alcoholic beverages, mixed swimming, coeducational classes in elementary and high schools, and most Western films and television shows. Vigilantes menaced couples demonstrating affection in public and warned women against

"immodest" dress or behavior. In July, Khomeini issued an edict banning the broadcasting of all music which, he maintained, "stupefies persons listening to it and makes their brains inactive and frivolous."

By the end of the summer of 1979 about forty publications in Iran had been closed or muzzled, a number of Western newsmen were expelled from the joyless country, and the Associated Press office in Teheran was shut down because of "biased and distorted" reporting. In August new press laws were issued, providing penalties for libeling religious leaders and exacting from foreign correspondents the pledge to report "only the truth."

Growing opposition to the Ayatollah's authority and the assassination of some of his closest aides by terrorists of the extreme left prompted him to crack down on antagonists. In August forces loyal to him raided the headquarters of two leftist groups that had grown disenchanted with his rule. In September government troops acting on his direct orders suppressed a Kurdish uprising in Iran.

Incensed by Khomeini's campaign against the left and by his cancellation of a gas pipeline contract, the Soviet government castigated him for "anti-Communist hysteria" and "religious fanaticism." Relations between Iran and the PLO also cooled when it appeared that Palestinians had been encouraging members of the Arab minority in Khuzestan to revolt against the Ayatollah's rule. On the other hand, the United States State Department appeared in the fall of 1979 to be making overtures to the Khomeini government to ensure continued oil supplies and to prevent Iran from falling under Soviet domination.

Economically, Iran under Khomeini seemed by the fall of 1979 to be going downhill. Some 3,000,000 people were unemployed, inflation was mounting, industrial and oil production had sharply declined, as had foreign trade, and investment was virtually nil. Iran's new "law for the protection and expansion of industry," under which most businesses were to be nationalized, did little to alleviate the situation, since many members of the managerial class, capable of running them, had left the country.

In early November 1979 militant student supporters of Khomeini, with the approval of the Ayatollah, seized the American Embassy in Teheran and held some sixty persons hostage in an effort to compel the United States government to extradite the Shah, who was undergoing medical treatment in New York City. The student action led to the resignation of Prime Minister Bazargan and of his government, which was provisionally replaced by Khomeini's Council of the Islamic Revolution pending ratification of the constitution.

Some aspects of the Ayatollah Ruholla Khomeini's life remain shrouded in mystery. It has been suggested that he has had two wives, and that the first, whom he married in 1928, bore him the son Mustafa and a daughter who died in infancy. After his first wife's death he was said to have married the daughter of a wealthy landowner from Gilan province who bore him another son and three daughters. Other sources insist that he was married only once, to a woman whose name is variously given as Quesiran, Khadijeh, or Khodsi. In any case, the Ayatollah is known to have four surviving children—three daughters, and his second son, Sayed Ahmed (or Hamid), who serves as his chief aide. In early 1979 he was reported to have fourteen grandchildren.

A tall, gaunt, robed figure, the Ayatollah Khomeini is said to have "the heart of a young man" despite his frail appearance. His black turban signifies that he is a lineal descendant of Mohammed. In a profile in the English edition of Le Monde, Paul Balta refers to his "white-bearded El Greco face and piercing mystic's gaze." Speaking neither English nor French, the Ayatollah, whose language is Farsi, communicates with Western visitors through interpreters. Although his public demeanor is serious, he is said to display a sense of humor in private. At his old one-story house in the center of Qom he subsists mainly on cheese, toast, fruit, rice, and yogurt. He spends many hours in prayer and meditation but also finds time to read news reports and political digests, and in France he watched televised soccer games with some interest. Responding to allegations that he exercised absolute dictatorial rule over his country, Khomeini told Oriana Fallaci in an interview in the New York Times Magazine (October 7, 1979): "Iran is not in my hands. Iran is in the hands of the people."

References: London Observer p9 Ja 28 '79 por; Macleans 92:28+ F 5 '79 por; N Y Times A p10 D 11 '78 por; A p4 Ja 30 '79 por; New Statesm 97:140+ F 2 '79 por; Newsweek 93:38+ Ja 29 '79 pors; 93:42+ F 12 '79 pors; Time 113:48+ Ja 29 '79 pors; 114:33+ Jl 16 '79 pors; Washington Post A p23+ Ja 21 '79 pors

Kimball, Spencer W(oolley)

Mar. 28, 1895- President of the Church of Jesus Christ of Latter-Day Saints. Address: b. 47 E. South Temple St., Salt Lake City, Utah 84108

The current head of America's richest, largest, and fastest growing home-grown church is the octogenarian "Prophet, Seer, and Revelator" Spencer W. Kimball, who became the twelfth president of the Church of Jesus Christ of Latter-Day Saints in 1973. Kimball was accorded that honor after thirty years of service in the church's governing Council of Twelve Apostles (usually called simply the Council, or Quorum, of the Twelve). The Mormons, as the Latter-Day Saints are commonly called, claim to be the pristine Christian church, possessor of the "restored Gospel" revealed to Joseph Smith, who founded the church at Fayette, New York in 1830. Deviating from the mainstream Christian norm, and living and working in a communal, close-knit, seemingly aloof way, the Latter-Day Saints were viewed as "a kingdom apart," hounded westward from state to state by their persecutors until they found a haven in the mountain fastness of the Great Salt Lake basin in what is now Utah, where they proceeded to "build up Zion." Even there, they were harassed by the federal government, until they renounced the practice of polygamy in 1890.

The most important change in the policy of the Church of Jesus Christ of Latter-Day Saints since its capitulation on the issue of multiple marriage eighty-nine years ago was the promulgation by President Kimball in 1978 of a "revelation" ending the exclusion of black males of African descent from priesthood, which had otherwise always been open to every "worthy" Mormon male twelve years and older. Besides the relief it brought to embarrassed white liberal Mormons and the opportunity it opened to the current relatively small number of Afro-American Mormons, Kimball's historic statement opened the way to further acceleration of the growth of the church's membership. At present that membership is estimated at 4,000,000, approximately four times what it was when

Kimball entered the Council of the Twelve Apostles in 1943. The church does not issue financial statements, but it is patently a billion-dollar organization, with especially strong holdings in the West and above all in Utah, where it is the dominant force on all levels of life. One of the symbols used by Mormons is the beehive, representing their hard-working, hard-tithing way of life and their system of mutual aid.

The sixth of eleven children, Spencer Woolley Kimball was born in Salt Lake City, Utah on March 28, 1895 to Andrew and Olive (Woolley) Kimball. The first Kimball on American soil was a Puritan wheelwright, Richard Kimball, a refugee from religious persecution in England who settled in the Massachusetts Bay Colony, in 1634. The first in the Mormon line of Kimballs was Spencer's paternal grandfather Heber Kimball (1801-1868), a contemporary of Joseph Smith and one of Mormonism's initial Twelve Apostles. Smith claimed to have discovered sacred writings dating back to pre-Columbian times which gave an account of the migration of Jewish tribes to the Americas and of a ministry by Jesus in the New World. That book, as translated by Smith and transcribed by his followers, is the *Book of Mormon,* which, along with later revelations, or discoveries, including the book *The Pearl of Great Price* (said to be sayings of Moses and Abraham), and the Bible, provide the scriptural basis for Mormonism.

Spencer W. Kimball's paternal grandmother was Ann Alice (Gheen) Kimball, the seventeenth of Heber Kimball's over forty wives. On the maternal side, his grandfather was Edwin Dilworth Woolley, the business manager for Brigham Young, the founding leader of the Salt Lake City community, and his grandmother was Mary Ann (Olpin) Woolley, Edwin's fourth wife. The practice of plural marriage brought mounting federal harassment in the 1880's: the church's property was seized, Mormon polygamists were disenfranchised by court order, and most of the church's leaders went "underground" to escape federal prosecution. National political leaders did not withdraw their opposition to statehood for Utah until the church officially ended the practice of plural marriage in 1890. Statehood followed six years later.

Spencer W. Kimball grew up in the Mormon frontier farming town of Thatcher, Arizona, where his father, a Mormon bishop, made a living as a farmer, carpenter, and salesman while serving as president of the Mormon "stake," or cluster of congregations (called "wards") there. The Arizona jurisdiction, called the St. Joseph Stake, took in the whole Gila Valley and its environs, including an Indian mission. Mormons put great importance on their work with the Indians, whom they believe to be descendants of a tribe of Israelites, called Lamanites, and Spencer W.

Kimball's youthful experiences in Thatcher filled him with a special interest in that work.

With their father away so often and so long, making the rounds of the St. Joseph Stake (which meant traveling some 200 miles through Arizona and New Mexico desert by horse and buggy), Spencer and his brothers and sisters did most of the farm work, loading hay, gardening, and milking the cows. In addition, Spencer helped his father with church correspondence, taking dictation in improvised shorthand and typing with two fingers. (He later taught himself to type properly.) On weekends he earned money playing piano with a schoolboy combo at various affairs, including dances at a gentile (that is, non-Mormon) dance hall in Safford, Arizona. Summers, he sometimes worked at a dairy in Globe, Arizona.

The Church of Jesus Christ of Latter-Day Saints was founded on the basis of the priesthood of the two orders of Aaron and Melchizedek. Like most devout male Mormons, Spencer W. Kimball became a member of the Aaronic priesthood at age twelve and of the Melchizedek priesthood at nineteen. Also in keeping with the Mormon tradition for young men, after graduating from the Latter-Day Saints Academy in Thatcher, in 1914, Kimball donated two years without pay to missionary work, or proselyting. As a missionary, he worked out of the headquarters of the Central States Mission in Independence, Missouri (in Mormon eschatology, the site where Jesus will establish the capital of his kingdom on his return to earth). At twenty he became president of the East Missouri Conference, with authority over twenty-five missionaries, all older than he.

On his return from his missionary assignment, in January 1917, Spencer Kimball matriculated at the University of Arizona. After one semester he dropped out and, having married, began to look for a steady job with which to support a family. He began as a clerk at the Citizens' Bank in Thatcher, was promoted to teller, and became assistant cashier when, in 1923, the bank was reorganized and renamed the Arizona Trust and Savings Bank. He was chief teller at the Bank of Safford, Arizona from 1923 to 1927, when he resigned to open the Kimball-Greenhalgh Agency, an insurance and real estate business, in partnership with Joseph W. Greenhalgh.

While running the agency, Kimball was involved in a dizzying round of other activities —some to augment his income and others in service to church or community. He hired himself out as a piano player and singer; directed the Sunday School chorus; was a member of the Safford City Council, the Chamber of Commerce, and the governing board of Gila College; served in executive positions in the Rotary Club, the Red Cross, and the Boy Scouts, helped organize, and was part owner of, local radio station KGLU, and served as secretary of the Gila Valley Irrigation Company. In the church he was both stake clerk and counselor to the president of the St. Joseph Stake, and when the stake was divided in two in 1938 he was named president of the new Mount Graham Stake.

Called to apostleship when a vacancy occurred in the Council of the Twelve in 1943, Kimball sold his home and business in Safford and moved with his family to Salt Lake City. As an apostle, Kimball had an office in the church's main office building, a block from Temple Square. There a constant stream of Latter-day Saints came to him to express "testimonies"; to confess sins that troubled them; to seek solace in sorrow; to ask advice about problems; to state grievances; to be married; or to resolve marital difficulties.

In addition, Kimball was sent to weekend stake conferences away from Salt Lake City, and beginning in 1945 much of his time was spent overseeing the church's work with the Indians. In his "service to Lamanites," he traveled extensively in Latin America as well as the United States. One of the projects closest to his heart was a student placement program initiated by him for Mormon Indian school children to live in white Mormon homes throughout Utah during the school year.

Kimball's first major overseas assignment was a tour of the ten Mormon missions in Europe, beginning in April 1955 in Germany and finishing in September 1955 at the dedication in Switzerland of the first Mormon temple outside of North America and Hawaii. The other countries on his itinerary included Great Britain, the Netherlands, Finland, Denmark, France, and Austria. In 1959 he visited the Mormon missions in Argentina, Uruguay, and Brazil, and in the early 1960's he made a world tour in the course of which he presided over the dedication of stakes in Australia and New Zealand. When the church divided its world missions into twelve areas in 1965, Kimball was assigned to supervise the seven missions in South America, and in 1969 he was reassigned to Great Britain.

In 1969 Bookcraft Publishers in Salt Lake City published Kimball's The Miracle of Forgiveness, a book that was based on his experience as a counselor to the troubled and that he "meant as a call to repentance and a guide on the road back from sin." A second book, Faith Precedes the Miracle, published by the Deseret Book Company in Salt Lake City in 1972, contained sermons delivered by Kimball over the years and selected and edited by his son Edward.

As the senior member of the Council of Twelve, Kimball was "invited, sustained, and ordained" in the presidency of the Church of Jesus Christ of Latter-Day Saints on December 30, 1973, following the death of President Harold B. Lee. Under his presidency the first Mormon temple east of the Rockies was dedicated, just outside of Washington, D.C. in 1974, and the following year a Church of Latter-Day Saints Visitors Center was dedicated across from Lincoln Center in New York City. On the occasion of the Manhattan dedication, Kimball was quoted by Kenneth A. Briggs in the New York Times (May 24, 1975) as saying that Mormons "have many philosophies different from other churches we know" and as warning that societies that allowed the family to disintegrate "went to early graves."

The Mormon stand on the family and related matters of morality are regarded as reactionary by birth-control advocates, feminists, and "gay rights" activists. While the church is concerned about its image among other Americans, it is not about to sacrifice its integrity for the sake of ecumenical popularity. In an interview with Dan L. Thrapp of the Los Angeles Times (October 5, 1974), Kimball reiterated the traditional Mormon refusal to join such organizations as the National Council of Churches and the World Council of Churches: "We have what we regard as the Truth, the whole capsule. We're not going to join other people who have different ideals and ideas, in order to make it uniform. They will move our way." In discussing the place of women in Mormonism, he said that 5 percent of the young women undertake missionary work, compared to 30 percent of the young men. He stressed "the importance of the woman's role in the family life, which is basic," adding, "We don't make them servants and we don't force them to work, or to leave off all the other things."

The church's disciplinary practices include rigid prohibitions against premarital or extramarital sex and strict dietary regulations, including proscriptions against alcoholic beverages, tobacco, and coffee and other caffeinated drinks. Mormon theology emphasizes free will and the importance of effort in salvation. Into traditional Christianity it incorporates such new elements as belief in a prior spirit life as well as life after death; in the efficacy of postmortem baptism by proxy, with living Mormons serving over and over as surrogates for ancestors or other dead persons; and in the ability of a married couple to have "spirit children" in the multi-tiered afterworld—if their marriage is sealed "for eternity." To enter the temple for the "sealing," one must be a Mormon priest, so that under the old dispensation an Afro-American could not "even properly go to heaven," as one black Mormon observed.

The former prohibition against priesthood for blacks of African descent was based on a disputed passage in The Pearl of Great Price suggesting that black Africans were descendants of Cain and therefore "cursed as pertaining to the priesthood." The prohibition did not extend to other races or ethnic groups of dark complexion; some Fiji Islanders and Dravidians in India were Mormons, for example. The offensiveness of the discriminatory practice became embarrassingly glaring with the rise of civil-rights consciousness, and it probably contributed to the failure of George Romney, a Mormon, in his try for the Republic Presidential nomination in 1967.

On July 10, 1978, the day following the rescinding of the controversial practice, a succinct letter sent to all Mormon officials and signed by Kimball and his two **counselors in** the First Presidency, declared. "We have pleaded long and earnestly . . . , spending many hours in the upper room of the Temple supplicating the Lord for divine guidance. He has heard our prayers and by revelation has confirmed that the long-promised day has come when every faithful, worthy man in the church may receive the holy priesthood . . . without regard for race or color." The number of Mormons immediately affected by the change was estimated variously at between two and four thousand.

As head of the Corporation of the President, Kimball is the legal owner of all assets of the Church of Jesus Christ of Latter-Day Saints. Those assets include eleven radio stations, two television stations, the Salt Lake City daily *Deseret News*, four insurance companies, several hotels, Brigham Young University in Provo, Utah, a sugar-beet company, controlling interest in a department store chain, a substantial portion of real estate in downtown Salt Lake City and 326,500 acres elsewhere, including valuable property in New York City. In addition to deriving profits from its holdings, the church receives 10 percent of the gross income of its members in tithes. Much of the current income is slated to go into the building of new temples in Seattle, Tokyo, Mexico City, and American Samoa and 600 other buildings in various countries. The young missionaries doing their service in the field currently number nearly 27,000.

While the influence of the Church of Jesus Christ of Latter-Day Saints is pervasive in Utah, and especially in Salt Lake City, the church does not openly engage in political activity. In economics, it advocates a combination of rugged free enterprise, cooperative effort, and mutual aid. One of the attractions of the church is the instant community it offers converts. For example, Mormons have their own welfare system, assuring sustenance for the needy and jobs for the unemployed.

Spencer Woolley Kimball and Camilla Eyring were married on November 17, 1917. They have four children, twenty-seven grandchildren, and fifteen great-grandchildren, concerning whom Kimball as said: "We anticipate their presence in eternity." The biography *Spencer W. Kimball* (Bookcraft, 1977) was written by Kimball's son Edward and his grandson Andrew.

Joking about his five-foot six-inch stature, Kimball once remarked, "I frequently find men thinner—seldom shorter." His voice is a rasp, the result of cancer surgery in 1957 in which one vocal chord and part of another were removed. Despite his bout with cancer, and an open-heart operation in 1973, Kimball is seemingly robust, with a bounce in his walk, a twinkle in his eye, and a busy daily schedule that begins at 7:00 A.M.

Sterling M. McMurrin, the prominent Mormon liberal who is dean of the graduate school at the University of Utah, has described Kimball as "a very spiritual person, not bureaucratic." Describing the Mormon prophetic mission as an ongoing process, Kimball testified at the church's April Conference of 1977: "Expecting the spectacular, one may not be fully alerted to the constant flow of revealed communication. I say, in the deepest of humility, but also by the power and force of a burning testimony in my soul, that from the prophet of the Restoration to the prophet of our own year, the communication line is unbroken, the authority is continuous, and light, brilliant and penetrating. continues to shine. The sound of the voice of the Lord is a continuous melody and a thunderous appeal. For nearly a century and a half there has been no interruption."

References: Los Angeles Times I p1+ Ja 1 '74, I p23+ O 5 '74 por; N Y Times p15 Jan 1 '74 por; Newsweek 91:67 Je 19 '78 por; Time 103:41 Ja 14 '74 por, 112:54+ Ag 7 '78 por; Kimball, Edward L. and Kimball, Andrew E. Spencer W. Kimball (1977); Who's Who in America (1978-79); Who's Who in Religion (1977)

Kirby, Robert E(mory)

Nov. 8, 1918- Corporation executive. Address: b. Westinghouse Electric Corp., Westinghouse Bldg., Gateway Center, Pittsburgh, Pa. 15222; h. 250 Tech Rd., Pittsburgh, Pa. 15205

After rising rapidly through management ranks, Robert E. Kirby became, in 1975, chairman and chief executive officer of Westinghouse Electric Corporation, the thirty-sixth largest corporation in the United States and its single largest supplier of nuclear power plants. Since then the affable but toughminded Kirby has effected a dramatic turnaround in the operations of the financially troubled electrical equipment manufacturer, once believed to be on the edge of bankruptcy. Today, thanks to its divestiture of money-losing businesses, judicious cost-cutting, strategic planning, and the introduction of firm financial controls, Westinghouse is once again on solid footing. Some problems still plague

Robert E. Kirby

the corporation, most notably the public backlash against nuclear power that has cut deeply into Westinghouse's operations in that field, and several highly publicized lawsuits against the company by public utilities angry over its failure to deliver promised uranium. Nevertheless, the company's prospects seem bright. In the words of Kirby himself, "When I look at the plans our business units have, even I get ecstatic."

Robert Emory Kirby was born in Ames, Iowa on November 8, 1918, the son of Robert Stearns and Ora (Walker) Kirby. When he was five he accompanied his family in a move to State College, Pennsylvania, where his father joined the Penn State University (then known as Pennsylvania State College) faculty as a professor of plant pathology. Expected to earn his own spending money as a boy, Kirby sold flowers and bags of peanuts on campus when he was only nine, and he and his father assisted in the first filming of Penn State football games at Beaver Stadium.

An omnivorous reader and bright student, Kirby skipped a grade in high school and entered Penn State University at a younger age than most of his classmates. There he played oboe in the symphony orchestra and first-chair clarinet in the Penn State Blue Band; his sports were varsity tennis and golf. Kirby formed a successful thirteen-piece jazz band which, in the words of a Westinghouse company biography, "continued in business years after its original members had graduated." Resisting a temptation to become a professional jazz musician, he took a job with the West Virginia Pulp and Paper Company in Tyrone, Pennsylvania after receiving his B.S. degree in chemical engineering in 1939. With-

in a year he became assistant superintendent of the mill. In 1943, during the height of World War II, he left West Virginia Pulp and Paper to join the United States Navy's highly secret radar corps. He was sent to Princeton for courses in electrical and electronic engineering, to Massachusetts Institute of Technology's radiation laboratory for an introduction to radar technology, and finally to Bell Labs for advanced radar training. Kirby served the duration of the war as a CIC and Atlantic Task Group electronics officer and was discharged in 1946 with the rank of lieutenant.

On his way home, Kirby chanced upon an article on high frequency heating, written by the head of Westinghouse Electric's electronics research department, that greatly impressed him. Visiting Westinghouse's Pittsburgh headquarters, he rejected the offer of a position with the company's research laboratories, but in 1946 he joined the staff of its industrial electronics division in Baltimore, for less money than he would have received in Pittsburgh. It was a choice that he later had no reason to regret, since he advanced so rapidly that he became manager of industrial electronics engineering in 1952.

Two years later, Kirby attended a sixteen-month program at Harvard Business School, obtaining his M.B.A. degree with distinction as a Baker Scholar in 1956. Back again in Baltimore with Westinghouse, he became manager of its ordnance department and, in 1958, advanced to the level of general manager of its electronics division. It was in that post that he began exercising the "people-oriented" management principles that characterize his managerial style to this day. "I used to go out and walk through the shop every day so people would have a chance to see me, talk with me, register a complaint if they had one on their mind," Kirby has said. "There's a tendency to get too far away from the people in your organization. The good manager makes sure this doesn't happen."

In July 1963 Kirby was preparing to leave Westinghouse to accept the presidency of a smaller company on the West Coast when Donald C. Burnham, the newly elected chairman and chief executive officer of Westinghouse, impressed by a presentation Kirby had made at a management meeting, asked him to remain as vice-president of engineering. After considering the offer for only one day, Kirby accepted. "I had a tremendous loyalty to Westinghouse and now I was being offered an opportunity to do something with it," Kirby has explained. "It was a much bigger challenge to me than the West Coast position, so I took it. It's a decision I have never regretted." A few months later, in 1964, he was named industrial group vice-president succeeding Donald C. Burnham. In 1966 he became a director and was promoted to executive vice-president, one of only two vice-presidents for the entire company, as a replacement for the late Ronald N. Campbell. As executive vice-president, Kirby held responsibility for approximately half of the company's lines, including construction, industrial products, and consumer products.

Making its first major structural change in sixteen years, Westinghouse restructured itself early in 1969 into four major units, each headed by a president. In the reorganization Kirby became president of the Industry and Defense Company, the largest and most diversified of the four new operating groups, whose products and services included sophisticated electronics for defense and space, transportation equipment, automation and control equipment for industry, elevators and other products for the construction industry, public systems, health care, and land development. In his new position Kirby had four executive vice-presidents heading subunits under him.

On September 26, 1974 Westinghouse announced that Robert E. Kirby would replace Donald C. Burnham as the company's chairman and chief executive officer early in 1975. It also disclosed that in the meantime, Kirby had been elected vice-chairman in charge of all the company's operations until Burnham's retirement. When, on February 1, 1975, Kirby officially assumed the duties of chairman and chief executive officer, Westinghouse found itself in an earnings slump, burdened with several money-losing enterprises that it had acquired during the merger-prone 1960's. The virtual absence of strategic planning from the top on down, and of financial controls exacerbated the situation. The situation appeared so critical that rumors circulated on Wall Street that Westinghouse was headed toward bankruptcy.

As a result, shortly before Kirby's election as chairman, the company undertook a major program of retrenchment and reorganization, in which Kirby played a major role. During the course of an interview with a writer for *Forbes* (May 15, 1975), he noted, "There haven't been any decisions made that Don [Burnham] and I didn't talk over thoroughly last year. . . . He wanted to make sure his potential successor agreed with everything he thought had to be done." Among the first retrenchments were a mail-order record business (including the Longines Symphonette Society), a low-cost housing subsidiary, the company's $600 million-a-year appliance division, and two European elevator subsidiaries. In January the company reorganized itself into three companies: Industry Products, Power Systems, and Public Systems, the heads of which, with Kirby, made up a new management committee. Kirby's strategy consisted of eliminating as much red ink as possible, centralizing divisional supervision, and instituting strict cost controls. "Our divestitures and closedowns over the past several weeks," he told Gene Smith of the New York *Times* (February 4, 1975), "have been a sort of clearing-of-the-

debt for the future. It was essential if we are to improve our profit margins, which we are determined to do."

Under Kirby's direction, limits of authority were established for all divisional managers, auditors routinely spot-checked sales contracts to assure their compliance with guidelines, and the number of divisions was trimmed from 144 to 37. Each unit, previously held to a single, rigid, company-wide growth or profit objective, now received goals appropriate to its particular situation. For the first time, the central management committee reviewed all policies of major importance. Finally, the company committed its capital budget to building productive capacity in what is after all its core business, electricity: motors, light bulbs, solid-state circuit breakers, computer control systems, and so on.

Those and other management strategies contributed to a mighty leap in Westinghouse's profits, from $28 million in 1974 to $165 million in 1975 and $223 million in 1977, although, unfortunately, a series of unforeseen circumstances somewhat soured those successes. Lawsuits against the company were filed by San Francisco's BART system because of the alleged malfunction of automatic train controls supplied by Westinghouse and also by some utilities for defects in steam turbine generators. In addition, the Securities and Exchange Commission began investigating the company's sale of its appliance division to White Consolidated Industries.

But by far the biggest problem facing Kirby was a series of twenty-seven lawsuits by American and Swedish utilities aimed at compelling Westinghouse to supply them with low-price uranium fuel. Beginning in 1966, Westinghouse salesmen, in an attempt to encourage the sale of nuclear power plants, had promised to supply utilities with uranium at fixed prices over an extended period of time. In 1973 the price of uranium began to skyrocket, from approximately $7 a pound to $40 a pound by 1976. If Westinghouse were to adhere to the agreements, it would suffer a $2 to $2.5 billion loss—an amount equal to its entire shareholders' equity.

As a consequence, in September 1975 Westinghouse announced it was legally excused from its contracts to supply uranium under certain provisions of the Uniform Commercial Code. "If Westinghouse were required to purchase all uranium required on the market and if the uranium market continues to deteriorate," Kirby said (New York *Times,* January 29, 1976), "the financial effect on Westinghouse could be severe." To further emphasize its point, the company contended that it was the victim of a worldwide uranium cartel—a charge that appears to be valid.

Nevertheless the utilities sued, initiating a long and costly series of still unresolved court battles. To deal with the situation, Kirby established a cash fund of $600 million to cover projected expenses, and the company began an extensive search for uranium ore throughout the West, Midwest, Alaska, and overseas. In July 1978 Kirby took personal charge of negotiating the uranium claims, "in hopes of extracting his company from lawsuits that once threatened its very existence," because, as a writer for *Business Week* (July 10, 1978) has pointed out, "The uranium cases have become a personal cause for Kirby." Estimates of the eventual cost of the claims to the Westinghouse corporation range from $700 million upward.

Another problem for Westinghouse is nuclear plant construction, which has been hurt by the Three Mile Island near-disaster and a general negative reaction on the part of the public to increased utilization of that form of energy. In 1978 there was only one domestic order for a new nuclear power plant, and in June 1979 the United States government questioned the safety of several Westinghouse-built reactors. When President Jimmy Carter proposed to halt breeder-reactor production in the United States in an effort to slow the proliferation of nuclear weapons, Kirby lodged a strong protest. Noting that breeder reactors promise energy resources three times as great as Middle East oil reserves, he commented at Westinghouse's annual meeting on April 27, 1977: "For a world concerned about energy shortages, it seems most unwise to fail to use these plentiful resources." He added: "The connection between the breeder program and possible nuclear weapons proliferation is so thin as to be insignificant."

An outspoken opponent of governmental caprice, Kirby blames environmentalists and utility regulators for delays in energy development and new plant construction. With regard to the federal government, he remarked during his 1975 interview with *Forbes*: "The real problem here is a government policy that cannot stand still. Some of these things require gigantic investments—in people, money, technology. But you can't get a firm guarantee from the Government. . . . The Government has screwed things up so badly that I'm not sure they are ever going to get private industry to help them."

On July 11, 1942 Robert E. Kirby married Barbara Anne McClintock. They had two daughters, Mary Linda, who is married to novelist Michael Memshaw, and Donna Susan, who is no longer living. Kirby holds memberships in the American Society of Naval Engineers, the Engineers Society of Western Pennsylvania, the Institute of Electrical and Electronics Engineers, the Pittsburgh Chamber of Commerce, Beta Theta Pi, and Kappa Gamma Psi. He has served as a trustee of both the University of Pittsburgh and the Pennsylvania State University Foundation, and as chairman of the visiting committee of the former's Graduate School of Business Administration. He is a deputy chairman of the Federal Reserve Bank of Cleveland. In 1976 Kirby was given an honorary doctorate of humanities by Thiel College, in Greenville, Pennsylvania.

An avid, low-handicap golfer, Kirby plays in several Pro-Am tournaments each season, and is an old friend of Arnold Palmer. His second major interest, music, is reflected by his honorary life membership in the American Federation of Musicians and his directorship of the Pittsburgh Symphony Society. He still plays jazz, listens to tapes of major bands, and keeps in touch with the world of music through such personal friends as bandleader Les Brown and Lionel Hampton. Addicted to crossword puzzles (especially those from the *Guardian* (Manchester) or the London *Times*) and to magic, Kirby once entertained Pasha Inonu, the former president of Turkey, with his card tricks. Since his responsibilities as chairman of Westinghouse require him to do a lot of traveling, he says "It's a vacation for me to be at home."

References: Bsns W p60+ Ja 31 '77 por; Forbes 97:34 F 15 '66 pors, 116:24 D 1 '75 pors, 119:66 My 1 '77 por; Fortune p146+ Ag '76 por; N Y Times p49 F 4 '75 por; Wall St J p6 S 27 '74; International Who's Who 1978-79; Who's Who in America 1978-79

Korman, Harvey

Feb. 15, 1927- Actor; comedian. Address: b. c/o Singer and Lewak, 10960 Wilshire Blvd., Los Angeles, Calif. 90024

One of American television's most gifted comics and character actors, Harvey Korman won four Emmy awards as straight man or "second banana" on the *Carol Burnett Show*, on which he was a fixture from 1967 to 1977, after helping to brighten up the proceedings on the *Danny Kaye Show* for three years. Capitalizing on his special forte for sketch comedy, Korman appeared on those programs in a broad spectrum of character roles, ranging from a Mexican bandit to a Viennese music professor. In recent years he has also made his mark in motion pictures with his diverting portrayals of menacing villains in Mel Brooks's comedies *Blazing Saddles* (1974) and *High Anxiety* (1977). "Harvey Korman is surprisingly free of all the usual mannerisms associated with comedians: brashness, one-liners, just plain *shtick*," David Johnson observed in *After Dark* (June 1974). "Instead, the king-sized comic actor's demeanor is low-key and serious and direct."

Of Russian-Jewish descent, Harvey Herschel Korman was born on February 15, 1927, on Chicago's North Side, to Cyril Raymond and Ellen (Blecher) Korman. His parents separated

Harvey Korman

when he was four, and his father, who had worked as a salesman, moved to New Orleans, where he became a soft drink company executive. Harvey and his younger sister, Faye, were raised by their mother, with the help of the father's alimony payments. "My childhood stunk," Korman recalled with his customary candor in an interview with Anthony Mancini for the New York *Post* (May 31, 1969). "We were poor, and there's the no-father bit."

At the urging of his seventh-grade teacher, Korman joined an after-school theatre workshop, the Jack and Jill Players, and his success with that group brought him some juvenile roles in industrial films. Later he acted in school productions at Chicago's Senn High School. At that time he was not especially interested in making a career of acting, but after attending Wright Junior College and serving a year and a half, in 1945-46, in the United States Naval Reserve, he enrolled in the Art Institute of Chicago's Goodman School of Drama and undertook four years of serious drama study.

After he left the Goodman School in 1950, Korman moved to New York City, hoping to establish a beachhead on Broadway, and for a time he shared a shabby apartment with an aspiring fellow actor named Tom Bosley. In November of that year he obtained a walk-on part in the memorable American National Theatre and Academy production of Robinson Jeffers' poetic drama *The Tower Beyond Tragedy*, starring Judith Anderson. Then, in December 1950 he was given a small role, as an Arab, in the City Center revival of George Bernard Shaw's *Captain Brassbound's Conversion*. "I figured this was going to be easy," Korman told an interviewer for *TV Guide*

(May 22, 1965). "Five months later I was selling candy bars in Radio City."

The job at the candy counter was to be only one of many such jobs that Korman held during the next decade while trying to launch his acting career. "I did all those corny struggling-actor things," he told David Johnson. "I did the cold-water flat and unemployment and running out of money and eating peanut butter sandwiches. . . . I worked a lot as a cashier, checker, host. I always liked to eat, so I made sure I got a job in a restaurant." He returned for a time to Chicago and worked in stock productions there and in Milwaukee, then tried New York again. "I didn't get on Broadway or off Broadway or anywhere near Broadway," he has recalled. Just before Christmas 1956 he was fired from the cast of *Uncle Willie*, starring Menasha Skulnik, during tryouts in Boston. He contemplated suicide, but shortly afterward he went into psychotherapy. Then he again moved back to Chicago and resumed repertory work.

In the 1950's Korman also traveled to California on some twenty different occasions, trying to break into television or Hollywood films. During one of those visits he was acclaimed for his performance, in a Santa Monica community theatre production, as Hamlet, a role he had first played at the Goodman School. But although his performance was praised by such film luminaries as Bette Davis, Charles Laughton, and Edward Everett Horton, it failed to advance his career. "The studios got interested in this brilliant young actor," Korman said in the *After Dark* interview. "They came out expecting to find a young, blond Adonis and, instead, found a kind of balding, aging Jew."

After more odd jobs, stock productions, and even a brief try at nightclub comedy—as part of a team called Marsh and Fields, a takeoff on Marshall Field's department store—Korman finally managed to break into television as a result of a minor role he had in a Chicago production of a play called *Mr. and Mrs.* Its director, Seymour Berns, who also directed television's *Red Skelton Show*, persuaded him to try his luck in California. Meanwhile, Korman and Donna Ehlert, a fashion model and charm school teacher whom he had met on a blind date in Milwaukee, were married, after a four-month courtship, on August 27, 1960. After settling in California, Korman made several appearances on the *Red Skelton Show* and other series, including *Dr. Kildare*, *Dennis the Menace*, and the *Donna Reed Show*, but his career again faltered, and his wife went back to modeling. As Korman described that period of his life in the New York *Post* interview: "Mostly I stayed home and made the beds and sat around the pool of the apartment and played gin rummy with some other bum while my wife was working."

Then in 1963, Berns recommended Korman for a slot in the supporting cast of the *Danny*

Kaye Show. Korman successfully auditioned for a role on the CBS series, becoming, at thirty-six, a regular performer on a television show for the first time. But at that point his age—and the lack of glamour that had worked against him earlier in his career—may have been assets. "If I had been three inches shorter [he's six feet four] or four or five years younger or just a little bit handsomer," he told Anthony Mancini, "I wouldn't have been any good for those skits. But Kaye's six feet one, so I could play parts where I could look down on him. Since I wasn't too young, I could play his boss. It all worked out."

Working with Danny Kaye, Korman proved adept at playing the straight man, not overshadowing the star but contributing his share of the comedy. In his skits with Kaye, Korman played scores of roles, including those of Nazi prison camp commandant, Gypsy fiddler, Canadian Mountie, and Count Dracula's butler, and he mastered the accents to match. The costumes and characterizations were often so good that his friends did not recognize him on the screen. According to a critic for the Washington *Post*'s *TV Channels* (September 6, 1964), Korman "can lose his own personality merely by changing the set of his shoulders and the swing of his walk. He is also an expert dialectician, a must for any actor working with the many-faceted Kaye."

"I can't tell a joke to save my life or do a dialect on command without hours of practice," Korman admitted to Anthony Mancini. "But I'm an actor doing comedy. I can be funny in a scene or situation." To help him master accents, he used a book that broke down languages phonetically. Playing a French waiter in one skit with Kaye, he had a single line— "*Oui, oui, Monsieur*"—to say three times. His delivery was so amusing that he got an ovation from the audience and special praise on the air from Kaye at the end of the show.

In 1967 Korman moved to the *Carol Burnett Show*, also on CBS-TV, where for the next ten years he cemented his reputation as a master of sketch comedy. The male-female combination allowed Korman to play a wider variety of roles. "Right from the start there was chemistry," Carol Burnett once recalled in an Associated Press interview that was published in the Toronto *Globe and Mail* (February 20, 1973). "We work very much alike. We think alike on most sketches. It's almost like a marriage." Korman and Miss Burnett, in fact, appeared as husband and wife in a number of their hundreds of sketches. Among their most hilarious skits were those spoofing old Hollywood movies or television soap operas. Commenting on Korman's talent, Tim Conway, another regular on the *Carol Burnett Show*, told the AP interviewer: "In sketch comedy I don't think anybody touches him. It's like a finely tuned racing car."

Analyzing his own success, Korman gives much of the credit to his training as an actor

and the approach it taught him. "I don't look for gags," he explained to Peter Andrews in an interview for the New York *Times* (October 3, 1976). "I look for characters. Even in the broadest sketch, I try to find out what kind of person I'm playing, what his problems are and what he's trying to do. The laughs will be there if you know the territory."

His accomplishments as a sketch comedian during his tenure with Carol Burnett brought Korman four Emmy awards from the National Academy of Television Arts and Sciences. The first two, presented for the 1968-69 and the 1970-71 seasons, were for "outstanding individual achievement" under a special classification. The third was for "outstanding achievement by a performer in music or variety" during the 1971-72 season, and the fourth was for the "best supporting actor in comedy-variety" in 1973-74. But even while being honored, Korman felt slighted by the academy. Noting that no precise category was designated for his first two Emmy awards, Korman told the *After Dark* interviewer: "I was in a catch-all thing. Arte Johnson and Ruth Buzzi and I were lumped in with *Wild Kingdom* and whatever else didn't have a specific category. So we fought for a category for variety performers and finally got it." Korman also recalled with some dismay that his second and third Emmy awards were not even presented on the regular televised ceremonies.

Discontented with his "second banana" role but reluctant to leave the *Carol Burnett Show*, Korman described his ambivalent feelings to Kay Gardella of the New York *Sunday News* (February 13, 1972): "One minute I'm telling people I'm sick of being a second banana, that I want to strike out on my own. The next time someone asks me, I think about how much safer it is to let the star carry the show, with all of its responsibilities. . . . What's best for me, I don't know. If I quit the show, I have an agreement with CBS whereby I bring a half-hour situation comedy to them starring Harvey Korman. But who is Harvey Korman? I've been playing characters for so long I don't know, nor does the audience."

In 1977 Korman finally decided to try a series of his own and was persuaded to switch from the CBS network to ABC-TV by Fred Silverman, who was then the latter's director. "There's only one Harvey Korman, and we wanted him very badly," Silverman had said in October 1976, according to Peter Andrews. "He is a fantastic comedy actor and a major reason for the success of the *Carol Burnett Show*. More importantly, he has the quality— the likeability—that you have to have to be a star on television."

But when a pilot of the *Harvey Korman Show* appeared on ABC-TV on May 19, 1977, it was generally panned. The half-hour situation comedy, produced by Korman's own company, Chrisma Productions, featured Korman as an aging, flamboyant actor supporting himself by giving acting lessons while trying to land star roles and deal with a rebellious grown daughter. The critic for *Variety* (May 25, 1977) described the comedy as "about two decades behind the times." He found the supporting cast "all stuck with typecast attitudes" and noted that Korman had to "carry the whole load by himself."

A second pilot, presented on January 31, 1978, introduced several modifications. The Korman character (Harvey Kavanaugh) was toned down, a new actress (Christine Lahti in place of Susan Lawrence) played his daughter, and an attempt was made to strengthen the father-daughter relationship. But critics generally concluded that Korman the sketch comedian had not adapted himself to the strictures of situation comedy. The reviewer for *Variety* (February 8, 1978) found the show "better this time out" but "still not precisely enough blended to suggest the transformation is completed." Much of the comedy was considered "too patently broad and revue-sketch farcical to fit comfortably into sitcom format." Marvin Kitman of *Newsday* (January 31, 1978), who had found the first pilot "embarrassing," detected "a number of improvements" in the second version but concluded that the show was "still badly conceived" and that the sitcom format left "little room for the Korman magic, which emerges in character roles."

When the show began a weekly run on April 4, 1978, Tom Shales wrote in the Washington *Post:* "The *Harvey Korman Show* . . . is such a poor attempt to exploit Korman's broad gifts for farce and comic characterization that it seems an act of willful sabotage." Viewers apparently agreed with those negative assessments. After a run of less than five months, the show went off the air on August 3, 1978.

Later that year Korman was well reviewed in a dramatic role in an NBC made-for-television movie, *Bud and Lou,* about the generally tragic private lives of the comedy team Abbott and Costello. In the two-hour production, presented on November 15, 1978, Korman portrayed Bud Abbott—who was an epileptic and, in later life, an alcoholic—while Buddy Hackett played Lou Costello. Reviewing the film for the New York *Times* (November 15, 1978), John J. O'Connor called Korman's performance "beautifully restrained and sympathetic, never sentimental."

Korman has also appeared in several feature films. He received some critical praise for his portrayal of what Judith Crist called a "blathering, slavering school principal" in the George Axelrod comedy *Lord Love a Duck* (United Artists, 1966), and he was also seen in the Paris-based American farce *Don't Just Stand There!* (Universal, 1968). Reviewing the comedy *The April Fools* (National General, 1969) in the New York *Times* (May 29, 1969), Vincent Canby included Korman's role among the "extraordinarily good supporting performances" that he considered "the best things in the movie."

Supporting roles by Korman and David Wayne were also singled out for praise by Lawrence Van Gelder of the New York *Times* (May 25, 1974) in a review of a generally lambasted musical version of *Huckleberry Finn* (United Artists, 1974). "Just when *Huckleberry Finn* is about to drown in its own treacle," Van Gelder wrote, "up bob Harvey Korman as the King and David Wayne as the Duke, and for half an hour or so, life on the Mississippi seems well worth living. . . . Aside from the all-too-few minutes when Mr. Korman and Mr. Wayne are on the screen—fleecing yokels and orphans, putting on airs, putting down lynch mobs and putting up with all the dullards around them—*Huckleberry Finn* . . . is a lavish bore."

That same year Korman was seen as the unctuous, land-grabbing lawyer Hedley Lamarr in Mel Brooks' manic spoof of Westerns, *Blazing Saddles* (Warner Brothers). Reviewing the film in the New York *Times* (February 8, 1974), Vincent Canby wrote: "Harvey Korman, a gifted comic actor . . . , tries very hard to be funny . . . and sometimes succeeds.. But it's apparent that he's hard put to keep up with the movie's restless shifting from satire to parody to farce to blackout sketch." In 1977 Korman again played the villain in a Mel Brooks spoof, *High Anxiety* (Twentieth Century-Fox), an affectionate takeoff on Alfred Hitchcock classics, especially *Vertigo*. As Dr. Charles Montague, a sadomasochistic psychiatrist at the Psycho Neurotic Institute for the Very, Very Nervous, Korman plots with Nurse Diesel (Cloris Leachman) to cheat wealthy patients out of their fortunes and to kill the hospital's new director, played by Brooks, when he catches on to their scheme. Korman also appeared in the comedy *Americathon* (United Artists, 1979) as the host of a telethon designed to save America from bankruptcy in the year 1998.

Unlike his television and screen characters, Harvey Korman leads a sedate and conventional private life. He and his wife still make their home in Southern California, where he enjoys golf, tennis, swimming, and jogging but seldom goes to parties. The Kormans have a daughter, Maria Ellen, and a son, Christopher Peter. Although Korman has also tried his hand as a director, having staged a few sketches for CBS-TV's *Steve Allen Comedy Hour* in 1967 and the *New Dick Van Dyke Show* in the early 1970's, he no longer feels driven to succeed in new endeavors. He told Guy Flatley of the New York *Times* (May 27, 1977): "I like to take a few months off, to read and to play. I don't need that constant pursuit and challenge." Notwithstanding his earlier ambition to achieve stardom on Broadway, he says: "The thought of doing a play on Broadway gives me the willies. It really fills me with terror." Considering himself deeply religious, Korman attributes his success in show business to "the power of prayer," although "it's not a denominational thing" with him. "I prayed so hard for my career . . ." he told Anthony Mancini of the New York *Post*. "But unless your heart is really in it, the prayer is not going to work."

References: After Dark 7:46+ Je '74 pors; N Y Post p29 My 31 '69 por; N Y Times II p25 O 3 '76 por; Toronto Globe and Mail p17 F 20 '73 por; TV Guide 13:24+ My 22 '65 por; Who's Who in America 1978-79

Kucinich, Dennis J(ohn) (kōō-sin'ich)

Oct. 8, 1946- Mayor of Cleveland. Address: b. City Hall, 601 Lakeside Ave. East, Cleveland, Ohio 44114

The youngest, and probably the most controversial, of American big-city mayors is the boyish-looking maverick Democrat Dennis J. Kucinich, who was elected to a two-year term as chief executive of financially troubled Cleveland, Ohio in November 1977, a month after his thirty-first birthday, and who survived a recall election nine months later. In his bid for reelection, Kucinich was defeated by Republican George V. Voinovich, whose term as mayor is scheduled to begin in January 1980.

An unmitigated practitioner of confrontation politics who has a flair for capturing media attention, Kucinich is regarded as a populist hero by his admirers and as a dangerous little demagogue or even a "lunatic" by his enemies. Kucinich established himself as the champion of Cleveland's blue-collar ethnics when he was a city councilman, beginning in 1970,

and the clerk of courts, in 1976 and 1977. As mayor he has continued stubbornly to oppose what he considers "ripoffs" of the "little guy" by the city's business "establishment," especially the banks, which he accuses of "systematically looting Cleveland's financial resources."

Kucinich's antagonization of the "Cleveland Set" and its partisans on the city council has not helped him in his efforts to solve the city's accumulated financial problems, which have brought Cleveland to the brink of bankruptcy. When the financial crunch came in December 1978, six Cleveland banks refused to renew $14,000,000 owed them by the city, and a mutinous city council rejected a financial rescue plan proposed by Kucinich. As a result, Cleveland became the first American city since the Great Depression to go into default.

The eldest of seven children in a Roman Catholic family, Dennis John Kucinich was born on October 8, 1946 in Cleveland, Ohio to Frank Kucinich, a truck driver of Croatian descent, and Virginia Kucinich, whose ancestry is Irish. Kucinich's brother Gary has followed him into politics and now serves as a Cleveland city councilman. The youngest brother, Perry, a psychiatric patient described by the Mayor as "extremely troubled," was recently charged with bank robbery. The Kuciniches were poor, and they moved frequently from one shabby home to another. "My background," Kucinich has said, as quoted by Edward P. Whelan in *Cleveland* magazine (December 1977), "gave me a first-hand chance to experience the deprivation which is only parlor conversation for the elite."

Despite his diminutive size, Kucinich went out for football at St. John Cantius High School, a small Polish parochial school in the white working-class West Side neighborhood in which he lived. As third-string quarterback, he was "cocky, gutsy, and aggressive," according to the former football coach at the high school. "Eight people would hit him and he'd get right back up." Kucinich also played the lead in the senior class play, *The Mouse That Roared*. He graduated seventh in a senior class of eighty-eight in 1964.

Leaving home at seventeen, Kucinich supported himself through odd jobs, including golf caddy. While earning a B.A. degree at Cleveland State University, he worked as a hospital technician and as a copyboy at the Cleveland *Plain Dealer*. Terence Sheridan (*New Times*, May 1, 1978) then a reporter for the *Plain Dealer*, remembers Kucinich as looking "like Dondi" and acting "like an attack Chihuahua."

As a boy, Kucinich "prayed to God" that someday he "would have a chance to be something, to do something important." By the time he started working for the *Plain Dealer* he had decided that politics would be his career, and he pursued his goal singlemindedly. He read widely on all aspects of Cleveland and its history, kept clipping files on local politics and politicians, attended all kinds of civic events, and spent all the time he could spare at city hall, talking to anyone he could buttonhole.

When Kucinich was growing up, Cleveland was changing rapidly. As industry moved to the Sun Belt or elsewhere and the upper-middle class moved to the suburbs—thus shrinking the city's tax base—poor whites from Appalachia, Hispanics, and poor blacks from the South moved into the city, expecting jobs but finding ever-worsening blight. In the summer of 1966 riots broke out in Hough, a black Cleveland ghetto, and lesser racial confrontations took place early in 1967. Alarmed, the local business and financial community allocated money for civic improvements and supported mayoral candidate Carl Stokes, a popular black, who won the 1967 election with the help of strategically placed campaign financing. When Kucinich took his M.A. degree in mass communications at Case Western Reserve University, the subject of his thesis was the media coverage of the confrontation between Mayor Stokes and city council president James Stanton.

Kucinich entered electoral politics in 1967, running unsuccessfully against the incumbent West Side city councilman John Bilinski, a supporter of Stokes. Two years later, with the help of an enthusiastic group of student volunteers, he edged out the sixty-four-year-old Bilinski by sixteen votes. During the campaign Kucinich had run as much against Mayor Carl Stokes, the first black mayor of a major city, as he had against Bilinski, and after his election he remained Stokes's arch-adversary, thus making himself a hero to the white ethnic groups—largely Hungarian, Slovak, and Polish—who made up the city's majority but who had felt ignored and virtually disenfranchised in the official preoccupation with civil rights for minorities. (Stokes, now a television newscaster for station WNBC-TV in New York City, has said that whatever else Kucinich is, he is "no racist.")

In 1971, when Stokes decided not to run for a third term as mayor, Kucinich bolted Democratic party ranks to support the candidacy of Republican Ralph Perk. Stumping against a "conspiracy" of "political bosses," Kucinich was a major force in rallying the ethnic support Perk needed for election. In 1972, when he supported the Presidential candidacy of George McGovern, Kucinich ran unsuccessfully for Congress in Ohio's 23rd District, comprised mostly of suburbs in Cuyahoga County, and he failed again in the same Congressional bid two years later. Meanwhile, in the city council Kucinich was a vociferous gadfly, exposing City Hall shenanigans and railing against the city's financial and political powers-that-be. In so doing he isolated himself from many of the other members of the council, but he became a household name in Cleveland.

During the mayoralty of Ralph Perk, from 1972 to 1975, Cleveland's drift toward bankruptcy accelerated. The population, 914,808 in 1950 and 750,689 in 1970, dropped to 650,000, a decline reflecting the movement of industry out of the city and the abandonment of housing by landlords and representing an annual loss in the tax base of $30,000,000. The sane solution to the city's short-term debt problem was to finance long-term bonds on the strength of increased property taxes—but that would have been unpopular. "In this dilemma," Alexander Cockburn and James Ridgeway wrote in New York's *Village Voice* (January 22, 1979), "Perk hit upon a simple solution: if you can't pay for the city, sell it off."

Cockburn and Ridgeway gave two examples of the selling of the city's assets: the transit system, with assets of $72,000,000 and net operating revenues of $28,000,000, was sold to a newly established Regional Transit Authority, dominated by businessmen and lawyers, for $8,900,000 in the form of loans to the system in addition to $1,100,000 for parking lots that had been thrown into the deal; Cleveland Stadium was leased out to "civic minded businessmen" who were to pay the city $370,000 in one year but who actually sent the city a check for less than $1,000.

In their study of the jumbled organization of city accounting dating at least from the early 1970's, Cleveland State University professors John Burke and Edrick Weld concluded that the city's accounting "predates Medici banking," so that it was not possible to see "if corruption existed at city hall, but since each account is so isolated from the other, effective cash management is impossible, leaving the system vulnerable." The accounting firm of Ernst & Ernst reported that upwards of $30,000,000 in capital and special funds was illegally used for operating expenses under Mayor Perk, and Hyman Grossman of Standard and Poor's has stated: "Cleveland had not been reporting its true financial picture for years. It's the same old problem of spending more than you take in and covering it with borrowing."

In 1977 Kucinich decided to challenge Mayor Perk. Aiming his campaign at his "people," the solid working middle class in the ethnic neighborhoods, he promised to end political patronage, to institute tax reform favorable to working people and cut out tax abatements for the expansion of big business downtown, to work for increased consumer protection and low-cost public transportation, and to trim government or at least minimize its expansion. But his stress was on the issue of the city-owned Municipal Electric Light and Power System.

Muny Light, as it is called, one of the eldest publicly owned utilities in the country, began going into deep debt in the 1960's. By 1970 it owed $20,000,000 to its creditors, chiefly to its rival, the privately owned Cleveland Electric Illumination Company (CEI). The city-owned company, which serves only 20 percent of Cleveland, including working-class neighborhoods on the West Side, buys most of its power from CEI. Mayor Perk had agreed to sell Muny Light to CEI for $158,000,000 and cancellation of its debt, but many Clevelanders opposed the sale, fearing the CEI would raise its rates if it became a monopoly. Kucinich pledged never to sell Muny Light.

In the nonpartisan primary of October 1977 Kucinich led the field, with State Representative Edward F. Feighan placing second and Mayor Perk finishing third. In the lively, vituperative runoff campaign against Feighan, who had the backing of the Democratic party, Kucinich made "power to the people" his slogan. He labeled his opponent a tool of party bosses and continued to pound away at his populist themes, especially Muny Light. In the November 8 election Kucinich narrowly defeated Feighan, with less than 52 percent of the vote.

Once in office, Kucinich set about fulfilling his campaign promises, or trying to. With the help of his political mentor, Sherwood Weissman (who, at forty-eight, was one of the oldest members of his city hall team), he put legal clout into the fight to save Muny Light, and, although the city council overrode his veto, he tried to hold the line on tax abatement. He also trimmed the city government payroll by laying off 300 employees; strengthened the Consumer Affairs Department; put $5,000,000—most of it from the Community Development budget—into desperately needed new sewers; personally directed the snow-removal teams—inadequate as they were—during the severe storms of early 1978; in a symbolic demonstration of the grassroots orientation of his administration, met with business leaders for breakfast at Tony's Diner, a small working-class West Side restaurant, rather than at the exclusive downtown Union Club; and turned down $41,000,000 from the federal government for a downtown monorail, declaring that what the city really needed was public transportation that would carry people between their homes and work.

When Terence Sheridan interviewed Kucinich for New Times, he asked the mayor what he considered his major achievement after four months in office. "Helping to make Cleveland the first big city in the nation which the establishment does not control," Kucinich replied. "We've set the stage to put Cleveland in the forefront of a new populist movement in America. We are recasting the mold of the New Deal." Sheridan commented, in an aside to the reader: "This is the Dennis Kucinich I remember, looking you straight in the eye and saying the most incredible things."

During his first year in office, Kucinich faced many problems, from police walkouts to his embarrassment over his brother Perry's bank caper and the arrest of his school board president for "mooning"—exposing his bare buttocks—from the rear of a car on a public highway. But the problem that first brought his mayoralty to a crisis point was the friction between him and Richard D. Hongisto, the police chief he had imported on the recommendation of his black safety director, James Barrett.

As a sheriff in San Francisco, Hongisto had earned a national reputation for his conspicuous, compassionate liberalism, including the championing of homosexual rights. Regarded with suspicion by the police in Cleveland when he first arrived there, Hongisto quickly became a popular figure, both in the police department and in the city generally. But it soon became apparent that the new police chief was as ambitious a politician and as astute a media manipulator as the mayor, and it looked as if he might be after his job. By March 1978 the police chief was accusing Kucinich of pressuring him to commit "unethical acts," which he later said included hampering a cleanup of the vice squad and assigning political favorites of Kucinich's to certain jobs within the police department. The mayor angrily fired Hongisto for insubordination during a televised news conference on March 24, 1978.

The firing of Hongisto unleashed a storm of previously suppressed animosity toward Kucinich and his administration, and soon petitions were being circulated for the recall of the mayor. Business leaders, disgruntled city employees, angry city councilmen, and other critics of the Kucinich administration regarded the mayor's adviser, Bob Weissman, as a kind of latter-day Rasputin and his youthful high-level appointees, drawn from the ranks of his campaign organization as "arrogant," "combative" and "inexperienced."

In April the mayor's director of human resources ordered three men to conduct an after-hours search of the office of her subordinate, the economic affairs commissioner. a Republican holdover, who was suspected of graft. When the incident became known, the newspapers touted it as Cleveland's mini-Watergate, and the city council ordered an investigation. That move strained the deteriorating relations between the mayor and the council to the breaking point, with Kucinich, in one speech, describing members of the council as "buffoons," "fakers," and "liars." The council retaliated by refusing to act on any appointments or other such actions initiated by the Mayor. By the time of the recall election on August 13, 1978, the mayor's ouster was supported by twenty-four of the thirty-three city council members, leaders of both the Republican and Democratic parties, the Teamsters union and the Cleveland AFL-CIO, and all three major Cleveland newspapers, including the *Plain Dealer*, which had supported his mayoral candidacy less than a year before. Nonetheless, the mayor squeaked through, winning the recall by 236 votes out of some 120,000 cast.

Mayor Kucinich's narrow victory hardly spelled a solution to his problems in governing Cleveland. When it became known that the city had over the years accumulated a $52,000,000 deficit in its bond fund accounts, Moody's Investors Service downgraded the city's bond rating and Standard and Poor's Corporation suspended its rating altogether. Those actions in effect ruled out the private investment market as a source of funds. On October 26 a local court ordered the city's bankrupt water department into receivership, and the nearly bankrupt school system was unable to open classes until the end of October because of the teachers strike.

Notes for $14,000,000 in short term loans owed by the city to six Cleveland banks came due in December 1978, and in addition the city owed $1,500,000 to its own treasury. On December 13 Kucinich presented the banks with a fiscal rehabilitation plan that included a mechanism for refinancing the loans. The plan called for an increase in the city's income tax, a multimillion-dollar bond issue that would be made possible by the fiscal strength created by the tax revenues, and a fiscal overseer. According to the consensus of news reports, the banks were ready to accept the report until the major bank, the Cleveland Trust Company, balked, refusing to roll over its loan to the city unless Kucinich agreed to sell Muny Light. The other banks followed the lead of Cleveland Trust, as did the city council under the leadership of George L. Forbes in a special session on the night of December 15-16, 1979. Accordingly, shortly after midnight on the morning of December 16, Cleveland officially went into default. (Bankruptcy would not occur unless and until the banks took the final step of calling in the notes.) "While many persons can share responsibility for this sad episode," the Cleveland *Plain Dealer* editorialized on December 16, "the major blame for the problem must rest with Mayor Kucinich." Kucinich said, "At least we didn't sell our soul."

Later Kucinich and the council compromised, agreeing to let the public vote on the issues of raising payroll taxes from 1 to 1.5 percent and the sale of Muny Light. The banks agreed not to call in their notes until after the referendum, scheduled for February 27, 1979. In the meantime, trying to avoid massive layoffs of city employees, the city was deferring payment of many of its bills, including $7,500,000 owed to state pension funds, and the funds were moving to put liens on city revenues.

The fierce opposition to him notwithstanding, Kucinich reportedly still has strong support in the ethnic wards that elected him, and expressions of approval come in by telephone and mail from other parts of the country. But he is, "to put it baldly, generally regarded as a lunatic," as Cockburn and Ridgeway point out in their *Village Voice* article. However, those writers insist, "he has in fact acted, as he says, on his belief that public institutions are viable and that government must not be surrendered to the private sector." At the polls on February 27, 1979 the voters vindicated Kucinich's faith in them, approving a 5 percent increase in the city income tax and the retention of Muny Light. But nine months later they turned him out of office, by approximately 94,400 votes to 73,505. George V. Voinovich, the victor in the election, said, "For the most part, people like Dennis. The thing they don't like is he hasn't been able to function." Kucinich attributed his political difficulties to his having "stepped on some big toes" and to what he regarded as the distortion of his record by the media in alliance with corporations on which they depend for advertising.

An "ageless kid wearing Buster Brown ties and suits that looked as if they had been yanked off a Robert Hall markdown rack," is the way Edward P. Whalen (*Cleveland*, December 1977) once described Mayor Dennis J. Kucinich, who is five feet six inches tall and weighs about 140 pounds. Kucinich lives with his wife, Sandra, a former Cleveland nightclub singer, in a modest house not far from the neighborhood where he grew up. A previous marriage ended in divorce.

"Dennis the Menace," as he is facetiously known, had part of his stomach removed years ago, and he still suffers from a chronic ulcer. The mayor is an avid reader who consumes a variety ranging from Freud and the *New York Review of Books* to comic books, and he is a movie buff who has seen *Star Wars* six times. A skilled ventriloquist, he keeps a dummy next to his desk at city hall to entertain visiting schoolchildren. The beleaguered mayor's sense of humor is as irrepressible as his cold-eyed doughtiness in standing up to his enemies. Interviewed on the ABC television network's *Good Morning America* show shortly after his recall election, Kucinich was asked if the newspaper headlines proclaiming him a lame duck were accurate. The mayor paused, then gazed directly into the camera and smiled. "Quack," he said.

References: Cleveland p113+ D '77 pors; Esquire 90:23+ D 5 '78 pors; N Y Times A p19 N 10 '77 por; New Times 10:24+ My 1 '78 pors; People 9:44+ My 15 '78 pors; Time 111:25 Ap 10 '78 por; Village Voice p11+ Ja 22 '79 por; Wall St J p12 Je 9 '78 por; Washington Post A p8 N 6 '79 por

Kyprianou, Spyros (kē-prē-ä′noo)

Oct. 28, 1932- President of the Republic
of Cyprus. Address: b. Kermia Building,
Office 202, 2nd Floor, 4 Diagoras St.,
Nicosia, Cyprus

As President of Cyprus, Spyros Kyprianou
faces some agonizing problems. His island
nation of 3,572 square miles, only part of
which is under his control, supports a population of about 640,000 people, 120,000 of whom
do not recognize his authority. Because of the
hostility between its Greek and Turkish ethnic
groups, Cyprus has been a focal point of
international tensions for nearly three decades,
fomenting discords that have twice brought
Greece and Turkey to the verge of war. After
years of intermittent but often bloody internecine violence, peace has been restored to
Cyprus, thanks to the presence of U.N. and
other foreign troops, but the island's fundamental problems remain. Whether Kyprianou,
formerly the Foreign Minister of Cyprus, will
prove any more successful in resolving them
than his predecessor, the venerated Archbishop Makarios III, remains to be seen.

Born on October 28, 1932 in Limassol, a port
and commercial center and the second-largest
town in Cyprus, Spyros Kyprianou is one of
the nine children of Achilleas Kyprianou, a
prosperous businessman, and Maria (Argon-
zov) Kyprianou. Raised in Limassol, where he
attended the local Greek Gymnasium for his
secondary schooling, Kyprianou went to England for his higher education. He studied
economics and commerce at the City of London College and law at Gray's Inn, which
granted him a diploma in comparative law.
Kyprianou was called to the bar in 1954.

Throughout Kyprianou's formative years, and
indeed for many decades before then, the
Greek community of Cyprus, numbering about
three-fourths of the island's population, was
agitating for independence from Great Britain.
(The British had taken Cyprus from Turkey
in 1878 and annexed it as a crown colony in
1914.) Even as a youth Kyprianou identified
himself with the Greek Cypriot national cause
—a commitment perhaps heightened by the
fact that his grandfather, Spyros J. Araouzos,
a former mayor of Limassol, had been one of
the early proindependence activists in the
period between the two world wars.

Although he was living abroad in 1950, when
the Cypriot independence struggle entered upon
a new and ultimately decisive phase, Kyprianou followed events in his homeland closely.
In that year Makarios III, whom he had known
since his school days in Limassol, was elected
archbishop and ethnarch (national leader) of
the Greek community of Cyprus. Commanding
virtually universal loyalty among the island's
Greeks, the beloved Makarios immediately
began an intensive campaign to achieve enosis,
the union of Cyprus with Greece, a goal
opposed by Turkey and the Turkish community of Cyprus, as well as by many
Britishers, who hoped to retain British sovereignty and military bases in the strategically
located island.

Living as he was in London, the capital of
the empire from which Greek Cyprus hoped
to free itself, Kyprianou was conveniently
situated for an active involvement in the independence movement. H. D. Purcell, in his
book Cyprus (Praeger, 1969), suggests that
Kyprianou's espousal of enosis as opposed to
independence per se, both then and later,
was politically motivated and not based on
firm personal conviction. In any case, in 1952
Kyprianou founded and became the first president of the National Union of Cypriot Students
in England (EFEKA), a post he retained until
1954. In February 1952, also, Makarios appointed him his London secretary.

In 1954, now a barrister-at-law, although
apparently more active as a pro-Cypriot journalist and lecturer than as a lawyer, Kyprianou
became the London secretary of the Cypriot
Ethnarchy, the national council of the Greek
Cypriot community. Charged with representing that community's views and interests in
Britain, he took on the responsibility in a
difficult period. That same year the Greek
government had openly endorsed enosis as
a solution to the Cyprus problem, and an
ongoing diplomatic impasse ensued. Greece
sponsored the cause of the Cypriot Greeks;
Turkey backed the demand of the Cypriot
Turks that the island be partitioned between
its two ethnic communities; and Britain sought
a compromise that would protect its own
interests.

When the Greek, Turkish, and British foreign
ministers proved unable to work out a mutually

acceptable formula, the situation deteriorated rapidly. In 1955 the Greek-backed EOKA guerrilla movement, commanded by Colonel George Grivas, began an underground war against the British in Cyprus, and as the fighting proceeded, the island's Greek and Turkish communities became so polarized that intercommunal warfare erupted in 1958. Meanwhile, as an official spokesman for a body sympathetic to EOKA, and as an activist involved in making contacts with Liberal and Labour parliamentary opponents of Britain's Conservative government, Kyprianou soon found himself unwelcome in England, and in June 1956 he was forced to leave. For a brief time he went to Greece, during which he was associated with the Panhellenic Committee for Self-Determination for Cyprus. From August 1956 to March 1957 he served as the Ethnarchy's New York representative, participating in U.N. General Assembly debates on the Cyprus Question and making private diplomatic contacts with U.N. delegates and with members of the United States State Department.

In March 1957 Kyprianou went back to Athens, but he was soon permitted to return to London as the Ethnarchy's representative. By late 1958 all factions were willing to make accommodations, and a relatively short period of negotiations, in which Kyprianou and Makarios represented Cyprus, led to the signing, in February 1959, of the Zurich-London Agreements. They granted Cypriot independence but maintained a military enclave for the British. The Turks of Cyprus were guaranteed the Vice-Presidency, 30 percent representation in the government and civil service, and veto power over legislation.

In April 1959 Kyprianou helped to found the moderately right-of-center National Democratic Front for Reconstruction (EDMA), committed to backing Makarios for the Presidency of Cyprus, and became a member of its central committee. On March 1, 1959 he had accompanied the archbishop, whom the British had expelled four years earlier, on his triumphal ceremonial return to Cyprus.

During the ensuing transition period, Kyprianou attended the Greek-Turkish-Cypriot conference in Athens, which drafted a series of tripartite accords that implemented the terms of the Zurich-London Agreements. In December 1959 Makarios was elected the first President of Cyprus, and on August 16, 1960, when the new republic officially became independent, he named Kyprianou his Justice Minister. A few days later, however, Makarios gave Kyprianou the foreign affairs portfolio instead.

Kyprianou, who was possibly the youngest man to head the foreign office of a European state in modern times, had to build his ministry almost from the ground up. While organizing and staffing a diplomatic service, he had, at the same time, to formulate a foreign policy for the new republic. Viewing Cypriot interests as aligned with those of the Arab states and the emerging nations of Africa, he worked from the outset to solidify ties with the third world. Equally concerned with Europe, he took Cyprus into the Common Market, and from April to December 1967, he served as president of the Committee of Foreign Ministers of the Council of Europe. Broadly internationalist in outlook, he often took a stand on developments in other countries. He called for intervention in South Africa and Rhodesia, for instance, and supported affirmative action policies in the United States.

Before long, however, Kyprianou was forced to turn his attention to domestic matters of more urgent import, for by 1963 fighting had broken out between the Greeks and Turks of Cyprus. He was often obliged to leave the island for visits to Athens, where he consulted with the Greek government, and in September 1964 he even journeyed as far afield as Moscow, to obtain Soviet military aid for the embattled Cypriot Greeks. A semblance of order was not restored until March 1964, when the United Nations sent a peace-keeping force to the island. Passions remained inflamed, however, and strife recurred throughout the 1960's. In 1967 Greece and Turkey, although both of them NATO allies, would have gone to war over Cyprus, had it not been for the mediation of President Lyndon B. Johnson's special envoy, Cyrus Vance.

During that turbulent period, as head of the Cyprus delegation to the U.N. Kyprianou effectively pleaded the Cypriot cause in the General Assembly and before the Security Council. He accompanied Makarios to conferences of the Commonwealth prime ministers and of the nonaligned nations, in addition to visiting European, African, and South American countries, as well as Japan, to obtain support for the Makarios government, then following a more moderate course than that of the extremist pro-enosis faction. As early as February 1964, while Kyprianou was in London, the police received reports that right-wing Greek extremists intended to assassinate him. Maintaining that Kyprianou's views were not "national" (i.e. pro-Greek), the Greek military junta finally demanded in late March 1972 that Makarios purge him from the Cabinet. Although the archbishop managed to resist Greek pressures for a few months, on May 5, 1972 Kyprianou was obliged to resign from his post as Foreign Minister of Cyprus.

For the next two years Kyprianou practised law. In July 1974, following a Greek-backed coup that overthrew the Makarios government, Turkish forces invaded Cyprus. War between Greece and Turkey was once more averted, but the Greek military junta collapsed and Turkish troops stayed on to garrison the areas in which the island's Turks were concentrated. In August 1974, in the aftermath of those events, Kyprianou met in a private capacity with the new Greek Prime Minister, Constantine Karamanlis, in Athens, and with Makarios in London; he then went on to New York City to head the island's delegation in the General Assembly debate on Cyprus. After Makarios resumed the Presidency of Cyprus in December 1974, Kyprianou stayed on as an ad hoc member of the Cyprus U.N. delegation, acting as a foreign policy adviser to the President and participating, unofficially, in talks with the Greek government. On May 12, 1976 Kyprianou founded a new right-of-center political party, the Democratic Front, with the backing of Makarios, who was seeking a counterbalance to his chief political adversary, Glafkos Clerides. Winning twenty-one out of thirty-five seats in the parliamentary election of September 5, 1976, Kyprianou succeeded Clerides as president of the House of Representatives. As such, he automatically became acting President of Cyprus.

Pledging himself to "faithfully follow the policies of our late great leader and President in all fields," Kyprianou on September 1, 1977 became caretaker President of Cyprus for the remainder of the archbishop's term. Although some observers expected him to meet with opposition in the election scheduled for February 1978, no contenders came forward. Consequently, on January 26, 1978 Kyprianou automatically became President of Cyprus in his own right for a five-year term.

Until 1977 Kyprianou had primarily been involved in foreign rather than domestic affairs. Despite the superficial impression conveyed by his smooth succession to the Presidency, his newly created Democratic Front seemed weak when compared to the three other parties: the Communists (AKEL), the Socialists, and Clerides' right-wing Democratic Rally. Knowing that he was the chosen successor of Makarios himself, however, the other parties refrained from opposing him, out of a concern for maintaining national unity and tranquillity in the period of uncertainty that followed the death of the revered father of the independent Cypriot republic. If there had been a contested election, it is by no means clear whether Kyprianou could have won, or at least could have won with enough strength to inspire public confidence. Once in office, however, Kyprianou took steps to solidify his position. He immediately began reshaping the Democratic Front to make it less dependent on Communist and Socialist support. Enlarging the Cabinet by creating several new portfolios, he appointed important political associates, rather than the nonpolitical specialists favored by Makarios, to high-level government posts.

Throughout his administration Kyprianou has displayed a decisiveness that has won the admiration of most Greek Cypriots. That firmness was most dramatically revealed in mid-December 1977, when his older son, Achilleas, a lieutenant in the Cypriot army, was kidnapped by pro-enosis extremists, who threatened to kill the youth if some of their imprisoned colleagues were not released. De-

claring himself ready to sacrifice his son "but never my country," Kyprianou refused to give in. All four of the Greek Cypriot parties, as well as the Cypriot people, rallied behind him, and when the political prisoners in question made clear that they would not accept their freedom in such circumstances, the kidnappers were forced to release the young man.

Kyprianou was equally forceful when, in February 1978, Egyptian commandos landed at Larnaca Airport in Cyprus and attacked a Cyprus Airways plane in an attempt to release hostages held by Arab terrorists. Insisting afterwards that he could not, under any circumstances, permit Cypriot sovereignty to be infringed, Kyprianou ordered his troops to open fire on the Egyptians. The bloody incident for a time imperiled the normally good relations between Cyprus and Egypt.

The main problem confronting the Kyprianou Presidency, however, remains the resolution of the long-standing and perennially vexing conflict between the island's Turks and Greeks. The Cypriot republic, with its extensive minority guarantees and unworkable constitution, died stillborn in the 1960's. It will probably never be resurrected, for in 1975 the Turks of Cyprus, protected by the Turkish army, severed their few remaining formal ties with Greek Cyprus and declared themselves independent. Moreover, since Turkey will never permit enosis, a goal that has been rejected by the Greek government as well, and by all but an ultra-rightist fringe in both Greece and Cyprus, that too seems not to be in the offing.

Recognizing that the island's economic well-being and ultimate viability would be irreparably harmed by a permanent partition between two small rival states, each supported by a foreign power, Kyprianou has accepted the concept of a Cypriot federation of some kind. Under it, Greeks and Turks will exercise full control over domestic affairs in their respective zones, but a central government will provide ceremonial unity as well as a basis for cooperation in spheres of mutual interest. Aided by such a structure, a sense of Cypriot nationality, overriding ethnic concerns, might eventually develop.

As the American foreign correspondent Nicholas Gage pointed out in the New York Times (April 23, 1978), federation is still a "bitter pill" for many Greek Cypriots to swallow, but Kyprianou's hand is strengthened by the fact that Makarios himself, shortly before his death, endorsed the same principle as a means of bringing peace to Cyprus. There are many roadblocks on the path to federation, however, including the certainty that massive population transfers on both sides will have to take place, and the difficulty of demarcating ethnic zonal boundaries acceptable to all parties. During 1978 Kyprianou met several times with Prime Minister Karamanlis of Greece and with Prime Minister Bülent Ecevit of Turkey, as well as with Raul Denktash, the

Turkish Cypriot leader, but despite their efforts, as well as those of President Jimmy Carter's Administration and U.N. Secretary-General Kurt Waldheim, few problems were solved. On May 19, 1979 Waldheim announced that the stubborn two-year deadlock on talks between Greek and Turkish Cypriot leaders had finally ended with their agreement to start intercommunal discussions in Nicosia on June 15.

In 1956 Spyros Kyprianou married Erasmia ("Mimi") Pagathrokliton, a native of Salonika, whom he met while they were both students in England. They have two sons, Achilleas and Marcos. Kyprianou is a smooth-featured, small, meticulously groomed man with wavy black hair and a shy smile. Although he has suffered from a serious heart condition for the past several years, he continues to be a hard worker who, it is said, draws upon deep reservoirs of nervous energy in times of crisis. For recreation, he swims, attends sports events, reads, and listens to music. His decorations include the Grand Cross of the Order of George I of Greece, the Grand Cross of the Federal Republic of Germany, the Grand Star of the Republic of the U.A.R., the Grand Cross of the Order of Boyaca of Colombia, the Grand Cross of the Order of Merit of Chile, the Grand Silver Cross of Austria, and the Order of St. Aekaterini of Sinai.

References: Current World Leaders 20:5+ N '77; N Y Times p3 F 17 '64 por, A p10 S 1 '77 por; International Who's Who, 1978-79; International Yearbook and Statesman's Who's Who, 1978; Who's Who in Europe, 1972; Who's Who in the World, 1974-75

Laxalt, Paul (Dominique)

Aug. 2, 1922- United States Senator from Nevada. Address: b. 326 Russell Office Building, Washington, D.C. 20510; h. 6660 Midhill Pl., Falls Church, Va. 22043

Senator Paul Laxalt is an anomaly in American politics. The first Republican to represent Nevada in the upper chamber since 1952, he was the only member of his party able to buck the foul winds of Watergate in 1974 to snatch a Senate seat previously held by a Democrat. In July 1975, when other Republican party regulars were lining up behind President Gerald Ford in his bid to be elected President in his own right, Senator Laxalt formed the Citizens for Reagan campaign committee. Further setting him apart from his colleagues is the ease and grace with which he propounds his staunchly conservative philosophy. His courtesy and unflappable, low-key manner during the most heated debates, including the long and rancorous battle over the Panama Canal treaties, have won him high praise even from his liberal opponents. Along with Reagan and Senator Barry M. Goldwater, Senator Laxalt has become the conscience of contemporary political conservatism in the United States.

The eldest of six children, Paul Dominique Laxalt was born in Reno, Nevada on August 2, 1922 to Dominique and Theresa (Alpetche) Laxalt, both French Basque immigrants. His father, a sheepherder, spent virtually all his time at his camp in the Sierras, while his mother managed the small family-style restaurant and hotel in Carson City. Paul and his younger brothers, Robert, John, and Mick, spent several weeks each summer on the sheep range with their father. Robert Laxalt, a writer who specializes in the history of the Basques, recalled those days in Sweet Promised Land (Harper, 1957), a biography of Dominique Laxalt. Both parents were strict with their children and instilled in them a "total respect for institutions and the family," in Paul Laxalt's words.

Laxalt attended the public elementary schools in Carson City and, after graduating from Carson City High School in 1940, enrolled at Santa Clara University in Santa Clara, California. His undergraduate education was temporarily interrupted in 1943 by a two-year tour of duty in the South Pacific as a medic in the United States Army. After the war, he resumed his education at the University of Denver, where he earned a B. S. degree and, in 1949, an LL.B. degree. Specializing in trial work, Laxalt practised law in his hometown of Carson City for about a year. He then ran successfully for district attorney of Ormsby County on the Republican ticket. In his four years as public prosecutor, he never lost a case, but notwithstanding his enviable record, he found himself temperamentally ill suited to the job. "My heart was always on the other side of the table," he explained to one reporter. He therefore returned to private practice in 1954.

Elected lieutenant governor in what was otherwise a Democratic sweep of state offices in 1962, Laxalt decided to take on the Democratic incumbent, Howard W. Cannon, for the United States Senate in 1964. In his campaign Laxalt came out strongly in favor of states' rights, assuring the voters that the influence of the federal government was being felt "too strongly" at the state and local levels. With a comfortable lead in the sparsely populated and largely Republican "cow counties" in the northern part of the state, Laxalt concentrated on heavily Democratic Clark County. Before the campaign heated up, he had openly backed Senator Barry M. Goldwater, the conservative Republican candidate for the Presidency, but when polls showed him pulling even with Cannon, he played down his support of Goldwater and quietly turned down offers of help from out-of-state Republicans. The first tally in November showed 67,336 votes for Cannon and 67,293 for Laxalt. Five weeks later, after a recount, Laxalt conceded to Cannon, having lost the contest by a mere 48 votes, in spite of Lyndon B. Johnson's landslide victory in the overwhelmingly Democratic state.

In nearly upsetting Senator Cannon, Laxalt had capitalized on the abuses of big government, an important issue in a state where the federal government controls 87 percent of the land. Few were surprised, therefore, when Laxalt drove home the same message in his victory over Grant Sawyer, the two-term Democratic incumbent, in the race for the governorship in 1966. As he prepared to take office on January 2, 1967, some Nevadans wondered how Laxalt, a devout Roman Catholic, could reconcile his beliefs with administering a state that derives the bulk of its revenue from gambling casinos, topless bars, and a brisk marriage and divorce traffic. "I was elected by all Nevadans of all faiths and creeds," Governor Laxalt declared, as quoted in the Washington Post (January 2, 1967). "And I'm not about to impose my religious views and will on the whole state."

Although he personally favored stricter marriage requirements, particularly a more reasonable waiting period, Laxalt declined to propose any new legislation along that line. He strongly opposed the elimination of the six-week residency requirements for divorce, however, because he did not want Nevada to be, as he put it, "in competition in the merchandising of divorces." To the surprise of some of his constituents, the governor approved continued appropriations for birth control clinics under existing public welfare programs.

One of Laxalt's top priorities as governor was to rid Nevada of the organized crime figures who had been flocking to the state ever since Bugsy Siegel opened the Flamingo, the first big casino hotel on the Las Vegas strip, in 1947. The solution to the problem, as Laxalt saw it, was corporate ownership of the gambling establishments. To that end, he pushed through the state legislature measures allowing corporations to invest in Las Vegas and requiring tighter state accounting rules for gambling control. One of the first big businessmen to take advantage of the situation was Howard Hughes, who took over six of the largest hotels. Encouraged by his success, other entrepreneurs followed suit and, by mid-1969, all but two of the eighteen largest hotels and casinos were owned by public corporations. "Undesirables don't like to associate with public ownership," Laxalt explained to William Greider in an interview for the Washington Post (December 15, 1968). "They prefer going behind the door on a cash basis."

Carrying out a campaign promise to force the casinos to shoulder a greater burden of the state's expenses, Governor Laxalt signed a bill that raised the gambling tax by an average of 20 percent. Seventy percent of the additional revenue generated by the increase was spent on education, including the establishment of a community college system, and government building programs. He also raised the state sales tax from two to three cents on the dollar. Always an advocate of law and order, Laxalt fired the warden on the spot when seven inmates escaped from the maximum security section of the Nevada State Prison and personally directed the manhunt until the last fugitive was captured.

Nevadans generally approved Laxalt's take-charge performance as governor, as well they might, since his only misstep was his well-meaning attempt to mediate an intracorporate dispute among Hughes' lieutenants. His popularity in a state where Democrats outnumber Republicans by more than two to one was not lost on the White House. President Richard Nixon saw in the bright, attractive Republican a chance to oust one of his most outspoken critics on Capitol Hill, Senator Howard Cannon, who was up for reelection in 1970. But despite Nixon's repeated urgings, Laxalt announced his retirement from politics, citing family considerations. Thus, at a point in his career when virtually any statewide office was his for the asking, Paul Laxalt chose to return to private law practice as the senior partner in the Carson City firm of Laxalt, Berry, and Allison. He also headed Laxalt Associates, the family corporation that built and managed Ormsby House, the first major casino hotel to be built in Carson City in nearly a century.

Recharged by his few years in retirement, Paul Laxalt decided to try again for the United States Senate in 1974. This time he aimed for the seat then held by Senator Alan Bible, who was retiring after twenty years on the Hill. As a Republican, he could not have chosen a more inopportune time to make his move. President Nixon's resignation in disgrace, President Gerald R. Ford's unpopular pardon of his predecessor, the controversial amnesty for draft evaders, and a bleak economic outlook, all militated against the election of a Republican. To ward off possible backlash, Laxalt decided to meet his opponent, Lieutenant Governor Harry Reid, a popular young Democrat who had never lost an election, head-on in a series of statewide television debates. As he had done in 1964 he campaigned as much against the federal government as against his opponent. Calling for reductions in government spending to curb inflation, he recommended, among other things, cuts in foreign aid, especially to "ungrateful two-bit countries" that "sell out to the highest bidder." As election day neared, the campaign debates turned increasingly acrimonious, with Reid playing up alleged connections between Laxalt and Howard Hughes, a heavy contributor to Nixon's tainted campaign treasury, and to other Watergate figures. Nevertheless, when the votes were counted, Laxalt came out on top, defeating his opponent by 626 votes. He was the only Republican to win a Senate seat formerly held by a Democrat.

Senator Laxalt first attracted national attention as the campaign chairman for Ronald Reagan, a Republican Presidential hopeful in 1976. According to most reports, it was Laxalt's idea to name Richard S. Schweiker, the affable, low-key junior Senator from Pennsylvania, as Reagan's running mate before the convention. The selection of a liberal Easterner to balance a ticket headed by a conservative Westerner—Reagan—was part of a carefully orchestrated attempt to derail Gerald Ford's election campaign, which had steadily been gaining strength. But the risky strategy backfired when dozens of Reagan delegates bolted. Except for that tactical error, Laxalt mounted a strong challenge to the incumbent President.

At the Republican National Convention in Kansas City, Laxalt drew sustained applause when he placed Reagan's name in nomination as "the man who can whip the irresponsible Congress into line." "I would dearly love to see Ronald Reagan debate Jimmy Carter," he added. "After one round of debating . . . he would have to go back to shucking peanuts." Yet, after his candidate lost to Ford on the first ballot, Senator Laxalt characteristically threw his wholehearted support behind his party's nominee. "Laxalt fought at Ronald Reagan's side to the bitter end," George F. Will observed in his column for Newsweek (May 1, 1978), "but never felt or provoked bitterness."

Since taking office in January 1975, Senator Laxalt has consistently received high marks from conservative groups, such as Americans for Constitutional Action and the National Association of Businessmen and low ratings from their liberal counterparts, Americans for Democratic Action and the AFL-CIO's Committee on Political Education. Domestically, he has concentrated on cutting the staggering federal budget by trimming waste from existing programs and turning down appropriations requests for "expensive experiments." For example, he condemned a bill sponsored by Senator Edward M. Kennedy that would have authorized the Labor Department to use general tax revenues to pay the health insurance costs of the unemployed as "short-sighted," "piecemeal," and "unjustifiably expensive." At the same time, however, he vigorously supported some federal social welfare programs and revenue sharing to help states pay escalating educational costs.

As another means of curbing inflation, he favored across-the-board tax reform to help the average taxpayer who was, in his words, being "nickeled and dimed to death by interest groups that profit from government largesse." Among other things, he opposed a limitation on earned income for persons on Social Security, supported tax credits for college tuition, and worked to close tax loopholes available to the wealthy. To encourage economic growth, he turned down requests for stiffer taxes on businesses, contending that the increases would cause business failures, provoke unemployment, and raise consumer prices. For similar reasons, he opposed the breakup of the big oil companies and led the floor fight against common situs picketing which would, in his view, lead to the elimination of the open shop and increase the number of crippling strikes.

Laxalt's biggest domestic concern, however, has been the rapid, unchecked growth of the federal government. In a widely circulated article for the National Review (April 15, 1977), he warned that "the momentum behind government growth is so strong and the resistance to it so weak that, unless effective action is taken soon, the growth of the government could become unstoppable." He traced that alarming trend to a "do-good impulse" in Congress that caused the federal budget to mushroom with appropriations for "undoubtedly well-intentioned but, just as undoubtedly, poorly administered" public assistance programs. To slow the pace, Laxalt has proposed that the annual percentage of increase in peacetime budgets not exceed the annual rate of growth in the gross national product over the previous three years.

An advocate of a strong national defense posture, Senator Laxalt mounted his first major legislative effort late in 1977 when he led the opposition to the controversial Panama Canal treaties. Convinced that American control of the canal was "absolutely necessary" for security purposes, he organized the more knowledgeable and articulate treaty opponents into a Panama Canal "truth squad" that visited seven key states in an effort to drum up last-minute support for retention of the canal. Appearing on television broadcasts paid for by contributions from various conservative groups and individuals, Senator Laxalt himself appealed to his fellow citizens to bombard wavering Senators with letters urging them to vote against the treaties, which gave control of the canal to Panama by the year 2000.

Despite the rancor and bitterness that marked much of the debate, Senator Laxalt maintained his reputation for fairness and courtesy throughout the proceedings. In fact, at one critical juncture, displaying the perspicacity that others on his side of the aisle seemed to lack, he rose above the battle long enough to vote against a treaty reservation which, in the worst tradition of turn-of-the-century gunboat diplomacy, would have granted the United States the right to dispatch troops anywhere in Panama without the consent of the Panamanian government. Although the Panama Canal treaties were eventually signed into law, no Senator emerged from the parliamentary struggle with a better image than Paul Laxalt. As a result, some conservatives have urged him to run for President in 1980, but he has brushed aside such suggestions. "The Presidency just has no appeal to me," he insisted to Adam Clymer, who interviewed him for the New York Times (April 17, 1978). "Not for a moment would I begin to seek it."

Paul Laxalt has been described as "a blend of true grit and amiableness." He is a handsome man, with brown eyes, closely cropped gray hair and, as one writer noted, "a round face . . . as placid as a mountain lake." He regularly visits his home state and, when he has a few days off, enjoys hiking and camping in its mountains. To keep in shape, he plays tennis as often as possible. Laxalt and the former Carol Wilson were married on January 27, 1976. He has six children—three of whom were adopted—from an earlier marriage to Jackalyn Ross Laxalt that ended in divorce in 1970.

References: Christian Sci Mon p2 Ja 22 '75 por; N Y Times A p5 Ap 17 '78 por; Almanac of American Politics, 1978; Douth, George. Leaders in Profile (1975); Who's Who in America, 1978-79; Who's Who in the West, 1978-79

Levine, Joseph E(dward)

Sept. 9, 1905- Motion picture producer. Address: b. Joseph E. Levine Presents Inc., 345 Park Ave., New York City, N.Y. 10022

Joseph E. Levine is often called the last of the movie moguls; actually he was the first of a kind. The golden age of Hollywood, with its traditional studio system of production, came to an end with the advent of television. Then, out of nowhere, it seemed, came the independent producers, the pioneer among whom was Levine, the master showman who invented saturation booking, a man with an instinct for what is saleable to the masses and for the kind of ballyhoo that will sell it.

Levine, a self-made tycoon, was a small-time exhibitor and distributor in New England until the late 1950's, when he began buying up foreign films, mostly Italian "spear and sandal" spectaculars and releasing them in the United States with promotional pizzazz under his Embassy Pictures logo. (In 1968, when the Avco Corporation bought into Embassy, the logo became Avco-Embassy; since 1974, when Levine left Avco-Embassy, his production company has been Joseph E. Levine Presents Inc.) Among the 500 or so pictures in which Levine has been involved as producer or presenter are

Hercules (1959), Two Women (1961), Boccaccio '70 (1962), Divorce Italian Style (1962), The Conjugal Bed (1962), The Sky Above, The Mud Below (1962), The Easy Life (1963), 8½ (1963), The Carpetbaggers (1964), Darling (1965), The Producers (1967), The Lion in Winter (1968), The Night Porter (1975), A Bridge Too Far (1977), and Magic (1978). His greatest box-office success was The Graduate (1967).

Of Jewish descent, Joseph Edward Levine was born on September 9, 1905 in Boston, Massachusetts, the youngest of six children of a Russian immigrant tailor. After his father died, when Levine was four, his mother remarried, but the second marriage lasted only three years. Growing up in poverty in a fatherless family in the slums of Boston, Levine sold newspapers, shined shoes, and at fourteen quit school to work full time in a garment factory and later as a traveling dress wholesaler, dress shop owner, and restaurant operator.

Beginning in 1937, when he bought the regional rights to a batch of old cowboy movies for $4,000, Levine was a film exhibitor —ultimately the owner of four movie houses and three drive-ins—and distributor, specializing in what he later described as "exploitation pictures where I could give vent to my peculiar talent." Among the early pictures he peddled was a sex-hygiene flick titled Body Beautiful, which made him "sick" but which nevertheless turned a profit. During World War II he made $50,000 by buying the rights to The Ravaged Earth (1942), a film about the Sino-Japanese war, and promoting it with a "swell ad" that he wrote himself: "JAP RATS WILL STOP AT NOTHING. SEE THIS—IT WILL MAKE YOU FIGHTING MAD." After the war he invested $20,000 in the distribution rights to Discovery (Film Classics, 1948), and when that documentary about the Antarctic expeditions of Admiral Richard E. Byrd failed commercially he recouped his money by selling it as an educational film.

Levine took his first step into big-time producing when he bought the Japanese monster movie Godzilla (Embassy, 1956) for $12,000, promoted it with $400,000 in borrowed money, and grossed $1,000,000 at the box office. In the first of many dealings with the Italian producers Carlo Ponti and Dino De Laurentiis, he bought the American rights to the Lux film Attila (1958), starring Anthony Quinn and Sophia Loren, for $100,000. Given $600,000 worth of exploitation, Attila grossed $2,000,000.

Levine established his place in the motion-picture industry with the Italian blockbuster Hercules (1959), starring the California weight-lifter Steve Reeves in the role of the mythological Greek strongman. By the time Levine attended a screening in Rome, the film had been rejected by every major studio in the United States. But Levine was attracted by its "glowing and vivid" colors and the heroic scale of its fight and harem scenes. His instinct told him that there was something in the film "for everybody," that there was "a potential fortune tied up in it." He bought the American rights for $120,000, spent another $120,000 for dubbing, sound effects, and titles, and then poured over $1,000,000 into promotion and advertising. "The way I operate," he said at the time, "you have to think of money as chips. If you think of it as money you're lost."

Laying out $375,000 for extra color prints, Levine was able to saturate-distribute Hercules, which opened simultaneously in 600 movie houses across the country. Ultimately, Hercules played in 11,465 theatres, was viewed by 24,000,000 people, and grossed about $5,000,000. Its success lured other independent American producers into the Italian motion-picture market, and a grateful Italian government decorated Levine with the Ordine del Merito della Repubblica.

Levine next imported the British crime film Jack the Ripper (1960), which he promoted with typical flamboyance. For a luncheon for exhibitors at the Plaza Hotel in New York, Levine "rented" $1,000,000 in cash from a Boston bank and had it shipped to New York in an armored car. He told William H. Manville in an interview for an article in the Saturday Evening Post (December 30, 1967): "At a banquet, you tell them you're going to spend a million on promotion, and they don't even look up from their plates. . . . I wanted to make it real to them, . . . We must have had . . . thirty armed guards in that room. When the time came . . . I actually held up the cash . . . and thumped it on the table in front of me. I said, 'You know what this is, it's $1,000,000, and the next time you see it, it will be working for you, advertising Jack the Ripper. . . .' It brought the house down. What's more, we got one of the best publicity breaks of the motion-picture business. We made every wire service and almost every newspaper, radio and TV station in the country." The armored car, the guards, and the insurance cost Levine approximately $5,000, but he estimated the value of the publicity the film received to be at least $1,000,000.

Later in the same year Levine presented a sequel to Hercules called Hercules Unchained (1960), which he promoted with neon signs depicting Hercules and with simulated Roman orgies featuring champagne fountains, toga-clad models eating grapes, and a live lion, when the film opened in New York City and Los Angeles. In England, where Levine also owned distribution rights, full-page ads for the motion picture appeared in newspapers.

Levine revolutionized the "art film" business in the United States with his unprecedented handling of the black-and-white Italian import Two Women (1961). Based on a novella by Alberto Moravia, the movie was directed by Vittoria de Sica and starred Sophia Loren and Eleanora Brown as a mother and daughter displaced from their home in Italy in World War II. Levine paid $300,000 for distribution rights in the United States and Canada after seeing only three minutes of rushes in Rome at the invitation of producer Carlo Ponti—footage that included the climactic rape of mother and daughter by Moroccan soldiers in a bombed-out church.

Predicting that Miss Loren would win an Academy Award for her performance, Levine mounted a promotional campaign accenting a still from the movie showing the actress in a torn dress, kneeling in the dirt and weeping with rage and grief. He took out a two-page ad in the New York Times and brought Miss Loren to New York for the picture's opening there and for radio and television interviews. While the film was doing capacity business at art houses in the big cities, Levine launched a promotional campaign for the star within the film industry itself, seeing to it that the movie appeared in those cities where members of the Academy Award jury resided, and placing ads in the trade press.

As Levine had predicted, Miss Loren became the first actress in a foreign language film to win the Oscar for best actress. After the Academy Awards, Levine released Two Women for saturation booking on the commercial circuit. He told Paul O'Neill in an interview for Life (July 27, 1962): "I nursed that picture like a baby. When Sophia won the Academy Award . . . it had been running for six months, but the public was still waiting. It made money before the Award dinner, but it's grossed a million since."

By the end of 1963, Embassy's annual net profits had reached $750,000, and Levine had become a stockholder in Paramount Pictures, with the purchase of 10,000 shares. Previously, Embassy had operated primarily as an importer and distributor; in 1963 the company began to undertake its own productions. The first results were The Carpetbaggers (1964) and Zulu (1964). The Carpetbaggers grossed $18,000,000, of which $3,000,000 (before taxes and office expenses) went to Levine.

Embassy's success with the 1965 British import Darling was surpassed by The Graduate (1967), in which Levine underwrote Mike Nichols in his first directorial effort. After packaging Harlow (1965) and Nevada Smith (1966) for Paramount Pictures, Levine in 1967 put an end to persistent rumors of a Paramount-Embassy merger by selling his Paramount stock, and shortly afterward he also sold stock he owned in Metro-Goldwyn-Mayer. In 1968 the Avco Corporation acquired Levine's Embassy Pictures for $40,000,000 in stock. Under the terms of the agreement between Levine and Avco, Embassy operated as a wholly-owned Avco subsidiary and Levine remained chief executive officer.

Levine gave Mel Brooks his start as a director with The Producers (1968); and later in 1968 Avco-Embassy released its first reserved-seat attraction, The Lion in Winter, Levine's own favorite among his productions. But, essentially a loner, Levine was restive under the restric-

tions inherent in the Avco-Embassy setup. "This is no business for big business," he complained to James Brady during an interview for New York (December 17, 1973). "It's an art form. You can't have countless meetings. Someone's got to have instinct. I never had a meeting in my life until I got here. Not because I was opinionated . . . but because I had confidence in my judgments."

After suffering losses in 1973, Avco-Embassy was reluctant to make big cash investments except for those Levine productions directed by Mike Nichols, of which there were two in addition to The Graduate: Carnal Knowledge (1971) and The Day of the Dolphin (1973). To no one's surprise, Levine resigned as chief executive on May 28, 1974. In his farewell press conference he said, "I'm not the executive type and I don't want to be one. I'm a wheeler-dealer who wants to buy or make movies and promote them, and that's what I'm going to do."

Levine formed his own production company, Joseph E. Levine Presents, with the understanding that Avco-Embassy would be offered distribution rights to his films on a first-refusal basis. The most formidable undertaking of Levine's career as a producer was A Bridge Too Far (1977), a $25,000,000 cinematization of Cornelius Ryan's best-selling World War II novel shot at 146 locations in Europe under the vigilant eye of its producer. In that instance, as with all the films he has produced with the exception of those directed by Mike Nichols, he reserved for himself the right to the final cut.

William Goldman wrote the screenplay for Magic, based on Goldman's novel of the same name. When Magic was released in November 1978, Levine announced that his future plans included a swashbuckler, also to be scripted by Goldman, and a screen version of Verna, the story of a young woman of mediocre voice who sang to the troops with the U.S.O. during World War II. Based on a story by Paul Gallico, Verna had already been dramatized on television, as a Public Broadcasting Service special, and Levine hoped to get Sissy Spacek, who starred in the television version, to play the lead in the movie.

Partly because he believes that "the theatre is a source of talent for films, and talent in the theatre must be encouraged," Levine has always been generous in his financial contributions to campus and repertory dramatic companies. Earlier in his career he also did some producing on Broadway, but he "doesn't care" about Broadway anymore. "I'm not spending all that time and money to please one guy [the critic]," he has explained. "He makes a decision and you're finished. In films we can lick the critics."

Joseph E. Levine stands five feet four inches tall and weighs more than 200 pounds. For more than four decades he has been married to the former Rosalie Harrison, who was a singer with Rudy Vallee's band. The Levines, who have two grown children, Tricia and Richard, live in New York City. The producer, who describes himself in his professional dealings as "a stubborn old Jew," has a reputation for *chutzpah* that belies a basic humility. After a recent private audience granted to him and his wife by the Pope in Rome, he said: "Imagine, a little newsboy from Boston going to see the Pope.... As we approached the Pope's chambers, I said to Rosalie: 'Remember when I proposed to you? I said to you, "Some day I'll take you way up with me." Well, you're up there now. This is as far as the car goes.'"

References: American Film p39+ S 79 por; Ladies' Home J 95:64+ Mr '78 por; Life 53:76+ Jl 27 '62 pors; New Yorker p55+ S 16 '67 por; Variety p3+ Je 28 '78; p5+ N 1 '78; Who's Who in America, 1978-79

Lougheed, (Edgar) Peter (lô'hēd)

July 26, 1928- Premier of Alberta, Canada.
Address: b. 307 Legislative Bldg., Edmonton, Alberta T5K2B6, Canada

Since becoming Premier of Alberta in 1971, Peter Lougheed has directed the fortunes of the rapidly growing western province of some 1,900,000 people that produces 86 percent of Canada's oil and 82 percent of its natural gas. Thanks to the royalties his government receives from the companies that exploit those resources, Premier Lougheed has been able to shield his province from sales and inheritance taxes, to reduce income taxes, to shift the costs of social services from property taxes to the general treasury, and to stimulate diversification in Alberta's economy. At the same time

he has sought a greater influence in Canada's national politics for his province, which, because of its small population, is limited to nineteen of the 264 seats in the national Parliament. In the process, Lougheed has become one of Canada's best-known provincial leaders and a potential national spokesman for the Progressive Conservative party, whose leader, Joseph Clark, became Prime Minister of Canada in May 1979.

Peter Lougheed was born on July 26, 1928 in Calgary, Alberta, to Edgar Lougheed, a lawyer, and his wife, the former Edna Bauld. He was christened Edgar Peter but later dropped the first name. His paternal grandfather, Sir James Alexander Lougheed, a lawyer for the Canadian Pacific Railway who came to Alberta in 1883, eventually established Alberta's most important corporate law firm, made a fortune in investments, served as a federal senator and Cabinet member, and became the only Albertan to be knighted. At the time of the Depression the family suffered reverses, and Peter Lougheed grew up in modest circumstances. But during the post-World War II oil boom in Alberta it prospered once more, and when Edgar Lougheed died in 1951, he left an estate of $3,100,000. One family friend has commented, with reference to Peter Lougheed's father: "I wouldn't call him exactly a weak man, but he sure as hell wasn't a strong one, and you soon learn that one of Peter's main drives is to restore the family name." Lougheed recalls that it was his mother who gave him "goals and objectives."

In the Calgary public schools he attended, Lougheed was an outstanding athlete, excelling in track and field, baseball, football, basketball, and hockey. His characteristic drive and ambition, which some observers attribute to his family's fluctuating fortunes, were soon evident. "I enjoy competition," he admits. "I guess it's the thing I enjoy most." At the University of Alberta he became president of Delta Upsilon fraternity and the student council and managed, despite his small size, to play two seasons as a punt returner for the Edmonton Eskimos of the Canadian Football League. He graduated from the University of Alberta with a B.A. degree in 1950, obtained his LL.B. from the same institution in 1952, and earned an M.B.A. degree at the Harvard Graduate School of Business Administration in 1954. Returning to Canada, he read law with the Calgary firm of Fenerty, McGillivray & Robertson and practised law with that firm in 1955-56, after his admission to the bar. In 1956 he joined the Mannix Corporation, a powerful Alberta conglomerate with interests in construction, engineering, energy, and other fields. Starting as a junior counsel and receiving an appointment as the firm's secretary soon thereafter, he became general counsel in 1958, vice-president in 1959, and a director in 1960.

In 1962 Lougheed left Mannix to practise law with the firm of Moore, Lougheed, Atkinson & Tingle. He also turned his attention to politics in an effort to revive the Progressive Conservative (PC) party, which was moribund after three decades of Social Credit (Socred) party rule in Alberta. Lougheed chose the PC, or Tories, over the Socreds because of his grandfather's connection with the former and his own liking for their "respect for the individual." After organizing a Lougheed Club among his friends, and conducting weekly meetings to plan strategy, finances, and other details, Peter Lougheed took over the leadership of the provincial PC organization at its Edmonton convention in March 1965. His next step was to garner grassroots support in preparation for his challenge to the Socreds.

The first opening for the PC came in the May 1967 provincial election, when Lougheed ran successfully in the Calgary West riding, and entered the Alberta legislature with five Tory colleagues. Although the Socreds still controlled all but ten of the sixty-five seats, the Conservatives had managed to increase their share of the vote from the 13 percent they received in 1963, when they had failed to win a single seat, to 26.3 percent, and they replaced the Liberals as the official opposition in the provincial legislature.

By 1971 the PC, under Lougheed's leadership, was ready to challenge the government of Harry Strom, who had succeeded the venerable Ernest Manning as Premier and leader of the Socreds in 1968. The Tories' elaborate platform vowed to promote industries with greater employment opportunities, to make government more democratic and responsive, and to grant more powers to municipalities. In particular, it pledged "to alter the present isolationist attitude of the outgoing Alberta Government and bring Albertans into the mainstream of Canadian life—performing a role of national leadership, not provincial reactionism." Lougheed's promise of "youth and vitality" and his effective use of television, to which the PC devoted 85 percent of its advertising budget, brought an upset victory in the election of August 30, 1971. The Tories took forty-nine of the seventy-five seats in the newly enlarged legislature, the Socreds found their representation reduced to twenty-five, the Liberals lost all three of their previous seats, while the left-leaning New Democratic party elected only one representative. As the leader of the strongest party in the Alberta legislature, Lougheed automatically became Premier.

Lougheed's victory reflected the transformation of Alberta from a rural, economically depressed province to an urban, highly prosperous one. Determined to redress past neglect by the federal government, which had been dominated by the populous eastern and central provinces, Lougheed and his constituents saw an urgent need to divert Alberta's economy from its dependence on the exploitation of energy resources and at the same time make those resources more profitable. Furthermore, they demanded greater autonomy within the Canadian Confederation and more influence in its administration.

Alberta's energy resources, which became enormously profitable as a result of the international oil crisis of 1973, placed the province in an unaccustomed but enviable economic position. "The East is used to us Westerners coming to them on bended knees," Lougheed observed in 1975. "Now we have some leverage, and we plan to use it." The pressure to take advantage of the situation was great, because forecasters believed that Alberta's easily tapped, conventional sources of oil might be productive for only another decade. Having worked briefly in Tulsa, Oklahoma during his student years in the 1950's, Lougheed has tried to safeguard Alberta from facing the type of decline suffered by Tulsa after the oil companies left. For continued prosperity, the province must, in his opinion, convert the demand for its provincially owned natural resources into diversification of the Alberta economy, thus reducing its dependence on primary, raw natural resource disposal.

A cornerstone of Lougheed's policy has been his demand that Alberta receive the world market price for its gas and oil. He has insisted that other Canadian provinces, which formerly shunned Alberta's energy in favor of cheaper foreign imports, must now pay what the traffic will bear, just as they expect to receive the going rate for their finished products. "If other regions of Canada are able to obtain fair market value for goods that can be easily replaced," he has asserted, "Alberta is surely entitled to ask for the same in regard to the sale of a resource which, once depleted, can never be renewed."

The British North America Act of 1867, which is Canada's Constitution, guarantees to each province control over its natural resources, but the federal government has tried to limit the scope of the law. On September 13, 1973 the administration in Ottawa imposed a forty-cent per barrel tax on oil exported to the United States, stipulating that its proceeds were to be used to mitigate the effects of rising energy prices in the eastern provinces. Lougheed called the maneuver "the most discriminatory action taken by a federal government against a particular province in the entire history of confederation." In November 1974 he denounced as "folly and lack of judgment" a decision by officials in Ottawa to phase out oil exports to the United States. A month later a federal decision not to allow the deduction of provincial royalties from taxable corporate income forced the Premier to reduce Alberta's levies on oil producers in order to keep the industry stimulated.

In 1976 Lougheed finally convinced the Ottawa government to permit domestic gas and oil prices to rise gradually to world market levels in order to stimulate domestic production and give Alberta additional revenue, but he has been less successful in winning federal support for some of his programs to diversify Alberta's economy. He was critical of Prime Minister Pierre Elliott Trudeau's failure to give full support to proposals made at the Western Economic Opportunities Conference in Calgary in July 1973. At that meeting Lougheed demanded federally backed credit and price supports for Alberta's farmers and called on Ottawa to lessen the province's high transportation costs by underwriting the expenses of western railway roadbeds as it does the construction and maintenance of highways and airports. Lougheed was even more dismayed by the federal government's refusal in 1974 to scrap, or limit in size, Petrosar, a large petrochemical complex that had been under construction since 1971 at Sarnia. To Albertans, Petrosar represented another coup for their industrial rival, Ontario, and, because of its great potential output, a threat to render impractical their own plans for developing local petrochemical installations.

In the face of such setbacks, Lougheed has concentrated on equipping Alberta to promote its own development through the expenditure and investment of the government's energy royalties. In August 1974 he engineered Alberta's purchase of Pacific Western Airlines for $36,000,000 as a means of guaranteeing access to adequate transportation in the province. He has also invested over $1 billion of Alberta's money in Syncrude, a gigantic project aimed at making feasible the exploitation of the oil sands along the Athabasca River, which was said to contain several times as much oil as the known total reserves of the rest of North America.

Lougheed's main campaign promise for the March 26, 1975 election—in which the PC won all but six of the seventy-five legislative seats and 63 percent of the popular vote—was the establishment of an Alberta Heritage Savings Trust Fund. Instituted in 1976 and financed with 30 percent of the government's annual energy revenues, the fund seeks to improve the quality of life in the province, to provide investment money for economic expansion and diversification, and to guarantee a source of revenue for a time when energy sources may be depleted. Up to 20 percent of the fund could be used for capital projects that offer social benefits but not financial returns. Another 15 percent might be allocated for purchase of securities of other provinces or of the federal government. But at least 65 percent of the money must be devoted to profitable investments in Alberta or to marketable, usually short-term, securities. By the spring of 1979 the fund had assets of over $4.8 billion.

Lougheed has denied that his "Alberta first" policies are tinged with separatism. "Alberta is very pro-Canadian," he has said. "All our demands really amount to is that the West

as a unit should become a new balance between the Ontario and Quebec axis. Instead of two major players, there will be three." Convinced that some constitutional revisions are necessary, he told a meeting of the Canada West Foundation in March 1978 that he favored allowing the provinces to appoint 40 percent of the members of federal regulatory agencies, restricting the central government's emergency powers, giving the provinces complete control of indirect taxation, and creating a court to settle jurisdictional disputes between the provincial authorities and Ottawa. Although he has expressed sympathy for French-speaking Quebec's desire for greater autonomy, the existence of Réne Lévesque's separatist government has caused him concern, and he has expressed the fear that Ottawa might use the Quebec crisis as what he has called "a convenient excuse to ignore our valid claims for a new deal in Confederation." He has criticized former Prime Minister Trudeau's plan to offer Quebec special status within Canada, preferring instead an arrangement under which all provinces would have the option to assume independently, or concurrently with Ottawa, a variety of powers that are now exercised exclusively on the federal level.

Within the context of Alberta's conservative politics, Lougheed is not an extremist. He describes himself as a "pragmatist," conservative on economic matters and "left-leaning" on social issues. Critics on the right, upset by his government's active involvement in the economy have dubbed him "Pinko Pete," but most of his opponents are from the political left. Liberals tend to distrust what they consider his non-intellectual approach. According to his biographer, Canadian Broadcasting Corporation correspondent Allan Hustak, whose book *Peter Lougheed* was published by the Canadian firm McClelland and Stewart in 1979, the Premier, "in his quest for dollar dynamism . . . appears to lack human and social reach."

Other critics have cited what they saw as Lougheed's preference for advisers recruited from among former school, sports, and business cronies. The Premier has also drawn criticism from students, who have demonstrated against his anti-inflationary restriction on expenditures for education, and from labor union spokesmen, who have attacked his stand that government employees have no right to strike. Alberta's Liberal party leader, Nick Taylor, referring to Lougheed's emphasis on technological development, has charged him with having a "Buffalo hunter mentality," while New Democratic party leader Grant Notley has questioned the wisdom of the Premier's emphasis on the petrochemical industry, given the oversupply of its products in North America, and has criticized him for failing to use the promise of cheap oil and gas as a means of bargaining for guarantees of improved and inexpensive transportation.

The Alberta Premier has also come under increasing fire from the Canadian media in recent years. In the CBC television drama *Tar Sands,* shown in September 1977, his role in the formation of Syncrude was portrayed so negatively that he sued the network for $2,700,000, charging an "unfair attack" on his character and reputation. Newspaper reports referring to Lougheed's excursions, including one taken in 1977 to promote Alberta's products in the Soviet Union, the Middle East, and Switzerland, prompted the Premier to reimburse airlines for some of the free transportation he had received.

Despite such attacks, Lougheed and the PC scored a major triumph in the March 1979 provincial election, which brought the party seventy-four out of seventy-nine seats in the legislature. Although that stunning victory thrust Lougheed into the national limelight as a potential Prime Minister, he has consistently played down that prospect, declaring on one occasion, "Why would I want to run Canada when I already run Alberta?" In the national elections of May 1979, which brought the Tories a plurality of 136 out of 282 seats, PC leader Joe Clark, a fellow Albertan and a close political associate of Lougheed's since the 1960's, succeeded Trudeau in the Prime Ministership.

Peter Lougheed, a trim, muscular man, is slightly under five feet eight inches tall, weighs 155 pounds, and has blue eyes, regular features, and medium length graying brown hair. "The King," as he is nicknamed, is not a brilliant debater, but he is an effective off-the-cuff speaker. According to Stanley Meisler of the *Los Angeles Times* (April 1, 1979), "although he speaks with a western twang and can sound folksy on the campaign trail, he . . . sounds in his speeches like a chairman of the board reading a dull annual report." Concerned with his image, he has mastered the art of using television to the best of his advantage, and in 1975 he had a film made about himself by the same experts who had provided United States President Richard Nixon with the same service three years earlier. To keep fit, the Premier jogs, skis, plays golf, and does pushups in his office. He also enjoys spectator sports and listening to symphonic music. With his wife, the former Jeanne Estelle Rogers, whom he met at the University of Alberta and married on June 21, 1952, Peter Lougheed has two sons, Stephen and Joseph, and two daughters, Andrea and Pamela.

References: *Canadian Forum* 58:6+ O-N '78; *Los Angeles Times* I p1+ Ap 1 '79; *Macleans* 85:30+ Ja '72 por; 88:19+ Jl '75 por; *Toronto Globe and Mail* p7 O 23 '75 pors, p37 N 30 '76 por, p38 F 24 '79 por; Hustak, Allan. *Peter Lougheed* (1979); *Canadian Who's Who,* 1973-76; *International Who's Who,* 1978-79; *Who's Who in Canada,* 1977-78

Ludwig, Daniel K(eith)

June 24, 1897- Shipping executive; financier. Address: b. National Bulk Carriers Inc., 1345 Ave. of the Americas, New York City, N.Y. 10019

America's richest man, the self-made shipping tycoon Daniel K. Ludwig, is probably the last of the true venture capitalists, an empire-building entrepreneur in the nineteenth-century tradition. Beginning with a single side-wheel excursion steamer purchased with a borrowed $5,000, the publicity-shy Ludwig amassed a fleet of individually owned ships that once ranked largest in the world and still ranks third. The keys to his success are two: his tactic of "rolling ships over" (chartering ships even before they were built, so that the charters could be used as collateral for loans for the building) and his virtual invention of the efficient supertanker.

Today Ludwig's multibillion-dollar National Bulk Carriers Inc. is a diversified multinational conglomerate embracing a range of ventures in twenty-three countries on six continents in addition to the flagship operation, the fifty-tanker fleet. The other interests include a chain of luxury hotels and other real-estate holdings, coal mining, oil and gas exploration, and savings and loan associations. The most ambitious of his current projects is a timber and wood pulp operation on 3.5 million acres in Brazil. On that tract of lush Amazonian jungle, larger than the state of Connecticut, Ludwig produces and processes his own timber, an exceptionally fast-growing variety, with a view to the shortage of sources for paper and other wood products expected in the mid-1980's.

An only child, Daniel Keith Ludwig was born on June 24, 1897 in South Haven, Michigan, on the southwest shore of Lake Michigan. Of mixed German, English, and Scottish ancestry, Ludwig is descended on the paternal side from a Hessian soldier who settled in Pennsylvania after the Revolutionary War. Daniel's grandfather, Charles Ludwig, built the now demolished Ludwig's Pier, four miles south of South Haven, out of which Daniel's father and four uncles worked as Great Lakes captains. His father was also a moderately successful investor in real estate.

"Nearly everyone has these antennae," Ludwig has said regarding his uncanny sensitivity to profit-making opportunities. "Most people just don't use them." Ludwig, a reserved loner in childhood, apparently began using those "antennae" early in life, at least by the age of nine, if one widely disseminated story about him is true. Saving money he earned by shining shoes and selling popcorn at a dance pavilion, he paid twenty-five or fifty dollars—reports differ on the exact amount—for a sunken twenty-six-foot boat deemed not worth salvaging by others, repaired it, and chartered it for more than $100.

Ludwig dropped out of public school in South Haven at the end of the eighth grade. After his parents separated, when he was fifteen, he moved with his father to Port Arthur, Texas, where he worked as a runner for a ship-chandlers firm while studying marine engineering in night school. Returning to Michigan after a year or so, he went to work for the Fairbanks, Morse marine engine company in Three Rivers, with a view to gaining the experience necessary for a marine engineer's certificate. While on installation assignments for Fairbanks, Morse in Alaska and the Pacific Northwest, he also contracted work on his own and was so successful that, at nineteen, he quit Fairbanks, Morse and went into business for himself.

His first major acquisition was the iron-hulled excursion boat Idlewylde, purchased for $5,000 on his father's signature. Recouping the purchase price and then some by selling the machinery and boilers, he converted the Idlewylde into a barge, bought several lesser barges of the wooden-hull variety, and several tugboats, and chartered the small fleet to A. I. Kaplan, who had cornered the blackstrap molasses market. For two years Ludwig hauled Kaplan's molasses up the Hudson River, through the Barge Canal, and across Lake Ontario to a Canadian distillery.

Through what Ludwig would later refer to only as a "misunderstanding," he came out on the short end of the deal with Kaplan. Accepting the experience as a lesson in shrewd trading, without hard feelings, he sold his barges to Kaplan and did general hauling of staves and lumber with his old tugboats, keeping just one step ahead of his creditors

as the shipping market slumped after World War I. "I had to hit on something or I was busted," he recounted in one of the rare interviews he ever granted, with Dero A. Saunders for Fortune (May 1957). What he decided to "hit on," he told Saunders, was oil transport, because he "saw the tanker boys getting three or four times as much for oil" as he was getting for hauling staves or lumber.

In 1921 Ludwig sold some of his dilapidated tugs, chartered the small tanker Anahuac from the War Shipping Board, and located a customer, a refinery in Fall River, Massachusetts with a Navy fuel-oil contract. The first oceangoing vessel he owned outright was the Wico, an antique tanker that was being scrapped by Standard Oil of New Jersey. Morris Schapiro, the Baltimore scrap dealer involved in that sale and numerous subsequent transactions with Ludwig, once observed. "He [Ludwig] knows where every piece of equipment being sold as scrap or surplus is. He is a brilliant man; it gets you all upset sometimes, the way his mind runs."

Pressed for cash by the Wico purchase, Ludwig took in a partner, who, wielding 51 percent of the stock, soon took over the business, leaving Ludwig with a settlement of $40,000 and the remnants of his tug fleet. With new associates, owners of a chain of gasoline stations in and around Boston, Massachusetts, Ludwig formed the American Tankers Corporation in 1925. As operational chief of the corporation, he bought the large tanker Phoenix from the War Shipping Board. The Phoenix was docked in Boston harbor with a cargo of gasoline one day in 1926 when an explosion below decks hurled Ludwig twenty-five feet, up through one deck and onto another. The accident fused three vertebrae in his spine, leaving him in constant pain so severe that he often had to conduct business lying flat on his back. A risky operation he underwent twenty-eight years after the accident ameliorated his back condition, but he reportedly still suffers some back pain and walks with a slight limp.

The low point of Ludwig's career occurred in the early 1930's, when he bought the coal ship Ulysses and converted it into the largest tanker then afloat; it operated at a loss for several years. Then, suddenly, his fortune turned upward. In the late 1930's he sold the Ulysses for $800,000—four times its value on the tanker market—to a whaling syndicate; established solid ties with three New York banks; and began to build his first really efficient staff, with a chain of command that included experienced, trusted deputies to watch over chartering, financing, and operating details. Previously he had tried to manage with an office boy, a part-time bookkeeper, and a part-time surveyor while he worked out of a borrowed New York City office, in which he did not even have a desk.

Ludwig's major innovation in ship financing was to apply to the tanker field the technique of borrowing against future lease income, a practice tantamount to buying a fleet with other people's money. That innovation emerged piecemeal, in a series of transactions, the first of which was a loan in 1936 from New York's Chemical Bank to buy several government-owned dry cargo vessels and convert them into tankers. A purer use of the technique occurred in 1938, when Ludwig assigned to the Bank of Manhattan (which later became the Chase Manhattan Bank) the charter on an existing ship, the *Phoenix*, in return for a loan to cover more conversions of dry cargo ships into tankers.

The Bank of Manhattan deal set the pattern for the tactic that insured the prosperity of Ludwig and his imitators. Using that tactic, the shipowner charters a tanker to a major oil company for, say, five or more years and then borrows from a bank an amount of money that will be more than covered by the charter price; the oil company pays the monthly charter cost directly to the bank, which takes its cut and deposits the remainder in the shipowner's account. This system is attractive to the banker, who has "two-name paper," backed by the credit of both charterer and shipowner, in addition to the security provided by the vessel itself. The shipowner, for his part, can borrow money on existing ships painlessly and use it to build new vessels, owned free and clear upon delivery, so that they in turn can be chartered for additional collateral.

After selling the original *Phoenix* to Stavros Niarchos of Greece (who went on to become a shipping tycoon in his own right), Ludwig gave a succession of other ships the name *Phoenix*, down to the present day. During World War II the United States Navy took over his facilities first in Little Creek, Virginia and later in Norfolk, Virginia. Finally, in a new, smaller yard in Welding, Virginia, he produced tankers totaling 438,000 tons, all of which were requisitioned by the government but returned to him at war's end. During the war Ludwig successfully pioneered the money-saving and time-saving shipbuilding techniques of welding hulls rather than riveting them and slipping ships sideways into the water instead of launching them bow-first—techniques that became standard in the industry.

Ludwig emerged from the war as the owner of America's fifth largest tanker fleet, with several ships as big as 18,000 deadweight tons (dwt), exceptionally large for the time. Never satisfied, he increased the tonnage of ships built at the Welding Shipyard during the immediate postwar years to as much as 30,000 dwt, the maximum possible at the yard, and he began to look abroad for a site where he could build even larger ships. Challenging the conventional wisdom in the industry at that time, which viewed big tankers as too "inflexible," he saw that operating costs did not rise with increase in size, that one giant ship could handle a given cargo more cheaply and efficiently than several small ships. He also knew that if he was to become a leader in international oil transport he must build and operate his supertankers under more advantageous economic conditions than those prevailing in the United States.

Ludwig found the conditions he was seeking in Japan, where the government was only too happy to make concessions in return for the employment opportunities he would offer. In 1951 he leased two building docks and one fitting-out dock in the Imperial Shipyard at Kure, Japan, where the world's largest battleship to date, the *Yamato*, had been built. The Japanese site offered several advantages in addition to the size of the ships that could be built there: the rent was nominal, the labor relatively cheap, and the government restrictions less stifling than in the United States; it cost $150 per dwt to build a ship at Kure, as contrasted with $300 in the United States. By registering his ships in "flag-of-convenience" countries such as Panama and Liberia, he gained the added advantage of inexpensive crews, low registration fees, less stringent safety regulations, and, most important of all, freedom from income taxes.

The Kure division of Ludwig's National Bulk Carriers was the major contributor to the emergence of Japan as the world's leading shipbuilder. The tonnage of the giant tankers and bulk carriers built at Kure began at 30,000 dwt in the early 1950's and progressively increased to 335,000 dwt in the late 1960's. Among the nontankers Ludwig built were carriers to haul ore from U.S. Steel's Cerro Bolivar iron mines in Venezuela, and the world's largest dredge, the 548-foot *Zulia*. Besides manning his ships with nonunion crews, mostly from the West Indies, Ludwig eliminated such frills as crew swimming pools and carpeting in captains' quarters, constructed thinner decks, and substituted exhaust pipes for funnels to reduce weight. Construction and maintenance costs were further lowered by the introduction of assembly-line and prefabrication construction methods and the use of interchangeable ships' parts.

Concurrently with the establishment of his shipbuilding base in Japan, Ludwig was beginning to diversify. Among the first of his diversification projects were Hato Vergareno, a 20,000-acre cattle ranch in Venezuela, and Panama Refining Inc., of Colón, Panama, a $22 million oil refinery which he has since sold. In the late 1950's he built the largest salt evaporation plant in the world, Exportada de Sal S.A., in Baja California, Mexico. Threatened with nationalization, he later sold the plant to the Mitsubishi Corporation for $50 million, but his ships continued to transport

Exportada's salt to Japan. In 1960 he founded Cítricos de Chiriqui S.A., a $25 million Valencia orange plantation on 10,000 acres of land in the interior of Panama; its sale to the Panamanian government was negotiated in 1976.

Ludwig never willingly sells stock in enterprises he controls, unless prudence or necessity so dictates. But two stockmarket deals he made in the 1960's increased enormously the cash reserves making possible his ventures in diversification. The 1.34 million shares of Union Oil of California stock bought by him in July 1963 for $100 million were sold nineteen months later at a profit of $46 million. Again, when the R. J. Reynolds Company acquired McLean Industries in 1969, it paid Ludwig $60 million for his McLean stock—five times what he had paid for it.

Ludwig's most ambitious diversification project is his vast natural resources domain on the Jari River, a tributary of the Amazon, in Brazil. Purchased for approximately $3 million in 1967, the Jari project now represents a total investment estimated at or near $1 billion. Uncannily anticipating the worldwide shortage of wood-product sources that is only now becoming imminent, Ludwig over a decade ago began planting vast stands of Caribbean pine trees and gmelina trees, which grow ten times faster than ordinary trees. Over the years he built a pulp and paper plant sixteen stories high and 200 yards long, a system of roads and a 150-mile railroad to transport the lumber from forest to plant, and towns for the workers. The $250 million processing plant was constructed at Ludwig's shipyard in Kure, Japan and transported by barge and tug across the Indian Ocean and up the Atlantic to a docking area built on the Jari River, 250 miles inland, by 2,500 workers.

The plant, which began operating early in 1979, is expected to have a daily output of 750 metric tons of bleached kraft pulp for paper and other products by 1981. In addition to the lumber operations, there is a 500-acre rice plantation and a huge open-pit kaolin mine. "If he succeeds," Louis Beman wrote in Fortune (November 1976) of Ludwig and the Jari project, "it will not be simply another profitable venture; it will be a historic achievement perhaps on a par with Cecil Rhodes's pioneering development of southern Africa—without the imperialism."

High-grade Ludwig coal is produced at the Clutha mines in Australia and United Pocahontas mines in West Virginia, and Ludwig is planning to construct a refinery in Scotland to process North Sea crude oil. The banking institutions under Ludwig's control are the Home Savings Association of Houston, American Savings and Loan of Utah, Southwest Savings and Loan of Phoenix, Westdale Savings and Loan of California, and European-American Securities Inc., a private merchant banking firm.

In the real estate field, Ludwig's construction companies have built tens of thousands of low-cost housing units in the United States, Latin America, and South Africa; Ludwig has investments in several high-rise office buildings; and he owns Princess Hotels International, a chain consisting of posh hotels in the Bahamas and Bermuda as well as the Sir Francis Drake in San Francisco and the Acapulco Princess in Acapulco, Mexico, where Howard Hughes suffered his final illness. According to recent reports, he may soon be selling the Princess chain, apparently because of the heavy financial demands of his massive Brazilian enterprise.

In addition to his position as chairman and director of National Bulk Carriers, Ludwig is president of two wholly owned subsidiaries, Sea Tankers Inc. and Universe Tankships Inc., and he is a director of the Kure Shipyard Division, Bahama Shipyards Ltd., on Grand Bahama Island, the American-Hawaiian Steamship Company, the Avco Corporation, and McLean Industries Inc. He is a member of the advisory board of the National Petroleum Council and of the Department of Defense's Military Petroleum Advisory Board and an adviser to the government on maritime policy.

The headquarters of National Bulk Carriers Inc. are in the Burlington House in New York City, a building in which Ludwig has a half interest. He still goes to his office there daily, and, despite his age and his back condition, he is reported to be in remarkably good health. A trim, gray-haired six-footer, he is an early riser, he neither smokes nor drinks, and he eats sparingly, displaying a partiality for bananas and buttermilk. He swims daily in a Burlington House pool and prefers walking to motorized transportation. If time or distance makes walking unfeasible, he will take a cab, or, preferably, public transportation. His habitual frugality and simplicity of lifestyle extend to his clothes, which are off-the-rack; he has been wearing the same black plastic raincoat for years.

Daniel K. Ludwig is reported to be "an exacting boss who does not tolerate mistakes by subordinates." Although he assiduously avoids the public eye and is impatient with small talk unrelated to business, Ludwig is not an eccentric recluse like the late Howard Hughes, with whom he is often compared. Associates describe him as talkative and friendly, and he maintains close ties with top officials of many major corporations. He has no hobbies, and he and his wife do little socializing, outside of dinner now and then with old friends like Kay Spreckles, Clark Gable's widow, and Ronald Reagan.

Ludwig's first marriage, to Gladys Madeline Ludwig, ended in divorce in 1937. By that marriage he has one child, a daughter. Shortly after the termination of his first marriage, Ludwig married his present wife, Ginger, who has a son by a previous marriage. According to the terms of his will, a substantial portion of Ludwig's estate will, upon his death, go to a cancer research foundation he established in Switzerland in 1970.

References: Biog N p307+ Mr '74 por; Fortune 55:171+ My '57 pors, 94:132+ N '76; New York 10:54+ N 28 '77 por; Time 96:76+ N 30 '70 por; Lamott, Kenneth. The Moneymakers (1969); Who's Who in America, 1978-79

Macdonald, Ross

Dec. 13, 1915- Writer. Address: b. c/o Alfred A. Knopf, Inc., 201 E. 50th St., New York City, N.Y. 10022; h. 4420 Via Esperanza, Santa Barbara, Calif. 93110

NOTE: This biography supersedes the article that appeared in Current Biography in 1953 under the name Kenneth Millar.

Ross Macdonald, who created the private eye-hero Lew Archer, has been justly credited with elevating the hard-boiled detective novel to the level of literature. For some time Macdonald had been regarded as the successor to Dashiell Hammett and Raymond Chandler in California-based detective fiction, but it was not until the late 1950's, when his mysteries began to carry autobiographical overtones, as well as elements of Freudian psychology and Greek myth, that he became recognized as a leading American man of letters. William Goldman was voicing a majority opinion when he once characterized Mac-

donald's work as "the finest series of detective novels ever written by an American."

Ross Macdonald is the nom de plume of Kenneth Millar, who was born on December 13, 1915 in Los Gatos, California to John Macdonald Millar, a Canadian newspaper editor and Scottish dialect poet, and Anne (Moyer) Millar, a nurse before her marriage and the daughter of an Ontario village storekeeper descended from Pennsylvania Dutch farmers. As a small child he moved with his parents to Vancouver, British Columbia, where his father worked for a time as a harbor pilot. When he was about three, the parents separated, and his mother, a partial invalid unable to support herself and her young son, took the boy with her to live at the homes of relatives in various parts of Canada. Later estimating that he had grown up in some fifty residences, Macdonald has recalled: "I felt uprooted from the time my parents separated." The missing father and the sense of exile from his true home—which, his mother constantly reiterated, was California—later evolved into literary themes for Macdonald, especially as they recalled the twice-exiled legendary king of Thebes in Sophocles' Oedipus tragedies.

A voracious reader, Macdonald considered his encounters with The Ancient Mariner, Oliver Twist, and Crime and Punishment among the "great events" of his boyhood. Other literary influences of his formative years included Sir Arthur Conan Doyle, Edgar Allan Poe, Stephen Leacock, Sigmund Freud, and the Black Mask magazine, where he first read the detective stories of Dashiell Hammett and Raymond Chandler. While attending St. John's, a boarding school in Winnipeg, in his early teens, he began to write prose and verse, including a narrative poem about Bonnie Prince Charlie. He and his mother finally settled at the maternal family home in Kitchener, Ontario, where he obtained his secondary education at the Kitchener-Waterloo Collegiate Institute and had his first story, a parody on Sherlock Holmes, published in the school magazine in 1931.

After graduating from high school in 1932, in the midst of the Depression, Macdonald spent a year working for his board as a farm laborer. He then entered the University of Western Ontario, aided by the proceeds of his recently deceased father's life insurance policy, but dropped out at the end of his junior year, after his mother's death. "I became quite depressed," he told an interviewer for Newsweek (March 22, 1971). "We were very close, very good friends, much closer than I realized before she died. She had kept my spirit alive all those years." He spent much of 1936 and 1937 abroad, cycling through the British Isles, France, and Germany, until an encounter with Nazi storm troopers along a parade route helped to persuade him to return home.

Back in Canada, Millar married, on June 2, 1938, Margaret Ellen Sturm, an aspiring writer, whom he had known in high school. That year, after obtaining his B.A. degree with honors from the University of Western Ontario, he went to summer school at the University of Michigan and studied modern European literature with W. H. Auden, who helped to stimulate his interest in detective fiction. He remembers Auden as "the most important single influence" on his life. After a year of graduate study at the University of Toronto he taught English and history from 1939 to 1941 at the Kitchener-Waterloo Collegiate Institute. During that period he also began to derive some income from free-lance writing, contributing short verses and stories to the Toronto weekly Saturday Night, for which he was paid one cent a word. The first substantial income for a Millar literary work was, however, generated by his wife. Launching her own career as a successful mystery novelist, Margaret Millar published her first book, The Invisible Worm, in 1941. Her success enabled her husband to quit teaching high school and accept a fellowship at the University of Michigan, which granted him an M.A. degree in English in 1943.

From 1944 to 1946 Macdonald was in the United States Naval Reserve, serving as a communications officer on an escort carrier in the Pacific and taking part in the battle for Okinawa. Discharged with the rank of lieutenant junior grade, he settled in Santa Barbara, California, where his wife and daughter had moved during his Navy service. He resumed his graduate studies at the University of Michigan in 1948 and obtained his Ph.D. degree there in 1951 on acceptance of his dissertation, "The Inward Eye: A Study of Coleridge's Psychological Criticism." "The leap from Coleridge . . . to the American detective novel is not so unlikely . . . as it first appears," Macdonald has said, as quoted in World Authors: 1950-1970. "Coleridge's American disciple Poe . . . invented the modern detective story and inspired Charles Baudelaire . . . [whose] Dandy . . . is one of the prototypes of the modern detective hero. . . ."

Meanwhile, partly motivated by his wife's continued success, Macdonald—still using his original name, Kenneth Millar—had begun to make his mark as a novelist. His first book, The Dark Tunnel (Dodd, 1944), a spy novel that he wrote while at the University of Michigan, dealt with the threat of Nazism and was described by critics as "breathtaking" and "a humdinger." Next came Trouble Follows Me (Dodd, 1946), written during his Navy service, in which a naval officer follows a murder trail from Hawaii to Detroit and then to San Francisco. It was praised for its realistic and nonstereotyped treatment of residents of Detroit's black ghetto in the smoldering aftermath of the race riots that beset the city in 1943.

For Alfred A. Knopf, Inc., which published most of his subsequent works, Macdonald next wrote Blue City (1947), a "Hammett-like novel of small-town corruption," and The Three Roads (1948), which dealt with the Oedipus theme. He then decided that he needed a pseudonym so that readers could distinguish the works of Kenneth Millar from the nine books that his wife, Margaret Millar, had published. Taking his father's first and middle names, Millar became John Macdonald. Then, to avoid public confusion with the established mystery writer John D. Macdonald, he randomly inserted the common Canadian name Ross between the first and last names, later dropping the name John altogether.

The first Millar novel published under the Macdonald name, The Moving Target (1949), introduced Lew Archer, private detective, who has since been the narrator of nearly all Macdonald novels. Although the novels abound with autobiographical allusions, Lew Archer —whose name was derived from Miles Archer, Sam Spade's murdered partner in Dashiell Hammett's Maltese Falcon—is not Macdonald's alter ego but a composite of several real-life detectives. Consistently a loner, Archer usually becomes involved in the beginning in what appears to be a simple and routine case but ultimately finds himself delving into the past to penetrate layer after layer of hidden relationships and tragic events.

The Moving Target also established California—especially Southern California—as the stage for Macdonald's fiction. Largely populated by relative newcomers lacking roots, California and its "rockslide culture" served as the perfect backdrop for novels emphasizing the alienation of individuals living without an established community value system. A persistent theme in Macdonald's works is the absence of human bonding in a technological society, and Archer's task often involves forging the links of relationship among estranged individuals. To do so, he must strip away the false fronts and ingenious masks that both the innocent and guilty have spent years devising to hide their true identities.

Through his protagonist, Lew Archer, Macdonald deals with corporate greed and technological destruction of the landscape in The Drowning Pool (1950); the impact of organized crime in The Way People Die (1951); and the guilt feelings of an idealistic son of wealthy parents in The Ivory Grin (1952). He treats "sex and sadism" in Find a Victim (1954) with "a nice sense of realism," according to a reviewer for Time (July 26, 1954); and exposes the decadence of contemporary Hollywood in The Barbarous Coast (1956). In Meet Me at the Morgue (1953), in which Lew Archer is not the protagonist, Macdonald explores the relationship between the psychological framework of the individual and the sociological framework of the community as he unravels the ramifications of a kidnapping.

During 1956-57 Macdonald experienced a personal crisis that he has described only as "seismic disturbances . . . in my life" and went with his family to the San Francisco Bay Area to undergo psychotherapy for a year. The experience marked a turning point in his life and career, enabling him to come to terms with his emotionally disrupted childhood. The result was a series of books—all within the detective genre—exploring rootlessness, the broken family, and the search for the lost father. "It took a good many years for me to get into my own background and see it and reflect it," he told Ed Wilcox of the New York Sunday News (November 21, 1971).

Returning to Santa Barbara in the summer of 1957, Macdonald taught creative writing in an adult education program and wrote some two dozen book reviews for the San Francisco Chronicle. His next novel, begun before he underwent psychotherapy, was The Doomsters (1958), a family saga featuring Lew Archer that marked, in his words, "a fairly clean break with the Chandler tradition" and enabled him to make his "own approach to the crimes and sorrows of life." He achieved what he termed a major "breakthrough" with The Galton Case (1959), in which Archer is assigned to locate a long missing father and solve a twenty-year-old murder. His purpose in writing the book was, as he told Clifford A. Ridley of the National Observer (July 31, 1976), to take the ancient Oedipus myth and "make it a modern myth in terms of my own biography."

Lew Archer is again excluded from Macdonald's The Ferguson Affair (1960), involving "blackmail, murder, organized robbery, mistaken identity, and kidnapping." He returns in The Wycherly Woman (1961) to solve a "wandering daughter" case; in The Zebra-Striped Hearse (1962), a Freudian "family fantasy"; in Chill (1964), involving a disappearing bride; in The Far Side of the Dollar (1965), a modern, inverted version of the myth of Ulysses and Penelope; in Black Money (1966), which combines international crime and academic intrigue; in Instant Enemy (1968), in which two teen-agers seek revenge against an insensitive adult world; and in The Goodbye Look (1969), a modern version of the tale of Pandora's box.

Macdonald's abiding interest in conservation is reflected in his highly praised The Underground Man (1971), in which Archer is called upon to solve an "ecological crime"—a man-made forest fire—as well as a related murder and kidnapping. Ecology is also the theme of Sleeping Beauty (1973), inspired by the 1967 oil spill near Santa Barbara, which examines the fragile relationship between the human and natural orders. In The Blue Hammer (1976), Archer's investigation of the mystery of a stolen painting leads him to uncover murder and intrigue.

Other books by Macdonald include a collection of short stories, The Name is Archer (Bantam, 1955), and a volume of essays, On Crime Writing (Capra Press, 1973), and he is the editor of William F. Nolan's Dashiell Hammett: a Casebook (McNally & Loftin, 1969). Several of his novels are included in his omnibus volumes Archer in Hollywood (1967), Archer at Large (1970), and Archer in Jeopardy (1979). Over the years he has written stories, essays, and reviews for magazines and newspapers. A motion picture version of Macdonald's The Moving Target was released by Warner Brothers in 1966 with the title Harper, starring Paul Newman, who was also featured in the film adaptation of The Drowning Pool (Warner, 1975). In mid-1979 filming was being completed on Double Negative, adapted from Macdonald's The Three Roads.

Much of the richness of a Macdonald novel may be attributed to the intricate plot and subplots that keep the precise nature of relationships and the identity of evil-doers unclear until the end. Yet Macdonald novels offer far more in literary quality than their clever and unexpected twists of plot. Unusual for detective fiction in that they inspire rereading, his books are highly stylized, relying heavily upon metaphor to evoke images of a distinctly intellectual nature. Although some critics have pounced on Macdonald for making Archer sound more like a Ph.D. in English literature than the modestly educated gumshoe he is supposed to be, he has gained the admiration of such leading contemporary novelists as Eudora Welty, who cites the "delicacy and tension" of his style, as well as his "spare, controlled narrative, built for action and speed," and the "almost unbroken series of sparkling pictures" that it conveys to the reader.

The Mystery Writers of America organization, of which Macdonald was president in 1965, has bestowed on him Edgar Allan Poe scrolls, in 1962 and 1963, and the Grand Master Award in 1974. His honors also include the 1965 Silver Dagger and 1966 Golden Dagger awards of the Crime Writers Association of London. Macdonald is a member of the Authors League of America, the Writers Guild of the American West, the Coral Casino of Santa Barbara, the American Civil Liberties Union, and the Sierra Club, and he helped to found the Santa Barbara chapter of the National Audubon Society. He is a Democrat.

Ross Macdonald and his wife, Margaret Millar, who are grandparents, had one daughter, Linda (Mrs. Joseph Pagnusat), who died in 1970. Unaffected by the adulation bestowed on him in recent years, Macdonald leads a simple life at his home in Santa Barbara's oceanside community of Hope Ranch. He spends three or four hours a day writing, filling spiral notebooks at a rate of about three pages a day while sitting in the same bedroom chair in which he has composed all of his books for three decades. He often works on several book ideas at once, sometimes obtaining his plots by attending local criminal trials.

A 200-pound six-footer, with blue eyes and graying black hair, Macdonald dresses casually and speaks softly with a trace of Scottish-Canadian accent. He prefers the tranquillity of the library in his hilltop home to the literary limelight and rarely ventures far from Santa Barbara, opting instead to spend his leisure hours bird-watching with his wife. But, as a dedicated conservationist, he has occasionally come out of his self-imposed seclusion to take part in protests against the encroachment of technology on the natural environment.

References: Esquire 101:148+ Je '72 por; N Y Times Bk R p1+ Je 1 '69 por; Nat Observer p17 Jl 31 '76 por; Newsday A p3 N 26 '74 por; Newsweek 77:101+ Mr 22 '71 pors; Contemporary Authors 1st rev vols 9-12 (1974); Contemporary Novelists (1976); Encyclopedia of Mystery and Detection (1976); Speir, Jerry. Ross Macdonald (1978); Who's Who in America, 1978-79; Wolfe, Peter. Dreamers Who Live Their Dreams: The World of Ross Macdonald's Novels (1976); World Authors: 1950-1970 (1975)

McIntyre, James T(almadge), Jr.

Dec. 17, 1940- United States government official. Address: b. Office of Management and Budget, Executive Office Building, Washington, D.C. 20503

The resignation of Bert Lance on September 21, 1977 as director of the Office of Management and Budget (OMB) in the executive office of President Jimmy Carter thrust James T. McIntyre Jr., a relatively unknown lawyer, into the national limelight. In his native Georgia, McIntyre had won distinction on the state level as director of the Office of Planning and Budget under the governorship of Carter and that of his successor. After Carter was elected President in November 1976 he invited his former state budget director to Washington to become deputy director of the OMB. With Lance's departure, McIntyre was named acting director, and on March 24, 1978, having obtained the Senate's unanimous confirmation, he took office as the sixth director of the OMB since its establishment in 1970.

McIntyre's responsibilities in his $57,500-a-year post include helping the President to prepare the federal budget, which projected expenditures of some $600 billion for fiscal 1981; supervising its control and administration and coordinating budget policy throughout the executive branch; formulating the fiscal program of the United States; and implementing the President's plans for reorganizing the government on a more economical and efficient basis. Although McIntyre does not consider himself a fiscal conservative he is concerned with fiscal responsibility and believes that government agencies should justify all expenditures, but without sacrificing real needs.

James Talmadge McIntyre, Jr. was born on December 17, 1940 in Vidalia, Georgia, an onion-growing and tobacco-marketing town that serves as a business center for a largely rural area. His parents still live in Vidalia. McIntyre's middle name was not derived from any relationship to Georgia's former Governor Eugene Talmadge or Senator Herman E. Talmadge. "I think I was named for a preacher," his father, James Talmadge McIntyre Sr., has said. McIntyre attended local public schools and Young Harris, a Methodist junior college in Young Harris, Georgia, of which Bert Lance's father was once president. He earned his B.A. degree from the University of Georgia, and in 1963 he received a J.D. degree from its school of law. To help finance his education, McIntyre worked during vacations as a clerk in a Macon drugstore and at an Atlanta post office.

After his admission to the Georgia bar, McIntyre practised law in Athens, Georgia, and in 1964 he joined the staff of the University of Georgia's Institute of Government. As general counsel to the Georgia Municipal Association from July 1966 to April 1970 he represented it on boards and commissions and helped to implement legislative programs for local governments. From 1970 to 1972, McIntyre was deputy to the state revenue commissioner, John A. Blackmon. Concurrently, he served in 1971 as legal counsel to the Reorganization and Management Improvement Study, established by Governor Jimmy Carter, whom he first met during the 1970 gubernatorial campaign. In 1972 Carter appointed him project director of his State and Local Government Coordination Study.

After the director of Georgia's Office of Planning and Budget resigned in October 1972, under fire for alleged misuse of state personnel and expense vouchers, Carter appointed McIntyre to take over the post. "His work on the local government study and with the state revenue department has been outstanding," Carter commented, as quoted in the Atlanta Constitution (October 11, 1972), "and I am completely confident that the same will be true in his new position." McIntyre played a key role in Carter's reorganization of Georgia's government and in his introduction of zero-based budgeting to the state. In addition to managing the state budget, he was responsible for directing state planning efforts, intergovernmental relations, management improvement, regional commissions, conservation of energy, promotion of the arts, and supervision of Georgia's coastal zone. George Busbee, Carter's successor as governor and an outspoken critic of his administration, demonstrated his confidence in McIntyre by reappointing him as budget director following his November 1975 election victory.

Shortly after his election as President in November 1976, Jimmy Carter invited McIntyre to Washington. Early in 1977 Carter formally nominated him to serve under Bert Lance as deputy director of the Office of Management and Budget, an agency in the Executive Office of the President and in March the Senate unanimously confirmed the appointment. Carter named McIntyre acting director of the OMB on September 21, 1977 after Congressional criticism of director Bert Lance's practices as a private banker prompted him to resign. As Jody Powell, the President's press secretary, explained, "Jim McIntyre has been intimately involved in the budget process since he got here. The President is quite confident of his ability to handle the ongoing processes there until a considered opinion can be made." Most commentators assumed that McIntyre would lead the OMB only temporarily. They expected Carter eventually to appoint as permanent director a well-known public figure like Robert S. Strauss of Texas, or a high-ranking executive in banking or industry, who could serve as a liaison between the White House and the business community.

On October 2, 1977 President Carter announced that he was completely satisfied with McIntyre's performance and indicated that he would not name a director until the budget for fiscal 1979—due in January 1978—was completed. Some observers, including James Reston of the New York Times, questioned Carter's decision to delay such an important nomination, and Democratic Senator William Proxmire of Wisconsin suggested that McIntyre might be violating the Vacancies Act, which prohibits persons from serving more than thirty days as the acting leaders of executive departments whose heads are subject to Senate confirmation. On December 27, 1977 President Carter announced the nomination of McIntyre as director of the OMB, praising him as "a professional in every sense of the word," and "a dedicated career public servant."

The appointment was described in the New York Times (December 30, 1977) as "puzzling, and somewhat disappointing," and some of McIntyre's friends questioned whether he was capable of replacing Lance as a spokesman for the Administration. An analyst for Business Week expressed doubt in an unsigned article that McIntyre could operate as an equal in an economic triumvirate that also included the chairman of the Council of Economic Advisers, Charles L. Schultze, and the Secretary of the Treasury, W. Michael Blumenthal, and suggested that the influence of the OMB would diminish under him. The same writer predicted that McIntyre would concentrate on the details of the budget and on government reorganization while Carter would be his own chief budget analyst and would thereby, in the opinion of at least one Capital Hill aide, be required to expend "an awful lot of political capital for nothing."

Some observers found the selection of McIntyre neither surprising nor politically risky. According to Time (January 9, 1978), the choice reflected the President's desire to have a competent technician in charge of the OMB after the flamboyant and controversial Lance. One former Georgia official explained: "My betting was on Jim from the very start after Bert left. You know, some Presidents don't like to talk figures and details. But Carter does . . . and he liked the way Jim McIntyre did things in Georgia." Political commentators generally recognized McIntyre's technical competence, which Stuart Eizenstat, the President's domestic policy adviser, described as "exceptional," and, according to Nation's Business (February 1978), the OMB director was a "lot more aggressive than most Washington pundits [seemed] to think." In a letter to the editor of the New York Times (January 16, 1978), Georgia's Governor George Busbee described McIntyre as a "lawyer-accountant-philosopher who has the ability to cut through the bureaucratic muck and mire and discern between actual program needs and mere empire building."

At the swearing-in ceremony in the Rose Garden of the White House on March 24, 1978, the President described his new OMB director as "something of an anomaly in the Carter administration—he's well qualified for the job he holds." In his own behalf, McIntyre had said earlier: "I want to run the sharpest, brightest agency in town. And there's a tremendous amount of talent in OMB that can enable me to do it." Although McIntyre, who tries to play down his Georgia background, considers his relationship with Carter "more professional than personal," he speaks his mind frankly to the President. "I don't mind telling him what I think," he told Jerome Cahill of the New York *Daily News* (December 28, 1977), "because that what he's got me around for."

Discussing what he considered the major responsibilities of the OMB under his direction, McIntyre told a reporter for *Business Week* (January 9, 1978): "We try to bring to the President's attention those programs that are of a big policy nature, have a big dollar impact, or are of special concern to Congress." The OMB chief elaborated on his principles in an interview in *Nation's Business* (February 1978). Although he doubted the feasibility of the President's earlier goal of balancing the budget by 1981, he asserted that budget deficits should not be permitted to become "a permanent feature on the economic landscape." He also said that public expenditures in the long run should not exceed 21 percent of the gross national product, and that the government should cut income taxes as inflation automatically increases its share of the incomes of individual taxpayers. Aware that the federal government "must meet critical national needs, particularly in human resources," McIntyre called for bold programs to generate private sector jobs, especially for minority groups and teenagers.

As quoted in *Forbes* (July 24, 1978), McIntyre estimated that "75 percent of the budget today is uncontrollable . . . , it encompasses spending formulas mandated by law and contract commitments made in previous years." He has also noted that "our society has become fragmented and highly consumed by the economic demands of individual groups" and that efforts to cut programs inevitably run into stiff opposition. Nevertheless, he has tried to reduce the budget deficit by limiting spending programs and continuing Bert Lance's plans for zero-based budgeting—that is, requiring federal agencies to recalculate their budgetary needs each year. Along with the President's other economic advisers, McIntyre has advocated the scaling down of Congressional appropriations for transportation and public works. In the spring of 1978 he helped to persuade Carter to reduce his proposed tax cut from $25 billion to $19.4 billion and to modify his plans for a system of national health insurance. While favoring the President's voluntary anti-inflation program, calling for co-

operation of business, labor, and government, McIntyre is opposed to direct government controls, which, he feels, "can't work in our complex society."

In February 1978 McIntyre announced that the OMB would establish, under the management of the Department of Defense, a Federal Procurement Data System and Data Center to monitor the approximately $80 billion annually spent on government contracts. He reported the following month that federal agencies would begin purchasing food according to the Agriculture Department's general specifications instead of special government standards that reduced competition among sellers and raised prices. Despite his efforts, McIntyre was not able to reduce the budget deficit to $40 billion for fiscal 1979, as he had predicted in November 1977. But he hoped to meet the President's goal of bringing the budget gap down from the $51 billion envisioned for 1979 to $37.5 billion in fiscal 1980 and to $17 billion in 1981.

Much of the responsibility for fulfilling President Carter's promise to make the federal government more efficient has fallen on McIntyre's shoulders. He assumed a leading role in formulating plans for a new Cabinet-level Department of Education and a Federal Emergency Management Agency. As proposed, the former would take over most of the education-related programs under the departments of Health, Education and Welfare, Housing and Urban Development, Agriculture, Defense, and Interior, and under the National Science Foundation. The latter would consolidate, at annual savings of up to $15,000,000, five existing agencies that deal with civil defense and disaster relief.

To cut red tape, McIntyre has announced, the OMB's Office of Federal Procurement Policy will coordinate the efforts of the General Services Administration and the Department of Defense to eliminate the multitude of procurement forms currently in use. He has assured state officals that the administration would simplify the planning requirements imposed on state and local governments seeking federal aid. In October 1978 President Carter named McIntyre head of the new National Productivity Council, established to increase efficiency in both the public and private sectors of the economy. A year later, McIntyre added to his tasks the overall responsibility for a new civil rights office set up in the OMB to coordinate action in government agencies.

Convinced that government could be made more effective and responsive to citizens by improving the morale and productivity of the federal work force, McIntyre has urged support of President Carter's program to revamp the civil service system and to make it easier to reward efficient employees and dismiss incompetent ones. He has also called for more incentive pay and fewer automatic increases for federal employees. While admitting that effective government reorganization could take several years, he feels that some progress has already been made.

Since taking office as OMB director, McIntyre has borne the brunt of much of the criticism leveled against the Carter administration's budgetary policies. Barton Biggs, the research chief of the investment banking firm of Morgan Stanley and Company, quoted in *Esquire* (May 23, 1978), described McIntyre as "a nice, naïve, not terribly bright lawyer from Georgia . . . without a questioning bone in his body" and criticized what he considered the OMB director's lack of concern about the budget deficit. Joseph Pechman, a Brookings Institution economist, charged that the 1979 budget contained "no significant new proposals for economizing," and Jack Carlson, chief economist of the National Chamber of Commerce and a former OMB official, complained that the OMB director lacked rapport with key Cabinet officials and predicted that there would be "no serious budget cutting with McIntyre there." Other critics charged that McIntyre lacked enough knowledge of federal programs to establish clear priorities for allocating limited budget resources and characterized him as an ineffective administrator overly concerned with details.

Despite such criticism, McIntyre's work in preparing the President's austerity budget for fiscal 1980 did much to enhance his reputation and prompted informed observers to describe him as the second most important man in Washington and "a backstage strongman of this Administration." In October 1979 McIntyre told reporters that, provided there was no tax cut, an expected increase in revenues in fiscal 1981 could bring the budget "very close to a balance" without sacrificing "the needs of the disadvantaged."

Although James T. McIntyre Jr. calls people by their first names on short acquaintance, he is not a backslapper and shuns the social life of the capital. The soft-spoken, slightly-built Georgian is different in personality and style from his predecessor, who was one of the most visible members of the administration. "He is a man of few words," a friend has commented, "but he makes those count." The OMB director is married to the former Maureen Ball, a non-practising veterinarian. With their three daughters they live on a five-acre farm in Clifton, Virginia. McIntyre is usually at his desk by 7:30 A.M. and often drives the family pick-up truck the twenty miles to his office in downtown Washington. He likes to work with his hands and has used some of his spare time to build a barn for the family's Arabian horses. He does his own plumbing and jokingly tells friends that "all you have to know is that water doesn't run uphill and that the hot water spigot is on the left and the cold on the right."

References: Bsns W p24+ Ja 9 '78 por; Nations Bsns 66:64+ F '78 por; N Y Times B p5 S 23 '77 por; Time 111:34 Ja 9 '78 por; Who's Who in America, 1978-79

McWhirter, Norris (Dewar)

Aug. 12, 1925 Writer; publisher. Address: b. Guinness Superlatives Ltd., 2 Cecil Court, London Rd., Enfield EN2 6DJ, Middlesex, England

Since its debut in 1955, the British *Guinness Book of Records* (known in the United States as the *Guinness Book of World Records*), compiled by Norris and the late Ross McWhirter, has become a worldwide best seller. Listing thousands of both obscure and well-known records on everything from staying awake (Roger Guy English, 288 hours) to the world's heaviest cat (42 pounds, 10 ounces), the Guinness book has sold 35,000,000 copies and has been translated into twenty-one languages, making it one of the best-selling books of all time. It has spurred thousands of would-be record-holders to try to get their names into its pages, launching a fad that *Sports Illustrated* has dubbed "Guinnessport."

As director of Guinness Superlatives Ltd., publisher of the world's most popular reference work, Norris McWhirter engages in voluminous correspondence and travels thousands of miles in order to keep the book up-to-date, a task he once shared with his collaborator and twin brother Ross, who was gunned down by Irish Republican Army terrorists in 1975. A stickler for accuracy, Mc-

Whirter insists on verification for each of the book's 15,000 entries—most of which he has committed to memory. In addition to compiling the *Guinness Book of Records*, McWhirter is the author or coauthor of a number of related books, including the *Dunlop Illustrated Encyclopedia of Facts* (Sterling, 1973) and the *Guinness Sports Record Book* (Sterling, 1976). He is also a television commentator for the BBC.

Norris Dewar McWhirter was born at 7:40 P.M. in London, England on August 12, 1925, the son of William Allan and Margaret (Williamson) McWhirter. His identical twin brother, Alan Ross, was born exactly twenty minutes later. Of Scottish descent, the McWhirters can trace their family tree back to 1696. Norris McWhirter's grandfather, William McWhirter, invented the voltameter and ammeter, and his father, William Allan McWhirter, was a distinguished Fleet Street newspaperman and publisher, the first Englishman to edit three national papers—the *Sunday Pictorial*, the *Sunday Dispatch*, and the *Daily Mail*. According to Norris McWhirter, his father "started 11 newspapers from scratch in the provinces and was managing director of both Northcliffe Newspapers, which he virtually founded, and the Associated Newspapers." An elder brother, Kennedy Graeme McWhirter, is a barrister.

Fascinated by facts from an early age, the McWhirter twins reportedly read scores of newspapers a week as youngsters, and their favorite book was *Whitaker's Almanack*. Both were educated at the public schools of Chesterton and Marlborough. From 1943 to 1946 the twins served in the Royal Navy, where they were separated for the first time in their lives. Norris was made a sub-lieutenant in the Royal Navy Volunteer Reserve, assigned to the second escort group in the Atlantic and was later assigned to a minesweeper in the Pacific; Ross was posted to a minesweeper in the Mediterranean. They met only once during the war, when their ships collided in Malta harbor. Later the twins attended Trinity College, Oxford, where Norris took his B.A. degree in international relations and economics and his M.A. in contract law in 1948. At Oxford they both belonged to the same record-setting relay team. As the slightly faster athlete of the two, Norris also competed abroad, in Scotland and Norway.

After graduating from Oxford the twins moved back to their parents' home. Norris worked as a freelance sportswriter and Ross covered rugby and tennis for the *Star*. The two continued the extremely close relationship of their childhood. One of their friends told Arturo F. Gonzalez of *Parade* magazine (September 5, 1976): "They had minds like Japanese calculators. They talked to each other in a code that only they fully comprehended. One would start a sentence and the other would finish it up. When you called them on the phone you never could really be sure which one you were talking to. I remember that Norris once had to make a quick trip to Paris and couldn't find his own passport, so he just took Ross'. Nobody noticed the difference." Another close friend observed that Norris "was the senior partner of the two. He was a better sprinter than Ross, and I've always felt that he was a little better in everything. My impression is that Ross tended to follow."

From 1951 to 1960 Norris McWhirter was a sportswriter for the *Star* and, from 1951 to 1967, for the London *Observer*. For a while he and Ross produced, a short-lived track magazine, *Athletics World*. In 1951 he became managing director of McWhirter Twins Ltd., a fact-gathering service for advertisers, newspapers, writers, yearbooks, and encyclopedias, and on his father's death in 1955 he became chairman of William McWhirter & Sons.

In 1954 the famous Anglo-Irish brewery known as Arthur Guinness, Son & Co., hired the firm of McWhirter Twins Ltd., to compile a book of records. According to the widely circulated story, Sir Hugh Beaver, managing director of Guinness, was fowl-hunting along the Irish coast when he and a companion disagreed over what was the fastest game bird. On discovering that the information was not available and that no book of superlatives or records existed, Sir Hugh commissioned the McWhirters to write one, thinking it might be used in pubs to help settle heated arguments. A subsidiary, Guinness Superlatives Ltd., in which McWhirter today holds a substantial interest and the title of managing director, was established to publish it.

Working around the clock, the McWhirter brothers assembled a slim, 198-page volume in sixteen weeks at a cost of $35,000. The first printing of 187,000 copies published in October 1955 in time for the Christmas rush, was an immediate success, and within four months the *Guinness Book of Superlatives* was England's number one best seller in the nonfiction category. Since 1956, when the McWhirters published a new, revised, and greatly enlarged edition, the *Guinness Book of Records*, as it is now titled, has been updated, revised and reissued at regular intervals. In Great Britain the publisher is Guinness Superlatives Ltd., the largest single market for the book, however, is the United States, where Sterling Publishing Company holds the hardcover rights and Bantam the paperback rights. Of the 4,500,-000 copies sold worldwide in 1978, almost 3,000,000 were sold in America.

Encouraged by the success of the *Guinness Book of Records*, Norris and Ross went on to write other books, many of them spinoffs of the Guinness work, but aimed at a juvenile audience. The first edition of the *Dunlop Book of Facts* (Dreghorn, 1964), prepared in collaboration with the Dunlop Rubber Company, was issued in 1964. Other titles include the *Guinness Book of Olympic Records* (Sterling, 1964); *Surprising Facts About Plants* (Franklin

Watts, 1972); *Surprising Facts About Kings and Rulers* (Franklin Watts, 1973); *Guinness Book of Amazing Achievement* (Sterling, 1975); *Guinness Sports Record Book* (Sterling, 1976); *Guinness Book of Surprising Accomplishments* (Sterling, 1977); *Guinness Game Book* (Sterling, 1978); and *Guinness Book of Startling Acts and Facts* (Sterling, 1978). In addition, the McWhirter twins collaborated on *Get to Your Marks* (Kaye, 1950). Norris has contributed to the *Encyclopaedia Britannica, Encyclopaedia Britannica Yearbook, Modern Athletics,* and the *Encyclopedia of Sport.*

As a television commentator, McWhirter covered the Olympic Games for the BBC for more than a decade, from 1960 to 1972. He also hosted *What's In the Picture* (1957) and, since 1972, *The Record Breakers,* a children's show based on the Guinness book. On May 6, 1954 he was public address announcer at the historic track meet at Iffley Road near Oxford, when Roger Bannister broke the four-minute mile. Anticipating Bannister's stunning success, McWhirter had carefully rehearsed his dramatic "crescendo-suspense" announcement in his bathtub the night before the race took place.

Encouraged by their growing public recognition, Norris and Ross McWhirter ventured into national politics. As staunch Conservatives, they opposed what they viewed as Great Britain's pervasive unionism, government bureaucracy, and permissiveness. In the late 1950's, according to a piece by Jerry Kirshenbaum in *Sports Illustrated* (July 30, 1979), they once "mischievously disrupted a ban-the-bomb rally by using a car with a loudspeaker on top to direct unsuspecting marchers into a field." In 1964 both men ran for Parliament on the Conservative ticket in different districts and lost, with each receiving, strangely enough, 19,000 odd votes.

After his defeat in the 1964 election Norris McWhirter left most of the political crusading to Ross. Nevertheless, as Kirshenbaum noted in his article, "Although Ross was more visibly involved in politics, longtime friends . . . know better than to downplay Norris McWhirter's role." Among Ross's more publicized battles were his 1973 attempt to stop the BBC from showing a 45-minute film about Andy Warhol that contained elements of nudity and homosexuality and a 1975 writ of injunction he succeeded in winning against striking ferry workers.

An outspoken foe of Irish Republican Army terrorists, Ross McWhirter once published a pamphlet entitled *How To Beat the Bombers* and offered $102,000 for the conviction of terrorists. On the evening of November 27, 1975 two IRA gunmen shot and killed him on the doorstep of his home in suburban London, less than a mile from the offices of Guinness Superlatives Ltd. Fifteen months later, on February 10, 1977, four IRA terrorists were given life sentences after being convicted of six killings,

including the murders of Ross McWhirter and Gordon Hamilton-Fairley, a noted cancer expert, a 1975 kidnapping, and a series of bombings. Deeply shaken by his brother's death, Norris McWhirter told the press, "To take action on one's principles is a very, very rare thing, and that's what Ross was doing . . . He was absolutely doing the right thing." In 1976 he wrote a book, *Ross: The Story of a Shared Life* (Churchill Press, 1976), about his life with his brother. In the opening paragraph of its Preface, Norris McWhirter wrote: "This account of my twin brother's life began as a piece of private therapy very soon after his assassination. That it has become a book at all is due to the insistence of friends who were determined that there should be something less remote than an unmarked grave, references in law books and a Memorial Fund."

After the violent death of Ross, Norris McWhirter briefly considered abandoning their pet project, the *Guinness Book of Records.* He had always felt, as he once put it, that he and his twin brother had looked upon their "individual experiences as collective." But eventually he decided against it. As he assured Arturo F. Gonzalez during the interview for *Parade:* "Not a day goes by here that we don't all miss Ross terribly, but I know he would want us to continue as we have, despite his being gone."

Norris McWhirter operates out of the top floor of a three-story building in the north London suburb of Enfield, which still has a mailbox bearing Ross McWhirter's name. There he continues to maintain the high level of accuracy that has characterized the *Guinness Book of Records* since its inception, through the judicious use of photographs, news clippings, and eyewitnesses to record-breaking events. He receives something like 20,000 letters a year, queries dozens of experts, and conducts firsthand research in hundreds of nonfiction books and periodicals. "You develop a technique in reading so that words like longest, shortest, biggest, and other 'ests' jump out at you," he has said. McWhirter disavows comparisons between himself and less scrupulously accurate predecessors such as Robert Ripley of *Believe-It-Or-Not* fame. "That Ripley," he told a writer for *People* (September 16, 1974), "used the greatest title in the world. His facts didn't have to be correct, just interesting."

Although the *Guinness Book of Records* contains records on nearly every subject imaginable, from yachting and pigeon racing to the art of running backwards, roughly one-fourth of it is devoted to sports. Still, it is the more quirky records, such as shoe-shining, and balancing on one foot that have aroused the most interest, a curiosity the publicity-conscious McWhirter encourages by issuing certificates and selling Guinness ties to record-breakers.

The tremendous success of the Guinness book has stimulated dozens of commercial spinoffs, such as greeting cards, cereal boxes, puzzles, notebooks, jump ropes, Dixie cups, and calendars. Guinness museums have sprung up in the Empire State Building and various other places. A television program with David Frost, a show at Radio City Music Hall, and a cartoon strip syndicated in some 100 newspapers have also showcased Guinness material.

"Guinnessport"—the sport of getting one's name into the Guinness Book of Records—has flourished in recent years, especially in the hospitable atmosphere of the United States. Its participants, according to Sports Illustrated, consist of "fraternity boys, failed athletes, assorted crazies, and maybe even some normal folk." Occasionally mass Guinness "olympics" are held in such places as New South Wales, London, San Antonio, and Los Angeles. "By acting as a kind of clearinghouse," McWhirter told Jerry Kirshenbaum, "the book is a catalyst for a lot of record-breaking. Nowadays, a record only has to be printed for somebody else to break it." Defending the inclusion of "crazy" entries in the Guinness Book of Records, McWhirter has said: "What many people don't realize is that only 3 % of the book is devoted to zany records. . . . Life isn't all frivolous, I know that. But it's not all serious, either. It's the same with records. There's room for all kinds."

On December 28, 1957 Norris McWhirter married Carole Eckert, a former student of gourmet cookery at the Cordon Bleu, whom he met on a skiing vacation. They have a daughter, Jane, and a son, Alasdair. McWhirter is a gray-haired, gray-eyed, and sharp-featured man, who stands five feet nine inches tall and weighs about 170 pounds. He is a member of the Royal Institution, the Association of Track and Field Statisticians, the Society of Genealogists, and a past member of the Sports Council. His clubs include the Caledonian, Vincent's (Oxford), and Achilles. He is a member of the Church of England.

Thirty years of compiling records and statistics have not quenched McWhirter's interest in the odd or unusual. He told one interviewer: "People are fascinated with extremes. They like to know what the steel brackets are around a given subject. . . . People crave delineation and points of reference. It's a matter of orientation, but it's also part of the natural competitiveness that most of us have."

References: People p45+ S 16 '74 pors; Sport Illus p55+ F 8 '65; Jl 30 '79 pors; Contemporary Authors vols 13-14 (1975); McWhirter, Norris. Ross: The Story of a Shared Life (1976); Who's Who, 1978-79

Menotti, Gian Carlo (mā-nôt′tē jän kär′lō)

July 7, 1911- Composer; dramatist; director. Address: b. c/o Thea Dispeker, 59 E. 54th St., New York City, N.Y. 10022

NOTE: This biography supersedes the article that appeared in Current Biography in 1947.

The most often performed living composer of opera is Gian Carlo Menotti, who has brought to traditional opera the realism and freshness of contemporary theatre. The Italian-born Menotti, who immigrated to the United States in 1928, was hailed as a neoromantic giant, a latter-day Puccini, when he came to prominence with the Broadway successes of his fifth opera, the macabre thriller The Medium, in 1946, and his sixth, the grim political tragedy The Consul, in 1950. Both of those operas have been given hundreds of performances in the major opera houses of the world, and they are considered modern classics, along with The Saint of Bleecker Street (1954) and Amahl and the Night Visitors (1951), which ranks close to A Christmas Carol as perennial Christmas fare. As atonal, aleatory, and electronic music came into vogue, Menotti's conventional techniques lost him some currency with many critics, but his general popularity has never

wavered. Menotti writes his own librettos, usually in English, provides his own orchestration, and directs productions of his works.

Besides operas, he has composed ballets, concertos for piano and violin, song cycles, and a symphony, among other musical forms. A cofounder of the Festival of Two Worlds, Menotti has resigned as artistic director and general manager but remains president of that annual multi-artistic event.

When his biographer John Gruen asked him what he would consider the most peculiar aspect of his style, Menotti replied: "I think I have contributed a very personal kind of recitative, beginning with *The Medium*, which I consider the fundamental work upon which I base all my other operas. The problem of the *parlar cantando* has always fascinated me. I felt somehow that no composer had yet solved the problem of making people talk and act a story in musical terms."

Gian Carlo Menotti, the sixth of eight children of Alfonso and Ines (Pellini) Menotti, was born in Cadegliano, a small town on Lake Lugano in Lombardy, northern Italy, on July 7, 1911. The family was well-to-do, enjoying income from a coffee exporting firm run by an uncle, Francesco Menotti, and—in absentia, by Alfonso Menotti—in Colombia, South America. It was also, as Gian Carlo told John Gruen, a family touched with "madness" here and there: for example, on the very day of his ordination, Francesco had left the Roman Catholic priesthood, and another relative, Liline Bianchini, who taught Gian Carlo to play the organ, had religious "hallucinations."

"This strain of madness in the Menotti family," John Gruen wrote in *Menotti, A Biography* (1978), "would place Gian Carlo in touch with the strange and disquieting factors upon which he would draw during his creative life. . . . Like his brother Pier Antonio, who introduced him to the staging of puppet shows, Gian Carlo adopted that pastime for his own. [Also] as a young boy, Gian Carlo was deeply religious, having been raised in the Catholic Church and guided by the religious zeal of Don Rimoldi, [the] odd and imaginative parish priest [who] allow[ed] the children of Cadegliano to come and play games in the church . . . to dance and sing."

The greatest influence was Ines Menotti, the dominant parent, who saw to it that her children were taught piano, violin, and cello and who organized evening chamber musicales, with the result that her favorite son, Gian Carlo, often fell asleep with the sound of music in his ears. From the age of five he was setting verse to music at the piano, and when he was eleven he wrote his first opera, *The Death of Pierrot*, which was performed as a home puppet show. Two years later he wrote his second childhood opera, *The Little Mermaid*, based on Hans Christian Andersen's fairy tale.

In 1924 Ines Menotti persuaded her husband to move the family to Milan, where she enrolled Gian Carlo in the Verdi Conservatory of Music. During three years in Milan he saw countless operas performed at Teatro alla Scala, popularly known as La Scala, and, as he told John Gruen, he developed "a voracious appetite for reading," especially of fairy tales from around the world, and for "the exotic, the theatrical, the occult, and the decadent."

When Menotti was seventeen his father's death and the collapse of the family's coffee shipping firm changed his life radically. With his mother he traveled to Colombia, where she tried in vain to rescue that end of the business. In the fall of 1928, before sailing back to Italy, Ines Menotti took her son (who at that time knew little English) to the Curtis Institute of Music in Philadelphia, armed with a letter from the wife of conductor Arturo Toscanini recommending him to Rosario Scalero, the school's celebrated professor of composition.

"The boy had some stuff in him, but he was most undisciplined and raw," Scalero later recounted. "Early on, I told him, 'Gian Carlo, if I am to teach you, we must come to an agreement, you and I. I promise you that I will be uncompromisingly severe. Do you promise to put in some very hard work, something you have never done before?' Well, Gian Carlo promised, and he abided by his agreement." Scalero, whose pedagogical system stressed the study and imitation of masterworks of the past, set his new pupil to writing motets and other pieces employing sixteenth-century counterpoint. Menotti felt he was undergoing "torture," but under Scalero's painful regimen he acquired self-reliance, resourcefulness, and thoroughness in learning and mastering the tools of composition.

The lifelong friendship between Menotti and the American composer Samuel Barber began at Curtis, where they were students together. After graduating, in 1933, they lived for several years in Austria, where, as Barber later recalled, they "wasted a lot of time going to wild parties" before settling down to work in a cottage in the rural village of St. Wolfgang, on Lake St. Wolfgang. There Menotti began to put on paper his first mature opera and one of the very few written in Italian, *Amelia al Ballo*, inspired by the Baroness von Montechivsky, one of the "very strange people" he had met in Vienna. At the time, opera was "very unfashionable," as Menotti recalled in one of his interviews with John Gruen. "And of course my teacher, Scalero, was always very scornful of opera. . . . I remember saying to myself, 'Well, I'll just write this one opera, and then I'll start composing all my symphonies, masses, and motets.' I guess *Amelia* was the beginning of my end."

Amelia al Ballo is a one-act *opera buffa* about a frivolous woman determined not to let her husband's murderous rage at being cuckolded stand in the way of her going to a gala ball; after dispatching husband to hospital and lover to jail, she attends the ball on the arm of the police chief investigating the case. The opera was translated into English by George Meade, and the English version, Amelia Goes to the Ball, was given its premiere in Philadelphia in 1937. The Italian version was first presented in San Remo, Italy a year later.

The success of Amelia Goes to the Ball at the Metropolitan Opera House and elsewhere led to a commission from the National Broadcasting Company for an opera for radio. For NBC, Menotti came up with another humorous one-act work, The Old Maid and the Thief, the story, set in a Pennsylvania town, of a "virtuous" spinster so smitten with her lodger, an attractive drifter, that she conspires to frame him as a criminal in order to keep him from moving on. That opera, broadcast in 1939, was later adapted for stage production.

Menotti's first attempt at "grand" opera was The Island God, which had its premiere at the Metropolitan Opera on February 20, 1942. In the libretto for The Island God, written in Italian by Menotti and translated into English by Fleming McLeish, the composer was concerned with a subject that has always fascinated him: the relation between faith and reality. Two men, religious skeptics shipwrecked on a Mediterranean island, come across the ruins of a Greek temple; in their despair they invoke the god worshiped there; and to their surprise they succeed in invoking him. The Island God was a resounding failure, perhaps one of the worst flops in the Met's history. While Menotti still thinks the idea of its libretto is a good one, he acknowledges that the opera was otherwise a youthful folly, heavy with "very bad Italian music," pretentious "noise." Faulty staging exacerbated The Island God's failure, in Menotti's view, and thereafter he insisted on directing his operas himself.

After writing his ballet Sebastian (1939) and his Piano Concerto in A minor (1945), Menotti returned to opera with the two-act chamber work The Medium (1946), which, like The Island God, is concerned with "whether belief was a creative power and whether skepticism could destroy creative powers." The plot of the opera had its origins in a séance Menotti once attended at the invitation of friends, where he was struck by the effectiveness of belief, or lack of it, in the area of the occult or supernatural. The title character of The Medium is Madame Flora, a fake spiritualist who, like the Sorcerer's Apprentice, cannot control the unseen forces she sets in motion. "Despite its eerie setting and gruesome conclusions," Menotti wrote in the liner notes for the Columbia recording of the opera, "The Medium is actually a play of ideas. It describes the tragedy of a woman caught between two worlds, a world of re-ality which she cannot comprehend and a supernatural world in which she cannot believe. [She] has no scruples in cheating her clients . . . until something happens which she herself has not prepared."

The Medium had its premiere at Columbia University in 1946 and it ran on Broadway, on a bill with the composer's one-act curtain-raising musical revue sketch The Telephone, for 211 performances in 1947. Four years later Lopert Films released a movie version directed by the composer. "From its ominous, crashing opening chords to its horrifying ending, this music drama never faltered or lost its grip on the audience," Joseph Sabin wrote of the The Medium in his contribution to The New Book of Modern Composers (1961), edited by David Ewen. . . . All of the elements that constitute Menotti's major contribution to the contemporary musical theatre are found at their best in The Medium: a naturalistic and musically adept handling of recitative, which blends imperceptibly into heightened melodic expression; a small orchestra employed with . . . consummate skill . . . ; a fully rounded dramatic treatment . . . ; melodic ideas of a more or less traditional character transformed by freely dissonant harmonic treatment and bizarre orchestral color; an intimacy of style and atmosphere more like the theatre than the opera house, but always translated into musical terms."

Menotti's ballet Errand into the Maze, a retelling of the story of Ariadne, was written for the Martha Graham Company in 1948. Between 1948 and 1955, the composer taught on and off at the Curtis Institute. After an abortive stint as a scriptwriter with Metro-Goldwyn-Mayer in Hollywood, he completed his first full-length opera, The Consul, a harrowing tragedy about political outcasts in a European totalitarian state seeking asylum through a foreign consulate but frustrated by its indifferent bureaucracy. "It carries on the tradition of the The Medium," Menotti has said of The Consul. "By that time my recitatives began to have a very definite style. Of course, thematically and musically The Consul is much stronger than The Medium."

The Consul opened in Philadelphia on March 1, 1950 and two weeks later it moved to Broadway, where it ran for 269 performances and won a Drama Critics Circle Award and a Pulitzer Prize. Its unequivocal triumphal reception in New York was repeated later in Europe, except in Italy. At La Scala it drew a tumult of boos and bravos that overflowed into the streets of Milan.

Again for NBC, Menotti wrote the one-act television opera Amahl and the Night Visitors, inspired by Hieronymus Bosch's painting "The Adoration of the Magi." The touching story of a crippled boy who is miraculously healed after he offers his crutches to the Three Wise Men as a gift for the Infant Jesus was first televised on December 24, 1951. Immensely popular, *Amahl and the Night Visitors* remained an annual NBC Christmas Eve presentation for thirteen years. In a survey of American opera companies and college and other groups covering the 1976-77 and 1977-78 seasons by *Opera News* (November 1978), *Amahl and the Night Visitors* in its stage-adapted form led all other contemporary operas in number of performances, with 587. *The Medium* was second, with 148.

After the pastoral peacefulness of *Amahl and the Night Visitors* Menotti turned again to what some critics called thunderous "verismo" in *The Saint of Bleecker Street,* a tragedy in three acts in an Italian neighborhood in New York City and dramatizing the conflict between cynical realism, personified in the unbelieving Michele, and mysticism, embodied in his sister, Annina, a stigmatic visionary who becomes a nun on her deathbed. Menotti has said that in *The Medium* and above all in the *The Saint of Bleecker Street* he was trying to express a duality in his own character: "I am definitely not a religious man. All the same I am haunted by religious problems. . . . The intense and incandescent faith which nourished my childhood and my adolescence have seared my soul forever. I've lost my faith, but it is a loss that has left me uneasy." First staged on Broadway in the 1954-55 season, *The Saint of Bleecker Street* was a commercial failure but a success with the critics, many of whom, like Menotti himself, viewed it as an improvement over *The Consul* melodically. It brought Menotti his second Pulitzer Prize.

The composer's *The Unicorn, the Gorgon, and the Manticore*—a "madrigal fable" about the three ages in the life of an artist—was given its premiere in Washington, D.C. in October 1956 and was presented by the New York City Ballet three months later. Even critics usually hostile to Menotti were enchanted by it.

The year 1958 was an eventful one in Menotti's career. On January 26, 1958 Samuel Barber's opera *Vanessa,* with libretto and stage direction by Menotti, had its premiere at the Metropolitan Opera. Five months later Menotti, in collaboration with the late Thomas Schippers, created the Festival of Two Worlds in Spoleto, Italy for the purpose of bringing together annually artists known and unknown, especially the young, from both sides of the Atlantic for the presentation of music, dance, poetry, drama, and other arts. In the years following, the festival proved such a boon to the town of Spoleto both culturally and economically that Menotti became—and remains—loved by the townspeople almost to the point of veneration.

Also in 1958, Menotti's opera *Maria Golovin,* about a man blinded outwardly by injury to his eyes and inwardly by jealousy, was given its world premiere at the Brussels World's Fair. That full-scale work is one of the composer's own favorites because he feels "very close to it," since it reflects "very much a part" of his own "suffering." But audiences did not share his point of view. After a cool reception in Brussels, in August 1958, *Maria Golovin* ran on Broadway for less than a week.

In 1959 Menotti provided librettos for operas by Samuel Barber (*A Hand of Bridge*) and Lukas Foss (*Introductions and Goodbyes*) and wrote the incidental music for Jean Cocteau's pantomime *Le Poète et Sa Muse.* During the same year, Menotti's *A Copy of Madame Aupic,* a nonmusical play, was staged in Paris, in an adaptation by Albert Husson. The protagonist of that comedy of manners is an art forger who attempts to apply his devious craft to life itself.

On March 3, 1963 NBC televised Menotti's mini-opera *Labyrinth,* a witty parable in which two newlyweds wander the halls of their hotel looking for the key to their room (life) only to find it at the exit desk (death). Also having their first performances in 1963 were the cantata *The Death of the Bishop of Brindisi* and the three-act comic opera *L'Ultimo Selvaggio,* translated by other hands into French as *Le Dernier Sauvage* and English as *The Last Savage.* French and American critics panned the latter—the story of a rich American girl who brings back the Abominable Snowman (actually the simple-minded servant of a maharajah who humors her) from India—but Italians applauded it. Smarting from the criticism of *The Last Savage,* Menotti abstained from writing conventional opera for several years.

Like *The Death of the Bishop of Brindisi, Martin's Lie* is built on recitative that is inspired in large measure by Gregorian chant. That one-act musical morality play about a medieval orphan killed by the Inquisition for hiding a heretic posing as his father, was given its premiere in Bristol (England) Cathedral in the spring of 1964. Some critics thought it was "maudlin," and Menotti conceded that "one day [he] will have to rework *Martin's Lie.*"

In June 1967 the Hamburg State Opera's production of Stravinsky's *The Rake's Progress,* with staging by Menotti, opened at the Metropolitan Opera House. According to Raymond Ericson of the New York *Times* (July 1, 1967), "He created a production that is up to Hamburg's high standards. He plays it straight. No tricks, no exaggerations, none of the opportunism he often demonstrates in his own works."

The following year Menotti wrote incidental music for Michael Cacoyannis' production of Shakespeare's *Romeo and Juliet* at France's Théatre National Populaire. At Christmas 1968 the Hamburg State Opera gave the first performance of his subtly polemical one-act children's opera *Help! Help! The Globolinks!,* about a group of children beleaguered by hostile aliens who communicate by electronic sounds—and who are finally destroyed by real violin music.

The Leper, a play with incidental music first performed at the Fine Arts Festival of Florida State University in Tallahassee in April 1970 is the most confessional of Menotti's works, an ambivalent polemic urging toleration of deviance only so long as it does not threaten the social order. John Gruen observes: "A careful reading of the play makes it clear that it is pitted mainly against the homosexual, or at least a certain kind of homosexual. This seems quite surprising, coming from Menotti. Although he has always refused to make any public statement about his private life, he has often said, when approached on the subject, 'My life is an open book; however, I don't like to leave it around.' "

Not many critics liked Menotti's The Most Important Man, an opera about racial conflict that was given its premiere by the New York City Opera on March 7, 1971, but the composer considers it one of his best works, on a par with The Saint of Bleecker Street, although difficult to cast. The opera Tamu-Tamu, commissioned by the Ninth International Congress of Anthropological and Ethnological Sciences and inspired by a news photo of a huddled Indonesian family cowering before the guns of soldiers, had its premiere in Chicago in 1973. Also in 1973, Menotti composed his Suite Number 62 for two cellos and piano.

Four new works by Menotti were given their world premieres in the summer of 1976: Landscapes and Remembrances, a cantata; The Hero, a bicentennial comedy; The Egg, his eighteenth opera, a companion piece to Martin's Lie; and his first symphony, The Halcyon. In the summer of 1977 the Festival of Two Worlds became a geographical reality with the first season of "Spoleto, USA" in Charleston, South Carolina. The night before the 1978 Festival of Two Worlds began in Charleston the composer attended the premiere of his twenty-five-minute opera The Trial of the Gypsy, performed by the Newark Boys Chorus at Lincoln Center.

Menotti's first attempt at an historical work of grand opera is La Loca, based on the tragic life of Queen Juana la Loca (Joan the Mad) of Spain, written as a fiftieth birthday present for Beverly Sills. Commissioned by the San Diego Opera, with funding by Lawrence E. Deutsch, La Loca had its world premiere in June 1979 in San Diego. Miss Sills sang the title role in six performances—presumed to be her farewell operatic appearances in New York City—with the New York City Opera beginning on September 16, 1979. The consensus of the mixed notices was that La Loca was inferior Menotti while allowing Miss Sills a tour de force performance.

Interviewers universally report that Gian Carlo Menotti is "charming" and that he looks far younger than his years. Menotti is a tall, slender man with an aquiline nose, piercing black eyes, and graying black hair. In the fall of 1973 he sold "Capricorn," the house he had long shared with composer Samuel Barber in Mount Kisco, New York, and bought "Yester House," a sixteenth-century mansion in the Lammermuir Hills of East Lothian, near Edinburgh, Scotland, where he composes and gardens. His entourage there includes a housekeeper, a butler, a secretary, and his adopted son, Chip. The composer also maintains an apartment in New York, and he retains his Italian citizenship.

References: N Y Daily News p3 My 19 '78 por; N Y Herald Tribune mag p36+ Ja 19 '64 por; New Yorker 39:49+ My 4 '63; Time 55:64 My 1 '50 por, 109:72+ Je 6 '77 por; Gruen, John. Menotti (1978); International Who's Who, 1977-78; Who's Who in America, 1978-79; Who's Who in Opera, 1976

Mihajlov, Mihajlo (mē-hī'lov)

Sept. 26, 1934- Yugoslav dissident; writer.
Address: c/o Mrs. Marija Ivusic,
3921 5th St. N. Apt. 2, Arlington, Va. 22203

"Arrested, tried, and bounced around from prison to prison," as he recently summed up his thirteen-year ordeal, the Yugoslav dissident and literary scholar Mihajlo Mihajlov has been in and out of jail since 1965 and is unable to publish his writing in his native country. The government has been particularly persistent in suppressing him because, unlike most other liberal critics of the Tito regime, Mihajlov has openly denounced the nation's one-party system. Although acknowledging in the 1960's that Yugoslavia was less repressive than the other Communist states, he has consistently maintained that so long as the Communist party possesses a monopoly of power, his country is totalitarian and vulnerable to a revival of Stalinist tyranny.

Mihajlo Mihajlov was born in Pancevo, Yugoslavia, near Belgrade, on September 26, 1934. His parents were Russian emigrés who met and married in Yugoslavia after leaving the Soviet Union during the famine that followed the Revolution. Mihajlov's father was an antifascist Partisan in World War II and for some years a director of the Yugoslav Scientific Institute. His mother, Vera Mihajlov, a former teacher, left Yugoslavia in the 1970's and joined her daughter, Marija Mihajlov Ivusic, in the United States, where

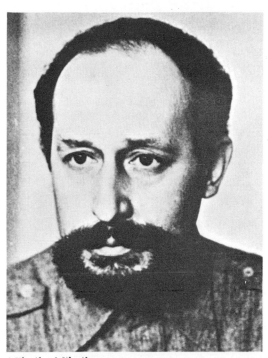

Mihajlo Mihajlov

non-Russian authors that reveal his rather extensive reading in modern Western literature.

During the summer of 1964 Mihajlov spent five weeks in Moscow and Leningrad under a cultural exchange program between Yugoslavia and the Soviet Union. He recounted his conversations with Russian writers in an essay published in two installments under the title "Moscow Summer 1964" in the January and February 1965 issues of the Belgrade literary periodical Delo. Discussing Soviet concentration camp literature, he wrote that the first death camps were established not by the Nazis but by the Soviets and that shortly before World War II Stalin committed genocide against peoples in regions along the Turkish-Iranian border. Mihajlov furthermore asserted that the process of de-Stalinization in the Soviet Union was far from complete and quoted a Moscow University student as saying that only Stalin's victims within the Communist party had been rehabilitated.

Yugoslav President Josip Broz Tito had himself attacked the Soviet Union following his break with Stalin in 1948. But in the early 1960's, as relations between Yugoslavia and the U.S.S.R. improved, the Belgrade government no longer looked favorably upon anti-Soviet statements. At a meeting with public prosecutors on February 11, 1965, Tito denounced Mihajlov as a "reactionary" and charged him with "defending Hitler's concentration camps." Although an injunction was issued to stop the sale of Delo, the Soviet ambassador to Yugoslavia formally protested the publication of the article, and soon afterward Mihajlov was arrested.

Accused of "damaging the reputation of a foreign state" and of mailing his banned article to a Rome publisher, Mihajlov went on trial on April 29, 1965 in the Zadar District Court. He argued that he had published only historical facts and that all forms of totalitarianism, such as death camps, whether Stalinist or fascist, were equally evil. On the following day the court found the author guilty of both charges and sentenced him to nine months in jail. But on June 23 the Supreme Court of Croatia, to which Mihajlov had appealed, dismissed his conviction on the charge of deriding the Soviet Union and suspended his sentence on the other charge. Some observers linked the reversal to the upcoming meeting in Yugoslavia of the International P.E.N. Club, a writers' organization.

His arrest, however, had cost Mihajlov his post on the Zadar faculty. He turned to writing full time, but could not get his articles published in Yugoslavia because their major thrust was a demand for the democratization of his country's politics. But the Western press welcomed his work. The American periodical, the New Leader, for example, published the Delo installments of "Moscow Sum-

they have both spoken out in Mihajlov's behalf.

After completing his high school education in Sarajevo, Mihajlov studied comparative literature at the philology faculty of Belgrade University and at the philosophy faculty of Zagreb University, receiving his degree from the latter institution in 1959. Following a period of service in the army, he worked in Zagreb as a translator, wrote for many Yugoslav periodicals, and lectured over the radio. Through those activities Mihajlov became known as an expert on Dostoyevsky and post-Stalin Soviet literature. In December 1963 he was appointed an assistant professor on the philosophy faculty of the Zadar branch of Zagreb University, where he taught Russian literature while working on his doctoral dissertation.

A collection of Mihajlov's literary, political, and philosophical essays, written over a period of five years, beginning in 1961, and translated by his sister into English, was published in 1968 by Farrar, Straus & Giroux under the title Russian Themes. In many of the essays Mihajlov uses the works of Russian writers as springboards for discussions of his own views on social and political issues. Apart from polemics, as Thomas Lask pointed out in his review in the New York Times (June 24, 1968), the pages of Russian Themes "are full of discerning summaries, pithy evaluations and sensitive responses to style." The essays of that collection and other writings of Mihajlov contain allusions to mer 1964" in March 1965. In June an additional segment, never published in Yugoslavia, appeared in that magazine. (The three segments were published by Farrar, Straus & Giroux in the book *Moscow Summer* in 1965.) Thereafter, he sent a stream of essays and open letters to Tito to the foreign press.

In "Why We Are Silent," an article published by the *New Leader* in August 1965 and reprinted in the Washington *Post* (September 5, 1965), Mihajlov presented his political views as those of a democratic socialist whose beliefs were based on Christian principles. He contended that true freedom existed neither in the West, with its private ownership of property, nor in the East, with its single-party regimes. He granted that Yugoslavia, where the Communist party had begun relaxing its controls over society in the 1950's, came closer than any other country to combining the political democracy of the West with the East's principle of material democracy. But Mihajlov warned that "every one-party system, whatever else may be said about it, is some kind of subspecies of Stalinism" and that a relapse into the worst excesses of totalitarianism was possible so long as the Communist party controlled all means of communication and barred non-Marxist ideas.

With the goal of breaking the Communist party's monopoly, in December 1965 Mihajlov wrote a draft proposal for an independent socialist magazine to serve as a nucleus for future opposition political groups. He circulated the manuscript among friends and, with about twenty supporters, planned to convene on August 10, 1966 an organizing conference for the magazine, to be called "Slobodni Glas" (The Voice of Freedom). Two days before the meeting he was arrested.

On September 22 and 23 Mihajlov was tried again in the Zadar District Court, for allegedly spreading false information about Yugoslavia in foreign publications and for distributing his banned "Moscow Summer 1964" essay. No mention of the projected magazine was made in the indictment. In 1966 the government was allowing expanded freedom of discussion, particularly after the July purge of dogmatic, hard-line Vice-President and Police Chief Aleksandar Rankovic. Liberals were permitted to argue for greater democracy within the party and for a reduction of its role in society. The journal *Praxis* was conducting controversial philosophical debates on Marxism. But the crackdown on Mihajlov, as viewed in the Western press, indicated that the authorities drew the line for permissible dissent at any challenge to the party's monopoly of political power. Many dissidents also believed that Mihajlov had gone too far and feared that he was jeopardizing recent gains by asking for more than could be expected. His reputation as an extremist limited his following.

When the prosecutor charged at Mihajlov's September trial that his motive for publishing in the West was monetary, the tense but articulate defendant replied, as quoted in the New York *Times* (September 23, 1966), "My personal experience is that with political articles one earns prison more easily than money." In the courtroom he also declared that only 6 or 7 percent of the Yugoslav population, those belonging to the Communist party, had rights, but he was not permitted to present to the court a written defense assailing totalitarianism. That statement was later published as "The Unspoken Defense" in *Russian Themes*.

While courtroom hecklers jeered him, Mihajlov was convicted of both formal charges and sentenced to one year in prison. Allowed to remain at liberty while appealing to the Croatian Supreme Court, he reported receiving threatening phone calls and letters and being followed through the streets by people who urged grocers not to sell him food. Having lost his appeal, he began serving his sentence on November 12 in the Sremska Mitrovca prison near Belgrade.

On April 17, 1967 Mihajlov was removed from jail and taken to the Belgrade District Court to face another trial. He was again accused of spreading false propaganda in the foreign press—the government simply chose a different group of articles from the one cited in his September 1966 indictment. Eric Bourne reported in the *Christian Science Monitor* (April 18, 1967) that even some official Communists regarded the new case as " 'stupid' and unnecessary." Although Mihajlov was also accused of supporting emigrés favoring separatism for Yugoslavia's republics, the prosecution's own witnesses confirmed that he had little sympathy for separatism.

In his defense Mihajlov told the court that nothing he had written violated his right of dissent as given by the Yugoslav constitution and that he sent his articles abroad only because no one in Yugoslavia would publish them. Richard Eder of the New York *Times* (April 18, 1967) recorded that when the judge asked the defendant why he did not go abroad to write, Mihajlov replied, "No, it would not be the same. When I write here in Yugoslavia, I am guaranteeing with my head everything that I write." The April trial brought Mihajlov a severe four-and-a-half year sentence minus time already served, a reduction in the number of visitors allowed him in prison, and a four-year ban on public activity following his release. Mihajlov appealed his conviction to the Serbian Supreme Court, which in October, as reported by the Washington *Post* (October 22, 1967), reduced his sentence by one year because two state psychiatrists found him "a psychopathic person not adequately prepared for social adaptation." The next month he was placed in solitary confinement after refusing to engage in forced labor.

Released from prison on March 4, 1970, Mihajlov continued writing articles for foreign publications. He did not alter his fundamental political views in the 1970's but devoted greater attention to the spiritual and religious aspects of freedom. In his essay "Two Convergences," published in 1971 and later reprinted in his *Underground Notes* (Sheed, Andrews & McMeel, 1976), he criticized Soviet physicist Andrei Sakharov's argument that the requirements of scientific-technical development would lead to democratization in the U.S.S.R. Mihajlov contended that freedom is an existential problem and that man opposes totalitarianism only when he "feels that by submitting to oppression he is losing his soul, his 'I.' . . . And that feeling is a religious one."

The beleaguered dissident was arrested again in October 1974. On February 25, 1975, during a year of severe repression in Yugoslavia that damaged its reputation as the most liberal Communist nation, he went on trial in Novi Sad on the usual charge of disseminating hostile propaganda in foreign publications. Three days later he was sentenced to seven years at hard labor and was again barred from public activity for four years following the completion of his sentence. In prison he began protracted hunger strikes in December 1975 and again in December 1976 to improve his living conditions. Meanwhile, human rights groups in the West petitioned Tito for his release.

To mark Yugoslavia's national day, the state freed Mihajlov and a group of other prisoners in a November 1977 amnesty. "I do not intend to be quiet," he announced upon leaving jail. Mihajlov attributed his release to the fact that the East-West Commission on Security and Cooperation in Europe was meeting in Belgrade at the time to discuss, among other things, compliance with the human rights provisions of the Helsinki agreements of 1975. In early 1978 he urged the delegates to make reference to the human rights issue in the conference's final document, a plea that failed.

Even when he was not in prison Mihajlov was unable to accept a standing offer, made in 1970, of an opportunity to carry on his academic work at Stanford University, because his government would not give him a passport. Early in 1974 he was also denied a passport to attend the annual meeting of the American Association for the Advancement of Science in San Francisco, to which he had been invited. The following August he wrote a letter to Tito in which he appealed, "Either enable me to live normally in this country or enable me to leave the country." Eventually successful in obtaining a passport, he visited the United States in the summer of 1978 to arrange for the publication of an autobiographical and political book and to collect material for another book, tentatively titled "American Summer." During his stay he wrote an article for the *New Leader* (July 31, 1978), "Notes of a Survivor: The Trials in That Other World," reflecting on the current wave of trials of dissidents in the Soviet Union, and a review for the *New York Review of Books* (October 26, 1978) of Dusko Doder's *The Yugoslavs,* calling attention to important Western misconceptions about Yugoslavia.

Because of an extensive crackdown on dissidents in Yugoslavia, Mihajlov prolonged his visit in the United States, where he lectured at dozens of universities and in 1979 began work on a new book, "Tyranny and Freedom," to be published by Harper & Row. In August 1979 Yugoslav authorities issued an arrest warrant for him, in an attempt, as some observers interpreted it, to discourage his return.

Groups of Mihajlov's supporters were arrested in Yugoslavia in August and November 1966. But, as reported in the Western press, he has not attracted a substantial following in his native country, and according to the *New York Times* (April 23, 1967), his compatriots were troubled by what they felt was "an excess in his style, an overly frenetic quality, a mournful fanaticism akin to that of Dostoyevsky's underground man." After meeting him in New York in June 1978, the editors of the *New Leader* wrote, "A short [five feet five inches tall], trim man, Mihajlov, remarkably, looks younger than his 44 years. He speaks English with relative ease and, rather than the bitterness one might expect, radiates a warm optimism." Yugoslavia's most famous dissident, Milovan Djilas, a former Vice-President who also spent many years in prison, had the highest praise for Mihajlov when, in 1974, he credited the son of Russian emigrés with the best of Russian qualities—openness, sacrifice, and sensitivity—in an unalloyed form.

References: Encounter 24:81+ Je '65; N Y Times p47 N 14 '74; New Leader 61:2 Jl 17 '78; Newsweek 68:42+ Ag 15 '66 por; Mihajlov, Mihajlo. Moscow Summer (1965), Underground Notes (1976)

Milgram, Stanley

Aug. 15, 1933- Psychologist; educator.
Address: b. Graduate Center, City University of New York, 33 W. 42nd St, New York City, N. Y. 10036

Widely known for his controversial work on obedience to authority, Stanley Milgram, the

Stanley Milgram

social psychologist, has examined such diverse aspects of attitude phenomena as conformity, crowd behavior, the effects of television violence on viewers, subliminal networks of human communication, and the experience of urban life. The titles of some of his papers—"The Urban Bystander," "The Familiar Stranger," "The Lost Letter Technique"—hint at the intriguing complexity of his work. His imaginative and innovative attempts to, in his words, "clarify and make visible the operation of obscure social forces so that they may be explored in terms of the language of cause and effect" have brought him a much wider audience than that usually reserved for research-oriented psychologists.

The son of immigrant East European Jews, Stanley Milgram was born in New York City, New York on August 15, 1933 to Samuel Milgram, a baker, and Adele (Israel) Milgram. He has an older sister, Marjorie, a housewife, and a younger brother, Joel, a professor at the University of Cincinnati. Milgram grew up in the Bronx, where he attended James Monroe High School. During his youth, he was, in his words, "always doing experiments." As he told one interviewer, "It was as natural as breathing, and I tried to understand how everything worked." One of his experiments won him the school's gold medal in biology. His extracurricular activities also centered around science. He served as president of the biology club and edited Science Observer, the school's science magazine, to which he contributed several articles, including a piece on the physiological and psychological effects of atomic radiation on the survivors of Hiroshima and Nagasaki. Following his graduation from high school in 1950, Milgram enrolled at Queens College

of the City University of New York in Flushing. There he held his experimental leanings in check to major in political science and to pursue his long-standing interests in art and music. An excellent student, he was awarded the Political Science Gold Medal and was elected president of the International Relations Club. Nevertheless, Milgram was 'dissatisfied with political science because of its 'philosophic emphasis.' "I was interested in the questions raised by Plato, Thomas Hobbes, and John Locke," he explained in his The Individual in a Social World (Addison-Wesley, 1977), "[but] I was unwilling to accept their mode of arriving at answers." After receiving his A.B. degree in 1954, he decided to switch to social psychology for his graduate work because that field, as he put it, "seemed to permit interesting questions to be raised and answered scientifically."

In the fall of 1954 Milgram entered Harvard University's Department of Social Relations as a Ford Foundation Fellow in the behavioral sciences. His mentors during his years at Harvard were Gordon W. Allport, the personality theorist, who gave him "spiritual and emotional support," and Solomon E. Asch, the social psychologist. Milgram was Dr. Asch's teaching assistant at Harvard and later worked with him as a research assistant at the Institute for Advanced Study, in Princeton, New Jersey. The stamp of Asch's work on group pressure and conformity is especially evident in Milgram's early experiments.

Milgram's dissertation, for which Harvard awarded him a Ph.D. degree in 1960, was an analysis of the national characteristics of two modern European countries: "Conformity in Norway and France." On the basis of experimental research conducted in the field from 1957 to 1959 under a fellowship from the Social Science Research Council, he concluded that the pressures for conformity were greater in the cohesive, group-oriented society of Norway than in France, with its long tradition of dissent and rebellion.

Milgram was an assistant professor of psychology at Yale University from 1960 to 1963, and it was there that he conducted what came to be his most famous and controversial series of experiments on obedience to authority, which brought him the annual sociopsychological prize of the American Association for the Advancement of Science in 1965. A book based on his experiments, Obedience to Authority; an Experimental View (Harper, 1974), was widely acclaimed by professionals and laymen alike. Nominated for a National Book Award in 1975, it has been translated into many languages, including Hebrew, German, French, Dutch, Japanese, Italian, and Swedish. In addition, the experiment and its shocking results inspired a play by Dannie Abse, The Dogs of Pavlov, and a television drama, The Tenth Level, broadcast by CBS in 1976. Nearly two decades later, the Milgram experiment, which has been replicated many times with the same results, continues to intrigue political scientists, psychologists, and philosophers.

Expanding on his earlier studies of conformity, Milgram sought, in his experiments, to examine a more humanly significant question: How far will one person go in hurting another at the behest of a recognized authority figure. Thus, into the purview of an experimental social psychologist came an aspect of human interpersonal relationships that was pertinent not only to the understanding of the experience of fascism, but also, as Milgram pointed out, to the interpretation of the Biblical story of Abraham, who was ordered by God to kill his son.

In Milgram's experiment, carried out under simulated laboratory conditions, a grey-coated technician asked each subject to administer a simple word-pair test to a learner, punishing each successive mistake with an electric shock of increasing intensity. The "electric shocks" were not real, but the "learner"—actually an actor—complained at the 150-volt level and feigned agony at 300 volts. Saying he would assume full responsibility for the outcome, the supervising technician told the subject to ignore the learner's protests and to continue to administer the shocks as directed. Contrary to the predictions of psychiatrists and psychologists, slightly more than 60 percent of the subjects tested obeyed the technician fully, leading Milgram to conclude that "a substantial proportion of people do what they are told to do, irrespective of the content of the act and without limitations of conscience, so long as they perceive that the command comes from a legitimate authority."

Extrapolating from his experimental findings, Milgram maintained that the propensity to obey was a "fatal" human flaw that "gives our species only a modest chance of survival." In an interview for Psychology Today (June, 1974), Milgram reminded Carol Tavris that examples of excessive obedience to authority could be found in all societies. "American democracy also has instituted policies that were severe and inhumane: the destruction of American Indians, the enslavement of blacks, the incarceration of the Japanese during the Second World War, Vietnam," he said. "There are always people who obey, who carry out the policies."

Milgram returned to Harvard University in 1963. For the next four years he taught psychology and served as executive director of the Comparative International Program in the Department of Social Research. During that period he developed some original experimental techniques for investigating communication systems. "The Lost Letter Technique," for example, examines attitudes in terms of deeds: would someone finding a letter addressed to "Friends of the Communist Party" be as likely to mail it as a letter addressed to, say, "Medical Research Associates" or to a private citizen? In another study, "The Small World Problem," Milgram considered the everyday remark, "My, it's a small world," and proved, in a series of experiments, that in terms of the structure of intermediate acquaintances, the social fabric of America is tightly knit.

After joining the faculty of the Graduate Center of the City University of New York, as a professor of psychology in 1967, Stanley Milgram took up the controversial issue of violence on television. With funding from CBS-TV, Milgram and fellow psychologist R. Lance Shotland designed experiments to discover whether or not "the depiction of antisocial behavior" on television stimulated "imitation in the larger community." Their research consistently supported the null hypothesis: there was no proved connection between exposure to television violence and an individual's propensity to commit violent acts. The results of those experiments, widely reported in the mass media, were published in Television and Antisocial Behavior; Field Experience (Academic Press, 1973).

Some of Milgram's most innovative work has been in the relatively new field of urban psychology. Although his academic interest in the subject may be dated from 1966, when he first taught an undergraduate seminar on the psychological study of cities, Milgram had been contemplating a study of social intrusion —that is, under what circumstances other people's business becomes one's own—since 1960. His notes on the subject prefigure the 1963 murder of Kitty Genovese, a young New Yorker who was repeatedly stabbed while at least thirty-eight bystanders ignored her pleas for help. Milgram reflected on the incident in "Murder They Heard," an article written in collaboration with Paul Hollander for The Nation (June 15, 1964).

The concern with human aggression that was so much a part of his studies of obedience and television surfaced again in his analysis of urban life. "A calculated and strategic indifference is an unavoidable part of our life in our cities," he wrote, "and it must be faced without sentimentality or rage. At most, each of us can resolve to extend the range of his responsibilities in some perceptible degree, to rise a little more adequately to our moral obligations."

Drawing on his own experiences as a resident of New York, Boston, and Paris, and as a visitor in small towns, Milgram raised questions about the comparative qualities of urban and rural life. In "The Experience of Living in Cities," a paper published in Science on March 13, 1970, he used the engineering concept of "overload" to explain the aggregate effect of the various stimuli that bombard the city-dweller and help shape his behavior. In a related paper, "The Familiar Stranger," Milgram looked into the fact that in an urban setting, people "often gain extreme familiarity with the faces of a number of persons, yet never interact with them."

Milgram has recently expanded his exploration of urban life to include cognitive maps. In an imaginative attempt to "plot a psychological variable onto the geography," Milgram tested the relative recognizability of a number of New York City locations to discover the "representation of the city that each inhabitant carries around in his head." First published in *American Scientist* (March-April, 1972) as "A Psychological Map of New York City," that study became the basis for a cover story in *New York* magazine. In a second, more elaborate, effort, "Psychological Maps of Paris," Milgram asked 218 Parisians to draw rough maps of the city, then examined each map in terms of common elements. He also asked his subjects to name familiar icons and to ascribe various qualities to the *arrondissements*. The maps, as Milgram describes them, are multidimensional: "They contain cognitive and also emotional and intuitive components, and a variety of procedures is needed to bring them to light."

Milgram believes that there is an art to experimentation, and the experiments he designs often have a dramaturgical quality. For example, in "The Image-Freezing Machine," a recent paper on the sociological and psychological effects of the ordinary camera, Milgram begins historically, reflecting on the prevalence and popularity of the photo-portrait in the nineteenth century. He considers photography as an act of exchange "that devalues the moment, as one trades the full value of the present instant for a future record of it." Then, describing several experiments conducted on the streets of midtown Manhattan, Milgram analyzes people's reactions to "giving away their image." Finally, he raises questions of broader social and psychological impact and speculates on the ways that photography helps to create the "universe of events" that it records.

On December 10, 1961 Stanley Milgram married Alexandra ("Sasha") Menkin, a psychiatric social worker. They have two children, Michele Sara and Marc Daniel. Standing five feet seven inches tall and of medium build, Milgram has irregular, almost sculpted features, inquisitive blue eyes, and brown hair. He is soft-spoken and unpretentious, and is constantly inquiring and self-observant in conversation. Uninterested in the play of ideas *per se*, he is, in his words, fascinated by "what is" as "a band on the broader perspective of what might have been."

In 1970 Milgram was elected a Fellow of the American Psychological Association and, in 1971, a Fellow of the American Association for the Advancement of Science. Awarded a Guggenheim Fellowship in 1972, he won a silver medal at the International Film and Television Festival of New York for his collaborative work on the documentary film, *The City*

and Self. He is a member of the Association of Independent Film and Television Producers. In 1977 he served as a consultant to the Polaroid Corporation and produced the report, "Photography as a Human Activity: Research for the Decade to Come."

References: *Psych Today* 8:74+ Je '74 por; *American Men and Women of Science* (1973)

Millar, Kenneth See Macdonald, R.

Moi, Daniel (Torotich) arap (moi)

1924- President of the Republic of Kenya. Address: b. Office of the President, Nairobi, Kenya

Some Third World nations have been torn apart by the strains entailed in handing on power from one administration or party to another. The pessimistic expectations of many observers of political developments in the East African Republic of Kenya, however, were proved unjustified when, in 1978, Daniel arap Moi, its Vice-President, peacefully succeeded to the Presidency vacated by the death of Jomo Kenyatta, who had ruled for fifteen years and had become a legend as the father of the Kenyan independence movement. Although he lacks Kenyatta's personal flamboyance and international reputation, Moi is an experienced and well-liked public figure who has been involved in the country's political life since the British colonial era. Building his administration on the ideals of intertribal harmony, good government, and economic development, he has done much to further Kenya's growing sense of unity and national purpose.

Torotich arap ("son of") Moi adopted the name Daniel when as a schoolboy he was baptized by Christian missionaries. He was born in 1924 into a farming family of the village of Kuriengwo (or, according to some sources, Sacho) in the Baringo district of the Rift Valley Province of western Kenya, about 150 miles north of Nairobi, the capital. One of the few top Kenyan politicians outside the Kikuyu and Luo tribes, he belongs to the Tugen subgroup of the Kalenjin tribal cluster, only recently perceived by Kenyans as comprising a single unit, whose membership amounts to nearly 2,000,000 out of Kenya's total population of about 14,000,000.

With the encouragement of the teachers at his first school, the African Mission School in Karbatonjo, Moi went to the highlands town of Kapsabet, the district headquarters of Baringo, where he continued his education at the African Inland Mission School, the Government African School, and the Kapsabet Teacher Training College. He became a teacher at the Government African School in 1945, advancing to the rank of head teacher the following year. Proving to be exceedingly popular with his students and their parents, he moved on to the post of headmaster of the Kabarnet Intermediate School in 1948 and to assistant principal of the Tambach Teacher Training College in 1949. He returned to Kapsabet in 1954 as headmaster of the Government African School, a position in which he remained until 1957.

Meanwhile, as a Kalenjin, Moi played no part in the terrorist Mau Mau rebellion of the early 1950's, which involved the Kikuyu, Kenya's largest tribal group. He was sympathetic, however, to the movement within the crown colony to gain independence from Great Britain, and at the height of the uprising he sheltered five Mau Mau rebels on his farm for several weeks. In October 1955, when the Rift Valley's British-appointed black representative to the Kenya Legislative Council resigned, Moi was named by the district councils to take his place. As provided in a plan introduced by Colonial Secretary Oliver Lyttelton to enlarge the role of Africans in the Kenya government, some 100,000 qualified blacks were permitted for the first time in the election of March 1957 to chose their own representatives. Voters chose Moi as one of the first eight blacks to be elected to the Legislative Council.

During the early years of his parliamentary career, according to Kenyan nationalist leader Oginga Odinga, in his book Not Yet Uhuru (1967), Moi was "influenced by the missions, overawed by settler power and making a slow adjustment to political trends and the need to make independent judgments." As Odinga

also noted, however, Moi was "a giraffe with a long neck that saw from afar." After some time as an unobtrusive backbencher acclimating himself to his new role and to the changing situation in independence-bound Kenya, he began to emerge as a political figure of some importance.

Because of the demands for increased representation of blacks in the legislature, its composition was changed, with the election of March 1958, to allow fourteen Africans, as well as fourteen Europeans, among the thirty-six elected members, who also included Asians and Arabs. In 1958 Moi, who retained his seat, joined with African and Indian fellow council members to form the multiracial Constituency Elected Members Organization, which boycotted meetings of the legislature to back up its demand for changes in Kenya's governmental system. Early in 1960 Moi was one of the African delegates to the Lancaster House Conference in London, which drafted a new Kenyan constitution, for the first time authorizing African political parties and granting blacks a majority in the Legislative Council.

Later that year, while again in England to attend a course given by the Commonwealth Parliamentary Association, Moi was elected assistant treasurer of the newly formed Kenya African Nationalist Union (KANU). Tom Mboya, a resourceful young Luo politician, headed that party until the release from prison in 1961 of its president-elect, Jomo Kenyatta, a Kikuyu leader who had been tried on charges of directing Mau Mau operations. In view of Kikuyu and Luo dominance in KANU, Moi feared that Kalenjin interests would not be well served. With majimbo (Swahili for "regionalism") as their rallying cry, Moi and the leaders of several other minority tribes soon withdrew from the party and founded the Kenya African Democratic Union (KADU), of which he was chairman for about a year.

After the general election of February 1961, in which KADU won ten seats in the enlarged Legislative Council compared to KANU's sixteen seats, Moi served for several months as parliamentary secretary to the Ministry of Education. In December he became Minister of Education. He represented Kenya at a pan-African education conference in Ethiopia in 1961 and at the Commonwealth Scholarship Conference in India in 1962. In a coalition Council of Ministers formed in 1962 of KADU and KANU members, Moi was named Minister for Local Government. Throughout 1962 he participated in the series of conferences, held under British auspices, that prepared Kenya for its transition to independence, successfully leading a fight to ensure that the new nation's government would be a federal system providing regional autonomy, to protect the minorities, rather than the highly centralized system desired by Kenyatta and the KANU delegates.

In the preindependence election of May 1963, Moi became the first president of the Rift Valley Region and also won a seat, from the constituency of Baringo North, in the House of Representatives in Kenya's new bicameral National Assembly. With an overwhelming majority of 105 parliamentary seats to KADU's twenty-two, KANU won control of the provisional government, and in December 1963, when Kenya finally achieved full independence, Jomo Kenyatta became its Prime Minister. In the shadow Cabinet that KADU, the parliamentary opposition, set up in true British fashion, Moi was designated Minister of Agriculture.

KADU's fortunes and political prospects declined rapidly, so that in November 1964, to forestall Kenyatta's plan to hold a national referendum to eliminate regionalism altogether, the party voluntarily dissolved itself. Most of its leaders, Moi included, joined KANU. In December, when he became President of the Republic of Kenya within the British Commonwealth, Kenyatta took several former KADU leaders into his Cabinet. Moi was sworn in as Minister for Home Affairs, an extremely important post that made him the head of Kenya's national police, a larger and militarily more potent force than the country's small army, and charged him with the responsibility for maintaining national security. In March 1966, according to Odinga, Moi helped to stage-manage the "American-style" KANU party convention in Limuru, handpicking some of the delegates. Within the KANU organization he was elected vice-chairman for the Rift Valley Province. While retaining his post as Minister for Home Affairs, in January 1967 he became Kenya's Vice-President, an appointive rather than an elective office, and vice-chairman of the KANU Parliamentary Group.

Overshadowed by the dominant presence of Kenyatta, who was known far and wide as *Mzee* ("the old man" or "the elder"), Moi, like the other members of the Kenyan government, attracted little attention in the West in the years that followed. Nonetheless, his considerable abilities were clearly apparent at home, and he soon became the most trusted non-Kikuyu adviser of Kenyatta. As Kenyatta's principal assistant, moreover, Moi handled much of the day-to-day business of the government.

On occasion, even earlier, it appeared that Moi bore the brunt of criticism that might otherwise have been directed at Kenyatta. In 1966, when he, as Home Affairs Minister, detained eight leaders of Oginga Odinga's opposition Kenya People's Union, he defended his action before the legislature with the argument, "Any government worth its salt must put the preservation of public security above the convenience of a handful of persons who are doing their utmost to undermine it." Virtually all foreign observers agree, nev-

ertheless, that during Moi's control of security matters Kenya had far fewer political prisoners and far less internal repression than almost any other African country in the postcolonial era.

Stretching the constitutional mandate of his Cabinet post, Moi also became involved in other spheres of government, most notably foreign policy, a development that was eased by the fact that the immigration department, which is part of the Home Affairs Ministry, has attachés or other officers in many of Kenya's foreign embassies. Moi was especially interested in intra-African affairs. Unlike most of his Cabinet colleagues, for a long time he supported friendly relations with Idi Amin, the truculent ruler of neighboring Uganda, even in the face of grave provocations. In 1967 he went to Egypt as Kenyatta's emissary to consult with President Gamal Abdel Nasser about United Arab Republic support of Somali guerrillas in northern Kenya in a long-simmering territorial dispute. He also traveled on government business to the United States, Germany, Taiwan, Japan, Lebanon, and Greece, and in 1976 he represented Kenya at the summit meeting of the Organization of African Unity, which tried unsuccessfully to hammer out a solution to the devastating civil war in Angola.

By 1975, with *Mzee* well into his eighties, the succession to the Presidency, a matter on which Kenyatta had never committed himself, was becoming a major question in Kenyan political circles. None of the President's Kikuyu intimates seemed strong enough to take his place, but Moi, known as "the father of the House" because he was the longest-serving member of the Kenyan legislature, also seemed eliminated from consideration by his non-Kikuyu status, which put him outside the country's main power establishment.

In October 1976 a group of Kikuyu politicians associated with Dr. Njoroge Mungai, Kenyatta's nephew, attempted to amend the constitutional provision permitting Moi in the event of the President's death to serve as interim President for ninety days pending a new election, but that move was defeated by another group led by Charles Njonjo, Kenya's attorney general and a paramount Kikuyu political figure, who has since emerged as one of Moi's key supporters. In 1977 it seemed likely that the same jockeying for the succession would characterize the scheduled KANU delegates' conference, but at the last minute Kenyatta canceled the meeting without offering any explanation.

In the small hours of the morning of August 22, 1978 Moi was awakened by a phone call from a government official who told him, "Your Excellency, come down to the State House. Kenya has lost its eyes!" Kenyatta was dead, and as provided by the constitution, Moi immediately became interim President, but many observers, both inside the country and abroad, feared that chaos would ensue and that the nation, like most of the emerging states of Africa, would not peacefully endure its first transfer of power. Kenyatta, who remained vigorous and in control until the end, had ruled with a firm hand for fifteen years, and no one, Moi included, seemed to possess assets approaching his political stature and public acceptance.

The country remained calm, however, and in the days following Kenyatta's state funeral, Moi swiftly solidified his position, especially as it became evident that he could count on the support of a triumvirate of top Kikuyu power brokers, Njonjo, Resources Minister Mbiyu Koinange, and Finance Minister Mwai Kibaki, whom he appointed to fill the now vacant Vice-Presidency. Moi did not appear to differ very much ideologically from the other possible Presidential contenders, with the exception of former Vice-President Odinga, who was, however, eliminated from the race for the nation's highest office on constitutional grounds, because he was not a member of the National Assembly.

Although Moi lacked Kenyatta's magnetism and indeed was regarded as a somewhat lacklustre personality, he had many other advantages. Like Kenyatta, he was a devout, committed Christian, known for his fairness, personal decency, sense of honor, and openness to the people. His long service in the legislature, dating back twenty-three years, made him one of Kenya's best-known political figures, and his incumbency of the Vice-Presidential office seemed to imply that he would have been Kenyatta's choice. Finally, and perhaps most significantly, he was not a Kikuyu, for while that tribe had long dominated Kenyan government and economic life, nearly 80 percent of the population belong to other tribal groups, and it was felt that Moi, unlike a Kikuyu President, would be able to enhance the nation's unity by cultivating a coalition of its smaller groups.

From the outset of his interim Presidency, Moi made it clear that he would keep Kenya on the same capitalist, moderately pro-Western course set by Kenyatta, a direction widely regarded as the source of the nation's stability and developing prosperity. Promising to root out corruption, nepotism, and ethnic cronyism in government, he also pledged himself to reform Kenya's land-allocation program, diversify its coffee-based agricultural economy, eliminate smuggling and other kinds of crime, and work for tribal harmony. "All Kenyans, including ministers and civil servants, are answerable to me," he declared at a large political rally, "but I am answerable to God. If I do not rule fairly I will be judged by God."

On October 6, 1978 some 1,600 delegates from forty-one KANU branches throughout the country, many of them wearing T-shirts imprinted with the words "Moi, the son *Mzee* loved," assembled at the Kenyatta Conference Center in Nairobi to elect Moi unanimously the head of Kenya's only political party. On October 14 he automatically became the country's second President. Retaining most of the Cabinet ministers who had served under Kenyatta, he repeatedly stressed the continuity between his administration and the preceding one, promising, "We shall build Kenya into a single monument to the everlasting memory of our father of the nation in the living spirit he himself taught us." Nevertheless, a feeling of uncertainty was reflected in a report in the New York *Times* (November 20, 1978): "President Moi remains something of an enigma. No one is absolutely sure what kind of President he will make—weak or strong, tolerant or autocratic, liberal or conservative." Most observers believe, however, that Moi has the ability to devise and implement workable, lasting solutions to Kenya's economic and social problems. His desire for reconciliation and his sense of confidence in office were underlined on December 12, 1978, when he announced the release of sixteen detainees, making Kenya one of the few African countries that have no political prisoners. The results of the general election in November 1979 justified Moi's self-confidence: while many legislators from the Kenyatta era were ousted, he retained his seat in the National Assembly, running for reelection without opposition in his own district.

A successful businessman, like many other Kenyan government leaders, Daniel arap Moi has extensive land holdings and owns the East African International Harvester distributorship. He is head of Kenya's Boy Scout organization, has served on the Rift Valley Education Board and the Kalenjin Language Committee, and was chairman of the Rift Valley Provincial Court. Preferring to lead a quiet private life, the President keeps his wife and several children out of public view. He is said to have been deeply influenced by the African Inland Church, one of Kenya's largest Protestant denominations, and is widely held to be puritanical because he denounces hippies and miniskirts and neither smokes nor drinks alcoholic beverages. In *Who's Who in Africa* (1973) he was described as "a big man with a ready laugh and an informal approach to life." Among his often-quoted aphorisms against materialism and acquisitiveness is: "One can accumulate enough wealth to buy a golden bed, but one cannot buy sound sleep with money."

References: *Africa* 86:17+ O '78 por; *Atlan* 248:8+ Je '79 por; *Guardian* p11 Je 11 '79 por; N Y *Times* N 20 '78; *Time* 112:54+ O 23 '78 por, 114:52+ N 15 '79 por; *Toronto Globe and Mail* p7 Ag 31 '79 por; *Africa Yearbook and Who's Who*, 1977; *International Who's Who*, 1978-79; *Who's Who in East Africa*, 1967-68; *Who's Who in the World*, 1978-79

Morrison, Toni

Feb. 18, 1931- Writer. Address: b. c/o Lynn Nesbitt, International Creative Management, 40 W. 57th St., New York City, N.Y. 10019

With the phenomenal critical and popular success of her 1977 award-winning novel, *Song of Solomon*, Toni Morrison's place in contemporary American literature was assured. Her two earlier novels, *The Bluest Eye* and *Sula*, although less successful at the cash registers of bookstores, were equally acclaimed for their emotional depth and lyrical, precise language, prompting reviewers to compare Miss Morrison with Vladimir Nabokov, Joseph Heller, and Doris Lessing, among others. All three of her novels draw on her background as a black woman born into poverty, but their larger concerns with interpersonal relationships and individual growth have a universal appeal. As a senior editor at Random House, since 1967, and a visiting lecturer in English at Yale University, Miss Morrison has devoted herself to the development of black literature, and she has become much sought after as a reader of her own works at public gatherings.

The second of the four children of George and Ramah (Willis) Wofford, Toni Morrison was born Chloe Anthony Wofford on February 18, 1931 in Lorain, Ohio, a steel town twenty-five miles west of Cleveland. During the worst years of the Depression her father worked as a car washer, welder in a local steel mill, and road construction worker, while her mother, a feisty, determined woman, dealt with callous landlords and impertinent social workers. "When an eviction notice was put on our house, she tore it off," Miss Morrison remembered, as quoted in *People* (January 2,

1978). "If there were maggots in our flour, she wrote a letter to [President] Franklin Roosevelt. My mother believed something should be done about inhuman situations."

In an article for the New York *Times Magazine* (July 4, 1976), Miss Morrison discussed her parents' contrasting attitudes towards white society and the inevitable effect of those conflicting views on her own perception of the quality of black life in America. Ramah Wofford believed that, in time, race relations would improve; George Wofford distrusted "every word and every gesture of every white man on earth." Both parents were convinced, however, that "all succor and aid came from themselves and their neighborhood." Consequently, Miss Morrison, although she attended a multiracial school, was raised in "a basically racist household" and grew up "with more than a child's contempt for white people."

After graduating with honors from high school in 1949, Toni Morrison enrolled at Howard University in Washington, D.C. She had chosen Howard, then an all-black institution, because she had assumed it would be "full of brilliant black students" who could stimulate and challenge her intellectually. "But that was not what the school was about," she said years later. "It was about getting married, buying clothes and going to parties. It was also about being cool, loving Sarah Vaughan (who only moved her hand a little when she sang) and MJQ [the Modern Jazz Quartet]. From birth to Howard, I had been required to show some discipline, exert some initiative, hold jobs (after age twelve) and solve problems. Howard required none of that. We were treated like defective kids on the one hand . . . and ladies of the night on the other." Miss Morrison devoted most of her free time to the Howard University Players, a campus theatre company she has since described as "a place where hard work, thought, and talent" were praised and "merit was the only rank." She often appeared in campus productions, and in the summers she traveled throughout the South with a repertory troupe made up of faculty members and students.

Miss Morrison took her B.A. degree in 1953 and then went on to Cornell University for graduate work in English, mainly because, as she put it, she had "nowhere to go." Ill-prepared for Cornell's rigorous program, she spent long hours in the library and, in 1955, on submission of what she now calls a "shaky" thesis on the theme of suicide in the works of William Faulkner and Virginia Woolf, she received an M.A. degree. After two years of teaching English "theory, pronunciation and grammar" to undergraduates at Texas Southern University in Houston, Texas, she joined the faculty of Howard University as an instructor in English, a post she held until 1964. While at Howard, she met and married a Jamaican architect and gave birth to two sons, Harold Ford and Slade Kevin.

Stifled by her marriage, Miss Morrison began to write fiction in the early 1960's. "It was as though I had nothing left but my imagination," she said in an autobiographical sketch submitted to Current Biography. "I had no will, no judgment, no perspective, no power, no authority, no self—just this brutal sense of irony, melancholy and a trembling respect for words. I wrote like someone with a dirty habit. Secretly. Compulsively. Slyly." She eventually drifted into a small, informal group of poets and writers who met once a month to read, discuss, and criticize each other's work. For awhile, Miss Morrison took the "old junk" that she had written in high school, but one day, finding herself without a sample of writing to take to the meeting, she dashed off "a little story about a black girl who wanted blue eyes" that was to be the genesis of her first novel.

In 1964 Miss Morrison resigned from Howard and, after a divorce, moved with her children to Syracuse, New York, where she took a job as a textbook editor for a subsidiary of Random House, the publishing conglomerate. There, partly to alleviate her loneliness, she developed the short story she had written at Howard into a novel. She sent an unfinished version to an editor at Macmillan, who encouraged her to complete the book. When that editor moved to Holt, Rinehart & Winston a few months later, he asked to see the manuscript again and, in 1969, Holt published The Bluest Eye, the story of two young sisters living in a tiny, provincial black community in Ohio in 1941 and their friendship with Pecola Breedlove, a homely, outcast little girl so mercilessly victimized by her parents and narrow-minded neighbors that she eventually retreats into insanity.

Described by Toni Morrison as a book about "the absolute destruction of human life because of the most superficial thing in the world—physical beauty," The Bluest Eye is, on one level, a treatment of the universal theme of the loss of innocence and on another, an indictment of the physical and emotional poverty of middle-class black life during World War II. "Miss Morrison expresses the negative of the Dick-and-Jane-and-Mother-and-Father-and-Dog-and-Cat photograph that appears in our reading primers, and she does it with a prose so precise, so faithful to speech and so charged with pain and wonder that the novel becomes poetry," John Leonard wrote in his review of the book for the New York Times (November 13, 1970). "I have said 'poetry.' But The Bluest Eye is also history, sociology, folklore, nightmare and music." Several other critics were also enthusiastic.

The Bluest Eye established Miss Morrison as a literate observer of contemporary black America, and she was often asked to write social commentary for mass market publications. As a senior editor at Random House's New York headquarters, to which she had been transferred in 1967, she took a special interest in black fiction. "I want to participate in developing a canon of black work," she told Sandra Satterwhite in an interview for a New York Post (January 26, 1974) profile. "We've had the first rush of black entertainment, where blacks were writing for whites, and whites were encouraging this kind of self-flagellation. Now we can get down to the craft of writing, where black people are talking to black people."

On the average, Miss Morrison edited six or seven books a year for Random House. The most well-received were the autobiographies of Muhammed Ali, the boxer, and Angela Davis, the black activist, and The Black Book, an eclectic collection of newspaper clippings, faded family photographs, dream books, documents, slave quilts, and other memorabilia. Troubled by the direction the "black power" movement seemed to be taking in the late 1960's, she had conceived the book as a kind of tribute to the "anonymous black man" that stressed the commonness of experience. "The one thing Elijah Muhammed has said that I agree with was, if you knew who you were, you would get off your knees," she explained to Dorothy Gilliam of the Washington Post at a party celebrating the publication of the book in March 1974. "What we have to do is reintroduce ourselves to ourselves. We have to know what the past was so that we can use it for now."

Toni Morrison's own writing career took another step forward in late 1973 with the publication by Alfred A. Knopf, Inc., of Sula, an examination of the intense, forty-year friendship between two women: Nel, who accepts the conventional mores and rigid moral code of the insular black community that is her hometown, and Sula, who defies them. Much of the largely favorable critical response to Sula focused on Miss Morrison's spare, precise language, economical, life-like dialogue, and totally convincing characterizations. To Sara Blackburn, who reviewed Sula for the New York Times Book Review (December 30, 1973), the main characters seemed "almost mythologically strong and familiar" and had the "heroic quality" of the characters of Gabriel García Márquez. Other reviewers, including Ruth Rambo McClain, in Black World, Jerry H. Bryant, in the Nation, and Fath Davis, in the Harvard Advocate, seconded Miss Blackburn's assessment and singled out for special praise Miss Morrison's masterful creation of Sula, a complex woman who is at once self-reliant, amoral, predatory, alluring, and completely ruthless.

But for Jonathan Yardley, the most fully realized character is the tiny black community of Bottom. "Toni Morrison is not a Southern writer, but she has located place and community with the skill of a Flannery O'Connor or Eudora Welty," he commented in the Washington *Post* (February 3, 1974). "Thus the novel is much more than a portrait of one woman. It is in large measure an evocation of a way of life that existed in the black communities of the small towns of the 1920's and 1930's, a way of life compounded of such ingredients as desperation, neighborliness, and persistence."

What was to Yardley a literary strength was viewed as a weakness by Miss Blackburn, who found in her New York *Times* review that Miss Morrison's fiction lacked "the stinging immediacy, the urgency" of her nonfiction. "Toni Morrison is far too talented to remain only a marvelous recorder of the black side of provincial American life," she wrote. "If she is to maintain the large and serious audience she deserves, she is going to have to address a riskier contemporary reality than this beautiful but nevertheless distanced novel." Miss Morrison responded to that criticism in her interview with Sandra Satterwhite by saying simply, "She's talking about my life. It has a stinging immediacy for me." The consensus of opinion came down decidedly in Miss Morrison's favor. *Sula* was named an alternate selection of the Book-of-the-Month Club, was published in condensed form in the January 1974 issue of *Redbook*, and was nominated for the 1975 National Book Award in the fiction category.

A visiting lecturer at Yale University since 1976, Miss Morrison teaches courses in creative writing and in the works of such black women writers as Angela Davis, Alice Walker, Gwendolyn Brooks, Bessie Head, Carolina Maria de Jesús, the Brazilian author, and occasionally, Toni Morrison. She herself feels a special kinship with the Latin American authors García Márquez and Miguel Asturias because they effectively combine myth and political sensitivity. She also admires John Gardner, James Dickey, Lillian Hellman, and especially Nadine Gordimer and Eudora Welty because those two women, in her words, "write about black people in a way that few white men have ever been able to write. It's not patronizing, not romanticizing. It's the way they should be written about."

Miss Morrison plans her novels in her head, so that when she finally sits down to write, she has, as she once put it, "already heard the dialogue, met the people, know their names." Admittedly disorganized and undisciplined, she writes impulsively and irregularly when she "[feels] the stride" and "[gets] the hook, the right metaphor for the scene." But her third novel, *Song of Solomon,* the personal odyssey of Malcolm Dead Jr.,

presented a different kind of challenge. "I had to think of becoming a whole person in masculine terms," she explained to Mel Watkins for a New York *Times Book Review* (September 11, 1977) profile. "I couldn't use the metaphors I'd used describing women. I needed something that suggested dominion —a different kind of drive."

The central metaphor in *Song of Solomon* is flying—"the literal taking off and flying into the air, which is everybody's dream." Inspired by his great-grandfather Solomon's escape from slavery a century earlier ("My great granddaddy could flyyyyyy. . . . He left everybody down on the ground and he sailed off like a black eagle. . . . He didn't need no airplane. He just took off; got fed up."), Malcolm, known as Milkman because his mother nursed him well past infancy, leaves his middle-class Midwestern home for the South, ostensibly to search for a secret cache of gold, but ultimately to find his family heritage.

When *Song of Solomon* was published by Knopf in 1977, it was inevitably compared to Ralph Ellison's classic *Invisible Man*, to Alex Haley's blockbuster, *Roots*, and to Maxine Hong Kingston's *The Woman Warrior*. A few reviewers quibbled about the occasional vanished character and the annoying subplots; most, however, were overwhelmingly enthusiastic. Perhaps the most rapturous was John Leonard, who declared in his paean for the New York *Times* (September 5, 1977) that *Song of Solomon* had been "a privilege to review." He was particularly taken by the evocative, poetic descriptions of places "where even love found its way with an ice pick" and where the "heavy, spice-sweet smell. . .made you think of the East and striped tents and the *sha-sha-sha* of leg bracelets." "From the beginning. . .Toni Morrison is in control of her book, her poetry," Leonard wrote. "Out of the decoding of a children's song, something heroic is regained; out of terror, an understanding of possibility and a leap of faith; out of quest, the naming of our fathers and ourselves. The first two-thirds of *Song of Solomon* are merely wonderful. The last 100 pages are a triumph."

In 1978 *Song of Solomon* received the National Book Critics' Circle Award as the best work of fiction in 1977, edging out John Cheever's *Falconer* and Michael Herr's *Dispatches*. It was the first novel written by a black author to be chosen as a full selection of the Book-of-the-Month Club since Richard Wright's *Native Son* in 1940. Because of the critical and commercial success of *Song of Solomon* (The paperback rights were sold for an estimated $150,000), Miss Morrison has cut down on her editorial work at Random House to make "a genuine commitment to writing and take the knocks."

Toni Morrison has been described as a "large-boned, substantial, sensual" woman with "honey-brown" skin, graying black hair worn in an Afro hairstyle, and large, arresting eyes. She shuns the literary cocktail party circuit, preferring to spend her evenings working at her desk. Her favorite recreation is gardening, a passion she indulges at her house in Nyack, New York, where she grows collard greens, cabbages, and strawberries. She also maintains an apartment in New York City. She still finds writing "difficult," but as she told Mel Watkins, "I look forward to it. It stretches you. . .[and] makes you stay in touch with yourself. I guess it's like going under water for me, the danger. Yet I'm certain I'm going to come up." Miss Mor-

rison is currently working on a love story based on Joel Chandler Harris' tale of the Tar Baby, a project that she admits could occupy her for years. "I rewrite all the way to the printer," she told one interviewer. "I'm never satisfied." In 1978 the PBS television series "Writers in America" devoted an entire segment to Toni Morrison.

References: N Y Times Bk R p48+ S 11 '77 por; N Y Times Mag p109+ Jl 4 '76 por, p40+ My 20 '79 por; People 8:84+ Ja 2 '78 por; Washington Post C p3 S 30 '77 por; Contemporary Authors vols 29-32 (1972); Who's Who in America, 1978-79

Mugabe, Robert (Gabriel) (mōō-gä'bä)

Feb. 21, 1924- Zimbabwe Rhodesian political leader. Address: c/o Zimbabwe African National Union, C.P. 743, Maputo, Mozambique

As head of the Zimbabwe African National Union, Robert Mugabe was the most militant of the black leaders in opposition to the white supremacist government of former Rhodesian Prime Minister Ian Smith. After Smith was replaced on May 31, 1979 by Bishop Abel T. Muzorewa under a new constitution that changed the country's name to Zimbabwe Rhodesia and ostensibly turned the government over to its black majority but left substantial power in the hands of the white minority, Mugabe vowed to fight on with his Mozambique-based guerrilla force for true black majority. "Genuine independence," he believes, "can only come out the barrel of a gun."

Since 1976 Mugabe has been aligned with Joshua Nkomo, leader of the more moderate Zimbabwe African People's Union, in the Patriotic Front. Backed by the Organization of African Unity and the neighboring "front line" states of Zambia, Tanzania, Mozambique, Angola, and Botswana, the Patriotic Front is also recognized by Great Britain and the United States as a force that cannot be disregarded in a Rhodesian settlement. Although most of Mugabe's support comes from outside of Rhodesia, he wields much influence among the guerrilla forces fighting within the country. Some observers regard him as the possible leader of a future socialist-oriented, nonracist, and nonaligned Zimbabwe.

The son of a village carpenter, Robert Gabriel Mugabe was born on February 21, 1942 at Kutama, northwestern Mashonaland, in the former British colony of Southern Rhodesia. He is a member of the Shona tribe, which now makes up over 75 percent of the population of Zimbabwe Rhodesia, and he belongs to the Zezuru clan. Educated in Roman Catholic mission schools in Kutama and Empenden, Mugabe began his career as a teacher at the Kutama mission in 1942, while still in his teens. In 1943 he moved on to the Dadaya mission, where he taught under superintendent Garfield Todd, who later became Prime Minister of Southern Rhodesia. Mugabe had his first clash with authority when he threatened to "box" Todd because of a deduction from his scanty teacher's pay. According to a profile in the London Observer (October 31, 1976), he "raised quite a hell of a row" before the amount deducted was restored. From 1946 to 1949 he taught at the Hope Fountain Mission.

In 1950 Mugabe went to South Africa to attend the University of Fort Hare, a training ground for black political leaders. There he qualified for a B.A. degree after a year's study, and it was there too that he first became seriously interested in politics. Returning to Southern Rhodesia, he obtained a teaching job in 1952 at the Drifontein Roman Catholic school in Umvuma, about ninety miles south of Salisbury. In 1953-54 he was a teacher in the government service, first at the Salisbury South Primary School and then in the midlands town of Gwelo. Mugabe moved to Northern Rhodesia (now Zambia) in 1955, to teach at the Chipembe Teacher Training College. From the autumn of 1956 until the spring of 1960 he was in Accra, Ghana. There he married, taught at the St. Mary Teacher Training College, and, most importantly, fell under the influence of the radical politics of President Kwame Nkrumah. According to *Who's Who in Africa (1973)*, his experience in Ghana gave him "a breadth of vision on African nationalism which few of his compatriots developed."

Back in Southern Rhodesia, Mugabe immersed himself in the nationalist struggle against the white supremacist government of Prime Minister Edgar Whitehead. In 1960-61 he was publicity secretary (or information minister) in Joshua Nkomo's newly formed National Democratic party (NDP), which sought to bring about "one man, one vote" rule by means of moral persuasion, civil disobedience, and propaganda abroad. Mugabe's education enabled him to bridge the gap between the grass roots peasantry and the intellectuals in the nationalist movement, and he insisted on involving the largely illiterate rural population in the drive for African rights and majority rule. "It will be necessary for graduates, doctors, lawyers, and others who join the NDP to accept the chosen leaders even if they may not be university men," Mugabe declared in a speech on June 11, 1960.

As its publicity secretary, Mugabe was charged with the task of announcing the NDP's initial assent to a new constitution on February 7, 1961, following a constitutional conference with British authorities at Salisbury. Although the constitution admitted blacks to the Southern Rhodesian parliament for the first time, Mugabe opposed it, since it granted fifty of the sixty-five parliamentary seats to whites, who comprised only about one twentieth of the colony's population. Largely as a result of Mugabe's influence, the constitution was rejected by an NDP congress at Bulawayo on February 17 and by an unofficial referendum organized by the party in July 1961—a few days before the predominantly white electorate approved it by a two-to-one margin.

After increasing restiveness among the black population led to the banning of the NDP on December 9, 1961, Mugabe became acting secretary general and publicity secretary of the Zimbabwe African People's Union (ZAPU), established in its place by Nkomo. Continued racial unrest led to a ban on ZAPU and the arrest of Mugabe and other nationalist leaders in September 1962. After his release in December, Mugabe went to Northern Rhodesia, where, in March 1963, he delivered a fiery speech at a meeting of the United National Independence party and was again arrested

along with his wife. He escaped the following month and fled to Dar es Salaam, Tanzania.

Meanwhile, the Rhodesian Front, which demanded independence for Southern Rhodesia from Great Britain on the basis of white minority rule, won decisively in the December 1962 elections. By that time the neighboring colonies of Northern Rhodesia and Nyasaland, with which Southern Rhodesia had been linked in the Central African Federation since 1953, were well on their way to becoming the independent black-ruled states of Zambia and Malawi, respectively. But the British authorities resisted Southern Rhodesian demands for independence, insisting that the white minority of that colony must first grant greater equality to the black majority.

A split in the leadership of ZAPU occurred in July 1963, when Mugabe, then still in Tanzania, joined with the Rev. Ndabaningi Sithole in breaking with Nkomo to form a more radical organization, the Zimbabwe African National Union (ZANU). In an interview in the New York *Times* (November 5, 1976) Mugabe recalled: "We broke with Nkomo . . . because we believed he was not for armed struggle [and] was half-hearted about it at the time." On his return to Salisbury in August 1963 Mugabe was named secretary general of ZANU, ranking second to party leader Sithole. He was immediately arrested again as a result of a speech he had broadcast from Dar es Salaam but was permitted to go free on bail.

As the highest-ranking African nationalist official then at large, Mugabe was interviewed by Robert M. Hallett of the *Christian Science Monitor* (August 19, 1964) at ZANU's modest Salisbury headquarters. "As far as we are concerned the time has come for African rule," he declared. "We are not for gradualism.... It is an insult to the African people. There is no compromise on the one-man, one-vote issue." He called for a "nonracial society," but one that must be ruled by the African majority. Although willing to negotiate with the British, Mugabe rejected what he called "useless talks" with Southern Rhodesia's white leaders. After delivering a speech in which he denounced the leaders of the Rhodesian Front as "dangerous cowboys" and ridiculed their wide-brimmed bush hats, Mugabe was once more arrested, in August 1964, and remained in detention or restriction for the next decade. With the African nationalist movement divided and in disarray, with its top leaders in prison, and with negotiations with British authorities a failure, Ian Smith—who had become Prime Minister in April 1964—unilaterally declared Southern Rhodesia (now called Rhodesia) independent of Great Britain on November 11, 1965.

During his years in confinement Mugabe became a convinced Marxist. Devoting much of his time to teaching young black political prisoners, he continued his own education by correspondence and private study. He was for a time an external student with the University of London, passed three law examinations, and eventually held a half dozen university degrees, in education, administration, economics, and law.

Meanwhile, black nationalist guerrilla forces began in the late 1960's to carry out raids against the Rhodesian government, considered an outlaw regime by the United Nations. The Smith regime responded with increasing repressions and adoption, in 1969, of a new constitution known as the "white man's charter." In December 1970 some of the lower echelon leaders of ZANU and ZAPU, while in confinement, proposed a merger of their organizations, suggesting that both Sithole and Nkomo step down to make way for a united front under Mugabe's leadership. Although it ended in failure, the attempt made clear Mugabe's acceptability to both sides. Later, Mugabe led a group of his fellow prisoners in an effort to depose Sithole as leader of ZANU, accusing him of "selling out."

Mugabe was among sixteen black nationalist leaders released by the Smith regime in early December 1974 at the urging of South African Prime Minister John Vorster and Zambia's President Kenneth Kaunda. Growing friction between Rhodesia and Zambia, as well as the overthrow, in April 1974, of Portugal's right-wing dictatorship, launching that country's African colonies of Angola and Mozambique on the road to independence, had caused Vorster to fear for his country's security and motivated him to enter negotiations with Kaunda and other African leaders. At Kaunda's invitation, Rhodesia's black leaders met at Lusaka, Zambia later in December and agreed to form a common front for negotiations with Smith under the African National Council (ANC), then Rhodesia's only legal black political organization, which had been founded by Bishop Abel Muzorewa in 1971.

Alone among the black leaders meeting at Lusaka, Mugabe refused to accept the unified ANC. His insistence on being acknowledged as leader of ZANU was rebuffed by Kaunda, who continued to recognize Sithole. After quarreling openly with Kaunda, Mugabe went briefly to Tanzania and then to Mozambique. There the new Marxist Frelimo government eventually permitted him to play a major role in organizing the thousands of young black Rhodesian exiles who began to cross the border into Mozambique in early 1975 to form a guerrilla force that became known as the Zimbabwe African National Liberation Army (ZANLA). Mugabe helped to establish three guerrilla training camps in Mozambique and directed guerrilla raids into Rhodesia, personally taking part in at least one of those skirmishes. His guerrilla constituents soon recognized him as the leader of ZANU. Mugabe's account of the nationalist struggles of that period was circulated in what became known as "The Mugabe Diary."

In the wake of the failure of South African-Zambian détente efforts in August 1975 and the breakdown, in March 1976, of constitutional talks beween Smith and Nkomo, a new peace initiative was begun in the summer of 1976 by United States Secretary of State Henry Kissinger, who was concerned about possible Soviet and Cuban intervention in the turbulent Rhodesian situation. On September 24, 1976 Smith announced that he accepted in principle the Kissinger proposals for black majority rule within two years. In preparation for the Geneva talks, Nkomo—who had broken earlier with Bishop Muzorewa—met with Mugabe at Maputo, Mozambique on October 5, 1976 to form a tactical alliance that would enable the two leaders to present a united front at the conference and eliminate the threat of future civil war between their rival nationalist organizations. Amid revolutionary fanfare, the Patriotic Front was announced at Dar es Salaam five days later and was promptly denounced by Sithole, who had never relinquished the leadership of ZANU.

But the Geneva conference, which opened on October 29, 1976 under the chairmanship of British U.N. delegate Ivor Richard, seemed doomed from the start. Hostility between the Patriotic Front leaders on the one hand and the delegations led by Muzorewa and Sithole on the other, precluded any semblance of black unity. While Smith insisted that the Kissinger proposals for a two-year interim racially mixed government dominated by whites pending adoption of a constitution based on majority rule must be accepted as a whole, Mugabe and Nkomo maintained that those terms were not binding, since they had not been party to them. Looking upon the Smith regime as illegitimate, even before the conference opened, the Patriotic Front leaders demanded that the theme at Geneva must be the immediate and total "transfer of power from . . . the United Kingdom . . . to the people of Zimbabwe" and declared their intention to "intensify the armed liberation struggle until . . . victory." Mugabe especially opposed the Kissinger proposal to leave the police and defense establishments in the hands of whites during the interim period. When the Geneva conference ended on December 12, 1976, the only principle that had been agreed upon was the setting of March 1, 1978 as the tentative date for black rule.

In April 1977 Mugabe engaged in talks about Rhodesia's future with visiting British Foreign Secretary David Owen in Dar es Salaam and was rebuffed in his argument that Smith and rival black nationalists be barred from future talks. A few months later, Owen presented his proposals for the vesting of executive power in a British commissioner and for an international peacekeeping force to all interested parties, but they were opposed both by Smith, unwilling to relinquish his authority, and by the Patriotic Front leaders, who demanded full power for their guerrilla forces. The talks were, for the time being, stalemated.

Toward the end of 1977 Smith entered negotiations with Sithole, Muzorewa, and Chief Jeremiah Chirau that resulted, on March 3, 1978, in what became known as the "internal settlement." Although it promised "majority rule" by the end of the year (later postponed to April 1979), it granted twenty-eight of the 100 parliamentary seats to whites for at least ten years, and it gave them the power of veto. United States Ambassador to the U.N. Andrew Young called it a "recipe for civil war" and a New York Times editorial (March 5, 1978) described it as "little more than a device for keeping real power in the hands of Rhodesia's small white minority." Addressing the U.N. Security Council in New York City later that month, Mugabe called the "internal settlement" a fraud perpetrated by the Smith regime "with the active assistance of African stooges and traitors."

Meanwhile, Mugabe and Nkomo, fearing that the "internal settlement" might leave them isolated, had resumed talks with Owen and other British officials at Malta in January 1978 and succeeded in narrowing the gap between their own positions and the Anglo-American proposals. In a meeting with Owen and United States Secretary of State Cyrus R. Vance at Dar es Salaam in April, Mugabe and Nkomo indicated that they might assent to British and American demands for an impartial U.N. force to ensure free elections in Rhodesia. Nor did they reject the prospect of taking part in a conference of all parties to the Rhodesian conflict, including the Smith regime. They continued, however, to insist on a dominant role for the Patriotic Front during the transition period.

Although several authorities have predicted an impending break in the tactical alliance between his Chinese-backed ZANU and Nkomo's ZAPU, supported by Cuba and the Soviet Union, Mugabe has denied the possibility. While conceding that some differences between the two organizations had arisen, he told Godwin Matatu in an interview in Africa magazine (October 1978) that "there are no differences of a nature that can split the Patriotic Front." Convinced of his strength, he asserted in his U.N. speech in the spring of 1978 that the Patriotic Front controlled over two-thirds of his country's territory and had the solid backing of the Zimbabwean masses.

Following national elections in April 1979 that were boycotted by the Patriotic Front, Muzorewa was inaugurated in May as Prime Minister under the new Zimbabwe Rhodesian constitution. Mugabe and Nkomo remained in determined opposition to the government and rejected amnesty offers but also indicated that they were receptive to a settlement more in line with Patriotic Front demands. In September 1979 Mugabe and Nkomo met in London under British auspices with Muzo-

rewa, Smith, and other leaders of the Salisbury government to discuss constitutional changes aimed at giving greater power to the black majority, but differences over proposed safeguards for the white minority and other matters remained as obstacles to settlement.

Robert Mugabe and his Ghanaian-born wife, the former Sally Heyaffron (or Sarah Haytron), had a son who died at the age of four, during his father's imprisonment. The ZANU leader operates his organization from a modest three-room flat in a rundown section of Maputo, Mozambique. According to Colin Legum and David Martin of the London Observer (October 31, 1976), Mugabe "is slightly built, his narrow head invariably drawn to one side between his hunched shoulders. He doesn't smoke or drink and . . . seldom smiles. . . . His gentle and diffident manner disguises a self-assured tough militant." Robert I. Rotberg, writing in the New York Times (May 1, 1978), noted that "Mugabe has always shunned the kinds of Sybaritic trappings . . . common among exiled liberationists. His asceticism and integrity are well known." And James MacManus of the Guardian (October 2, 1976) referred to "the mystique which he has deliberately created around his person." Self-described as a "Marxist-Leninist-Maoist," Mugabe is also said to be a devout Roman Catholic, but he rejects the traditional tribal loyalties that have been a dominant force in Africa for centuries.

References: Guardian O 2 '76; London Observer p7 O 31 '76 por; People 11:36+ My 7 '79 por; Africa Contemporary Record, 1976-77; Africa South of the Sahara, 1978-79; International Who's Who, 1978-79; Who's Who in Africa (1973)

Murphy, Thomas A(quinas)

Dec. 10, 1915- Corporation executive; Address: b. c/o General Motors Corp., 3044 W. Grand Blvd., Detroit, Mich. 48202

Once described in Nation's Business (March 1978) as "the flywheel for the world's largest manufacturing firm," Thomas A. Murphy became chairman of the board of directors of the General Motors Corporation in December 1974, following the retirement of Richard C. Gerstenberg. Murphy had been groomed for that position after serving for three decades in the financial department of GM. In 1970 he became vice-president and group executive of the car and truck division, and in 1972 he was named vice-chairman of the board. At the time that Murphy took office as board chairman, GM was beset by troubles, as a result of the international oil crisis and a business recession. Sales were in a severe slump and profits were down, partly because Americans were

Thomas A. Murphy

becoming interested in smaller, more fuel-efficient automobiles, whereas GM had built its reputation on the "big car." But under the leadership of Murphy and GM president E. M. Estes the corporation's profits have increased with each successive year. Murphy and Estes have directed the successful "downsizing" of the entire General Motors fleet, and the development of smaller models, such as the now discontinued Chevrolet Chevette. "I have a hard time figuring out why anyone would buy anything but a GM car," Murphy told the interviewer for *Nation's Business*. In 1978 enough people agreed with him to give General Motors a commanding 60.2 percent of the domestic automobile market.

Of Irish and German ancestry, Thomas Aquinas Murphy was born in Hornell, New York on December 10, 1915 to John Joseph and Alma (O'Grady) Murphy. He grew up in modest circumstances in Buffalo, where the family moved when he was six, and in Chicago, where his father was relocated by his firm, the City Products Company. Murphy attended St. Leo High School in Chicago, where he played on the basketball team and graduated in 1932, at the nadir of the Depression. Unable to afford college, he found it hard to find any jobs, except for some seasonal work in the summers of 1932, 1933, and 1934 in a Cicero, Illinois icehouse owned by City Products.

Murphy believes that those bleak years formed an important part of his "maturing process" since, as he told an interviewer for *Newsweek* (July 4, 1976), they made him appreciate that "getting a job was important—that it was something you had to get, and after you got it, you had to work to keep it." Finally, determined not to be an "ice jockey"

all his life, Murphy took the advice of a co-worker at the icehouse and used his savings to enter the University of Illinois in the fall of 1934. Uncertain about his career plans, Murphy at first considered going into physical education, and it was not until the last minute, when he was face-to-face with the registrar, that he made up his mind to major in commerce. At the university he played guard and tackle on the "B" football team, and he graduated with a B.S. degree in accounting in 1938.

Shortly after leaving the university, Murphy began his long association with General Motors as a clerk on the comptroller's staff in the Detroit offices, but only two weeks later was transferred by the company to its financial staff offices in New York City. His career with GM was interrupted in 1943, when he was drafted into the United States Naval Reserve. Discharged in 1946 as a lieutenant junior grade, Murphy returned to the financial staff in New York and began his climb up the corporate ladder, serving successively as an accountant and statistician and as supervisor of corporate forecasts and financial analysis. In 1954 he became director in charge of analysis of corporate and divisional pricing; in 1956 he was promoted to director of the financial analysis section in the treasurer's office in New York; and in 1959 he was named assistant treasurer. Murphy returned to Detroit in 1967 after being elected comptroller of GM, and reached the pinnacle of the financial staff in November 1968, when he became treasurer.

Continuing his rise through GM's upper echelons, in March 1970 Murphy was chosen by board chairman James M. Roche to become vice-president and group executive of the car and truck division, a post that usually went by promotion to the general manager of one of General Motors' car divisions. Having worked exclusively on the financial end during his years with GM, Murphy was somewhat intimidated by his new responsibility. He told Roche, as quoted in the New York *Times* (March 24, 1974): "I'm a bookkeeper. I don't know the first damn thing about running a plant." But the board chairman told him not to worry and assured him that the board of directors was confident that he could do the job.

When Roche reached the mandatory retirement age of sixty-five in December 1971 and was replaced by vice-chairman Richard C. Gerstenberg, Murphy was promoted to the vacant vice-chairmanship, effective January 1, 1972, over the heads of several executives with greater seniority. "Never in recent years has it been [possible] to pinpoint a man so early who appeared destined for the top rung of the world's greatest industrial empire," Jerry M. Flint wrote prophetically in the New York *Times* (December 12, 1971). "In the lower ranks of General Motors, it's expected that when the need appears, in three years and barring unforeseen troubles, he'll have the job at the top." As vice-chairman, Murphy took charge of the financial and overseas aspects of GM's operations, and he also served on the corporation's finance and executive committees.

In November 1974 Gerstenberg retired, and as expected, Murphy was chosen to succeed him as board chairman and chief executive officer, effective December 1. The GM board of directors named two vice-chairmen to replace Murphy and created a fourth executive vice-presidency, thus expanding the team that assumed leadership at a time of serious financial difficulty for the nation's number one automaker. The growing energy crisis had hurt GM more than its competitors, slashing sales by 26 percent over the previous year. Profits during the first half of 1974 had plummeted 70 percent. Observers traced the decline to the public's growing aversion to energy-inefficient "big cars," a corner of the market that had become a GM specialty, and to the inflated prices of automobiles in general.

At his first news conference as GM chairman, in December 1974, Murphy identified "lack of consumer confidence" as the major factor in the industry's sales decline and criticized government officials, the news media, and competitor Henry Ford II for their pessimistic assessments of the economy, which he felt exacerbated the situation. Robert Lindsey of the New York Times (December 3, 1974) quoted Murphy as saying: "We're going to turn this thing around because we have the will and the wherewithal to do it if we join in a common effort to beat inflation and, at the same time, climb out of this recession." At the same conference Murphy endorsed—although not very enthusiastically—a proposal made by Henry Ford II for an increase in the federal gasoline tax as a means of encouraging conservation. "If in the judgment of the administration it looks like a gasoline tax is necessary," he said, "I think we ought to consider it."

Although in February 1975 GM laid off a number of workers, raising the unemployment rate of its labor force to 36 percent, Murphy was more optimistic about the year ahead than most auto industry executives. Looking toward the end of the year, Murphy told a reporter for the New York Times (February 13, 1975): "We believe this country will be much further along the road to full recovery than the President's recent economic report indicated."

At GM's annual shareholders meeting in Detroit in May 1975, Murphy predicted a "turnaround year for our economy and our business." In answer to allegations by shareholders concerning reports of questionable political activity by GM and other major corporations, Murphy conceded that GM had contributed to the two major parties in Canada in the "five-figure" range and pointed out that in Canada corporate gifts are part of the normal political process just as individual contributions are in the United States. "In Canada

we conduct ourselves as a Canadian company," he explained, as quoted in the Wall Street Journal (May 27, 1975). Murphy also admitted that GM had made a $125,000 contribution to the South Korean Defense Fund, whose purpose, he said, was not to support any political party but "to develop understanding of free enterprise and combat Communism."

Meanwhile, the introduction of smaller vehicles had become a prime component of GM's marketing strategy, and in 1975 six new small car lines were made available to the public. In August of that year Murphy announced that GM would spend a record $15 billion by the end of the decade, most of it earmarked for the development of small cars. For 1976 the corporation offered the Chevette minicar, developed through the efforts of GM president E. M. Estes from GM models available abroad. That car was intended to compete directly with gas-efficient imports, and Murphy predicted a substantial increase in domestic automobile sales along with the expected decline in sales of foreign cars.

Even the sanguine Murphy was surprised by the stunning comeback made by the industry in 1976, when GM reported first-quarter earnings of $800,000,000, as compared with $59,-000,000 for the same period in the previous year. But although Murphy had based his predictions largely on prospects for sales of smaller cars, much of the GM recovery could be attributed to sales of its traditional big cars. Despite his high hopes for the Chevette, sales of that model were running at only half the anticipated rate as of mid-1976. Nevertheless, Murphy felt that the development of the Chevette was a positive achievement for GM. "It demonstrated our capability to ourselves," he told William K. Stevens of the New York Times (August 29, 1976). "More importantly perhaps for the long run, it demonstrates our capability and our dedication to a lot of our critics." In the fall of 1976 the 1977 models of such well-known large cars as the Oldsmobile Delta 88 and the Chevrolet Impala were "downsized"—made shorter and lighter—as part of GM's continuing program to achieve federally mandated levels of fuel efficiency, thereby placing GM significantly ahead of its competitors in meeting the new government guidelines.

By the end of 1977 GM's share of the domestic automobile market had risen to 56 percent, and Murphy forecast a record year for 1978. A particularly bitter winter had caused a temporary slackening of the sales pace, but in May 1978 sales of GM cars picked up strongly, and Murphy told the shareholders meeting that he was holding to his prediction. At that same meeting the GM management was faced with accusations that the corporation was cooperating with the white supremacist government of South Africa. At issue was a report drawn up by GM's South African subsidiary outlining the probable actions of that country's government in the event of a national crisis and how those actions would affect GM. "We are not working with the South African government," Murphy told the shareholders, as quoted by Reginald Stuart of the New York Times (May 20, 1978). "That contingency plan is a General Motors document."

On occasion Murphy has been highly critical of certain actions by the federal government. In April 1977 he characterized as "unnecessarily drastic" and "completely inconsistent with . . . President [Carter's] position on inflation and energy" a decision by the Environmental Protection Agency to determine by 1980 what levels of nitrogen oxide auto emissions could safely be permitted. That same month he described as "simplistic, irresponsible, and shortsighted" a Carter administration proposal to slap additional taxes on large "gas guzzler" vehicles. Although he later toned down his remarks, Murphy maintained that such a tax would penalize large families requiring larger vehicles. On the other hand, he endorsed President Jimmy Carter's anti-inflationary program for voluntary wage and price restraints. At an April 1978 meeting between the President and sixteen business leaders, he promised that GM would use "maximum discipline" to minimize costs and hold down price increases and added: "If it's good for the country, it's good for General Motors"—reversing the emphasis in a similar statement made some decades earlier by the late GM president Charles E. Wilson. Later in the year Murphy rebuked critics of the Carter plan, declaring that the President's battle against inflation "not only has a distinct possibility of succeeding—it can succeed, it must succeed."

Record second-quarter earnings for GM seemed to confirm Murphy's earlier predictions that total car and truck sales in the United States would exceed 15,000,000 in 1978. By the end of the year, GM sales accounted for more than 60 percent of that total, a goal that Murphy had set for the firm three years earlier. Sales were still going strong as 1979 began, and first-quarter earnings for the year amounted to a record $1.26 billion. With the GM share of the domestic market so formidable, the company was increasingly preoccupied with foreign sales, which had lagged seriously behind those of the Ford Motor Company. The key to GM strategy in its quest for first place on the international market is the continuing development of a "world car," combining European efficiency and American comfort.

At the May 1979 shareholder's meeting in Detroit, Murphy asserted that the economy still had "considerable forward momentum" and expressed confidence that there would not be a recession as some had feared. He again defended GM's South African operations, observing that the problem of racial separatism would "have to be solved in South Africa" and that it was inappropriate for GM to interfere in the politics of a foreign nation. Proposals to restrict or end GM operations in South Africa were overwhelmingly defeated. At the meeting Murphy backed the President's proposed decontrol of oil prices, declaring: "We have no immediate and reasonable alternative if we are to spur both the development and the conservation of oil." He also urged leaders of the United Auto Workers to "give some heed" to President Carter's economic guidelines when they begin negotiations in the summer of 1979 for a new three-year contract with the major automakers.

In August 1979 Murphy gave President Carter "reasonable marks" for his handling of the country's economic and energy problems but predicted that production of new passenger vehicles for the year would be sharply reduced from earlier estimates. He emphatically argued against proposals for government aid to GM's ailing competitor, the Chrysler Corporation, declaring that such assistance would present "a basic challenge to the free enterprise system." Instead he urged a complete review of federal regulations governing such areas as fuel economy and clean air that have forced heavy expenditures by the auto industry.

In addition to fulfilling his role as board chairman and chief executive officer, Murphy is chairman of GM's finance committee and serves on its executive and administration committees. He is a member of the corporation's policy groups for energy, engineering, industrial relations, public relations, marketing, personnel administration and development, product, research, service, and overseas. Murphy holds honorary doctorates from New York University, Fordham, the University of Detroit, and other institutions. One of the ten highest-paid executives in the United States, he reported an income of $975,000 for 1977, from his salary, bonuses, and stock options.

Since June 7, 1941 Thomas A. Murphy has been married to the former Catherine Rita Maguire. The Murphys, who are grandparents, have two daughters, Catherine (Mrs. Edward Rowan) and Maureen (Mrs. Donald Fay), and a son, Thomas Aquinas. They divide their time between a New York City apartment, a house in the fashionable Detroit suburb of Bloomfield Hills, and a vacation home in Florida. Murphy was described by Robert Irvin of the New York Times (September 8, 1974) as "tall, blue-eyed, and silver-haired." He "wears large, dark-rimmed glasses and favors the traditional GM upper echelon attire—a dark, pinstriped suit." According to Newsweek (July 4, 1976), he runs the corporation "from behind one of the untidiest desks in American industry—a litter crowned by a plaque imploring 'Bless this Mess.'" His wry, self-effacing wit, and easy relationship with the media contrast sharply with the more aloof corporate demeanor of some other GM executives. Murphy is a practising Roman Catholic, active in church fund-raising campaigns. He enjoys golf, but says he plays it "horribly," and exercises daily on a stationary bicycle. A compulsive reader, he admits to being a fan of Charles M. Schulz's comic strip *Peanuts*, from which, he says, "you can learn things . . . you can't get anywhere else."

References: N Y Times III p5+ D 12 '71 por; III p9 S 8 '74 pors; Nations Bsns 66:62+ Mr '78 pors; Newsweek 88:16 Jl 4 '76 por; Time 111:70 Mr 27 '78 por; Wall St J p1+ S 30 '74 por; Who's Who in America, 1978-79

Muzorewa, Abel T(endekai) (mū-zōr-ā′wə)

Apr. 14, 1925- Prime Minister of Zimbabwe Rhodesia. Address: b. Prime Minister's Office, Causeway, Salisbury, Zimbabwe Rhodesia; h. 8 Chancellor Ave., Salisbury, Zimbabwe Rhodesia

With the advantage of a clerical office that commands great respect in a country bearing a strong Christian missionary imprint, Abel T. Muzorewa became a major black nationalist leader in Rhodesia, though he was a relative political novice notably lacking in guile. In 1968 he was elected the first black Rhodesian Bishop of the United States-based United Methodist Church; in 1971 he acted as a proxy for jailed nationalist leaders; and soon afterward he established his own organization to combat the rule of the African nation's 250,000 whites over its 6,700,000 million blacks. After being involved in years of intranational

ist squabbling based more on personal and tribal rivalries than ideological differences, in 1978 Bishop Muzorewa emerged as the leading black signer of a constitutional agreement with the white government that provided for majority rule and as a member of a transitional government. Following an election on April 21, 1979, in which his party won a majority in Parliament, he became the first black Prime Minister of his country. He took his oath of office as successor to Ian D. Smith on May 29 and proclaimed the new state of Zimbabwe Rhodesia at midnight May 31.

Abel Tendekai Muzorewa was born to Christian parents on April 14, 1925 at the Old Umtali Methodist Centre, an American Methodist settlement near the city of Umtali in eastern Rhodesia. He was the oldest in a family of nine surviving children. His father, Haadi Philemon Muzorewa, was descended from members of the Makombe tribe, whose historic home was Mozambique. His mother was given the name Takaruda at birth and the name Hilda at baptism. Her father belonged to one of the royal families of the Wajindwi tribe. On both sides of his family Muzorewa's ancestors had been landholders who were evicted from their farms by white settlers.

"Discipline, sharp temper, humour—those words summarize my upbringing," Muzorewa wrote in his autobiography, *Rise Up & Walk* (Abingdon, 1978). "Add regular Bible lessons plus churchgoing, and you have the ingredients which have moulded my character." For some years his boyhood home was the village of Chinyadza, to which his father, who had been a pastor-teacher, moved his family after deciding to try to make a living as a farmer. Muzorewa attended a mission school there until the age of thirteen when he was sent to the Old Umtali boarding school, which he considered the best in the country. Beginning in early 1944 he taught in lower primary schools for about three years before he received an appointment as lay evangelist to the Nyadiri East Circuit in the Mtoko district. While preaching and offering guidance to his five small congregations, he decided to become a minister.

In 1952 Muzorewa graduated from the Hartzell Theological School at the Old Umtali mission. On being ordained a minister of the United Methodist Church, he was given as his first assignment the post of assistant conference evangelist. From 1955 to 1958 he served as village pastor of Chiduku North Circuit, during a period when Africans were beginning to express nationalist feelings. The young minister's own political awakening occurred in 1957 while he was attending a meeting relating to the formation of the African National Congress at which he heard a leader of the white supremacist Dominion party say, "I do not believe an African will go to heaven."

Under a scholarship awarded by his church Muzorewa went to the United States in 1958 for additional theological training. He first enrolled as a special student in the Missouri School of Religion in Columbia and the following year entered the Central Methodist College in Fayette, Missouri, where he concentrated on philosophy as well as religion. After obtaining his B.A. degree in 1962, he transferred to Scarritt College for Christian Workers in Nashville, Tennessee to study for his M.A. degree, which was awarded in 1963.

When he returned to Rhodesia in June 1963 to become pastor and station chairman at Old Umtali Centre, Muzorewa realized with approval that during the years he had been away political concern among Africans had intensified considerably. He was disturbed, however, by the split in leadership of the nationalist effort, as rivalry grew between the ZANU (Zimbabwe African National Union) and the ZAPU (Zimbabwe African Political Union). His own ministry reflected his commitment to the African liberation struggle, and in 1964 he became politically involved in protesting the deportation of Bishop Ralph Dodge of the United Methodist Church, who had opposed some of the repressive and discriminatory policies of the Salisbury government. Having specialized at Scarritt College in Christian education and the ministry to youth, Muzorewa decided in 1965 to give up his position in Old Umtali for full-time youth work. Later in the year he accepted the appointments of youth secretary of the Christian Council and traveling secretary for the Student Christian Movement. In that dual post he encouraged church involvement in political activity.

At the African Central Conference meeting in Botswana in August 1968, Abel T. Muzorewa was elected to succeed Ralph Dodge as bishop of the United Methodist Church, becoming the first African leader of a major denomination in Rhodesia. His advocacy of black, or Zimbabwean, interests soon earned him the enmity of the white-minority regime of Prime Minister Ian Smith, leader of the Rhodesian Front party, who in 1965 had unilaterally declared Rhodesian independence from Britian rather than accept London's plan for eventual black rule. In September 1970 the government barred Muzorewa from the country's tribal trust lands, where more than three-quarters of his church's 55,000 black Rhodesian members lived. But the bishop refused to stop criticizing the regime's racial policies after the ban, asserting that "where a government encourages separatism in people, we think this is encouraging hatred."

Because he had stood aside from Rhodesia's faction-ridden black nationalist politics, Muzorewa was regarded as a potential unifier of the movement against a November 1971 British-Rhodesian agreement providing for a gradual transition to majority rule over a period of decades in exchange for an end to London's economic sanctions against Smith's government. Jailed nationalist leaders Joshua Nkomo and the Reverend Ndabaningi Sithole, leaders respectively of the feuding ZAPU and ZANU,

both outlawed, asked Muzorewa to organize a consolidated opposition to the plan. In December 1971 the Bishop created a new African National Council (ANC), and within a few months it had aroused such strong black antagonism to the plan that Britain scuttled the proposal.

The established nationalist leaders regarded Muzorewa as their figurehead and expected him to cease his political activities after carrying out the campaign for which ANC had been formed. But in March 1972 the ANC announced that with Muzorewa as president it would continue as a permanent political action group, seeking universal suffrage. It declared itself in its manifesto to be "the one sole voice and instrument of the African masses of Zimbabwe." Unlike the ZANU and ZAPU, which had formed guerrilla forces outside of the country, it eschewed violence. For that reason the ANC became the only legal black nationalist organization in Rhodesia.

Although he is said to possess neither forcefulness nor dynamism, Muzorewa became a popular leader among Rhodesia's blacks, particularly in urban centers such as Salisbury. Because of his status as a newcomer to the political scene and his lack of cunning, many believed that he did not have the overweening ambitions that had divided the black nationalists' ranks. His church position, moreover, was a crucial asset among the country's heavily Christianized blacks. His membership in the Shona-language tribal group, comprising about 85 percent of the black population, also helped him. Nkomo had been the father of black resistance in the 1950's and was the shrewdest of the nationalist leaders, but he suffered the disadvantage of being in the Ndbele-speaking minority.

In December 1974 Muzorewa's organization united with ZANU and ZAPU in a new African National Council, while the Smith regime released Nkomo and Sithole after more than two years of incarceration. The release resulted from the efforts of neighboring Zambia and South Africa to bring the nationalists and the Smith government together for a negotiated constitutional settlement to avoid the civil war threatened by stepped-up ZANU and ZAPU guerrilla activity. As part of the move toward Zimbabwean unity, Muzorewa for the first time endorsed guerrilla warfare as a last resort.

Muzorewa was made president of the enlarged ANC, to serve until a congress could be held to elect a new leadership. However, black unity collapsed before tribal and personal conflicts, and believing that the ANC congress scheduled for June 1975 would prove to be divisive rather than unifying, Muzorewa vetoed plans for its convening. Political observers have pointed out that it was generally believed that Nkomo would have wrested leadership of the organization from the bishop. In the face of Zimbabwean divisions and Smith's announcement in August that he would never hand over power to any black majority government, an August 26 conference between the Prime Minister and the nationalists was doomed to failure.

To challenge Muzorewa's leadership of the nationalist movement, Nkomo withdrew from the ANC in September 1975. When he and Smith agreed the following December to negotiate, Muzorewa, previously considered the most moderate of the nationalists, denounced the talks from a self-imposed exile in Zambia and took the militant view that war was inevitable. After the Smith-Nkomo talks collapsed in March 1976, Muzorewa and his rivals intensified their jockeying for preeminence in anticipation of a British-sponsored Geneva Conference on Rhodesia called for late October 1976. In September Sithole withdrew from the ANC and later formed his own ANC. Muzorewa's group then became known as the United African National Council, or UANC. When the bishop returned from his fourteen-month voluntary exile in early October, he received an enthusiastic reception from more than 100,000 people in Salisbury that overshadowed the welcome earlier given to Nkomo. To outflank the bishop, Nkomo formed an alliance with guerrilla leader Robert Mugabe known as the Patriotic Front.

The October Geneva Conference, spurred by Smith's acceptance the previous month of United States Secretary of State Henry A. Kissinger's proposal for black majority rule after two years, was marked by disputes between Muzorewa and the Patriotic Front leaders. All three, however, rejected Smith's demand for white control of the army and police during the two-year interim period. The conference collapsed in January 1977. Soon afterward Muzorewa found himself isolated within the framework of African nationalist politics when later in the month the presidents of the five neighboring black-controlled nations —Zambia, Tanzania, Botswana, Mozambique, and Angola—threw their backing to the Patriotic Front's guerrillas.

At about the same time, however, Smith indicated an interest in negotiating with Muzorewa, who eventually, in November 1977, agreed to constitutional negotiation after Smith accepted universal suffrage as the basis of talks. Muzorewa was joined by two lesser black leaders: Sithole, who had lost control of ZANU to Mugabe, and Chief Jeremiah Chirau, a tribal chief with no record of opposition to the Smith government. None of the three commanded any guerrilla forces.

On March 3, 1978, the four negotiators signed an agreement for installing a black majority government by the end of the year. During an interview with correspondent Lee Griggs of Time (March 20, 1978), Muzorewa stated that the agreement was not perfect but added, "It was the best we could get, and the important thing is that we now have a basis for the transfer of power." His comment reflected the fact that though the new government was to take over December 31 following elections open to all citizens over eighteen, the settlement included strong safeguards for whites. Twenty-eight seats in a 100-member legislature were to be guaranteed to whites, for example, and 25 percent of the Cabinet appointments would also be reserved for whites.

A transitional government was to be headed by Muzorewa and the three other parties to the settlement acting by consensus as an Executive Council with a rotating chairmanship. Beneath it the agreement established a Ministerial Council of an equal number of blacks and whites. The interim government was charged with considering the release of political prisoners and eliminating racial discrimination. Despite his reservations about the pact, Muzorewa, who was expected to become the first Prime Minister under the new government, vigorously defended the settlement. Justifying its guarantees for whites at a March 19 Salisbury rally of 150,000 blacks, he was quoted by John F. Burns in the New York Times (March 20, 1978) as saying that keeping whites in Rhodesia would prevent it from becoming "a nation of beggars and paupers. . . . We want to insure that Zimbabwe will have bridges and roads and employment."

Bishop Muzorewa and other supporters of the internal settlement immediately faced substantial international opposition. Regarding it as a fraud, black African nations blocked a scheduled March 10 appearance before the United Nations Security Council by the bishop to reply to Nkomo and Mugabe, who the previous day had told the council that the pact was a device for perpetuating white rule. The United States and Britain, believing that no agreement could work without Patriotic Front endorsement, refused to back the settlement. After the Executive Council was sworn in on March 21, 1978, Muzorewa suffered political setbacks within Rhodesia as internal conditions deteriorated and as incidents occurred that threatened his standing among Zimbabweans.

Whites who favored the settlement, moreover, increasingly lost confidence in Muzorewa's ability to persuade the guerrillas to abandon their warfare. The March agreement led to an intensification of the fighting by Nkomo's Zambia-based and Mugabe's Mozambique-based forces. By July whites and pro-government blacks were reported to be not safe beyond a twelve-mile radius of Salisbury. In September, 1,490 members of the shrinking white population left Rhodesia, a one-month record. Because of the deteriorating military situation the Executive Council on October 20 reluctantly agreed to an Anglo-American plan for an all-parties conference, but Nkomo and Mugabe rejected the idea. With 60 percent of the country under martial law, the Executive Council, after initial opposition by the bishop, decided on November 15 to postpone elections until April 1979.

In that election Muzorewa's party won 67 percent of the popular vote and fifty-one of the seventy-two seats reserved for blacks in Parliament. Among the problems that the new Zimbabwe Rhodesia government faced were the continuing civil war, which Prime Minister Muzorewa's offers of amnesty to Patriotic Front guerrillas failed to halt, and the refusal of the United States and Great Britain, along with some other nations, to grant diplomatic recognition. As part of his effort to gain recognition, Muzorewa joined Patriotic Front leaders in a British-sponsored conference in London, beginning in September 1979, to seek agreement on a constitution for actual black majority rule and on issues regarding the country's social and political restructuring.

While in theological school, Abel T. Muzorewa courted Maggie Rutendo Chigodora, whom he married on August 11, 1951. Their children are Blessing Tendekai, Philemon Dairai, Wesley Tanyaraduzwa, Charles Scarritter Chido, and Charity Rufaro. Muzorewa is a trim man,

standing five feet two inches tall. According to June Goodwin of the *Christian Science Monitor* (August 28, 1978), he is "perhaps the most likeable of the internally based politicians" among the Zimbabweans. He enjoys whatever time he can spend at his farm in Dowa, some sixty miles from Salisbury, where he pursues his hobby of breeding chickens and hogs. He holds an honorary Doctor of Divinity degree from Central Methodist College, and in 1973 he won a U.N. Award for Outstanding Achievement in Human Rights for his opposition to minority rule in Rhodesia.

References: London Observer p7 O 31 '76; N Y Times A p3 Mr 22 '78 por; People 9:47 My 15 '78 por; Time 113:31 My 7 '79 por; Toronto Globe and Mail p27 Mr 27 '78 por; International Who's Who, 1978-79; Muzorewa, Abel T. *Rise Up & Walk* (1978); Who's Who in the World, 1974-75

Nelson, Willie

Apr. 30, 1933- Singer; musician; composer.
Address: b. c/o Columbia Records, Press and Public Information, 49 Music Square W., Suite 500, Nashville, Tenn. 37203

Perhaps not since the late Hank Williams has there been as distinctive and renovative an artist in country music as the composer and performer Willie Nelson, who created

the "Austin sound" and is worshiped by his fans as the "King of Country Music." In the 1960's, such Nelson compositions as "Crazy" and "Night Life" became country standards— as recorded by other singers. But since 1972, when Nelson left Nashville, Tennessee, the the country music capital, to strike out on his own, he has become, in the words of John Rockwell of the New York Times (August 8, 1975), "the acknowledged leader of country music's 'left wing,' working to cleanse Nashville of stale excesses by bringing it up to the present and back to its own folkish roots." Nelson has attracted an entirely new audience—the young aficionados of rock 'n' roll, who had been intimidated by the "red-neck" image of country music. As a result, his recordings sell by the millions, his concerts are routinely sold out, and his annual Fourth of July "picnics" attract as many as 100,000 fans. As Mick Martin observed in the September 15, 1978 edition of the Sacramento *Union*, "The magic of Willie Nelson transcends all boundaries and prejudices."

Willie Nelson was born on April 30, 1933, during the depths of the Great Depression, in the small Texas farming community of Abbott, some sixty miles south of Fort Worth. (Some sources give Fort Worth as his birthplace and March as the month of his birth.) When Willie was a small boy, his mother went off to find a job, never to return, and his father, Ira D. Nelson, eventually remarried and opened Willie's Pool Hall in Austin, Texas, which he ran until his death in late 1978. Willie and his older sister, Bobbie, were raised by their grandparents and aunts in Abbott, where he helped to earn his keep by picking cotton after school. His grandfather, a blacksmith by trade and a devoted amateur musician, gave him his first guitar and rudimentary musical instruction—the only training Nelson ever received. By the time he was ten, Willie was playing at local dances, along with Bobbie, who had taken up the piano, and who is still a member of her brother's band. At thirteen he had his own musical group.

"I have no negative memories about growing up," Nelson told Pete Axthelm of *Newsweek* (August 14, 1978). "It was being grown up that started to be a problem." In 1950 he dropped out of high school and left Abbott to join the Air Force. Discharged for medical reasons after eight months, he went to Waco, Texas where, intent on a career in agriculture, he briefly studied at Baylor University. About that time he married a sixteen-year-old Cherokee Indian waitress named Martha Matthews, by whom he had a daughter, Lana. But that stormy marriage eventually broke up. Meanwhile, between doing odd jobs, such as working as a janitor and as a door-to-door salesman of Bibles, encyclopedias, vacuum cleaners, and sewing machines, Nelson wrote songs and performed on the Jacksboro strip outside Fort Worth at rowdy bars and at honky-tonks with names like County Dump and Bloody Bucket, where the performers had to be shielded from flying cans and bottles by chicken wire fences. For a time he taught at a Baptist Sunday school—until its officials objected to his performances in honky-tonks. He also tried his luck in Oregon but had to content himself with a job as a plumber's helper. In the late 1950's he worked as a disk jockey for radio stations in Houston, San Antonio, and Fort Worth, and it was during those years that his music began to attract attention.

Nelson sold his first song, "Family Bible," for $50 just to feed his family. Like many of his later compositions, it was destined to become a country classic. In 1959 he wrote "Night Life," a song that was eventually recorded by more than seventy artists and sold over 30,000,000 copies. In 1961 Nelson sold the copyright to "Night Life" to three Houston businessmen for $150, bought a second-hand Buick, and left Fort Worth for Nashville, hoping to become a country music star.

In Nashville, Nelson married again, this time singer Shirley Collie, and that union, although also turbulent, lasted nearly a decade. While performing at Tootsie's Bar, a hangout for aspiring songwriters, Nelson came to the attention of singer Hank Cochran, who signed him up with Pamper Publishing, of which Ray Price, a leading Nashville vocalist and bandleader, was part-owner. Price soon hired Nelson as bass guitarist in his band, and by adopting "Night Life" as his theme, became one of a number of country stars who in the early 1960's scored a major success with a Willie Nelson song. Patsy Kline, one

of Nashville's leading female performers, made Nelson's "Crazy" a big hit of 1961, and Faron Young did the same thing with "Hello Walls." Another Nelson classic, "Funny How Time Slips Away," written in 1961, has been recorded more than eighty times.

But Nelson's own efforts to record his songs proved disappointing. A few early successes, such as the 1962 hit "Touch Me," which reached the top ten, and "Willingly," which he sang with his wife, Shirley, were followed by a number of RCA albums that failed to sell. "My music was not exactly what you'd call country music," Nelson explained to Wayne Robins of *Newsday* (January 22, 1975). ". . . We were just doing too many new things for the country audiences to accept right away." Nashville in the 1960's was a poor environment for the unorthodox, since it had become the leading regional recording center outside of New York and Los Angeles, and albums were being ground out on an assembly line formula. In competition with the new "studio sound" of florid orchestral arrangements and diluted rhythms, the free-wheeling, honky-tonk spirit of Nelson's music could not have been more out of place.

Nor were Nashville's production methods suited to Willie Nelson's material and style. Performers were expected to work with musicians hired by the studio. "You'd walk into the studio and they'd put six guys behind you who'd never seen your music before," Nelson explained to Al Reinert in the New York *Times Magazine* (March 26, 1978). Nelson preferred working with his own band, comprised of musicians whom he had known for years. But as Nelson told Wayne Robins, "It just wasn't an accepted thing to make records with members of your own band." Thus hampered by a system that would not accommodate his special musical personality, Nelson found only a limited audience during his years in Nashville.

Yet those years were not without their rewards. Nelson received substantial royalties from his songs; he was one of the few country musicians able to make frequent appearances in Las Vegas; and the Grand Ole Opry, the nation's blue-ribbon showcase for country music talent, made him a company member in 1964. He also appeared regularly on Ernest Tubb's syndicated country music television show, often singing the sacred song featured on the program. In 1967 Nelson introduced audiences to Charlie Pride, country music's first black singer, whose career skyrocketed while Nelson's was still foundering in Nashville.

In the late 1960's a hog-raising venture that Nelson had started on a farm near Nashville failed, just about the time that his second marriage began to break up. Then, toward the end of 1969, his house in Nashville burned to the ground, and all he was able to salvage was a sack of marijuana and an old guitar. The event was a watershed in Nelson's life. In the words of Pete Axthelm of *Newsweek*, "In 1970 Willie surveyed the ashes of his Nashville house, his two marriages, and his dozen or so flop albums—and decided to go home to Texas." He moved to Austin and worked on *Yesterday's Wine*, his last album produced in Nashville. Released in 1971, it became the first country music "concept album": a style long familiar to the world of rock music, in which the lyrics and music in each song are part of an overall theme or story. Nelson considered it the finest of his Nashville creations, and when it failed to sell, like his previous albums, it fortified his determination to abandon Nashville.

At the time that Nelson moved to Austin, its Armadillo World Headquarters had already begun to acquire a reputation as the refuge for Nashville expatriates dissatisfied with the country music mainstream. Those musicians, who came to be known as "outlaws," were country music's "counter-culture," rejecting the conservative image of Nashville for the dress, hairstyles, and taste for drugs associated with rock music. Nelson soon was in the vanguard of the "progressive country" movement in Texas. After he bought a second-hand Greyhound bus, he and his band toured dance halls and country fairs throughout the South and Southwest, where they became increasingly popular. On July 4, 1973 he staged the first of several annual country music festivals in Dripping Springs, Texas that featured such other prominent "outlaws" as Kris Kristofferson, Billy Joe Shaver, and Waylon Jennings, in addition to more traditional country stars. The audience was no less an unusual blend of the "red-neck" and the radical "hippie" contingents of country music. In recent years the more radical elements have tended to predominate at those festivals.

With the failure of *Yesterday's Wine*, Nelson decided to leave RCA. In 1973 he signed with Atlantic Records of New York City after receiving encouragement from its vice-president, Jerry Wexler. That year Wexler produced Nelson's *Shotgun Willie* album, described by Al Reinert as "the first album to catch any of the flavor of Nelson's live performance sound." It was also the first of Nelson's albums to succeed commercially. Within six months, its total sales outnumbered those of all his previous albums combined, and in November 1973 the Nashville Songwriters Association elected Nelson to its Hall of Fame.

In the spring of 1974 the album *Phases and Stages*, another joint effort of Nelson and Wexler, was released, and it also became a major financial and critical success. The second of Nelson's concept albums, it depicted the collapse of a marriage from the viewpoint of both the wife and the husband. "Unlike most concept albums, this one never forces the idea or relies on gimmicks," Loraine Alterman wrote in the New York Times (May 19, 1974). "Both the music and lyrics Nelson has written touch us directly because of their genuine concern for the situation that in one form or another strikes many people." The album sold over 400,000 copies, and one of its numbers, "Bloody Mary Mornings," became very popular as a single.

After Atlantic phased out its country music line, Nelson formed his own company, Lone Star Records, and signed a distribution agreement with Columbia Records. His album *Red Headed Stranger*, released in mid-1975, continued the "concept" approach and was even more personal in its content than its predecessors. It was intended, according to Nelson, as a combination of original compositions and "old songs [he] always liked and wanted to go into the studio and record." John Rockwell wrote in the New York Times (August 8, 1975): "What Mr. Nelson has done . . . is to keep the music naturally simple and to link the songs with short recurrent refrains and flashbacks to earlier material. The result is somewhat like Kurt Weill did in his collaboration with Bertolt Brecht, although, of course, the actual idioms are very different." *Red Headed Stranger* told the story of a wandering preacher and the lessons he learned in his travels. One of its selections, "Blue Eyes Crying in the Rain," brought Nelson—who had received five previous Grammy nominations—the 1976 Grammy Award for the best country performance on a single. The album eventually "went platinum," that is, it sold more than 1,000,000 copies. Universal Pictures has indicated an interest in developing its theme into a motion picture.

In his home state, Nelson has become almost a cult figure. The Texas state legislature unanimously declared July 4, 1975 "Willie Nelson Day." By 1976, "Williemania" was in full swing. Seven Nelson albums appeared that year on the charts of *Billboard* magazine, which named *The Sound in Your Mind* the country album of the year. He recorded *Wanted: The Outlaws* with Waylon Jennings, another progressive country musician who benefited from the Austin renaissance. A collection of duets and solos, it sold even more swiftly than *Red Headed Stranger*. Among other honors, Nelson and Jennings won the 1976 Country Music Association award for album of the year, and their "Good Hearted Woman" was named single of the year.

Among Nelson's recent albums are *Troublemaker* (Columbia, 1976); *To Lefty from Willie* (Columbia, 1977), dedicated to the late singer-composer Lefty Frizzell; *Waylon and Willie* (RCA, 1978); *Willie and Family Live* (Columbia, 1978); and *One for the Road* (Paradise, 1979), with Leon Russell. *Stardust* (Columbia, 1978), his own favorite and perhaps his most unusual album, consists of a series of venerable pop standards by such masters as Irving Berlin, George Gershwin, Duke Ellington, Kurt Weill, and Hoagy Carmichael, performed in Nelson's inimitable country blues manner. Carl Arrington of the New York *Post* (May 5, 1978) cited Nelson's "clear and variable country baritone" and commented, "Willie's phrasing is distinct from the styles of most other country artists. He leaves off the twang and paces his vocals behind the beat in a fashion that resembles that of one of his idols, Frank Sinatra."

Nelson's television credits include performances on such programs as the variety show *Austin City Limits*, presented on PBS-TV in March 1975. He maintains a grueling concert schedule, spending as many as 250 days a year on the road. In September 1978 he gave a performance on the White House lawn for the National Association for Stock Car Auto Racing. Although President Jimmy Carter was detained at the time by Middle East negotiations at Camp David, Nelson sang some impromptu duets with First Lady Rosalynn Carter, who, like the President, is a Nelson fan of long standing. In May 1979 Nelson presented Carter with a special Country Music Association award.

Nelson, who has formed a production company with two partners, has been involved in several film projects, including Columbia-Universal's forthcoming "The Electric Horseman," in which he appears with Jane Fonda and Robert Redford. He bought the Pedernales Country Club near Austin in the spring of 1979 as a permanent site for his July festivals. In October the Country Music Association awarded him top honors as entertainer of the year.

Willie Nelson was described by Stephanie Mansfield in the Washington *Post* (April 25, 1978) as "a five-foot-eight-inch . . . Gabby Hayes look-alike with a fondness for baggy jeans, green and yellow imitation Adidas, worn T-shirts and shoulder-length strawberry hair tied Tonto fashion with a faded bandana." From his three marriages, Nelson has five children and four grandchildren. When not on tour, he lives with his third wife, Connie, a former lab technician whom he married in 1972, and his two youngest children, Paula Carlene and Amy, in a three-story Swiss chalet that he built in the foothills of the Colorado Rockies after his ranch house outside Austin became constantly overrun by fans. The couple also have a house at Malibu Beach, California. Nelson has real estate holdings in Texas and owns controlling interest in a record label and a music publishing company. He is an enthusiastic reader of Edgar Cayce and Kahlil Gibran, and an avid jogger. Generally soft-spoken and self-possessed, Willie Nelson is also known for a quick temper that can be set off by such inanimate adversaries as locked doors and intrusive tele-phones. His broad, winning smile has been characterized as "beatific," "radiant," and "straight out of Huckleberry Finn."

References:: N Y Sunday News Mag p5+ F 4 '79 por; N Y Times Mag p20+ Mr 26 '78 pors; Newsweek 92:52+ Ag 14 '78 pors; Time 110:86+ S 19 '77 por, 112:81+ S 18 '78 pors; Brown, Len and Friedrich, Gary. Encyclopedia of Country and Western Music (1971); Illustrated Encyclopedia of Country Music (1977); Malone, Bill C. and McCulloh, Judith, eds. Stars of Country Music (1975); Shestack, Melvin. Country Music Encyclopedia (1974); Stambler, I. and Landon, G. Encyclopedia of Folk, Country and Western Music (1969); Who's Who in America, 1978-79

Nyad, Diana

Aug. 22, 1949- Athlete. Address: c/o Uptown Racquet Club, 151 E. 86th St., New York City, N.Y. 10028

The former women's world marathon swimming champion Diana Nyad drew the full attention of the mass media to the obscure sport of long-distance swimming with her unsuccessful but nonetheless admirably herculean attempt to swim the shark-infested, current-swept distance from Cuba to Florida in July 1978. A year later, in August 1979, she became the first person ever to swim from the Bahamas (specifically, North Bimini Island) to the United States (Juno Beach, Florida). As a professional marathon competitor, beginning in 1970, Miss Nyad set several world records, but the general public did not become aware of her until 1975, when she quit racing and launched a new career as a solitary endurance swimmer with a circuit of Manhattan. In addition to swimming, Miss Nyad plays squash, in which she ranks thirteenth among women players nationally. Miss Nyad's physical strength, coupled with her dedication and drive, mark her as as one of the foremost women athletes of our time.

Diana Nyad was born Diana Sneed in New York City on August 22, 1949 to the former Lucy Curtis and William Sneed, a New York stockbroker. Writing in Sports Illustrated (December 6, 1971), Dan Levin described Miss Nyad's mother as a "gracious, almost stately woman, with a sort of vaguely society manner." When Miss Nyad was three her parents were divorced, and her mother married Aristotle Zason Nyad, a Greek land developer. That second marriage ended about eight years later.

Despite a nascent penchant for inventive practical joking, Miss Nyad was a child who, as she recalled in an interview with Joyce Wadler of the New York Post (October 11, 1975), "took life seriously even then" and "didn't want to waste any time." With her half-brother and half-sister, she was raised in Fort Lauderdale, Florida. At the Pine Crest School, a private school in Fort Lauderdale, she began swimming seriously in the seventh grade, under the tutelage of Jack Nelson, who was her geography teacher as well as the coach of the swimming team.

"He [Nelson] knew a thing or two about mind over matter and dedication," Dan Levin wrote in his 1971 Sports Illustrated article, "and Diana Nyad met him at an impressionable time." Levin quoted Miss Nyad: "Coach Nelson became sort of a father figure to me. I respected him more than anyone I've ever known." She especially took to heart his dictum, "If you put your guts into something, you'll get it."

When Miss Nyad was in the ninth grade she finished a close second in the 200-meter backstroke race at the Florida senior regional championship meet, and during the following three years she won the 100-yard backstroke at six state meets. She dreamed of competing in the Olympics in Mexico City in 1968, but that dream evaporated when she contracted endocarditis, a virus infection of the heart, two years before the Olympics, in 1966, when she was sixteen and finishing her eleventh year at the Pine Crest School. After a summer of quarantined bed rest, she resumed her swimming routine gradually, over a period of several years.

Originally, Miss Nyad wanted to be a surgeon. After graduating from Pine Crest School in June 1967—with the slogan "Great Marks Are Soonest Hit" beside her yearbook picture —she enrolled at Emory University in Atlanta, Georgia as a premedical student. At that time

she was, she has said, "a real basket case" whose "adolescence was misplaced and came late." The dean of women at Emory failed to see the humor in some of her pranks (such as parachuting from a fourth-floor dormitory window), and during her sophomore year she was asked to leave. "It was kind of scary being kicked out of college," she has reminisced. "I wasn't ready for a life of work yet. I wasn't confused, but they'd had such warped impressions of me at Emory that I'd begun to wonder if maybe there really wasn't something wrong with me."

During the months following her expulsion from Emory University, Miss Nyad traveled across the United States and to Europe, worked as a lifeguard and waitress, and filled notebooks with therapeutic ruminations. In January 1970 she applied for admission to Lake Forest College in Lake Forest, Illinois, where she was readily accepted. Two important members of the administration at Lake Forest were aware of her reputation as a swimmer: Gordon White, the director of financial aid, and Karl Sutter, the swimming coach.

At Lake Forest, Miss Nyad took part in dramatics, played varsity tennis, and switched her major from premed to English and French. "I was very excited about physics and chemistry," she has recalled, "but I was really just using my memory. I wasn't getting the kind of release I'd gotten from theatre work, or even from playing the piano and trumpet in high school." She was an "A" student at Lake Forest, and she graduated Phi Beta Kappa.

A lasting ill effect of Miss Nyad's bout with endocarditis was a reduction in her swimming speed. As Coach Sutter observed: "She stood out as a person with tremendous mental toughness and more desire than anyone I'd ever coached, but judging from her workouts, she seemed more promising as a distance swimmer than a sprinter." She was persuaded to venture into the marathon swimming circuit by Buck Dawson, the executive director of the International Swimming Hall of Fame in Fort Lauderdale. "He had seen me grow up," she told Julia Whedon in an interview for an article in the New York Times Magazine (June 18, 1978), "seen the difficulties I had had after the endocarditis, and was sensitive enough to know exactly what marathon swimming and I would do for each other."

Miss Nyad began training for marathon swimming in the spring of 1970 and launched her career as a long-distance swimmer in July of the same year. In her first race, an international ten-miler across Lake Ontario, she finished tenth, behind nine men, and set a women's ten-mile record (four hours, twenty-three minutes). Regarding that race she later said during her interview with Julia Whedon: "The five-minute signal was given, all the great bears were greased, which rendered them even greater bears, and the ten-second countdown began. Everyone was supposed to wait for the

'Zero,' of course, but I learned that day a pattern of takeoff was quietly assumed in all races. The Egyptians barreled down the beach at 'Ten'; the Argentinians and Syrians were on their heels at about 'Eight'; the Europeans gave it to a fair 'Three'; and the Canadians and Americans would not budge an inch until the 'Zero' and the gun sounded forth simultaneously."

She went on to describe how she, "a swimmer who had always raced in very civilized manner," responded to "this alarming chaos": "Every time I was shoved headlong from the back, I gave an abrupt elbow in the ribs to the side. And for every Egyptian who ducked me five feet under to push himself ahead into free swimming space, I issued a return kick where it would be remembered most."

Over the following five years Miss Nyad swam distances ranging from twenty-two miles to fifty miles in the Suez Canal, the North Sea, the Nile, the Paraná River in Argentina, the Caribbean, Lake Ontario, the Coral Sea, and the Bay of Naples. In the fall of 1975 she swam the twenty-six unspeakably turbid miles around Manhattan in a record seven hours and fifty-seven minutes.

"I want to do something unprecedented in the world of sports," Miss Nyad once told a reporter, "something so outrageously difficult it would go unmatched for many, many years to come." In keeping with that desire, she attempted a 103-mile swim from Cuba to Florida, an event for which she began training a year in advance, in 1977. Her daily regimen in the first six months consisted of running twelve miles at speeds averaging less than seven minutes a mile, skipping rope for an hour, and playing squash for four hours, and she worked with weight machines twice weekly. During that initial training period she told Emily Greenspan, who was preparing an article on her for Us (May 30, 1978): "My triceps are aching so much that I just want somebody to grab them and hold them. But I don't have any problem sticking through a workout. I'm excited that I'm capable of pushing so hard and putting myself through such pain to reach my goal."

The last months of training consisted of swimming eight, ten, sometimes twelve hours a day. Before Miss Nyad left for Cuba there were problems of raising money for the venture (most of which eventually came from the Colgate-Palmolive Company), including the building of the motorized, pontoon-mounted "shark cage" within which she would swim, for protection from Portuguese men-of-war as well as from sharks. Afterwards, there were problems with the Cuban government, causing a delay in the timing of the swim. It was originally planned for the middle of July 1978, when the winds and water would be gentlest. Instead she was unable to set off from Ortejaso, Cuba until August 13, and choppy seas, abetted by stinging jellyfish and a swelling of

her lips and tongue, turned her dream of winning her "personal Olympics" into a nightmare. Forty-two hours and seventy miles out, she was hopelessly far off course, with Key West still at least sixty miles away. Finally persuaded by her crew to quit, she was pulled from the water in tears. "I've never been so tired in my life," she said. "I'm feeling pains I've never felt before."

Miss Nyad's first attempt to swim from the Bahamas to Florida ended abruptly on August 4, 1979, when she was stung by a Portuguese man-of-war twelve and a half hours out. In her second, successful attempt, on August 19 and 20, she swam the eighty-nine miles in twenty-seven hours and thirty-eight minutes.

Marathon swimming is perhaps the most punishing of all sports, both physically and spiritually. The swimmer is given feedings of high-energy drink at frequent intervals, usually once an hour, and yet twenty pounds can be lost in the course of a single swim and hospitalization and intravenous feeding are usually necessary afterward. The "loneliness of the long-distance runner" seems minor in comparison with the painful isolation experienced by the marathon swimmer, half-blinded by blurred goggles and deafened by several bathing caps (for warmth). The hours spent in cold, rough waters can be overwhelming, taking one across the threshold to a state of limbo comparable to an LSD trip. "My memory delves back into my childhood, to even as early as two years old," Miss Nyad once said. "Marathon swimming produces the same effects as floating in a sensory deprivation tank and magnifies them a hundredfold." She told David Zinman of Newsday (August 24, 1978): "You drop into a hypnotic trance. . . . A lot of childhood and sexual images go through my mind—quick dreamlike flashes that come like a picture on a movie screen. When I've finished a swim, I feel I know myself better." In the constant battle to stay alert, and to forget the pain, she uses the trick of counting her strokes to choruses of "Row, Row, Row Your Boat" and other songs.

The details of Miss Nyad's achievements, failures (the English Channel was one), Spartan lifestyle, and rigorous training are given in her autobiography, Other Shores (Random House, 1978). Mary Gordon, who reviewed the book for the New York Review of Books (December 21, 1978), felt "disappointment" at learning more about the workouts than about "the motives and emotions" of the swimmer. But Jim Fixx, the runner, considered Other Shores "a testimony to the durability of the human spirit . . . vividly told," and Jonathan Yardley, the swimmer, wrote in Sports Illustrated (September 18, 1978): "Though her prose can get excessively heroic (and it is, incidentally, her own prose), at its best the book provides a fascinatingly detailed view of the swimmer's life." In Library Journal (September 15, 1978), Francine Fialkoff wrote: "Even for readers not particularly interested in athletics, Nyad's determination and enthusiasm make this book intriguing and inspirational."

Miss Nyad herself was not entirely happy with her autobiography, as she noted in the preface to the book: "However delighted I was with some aspects of [the manuscript], I was appalled to discover that the persona of the book, myself, came across as such an overly dramatic braggart. . . . It seems I am simply not given to understatement. My world view is dramatic. Every minute seems like the most important minute of my life."

Diana Nyad is five feet six inches tall, weighs about 135 pounds, and has brown hair and brown eyes. Her lung capacity has been measured at 6.1 liters—extraordinarily large. Joyce Wadler in her New York Post article describes Miss Nyad as "open, direct, articulate, very, very high-powered." The swimmer speaks several foreign languages and plays several musical instruments. She had done

postgraduate work in comparative literature at New York University and is thinking of going to law school. "What interests me about marathon swimming is that it tests the human spirit," Miss Nyad wrote in Other Shores. "It is a sport of extremes. The real issue behind reaching the other shore is neither talent nor preparation nor the outwitting of an opponent. The real issue is the strength of the human will and the ability to focus that will under the most unimaginable of circumstances." But on reaching Juno Beach on August 20, she told the cheering crowd of another reason for her success: "I prayed to the man-of-war god."

References: N Y Post p21 O 11 '75; N Y Times p26+ Je 18 '78 pors; New Times 10:66+ Je 26 '78 pors; Newsday p4+ Ag 24 '78 pors; People 10:27 Ag 28 '78 pors; Sports Ill 35:38+ D 6 '71 por, 49:22+ Ag 28 '78; Today A p5 Ag 6 '79 por, A p1+ Ag 21 '79 por; Nyad, Diana. Other Shores (1978)

Olivier, Laurence (o-liv'ē-ā)

May 22, 1907- British actor; director. Address: h. Number 4, Royal Crescent, Brighton, England

NOTE: This biography supersedes the article that appeared in Current Biography in 1946.

Great resources of imagination, daring, technical skill, and other essentials to creativity as an actor, director, and producer have combined to make Laurence Olivier probably the world's finest interpreter today of the works of Shakespeare and Chekhov and of many contemporary dramatists. Even before his decade (1963-73) as the founder director of the National Theatre of Great Britain, he had been a powerful influence in the English theatre, having enriched the stage since the 1920's with a repertoire of remarkably varied and numerous characters. Lord Olivier, as he became in 1970, prefers the stage to the screen, but he owes his international renown to his performances in some fifty films, both British and American, over as many years. He has several Academy of Motion Picture Arts and Sciences Awards, including an honorary Oscar for his "lifelong achievement in films," presented in 1979.

Born in Dorking, Surrey, England on May 22, 1907 and christened after Laurent Olivier, a sixteenth-century Frenchman and his family's earliest known ancestor, Laurence Kerr Olivier was the third child—second son—of Gerard Kerr Olivier, an Anglo-Catholic clergyman, and Agnes (Crookenden) Olivier. "I spent most of my stupid youth being terrified of my father," the actor told interviewer Kathleen Carroll of the New York Sunday News (November 30, 1975), but his terror would seem to have been well founded, at least, according to his sister, Sybille, who has described the Reverend Mr. Olivier's wrath as "a storming, raging tornado which he'd turn on Larry in a way he never did on our brother Dickie and me." From his mother, the center of his boyhood world, he acquired much of his sense of fun, reflected later in his ability to discover elements of humor even in so tragic a figure as King Lear.

His father's theatrical flair in preaching fascinated Olivier, as did the drama and ceremony of the High Church service. When he began playacting at about the age of five he dressed up to simulate the vestments his father wore in church. A few years later, with the help of his father, he fashioned a small stage on which he sang, danced, and acted out stories. The Reverend Mr. Olivier secured the post of assistant priest at St. Saviour's Church in London in 1912 and the following year enrolled his son in a class for small boys at the Francis Holland Church of England School for Girls, near their Pimlico home. In 1916 Olivier was accepted at the fourteen-pupil choir school affiliated with the Church of All Saints in London. There he came under the influence of Geoffrey Heald, a priest devoted to the theatre who led the choir and directed student plays. The actress Dame Sybil Thorndike, a longtime friend of the Olivier family, credited Heald with having "sowed the seeds in Larry that made him bold and adventurous in his work."

After portraying a policeman in a harlequinade at All Saints, Olivier demonstrated the strength of his stage personality and his grasp of complex character as Brutus in *Julius Caesar*. Other Shakespearean roles that he played under Heald's direction were Maria in *Twelfth Night* and Katherine in *The Taming of the Shrew*. At St. Edward's, Oxford, the public school that he attended from 1921 to 1924, Olivier appeared as Puck in *A Midsummer Night's Dream*. Although his performances had always received praise, Olivier gave no serious thought to a stage career until 1924. Saddened by the death of his mother four years earlier and then by the departure of his brother to work on a plantation, he told his father that he would like to follow Richard to India. "Don't be a fool," the Reverend Olivier replied. "You are going on the stage."

In response to Olivier's application for a scholarship to the Central School of Speech Training and Dramatic Art in London, Elsie Fogerty, the founder and director of the school, awarded him tuition and a stipend to meet some of his living expenses. Between terms he worked as an assistant stage manager and general understudy at the St. Christopher Theatre in Letchworth, making his professional acting debut there, as Lennox in *Macbeth*, during the Easter holidays in 1925. Supernumerary chores in Sunday night benefits on London's West End provided further experience. Upon completion of his training at Fogerty's, he was awarded the Dawson Milward Cup as the best actor in his class.

It took Olivier three years to pay the dues that the English theatre traditionally exacts from beginners. He progressed from mere walk-ons, such as sharing with the future film director Carol Reed the task of carrying Sybil Thorndike's train in a London production of *Henry VIII*, to bit parts and then to leads, including the role of Tony Lumpkin in *She Stoops to Conquer* during his first season, in 1926, with the Birmingham Repertory Company. In January 1928 Sir Barry Jackson, the director of the Birmingham Repertory Company, leased the Court Theatre in London to present five "experiments." In *The Adding Machine* by Elmer Rice, Olivier had the minor part of the Young Man, for which he perfected an American accent. He was singled out for his electrifying characterization of Malcolm in the modern-dress version of *Macbeth*. Then, after essaying the relatively unrewarding role of Martellus in George Bernard Shaw's *Back to Methuselah*, he played the fiercely patriotic Saxon king in Tennyson's epic verse drama *Harold*. He also played the Lord in the prologue of a modern-dress version of *The Taming of the Shrew*.

Almost immediately, Sir Barry engaged Olivier for the part of the squire's son in *Bird in Hand*, a comedy by John Drinkwater that was then chalking up a long run at the Royalty Theatre in London. Towards the end of 1928, to gain the attention of producer Basil Dean, who was known to be looking for a virile young actor to star in his stage adaptation of the novel *Beau Geste*, Olivier agreed to appear as Captain Stanhope in two tryout performances of *Journey's End*, R. C. Sherriff's play about World War I. Olivier had not underestimated the effectiveness of *Journey's End* as a showcase: after seeing his sensitive portrayal of the fatigued front-line officer, Dean signed him to play the title role in *Beau Geste*. When *Beau Geste* closed in disaster, Dean quickly threw together another lavish production, *The Circle of Chalk*, in which Olivier, as a Chinese prince, was cast opposite Anna May Wong; it also flopped. In April 1929 a fling at domestic comedy, *Paris Bound*, fared no better, and in June of that year, despite affirmative notices, *The Stranger Within* proved a box-office dud.

Those four consecutive fiascoes were followed by the New York edition, in which Olivier had a role, of the London hit *Murder on the Second Floor*. On Broadway the English import foundered after a run of only five weeks. Returning home, he landed an excellent role in *The Last Enemy*, a drama by Frank Harvey, but it, too, failed. The London *Observer* critic Ivor Brown commiserated with the actor, affirming that Olivier had given "consistently brilliant performances in consistently ill-fated plays." The string of seemingly jinxed vehicles was broken in 1930 when Noel Coward talked Olivier into joining Gertrude Lawrence and himself in a comedy that he had written called *Private Lives*. It created a sensation, first in London, and later in New York.

London's drama critics, commenting on Olivier's strong supporting role in 1933 in *The Rats of Norway* by Keith Winter, were struck by the "sincerity" of his acting. Later in 1933 he was back on Broadway, this time in Jed Harris' lauded production of *The Green Bay Tree*. Next he partnered Ina Claire when she tried, unsuccessfully, to duplicate in London the triumph she had scored in New York as the heroine of S. N. Behrman's *Biography*. Twice during 1934 Olivier assumed roles that had been earmarked for others, replacing Ralph Richardson as Bothwell in *Queen of Scots* and Brian Aherne in the colorful role of Tony Cavendish in *Theatre Royal*.

For Olivier, 1935 got off to an inauspicious start with short runs of *The Ringmaster* and *Golden Arrow*. Much more heartening was the public's reaction to a revival the following autumn of *Romeo and Juliet*. During the seventh week of its run of nearly six months at the New Theatre, Olivier switched his role of Romeo with John Gielgud's Mercutio. In May 1936 Olivier and Ralph Richardson coproduced and costarred in *Bees on the Boat-deck*, a comedy by J. B. Priestley that drew mixed reviews. Later that year, feeling the need, as he phrased it, "to start life all over again," Olivier concentrated on the classics at England's Old Vic. In January 1937 he opened there in *Hamlet*, giving a performance that, it has been said, "laid the foundations for his becoming a truly great actor." During his two prewar seasons with the company he evidenced an amazing versatility: besides Hamlet, he played Sir Toby Belch in *Twelfth Night*, the title roles in *Henry V*, *Macbeth*, and *Coriolanus*, and Iago to Ralph Richardson's Othello.

Three Hollywood films, as well as the New York stage ventures *No Time for Comedy* with Katharine Cornell in 1939 and his own critically deplored production of *Romeo and Juliet* in 1940, kept Olivier in the United States just before and after the outbreak of World War II. When he returned to England in January 1941, he applied for a commission in the Fleet Air Arm and was designated a second-line pilot. But denied a combatant role in defense of his country, he responded to a demand for his services in morale-boosting movies and radio broadcasts. In June 1944, when the board of governors of the Old Vic asked Ralph Richardson to help resuscitate the war-disbanded London troupe, he turned for assistance to Olivier and John Burrell. During the next five years, with especially stunning productions of *Arms and the Man*, *Peer Gynt*, *Richard III*, *Henry IV*, parts I and II, *Oedipus*, *King Lear*, *The Skin of Our Teeth*, *The School for Scandal*, and Jean Anouilh's *Antigone*, the codirectors "raised the company"—in the words of the Olivier biographer John Cottrell—"to an unprecedented peak of popularity and prestige."

In the wake of his departure from the Old Vic in 1949, Olivier staged the London offering of Tennessee Williams' *A Streetcar Named Desire* with Vivien Leigh in the role of Blanche Du Bois. He then reactivated Laurence Olivier Productions, Ltd., which two years earlier had imported the American comedy *Born Yesterday* to the West End and afterward had sponsored the hit presentation at Wyndham's Theatre of *Daphne Laureola*, starring Edith Evans. To gratify his long-simmering ambition to be an actor-manager, between 1950 and 1957 Olivier introduced to London audiences Christopher Fry's elegant verse comedy *Venus Observed*, Gian Carlo Menotti's harrowing opera *The Consul*, and Australian playwright Ray Lawler's drama *Summer of the Seventeenth Doll*.

After directing and appearing in the Fry work, which had been written specifically for him, Olivier costarred with Vivien Leigh in productions of Shaw's *Caesar and Cleopatra* and Shakespeare's *Antony and Cleopatra* that were performed on alternate nights at the height of the tourist-thronged Festival of Britain in 1951 and later were transferred to the Ziegfeld Theatre in New York for a limited run. In 1953 Terence Rattigan supplied the Olivier-Leigh team with his "occasional fairy tale," *The Sleeping Prince*, which was set at the end of the Edwardian era and dealt with a rather humorless European noble in amorous pursuit of an American chorus girl. Roles of greater substance challenged Olivier and Miss Leigh at the Shakespeare Memorial Theatre in 1955: Malvolio and Viola in *Twelfth Night*, the would-be king of Scotland and his conspiring wife in *Macbeth*; and the battle-weary Roman general and his dishonored daughter in *Titus Andronicus*. Olivier's lisping, lightfooted Malvolio was highly praised for its originality, his chillingly low-keyed Macbeth cited as "the best . . . of our time," and his pathetic Titus hailed as "an unforgettable concerto of grief."

As the fifth-rate vaudevillian Archie Rice of John Osborne's scalding repudiation of "the system," *The Entertainer*, Olivier gave in 1957 what is now conceded to have been "his greatest performance outside the classics." For their portrayals of the lecherous Archie and his long-suffering wife, Olivier and Brenda de Banzie won the London *Evening Standard* Drama Awards as the year's best actor and actress. If Osborne's use of a seedy music hall comic as a metaphor for a deteriorating England was largely lost on American audiences, Olivier's *tour de force* was not: during *The Entertainer*'s limited engagement at the Royale Theatre in New York in 1958, he took his curtain call to thunderous applause.

With his reinterpretation of the title role in *Coriolanus*, Olivier contributed immeasurably to the Shakespeare Memorial Theatre's centennial season in 1959. The following year London audiences saw him as Berenger in a production of Eugene Ionesco's *Rhinoceros* directed by Orson Welles. At the St. James Theatre in New York he costarred in 1960 with Anthony Quinn in *Becket* by Jean Anouilh. Later, on tour, he exchanged the part of the tormented Archbishop for the role Quinn had vacated, the roistering king, Henry II, a character he continued to play when producer David Merrick brought the *Becket* road company back to Manhattan in May 1961 for a three-week booking. Olivier did not appear again on the commercial stage until he performed in the satirical comedy *Semi-Detached* in London during the winter of 1962-63.

Having meanwhile accepted the stewardship of the Chichester Festival Theatre, England's first arena-type auditorium, Olivier directed the three plays that comprised the inaugural program in the summer of 1962. His masterly presentation of *Uncle Vanya*, in which he also played Dr. Astrov, paved the way for his appointment in August 1962 as head of Britain's planned National Theatre. He continued as Chichester director until 1965. During the ten years that he occupied the command post at the National, he had to cope not only with the administrative problems endemic to an organization partly dependent on government subsidy, but also with the dilemma of dividing his artistic labors to the satisfaction of press and public, sponsors and subordinates. On one of the rare occasions when the directorial reins were in his hands, he supervised a consummate production of *The Three Sisters*. His few National roles included the title characters in *Othello* and *The Master Builder*, Captain Edgar in *The Dance of Death*, Shylock in *The Merchant of Venice*, and James Tyrone in *Long Day's Journey into Night* —portrayals that revealed him to be at the peak of his histrionic powers. The director Tony Richardson was among those who lamented Olivier's expenditure of time and energy on the minutiae of theatre management. "No one should allow Larry to do anything but act," he argued. "Few, if any, can do that so well."

Although Olivier was plagued intermittently by physical ills (a bout with cancer that surgery and X-ray treatments helped him to win, appendicitis, bronchial pneumonia, and a mild thrombosis), he did not surrender leadership of the National company until November 1973. Then, with Peter Hall at the helm, he remained a member of the troupe for several months, acting in Eduardo de Filippo's farce *Saturday, Sunday, Monday* and Trevor Griffiths' play *The Party*. In the latter—on March 21, 1974—he made what may have been his last stage appearance.

A short while later he fell victim to a muscle-wasting disease called dermatomyositis. He recovered sufficiently to resume his career, but in the less arduous media of television and motion pictures.

"At first I was frightfully snobbish about films," Olivier has been quoted as saying. His attitude presumably stemmed from the mediocrity of his early movies, the least objectionable of which were the melodrama *The Yellow Ticket* (Fox, 1931), *As You Like It* (Fox, 1936), and the sixteenth-century romance *Fire over England* (United Artists, 1937). Exposure, however, to the perfectionist methods of movie director William Wyler on the set of *Wuthering Heights* (United Artists, 1939) caused Olivier to raise his estimate of the motion picture's potential as an art form. The portrayal of Heathcliff that Wyler wrested from him brought Olivier an Academy Award nomination as best actor. The following year his interpretation, under Alfred Hitchcock's direction, of the moody Maxim de Winter in David O. Selznick's production of *Rebecca* (United Artists) catapulted him again into the Oscar competition. In 1940 he was seen to advantage in *Pride and Prejudice* (MGM), an adaptation that retained much of the unique comic flavor of Jane Austen's novel.

One of the films in which Olivier appeared during World War II to bolster the spirits of his countrymen was *That Hamilton Woman* (United Artists, 1942), in which he played Lord Horatio Nelson. His major undertaking of the war years, the spectacular color film *Henry V* (Two Cities, 1944; United Artists, 1946), drew countless encomiums, such as the appraisal in *Life* (May 20, 1946), "Both scholars and the ordinary public will rejoice . . . for Olivier has presented Shakespeare with a magnificence and a spaciousness worthy of the poet's language." Besides proving to be a financial success, the film won Olivier a special Academy Award "for his outstanding achievement as actor, producer, and director" and selection by the New York Film Critics as best actor of the year, among other honors.

With his screen version of *Hamlet* (Two Cities, 1948) Olivier matched the excellence of *Henry V* in production, direction, and acting. Describing the film as "a sternly beautiful job, densely and delicately worked," James Agee went on to say in his review for *Time* (June 28, 1948), "A man who can do what Laurence Olivier is doing for Shakespeare is certainly among the more valuable men of his time." *Hamlet* won the 1948 Venice Film Festival's International Grand Prize and several Oscars, including one to Olivier for his performance in the title role. After playing a bit part in *The Magic Box* (Rank, 1952) and leads in the commercial calamities *Carrie* (Paramount, 1952) and *The Beggar's Opera*

(Warner Brothers, 1952), he returned to Shakespeare filming as producer, director, and star of *Richard III* (Lopert, 1956), in which he portrayed the malignant Crookback as both humorous and ferocious. The British Film Academy gave him and the picture three awards.

Olivier also directed *The Prince and the Showgirl* (Warner Brothers, 1957), the screen version of Rattigan's *The Sleeping Prince*, costarring with Marilyn Monroe. Another stage role that he transferred to the screen was Archie Rice in Tony Richardson's somewhat flawed presentation of *The Entertainer* (Bryanston, 1960). He gave a delightfully smooth and unselfconscious characterization of General Burgoyne in Shaw's *The Devil's Disciple* (United Artists, 1959) and what Stanley Kauffmann called "an impeccably patrician performance" as the corrupt Roman General in *Spartacus* (Universal-International, 1960). Throughout the 1960's he continued to demonstrate his versatility as the decadent priest in *The Power and the Glory* (Paramount, 1961), the seedy schoolmaster in *Term of Trial* (Warner Brothers, 1963), the police inspector in *Bunny Lake Is Missing* (Columbia, 1965), the title character in *Othello* (Warner Brothers, 1966), and the Mahdi, the nineteenth-century Moslem leader, in *Khartoum* (United Artists, 1966).

During 1969 Olivier made guest, or cameo, appearances in *David Copperfield* (Twentieth Century-Fox), *The Battle of Britain* (United Artists), and *Oh! What a Lovely War* (Paramount). His later subsidiary roles included those in *Nicholas and Alexandra* (Columbia, 1971); *The Three Sisters* (American Film Theatre, 1976), of which he was also co-director; and *A Bridge Too Far* (United Artists, 1977). Meanwhile, his performance in *Sleuth* (Fox-Rand, 1973) as the mercurial mystery writer Andrew Wyke, one of his finest comedy roles on the screen, earned him the New York Film Critics' best-actor designation. He also won an Oscar nomination for that portrayal and for his superb evocation of evil as the sadistic ex-Nazi adversary in *Marathon Man* (Paramount, 1976). His characterization of a relentless tracker of German war criminals, for which he again earned an Oscar nomination, was equally convincing in *The Boys from Brazil* (ITC), one of his two 1978 releases. In the other, *The Betsy* (Allied Artists), he played an oversexed tycoon of the American automobile industry. He headed the cast of George Roy Hill's slight and sentimental comedy of 1979, *A Little Romance* (Orion), portraying a distinguished-looking French pickpocket who masquerades as a diplomat.

British television viewers saw Olivier in "live" performances of *Macbeth* in 1938 and Ibsen's *John Gabriel Borkman* in 1958. In appearances on American TV he won Emmy awards for his portrayal of the Gauguin-like painter in *The Moon and Sixpence* (1959), James Tyrone in the British-made *Long Day's Journey into Night* (1973), and the eminent barrister in *Love Among the Ruins* (1975). Another of his important TV roles was Nicodemus in director Franco Zeffirelli's epic *Jesus of Nazareth* (1977). Joining Granada Television in 1976, he produced a series of plays of his own selection. He was seen in some of them in the United States—as Big Daddy in Tennessee Williams' *Cat on a Hot Tin Roof* (1976), as the alcoholic Doc in William Inge's *Come Back Little Sheba* (1977), and as the homosexual Harry Kane in Harold Pinter's *The Collection*.

Despite his precarious health, the blue-eyed actor remains hardy-looking, energetic, and enthusiastic about his future acting commitments. He and the actress Joan Plowright have been married since March 17, 1961 and have three children: Richard Kerr, Tamsin Agnes Margaret, and Julie Kate. They live in a Regency house at the Channel's edge in the resort town of Brighton. Olivier's two previous marriages ended in divorce. By his first marriage, from 1930 to 1940, to the actress Jill Esmond, he has a son, Simon Tarquin. On August 30, 1940 Olivier married the actress Vivien Leigh, from whom he was divorced on December 2, 1960.

When he was knighted by King George VI in 1947, Laurence Olivier became the youngest actor ever to receive such an honor. In 1970 when, as a reward for his "services to the theatre," Queen Elizabeth II made him a peer of the realm, thus entitling him to a seat for life in the House of Lords, he became the first actor in history to attain that distinction. The largest of the auditoriums in the National Theatre's Thames-side complex bears his name.

References: Barker, Felix. The Oliviers (1953); Cottrell, Joan. Laurence Olivier (1975); Gourlay, Logan. Olivier (1974); Morley, Margaret. The Films of Laurence Olivier (1978)

O'Neal, A(rthur) Daniel, (Jr.)

May 15, 1936- Government official. Address: b. Interstate Commerce Commission, 12th St. and Constitution Ave., NW, Washington, D.C. 20423; h. 1905 Torregrossa Ct., McLean, Va. 22101

The apparent success of the 1978 airline deregulation has increased pressures for the removal of government controls over the trucking and railroad industries. At the center of those pressures, some of them exerted by

A. Daniel O'Neal

anti-inflation tacticians, is A. Daniel O'Neal, chairman of the ninety-two-year-old Interstate Commerce Commission, which regulates the nation's railroads and trucking companies. Since taking over the ICC chairmanship from George M. Stafford in 1977, O'Neal has moved to revitalize his once lethargic agency and loosen its regulatory grip. As chairman, he has attempted to steer a middle course between advocates of immediate, sweeping deregulation and supporters of the status quo. In his work, moreover, toward administrative and other reforms in line with changing economic and social conditions, O'Neal, a lawyer from Seattle, has lived up to the reputation as a progressive that he had acquired as transportation counsel to the Senate Commerce Committee. In October 1979 he announced that when his ICC term expired on December 31, 1979, he would not seek reappointment, but instead would leave government service, probably to return to his law practice.

Arthur Daniel O'Neal Jr. was born on May 15, 1936 in Bremerton, Washington, the son of Arthur Daniel and Louise Ragna (Nordahl) O'Neal. He attended Whitman College in Walla Walla, Washington, where he was a member of the Phi Delta Theta social fraternity, majored in mathematics, and earned his B.A. degree in 1959. During a four-year stint in the Navy he was assigned to destroyers in the Pacific and served for a time in waters off Vietnam. On his release from military duty in the rank of lieutenant (j.g.) in 1963, he entered the University of Washington Law School. He was awarded a J.D. degree and admitted to the Washington State bar in 1965.

As soon as he left law school, O'Neal went to Washington, D.C. as a staff counsel to the Senate Commerce Committee, headed by Democratic Senator Warren G. Magnuson of the state of Washington, which has jurisdiction over transportation legislation. Occupying a wing of the Old Senate Office Building known as "Maggie's Alley" after the veteran Senator, the committee staff has traditionally attracted smart, independent, aggressive professionals, often from the state of Washington, who exercise considerable influence over new legislation. O'Neal spent a year on the staff handling routine chores but then moved in 1967 to Magnuson's own office as a legislative assistant.

With an eye on Magnuson's 1968 reelection campaign, O'Neal worked on constituent services and bills that reinforced the Senator's growing reputation as an advocate of consumer interests. Following Magnuson's victory, O'Neal returned to the Commerce Committee staff in 1969 as counsel to the surface transportation subcommittee. When a correspondent for *Business Week* (April 4, 1977) asked about his choice of assignment, he explained, "I sure didn't study anything about it in school. But the slot was open, and I wanted back on the committee. Anyway, the area is important."

O'Neal served as surface transportation counsel until 1971, when he became the committee's transportation counsel. In 1970 he wrote the final Senate version of the legislation establishing a passenger rail system under the National Railroad Passenger Corporation, which he optimistically hoped would eliminate financial losses in passenger transportation by doing away with competitive duplication and changing management. When the government-sponsored service went into operation in the spring of 1971, its original nickname, Railpax, was changed to Amtrack. O'Neal was also coauthor of "A Study of the Penn Central and Other Railroads," published by the United States Government Printing Office in 1972, and a 1973 Senate report "The Penn Central and Other Railroads." By 1973 he had become a leading expert on water, truck, and rail transportation.

At the recommendation of Senator Magnuson, on March 6, 1973 President Richard Nixon nominated O'Neal to the eleven-member Interstate Commerce Commission to replace Rodolfo Montejano, a temporary appointee, as one of the five Democratic members. A month later the Senate confirmed O'Neal's appointment. Established in 1887, the ICC is the federal government's oldest regulatory agency. As additional legislation broadened its jurisdiction over the years, the commission became responsible for regulating interstate surface transportation that included trains, trucks, buses, inland waterways, coastal shipping, and, for a time, oil pipelines. The commission certifies carriers seeking to provide service, controls rates, rules on the adequacy of service, and performs other functions that are intended to insure adequate, nondiscriminatory service at fair and reasonable rates. By 1973, however, it had acquired a reputation as one of the least effective of the regulatory agencies—slow-moving, tradition-bound, and insensitive to consumer needs.

As an ICC member O'Neal was considered a progressive, or, according to *Forbes* (July 1, 1977), "the closest thing the ICC ever had to a consumer advocate." During 1976, for example, he gave a number of speeches attacking the lack of public participation in the commission's dealings with truckers and shippers. However, Richard Briggs, vice-president of the Association of American Railroads, told Ernest Holsendolph of the New York *Times* (April 9, 1978), "I can remember when Dan O'Neal was one of those 11 [commissioners]. Like the others, he would file those wordy dissents that sometimes had little to do with the real issues."

Only after the Democrats regained control in Washington by Jimmy Carter's election in 1976, did O'Neal have a chance to influence the commission's policies and practices substantially. Appointed by the newly inaugurated President Carter, he succeeded George M. Stafford as chairman of the ICC in April 1977. With speed uncharacteristic of ICC officials he ordered a quick outside study of the commission's operations and sent a report to Carter in mid-1977 criticizing the agency for its "lack of a strong policy planning entity and [for] communications and structural imbalances." The report also found that the ICC had been taking "narrow, legalistic, judicial approaches to problems which require decisions based on sound economics and practical analyses."

Acting decisively on the findings of the study, O'Neal established a policy-planning bureau, a data-processing unit to keep track of the 18,000 common carriers regulated by the ICC, and offices to deal with minority entrepreneurs, small businesses, and consumer concerns. Enforcement of the agency's ethical code was tightened to bar improper contacts between ICC staff members and parties interested in a case before the commission. In agreement with the White House, the number of commissioners was reduced from eleven to seven.

Reaction to O'Neal's administrative reforms was generally positive, as Holsendolph reported in his New York *Times* article. "I have spent 30 years dealing with this industry and the way well-heeled trucking companies are given privileges," Leaman McCoy, a black trucking executive, told him. "But only now can I say that minorities and other small companies are getting attention thanks to the small business office that Dan O'Neal has set up." Holsendolph also quoted Repre-

sentative Millicent Fenwick, a New Jersey Republican and member of the Small Business Committee, as saying, "I like the new atmosphere down there. I'm not satisfied that adequate regulatory reform has occurred yet, but under O'Neal they are moving in that direction."

The most urgent issue facing O'Neal was, in fact, not administrative reform but deregulation. By 1977 a coalition of liberals and conservatives had begun to call for less government control over the transportation industries so that companies would be freer to provide service and set rates in competition with one another without sanction from Washington. Alfred E. Kahn, then chairman of the Civil Aeronautics Board, pushed through partial deregulation of the airline industry in 1978 and saw fares drop and profits soar with dramatically increased passenger volume. Kahn's success increased pressure on the ICC for similar action although critics maintained that such generally happy results could not be expected from deregulation of surface transportation.

In an interview for *Forbes* (July 1, 1977), soon after he had taken over the ICC chairmanship, O'Neal expressed a cautious attitude toward deregulation: "Regulation is a very imperfect system. Unfettered competition is also imperfect. We need to try to find the best mix." But he recognized the pressure for deregulation: "Jimmy Carter didn't put any conditions on the job, but I feel implicitly that if the commission fails to act, the White House will feel disposed to introduce legislation." The issue of deregulation centered primarily on trucking, which had been subjected to ICC control in 1935 in an effort to eliminate cutthroat competition and end price discrimination against small shippers. Under the regulatory system the ICC certified carriers to provide service for specific products along defined routes. Applicants for certification had to show that a public need existed for their services and demonstrate that carriers serving the route would not be hurt by additional competition. The certified carriers could set their rates collectively with ICC approval, which was normally granted for rate proposals reflecting the carriers' average operating efficiency. As more efficient operators, the eight largest truck lines have shown a highly profitable average return of over 20 percent on equity in the past eight years.

Deregulation proponents, including President Carter and Senator Edward M. Kennedy, argue that competition would cut shipping rates and drive out inefficient companies. The American Trucking Associations and the Teamsters Union contend, however, that deregulation would not lead to lower rates and increased volume and profits, but would cause confusion in the industry, cut off service to smaller communities, and force out so many competitors that rates would rise.

Chairman O'Neal's first response to those pressures was to conduct a series of regional hearings in 1977 to receive complaints and recommendations concerning the trucking industry. The hearings led to an ICC staff study recommending administrative changes to promote competition in the industry. From the staff recommendations O'Neal drafted his own proposals, which were presented to the ICC on October 31, 1978, after Transportation Secretary Brock Adams had criticized the commission's lack of progress toward deregulation. The proposals would, in effect, deregulate all truckers except less-than-truckload carriers, loosen controls even for that traffic, and establish a range within which companies could adjust prices without ICC review.

Although initial ICC reaction to its chairman's proposals was cool, in late November the commissioners took the major step of permitting companies that haul their own goods by truck to transport goods for other shippers. Further ICC decisions provided that a new truck line seeking permission to operate need only show that it will "serve a useful public purpose," that truckers should not receive a greater return on equity than manufacturers, and that a carrier may contract to haul the goods of more than eight shippers, the old limit imposed by the ICC. In another move to stimulate competition, in February 1979 the commission announced it would give preference to applicants for certification who promise to provide service at cut rates.

"We're changing the whole ball game," O'Neal was quoted as saying in Business Week (November 27, 1978), and according to Fortune (December 18, 1978), wits in the trucking industry were joking about the "ICC's going out-of-business sale." Some truckers and Teamsters Union President Frank E. Fitzsimmons have called for O'Neal's resignation, but reaction from the Carter Administration has been favorable. O'Neal and the Administration agree, however, that legislative changes will also be necessary to promote deregulation. In early 1979 both the Administration and Senator Kennedy were reported drafting bills for presentation to Congress and the American Trucking Association was framing its own defensive deregulation proposal.

While deregulation of trucking seems likely to lower rates, United States railroads seek deregulation on the other hand to permit rate increases. The reason lies in the railroads' meager profits, which average a sickly 0.6 percent on investment. Legislation passed in 1976 provided that the ICC should regulate rates only where railroads have "market dominance," but to the annoyance of Transportation Secretary Adams, who had supported the railroad bill as a Congressman, the commission has left 50 percent of the railroads'

business tightly regulated. According to railroad spokesmen, ICC policies allow the companies freedom to change rates only in markets where they would lose too much traffic to truck or barge competition if rates were raised.

In an article for Forbes (November 27, 1978) on the pros and cons of railroad deregulation, James Cook quoted O'Neal as explaining, "The railroads would like to have freedom to increase rates on those commodities for which they do not have competition or adequate competition—coal and other bulk commodities. . . . We have a statutory mandate from Congress to see that captive shippers are not overcharged." Nonetheless, the ICC is reassessing its definition of market dominance under O'Neal's leadership at a time when the Transportation Department has proposed that Congress provide railroads with a 7 percent "zone of reasonableness" within which they could adjust their rates to shippers without ICC approval. As in trucking, President Carter is pressing to end most ICC controls over the railroad industry.

The Carter government's bright, articulate defender of ICC efficiency has been described in the press as "boyish-looking" and, according to Time (February 5, 1979), is "a soft-voiced, informal lawyer (he wears short-sleeved shirts even in January)." While serving in the Navy, on August 5, 1961 A. Daniel O'Neal married Diana Gay Reedy. They have four children: Daniel Stewart, Reed Kazis, David Christopher, and Beth Marie. O'Neal is a Protestant.

References: Bsns W A p84 Ap 4 '77 por; N Y Times III p1+ Ja 7 '79 por; Who's Who in America, 1978-79; Who's Who in American Politics, 1977-78

O'Neill, Gerard K(itchen)

Feb. 6, 1927- Physicist; educator. Address: b. Department of Physics, Princeton University, Princeton, N.J. 08540; h. 127 McCosh Circle, Princeton, N.J. 08540

For decades space colonies were only a dream of science fiction writers, but they entered the realm of possibility in the mid-1970's with the publication of Gerard K. O'Neill's The High Frontier. That work won for him the Phi Beta Kappa award as the best science book of 1977 and popularized his way of looking at near-earth space "not as a void, but as a culture medium, rich in matter and energy." A specialist in high-energy particle physics and the inventor of the colliding-beam storage ring, O'Neill has been a physics professor at Princeton University since 1954.

Gerard K. O'Neill

He first realized the technical feasibility of space colonization, or as he prefers to call it, the "humanization" of space, in 1969. Over the next few years he drew up the blueprints for increasingly elaborate self-supporting space habitats that could be constructed entirely from lunar and asteroidal raw materials and powered by solar energy.

"It is mainly civil engineering on a large scale, in a well-understood, highly predictable environment," O'Neill told a Congressional committee investigating the subject in July 1975. Arguing his case with contagious enthusiasm, he describes space settlements as the obvious solution to such seemingly intractable earthly problems as overpopulation and fossil fuel depletion, and he estimates that the payback from potential space manufacturing is virtually limitless. O'Neill readily admits that his conceptions are, as he once put it, "very rich in future shock," but he reminds skeptics that the "breakout" from a planet into a space colony is "almost inevitable" and is ultimately "the difference between success and failure for intelligent life."

Gerard Kitchen O'Neill was born in New York City, New York on February 6, 1927, the only child of Edward Gerard O'Neill, a lawyer, and his wife, Dorothy Lewis (Kitchen) O'Neill. Raised in Connecticut and in upstate New York, he attended the Newburgh Free Academy in Newburgh, New York, where he edited the school newspaper. In his spare time he earned pocket money by broadcasting the news for a local commercial radio station.

O'Neill graduated from high school in 1944 and immediately enlisted in the United States Navy. After being trained as a radar technician, he was shipped to the western Pacific in the closing days of World War II.

Following his discharge in 1946 with the rank of radar technician II, O'Neill enrolled at Swarthmore College in Swarthmore, Pennsylvania to study physics and mathematics. Having seen at firsthand the role played by physicists in the war, he was determined, as he told Current Biography, to use the power of increased knowledge of the natural world "for human benefit rather than for weapons." After taking his B.A. degree, Phi Beta Kappa, in 1950, he began his graduate study at Cornell University in Ithaca, New York on an Atomic Energy Commission fellowship. Four years later, on submission of his doctoral dissertation on the scattering of 14.8 MeV neutrons, he obtained his Ph.D. degree in physics.

That same year—1954—O'Neill joined the Princeton University faculty as a physics instructor. Undiscouraged by the skepticism of his colleagues, he began investigating techniques for increasing the collision energies of atomic beams from particle accelerators. After about two years' research, he came up with a design for a special storage ring—an annular vacuum chamber in which scientists could store electrically charged atomic or subatomic particles, then cause them to collide head-on, thus releasing greater energy. Gradually he convinced other physicists of the efficacy of his scheme, and, in 1959, with financial support from the Office of Naval Research and the Atomic Energy Commission, he and Dr. Wolfgang K. H. Panofsky of Stanford University oversaw the construction of two particle storage rings at Stanford. In 1965, using charged electrons, O'Neill finally demonstrated his colliding-beam theory, which has since become a principle of high-energy physics. Later that year he was named full professor of physics at Princeton.

Always fascinated by space exploration, O'Neill applied for the United States astronaut corps when NASA opened the program to civilian scientists in 1966. "The space age is perhaps the most exciting moment for man in many centuries," he said, in explaining his decision to Richard K. Rein, who interviewed him for a People magazine (December 12, 1977) profile. "To be alive . . . and not take part in it seemed terribly myopic." After undergoing months of intensive training and testing, he was selected as a finalist, but a few weeks later NASA discontinued the program. O'Neill recovered from his initial disappointment with characteristic resilience and returned to research and teaching at Princeton.

In 1969, as campus demonstrations against the Vietnam war mounted, O'Neill found himself teaching an introductory physics course to several hundred freshmen, most of whom were disenchanted with what they viewed as the irrelevance of the natural sciences. To answer some of his own questions about the value of science and technology and, in his words, "to explore for the students whether it was, in fact, useful and productive and 'right' to be going into technical fields," he discarded "the classical physics problems of pushing frictionless elephants up inclined planes" in favor of a comprehensive examination of the Apollo lunar-landing program and its beneficial technological spinoffs. In addition, he invited about a dozen of the brightest, most ambitious physics majors to attend an extra weekly seminar in which they would jointly consider ways to expand technological growth, but only in a beneficial fashion.

By chance, the first question O'Neill posed was, "Is the surface of the planet earth really the right place for an expanding technological civilization?" As the students enthusiastically looked into all aspects of the problem, it became increasingly obvious to them and to their teacher that the logical solution was to live not on earth, or indeed on any planetary surface, but in space itself, on artificial planets. Now as intrigued as his students, O'Neill devoted every spare hour to "working out the numbers," as he put it. Within a year, he and his students—even though they had deliberately restricted themselves to existing 1970's technology—had designed a kilometer-long, rotating cylindrical habitat, constructed almost entirely of processed lunar rock, that used solar energy to sustain life in a sealed ecological system.

O'Neill postulated that the ideal location for the first habitat was a point about equidistant from the earth and the moon known as Lagrange 5, or L5. (The point was named for Joseph Louis Lagrange, the eighteenth-century French mathematician who first identified the five stable locations where lunar and terrestrial gravitational and centrifugal forces cancel each other out.) He eventually revised his design to place the habitats in kidney-shaped orbits about L4 or L5. Having made a thorough analysis of the findings of the Apollo lunar surveys, O'Neill concluded that the moon could supply 98 percent of the raw materials needed to construct the prototypical cylinder: aluminum, titanium, and iron for the structural shell; silicon for the huge windows; moon "dust" for arable soil; and oxygen for atmosphere and rocket fuel. Only carbon, nitrogen, and hydrogen would have to be brought up from earth on the space shuttle and eventually, he added, those elements could be extracted from the mineral-rich asteroids.

Using conventional strip-mining techniques, a small team of men would collect chunks of lunar ore and load them into buckets on a "mass driver," a kind of electromagnetic catapult that would pitch a load of lunar "bricks" to a mobile "mass catcher" in space at one-second intervals. The accumulated material would be ferried from the mass catcher to an orbital processing plant, then to a construction module in orbit at L5, where about 1,000 galactic hardhats, applying modified earthbound bridge- and ship-building methods, would assemble a gigantic hollow cylinder. After considerable experimentation, O'Neill had selected the cylinder as the most effective geometrical shape for human habitation in space because it afforded the maximum inner surface at full artificial gravity. Only near the hemispherical end-caps would near-weightless conditions occur. By attaching each colony to a counter-spinning twin cylinder, O'Neill forestalled the effects of gyroscopic tugging and, at the same time, insured that one end-cap was always pointing toward the sun for an uninterrupted flow of solar power.

To make his new world much more than a space station, O'Neill divided his cylinder into six longitudinal strips of alternating "valleys," with meadows, forests, streams, and villages, and "solars"—blue-tinted, reinforced glass windows through which the inhabitants could see the sun's reflection in the mammoth external aluminum mirrors that opened and closed to simulate the diurnal cycle. In interview after interview O'Neill repeated his determination to make the habitats as "earthlike as possible, rich in green, growing plants, animals, birds, and other desirable features of attractive regions on earth." Indeed, designs for larger habitats (theoretically, there is no limit to their size) are reminiscent of sections of the southern California coastline, or the Swiss Alps and one model, Island Four, is large enough to accommodate an island the size of Bermuda.

As O'Neill envisions it, life aboard the space habitats would be almost idyllic and certainly more pleasant than in most places on earth. "In a space colony, the basic human activities of living and recreation, of agriculture, and of industry could all be separated and non-interfering, each with its optimal gravity, temperature, climate, sunlight, and atmosphere, but could be located conveniently near to each other," he has explained, as quoted in Space Colonies (Penguin, 1977). Crops, for example, could be grown in climate-controlled, pest-free environments or in aeroponic nutrient fogs in external agricultural pods fastened to spokes radiating out from the end-caps. Similarly, heavy industry could be carried out in non-rotating external factories. At that time—the mid-1970's—O'Neill estimated that Island One, which is designed to house 10,000 people, could be ready for occupation in about fifteen years at a cost no more than the Apollo project's.

For O'Neill, space habitats would provide the solution to many of the earth's most pressing problems, among them, the energy shortage, overpopulation, pollution, and potentially irreversible environmental damage. Moreover, a cooperative international effort to establish a beachhead in space could have, in his words, a "real stabilizing effect on world tensions." More importantly, however, O'Neill believes that there is "reason to hope that the opening of a new, high frontier will challenge the best that is in us, that the new lands, waiting to be built in space will give us new freedom to search for better governments, social systems, and ways of life."

Eager to communicate his ideas to others, O'Neill repeatedly submitted a detailed article describing his space habitats to several scientific journals and to such reputable popular magazines as the *Atlantic,* but each time, he was rebuffed. Finally, in the spring of 1974, he persuaded the Point Foundation, a small San Francisco-based organization managed by the publishers of the *Whole Earth Catalog,* to put up $600 for a conference to be held on the Princeton University campus in May 1974. The conference, which was covered by Walter Sullivan, the New York *Times's* science correspondent, generated so much interest in O'Neill's cities in space that *Physics Today* devoted much of its September 1974 issue to the topic.

Although the public's response to the idea was overwhelmingly enthusiastic, some of O'Neill's colleagues scoffed at his "happy valleys." Freeman Dyson, a prominent physicist who has himself designed self-sufficient starships, complained that O'Neill's habitats were "too big," "too sanitized," "too expensive," and "completely unappealing." Others questioned the durability of the hull under exposure to cosmic ray bombardment and solar particles, the unknown long-term physiological effects of rotation, and even the wisdom of maintaining a controlled, enclosed ecosystem.

Constantly reevaluating and revising his scheme as new problems were considered and solved, O'Neill gradually shifted his emphasis from population pressure relief to the supply of clean, inexhaustible, and inexpensive energy in the form of low-density microwaves beamed to earth from satellite solar power stations in geosynchronous orbits. To avoid the prohibitive lift-costs, O'Neill proposed that the satellites be built from processed lunar ore at orbiting construction "shacks" juryrigged from spent shuttle fuel tanks. He estimated that in about fifteen years, the energy furnished by those satellite stations would exceed the total capacity of the entire Alaskan north slope oil fields.

As other examples of potentially profitable space industries, O'Neill listed the production of orbital chemical processing plants, turbogenerators, mass drivers, optical and radio telescopes, and the construction of enormous research vessels to explore the outer reaches of the solar system and of larger and more elaborate cylindrical, spherical, and circular habitats to house the growing number of space workers. O'Neill and dozens of his colleagues from all fields of applied science worked out a detailed, step-by-step program for space manufacturing from nonterrestrial materials during three successive, NASA-funded summer study programs, in 1975, 1976, and 1977, at the space agency's Ames Research Center in Mountain View, California.

The ambitious space manufacturing program outlined by O'Neill in his book *The High Frontier* (Bantam, 1978) hinged on the development of the reusable space shuttle, which was successfully tested in free flight in 1977, and on the construction of a working model of the mass driver. Using techniques originally devised for magnetically levitated mass transit trains, O'Neill designed a launching machine in which magnetically suspended buckets are accelerated along a track by superconducting electromagnetic coils. When the buckets are decelerated, their payloads carry on. In 1977 O'Neill, then on sabbatical leave at M.I.T. as Hunsaker Professor of Aerospace, Dr. Henry Kolm, an M.I.T. physicist, and several graduate students built a working scale model mass driver from scrap. In tests at Princeton and at the Ames Research Center, the model pushed a one-pound bucket to eighty-five miles per hour in one-tenth of a second for an acceleration of thirty-five G's.

In 1978 Congress enacted the High Frontier Feasibility Act, an amendment introduced by Senator Harrison Williams to the Authorization Act of the National Science Foundation. It calls for an intensive study of "the use of lunar or asteroidal materials for building large orbital structures to relay solar energy to Earth." A second, larger mass-driver is in construction at Princeton, with continuing support from NASA. To provide an alternative source of research support, O'Neill also founded at Princeton the Institute for Space Studies, a nonprofit organization funded by private donations.

Slim and youthful-looking, Gerard K. O'Neill stands six feet tall and weighs 151 pounds. He has a handsome, unlined, fine-boned face, blue eyes, and brown hair cut in a modified Beatle style. On weekends he unwinds by sailing, hiking in the mountains, or flying his single-engine Piper Cherokee. He particularly enjoys gliding and is one of a handful of glider pilots to hold the International Diamond Badge for soaring. O'Neill and his wife, the former Renate ("Tasha") Steffen, whom he married on April 19, 1973, live in a four-bedroom ranch house in Princeton, New Jersey. Mrs. O'Neill is the treasurer of the Space Studies Institute. He has three children—Janet Karen, Eleanor Edith, and Roger Alan—from an earlier marriage, to Sylvia Turlington O'Neill, that ended with the couple's divorce in 1966.

References: *Family Circle* p34 Mr 1 '78; *Harpers* 251:66+ Ag '75; *People* 8:123+ D 12 '77 pors; *Smithsonian* 6:62+ F '76 por; Brand, Stewart. *Space Colonies* (1977); *Who's Who in America,* 1978-79

Perdue, Frank(lin Parsons)

1920- Farmer; businessman. Address: b. Perdue Farms Inc., P.O. Box 1537, Salisbury, Md. 21801

By using up-to-date scientific methods in the production of processed broilers and roasters and the techniques of Madison Avenue promotion in their marketing, Frank Perdue transformed his family chicken farm into the fourth largest integrated processor in the United States. As chairman and chief executive officer of Perdue Farms Inc., he heads a multistate East Coast business with annual sales in excess of $150,000,000. A by-product of his involvement in every phase of Perdue Farms operations is the celebrity that fell to him when he began delivering the sales pitch for his broilers on TV commercials that introduced brand identification in the marketing of fresh poultry.

The only child of Arthur W. and Pearl (Parsons) Perdue, Franklin Parsons Perdue was born in 1920 in Salisbury, in the Maryland part of the Delmarva Peninsula, which also includes portions of Delaware and Virginia. One of his ancestors was Henri Perdeaux, a French Huguenot explorer who left Europe in search of Martinique, but landed at a site on the Maryland coast now called Ocean City and in the 1660's settled at Snow Hill, not far from Salisbury. Among the descendants of Perdeaux who did not remain on the East Coast was, probably, a member of the family that gave its name to Purdue University in Indiana.

About the time of Frank Perdue's birth, his father, who was known as Mr. Arthur, gave up his job as a Railway Express agent because the company wanted him to move to a station away from Delmarva. With the help of his wife he built a small coop to house fifty Leghorn chickens that he bought for $5 and was soon selling table eggs. As he expanded his market with shipments of white eggs to New York and other cities, he earned enough money to build a new chicken house every year or so. Practising small economies such as mixing his own chicken feed during the Depression and salvaging leather from his old shoes to make hinges for the coops, he stayed out of debt and prospered.

During his childhood Frank Purdue had some fifty chickens of his own to look after, earning money from their eggs. He worked along with his parents, not always enthusiastically, to feed the chickens, clean the coops, dig the cesspools, and gather and grade the eggs. A shy, introverted country boy, he went to one-room schools with half a dozen other local pupils until he was old enough to attend Salisbury High School. There, and later at Salisbury State College, a small teachers' college, he was a mediocre student. Playing table tennis appealed to him more than studying, and if his ability had been equal to his enthusiasm, he might have tried to become a professional baseball player. After two years of college, in 1939 he decided to return to the farm and work with his father.

Soon afterward the family enterprise met with a setback that led to a change of product. Leukosis, an infectious chicken disease, decimated the flock of 2,000 Leghorns. Mr. Arthur and his son turned to the hardier breed of New Hampshire Reds, and with an initial purchase of 800 they shifted from egg production to broiler production. The market for Delmarva broilers, already sizable, grew considerably during World War II, when meat prices soared. The Perdues hatched their own chicks by the thousands, raised them to maturity on a special feed mixture, and sold them at the Delmarva broiler auction near Selbyville, Delaware. Some of the Perdue broilers were processed by Armour Company and by Swift & Company.

In several ventures outside the poultry industry—a nightclub business, an oyster business, and Ocean City resort business—Perdue paid the price of overconfidence and credulity. Learning from his mistakes, he became a shrewd businessman. "The prime ingredient of success is fear," he has said, as quoted in the Washington Post/Potomac (May 11, 1975). ". . . I'm talking about the kind of fear that made me thorough. You should have enough fear to always second-guess yourself." His practice of running scared eventually set the family business on a course of rapid expansion.

When Frank Perdue became president of Perdue Farms Inc. in 1952, the company was averaging revenues of $6,000,000 a year from sales of 2,600,000 broilers. The business continued to thrive at a modest rate for several more years until, in 1958, it surged ahead in growth with the building of a huge new facility at Salisbury. The complex consists of a feed mill for mixing grain, machinery that manufactures meal and oil from soybeans, and enormous cylindrical storage bins that cast long shadows over an expanse of low-lying hatcheries. Approximately 16,000,000 bushels of soybean and corn are processed each year at the Delmarva plant, which has a total storage capacity of 11,200,000 bushels. Meal not used for Perdue Farms Inc. is sold, as is all the soybean oil that is produced.

Perdue Farms Inc.'s annual revenues from sales exceeded $35,000,000 by 1967. Sources of profit in the chicken business, however, were shifting from growing and supplying to processing. Ordinarily processors realized a profit of about ½c per pound, but in 1967, as Perdue recalled in an interview for Business Week (September 16, 1972), "processors were paying us 10c per lb. for what cost us 14c to produce. Suddenly, processors were making as much as 7c per lb." A cautious, conservative planner, Arthur Perdue had not been eager for expansion, and Frank Perdue himself was reluctant to enter poultry processing. But yielding to economic forces, he decided upon an integrated operation of hatching eggs, delivering the chicks to contract growers and supplying the feed and litter, processing the broilers, and providing immediate shipment to market.

In 1968, therefore, Perdue bought a plant in Salisbury that once housed a Swift & Company operation, renovated it, and equipped it with machines capable of processing 14,000 broilers an hour. He used computers to devise feeding formulas for each stage of growth so that with less feed he could produce more meat on his chickens than ever before. He hired geneticists who taught him how to breed larger-breasted chickens and veterinarians to keep his flock healthy.

To keep pace with the increased demand for his broilers, in 1971 Perdue invested $7,000,000 or more in a new, larger plant in Accomac, on Virginia's Eastern Shore, capable of processing 28,000 birds an hour. In 1976, when at a cost of $17,000,000 he opened a hatchery and a third processing plant in Lewiston, North Carolina, Perdue's company had more than 3,100 salaried employees, as well as 750 contract growers on the Delmarva Peninsula and 150 in North Carolina. At that time the combined production of broilers from the three plants reached 1,900,000 a week and the total output of all types of chickens, including cornish hens and breeder fowl rose to 2,000,000 a week. The figure for processed poultry increased after the opening of a fourth processing plant in Felton, Delaware in 1977 and a plant for the processing solely of roasters in Georgetown, Delaware in January 1979.

Every chicken and chicken part carrying a red and yellow Perdue identification tag is guaranteed as a quality product that has been subjected to a second inspection by company graders after agents of the United States Department of Agriculture have passed it as Grade A. Shoppers in butcher stores and supermarkets recognize a Perdue chicken not only from its brand name, but also from its golden-yellow color, which is obtained by enriching the feed with xanthophyll, derived from marigold petals and other natural sources. Replying to charges that the yellow color is merely a cosmetic come-on, Perdue pointed out, as Myra MacPherson quoted him in the Washington Post/Potomac (May 11, 1975), "In order to keep that yellow cover we do not over-scald, which toughens the bird, and we do not beat off that outer skin, which means the bird is less susceptible to deterioration. The gentler you handle a chicken the fresher and tenderer it will be —and if we don't handle it gently our yellow trademark will get knocked off."

Unlike some other processors of poultry, moreover, Perdue ships his chickens to the market fresh, packed in ice, not frozen. He has explained that he has "a moral problem with freezing," believing that the best chicken cannot be a frozen one. One of the reasons that Perdue has flourished in the risky marketing of a mass-produced perishable commodity is that his operation is regional. The location of his plants, in the Delmarva Peninsula and North Carolina, enables him to deliver his product within several hours or overnight to the densely populated towns and cities of the East Coast, particularly New York City, which consumes more Perdue chickens than any other brand.

Although Perdue insistently attributes his success to a superior product, he admits that the company's phenomenal increase in sales owes much to advertising. But he did not invest in advertising until he was sure of the quality of his wares. "Nothing," he has said, "will destroy a bad product quicker than good advertising." When he decided in 1968 to tag his processed broilers, he spent $50,000 for radio ads to infiltrate the previously anonymous fresh poultry industry with the name of Perdue. Before deploying television in his marketing campaign, he gave himself a crash course in advertising. Then, in 1971, with characteristic thoroughness and with a preparation of months of reading and research, he went to New York to interview the executives of more than forty advertising agencies.

The firm that Perdue chose, Scali, McCabe, Sloves Inc., deluged the New York area with radio, television, newspaper, and subway ads, largely centered on the chairman of the company himself. According to a Perdue Farms survey, local brand recognition had risen to 51 percent after several months. As reported in *Business Week* (September 16, 1972), "In one month alone some 10,000 New Yorkers contacted Perdue for a list of stores selling his chickens, while 22,000 customers who have written him to praise, criticize, or satisfy their curiosity about his business have received his free 59-page cookbook." As the publicity blitz spread out from New York to major cities in New England, New Jersey, Pennsylvania, and other states, Perdue funneled more and more dollars into advertising until by the spring of 1974, as Bill Paul disclosed in the *Wall Street Journal* (May 13, 1974), "his yearly ad budget [had] grown to about $1 million."

Much of that budget paid for brief, but highly effective television commercials, some of which won advertising awards for Scali, McCabe, Sloves Inc. Perdue backed away at first from the ad agency's inspired idea of making him the star of his own commercials. In the beginning he was nervous and awkward before the camera, having had no performing experience, even in a school play. But the very fact that he lacked professional slickness and matinee idol charm made him all the more convincing to prospective customers.

Television viewers see Frank Perdue as a 165-pound six-footer whose spareness, bald head, lean lips, prominent nose, and occasionally droopy-eyed expression give him a somewhat wizened appearance. "It takes a tough man to make a tender chicken," he asserts with a nasal twang and a nononsense matter-of-factness. To reach the Latin market he struggles with the same message on United States Spanish television: "Le necesita un hombre fuerte para hacer un pollo tierno." In one of his commercials he informs his listeners, "My chickens eat better than you do. A chicken is what it eats. If you want to start eating as good as my chickens, take a tip from me—eat my chickens." Reiterating his claim that his product is the best, he boasts, "The Perdue roaster is the master race of chickens," and in another ad he assures his buyers, "If you're not completely satisfied with my chicken, you can always write to me—the president of Perdue—and I'll give you your money back. If you buy some government-approved chicken, and you're not completely satisfied, who do you write? The President of the United States? What does he know about chickens?" Some of his TV commercials —such as his advice to housewives, "If your husband is a breast or leg man, ask for my chicken parts"—have equivalents in advertising posters.

Diversification into some related business like turkey or prepared chicken is not necessarily out of the question for Frank Perdue, but he fears that too much expansion may weaken his control of operations and compromise quality. He agrees with Andrew Carnegie's dictum, "Put all your eggs in one basket and watch that basket." He is, accordingly, intensely concerned with all aspects of his business, maintaining standards by spot-checking his plants and hatcheries and monitoring the condition of his product at retail and wholesale outlets. The greater part of his time is spent on details of marketing, sales, and advertising and on such public relations chores as touring supermarkets to talk with shoppers.

Frank Perdue is an urbane, aggressive, and direct man who is said to guard his feelings. Not much information appears in the press about his private life, but according to the New York *Sunday News* (November 14, 1976), "He has recently separated from his wife of over thirty years, whom he met while a college student." He has four children, a son and three daughters. In addition to his lakeside home in Salisbury, he owns a condominium apartment in Ocean City. His clothes are fashionable, expensive, and often casual, and for recreation he sometimes flies down to a Caribbean resort to play tennis.

References: Bsns W p113+ S 16 '72 por; Esquire 77:113+ Ap '73 por; N Y Post p33 O 27 '77 por; N Y Sunday News p94 N 14 '76 por; N Y Times III p5 S 12 '76 por, D p3 Ag 2 '78 por; Wall St J p1+ My 13 '74 por, p1+ Ja 24 '75; Washington Post/Potomac p14+ My 11 '75 pors

Pereira, William L(eonard) (per-ā′rə)

Apr. 25, 1909- Architect; regional planner.
Address: b. William L. Pereira Associates, 5657 Wilshire Blvd., Los Angeles, Calif. 90036

"To design plans to satisfy the future," one of the objectives in regional planning of the California architect William L. Pereira, means a reversal of the practices of the past that have resulted in haphazard, sprawling growth of cities and misuse of open land throughout the country. His master plans for such tremendous development projects as the Irvine Ranch in California and Houston Center in Texas have required more than the know-how and aesthetic perception of an architect or the ability to coordinate the buildings of other architects. Pereira's Los Angeles firm is known internationally for its scholarly, exhaustive research on the economic, environmental, and many other forces involved in assuring orderly direction of growth, functional reliability, and values beyond the fashions and technology of the hour.

William L. Pereira

William Leonard Pereira was born in Chicago, Illinois on April 25, 1909 to Saul and Leah Pereira and grew up in a comfortable home on Lake Shore Drive on the city's North Side. A typographer, his father shared a partnership with a brother in a printing business. Another of William Pereira's uncles was an architect whose example seems to have influenced the vocational decisions not only of Bill, but also of his brother, Hal Pereira, a motion picture art director and art consultant who became a member of the American Institute of Architects even though his formal education in architecture was limited.

At the age of six, under the instruction of his grandfather, Pereira began to acquire the skill that eventually made him an intercollegiate fencing champion. Other boyhood pastimes that grew into abiding recreational interests were sailing on Lake Michigan and horseback riding. But as far back as he can remember his foremost enthusiasm was architecture, an absorption that led him to extensive reading in history and biography. His talent as a draftsman emerged early in the sketches he made of whatever he found visually interesting, especially buildings. At Senn High School in Chicago he used his ability to draw in illustrating student publications and making posters and theatrical sets.

When Pereira was fourteen, the death of his uncle brought about the collapse of the family printing enterprise. To help out financially, the teenager worked during summer vacations as a riding master at a boys'

camp and during the school year free-lanced as an architect's assistant, making illustrations and watercolor sketches of projected buildings. Also while in high school he assisted the stage designer Frank Cambria in creating elaborate sets for theatrical productions.

His resourcefulness in handling a similar assortment of jobs—such as training horses, painting scenery, and sketching for a mimeograph service—enabled Pereira to work his way through the University of Illinois. There he underpinned his major subject, architecture, with intensive study in physics on light and color. His student design for a sports palace won him the first medal of the New York Beaux Arts School of Design. Graduating with a B.S. degree in 1930, he launched his career at a time when the onset of the Depression was severely curtailing opportunities for fledgling architects.

A few months after leaving college, however, Pereira joined the Chicago architectural firm of Holabird & Root, which assigned him to work on plans for a multibillion-dollar public redevelopment project. He also took part in drafting the master plan for the 1933 Chicago World's Fair. Attending the atelier sessions conducted by members of the fair's board of design, including John Holabird, Pereira encountered new ways of thinking about architecture, such as the theories of Frank Lloyd Wright, that had a decisive impact on his later work. The fair advanced his career in other ways: he won more than a score of its industrial-design competitions, and after opening a private practice of his own in 1932, he worked directly on several of the exposition's buildings. According to Newsweek (May 7, 1962), "By 25, he had designed structures in 26 states." Many of those designs were for the theatre chain of Balaban & Katz.

Paramount Pictures, of which Barney Balaban became president in 1936, held the controlling interest in that Midwest theatre empire. Because of his elegant movie house designs, Pereira was offered the opportunity in 1938 to submit sketches for a new studio in Hollywood for Paramount. In preparing his designs he made so thorough a study of the way films are produced that Paramount not only awarded him the architectural contract, but hired him as an art director. With similar painstaking research he had some years earlier designed the Lake County Tuberculosis Sanatorium in Waukegan, Illinois, for which in 1944 he received a citation from the Museum of Modern Art.

Although Pereira did not immediately abandon his Midwest architectural practice, he concentrated his attention increasingly on work in connection with the film industry. In 1942 he shared an Oscar with other special effects experts for work on Reap the Wild Wind (Paramount), a Cecil B. DeMille spectacular that featured an underwater fight scene between a man and a giant squid. For RKO-Radio he produced the crime-mystery melodrama *Johnny Angel* (1945), starring George Raft, and the romance *From this Day Forward* (1946), starring Joan Fontaine.

Meanwhile, as a California architect, in 1946 Pereira won awards from the American Institute of Architects for his designs of the Motion Picture County House and Hospital and for the Pan Pacific Theatre. Faced in time with having to choose between film making and architecture, he opted for the latter and in 1949 joined the faculty of the University of Southern California as professor of architecture, a post that he held until 1957. With a view to expanding his practice, in 1950 he invited Charles Luckman who had been his classmate in engineering and architecture at the University of Illinois, to form a partnership with him. Some months earlier Luckman had resigned as president of Lever Brothers, where his salesmanship had earned him the reputation of the wonder boy of the soap business.

One of the first undertakings of the Los Angeles firm of Pereira & Luckman was the design for the $12,000,000 pilot plant of the CBS Television City in Hollywood. Built specifically for television production, that unit, the first of six planned for the center, has a core of four studios, each with a floor space of 12,000 square feet, which can be expanded when more space is needed because the walls are made to be moved outward to allow for additional construction. CBS dedicated that first facility of Television City in November 1952.

Within five years after Luckman had joined Pereira in architectural practice, as reported in *Time* (September 6, 1963), the partnership "exploded from an office with a dozen architects and a $15 million volume of business to a firm with about 400 employees and more than $500 million worth of work on the boards." They designed, among other functionally diverse structures, a suburban San Diego hospital notable for its efficiency, two enormous tanks duplicating undersea conditions for Marineland of the Pacific, and a 450-room hotel for Disneyland. Their specialty became the master planning of building complexes, such as the rocket-launching installations at Cape Canaveral (later Cape Kennedy) in Florida; the United States air and naval bases construction in Spain; the Los Angeles International Airport; jet bases in California for Lockheed, North American, Northrop, and Convair; the Santa Barbara campus of the University of California; and the National Bureau of Standards laboratories at Boulder, Colorado.

Apparently, however, Pereira became concerned that by undertaking so large a volume of planning and building in its worldwide operations, Pereira & Luckman might be compromising quality. "It was like working in a factory," he recalled, as quoted in *Time* (September 6, 1963). ". . . I don't say we were doing inferior work; I just know I wasn't doing my best." Soon after Pereira withdrew from his partnership with Luckman in 1958 and set up his own firm, William L. Pereira Associates, the Lockheed Aircraft Company engaged him to master plan its 200-acre, $50,000,000 research center at Saugus, California. In 1959 he was awarded the contract to design the long-discussed Hollywood Film Museum, to be dedicated to the movie, television, radio, and recording industries. He contributed also to the Los Angeles cultural expansion program as designer of the $11,-500,000 Los Angeles County Museum of Art. That monumental complex of three pavilions located on Wilshire Boulevard, the largest museum in the West, opened its doors to the public in the spring of 1965.

While the museum was being built, the architects of Pereira Associates were planning the transformation of huge tracts of undeveloped land not far away. For Santa Catalina Island's 47,000 acres, then largely owned by Philip K. Wrigley, head of the chewing gum company, Pereira envisioned the emergence of urban centers that would retain the charm and livability of towns of an earlier era under modern conditions. His master plan for Mountain Park, an 11,300-acre area of mountains and canyons within the city limits of Los Angeles, included the construction of ten or eleven villages strung along the slopes of hills, with houses, schools, research and light-industry plants, and civic and shopping centers so conveniently situated that transportation by car would be unnecessary. Pereira hoped that such a community, carefully built up over two or more decades, would influence the redevelopment of Los-Angeles as a whole on a human scale.

Nowhere has Pereira applied his theories of orderly, balanced land development more spectacularly than in the ambitious master planning of the Irvine Ranch, some 93,000 acres of privately owned open land in Orange County, Southern California. The Irvine Company hired him in 1960 to draw up the overall scheme for that project, one of the largest land development programs in the United States, after he had recommended a section of the Irvine Ranch as a site for a new branch of the University of California. His plan called in part for the creation of a town of 100,000 people centered on a 1,000-acre campus for 27,000 students and including a variety of housing for different income levels, hotels, theatres, and other amenities and cultural resources to be shared by students and townspeople, as well as an industrial park. Besides surrounding urbanized communities, mainly along or near the coast, Pereira's design provides for the utilization of 20,000 acres for agricultural purposes and for the reservation of 30,000 acres of mountain wilderness for recreation and wildlife preservation. By 1980, he predicted, as many as 300,000 people would live and work on the Irvine Ranch.

Another mammoth-scale undertaking that Pereira has designed is the thirty-two-square-block "Houston Center," a $1.5 billion project funded by the Texas Eastern Transmission Corporation. According to *Newsweek* (November 9, 1970), the seventy-five-acre "minicity," expected to be opened in 1990, "may well be the largest urban development anywhere to be completely financed by private capital."

Pereira's innovative concepts have attracted considerable attention in both mass circulation magazines and professional journals. One of his most controversial buildings has become a San Francisco landmark—the $32,000,000 Transamerica Corporation building, a forty-eight-story, white-walled elongated pyramid, the tallest pyramidal office building in the United States. When Transamerica announced its plan for the new building in the late 1960's, various San Francisco civic groups and environmentalists protested that the structure would be unsuitable to the city's skyline. Some called it a dunce cap. But the corporation decided to go ahead with Pereira's design because it wanted a building that would make Transamerica more widely known and give it a distinctive image. Because of its unusual foundation and pyramidal form, the towering Transamerica building, which had its formal opening in 1973, is said to be able to withstand any earthquake that might strike the city. In the late 1970's construction began on another of Pereira's office buildings for San Francisco, the nineteen-story northern California headquarters for Pacific Mutual Life Insurance. Among its remarkable features are openable windows and many balconies, attractions that its fresh-air-loving architect revived from the pre-World War II era.

The pyramidal form was also the one Pereira chose in designing a $90,000,000 luxury hotel and conference center for Sheikh Khalifa bin Hamad al-Thani, the Emir of Qatar. Scheduled for completion in 1978, the center includes an auditorium, theatre, ballroom, restaurants, shops, and gardens. Its location on the Persian Gulf at the northern edge of the harbor of Doha is not far from an area where additional structures, now on the drawing boards of Pereira Associates, are expected to be built. Among earlier overseas projects that the architects of Pereira's firm master-planned were a new town in the Ivory Coast of Africa and an urban center in Taipei, Taiwan.

Regarded in the press as a scholar as well as an artist, throughout his career Pereira has contributed notably to the architecture of the academic community. His designs of campus structures include those for the University of Missouri, Brigham Young University, Pepperdine University in Malibu, Occidental College in Los Angeles, and the University of Southern California. In addition to buildings for the University of California campuses at Santa Barbara, Los Angeles, and Irvine, he designed the much-discussed central library of the university's San Diego campus.

To make the library the centerpiece of the San Diego school, Pereira placed it in the middle of the heavily wooded 1,000-acre campus. At present it stands in isolation because of delay in the construction of the buildings that Pereira had intended to surround it in his master plan of the 1960's. James Britton, who wrote in the *AIA Journal* (August 1977) of the library's "poetic force" and "sculptural character," quoted Pereira as saying, "The spheroidal form is unusual and could be expected to establish a more powerful image for the university center than a tower or cube." At the dedication of the library in 1970, the architect also explained, "If it appears to some that the design of this library building conveys the idea that powerful and permanent hands are holding aloft knowledge itself, and offering to future generations wisdom and hope with conviction—I can only say in all humility that is what we meant to do, as a dividend of spirit beyond the library's practical capacity as a functional building."

During 1971 Pereira was architect in residence at the American Academy in Rome. He served as a member of the President's National Council on the Arts from 1965 to 1968, chairman of the California Governor's Task Force on Transportation in 1967-68, and adviser to the Aeronautics and Space Engineering Board in 1969. He is a member of the board of directors of Urban America, Inc., and of the advisory committee of the board of directors of Crocker-Citizens National Bank. The American Institute of Architects, of which he is a fellow, has presented Pereira with many honor and merit awards. His other tributes include the decoration of commander of the Order of the Ivory Coast, Man of the Year award for 1967 of the Los Angeles Chamber of Commerce, and honorary degrees from Otis Art Institute and Art Center College of Design. He belongs to the Gargoyle Society and the Society of American Military Engineers.

William L. Pereira stands six feet tall and has blue eyes, iron-gray hair, and, according to *Time*, "an actor's dash." His wife, Margaret (McConnell) Pereira, whom he married on June 24, 1934, was formerly a fashion artist for Marshall Field's in Chicago and a photographer's model. During their courtship she went to Hollywood to act in a few movies, and while visiting her there Pereira realized that California was the place where he wanted to work. The Pereiras have two children, William L. Jr. and Monica. One of their homes, in the Hancock Park district of Los Angeles, was designed by Pereira himself in a variety of styles that accommodate mahogany and glass, an L-shaped pool, patios, and palm trees.

References: Los Angeles Times II p1+ Ap 6 '59 por, II p1+ Ap 7 '59; Newsweek 59:90+ My 7 '62; Time 67:90+ F 27 '56 por, 82:68+ S 6 '63 pors; American Architects Directory (1970); International Who's Who, 1978-79; Who's Who in America, 1976-77; Who's Who in California, 1968

Rafshoon, Gerald (Monroe)

Jan. 11, 1934- Advertising executive; political media expert. Address: b. Rafshoon Communications, 1612 K St., Suite 508, Washington, D.C. 20006

As the media strategist who has handled Jimmy Carter's public relations since 1966, the fast-talking and irreverent Gerald Rafshoon both planned and administered Carter's victorious campaigns for the Georgia governorship, the Democratic Presidential nomination, and the American Presidency itself. In 1978 the Atlanta advertising man was made Carter's assistant for communications. Rafshoon is seen by some as a kind of éminence grise behind Carter, a man who can induce the nation's chief executive to act or not to act on the basis of the presumed impact of his conduct on public relations. (The slang

infinitive "to rafshoon" is currently in vogue in Washington.) Rafshoon views himself in more modest terms, although he would probably concede that he is one of the foremost political media experts in the United States. In September 1979 he returned to his private firm, Rafshoon Communications, in Washington, to work for the Carter Presidential campaign. His Atlanta agency was sold in April of that same year.

The son of Jack and Helen (Goodman) Rafshoon, and the grandson of Jewish immigrants from Minsk in Belorussia, Gerald Monroe Rafshoon was born on January 11, 1934 in Brooklyn. His father, who had been a private detective, entered the Army Air Corps during 1942 and stayed on in the Air Force when World War II ended, eventually attaining the rank of captain in the air police. Rafshoon's parents were divorced in the late 1950's. His mother and his older brother, Charles, both live in Atlanta, and his father, with whom he had no contact during the final decades of his life, died in 1973.

Growing up at Air Force bases where Jack Rafshoon was stationed—in Marfa, Texas, Long Beach, California, Hickam Field, Hawaii, Colorado Springs, and Sumter, South Carolina— Gerald Rafshoon had a rootless and lonely childhood. Since Jewish families were rare among career military personnel, he often felt himself to be an outsider, while as the perennial new kid on the block, smaller than his peers and not athletically inclined, he was often rejected by the boys and spent most of his time reading or playing with girls. His unhappiness was compounded by his troubled relationship with his father, whom he has described as a "mean man." Gerald Rafshoon developed his mordant wit in his many arguments with him.

In the autumn of 1951, after completing high school in Los Angeles, Rafshoon enrolled in the University of Texas at Austin, not far from Bergstrom Air Force Base, where his parents were then living. Taking Navy ROTC courses and majoring in journalism, he supported himself by selling ads for the Daily Texan, the campus paper, which had a circulation of almost 25,000. Through his association with the Daily Texan, Rafshoon began his lifelong friendship with the writer Willie Morris, who later became editor of Harper's magazine. During his senior year, in what amounted to his public relations debut, Rafshoon ran Morris' successful campaign to win election as the Texan's editor.

After receiving his Bachelor of Journalism degree in 1955, Rafshoon took a job writing advertising copy, at $50 a week, for KTBC, an Austin radio station owned by Lyndon B. Johnson. There he shared a desk with newswriter Bill Moyers, who later became Johnson's Presidential press secretary. In 1956 Rafshoon went on active duty in the United States Navy as a lieutenant, junior grade, serving as communications officer on a tanker in the Mediterranean. When he completed his naval tour of duty in 1959, he settled in Atlanta, Georgia, working as an advertising copywriter for Rich's, the city's largest department store. Soon after that move, he became regional manager of advertising and publicity for Twentieth Century-Fox, with the responsibility of conducting the southern promotional campaigns for such films as the Richard Burton-Elizabeth Taylor *Cleopatra* epic.

Three years later, in 1963, Rafshoon opened his own advertising agency, with a chain of southern movie theatres as his first client. Although a small enterprise by Madison Avenue standards, Gerald Rafshoon Advertising, Inc., based on the eighth floor of an office building on Atlanta's West Peach Tree Street, grew steadily as its founder gained both national prominence and a reputation for promotional expertise. By 1975 it had some twenty clients, among them Sears Roebuck, with an annual billing of $7 million, a figure that had increased to $20 million by 1977.

In the summer of 1966, meanwhile, when his firm still had a long way to go, Rafshoon happened to hear a commercial for an almost unknown state senator named Jimmy Carter, who was running in Georgia's Democratic gubernatorial primary. "I was impressed by how bad Carter's advertising was," Rafshoon has said, as quoted by Kandy Stroud in *How Jimmy Won* (Morrow 1977). "I'll never forget hearing a jingle on the radio . . . 'Jimmy Carter is his name. Jimmy Carter is his name.' No one knew who the hell Jimmy Carter was anyway, so what good was it to sing 'Jimmy Carter is his name'?"

Rafshoon phoned his friend Hal Gulliver, now the editor of the Atlanta *Constitution*, whom he knew to be closely associated with Carter, offering to help, and Gulliver arranged a meeting between Rafshoon and Carter, for which the advertising executive worked up a 120-page presentation. Although Carter's associates were not impressed, Carter himself *was*, both by the presentation and by Rafshoon's personal qualities. The admiration was mutual, especially after the two men got to know each other better during a weekend Rafshoon spent at the Carter home in Plains, Georgia. As a result, Rafshoon took over Carter's advertising, spending the $70,000 that remained in the campaign chest entirely on television and using a *cinéma vérité* technique never before seen in Georgia politics.

Although Lester Maddox went on to become governor, Rafshoon's media magic had been clearly demonstrated, for Carter finished third in the six-man race, rather than last, as Georgia politicians had predicted when the primary began. Almost at once, Carter started planning his next assault on the Georgia governorship by organizing a high-powered campaign team that included Rafshoon, Hamilton Jordan, Jody Powell, and Robert Lipshutz, all

of whom have remained with him ever since. Put in charge of Carter's advertising, Rafshoon took a second mortgage on his house to help finance the campaign and threw himself into his work with alacrity and enthusiasm.

Rafshoon's approach to the use of media was once again vindicated, since Carter won both the Democratic primary and the November 1970 gubernatorial election. But several episodes during the campaign led some observers to conclude that Rafshoon was not above playing "dirty pool" when the situation warranted it. He has denied any involvement in those incidents, but some writers claim to detect his "fingerprints."

The incidents arose from the circumstance that Carter's most formidable primary opponent, former Governor Carl Sanders, was widely regarded as a liberal. He was thus expected to capture the state's growing black vote, a likelihood that Rafshoon could not directly counter, since he was presenting Carter as a downhome farmer with appeal for Georgia's rural whites. Midway through the campaign a black attorney, C. B. King, unexpectedly cast his hat into the ring. By providing the new contender with the services of his agency gratis, Rafshoon enabled King to pull the black vote away from Sanders, thus clearing Carter's path to the State House. Later in the campaign it was alleged that Rafshoon was responsible for circulating a photo showing Sanders in a convivial situation with some blacks.

Carter's gubernatorial victory in 1966 brought Rafshoon several new clients, including the State of Georgia. Remaining as interested in politics as in advertising, by mid-1971 he and several other Carter associates had concluded that their man was Presidential timber, and in 1972 they attended the Democratic National Convention in Miami with the hope of getting him the party's Vice-Presidential nomination.

As they realized afterwards, they had been naïve, for candidate George McGovern was unwilling even to consider Carter, who had delivered the nominating speech for his rival, Henry Jackson. Yet they reasoned that things had worked out well, since Carter's political prospects might have been blighted permanently if he had gone down to defeat with the Democratic nominee in the November election. Meanwhile, convinced more than ever by their visit to Miami that Carter held far more potential than anyone else on the Democratic Presidential horizon, Rafshoon, Jordan, and Peter Bourne met with the governor in Atlanta, mapping a detailed strategy that could gain him the party's nomination in 1976.

Jimmy Carter's famous end-run for the Democratic Presidential nomination was brilliantly planned and executed. That it succeeded despite Carter's many presumed weaknesses at the outset not only testified to the merits of the candidate but also represented a promotional triumph for Rafshoon. Those presumed weaknesses had included Carter's southern origin and fundamentalist piety; his obscurity outside his home state; his lack of experience in national politics and foreign affairs; and his lackluster speaking style. The long uphill battle for the nomination, as James Wooten pointed out in Esquire (March 13, 1979), was "the most harrowing chapter in Rafshoon's life," for "he was embarking on what many considered a fool's errand—selling as unlikely a candidate as the country would ever see."

By the time Rafshoon had finished, however, Carter's strengths had been projected forcefully, and even his apparent deficiencies had been transmuted into virtues. Many members of the American public, cynical about old-line politicians in the post-Watergate era, eagerly turned to the soft-spoken, upright, small-town boy who unapologetically professed all the old verities. Rafshoon was not a mere salesman, nor was he simply an "image engineer," as John Osborne saw him in the New Republic (September 9, 1978). Rafshoon sensed that Carter was a winner because he suited the country's mood at the time. More than that, there was a special chemistry between the candidate and the advertising man because Rafshoon believed fervently in Carter and wanted to further his cause. As he has often explained, he did not "create" the candidate, but articulated and explained him as only one who knew him well could do—selecting or emphasizing certain traits, perhaps, but not molding him in accordance with some preconceived notion.

Equally important, Rafshoon knew that Carter's informal style and likable presence could be "sold" on television. Since that medium had become the single most efficient means of placing a new product or presenting a new idea before the greatest number of people in the briefest possible time, television was exactly what the situation required. After all, Carter had barely two years—from December 1974, when he announced his candidacy, to July 1976, when the Democratic convention was scheduled to take place—to become a figure of national stature. To accomplish that, he would have to win a goodly number of the thirty state primaries he was entering, many in areas where he had never been heard of.

Allocating 85 percent of Carter's $2.3 million advertising budget to television, Rafshoon organized and conducted a highly effective media campaign, in which, as was pointed out in Dun's Review (August 1976), he "played the candidate and not the advertising—no slogans, no gimmicks and very little, if any, slickness." Many hours of work and analysis were invested in the making of each commercial, and the placement of messages in particular time-spots was geared to the presumed audiences. One message was aimed at the senior citizens mesmerized by the Lawrence Welk Show, another at the blue-collar audiences of Hee Haw and All in the Family, still others at the liberals addicted to Maude, the professionals who watch Today, and the housewives who tune in on the daytime soap operas. Moreover, Rafshoon had his time buyers concentrate on frequency rather than scope of audience (that is, he preferred six spots with 35,000 viewers each to one with 200,000 viewers) and on off-hours rather than the more expensive prime time.

The aim throughout, as Joseph Lelyveld noted in the New York Times Magazine (March 28, 1976) was "to insure that Carter would have more to say—at least appear on TV to have more to say—on more questions than any of his rivals." Thus, when critics complained that they found some of Carter's carefully filmed but nonetheless impromptu statements too diffuse, Rafshoon adroitly tacked new beginnings and endings onto the same messages, such as the words "Jimmy Carter on the issue of . . ." and "If you agree with Jimmy Carter on. . . ." He thus convinced viewers that the candidate had said something concrete.

Rafshoon's ingenuity was rewarded when Jimmy Carter won the Democratic Presidential nomination. In only two years he had helped a relatively obscure man from Plains, Georgia to become one of America's foremost political figures. With a far larger budget and a candidate who was no longer an unknown, Rafshoon now used the same methods, and even many of the same commercials, that had been honed in the primaries in the campaign that followed against the Republican candidate, Gerald R. Ford. But although the final stage in Carter's battle for the Presidency was hard-fought to the finish, the challenges for Rafshoon were on a lesser order of magnitude. It was, therefore, somewhat anticlimactic.

When Jimmy Carter won the American Presidency on November 2, 1976, he offered Rafshoon a job on the White House staff, but Rafshoon turned it down, agreeing only to serve occasionally as an unofficial adviser. Instead, he became a political consultant in Washington, in partnership with pollster Patrick Caddell. Later in 1977, after handling two losing clients—Henry Howell, who was seeking the governorship of Virginia, and Mario Cuomo, who was competing in the New York mayoral primary—he decided to leave politics. He opened Rafshoon Communications, a public relations firm in Washington, and for a short time he also engaged in film production and the packaging of television specials through Rafshoon Productions, based in Hollywood.

Meanwhile, Carter's Presidency, which had begun on a note of euphoria, ran into difficulties. A dearth of solid achievements and a widespread impression that the White House was staffed by bumblers brought about a sag in the President's popularity, and he found it increasingly difficult to muster support for his programs Hoping to reverse that trend, in May 1978 Carter appointed Rafshoon his assistant for communications.

To free himself of possible conflicts of interest in the $56,000-a-year post, Rafshoon put his Washington and Atlanta business enterprises into a blind trust. Although he carefully cultivated a low profile, avoiding interviews and describing himself simply as another White House "hand," many observers assumed his role to be that of "chief of staff in all but name"—Carter's "number-one hatchetman," charged with putting the administration's confused affairs in order. Since Rafshoon was generally regarded as the most sophisticated member of Carter's inner circle of Georgians, it was also suggested that his public relations function might impinge on the President's integrity as the nation's chief policymaker.

Rafshoon was quick to deny such allegations, repeatedly insisting that Carter would not only reject any advice to pursue a policy for its image value but would regard the very suggestion as ridiculous. Such views persisted, however, since the line between the manipulation of image and the creating of an image through Presidential action is a fine one indeed. Rafshoon's mandate to refurbish Carter's public image inevitably entailed overall management of many aspects of administration activities, including the clearing of all public appearances and statements by top officials, the supervision of speechwriters and photographers, and liaison with the news media.

In the months after his appointment, in the wake of such false starts as the President's rambling energy message on June 23, 1978, Rafshoon took several measures to set the Carter administration on the right course. He was involved, for instance, in the events leading to the resignation of Midge Costanza, the President's adviser on women's affairs, the public rebuke of U.N. Ambassador Andrew Young, and the President's memo on drug use that followed an incident involving the White House aide Dr. Peter Bourne. He also coached Carter for his press conferences. Rafshoon's efforts, when added to such solid achievements as the Israel-Egypt peace treaty and the widespread public desire to have confidence in the nation's President, led to a turnaround in Jimmy Carter's popularity ratings early in 1979, although they plummeted again later in the year.

Gerald Rafshoon was married in April 1956 to Betty Gumbiner of Shreveport, Louisiana, from whom he was divorced in 1976. They have three daughters and a son. After a lengthy friendship with the television personality Barbara Howar, Rafshoon married the wealthy Atlanta widow Eden White Donohue in March 1978. Rafshoon is an informal, gregarious, and witty man who generally dresses in open-neck shirts and wears his hair unkempt. In Washington he worked out

of Richard Nixon's former sanctum in the Old Executive Office Building across the street from the White House, a locale that provided an outlet for Rafshoon's sardonic humor. When tensions ran high, he sometimes relaxed his staff by striking a "Presidential" pose on a gaudy papier-mâché throne, topped by a two-headed eagle.

References: Esquire 91:25+ Mr 13 '79 por; Macleans Ja 1 '79 pors; N Y Times Sunday Mag p96+ Mr 28 '76 por; Stroud, Kandy. How Jimmy Won (1977)

Rey, Fernando

Sept. 20, 1917- Spanish actor. Address: b. c/o Paul Kohner, Inc., 9169 Sunset Blvd., Hollywood, Calif. 90069; h. Orense 62, Madrid 20, Spain

A favorite of his compatriot Luis Buñuel, who first cast him in Viridiana, Fernando Rey is one of Spain's few internationally known film actors, with more than one hundred pictures to his credit during his three-decade career. Earlier typecast in leading-man roles in Spain and Latin America, the cosmopolitan and multilingual Rey first won worldwide recognition in 1971, as the silken but deadly drug trafficker in The French Connection. He went on to consolidate his international reputation in such recent Buñuel films as The Discreet Charm of the Bourgeoisie and That Obscure Object of Desire. Pauline Kael of the New Yorker has .called Fernando Rey "probably the most believable man of the world in contemporary movies," an opinion that is obviously seconded by reviewers and filmgoers.

Fernando Rey was born Fernando Casado Arambillet on September 20, 1917 to Fernando Casado Veiga and Sara d'Arambillet Rey in La Coruña, a major seaport and the largest city in Spain's northwest Galicia region, which is largely Celtic in origin. He has a younger sister, Elvira. The father was a Spanish Army colonel who remained loyal to the Republic when General Francisco Franco and his insurrectionists rose up against it in 1936, a choice that earned him a death sentence when the Civil War ended. That sentence was later suspended, and he died in 1972.

Because the Casado family was related to wealthy shipping interests, Fernando Rey had a privileged childhood. He was a timid child, awed by the tales of mystery spun by his nanny and other household servants, who were nurtured in the folklore of that foggy maritime region. Although he sometimes mingled with playmates, he more often than not stayed indoors, inventing imaginary travel itineraries or operating the toy electric train that he believes was one of the first of its kind in Spain.

Fernando Rey went to school for the first few years in La Coruña, until his father's transfer to a new military post took the family to the nearby coastal province of Asturias. Later, they moved to the historic inland city of Segovia in Castile, where he took his secondary level or *bachillerato* entry exam. Rey proved to be an apt student under his father's understanding supervision. His final move with the family brought him to Madrid, where he studied at the Donoso Cortés Academy and took his *bachillerato* exams at the Instituto Cardenal Cisneros. By that time King Alfonso XIII's abdication had led to the proclamation of the Second Spanish Republic, and Fernando Rey's initial ambition to enter the Navy was thwarted by the shutdown of the Naval Academy.

An aptitude for mathematics prompted Rey to enter the University of Madrid's School of Architecture instead, but after flunking the first couple of drafting exams like many other freshmen, he decided to take a detour around the tougher Madrid test board by taking his next examination in Salamanca. It was in that ancient university city that he noticed the first ominous signs of the approaching Civil War. He returned to Madrid in 1936, just about the time that the conflict broke out, and spent much of the next three years in trenches and on battlefields across the country. Rey wound up with his father at general staff headquarters when the Franco victory in 1939 ended the war and, with it, the Spanish Republic.

His father was imprisoned, and the fate of his mother and sister was still unknown, but Fernando Rey refused to flee abroad with the hundreds of thousands of other Republican refugees, although he was forced to pawn or sell many of the family belongings to survive. In 1940 he answered an ad for movie extras, only to learn to his disappointment that Oriental features were required for the film, which was entitled *Los cuatro Robinsones* (The Four Robinsons) and directed by Eduardo García Maroto for the Cifesa studios. A sympathetic production chief who happened to know his father recognized him, and Fernando Rey found himself unexpectedly portraying an Englishman. In his student days, Rey had acted as a film extra in *Nuestra Natacha* (Our Natasha), under Benito Perojo, and thus had some experience to draw on.

After *Los cuatro Robinsones*, Fernando Rey became an extra in a succession of Spanish films such as *La gitanilla* (The Little Gypsy Girl), *El Rey que rabió* (The Furious King). and others, telling himself that it was only a temporary expedient until his economic situation improved. By answering an ad during that period, however, he found himself drawn into the specialized craft of voice dubbing for the sound track of foreign films to be shown in Spain. His first dubbing part was the voice of Tyrone Power in *Lloyds of London*. Later he became famous among Spanish moviegoers for his dubbing of Laurence Olivier. In a special chapter of his book of film essays entitled *El cine y el momento* the celebrated prose stylist Azorín praised Fernando Rey's ingratiating and unaffected voice, regretting only that he did not appear on screen. Rey told Miguel Acoca of *Newsweek* (April 9, 1973) that it was from watching those players on the screen while he dubbed in their dialogue that he learned the art of acting. Eventually, however, World War II made imports of films from the United States more difficult, and voice-dubbing jobs in Spain became more and more scarce.

Eventually an actor friend working at the Teatro Español in Madrid tipped Rey off to an uncast role in a production of Guillén de Castro's play *Las mocedades del Cid* (The Youth of the Cid), and Rey successfully tried out for the part. From the Teatro Español he went on to a theatrical company being formed by Francisco Melgares. There he earned the admiration of the drama critic Alfredo Marquerie, who wrote such a glowing review that the producer Arturo Serrano hired him as the leading man for a play in Barcelona. Over the next couple of seasons Fernando Rey appeared on the Spanish stage in works by Torrado, Foxá, Arniches, Jardiel Poncel, and others.

Despite his success in Spain's legitimate theater, Rey was not happy with that taxing medium, which then as now exacted from its overworked actors two performances a day, and sometimes three on Sunday. Anxious to return to motion pictures, he played his first important role in a film about the Spanish-born Empress Eugénie entitled *Eugenia de Montijo*, which was directed in Seville by José López Rubio in 1944. (López Rubio recalls that he chose Rey for that movie because of the young actor's poise, good manners, and imposing figure.) Although he returned occasionally to the theater until 1968, when he portrayed the title role of Beckett in the Jean Anouilh play, Fernando Rey was seen mainly on the screen. The latter half of the 1940's brought him roles in a broad range of Spanish period films, largely produced by Cifesa, such as *Los últimos de Filipinas*, *Misión blanca* (White Mission), *Reina Santa* (Holy Queen), *La Princesa de los Ursinos*, *Don Quijote de la Mancha*, *Locura de amor*, and *Aventuras de Juan Lucas*. *Locura de amor* (1948), sometimes entitled *The Mad Queen* in English, proved a resounding box-office success in Latin America as well as in Spain, and marked the beginning of major international movie careers for several of its stars, including Aurora Bautista, Jorge Mistral, and Sara Montiel. *Agustina de Aragón*, a costume epic about the Spanish uprising against Napoleon, in which Rey starred with Aurora Bautista in 1950, has since become something of a cult classic among young film buffs in Spain.

Fernando Rey's widening fame as an actor in the Spanish-speaking world brought him an invitation in 1950 to visit Mexico, where he costarred with María Félix in a film version of Blasco Ibáñez' *Mare Nostrum*. Despite tempting offers to remain in Mexico and his own inclination to settle in Italy and work in its emerging postwar film industry, Rey chose to return to Spain, which was then undergoing one of its periodic movie crises. Roles were far from abundant, but he made *Cielo negro* (Black Sky) in 1952 and the following year was heard as "the voice" in *¡Bienvenido, Mr. Marshall!* (Welcome, Mr. Marshall), the first major picture of Spanish director Luis G. Berlanga, which won a prize at the 1952 Cannes Film Festival. That same year he appeared in *Cómicos*, directed by J. A. Bardem, which also strengthened hopes for a new type of artistic motion picture in Spain. Fernando Rey made several movies over the next few years with Berlanga and Bardem, the *enfants terribles* of Spanish filmmaking during that decade, including *La venganza* (Revenge) in 1957 and *Sonatas* in 1959.

Meanwhile, Rey continued accepting roles in more conventional Spanish pictures such as the classic *El Alcalde de Zalamea* (The Mayor of Zalamea), *Un marido de ida y vuelta* (A Round Trip Husband), and *El amor de Don Juan* (The Love of Don Juan) during the mid-1950's. He was also offered roles in foreign coproductions including *Tangier Assignment*, *Una aventura de Gil Blas* (An Adventure of Gil Blas), and *Les Bijoutiers au Clair de Lune* (Heaven Fell That Night)

that provided him with his first opportunity to work with such well-known European directors as Roger Vadim. The early 1960's brought him contracts for such movies of the Cecil B. De Mille persuasion as *Fabiola*, *The Last Days of Pompeii*, *Rebellion of the Slaves*, *Shéhérazade*, and *Goliath and the Giants*, followed by a string of spaghetti westerns that did nothing to fortify his self-esteem.

Just when his ego needed bolstering most, because he seemed unable to break out of mediocre Spanish and foreign films, Fernando Rey received an offer from Luis Buñuel to appear in *Viridiana*, the first picture the iconoclastic director had made in Spain since the 1930's. Reportedly, Buñuel had seen Rey in a movie role that required him to die on horseback, and had admired the way the actor lay dead. Rey's poignant creation of the demanding figure of Don Jaime in *Viridiana* earned him the praise of critics everywhere, including Washington *Post* reviewer Leo Sullivan (August 25, 1962), who hailed that picture as "a film of magnificent splendor," in which director Buñuel demanded and got from Fernando Rey "the image of gentleness, self-indulgence, and cruelty that establishes the bizarre nature of the picture." *Viridiana* shared the Golden Palm Grand Prix at the 1961 Cannes Film Festival.

Some five years after appearing in *Viridiana*, during which time he made nearly two dozen Spanish movies and foreign coproductions, Fernando Rey was approached by Orson Welles, who asked him to play the role of Northumberland in *Falstaff* (also released as *Chimes at Midnight*). That relationship, begun in 1966, led to a project for directing several films with Welles, including *The Survivors* and *Treasure Island*, that was never consummated because of financing difficulties. After *Falstaff*, which was filmed in Spain with Spanish extras, Rey appeared in a dozen more Spanish and foreign motion pictures of the late 1960's, among them such American films of no special distinction as *Run Like a Thief*, *Navajo Joe*, *Beyond the Mountains*, *Guns of the Magnificent Seven*, *Villa Rides*, *Land Raiders*, and *The Adventurers*, as well as Federico Fellini's *Satyricon* (1969). He then returned to work with Buñuel in 1970 as Don Lope in *Tristana*. His starring role in that fairly free adaptation by Buñuel of the novel by Benito Pérez Galdós brought Rey to the attention of a much wider international audience.

When *Tristana* was released in 1970, critics searched for superlatives to describe Fernando Rey's portrayal of the aging and complex Don Lope. "Superb," "marvelous," and "splendid" were among those most used by reviewers after the film opened in New York City in late September of that year and in London a year later. Rey was less fortunate in his choice of his next few roles, among them that of a lighthouse keeper in Kirk Douglas' 1971 production of *The Light at the Edge of the World.* He was acclaimed, however, as a European character actor of the first rank with his interpretation of Charnier, the suave drug smuggler in *The French Connection,* which William Friedkin directed in 1971 for Twentieth Century-Fox. Virtually all the American reviewers made some room for favorable mention of what a *Variety* critic (October 6, 1971) called "an auspicious debut in a major American film."

Among the enthusiasts was Stephen Farber, who noted in the New York *Times* (November 21, 1971): "Fernando Rey as the French master criminal Charnier, is the epitome of Old World grace and cultivation, his elegance concealing a slight trace of decadence that makes him an almost Jamesian villain." In seeking to explain what made *The French Connection* so credible, Stanley Kauffmann wrote in *The New Republic* (October 31, 1971): "One very big reason that we believe is the acting [of] Fernando Rey." When the less successful sequel, *French Connection II,* directed by John Frankenheimer, appeared in 1975, American reviewers welcomed the reappearance as the urbane drug czar of "the great Fernando Rey," as David Sterritt called him in the *Christian Science Monitor* (June 23, 1975).

His next role for Luis Buñuel, in 1972, found Rey again involved with drugs, this time as the heroin-smuggling envoy from a mythical Latin American republic in *The Discreet Charm of the Bourgeoisie.* Nobody who had seen the film or read its laudatory reviews was surprised when it accumulated more than its share of honors by the year's end. The National Society of Film Critics named *The Discreet Charm of the Bourgeoisie* the best movie of 1972 and singled out Luis Buñuel as the best director. The film also won an Oscar from the Academy of Motion Picture Arts and Sciences as the best foreign-language picture of the year. Rey, who had just finished filming *La Chute d'un Corps (A Body Falls)* with Marthe Keller for French director Michel Polac, was reportedly delighted with the Oscar. His gratification became complete when he was awarded the grand prize at the 1972 San Sebastian Festival in Spain as best actor of the year for his role in *La Duda* (Doubt).

Roles in both Lina Wertmuller's *Seven Beauties* and Mauro Bolognini's *La grande bourgeoise* kept Rey busy in 1975—a year in which he also appeared to advantage in the Franco-Italian production *Cadaveri excellenti* (Splendid Corpses) and *French Connection II.* In *Seven Beauties* he appeared briefly but unforgettably as a Spanish anarchist confined in a Nazi prison; in *La grande bourgeoise* he portrayed an Italian Socialist professor whose son and daughter conspire in a murder that the father is bound by his conscience to denounce to the police, despite the family tragedy that ensues. Both performances brought Rey further acclaim, which was sustained in the following year for his interpretation of the father of the character portrayed by Geraldine Chaplin in the Carlos Saura film *Elisa, vida mia* (Elisa, Darling).

Even more impeccable and masterly was Rey's performance as the middle-aged Mathieu enamored of the seductive and much younger Conchita in Luis Buñuel's *That Obscure Object of Desire* (1977). After the film closed the fifteenth New York Film Festival, Vincent Canby wrote in the New York *Times* (October 9, 1977) that Fernando Rey "at this point in his career, is virtually a projection of Buñuel's artistic personality—gentle, polite, self-aware incapable of the superfluous gesture." And Judith Crist, in her account of that festival for the New York *Post* (October 10, 1977) called *That Obscure Object of Desire* a festival in itself, and characterized Rey as "that epitome of fiftyish suavity."

Since that Buñuel triumph, Fernando Rey has completed *Quintet,* which was filmed in Canada by Robert Altman and released in early 1979 by Twentieth Century-Fox. Rey had the role of Grigor, the adjudicator for a group of players of a mysterious game called quintet, whose several metaphorical meanings include life and art. He has also finished a series for Spanish television about the opera houses of Europe. A Swedish film with English dialogue, *The Assignment,* directed by Mats Arehn and costarring Fernando Rey, was released in Europe in 1978.

Fernando Rey is an indolent golfer and fisherman who often settles for reading a book from his extensive library or puttering with his stamp collection instead of venturing out-of-doors. He and his wife, the Argentine actress Mabel Karr, whom he married in 1960, make their home in a spacious Madrid apartment that is decorated with paintings by contemporary Spanish artists and art objects accumulated during their travels. They also have a vacation home on the Balearic island of Ibiza. Their daughter, Mabel, who is married to the Paraguayan soccer player, Fleitas, of the Royal Madrid team, is the mother of two children; their son, Fernando, is a medical student. Miguel Acoca reported in his *Newsweek* interview that Rey still views himself as "a dreamy, musing, insecure person," a self-image that flatly contradicts the film producer Phil D'Antoni's characterization of him as "the last of the Continental guys. They don't make them like that anymore."

References: N Y Post p22 Je 7 '71; N Y *Sunday News* II p89 Ja 17 '71 por; NY *Times* II p17 F 4 '79 por; *New Yorker* 53:128+ D 19 '77; *Newsweek* p49+ Ap 9 '73 por; *Variety* 260: 66 N 18 '70; *Who's Who in Hollywood, 1900-1976*

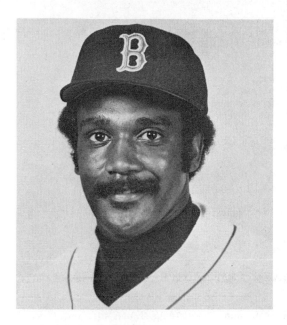

Rice, Jim

Mar. 8, 1953- Baseball player. Address: b.
Boston Red Sox, 24 Yawkey Way,
Boston, Mass. 12215

The most powerful hitter in the American
League is Jim Rice, the designated hitter and
leftfielder of the Boston Red Sox. In his first
four full seasons with the Hub city team, the
righthanded slugger from South Carolina averaged thirty-three home runs, 110 runs batted in,
and .306 at the plate. His home-run tally has
risen each year, and in 1978 his 406 total bases
—giving him a slugging percentage of .600—
were the most by an American Leaguer since
Joe DiMaggio's 418 in 1937. At the end of the
1978 season Rice was voted the Most Valuable
Player in the league, and a contract signed
with Boston in January 1979 made him the
highest-paid player in the league. Going into
the 1979 season, his major-league totals were
644 games, 2,533 times at bat, 398 runs, 775
hits, 110 doubles, forty-three triples, 133 home
runs, and 453 runs-batted-in.

"[The Red Sox] can be down six runs in the
ninth inning, but if Rice still has a chance to
bat, nobody leaves," one Sox fan has observed.
"What the crowd waits to see," according to
a reporter for *Time* (June 12, 1978), "is one
of the smoothest righthanded swings in recent
baseball memory. With his bat held letter high
and his head arched over a cocked shoulder,
Rice explodes with a compact swing." Rice has
compared his swing to the movement of a
rattlesnake, coiling and then "springing out":
"My strength comes from my wrists and legs.
But then I bring my left shoulder back so
that all my momentum jumps out to the
ball."

The fourth of nine children of a factory
supervisor, James Edward Rice was born in
Anderson, South Carolina on March 8, 1953 to
Mr. and Mrs. Roger Rice. Rice was an all-round
star athlete at Westside and Hanna high
schools in Anderson. "I wanted to play pro
basketball," he recounted in an interview with
Mark Ribowsky for *Sport* (July 1978), "but I
never got tall enough. Football was okay.
Everyone wanted me—Nebraska, Michigan,
Tennessee, Iowa. But after I played in the
Carolina Shrine game I said, 'Who needs four
years of college?' The Red Sox drafted me in
'71 and sent their Carolina scout to my house
with $45,000. That decided it for baseball."

Rice's progress in the minor leagues was
slow at first. With Williamsport (Pennsylvania)
in 1971 he hit for .261 and ninety-one total
bases in sixty games, and with Winter Haven
(Florida) the following year he averaged .291
and hit for 240 total bases in 130 games. With
Bristol (Rhode Island) in 1973 he led the
Eastern League with a .317 batting average,
and he hit for a total of 254 bases in 119 games.
Finishing the 1973 season with Pawtucket
(Rhode Island), he hit for a .378 average and
twenty-eight total bases in ten games. In 117
games with Pawtucket the following season he
had a .337 average and 249 total bases.

Called up to Boston for twenty-four games
at the end of the 1974 season, Rice tallied
a batting average of .269 and hit fourteen
singles, two doubles, one triple, and one home
run. In his first full season with Boston, in
1975, his average was .309 and he hit twenty-
two home runs, twenty-nine doubles and four
triples. An injured left hand kept him out of
the 1975 World Series, which the Red Sox lost
to Cincinnati.

With Boston, Rice was more often than not
the starting leftfielder until the beginning of
the 1976 season, when he became designated
hitter. While he was getting used to the hit-
and-sit routine of designated hitting, his average slumped a little, to .282, and he led the
American League in strikeouts, with 123, but he
maintained his power hitting, with twenty-five
doubles, eight triples, and twenty-five home
runs in 153 games. He finally came into his
own in 1977, leading the American League in
home runs, with thirty-nine, total bases, with
382, and slugging average, with .593. His batting average in 1977 was .320. In the 1977 All-
Star game he singled once in two times at bat.

"It is power, lean-muscled, quick-wristed
power, that stirs excitement when Jim Rice
comes to the plate," read the story that appeared in *Time* early in the 1978 season. "In
Fenway Park, where the fans have a connoisseur's appreciation of the slugger's art, the
cheers begin when he strides to the on-deck
circle. Rice has sparked Boston to its best
start since 1946, when Ted Williams and Dom
DiMaggio returned from World War II to win
the first Red Sox pennant in almost three
decades."

Again in 1978 Rice led the league in home runs (forty-six), total bases (406), and slugging (.600), and in addition he was first in hits (213), triples (fifteen) and runs-batted-in (139). His .315 batting average ranked third in the league. In the 1978 All-Star game he went hitless in four times at bat. He won easily over pitcher Ron Guidry of the New York Yankees in the voting for the American League's Most Valuable Player in 1978, taking twenty first-place ballots and eight second-place mentions to outdistance Guidry by sixty-one points in the Baseball Writers Association of America poll. In 1979, when Boston finished third in the American League East with a 91-69 record, Rice hit thirty-nine homers, batted in 130 runs, and had an average of .325.

On January 9, 1979 Rice signed a seven-year, $5,400,000 contract with the Boston Red Sox—the largest in American League history and the second largest in major-league history. The contract ties Rice to the Red Sox through the 1985 season at an average salary of $770,000 a season, a figure exceeded only by Pete Rose of the National League's Philadelphia Phillies, who makes $800,000 a year.

In a dispatch from Winter Haven, Florida on the occasion of an exhibition game with the Minnesota Twins, Rice was quoted in Newsday (April 1, 1979) as intending not to swing "at bad pitches so much, so the pitcher has to come to me. You've got to make them throw strikes and most of them don't want to." Red Sox rightfielder Dwight Evans commented that he did not blame the pitchers. "Jim is awesome and he's going to get better. It wouldn't surprise me if he hit seventy-five homers some year. But I don't think anybody can look at Jim Rice and learn from his swing. It's raw talent."

In the same dispatch, Don Zimmer, the Red Sox manager, was quoted as saying of Rice, "He's got burnt four or five times and he's wary [of the press], but he's a hell of a guy. If a man had to manage twenty-five Jim Rices, and I'm not talking about anything to do with playing ability, a man would have no problems. My job is out here on the field and you couldn't ask for any more than what you get from Jim Rice."

Zimmer retold his favorite story about Rice, about the slugger breaking a bat without even touching the pitch, by the sheer force of his swing. "People still don't believe it. But it happened. I was coaching third base in Detroit and I guess it was 1975. He tried to check on a low outside breaking ball. He was left with about ten inches of bat in his hands. The rest of it almost reached the Tigers' dugout."

Rice's election to the American League All Star team for the third consecutive year meant "a little more" to him that year (1979) because he had "been a regular outfielder for most of the year," he told a reporter just after the team's roster was announced, early in July 1979. At that point in the season he had twen-ty-one home runs, sixty-four runs-batted-in, and a .325 batting average. Although a worsening of the astigmatism in his right eye—for which he had been wearing corrective contact lenses or glasses for more than a year—had been giving him trouble in the field (but not, he said, at the plate), he had committed only three errors.

Although Rice has had to work hard at his fielding, his hitting is, as he has said, "a natural thing" for him and not something he had to develop. "God gave me the ability to hit a ball hard, so I never mess around with theories of hitting. I don't try to understand what I'm doing. For example, I never guess on a pitch because I'm confident no pitch is gonna get by me. Also I don't try to pull because I'm so strong that I can hit pitches to rightfield harder and deeper than most lefthanded hitters. I usually just try to meet the ball, meet it *hard*. By doing this, I can concentrate on getting my hits and still bust enough out of the park." He was quoted in the same vein in the *Time* article: "I don't know how many home runs I can hit, and I don't care. I just want to get hits, and the homers will be there. People forget that the first thing a home run is, is a hit."

A soft-spoken man with a dignified manner, Rice keeps his own counsel and is especially guarded with the press. His rules with reporters are: "No personal questions. No questions about teammates. If you want to talk about baseball, fine, but that's it." Red Sox broadcaster Ken Harrelson, a former teammate and still a friend and golfing partner of Rice, told Ron Fimrite of *Sports Illustrated* (April 9, 1979): "Jimmy is almost too good to be true. He's a kind of Frank Merriwell. I have a twelve-year-old son, and I just hope he can grow up to be the person Jim Rice is. Jimmy is such a good kid—except for this one thing with the press. If he could only cultivate or tolerate the media better. He's so thoughtful with everybody but writers. As a former player, I know what the media can do for you. The press made a personality out of me. If only Jimmy could portray himself to the writers the way he really is, if he could only get that charisma across." Fimrite quoted Rice's lawyer, Tony Pennacchia: "Jimmy has a smile that will make you melt and a frown that will make you cringe."

Jim Rice and Corine Gilliard, his girlfriend since high school, were married in 1972. With their son, Chauncy, they live in the Boston suburb of Peabody during the baseball season and in Anderson during the off-season. They take junior college classes together for self-improvement. Rice's favorite recreation is golf, in which he has a handicap of fourteen and a powerful drive; he and Bruce Lietzke won the Tucson Pro-Am in 1977. His tastes, in muted-tone automobiles as in vested suits, is conservative. In addition to his income from baseball, Rice earns money endorsing the frankfurters sold in Fenway Park, sporting goods, and other products and doing public relations work for the Southern Bank and Trust Company in Greenville, South Carolina. But he lets nothing distract him from his job that has made him a millionaire. As a reporter once observed, "He's a worker, as close as the team comes in spring training to having a 9-to-5 laborer."

References: Christian Sci Mon p10 Je 28 '78 por; Newsday p10+ Ap 1 '79 por; Sport 67:14+ Jl '78 pors; Sporting News p3 My 27 '79 por; Sports Illus 50:53+ Ap 9 '79; Baseball Register, 1978

Ritt, Martin

Mar. 2, 1920- Actor; motion picture director, producer. Address: b. c/o International Creative Management, 8899 Beverly Blvd., Los Angeles, Calif. 90048

"You've always got to be willing to pick up the tab for what you believe in," insists film director Martin Ritt. "That's the mark of a man." One of many Hollywood artists blacklisted during the McCarthy era, Ritt is a loner with an ethic, an individual at odds with the system, and the heroes of his films tend to be the same sort of people. They are, according to Sheila Whitaker in her *The Films of Martin Ritt*, (1972), "outside the dubious moral values of a society which resents their separate existence and insists on conformity to its values." From the black man who befriends a white

down on his luck in *Edge of the City* (1956) to the drab hillbilly woman who becomes a defiant union organizer in *Norma Rae* (1979), Ritt's protagonists pay the price of nonconformity.

Martin Ritt was born in New York City on March 2, 1920, to Morris and Rose Ritt. As a first-generation Jew growing up on the Lower East Side, Ritt found little in his immediate environment to encourage an interest in social questions or in the arts. His tough ghetto neighborhood was more likely to produce street fighters than film artists, and his immigrant parents were devoted not to politics but to money. As a result, Ritt went through DeWitt Clinton High School unscathed by scholarship. "He was," Aljean Harmetz wrote in the New York *Times* (February 25, 1979), "a jock—a barrel-chested, tough battering ram with bruised knuckles whose goal, if he had one, was to coach football when he was too old to play it."

Ritt's interest in athletics persisted during his years as a student at Elon College in North Carolina, where he was both a running guard and a boxer, but by the time he left Elon, his goals had changed. He now wanted to be a lawyer, and his experience of the world had enlarged to include the American South, a region that would provide the setting for many of his films. The real awakening of Martin Ritt, however, came upon his return to New York City. He was studying law at St. John's University, in Brooklyn, when he met actor-director Elia Kazan and decided to join his new friend in Lee Strasberg's Group Theatre, the famous company dedicated to the production of social dramas and to Stanislavsky's techniques of naturalistic acting. The jock, Ritt later recalled, turned "actor and overdosed on the class struggle."

It was, nonetheless, Ritt's athletic background that initially won him his berth with the Group Theatre, for his first job was to teach Luther Adler how to box for his leading role in Clifford Odets' *Golden Boy* (1937). Ritt also won a small part in the play itself. "I had exactly two lines," he told Ralph Hicklin in an interview with the Toronto *Globe and Mail* (March 30, 1967). "Remember the guy who runs in to announce that Joe has won his fight by a knockout? That was me." Eventually he became an understudy to John Garfield, and an associate not only of Kazan, Strasberg, and Adler, but also of Harold Clurman, Frances Farmer, Lee J. Cobb, Sylvia Sidney, and Franchot Tone. Ritt went on to appear in *Plant of the Sun* (1938), *The Gentle People* (1939), *Two on an Island* (1939), and other Group Theatre productions before leaving to join the United States Army Air Force during World War II.

As a member of the armed forces, Ritt continued to act, appearing in the George Cukor film of the Army Air Force's *Winged Victory* (1944), and he began to direct as well, making his debut with a theatre production of *Yellow*

Jack. After his discharge from military service, he returned to Broadway, where he performed in an occasional play, but found that he was not making a living as an actor and that his chances seemed much better as a director. He assumed that role in the production of plays like *Mr. Peebles and Mr. Hooker* (1946), *The Big People* (1947), and *Set My People Free* (1948). Then he entered the exhilarating world of live television, where he acted in over 150 teleplays and directed at least 100 others. Ritt found live television during its golden age an adventure, an opportunity for a bold man to do anything he wanted to do, but his sense of freedom was shortlived. In 1951 he was suddenly dismissed from CBS, a victim of the notorious television blacklist. "One day I was working," he has said, "and the next day I was out on my ass."

Martin Ritt had joined the Communist party, U.S.A., while still an idealistic youth, but he had left it by the end of the war. He told Rex Reed (New York *Sunday News,* October 10, 1976): "I didn't think it was any more sinful than joining the priesthood or being any other kind of evangelist. It had to do with beliefs for what could save the world. When I no longer believed . . . , I dropped out." Ritt *had* been a Communist, but the immediate cause of his dismissal was not his former Party membership; it was a Syracuse grocer's accusation that he had given money to Communist China. The charge was trivial, but devastating. Ritt lost the *Danger* series he had been directing, he lost the title role of Marty, which Paddy Chayefsky had written for him, and he lost any chance of working in television again.

The next four or five years were lean ones for Ritt and his family. He taught at the Actor's Studio, the educational extension of the Group Theatre, where his students included Paul Newman, Joanne Woodward, Anthony Franciosa, Lee Remick, and Rod Steiger; he won an occasional role on Broadway, including that of Shem in Odets' *The Flowering Peach* (1954); he played the horses with some success; and his wife sold space in the Yellow Pages. They survived, and Ritt later said, "I went on to do better work than I had before."

Prominent among that better work was his direction of Arthur Miller's *A View from the Bridge* (1955). Ritt's supervision of that contemporary tragedy of destructive sexual passion won him the favor of the critics, but the real turning point in his career came the following year when he directed Robert Alan Aurthur's *A Very Special Baby,* an assignment that led to his debut as a screen director in *Edge of the City* (MGM, 1956), which Aurthur adapted from his own teleplay.

The story of Axel Nordmann (John Cassavetes), a young misfit who has deserted from the army and resents all authority, and of Tommy Tyler (Sidney Poitier), the sympathetic black dockworker who has the courage to befriend him, *Edge of the City* is Ritt's first film dramatization of the outsider theme that characterizes most of his best work. The first of his many explorations of race relations, it was praised for the humane and unselfconscious treatment it gave what was then a bold subject. "The scene," observed Colin Young (*Film Quarterly, Spring,* 1959), "is between two human beings, one lost and the other certain, rather than one white and the other black, and when the gulf is closed between them it is only accidentally important that one is a Negro." *Edge of the City* is further distinguished by the sensitivity of its acting, with Cassavetes and Poitier offering the first in the long series of memorable screen performances inspired by Martin Ritt.

After *Edge of the City,* Ritt never returned to the theatre. He later explained to Bernard Drew of the White Plains *Reporter-Dispatch* (April 16, 1974): "The stage director is the third man on the totem pole—the writer and star are much more important . . . it doesn't compare with directing a film where you're it." The screen, he had discovered, offered him the freedom to dramatize his own values. Although there were limits to that freedom, imposed by the studios and their fear of offending public taste with bold themes and uncompromising realism, Ritt was prepared to do quiet battle. He was willing to earn the right to make his pictures his way by creating a succession of box office hits that would give him the control he desired.

The result was years of compromise, a series of flawed films beginning with *No Down Payment* (Twentieth Century-Fox, 1957). That portrait of what a critic for the New York *Times* (October 31, 1957) described as a "sub-division society living on the installment plan in an age of conformity" was noteworthy for its social criticism and for its introduction of Joanne Woodward to the screen, but its studio ending, contrived and moralistic, rendered it little more than an interesting failure.

The Long Hot Summer (Twentieth Century-Fox, 1958), loosely adapted from William Faulkner's *The Hamlet,* is the story of Ben Quick (Paul Newman), an unprincipled maverick who wanders into a Mississippi town and disrupts the already turbulent life of its first family. The film has the look and feel, according to Bosley Crowther in the New York *Times* (April 4, 1958), "of an afternoon storm making up above the still trees and sun-cracked buildings of a quiet Southern town on a hot day. That look and feel reflect the sexual and emotional tensions among the characters, but the storm never comes." For as Douglas McVey (*Films and Filming,* December, 1964) observed, the movie goes "nursery story ('And so they all lived happily ever after')" at the end, another victim of the studio system.

Such studio compromises continued in *The Sound and the Fury* (Twentieth Century-Fox, 1959) and *The Black Orchid* (Paramount, 1959). The first was a screen version of Faulkner's famous novel, in which Joanne Woodward plays an illegitimate child, a restless rebel against her Southern family and the past. The second was a portrait of a frustrated relationship between a widow (Sophia Loren) and a widower (Anthony Quinn) in a poor Italian neighborhood of New York. Both received mixed reviews, and both were criticized for their endings, The Black Orchid for what a New York Times critic (February 15, 1959) called its "soap opera" conclusion and The Sound and the Fury for subscribing to what Archer Winsten in the New York Post (March 29, 1959) described as "Hollywood's most deeply held doctrine, namely that men and women who fight most fiercely must eventually love each other the most."

The nadir of Ritt's career came with Five Branded Women (Paramount, 1960), a tale of crime, punishment, and guerrilla warfare during the Nazi occupation of Yugoslavia. Dismissed by one reviewer as a "disappointment" and by another as a "shoddy piece of work," it is the only Ritt film that the director himself despises. "I don't even mention it in my credits," he told Tom Topor during an interview for the New York Post (March 12, 1979). He had chosen his other projects because they moved him emotionally, but he made the mistake of doing Five Branded Women solely for the money.

Ritt redeemed himself, in the eyes of some reviewers, with Paris Blues (United Artists, 1961), a study of expatriated jazz musicians in Paris; faltered momentarily in Adventures of a Young Man (Twentieth Century-Fox, 1962), a rambling adaptation of Hemingway's Nick Adams stories; and finally triumphed with Hud (Paramount, 1963). A contemporary western promoted as a portrait of "a man with a barbed-wire soul," Hud is really the story of Lon Bannon, a young man confronted with two strikingly different lifestyles, in the persons of his uncle Hud and his grandfather Homer—the one, an immoralist who cares only for himself, and the other, an honorable man of old-fashioned principle and integrity. Lon finally chooses Homer's values over Hud's, but it is not a victory easily won, since Hud is as attractive as he is unprincipled. He is, as Richard L. Coe observed in the Washington Post and Times Herald (May 29, 1963), the American ideal, "straight out of the TV ads," revealed at last for what he is, in all his weakness, selfishness, and arrogance.

Ritt had finally made a totally uncompromised film with an ending praised for its honesty, for Homer dies, Hud is unrepentant, and Lon must make his way alone in the world. Judith Crist, writing in the New York Herald-Tribune (June 2, 1963), condemned the Hollywood formula by which the evil are punished and the good rewarded and found the distinction of Hud to reside in its presentation of "an unpleasant truth about people, without the pretty packaging, without the confines that easy answers and penny-ante analysis provide, without the slightest sweetness to satisfy our sentimental yearnings."

Ritt's The Outrage (MGM, 1964), which dramatized four different accounts of a rape, was Rashomon reset in the West and reduced, at the end, to farce, but his The Spy Who Came In From the Cold (Paramount, 1965) was, according to Judith Crist in the New York Herald Tribune (December 24, 1965), "the ultimate anti-romantic statement on espionage"— a somber, brooding portrait of an alienated agent (Richard Burton) who discovers that he, like those he is supposed to be defending, is a victim of a deceitful, corrupt society, and who walks out on it in the "ultimate defection."

In Hombre (Twentieth Century-Fox, 1967), the Stagecoach-like story of a white man (Paul Newman) raised by Indians and now at odds with his own race, Martin Ritt faltered momentarily. The same slackening seemed evident in his The Brotherhood (Paramount, 1969), an understated study of the Mafia, in which an aging mobster who clings to the old immigrant ways of honor and vengeance finds himself in conflict with the organization and with his younger brother.

Then came The Molly Maguires (Paramount, 1970), the box-office failure that Ritt nevertheless considers one of his best films. It is a portrait of two men, one of whom is a bitter, rebellious miner who leads the Molly Maguires, a terrorist organization struggling for just and humane treatment in the coal mines of Pennsylvania in the 1870's. The other is a Pinkerton detective who infiltrates their ranks and betrays them. Although some critics complained of its impersonal tone and pervasive somberness, Gary Arnold of the Washington Post (May 16, 1970) called the film "beautiful to behold, a serene but breathtaking evocation of the American past," and Louise Sweeney of the Christian Science Monitor (February 11, 1970) said: "Ritt makes you feel the black dust of the mines seeping into every pore, and the sense of trapped futility that went with life in the grimy poverty of a mining town."

After the "impressive failure" of The Molly Maguires, Ritt directed James Earl Jones in The Great White Hope (Twentieth Century-Fox, 1970), a stage-bound screen version of the biographical Broadway hit in which Jack Jefferson (Jack Johnson), the first black to become heavyweight boxing champion of the world, is harassed and humiliated by the white establishment because of his involvement with a white woman. Then Ritt achieved his biggest success since Hud with Sounder (Twentieth Century-Fox, 1972). With such comments as "flawless," "a lyrical, moving tribute to black experience," "touching and heartening," "a missing chapter from The Grapes of Wrath," Sounder received an enthusiastic response from critics and audiences alike. The simple story of a family of southern black sharecroppers during the Great Depression who are struggling to survive after the father's imprisonment for stealing a ham to feed his loved ones, *Sounder* is a tribute to what Louise Sweeney of the *Christian Science Monitor* (September 25, 1972) called "warmth and indomitable spirit in the face of a dehumanizing system."

Sounder seemed to signal a change in Martin Ritt's outlook. He continued to explore social themes and the alienation of the outsider, but his work grew warmer and more optimistic, and he spoke, in the Aljean Harmetz New York *Times* interview, of the "affirmation about struggle" at the heart of his films. That affirmation irradiates *Pete 'n' Tillie* (Universal, 1972), a tragicomedy about a middle-aged couple whose marriage is threatened by the death of their son, and is also present in *Conrack* (Twentieth Century-Fox, 1974), a somewhat simplistic and old-fashioned film in which an idealistic Southern white (Jon Voight) accepts a teaching position on a South Carolina island and meets the challenge of educating a group of black children devastated by ignorance of the world outside. *Conrack*'s reviews were mixed, but Pauline Kael in her *New Yorker* column (March 11, 1974) praised the film as "the tale of an unrepressed man fighting a slowly dying system of repression."

In Ritt's next film, *The Front* (Columbia, 1976), he chose to address the most painful episode of his life in comic terms rather than in the grim manner one might have expected. Counterbalancing viciousness with tenderness, he tells the story of a loser (Woody Allen) who fronts for several television writers blacklisted during the McCarthy era, representing and selling their work as his own, until at last he too is called before the House Un-American Activities Committee and forced to take a stand. *The Front* was followed by *Casey's Shadow* (Columbia, 1978), an affectionate portrait of an impoverished Cajun horse trainer with three sons and a quarter horse that holds the promise of racing fame and fortune. And then came the highly acclaimed *Norma Rae* (Twentieth Century-Fox, 1979). An optimistic celebration of an uneducated Southern girl who has her consciousness raised when she attempts to organize her fellow textile workers into a union, the film pays homage to what Kathleen Carroll, in reviewing it for the New York *Daily News* (March 2, 1979), called "spunky courage and natural resilience, the ability to survive anything." Suggested by actual events at a J. P. Stevens textile plant, the film benefits immensely from the extraordinary performance of its star, Sally Field.

Known as an actor's director, Ritt genuinely loves and respects performers. Jon Voight has said that "[Ritt] always gives you something actable. He directs the way he plays tennis, with a nice, clean touch. He doesn't overrun the ball, doesn't make the grandstand play, the extra frill." He directs his camera the same way he directs his actors—with restraint, without flashy angles and editing. And he prefers a similar simplicity in the stories he tells, choosing the linear or sequential plot over the fragmented narrative that has lately come into favor.

Martin Ritt is a husky man with a bulldog head and manner, who is addicted to jumpsuits, race horses, and tennis. Bess Winakor, who interviewed him for the New York *Post* (April 8, 1975) reported that he "talks short. Staccato. To the point. Lean and spare like the movies he directs." Tough-minded and unconventional, he is, in the words of John Le Carré, as quoted in the New York *Herald Tribune* (April 4, 1966), a man "apart not because he's a power man or vain but because in a painful and ambitious life he has learned that his own judgment is the only one he can trust."

References: Action 27+ Mr/Ap '71 pors;
N Y Times II p5 Je 1 '58 por;
N Y Times II p1+ F 25 '79 pors;
N Y Sunday News L p5 O 10 '76 por;
Toronto Globe and Mail p10 Mr 30 '67 por;
White Plains Reporter-Dispatch p18 Ap 16 '74 por; Whitaker, Sheila. The Films of Martin Ritt (1972)

Rowse, A(lfred) L(eslie)

*Dec. 4, 1903- British historian; author; poet.
Address: h. "Trenarren House," St. Austell, Cornwall, England*

Recognized as one of the most brilliant and readable of contemporary authorities on Elizabethan England, the Oxford scholar A. L. Rowse is also known as an immensely controversial literary biographer and as an accomplished poet and memoirist. A resident scholar at All Souls College for nearly half a century, Rowse has written more than forty books, including the trilogy *The Elizabethan Age* (1950-71), some studies of William Shakespeare, and several works about his native Cornwall. Historian J. H. Plumb has said of Rowse: "Outspoken, fearless, at times alive with hate, at others generously responsive, he is one of England's most interesting literary figures."

Alfred Leslie Rowse was born in St. Austell, Cornwall, on December 4, 1903, the youngest of the three children of Richard Rowse, a clay worker, and the former Ann Vanson. He grew up in the nearby village of Tregonissey. His father supplemented his wage as a laborer in the local china-clay works with the income he derived from Tregonissey's small general store. Rowse believes that he inherited from his father's side of the family "a certain pugnacity . . . , shortness of temper, [and] a gift for music."

A. L. Rowse

An imaginative, timid child, Rowse was "awkward, . . . hopeless at games," but at the same time self-willed, determined, and intensely inquisitive. "Nothing gave me greater pleasure as a small child than to get my father, when he was in a good humor, to tell me about the 'old days' in the village," he has recalled. "I suppose it was the first beginnings of the historical sense in me: that peculiar, razor-edge sensation, at once a joy and a grief, for life that was gone and was so valued because irrevocable."

At the Carglaze Elementary School Rowse showed precocious ability from the first, learning to read at the age of four. Not long afterwards, he began "a continuous and persistent effort to speak correct English." Unapologetic about his early attempts at self-improvement, Rowse has described himself as "a proletarian who appreciates and has an altogether higher respect for the standards, the culture, the sense and ability of the upper classes." It was the oddity of being an "exceptionally sharp and sensitive lad in a very ordinary working-class home" that set him on his long and lonely path.

During his childhood, Rowse regularly attended services and Sunday school sessions at the Anglican church, which, he remembers, was "in some ways, certainly aesthetically, . . . the chief influence" in his early life. It was there that he "hinged on to the civilization of the past, to history." Endowed with an exceptional singing voice, he earned some local fame, as well as pocket money as a soloist in the church choir. He took his religion very seriously; by the time he went to college, however, he had come to the conclusion that

Christianity was "a world of illusion . . . a social phenomenon, to be studied and understood anthropologically."

At eleven years of age, Rowse became the first in his village to win a scholarship to the secondary school in St. Austell. The "clever, ambitious, comically fat boy" was consistently first in his class, despite his detestation of mathematics, physics, and chemistry. He won essay and story competitions, served as school librarian, secretary of the debating society, and joint editor of the school magazine, sang in school concerts, acted in plays, and was eventually appointed "head boy." But despite his varied activities he became increasingly conscious of the loneliness that was to be his destiny and to resent the fact that it was his "nature and fate to be forever outside."

Meanwhile, Rowse's horizons were broadening. He was acquiring a small library in his almost bookless home, including works by Daudet, Hardy, Swift, and the Cornish author Sir Arthur Quiller-Couch, who later became his friend. In his late teens he developed a sympathy for socialism—surprising in view of his low opinion of the proletariat, but influenced, in his own words, by his reading, by "the generous impulses of a youngster for those who had had a raw deal in life," and by anger at those "more fortunate and more selfish." As a poet he scored his first success in 1921, when a sonnet of his appeared in the annual anthology Public School Verse.

During his last year at school Rowse, with the encouragement of his headmaster, expended almost superhuman efforts to gain scholarships to Oxford University. Eventually, despite illness and other problems, he succeeded, winning a Cornwall county scholarship, an open scholarship to Christ Church College, Oxford, and another offered by the Drapers' Company of the City of London. He was the first member of his school to win a university scholarship, and his achievement was reported in the national newspapers.

Entering Christ Church College, Oxford, in October 1922, Rowse expected to read English, but was persuaded to switch to history. In spite of his dedication to work, Rowse engaged in a variety of extracurricular activities through which he met such distinguished contemporaries at Oxford as Lord David Cecil, Harold Acton, and Graham Greene. He continued to write verse, published in Oxford Poetry and elsewhere, and devoted considerable time to the university's Labour Club, eventually becoming its secretary and chairman. Although he remained a "fanatic and proselytizer outside," he was increasingly a skeptic within. His historical reading increased his doubts about politics and humanity in general, and he asked himself: "Was there any objectivity, . . . any truth to be found?"

This intellectual crisis and constant overwork did further damage to Rowse's health. During the summer of 1923 he was gravely ill with a perforated appendix and peritonitis, and over the next few years he suffered intermittently from ulcers. In the summer of 1925 he graduated with a first class honors degree in modern history. A greater honor soon followed, when Rowse became the first member of the working class ever elected to a fellowship at All Souls. That institution, founded in 1437, permitted its fellows to pursue their own interests while enjoying a small stipend and the benefits of membership in one of the most select clubs in the world. Oxford conferred an M.A. degree on Rowse in 1929 and a D. Litt. degree in 1953.

At All Souls, Rowse soon became accustomed to the "upper-class mode of life." His circle of acquaintances widened dramatically over the next few years, and he met among others John Masefield, John Buchan, Lady Ottoline Morrell, C. K. Ogden, Robert Bridges, H. G. Wells, Gilbert Murray, and G. D. H. Cole. Traveling abroad for the first time, he visited France, Germany, and Austria.

After his recovery from surgery for a perforated ucler in 1926, Rowse returned to All Souls and established what became a regular pattern of life, combining tutoring, examining, and lecturing with the writing of reviews, articles, poems, and books. In 1929 he became Labour party candidate for Parliament in the Penryn-Falmouth constituency of Cornwall. His outrage at Tory economic policies, and later the government's attempts to appease Hitler, motivated him to remain in the Labour party. Rowse stood for election in 1931 and 1935, and in the latter year he came within 3,000 votes of success. In 1941 he left the political arena at the insistence of his doctors.

In 1929 he came to know T. S. Eliot, who solicited political articles from him for the Criterion and later, as a director of the publishing house of Faber & Faber, published his poetry. That same year he met Adam von Trott, a young German aristocrat. Rowse says that "this was an ideal love affair, platonic in the philosophic sense." (Adam von Trott eventually became a diplomat and a hero of the anti-Nazi Resistance, and was executed for his part in the attempt to assassinate Hitler.)

Rowse's first book, On History (Routledge, 1927), an essay on historical materialism, was followed by some political pamphlets. The first of his works to attract international attention was Sir Richard Grenville of the Revenge (Cape; Houghton, 1937), an exciting and well-received biography of the Elizabethan sea captain. His Tudor Cornwall (Cape, 1941), the product of twelve years of research, rated a two-page review in the London Times Literary Supplement (September 27, 1941), where it was said to enable the reader "to see the very life of the Cornish people of the Elizabethan age with an intimacy that has not yet been attained for any other society of Englishmen of that time."

Commenting on Rowse's first collection of verse, Poems of a Decade: 1931-1941 (Faber, 1941), Raymond Mortimer observed in the New Statesman (October 4, 1941): "Not only is he, in a good sense, an intellectual poet, but his volume can be read as the history of an intellectual." Poems Chiefly Cornish (Faber, 1944) was praised by critics for its sensibility and intelligence, but found lacking in imaginative intensity, and there was a mixed reception also for Poems of Deliverance (Faber, 1946) and Poems Partly American (Faber, 1959). Rowse has noted with some distaste: "Because a man is well-known as an historian, his poetry is totally neglected." His most recent volume of verse is The Road to Oxford (Cape, 1978), of which Kathleen Raine wrote in Country Life (April 6, 1978): "These are poems that might have been written at any time in the past hundred years or more; they recall now Housman, now Hardy. . . . They are not paper currency but the incorruptible metal of all that is in the English language traditional and enduring. He writes in that pure English now used only by an educated minority."

It is as a historian that Rowse's reputation is most secure. His The Spirit of English History (Cape, 1943; Oxford, 1945), a one-volume history of England, seemed to A. J. P. Taylor, writing in the Manchester Guardian (December 10, 1943), "fascinatingly readable, a triumph of restraint and artistry." It was followed by The English Spirit (Macmillan: London, 1944; New York, 1945), a volume of historical and literary essays; The Use of History (English Univ. Press, 1946; Macmillan, 1948), a text in the 'Teach Yourself History Library," edited by Rowse; and The End of an Epoch (Macmillan, 1947), a collection of political essays.

Rowse's magnum opus, the trilogy The Elizabethan Age, was received with general enthusiasm. Its first volume, The England of Elizabeth (Macmillan, 1950), was widely admired for its author's learning and vivid prose. H. R. Trevor-Roper, writing in the New Statesman (January 13, 1951), found in it an "intemperate, sometimes irritating impressionism" and an "intellectual arrogance," but concluded that the book was, despite those objections, "by far the best and most scholarly account of Elizabethan society."

The trilogy's second volume, The Expansion of Elizabethan England (Macmillan, St. Martin's, 1955), which deals mainly with Elizabethan exploration and conquest, also had an overwhelmingly favorable reception. It was fifteen years before the third volume appeared, in two parts, as The Elizabethan Renaissance (Macmillan; Scribner, 1971-72). The first part, subtitled The Life of the Society, examines the mores, superstitions, and mental attitudes of the Elizabethans and shows how these were affected by influences from abroad; the second part, The Cultural Achievement, deals with the art of the period and its religious, philosophical, and scientific thought.

Although few would dispute Rowse's standing as one of the greatest living authorities on Elizabethan England, a number of his colleagues have criticized his intensely personal style, and his dislike of the paraphernalia of historical scholarship. Rowse's approach to historiography derives partly from the fact that he admires G. M. Trevelyan, who believed that the writing of history was as much a literary as a scholarly activity. It was therefore fitting that Rowse was invited to give the first Trevelyan Lectures at Cambridge University in 1958. Published as *The Elizabethans and America* (Macmillan; Harper, 1959), those lectures give an account of what led up to the settlement of British America as the prime extrapolation of the Elizabethan age.

J. B. Conacher once wrote in the *Canadian Historical Review* (September 1956): "Rowse's whole approach to history is biographical. He delights to dip into family records." This approach is nowhere more effective than in his two-volume history: *The Early Churchills: An English Family* (Macmillan, Harper, 1956), and *The Later Churchills* (Macmillan, 1958), published in the United States by Harper as *The Churchills: From the Death of Marlborough to the Present* (1958). Commenting on the first volume in the *Saturday Review* (October 6, 1956), L. B. Wright observed that "few books dealing with this period contain so much material of compelling interest." Other works of family history and biography by Rowse include *Ralegh and the Throckmortons* (Macmillan, 1962), issued in the United States later that same year by Harper as *Sir Walter Ralegh, His Family and Private Life*, and *The Byrons and Trevanions* (St. Martin's, 1979).

Always as passionately interested in literature as in history, Rowse has published several controversial literary biographies, beginning with *William Shakespeare; A Biography* (Macmillan, Harper, 1963). That book incorporated his solutions of several long-standing mysteries, including the dating of the sonnets and the identity of the man to whom they were addressed—the Earl of Southampton, Shakespeare's patron. His findings brought opposition from literary scholars, who objected to his application of historical method to their province. But the book sold well.

In *Shakespeare the Man* (Macmillan, Harper, 1973) Rowse went on to establish the identity of the Dark Lady of the sonnets as Emilia Lanier, daughter of an Italian musician at Elizabeth's court. Another study by Rowse about the Bard and his times is *Shakespeare the Elizabethan* (Weidenfeld, Putnam, 1977). He has edited *Shakespeare's Sonnets* (Harper, 1964, 1973) and a three-volume complete *Annotated Shakespeare* (Potter, 1978). Among his biographies of literary figures are also *Christopher Marlowe: His Life and Work* (Harper, 1964), *Jonathan Swift: Major Prophet* (Thames, Scribner, 1975), *Matthew Arnold: Poet and Prophet* (Thames, 1976), and *Milton the Puritan* (Macmillan, 1977).

Rowse claims "a wholly Cornish temperament." His Celtic heritage accounts for his sympathy with "Latin peoples and their culture," as well as "a certain distaste for . . . Puritan idealism." He has published stories, poems, and essays with Cornish settings and themes, as well as a lively and affectionate history, *The Cornish in America* (Macmillan, 1969). Scribner changed the title of the book to *The Cousin Jacks* (1969) for American readers.

A more recent preoccupation is with the history of sexual mores and attitudes. *Simon Forman: Sex and Society in Shakespeare's Age* (Weidenfeld, 1974) is a biography of an Elizabethan astrologer, physician, and womanizer, drawing on Forman's own diaries and notes. His *Homosexuals in History* (Macmillan, 1977) deals with such historic personalities as James I, Frederick the Great, Leonardo da Vinci, and Oscar Wilde. Rowse also wrote *The Tower of London in the History of the Nation* (Weidenfeld, Putnam, 1972) and similar works about Windsor Castle and Oxford. He translated and completed Lucien Romier's *History of France* (Macmillan, St. Martin's, 1953).

Over the years, Rowse has devoted considerable time to writing his personal history. The first volume of his autobiography, *A Cornish Childhood* (Cape, 1942; Macmillan, 1947), written with humor and sensitivity, became a best seller. It was followed by *A Cornishman at Oxford* (Cape; Verry, 1965) and *A Cornishman Abroad* (Cape, 1976). In *All Souls and Appeasement* (Macmillan, 1961), which was released in the United States under the title *Appeasement: A Study in Political Decline* (Norton, 1961), the author discusses his political attitudes and activities during the 1930's, when some of his most eminent colleagues favored appeasement of Nazi Germany. In a lighter vein, *Peter, the White Cat of Trenarren* (Joseph, 1974) is a charming biography of Rowse's four-legged companion of sixteen years, followed by *Three Cornish Cats* (Weidenfeld, 1979).

In 1974 Rowse relinquished his All Souls fellowship and retired to Trenarren House, a stone Georgian manor house overlooking St. Austell Bay, a few miles from his birthplace. Rowse is a Fellow of the British Academy and of the Royal Society of Literature, and he has honorary doctorates from the University of Exeter and the University of New Brunswick, Canada. He was president of the English Association in 1952 and of the Shakespeare Club at Stratford-upon-Avon in 1971-72. Rowse served as the British Academy's Raleigh Lecturer in 1957 and the Beatty Memorial Lecturer at McGill University in Montreal in 1963, and he has been a visiting professor at the University of Illinois and the University of Wisconsin. In the 1960's he pursued his Shakespearian studies as a senior fellow of the Huntington Library, located in San Marino, California.

A. L. Rowse, who has been described as "owlish" and as "a lively, thickset bachelor with piercing green eyes," enjoys gardening, visiting historic places, and listening to music. He is a member of the Athenaeum Club. Garrett Mattingly, writing in the New York *Herald Tribune Book Review* (November 15, 1959), called him "one of the most distinguished . . . , versatile, and wide-ranging" scholars, endowed with "the insights of a Celt and a poet." And Auberon Waugh, after visiting Rowse at Trenarren, observed in the New York *Times Book Review* (June 26, 1977): "He says he is happy alone, and I expect he is. . . . There is something elemental and heroic in his boastfulness, his certainty and his cosmic tactlessness. To understand how there is also something profoundly endearing . . . one needs to meet the old man for oneself."

References: Contemporary Authors 1st rev vol 1-4 (1967); International Who's Who, 1978-79; Rowse, A. L. A Cornish Childhood (1942); A Cornishman at Oxford (1965); A Cornishman Abroad (1976); Twentieth Century Authors (First Supplement, 1955); Who's Who, 1979

Salk, Lee

1926(?)- Psychologist. Address: b. Cornell University Medical College, 1300 York Ave., New York City, N.Y. 10021

"The other Dr. Salk" is Lee Salk, a child psychologist, the younger brother of Dr. Jonas Salk, the discoverer of the polio vaccine. Lee Salk is professor of psychology in pediatrics at Cornell University Medical College and a consultant in pediatric psychology at the New York Hospital-Cornell Medical Center as well as the Payne Whitney Psychiatric Clinic and Lenox Hill Hospital, all in Manhattan. Salk writes the column "You and Your Family" for *McCall's* magazine, and he is the author of *What Every Child Would Like His Parents to Know* (1972), *Preparing for Parenthood* (1974), and *Dear Dr. Salk; Answers to Your Questions About Your Family* (1979), among other books.

Salk writes in language the layperson can understand while earning the respect of his professional peers, especially for his work in relating the conditions of birth and infancy to later psychological health and illness. "He has become the dominant figure in the growing new specialty called pediatric psychology, working out of the New York Hospital-Cornell Medical Center," a writer for *Life* (April 21, 1972) observed. "But he also has a flair for showmanship and he turns up frequently in the mass media, ebulliently discussing what science has learned about how kids get hung-up."

Lee Salk was born in New York City some fifty-three years ago, the youngest of three sons of Daniel B. Salk, who was employed in the garment industry, and Dora (Press) Salk. With his brothers, he grew up in the Bronx. After taking his Ph.D. degree in psychology at the University of Michigan, in 1954, he taught in the Department of Psychiatry at McGill University in Canada for several years before joining the staff of Elmhurst Hospital in Queens, New York City.

At Elmhurst Hospital, Salk studied the maternal heartbeat as an imprinting stimulus and invented the "Securitone," a device that reproduced the sound of a normal maternal heartbeat. In sixteen weeks of experiments Salk and his associates found that when the sound of the Securitone filled a nursery the babies were more likely to gain weight and less likely to cry (except when hungry) or suffer stomach upset or respiratory trouble. At a World Federation for Mental Health symposium in 1960 Salk urged that pediatric researchers investigate more thoroughly the trauma of birth, when "the rhythmical sensation [the newborn infant] had been exposed to from the moment sense organs began to function" ends and the infant is "exposed to unfamiliar, dissonant, non-rhythmical sounds." In a paper delivered before the New York Academy of Sciences in 1962 Salk discussed the importance of the intrauterine environment in general and the maternal heartbeat rate in particular in the later development of the response apparatus. He asserted that imprinting helps bring the developing organism into proximity with conditions favoring survival, sets the pattern for later learning, forces the organism to seek sensory stimuli, and enhances the development of appropriate behavior patterns through associative learning.

During the 1960's Salk moved from Elmhurst Hospital to Lenox Hill Hospital in Manhattan and from there to Cornell University Medical College. In 1968 he published in volume 29 of *Diseases of the Nervous System* the paper "On the Prevention of Schizophrenia," in which he stressed an environmental approach. Citing instances of autism in children who had been very premature incubator babies, and explaining the process of imprinting in the animal kingdom, he suggested that autism may result from sensory deprivation and the lack of tactile and kinetic stimulation in early infancy, rather than from organic factors.

How Salk translates and adapts professional jargon to everyday language and situations can be seen in a *McCall's* column in which he reassured the parents of a premature son who wondered, "Now that he is home with us, should he be treated with any special care and attention?" Salk answered, "It is not necessary for you to treat a premature baby with any more special care and attention than you would an infant born after a full-term pregnancy. I think it is essential to give your son —or any baby—as much cuddling, love, and stimulation as he requires. In this way he will develop a trusting relationship with you and will flourish emotionally. Babies who get a great deal of cuddling, both premature and full-term babies, seem to be more outgoing and friendly and more independent later on."

In their book *How to Raise a Human Being; A Parents' Guide to Emotional Health from Infancy through Adolescence* (Random House, 1969), Salk and Rita Kramer suggested "certain kinds of experiences that serve not only to avoid some of the causes of emotional illness but also to provide for the greatest possible degree of healthy development for each child in terms of his own potential." "Again and again," a reviewer in *Harper's Magazine* (October 1969) observed, "the book returns to that haunting series of studies made not long ago of the dire effects of being institutionalized— deprived, that is, of the mothering adult figure —upon young babies." The main points of the book as seen by C. E. Wadsworth in the *Library Journal* (October 1, 1969) were "that [the] infant's cries for attention should always be responded to quickly so that the baby will learn to trust adults, and that the toddler must learn limits to his actions—by spanking if necessary—or it will be impossible to develop self-discipline later."

In a study published in *Professional Psychology* (summer 1970) Salk described the purposes and functions of a psychologist in a pediatric setting. The possible contributions of the psychologist he enumerated included

prompt screening, early diagnosis of learning and developmental problems, the transmission of current behavioral knowledge to the pediatric staff, and sensitization of the staff to the emotional needs of children so as to lessen "the traumatic nature of medical procedures and hospitalization."

The dry description given in the professional journal was fleshed out in the 1972 article on Salk in *Life:* "Salk roams the pediatric corridors, where a knowledge of behavior is often needed on the spot. There are jittery children to be calmed or anguished parents to be consoled, and sometimes a distraught, overworked nurse to be reassured. Salk also does intellectual and emotional evaluations needed to diagnose degrees of brain damage. Often he is a psychological handyman. He might help a nurse deal with a five-year-old boy who has a grown man's sex drive, thanks to hormone shots he needs to live. Or he might chastise residents he has heard chatting casually on an elevator filled with parents about a child who is 'going downhill fast.'" Salk was quoted: "A child in crisis wants to hold your hand. With a dying patient in particular, there is that horrible, distressing loneliness at the end. Words won't do it. But human touch can tell him he is not so alone."

The title of Salk's book *What Every Child Would Like His Parents to Know* (McKay, 1972), was completed in the subtitle: *To Help Him with the Emotional Problems of His Everyday Life*. In the book Salk covered much of the same ground he and Rita Kramer had gone over earlier: don't be afraid of spoiling a baby under the age of nine or ten months, whose dependency needs are massive, but lay down disciplinary guidelines after he begins crawling and exploring on his own. Reward and punishment should involve the bestowal and withdrawal (briefly) of love, he advised, and not of material possessions. Material rewards and punishments will make the child "thing-oriented," he warned.

Running through Salk's *Preparing for Parenthood: Understanding Your Feelings About Pregnancy, Childbirth and Your Baby* (McKay, 1974) was the theme that it is better for parents to recognize any ambivalent feelings they might have about pregnancy and parenthood than to hide or rationalize them. "Too many people have a stereotyped picture of parenthood," he wrote, "which emphasizes the joys and deemphasizes the potential problems." In one chapter he admonished the father to participate as much as possible in the pregnancy, by reading and by other means of learning about childbirth and childcare. In others he dispensed advice on such matters as the handling of an older child when the new baby arrives, the parents' need to organize a life of their own away from the baby, and the "when" and "how" of discipline.

Salk won custody of his own two young children in a landmark court decision when he and his wife Kerstin were divorced in 1975. "I thought I knew the extent of the anguish that divorce could inflict on both parents and children," he wrote in the preface to his *What Every Child Would Like Parents to Know About Divorce* (Harper & Row, 1975). "But it was not until I myself experienced, together with my children, the terrible realities of getting 'unmarried' that I fully understood how deeply this experience reaches into the very heart of one's existence, testing all of one's strengths and revealing all of one's weaknesses as a human being." In the book he discussed in simple language such profoundly complicated psychological events as separation anxiety, the trauma of grief and loss, self-destructiveness, denial in fantasy, the reality principle, and regressive behavior.

Questions and answers from Salk's *McCall's* magazine column formed the basis for much of *Dear Dr. Salk* (Harper & Row, 1979). In that book Salk answered questions about such problems as planning family size, sibling rivalry, stepsibling rivalry, toilet training, masturbating, bed-wetting, watching too much television, and Santa Claus. On the last mentioned point he wrote: "I think it is crucially important for parents to be honest with their children. . . . I believe it is best to tell children that Santa Claus is a make-believe person and that both children and grownups pretend he brings presents at Christmas time. Children

are delighted that grownups can engage in make-believe also." In addition to the wide readership of his books, Salk reaches a television audience, through his regular appearances as a commentator on the local evening news on WNBC-TV in New York City.

Short, bald, bespectacled Lee Salk lives with his daughter Pia, a grade-schooler, and his adolescent son Eric in a duplex apartment on Park Avenue in Manhattan. When possible, Salk arranges his schedule so that he can be working at home when his children arrive from school. When the children are not in school they often travel with him on business trips, and the three go skating together at Rockefeller Center in the winter.

Salk has served as president of the Society of Pediatric Psychology and the American Psychological Association's section on clinical child psychology. Among the honors he has received are a citation from the Society of Pediatric Psychology and the Pearl Merrill Award "in recognition of his distinguished contribution to the field of pediatric psychology and for his warm understanding of the needs of the human family."

References: Life 72:73+ Ap 21 '72 pors; N Y Daily News p4 O 9 '75 por; People 9:55+ Je 19 '78 pors; Authors in the News vol 1 (1976)

Sarkis, Elias

July 20, 1924- President of the Republic of Lebanon. Address: Palais de Baada, Beirut, Lebanon

The only Christian President in the Arab world is the moderate Elias Sarkis, the technocratic chief executive of religiously pluralistic Lebanon, which was once a paragon of Muslim-Christian accord, and is now a savaged surrogate in the Arab-Israeli conflict. When Sarkis, former governor of the Bank of Lebanon, took office in 1976, the fighting in Lebanon still seemed largely a civil war between rival domestic factions, although those factions were supported by outside powers. It soon escalated, however, as a Syrian "peacekeeping" force became less than peaceful and Israel launched retaliatory attacks on "guerrilla bases" of the Palestine Liberation Organization located within Lebanon. By October 1978 the capital city of Beirut was—as a fleeing Lebanese Christian described it—a flaming "second Stalingrad," occupied within by Syrian troops searching out and destroying right-wing Christian militiamen and bombarded from without by Israeli warships in a paradoxical gesture of Jerusalem's support for the Christians.

By December 1, 1978 rebuilding had resumed in the predominantly Christian section of eastern Beirut, but in the meantime most foreign companies had withdrawn their non-Lebanese employees, and only 100 out of

450 business and industrial enterprises had resumed operation.

The oldest of three sons of a struggling Maronite shopkeeper, Elias Sarkis was born on July 20, 1924 in the Lebanese mountain village of Shibaniyah, twenty-two miles east of Beirut. At that time Lebanon, along with Syria, which borders it on the north and east, was a newly created national entity, administered under French mandate in accordance with the treaties that dismembered the Ottoman Empire at the end of World War I.

As a child, Sarkis had to work at odd jobs for his pocket money, and after graduating from high school in Beirut he took a full-time job as a clerk in a railroad office. Lebanon was then in the process of obtaining national autonomy; its independence, proclaimed in 1941, was confirmed in a National Pact worked out with Free French representatives in 1943 and became fully effective with the withdrawal of French troops three years later. The nation's constitution, promulgated during the French mandate, in 1926, and later amended, established a unitary republic with an indirectly elected president, a unicameral legislature elected through universal suffrage, and an independent judiciary. The National Pact of 1943, reflecting the balance of religious groups within the population at that time, provided for the sharing of executive and legislative functions in the ratio of six Christians to five Muslims. Thus, the President is a Maronite Christian, elected by a two-thirds majority of the Chamber of Deputies; the Prime Minister is a Sunni Muslim, appointed by the President after consultation with religious and political leaders; the President of the Chamber of Deputies is a Shia Muslim; and seats in the Chamber of Deputies are filled through a system of proportional representation based on religious groupings.

When Sarkis had saved enough money he quit his job and enrolled at the Université Saint Joseph, a Jesuit institution in Beirut, where he received his law degree in 1948. Following the deposition of Lebanon's first President, Bichara el-Khoury, in 1952, Sarkis was appointed a judge in the government's Audit Office in the administration of President Camille Chamoun, in 1953.

Meanwhile, pan-Arab nationalism was surging throughout the Middle East under the leadership and example of President Gamal Abdel Nasser of Egypt. The surge reached flood point in 1958, when the monarchy in Iraq was overthrown in a revolution led by the Iraqi army and revolts shook other pro-Western governments, including the Chamoun regime in Lebanon. The United States sent troops into Lebanon (at the request of Chamoun), as well as Jordan, thereby serving notice to Nasser and other leaders of the Arab bloc that it would fight to protect its remaining spheres of influence in the Arab world.

Sarkis rose to political prominence in the wake of the insurrection of 1958. General Fuad Chehab, who succeeded Chamoun as President, assigned him to a reform committee, and in 1959 he named him director of the Cabinet of the Presidency. As Cabinet director, Sarkis created the Deuxiéme Bureau, a top-level team of army officers charged with holding the country's political factions in check.

Charles Hélou, who became President in 1964, retained Sarkis in his post and, in 1967. after the Intrabank crash threatened the country's financial institutions, made him governor of the Bank of Lebanon. As head of the central bank, Sarkis helped to restore Lebanon's importance as an international financial center. In a bid for the Presidency in 1970, he lost to Suleiman Franjieh.

Sarkis was still at the Bank of Lebanon in 1975, when civil war, brewing for two years, broke out in Lebanon, pitting Muslims, leftists, and Palestinian refugees against the Christian community and its allies. Muslim Lebanese resented the privileged position of Christians, who no longer constituted a majority of the population but still enjoyed their fixed numerical advantage in the Chamber of Deputies and their traditional claim to the Presidency; leftists hoped to replace Lebanon's confessional system with a strictly secular state; Christians wanted to curb the Palestinians, who added to the Muslims' numbers and brought trouble with Israel; and the refugees feared the consequences of a Muslim defeat. Neighboring Syria, a hulking kibitzer, at first supported the Muslim cause but switched to the Christian side to prevent the victory of radicals intent on war with Israel. By early 1976 Lebanon was in shambles, and on April 24 the Chamber of Deputies forced a reluctant Franjieh to sign a constitutional amendment moving the upcoming Presidential election forward by several months.

In the first press conference he ever gave. Sarkis announced his candidacy to succeed Franjieh on April 29, 1976. Despite his self-effacement—his supporters had difficulty even finding a photograph of him to use on posters —and allegations by his chief opponent, Raymond Eddé, that he was a Syrian pawn, he easily won the presidency, obtaining the necessary two-thirds majority in the second round of voting in the Chamber of Deputies on May 8, 1976. Sixty-six members voted for him, three handed in blank ballots, and twenty-nine Eddé backers boycotted the process. Prime Minister Rashid Karami, a conservative Muslim, described Sarkis' election as an act of national reconciliation through which "all of Lebanon has again become one family." Sarkis promised to try to rebuild national unity by bringing rival factions to an agreement, but he warned that he would seek other alternatives if negotiations failed.

While Suleiman Fanjieh stubbornly remained in the Presidential palace to the end of the full term to which he had been elected, Sarkis began talking with leaders of the contending factions. When his discussions with Kemal Jumblatt, leader of the Druze sect of Muslims, and Yasir Arafat of the Palestine Liberation Organization came to naught, a Syrian "peace-keeping" force intervened, at first actually in behalf of the beleaguered Christians. On June 10, 1976 the Arab League dispatched a multination peace-keeping force to Lebanon, but the fighting went on. The President-elect continued to meet with representatives of the warring parties and with leaders from neighboring states, including Premier Abdel Salam Jalloud of Libya, President Hafez al-Assad of Syria, and Anwar Sadat, who had become President of Egypt following the death of Gamal Abdel Nasser.

Sarkis was inaugurated on September 23, 1976 in Shtoura, a resort town in the Bekaa Valley, where Syrian forces were in control. Sixty-seven of the ninety-eight members of the Chamber of Deputies attended the ceremony, which took place in the Park Hote' in Shtoura, but Jumblatt, Karami, and others refused to enter "occupied territory." In his inaugural address, President Sarkis described "Lebanon's sovereignty, the unity of its land and the unity of its people" as "sacred" and expressed "an unshakable faith in the ability of the people to build a new Lebanon based on fraternity, unity, and opposition to any form of partition." Unlike his predecessor, he expressed support for the Palestinians and promised to "spare no effort to help the Palestinian commando movement regain its homeland." Finally, he praised Syria and said that her military actions were "based on the will of Lebanon's constitutional authority."

After Syria opened a major offensive against the Palestinians, on September 28, 1976, King Khalid of Saudi Arabia called for a peace conference. On October 16, Sarkis, Arafat, Assad, Sadat, and Sheikh Sabah al-Salem al-Sabah of Kuwait met with Khalid in the Saudi capital of Riyadh. Two days later the participants signed a compact that put Sarkis in charge of a greatly increased Arab League peace-keeping force composed mostly of Syrian troops. The agreement directed the peace-keeping force to separate the combatants and induce them to turn over their heavy weapons; ordered the warring parties to withdraw to the positions they held before the war; and instructed the Palestinian guerrillas in Lebanon to abide by the Cairo agreement of 1969, which restricted them to refugee camps and to the Arkub section in the southeast.

President Sarkis put a neutral Muslim in command of the Arab League peace-keeping force, and in a radio and television address to the nation on November 7, 1976 he asked that the force be met with "fraternity" and an understanding of its "noble purpose." "We have had enough bloodshed, destruction, waste of effort, and loss of opportunity," he said. At a meeting on November 9, 1976 Sarkis persuaded two Christian leaders, Pierre Gemayel of the far-right Phalangist party and Camille Chamoun of the National Liberal party, to accept amicably the presence of Syrian troops in the Christian areas of Beirut and its suburbs.

With some degree of peace and order restored, Sarkis turned his attention to forming an efficient government team composed largely of technocrats, or apolitical experts, and on December 9, 1976 he named Salim Ahmad al-Huss Prime Minister of a Cabinet composed of four Christians and four Muslims. In January 1977 he imposed a temporary program of press censorship, and in the following months he devoted much of his attention to controlling right-wing Christian leaders, especially after the assassination of Kemal Jumblatt deprived the left of its chief spokesman. When, in March 1977, Sarkis named a neutral Maronite to replace a rightist as commander of the Lebanese army, Chamoun protested, but Sarkis refused to relent. As one of his supporters pointed out, the President was trying to establish de facto the authority of his new government, and capitulation to Chamoun "would have been interpreted as an abdication." Chamoun and other Christian leaders of like mind were in agreement with Sarkis on such other matters as the expulsion of Palestinians who had entered Lebanon illegally after 1969.

High on Sarkis' agenda was the reconstruction of Lebanon's shattered economy. When he warned the international banking firms, whose presence had made Beirut a financial center, to reopen by January 17, 1977 or not at all, several complied. The government made 7 percent loans to businessmen through the National Bank of Industrial and Touristic Development and obtained promises of desperately needed additional funds from the World Bank, Saudi Arabia, Kuwait, the United Arab Emirates, and the United States. The Reconstruction and Development Council, established on March 21, 1977, took on the responsibility of returning war refugees to their homes and providing them with handicraft employment. By the end of the year overseas telephone service for businesses in Beirut had been restored, the airport had reopened, and plans for the rebuilding of Beirut's commercial center and port had been completed.

Problems outpaced the progress, however, Inflation was high and going higher, foreigners were reluctant to invest in the strife-torn country, and Sarkis' call for a summit meeting of Arab leaders to discuss the nation's future went unanswered. Worst of all, the warring factions, far from laying down their weapons, struck at each other viciously and for all practical purposes partitioned Lebanon into Christian, Muslim, and Palestinian sections.

In southern Lebanon the fighting between Christian militiamen, backed by Israel, and Palestinian guerrillas was out of control, and an Israeli invasion of the south launched on March 14, 1978 created a crisis there. The Israelis were retaliating for a Palestinian attack along the Haifa-Tel Aviv road, but Sarkis charged that Israel's refusal to allow Arab peacekeeping forces to take positions near the border was the root of the problem.

Under pressure from the United States the Israelis agreed to surrender their strategic posts in Lebanon to a United Nations interim force. At the urging of U.N. Secretary General Kurt Waldheim and Syria's Assad, Sarkis sent a fledgling Lebanese army of 600 men to take up positions beside the United Nations contingent in the south in a symbolic act of national sovereignty. Sarkis' prestige suffered a humiliating blow when the small Lebanese detachment was denied access to the sovereign Lebanese territory in the south by Israeli-supported Christian militiamen.

Lebanon's inability to assert its sovereignty in the south of its own country apparently gave Syria second thoughts about the wisdom of supporting the Sarkis government. Lebanese and Syrian troops clashed briefly in early February 1978, and two months later Syrian soldiers attempting to quell an outbreak of fighting between Christian and Muslim militiamen in Beirut directed the brunt of their attack against the former. On April 19 Sarkis accepted the resignation of Prime Minister al-Huss and his Cabinet, which was considered too cooperative with Syria, but he reinstated the Cabinet nine days later, after failing to form a unified replacement for it.

On June 13, 1978 Tony Franjieh, son of the former president and a pro-Syrian Christian leader, was assassinated, in an incident in which his wife, his baby daughter, and thirty-one other persons were also killed. It was generally assumed that the killings were done by Phalangists, the far-right faction among the three Christian groups. Later in the same month more than two dozen Christian rightists were slaughtered, in apparent retaliation, and on July 1 Syrian soldiers in the Arab League force began to attack Christian militia units in and near Beirut. Bitter fighting continued until a cease-fire was achieved on July 6, a few hours after Israeli war planes roared over the Muslim section of west Beirut as a warning that the government of Prime Minister Menachem Begin would not allow the extermination of Israel's Christian allies.

On July 6, 1978, in the midst of the crisis, Sarkis threatened to resign, and he repeated the warning three days later, stating that he could see no point in continuing in office if the opposing sides would not cooperate with him. According to close observers, the President especially wanted Syria to withdraw its demands that he punish pro-Israeli Christian soldiers and that he increase the Muslim role in the army. Camille Chamoun denounced Sarkis for his readiness to abandon Lebanon in its darkest hour, and President Assad of Syria asked the President to make up his mind quickly so that an alternative leadership could prepare to face the nation's problems. Other Christian and Muslim leaders as well as representatives of the United States, Great Britain, France, Germany, and Saudi Arabia asked Sarkis to remain in office, and on July 15 the President announced his decision to stay. He once again called on the Lebanese to accept the Arab peacekeepers, and he warned that "violence will continue to threaten security, the state, legitimacy, and lives of innocent people as long as hundreds of thousands of [unauthorized] people continue to possess weapons and as long as tens of thousands of fighters remain."

Lebanon's shaky peace began to totter in August and collapsed completely in September, as Syrians and Christians again clashed in Beirut. Between September 24 and October 4 about 400 people died and approximately 1,200 were wounded in fighting that devastated the Christian section of the capital. On October 2 Sarkis called for a new "security plan" that would put the Lebanese army in charge of the Christian districts of the capital and restrict Syrian soldiers to Muslim areas. After conferring unsuccessfully with President Assad in four rounds of talks between October 6 and 9, he consulted with the leaders of Saudi Arabia, Jordan, and the United Arab Emirates. Returning to Damascus he reached an agreement with Assad on October 12, and the Sarkis-Assad accord was given wide Arab approval at a meeting in Beirut of representatives from Syria, Saudi Arabia, Kuwait, the United Arab Emirates, and Qatar on October 16. In keeping with the provisions of the accord, the Lebanese army was deployed in Beirut, the Syrians began the process of turning over their strongholds near the city's Christian quarter to troops from other Arab states, and the Sarkis government drew up plans to discourage citizens from cooperating with Israel.

Reporting from Beirut at the height of the fighting there, David Hirst of the *Guardian* (October 8, 1978) blamed the crisis in Lebanon partly on the inability of the United States "to bring its tyrannical Israeli protégé to discuss peace on terms which they [the Arab states] can at least contemplate." Hirst continued: "But the Lebanese, many of them now believe, could be the victim of something far more sinister than that. For in their view it is precisely because of America's inability to solve the main problem of the Middle East—the Arab-Israeli conflict—that it has to look for an alternative solution. It has been Lebanon's mission to furnish it. Paradoxically, this is the one thing on which the most bitter enemies, Palestinians and right-wing Christians, now agree. In its extreme form, the alternative solution is thought to call for the complete dismemberment, through civil war, of the existing Lebanese polity. In the resulting carve-up, the Christians would get their mini-state, 'Marounistan' [and] the Syrians (suspected by both Palestinians and Christians to be a party to the conspiracy) would annex their share, while the Palestinians . . . would be fobbed off with a homeland of sorts in the south."

As of December 1978, much of Lebanon's business, banking, and industry, which were concentrated in Beirut, were at a standstill, leaving 90,000 workers unemployed. As one small businessman-industrialist told Marvin

Howe (New York Times, December 6, 1978), "Everybody's waiting now until the new year to make any new investments because we are afraid there will be a new Arab-Israeli war after the signing of the Israeli-Egyptian peace treaty." Howe commented, "Many Lebanese predict that such a conflict would take place in Lebanon because most of the forces are here and there is no strong central authority to resist."

Elias Sarkis is a tall, quiet man of swarthy complexion and solemn, brooding visage. The first Lebanese President not born into one of the nation's leading families, he is unassuming and simple in his ways, unspoiled by the perquisites of office. A bachelor who is accustomed to solitude, he eschews the Beirut social scene as assiduously as he shuns publicity. "He belongs neither to an aristocratic circle nor to a specific social stratum," a friend has said. "He has moved up the ladder from the bottom rung." Sarkis, who has a mountainside home at Hazmieh, finds recreation in reading, listening to classical music, hunting pheasant, and growing roses.

References: N Y Times p3 My 10 '76 por; Washington Post A p1 S 23 '76 por; International Who's Who, 1978-79

Sawhill, John C(rittenden)

June 12, 1936- Educator; economist; administrator. Address: b. Elmer Holmes Bobst Library, 70 Washington Square South, New York City, N.Y. 10012

An appetite for challenges, sharpened on large-scale managerial undertakings in finance and government, sustained John C. Sawhill in bringing off, as president of New York University, what Edward B. Fiske of the New York Times considers to be "perhaps the most dramatic rescue operation in the history of American education." His six-month supervision of the Federal Energy Administration in the wake of the 1973-74 Arab oil embargo had ended with a split on policy matters with the Ford Administration, but earned him a reputation as a forthright, hard-working public servant. When he assumed the presidency, in 1975, of the gravely deficit-ridden New York University, the country's largest private institution of higher learning, he initiated a wide range of cost-cutting and income-generating measures that achieved a balanced budget within two years. He has, moreover, introduced intercollegiate academic programs to enlarge the university's educational offerings, especially in the humanities. President Sawhill is also professor of economics and the first holder of the David B. Kriser Professorship in the Humanities at NYU. In the summer of 1979 Sawhill took a leave

of absence from NYU to become Deputy Secretary of Energy in the Administration of President Jimmy Carter, serving as second in command to Charles W. Duncan Jr., newly appointed Secretary of Energy.

The oldest of the four children (two sons and two daughters) of James Mumford Sawhill, a corporation executive, and Mary Munroe (Gipe)

Sawhill, John Crittenden Sawhill was born in Cleveland, Ohio on June 12, 1936. The family soon afterward moved to Baltimore, where John Sawhill attended private schools, preparing for college at Gilman School. While a student at Princeton University's Woodrow Wilson School of Public and International Affairs, he wrestled, played intramural hockey, won poker games, and was a member of Colonial, a prestigious eating club. After he had graduated *cum laude* with a B.A. degree in 1958, he worked for two years in the underwriting and research departments of the investment brokerage firm of Merrill, Lynch, Pierce, Fenner and Smith.

To equip himself further for a Wall Street career, Sawhill enrolled in New York University's Graduate School of Business Administration in 1960 to earn a Ph.D. degree in economics, finance, and statistics. During his three years of study there he was employed as assistant to the dean and instructor in 1960-61 and later as assistant dean and assistant professor. He also worked as senior consulting economist for the House Committee on Banking and Currency of the United States Congress. From 1963 to 1965 Sawhill was director of credit research and planning for the Commercial Credit Company in Baltimore, a firm providing a variety of financial services. Then for three years he was a senior associate for McKinsey and Company, a management consulting firm in Washington, before returning in 1968 to Commercial Credit, where he advanced to senior vice-president the following year.

In an interview for the New York *Post* (May 12, 1975) Sawhill recalled the day he received a telephone call from the White House offering him an appointment in the Republican executive office: "I was a Democrat and I had never met President Nixon—although I had voted for him. . . . I believed in his philosophy of returning power to the states." He therefore gave up his $100,000-a-year job to accept in April 1973 a post as one of the four associate directors of the Office of Management and Budget. In his $38,000 position Sawhill had responsibility for programs relating to energy, science, and natural resources. As part of his work, he consolidated and reviewed the budgets for the Interior Department and Agriculture Department and four additional major federal agencies.

Energy became an area of increasing concern to Sawhill when the embargo imposed by the Arab oil-producing nations on petroleum exports to the United States in the fall of 1973 intensified a fuel shortage crisis that the new Federal Energy Office, under the direction of John A. Love, failed to relieve. In early December, after announcing the resignation of Love, President Richard Nixon signed an executive order officially establishing the FEO within the White House and named Deputy Treasury Secretary William E. Simon as its administrator, with Sawhill as his deputy director. The Agency's most important tasks were preventing fuel shortages through a mandatory allocation program and regulating the price of domestic crude oil. The FEO was also charged with policy development for all forms of energy. To carry out its function, within two months Sawhill and Simon increased the staff from some 200 to more than 3,000 employees.

When Simon was made Treasury Secretary in mid-April 1974, the President chose Sawhill to replace him as FEO chief. Nixon's selection of Sawhill as the new "energy czar" came as a surprise to some Washingtonians. He had demonstrated considerable independence of the White House in January by publicly contradicting the President's prematurely optimistic assessment of the energy crisis in his State of the Union message. But Sawhill's bipartisan popularity on Capitol Hill, resulting from his openness and his willingness to listen to the problems of individual Congressmen, as well as the need for administrative continuity in the FEO, tipped the balance in the deputy director's favor. The post took on additional importance in May, when the President signed a bill converting the FEO into the Federal Energy Administration, a temporary independent executive agency with new authority to impose conservation measures, prohibit unreasonable profits, collect data from industry, and plan "Project Independence"— the Administration's effort to reduce United States reliance on foreign energy sources.

Although the Arab embargo had ended in March 1974, the danger remained of both short-term fuel shortages and of vulnerability to future decisions of foreign oil suppliers. In an interview with *U.S. News and World Report* (May 20, 1974), Sawhill described the two basic components of his program to meet those threats: "One is the effort to bring on new [domestic] energy supplies; the other is conservation." To foster continuation of the conservation habits that had prevailed during the embargo period, Sawhill's agency offered consumers energy-saving advice for the coming warm weather. He urged automobile manufacturers to produce more gas-efficient cars, warning that compulsory standards would be imposed if voluntarism failed. The FEA also asked all big businesses to cut down on energy use.

Sawhill acknowledged that rapid development of domestic energy resources called for modification of environmental legislation. Air pollution laws, for example, would have to be amended to permit factories and power plants to burn 50 percent more coal. Believing that higher fuel prices would stimulate increased domestic fuel production, he advised the Senate Commerce Committee that the rising cost of oil products "serves a useful economic function." He rated the deregulation of natural gas prices his number-one legislative priority and lobbied in Congress for a deregulation bill. In a June memo to the White House Sawhill proposed a gradual phasing out of the FEA's petroleum allocation and price control authority, and the next month he told the Western Governors Conference, as reported in the New York Times (July 30, 1974), that "consumers are just going to have to live with these higher energy costs."

Gerald R. Ford's succession to the Presidency in mid-1974, following Nixon's resignation, did not end the outspokenness of Sawhill on policy matters. In September he opposed as inflationary the rapid deregulation of domestic oil prices favored by Interior Secretary Rogers C. Morton and Treasury Secretary Simon. Emerging as an advocate of mandatory conservation, during a TV appearance on October 2 Sawhill proposed an increase in the federal gasoline tax, a step that President Ford opposed. A few days later Morton, who placed less emphasis than Sawhill on conservation, became the new overall energy boss upon his appointment as head of the just-created Energy Resources Council. At an October 29 press conference Ford announced the forced resignation of Sawhill, who, however, remained in his post until mid-December and then served as a consultant to his successor, Frank Zarb, for two months.

While Sawhill was winding up his service in the Ford Administration, a committee of New York University's board of trustees interviewed him and almost 400 other candidates in their search for a successor to President James M. Hester. Joseph Taggart, dean emeritus of the Graduate School of Business, under whom Sawhill had been assistant dean, intervened with key trustees on behalf of his former aide. Sawhill's position was further strengthened by the fact that, like other private universities, NYU suffered serious fiscal difficulties in the 1970's and needed an administrator like Sawhill with a background in business and corporate management. On April 21, 1975 the university named Sawhill its next president. After working with Hester during a transitional period, he assumed his full duties on September 1 and was invested as NYU's twelfth president in November.

As president-designate, Sawhill had summed up the immediate challenge of his job in an interview with Iver Peterson of the New York Times (July 31, 1975): "My main task at this point is to put the university on a sound financial basis and to install an effective management system." In the late 1960's previously generous federal funding began drying up as NYU was in the midst of a massive upgrading program to meet stiffening competition from the low-tuition State University of New York and the no-tuition City University of New York. The resulting $8,000,000 budget deficits in academic years 1971-72 and 1972-73 had been followed by the sale of the institution's uptown campus in the Bronx. At the time of Sawhill's appointment the university had an apparent $3,000,000 deficit for 1974-75 and a projected $5,000,000 deficit for 1975-76. Its continued existence as a private institution seemed endangered.

Soon after taking office Sawhill sharply cut the central administration's budget, imposed spending limits on each of the university's schools, and pared both academic and nonacademic payrolls. Other economy measures included the trimming of energy costs, consolidation of computer operations, automation of the telephone system, and development of a more economical classification system for clerical jobs. Sawhill sold unprofitable university real estate, placed more emphasis on fixed-income securities, and made sure that cash reserves were constantly invested. He streamlined the university's organizational chart, eliminating the chancellor's office and giving clear lines of responsibility to the vice-presidents reporting to him. In 1976 Sawhill helped to engineer the sale of the C. F. Mueller Company, owned by a corporation whose income went entirely to the NYU School of Law, for $115,000,000. The School of Law was legally entitled to all of the proceeds of the sale, but the president worked out an agreement with the School of Law dean whereby $47,500,000 went to the university as a whole, nearly tripling its endowment. A fund-raising campaign launched by Sawhill had netted $90,000,000 by the spring of 1979.

The fruit of Sawhill's efforts was a balanced NYU budget in 1976-77. But because NYU had suffered declining enrollments in the early 1970's, the president tried to link economy goals with improvement of academic quality through consortial arrangements that would reduce duplication of services while widening the scope of educational resources available to the students. In 1977 NYU, Columbia, and City University initiated a program to enable some of their doctoral students to take courses at each school. During the same year NYU, Cooper Union, and the New School for Social Research linked their libraries through central-computer cataloging and coordinated purchasing, and arranged for the sharing of the collective facilities by the three student bodies and faculties. The following year the Hebrew Union College-Jewish Institute of Religion began construction of a new home on the NYU campus as part of a course-and-library sharing arrangement between the schools.

Since Sawhill regarded improvement of the quality of student life as particularly important in increasing enrollment, he spent considerable time talking to students about their needs. The student-affairs budget was the only one sizably increased after his appointment. The Loeb Student Center and the Judson Hall dormitories were renovated at a combined cost of $660,000. From a low of 38,577 in 1972-73, enrollment rose to 43,000 in 1978-79.

Shortly before his formal investiture, in which he deplored the diminishing importance of the humanities at institutions of higher learning, Sawhill contended in a piece for the New York Times (November 16, 1975) that universities must train people not only in specialized skills but "for a moral and civilized life." In a later article for *Harper's* (February 1979), "The Unlettered University," after pointing out the deficiencies of career-directed studies alone, he wrote, "The universities must reassert the balance between the transient interests of a particular society and the enduring truths of civilization. Universities must cease doing the work of government and industry and reclaim their position as the agency that instructs and enlightens these institutions in how best to function for the benefit of all." Sawhill's work toward strengthening liberal arts programs includes the establishment of the New York Institute for the Humanities.

NYU's president has been deeply involved in the civic life of New York City. In 1977 New York Governor Hugh Carey appointed him a public member of the state's Emergency Financial Control Board, created to oversee the city's troubled financial affairs. Since June 1978 he has been conducting meetings in his apartment with a changing group of the city's leading businessmen, labor leaders, and academicians who have become an informal long-range planning group for Mayor Edward Koch. Still concerned with energy conservation, Sawhill was principal author of "Energy—Managing the Transition," a 1978 study prepared for the Trilateral Commission, and he serves on advisory boards to the Federal Power Commission and the New York State Committee for Jobs and Energy Independence. He also serves on the committee on energy of the Aspen Institute for Humanistic Studies and is a director or trustee of several educational and other professional associations, as well as of a number of business organizations, including Automatic Data Processing, Consolidated Edison, and Philip Morris Incorporated. He belongs to the Adirondack League and the Century, among other clubs. His church is the Presbyterian.

John C. Sawhill married Isabel Van Devanter on September 13, 1958, and they are parents of a college-age son, James Winslow Sawhill. In New York, John Sawhill's home is a penthouse apartment overlooking Washington Square, but the Sawhills have retained their Georgetown townhouse in Washington, where Mrs. Sawhill, an economist who earned her Ph.D. at NYU in 1968, is employed as director of the National Commission on Employment Policy. Sawhill is a 155-pound, athletic-looking six-footer; he has brown eyes and brown hair. A self-described "workaholic" and "tough manager" who prefers strenuous forms of relaxation, he begins the day with a two-mile run and is likely to fill any gap in his work schedule with bicycle riding, skiing, or playing squash or tennis.

References: Biog N p945 Ag '74 por;
N Y Times p73 Ap 19 '74 por, p1+ Ap 22 '75;
N Y Times Mag p21+ Ap 30 '78 pors;
People 4:20+ S 8 '75 pors;
Time 105:81 My 5 '75 Por;
Who's Who in America, 1974-75

Schickele, Peter (shik'il-ē)

July 17, 1935- Musician; composer. Address:
b. c/o Harold Shaw, Shaw Concerts Inc., 1995
Broadway, New York City, N.Y. 10023

Traditional musical boundaries are anathema to the irrepressible and antic Peter Schickele, who maintains an easygoing relationship between the serious composer that he actually is and the fictitious Professor Schickele, the zany head of the Department of Musical Pathology at the nonexistent University of Southern North Dakota at Hoople. Schickele's clowning disposition is given free rein in the persona of Professor Schickele, a deadpan travesty of stuffy musicologists. He is the discoverer and sole exegete of the long-lost works of P.D.Q. Bach, the "last but least" of the children of J. S. Bach. In that persona, Schickele has for fourteen years been convulsing concert-hall and college audiences across the United States with his mock productions of eighteenth-century baroque music, composed by the real Schickele, with ample borrowings from virtually every other composer who ever lived. Schickele's spoofs, done full-scale with his New York Pick-Up Ensemble or larger orchestral and choral contingents and rife with shameless puns and explosive visual jokes, might be described as a cross between the British Hoffnung Festival, Anna Russell's lampooning of the Wagner Ring Cycle, Victor Borge's self-derisive piano recitals, and the late band leader Spike Jones's slapstick renditions of romantic popular songs. "Few forgotten composers of the past," the musicologist Newell Jenkins once observed, "deserve their oblivion as richly as does P.D.Q. Bach."

Schickele devotes only about half of each year to P.D.Q. Bach. Outside of his Professor Schickele persona, he is a serious composer of music for orchestra, chamber ensemble, organ, piano, other instruments, and voice. He has written numerous film scores and music for several theatrical productions, including the Broadway hit *Oh! Calcutta!*, and he has composed and arranged for Joan Baez, among other pop and folk recording artists. As a performer, on the piano, bassoon and other instruments, he has played with his own rock 'n' roll combo as well as with the St. Louis Symphony, the Los Angeles Philharmonic, the Boston Symphony, and other orchestras. Recordings by him are available on the Vanguard label, and the Theodore Presser Company of Bryn Mawr, Pennsylvania publishes his scores.

Peter Schickele was born in Ames, Iowa on July 17, 1935 to Rainer W. Schickele, a German-born agricultural economist, and Elizabeth (Wilcox) Schickele. With his younger brother, David, a film maker and amateur violinist, Schickele grew up in Ames, in Washington, D.C., and in Fargo, North Dakota. Schickele's interest in music was always combined with a love of theatre; indeed, his first aspiration was to become an actor. In childhood he ran what he called the Nitso Theatre in the basement of his home, putting on skits inspired by westerns and serials seen at local movie houses, and later he acted in community theatre productions.

The records of Spike Jones, the late clown prince of band leaders, had an early, crucial influence on Schickele. "I remember being in a record store and hearing a very soupy, sentimental ballad," Schickele recounted in an interview with Allan Kozinn for the New York *Times* (December 25, 1977). "Being a ten-year-old, I thought there was nothing worse than soupy, sentimental ballads, but all of a sudden there was a gunshot, and the music took off into a Dixieland kind of thing. It was my introduction to Spike Jones, and I completely fell over myself for his records."

Schickele first studied music theory with Sigvald Thompson, the conductor of the Fargo-Moorhead Orchestra. He played bassoon in that orchestra, also doubling on strings in local bands, including his own, Jerky Jems and his Balmy Brothers. After graduating from high school in Fargo, he majored in music at Swarthmore College and studied one summer with composer Roy Harris in Pittsburgh.

Schickele's favorite music in college included the recordings of such pop singers as Ray Charles and Elvis Presley as well as of performances of the works of Hindemith, Bartók, and, above all, Stravinsky. "From the beginning," he told Allan Kozinn, "I felt a tug between classic music and certain forms of popular music. When I was at Swarthmore I used to draw a lot of puzzled looks because even though I was the most serious musician there—I was *the* classical composer

—I would go to the student lounge and play Elvis, Fats Domino, and the Everly Brothers on the juke box."

In 1957 Schickele took his B.A. degree at Swarthmore and matriculated at the Juilliard School in New York City, where he studied composition with Vincent Persichetti and William Bergsma and became a teaching fellow. While working for his M.S. degree at Juilliard, Schickele cofounded the Composers Circle, which over a period of five years held workshops and presented concerts that included works by members of the group. Schickele's output in the late 1950's and early 1960's included *Celebration with Bells*, *Fantasy* (strings), *Invention* (piccolo, strings, and other instruments), *Requiem* (strings), and *Serenade*, among other compositions for orchestra; *Pavilion Piece*, for marching band; three sonatinas and some dozen other pieces for piano; *Variations on a Medieval Theme* and *Canzona* for organ; *The Flow of Memory Songs* for Baritone, Bassoon, and Trombone, and *Two Pleasant Songs*, for solo voice; *After Spring Sunset*, *The Birth of Christ*, *Mass for Men's Voices*, *Two Prayers*, *Three Choruses from Cummings*, and several other compositions for chorus; and many pieces of chamber music, including *Liturgies*, *Piano Concerto No. 1 in G Major*, *String Trio*, *Trio Serenade*, and *Three Scenes for Five Instruments*.

After taking his M.S. degree, in 1960, Schickele spent a year on a Ford foundation grant as a composer-in-residence in the Los Angeles, California public school system and another year as a teacher at Swarthmore before returning to Juilliard as a teacher of extension courses. In one of the Composers Circle concerts, in 1961, Schickele played his *Serenade for Piano*, the last movement of which, incorporating a rock 'n' roll mode, offended one of his Juilliard colleagues, who told him it "doesn't belong in a concert hall." "I found that attitude very constricting, and I began to feel the same about teaching at Juilliard," Schickele recounted in the New York *Times* interview with Allan Kozinn. "I found that I was spending all my time composing and I was not preparing my classes. Also, I was waiting to see whether P.D.Q. Bach was going to get off the ground, and if it did, I wanted to be free to go on the road."

The genesis of P.D.Q. Bach began as a lark in 1953. Schickele, his brother, and a musician friend were playing around with two tape recorders, multiplying musical sounds, when Schickele came up with the *Sanka Cantata*, inspired by Johann Sebastian Bach's *Coffee Cantata*. The *Sanka Sonata* was to become the first of the newly "discovered" works of P.D.Q. Bach, previously known only "from police records and tavern IOU's." In the chronicle subsequently fabricated by Schickele, the discovery took place when Professor Schickele was touring a Bavarian castle and stumbled upon the manuscript, which was being used by the caretaker as a percolator strainer.

Six years passed before another work by P.D.Q. Bach came to light. That composition was the *Concerto for Horn and Hardart*, performed by Schickele (on the Hardart) and fellow students at Juilliard to fill the second half of the program when a scholarship recital ran too short. The concert-grand Hardart is a gigantic four-wheeled wind percussion-explosion instrument worthy of a Rube Goldberg. "Automated during the Industrial Revolution," it later became obsolete. As reconstructed by Professor Schickele, it is a nine-foot contraption consisting of an odd assortment of ocarinas, tonettes, kazoos, mixing bowls, buzzers, bells, balloons (to be exploded on cue), and bottles. Like a Horn and Hardart Automat, it has a coffee spigot and a series of coin-operated windows offering a choice of sandwiches and pastries. The Professor points out that the third movement of the *Concerto for Horn and Hardart*, "Menuetto con Panna e Zucchero" (Minuet with Cream and Sugar), is dance music that could only have been written by a composer with one leg shorter than the other.

New pieces by P.D.Q. Bach were introduced annually at humorous concerts at the Aspen (Colorado) Music School organized by Schickele and Jorge Mester, (now the conductor of the Louisville Orchestra). When the P.D.Q. Bach repertory was of sufficient size and quality, Schickele and Stephen Schmidt, then his partner, prepared to unleash "the oddest of J. S. Bach's twenty-odd children" on the general public. The grand unleashing came with "An Evening with P.D.Q. Bach," a concert given at Town Hall in New York City on April 24, 1965 by Professor Schickele and a chamber orchestra under the direction of Jorge Mester. The soloists included Schickele; John Ferrante, countertenor; Ralph Froelich, French horn; and Leonid Hambro, piano and harpsichord.

The evening at Town Hall began with Schickele making his entrance by swinging from balcony to stage by rope, and the concert opened with the *Concerto for Horn and Hardart*, followed by *Iphigenia in Brooklyn*, a "cantata for bargain countertenor, trumpet mouth piece, three double reeds, wine bottle, string quartet, and harpsichord." Narrating as well as performing, Professor Schickele observed that P.D.Q. Bach wrote for such exotic instruments "out of an overdeveloped sense of tonal color, or else sheer perversity." After the intermission came the *Gross Concerto for Divers Flutes* (fipple, globular, and transverse), and the concert ended with the *Sinfonia Concertante*, a "battle to the death" for lute, balalaika, bagpipes, ocarina, left-handed sewer flute, and double-reed slide music stand.

Before sending the members of the audience on their way, Professor Schickele assured them that the search for more P.D.Q. Bach compositions would go on unabated, in the hope "that the latest score can't possibly be as bad as the one before." "So far," he noted, "every new piece has lived up to the previous low standard." When the Vanguard Recording Society issued a recording of the Town Hall concert *(An Evening with P.D.Q. Bach)*, Howard Klein, writing in the New York *Times* (December 12, 1965), noted the rarity of court jesters in the palace of serious music and commented, "How good it is to have musical pomposity punctured."

In a second major P.D.Q. Bach program in New York City, at Philharmonic Hall on December 28, 1966, Professor Schickele introduced P.D.Q.'s oratorio *The Seasonings* and the Professor's own *Unbegun Symphony*, so called because he "never got around to writing" the first two movements. In his narration on that occasion he divided the career of P.D.Q. Bach into three periods: the initial plunge, the soused period ("by far the longest"), and contrition.

New P.D.Q. Bach programs became an annual holiday tradition for music lovers in New York City; the successive productions were giggled, guffawed, and hissed at by large audiences from Maine to California; and Vanguard Records kept pace with its recordings of the concerts: *An Hysteric Return, Report from Hoople, P.D.Q. Bach's Half-Act Opera "The Stoned Guest," The Wurst of P.D.Q. Bach, The Intimate P.D.Q. Bach*, and *Portrait of P.D.Q. Bach*.

Concurrently, the more serious Schickele wrote the scores for the television films *The Sounds of Alienation* (CBS, 1966), *Three Riddle Films* (Sesame Street, 1969), and *Where the Garbage Goes* (Sesame Street, 1969), and the scores for the motion pictures *Song of Innocents* (Electric Circle Film Workshop, 1964); *Poland* (International Film Foundation, 1964); *Israel* (International Film Foundation, 1965); *The Crazy Quilt* (Walter Reade-Sterling, 1965); *Big People, Small People* (Sterling Educational Films, 1967); *Someday* (Sterling Educational Films, 1967); and *Funnyman* (New Yorker Films, 1967). Regarding *The Crazy Quilt*, *Time*'s critic wrote that the music "flows so congruously out of the images that the spectator sometimes feels he must be seeing with his ears," and Brendan Gill of the *New Yorker* described the score as "admirably bold and delicate." Others noted that in contrast to the P.D.Q. Bach compositions, which are often cacophonous, Schickele's serious music tends toward pastoral serenity.

In 1967 Schickele formed the Open Window, a chamber-rock-jazz trio described as a "pop-classical ensemble," with composer-performers Stanley Walden and Robert Dennis. The group wrote music and lyrics for the erotic Broadway musical *Oh! Calcutta!*, and with the Louisville Orchestra it recorded *Three*

Views from the Open Window (Vanguard, 1968). One of the "views" was "The Fantastic Garden," composed by Schickele. Vanguard also released *The Open Window* (1969) and Schickele's own *The Good-Time Ticket*, consisting of his instrumental interpretations of six of his own songs and six by others, including the Beatles and Bob Dylan. In the late 1960's Schickele also arranged the music for Joan Baez's Vanguard LP's *Noël* and *Joan*, and he composed as well as arranged the music for her Vanguard album *Baptism*. During the same period he arranged the music for Buffy Sainte-Marie's Vanguard recordings *Fire, Fleet and Candlelight* and *Illuminations* and the Vanguard releases of Mimi and Richard Farina's *Memories* and Jeff Monn's *Reality*.

Schickele's most important cinematic contribution was his score for *Silent Running* (Universal, 1972), a futuristic tale with an ecological message. Reviewing the Decca recording of that film score, a critic for the New York Times (August 27, 1972) described it as "very inventive" and "visionary." Schickele wrote the music and some of the lyrics for a new adaptation of the Jacobean comedy by Beaumont and Fletcher, *The Knight of the Burning Pestle*, performed at New Haven's Long Wharf Theatre in 1974. On the occasion of America's Bicentennial he composed *American Birthday Card* for the St. Louis Symphony Orchestra, and he wrote *American History Lesson: A Musical Antidote to the Bicentennial*, consisting of five operatic skits, including the unusual *Hornsmoke*, in which human voices are replaced by a brass quintet.

Meanwhile, the intrepid Professor Schickele, ignoring the complaints of a few critical curmudgeons that his "crude," "sophomoric" joke was wearing thin, continued to come up with P.D.Q. Bach manuscripts. They included the *Echo Sonata* ("for two unfriendly groups of instruments"), *Pervertimento* ("for bagpipes, bicycle, and balloons"), *Pertückenstück* ("Hair Piece," from *The Civilian Barber*), *Schleptet* ("in five short movements, or as P.D.Q. called them, shots"), and *Concerto for Piano vs. Orchestra* (in the finale of which the piano bench explodes).

Proof against charges of hoax were proffered to a grateful public in Professor Schickele's *The Definitive Biography of P.D.Q. Bach* (Random House, 1976), which had all the trappings of a scholarly biography, including a mock index and an annotated catalogue of the music of P.D.Q. Bach. Harvey E. Philips observed in the National Review (October 29, 1976) that the book earned Schickele the right to "take his place on the left hand of Sir Donald Tovey and on the right hand of each of the Brothers Marx."

In his review of the initial P.D.Q. Bach concert of the 1978-79 season, at Lincoln Center, Allen Hughes of the New York Times (December 28, 1978) struck a serious note,

observing that clowning "comes naturally" to Schickele, as does "the stringing together, in incongruous juxtaposition, of elements from the Baroque, Classical, Romantic, and current pop repertoires." Schickele himself has told interviewers that his style, especially in his serious music, is influenced by folk, rock, and jazz as much as it is by traditionally "good" music and that he believes music schools should be more open to change. "You can't regard such things as a symphony or a string quartet as timeless," he has pointed out. "They aren't. They didn't exist before 1750. . . . Music schools should be set up and be large enough to encompass people working in many different areas, from jazz to classical music."

But his spoofing of the music of Bach and Mozart is done from a position of love of those composers, as he told Jo Ann Levine when she interviewed him for the Christian Science Monitor (August 16, 1976): "Eighteenth century music has a well defined style, so that you can depart from it. The problem is doing a satire on contemporary music. [Also] I like that music. I would have been tired of doing it a long time ago if I didn't like it."

Burly, blue-eyed Peter Schickele has an easygoing manner that matches his unhurried speech patterns but not his thought processes. The latter, according to Jo Ann Levine, "derail his conversation from one track to another, or just send it zooming downhill." Schickele and Susan Sindell, a children's dance teacher, were married on October 27, 1962 and have two children, Karla and Matthew. The Schickeles live in a brownstone in Brooklyn, and they have another residence in Woodstock, New York.

References: Christian Sci Mon p14+ Ag 16 '76 pors; N Y Daily News p128 D 2 '76 por; N Y Times II p17+ D 25 '77 por; Anderson, Ruth. *Contemporary American Composers* (1976); Slonimsky, Nicholas. *Baker's Biographical Dictionary of Musicians* (1971); *Who's Who in America, 1978-79*

Schlesinger, Arthur M(eier), Jr. (shlā′ zing-ər)

Oct. 15, 1917- Writer; educator; historian.
Address: b. City University of New York,
33 W. 42d St., New York City, N.Y. 10036

NOTE: This biography supersedes the article that appeared in Current Biography in 1946.

The historian, best-selling author, and political sage Arthur M. Schlesinger Jr. is a premier exponent of mid-twentieth-century liberalism. As a founder and vice-chairman

Arthur M. Schlesinger Jr.

of Americans for Democratic Action, he propounded a political philosophy that combined idealism and pragmatism. The author of over a score of books, he presented his "politics of hope" in his scholarly, yet popular, histories and biographies, including the Pulitzer-prize-winning *The Age of Jackson* and *A Thousand Days*, that attracted the attention of some of the most eminent liberal politicians of his time. He was an adviser to several Democratic Presidential aspirants and served in the White House as a special assistant to President John F. Kennedy. Out of the political spotlight since the late 1960's, he has devoted himself to writing and teaching at the City University of New York, where he is Albert Schweitzer Professor of Humanities.

Arthur Bancroft Schlesinger was born on October 15, 1917 in Columbus, Ohio, the elder of the two sons of Arthur Meier and Elizabeth (Bancroft) Schlesinger. He eventually changed his middle name to that of his father because, as he put it years later, "at that point I wanted to be Arthur Schlesinger Jr." His father, a prominent historian, spearheaded an effort to extend the concerns of historians beyond the study of politics, wars, and diplomacy; his mother, a descendant of George Bancroft, the distinguished American historian, was a leading suffragist.

"Young Arthur," as Schlesinger was known, spent his early childhood in Iowa City, Iowa, where his father was for five years a member of the faculty of the University of Iowa and, after the elder Schlesinger accepted an appointment to Harvard University's history department in 1924, in Cambridge, Massachusetts. He attended the public schools there, and completed his secondary education with two years at Phillips Exeter Academy in New Hampshire. His education was rounded off by a world tour with his parents and his brother Thomas.

On his return to the United States in 1934, Schlesinger enrolled at Harvard University, where he specialized in American history and literature. He earned his B. A. degree, *summa cum laude*, in 1938. His senior honors thesis, *Orestes A. Brownson: A Pilgrim's Progress*, a biography of the nineteenth-century New England journalist, novelist, and theologian, was published by Little, Brown the following year. Schlesinger spent a year at Cambridge University on a Henry Fellowship and then returned to Harvard for graduate school. Because of his three-year appointment to the prestigious Society of Fellows, he was able to avoid the "Ph.D. mill," as he called it, and concentrate on an in-depth study of Jacksonian democracy.

In 1941, after spending two years in research, Schlesinger delivered an important series of lectures on Andrew Jackson and his times at Boston's Lowell Institute. Drawing on those lectures, he wrote, in five months, *The Age of Jackson* (Little, Brown, 1945), an exhaustive analysis of Jacksonian democracy as a political and intellectual movement that rejected earlier interpretations linking Jacksonian Democracy with western expansion and identified as its core a coalition of intellectuals and workers in the Northeast, who were determined to check the growing power of business. Although Schlesinger denied that the book was an apologia for the New Deal, its organization revealed his interest in contemporary politics, and its effect was to legitimatize Franklin D. Roosevelt's policies as a continuation of the American reform tradition. *The Age of Jackson* sold more than 90,000 copies in its first year and won the 1946 Pulitzer Prize for history.

During World War II Schlesinger spent one year working as a writer in the Office of War Information in Washington, D.C., and another one in the Office of Strategic Services. He went overseas in the spring of 1944 and eventually became deputy chief of the O.S.S. reports board in Paris. After the war, Schlesinger returned to Washington, where he established himself as a freelance writer specializing in political affairs. For about a year he contributed articles to the *Atlantic*, *Fortune*, *Life*, and the *New Republic*, among other publications, and worked intermittently on a projected series of books about Franklin Roosevelt's administration. Then, late in 1946, he accepted a tenured position as an associate professor in Harvard's history department, a plum for a twenty-nine-year-old scholar who had never taken an advanced degree.

In 1947 Schlesinger helped to found Americans for Democratic Action, a militantly liberal organization established to provide talent and ideas to implement the unrealized social goals of the New Deal. With the publication of *The Vital Center; The Politics of Freedom* (Houghton Mifflin) two years later, he emerged as a leading spokesman for Democratic liberalism. Basing his political arguments on his father's faith in reasoned democracy and distrust of absolutisms and on the doctrines of theologian Reinhold Niebuhr, Schlesinger contended that true democracy implied the acceptance of human imperfection. "Problems will always torment us," he wrote, "because all important problems are insoluble: that is why they are important. The good comes from the continuing struggle to try and solve them, not from the vain hope of their solution." Strengthening his commitment to the Democratic party, Schlesinger agreed to work as a consultant to the Economic Cooperation Administration, which oversaw the implementation of the Marshall Plan, and to the Mutual Security Administration during Harry S. Truman's Presidency.

The decade of the 1950's was an especially productive period for Schlesinger, who became a full professor in 1954. In spite of his heavy teaching load, he wrote scores of articles for general magazines and scholarly journals and collaborated with Richard H. Rovere on *The General and the President and the Future of American Foreign Policy* (Farrar, Straus, 1951), an analysis of the national schism brought about by President Truman's recall of General Douglas MacArthur in 1951. He also somehow managed to find the time to complete the first three volumes of *The Age of Roosevelt: The Crisis of the Old Order, 1919-1933; The Coming of the New Deal;* and *The Politics of Upheaval,* published by Houghton Mifflin in 1957, 1958, and 1960, respectively.

In all those works, but especially in *The Age of Roosevelt,* Schlesinger de-emphasized the role of class conflict in American history and encouraged the development of "a spirit that aims not to indict any group in the community as a special obstacle to change but rather to rally men of good will in all groups behind programs designed to improve life in America for all Americans."

Roosevelt epitomized the pragmatic liberalism favored by Schlesinger and illustrated his theory of the efficacy of heroism. "The heroic leader has the Promethean responsibility to affirm human freedom against the supposed inevitabilities of history," Schlesinger wrote in his essay "On Heroic Leadership." "As he does this, he combats the infection of fatalism which might otherwise paralyze mass democracy. Without heroic leaders, a society would tend to acquiesce in the drift of history."

Schlesinger put his political theories to practical use in 1952, when he persuaded W. Averell Harriman, a leading candidate for the Democratic Presidential nomination, to surrender his delegates to Adlai E. Stevenson, the liberal governor of Illinois. In so doing, he enabled Stevenson to capture the top spot on the ticket. In that year and again in 1956 he advised Stevenson to adopt a more aggressive campaign style, but the urbane and erudite Democrat was unable to defeat the enormously popular Republican candidate, Dwight D. Eisenhower.

Hoping to block the nomination of a Southern conservative in 1960, Schlesinger impartially advised three chief contenders for the Democratic nomination—Stevenson, John F. Kennedy, and Hubert H. Humphrey. The professor, who confessed that he was "nostalgically for Stevenson, ideologically for Humphrey, and realistically for Kennedy," finally cast his lot with Kennedy after the Massachusetts Senator showed superior strength in the primaries. His main contribution to the Kennedy drive was *Kennedy or Nixon: Does It Make Any Difference?* (Macmillan, 1960), in which he contended that the election boiled down to a choice between idealism and materialism.

Because he was, as he put it, tired of "being upstairs writing the speeches while the political decisions were being taken elsewhere," Schlesinger took a two-year leave of absence from Harvard to join President Kennedy's inner White House circle as a special assistant in January 1961. His duties were unspecified, but among other things, he acted as Kennedy's liaison with Adlai Stevenson, the recently appointed American Ambassador to the United Nations; as his main contact with liberals and intellectuals; as his adviser on Latin American and cultural affairs; and as his resident "court philosopher." According to Theodore Sorensen, the President's special counsel, Schlesinger also served as "a lightning rod to attract Republican attacks away from the rest of us." In Oval Office conferences he was especially valued for his historian's perspective. Convinced that Fidel Castro's influence in Latin America was on the wane, he was one of the few administration officials to oppose the disastrous Bay of Pigs invasion.

Exhilarated by the supremely confident atmosphere of the Kennedy White House, Schlesinger resigned from Harvard when his leave of absence expired in 1962. His belief in the energizing effect that Kennedy exercised on the country is perhaps best illustrated by the euphoric introduction he wrote for *The Politics of Hope* (Houghton Mifflin, 1963), an eclectic and provocative collection of essays and articles written over the previous ten years. He remained on the White House staff after President Kennedy's assassination in November 1963, but submitted his resignation two months later. "The exhilaration came from working with Kennedy," he explained to the press. "With Kennedy gone, it was no longer exhilarating."

At Kennedy's request, Schlesinger had begun keeping a journal after the Cuban debacle. That 400-page notebook became the basis for *A Thousand Days: John F. Kennedy in the White House* (Houghton Mifflin, 1965), a personal memoir of Kennedy's tenure. Pre-publication excerpts in *Life* magazine disclosing confidential information, including a report that Kennedy intended to dismiss Secretary of State Dean Rusk after the 1964 national election, provoked considerable dispute, and even some old friends, like Hubert Humphrey, denounced Schlesinger for undermining the effectiveness of an incumbent Cabinet officer. The ongoing controversy generated tremendous interest in the book and assured it a place on the best-seller list, even though the critical response was not entirely favorable. *A Thousand Days* won for Schlesinger a second Pulitzer Prize, for biography, and a National Book Award for history and biography.

Schlesinger spent the first few months of 1966 at the Institute for Advanced Study in Princeton; he then joined the faculty of the City University of New York as Albert Schweitzer Professor of Humanities. Like many intellectuals during the last half of the 1960's, he devoted a great deal of attention to the continuing war in Vietnam At first opposed to unilateral American troop withdrawal because he felt it would encourage Chinese militancy and lead to a "deep profound disaster" for the other independent Southeast Asian nations, Schlesinger became increasingly concerned as mounting American involvement transformed the struggle into an "unwinnable" war. As early as October 1966 he proposed a "middle course" of de-escalation and negotiation.

Yet even during the most heated moments of the raging Vietnam debate, Schlesinger refused to ascribe the blame to a specific government policy or to a particular individual. "Vietnam is the triumph of the politics of inadvertence," he wrote in *The Bitter Heritage: Vietnam and American Democracy, 1941-1966* (Houghton Mifflin, 1966). "We have achieved our present entanglement, not after due and deliberate considerations, but through a series of small decisions. It is not only idle but unfair to seek out guilty men." He bore down especially hard on revisionist political analysts who accused the United States of conducting a deliberately aggressive foreign policy.

In a subsequent article—"The Necessary Amorality of Foreign Affairs," (*Harper's*,

August 1971)—Schlesinger blamed the Vietnam quagmire on the fanatic moralism of both the left and the right. Because "the raw material of foreign policy is, most of the time, morally neutral or ambiguous," he argued that the "safest basis for foreign policy lies not in attempts to determine what is right or wrong but in attempts to determine the national interest." But the probable primary motive for American involvement in Vietnam was, in his view, "the insistence on seeing the civil war in Vietnam as above all a moral issue." Although Schlesinger admitted that moral considerations must be brought to bear on certain questions of foreign policy, such as war crimes, nuclear arms, world poverty, and racial injustice, he contended that they should not supersede the idea of national interest which, when "realistically construed," automatically insured "enlightened rather than greedy policy."

As an enthusiastic supporter of Senator Robert F. Kennedy's Presidential candidacy in 1968, Schlesinger was shocked and angered by Kennedy's assassination after his victory in the California primary in June 1968. "What sort of people are we, we Americans?" he asked a commencement audience at the City University of New York the next day. "We are today the most frightening people on this planet. . . . The atrocities we commit trouble so little our official self-righteousness, our invincible conviction of our moral infallibility. . . . We must uncover the roots of hatred and violence and, through self-knowledge, move toward self-control." He analyzed violence as a peculiarly American way of life in greater depth in *The Crisis of Confidence: Ideas, Power and Violence in America* (Houghton Mifflin, 1969), a collection of essays that questioned American ideals, values, and policies in the 1960's.

Although he has always championed open political debate and has fought for intellectual freedom around the world, Schlesinger has, on occasion, chastised the more vocal critics of the United States government. By "substituting slogans for sense and rage for reason," he argued, those dissidents degraded the level of public discussion and prepared the way for "a new McCarthyism." He also condemned several prominent New Left historians who tried to "manipulate, distort, and fabricate evidence to serve the interests of their own politics."

Appalled by the abuse of Presidential power, particularly warmaking power, by Lyndon B. Johnson and Richard Nixon, Schlesinger wrote *The Imperial Presidency* (Houghton Mifflin, 1973), a detailed study of the gradual assumption of power by the executive branch that, in his view, threatened the Constitutional system of checks and balances. He attributed the expansion of Presidential power to the executive's increasingly independent conduct of foreign policy. Nixon, in particular, concentrated power in the White House to such a degree that he was an absolute monarch on issues of war and peace. To restrain the "runaway Presidency" without weakening the office, Schlesinger recommended finding a middle ground. "The problem is to devise a means of reconciling a strong and purposeful Presidency with equally strong and purposeful forms of democratic control," he said. "We need a strong Presidency—but a strong Presidency *within* the Constitution."

Several reviewers accused Schlesinger of underestimating the ways in which Roosevelt and Kennedy arrogated new powers to the Presidency and of playing partisan politics. Readily conceding that *The Imperial Presidency* had its topical and polemical aspects, he argued that its release, coinciding with the Senate's investigation of the Watergate scandal, was fortuitous. In his opinion, Watergate was "the healthiest thing to have happened to the Presidency in many years." Noting that only the "condign punishment" of President Nixon would "deter future Presidents from illegal conduct," he added that, historically, "exposure and retribution inoculate the Presidency against its latent criminal impulses for about half a century" and advised the American people "to go on the alert and start nailing down everything in sight" around the year 2023.

Schlesinger disclaimed all rumors of a return to government service under President Jimmy Carter, whom he has described as the most conservative Democratic President since Grover Cleveland. "I'm really a writer," he told one reporter. "I prefer to be responsible for myself." His self-image reflects his perception of his academic discipline. "History," he wrote in "The Historian as Artist" in 1963, "has always seemed to me primarily an art, a branch of literature, a minor branch perhaps, subject to its own rules, concerned with its own issues, but committed nonetheless to the written word, and therefore a literary enterprise."

In the mid-1970's Schlesinger devoted much of his energy to a biography of Robert Kennedy, who was, in his opinion, the most creative man of his time, and one who, had he lived, might have changed history. Drawing on Kennedy's personal papers, interviews with Kennedy associates, published sources, and his own recollections, Schlesinger wrote a monumental volume of more than a thousand pages. Published by Houghton Mifflin in September 1978, *Robert Kennedy and His Times* became an immediate best seller. In general, the critics were enthusiastic. Most of them discounted Schlesinger's admitted admiration for his subject and focused instead on the lucidity, exhaustiveness, attention to detail, and eloquence with which he handled his material.

A trim man of medium height, Arthur Schlesinger has receding, graying brown hair, and lively brown eyes framed by horn-rimmed spectacles. He habitually sports a large bow tie. For recreation he attends parties, plays tennis, and goes to the movies. A facile writer, Schlesinger regularly turns out as many as 5,000 words a day. He has resumed work on *The Age of Roosevelt* and recently succeeded Judith Crist as the regular movie critic for the *Saturday Review*. Having written movie reviews for *Show* and *Vogue* in the 1960's, he returned to that task with "unalloyed pleasure." He makes his home in an East Side Manhattan townhouse with his wife, the former Alexandra Emmet, whom he married on July 9, 1971. They have two sons, Robert Emmet Kennedy and Peter Cushing Allan. He also has four children—Stephen Cannon, Katharine Kinderman, Christina, and Andrew Bancroft from his marriage, in August 1940, to Marian Cannon, a writer and illustrator of children's books and daughter of the renowned Harvard physiologist, Walter B. Cannon. That marriage ended in divorce in 1970.

References: Biog N p351 Mr '74 pors; N Y Post p25 Ap 3 '61 por, p25 Ap 4 '61 por, p39 Ap 5 '61 por, p25 Ap 6 '61 por, p37 Ap 7 '61 por, p28 D 5 '65 por; N Y Times Mag p30+ N 21 '65 pors; Newsday mag p17+ O 29 '78 pors; R of Politics 39:3+ Ja '77; Time 86:54+ D 17 '65 pors; Washington Post E p1+ O 20 '78 pors; Anderson, Patrick. The Presidents' Men (1968); Cunliffe, Marcus, and Winks, Robin W., eds. Pastmasters (1969); Ross, Mitchell S. The Literary Politicians (1978); Who's Who in America, 1978-79

Schuller, Robert H(arold)

Sept. 16, 1926- Clergyman. Address: b. Garden Grove Community Church, 12141 Lewis St., Garden Grove, Calif. 92640

A "theology of self-esteem" comprehensible and attractive to the unchurched is the chosen ministerial province of Robert H. Schuller, the Reformed Church in America minister who invented the drive-in church when he founded his Garden Grove Community Church near the Santa Ana Freeway in Orange County, California a quarter of a century ago. On what he describes as his "twenty-two-acre shopping center for Jesus Christ," the Rev. Dr. Schuller preaches every Sunday to nearly ten thousand people, some sitting in traditional pews in a futuristic glass-walled church building and the rest parked in cars, with their radios tuned to 540 on the local AM dial. Later a syndicated videotape of the service is beamed under the title *The Hour of*

Robert H. Schuller

Power to an audience of 3,000,000, the largest regular religious congregation of its kind.

Dr. Schuller's relentlessly positive message of "possibility thinking," typified by such mneumonic slogans as "Put a soul in your goal" and "Turn your scars into stars," is transmitted through his weekly sermon, his syndicated NEA newspaper column "It's Possible," and a score of books, including *God's Way to the Good Life* (Eerdmans, 1963), *The Future is Your Friend* (Eerdmans, 1964), *You Can Become the Person You Want to Be* (Hawthorn, 1973), *Positive Prayers for Power-Filled Living* (Hawthorn, 1976), and *Peace of Mind Through Possibility Thinking* (Doubleday, 1977). In answer to those theological purists who accuse him of being "shallow," Schuller points out that he is not "*narrow*-casting," or engaged in dialogue with specific individuals, but rather "*broad*casting" to a mass audience that includes "those people who are flipping dials . . . in pain, and dying."

The youngest of five children in a farm family of Dutch descent, Robert Harold Schuller was born to Anthony and Jenny (Beltman) Schuller on September 16, 1926 in Alton, Iowa. By the age of five he had decided to become a minister, in part to fulfill the dream of his father, a minister *manqué*. At Newkirk High School in nearby Newkirk, Iowa, Schuller found mathematics difficult, but debating and dramatics came naturally to him, and he was always a good singer. He graduated from high school in 1943.

At Hope College in Holland, Michigan, an institution with a predominantly Reformed Church governing board, Schuller majored in psychology and history, won an oratorical prize, and was a member of the debating team. Upon receiving his B.A. degree, in 1947, he entered Western Theological Seminary, also in Holland. His proudest achievements at the seminary were the compilation of a topical and scriptural index to John Calvin's *Institutes of the Christian Religion* and a first prize in preaching delivery.

After taking his B.D. degree, in 1950, Schuller became pastor of the Ivanhoe Reformed Church in Chicago, Illinois. Under him, the Ivanhoe congregation grew within a five-year period from thirty-eight to 400 members, just about the limit of its growth potential. In 1955 Schuller gladly accepted a call from the Reformed Church's Board of Domestic Missions to establish a congregation in sprawling Orange County, California, where aerospace and electronics industries as well as retirement communities were flourishing.

Arriving in Garden Grove with a stake of $500, the prospect of a $4,000-a-year salary, a new two-manual electric organ bought on credit, and a resolute goal of "putting strong wings on weary hearts" (now his letterhead slogan), Schuller practised "possibility thinking" in his very manner of choosing a place for conducting services. He made a list of nine possibilities, from "renting an Elks Hall" to "pitching a tent," and settled on the eighth: "renting a drive-in theatre." Meanwhile, he opened a bank account under the name Garden Grove Community Church because he knew the name "Reformed" would hardly "bring the unchurched people rushing in," and that was the group he was aiming at.

Schuller rented the Orange Drive-In Theatre near the Santa Ana Freeway for $10 a Sunday; with a hammer and saw, built his first altar and a fifteen-foot cross; and took out an ad in the local newspaper stressing the slogan "Worship as you are/In the family car." He purposely did not mimeograph a Sunday morning bulletin because he was, as he explains in *Your Church Has Real Possibilities* (G/L Publications-Regal Books, 1974), "insistent upon creating a success image in the very beginning." No bulletin at all was, to his mind, preferable to anything less than a well-printed one. When money began to flow in, the printing allocation would be a top priority. "You can spoil the whole 'money tree,'" Schuller still advises fund-raisers, "if you give the impression that you are having financial problems."

With Schuller standing atop the theatre's refreshment stand, the first open-air service at the Orange Drive-In took place on March 27, 1955. It attracted worshipers in seventy-five cars and yielded an offering of $86.79. Schuller's wife, Arvella, recalled the occasion in an interview with Marshall Berges for the *Los Angeles Times* (December 12, 1976): "There was no stained-glass window, no gold cross, no choir, no props, just a microphone and Bob standing alone on a sticky tarpaper roof. He had to dip into his own imagination and become an entertainer, an inspirer. Call it theatrical presence and you won't be far wrong."

During his first year in Garden Grove, Schuller rang some 3,500 doorbells and began compiling his "all-important" mailing list, a tool described by him as "the first line of publicity," the "way to build a church." His recruitment drive went into high gear when Norman Vincent Peale, the best-selling exponent of "the power of positive thinking," deigned to share Schuller's unusual pulpit as a guest speaker. In his letter of invitation to Peale, Schuller had described his church thus: "It is the largest church in Orange County, with parking for 1,700 cars. Everyone who comes has a soft upholstered seat by an open window, with a view of the blue sky and orange trees that encircle the property. On a spring morning, the fragrance of orange blossoms saturates the area and literally creates a heavenly aroma. And while we worship, the soft sunlight streams into our assembly. We are located on the busiest road in the state of California. Assuming that every parking space is filled, we are talking about a potential audience of nearly 6,000 people!"

In his sermon at the drive-in theatre, Peale stressed not "what sinners you are" but "what great people you can become if you only let His Holy Spirit of faith, hope, and love fill every ounce and fibre of your being." Schuller later commented: "That sermon by Dr. Peale changed my style from 'preaching' to 'witnessing.' Until that moment, I looked upon the job of a sermon to be fundamentally directed to generate a sense of guilt in guilty hearts! What I failed to realize was that unchurched people, who have no vital relationship with God, have a much deeper sense of guilt than we Christians realize. It is this sense of guilt that keeps them out of the church, the same way an overweight man avoids stepping on a bathroom scale!" Peale had "shocked" Schuller into realizing, for the first time, that "Jesus never called a human being a sinner."

The drive-in church was born of necessity, "because we had no other place to go," as Schuller related in the interview with Marshall Berges. "In time we expanded to a separate walk-in church but kept the drive-in because some of the congregation were physically handicapped, able to attend services only in cars, and others simply didn't want to dress up on Sunday. It took me quite a while, hurrying back and forth to conduct services at separate locations, before I saw the possibility of putting the two churches together."

His dream, Schuller told Berges, was to combine outdoor and indoor services in a structure designed by Richard Neutra, an architect who espoused the principle of "biorealism," based on the belief that God has provided human beings with a built-in tranquilizing system that is triggered by response to nature. But the congregation was sharply divided over the idea, with some members accusing Schuller of being "on an ego trip" and trying to build a "monument to himself." "It was a very depressing experience for me," Schuller recalled. "For two terrible years I kept thinking I'd be happy if somehow, by an act of God, I could be relieved of all responsibility. [But] a sense of responsibility comes out of my Iowa background. People can find smarter ministers than I am, but none who are more responsible. When you grow up on an Iowa farm, nothing . . . can interfere with getting your job done."

So, "caught between a rock and a hard place," with "the only escape either success or a fatal heart attack," Schuller "chose success." "It may sound simplistic, just as I suppose many of my sermons do, but the truth often is simple and straightforward. I sat down and wrote a commitment to myself: 'When faced with a mountain, I will not quit. I will keep on striving until I climb over it, find a path through it, tunnel under it, or simply stay and turn the mountain into a gold mine.'"

Finally prevailing over the dissidents in his flock, Schuller worked closely with Neutra in planning the building of a walk-in, drive-in church on twenty-two acres half a mile down the freeway from the drive-in theatre. "The secular and the sacred must be integrated in architecture, we both agreed," Schuller has explained. "Therefore we deliberately designed clear glass windows so people seated in the pews can see 'the world out there.' A religious experience that is experienced in the sanctuary does not seem totally divorced from daily life if, out of the corner of your eye, you can see a jet-liner gliding through the sky at the moment that you experience Christ coming into your life."

The structure completed by Neutra in 1961 is a sweeping glass church seating 1,700 and accommodating about the same number of standees. On an asphalted area nearby another 1,600 or so people can hear the service by car radio, amidst landscaping that includes fountains, pools, and a garden. In 1968 another major building was dedicated: the Tower of Hope, a fourteen-story office building topped by a chapel that is open to the public daily. In addition to office space, there are classrooms where more than 2,000 children attend Sunday school, and a telephone counseling service is offered twenty-four hours a day nationwide at a telephone number translated by Schuller and his associates as (714) NEW HOPE. The tower is topped by a ninety-foot neon cross, which is visible from the "Matterhorn" in the Disneyland amusement park, a few miles away. A spectacular $15,000,000 "Crystal Cathedral" designed by Philip Johnson and John Burgee is now under construction at the Garden Grove Community

Church. Slated for completion in 1980, the 10,000-window cathedral will seat 4,000 of Schuller's followers.

Also in the Garden Grove Community Church complex is the headquarters of the Robert Schuller Televangelism Association Inc., which has been taping *The Hour of Power* for television since 1970 and now syndicates it to approximately 200 stations in North America, Australia, and New Zealand in addition to the Armed Forces network. Down the freeway, at the original drive-in site, is the Robert H. Schuller Institute for Successful Church Leadership. The institute offers four-day seminars in church-building for clergymen based on principles similar to those proven effective in retailing: accessibility, surplus parking, inventory geared to demand or need ("Find a hurt and heal it"), service by a trained laity, visibility, possibility thinking, and good cash flow. Schuller advises his colleagues of the cloth to deal with controversial social, political, or theological issues not in the pulpit but in a setting where dialogue is possible.

A typical *Hour of Power* begins with the choir singing; a beaming, majestically robed Schuller steps to the pulpit and presses buttons that send geysers of water shooting from a dozen fountains and roll back two large glass wall sections fronting the outside parking area to bring the automobile audience into an unobstructed line of vision with the pulpit; then, arms raised, Schuller intones, "This is the day God has made. Let us rejoice and be glad in it!" The hour is filled with traditional hymns, such as "How Firm a Foundation" and "O God Our Help in Ages Past"; talks with guests ranging from average Americans with an edifying Christian story to tell to a bishop who escaped martyrdom under Idi Amin in Uganda and a minister caught in the crossfire in troubled Belfast, Ireland; and the *pièce de résistance*, Schuller's message, a sermon on a subject such as hope in the face of adversity, the fearlessness implicit in the "Our Father," the family as "therapeutic fellowship," self-love as a "dynamic force for success," and turning "stress into strength."

Giving no quarter to the negative, Schuller concentrates entirely on draining out "the dirty stuff," the "core of guilt that keeps a person from loving himself." Differentiating himself from Fundamentalists and Born-again Christians, Schuller told Janet Chase-Marshall in an interview for *US* (February 6, 1979), "In my theology of self-esteem, real salvation is to recover your dignity as though you had never lost it." Defending himself against the charge of superficiality made by some critics, Schuller told the editor of *Current Biography* in a written statement: "I am in fact communicating previously uncharted and systematic theological principles which I publicly verbalize in a practical manner and in helpful human terms rather than a professional theological jargon." He went on to say that he was planning to develop a systematic theology in four volumes, devoted to the theologies of self-esteem, communications, social ethics, and economics. "All of these would have their source and their force in the dignity of the individual person."

Schuller and Arvella de Haan were married on June 15, 1950 and have five children, Sheila, Robert, Jeanne, Carol, and Gretchen. The Schullers live in Garden Grove, in a house built on two landscaped acres lush with foliage, and they have a vacation cabin in Big Bear, California and a one-bedroom cottage at Laguna Beach, California. To keep in trim, Schuller jogs every morning, and his recreations include gardening and deep-sea fishing. He is a Republican and a Rotarian, and his honors include three Freedom Foundation awards and several honorary doctorates.

Dr. Schuller is a trim six feet one and a half inches tall, weighs 197 pounds, has gray hair, lively brown eyes, and a smile that, on television at least, never seems to quit. Writing in the *Christian Century* (May 4, 1977), Browne Barr described Schuller as "a decent, warm, ordinary, and enthusiastic human being," adding: "Robert Schuller's gift to today's church is to be found largely in his genius for winning a hearing from the unchurched. Regardless of our theology or our politics or our location, we can learn from him. Most of us have been preaching the gospel to ourselves long enough."

References: Los Angeles Times II p1 Mr 17 '75, mag p44+ D 12 '76 pors; New West p33+ Ap 24 '78 por; Sat Eve Post 250:54+ Ap '78; Time 105:38 F 24 '75 pors; Who's Who in America, 1978-79

Schwartz, Arthur

Nov. 25 1900- Composer. Address: b. c/o American Society of Composers, Authors, and Publishers, 1 Lincoln Plaza, New York City, N.Y. 10023

No writing team was more closely identified with the development of the revue in the American musical theatre than that comprising the composer Arthur Schwartz and the lyricist Howard Dietz. Schwartz and Dietz's most elegant collaborations were perhaps their earliest, including *The Little Show* (1929), *Three's a Crowd* (1930), *The Band Wagon* (1931), *Flying Colors,* (1932), and *Between the Devil* (1937). "Though his music has always shown great variety, Schwartz's most distinguished ballads

Arthur Schwartz

in any respectable family, he insisted that his younger son follow in his legal footsteps. Consequently, Schwartz received no training in music (outside of a class in harmony when he was in college); he taught himself to play first the harmonica and then the piano, and by the age of fourteen he was good enough at the piano to work as an accompanist at a silent movie house in Flatbush. From an early age he was also inventing tunes and making up ditties.

After graduating from Boys High School in Brooklyn in 1916, Schwartz, who was interested in literature and theatre as well as music, majored in English at New York University. As an undergraduate, he wrote for the college newspaper and composed marches for the band and a football song. He took his B.A. degree at NYU in 1920, his M.A. degree in literature at Columbia University in 1921, and his law degree at Columbia in 1924. While working for the law degree he taught high school English in the New York City public school system, and after his admission to the bar he practised law in New York City for four years.

In 1923, while still a law student, Schwartz published his first song, "Baltimore, Md., You're the Only Doctor for Me." The following year he and the lyricist Lorenz Hart—who had already begun collaborating with composer Richard Rodgers but was still an unknown— were counselors together at the Brant Lake Camp for boys in the Adirondack Mountains. Together they wrote songs for camp shows, including "I Know My Girl by Her Perfume," which later graduated to the vaudeville stage, and "I Love to Lie Awake in Bed," which was heard on Broadway five years later with different lyrics ("I Guess I'll Have to Change My Plan").

In the 1920's the best opportunities for aspiring writers for the musical stage were the medleys of song, dance, and skits known as revues—shows more sophisticated and structured than vaudeville without the cohesive "book" of an operetta or musical comedy. Among the revues the easiest of access to the young composer or lyricist was the "little" or "intimate" variety, more wittily crafted and modestly mounted than the frothy Broadway extravaganzas of Florenz Ziegfeld, Earl Carroll, and George White. A pioneer among the intimate revues was the Off-Broadway *Grand Street Follies*, the 1926 edition of which included three. compositions by Schwartz: "If You Know What I Mean" (words by Theodore Goodwin and Albert Carrol), "Little Igloo for Two" (words by Agnes Morgan), and "Polar Bear Strut" (words by Theodore Goodwin). To the 1927 revue *The New Yorkers*—not to be confused with Cole Porter's 1930 show of the same name—Schwartz contributed "Floating through the Air" (words by Henry Myers), among other songs.

For several years Schwartz lacked the confidence to compose full time, as he recounted

are frequently marked by a brooding soulfulness that is perhaps matched only by some of Cole Porter's work," Stanley Green observed in *The World of Musical Comedy* (1968). "Dietz's lyrics are characterized by their brittle wit and subtle poetic imagery [and] contain a keenness and originality that make them ideally suited to Schwartz's music." Writing in *High Fidelity* (September 1976), Gene Lees described the combined work of Schwartz and Dietz as "urbane, intelligent, warm, witty, lovely, and, above all, civilized."

Among Schwartz and Dietz's best known compositions are "Dancing in the Dark," "Louisiana Hayride," "I See Your Face Before Me," "By Myself," "If There Is Someone Lovelier Than You," "You and the Night and Music," and "That's Entertainment" (written for the movie version of *The Band Wagon*). Schwartz's major collaborator other than Dietz has been Dorothy Fields, with whom he wrote the scores for the musical comedies *Stars in Your Eyes* (1939), *A Tree Grows in Brooklyn* (1951), and *By the Beautiful Sea* (1954). "Whatever the reasons for Schwartz's somewhat fever-chart graph line of writing," Alec Wilder wrote in *American Popular Song: The Great Innovators, 1900-1950* (1972), "his published record contains some of the finest American songs in existence. He remains stylistically as mysterious and elusive as Irving Berlin. And so, one can only say only that quality was his style. And that's plenty."

Arthur Schwartz was born in Brooklyn, New York on November 25, 1900, the second son of Solomon and Dora (Grossman) Schwartz. Solomon Schwartz, a lawyer, allowed his older son a musical education but forbade the same to Arthur; believing that one musician was enough in an interview with Gene Lees for *High Fidelity* (September 1976): "You see, I never had any music lessons in my life, and that worried me very much, because I was just an intuitive writer. I learned how to do everything myself—not orchestrate, especially, but I do write my own piano parts. But I felt it was very risky for me to compete with educated musicians like [Cole] Porter. How dare I think I could compete with such people?"

However, with the encouragement of Lorenz Hart (who was by then solidly teamed up with Richard Rodgers), Schwartz finally abandoned his law practice to concentrate on songwriting, in 1928. For a brief time after taking that decisive step, he contented himself with anonymous assignments as a ghostwriter, show "doctor," and creator of vaudeville scores. Then, fortunately, he formed his partnership with Howard Dietz, the director of publicity at Metro-Goldwyn-Mayer studios and a part-time lyricist.

Among the first fruits of the Dietz-Schwartz collaboration were "I Need You So" in the 1929 edition of the *Grand Street Follies* (which had moved uptown to Broadway) and "I'll Guess I'll Have to Change My Plan," "I've Made a Habit of You," and "Hammacher, Schlemmer, I Love You" in *The Little Show*, which opened at the Music Box in April 1929. The pair wrote "Lucky Seven" and most of the other songs for *The Second Little Show* (1930). Their most memorable contribution to *Three's a Crowd* (1930) was "Something to Remember You By." The cast of *Three's a Crowd*, like that of the first *Little Show*, was headed by Clifton Webb, Libby Holman, and Fred Allen.

The Band Wagon (1931), produced by Max Gordon and starring Fred and Adele Astaire, combined the best features of the smart little revues on the one hand and such lavish productions as the *Ziegfeld Follies* on the other. The score by Dietz and Schwartz, possibly the best ever written for a revue, included "Confession," "Miserable with You," "New Sun in the Sky," "High and Low," "I Love Louisa," and the singular "Dancing in the Dark," probably Schwartz and Dietz's greatest song. Regarding the latter, Schwartz has recalled that during rehearsals for *The Band Wagon* he was asked to compose a "dark song, somewhat mystical, yet in slow, even rhythm." Feeling inspired when he awoke the following morning, he went immediately to the piano and played the melody of "Dancing in the Dark" from beginning to end without hesitation. "*Mirabile dictu*," Olin Downes wrote in his review of the 1931 production in the New York *Times*, "we have a composer whose melodic vein is not only graceful but characterized at its best by refinement and artistic quality." The Dietz-Schwartz score for *Flying Colors* (1932), another Max Gordon revue, included "Alone Together" and the exuberant chorus number "Louisiana Hayride."

Dietz and Schwartz's first musical with a book was *Revenge with Music* (1934), an adaptation of Pedro de Alarcón's Spanish novel *El Sombrero de Tres Picos* (The Three-Cornered Hat). The score for that production included the enduring favorites "You and the Night and the Music" and "If There is Someone Lovelier than You." The latter, perhaps the purest of all Schwartz's ballads, was developed from a song Schwartz and Dietz had written for the radio serial *The Gibson Family*.

After collaborating on the revue *At Home Abroad* (1935), Schwartz and Dietz scored their second "book" show, *Between the Devil* (1937), a farce about the complicated life of a bigamist with one wife in England and another in France. Outstanding among the songs in *Between the Devil* were "I See Your Face Before Me" and "By Myself." Running on Broadway concurrently with *Between the Devil* was another "book" musical with music by Schwartz (and lyrics by Albert Stillman)—*Virginia*.

When Dietz's executive duties at MGM became more burdensome, Schwartz found a new and equally felicitous partner in Dorothy Fields, with whom he wrote the score for the musical comedy *Stars in Your Eyes* (1939), a satiric look at Hollywood that included the songs "This Is It" and "The Lady Needs a Change." In the New York *Times* for July 7, 1940, Benjamin Welles noted: "Schwartz's chief gift, in the view of theatre technicians, professional critics, and the public at large, is a tremendous freshness, a boundless variety of musical expression."

From 1939 to 1946 Schwartz worked in Hollywood, writing songs for motion pictures with Frank Loesser and Leo Robin, among other lyricists. Among the films for which he wrote complete scores were *Thank Your Lucky Stars* (Warner, 1943) and *The Time, the Place, and the Girl* (Warner, 1946). He produced the musical *Cover Girl* (Columbia, 1944) and the cinematic biography of Cole Porter, *Night and Day* (Warner, 1946).

Schwartz returned to the stage as the composer, with Ira Gershwin as lyricist, of *Park Avenue* (1946). With his old partner, Dietz, he scored the revue *Inside U.S.A.*, a celebration of the several states that ran for more than a year in 1948 and 1949, and with Dorothy Fields he wrote the musical comedies *A Tree Grows in Brooklyn* (1951) and *By The Beautiful Sea* (1954). With Dietz once again as his lyricist, Schwartz scored the musical comedies *The Gay Life* (1961), based on Arthur Schnitzler's Viennese bedroom farce "Affairs of Anatol," and *Jennie* (1963), based on the life of actress Laurette Taylor.

In his book on the great innovators in American popular song, Alec Wilder wrote that he found little of interest in Schwartz's work in the ten years following *A Tree Grows in Brooklyn*, with its "lovely" ballad "Make the Man Love Me." "Not until 1961, in *The Gay Life*, was there, for me, a return of Schwartz's brilliance," Wilder wrote. He quoted his friend James Maher's observation on the failure of *The Gay Life*: "The music was tasteful, full of melodic invention, sophisticated, and, in another era, may well have found a wide audience outside the theatre. But it never had a chance to find such an audience. The rock era closed the door on all such music and its mature sensibilities."

In the score of *The Gay Life* Wilder particularly liked "Something You Never Had Before," which he listed "among the great theatre songs," and the "marvelous" romantic ballad "For the First Time." "There is such sadness in the renaissance of Schwartz's high style just at the point when good taste became an obsolete phrase. . . . The extraordinary score was written thirty-eight years after Schwartz had published his first song, 'Baltimore, Md., You're the Only Doctor for Me.' I don't know of any writer who rose to such heights after such a long writing career except Kern." But, unfortunately, "the handwriting of the Beatles was on the wall."

"The striking irony in the career of Arthur Schwartz," Stanley Green wrote in his 1968 book on American musical comedy, "is that in spite of the high quality of his melodic creations for such book musicals as *Revenge with Music*, *Virginia*, *Between the Devil*, *Stars in Your Eyes*, *Park Avenue*, *The Gay Life*, and especially *A Tree Grows in Brooklyn*, the composer's only commercial successes have been the revues he wrote in partnership with Howard Dietz. The fault has seldom been his or his lyricist's; in almost every case it has been the librettist who has somehow failed to supply a script worthy of its score. Thus, at this writing, Schwartz remains a composer looking for a good librettist—just as in the mid-Twenties he was a composer looking for a good lyricist. To date, the contributions of Dietz and Schwartz to the revue form are still their most significant collaborative achievement in the development of the musical theatre. Chiefly due to their efforts, the revue reached a peak of perfection that has never been surpassed. Indeed, in the event that this form of entertainment ever does return to its former eminence, it will need the very qualities of smartness, originality, wit and melody that have so distinguished the works of Howard Dietz and Arthur Schwartz."

In 1976 RCA issued the album *From the Pen of Arthur Schwartz*, on which the composer can be heard singing a wide selection of his own songs. Two of the songs were written with Leo Robin: "A Rainy Night in Rio" and "A Gal in Calico." The others, all written with Howard Dietz, include "Love is a Dancing Thing," "Triplets," "A Shine on My Shoes," and "By Myself." On the occasion of the LP's release, Gene Lees wrote in *High Fidelity*: "This title will communicate little to a generation deprived, through current radio programming and practice and the not-so-benign neglect

of the record industry, of the opportunity to know Schwartz's marvelous music. . . . As a composer of lovely and even haunting melodic contours, Schwartz, I feel, is close to Jerome Kern. In fact, in one specific sense, I rate him somewhat more highly: Kern sometimes reaches awkwardly for harmonic effects. . . . Schwartz never does that sort of thing. He never makes you aware of the craft."

In January 1979 the Manhattan Theater Club produced the cabaret revue *Dancing in the Dark*, built around thirty-four of Schwartz's songs, including "Never Marry a Dancer," "I Can Never Get Anywhere on Time," and two new compositions, "Love Should Be Free" and "The Jog." On the evenings of March 19 and 20, 1978 three singers performed a concert of songs by Schwartz in the "Lyrics and Lyricists" series at the 92nd Street Y.M.-Y.W.H.A. in Manhattan. The lyricists represented included Maxwell Anderson and E. Y. ("Yip") Harburg. *Look Who's Dancing*, a new version of *A Tree Grows in Brooklyn*, with a revised book by Mary O'Hagan, Schwartz's wife, and eight additional songs with words as well as music by Schwartz himself, was performed at the Berkshire Music Festival in Stockbridge, Massachusetts in the summer of 1978.

Arthur Schwartz's first wife, the actress Kay Carrington, died in 1954. By his first marriage he has a grown son, Jonathan, a novelist and a disc jockey on radio station WNEW in New York City. With his present wife, Mary, Schwartz lives in London, but he returns to the United States monthly to attend to his duties as a director of ASCAP. Like many another interviewer, Gene Lees of *High Fidelity* "had real trouble handling the fact" that Schwartz will soon be an octogenarian. "Tall, black-haired, assured, gracious, he is strikingly handsome. . . ." Lees wrote. "His speaking voice is a warm baritone, his enunciation upperclass East Coast."

References: High Fidelity 26:20+ S '76 por; N Y Times IX p1+ Jl 7 '40; N Y Times C p3 Ja 5 '79; Ewen, David. Great Men of American Popular Song (1972); Gottfried, Martin. Broadway Musicals (1979); Green, Stanley. The World of Musical Comedy 1968; Stambler, Irwin. Encyclopedia of Popular Music (1965)

Schwarzenegger, Arnold (schvarz″ən-ek′ ər)

July 30, 1947- Bodybuilder. Address: b. c/o Simon & Schuster, Simon & Schuster Bldg., 1230 Ave. of the Americas, New York City, N.Y. 10020

By bodybuilding standards, Austrian-born Arnold Schwarzenegger probably has the

Arnold Schwarzenegger

world's most perfect male physique; by any standards, he is a premier figure in the history of the sport, or art, of developing muscle for aesthetic purposes. A former Mr. World title-holder, five times Mr. Universe, and six times Mr. Olympia, Schwarzenegger retired from competition in 1975 because, he says, he "wasn't giving the others a chance." Besides a prize-winning physique, Schwarzenegger brought to his chosen field of endeavor the more exceptional asset of an engaging personality, which remains identified with the world of muscle through his activities as entrepreneur, showman, and movie strong man. As bodybuilding's first real promoter-star, the "Austrian Oak" has done more than any other individual to gain wide acceptance for that misunderstood sport, once regarded by outsiders as the freakish, "low camp" pastime of pea-brained, sexually suspect blue-collar brutes.

Arnold Schwarzenegger was born on July 30, 1947 in Graz, Austria, and he grew up in the nearby village of Thal, where his father, Gustav, a former champion ice curler, was then police chief. Through his mother, Aurelia, he is descended from Russian peasant stock. He had an older brother, a champion boxer, who died in an automobile accident.

Raised a Roman Catholic, Schwarzenegger attended Sunday Mass with his parents during childhood, and he was reared under strict paternal discipline. "My father always acted like a general, checking to see that I ate the proper way, that I did my studies," he recalls in his autobiography-cum-training manual *Arnold: The Education of a Body Builder* (Simon & Schuster, 1977), written with Douglas Kent Hall. His was "a physical family," he

says, "oriented toward training, good eating, and keeping the body fit and healthy." Originally a sickly child, he improved in health as he participated in sports and especially after he began playing soccer. By the age of twelve he was a wing for the Graz Athletic Club, considered the second-best team in the city.

"From the time I was ten years old, I wanted to be the very best in something," Schwarzenegger told Elizabeth Kaye in an interview for an article in *Family Health* (December 1977). "Even when I was that age, I would daydream about leaving Austria and coming to America." What he would be "the very best in," he decided, was bodybuilding, discovered by him when, at fifteen, he began lifting weights to develop his legs for soccer. "Once I decided I wanted to do it," he has said, "I learned up about the body, how it works, how each muscle can be worked. I felt like Leonardo da Vinci; I was a sculptor shaping the body." Soon he dropped out of other sports to devote his full attention to his new-found interest, training six days a week and continuously increasing the weight he lifted and the length of his training sessions. He pored over American magazines like *Muscle Builder* and *Mr. America* and assiduously followed the adventure films of strong men-actors Steve Reeves, Gordon Mitchell, Brad Harris, Mark Forest, and, above all, Reg Park. His parents, alarmed at his obsession, forbade him to spend more than three nights a week at the gym. To circumvent their curfew, he set up his own gym in an unheated room at home, where he trained even on the coldest days in winter, when the temperature dropped below zero.

In 1965 Schwarzenegger graduated from secondary school and enlisted in the Austrian army, where he was given the time and opportunity to follow his athletic bent. "I won the Austrian and European curling championships," he later recounted, "but I also realized there was no future in curling. I began going to the gym just to do power lifting and bodybuilding." After winning the Austrian junior Olympic weight-lifting championship, he realized that "the human body is not made to do the Olympic lifts," and that those lifts were injuring him. He continued to do some power lifting, but he concentrated on bodybuilding, working on all of his muscles and not just those stressed in Olympic events. In 1965 he won the title of Junior Mr. Europe in the junior division of the Mr. Europe competition in Stuttgart, Germany, where he met the Sardinian bodybuilder Francesco Columbu, who became his best friend.

Of his year in military service Schwarzenegger later wrote, "For me the Army was a good experience. I liked the regimentation, the firm, rigid structure. The whole idea of uniforms and medals appealed to me." After his discharge he managed a health and body-building club in Munich, and it was there that he developed many of the innovative training techniques that were to win him wide respect and emulation among bodybuilders. They included the "split routine," in which the upper and lower parts of the body are trained in two separate sessions, one mornings and the other evenings, and "muscle shock," overdoing a specific routine in such a way as to get the muscles past the pain barrier, to new heights of development. During the same period he won the titles of Best Built Man of Europe and Mr. Europe and the International Power-lifting Championship, all in 1966. Also in 1966, he finished second in the National Amateur Bodybuilding Association's Mr. Universe competition, in London. The following year he won the NABBA amateur title, and in 1968 he won the professional title.

In the period between his winning his first and his second Mr. Universe titles Schwarzenegger met his idol, Reg Park, and made an exhibition tour of England and Ireland with him. Working with Park helped him both professionally and personally, as he recounts in his autobiography. "One inspiring thing was that his body tuned in the same way mine did. We both liked the heavy, heavy workouts with barbell sets and not so much with dumbbells. ... There were so many things to talk about that still seemed mysterious. Such as how different bodybuilders had to do different exercises for different body parts. According to Reg, the reason was body structure. It was obvious, for example, that a guy with short legs had to do fewer squats.... You have to try out certain things and find out what is best for your own body."

Park also made him "want to become a better person." "It was a bad time. Now, looking back on it, I'm embarrassed. I was nothing more than a punk, a big bully throwing my weight around. I had fights almost every day ... all connected with my need to emphasize my masculinity, my superior size and strength. But when I'd finished my tour with Reg ... I became so content to work hard and drive myself to the top that the whole business of fighting and acting out the macho role went away."

At the invitation of the California muscle entrepreneur Joe Weider, the owner of Weider Enterprises and publisher of Muscle Builder and Mr. America magazines, Schwarzenegger came to the United States in 1968 for the International Federation of Bodybuilding's Mr. Universe contest in Miami, Florida. After the contest (in which he placed second to Frank Zane), he remained in the United States under Weider's patronage. "My desire, which I knew I could accomplish, was to train one whole year and beat everybody in America," Schwarzenegger relates in his autobiography. "My part of the agreement was to make available to Weider information about how I trained. He agreed to provide an apartment, a car, and to pay me a weekly salary in exchange for my information and being able to use photo-graphs of me in his magazine. But the main thing I had was time, the freedom to stay and train four or five hours a day and compete in next year's IFBB Mr. Universe contest in New York."

Schwarzenegger settled in California, which he still regards as a "bodybuilder's paradise," and from his home in Santa Monica he traveled daily to Gold's Gym in Venice, where he worked out with some of the best bodybuilders in the world. In 1969 he won the IFBB Mr. Universe contest, placed second to Sergio Oliva in his first IFBB Mr. Olympia contest (considered the "superbowl of bodybuilding"), and again won the NABBA Mr. Universe contest. In 1970 he bested Reg Park in London to claim his fifth and final Mr. Universe victory, captured the Mr. World title in Columbus, Ohio, and won his first Mr. Olympia in New York. (No one has equaled his remarkable feat of capturing all three major titles in one year.) He continued to win the Mr. Olympia title annually until 1975, when he retired. "By then I had gotten the physical development I wanted," he has explained, "and my ego wasn't being satisfied anymore from winning."

The judging of a bodybuilding contest is done in three stages, the first two of which take place privately under bright lights on the afternoon of the event, when the judges look first for overall proportion and then for the mass and contoured "cut" of muscles. The public views only the third stage, the posing competition which takes place in the evening under stage lights. In the posing competition each contestant, his body glistening with oil, spends ninety seconds putting his body in various positions calculated to make the muscle groupings flex, bulge, and ripple. As a competitor, Schwarzenegger was known for using questionable, if officially permissible, tactics to "psych out" his rivals, but he could, when winning, be gracious as well. As Richard Schickel observed in Time (January 24, 1977), "Schwarzenegger numbers among his many gifts the ability to let losers down lightly, with tact, delicacy, and psychological acuity."

Schwarzenegger's dream of becoming an actor was finally realized in Stay Hungry (United Artists, 1976), Bob Rafelson's cinematization of the novel by Charles Gaines. The comedy-melodrama, set in Birmingham, Alabama, starred Jeff Bridges as an eccentric scion of Southern gentry. He is used as a front man by unscrupulous real-estate developers trying to acquire the site of a health club used by a contingent of bodybuilders led by one Joe Santo. As Santo, Schwarzenegger received much better notices than the film itself. Jack Kroll of Newsweek (May 17, 1976) called him "surprisingly good as the muscle man with heart—and pectorals—of gold." Writing in the Wall Street Journal (May 3, 1976), Joy Gould Boyum described him as radiating "assurance and appeal," and Bryan Johnson of the Toronto Globe and Mail (August 17, 1976) credited him with a "believably natural performance." For his performance, he received a Golden Globe award for best new actor.

Meanwhile, Charles Gaines and photographer George Butler had come out with *Pumping Iron*, (Simon & Schuster, 1974), a photojournalistic study of bodybuilding in which they concentrated on preparations for a Mr. Universe competition. The book turned out to be a surprising best seller, with 93,000 copies sold in successive printings. "People have no idea, not the remotest notion," George Butler commented, "[that] bodybuilding is a giant underground obsession. Already it's the ninth largest spectator sport in America and growing all the time. Potentially, Arnold Schwarzenegger could be a folk hero on a par with Bruce Lee or Muhammad Ali."

Like the book, the documentary film *Pumping Iron* (Cinema 5, 1977), directed by Butler and Robert Fiore, had an amazingly wide appeal. "The film gets to the essence of a process of muscle building which is more miraculous than plastic surgery or transplants," Joseph Gelmis wrote in *Newsday* (January 16, 1977). "It is this: The bodybuilder *wills* his metamorphosis, endures daily pain in exchange for controlled muscle growth, sculpts his own body into a work of living art by the exercise of mind over matter." Nik Cohn of *New York* (January 24, 1977) observed: "All of this would be intriguing, no more, if it were not for the presence of Schwarzenegger himself, who lights up the film like neon every time he comes on-screen. Blond and Germanic, muscular beyond all conceiving, he looks like a walking incarnation of the Mighty Thor, the Marvel Comics superhero. Yet his physical power is balanced by great humor, prodigious charm—that same mixture of sweetness and sass, mock arrogance and mock innocence, that Ali once possessed." Other critics wrote in similar vein, describing Schwarzenegger as "charismatic" and "bright," "the first personality since Bruce Lee who might become a unique and credible *physical* star."

Schwarzenegger, who reportedly holds a bachelor's degree in business administration from the University of California at Los Angeles, numbers among his business enterprises mail-order training courses in bodybuilding and physical fitness, a line of training clothes and equipment, endorsements of food supplements and other products, seminars and other paid public appearances, a company that produces bodybuilding competitions, and investments in real estate. *Arnold: The Education of a Body Builder* has sold more than 150,000 copies in hardcover, and a paperback edition has been issued by Pocket Books. In November 1979 Simon & Schuster published his *Arnold's Bodyshaping for Women*, written with Douglas Kent Hall. Schwarzenegger has a contract with Paramount and has appeared on TV as a commentator for ABC's *Wide World of Sports.*

Arnold Schwarzenegger is six-feet two inches tall and weighs about 230 pounds. His top-form measurements, in inches, are as follows: arms, twenty-two; chest, fifty-seven; waist, thirty-four; thighs, twenty-eight and a half; and calves, twenty. Schwarzenegger still works out for one hour each day. He dates frequently, expressing a preference for "smart, intellectually aggressive women," and his other leisure-time pursuits include tennis, diving, archery, and hunting wild boar. His automobile is a silver Mercedes with fur-covered bucket seats. Bodybuilding's superstar still makes his home in Santa Monica, and he has a winter house in Palm Springs, California. He regularly visits his relatives in Austria but says, "There is no place in the world where I feel as comfortable as in America."

References: N Y Sunday News p7 S 5 '76 pors; N Y Times p12 My 8 '76; New Times 7:71+ O 15 '76 pors; Newsweek 92:17 Jl 17 '78 por; Sports Illus 41:107+ O 14 '74 pors; Schwarzenegger, Arnold, with Hall, Douglas Kent. Arnold: The Education of a Body Builder (1977)

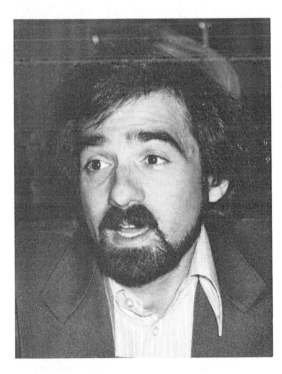

Scorsese, Martin (skōr′sā-sə)

Nov. 17, 1942- Filmmaker. Address: c/o United Artists, 10202 W. Washington Blvd., Culver City, Calif. 90230

Working with increasingly diversified locales and genres—as evidenced by *Mean Streets*

Alice Doesn't Live Here Anymore, and *New York, New York*—the director Martin Scorsese has forged a controversial, deeply personal style of filmmaking characterized by subjective realism, an involvement with the theme of the outsider, and a pervasive undercurrent of violence. In a quasi-documentary idiom sometimes employing vertiginous camera angles and surreal interludes and always enriched by music, Scorsese explores the inner conflicts of his characters without romance or cynicism, but with an empathy that makes his films painful to watch. A movie buff who is thoroughly versed in Hollywood's conventions, Scorsese demonstrates a mastery of cinematic devices, without totally succumbing to the motion picture industry's prevailing concern with pleasing the audience.

Martin Scorsese was born on November 17, 1942 in Flushing, Queens, New York, where his parents, Charles and Catherine (Cappa) Scorsese, had recently moved from their native Little Italy in Manhattan. They both had jobs in the garment district, but because of financial straits, apparently, they returned to their former home in New York City's Lower East Side when Martin was eight. Remaining there until the age of twenty-four, he came to know thoroughly the flavor and rhythm of life in that confined Italian community.

Poor health, specifically asthma, prevented Martin Scorsese from joining his older brother, Fred, and other boys of the neighborhood in sports, street fights, and work at odd jobs during the summer. In the macho world of Little Italy, his physical frailty made him an outsider, a role he was to examine repeatedly in his films. To relieve his loneliness and idleness, his father took him to the movies. Afterward the boy would sketch motion picture scenes of his own on drawing pads. "There's a great similarity in the way I look at reality and the things I saw in the musicals and the dark 'noir' films of the '40s," he told David Sterritt in an interview for the *Christian Science Monitor* (May 1, 1978). "My reality and film reality are interchangeable. They blend."

Raised a devout Roman Catholic, Scorsese attended a Catholic grade school and at fourteen, with the intention of becoming a priest, enrolled in a junior seminary on the Upper West Side. On being expelled at the end of the year—"for roughhousing during prayers," according to one account of the incident—he transferred to the Cardinal Hayes High School in the Bronx. He did not abandon the idea of renewing his study for the priesthood until he found in filmmaking what he has called his "true vocation." In several press interviews he disclosed that he stopped attending Mass after he heard a priest endorse the Vietnam War as a holy cause. His struggle with persistent feelings of guilt generated by Catholic moralism is depicted in some of his earliest films and at times underlies the dramatic tension in his later work.

After he failed the examination for Fordham College's divinity program, Scorsese entered New York University, planning to major in English. But as soon as he discovered the film department of the university's School of the Arts, he began to devote himself to the fundamentals of filmmaking and was soon turning out films that won awards from the Edward L. Kingsley Foundation, the Screen Producers Guild, and the Brown University Film Festival. While studying to obtain his B.S. degree in film communications in 1964 and his M.A. degree in 1966, he taught in NYU's film department as assistant instructor from 1963 to 1966. He returned to the NYU faculty in 1968 to teach film until 1970.

Among Scorsese's award-winning student films were "What's a Girl Like You Doing in a Place Like This?" (1963) and "It's Not Just You, Murray" (1964). His fascination with violence emerged particularly in the blood-drenched, six-minute color film "The Big Shave" (1967-68), described by its sponsor, the Belgian Cinémathèque, as a "brief American nightmare." In 1968, while still an instructor at NYU, Scorsese wrote and directed his first feature film, *Who's That Knocking At My Door?* (Brenner Associates), about the struggle of a young Italian, J.R., to reconcile his rigid Catholic sexual mores with the actualities of Little Italy. The film introduced Harvey Keitel, an actor who became part of an informal Scorsese ensemble. To attract a distributor for his low-budget production, Scorsese was forced to add an explicit, though psychologically doubtful, sex scene, but the film attracted considerable critical interest. While some reviewers agreed with William Wolf of *Cue* (August 19, 1972), who thought it "a sophomoric cinematic exercise," others praised the vivid depiction of a visual and aural environment and the underlying authenticity of feeling.

A later movie on which Scorsese worked while at NYU, *Street Scenes* (1970), documents an anti-Vietnam War demonstration in New York City. He was associated, as supervising editor and assistant director, with another documentary, *Woodstock* (Warner Brothers, 1970), an account of the gathering in 1969 of a half-million rock music fans in the Catskills, which was directed by Michael Wadleigh, the photographer of *Who's That Knocking At My Door?* Somewhat reminiscent of *Woodstock*, *Medicine Boy Caravan* (Warner Brothers, 1971), of which Scorsese was associate producer, chronicles a cross-country bus junket of music-loving, long-haired San Franciscans. He also did some editing on the music documentary *Elvis on Tour* (MGM, 1973). His other early work included making television commercials in England in 1968 and editing news for CBS-TV.

In 1972 the producer Roger Corman hired Scorsese to direct his low-budget exploitation film *Boxcar Bertha* (American International), based on the life story of an unhappy vagrant young woman during the Depression. A reviewer for *Variety* (May 3, 1972) summed up that potboiler with the verdict: "Whatever its intentions, *Boxcar Bertha* is not much more than an excuse to slaughter a lot of people." It was, however, compared not unfavorably to *Bonnie and Clyde,* and Arthur Winsten pointed out in the New York *Post* (August 17, 1972) that Scorsese "is very strong with the crucifixion that does place this picture off by itself."

Admonished by his mentor, the movie director John Cassavetes, for wasting his time and talents on *Boxcar Bertha,* Scorsese resolved to pursue his own film ideas. In 1973 he filmed *Mean Streets* (Warner Brothers), based on a script he had written with Mardik Martin seven years earlier about the relationship between a small-time hood, Charlie, and his reckless friend Johnny Boy, both of whom are caught up in the criminal world of Little Italy. Torn between loyalty to his friend and the desire to get ahead in the Mafia, Charlie sacrifices his epileptic girl friend and Johnny Boy. Scorsese appears in a cameo role as the gunman who shoots Johnny Boy and the girl. He adopted Cassavetes' improvisational techniques to direct Harvey Keitel as the hood and the then unknown Robert De Niro, who also grew up in Little Italy, as Johnny Boy. In the screen credits, Scorsese thanked his California analyst, presumably for giving him insight into the characters.

Mean Streets won widespread acclaim after its release at the 1973 New York Film Festival. In a long laudatory review in the *New Yorker* (October 8, 1973) Pauline Kael called it "a true original of our period, a triumph of personal filmmaking." She wrote, "What Scorsese, who is thirty, has done with the experience of growing up in New York's Little Italy has a thicker-textured rot and violence than we have ever had in an American movie." Martin Knelman described it in the Toronto *Globe and Mail* (December 28, 1973) as "a brutally unforgettable street drama about a kind of life that is not at all remote or exotic, but it has the imagination and the spell of a visionary work." Representative, on the other hand, of some criticism of the documentary style was Richard Schickel's complaint in *Time* (November 5, 1973): "One leaves the film with the sense of having endured a class in social anthropology rather than an aesthetic experience."

Too grim for most moviegoers, *Mean Streets* was not a box office success. Hollywood recognition of Scorsese's potential, however, brought him studio sponsorship and funding for his next movie, *Alice Doesn't Live Here Anymore* (Warner Brothers, 1975). A strong departure from his previous work, that "woman's movie" was based on Robert Getchell's television screenplay about a mediocre singer who seeks a career in the music world after she is suddenly widowed. Ellen Burstyn, who owned the film property and gave an Oscar-winning performance as Alice, was acknowledged to have contributed substantially to shaping the film, as was Scorsese's then girl friend, Sandy Weintraub, its associate producer. But the hand-held camera sequences, the homage to *The Wizard of Oz* in the opening of the film, the violent interlude with Alice's sadistic lover, and the pivotal role of friendship in the story, all reflect Scorsese's directorial vision.

Overall critical response to *Alice* was mixed. Several reviewers agreed with Steven Farber of the New York *Times* (March 30, 1975), who wrote, "Although dressed up to look modern, *Alice* is just another Technicolor advertisement for cotton candy romance." Other critics shared the delight of Richard Gelmis in *Newsday* (January 30, 1975): "It's humane. It's poignant. It's funny." Several rejected the happy ending as "wrongheaded," but Diane Jacobs in *Hollywood Renaissance* (1977) saw it as appropriate to "a transcendent comedy." The film confirmed her view that "Scorsese's study of Middle Americans today concentrates on their humor, their tenacity, their ability to help each other survive and, just maybe, ameliorate." Audiences loved the movie, which was a solid box office hit, making Scorsese a "bankable" director.

During 1973 Scorsese also made a forty-five-minute documentary of an after-dinner conversation with his parents. His affectionate portrait of them is realized through family reminiscences and a demonstration of his mother making spaghetti sauce. *Italianamerican* received a standing ovation when it was premiered at the 1974 New York Film Festival, at which his mother blew kisses to the audience. It was later shown on public television as part of a PBS series, *Storm of Strangers.*

Scorsese took a huge commercial risk with his next film, *Taxi Driver* (Columbia, 1976), a compelling case study of an ex-Marine taxi driver who becomes a sociopath and is driven by loneliness and rejection to "cleanse" himself and New York City in an orgiastic massacre. Both the director and De Niro, who played the title character, admit to having identified with the alienated cabbie of Paul Schrader's script.

Much critical controversy surrounded the bloody climax of the film, in which the taxi driver murders the pimp, the customer, and the intruders into the room of a teenage prostitute he is trying to reform. Although the color of that sequence was desaturated to avoid an X rating, reviewers in general were unnerved by Scorsese's depiction of butchery. Several considered it an amoral glorification of violence. Diane Jacobs commented, "A pictorial affection for violent death gets out of control and dulls the impact of a still extraordinarily forceful psychological study." The trick ending, in which the taxi driver is hailed as a hero for gunning down mobsters, also provoked considerable censure.

Audiences, on the whole, seconded the approval of David Sterritt, who called *Taxi Driver* "the nastiest masterpiece in years" (*Christian Science Monitor*, February 19, 1976), and Pauline Kael, who contended, "No other film has ever dramatized urban indifference so powerfully" (*New Yorker*, February 9, 1976). Abroad, *Taxi Driver* won the Golden Palm grand prize at the Cannes Film Festival in 1976 and boosted the sales in Rome of the gun, a .44 magnum, used by the taxi driver.

Venturing into an entirely different genre for his next film, Scorsese set out to recreate a lavish Hollywood-style musical of the 1940's, replete with flashy production numbers and a romantic story line about two ambitious musicians who meet, marry, and break up. During the filming of *New York, New York* (United Artists, 1977) Scorsese grew more interested in exploring the troubled relationship between the musicians, played by Liza Minnelli and Robert De Niro, than in making a Hollywood extravaganza. Through lengthy sessions of improvisation recorded on videotape, Scorsese and his actors rewrote the script to focus on the conflict between career and love that keeps the couple apart. "My light frothy musical turned out to be my most personal film," Scorsese said in an interview for *Newsweek* (May 16, 1977).

The $8.7 million *New York, New York* impaired Scorsese's reputation with most critics. In a review called "The Director Suffers Most" Joy Gould Boyum in the *Wall Street Journal* (July 18, 1977) lamented, "Still another gifted young filmmaker has succumbed to that current pandemic of the movie world, cloying and crippling nostalgia." Stanley Kauffmann of the *New Republic* and Penelope Gilliatt of the *New Yorker* also lambasted *New York, New York*. But the movie mustered a respectable troop of defenders who thought it first-rate entertainment.

While still at work on *New York, New York*, Scorsese took time out to direct *The Last Waltz* (United Artists, 1978), a documentary-type tribute to the rock group called The Band on the occasion of its "last" concert on Thanksgiving Day, 1976. Assembling six of Hollywood's top cinematographers, including Vilmos Zsigmond and Laszlo Kovacs, Scorsese filmed the first 35mm rock movie. "The coverage is nearly perfect and puts to shame all those murky rock movies of the past," Chris Hodenfield wrote in *Rolling Stone* (June 1, 1978), an assessment shared by a host of critics. Some reviewers found fault

with Scorsese's interrupting the concert footage with interviews of the musicians, which the director himself reportedly included only grudgingly, but the movie fared well at the box office.

In an effort related to his recent moviemaking, Scorsese staged a theatrical showcase for Liza Minnelli eventually called *The Act,* a spinoff of *New York, New York.* Although the bill gave him sole directorial credit, production and other problems had led him to turn the final doctoring and polishing over to Gower Champion before the musical opened on Broadway in late October 1977. Among Scorsese's current projects is a film about the boxer Jake La Motta, to be portrayed by De Niro.

During his years at NYU, Martin Scorsese met and, on May 15, 1965, married Laraine Marie Brennan. By that marriage, which ended in divorce, he has a daughter, Catherine Terese. He has another daughter, Domenica Elizabeth, by his second marriage, to the writer Julia Cameron in the mid-1970's. He was also divorced from his second wife, and on September 30, 1979 he married Isabella Rossellini, daughter of the actress Ingrid Bergman and Roberto Rossellini, the late Italian film director.

The word "workaholic" has often been used in the press in reference to Scorsese, who admits to having a compulsive drive that impels him from one film to the next. He is the wiry, dark-haired, bearded man seen as the psychotic passenger in *Taxi Driver.* Although essentially intense and serious, he is not without humor in regard to his work. When William Wolf, interviewing him for *Cue* (March 3, 1975), asked about his next movie, Scorsese responded, "I want to make the New Testament on 16mm with the Jefferson Airplane doing the score. After all, I must do one religious picture."

References: After Dark 8:36+ Mr '76 *pors; Guardian* p6 Ag 9 '76 *por; N Y Sunday News* III p7 Ag 17 '75 *por; N Y Times* II p17+ D 16 '73 *por,* II p1+ Mr 30 '75 *por; N Y Times Mag* p34+ F 8 '76 *por; New York* 8:48+ S 8 '75 *por; Rolling Stone* p36+ Je 16 '77 *pors;* Jacobs, Diane. *Hollywood Renaissance* (1977); *Who's Who in America, 1977-78*

Seymour, Lynn

Mar. 8, 1939- Canadian dancer. Address: b. Bayerische Staatsoper, Maximilianstrasse, 8000 Munich, Germany

For more than twenty years, most of them spent with the Royal Ballet, Lynn Seymour

Lynn Seymour

has danced leading roles in classical and contemporary ballets, with rare expressiveness and individuality. A self-styled "natural choreographer's moll," she has had more ballets created for her than any other Royal Ballet dancer except Dame Margot Fonteyn. She is best known for her emotional interpretations of Kenneth MacMillan's traumatized heroines in his *Romeo and Juliet*, *Anastasia*, *Manon*, and *Mayerling*, and her passionate portrayal of Natalia Petrovna in Frederick Ashton's *A Month in the Country*, but her range is enormous, encompassing sixty-odd works by such disparate choreographers as Petipa, Balanchine, Robbins, and Tetley. Late in 1978 Miss Seymour became artistic director of the Bayerische Staatsoper. There she has combined administrative duties with performances as the prima ballerina.

Lynn Seymour was born Lynn Berta Springbett on March 8, 1939 in Wainwright, Alberta, Canada, the daughter of E. V. Springbett, a dentist, and his wife. The family moved to Esquimalt, British Columbia, a seaport near Vancouver, during World War II and it was there that Lynn Springbett first saw performances by the Ballet Russe de Monte Carlo and the Sadler's Wells Ballet. "Passionate" about the ballet ever since, she began her formal training at the age of nine in the Vancouver studio of Jean Jepson, a teacher who imbued her students with "a love for dance." "I mean, it wasn't your 'holy' bit," she explained to John Gruen in an interview for his book *The Private World of Ballet* (1975). "More workmanlike, really. Her classes weren't airy-fairy at all. She taught one about the gypsy side of it all, which was rather romantic. She taught us to work hard—it wasn't about being an ethereal creature."

Within two years, Lynn Seymour was ready for the more technically demanding classes taught by Nicolai Svetlanoff. A dedicated student, she often went to the studio alone to practise and regularly took company class with whatever touring troupe happened to be performing in Vancouver. At Svetlanoff's suggestion, she auditioned for Ailne Phillips and Frederick Ashton, associate directors of the Sadler's Wells Ballet, during that company's visit to Vancouver in 1953. She was immediately offered a scholarship to continue her training in London at the Sadler's Wells Ballet School. There she took a rigorous program of academic and dance classes and perfected her developing technique under the demanding scrutiny of Winifred Edwards.

In 1956 Lynn Seymour was assigned to the corps de ballet of the Covent Garden Opera Ballet, which, in her words, "was about the last thing they could do with you." She spent a year with that company, appearing in its productions of *Hansel and Gretel*, *Rigoletto*, *The Bartered Bride*, and *The Marriage of Figaro*, and then joined the Royal Ballet's touring company, a smaller and younger group with a more experimental repertory than the parent organization. After spending several months in touring the provinces, she returned to London to learn a leading role in Kenneth MacMillan's *The Burrow*, a new one-act ballet loosely based on *The Diary of Anne Frank*. On the strength of her performance in that ballet, she was promoted to soloist. It was at about this time that she adopted the surname Seymour, a change suggested by MacMillan.

During an extended tour of Australia in 1958 Miss Seymour danced the roles of Dawn in *Coppélia*, a lead Wili in *Giselle*, and the White Skater in Ashton's *Les Patineurs*, as well as soloist parts in *Les Sylphides* and in Andrée Howard's *La Fête Étrange* and *Veneziana*. Her first attempt at the dual role of Odette/Odile in *Swan Lake*, at a performance in Melbourne, so impressed the company's assistant director that he immediately arranged her Covent Garden debut in that classic. Partnered by Donald MacLeary, she captivated the dozens of critics who attended the sold-out performance on May 6, 1959. Clive Barnes spoke for his colleagues in his ecstatic review for the *Spectator*: "From her first entrance, swooping in with the untroubled dignity of a young Russian, she instantly showed that rare ballerina quality, recognizable, but elusive. . . . Even at this early stage there is an individuality about her movements that sets her apart."

Many balletomanes saw in the soft, melting movements of Miss Seymour's sensitively interpreted Odette an astonishing resemblance to the young Margot Fonteyn. Her portrayal of Odile, the alluring seductress, was emotionally accurate, but stylistically weak, mainly because of technical deficiencies. Critics noticed, among other things, "uneven" and "blurred" technique, "fussily executed" transitional steps, and a tendency to flag in the virtuoso Black Swan variations. Perhaps for those reasons, Miss Seymour stopped dancing *Swan Lake* in the mid-1960s, except for a single performance with American Ballet Theatre in 1976. "It's been drummed into me that my technique is shoddy," she admitted to John Gale, who interviewed her for a Toronto *Globe and Mail* (June 5, 1965) profile. "As you get older you get more full of fear and doubt. When it comes to the classics, I fear that I'll be the shame of the opera house. I like best doing ballets that I created."

In April 1960, not long after she was advanced to the rank of principal dancer in the Royal Ballet, Lynn Seymour created the role of the Bride in MacMillan's version of *Le Baiser de la Fée*. But it was her affecting portrayal of the violated young girl in his *The Invitation*, a psychological ballet tailor-made for her which had its première at the New Theatre in Oxford, England on November 10, 1960, that confirmed Lynn Seymour as a dramatic dancer of enormous talent. Her transformation from a dewy-eyed adolescent just awakening to an idyllic romance with a sensitive boy to a disillusioned young woman emotionally shattered by a brutal rape, astounded audiences and critics alike. In reviewing the American première of the ballet for the *Christian Science Monitor* (May 7, 1963), P. W. Manchester applauded Miss Seymour for giving "one of the towering danceractress performances of our time." Allen Hughes, writing in the *New York Times* (May 11, 1963), concurred: "[Her performance] was touching and agonizing and as real as any that an actress could make. Nothing was exaggerated; nothing was underdone."

Despite a series of illnesses and injuries that included a torn Achilles tendon and a bout with the flu that prevented her from dancing in the première of MacMillan's *Symphony*, Miss Seymour added a number of ballets to her repertory in the early 1960's, among them *Napoli Divertissement*, *La Boutique Fantasque*, and revivals of Ashton's *Birthday Offering* and *Cinderella* and of MacMillan's *Danses Concertantes* and *Solitaire*, a witty, semiabstract ballet in which she revealed an unexpected comic flair. MacMillan chose Miss Seymour and Christopher Gable, a frequent partner, to dance a central pas de deux in his lyrical *Images of Love*, and Ashton, sensing her willingness to subordinate technique to total expressiveness, tapped her for the pivotal role of the Young Girl in his *The Two Pigeons*.

Notwithstanding her aversion to the romantic classics, Miss Seymour also tackled the technically taxing title roles in *La Sylphide*, *La Bayadère*, *The Sleeping Beauty*, and *Giselle*. "They're very demanding and not that rewarding," she said, as quoted in *Quest/79* (July-August, 1979). "But the classics are important as a measuring rod. For me those roles are like medicine. You know they're good for you." She was particularly effective as the frail peasant girl in *Giselle*. Although the solidly built dancer seemed at times to be more "earthbound" than impalpable as Giselle's spirit, most critics conceded that the emotional depth of her interpretation transcended occasional lapses in technique.

Because he never asked her to play, as she once put it, "a wafty, off-this-earth character," Miss Seymour naturally gravitated toward MacMillan's ballets. Like him, she is fascinated by themes of alienation and frustration, by "those strange dark areas of life." In 1964 MacMillan worked closely with Miss Seymour in creating the role of Juliet for his full-length version of *Romeo and Juliet*. He saw Juliet as the ballet's motive force—a headstrong, passionate young woman who defies the conventions of her society. Although that interpretation was ideally suited to Miss Seymour, Dame Margot Fonteyn, partnered by Rudolf Nureyev, danced the role in the ballet's première in February 1965. In subsequent performances Miss Seymour and her partner, Christopher Gable, danced with more passionate abandon than Fonteyn and Nureyev and stressed the dramatic elements of the choreography.

Over the years Miss Seymour matured into "the most sensual of Juliets," in Anna Kisselgoff's opinion, and "the most truly Shakespearean," in Alexander Bland's. Lending additional impact to her masterful characterization were the emotional nuances of her gestures and attitudes in the nondance moments. "Her way of tossing her head—only slightly—hither and yon and letting her hands, like agitated butterflies, take off from the swaying stalks of her arms is utterly moving," John Simon wrote in his review of a performance of *Romeo and Juliet* for *New York* magazine (April 23, 1976). "With the passage of years, some of her adorable kittenishness seems less spontaneous, but she has grown in inner resources that spend themselves in fireworks of feeling."

Dissatisfied with the dwindling opportunities available to her as one of about a dozen accomplished ballerinas in the classically oriented Royal Ballet, Lynn Seymour left the company in 1966 to join Kenneth MacMillan, who had just taken over as the ballet director of the Deutsche Oper, in West Berlin. Just four months after her arrival, Miss Seymour led the company in three acclaimed MacMillan productions, including *Concerto*, a plotless ballet of pure dance. For most of the following year, however, she was sidelined with a succession of illnesses, ranging from acute glandular fever to thrombosis in her right shoulder. She recovered sufficiently to dance the grueling role of Anna Anderson, an apparently deranged woman beset by hallucinations who claims to be the youngest daughter of Tsar Nicholas II, in the première of MacMillan's *Anastasia*, a one-act psychological ballet. She later danced in his *Olympiade* and in his productions of the romantic classics

When MacMillan returned to the Royal Ballet in 1970 as its director and resident choreographer, Miss Seymour reestablished her relationship with that company as a guest artist. "My first allegiance is to the [Royal]," she said, "but this gives them and me more freedom." Capitalizing on Miss Seymour's gift for building a role over three long acts, MacMillan immediately set to work on a full-length version of *Anastasia*. The new ballet followed Anastasia from a carefree childhood through a debutante ball to the ward of a mental hospital where, as Anna Anderson, she recalls the characters and events of her life and fights for recognition as the sole survivor of the Imperial family.

Miss Seymour headed a star-studded cast that included Svetlana Beriosova, Derek Rencher, Antoinette Sibley, and Anthony Dowell in *Anastasia's* world première in July 22, 1971. The critical reception was generally lukewarm, but reviewers were virtually unanimous in their praise of Miss Seymour's stunning portrayal. As Mary Clarke observed in a review of a later performance for *Dancing Times* (March 1975): "That first, tomboy entrance on roller skates, the little face brimming with mischief and happiness catches the heart and Seymour never lets you go. Her total involvement with the family pleasures and worries of the first act, her shy, yet proud coming-out ball . . . and the final torments of Anna Anderson, are built into what is now surely one of the great performances of twentieth-century ballet."

Among the many other ballets new to Miss Seymour's Royal Ballet repertory were Jerome Robbins' *Dances at a Gathering* and *The Concert;* Glen Tetley's abstract *Laborintus;* the "Friday" pas de deux in Ashton's *Jazz Calendar;* the circusy *Side Show;* MacMillan's *The Four Seasons* and the "Celebration and Prayer" movement in his Japanese *Rituals;* and *Brahms Waltzes,* a solo that Ashton choreographed in the manner of Isadora Duncan especially for her. She also created the roles of Mary Vetsera, in MacMillan's *Mayerling* and, partnered by Anthony Dowell, the courtesan Manon Lescaut in his *Manon.*

Dowell was also her partner in Ashton's *A Month in the Country,* a one-act ballet inspired by Turgenev's play. Miss Seymour was eloquent and mercurial as Natalia Petrovna, the capricious wife whose dull existence is enlivened, then shattered by an affair with her son's tutor. Of her performance in that ballet, John Percival wrote in the Toronto *Globe and Mail* (February 24, 1976): "Who else could convey in a movement such a delicate balance of flirtatiousness and boredom when she responds to Rakitin's admiration? And who, from such a deliciously comic beginning, could go to such bitter anguish at the end? . . . Like Fonteyn's Marguerite, Seymour's Natalia Petrovna shows a great dancer at full stretch. The genius which Kenneth MacMillan first revealed in young Seymour is in full flower, and you will go a long way before finding a dance actress to beat her."

Miss Seymour expanded her repertory still further through guest appearances with the London Festival Ballet, the Stuttgart Ballet, the National Ballet of Canada, the Alvin Ailey American Dance Theatre, and American Ballet Theatre, dancing leading parts in such ballets as John Cranko's *Romeo and Juliet,* Roland Petit's *Kraanerg,* Antony Tudor's *Pillar of Fire,* and Ailey's *Flowers,* a rock ballet based on the life of Janis Joplin. As a regular guest artist with such varied companies, Miss Seymour has danced with some of the finest premiers danseurs in the world, including Rudolf Nureyev, Ivan Nagy, Egon Madsen, Peter Martins, Alain Dubreuil, Desmond Doyle, and David Wall. Many critics thought that her partnership with Christopher Gable, in the mid-1960's, was on par with that of Alicia Markova and Anton Dolin or Fonteyn and Nureyev. Because he has, in her words, "such marvelous force" that he "sustains the whole performance," Nureyev remains a favorite partner.

In the mid-1970's Miss Seymour decided to try her hand at choreography. Her earliest efforts, *Breakthrough* and *Two's Night Ride,* which she has described as "a very sensual encounter," were performed at Royal Ballet workshops. Later works—*Rashomon, The Court of Love,* and the semiautobiographical *Intimate Letters*—were incorporated into the Royal Ballet's repertory and *Gladly Badly Sadly Madly,* the result of a collaboration with the American choreographer Robert North, was produced by the London Contemporary Dance Theatre.

Rashomon, The Court of Love, and *Intimate Letters* were among the ballets Miss Seymour scheduled for presentation during her first season as director of the Bayerische Staatsoper in Munich, Germany. Attracted by the opportunity to direct and choreograph as well as perform, she signed her two-year contract in October 1978 and took over the administration of the seventy-member company a few weeks later. The opening-night audience, already annoyed because Miss Seymour had snubbed such beloved Munich dancers as Konstanze Vernon and Peter Breuer and invited Richard Cragun, a principal dancer with the Stuttgart Ballet, to partner her in *Romeo and Juliet,* responded rudely to a mixed program that included an undistinguished performance of Harald Lander's *Etudes,* Youri Vamos' *I Want You To Be Well,* and *Intimate Letters.* According to Horst Koegler of *Dance* (March 1979), *Intimate Letters* showed "such utter misunderstanding of [Leos] Janácek's music that people didn't only boo, but just laughed the ballet off the stage." He added, "There is now such a hostile climate in Munich that her chances for survival look dim."

Physically, Lynn Seymour is the antithesis of the stereotypical fragile, long-limbed ballerina. Standing five feet four inches tall, she is, as one interviewer remarked, as "sweetly rounded" as any Degas dancer. She has a round face, a button nose, large brown-black eyes, and short black hair. In spite of the intermittent aches and pains and the recurrent injuries, Miss Seymour claims to derive a sense of well-being from dancing. "Sometimes, of course, the constant drill of rehearsal makes you feel like a punch-drunk boxer," she said in one recent interview. "But such intense concentration is also a form of meditation. You come out of yourself and face problems that may have seemed beyond your control—like turns that haven't worked well."

To unwind, the dancer reads, listens to music, goes to the movies, and watches television, particularly *The Muppet Show.* Miss

Seymour, who married Philip Pace, a photographer, on January 7, 1974, lives in an Edwardian house in the Chiswick section of London with her three sons—Jerzy and Adrian, the twins, and Demian. An earlier marriage to Colin Jones, a dancer turned photojournalist, ended in divorce. In 1976 Miss Seymour was named a Commander of the Order of the British Empire.

References: Dance 37:55+ Je '63 pors; Dancing Times 66:21+ O '75 pors; Toronto Globe and Mail mag p12+ Je 5 '65 pors, p35 F 12 '77 pors; London Observer p11 F 29 '76 pors; Macleans 76:16+ Ag 10 '63 pors; N Y Times p42 My 3 '76; Gruen, John. The Private World of Ballet (1975); International Who's Who, 1978-79; Who's Who, 1979

Shannon, William V(incent)

Aug. 24, 1927- United States Ambassador to Ireland; journalist; author. Address: b. Embassy of the United States, 42 Elgin Rd., Ballsbridge, Dublin 4, Ireland; h. The American Residence, Phoenix Park, Dublin 12, Ireland

William V. Shannon, the United States Ambassador to Ireland, was once described by Brock Brower of *New York* magazine (October 21, 1974) as "a voice from Washington that speaks with moral seriousness about politics."

The son of an Irish immigrant, Shannon had behind him a career of more than a quarter of a century as a reporter, editor, and columnist, first with the New York *Post* and more recently with the New York *Times,* when President Jimmy Carter nominated him to his present diplomatic post in June 1977. In addition to his journalistic pieces on international affairs, domestic politics, and the environment, Shannon is the author of a definitive history of the Irish in the United States and of a biography of the late Robert F. Kennedy. He has acquired a reputation as an astute observer of the Washington scene, especially during the troubled Presidency of Richard Nixon.

William Vincent Shannon was born in Worcester, Massachusetts on August 24, 1927, one of the five children of Patrick Joseph Shannon, a carpenter who emigrated from Ireland in 1910 and settled in Worcester, and of Honora Agnes (McNamara) Shannon. His brother, John J., and his sisters, Mary (Mrs. Warren J. Willett), Margaret (Mrs. Robert McLoughlin), and Clare (Mrs. John E. Graham), still live in Worcester. Interested since boyhood in public affairs, Shannon credits his brother and some of his teachers with inspiring him to become a historian and journalist. He was educated in Worcester public schools, and at South High School, from which he graduated in 1944, he took part in dramatics and public speaking and edited the senior yearbook. He then studied on a Theodore and Mary Ellis scholarship in history at Clark University in Worcester, where his extracurricular activities included debating, dramatics, and serving as president of its international relations club. In 1947 he obtained his B.A. degree from Clark University *magna cum laude.*

Continuing his studies at Harvard University, Shannon remained there for an additional year of graduate work after obtaining his M.A. degree in history in 1948. Arthur M. Schlesinger Jr., one of his Harvard professors, remembered him more than a decade later as "the most brilliant student" he ever had. In 1949, while a research associate at the Massachusetts Institute of Technology, Shannon served as associate editor of Elting E. Morison's eight-volume *Letters of Theodore Roosevelt* (Harvard Univ. Press, 1951-54). From 1949 to 1951 he did free-lance writing in Washington, D.C. for such liberal weeklies as *Commonweal* and the *New Republic*. He was also a reporter on the staff of the political columnist Robert S. Allen, assigned to matters of the State Department, and he contributed the chapter on Massachusetts to the volume *Our Sovereign State* (Vanguard, 1949), an indictment of state governments, edited by Allen.

With Robert S. Allen, Shannon collaborated on the book *The Truman Merry-Go-Round* (Vanguard, 1950), a collection of anecdotes and sketches about life in Washington that was somewhat critical of the administration of President Harry S. Truman. Although the book was not financially successful, it evoked some favorable comment. Writing in the *New Republic* (November 13, 1950), A. H. Uhl called it "a welcome political purgative" and "a fighting indictment of the shoddy and anemic reporting that floods out of Washington each day." And Bert Andrews, appraising it for the *Saturday Review of Literature* (October 14, 1950), found it "entertaining" and "interesting" but added the proviso that "it should be taken with a large grain of salt."

From 1951 to 1957 Shannon was Washington bureau chief and correspondent for the New York *Post*. He joined its staff on the day, in April 1951, before President Truman dismissed General Douglas MacArthur, and he later covered the MacArthur Senate hearings. In a column for the *Post* (August 1, 1961), reviewing his work of the preceding decade, Shannon remembered that he had "as exciting a debut as any political writer could desire." He felt that the Truman-MacArthur disagreement over Korean war strategy and the broader United States foreign policy issues of that time "ranked in importance with the debates on the League of Nations in 1919-20 and on neutrality and intervention in 1939-40" and concluded that he would always be grateful for having had "a front row seat when this history was being made." Shannon accompanied Adlai E. Stevenson on his 1952 Presidential campaign which, he recalled, "had a moral unity and an esthetic integrity that few human experiences of any kind have."

In his column on national affairs, which he wrote for the New York *Post* from 1957 to 1964, Shannon expounded a liberal but staunchly anti-Communist viewpoint. He castigated the administration of President Dwight D. Eisenhower for "not mobilizing the full energies of the American people in fighting the political cold war," and in the early 1960's he criticized Senator J. William Fulbright and others for their efforts to ease cold-war tensions. According to editor James A. Wechsler, writing in the New York *Post* (March 30, 1964), Shannon seemed to adhere to the view "that the conflict between East and West remains a holy war and that nothing has happened in the post-Stalin world to change any basic dimensions of the struggle."

On the other hand, Shannon resolutely supported the civil rights struggle. He considered his coverage of sit-in demonstrations in the South during the spring of 1960 to be "the most deeply moving emotional experience" of his first ten years with the New York *Post* and praised the "gallantry and idealism" of the black students who took part in them. Shannon also claimed credit for having "played at least a small part . . . in blocking the respective careers of Joseph McCarthy and Richard Nixon." As for John F. Kennedy, he was sympathetic but skeptical. Warning against a Kennedy personality cult, he asserted in early 1961 that it "can only lead to an unhealthy disillusionment" as the President "engages in the awkward shifts, evasions, and compromises that inevitably accompany the exercise of great power."

In his book *The American Irish* (Macmillan, 1964; rev. ed., 1966) Shannon tried to present a definitive historical study of the Irish in the United States in such areas as politics, literature, the performing arts, sports, and law enforcement with special emphasis on the role of the Roman Catholic Church. "My principle in organizing this book has been to emphasize those activities in which the presence of the Irish has made a significant difference," Shannon wrote in his preface. The book took him a long time to complete, and he had been ready to abandon it at one point, but he finally finished it at the urging of his wife, who told him: "Look, it's like a pile of wet laundry down in the cellar. You just have to pick it all up and iron it."

The critical reception of *The American Irish* was generally favorable. "It will take considerable scholarship and good writing to undermine Shannon's positions, . . ." Paul Gavaghan wrote in *America* (February 1, 1964). "Although the author applies modern-day liberal standards to eras that never heard of them, . . . most of his judgments will stand the test of time." J. F. Powers, in *Book Week* (January 12, 1964), cited Shannon's skill in compressing a short history of Ireland into "one of the best chapters in the book" and praised his digests of the principal works of such writers as F. Scott Fitzgerald, James T. Farrell, Eugene O'Neill, and John O'Hara.

He felt, however, that the "good guys"—as compared with such "villains" as Senator Joseph R. McCarthy and Father Charles E. Coughlin—emerged as rather dull and colorless in the book. "They couldn't very well be left out of their own history," he wrote, "but the truth is they haven't helped the book by their presence. This was one of the literary difficulties confronting the author, and it remains one for the reader."

In 1964 Shannon left the New York Post and joined the editorial board of the New York Times, a move prompted in part by his desire to be a more influential writer. He felt that, although his New York Post column appeared in newspapers in various American cities, it had little impact in Washington, D.C. He therefore welcomed the opportunity to go to the Times as an editorial writer on national affairs. Shannon lived with his family in New York City until 1967, when, partly because of the high cost of living, he returned to Washington. In addition to contributing unsigned editorials, he began in 1968 to write occasional columns under his own name, his first in almost four years, filling in on the Op-Ed page when such regulars as Russell Baker, James Reston, or Tom Wicker were on vacation.

In his next book, The Heir Apparent; Robert Kennedy and the Struggle for Power (Macmillan, 1967), Shannon presented a political biography that was, according to a reviewer for Time (October 6, 1967), "often severely critical" but "always dispassionate in its analysis and at times sympathetic." Reflecting a consensus of critical opinion, Eliot Fremont-Smith of the New York Times (September 23, 1967) called it "doubtless one of the most honest and balanced" of the books written about Robert F. Kennedy in that pre-election year. Cabell Phillips, in the New York Times Book Review (October 29, 1967), found the book informed "with the professional's understanding of politics and the political mentality," while V. S. Navasky, reviewing it for Book World (October 22, 1967), observed that Shannon had provided "sound, Times-depth sketches of state and local politics and politicians, and the contexts and environments" in which Kennedy had to operate. Among the few negative reviews was that of Raymond A. Sokolov, who suggested in Newsweek (October 2, 1967) that Shannon "never really gets under the surface tensions of his hero."

Meanwhile, Shannon continued to write his New York Times columns, in which he proved to be far more outspoken than he had been as an editorial writer. Opposed to Richard Nixon ever since the notorious "Checkers speech" of 1952, and convinced even at that early date that "we had a real con man here," Shannon kept a watchful eye on Nixon's Presidential administration, and it was he

who alerted the Times home office in New York City about the Watergate scandal. Before Nixon's resignation, Shannon supplied the text for a volume of 102 photographs by Stanley Tretick, called They Could Not Trust the King; Nixon, Watergate, and the American People (Collier Books, 1974), with a foreword by Barbara W. Tuchman. Although the text was merely incidental to the pictures, a reviewer for the New Yorker (February 4, 1974) gave Shannon credit for pulling "the loose ends together" and making "a coherent narrative of all that has happened thus far, combining this with a sharp, humane, and often witty comment."

In early May 1977 President Jimmy Carter notified the office of Senator Edward M. Kennedy of Massachusetts that Shannon was his choice for the United States Ambassadorship to Ireland, being vacated by Walter J. P. Curley Jr. Formally nominated by the President on June 20, and confirmed by the Senate on the following day, Shannon took up residence with his family at the 200-year-old ambassadorial mansion in Dublin after being sworn into office on July 11, 1977. At President Carter's urging, Shannon has, among other matters, familiarized himself with the problems of strife-torn Northern Ireland, and he has consulted with Irish Prime Minister John Lynch about steps that might be taken by the United States to help establish peace in Ulster.

A consultant on American politics and a regular contributor to the Economist of London from 1956 to 1964, Shannon was also for several years the Washington columnist for Commonweal magazine. He was on leave of absence from the New York Post in 1961 and 1962 as a fellow-in-residence at the Center for the Study of Democratic Institutions at Santa Barbara, California, where he took part in Robert M. Hutchins' "American Character" project, which studied the changing "moral character of American society." Shannon's specific assignment was to work on problems of ethics in politics. He was chosen by the Alicia Patterson Fund as a traveling fellow in 1969-70 to study political institutions in Great Britain.

Shannon has contributed articles to the Dictionary of American Biography, Notable American Women, Catholic University Law Review, New York Times Magazine, Harper's, Atlantic Monthly, New Statesman, Partisan Review, American Heritage, and other publications. He has lectured at such universities and colleges as Yale, Princeton, Mount Holyoke, Oberlin, Indiana University, Union Theological Seminary, Pennsylvania State University, American University, Georgetown, and the University of North Carolina. Before he became Ambassador to Ireland, he was a lay member of the advisory committee on social development and world peace of the

United States Catholic Conference and a lector at Epiphany Catholic Church in Washington, D.C. He became an associate fellow of Morse College, Yale University, in 1966; a director of the American Irish Foundation in 1969; and a trustee of Clark University in 1975; and he served as national alumni chairman of Clark University's capital fund drive in 1976-77.

Among Shannon's honors are the 1951 New York Newspaper Guild's Page One Award for national coverage and the Edward J. Meeman Award of the Scripps-Howard Foundation, presented to him for his writings on conservation in 1968 and 1976. He has honorary doctorates from Clark University, the College of New Rochelle, Boston University, and Sacred Heart University in Bridgeport, Connecticut. In 1975 the Eire Society presented him with its gold medal, for service to literature.

William V. Shannon and Elizabeth McNelly, a writer, who is a fifth-generation American of Irish descent, were married on August 5, 1961. They have three sons: Liam Anthony, Christopher Andrew, and David Patrick. According to Nan Robertson of the New York

Times (March 16, 1978), the Shannons "are outdoorsy folk" who enjoy the sixty-eight acres of lawns, orchards, and gardens surrounding the American Embassy in Dublin. Shannon, who is six feet tall, weighs 160 pounds, and has gray hair and hazel eyes, has, according to Brock Brower, "a very correct manner, a soft Irish voice that he never quite lets lilt, . . . and an approach to people that is sweetly, elegantly shy." He can run a mile in eight minutes and jogs one and three-tenth miles around the embassy grounds every morning before breakfast. His other recreations include growing roses, reading, and fishing. He is a member of the Cosmos and National Press clubs in Washington, D.C., the Century Club in New York City, Phi Beta Kappa, and Sigma Delta Chi, the honorary journalism fraternity.

References: N Y Post mag p9 Ag 6 '61 por; N Y Times A p9 My 6 '77 por, C p1+ Mr 16 '78 pors; New York 7:60+ O 21 '74; Time 77:72 Mr 10 '61 por; Contemporary Authors 1st rev ed vols 9-12 (1974); Who's Who in America, 1978-79

Shepard, Sam

Nov. 5, 1943- Playwright; actor; musician. Address: b. c/o Lois Berman, 250 W. 57th St., New York City, N.Y. 10019

The extraordinarily prolific Sam Shepard is a genuine American original, an unconventional playwright who has insisted that the

theatre accept him on his own terms—and prevailed. Shepard's independent vision and daring imagination made him a cult figure on Off Off Broadway's pass-the-hat circuit in the 1960's, when he won numerous Obie awards for his quasi-surreal one-act plays. Even after his first full-length play, the apocalyptic, counter-cultural fantasy *Operation Sidewinder*, had its premiere at Lincoln Center in 1970 the critical establishment continued to view him as an "undisciplined," "obscure," or even "obscurantist" *enfant terrible*. Only with his *Curse of the Starving Class* (1977) and *Buried Child* (1978), his superficially farcical but at the same time profoundly mournful epitaphs for the American family as an institution, has the critical establishment accepted him unequivocally as a major, enduring creative talent in the theatre. In addition to writing plays, Shepard has done some acting, most notably in the film *Days of Heaven* (1978), and he has played the guitar and drums professionally. His rock 'n' roll combo, the Holy Modal Rounders, provided the music for some of his stage productions in the early 1970's.

The macabre landscape of a Shepard play is a nightmarish America where myth collides with reality. "Mr. Shepard is a playwright of the American frontier," the critic Mel Gussow has observed, "but his plays generally take place in confined, even claustrophobic rooms. These plays . . . form an abundant body of work, one of the most sizable and tantalizing in the American theatre."

Referring to the best of that work, John Simon has written: "It is powerful, obsessive stuff, intensely theatrical, not always disciplined but always wildly poetic, full of stage images and utterances replete with insidious suggestiveness even if they don't yield unequivocal meanings." Many of Shepard's plays have been published by Bobbs-Merrill.

Sam Shepard was born on November 5, 1943 in Fort Sheridan, Illinois to Samuel Shepard, a career army man, and Jane Schook Rogers. As his father's military assignments changed, the family moved to South Dakota, to Guam, and elsewhere, finally settling in Duarte, California, on a farm where they grew avocados and raised sheep. After graduating from high school in Duarte, Shepard studied agricultural science for a year at San Antonio Junior College before turning to the theatre.

Shepard entered the theatrical world as an actor with a troupe called the Bishop's Company Repertory Players, which toured church communities around the country with plays suitable for religious audiences. "The religious cover was a phoney," Shepard confessed to Michael White when White interviewed him for the *Guardian* (February 20, 1974). "We were really a bunch of frustrated actors who couldn't find a niche."

In 1963 Shepard left the Bishop's Company to seek his fortune as an actor in New York City. To support himself, he took a job as a busboy at the Village Gate, the Greenwich Village cabaret, where Ralph Cook, founder of Theatre Genesis, was headwaiter. Shepard had been trying his hand at poetry, in the then fashionable "Beat" style, and Cook encouraged him to write for the Off Off Broadway theatre. The latter is the New York theatre's noncommercial avant-garde, encompassing at the time such experimental companies—most of them in storefronts, lofts, church basements, and other makeshift sites in Manhattan's East Village—as Theatre Genesis, Cafe Cino, the American Place Theatre, the Open Theatre, the Judson Poets Theatre, and the Cafe La Mama Experimental Theatre Club.

Following Ralph Cook's suggestion, Shepard began turning out one-act plays at a furious pace. Most of the early, rough-hewn plays were actually impressionistic mood pieces expressing with fractured pop-art wit the broodings of a free sensibility awaking to social forces inimical to it. The first to be produced were *Cowboys* and the *Rock Garden*, directed by Cook in a Theatre Genesis production at St. Marks-in-the-Bouwerie Church in October 1964. The last scene of *Rock Garden* was later incorporated into the multi-authored "erotic" Broadway musical *Oh! Calcutta!*

Later in the 1964-65 Off Off Broadway season the Cafe La Mama Experimental Theatre Club staged Shepard's *Up to Thursday, Dog,* and *Rocking Chair.* In retrospect, Shepard has described *Up to Thursday* as "a bad exercise in absurdity" and summarized *Dog* as being "about a black guy—which I later found out it was uncool for a white to write about."

An important milestone in Shepard's career was the decision of Richard Barr, Clinton Wilder, and Edward Albee to include *Up to Thursday* in their New Playwrights series at the Off Broadway Cherry Lane Theatre in February 1965. Three plays by Shepard produced in the 1965-66 season, *Chicago, Icarus's Mother,* and *Red Cross,* won Obie awards (*Village Voice* citations for Off and Off Off Broadway excellence), and *Chicago* was included in *Six From La Mama,* a program of one-act plays presented at the Martinique Theatre in April 1966. *Chicago,* in which a young man stands in a bathtub delivering a monologue about the life swirling about him, typified the angry-young-man theatrical pieces Shepard was creating at the beginning of his career.

A Rockefeller Foundation grant in 1967 and a Guggenheim grant in 1968 gave Shepard the freedom to write full time. His first two-act play, *La Turista,* was given its premiere at the American Place Theatre, then based in St. Clement's Church, in March 1967. On that occasion, Shepard exercised the option of not inviting critics, explaining that he did not see "why everything [has] to be evaluated in terms of success or failure."

Forensic and the Navigators and *Melodrama Play* earned Shepard another Obie at the end of the 1967-68 season. Paired with John Guare's *Muzeeka,* a revival of Shepard's *Red Cross* played to a mixed reception at the Provincetown Playhouse in the spring of 1968. Among the positive reviews was that of Clive Barnes in the New York *Times* (May 28, 1968). After describing Shepard's work in general as an attempt to sever "an umbilical connection with the past," Barnes wrote: "As a result, a play like *Red Cross,* set presumably in some casualty station of the mind, is mysterious simply because it does not play the nice game of drama according to our rules. Two people are arguing in adjacent beds, and we ask, who are they? They tell us what they are doing and how they are feeling, but never for a moment who they are. It is like meeting someone at a party whom you can't quite place. The results that Mr. Shepard gets are very, very funny. But much more than funny, they are stealthily disturbing."

London audiences became acquainted with Shepard's work through Off and Off Off Shaftesbury Avenue productions of *Melodrama Play, Chicago,* and *La Turista* in the late 1960's. In a dispatch to the New York *Times* (April 13, 1969), Charles Marowitz reported that those London critics who were "not wholly dismissive" of *La Turista* agreed on one main point—"the play is baffling." Marowitz went on to observe: "But Shepard is not so much obscure as he is disjointed. His is a quirky, fey, mildly Saroyanesque turn of mind which trusts its changes of direction as totally as the traveler trusts the instincts of the burro carrying him through the foothills of a foreign countryside. . . . If one hadn't seen *Chicago* and read other Shepard plays, *La Turista* would be a perfect case of the emperor's new clothes. But there is a consistency in Shepard and a richness of texture which encourages one to suspend judgment. He is a writer with a cool, idiosyncratic style and one waits to see what he will ultimately deliver."

Michelangelo Antonioni hired Shepard to help write the script for his first American film, *Zabriskie Point* (MGM, 1970), a strident polemic about the radicalization of a "flower child" that was, as one reviewer observed, "bad enough to give anti-Americanism a bad name." The experience was an unhappy one for Shepard, as he told Michael White in the *Guardian* interview: "Antonioni wanted to make a political statement about contemporary youth, write in a lot of Marxist jargon and Black Panther speeches. I couldn't do it. I just wasn't interested."

The influence of Shepard's cinematic stint was evident in both the form and the content of his first three-act play, *Operation Sidewinder*, which was given its premiere at the Vivian Beaumont Theatre by the Repertory Company of Lincoln Center in March 1970. Set in the Hopi Indian country of the American Southwest, and featuring a secret Air Force computer project, a giant mechanical rattlesnake that runs amok, *Operation Sidewinder* delineates the dehumanization of the American spirit in twelve grotesquely satirical scenes, ending with an atomic holocaust. In the Lincoln Center production the scenes were divided by rock music interludes provided by the Holy Modal Rounders, a group described as a "hippie combo" that included Shepard himself.

Even ordinarily sympathetic critics found fault with *Operation Sidewinder*. Jack Kroll of *Newsweek* (March 23, 1970), for example, had this to say: "His plays are rituals of confrontation . . . often richocheting like esthetic shrapnel into the spectators to sting them with signs of the perversity that has taken hold in *their* lives. As in contemporary life itself, in a good Shepard play you can't tell where the horror ends and the joke begins. . . . But in *Operation Sidewinder* the energy has congealed in a half-slick pop machine with the feel of celluloid and the clackey sound of doctrinaire contemporaneity." In retrospect, Shepard himself concedes that the play deserved to fail because he was mistaken in trying to apply film technique to the stage. "That single frame editing kind of thing doesn't work on stage," he said in the *Guardian* interview. "It was very static."

A considerably warmer reception greeted *The Unseen Hand* when that science-fiction western—in which an interplanetary fugitive raises three outlaws from the dead—was given its premiere at the Astor Place Theatre the following month. In the New York *Times* (April 2, 1970), Clive Barnes was facetious, describing Shepard as "perhaps the first person to write good disposable plays. . . . Like Kleenex, he may well overcome." Marilyn Stasio, writing in *Cue* (April 11, 1970), was effusive: "Shepard is an awesomely talented writer with a freedom fixation. . . . Once you accept the basic 'flight patterns,' his outlandishly funny but dead-earnest plays seem perfectly logical within their own zany, surrealistic terms of reality." Later, reviewing a London production of *The Unseen Hand* for the *New Republic* (April 21, 1973), Robert Brustein wrote of Shepard: "He continues to confront American popular culture with a kind of manic exuberance—not exalting its every wart and pimple, like Andy Warhol, but nevertheless considerably turned on, like many of his generation, even by its more brutalized expressions. In a degenerate time, this may be a strategy for survival, and it certainly sparks the energy of *The Unseen Hand*."

In 1971 Shepard moved to England, and he remained there for four years, living in Hampstead. One of his own favorites among his plays, *The Tooth of Crime*—a two-act musical fantasy about an Arizona outlaw-rock star whose "turf," both in music and along the freeways, is taken over by a young gypsy upstart—had its premiere in London in 1972 and its first American production the following year. Critics on both sides of the Atlantic generally tended to see beneath "the fresh and zippy jargon" a reiteration of "ancient myths" and a "deeply old-fashioned" message. As T. E. Kalem noted in *Time* (November 27, 1972), in order to glean what *The Tooth of Crime* is basically about the playgoer must understand Shepard's continuing theme: "Fast cars, mechanical gadgetry, chrome, and plastic values form a symbolic veneer under which, he seems to be saying, older American ideals are shriveling."

Other critics have described Shepard's continuing theme in terms of the degradation or displacement of the artist (seen as the natural hero) in our culture and of the corruption of innocence, a message certainly evident in *Geography of a Horse Dreamer*, a "mystery in two acts" about a young cowboy whose ability to pick horse-race winners when he dreams diminishes when gangsters try to exploit his powers. The premiere of *Geography of a Horse Dreamer* was directed by Shepard himself at the Royal Court's Theatre Upstairs in London in February 1974 and the first American production was directed by David

Schwelzer at the Yale Repertory Theatre the following month. Reviewing a revival of the play, Edith Oliver of the New Yorker (December 22, 1975) called it "one more work of Sam Shepard's incomparable imagination."

After returning to the United States, late in 1974, Shepard settled in California and became playwright-in-residence at the Magic Theatre in San Francisco. When Bob Dylan and his band toured the Northeast with their Rolling Thunder Revue in 1975, Shepard, at Dylan's request, went along as scriptwriter for a projected film of the tour. The film never materialized, but the tour was wittily chronicled by Shepard in words and pictures in Rolling Thunder Logbook (Viking, 1977).

In April 1975 Action, first staged in London the year before, opened at the American Place Theatre, on a bill with Killer's Head, in its world premiere. Killer's Head is a brief, jarring exploration of a man's mind as, the moment before he is executed in the electric chair, his stream of consciousness flows out of habit to plans for the morrow to which he will not awaken. Action, a more substantial work, is a study in inertia, or inaction, set in a dimension where there is "no sound, no time," a "cold space" where four humanoids are celebrating (or uncelebrating) Christmas. "His language reminds us of Pinter," Clarke Taylor observed in After Dark (June 1975); "his landscape of Beckett."

The stifling of creative freedom is again suggested in the musical play Suicide in B-Flat, introduced by Robert Brustein at the Yale Repertory Theatre in 1976. In that "mysterious overture," police investigate the apparent suicide of Niles, a jazz musician who is "playing dead" just as he once "played alive" and who at one point says, "We've all lost our calling." The Magic Theatre in San Francisco in 1976 staged the premiere of Shepard's Angel City, his first clearly autobiographical play, a scathing satire on the temptations that Hollywood sets before young writers.

More theatrically conventional than his previous work was Shepard's bitter three-act tragicomedy Curse of the Starving Class, in which a self-destructive society is reflected in the dissolution of a Southern California farm family. Because of its descent into gross vulgarity, the play stirred controversy when it had its world premiere in London in 1977 and its American premiere in New York City in 1978, but it was generally recognized as a major step forward in Shepard's career. In Cue (March 18, 1978) Marilyn Stasio advised her readers that "you must go with all your wits about you" to appreciate how Shepard opens the play "sneakily, under the false pretense of being a half-satiric, half-serious domestic drama" and then "rips away the dramatic trappings to reveal the inner darkness. It's a hellish place; violent, brutish, and ugly. Like Walt Whitman gone berserk, Shepard sings America in flames. . . . These

people are real and poignant and damned." Curse of the Starving Class brought Shepard his seventh Obie, for Best Play/Best New American Play.

Shepard's Buried Child—another horrific three-act tragicomedy about a decayed rural American family, this an ingrown one harboring guilty secrets of incest and infanticide —opened Off Off Broadway, at the Theatre for the New City, in October 1978 and moved Off Broadway, to the Theatre de Lys, two months later. Even more lucid and accessible than Curse of the Starving Class, Buried Child became Shepard's first real success, as the commercial theatre defines success, in terms of box-office receipts and the endorsement of the critical establishment. Among the rave reviews was that of John Simon in New York (November 27, 1978): "This tale of a silent American farm family that seems to go crazier by the minute—but with a craziness containing both sardonic bite and the gift of holy terror—bears some resemblance to Pinter's Homecoming, which, in my estimate, it surpasses. Here, as in other Shepard works, the effect is rather as if Pieter Bruegel and Hieronymous Bosch had set about improving a Grant Wood canvas, until rustic creepiness grew into manic vitality and visionary madness." On April 16, 1979, the day after it ended its Off-Broadway run, Buried Child won the Pulitzer Prize for drama.

Cowboy Mouth, a rock 'n' roll play written by Shepard and singer-poet Patti Smith and first staged in New York City in 1971 with Shepard himself in the leading role, was given a revival at the Horseshoe Tavern in Toronto, Canada in November 1978. Shepard's Seduced, a two-act fantasy about an ailing eccentric recluse, a character apparently suggested by the late Howard Hughes, opened to mixed notices at the American Place Theatre in February 1979. John Simon (New York, February 19, 1979) attributed the failure of Seduced to an ill-advised effort at Grotowskian "poor theatre" and to Shepard's straining for "a blend of realism and absurdism that comes off only very sporadically."

The versatile, photogenic Shepard turned actor for film director Terrence Malick's Days of Heaven (Paramount, 1978), in which he played an affluent farm owner duped into a tragic marriage with a migrant worker. Critics generally agreed that Shepard was "excellent," "a minor revelation," in portraying the ill-starred farmer with "laid-back grit." "The real surprise of the film," Annette Insdorf wrote in Take One (November 1978), "is playwright Sam Shepard, who creates in his first screen role the most sympathetic, believable, and sustained character."

As a playwright, Shepard is interested in myth and indifferent to "ideas which speak only to the mind." "Myth speaks to everything at once, especially the emotions," he has said. "By myth I mean a sense of mystery and not necessarily a traditional formula. A character for me is a composite of mysteries." He considers theatre and writing "a home" where he brings the adventures of his life and sorts them out, "making sense or nonsense out of mysterious impressions." "I feel that language is a veil hiding demons and angels which the characters are always out of touch with. Their quest in the play is the same as ours in life—to find those forces, to meet them face to face and end the mystery."

Sam Shepard is a tall, soft-spoken, unaffected man whose typical attire includes turtleneck sweaters, jeans, and boots. By temperament he is amiable with a free-wheeling life style, but as his fame has increased he has become increasingly reclusive, protecting his privacy in the manner of a Salinger. Shepard and the actress O-Lan Johnson Dark who were married on November 9, 1969, have a son, Jesse Mojo. In addition to his home in Marin County, California, Shepard owns a farm in Nova Scotia where he grows alfalfa and wheat. When in England, he ran greyhounds bred by him at the Walthamstow and Birmingham tracks.

According to a recent published report, this "prophet of technological mysticism" (as Martin Gottfried has dubbed him) has been steeping himself in the teachings of Georgi Gurdjieff. From time to time Shepard has practised Jack Kerouac's method of jazz-sketching with words in the same way that a musician jams with his instrument. "After periods of this kind of practice," he has said, "I begin to get the haunting sense that something in me writes but it's not necessarily me."

Regferences: Biog N p695 Je '74 por; Guardian p8 F 20 '74 por; Washington Post p1+ Ja 14 '79 pors; Notable Names in the American Theatre (1976); Who's Who in America, 1978-79; Who's Who in the Theatre (1979)

Silberman, Charles E(liot)

Jan. 31, 1925- Author. Address: b. 535 E. 86th St., Apt. 2A, New York City, N.Y. 10028

Over the past fifteen years Charles E. Silberman has combined the talents of an investigative journalist, a perceptive social analyst, and an enterprising researcher to produce national best sellers on three of America's most pressing domestic problems. His latest work, *Criminal Violence, Criminal Justice*, is a provocative, exhaustive examination of crime and punishment in the United States. Earlier, he scrutinized public education in *Crisis in the Classroom* and race relations in *Crisis in Black and White*. Each of those three books—the result of years of painstaking research undertaken with the generous funding of a major foundation—won wide critical acclaim.

In addition to his three major works, Silberman has written, in collaboration with the editors of *Fortune*, *The Myths of Automation* (Harper, 1966), a collection of seven articles on technology and the labor market that had previously appeared, in a slightly different form, in *Fortune* magazine, and he has edited *The Open Classroom Reader* (Random, 1973).

Charles Eliot Silberman was born in Des Moines, Iowa on January 31, 1925, one of the two sons of Seppy Israel Silberman, a salesman, and Cel (Levy) Silberman, a camp director. Reared in New York City, Silberman attended DeWitt Clinton High School in the Bronx, where he was the news editor of the student newspaper. He graduated from high school in 1941 and immediately enrolled in the liberal arts program at Columbia University. From June 1943 to June 1946, he served with the United States Naval Reserve, rising from apprentice seaman to lieutenant (j.g.). He took his B.A. degree from Columbia in October 1946, but remained at the university for three years of graduate work in economics. During that time he worked as a tutor in economics at the City College of New York and as a research assistant in economic history at Columbia.

In 1949 Silberman joined Columbia's faculty as an instructor and lecturer in economics.

Four years later, when his wife became seriously ill and her medical bills outstripped his salary, he decided to switch to a more lucrative writing career. Hired in 1953 as an editor by *Fortune*, a leading business magazine, he wrote about economics and business, governmental economic policy, automation, corporate finance, consumer behavior and, eventually, social problems.

Silberman's first book was the outgrowth of an examination of urban problems commissioned by *Fortune*. "The more I probed," he wrote afterward, "the more apparent it became that just about every urban problem was bound up in some way with the problem of race and racism." After the publication of "The City and the Negro" in the March, 1962 issue of *Fortune*, the public affairs division of the Ford Foundation made a grant of $23,000 to Columbia on Silberman's behalf, enabling him to take a leave of absence from *Fortune* to complete his research and write *Crisis in Black and White*, which was published by Random House in the spring of 1964, at the height of the civil rights struggle.

In the opening chapter, Silberman declared that a solution to the race problem was "not only the most urgent piece of public business facing the United States," but also "the most difficult." Speaking with the no-holds-barred frankness that was to become the hallmark of his work, he admitted that he had deliberately set out to "offend and anger" both blacks and whites because the truth about American race relations was, in his words, "too terrible" not to offend them. Whites, Silberman argued, must bear "the shame" of slavery as well as the blame for the present "racist society," which, he contended, must be transformed for reasons of "political self-interest" and "because it is the only right thing, the only decent thing, to do." Buttressing his inflammatory statements with statistical data, he conceded that "the behavior of a good many Negroes does help perpetuate white prejudice." Negroes are, in general, less ambitious, more sexually promiscuous, and less family-oriented than whites, Silberman wrote. The crime rate among blacks is substantially higher than that among whites, and black students do less well in school and score lower on I.Q. tests than their white counterparts. Furthermore, he added, blacks have, to a large extent, failed to advance in American society, especially in business and the professions.

But rather than manifesting any intrinsic racial inferiority, Silberman emphasized, these statistics reflect the consequences of "350 years of white oppression" and illustrate the demoralizing effects of living under "a system designed to destroy ambition, prevent independence and erode intelligence." To "restore to the Negro the dignity, the initiative and the ambition of which his countrymen . . . have traditionally deprived him" and thus

achieve a peaceful solution to the racial problem, Silberman recommended, among other things, giving blacks the political, social and economic power to influence the decisions that affect them and admitting Negro children to elementary schools at the age of three or four, instead of the traditional five or six, to make up for the cultural deprivation of the slums.

Crisis in Black and White provoked considerable controversy. To some, among them Godfrey Godsell, who reviewed the book for the *Christian Science Monitor*, and Calvin Trillin, who appraised it for *Book Week*, it was "solid and persuasive," a "perceptively accurate diagnosis" of American race relations.

Black spokesmen, from Whitney M. Young Jr., the executive director of the National Urban League, who called the book "exciting and meaningful," to the Black Muslim leader Malcolm X, who prized it because it went "straight to the historical roots of the problem," joined in the general applause. But Saunders Redding, a specialist in black history, was highly critical of Silberman's "confused and confusing" work. Writing in the New York *Times Book Review* (May 31, 1964), he dismissed *Crisis* as "a muddle of history, anthropology, sociology, social psychology and today's headlines; a welter of speculations, opinions and conclusions; a jumble of truths, halftruths and untruths." Worst of all, he added, Silberman's "distorted history" gave the impression that "justice and equality when they come will be a special dispensation for which Negroes are unworthy." Notwithstanding his criticisms, Redding admitted that the book "had positive values" because it reflected "the kind of social and moral commitment that is badly needed." *Crisis in Black and White* won the Four Freedoms Literary Award and the National Conference of Christians and Jews Superior Merit Award.

Silberman returned to his editorial duties at *Fortune* after the publication of *Crisis in Black and White*, but in 1966 he took another leave of absence to direct a $300,000 educational research project commissioned and funded by the Carnegie Corporation of New York. Three and one-half years of research and writing, including visits to 250 schools by Silberman and his staff, produced his second major work, *Crisis in the Classroom; The Remaking of American Education* (Random, 1970)—a book that went far beyond its original goal of examining teacher education to analyze what was wrong with American schools at all levels, from the elementary school to the university, and to suggest ways to improve them.

In his wide-ranging indictment of American education, Silberman charged the public school system with the "mutilation" of children's spontaneity and "sense of self." Most American schools, he wrote, are "grim, joyless places," where teachers and principals, in an unconscious display of "contempt . . . for children as children," slavishly follow an "intellectually sterile and esthetically barren" curriculum and maintain discipline by strictly enforcing "oppressive and petty" rules and regulations. Even in schools in middle- and upper-class neighborhoods, that authoritarian "preoccupation with order and control" effectively crushed students' curiosity and their ability and desire to think and act for themselves, resulting in a type of education that Silberman considers merely training for docility.

Blaming the unfortunate state of affairs on the "mindlessness" of teachers and school administrators, Silberman complained. "It simply never occurs to more than a handful [of them] to think seriously or deeply about the purposes or consequences of education." Nevertheless, he insisted that public schools in the inner cities as well as in the affluent suburbs could be reorganized to "facilitate joy in learning and esthetic expression and to develop character." To that end, Silberman recommended a radical reordering of priorities and a change to the "informal" or "open" classroom, then in wide use in Great Britain and in a handful of progressive schools in the United States. As might be expected, Crisis in the Classroom attracted a great deal of attention among educators and social critics. Voicing the opinion of most of his colleagues, Dr. John Fischer, the president of Columbia University's Teachers College, called it "one of the best studies in education that has appeared in the last twenty years." Ronald Gross, who reviewed the book for Book World (November 1, 1970), agreed that it was "the best diagnosis and prescription for American education available between hard covers," but, like some educators, he criticized Silberman for failing to confront the issue "that schooling is determined not just by intelligence or its lack, but by the vital economic and political interests of those who control it." Although he found little fault with Silberman's "thorough and well-informed" argument, Martin Duberman was a bit perturbed by Silberman's "abstract, compulsive search for the Holy Grail of 'right balance' between children's freedom in the classroom and direction by teachers."

Like its predecessor, Crisis in the Classroom was a best seller, and it won six national awards, including the 1971 John Dewey Award from the United Federation of Teachers, and the National Council for the Advancement of Education Writing award for the book published in 1970 that contributed most to the public understanding of education. Moreover, it brought Silberman such an avalanche of mail from concerned parents and teachers that he quit his job at Fortune in 1971 to devote all his time to lecturing and writing on informal education as a recipient of a Field Foundation fellowship.

In 1972 Silberman was hired by the Ford Foundation to head its Study of Law and Justice, a $537,000 research project that culminated in his most recent book, Criminal Violence, Criminal Justice, published by Random House in November 1978. Believing that most crime studies are "stale and shallow," Silberman and his staff, supported by a fifteen-member advisory board of judges, lawyers, scholars, and criminologists, studied the literature, conducted field research in police stations, courtrooms, jails, reform schools, and group homes, and interviewed criminals, policemen, attorneys, parole officers, prison guards, and judges. After six years of intensive research, Silberman concluded, as he wrote in his foreword, that "most of what is believed about crime and about the criminal justice system is false or irrelevant." "My goal is not simply to correct errors and clear up misunderstandings," he added. "It is to change the way Americans think about criminals and crime and about the operation of our system of criminal justice."

Historically, violence is "as American as Jesse James," Silberman observed, and criminal behavior is "endemic in every sector of American society." (While he was working on the book, Silverman's home and that of his son and daughter-in-law were burglarized.) But since the early 1960's, the country has been "in the grip of a crime wave of epic proportions." Increasingly, the most feared violent crimes are committed largely by young, poor minority group members—a fact that Silberman attributed to the dehumanizing environment of inner-city slums. Theft "is in the very air that lower class youngsters breathe," he explained. But young black men commit a disproportionately high percentage of those violent crimes—several times higher than other, statistically poorer, minorities, such as Puerto Ricans and Mexican-Americans. Although blacks comprised just 11.5 percent of the population in 1976, Silberman reported, "59 percent of those arrested for robbery were black . . . , more than half those arrested for murder, nearly half those arrested for rape, and two-fifths of those arrested for aggravated assault were black."

The reason for the recent explosion of black violence, Silberman argued, is neither genetic nor cultural. (The homicide rate in Africa is "about the same as in Western Europe.") Violence is "something black Americans learned in this country," the result of slavery, oppression, and racial discrimination. "When one reflects on the history of black people in this country," Silberman added, "what is remarkable is not how much, but how little black violence there has always been." In the past fifteen years, however, young blacks have begun to act out the long-standing hatred of whites that had for generations been sublimated in fantasy, myth, and other cultural devices. "After 350 years of fearing whites, black Americans have discovered that the fear runs the other way, that whites are intimidated by their very presence," Silberman wrote. "It would be hard to overestimate what an extraordinarily liberating force this discovery is." He is quick to add, however, that "to excuse violence because black offenders are the victims of poverty and discrimination is racism of the most virulent sort; it is to continue to treat black people as if they were incapable of making moral decisions or of assuming responsibility for their own actions and moral choices."

Shattering a long-held myth, Silberman maintained that his research proves there is no reason to believe that stricter law enforcement and tougher sentencing would noticeably reduce crime. Although they often appear to be inefficient and unjust, the criminal courts work remarkably well. They are neither hamstrung by Supreme Court decisions protecting defendants' rights nor more lenient than they used to be. Furthermore, he denied that disparate sentencing practices and plea bargaining undermined the administration of justice. "Most important of all," Silberman wrote, "it is not true that the guilty escape punishment. . . . Most of those who should be convicted are convicted, and most of those who should be punished are punished."

Silberman's major criticism of the courts was that while they effectively mete out justice, "almost none of them appears to do justice." Most "undermine respect for law—not by their results, but by the shabby, haphazard way in which they are run." He was especially critical of the juvenile courts, which, he argued, are too harsh on juveniles charged with such relatively minor offenses as "incorrigibility," "ungovernability," and truancy, and too easy on those who commit serious crimes. He also came down hard on the prison system, where violence against inmates by guards has been replaced by violence by inmates against one another, especially by black prisoners, who have become "the dominant caste," against whites.

Although he readily conceded that there are "no easy or cheap solutions" to the problem of violent crime, Silberman suggested as possible short-run answers the establishment of community-controlled renovation and self-help projects to improve living conditions in the cities and the development of more humane correctional methods. But he emphasized that if criminal violence was to be reduced to "a tolerable level," poverty, inequality, and racial discrimination "must be eliminated as significant factors in American life."

Most critics agreed with Silberman that *Criminal Violence, Criminal Justice* was "a gloomy book," but virtually all of them recognized its importance to the study of criminology. "Thorough," "provocative," and "almost lyrically well-written," its greatest contribution, according to most reviewers, was its astute analysis of the relationship of poverty to crime and of race, culture, and crime. One of the few dissenting voices was that of Roger Wilkins, who commented on the book for the New York *Times* (March 6, 1979). In an otherwise favorable appraisal, he questioned Silberman's "failure finally to come fully to grips with the issue of racism —the force that may make this set of problems insoluble."

An enthusiastic and energetic man with blue eyes and a full head of curly gray hair, Charles Silberman stands six feet one inch tall and weighs 182 pounds. He keeps in trim by playing tennis and jogging. He and his wife, Arlene (Propper) Silberman, a free-lance writer, were married on September 12, 1948. They have four sons, David, Richard, Jeffrey, and Steven. After having lived in Mt. Vernon, New York for fifteen years, the Silbermans recently moved to Manhattan's Upper East Side. The new location makes it easier for the pair to indulge their passion for concerts, plays, and ballets. An active Jewish layman, Silberman is a director of the Synagogue Council of America and the Institute for Jewish Policy Planning and Research.

References: Newsweek 77:60+ My 3 '71 por, 92:134 O 23 '78 por; People 11:45+ F 19 '79 pors; Pub W 214:8+ O 16 '78 por; Time 96:57 N 2 '70 por, 112:76+ N 6 '78 por; Who's Who in America, 1978-79

Simon, Herbert A(lexander)

June 15, 1916- Economist; psychologist; computer scientist. Address: b. Department of Psychology, Carnegie-Mellon University, 500 Forbes Ave., Pittsburgh, Pa. 15213

In awarding Herbert A. Simon of the Carnegie-Mellon University the Nobel Prize in Economic Science in the fall of 1978, the members of the Swedish Academy of Sciences cited "his pioneering research into the decision-making process within economic organizations" and acknowledged that "modern business economics and administrative research are largely based on Simon's ideas." Challenging classical economic theory, Simon contends that in a complex world, businessmen lack enough information to make decisions that maximize profits; they therefore merely seek to reach satisfactory targets. Simon's interest in decision-making has also led him into the fields of political science, psychology, and computer science. He has pioneered in developing the computer simulation of thought and has used the results to study the human cognitive processes. Small wonder that the Swedish Academy of Sci-

Herbert A. Simon

ences has described Simon as "one of the greatest of interdisciplinary researchers," and that Richard M. Cyert, the president of Carnegie-Mellon, has said that he is "the one man in the world who comes closest to the ideal of Aristotle or a Renaissance man."

Herbert Alexander Simon, the younger of Arthur and Edna (Merkel) Simon's two sons, was born in Milwaukee, Wisconsin, on June 15, 1916. He attended Milwaukee's public schools, where he found his studies interesting but unchallenging. Meanwhile, as he recalled in an interview with Jeffrey Zaslow for the *Pittsburgher* magazine (February 1979), his father, an electrical engineer, and his mother, an accomplished pianist, taught him that curiosity is the beginning of all science, and the Simon household was run on that conviction. If there was a question or phenomenon the Simons failed to understand, they immediately set out to find the answers and reasons.

When he entered the University of Chicago in 1933, Simon had already decided to be the type of social scientist who applies the same rigorous methodology to his discipline that is employed in the "hard" sciences. His career specialization was more sharply defined when he made an undergraduate field study of the administration of Milwaukee's recreation department, a study that focused his attention upon the process of decision-making in organizations.

After receiving a B.A. degree in political science from the University of Chicago in 1936, Simon became an assistant to Clarence E. Ridley of the International City Managers' Association. In that post he carried out investigations in the field of municipal adminis-

tration, and from 1939 to 1942 he engaged in similar work as director of administrative measurement studies in the Bureau of Public Administration of the University of California at Berkeley. In 1942 he joined the political science faculty at the Illinois Institute of Technology, where he remained for seven years. After submitting a dissertation on decision-making in organizations, Simon obtained his Ph.D. degree in political science from the University of Chicago in 1943.

That dissertation, with modifications and additions, was published by Macmillan in 1947 under the title of *Administrative Behavior; a Study of Decision-Making Processes in Administrative Organization.* In that first seminal study, Simon sharply attacked the sterility of existing administrative theory, primarily in public administration, but not neglecting commercial, industrial, military, and private nonprofit organizations. As Chester I. Barnard explained in his foreword to the book, Simon's objective was to construct a set of tools—a set of concepts and a vocabulary—suitable for describing an organization and the way an administrative organization works. "If any 'theory' is involved," Simon himself pointed out, "it is that decision-making is the heart of administration, and that the vocabulary of administrative theory must be derived from the logic and psychology of human choice."

Building upon his belief in the centrality of the decision-making process in administration, Simon accomplished much of his most influential work over the next ten years. In 1949 he became a professor of administration at the Carnegie Institute of Technology's newly established Graduate School of Business Administration. There during the following decade Simon and his associates, aided by Ford foundation grants, conducted field studies involving observation of decision-making in about ten companies and ran laboratory studies to observe the process under controlled experimental conditions that simulated company environments.

By the mid-1950's Simon had come to the conclusion that in the complex economic organizations of today, individuals cannot possibly process or even obtain all of the information relating to the decisions they must make. He therefore maintained that instead of seeking the most advantageous possible decisions, companies merely try to set goals that represent reasonable achievement levels or minimally acceptable targets, a course of action that he called "satisficing" behavior. In the second edition of his *Administrative Behavior* (1957), Simon spelled out the theoretical implications of his conclusions, noting that classical economic theory subscribes to the belief that the decision maker, known as "economic man," is omniscient and therefore capable of making decisions that maximize profits. Rejecting this construct as unrealistic, he offered in its stead what he referred to as "administrative man," who "satisfices— looks for a course of action that is satisfactory or 'good enough.' "

Defending his controversial conclusions two decades later in a retrospective interview for *Newsweek* (October 30, 1978), Simon recalled that "there was no strong tradition of empirical observation in economics. . . . Economists never thought about watching how men really worked." Although most economists at that time rejected his theories, Simon was not disturbed. "Prominent American economists do not agree," he told Cable Neuhaus of *People* (January 15, 1978). "But they are mistaken." Meanwhile, economists specializing in business operations gave his ideas considerably more credence, and he greatly influenced teaching methods in business schools.

During the mid-1950's his work took a crucial turn. After deciding that the understanding of administrative decisions required a more adequate theory of problem-solving, around 1954 Herbert A. Simon, along with Allen Newell of the Rand Corporation, decided that the right way to study problem-solving was to simulate it with computer programs. They presented to an experimental subject a well-structured problem in logic that required fundamental reasoning processes for its solution. The subject was asked to verbalize his reasoning while solving the problem, after which the basic elements of reasoning were coded onto a program for computer simulation. The program made no specific reference to the subject matter of the problem, but had as its objective the enabling of the computer to solve any problem stated in a certain general form. In short, Simon and Newell were trying to make the computer simulate intelligent, adaptive thought rather than merely perform rote, stereotyped procedures involving no discrimination. Since computers record their own steps, success would provide valuable insight into human thought processes.

Simon regards December 15, 1955 as the most exciting day of his career. "We were working on a logic theorist program, and we finally got it running," he told Jeffrey Zaslow during the *Pittsburgher* interview. "It was then that we knew we had a program that could solve problems in a humanoid fashion." Using general reasoning processes, the computer had solved the same problem as the human subject. That successful experiment was the first example of what was later to be called "artificial intelligence." Subsequently, Simon worked on programs that enabled computers to replicate more complex forms of human thinking. With J. R. Hayes, for example, he developed the "Understand" program, under which computers could cope with poorly structured problems that required an identification and definition of the problem before the application of its problem-solving abilities.

After achieving his initial programming success, Simon continued to investigate the artificial simulation of human thought processes. As a result, his work fell primarily within the academic disciplines of psychology and computer science, although his fundamental intellectual concern remained the area of decision-making. Official recognition of that fact came in 1966, when he became Richard King Mellon University Professor of Computer Science and Psychology at Carnegie-Mellon University (formerly the Carnegie Institute of Technology).

Convinced that psychological research can be greatly advanced by studying how computers simulate human thinking, Simon has reached some basic conclusions about thought processes. The ability to create artificial intelligence, he argues, demonstrates that the mind is an information-processing machine. "My mind works according to laws and mechanisms, not some mysterious mind fluid," Simon told a writer for *Time* magazine (October 30, 1978). Furthermore, he contends, the ability of computers to solve problems using no more than the known, simple elements of human thinking demonstrates that subconscious thought follows the same principles as conscious thought. On the practical plane, Simon contends that by using the information gained about thought through charting the workings of artificial intelligence, people can be taught to be more efficient problem solvers.

His experience with artificial intelligence gave Simon the reputation of being what he called a "technological radical" in the computer science field. John Kobler quoted him in the *Saturday Evening Post* (May 4, 1968) as saying that "in our time a computer will do anything a man can do. They can already read, think, learn, create." He and his associates have programmed computers to play chess, prove thirty-eight out of fifty-two theorems from Bertrand Russell's *Principia Mathematica*, and discriminate between geometrical shapes. In the revised edition of his book *The New Science of Management Decision* (Prentice-Hall, 1977), Simon wrote that "we should avoid the simple assumption that the higher-status occupations, and those requiring the most education, are going to be the least automated. There are perhaps as good prospects technically and economically for automating the job of a physician (but not a surgeon), a corporate vice-president, or a college teacher as for automating the job of the person who operates a piece of earth-moving equipment."

As the most celebrated faculty member at Carnegie-Mellon University, Simon has helped shape the teaching methods at its internationally renowned Graduate School of Industrial Administration. Carnegie-Mellon has challenged the Harvard Graduate School of Business Administration's case study approach with an attempt to provide businessmen with the basic tools they need to learn on their own, an approach that reflects Simon's interest in enhancing the efficiency of overall problem-solving ability. He told a writer for *Business Week* (December 5, 1970) that "if we could somehow teach . . . [the] capacity to learn independently, we wouldn't have to teach the manager anything else." Carnegie-Mellon was one of the earliest advocates of management's use of the computer, and Simon was one of the founders of the university's computer center, rated third in the United States. Simon, who was associate dean of the Graduate School from 1957 to 1973, is the only Carnegie-Mellon faculty member to belong to the university's board of trustees.

Simon's extraordinary intellectual versatility and curiosity are demonstrated by the variety of courses he has taught. They include not only political science, economics, psychology and computer science, but also an undergraduate history course on the French Revolution he took on in 1977. With more than fifteen books and over 500 articles to his credit, he has received honorary degrees from McGill University in Canada, Lunds Universitet in Sweden, and Erasmus Universiteit Rotterdam in the Netherlands, and from three American schools. He won the Distinguished Science Contribution Award from the American Psychological Association in 1969 and the A. M. Turing Award from the Association for Computing Machinery in 1975. He served as chairman of the National Research Council's Division of Behavioral Sciences from 1968 to 1970 and was a member of the President's Science Advisory Committee from 1968 to 1972.

Herbert A. Simon married the former Dorothea Pye, who is now a research associate in Carnegie-Mellon University's psychology department, on December 25, 1937. They live in an eleven-room red-brick house in the Squirrel Hill area of Pittsburgh. The Simons have three children, Kathie, Peter, and Barbara. Simon overflows with ideas and opinions on all subjects. Fond of debating, he sometimes takes both sides of an issue, just for amusement. Simon also enjoys playing the piano, painting, mountain climbing, walking, traveling, and acquiring foreign languages. Indifferent to some of the earthbound details of everyday life, he settles for a snack unless his wife is present to cook dinner and call him to the table. He is so forgetful that he occasionally misses classes. "Isn't absent-mindedness part of the job description?" he asked Cable Neuhaus during the interview for *People*. His deep commitment to Carnegie-Mellon is demonstrated by the fact that for years he has turned over part of his salary to the university. He is a Democrat and a Unitarian.

References: N Y Times III p5 N 26 '78 por; People 11:52+ Ja 15 '79 pors; American Men and Women of Science: Social and Behavioral Sciences, 1978; Who's Who in America, 1978-79

Skinner, B(urrhus) F(rederic)

Mar. 20, 1904- Psychologist; educator.
Address: h. 13 Old Dee Rd.,
Cambridge, Mass. 02138

NOTE: This biography supersedes the article that appeared in *Current Biography* in 1964.

A rigorous scientist who has applied his carefully wrought brand of "radical behaviorism" to broad and pressing social problems, B. F. Skinner is one of the most controversial living figures in the field of psychology. Skinner, a professor emeritus at Harvard University since his official retirement in 1974, has sometimes been dismissed as a "rat psychologist" because of his experimental orientation, but his interests cover a broad spectrum, including linguistics, education, psychotherapy, and social psychology. In 1958 he was cited by the American Psychological Association, which bestowed upon him the Distinguished Scientific Contribution Award, as "an imaginative and creative scientist, characterized by great objectivity in scientific matters and by warmth and enthusiasm in personal contact." Outspoken and passionate in his defense of the application of

scientific methods to social ills, Skinner has been widely attacked for advocating the control of human behavior. But nearly half a century of innovative research, teaching, and problem-solving has left B. F. Skinner with the conviction that man can shape his own destiny "because he knows what must be done and how to do it."

Burrhus Frederic Skinner was born on March 20, 1904 in the small railroad town of Susquehanna, Pennsylvania, to William Arthur Skinner, a lawyer with unfulfilled political ambitions, and Grace Madge (Burrhus) Skinner. His only sibling, a younger brother, Edward James, died in the early 1920's. In the first volume of his projected three-volume autobiography, *Particulars of My Life* (Knopf, 1976), Skinner has described his "warm and stable" childhood shaped by the pleasures as well as by the constraints and inhibitions of small town life in pre-World War I America. An industrious and inquisitive child, he was fascinated by gadgetry and mechanics. "I was always building things," he wrote years later. "I made tops, diabolos, model airplanes driven by twisted rubber bands, box kites and tin propellers which could be sent high into the air with a spool-and-string spinner. I tried again and again to make a glider in which I myself might fly."

In 1922 Skinner graduated from Susquehanna High School, ranked second in a class of seven, then enrolled at Hamilton College, a small men's school in Clinton, New York. Uncertain of his career choice, he majored in English language and literature, with classical and romantic languages as his minor subjects. He had written poetry and short stories throughout his youth and at Hamilton he contributed to the campus literary and humor magazines. Between his junior and senior years, he attended the Summer School of English at Bread Loaf, near Middlebury, Vermont, where he was encouraged in his literary ambitions by Robert Frost. Having been elected to Phi Beta Kappa and having been awarded the Hawley Greek Prize, he took his A.B. degree in 1926.

Heartened by Frost's interest in his work, Skinner spent the year following his graduation writing fiction—mostly short stories—at his parents' home in Scranton, Pennsylvania. "I discovered," he said later, "the unhappy fact that I had nothing to say." As a result of that "disastrous" experiment, he abandoned his hopes for a writing career, though he eventually recognized in his predilection for literature a latent interest in human behavior. Inspired by Bertrand Russell's articles on behaviorism, he read John B. Watson's seminal *Behaviorism* and other books and articles on the relatively new theory and, in 1928, decided to take graduate work in psychology at Harvard University. He was awarded his M.A. degree by that institution in 1930 and his Ph.D. degree a year later.

At Harvard, Skinner was never tempted by Gestalt psychology, much in vogue at that time, or by clinical or abnormal psychology, and he remained relatively uninfluenced by the "science of mental life" championed by Dr. Edwin G. Boring, who was the director of the university's psychological laboratory. "I was determined to become a *scientific* psychologist!" he wrote in his autobiography, and he purposely limited himself, like Watson, to examining the observables to explain behavior.

Skinner's experimental orientation led him, early on, to make the psychology department's machine shop the center of his activity, and it was there that he developed, largely by trial and error, what came to be known as the "Skinner box": a controlled environment for observing and recording patterns of behavior. Working with rats, he shunned the complicated mazes favored by most researchers for a simple box and a simple task (usually, pressing a lever to receive a pellet of food) in which a few variables could be described and measured.

Whereas Pavlovian (or instrumental) conditioning concentrated on the reflective behavior of an animal, Skinner's experiments focused on the spontaneous behavior of an organism in response to its environment. Skinner called that kind of behavior "operant," and when it was positively reinforced by a reward, or negatively, by a punishment, "operant conditioning." He distinguished it from automatic "respondent" behavior, such as Pavlov had studied in his famous experiments with dogs, and in so doing, brought to psychology an established methodology for the investigation and analysis of the interaction of an organism with its environment. His first book, *The Behavior of Organisms* (Appleton, 1938), is a record of some of his early systematic observations.

After receiving his doctorate, Skinner remained at Harvard for five more years to do research in experimental psychology, first as a National Research Council Fellow, then as a Harvard Junior Fellow. In 1936 he moved on to the University of Minnesota, where he was an instructor during the academic year of 1936-37, an assistant professor from 1937 to 1939, and an associate professor from 1939 to 1945. He was awarded a Guggenheim Fellowship for the academic year 1944-45 to investigate the relatively undeveloped field of verbal behavior, which he defined as "the actual behavior of the individual in emitting speech."

From the beginning of his career, Skinner believed that there could be a science of behavior independent of neurological or physiological hypotheses and free from such mentalistic concepts as "mind" or "thinking." By relying wholly upon observable and testable features for his data, Skinner came to be known as a radical behaviorist, and while his antitheoretical bias disturbed many psychologists, it was largely consonant with the contemporary philosophy of science. Skinner assumes that behavior is subject to law, but any inferences as to why this is so, apart from what can be observed, cannot be proved, and therefore should not be made.

The advent of World War II provided Skinner with a unique opportunity for practical application of operant conditioning. In 1940, with the bombing of Warsaw by the Nazis fresh in his memory, he began experimenting with pigeons, which he believed could be trained to guide missiles, such as bombs or torpedos, to intercept and destroy enemy aircraft. He received support from the Office of Scientific Research and Development and, in 1943, a $25,000 government contract, awarded to General Mills, Inc., which had taken an interest in his so-called Project Pigeon, to develop the unconventional homing device. Trained to peck at the center of a target image, the birds were to be placed in the nose of a missile behind a ground-glass plate carrying electricity. The missile's guidance system was to be controlled by electrical impulses generated by the pecking of the pigeons. Although tests proved that the plan was feasible, it was never put into practice.

From 1945 to 1948 Skinner was a professor of psychology and chairman of the department of psychology at Indiana University in Bloomington, Indiana. Although his time-consuming administrative responsibilities occasionally interfered with his research, it was a productive period for Skinner that saw the emergence of a behaviorist movement based on his experimental work. In the spring of 1946 he helped to organize a conference on the analysis of behavior which proved so successful that it became an annual event and, in time, a division of the American Psychological Association. A periodical devoted to the latest research, the *Journal of the Experimental Analysis of Behavior* was established in 1958.

Skinner first gained the attention of the general public in October 1945, when he published an article in the *Ladies' Home Journal* describing the uses and advantages of the "air-crib" that he had built for his second child, Deborah, who spent much of her first two years in that mechanical baby-tender. That device—a crib-sized, air-conditioned, soundproof box with a sliding window of safety glass—was designed to provide an optimum environment for a growing baby, who could sleep or play in it without the benefit of clothing or blankets. The device generated a good deal of public interest, and there were even several attempts to manufacture and market it, most notably, as an "Heir Conditioner." Several prominent pediatricians and child psychologists, however, expressed their reservations about its usefulness, and many laymen inevitably confused the baby-tender with the Skinner box. Years later, Skinner defended his invention in an interview with Tom Zito for a Washington *Post* (April 26, 1946) profile: "The whole idea was to provide the child with a very comfortable, stimulating environment. . . . There were all sorts of things hanging down to provide tactile and visual stimulation. It was really just a special sort of crib."

Skinner returned to Harvard in 1947 as the William James Lecturer and was appointed a regular faculty professor in 1948, the year his controversial novel, *Walden Two* (Macmillan) was published. Conceived and written just after World War II, it is the story of a Utopian community founded on behaviorist principles. Originally titled "The Sun Is But a Morning Star," after a quotation from Henry David Thoreau, *Walden Two* encountered a mixed critical reception. Some reviewers applauded Skinner's effort as, in the words of Charles Poore, who commented on the book for the New York *Times*, "a brisk and thoughtful foray in search of peace, mind, security, and a certain balm for burnt-fingered moderns." Others were repelled by the implications of Skinner's theories. An editorial in *Life* magazine (June 28, 1948) denounced *Walden Two* as a "slander on some old notions of the good life" and as a "corruption" of Thoreau's *Walden*, and Joseph Wood Krutch, in his *The Measure of Man* (1954), accused Skinner of attempting to "perfect mankind by making individual men incapable of anything except habit and prejudice."

Walden Two has been reprinted many times in the past thirty years and the debate over its merit still smolders, particularly on college campuses. In an interview with Michael Hollingshead for *Omni* (September 1979), Skinner confessed that at the time he wrote the book he was "guessing." "I described a world of minimal consumption and minimal pollution and maximal socializing and opportunity for creative behavior," he explained. "It substitutes direct interaction for economic exchanges and police action. . . . It's a world so designed that the behaviors needed to keep it going are automatically reinforced." Several communes, including Twin Oaks in Virginia, and East Wind in Missouri, have been organized according to the guidelines set down in *Walden Two*. Skinner recently visited Twin Oaks and, when questioned about its high turnover, he agreed that all of the inhabitants were not "good behaviorists." Nevertheless, he contended that those who left the commune were in "much better shape than when they arrived." "It's a therapeutic experience for many people who learn how to get along well enough to adjust to the outside world, which is where they may eventually prefer to be," he said.

Skinner continued his laboratory research throughout the 1950's, and his experiments with pigeons, described in *Schedules of Reinforcement* (Appleton-Century-Crofts, 1957), which he wrote with Charles B. Ferster, is considered by many research psychologists to be a model of the experimental analysis of behavior. But his major work dealt with contemporary social issues. After writing *Walden Two*, Skinner felt, in his words, "satisfied that I had solved the major problems inherent in the control of human behavior." Specifying those problems and elaborating upon their solution have provided the focus for Skinner's interest in the ensuing three decades.

One of his first teaching assignments at Harvard was a course in human behavior, a subject for which there was no adequate textbook. To fill that void, he wrote *Science and Human Behavior* (Macmillan, 1953), in which he extrapolated behaviorist principles and theories to the study of a more complex organism—man—and his environment and considered individual and group behavior, as well as the roles of such "controlling agencies" as government and religion. In his reasoned review of the book for *Ethics* (July 1953), Harry Prosch wrote that it presented a "strong, consistent, and all but exhaustive case for a natural science of human behavior."

Two disparate fields touched by the broader implications of Skinner's work were linguistics and education. Always fascinated by the nature and structure of human speech, he had, over the years, taught a course on the psychology of literature, published an article about Gertrude Stein and automatic writing in the *Atlantic Monthly*, tried to predict alliterative tendencies in Shakespeare and Swinburne, and experimented with the epistemology of vocabularies. In 1957 *Verbal Behavior*, the long awaited analysis of language that Skinner had begun while still a Junior Fellow at Harvard, was published by Appleton-Century-Crofts. True to form, *Verbal Behavior* presented a view of language derived from the laws of operant conditioning established by his studies of the behavior of animals. Although Skinner's view has never been widely accepted by linguists, among them Noam Chomsky, who attacked it in the widely praised *Language* (1959), Dr. James A. Dinsmoor observed in an article for *The Handbook of General Psychology* (1973) that "students of conditioning supposed that Skinner had successfully breached and probably overrun the last citadel of circular or mentalistic explanation."

An even more influential development was Skinner's application of behavioral techniques to educational technology. He first became interested in teaching machines and so-called "programmed instruction" after he had visited one of his daughter's arithmetic classes in elementary school and had seen, as he later told an interviewer, "minds being destroyed." Years earlier, he had discovered that he could teach pigeons to play ping-pong by rewarding each correct move with a kernel of corn. He reasoned that the step-by-step techniques of "reinforced" learning were equally applicable to human beings, with the correct answer serving as the reward.

After testing his first teaching machine in his own basic psychology course, Skinner set up programmed learning sessions in several local schools. As he had expected, the students, proceeding at their own paces, learned faster with the machines than with more conventional classroom methods. He discussed the application of behaviorism to education in *The Analysis of Behavior; A Program for Self-instruction* (McGraw-Hill, 1961), written in collaboration with James G. Holland, and *The Technology of Teaching* (Appleton-Century-Crofts, 1968). Although his methods have not of themselves created a revolution in education, many educators and social psychologists believe that Skinner was primarily responsible, for the formulation of "a detailed rationale for such behavioral engineering."

In 1958 Skinner succeeded Boring as the Edgar Pierce Professor of Psychology at Harvard, where he remained, apart from holding a number of visiting professorships, until his retirement in 1974. In 1971 he published his most popular and controversial work, *Beyond Freedom and Dignity* (Knopf), which was followed three years later by *About Behaviorism* (Knopf). He argued that if the human environment were properly managed and organized, the relevance of or need for such notions as "freedom" or "dignity" would vanish. Denying the existence of an autonomous "inner being" in man, he argued for a "technology of behavior" and an acceptance of the concept of "control" as applied to social issues. "Freedom" was, in any case, illusory, since everyone was subject to a subtle and complex system of cultural and environmental rewards and punishments. Commenting on the Skinnerian approach to "social engineering" in the *New Republic* (August 1979), Christopher Lasch, the sociologist, observed: "[Skinner] scandalized liberals by carrying their own premises to unpalatable conclusions. He makes explicit what other progressives prefer to ignore: that the therapeutic morality associated with twentieth-century liberalism destroys the whole idea of moral responsibility, and that it culminates . . . in the monopolization of knowledge and power by experts."

Professor emeritus at Harvard since his retirement, B. F. Skinner is the recipient of the National Medal of Science (1968), the Gold Medal of the American Psychological Association (1971), the Joseph P. Kennedy Jr. Foundation Award (1971), and many other awards. He is a Fellow of the Royal Society of Arts and a member of the National Academy of Sciences, the American Philosophical Society, the American Academy of Arts and Sciences, the American Psychological Association, and professional psychological societies abroad.

On November 1, 1936 B. F. Skinner married Yvonne ("Eve") Blue. They have two daughters, Julie (Mrs. Ernest Vargas), a psychologist, and Deborah (Mrs. Barry Buzan), an artist. Skinner is five feet ten inches tall, weighs about 155 pounds, and has blue eyes and gray hair. For recreation, he prefers indoor gardening, watching old movies on television, and reading the mysteries of Agatha Christie. Before his eyesight began to fail, he played the organ and tinkered in his carpentry workshop.

Skinner claims to apply the principles of operant conditioning to his own life. "I arrange a world in which behaviors I want to strengthen are reinforced," he told Joy Horowitz in an interview for the Los Angeles Times (February 21, 1979). "I apply my own analysis to my own behavior. I never assumed that I was not like my pigeons. I'm sure I am—and very much more complicated, I hope. But as I designed an environment to get some behavior out of my experimental organisms, so I work on the environment to get my own behavior out in ways that are reinforcing to me. That's all there is to it." Skinner has recently voiced concern about the energy problem, nuclear proliferation, and pollution, and he continues to emphasize that "the great danger is not that science will be misused by despots for selfish purposes, but that so-called democratic principles will prevent men of goodwill from using it in their advance toward humane goals."

References: Los Angeles Times II p1+
F 21 '79 pors; Omni 1:76 S '79 por;
Schellenberg James A. Masters of Social
Psychology (1978); Weigel, John. B. F. Skinner
(1977); Who's Who in America, 1978-79

Stabler, Ken

Dec. 25, 1945- Professional football player.
Address: b. Oakland Raiders, 7811 Oakport St.,
Oakland, Calif. 94621

After holding out for a week, Ken ("the Snake") Stabler, the Oakland Raiders' $342,000-a-year quarterback, reported to the Raiders' training camp in Santa Rosa, California in July 1979. The left-handed Stabler went to the Raiders from the University of Alabama in 1968, moved into the starting quarterback position in 1973, and led the team to its first National Football League championship two years later. Hampered by injuries affecting his distance passing, he slumped in 1978 and the Raiders did likewise, failing to make the playoffs for the first time in seven seasons. His acrimonious holdout in 1979 followed what he called "over-the-shoulder remarks to the media" by Al Davis, Oakland's managing general partner, regarding the distribution of blame for the team's sudden decline. "He says I get paid to take the criticism," Stabler commented, "but I don't think it has to be done in the press."

Over the years Stabler accrued a reputation for high living and hard drinking off the field, but at the same time he earned fame for his brilliance and equanimity as a field general. In his youth he was known as a slithery runner (hence his nickname) as well as an accurate thrower of delayed passes, but in pro ball his forte, aside from cool play calling, has been, far and away, his passing. He has an uncanny ability to slice the defense with precise, last-minute touchdown spirals, like someone throwing darts at balloons suddenly appearing out of nowhere. "I don't throw nearly as hard as Bradshaw, Pastorini, Bert Jones, those guys," he has said. "They've got shotguns. My thing is timing and reading defenses. I like to throw the ball over people. You've got to be patient. You just can't go out and smoke it. You have to take what the game will give you."

Ken Michael Stabler was born to Mr. and Mrs. Leroy Stabler on December 25, 1945 in the farming, fishing, and timber town of Foley, Alabama. His father was an auto mechanic who managed a Chevrolet service, his mother was a registered nurse. A natural all-round athlete, Stabler received attractive offers from major league baseball teams when he graduated from high school, but he chose instead to play football at the University of Alabama in Tuscaloosa.

At the University of Alabama, Stabler became, in the words of Coach Paul ("Bear") Bryant, "the best college quarterback I ever saw [in] his junior year." That year Stabler led the Crimson Tide through an undefeated season to victory over Nebraska in the Sugar Bowl. "I thought I was pretty hot stuff, the MVP in the Sugar Bowl and a senior coming back for another year as the regular quarterback . . . ," Stabler recounts in Super Bowl; The Autobiography of Ken "The Snake" Stabler (Pinnacle Books, 1977), written with Dick

O'Conner. "I was running around, drinking, not studying, and not living up to my responsibilities. I was the quarterback and the leader of that team and I wasn't doing the job."

Stabler straightened out fast, after he was suspended by Bryant and admonished in a telegram from Joe Namath, the Alabama quarterback who preceded him to pro fame, that Bryant "means it." Stabler credits Bryant with saving him from a career "pumping gas somewhere." "Bryant taught me about self-sacrifice, discipline, and doing what you're supposed to be doing in order to win. You depend on others and others depend on you. I learned you have a certain obligation to your teammates."

Selected by Oakland in the second round of the 1968 draft, Stabler arrived at the Raiders' camp following a serious knee operation. He was on the injured reserve list throughout the 1968 season, and he was still hobbled by his bad knee when he reported to camp for the 1969 season. Discouraged by marital problems in addition to his physical condition, he packed his bags and left. "I didn't even tell anyone," he recounted in an interview with Ralph Barbieri for *Sport* (October 1975). "I just busted out. I went back to Tuscaloosa and really raised hell. The Raiders finally managed to get hold of me, [but] I sat out the whole year, got a divorce, and finally got to thinking. . . . What the hell was I going to do? Sell something? Hell, I couldn't sell anything; someone would tell me they didn't want it and I'd probably say, 'Fine, let's go get a drink.'" He returned to the Raiders with the determination to persevere and to win that he retains to this day.

Stabler saw a little action in 1970, more in 1971, and still more in 1972, when he came off the bench with a minute left in the playoffs and ran thirty yards for the touchdown that put Oakland ahead of Pittsburgh. But he was unhappy with his uncertain position on the Oakland roster, and when the nascent Birmingham Americans of the World Football League made him an attractive offer, he accepted it, in April 1973. He was to begin playing for Birmingham in 1976, but in the meantime the World Football League died aborning.

Four games into the 1973 season Stabler finally succeeded Daryl Lamonica as starting quarterback. In 1973 he led the Raiders to the title in the AFC-West with the best all-round quarterbacking performance in pro football that year: he topped the AFC in passing, completing 163 of 260 throws for 1,997 yards, fourteen touchdowns, and only ten interceptions, and he broke Sammy Baugh's three-decade-old record for single-game passing efficiency with a percentage of 86.21 against the Baltimore Colts.

The following year the Raiders racked up a 12-2 record as Stabler completed 57.4 percent of his passes for 2,469 yards and twenty-six touchdowns. With twenty-five seconds to go in the playoffs against the Miami Dolphins, he completed the game-winning touchdown pass in dramatic fashion, as he was falling to the ground. The *Sporting News* named him Player of the Year and the Associated Press cited him as the National Football League's Most Valuable Player.

In the 1975 off-season Stabler again underwent knee surgery. Despite the bad knee, he completed 58.4 percent of his passes for 2,296 yards and sixteen touchdowns in 1975. The following year he led the Raiders to their best record ever (13-1) and their first Super Bowl while compiling a completion percentage of 66.7, the highest in pro football since Sammy Baugh's 70.4 in 1945. In addition, his twenty-seven touchdown throws were the most in the NFL since Daryl Lamonica's thirty-four in 1969. In the Super Bowl, Stabler and the Raiders trounced Fran Tarkenton and the Minnesota Vikings, 32-14. Following the Super Bowl victory, Stabler was awarded the Hickok Belt as professional Athlete of the Year.

As of the end of the 1976 season, Stabler had quarterbacked high school, college, and professional teams to a total of ninety-nine victories, seventeen defeats, and two ties, for a winning percentage of .847. In 1977 he led the Raiders into a tie with the Atlanta Falcons for first place in the AFC-West.

In the *Christian Science Monitor* (November 11, 1977) Phil Elderkin observed, "For those who believe that sight is a faculty and seeing is an art, Stabler falls into the latter category. He often finds openings for his passes where only seconds before none seemed to exist." Elderkin quoted Al Davis, the Raiders' managing general partner: "Kenny Stabler is the most accurate passer of all time. Short or deep, he's better than any of the oldtimers or any of his contemporaries. The big thing is that he always throws the ball where his receivers can do something with it. Stabler is the best because nobody taught him how. He was born with that kind of ability and very few have it. I like quarterbacks who can stand back and wait for openings—who can hold the ball and not panic, and then hit their receivers after they've made their break. That way the defense is always trailing the play and almost never gets the interception."

Davis changed his tune the following year, when a split tendon in Stabler's left ring finger and a jammed left elbow prevented him from throwing long passes. Oakland slumped to 9-7 as Stabler threw only sixteen touchdown passes, none of them longer than fifty yards, and was intercepted thirty times. Bay Area sportswriters, most of whom were not aware of the extent of his physical problems, tended to blame his decline on the field on his carousing in private life.

Resenting the questioning of his lifestyle, Stabler stopped talking to reporters. Recently, after resuming communication with the press, he told John Reid of *Sports Illustrated* (August 6, 1979): "Hell, my lifestyle hasn't changed in twenty years. It was all right when we won the Super Bowl, but then we lost some games, and all of a sudden I'm a fat drunk, out of shape, overweight, and all that." He went on to say that he had no intention of changing his ways. "People say, 'You can't do those things as you get older.' Well, if I can't, and it hurts my game, I'll get out. But I'm not going to let football control my entire life. I play and I work as hard as I can, and in the off-season I do the things I like to do. That's not going to change."

A curious incident involving the press took place in January 1979, when Bob Padecky of the Sacramento *Bee* went to Gulf Shores, Alabama, where Stabler lives, to interview him. Padecky was detained by police after they found a key case containing cocaine under the fender of his car. Padecky was released after the police came to the conclusion that he had been "framed." As for his relations with Al Davis, Stabler stopped talking to Oakland's managing general partner after reading remarks by him that he considered pejorative. One of the remarks was, "If you've got to find someone to blame [for the Raiders' decline], then blame Stabler. He makes the most money, and he's paid to take that kind of pressure." In the course of responding to Davis's remarks, Stabler criticized several of his teammates, thus exacerbating his estrangement from the team. Demanding to be traded, he stayed home in Alabama until July 19, 1979, when he finally reported for training. Going into the 1979 season, Stabler's career totals in professional football were 1,182 passes completed for a percentage of 59.6 and 15,463 yards.

Redheaded Ken Stabler is six feet three inches tall, weighs about 215 pounds, and speaks with a soft drawl. He was married twice, to Isabel Clarke, whom he met at the University of Alabama and by whom he has a daughter, Karen, and to Debbie Fitzsimmons. Both marriages ended in divorce. A self-described "hell-raiser," Stabler numbers among his recreations drinking beer in honky-tonks, drag racing, and speedboat racing. He owns several boats and numerous cars, pickup trucks, and dune buggies. In addition to his homes on San Francisco Bay and Mobile Bay, the Oakland southpaw owns shares in three luxury apartment complexes in Alabama, and he runs a football camp for boys in Marion, Alabama.

In an interview with Jack Fincher for *Sports Illustrated* (December 1977), Stabler said that after he retires as a player he would like to concentrate on coaching young boys. "But I wouldn't like to coach higher. I like to stay out late, drink, and chase the women, and that'll get you into trouble in high school and college. As for the pro level, after you've lived with the constant pressure of winning,

why go . . . right back into the same thing? . . . Not that I mind it. But when I retire I want to get away from all that."

References: People 8:83+ N 14 '77 pors; *Sport* 61:55+ O '75; 65:18+ D '77 pors; 69:24+ Je '79 pors; 69:45 Ag '79; *Sports Illus* 47:88+ S 19 '77 pors, 50:42+ Ap 23 '79 por, 51:12+ Ag 6 '79; *Stabler, Ken and O'Conner, Dick.
Super Bowl* (1977)

Steinbrenner, George Michael 3d

July 4, 1930- Industrialist; baseball executive. Address: b. New York Yankees, Yankee Stadium, 161st St. and River Ave., Bronx, N.Y. 10451

The person most responsible for the restored glory of the New York Yankees is the adventurous, extraordinarily energetic shipbuilding magnate George Steinbrenner, who bought into the world's best-known sports franchise in 1973 and is now its principal owner. Once professional baseball's perennial champions, the Yankees went into eclipse in 1965 and remained there until 1977, when "the best team that money can buy" won its first pennant in thirteen years and its first World Series in fifteen. Doubts about the durability of the championship muscle developed through Steinbrenner's lavish, astute shopping in baseball's free-agent market were dispelled in

1978, when the New York team again took the American League pennant and the World Series. But the doubts began to gather again in 1979, when the Yankees slumped miserably; despite a late-season surge, they finished in fourth place in American League East, midway in the standings between the pennant-winning Orioles and last-place Toronto.

Steinbrenner is chairman of the board of the American Ship Building Company, which had an estimated $180 million in sales in 1978. His other ventures include political fundraising (which involved him in a felony conviction in the time of the Watergate scandal), the backing of Broadway plays, an interest in the Chicago Bulls basketball team, ownership of the thoroughbred Kinsman Stud Farm in Florida, and extensive holdings in banking operations and Florida real estate.

The scion of a Great Lakes shipping family, George Michael Steinbrenner 3d was born in Rocky River, Ohio on July 4, 1930—a date the patriotic significance of which is not taken lightly by the Yankee owner, an old-fashioned, unabashed flag-waver. His mother, Rita (Haley) Steinbrenner, who was of Irish descent, imbued him, he says, with compassion for the underdog; his father, of German ancestry, instilled in him a perfectionist will-to-win. "Always work as hard as, or harder than, anyone who works for you," was the constant imperative of the father, a former intercollegiate track champion who had George running hurdles when he was twelve. When George lost in a meet, Henry Steinbrenner lost no time in coming down from the stands to ask, "What the hell happened? How'd you let that guy beat you?" Trained to be self-reliant, George Steinbrenner earned his own pocket money delivering eggs in Bay Village, the suburb of Cleveland in which he grew up. He told Tony Kornheiser (New York Times Magazine, April 9, 1978) that he "never really appreciated" his father when he was growing up but that now he "can't give enough credit" to him. "Anything I ever accomplish I owe to him," he said in the same interview.

At Culver (Indiana) Military Academy, Steinbrenner was an all-round athlete; and at Williams College in Williamstown, Massachusetts he ran hurdles on the track team and was president of the glee club. In addition to his academic subjects he studied voice for three years. After taking his B.A. degree at Williams, in 1952, he served in the United States Air Force, as an aide to the commanding general at Lockbourne Air Force Base in Columbus, Ohio, where he ingratiated himself with his superiors by setting up a varied sports program that contributed to a diminution of AWOL's. His favorable standing helped him to get permission to set up a food service business on the base, as his friend Pete Smythe, a Cleveland industrial realtor, recounted to Everett Groseclose of the Wall Street Journal (June 25, 1975): "For George,

the word has never been day dreaming—it's day scheming. George got to sitting around trying to come up with a way to make money. and what he came up with was a sort of early-day coffee cart. He got a kind of franchise—well, you know how government workers are about coffee breaks—it saved time and made the whole operation on the base more efficient." Using six pickup trucks, Steinbrenner's food franchise served approximately 16,000 military and civilian personnel.

Following his discharge from the Air Force and a year of postgraduate study at Ohio State University, Steinbrenner was an assistant football coach, first at Columbus (Ohio) High School, then at Northwestern University, and finally at Purdue University. In 1957, at his father's request, he joined the original family business, the Kinsman Marine Transit Company, which at that time had a fleet of five ships engaged in bulk carrying on the Great Lakes.

During Steinbrenner's tenure as treasurer of Kinsman Marine Transit, he made his first venture as a sports entrepreneur: with Albert W. Bernstein, owner of the Pewter Mug restaurant in Cleveland, and others, he formed a partnership in 1960 to buy the Cleveland Pipers, a semipro basketball team. The attempt to turn the Pipers into a professional team was a failure that cost Steinbrenner a reported $250,000, money that he had raised by sale of his stock in the shipping company. When the team folded in 1962 with a debt of $125,000, he was advised to go into bankruptcy. His reputation as a businessman of his word dates back to his decision not to follow that advice: assuming the entire financial burden, he paid off all nine of his partners and then, over a period of three years, paid every debt the Pipers owed.

At the same time, the Kinsman Marine Transit Company was also in financial trouble. including tax problems. In order to succeed his father in the presidency of the company when the elder Steinbrenner retired in 1963. George Steinbrenner had to buy in, because the company was up for sale. Unable to obtain a loan for a down payment in Cleveland, Steinbrenner found a New York bank that was receptive to his argument that lake shipping had a future. "He was a supersalesman when he believed in something," an associate told Harry Stainer of the Cleveland Plain Dealer (April 6, 1974). "And he firmly believed that ships could always transport bulk cargo cheaper than the railroads."

On the strength of the bank loan, Steinbrenner took over Kinsman Marine Transit and soon had it operating in the black. He then joined a syndicate of investors headed by Thomas H. Roulston, president of Roulston & Company, a Cleveland brokerage firm, that bought a substantial block of stock—470,000 out of 1,197,250 outstanding shares—in the American Ship Building Company. To avoid a threatened proxy fight, American Ship's board of directors elected Steinbrenner president in 1967. Kinsman Marine Transit became a subsidiary of American Ship Building, and Steinbrenner's father returned from retirement to head the subsidiary. American Ship fared well under Steinbrenner: it completed the fiscal year ended September 30, 1968 with a net operating income of approximately $900,000, or sixty-seven cents a share on sales of $45.3 million, and in recent years those figures doubled. The company's subsidiaries in addition to Kinsman Marine Transit include a Great Lakes tugboat company, stevedoring operations in four cities, and several shipyards, including one in Tampa, Florida set up for the making of offshore oil drilling rigs and the repair of tankers. American Ship became the dominant grain carrier on the Great Lakes when it bought out its major competitor, the Wilson Marine Transit Company, in 1972. The United States Department of Justice filed an antitrust suit as soon as the sale was transacted, but later the department agreed to a federal court settlement of the matter.

About the time that Steinbrenner took over American Ship, Congress was beginning to consider amending the Merchant Marine Act of 1936. "From the start I knew the secret for American Ship was to get the Great Lakes included in the maritime act to get the Great Lakes in there so they could get their share of assistance," Steinbrenner has said. "I saw that the whole Great Lakes fleet had to be rebuilt, and the only way this could be done was with help." For three years Steinbrenner lobbied for legislation that would qualify the construction of Great Lakes vessels for federal benefits, especially tax considerations.

In the course of his lobbying, Steinbrenner became friendly with Senator Edward M Kennedy and other prominent Democratic politicians. Asked to chair the Democratic Congressional Dinner, the party's chief annual fundraising event, he did so for two years Under his chairmanship the dinner drew contributions totaling a record-breaking $803,000 in 1969 and surpassing that figure by $200,000 the following year.

Some Democratic leaders had advised Steinbrenner not to chair the Democratic dinners because they anticipated "vindictiveness" on the part of the Republican Administration of President Richard Nixon. American Ship was vulnerable to governmental pressure in several matters, including anti-trust litigation, a Department of Labor investigation of the company's working conditions and safety standards, and the negotiation of a settlement of a $5.4 million cost over-run on a government contract for the construction of an oceanographic survey ship.

According to later Senate testimony, pressure was as a matter of fact put on Steinbrenner to contribute to President Nixon's re-election campaign in 1972. The agent of the pressure, according to the testimony, was Herbert W. Kalmbach, Nixon's personal attorney, who met with Steinbrenner in behalf of the Committee to Reelect the President. Sheldon B. Guren, a realty investor who is a business associate and close friend of Steinbrenner's, has said, as quoted by Everett Groseclose in his Wall Street Journal article: "I know that the pressure was clearly and subtly exerted. . . . The price was clearly articulated, a significant round number, it was said. All the politicians and anybody in business in a substantial way can imagine the pressures."

Steinbrenner contributed $75,000 of his own money and $25,000 of his company's money— in the guise of executive bonuses—to the Nixon campaign, and he also made illegal contributions to the campaigns of Senator Vance Hartke and Senator Daniel Inouye. After plea bargaining, he faced a federal felony charge of conspiring to make illegal campaign contributions and a federal misdemeanor charge of accessory after the fact to violation of the federal campaign contributions law. Pleading guilty in federal district court in Cleveland in August 1974, he was fined $10,000 on the felony charge and $5,000 on the misdemeanor charge. In addition, his company was fined $10,000 on each of two felony counts.

Much more painful than the federal penalties was the one imposed on Steinbrenner by Commissioner of Baseball Bowie Kuhn on November 27, 1974: a two-year suspension from activity in professional baseball. Twenty-two months before, in January 1973, Steinbrenner had headed a group that bought the New York Yankees from the Columbia Broadcasting System for $10 million. In succeeding years he bought out his partners, acquiring 55 percent ownership. During those years the value of the Yankees rose 150 percent, to $25 million; the club's annual receipts reached $12 million; and the Yankees became the first team in the history of the American League to draw an annual attendance of two million both at home and on the road.

The rebuilding of the Yankees began with the acquisition by trade of outfielder Lou Piniella in 1973; it continued with the acquisition, also by trade, of infielder Chris Chambliss and pitcher Dick Tidrow in 1974; it accelerated with the signing of pitcher Catfish Hunter, a free agent, at the end of 1974, and the acquisition by trade of outfielder Mickey Rivers, pitcher Ed Figueroa, and infielder Willie Randolph in 1975.

The flow of Steinbrenner's money became a torrent in 1976, when slugger Reggie Jackson and pitcher Don Gullett were signed in the free agent draft. In the same year, pitcher Ken Holtzman was obtained by trade, and in 1977 pitcher Ron Guidry was brought up from the Yankee's farm system and infielder Bucky

Dent was acquired by a combination of trade and cash. Pitcher Mike Torrez, obtained by trade in 1977, left the Yankees the following year, to sign as a free agent with Boston.

Relief pitcher Rich Gossage was obtained in the free-agent market before the 1978 season. Rounding out the world championship team redivivus were four veterans already on hand when Steinbrenner took over the New York franchise: catcher Thurman Munson, relief pitcher Sparky Lyle, infielder Graig Nettles, and outfielder Roy White.

Under president and general manager Gabe Paul and manager Billy Martin, the Yankees won their thirty-first American League pennant in 1977, and they went on to defeat the Los Angeles Dodgers in the World Series. Disagreement between Steinbrenner and Paul culminated in the winter of 1977-78 in the departure of Paul—for the Cleveland Indians— and the naming of Al Rosen to replace him. In 1978 tension between Martin and Reggie Jackson led to a feud between Martin and Steinbrenner, who sided with Jackson and brought in Bob Lemon to replace Martin as manager in mid-season. (A Miller Lite beer television commercial in which Steinbrenner jestingly told Martin he was fired was made two weeks before the actual firing, but it hit the air, unfortunately, at the time of the firing itself. A week later, Steinbrenner announced that Martin would be coming back—"in 1980.") Despite the turbulence, New York again won the pennant and again defeated the Dodgers for the world championship.

In the free-agent draft of 1978 the Yankees signed Boston pitcher Luis Tiant and Los Angeles hurler Tommy John to contracts totaling $900,000 and $1.2 million, respectively. The price paid for John was roughly the same as that expended earlier for reliever Rawly Eastwick. It exceeded Andy Messersmith's $333,333 but fell below the value Steinbrenner put on several other pitchers: Catfish Hunter ($3.2 million), Don Gullett ($2.1 million), and Rich Gossage ($2.1 million).

The addition of starters John and Tiant gave the Yankees a formidable pitching staff, with Ed Figueroa, and Catfish Hunter also in the front rank, Jim Beattie, Dick Tidrow, and Ken Clay backing them up, and Gossage in the bullpen. Commenting on the acquisition of Tiant and John, Commissioner Bowie Kuhn expressed the fear that "this process will develop a group of elite teams with potentially great damage to competitive balance."

Billy Martin, rehired as manager of the Yankees on June 19, 1979, was again fired four months later, after the disappointing 1979 season. In the wake of allegations that Martin lied about an incident in a Bloomington, Minnesota hotel in which he reportedly punched a salesman in the face, Steinbrenner announced that Martin would be replaced by Dick Howser. To prepare for 1980, Steinbrenner again went on a player-buying spree.

As an "angel," Steinbrenner invested in, among other shows, the Broadway hits *Applause* and *Two for the Seesaw* and national tours of *Funny Girl, On a Clear Day,* and *George M.* Regarding the last mentioned, one of his political friends, Speaker of the House Thomas P. ("Tip") O'Neill has said: "George put that show in every city in the country, not so much to make money but to get people waving the flag again. He did it right after Vietnam." Steinbrenner's philanthropies and civic-improvement activities are legion.

The Yankee owner is a husky man of meticulous grooming, with a head of hair always so perfectly in place that observers occasionally mistake it for a toupee. His favorite wardrobe color is, like his eyes, blue. He wears Bill Blass shirts, partly because they are American designed and made, and he will not buy a foreign automobile. Patriotic to the point of sentimentality, he views the Yankees as the essence of Americana, like "apple pie and hot dogs" and as "something to be revered and respected." "I feel good about winning one for New York," he told Tony Kornheiser. "This is the greatest city in the world and its people are the greatest people in the world. And I just hope they like me." On the latter point he is not sanguine, however: deploring the fact that he too often projects a "Simon Legree image," he says, "I'm the heavy. I don't like it, but I don't know how to change it."

George Steinbrenner and Elizabeth Joan Zieg were married on May 12, 1956 and have four children: Henry G. 3d, Jennifer Lynn, Jessica Joan, and Harold Zieg. Several years ago the Steinbrenners moved from Cleveland to Tampa, where the American Ship Building Company has a major facility. Much of George Steinbrenner's time in Florida is spent at his stud farm near Ocala and at Florida Downs, outside of Tampa, where he races his thoroughbreds. When in Cleveland he socializes with his cronies at the downtown Pewter Mug restaurant, and in New York he frequents such elite watering holes (though he barely drinks—he sips) as "21" and Elaine's and takes in theatre, ballet, and opera. Wherever he is, whether at work or play, he moves at a pace described by those trying to keep up with him as "furious." Temperamentally mercurial, the Yankee owner impresses most outsiders as "charming," but insiders often find him to be "imperious," "impatient," and "tough." He says he accepts "tough" as long as it is qualified with "but fair." A close friend sees him as an "empire builder" born a little too late, when "most of the world has already been parceled out."

References: Biography News p706 Je '74; New York 10:32+ Ag 15 77 pors, 11:39+ Ap 17 '78 pors; Newsday p2+ F 3 '74 pors; Sports Illus 47:122+ O 10 '77 pors; Linn, Ed. Inside the Yankees (1978)

Steptoe, Patrick C(hristopher)

1913(?)- British physician. Address: b c/o
Hutchinson Publishing Group, Ltd., 3 Fitzroy
Sq., London W1P 6JD, England

The first authenticated birth of a laboratory-
conceived baby has brought international
fame to British gynecologist Patrick C. Steptoe, whose delivery of Louise Brown in Oldham, England on July 25, 1978, capped twelve
years of research. Dr. Steptoe pioneered the
technique for aspirating ripe eggs from would-
be mothers' ovaries and the procedure for
reimplanting the embryos in their wombs
following in vitro fertilization of the eggs.
His collaborator in those efforts was Dr.
Robert G. Edwards, the Cambridge University physiologist who developed the method
for the in vitro fertilization of human ova.
Dr. Steptoe currently works at the Oldham
General and District Hospital near Manchester,
England, but he and Edwards intend to open
a clinic in Cambridge where, after further
experimental work, they expect to help scores
of women who, like Louise Brown's mother
have defective Fallopian tubes. A second
"test-tube baby"—a boy—was born in Glas-
gow, Scotland in mid-January, 1979.

Patrick Christopher Steptoe was born in
1913 (some sources say 1915) in a village in
Oxfordshire, England, where his father was
the organist in a local church and his mother
was a social service worker involved in family
planning. Later in life Steptoe gave his "remarkable" mother credit for instilling in him
the quality of perseverance that became so
crucial to his work. In an interview for the
Washington Post (October 12, 1978) he told
Myra Macpherson, "She used to say opposi-

tion, obstructions and setbacks are really
challenges, that you should see them as opportunities for progress and development."

In his youth Steptoe studied music, but
he eventually decided to pursue a medical
career. Specializing in obstetrics and gynecology, he trained at the University of London's
St. George's Hospital Medical School and
at hospitals in Dublin, Ireland. He received
a "conjoint diploma" in 1939 and shortly
thereafter was admitted to the Royal College of Surgeons and licensed to practise
by the Royal College of Physicians. That
same year, Steptoe volunteered for active
duty in the Royal Navy Reserve. Called up
a few months later, he was taken prisoner
by the Italians after his ship was sunk in
the Battle of Crete in the spring of 1941.
Because he was a doctor, he was allowed
to move freely about the prison camp. Taking advantage of his situation, Steptoe helped
a number of his fellow inmates to escape.
When, in late 1942, his captors learned of
his involvement in the escapes, they put him
in solitary confinement, but he was exchanged
a few weeks later.

Returning to London, the young doctor
completed several years of postgraduate work
in his specialty and became a member of
the Royal College of Obstetricians and Gynecologists in 1948. In the late 1940's Steptoe moved to Manchester, the big industrial
center in Lancashire, where he set up his
practice. "London was such a rat race after
the war," he explained to Myra Macpherson
"So many of us discharged, trying to take
up careers again. Must have been 500 of us
young gynecologists trying to get a foot-
hold." In about 1951 he began working at
the Oldham General and District Hospital
in Oldham, a mill town a few miles northeast of Manchester. There he studied methods of sterilization and the problems of infertility.

In the course of his research, Dr. Steptoe
perfected the use of the laparoscope, a narrow, hollow foot-long tube with a built-in
optical fiber light and telescopic eyepiece
that could be inserted into the abdominal
cavity, which had been inflated with an
inert gas to provide working room, through
a small incision near the navel. The instrument was to become a major aid in determining the causes of infertility and in performing sterilization surgery. At the time,
however, the president of the Royal College
of Obstetrics and Gynecology expressed reservations about its use. "All they saw was
the difficulties," Steptoe said in the Washington Post interview. "In those days it was
done under local anesthesia and they saw
the hot lights which were used for two or
three minutes and it was a smash and a
grab and they said 'no.' But it was a marvelous idea. Brilliant. It was just a matter
of those bad things being replaced and adapt-

ing the technology." Steptoe worked for five years before publishing his first paper on laparoscopic surgery in 1965.

In 1966 Steptoe joined forces with Robert G. Edwards, the Cambridge University physiologist who had developed a technique for fertilizing human eggs in the laboratory, in an effort to help women with defective Fallopian tubes become pregnant. In healthy women, the Fallopian tubes, or oviducts, each month carry egg cells from the ovaries to the uterus, and it is in the tubes that the eggs are fertilized by sperm. The doctors hoped to bypass the oviducts' function in the reproductive process by fertilizing the egg *in vitro,* or in a laboratory dish, and then reimplanting the resulting embryo in the uterus. Edwards had previously worked with ovaries excised for medical reasons, but Steptoe, with his laparoscope and a suction needle, was able to select and remove a mature egg from a woman's ovaries at the appropriate moment in her monthly cycle. Since an estimated 20 to 50 percent of women unable to bear children can attribute their problem to absent, defective, or blocked oviducts, Steptoe and Edwards had no difficulty in attracting volunteer couples.

Their first major breakthrough came in the fall of 1968, when Edwards succeeded in fertilizing human ova extracted by his colleague. Each extracted egg was placed in a Petri dish containing blood serum, nutrients, and sperm, usually obtained by masturbation. As soon as a single spermatozoon penetrated the egg, it was transferred to another dish of life-sustaining solution, where it divided into a cluster of cells. The next step was to reimplant the fertilized egg in the uterus. At first the eggs grew in the laboratory to only eight or sixteen cells, a stage believed insufficiently mature for implantation. It was not until 1970 that a fertilized egg reached the blastocyst stage of about 100 cells—the point in the reproductive process, about four and one-half days after fertilization, at which the embryo normally leaves the oviducts for the uterus. In outlining the results of their research at a press conference in Washington, D.C. in December 1970, a jubilant Steptoe told reporters, "We have been able to complete all the developments that normally take place in the oviducts."

The first implantation of a fertilized egg into a would-be mother's womb was made in 1972. After carefully examining the blastocyst for possible genetic defects, Dr. Steptoe placed the embryo in the uterus with a tiny plastic tube inserted through the cervix —a nonsurgical procedure he himself had devised. But because the inserted embryo failed to lodge properly in the uterine wall, none of the approximately thirty women who had become pregnant carried it beyond ten weeks at the most. Some scientists speculated that prolonged culture in the laboratory was responsible for the problem, but Steptoe and Edwards were inclined to disagree, noting that microscopic monitoring proved the embryos developed normally in the artificial environment. Concluding that the follicular stimulating hormone injections given to induce "superovulation," or multiple egg production at a predictable time, interfered with the normal reproductive signaling system, they set out to correct the problem.

Steptoe and Edwards also faced difficulties outside the laboratory. As news of their research spread throughout the scientific community in the early 1970's, clergymen, scientists, and others attacked them for degrading the procreative process by transferring its most crucial step to the test tube, for allegedly destroying the embryos that they did not implant, and for risking the birth of chromosomally-damaged babies. Genetic engineering of "babies to order" and the hiring of "surrogate mothers" to carry the fetuses of other women to term were among the ominous social implications foreseen. No less an authority than Dr. James D. Watson, who as the codiscoverer of the molecular structure of DNA won the Nobel Prize for Medicine in 1962, denounced their research.

In Great Britain, Members of Parliament demanded an investigation, and the British Medical Research Council, contending that more research on subhuman primates was needed, turned down a request for funds. The Ford Foundation, which was more interested in research to curb population growth, also cut off direct funding. Financing their research with Steptoe's earnings from legal abortions, the two doctors continued their work at Dr. Kershaw's Cottage Hospital, a small hospital in Oldham with woefully inadequate research facilities. Feeling progressively beleaguered, they refused to publish progress reports on their research, and thereby attracted even more criticism from their colleagues.

Their fortunes took a turn for the better after Lesley Brown, a healthy, thirty-year-old woman who was unable to conceive because of blocked oviducts, was referred to Dr. Steptoe in 1976. After surgically removing Mrs. Brown's Fallopian tubes, which blocked access to her ovaries, Dr. Steptoe on November 10, 1977, extracted a mature egg from one of her ovaries. Edwards immediately fertilized it with the sperm of her husband, Gilbert John Brown. Encouraged by the preliminary results of Dr. John Marston's experiments with Rhesus monkeys suggesting that fertilized eggs as small as two cells could survive in the uterus, Dr. Steptoe decided to reimplant Mrs. Brown's ovum at the eight-cell stage, just two-and-a-half days after fertilization. Apparently as a result of that procedural modification, the fetus thrived, and, in June 1978, Mrs. Brown entered the Oldham District and General Hospital's maternity ward, where doctors monitored her around the clock.

A few weeks before her baby was due, Mrs. Brown developed a slight case of toxemia, which could have led to a stillbirth. As a precaution, Dr. Steptoe delivered the slightly premature baby, a healthy five-pound twelve-ounce girl later named Louise Joy, by Caesarian section on July 25. Exultant over their success, Steptoe wrote in a copyrighted article published in *Newsday* (August 16, 1978): "The baby is everything we have strived for for nine years. . . . Now the way is open and there is hope for women all over the world."

At a press conference on July 27, both scientists were reluctant to discuss the details of their research before publishing their results in a medical journal, but Dr. Steptoe assured reporters that, after a reasonable length of time needed to perfect the procedure, laboratory-conceived babies would become a common occurrence. Responding to the predictable religious and ethical objections to their work, Steptoe asserted that he and Edwards were not interested in the creation of life, or in "baby farms," surrogate mothers, or genetic manipulation, but were merely trying to help infertile couples. "To me it is religious for [a] couple to be so strongly motivated, to do all the things they have to do to get a baby," he said in a subsequent interview. "It's just as religious an act to conceive a baby by transferring. People try to mix up sex and this sort of thing. All we've done is to assist." Steptoe however, is the first to admit that the procedure itself has "tremendous potentialities" as a tool for studying the origins of life, finding the causes of, and possibly the cures for, such genetic abnormalities as mongolism, and developing new methods of contraception. "Once you learn how a system works," he explained to one reporter, "you can learn how to upset it."

In October 1978 Dr. Steptoe became embroiled in still another controversy when the Barren Foundation, a Chicago-based fertility research organization, cancelled the presentation of its award to the doctor. Dr Jay Gold, the chairman of the Foundation's medical advisory council, said the decision was based on the failure of Steptoe and Edwards to publish in a reputable scientific journal "information to substantiate claims made in the lay press." Other members of the council questioned the medical ethics of selling the story to the mass media. (According to several published reports, Steptoe had signed a six-figure contract with the *National Enquirer*, a sensationalistic tabloid.) The doctor, who was then traveling in Australia, told reporters he was "offended and surprised" by what he called "the most utterly disgraceful exhibition of bad manners [he had] ever come across in the scientific world." Steptoe maintained that he had rejected an offer from the *Enquirer* and denied having made money from the highly publicized birth. He admitted, however, that he had advised the Browns to negotiate an exclusive world print rights agreement with Associated Newspapers for an estimated $600,000 to protect them from an onslaught of reporters.

As to the validity of his and Edwards' achievement, Dr. Steptoe revealed that films of Louise Brown's birth taken by the information agency of the British government clearly showed that Mrs. Brown's Fallopian tubes had been removed some months earlier. Furthermore, he reminded his critics that most scientists did not publish their findings until from six months to a year after the completion of research. "We haven't published the details of our recent developments and our modifications of technique for the simple reason that we did want to have more than one baby born by this means," he explained on the December 3, 1978 edition of NBC's *Meet the Press*. "We wanted to show that it could be done, that we had done it, and that it could be repeated. . . . There is a great deal of data that has to be analyzed before you can publish. Otherwise, you could easily mislead people, and we would, in fact, be doing them a disservice if we published too soon." He and his colleague Dr. Edwards described their procedure and its results fully at a January 26, 1979 meeting of the Royal College of Obstetricians and Gynecologists in London and at a conference of the American Fertility Society in San Francisco, California a week later. The two have also contracted with a British television production company for a documentary program and with the Hutchinson Publishing Group, Ltd. for a book on the subject.

The New York Fertility Foundation presented Dr. Steptoe with a citation of achievement on December 1, 1978. At a Manhattan press conference the day before, Steptoe reported that Louise Brown's birth was the result of a method that produced pregnancy in only 1 percent of the cases, but that subsequent modifications in the technique had increased the success rate to 10 percent and he envisioned an eventual 50 percent success rate. At that particular time, he said, several women in Great Britain were pregnant with babies conceived *in vitro*. Because laboratory fertilization can be accomplished with a far lower sperm count than that required for natural conception, Steptoe said the procedure could be used to overcome male as well as female sterility.

Since the birth of Louise Brown, Steptoe has received more than 1,000 letters from couples seeking his help, but he can see no more than 300 patients each year. Officially retired from the National Health Service, he is continuing to work at his temporary laboratories until construction of his new clinic near Cambridge, paid for by Associated Newspapers, is completed.

Myra Macpherson described Dr. Patrick Steptoe as being "perfect for his role: silver-haired, blue eyes twinkling behind horned-rimmed glasses, a reassuring, gentle manner, a Rex Harrison emphasis, and a lift to certain words in his sentences." A man of many interests, Steptoe gives occasional piano and organ recitals, goes to movies, plays, and operas, and takes in a cricket match when-

ever he can. He and his wife, a former actress with the Old Vic, have a son and a daughter. He readily admitted to Miss Macpherson that the publicity surrounding Louise Brown's birth had disrupted his life and told her that he was "just waiting for things to settle down."

References: N Y Times A p1+ Jl 26 '78 por, A p16 Jl 27 '78; Newsweek 92:66+ Ag 7 '78 por; Time 112:58+ Jl 31 '78 por; Washington Post A p1+ Jl 27 '78, D p1+ O 12 '78 por

Stewart, Rod

Jan. 10, 1945- Musician; recording artist.
Address: b. c/o Warner Brothers Records,
3300 Warner Blvd., Burbank, Calif. 91510

Rock music's reigning male sex symbol, raucous, raspy-voiced Rod Stewart, began his career in the mid-1960's with various groups, notably two led by Long John Baldry, in his native England. In the late 1960's he was the lead singer with the Jeff Beck Group, from which he went into a seven-year association with The Faces. His ascent to superstardom might be dated from 1971, when his album *Every Picture Tells a Story*, with its hit single "Maggie May," shot to the top of the charts in both England and the United States (where he now lives). Since then Stewart has had a succession of hits, including the gold (million dollar-earning) albums *Never a Dull Moment* and *Atlantic Crossing* and the

platinum (million copy-selling) LP *Night on the Town*. His 1979 release *Blondes Have More Fun* also went platinum and spawned the hit single "Da Ya Think I'm Sexy?"

Stewart's rough but expressive tenor voice is one of the most distinctive in current pop music. In concert Stewart is a colorful performer, known for his dyed-blond haystack head of hair, his makeup, his outrageously foppish costumes, including skin-tight pink pants, and his penchant for low comedy and broad melodrama; he is also energetic, leaping about as if he were playing soccer. In fact, he was once a professional footballer and is still an amateur one, along with his friend and fellow rock star Elton John, and earlier in his career the dominant image he projected was that of a tough street "jock." That "macho" image still comes through, but subtly, in a wink, a tongue in cheek, or the studied disarray of his elegant attire as he struts about the stage. The result is a paradoxical persona—the effeminate roustabout, the womanizing dandy. Reviewing *Blondes Have More Fun* in the Washington *Post*, Harry Sumrall credited Stewart the lyricist and performer with a "sense of sloppy sophistication." In his "finely crafted" compositions, Sumrall wrote, "melodies, rhythms, and harmonies all seem rough around the edges, yet they are tightly controlled."

Roderick David Stewart was born on Archway Road in the Highgate section of North London on January 10, 1945, the fifth child of Scottish-born Bob and Elsie Stewart, the proprietors of a small tobacco-newspaper-confectionery store. One of his earliest memories is of the pictures of Scottish soccer players that his brothers had on their walls, and another is of the family gathering around the piano for sing-a-longs, in which his brother Don would do Al Jolson impersonations. Jolson's brash performing style appealed to Rod; growing up, he saw the films *The Jazz Singer*, *The Jolson Story*, starring Larry Parks, and *Jolson Sings Again*, and in adolescence he began collecting a complete library of Jolson records, which he still owns.

At the William Grimshaw Secondary Modern School in Hornsey, Stewart captained the soccer team, and he later played on the Middlesex Schoolboys Team. In 1961 he signed a professional contract with the Brentford Football Club, but his love of music ultimately prevailed over his love of soccer. He had been playing guitar and banjo at school events from his early teens, and three of his schoolmates, Ray and Dave Davies and Pete Quaife, later became members of the rock group the Kinks.

Stewart took part in the Aldermaston "Ban the Bomb" marches of the early 1960's, often leading the protesters in song. At first the music to which he aspired was the topical folk variety exemplified by Ewan McColl, Alex Campbell, the Thames Side Four, Ramblin' Jack Elliott, Woody Guthrie, and especially Derroll Adams. Later he was attracted to rhythm and blues, and the single most enduring influence on him was the "soul"-based singing of the late Sam Cooke.

While working at grave-digging and other jobs, Stewart frequented the clubs in and around London where the Rolling Stones, the Who, the Yardbirds, and other young rock or rhythm and blues groups could be heard. In 1963 he began playing part-time harmonica with the rhythm and blues combo the Five Dimensions, and the following year he joined Long John Baldry's Hootchie Coochie Men as a vocalist. During his tenure with Baldry's group he was given the nickname "Rod the Mod," because of his dandyish style of dress and grooming, and he began to attract attention with his detached performing style, which he originally adopted as a refuge from stage fright. The first single under his own name was the Decca release "Good Morning Little Schoolgirl," with "I'm Gonna Move to the Outskirts of Town" on the flip side.

After Baldry disbanded the Hootchie Coochie Men, Stewart did some gigs with the Soul Agents before rejoining Baldry in a new group, Steampacket. While with Steampacket, he recorded two singles for Columbia Records. One was "The Day Will Come," backed by "Why Does It Go On," and the other was a cover of Sam Cooke's "Shake," with "I Just Got Some" on the B side. Following the dissolution of Steampacket, he sang briefly with Shotgun Express and then entered the most important stage of his early career, his association with Jeff Beck.

It was as a member of the Jeff Beck Group that Stewart began to attract a following in America, which the group successfully toured in 1968. Equally successful was the album by the group released by Columbia at the end of the tour, Truth, for which Stewart and Ron Wood wrote several songs. The group returned to the United States for an engagement at the Fillmore East Theatre in New York City in January 1969, and later that year they re-corded the LP Beck Ola (Columbia), which represented a shift from blues to "heavy metal."

When Beck broke up his band, Stewart and Wood joined The Faces (originally, The Small Faces), and they remained with that group for seven years, until it split up in 1976. As lead singer with The Faces, Stewart enhanced his reputation in the United States, which the group toured often. "A reputation for beer, football, cockney humor, and parties appeared very British and gained a strong cult following for The Faces," Tony Jasper observed in Rod Stewart (1977).

The seven albums Stewart made with The Faces, including A Nod's as Good as a Wink to a Blind Horse (Warner Brothers, 1972) and Coast to Coast Overture (Mercury, 1974), tended to be overshadowed by Stewart's solo discs. The first of his solo LP's was An Old Raincoat Won't Ever Let You Down (Vertigo, 1970), released in the United States as The Rod Stewart Album, a mixture of original compositions and covers of blues, folk rock, and traditional melodies demonstrating Stewart's broad musical range. Richard Cromelin wrote in his book Rod Stewart (1976): "The record is somewhat tentative in feel . . . but it immediately marked Stewart as an innovator in rock singing technique and an effective reviver of several neglected musical directions." Stewart's second solo album, Gasoline Alley (Vertigo, 1970), was reissued together with the first in a double package by Mercury Records in 1976.

Stewart's status as a rock star was clinched when his album Every Picture Tells a Story (Mercury, 1971) hit the top of the LP charts on both sides of the Atlantic and the track "Maggie May" did the same on the single charts. "Maggie May" was written by Stewart in collaboration with arranger Martin Quittenton. The other cuts on the album included the hymn "Amazing Grace," songs by Bob Dylan, and soul music. Richard Cromelin noted that the album had "an assurance and authority that lent a new dimension and power to his [Stewart's] basic ingredients" and that "Stewart exploits the raw, earthy qualities of his style as well as he ever has."

When Stewart and The Faces performed at Madison Square Garden in November 1971, Don Heckman of the New York Times (November 28, 1971) wrote: "The support it [The Faces] provides the lead singer is only minimally effective. But Stewart doesn't need much help. He has the almost hypnotically appealing stage presence of a Mick Jagger; one watches his strutting cock-of-the-walk antics even while he isn't singing. And his voice—slightly hoarse-sounding, but ringing with a crackling masculine authority—is an unmistakably original expression."

Stewart's Mercury solo singles "You Wear It Well"/"Lost Paraguayos" and "Angel"/ "What Made Milwaukee Famous (Has Made a Loser Out of Me)" were issued in 1972. Reviewing *Never a Dull Moment* (Mercury, 1972), Stewart's fourth album, in the New York *Times* (September 24, 1972), Lorraine Alterman described the recording artist as "a master of phrasing and control" who "projects all of the passion or irony or hurt that belongs to each set of lyrics." Like *Every Picture Tells a Story*, *Never a Dull Moment* went "gold," surpassing $1,000,000 in sales. Meanwhile The Faces continued to build their reputation for unpredictable performances, adding a circus trapeze and high wire act to their act in the latter half of 1972. In December 1972 Stewart appeared in a London revival of the rock opera *Tommy*, singing "Pinball Wizard."

The compilation *Sing It Again, Rod* (Mercury, 1973) included a "cover" of Tim Hardin's "Reason to Believe" that received much air play. The solo album *Smiler* (Mercury, 1974) contained compositions by Stewart in collaboration with Quittenton and Wood, selections from the works of Bob Dylan, Chuck Berry, Paul McCartney, Sam Cooke, and Elton John, and an instrumental version of Lerner and Loewe's "I've Grown Accustomed to Her Face." Of the album Tony Jasper wrote in his book on Stewart: "Rod performed this variety of songs with great skill and gave practical evidence of the remark that he could sing 'anything, virtually everything.'"

But some critics and fans wondered if the "working-class kid" might not be losing his "earthy" quality in the *dolce vita* of show business in which he was becoming immersed, and there was a similar reaction in some quarters to his next solo album, *Atlantic Crossing* (Warner Brothers, 1975). Among the cuts on *Atlantic Crossing* was "Sailing," which was a massive hit in England. After leaving The Faces Stewart recorded *A Night on the Town* (Riva, 1976), which included four songs written by him, the best of which were "The Killing of Georgie," about the death of a New York homosexual friend of his, and "Tonight's the Night." The latter became a major hit despite the restricted radio play resulting from the explicit language used in describing a girl losing her virginity.

With a new back-up group he organized—a group consisting of pianist Kevin Ravinger, bassist Phil Chen, and guitarists Gary Grainger, Billy Peek, and Jim Cregan—Stewart cut *Footloose and Fancy Free* (1977). Also in 1977 Private Stock brought out *A Shot of Rhythm and Blues*, containing songs recorded between 1964 and 1966. That album became the subject of a legal battle, with Stewart claiming that the tracks had been intended for demonstration only.

On his most recent tracks Stewart, whose rapport with his musicians gives his recordings a festive air of easy give-and-take, is backed by a group that includes Carmine Appice on drums and Nicky Hopkins on piano. *Blondes Have More Fun* (Warner Brothers, 1979) sold better than any previous Stewart album, and its cut "Da Ya Think I'm Sexy?" became the fastest-selling single in Warner Brothers history. In his review in the Washington *Post* (January 17, 1979), Harry Sumrall wrote: "The record is imbued with the character and vocal style that are Stewart's alone. [It] bristles with a rough-edged excitement and energy that are the equals of his earlier work. Whether prancing away on the disco-like 'Da Ya Think I'm Sexy?' boogeying on 'Blondes Have More Fun,' or playing the part of the ragtag crooner on 'The Best Days of My Life' Stewart [draws] the listener into the spirit of enjoyment that he obviously brings to and takes from his music."

Stewart sold out Madison Square Garden in New York City when he performed there on four successive nights in June 1979. John Rockwell wrote in the New York *Times* (June 7, 1979): "He gave an old fashioned rock-and-roll show, and it was a humdinger. . . . He pranced and strutted about the stage with real enthusiasm, and the enthusiasm was contagious. [He] is a lithe and extremely sexy man [who] also happens to be about the best male singer in rock, with a fervent, husky, plaintive tenor that he phrases with real musicality. His band is a confident one, and his tunes are catchy and melodic. . . . [Stewart] doesn't approach the great work of the Beatles, the Rolling Stones, Bob Dylan, Neil Young, and so on. But as an entertainer he has few peers."

Rod Stewart and Alana Collins Hamilton, the ex-wife of the actor George Hamilton, were married in April 1979. They have a daughter, Alana Kimberly. Before his marriage, Stewart had had a succession of affairs, including a two-and-a-half-year ménage with Britt Ekland, beginning in 1975. A $15,000,000 breach-of-trust suit filed by Miss Ekland was settled out of court, with a reported $500,000 property settlement.

The Stewarts live in Rod's chateau-like mansion in Holmby Hills in Los Angeles County, California, which is decorated in the singer's favorite style, art nouveau, and includes a game room containing a collection of animal horns and tusks. Also in the game room is a fifteen-foot television screen on which Stewart plays over and over the tapes of soccer games sent from England by his father. Once a week he plays soccer in a Beverly Hills park. "My passions are soccer, drinking, and women, in that order," Colin Dangaard and Daphne Davis quoted Stewart as saying in *Us* (May 20, 1979). His other interests include vintage automobiles.

References: Newsweek 80:75+ S 11 '72 por; People 11:80+ F 5 '79; Rolling Stone p53+ N 6 '75 pors, p46 Ap 6 '78 pors; Time 102:99+ N 12 '73; Cromelin, Richard. *Rod Stewart* (1976); Stambler, Irwin. *Encyclopedia of Pop, Rock, and Soul* (1977)

Stigwood, Robert (C.)

1934 (?)- Theatre, motion picture, television, and record producer. Address: b. The Robert Stigwood Organisation Inc., 1775 Broadway, New York City, N. Y. 10019

Australian-born Robert Stigwood, the enigmatic impresario with the Midas touch, has built up a vast international entertainment empire by merging rock music with other performing art forms, namely theatre, motion pictures, and television. A rock promoter in England in the 1960's, he helped to manage the Beatles and launched the careers of such successful groups as Cream and the Bee Gees. Late in the decade he established a profitable cross-over pattern in which a record album pre-sold a theatre production or a motion picture and vice versa. His biggest hits, all helped along by razzle-dazzle promotion, have included *Jesus Christ Superstar, Tommy, Saturday Night Fever, Grease,* and *Evita.* By a conservative estimate, the Robert Stigwood Organisation, largely due to the phenomenal sales of the RSO record company, grossed an estimated $300,000,000 in 1978.

Robert C. Stigwood, whose roots are Scottish-Irish-German Protestant, was born in 1934 in Adelaide, the capital of South Australia. His father, an electrical engineer, and his mother, who ran a nursing home, were divorced when he was twelve years old. A self-possessed child, Stigwood showed an early interest in local amateur theatre productions. At the age of fifteen he converted to Catholicism because he was, as he put it, "attracted by the mystery" and enrolled at Sacred Heart College, a boarding school. "I decided to become a priest somewhere around the age of eighteen," he

said, as quoted in *Newsweek* (July 31, 1978). "But I had a party and changed my mind the next day and had to return the presents." More interested in amateur hypnotism than in his studies, he dropped out of Sacred Heart before graduating.

Stigwood spent about three years working as a copywriter in an Adelaide advertising agency, but he eventually wearied of dreaming up "wonderful things to say about refrigerators." In the late 1950's he took a tramp steamer to India, then hitchhiked to London. When he finally arrived at his destination three months later, he had just thirty shillings in his pocket. He found lodgings with other expatriate Australians in "Kangaroo Valley" in the Earl's Court section of London and took a series of odd jobs that included a stint as a theatre manager in the provinces.

Back in London in 1962, Stigwood started a small talent agency "in a cupboard in Charing Cross Road." As he recalled in an interview with Anthony Haden-Guest for *New York* magazine (January 30, 1978): "Commercial television had just started in London. The big agents were ignoring it. In the space of a few years, I suppose I was handling half the casting for all English commercials. Then I found I was handling some good legitimate talent. My first break was with John Leyton." Stigwood cast Leyton, a young actor-singer, as a pop star in the television series *Harper West One.* Unable to persuade the three major British recording companies (EMI, Decca, and Pye) to record Leyton, Stigwood himself produced a single, "Johnny Remember Me," then talked the producer of *Harper West One* into letting his client sing the song on the show. Attracted by the free national exposure, EMI agreed to distribute the disc, which soared straight to the top of the British pop charts and sold 1,000,000 copies. With that early example of his characteristic cross-media marketing techniques, Stigwood had become Britain's first independent record producer.

Within a few months Stigwood had five records in the Top Fifty, but he suffered reverses and in March 1965, in debt to the Rolling Stones and to EMI, he liquidated his company. While maneuvering a comeback, he kept his hand in pop music promotion by acting as the business manager of the Graham Bond Organization, one of the more successful British pop groups in the mid-1960's. In January 1967 he merged his new company with NEMS Enterprises, the conglomerate that controlled the Beatles, and became its managing director, a post he shared with Brian Epstein, the Beatles' personal manager. When Epstein died of a drug overdose later that year, Polygram B. V. Records, the recording arm of the German-Dutch electronics consortium, Siemens and Philips, offered to bankroll Stigwood as he attempted to exercise his £500,000 option to take over NEMS. The Beatles, however, stubbornly resisted, and in November 1967 Stigwood pulled out of NEMS to set up his own company, the Robert Stigwood Organisation. He took with him the Graham Bond Organization and Cream, a supergroup composed of Ginger Baker and Jack Bruce, formerly with the Bond group, and Eric Clapton, one of the best guitarists in the country. At about that time, Stigwood signed the Bee Gees, fellow Australians who had arrived in England just as their first single, "Spicks and Specks," was attracting attention in Europe.

According to a report in the London *Times* (October 31, 1967) the Robert Stigwood Organisation intended to form a "new international entertainment organization," with branches in the United States, France, and other countries, and expand its interests outside the music industry to films, television and theatre. Stigwood snapped up the British rights to *Hair*, the American tribal love-rock musical, but production was delayed because the Office of the Lord Chamberlain, shocked by its obscenity and its brief nude scene, refused to license it. When the Lord Chamberlain's right of censorship was fortuitously abolished six months later, Stigwood immediately opened the play. An unqualified success, *Hair* played to full houses in London for some six years. He also presented *Oh! Calcutta!*, Kenneth Tynan's nude musical, *The Dirtiest Show in Town*, which enjoyed a two-and-one-half-year run, and a British version of the popular musical comedy *Pippin*. Entering the television arena, Stigwood bought a small writers' talent agency from Beryl Vertue, whose clients included the authors of two successful British series, *Till Death Do Us Part* and *Steptoe and Son*. Having thereby acquired the rights to those properties, he sought out Norman Lear, an enterprising television producer, who Americanized the characters and plots into the long-running *All in the Family* and *Sanford and Son*. By mid-1978 those two shows alone had earned Stigwood more than $5,000,000 in licensing fees and profit-sharing arrangements.

Even greater profits were generated by an earlier Stigwood coup. In 1970, after hearing a predistribution acetate of the score, he snared the performing rights to the phenomenally successful rock opera, *Jesus Christ Superstar*, in its concert, stage, and screen forms. The work of two young Britons, lyricist Tim Rice and composer Andrew Llyod Webber, *Jesus Christ Superstar* is unique in show business annals because it was the first Broadway musical to be based on a recording. With the sale of over 3,000,000 albums and tapes and an advance ticket take of more than $1,000,000, it was an ironclad smash hit even before rehearsals had begun.

But before Stigwood's production of *Jesus Christ Superstar* opened on Broadway, dozens of unauthorized versions of the play were mounted around the country and Stigwood became heavily involved in litigation to protect his rights. His own concert version of *Superstar* premiered on July 12, 1971 at the Civic Arena in Pittsburgh, Pennsylvania and grossed $1,200,000 in its first four weeks. With a picket contingent of several religious denominations parading outside, the show finally opened at the Mark Hellinger Theater in New York City on October 12, 1971 to mixed reviews. Most critics conceded that the elaborate $700,000 production, staged by Tom O'Horgan, the avant-garde director of *Hair* and *Lenny*, would be a commercial success despite its artistic failings. Many preferred the album, already a rock classic, to the spectacular theatrical extravaganza.

Clive Barnes, writing in the New York *Times* (October 13, 1971), pronounced it "brilliant but cheap" and a reviewer for the trade paper *Variety* (October 13, 1971) called it "a miracle play in terms of a circus parade." Nevertheless, the play was nominated for five Tony awards. After a respectable Broadway run of 720 performances, *Jesus Christ Superstar* closed on June 30, 1973.

The *Superstar* industry thrived throughout the early 1970's as Stigwood formed road companies to present the play on the West Coast and in Britain, Denmark, West Germany, France, Italy, and Australia. A film version of *Jesus Christ Superstar*, photographed on location in Israel under the direction of Norman Jewison, was released by Universal in June 1973. Like its parent play, the motion picture drew conflicting reactions, ranging from "a real zinger" to "one of the true fiascos of modern cinema."

In the interim before producing his second multimillion-dollar-grossing rock opera film, *Tommy*, Stigwood mounted a Young Vic production of Rice and Webber's popular rock cantata for children, *Joseph and the Amazing Technicolor Dreamcoat*, and produced *Rachel Lily Rosenbloom and Don't You Ever Forget It*, a campy vehicle for Bette Midler that closed during previews. Originally a concert recording by The Who, *Tommy* had been turned down by every major motion picture studio until Stigwood sought private financing. Coproduced and directed by Ken Russell, who also wrote the screenplay, *Tommy* (Columbia, 1975) was hailed by Los Angeles *Times* entertainment editor Charles Champlin, among others, as "an overwhelming, thunderous, almost continuously astonishing achievement, coherent and consistent from first frames to last." Other Stigwood ventures in 1975 included *Beacon Hill*, the short-lived CBS dramatic series inspired by *Upstairs, Downstairs*, and *Death Scream*, a star-studded made-for-television movie.

In 1976 Stigwood was named International Producer of the Year by ABC Interstate Theaters, Inc. That same year he became a director of Polygram, his silent partner for almost a decade, while retaining full control of RSO. In what a writer for *Fortune* magazine called "a shrewd and shabby venture," Stigwood purchased for $500,000 the negative of a quickie Mexican exploitation film about cannibalism among plane crash survivors, dubbed in English dialogue, inserted some stock footage, and added a new musical score. Released by Paramount in mid-1976 as *Survive!*, the film grossed $40,000,000 worldwide. Later that year Stigwood presented *Bugsy Malone* (Paramount), a satire of 1920's gangster movies, and a television adaptation of John Osborne's *The Entertainer*, featuring Jack Lemmon in the title role.

Capitalizing on discomania, Stigwood scored his first triumph of 1978 with *Saturday Night Fever* (Paramount), the motion picture that made John Travolta, whom he had astutely signed to a $1,000,000 three-picture deal, an international star. Stigwood conceived the idea for *Saturday Night Fever* in 1976, after reading a piece in *New York* magazine about a young blue-collar worker from Brooklyn who only came alive in discotheques. He immediately bought the story rights, put up $2,500,000 for initial production expenses, and hired the Bee Gees, then making a comeback as a disco group, to compose and record the music. The double soundtrack album, strategically released by Stigwood's own RSO label two months before the film, was the fastest-selling LP in pop music history and spawned a handful of chart-topping singles. By July 1978 it had sold an incredible 22,000,000 copies, grossing more than $285,000,000. The LP eventually won for the Bee Gees a Grammy award for album of the year.

Released amidst a publicity blitz in December 1977, *Saturday Night Fever* did especially well at the box office during the lucrative holiday season. In its first six months of commercial release the film grossed $107,000,000, 45 percent of which went directly to Stigwood. Directed by John Badham, it received unexpectedly favorable notices and an Academy Award nomination for John Travolta. Stigwood followed up that blockbuster with *Grease* (Paramount, 1978), an adaptation of the long-running Broadway musical about ducktailed teenagers in the 1950's, starring Travolta and country-pop singer Olivia Newton-John. Despite its downbeat notices, the film prospered at the box office. Travolta's third motion picture for Stigwood, *Moment By Moment* (Universal, 1978), a romantic drama costarring Lily Tomlin, the comedienne, was both a critical and commercial disaster. Summing up his colleagues' opinions, Charles Champlin conjectured that "all those in favor of *Moment By Moment* could convene in a Pinto."

Over in England, however, Stigwood had the compensatory pleasure of reaping acclaim from another project he had presided over since its infancy—*Evita*, a spectacular rock opera based on the life of Eva Perón, the wife of the late Argentine dictator Juan Perón, composed by the team that had created *Jesus Christ Superstar*. With the pre-released cast album riding high on the charts, *Evita*, which was staged by Harold Prince, the leading director of musicals

in the United States, opened in London to critical accolades on June 21, 1978. *Evita* came to Los Angeles, California for its sold-out American première at the Dorothy Chandler Pavilion on May 8, 1979. Commenting on that performance for the Los Angeles *Times*, Sylvie Drake agreed that *Evita* was a "musical phenomenon." It was "not flawless," she emphasized, but it possessed "at least three vital ingredients: tremendous scope, a remarkable score, and the directorial genius of Prince." That same month Stigwood's highly praised serial version of Muriel Spark's *The Prime of Miss Jean Brodie* was introduced to American television viewers by the Public Broadcasting Service.

A monumental flop in Stigwood's otherwise banner year was the ballyhooed *Sergeant Pepper's Lonely Heart's Club Band* (Paramount, 1978), a $12,000,000 fantasy inspired by the Beatles' historic album of the same name, and featuring more than two dozen of their songs. Stigwood had been toying with that project, which he has called "my ultimate musical," since 1974. To attract the free-spending teenage market, he cast rock guitarist Peter Frampton and the Bee Gees in the leading roles and surrounded them with such high-powered groups as Aerosmith and Earth, Wind and Fire. The film's real subject, however, as David Ansen of *Newsweek* (July 31, 1978) pointed out, was "the venal music mogul B.D. Brockhurst . . . a send-up of Stigwood himself, fangs bared and greed showing." Stigwood has been variously described in the trade press as "a shark," "a benign autocrat," a power-broker who "gives people opportunities they never had before," and "a big-time gambler" attuned to mass tastes. His usually accurate reading of the public's mind failed him with *Sergeant Pepper*. Not even the soundtrack LP sold well, and more than 2,000,000 copies were returned to RSO.

Stigwood recouped RSO's losses with huge sales of records and tapes by such artists as the Bee Gees, Cream, Blind Faith, Andy Gibb, Samantha Sang, Eric Clapton, and Yvonne Elliman. In the first half of 1978 RSO dominated *Billboard's* "Hot 100" singles list and held down the number one spot for twenty-six weeks. By the year's end, RSO had been accorded more platinum records for singles sales than the entire industry had rated in 1977. In January 1979, at the suggestion of the Bee Gees, Stigwood masterminded a televised rock spectacular as a benefit for UNICEF. At that 1979 concert, each of the performers, among them, the Bee Gees, Rod Stewart, and John Denver, turned over to the United Nations the rights and royalties to one song.

A man of average height and build, Robert Stigwood has graying blond hair, baby-blue eyes, a ruddy complexion, and a certain elegance of manner. Associates say he is somewhat shy and private and has a "Victorian sense of honor." He runs his twenty-nine division empire like a family firm and relies for advice on a small, closely-knit group of aides to whom he is, as one reporter put it, "sugar daddy, best friend, guru, and toastmaster." He recently set up a generous profit-sharing plan for all employees. He has been known to give friends and employees expensive gifts and loves to throw lavish promotional parties, such as the highly publicized bash for *Tommy*, at which guests consumed $14,000 worth of lobster in a rented New York City subway station.

Stigwood works such long hours that he can only infrequently indulge in his favorite recreations—cooking, swimming, playing tennis, and sailing on his luxury yacht. A bachelor, he divides his time between a triplex apartment on Central Park West in New York City, a $15,000-a-month mansion in Beverly Hills, California, and "Wreck House," a nineteenth-century estate in Bermuda. "I'm lucky, I suppose," Stigwood told Steven Gains in an interview for the New York *Daily News* (March 27, 1977). "It's luck, timing, judgment—all those factors. I don't plan any of it. . . . I don't have any goal, really. Some days I do, some days I don't. I really just enjoy what I do. I'm having a terrific time. I never set out to set the world on fire or anything."

References: New York 11:50+ Ja 30 '78 por; N Y Daily News III pl Mr 27 '77 por; Newsweek 91:40+ Ja 23 '78 por, 92:40+ Jl 31 '78 pors; International Motion Picture Almanac (1979); Nassour, Ellis. Rock Opera (1973)

Sullivan, William H(ealy)

Oct. 12, 1922- Former United States diplomat.
Address: b. c/o "Arden House," Harriman,
N.Y. 10926

When Iranian radicals shot their way into the United States Embassy in Teheran on February 14, 1979, Ambassador William H. Sullivan directed a cool and measured response that may have meant the difference between life and death for its American staff members. No stranger to highly charged situations during his thirty-two year career in the Foreign Service, Sullivan directed the United States secret bombing campaign while serving as Ambassador to Laos in the 1960's and deputized for Henry A. Kissinger during the Vietnam peace talks in 1972 and 1973. He earned the enmity of American liberals for his staunch defense of President Richard Nixon's Southeast Asia policy. In 1977 Sullivan was appointed Ambassador to Iran by President Jimmy Carter, succeeding Richard Helms, but his close association with the Shah led to his recall in April 1979 to open the way for better United States relations with the new Iranian regime. After resigning from the Foreign Service in April 1979, Sullivan became president of the American Assembly, a study group associated with Columbia University, that meets at Arden House in Harriman, New York to discuss governmental, economic, and other social problems.

William Healy Sullivan was born on October 12, 1922 in Cranston, Rhode Island, the son of Dr. Joseph W. Sullivan, a dentist, and Sabina (Foley) Sullivan. After attending Cranston High School, he went on to Brown University, from which he graduated in 1943 with a bachelor of arts degree in political science and a Phi Beta Kappa key. He then enlisted in the United States Navy, serving as a line officer aboard minesweepers and destroyers in the Atlantic, Mediterranean, and Pacific. In 1946 he was discharged as a lieutenant junior grade.

While working on the undergraduate newspaper *Brown Daily Herald*, Sullivan planned to become a foreign correspondent, but he scrapped those plans when one of his professors asked him, "Why don't you do something responsible?" At the professor's urging he entered the Fletcher School of Law and Diplomacy at Tufts University in 1946, where he concentrated on Latin American studies. Following his graduation in 1947 with a M.A. degree, he joined the United States Foreign Service.

Sullivan's early Foreign Service career followed the typical pattern of the broad range of assignments given by the State Department to a junior officer. He served as a consular officer in Bangkok from 1947 to 1949 and then spent a year as an economic consular officer in Calcutta. Transferred to Tokyo in 1950, he was assigned as a political adviser to General Douglas MacArthur. Upon his transfer to Rome in 1952, he was assigned similar responsibilities with the staff of NATO's Southern Forces. Sullivan's last European post was The Hague, where he served as a political officer from 1955 to 1958.

Returning to Washington in 1958, Sullivan became Officer-in-Charge of Burmese Affairs at the State Department. Named United Nations Adviser for the Bureau of Far Eastern Affairs in 1960, he became involved in preparations for the 1961-62 Geneva conference called to protect Laotian neutrality. There he caught the attention of W. Averell Harriman, who headed the United States delegation. "It took me just a couple of discussions with Sullivan to realize he was not an ordinary man," Harriman recalled in an interview with Time (February 19, 1973). Impressed with what he called Sullivan's "Irish ability to see the other fellow's point of view," Harriman asked that Sullivan be designated deputy United States representative to the Geneva conference. The State Department protested that several other delegation members outranked Sullivan, then only a middle-grade Foreign Service officer, but Harriman got his way by threatening to send those senior officers home. As acting head of the United States delegation, Sullivan caused a stir by telling the representatives of the People's Republic of China that they could not hope to provoke a Soviet-American war over Laos to promote their own ends.

Following the Geneva conference Sullivan continued to work on Southeast Asian affairs as special assistant to Harriman, then Undersecretary of State for Political Affairs, and, in 1964, as chairman of a high-level interagency committee on Vietnam. In July 1964 he was sent to Saigon as executive assistant to Ambassador Maxwell T. Taylor, and in December of that year President Lyndon B. Johnson appointed him as Ambassador to Laos. Officially neutral after the Geneva conference, that country nevertheless faced a strong Communist insurgent movement and served as a conduit for North Vietnamese assistance to Communist guerrillas in South Vietnam. In commenting on his appointment during a press interview, Sullivan said, "To me Laos is a perfect example of the critical problems we face internationally. Whether small nations without resources or a large army can preserve their peace and independence is the critical issue."

United States policy in Laos was then committed to supporting the ostensibly neutralist government of Prince Souvanna Phouma against the Communist insurgents backed by North Vietnam and to impeding by steady bombardment the flow of Communist war materiel down the Ho Chi Minh trail to South Vietnam. The extent of American support was not officially acknowledged until 1970, after Sullivan told a Senate committee that as Ambassador in Vientiane he approved or disapproved bombing targets in Laos recommended for American air strikes by the Laotian government or the United States Air Force. He also supervised all United States agencies in Laos, including an extensive CIA operation and seventy-two military attachés. Commenting on Sullivan's testimony, Senator Stuart Symington said that the Ambassador had become virtually "a military proconsul."

Known for their persuasiveness and wit, Sullivan's cables from Vientiane were the only Foreign Service reports read regularly, and with some delectation, by President Johnson. The following example, as quoted by Time (February 19, 1973), demonstrates Sullivan's freedom from the operational controls ordinarily imposed by the State Department: "After you read this report, you will no doubt want to dispatch instructions. Please resist. We have all the instructions we will ever need. I will be reporting my actions."

In 1968 Sullivan's role expanded from warmaking to peace-making, when Washington instructed him to deal with his North Vietnamese counterpart in Vientiane in the search for a mutually acceptable site for the Vietnam peace talks. With Nixon installed in the White House, he returned to Washington in April 1969 as deputy assistant Secretary of State for East Asian and Pacific affairs and as chairman of the National Security Council's ad hoc committee on Vietnam. In the latter position he developed American policy proposals for the Paris peace talks and in 1971 broached the "leopard spot" stand-still concept, which was eventually adopted as the basic rule governing the ceasefire.

At the Paris talks in 1972 and 1973 Sullivan acted as chief deputy to Henry A. Kissinger, the President's National Security Adviser, and headed the "tandem negotiations" that covered the technical details of the ceasefire, including the machinery for prisoner exchange and truce supervision. When Kissinger announced in October 1972 that "peace is at hand," he noted that the protocol governing ceasefire supervision was so complex that "as far as I can tell, only my colleague, Ambassador Sullivan, understands completely."

After the ceasefire agreements were finally signed on January 27, 1973, Sullivan moved to the forefront of American efforts to improve their effectiveness and to work out a similar arrangement for Cambodia, then being subjected to daily bombing attacks by American war planes. When asked what legal authority permitted the bombing without Congressional approval, he replied at a Capitol hearing, "For now, I'd just say the justification is the re-election of President Nixon." Some antiwar activists regarded Sullivan as one of the President's worst apologists because of that and similar statements, but other, more charitable observers noted that he was, after all, a disciplined professional obliged to operate under Administration guidelines.

Although Sullivan had been nominated as Ambassador to the Philippines by President Nixon in April 1973, his ongoing preoccupation with the unsettled situation in Indochina kept him from reaching Manila until August. The prime accomplishment of his four-year tour of duty was the extension of American leases for military bases in the Philippines, a considerable achievement in view of his occasionally rocky relationship with President Ferdinand Marcos and his often imperious wife. When, for example, Sullivan once asked why more was not being done to aid the country's poor, Mrs. Marcos replied, "I don't know what else we could have done." "You could try feeding them cake," Sullivan retorted.

When, in one of his first diplomatic appointments, President Jimmy Carter nominated William H. Sullivan in April 1977 to succeed Richard Helms, the former CIA Director, as Ambassador to Iran, the nomination was criticized by some liberals because of Sullivan's role in Vietnam. According to the Nation (July 30, 1977), the Senate Foreign Relations Committee would have rejected Sullivan, had Averell Harriman not actively intervened in his behalf. Sullivan took up his Teheran post in June 1977, when Iran was in the midst of a wide-ranging modernization drive launched by Shah Mohammed Riza Pahlevi with the aid of his country's vastly expanded oil revenues. Beginning with the Nixon Administration, American policy had supported that effort because of the Shah's unimpeachable record as a pro-American force in the troubled Middle East. As it developed, however, American influence in Iran could be exercised on only a limited scale. Time (February 26, 1979) quoted Sullivan as having said in 1977, "We ran Laos, but in Iran, which is tremendously important to us, there's not much we or anyone can do."

Acknowledging his sketchy background in Iranian affairs, Sullivan once told a fellow diplomat, according to Newsweek (January 29, 1979), "I make no pretense of understanding these people. I find the Iranians a lot more inscrutable than Asians." He moved to establish a close relationship with the Shah, however, and, as he explained to Nicholas Gage of the New York Times (November 13, 1978), "He lays out his views and asks my opinion. But I don't go up there and tell him how to run things." Critics have charged that his preoccupation with the Shah, an established American practice, initially led Sullivan to reinforce his predecessor's ban on Embassy contacts with opposition politicians and to assign low priority to contacts with Iran's student, intellectual, and religious leaders. The United States Embassy was therefore unable to judge the depth of opposition generated by the de-

stabilizing modernization campaign at a time when the Shah might have been persuaded to defuse it.

Even when the Shah's regime started to topple in the fall of 1978, Sullivan played down the strength of the opposition. He told one journalist, as quoted in Newsweek (February 26, 1979), that the anti-Shah protesters were "just a bunch of out-of-work young men with nothing better to do." Nevertheless, he instructed his staff to establish contacts with opposition leaders while continuing to meet with the Shah on an almost daily basis to assure him of Washington's support for his efforts to restabilize Iran.

The Shah's enforced departure from Iran into exile in January 1979 was followed by a turbulent period when the Muslim religious leader Ayatollah Ruholla Khomeini dominated the political scene, and when armed guerrillas of various political persuasions roamed the streets of Teheran and other Iranian cities. On February 14 a guerrilla band shot its way into the American Embassy, possibly on the misunderstanding that Iranian secret police agents had taken refuge there. Sullivan reacted cooly, ordering the Marine security guards to cease resistance and take refuge with other staff members in a secure area. At Sullivan's telephoned request, forces loyal to Khomeini arrived and relieved the siege. "An interesting Valentine's Day" was Sullivan's low-keyed and ironic reaction, but in spite of his underplaying of the incident, Embassy staff members credited him with having averted heavy American casualties.

In February 1979, spokesmen for Mehdi Bazargan, Iran's new Prime Minister, made clear that Sullivan had become a liability for the United States in Teheran because of his close relationship with the Shah. Responding to those hints, President Jimmy Carter announced in late April that Sullivan would be replaced by Walter Cutler, a career diplomat who had been Ambassador to Zaire since 1975. Sullivan returned to the United States for consultations and a well-earned vacation, and it was soon announced that he had been named to the presidency of the American Assembly, the social science study group associated with Columbia University.

The adjective most often used to describe William H. Sullivan is "cool," but observers are quick to point out that his sangfroid is leavened with a genial Irish wit. A well-built man standing five feet eleven inches tall, he looks like a Hollywood scriptwriter's concept of a diplomat, with his silver hair, bushy eyebrows, blue-gray eyes, and conservative suits that never seem to lose their crease. To maintain his trim waistline, he enjoys ice skating and swimming. His Foreign Service career has helped him to acquire fluency in French, Italian, and Dutch. Sullivan was married in 1947 to Marie Johnson, one of his classmates at the Fletcher School of Diplomacy. Their four children, Anne, John, Mark, and Margaret, have all grown to adulthood.

References: Newsweek 93:34 F 26 '79 por; N Y Times p3 F 6 '65 por, p2 Ap 30 '68 por, p12 Ja 29 '73 por, A p12 N 13 '78 por, A p16 F 15 '79 por; Time 101:20+ F 19 '73 por, 113:32 F 26 '79 por; International Who's Who, 1978-79; Who's Who in America, 1978-79; Who's Who in the World, 1978-79

Summer, Donna

Dec. 31 1948- Singer. Address: b. c/o Casablanca Records & Filmworks, 8255 Sunset Blvd., Los Angeles, Calif. 90048

No performer is more closely identified with the mainstream emergence of synthesizer-based "disco" music—a propulsive form of recorded dance music sometimes lumped together with "sex rock"—than the singer and songwriter Donna Summer. The current deep-throbbing, erotic discotheque sound was only a subcultural phenomenon until 1975, when Miss Summer's aphrodisiacal "Love to Love You, Baby" (the title track of her first album) became the landmark anthem of the disco revolution. Now, with six gold (million dollar-earning) albums, a platinum (million copy-selling) one, and many hit singles, including the Grammy-winning "Last Dance for Love," behind her Donna Summer is beyond any doubt a superstar—the first to come out of disco, a musical genre so dependent on the depersonalized electronic wizardry of the recording studio that individual achievement often goes unnoticed. But,

with her full, ringing voice and the wide range of her repertoire, she transcends her original identification with disco, as she herself has pointed out: "I do not consider myself a disco artist. I consider myself a singer who does disco songs. What I like to do is expose my market to other parts of music."

Miss Summer's close collaborators from the beginning of her recording career have been the Munich-based producers and arrangers Giorgio Moroder and Pete Bellotte, who helped to develop the heavily electronic sound known as Eurodisco, which was introduced into the United States chiefly through the East Coast homosexual community. In a review in Rolling Stone of Miss Summer's fifth album, Once upon a Time, Stephen Holden looked back over the earlier years of the collaboration: " 'Love to Love You, Baby' fused Barry White's pseudo-orgasmic approach with the synthesized style heralded by the Silver Convention's 'Fly, Robin, Fly.' 'Love to Love You, Baby' not only paved the way toward a more blatant eroticism, it exhibited a nearly total fragmentation of narrative musical structure and signaled disco's break from short radio forms to longer, more organic structures. In their next two albums with Summer, Moroder and Belotte padded the chant with a diaphanous gloss and fluffed out the fantasy of perpetual gratification with love-comic scenarios. I Remember Yesterday finally revealed Summer as not just a centerfold gasp but a brassy pop/soul stylist."

One of seven children in a lower-middle-class black family, Donna Summer was born LaDonna Andrea Gaines on December 31, 1948, in Boston, Massachusetts. Her father, Ernest Gaines, a strong believer in discipline and self-motivation, worked at several jobs. "He struggled like hell to keep our house," Miss Summer recounted to Elliott Mintz when he interviewed her for Penthouse (July 1979). "He was a real dominating father but a very good father. He was a butcher during the war; so we always had meat. He was also an electrician and a janitor, and in his spare time he took care of buildings." She told Mintz that even as a child she "knew she was going to be something," and in other interviews she has suggested an implicit belief in a providence at work in her life, relieving her of worry about what the future holds.

Growing up in an ethnically mixed neighborhood in Boston, Miss Summer "didn't know what the word [racial] meant" until she was older. Mahalia Jackson was among her childhood idols, and her first training ground in singing was in choirs, at the Grant A.M.E. Church and other Boston churches. Later she sang in a classical chorale, and when she was about sixteen she became lead singer with a Boston rock 'n' roll group called Crow. While singing with Crow she "went through a pretty heavy drug scene," as she recalled in the interview with Elliott Mintz. "I finally went so far that when I was eighteen I said, 'Enough!

God did not intend me to live my life this way!' And so I quit, abruptly, after two years, and I really haven't indulged in drugs since. Now I'm unusually sensitive to any type of drug or medication. I have a hard time taking Tylenol."

Over the fierce opposition of her father, Donna Summer left Boston in the spring of 1967, less than a month before she was to have graduated from high school, to join a German touring company of the rock musical *Hair*, in which she sang Sheila, the role created by Melba Moore on Broadway. After the show ended its run, she remained in Europe, for a total of eight years, modeling and singing in Vienna Volksoper productions of *Showboat* and *Porgy and Bess* and German productions of *Godspell* and *The Me Nobody Knows*.

Miss Summer also worked as a backup singer at the Musicland recording studios in Munich, where the driving, deep-bass Euro-disco sound, dominated by synthesizers, was being created. There she met Giorgio Moroder and Pete Bellotte, owners of Oasis Records. The three began to work on songs together and came up with two singles that became European hits for Miss Summer—"Hostage" and "Lady of the Night." Inspired by the success of a revival in England of the breathy 1969 recording "Je t'aime," they tried a three-minute version of a libidinous song written by Miss Summer, "Love to Love You, Baby," consisting mainly of repetitons of the title line in varied orgasmic moans and gasps. That brazenly torrid departure from the more innocent image Europeans had of Miss Summer probably contributed to the failure of the record on the Continent (except in Paris).

In the United States, where Miss Summer was as yet unknown to the general public, the Oasis label was leased for distribution to Neil Bogart's Casablanca Records, based in Los Angeles. When Bogart played the three-minute Oasis version of "Love to Love You, Baby" at a private party at his home the guests could not get enough of its hypnotic lubricity and asked that it be played over and over. Deciding to gamble on a full-sided version for Miss Summer's first Casablanca album, Bogart asked Moroder for a new track, expanded to seventeen minutes.

Recalling the recording of "Love to Love You, Baby," Miss Summer has said that she "knew how it had .to be done" but, never having attempted anything so openly ecstatic before, she was "embarrassed" and had to be left alone in the studio with the lights dimmed before she felt free enough to go into the heavy breathing and the feigned orgasm. She approached the song as an "acting piece," she told Elliott Mintz, and her acting was convincing. "My song conjured up physical fantasies for people. My acting was done well, and people believed the story I was acting."

By adding a touch of American "soul" to the electronic sound pioneered by such groups as Germany's Kraftwerk, "Love to Love You, Baby" not only gave a new intensity to Euro-disco but vastly expanded the market to which it appealed. Following the release of the album *Love to Love You, Baby* in 1975, the title track became a favorite not only of the undulating, gyrating dancers in "gay" discotheques and black and Latin dance halls but also of listeners to late-night pop radio, where soft-core pornographic music had gained acceptance. Within six weeks 400,000 albums had been sold, and on Valentine's Day of the following year the album hit the top of *Billboard* magazine's "Hot 100" list.

"Without 'Love to Love You' I undoubtedly would have stayed in Germany," Miss Summer told Pat Snyder when he was writing an article on her for the Toronto *Globe and Mail* (October 21, 1978). "I'd sworn to my mother, 'When I come back to this country, Mommy, I'll be somebody.' Until that song there really wasn't any reason to come back."

Not having watched *Love to Love You, Baby* as it climbed the American charts, Miss Summer was unaware that the album was already number one when she arrived back in the United States in 1975. She was shocked at the wild adulation of the crowds that greeted her when she disembarked from the plane, and the explosion of her fame as the "disco sex goddess" nearly precipitated a nervous breakdown. As was noted in the introduction to the *Penthouse* interview, "Traumatized by the frenzy and the new identity imposed on her, she went through periods of forgetting her name, developed a chronic ulcer, and occasionally checked into hospitals for a week at a time. To this day she admits that her greatest fear is of losing control of herself, mentally and emotionally."

The stylized sexuality and disco metronomics of "Love to Love You, Baby" were sustained in the 1976 albums *A Love Trilogy* and *The Four Seasons of Love*. Like *Love to Love You, Baby*, both albums quickly "went gold," with *The Four Seasons of Love* comprising four full-side cuts, including "A Spring Affair," which did very well as a single. "By the time of 'A Spring Affair,' it was enough," she told Mikal Gilmore in her *Rolling Stone* interview. I couldn't go on singing these soft songs. I've sung gospel and Broadway musicals all my life, and you have to have a belting voice for that. And because my skin is black, they categorize me as a black act, which is not the truth. I'm not even a soul singer. I'm more a pop singer."

The hit single "I Feel Love" was a cut from the 1977 album *I Remember Yesterday*, a wide-ranging sampler of twentieth-century pop styles described by Ken Tucker in *Rolling Stone* (August 11, 1977) as "the luxurious stretching out of a performer just beginning to realize her strengths and possibilities," an album "clearly meant" to "move Summer as both a singer and songwriter beyond the disco classification" and one which "succeeds with ease." Miss Summer herself was not satisfied with the "popcorn tracks" of *I Remember Yesterday*. The first album she felt she could "really say is a part of" her was the later 1977 release *Once Upon a Time*, a four-sided erotic mock opera in which Miss Summer is a campy sci-fi Cinderella.

John Rockwell of the New York *Times* (December 9, 1977) saw in *Once Upon a Time* proof that Miss Summer had "overcome the novelty success" of *Love To Love You, Baby*. In his review in *Rolling Stone* (January 12, 1978), Stephen Holden called the "erotic Muzak" of Moroder and Bellotte "the music of the brave new world—music with a capacity to suggest comic-book erotic/astral configurations limited only by the studio and the synthesizer technologies that. produce and reproduce it."

Also in 1977, Columbia Pictures released *The Deep*, for which Miss Summer wrote and sang the theme song. For her role as an aspiring disco singer using her wiles on a discotheque disk jockey in the Motown-Casablanca Records and Film Works motion picture *Thank God It's Friday* (1978)—a critical dud but a commercial blockbuster—Miss Summer wrote the hit single "Last Dance for Love," for which the National Academy of Recording Arts and Sciences presented her with its award for best female vocalist of 1978 in rhythm and blues. In his article in the Toronto *Globe and Mail*, Patrick Snyder observed that "Last Dance for Love," along with Miss Summer's chart-topping cover of Jimmy Webb's "MacArthur Park," first recorded by Richard Harris in the late 1960's, "reveal a strong, clear voice that no one listening to her early records would have expected." He quoted the singer: "My first hit was like making up your face not to look like you and having people believe that's what you looked like. Little by little we've taken the makeup off."

The 1978 release *Live and More*—which included songs by such popular music masters as Gershwin and Ellington—became a "double platinum" album, selling more than 2,000,000 copies. Miss Summer wrote or collaborated in the composition of eight of the fifteen songs on the album *Bad Girls*, which was released in April 1979 and shot to the top of the charts the following month. One of its cuts, the rock-disco hybrid "Hot Stuff," quickly became the hottest song in discos across the United States, and the title cut rose to the top of both *Variety's* Singles chart and the Airplay chart in July 1979.

Spectacle—including sensual choreography and glamorous costumes costing about $70,000 a year—is an an important aspect of the act that Miss Summer regularly takes to clubs in Las Vegas and Lake Tahoe and on concert tours elsewhere. Her concert repertoire ranges from her bawdy, strutting rendition of "If You've Got It, You'd Better Flaunt It" through a rocker-style "My Baby Understands" to a

performance of "Love to Love You, Baby" in which she pretends to make love to the microphone, the sequins on her dress sparkling as she rotates her pelvis.

Reviewing a performance by Miss Summer in the Maple Leaf Concert Bowl in Toronto, Canada, Katherine Gilday of the Toronto *Globe and Mail* (October 23, 1978) thought the "best number of the night" was "If You've Got It, You'd Better Flaunt It," in which the singer seemed "a cross between a female impersonator and Tina Turner on Valium." Regarding "Love to Love You, Baby," Miss Gilday wrote, "Somehow it never felt lewd. There was, in fact, a sort of inspirational grandeur about Summer's movements here—as if she were a true priestess of the body. The rest of the night, though, it was straight showmanship, with not too many qualities mitigating the pervasive bad taste, musically and theatrically. Donna was the dream come true of the upwardly mobile set in that almost as much attention was devoted to her wardrobe as to her songs." In *Time* (December 4, 1978), Jay Cocks gave this description: "Arms flung wide, blowing kisses like confetti, Donna sashays around the stage in glittering costumes, exhorting the audience ('You are beautiful'), joshing the band, trading prefabricated bitchiness with her backup singers, who undulate at sharp angles like clockwork Nefertitis when Donna wraps herself around a lyric."

Miss Summer tours under the management of Susan Munao. Her regular backup singers are three of her sisters, and in many of her concert performances she has been accompanied by a group called Brooklyn Dreams, of which the lead guitarist is Bruce Sudano, with whom she has been romantically involved for more than two years. Her last name is the anglicized form of the surname of her ex-husband, Helmut Sommer, an Austrian actor in the German *Hair* troupe from whom she was divorced in 1974. By the marriage to Sommer she has a daughter, Mimi.

In his article in *Rolling Stone*, Mikal Gilmore described Miss Summer's tall frame as "muscular," her face as "less angular than in album photos," and her nose as "puggish." Miss Summer lives in a twenty-five-room house she recently bought in Beverly Hills. Her offstage life apparently contrasts sharply with her on-stage image. "I don't smoke, drink, snort cocaine, take Quaaludes, or sleep around town," she once told a reporter. The singer takes astrology and faith healing very seriously. Professionally, she considers herself at a crossroads; in the future, if she has her way, she will be doing much more serious acting. On the side, she would like to do some fabric designing, one of her favorite pastimes since childhood.

"I'm always slightly depressive," Miss Summer told Elliot Mintz in the *Penthouse* interview. "My whole life is work, and it's always been work. Even when I'm home relaxing, I'm playing the piano or singing. I've always got to be doing something recreative or constructive." Mintz asked her why. "I think it comes from the fear of dying, in the sense that I feel God gave me a reason to be here," she answered. "I'm very religious in the sense that I think there is life after death and that everyone has a karmic debt to pay back; and whatever that is, I want to pay it back before I go. I want to do things for other people— and I'm getting to be in a position where I can." Her long-range goal, she said, was to set up a community center in South America that would be philanthropic without being exploitative, that would let the people "retain a sense of themselves." Her accountants are always telling her that she is spending too much money, she said. "I'm not afraid of tomorrow, and I'm not afraid to be hungry. I can risk whatever money I have because I know that with my intelligence, with my strength, I will get back to where I was."

References: After Dark 9:39+ Ap '77 pors; Ebony 32:33+ O '77 pors; Rolling Stone p11+ Mr 23 '78 pors; Toronto Globe and Mail mag p8+ O 21 '78 pors; Penthouse 10:86+ Jl '79 pors; Who's Who in America, 1978-79

Swados, Elizabeth (swā′dōs)

Feb. 5, 1951- Composer; writer; director.
Address: h. 112 Waverly Place,
New York City, N.Y. 10011

An eclectic composer who draws on everything from Indian ragas to Japanese No chants, American Indian laments, salsa and disco rhythms, and the songs of birds, Elizabeth Swados has dazzled New York theatre audiences with her masterful and innovative scores for productions of plays by other artists as well as with her own free-wheeling, idiosyncratic musical entertainments. Miss Swados first came to prominence Off Off Broadway at the La Mama Experimental Theatre Club during the early 1970's, where she and the Ro-manian-born director Andrei Serban created highly acclaimed adaptations of Medea, Electra, The Trojan Women, and The Good Woman of Setzuan. Later Miss Swados and Serban moved uptown to Lincoln Center, where she scored his versions of The Cherry Orchard and Agamemnon. In 1977 she struck out on her own, creating a delightful Off-Broadway musical pastiche entitled Nightclub Cantata. Her most ambitious creation to date has been the hit Broadway show, Runaways, a collage of songs and monologues about adolescents estranged from their families. Miss Swados conceived the idea for that production, wrote the book, composed the music, choreographed it, and directed it, a feat that won her five Tony award nominations in 1978.

Elizabeth Swados, whose family background is rich in actors, writers, and musicians, was born in Buffalo, New York on February 5, 1951, the only daughter of Robert O. and Sylvia (Maisel) Swados. Her father, who is now vice-president of the Buffalo Sabres hockey team and president of the board of trustees of the Studio Arena Theater in Buffalo, originally trained to be an actor and considered a stage career before becoming a lawyer. Her mother was an actress and a poet who at one time wrote for the liberal New York daily newspaper of the 1940's, P.M. Her maternal grandfather was a concertmaster and violinist in Russia, and her paternal grandmother was a concert violinist. Harvey Swados, the late novelist, journalist, and short story writer, was her second cousin. The Swados family, originally from Vilna, Lithuania, used to spell their name Swiadisch. Miss Swados has one brother, eight years her senior, who lives in New York.

"They were strong, giddy Jewish people, very huggy-kissy," said Elizabeth Swados in describing her family to Mel Gussow of the New York Times Magazine (March 5, 1978), "an extraordinarily loving, passionate brood, moody and dramatic. You had to be careful." She has also characterized her family as troubled and eccentric. Her violinist grandmother had to have a lobotomy, and the composer has recalled that her parents fought constantly during her childhood. In 1974 her mother committed suicide. "A family's history has an enormous effect on an individual," Miss Swados told Gussow. "Those demons certainly exist in me. There is pain. But the lucky thing is that they are a great help, a source of enormous energy and inspiration. . . . People in my family have gone both ways —off the deep end, or, like my father, using his energy to accomplish things, to be productive, and giving. It's a fight. It's probably made me stronger than most people who come from sedate families."

As a child Elizabeth Swados was solitary, independent, creative, and rebellious. She ran away from home several times, the first time at the age of five. At home she lived in a world of imagination that she filled with paper cutouts, made-up stories, and especially music. At five she started playing the piano and at ten the guitar, and soon she was composing music on both. At the age of twelve she began performing as a folk singer, emulating her idol, Joan Baez, and as a teen-ager she amassed a collection of rejection slips from the New Yorker for her short stories.

At sixteen Miss Swados entered Bennington College, where she studied creative writing and music under Henry Brant. There she first encountered Far Eastern music, which intrigued her so much that she composed, much to the consternation of the music department, a symphonic overture in which thirty actors imitated a Balinese monkey chorus. She also gained distinction at Bennington by getting her picture published nationally as the first woman to live with a male student when the college went coed. "In a short period of time," remarked Mel Gussow, "she seemed to try everything: commune life, vegetarianism, and drugs." For a school work project Miss Swados signed up with Appalachia Volunteers, Inc., and lived for four months with a mining family in Stephenson, West Virginia. While there she tutored children in reading, started a young people's newspaper, organized drama groups, and led a public protest against black-lung disease. Meanwhile, she continued her folk singing in Buffalo and New York City coffeehouses and spent two summers singing with Pete Seeger aboard his sloop Clearwater on the Hudson.

Miss Swados began composing theatre music at Bennington and eventually dropped out of college to continue at the avant-garde La Mama theatre in the East Village, where she met Andrei Serban. They first worked together on Serban's audacious adaptation of Medea, for which Miss Swados created a musical score that incorporated a number of Far Eastern influences. But her contribution did not stop there. For Serban, drama is primarily ritual, and he is willing to sacrifice psychological nuances for sights and sounds that evoke powerful emotions in his audience. His Medea was presented not in English but in a combination of the original Greek of Euripides and the Latin of Seneca—with the words chosen for their sounds, not for their meanings, by Miss Swados. She also helped to drill the performers in the rhythms and tones they were to produce in pronouncing them.

A much garlanded Off Off Broadway production, Medea won for Miss Swados, who was then twenty years old, a 1972 Village Voice Obie for her score. (When submitted to Bennington, the score also won Miss Swados her B.A. degree in absentia.) While touring Europe with the play, she met the celebrated British director Peter Brook and joined his International Theater Group as musical director and composer. That year she toured with them in Africa, where they performed improvisational theatre in tiny villages and recorded the songs and stories of the natives. In the United States the following year with Brook, she worked with El Teatro Campesino in California, an American Indian troupe in Minnesota, and the National Theatre of the Deaf in Waterford, Connecticut. With Serban she collaborated on their second Greek drama, Electra, which was first performed at the 1973 October Festival at Bordeaux, France.

Back at La Mama with Serban in 1974, Miss Swados created the music and sound for a third Greek drama, The Trojan Women, which was performed at the rate of two plays per night in repertory with Medea and Electra in a program entitled Fragments of a Trilogy. Together the three plays comprised a compendium of the musical influences that the composer had encountered in her studies and travels—Oriental and African music, songs of Eastern Europe and the Middle East, and American Indian laments, as well as the use for sound effect of Mayan, Aztec, and other ancient Indian languages. "Though we understand scarcely a word—proper names excepted," wrote Walter Kerr of The Trojan Women in the New York Times (January 25, 1976), "we are fully present: drum beats, the whole instrumentation that composer Elizabeth Swados has so pulsingly and powerfully supplied [for] the holocaust, become our words, fusing with the animal-like bursts of anger and pain that come from the actors' throats."

Serban and Miss Swados next worked together on an adaptation of Bertolt Brecht's acerbic comedy, The Good Woman of Setzuan, which was first presented at La Mama in February 1975. Using a small musical ensemble, in which she herself played piano and guitar, Miss Swados created a lively, melodic score for the play. "The frolicsome journey is enlivened by Elizabeth Swados's score," wrote Mel Gussow (New York Times, January 27, 1976) in a typically admiring review. ". . . . The songs have a Weill touch . . . but also their own sweet-and-sour flavor—sounding something like an Oriental version of American jazz."

Eager to use what she had learned about theatre from Serban in a work of her own, Miss Swados conceived, composed, and directed a cabaret revue entitled Nightclub Cantata, in which she performed as one of its eight actors. Nightclub Cantata consisted of about twenty gracefully interwoven poems and narratives by such authors as Sylvia Plath, Delmore Schwartz, and Pablo Neruda, as well as Miss Swados herself, set to a startling range of music that included calypso, raga, rock, folk, ragtime, and various exotic sounds, including bird calls. First performed at the Lenox Arts Center in the summer of 1976, Nightclub Cantata opened Off Broadway at the Top of the Gate on January 9, 1977 to generally enthusiastic reviews. Alan Rich (New York, January 31) wrote that he "liked virtually everything about the show," and Clive Barnes (New York Times, January 10) called it "the most original and perhaps the most pleasurable form of nightclub entertainment I have ever encountered." Nightclub Cantata brought Miss Swados her second Obie, as well as an Outer Critics Circle Award, and road companies carried the show to Boston, Washington, and Europe. A London production was scheduled for the fall of 1978.

When Joseph Papp commissioned Andrei Serban to mount two productions for the Vivian Beaumont Theater at Lincoln Center in 1977, the Romanian director again turned to Miss Swados to compose the music. For The Cherry Orchard, which opened on February 17, 1977, Miss Swados wrote mazurkas, polonaises, and waltzes. More extensive was her contribution to Agamemnon, which was, according to the program notes, "conceived" by Serban and Miss Swados "using fragments of the original Greek and Edith Hamilton's translation." The drama was so dominated by the chorus, coached by Miss Swados, that several reviewers compared the production to an oratorio without arias. Like The Cherry Orchard, Agamemnon was greeted with a mixed reception. One reviewer, Martin Gottfried of the New York Post (May 19, 1977), found the chorus overwhelming. "They sometimes sound like natives in a 'King Kong' movie, sometimes like prayer chanters in a synagogue, and altogether like the showy bombast of Orff's flashy primitive cantata, 'Carmina Burana,'" he complained. The often exigent Stanley Kauffmann of the New Republic (June 11, 1977), on the other hand, found much to admire. "The barbaric-gentle quartertones, the dramatically used instruments (especially flutes and drums), the overlay of august song are inseparable from the whole," he wrote. "Does Swados write Attic music? No one on earth knows. But if the Theater of Dionysus didn't have music as good as this, the Athenians were deprived."

When Nightclub Cantata closed in May 1978, Elizabeth Swados began working on the idea that would eventually become Runaways, levying partly on her own stormy experiences as a child and adolescent. Sponsored by Joseph Papp's Public Theatre, she spent several months interviewing adolescents and using the material she had collected to write the songs and monologues for the show. In her search for actors she shunned professional schools and went to storefront cultural centers, alternative schools, recreation centers, and public high schools. The result was a cast recruited from a diversity of New York ethnic and social backgrounds. A few were professionals, and most had had some sort of previous acting experience. Ranging in age from their early teens to their early twenties, they included an accomplished New York subway graffiti artist, a skateboard champion, and a deaf and dumb boy who used sign language.

Set in a playground with a large coop full of live pigeons in the background, Runaways had its youthful actors performing loosely connected songs, dances, and monologues on such subjects as suffering child abuse, being a child prostitute, surviving parents' quarrels, and making it on the streets. "One of Swados' most effective devices is to undercut the toughness of her runaways with reminders that they are still, after all, only children," observed Allan Wallach in Newsday (March 10, 1978) after the play opened at the Public Theatre Cabaret on March 9, 1978. "When a frail girl who looks as if she's no more than fourteen or fifteen sings about being a prostitute, pianist Judith Fleisher accompanies her on a toy piano. At other times a lullaby or a nursery tune is used for a song of loneliness or despair. The effect is an unsettling mingling of harshness and innocence." Critics were nearly unanimous in their enthusiasm. "In the year 1978," declared Clive Barnes in the New York Post (March 10, 1978), "[Runaways] is perfectly essential seeing—for itself, for the way it has been done, and for what it is crying in the wind."

So that it could reach a wider audience, in May the show moved uptown to Broadway's Plymouth Theatre, with an enlarged cast. Reviewed again by the city's drama critics, Runaways still received excellent notices, although several members of the press thought it had worked better in the intimacy of a small theatre. A few felt that the show's anti-establishment, anti-adult viewpoint and deliberate air of inspired amateurism were not appropriate to the hustling commercialism of the Broadway stage. Marilyn Stasio, for example, who liked the show downtown, drastically revised her opinion when she saw it at the Plymouth. "Runaways is Sesame Street at $17.50 a ticket," she lamented in Cue (May 27-June 9, 1978), "and I don't know who should be more offended by it, audiences or stage professionals." Still, the majority of critical opinion was obvious when Miss Swados became the first person ever to get five Antoinette Perry nominations for one show—for best musical, musical score, direction of a musical, choreography, and musical book. Columbia Records has released a recording of *Runaways*, and Twentieth Century-Fox has purchased the film rights.

Freely adapted from Michael Herr's powerful book of Vietnam combat reportage with the same title, Miss Swados' *Dispatches*, a "rock-war musical," opened in the Cabaret of Joseph Papp's Public Theater on April 6, 1979. The show was acted, sung, and danced by eleven youthful performers on a bare stage to the accompaniment of seven musicians seated on an elevated platform. Critics were so divided on the merits of *Dispatches*, a difficult and adventurous work, that reviews ranged from rapturous in Newsweek to condemnatory in New York magazine

Miss Swados has written a children's book entitled *The Girl With the Incredible Feeling* (Persea Books, 1977), composed a *Sylvia Plath Song Cycle* (1973) and *The Conference of the Birds* (1973), and has written the music for several *Camera Three* CBS-TV shows. She is currently reworking her musical version of Lewis Carroll's *Alice in Wonderland*, and is working on a short jazz opera about prostitutes, their clients, and their pimps. Miss Swados has taught at Carnegie-Mellon University (1974), Bard College (1976-77), and Sarah Lawrence (1976-77). She has been the subject of a documentary film that also has the title of *The Girl With the Incredible Feeling*.

About five feet one inch tall and very slender, Elizabeth ("Liz") Swados is often called "waif-like," because of her huge eyes, waist-length brown hair, and generally somber expression. On her left hand is a small tattoo consisting of two intertwined halves of triangles, and she has other small tattoos on her leg and shoulder. She habitually wears her guitar pick on the small finger of her left hand. A woman of divergent moods, Miss Swados is prodigiously energetic and has a fun-loving, self-satiric streak. She is said to have a fierce temper, and often directs her anger at herself when she is dissatisfied with her work. She has been known to slam her fist through her guitar and regularly smashes tape recorders. "I'm not advocating that," she told Gussow in the New York *Times Magazine* interview. ". . . [But] I can choose to be unstable. I have all the makings for a nervous breakdown, but I want to *do* a lot of things. I work most of the time. The way to survive is to work and to live entirely in the moment." In Manhattan Miss Swados lives in a Greenwich Village coach-house apartment that she shares with her dog, a poodle named Mushroom. She also rents a house in Woodstock.

References: BMI p27+ no. 2 '78 por; N Y *Daily News* p58 Ja 6 '77 por, p5+ Mr 5 '78 por; N Y *Post* p34 Je 2 '78 por; N Y *Times Mag* p19+ Mr 5 '78 pors; *People* 7:91+ Mr 7 '77 pors; *Who's Who in America, 1978-79*

Swearingen, John E(ldred)

Sept. 7, 1918- Corporation executive. *Address:* b. Standard Oil Co. (Indiana), 200 E. Randolph Dr., Chicago, Ill. 60601; h. 1420 Lake Shore Dr. N., Chicago, Ill. 60610

John E. Swearingen is a self-made man who scrambled up through the ranks of the Standard Oil Company (Indiana) to become its chief executive officer in 1960 and chairman of the board five years later. In little more than a decade he transformed that modest, domestically oriented enterprise, the sixth largest American oil company, into a corporate hustler with international clout. Elected chairman of the American Petroleum Institute in 1977, he has become the chief spokesman for the oil industry during the most trying period in its history. Swearingen, who has often expounded the prevailing industry opinion that taxation and government regulation will not solve the energy crisis, refuses to believe that "a small group of people in Washington can decide for 210,000,000 people better than they can for themselves."

John Eldred Swearingen was born in Columbia, South Carolina on September 7, 1918, the son of John Eldred and Mary (Hough) Swearingen. He entered the University of South Carolina in Columbia when he was only sixteen and received his B.S. degree from that institution in 1938. Swearingen then went on for graduate study in engineering to Carnegie Institute of Technology in Pittsburgh (now incorporated into Carnegie-Mellon University). Equipped with his M.S. degree, he joined the Standard Oil Company (Indiana) in 1939 as a chemical engineer in its Whiting, Indiana research laboratories, where he held increasingly responsible positions. In 1947 he was transferred to the manufacturing department of its subsidiary, Pan American Petroleum Corporation, in Tulsa, Oklahoma, and advanced through its management ranks so quickly that he was named a director in 1951.

Later that same year Swearingen returned to Standard Oil Company (Indiana) as general manager of production. He was named vice-president for production in 1954 and, as such, coordinated the crude oil production, pipeline, and purchasing activities of the company's several subsidiaries. When he moved up to executive vice-president two years later, he assumed the additional responsibility of overseeing the manufacturing, sales, and distribution operations. Working closely with Frank O. Prior, Indiana Standard's chief executive officer, Swearingen realigned and consolidated the subsidiaries, stepped up oil exploration, and began trimming the company's ever increasing work force.

After he became president of Indiana Standard in 1958, Swearingen accelerated his tough-minded program of cutting costs. By stepping up the installation of labor-saving devices in company refineries and completely automating certain operations, he cut the number of employees from 52,000 in 1956 to 43,000 by the end of 1959 and saved some $80,000,000 in wages. To eliminate excessive duplication of effort, he concentrated all research activities in one plant, coordinated marketing and accounting procedures, and streamlined sales operations. Moreover, he decreed that all Indiana Standard products, even those manufactured and marketed by subsidiary units, be sold under the parent company's torch and oval shield emblem. But Indiana Standard's slow but steady progress under its new president was impeded by occasional labor problems. Swearingen's unwavering insistence on the company's right to determine work rules provoked five crippling strikes, including one that lasted 241 days, in 1959 alone, but Standard eventually prevailed in all five disputes.

Swearingen succeeded Frank Prior as chief executive officer in 1960 and became chairman of the board in 1965. At the time of his first promotion, profits were down sharply because of a temporary oversupply of petroleum products, low gasoline prices, and a general economic recession. Although Indiana Standard had for years been the dominant oil company in the Midwest, Swearingen immediately began a massive remodeling operation to improve the company's position in the industry and, at the same time, substantially increase its profit ratio. In 1960, for example, the company's net profit per dollar of sales was just seven cents as opposed to twelve and sixteen cents for such rivals as Gulf and Texaco. "Let's face it. In many respects, this is a second-rate company," Swearingen said, as quoted in Forbes magazine (June 1, 1961). "This company has just not kept pace with the oil business or with other companies in the past ten years."

Swearingen's blunt appraisal called attention to Indiana Standard's chronic problem: not enough supplies of crude oil. It produced less than half of the 636,000 barrels of crude that it refined and marketed daily in 1960 and its modest crude oil reserves totaled a mere 2,300,000 barrels compared to Texaco's 15,-000,000 and New Jersey Standard's 29,000,000. To solve the problem, Swearingen expanded domestic exploration and production of crude oil by leasing drilling rights in offshore Louisiana, Alaska, and other areas. He dispatched drilling crews to the Persian Gulf, where large offshore reserves were discovered, and to Argentina, Pakistan, Ecuador, Ghana, Mozambique, Canada, and other promising locations. By 1970 fully 40 percent of Indiana Standard's crude oil supplies came from its own overseas fields, up from 15 percent in 1960.

Swearingen significantly increased production in the company's refineries abroad and began marketing operations in Australia and Europe. For instance, at his behest, the company bought 700 service stations as Standard outlets in Italy. While he conceded that playing "catch-up" in the international oil race was both expensive and risky, Swearingen maintained that there was a greater possibility of gain from overseas operations. By 1971 $865,000,000 of the company's $3.4 billion assets were outside the United States, an investment that increased dramatically in the mid-1970's with major drilling operations off the coasts of Japan and the Philippines and in the Montrose fields in the North Sea.

At home Swearingen continued the judicious cost-cutting and sweeping organizational changes that he had begun in the 1950's. He trimmed the number of employees by almost 25 percent, so that by 1963 the total wage and benefit costs, despite sizeable pay hikes, were $17,000,000 less than they had been in 1957. To reduce duplication of functions and operations, he consolidated twenty-six Midwest divisional offices into eight regional headquarters and merged domestic refining and marketing operations under the American Oil Company, a subsidiary that sells Standard and American brand products.

Because he believes that "there's no point in retaining business where you're just trading dollars," he cut back on less profitable retail operations by, for example, closing dozens of low-volume service stations and building new ones in better locations. Despite 13 percent fewer outlets, sales jumped 14 percent.

Indiana Standard stepped up manufacture of its petrochemical products and even branched out into roadside restaurants and, through its wholly owned subsidiary, Imperial Casualty Indemnity Company of Omaha, into private automobile insurance. Although eager to improve the company's substandard rate of return, Swearingen opted for "careful planning for the long pull" rather than short-term benefits "which improve the present at the expense of the future." Under his leadership, Indiana Standard showed a slow, but steady annual increase in net income and in dividends, so that by the time of its seventy-fifth anniversary in 1964 the company, with assets of $3.2 billion, was the sixth-largest oil company in the United States. Earnings had increased in each of the previous five years and in 1963 were 55 percent higher than they had been five years before. Dividends went up fifty percent over the same period. To Swearingen, profit increases provide the best test of a corporation's contribution to society. "It's a simplification," he told John J. Abele of the New York Times (June 14, 1964), "but we're in business to make money, not sell oil."

Swearingen elaborated on that theme in a speech he delivered at DePauw University in Greencastle, Indiana in November 1965. He told his audience that although the federal government has a "vital interest in corporate profitability," which he defined as "the creative force in our economy," most government officials equated profit with "private greed." Moreover, that "simplistic attitude" was reflected in the bargaining demands of organized labor. "Once the essential role of profits in a nation officially dedicated to individualism and a free economy is conceded, one comes close to an admission that a great number of things the government has been doing for a long time are simply wrong," he argued. "The logic for punitive taxation, for over-regulation, for governmental competition with private business, for wholesale interference with the workings of the economy, largely disappears."

On several occasions during Swearingen's executive tenure, Indiana Standard tangled with the Washington bureaucracy. In the early 1960's, for example, the Justice Department, charging a violation of antitrust laws, brought suit when Indiana Standard purchased the Honolulu Oil Corporation's production properties for $385,000,000. (The company was eventually absolved of monopoly charges in federal court.) Contending that "the businessman is trapped in the middle" of conflicting government regulations, Swearingen has repeatedly called for the clarification of antitrust laws. "For the last two decades, no legal counsel has been in a position to advise his employer accurately as to the precise limitations and restrictions of existing statutes," he said, as quoted in the New York *Herald Tribune* (November 12, 1961). "What is legal one day becomes the subject of prosecution the next."

Indiana Standard entered the decade of the 1970's in a rather enviable position, ranking third in natural gas production, fourth in gasoline, and sixth in crude oil. To strengthen Standard's position still further, Swearingen moved in 1971 to merge the Midwest Oil Corporation of Denver, then 68 percent controlled by Indiana Standard, with the Amoco Production Company, a subsidiary. When ten of the thirteen Midwest directors balked at the merger terms, Swearingen promptly dismissed all ten; then he and the remaining directors approved the plan.

A few years later, in November 1974, Swearingen tried to acquire Occidental Petroleum, the eleventh-largest oil company in the United States. Occidental was especially attractive to Indiana Standard because of its sizable foreign oil reserves, coal properties, and diversified chemical and fertilizer operations. Swearingen proposed to Armand Hammer, Occidental's chairman, that Standard acquire all of Occidental's shares in exchange for Standard stock. Contending that the takeover would be "anticompetitive," Occidental filed suit December 3, 1974 to prevent the acquisition. In testimony before a Senate subcommittee that was looking into the proposed merger, the largest in history, Swearingen countered that Standard's more efficient management could bring about a more rapid and efficient utilization of Occidental's energy resources. After weeks of investigations by the Securities and Exchange Commission and the Federal Trade Commission and considerable adverse publicity, Swearingen quietly dropped the proposal.

Less affected by the Arab oil embargo of the winter of 1973-74 than his competitors, who were more dependent on Mideast crude supplies, Swearingen advised the oil industry to "economize and husband supplies." To encourage more domestic oil exploration off coastal areas and in the oil-rich Alaskan wilderness, he called for a compromise between environmentalists, who had held up drilling in several promising locations for months, and energy producers. Without substantial increases in domestic crude production, he warned, the United States foreign trade deficit for 1975 could amount to $10 billion from energy imports alone. For that reason, he opposed a Congressionally endorsed rollback of domestic crude oil prices that would cost the oil industry millions of dollars in annual revenue. Indiana Standard stood to lose approximately $100,000,000 a year that could have been funneled into the exploration and development of new oil fields.

Swearingen labeled President Jimmy Carter's high-priority energy conservation package "one-sided" and "naïve." Speaking on NBC-TV's *Meet the Press* on April 25, 1977, Swearingen pointed out that Carter's energy program "will leave the [oil] industry with less money to drill wells and increase supplies than the industry currently has." "If you really want to accelerate domestic production," he added, "the industry has to be given the money to do it." To generate the revenue needed to increase domestic drilling operations and shale oil production, he suggested an immediate thirty-cents-per-gallon hike in gasoline prices. "People are paying higher oil and gas prices in Europe and you're not seeing any revolution there," he told Dan Dorfman of *New York* magazine (June 6, 1977). When questioned about the resulting hardship to lower-income familes, he replied, "I'm sympathetic to poor people, but for heaven's sake, let's not ruin our future to take care of a relatively few people when we can handle the [energy] program in another way. . . . What is a man on relief doing owning an automobile? Let's not let our sympathies run away with us."

When President Carter accused the oil companies of capitalizing on the energy shortage by overcharging consumers, Swearingen publicly denied the charge, which he belittled as simply an "emotional appeal to defend a tax program that isn't defensible." Although he acknowledged that there was room for compromise in the kind of incentives needed to stimulate oil and gas production, Swearingen disagreed with the independent producers who wanted immediate deregulation of oil and gas prices. In mid-November 1977, in one of his first speeches as chairman-elect of the American Petroleum Institute, he conceded that "ultimately we have to free the price of oil from controls." "But," he added, "there's no point in giving the industry cash at a rate it can't spend. I think five years is a reasonable phaseout for controls." In his opinion, it was more important for the oil companies to make a concerted, united effort to solve their common problems. "We need a renewed desire on the part of all elements of the industry to work together rather than go off in different directions," he said.

In contrast to some of its larger competitors, such as Exxon, the world's biggest oil company, which registered a disappointing bottom line in 1977, Indiana Standard reported record net earnings of $1.01 billion on sales of slightly more than $13 billion. Swearingen attributed the impressive gains to unexpectedly high yields from overseas drilling operations, higher natural gas prices in the United States and Canada, and expanded domestic markets. Only the petrochemical division made less money in 1977 than it had in 1976.

John Swearingen married the former Bonnie L. Bolding, a stockbroker, on May 18, 1969.

They live in an elegant apartment on Chicago's Lake Shore Drive. He has three grown daughters from an earlier marriage. Because of his crowded business calendar, Swearingen has little time for his favorite recreations, big-game hunting and golf. Although one of the highest-paid executives in the country, with an annual salary hovering around the half-million-dollar mark, he shuns the jet set crowd. "I have nothing to gain from it and nothing to contribute to it," he told one interviewer. A staunch Republican, he respected former President Richard Nixon for "his efforts to set the country on a path I think is sensible." Swearingen admires a man who "believes in what he's doing" and "achieves actively and successfully his objectives." "The thing I don't admire is a man who tries to be on all sides of the question," he once told a reporter for *Women's Wear Daily* (August 17, 1970). "In a man, I value sincerity and achievement. In a woman, it's sincerity and understanding."

References: Time 82:100 N 1 '63 por; Women's Wear Daily p5 Ag 17 '70 por; Who's Who in America, 1978-79; Who's Who in Finance and Industry, 1977-78

Thompson, James R(obert)

May 8, 1936- Governor of Illinois. Address: b. Office of the Governor, State Capitol, Springfield, Ill. 62706; h. Governor's Mansion, 5th and Jackson Sts., Springfield, Ill. 62706

After just two years as governor of Illinois, the only elective office he ever held, James R. ("Big Jim") Thompson was already being talked about as a possible candidate for the Republican Presidential nomination in 1980. At the time he succeeded Dan Walker in the governor's mansion in January 1977, Thompson had to his credit an impressive record as a tough United States attorney, taking on the formidable machine of the late Mayor Richard J. Daley of Chicago and cracking down on corrupt public officials of both the Republican and Democratic parties. A self-proclaimed pragmatist who shuns the traditional labels of liberal and conservative, Thompson has referred to Illinois as "the state that works." He demonstrated a talent for compromise when, soon after his arrival in Springfield, he worked out a *modus vivendi* with Chicago officials for a mass transit and highways program, and he steered a tough anti-crime bill and plan for a balanced state budget through the Democratic-controlled Illinois General Assembly. The citizens of Illinois recognized those and other achievements by re-electing him to a four-year term in November 1978.

James R. Thompson

James Robert Thompson was born in Chicago on May 8, 1936 to Dr. James Robert Thompson, a pathologist, and Agnes Josephine (Swanson) Thompson. Growing up in middle-class Garfield Park on the city's west side, he became precociously interested in politics, and at eleven he announced for the first time his intention to become President of the United States—an ambition that he has never disavowed since. In high school he pinned down the year, writing in his yearbook: "1984, President of the U.S."

After completing high school, Thompson undertook prelaw studies at the University of Illinois in Chicago from 1953 to 1955 and at Washington University in St. Louis in 1955-56. He then entered Northwestern University Law School, where he obtained his J.D. degree in 1959. Admitted to the Illinois state bar that same year, he served for the next five years as an assistant on the prosecutorial staff of the state attorney for Cook County. From 1964 to 1969 he was an associate professor at Northwestern University, teaching criminal law. While serving in 1969-70 as an assistant attorney general of the state of Illinois he headed the criminal division and then the department of law enforcement and public protection in the attorney general's office. In 1970 he became first assistant to the United States Attorney for the Northern District of Illinois.

During the 1960's Thompson served on a number of committees, including one to revise the Illinois criminal code and another to draft legislation for the defense of the indigent, and he was on the board of directors of the Chicago Crime Commission. From 1964 to 1967 he was a member of the Chicago's mayor's committee to draft legislation to combat organized crime, in 1966 he was an adviser to the President's commission on law enforcement and administration of justice, and in 1967 he served on the President's task force on crime. In 1964 he qualified as a member of the bar of the United States Supreme Court. From 1962 to 1964 Thompson was codirector of a criminal law course for Chicago police and industrial security personnel. He has lectured at Michigan State University, the Davis campus of the University of California, and other institutions.

Appointed United States Attorney for the Illinois Northern District in November 1971, Thompson soon tripled its small prosecutorial staff, long accustomed to handling merely routine legal matters, and turned it into a virtual juggernaut aimed at crooked politicians and police. During his four years in the post he rose from being an obscure federal prosecutor to what David S. Broder of the Washington *Post* (June 5, 1973) described as "the busiest, boldest, best-publicized officeholder in the Midwest—and, perhaps, the brightest new political star." Of over 300 indictments, Thompson obtained convictions in 90 percent of the cases. He successfully prosecuted hundreds of public employees on charges of corruption, including Mayor Richard J. Daley's press secretary, several Chicago aldermen and state legislators, nineteen employees of the Cook County assessor's office, and over fifty policemen.

Thompson's prosecution of one Chicago officer accused of gratuitous brutality against a black youth resulted in the first civil rights conviction against a policeman in the city's history. He also prosecuted Edward J. Barrett, a former clerk of Cook County and a staunch Daley lieutenant, for bribery and income tax evasion. But by far the biggest fish caught in Thompson's net was former Governor Otto Kerner, who, at the time of his 1973 conviction on seventeen counts of income tax evasion, fraud, perjury, bribery, and conspiracy in connection with a much-publicized racetrack scandal, had been serving on the United States Circuit Court of Appeals for the seventh district. Judge Kerner was sentenced to three years in prison and fined $50,000.

In addition to making a vigorous assault on crime and political corruption, Thompson prosecuted corporate violators of antipollution standards. With his 1973 suit against United States Steel, accusing that corporation of permitting its plant in Waukegan, Wisconsin to pollute Lake Michigan, he successfully concluded the first joint federal-state attempt to use the courts to protect the environment.

As a result of his accomplishments as a federal prosecutor, Thompson was invited to head President Richard Nixon's new narcotics enforcement administration, but he turned down the offer. In 1975 he left his post as United States attorney and became a counsel with the Chicago law firm of Winston & Strawn, where he remained until early 1977. Meanwhile, his reputation as a relentless and incorruptible government prosecutor kept him in the public eye, giving him an image of "Mr. Clean" in his home state, at a time when Republicans in Washington were sinking in the mire of Watergate. To a party sorely in need of candidates untainted by scandal, he seemed the perfect candidate for governor in 1976. In the March primary, Thompson won the Republican nomination with 86 percent of the vote. His opponent had been expected to be the incumbent Governor Dan Walker, the feisty anti-Daley Democrat who had headed the official investigation of the violence at the Democratic National Convention in Chicago in 1968. But Walker lost his bid for renomination to Illinois Secretary of State Michael J. Howlett, Mayor Daley's handpicked candidate. Howlett's resemblance to the veteran Chicago mayor seemed to do his candidacy little good downstate and in the suburbs, where the name Daley was considered by many voters as synonymous with heavy-handed patronage because of his tight control of the Cook County political machine.

Also working in Thompson's favor was Daley's unsuccessful attempt to purge black Congressman Ralph H. Metcalfe during the primary campaign. Metcalfe had split with the mayor over alleged police brutality in Chicago's black community and, after surviving the primary, refused to make peace with City Hall. Although Metcalfe declined to endorse Thompson openly, he turned his back on Howlett's candidacy, and many black campaign workers gave their support to Thompson.

Although the usual term of a governor of Illinois had been four years, the 1976 election was for a two-year term, which the state legislature had temporarily established so that future gubernatorial races would not coincide with Presidential elections. The election of November 2, 1976 resulted in a landslide victory for Thompson, who received some 65 of the vote, winning by a record margin of nearly 1,400,000. In addition to obtaining about 60 percent of the Roman Catholic and Jewish votes and substantial majorities downstate and in the suburbs, Thompson also garnered an impressive 38 percent of the vote in Chicago's black precincts. As a byproduct of Thompson's decisive victory, Gerald R. Ford scored a narrow majority of the Illinois vote over Democrat Jimmy Carter in the Presidential race.

In an interview in the U.S. News & World Report (November 15, 1976), Governor-elect Thompson commented: "I thought that people were fed up with politicians who made promises and then didn't perform, so I went to the people and said, 'Look I can't make promises that involve legislative action when I don't even know who's going to sit in the legislature. I'll tell you my intentions and my plans and my hopes, but I won't promise.' " Asked whether he might enter the Presidential race in 1980, Thompson asserted: "I'm not going to suggest myself as a national figure until I perform in Illinois."

Thompson, whose assumption of the governorship in January 1977 coincided with Jimmy Carter's accession to the White House, had much in common with the President. Both had been thrust into a complex administrative position with little political experience, and both faced the threat of becoming bogged down on too many issues at once. Aware of the danger of spreading himself too thin, Thompson singled out two key issues: a balanced budget and a comprehensive anticrime bill. Reducing his predecessor's budget by $70,000,000, Governor Thompson stumped the state with a series of eighteen "chalk talks" to justify his lean $10 billion budget. Although his proposals for curtailing the state's education expenditures evoked some criticism, the governor's frugality was well received by disgruntled taxpayers and members of the legislature.

The governor's so-called "Class X" crime bill also struck a responsive chord among his constituents. Contending that "it's time to put to rest the notion that prisons are for rehabilitation," Thompson asserted that their main purpose was to separate criminals from the rest of society and to deter others from crimes. The new legislation provided stiff mandatory sentences without chance for parole for "class X" felons—those convicted of rape, arson, the sale of hard drugs, or armed violence. Stalled during the regular session of the Legislature, the bill was passed during a special session in October 1977. Earlier that year Thompson had signed a bill providing for the death penalty for adults convicted of any of sixteen categories of murder after mitigating circumstances had been considered.

If Governor Thompson pleased conservatives in guarding the public pursestrings and cracking down on crime, he drew angry denunciations from the right on other issues. He endorsed the Equal Rights Amendment, lobbying unsuccessfully for its ratification by the state of Illinois. He vetoed a measure that would have cut off state funding of abortions for the poor, despite advice from political strategists that such a proabortion stance might doom his Presidential aspirations. And he vetoed a bill, sponsored by conservatives, that would have legalized the intrastate sale and use of the controversial drug Laetrile, which some believe to be helpful in the treatment of cancer. Both vetoes were overridden.

A major accomplishment of the Thompson administration was its settlement of a fifteen-year feud between the state and Chicago over the disposition of transportation funds. Thompson arrived at a compromise with Michael A. Bilandic, who became acting mayor of Chicago after Mayor Daley's death in December 1976. Bilandic settled for half the freeway mileage City Hall had been demanding, and the governor agreed to build just one of the two subway tubes the state had planned for the city. To please downstaters, Thompson also agreed to rebuild roads in the southern part of the state. The compromise released some $1 billion in federal funds, and it provided for an estimated 40,000 new jobs.

His early victories on the budget, the crime bill, and the transportation compromise, as well as the rapport he established with key labor leaders and the Roman Catholic hierarchy, served to enhance the stature of Governor Thompson, who in 1978 found himself in the unique position of having to stand for reelection after just two years in office. Although Thompson, who faced no opposition in the 1978 Republican primary, was seen as virtually certain of victory in his bid for a four-year term as governor, his Democratic opponent, state comptroller Michael J. Bakalis, found him vulnerable on several fronts. The governor's often repeated desire to become President, coupled with his frequent trips out of state to speak to groups that might prove helpful in a national contest, left him open to the charge that he was using Springfield as a steppingstone to the White House.

While keeping his 1976 campaign promise not to raise taxes, Thompson resisted demands for a tax cut, a step for which there had been a growing clamor in the wake of California's tax-slashing Proposition 13. During the summer of 1978 the governor vetoed a state measure, supported by Bakalis, that sought to rebate part of the taxes paid by middle-income home owners, and another, sponsored by conservative Republicans, that would cut taxes in proportion to the rise of inflation. He argued that such measures would be unduly costly and would necessitate reductions in essential services.

Instead, Thompson proposed putting the question directly before the people in an advisory referendum—since Illinois law forbids binding referenda. Voters were asked whether they favored "ceilings on taxes and spending by the State of Illinois, units of local government, and school districts." To get the 589,000 petition signatures needed to place the measure on the November ballot, referendum organizers paid party workers $100 for every 750 names they collected. Inevitably, Democrats challenged the petitions in court, charging that they carried fictitious names and some names lifted from obituaries. Bakalis, who called the proposed referendum "Proposition Zero," maintained that it was "nothing but a ruse . . . to deceive the voters." Although the governor was not personally implicated in the alleged improprieties, the specter of Mayor Daley and shady Chicago politics haunted the Republican candidate and boosted Bakalis' position in the polls. Nevertheless, Illinois voters reelected Thompson on November 7, 1978 by a margin of over 600,000 votes.

Thompson has written articles for professional journals and he is coauthor of four textbooks, including the two-volume *Cases and Comments on Criminal Justice* (Foundation Press, 1968-74), on which he collaborated with Fred E. Inbau and Claude R. Sowles. He has served on the board of editors of the *Criminal Law Bulletin* and from 1965 to 1969 he was assistant to the editor in chief of the *Journal of Criminal Law, Criminology, and Police Science*. A member of the American Bar Association and past chairman of the criminal law section of the Illinois Bar Association, Thompson also served from 1967 to 1969 as vice-president of Americans for Effective Law Enforcement.

During the 1976 campaign James R. Thompson married Jayne A. Carr, a lawyer. She had been one of his students at Northwestern, later worked for him as a law clerk in the state attorney general's office, and more recently practised civil law with a Springfield firm. The couple's first child, Samantha Jane, was born in August 1978. Thompson, who stands at a towering six feet six inches and weighs about 220 pounds, keeps fit by lifting weights and playing racquetball, and he is as much at home in flannel shirts and denim, shaking hands at county fairs, as he is in a suit and tie, discussing bond ratings in boardrooms.

When time permits, Governor Thompson attends the theatre and reads spy novels, especially those of Howard Hunt and John D. MacDonald. An antiques enthusiast, he collects inkwells and Victorian furniture, and he has installed a Jenny Lind cradle and antique toys in the nursery of the Governor's mansion. The household includes an Irish setter named Guv and a Collie called Sam. In his office, the governor keeps a wall plaque inscribed with a quotation from his hero, Theodore Roosevelt: "Aggressive fighting for the right is the noblest sport the world affords." He is a Presbyterian.

References: Christian Sci Mon p6 Ap 20 '77 por; N Y Times A p18 S 28 '77 por; New Republic 177:16+ D 24-31 '77; Almanac of American Politics, 1978; International Who's Who, 1978-79; Who's Who in America, 1978-79

Trilling, Diana

July 21, 1905- Writer.
Address: h. 35 Claremont Ave.,
New York City, N.Y. 10027

In a sharp exchange with the poet Robert Lowell after the insurrection at Columbia University in 1968, Diana Trilling defended her claim of being a liberal with the argument: "I did my best to see the truth, and ... I did my best to look beneath the appearance of things, especially the things which announced themselves as virtues." Mrs. Trilling is a rationalist and a moralist of firm opinions, including the view that "no one can call himself a liberal who is not an anti-Communist." Her close analysis of motivations and implications of political behavior is part of the scrutiny of literature and society that she has made in critical essays distinguished by "a fine, clear, scrupulous prose," to quote Granville Hicks's appraisal. A selection of her early book reviews, for the *Nation*, appeared in *Reviewing the Forties* (1978), and some of her other essays, provocative and occasionally caustic articles contributed to periodicals, were collected in *Claremont Essays* (1964) and *We Must March My Darlings* (1977).

Diana Rubin Trilling was born in New York City on July 21, 1905, the youngest of the three children (a son and two daughters) of Joseph Rubin, a manufacturer, and Sadie Helene (Forbert) Rubin. During her growing years she lived in Manhattan, Brooklyn, and Westchester. As a student at Erasmus Hall High School in Brooklyn, she has recalled, her single accomplishment in extracurricular activity was to oppose corruption in the two-party system of student government by help-

ing to organize a third party, which had a black candidate for president of the student body. In 1921, having "won a family battle," she left New York to enroll in Radcliffe College, where she chose fine arts as her major subject. With music her minor subject, she became a member of the Choral Society and was also professionally engaged for a choir to illustrate the Lowell Institute lectures on the history of choral music given by Harvard's Professor Archibald Davison. In her junior year she won an honorary, or nonstipend, scholarship, and in 1925 she obtained her B.A. degree *cum laude* with special distinction in fine arts.

Although her academic background is an important part of the intellectual equipment that Diana Trilling brings to bear on whatever subject she considers, it remained a largely untapped resource for a time after her graduation, when, unable to find work in the New York art world, she took a job with the National Broadcasting Company. "Fortified by what many people even then considered the best education available to women in this country," she wrote in an essay in *We Must March My Darlings*, "I earned a modest weekly paycheck shepherding five child actors, a dog, a cat, a singing policeman, and an organ grinder plus monkey on publicity tours to promote the sale of a shoe leather that was being widely advertised on radio."

On June 12, 1929 Diana Rubin married Lionel Trilling, who was then lecturing in English at Hunter College in Manhattan and was soon to begin his long association as a teacher with Columbia University. Illness had prevented her from continuing in the singing career for which she had trained, and she was feeling the need of finding some other occupation just at a time when, during 1941, the literary editor of the *Nation* asked Lionel Trilling to recommend someone to write unsigned paragraphs on books that did not warrant full-length reviews. Diana Trilling, who tentatively proposed herself, has recounted, "I did my first little unsigned bits in a panic, and then my first signed review in total terror."

Within a year at the *Nation*, Mrs. Trilling had earned a regular column of her own devoted to criticism, "Fiction in Review," for which she read a new novel just about every day. Many of the books she reviewed were mediocre efforts by writers who have remained obscure; others were by newcomers whose reputations have grown over the years, such as Saul Bellow, Truman Capote, and Jean Stafford; and still others were by established authors like Jean-Paul Sartre, John Dos Passos, and Sinclair Lewis. Bringing to her work for the *Nation* the advantage of extensive and perceptive reading, much of it presumably acquired after her marriage to Lionel Trilling, she showed herself to be discerning of genuine talent in an unknown novelist and uncowed and unimpressed by the mere celebrity of any writer.

A selection of Diana Trilling's reviews that appeared in the *Nation* between September 5, 1942 and June 25, 1949 were collected in *Reviewing the Forties* (Harcourt, 1948), whose title suggests Mrs. Trilling's recognition of the connection between a literary work and its social context. "As a critic, Diana Trilling has range," Paul Fussell pointed out in his introduction to her book; "she is not satisfied to leave literature sitting there uninterpreted in its fullest psychological, social, and political meaning, for she perceives that 'literature is no mere decoration of life but an index of the health or sickness of society.'" Although James Atlas expressed a lack of enthusiasm in the *New Republic* (October 28, 1978) for what he called the "ideas" that preoccupied Diana Trilling in some of her later essays, he liked *Reviewing the Forties*: "But these are reviews, and whatever ideas appear in them are incidental to her purpose, which was to evaluate new books. In this, Mrs. Trilling was a master, one of the critics responsible for the authority *The Nation* enjoyed in those days." The personal flavor of her appraisals were appropriate moreover to the magazine's lively, direct style. She began one review, for example: "I find it difficult to determine how much of my distaste for Eudora Welty's new book, *Delta Wedding*, . . . is dislike of its literary manner and how much is resistance to the culture out of which it grows and which it describes so fondly."

Among the novels that Mrs. Trilling reviewed for the *Nation*, in 1944, was D. H. Lawrence's *The First Lady Chatterley*, an early version of *Lady Chatterley's Lover*. Her special interest in Lawrence led in 1947 to her editing *The Portable D. H. Lawrence* (Viking), for which she wrote an introduction analyzing the emotional premises of Lawrence's writing and their sources in the experiences of his childhood; his rejection of the modern "civilized" consciousness for "the dark gods of the blood"; the nature of his place in twentieth-century letters. About a decade later she returned to the English author with *The Selected Letters of D. H. Lawrence* (Farrar, 1958), which she edited for the Great Letters Series with an introduction that offered a new set of perceptions about Lawrence, about his literary intentions, his relationships with those around him, and the complexity of his notion of sexuality.

Mrs. Trilling gave up her column for the *Nation* in 1949 to spend more time on freelance criticism. Over the years she has contributed to an exceptionally wide range of American and British periodicals, reaching a highly diversified readership. *Partisan Review* carried several of her articles in the early 1950's: "Men, Women, and Sex," a long review of Margaret Mead's *Male and Female*, in April 1950; "A Memorandum on the Hiss Case," loosely a review of *Seeds of Treason* by Ralph de Toledano and Victor Lasky, in May-June 1950; "A Communist and His Ideals," in July-

August 1951. In January 1953 the same magazine published "From an Autumn Journal," her lively rumination on such diverse concerns as the needs of a four-year-old son, differences in the treatment of little boys and little girls in current acculturation practices, the perfunctory attitude of some physicians toward patients who will probably not know enough to raise questions, and Adlai E. Stevenson's defeat by Dwight D. Eisenhower.

Moving steadily toward a comprehensive attention to many aspects of contemporary life, Mrs. Trilling discussed problems unique to women, decades before the women's movement; the decay of the ethic of social responsibility; radical politics, especially the conflict between commitment to the liberal tradition and commitment to the Communist party. From 1957 to 1959 she wrote a column, "Here and Now," for the *New Leader*, for which she also substituted briefly as theatre critic, and for a short period she contributed pieces to the editorial page of the New York *Herald Tribune*.

Thirteen of Mrs. Trilling's articles, published during the preceding two decades in *Partisan Review*, the *American Scholar*, and other periodicals, were collected in 1964 in *Claremont Essays* (Harcourt; Secker & Warburg, 1965). The title refers to the street on which the writer lives, Claremont Avenue in the Columbia University neighborhood. "This short street is a causeway of liberal culture," a reviewer for *Newsday* (March 16, 1964) noted. "This is Mrs. Trilling's milieu and her book breathes the red-brick air of upper Manhattan on every page." In his comments for the New York *Times Book Review* (March 15, 1964) the British critic Frank Kermode called Diana Trilling "Arnoldian," placing her among those "intellectuals who labor to understand the current of ideas, and to examine with wisdom not only the art but also the main public issues of their times." Edward Albee, Norman Mailer, Alger Hiss, Enrico Caruso, Marilyn Monroe, and Britain's scandal-plagued John Profumo are among the men and women on whom she focuses in her observations about the cultural climate.

In the spring of 1971 Diana and Lionel Trilling went to Cambridge, Massachusetts to spend nearly nine weeks on the Radcliffe campus, residing in the dormitory in which Mrs. Trilling had lived during her senior year. The three-part record of her impressions, a rather dismal assessment of women's liberal education, gave its ironic title, "We Must March My Darlings," a quotation from Walt Whitman's "Pioneers! O Pioneers!," to the collection of essays in which it was later included. Mrs. Trilling contracted with Little, Brown & Company for the book's publication. But when she refused to delete or modify passages in an essay, "Liberal Anti-Communism Revisited," that the company considered unacceptably critical of another of its authors, Lillian Hellman, the publisher canceled the contract. Little, Brown had published Miss

Hellman's *Scoundrel Time,* a memoir of the McCarthy "witch-hunting" period of the 1950's, which disapproved of political views of the Trillings that differed from her own. One of the related passages in Mrs. Trilling's manuscript that was deemed offensive by the publisher read: "... the issues ... have continued to divide the intellectual community with ever-increasing acuteness, albeit with always-diminishing intellectual force. The most recent document of the division is Lillian Hellman's *Scoundrel Time.*"

Because of the attention that the controversy received in the press, when Harcourt Brace Jovanovich published *We Must March My Darlings: A Critical Decade* in 1977, it came "trailing clouds of scandal," as Thomas R. Edwards remarked in the New York *Times Book Review* (May 28, 1977). "Trilling brings to the peculiar confusions of our time a moral and intellectual disposition that is strong and clear," Edwards wrote in his review. "Like what she says or not, one always knows who and where she is, what standards of judgment she applies to the case at hand."

One stand taken by Diana Trilling that Edwards questioned related to her association with the American Committee for Cultural Freedom, an antitotalitarian group composed primarily of writers, of which she was a member of the executive board and its chairman from 1955 to 1957. The American Committee was an "independent affiliate" of the Congress for Cultural Freedom, an international organization based in Paris and financed, as was disclosed a decade or so later, by the CIA. The American Committee, alone among the various national committees, received no government funds; the CIA cannot legally spend money on American projects. Mrs. Trilling reported, however, on one meeting of the American executive board at which she was present, when, faced with its inability to pay the next month's office rent, the board acquiesced in an appeal by its then chairman Norman Thomas to Allen Dulles, director of the CIA, who responded with a check for $1,000. No one present protested what she acknowledged to be a "breach of legality." She asked, moreover, whether there was any reason to protest, since the CIA at that time was not known as a usurper of authority. Edwards, however, criticized her for maintaining an unrepentant posture while deploring other breaches of legality.

The spirited essays in *We Must March My Darlings* also explore the social implications of the assassination of President John F. Kennedy, Timothy Leary and the drug culture, the 1968 Students for a Democratic Society uprising at Columbia University, Women's Liberation, society's treatment of homosexuals, and other issues. Some reviewers praised her attack on the cult film *Easy Rider* and admired her skillful synthesis of social and literary criticism in her treatment of D. H. Lawrence, Philip Roth, Nigel Nicolson, Norman Mailer,

and others. On the negative side, Alfred Kazin, who attacked Lillian Hellman in *Esquire* (August 1977), regretted that he could not rejoice in Diana Trilling as an ally: "Alas, Mrs. Trilling is not likely to persuade anyone not already in agreement with her. She is a heavy, totally humorless writer, with a mannered style and an abstract vocabulary."

The charge that she is a humorless writer is not one that Diana Trilling hears without demur. When asked recently whether there were any published misstatements about her that she would like to have corrected, she replied, "That I am humorless—but how correct that without humorlessness? That I am unsympathetic to the young—but how correct that without piousness?" Another complaint of Kazin's was that "there is nothing in *We Must March My Darlings* that tells us anything concrete about Diana Trilling, her honest troubles as a human being or the famous husband to whom she was married for forty-five years." But in a memoir, "Lionel Trilling, A Jew at Columbia," in *Commentary* (March 1979), Mrs. Trilling, who has been a widow since 1975, wrote movingly of the early years of her marriage and of the experiences at Columbia of a young teacher who was to become one of America's most distinguished men of letters. In 1979 Harcourt Brace Jovanovich published her edition of a collection of ten of her husband's essays, *The Last Decade: Essays and Reviews, 1965-75.* Diana and Lionel Trilling have one son, James Lionel Trilling.

Diana Trilling is five feet five inches tall, weighs 136 pounds, and has brown hair and brown eyes; her published photographs, like her writing, suggest a woman of thoughtful and buoyant disposition. Listening to music, especially opera, is her chief recreation. Since 1976 she has been a member of the American Academy of Arts and Sciences and for several years has served on the editorial board of the *American Scholar.* She was a Guggenheim fellow in 1950-51, and more recently under a grant from the Rockefeller Foundation and the National Endowment for the Humanities, she has been working on an oral history of aspects of New York culture.

References: Contemporary Authors 1st rev vols 5-8 (1969); Who's Who in the East, 1975-76; Who's Who in World Jewry (1972)

Troyanos, Tatiana

Sept. 12, 1938- Singer. Address: b. c/o Columbia Artists Management, Inc., 165 W. 57th St., New York City, N.Y. 10019; h. 98 Riverside Drive, New York City, N.Y. 10024

After living and performing in Europe for a decade because its prestigious opera houses

Tatiana Troyanos

offered her the important roles that she had been denied in the United States, the New York-born mezzo-soprano Tatiana Troyanos returned to America permanently in 1975. Since making her Metropolitan Opera debut as Octavian in *Der Rosenkavalier* on March 8, 1976, she has become recognized as one of perhaps a half-dozen American mezzo-sopranos who have outdistanced all competitors in their field. Her powerful, miraculously even, velvety, and pliant voice can cope with roles as diverse as Bizet's sultry Carmen, Handel's florid Ariodante, Berg's lesbian Countess Geschwitz, and Bellini's Romeo, and her figure is svelte enough to qualify her as perhaps the operatic world's most persuasive exponent of trouser roles. Although she could have comfortably remained at her home base, the Hamburg State Opera in Germany, Miss Troyanos harbors few regrets about her return. "After all," she has said, with some deference to the fact that she has Greek and German origins, "I'm basically American." Having met and conquered all the challenges on which she seems to thrive, the once driven and ambitious singer feels that she has earned her dues and can now relax occasionally, even as she continues to develop a career that hints at future greatness.

Tatiana Troyanos was born on September 12, 1938 in New York City to a Greek father from the island of Cephalonia in the Ionian Sea, who now lives in Brooklyn, and a German mother from Stuttgart, who lives in New Jersey. Both of her parents possessed fine singing voices but had little else in common; they are now divorced. The father, whose relatives in Greece included a sculptor and an architect, was in the restaurant business.

Her first home was near the present site of the Metropolitan Opera House, but she moved during her girlhood to Forest Hills in Queens, where she continued piano lessons and sang in the high school chorus, and in church choirs. During those fortunate years she had her first exposure to opera, as a standee at the Met. Impressed by her vocal potential, an interested teacher at Forest Hills High School took Tatiana to the Juilliard School in Manhattan for an audition. Awarded a scholarship, she helped to defray expenses by working as a secretary at the publishing firm of Random House, and as a waitress in summer hotels.

Disapproving of the opera department at Juilliard because it used professionals instead of students in its productions, Tatiana Troyanos concentrated on lieder and oratorio singing. When a dean refused her permission to switch from her assigned vocal teacher to another, Hans Heinz, who was highly regarded by her fellow students, she left the school. Later she was able to study privately with Heinz and has continued to do so throughout her career.

After leaving Juilliard, Miss Troyanos sang in musicals in summer stock and was a singing nun in the chorus of the original Broadway production of Rodgers and Hammerstein's *The Sound of Music* for many months. In 1963, after having auditioned all around the town, she was hired by the New York City Opera, where she made her debut as Jocasta in Stravinsky's *Oedipus Rex*. After a season and a half, when a promised *Carmen* was taken away from her and given to another singer, she left the company. Risking a loss of financial support from the Martha Baird Rockefeller Foundation, she took off for Europe the following year for a round of auditions, but when she returned with three contracts from Frankfurt, Zurich, and Hamburg awaiting her signature, the Foundation paid for her trip.

When, in 1965, her idol, Risë Stevens, the Metropolitan Opera's great Carmen of the 1940's and 1950's, heard Tatiana Troyanos sing the gypsy song, she was so impressed that she arranged an audition with Rudolph Bing, but the small roles he offered her at the Met could not, Miss Troyanos was convinced, lead to anything else. Finally, at the urging of Hans Heinz, she signed a contract with the Hamburg State Opera for the 1965-66 season, thus ending months of indecision. She went off to Europe with her sights set on the big roles but had to settle for such lesser ones at the beginning as Lola in Mascagni's *Cavalleria Rusticana* and the camp follower Preziosilla in Verdi's *La Forza del Destino*. She also remembers her Suzuki in Puccini's *Madama Butterfly*, which was so bad that the director warned her that she would have to improve or quit. Rolf Liebermann, the Hamburg Opera's famous Intendant, patiently and slowly led her into bigger roles within his repertory company. She sang *Carmen* in an old Wieland Wagner production and then went on to tackle other important roles, such as Cherubino in Mozart's *Le Nozze di Figaro*, Marina in Mussorgsky's *Boris Godunov*, Dorabella in Mozart's *Così Fan Tutte*, and Octavian in Richard Strauss's *Der Rosenkavalier*, which was to become one of her specialties. In 1969, when she undertook the taxing role of the prioress Jeanne in the world premiere of Krzysztof Penderecki's *The Devils of Loudun*, she had to carry a pitch pipe onstage to help her negotiate the music's difficult intervals.

Tatiana Troyanos achieved her first big European success at the 1966 Aix-en-Provence Festival, when she sang the trouser role of the Composer in Richard Strauss's *Ariadne auf Naxos* in a performance that starred the French soprano Régine Crespin. Impressed by her singlemindedness and hard work, Liebermann had recommended her to the festival's director in spite of the fact that she had never sung the role before and knew no French. A year later, when the Paris Opera needed a replacement for Cherubino in a gala performance of *Le Nozze di Figaro*, she was summoned again. In the audience that night was Herbert von Karajan, who not only assured her that she would have an international career but also invited her to join him when he directed Mozart's *Coronation Mass* in Rome for the Pope. Her eager impetuosity sometimes led her, however, to undertake more than she could handle. Miss Troyanos recalls a production of *Der Rosenkavalier* to which she came inadequately prepared and a Schoenberg's *Erwartung* under Sir Georg Solti that she negotiated only with difficulty. Part of the secret of success, she came to realize, lay in knowing when to say "no." And with the blessing of Rolf Liebermann, she entered the international circuit, including Covent Garden, Edinburgh, Berlin, Munich, and Vienna.

While based in Europe, Tatiana Troyanos had come back home from time to time to work with Hans Heinz and to perform. When the Hamburg Opera visited New York City in 1967 she appeared as the bearded Baba in Stravinsky's *The Rake's Progress*, made her debut with the New York Philharmonic in 1970 in a concert version of *Oedipus Rex*, and sang Charlotte in Massenet's *Werther* with the Chicago Lyric Opera in 1971. Her other commitments included *Der Rosenkavalier* in Los Angeles, Purcell's *Dido and Aeneas* and Donizetti's *Lucrezia Borgia* in Dallas, and Berlioz' *The Damnation of Faust* with the Cincinnati Symphony under Thomas Schippers. The performance that brought her the most national publicity, however, took place on September 14, 1971 at the opening of the new Opera House at the Kennedy Center in Washington, D.C., when she performed the title role in the first fully staged production in the Western hemisphere of Handel's *Ariodante*. Unknown to many in the audience and singing opposite the celebrated Beverly Sills, she overshadowed her formidable colleague in a role originally written for a male castrato but usually sung by a tenor. "Her voice," Richard D. Fletcher wrote in the Washington *Post* (September 18, 1971), "has grown in size with no loss of the velvety smoothness for which we remember her. Her execution of the vocal ornamentation was brilliant, bringing her several thunderous ovations."

In yet another trouser role and again singing in tandem with Beverly Sills, Tatiana Troyanos made her Boston debut in June 1975, when she appeared as Romeo in Sarah Caldwell's production of Bellini's *I Capuleti ed i Montecchi*. That October, during her first season with the San Francisco Opera, she undertook the title role in Monteverdi's *L'Incoronazione di Poppea* and sang Adalgisa to Montserrat Caballé's Norma. With the greatest of ease, she then managed the transition from Druidic Gaul to Elizabethan England by singing in Donizetti's *Anna Bolena* in Dallas.

Rather belatedly, Tatiana Troyanos made her Metropolitan Opera debut on March 8, 1976 as the seventeen-year-old cavalier Octavian in *Der Rosenkavalier*, a role she had performed many times under such notable conductors as Karl Böhm and Josef Krips. At the Metropolitan it was James Levine, one of her fellow students at Aspen, Colorado in 1962, who greeted her on the podium. According to Speight Jenkins of the New York *Post* (March 9, 1976), she was "the star of the show. The most aristocratic Octavian at the Met in years, she splendidly acted a girl playing a boy (and sometimes playing at being a girl). Never did she overdo; she moved gracefully, and her hauteur could have only belonged to someone in the nobility. Vocally, the role seemed perfect for her. She has a large, warmish lyric mezzo-soprano with perfect control and an even, balanced sound throughout . . . and her singing of the trio and the final duet was perfection itself." In that he was in agreement with the soprano Evelyn Lear, who sang her first Marschallin opposite Troyanos in Berlin in 1971 and who calls her "the greatest Octavian in the world," and with no less an authority than Elisabeth Schwarzkopf, who once sent her a card of congratulations after witnessing her Octavian in Vienna. Her next role at the Met was another of her specialties, that of the Composer in Ariadne auf Naxos, and when the company ended its season at Lincoln Center in 1976, she sang Carmen on its spring tour.

When Verdi's *Aïda* became the first opera to go past the six-hundred performance mark at the Metropolitan, Tatiana Troyanos was in the cast as Amneris, a role she had only recently learned. In the complex personality of the vengeful princess she sees "a great deal of softness and warmth," subtleties she tries to underscore in her interpretation. Of her performance Speight Jenkins, writing in the New York *Post* (November 30, 1976) observed: "In the first three acts her musicianship, convincing acting, and striking beauty did not compensate for a lack of overall heft of voice and specific power in the lower register. In the Judgement Scene, however, she pulled out all the stops. Though it was not in the grandest Italian manner, the richness of tone, evenness of sound and musical and dramatic intellect made the whole scene more than memorable. In short, Miss Troyanos proved that even in a role not ideally suited to her talents, her artistry would carry the day."

In another debut, equal in European importance to her bow at the Metropolitan Opera House, Tatiana Troyanos made her first operatic appearance at Milan's La Scala on January 18, 1977 as Adalgisa in *Norma* opposite Montserrat Caballé. To do so, she had to cancel a previous commitment to performing in Mahler's *Das Lied von der Erde* in Seattle. That La Scala *Norma* had the added distinction of being the first live performance of an opera to be broadcast by satellite throughout the world. In between her many engagements she somehow found time enough to record Purcell's *Dido and Aeneas* in London for Erato records. By the middle of 1979 she had become one of the busiest of all operatic recording artists, with performances on the RCA Victor Red Seal, Deutsche Grammophon Gesellschaft, London, and Columbia labels.

To considerable critical acclaim, on March 18, 1977 Miss Troyanos created the role of the lesbian Countess Geschwitz in the first Metropolitan Opera production of the truncated version of Alban Berg's *Lulu*. As with all her roles, she had carefully thought out the assignment in advance, so that it came as no surprise when she discussed the character so articulately with Gary Lipton in *Opera News* (April 2, 1977). "It is she who seems to get all the sympathy in the end because she is the only one who truly loves Lulu," Miss Troyanos explained. "She gives everything because she has nothing to gain by not doing so. No man has risked so much for Lulu—fortune, name, safety, even health. The audience must feel the intensity of this love. Geschwitz is interesting to play. You look at a part for what you can get out of it and give to it."

A spate of engagements in the spring and summer of 1977 kept her busy. In May there were two performances of the Verdi *Requiem* with the Houston Symphony; two *Normas* in the same month opposite Beverly Sills at the San Antonio (Texas) Grand Opera; in June there were several *Rosenkavaliers* in Paris; in August she sang Sesto in Mozart's *La Clemenza di Tito* at the Salzburg Festi-

val; and in September of that year she was Eboli in Verdi's *Don Carlo,* sung in the original French with the Canadian Opera in Toronto, Canada.

In her first Carnegie Hall recital on March 16, 1978 Miss Troyanos avoided time-worn items in favor of four songs by Schubert, five from Hugo Wolf's *Spanisches Liederbuch,* and the *Four Songs* of Alban Berg's Opus 2. Equally off the beaten path, her four arias came from Handel's *Ariodante,* Mozart's *La Clemenza di Tito,* and Tchaikovsky's *Jeanne d'Arc.* Despite problems with the delivery of some songs, a critic for *Musical America* (July, 1978) found "a more than ample measure of the variety, the control, and the dramatic projection of the meaning of the text that characterize the true Lieder singer."

One of Troyanos' most successful portrayals is that of Santuzza, the rejected and love-sick heroine of Mascagni's *Cavallería Rusticana,* a role she has sung both on the stage and on television and in which she says she has been influenced by the films of the emotionally volcanic Italian actress Anna Magnani. Writing of her first Met performance of the verismo role in the *Christian Science Monitor* (April 20, 1978), Thor Eckert Jr. called it "stunning on just about all counts. Rarely has a Santuzza so looked the part— the embodiment of a striking, fiery, brash, impetuous Sicilian peasant girl."

"Radiant both to hear and to behold," as one enraptured New York critic, Alan Rich, put it, Tatiana Troyanos sang the role of Venus on the opening night, in late September, of the Metropolitan Opera's 1978-79 season. Although she now tries to limit herself to forty performances a year, that season turned out to be as hectic as the preceding one, with engagements as Princess Eboli with the Miami Opera in January 1979; as the Composer with the Met on February 13, 1979; as a soloist in Schönberg's *Gurrelieder* with the Boston Symphony in the early spring of 1979; as Romeo in a concert performance of *I Capuleti ed i Montecchi* with the American Opera Society under Eve Queler at Carnegie Hall on May 13, 1979; and, again as Romeo, with the Washington Opera in the Bellini work on April 29, 1979. One of the dazzled critics in the audience in Washington was Robert Jacobson of *Opera News* (July 1979), who reported that her Romeo "became pure Lord Byron—a dashing romantic hero in boots and cape with flowing hair and flashing eyes. More than that, she conjured up the essence of bel canto through her magically even emission of opulent mezzo tone, the extravagantly long line, her range of tonal coloration, her ringing high notes, and her total grasp of the role, moving and riveting in the tomb scene."

One of the factors lending such credibility to Tatiana Troyanos' appearance in trouser roles is her appearance: tall, slim, and long-legged, she has an elegantly sculptured face, of which the most important feature is her large dark eyes, accentuated with liner make-up. Critics have often commented on her grace of movement, and according to journalists, one of the joys of interviewing her is the sound of her deep, throaty laugh. At last report she was sharing an Upper West Side apartment with Schatzie, a grey and brown mongrel that she rescued from a dog pound in Germany. Although Miss Troyanos has not ruled out the possibility of marriage, she feels that it is difficult to reconcile with the claims of a busy career. To keep fit she walks, bikes, rides, swims, waterskis, and abjures the German beer she once loved. Since she is a confirmed moviegoer, she enjoys living in New York City, among other reasons, because it is the acknowledged film capital of the world. Her recorded roles include Carmen, Clairon in Richard Strauss's Capriccio, Dorabella, Cherubino, Judith in Bartók's Bluebeard's Castle, the tormented nun in The Devils of Loudon, Jocasta, and Dido. Her recording schedule for 1979 includes Norma and La Gioconda.

References: After Dark 8:59+ N '75 por; N Y Times II p17 Mr 7 '76 por; Newsday II p4+ F 22 '76 por; Newsweek 87:78 Mr 22 '76 por; Opera News 40:21+ Mr 20 '76 por; Who's Who in Opera, 1976

Tuckwell, Barry (Emmanuel)

Mar. 5, 1931- Musician. Address: b. c/o The Carson Office, 119 W. 57th St., New York City, N.Y. 10019; h. 21 Lawford Rd., London NW 5, England

The world's premier horn player, Barry Tuckwell became the first to make a career of playing that instrument almost exclusively as a soloist and chamber musician after spending some twenty years as a member of Australian and British orchestras. On his own since 1968, he has given some 200 concerts annually with orchestras and chamber groups throughout the world. He has recorded more music for the horn than any other player, and his albums —on the RCA, CRI, Angel, London, and Argo labels—include concertos and chamber works by both classical and contemporary composers.

The horn, erroneously referred to in English-speaking countries as the "French" horn, has been described by Tuckwell as "inherently treacherous." Regarded by some connoisseurs as the most beautiful-sounding orchestral instrument, it is also probably the most murderously difficult, and few performers have attained Tuckwell's standard of excellence in playing it. Winthrop Sargeant wrote about Tuckwell in a profile in the New Yorker (March 14, 1977): "He almost never misses a note. His agility might be compared to that of a coloratura soprano. His tone is rich, and variously colored and shaded. His legato exhibits a singing line and a faultless feeling for accent and phrasing. His staccato attacks, made with the help of the tongue, are firm, and where desired remarkably rapid, and his articulation has enormous variety. All these qualities have caused him to be called, with some justice, the Jascha Heifetz of the horn."

Descended from Welshmen who had immigrated to Australia three generations earlier, Barry Emmanuel Tuckwell, the younger of two children of Charles Robert and Elizabeth Jane (Hill) Tuckwell, was born on March 5, 1931 in Melbourne, Australia. He comes from an intensely musical family, all of whose members, it is said, were endowed with perfect pitch. His father was a professional pianist and organist, his mother also played the piano, and his sister, Patricia, who is married to Lord Harewood, a cousin of Queen Elizabeth II, was a violinist.

Able to read music before he could read words, Tuckwell studied the piano and the violin as a child. As a member of the choir at St. Andrew's Cathedral in Sydney, where his family moved when he was four, he briefly showed an interest in the organ, although his legs were at that time too short to reach the pedals. When he was thirteen, he was introduced to the horn by a friend, who gave him some instruction on how to play it. After he discovered his natural affinity for the instrument, he won a scholarship to study with Alan Mann at the Sydney Conservatorium of Music. "I progressed very rapidly," Tuckwell has recalled. "I could read horn music easily, because there was only one note at a time and the pace was usually slow. I found that the instrument was the most natural thing in the world for me. I can't imagine how anybody who hasn't got perfect pitch can play the horn. I had perfect pitch and the physical makeup for horn playing, and everything went smoothly." In an interview with Patricia Burstein in *People* magazine (January 8, 1978) Tuckwell reflected: "It was an important age to find something. I was not bright academically and I was on the verge of being a juvenile delinquent." Within six months after beginning his formal studies, Tuckwell was able to obtain paying jobs as a horn player.

After leaving school in 1947, at the age of fifteen, Tuckwell auditioned for and obtained the position of third horn and assistant first horn in the Melbourne Symphony Orchestra where he was the youngest player. Six months later he was engaged by the Sydney Symphony, with which he had already played as a student. There, under the direction of conductors such as Sir Eugene Goossens and Otto Klemperer, he learned the then seldom played symphonies of Bruckner and Mahler as well as the standard classical works and a number of contemporary compositions. After two years with the Sydney Symphony, Tuckwell went to England in 1950 and there attended concerts by such renowned conductors as Wilhelm Furtwängler, Erich Kleiber, and Bruno Walter. He visited the phenomenal British horn player Dennis Brain, whom he credits with influencing him profoundly, along with Gottfried von Freiburg, the longtime first horn of the Vienna Philharmonic, and the American pop trombone player, Tommy Dorsey. "I would say that I learned virtuosity from Dennis Brain, and also facility and security; sound from Freiburg; and beauty of melody—that singing sound—from Dorsey," Tuckwell told Winthrop Sargeant.

While awaiting answers to his job applications to various orchestras, Tuckwell took a summer job with a small and underrehearsed ensemble of thirty musicians who played light classics at Buxton Spa. Then he was offered the position of assistant first horn with the Hallé Orchestra of Manchester, whose music director was Sir John Barbirolli. He remained with the Hallé from 1951 to 1953, touring extensively and playing in as many as 250 concerts a year. In 1953-54 he played third horn with the Scottish National Orchestra under composer-conductor Karl Rankl, a former pupil of Arnold Schoenberg. Next he spent one season, in 1954-55, playing first horn with the Bournemouth Symphony. Finally, in 1955, at the age of twenty-four, he obtained the position of first horn with the London Symphony Orchestra, where he remained until 1968. He also served for several years as chairman of the London Symphony's board of directors.

For about a decade, beginning in the early 1960's, he was a professor of horn at the Royal Academy of Music, in London, of which he is an honorary member. Apart from giving occasional master classes, at Harvard University and in Europe, Tuckwell no longer teaches. "It is very difficult work, I think," he said in 1975. "It's so exhausting. Playing concerts is far easier."

Although Tuckwell was primarily an orchestral musician from 1947 until 1968, he had experience as a soloist dating back to his early days in Australia. Later, in England, after he had played with the English Opera Group under the direction of Benjamin Britten at the Aldeburgh Festival, the latter invited him to play at the lunchtime recitals at London's Royal Court Theatre, where young musicians were introduced to the public. In the mid-1950's Tuckwell performed as a soloist with the London Mozart Players under the direction of Harry Blech and toured East Germany with them. In 1963 he took part in the first Anglo-Soviet Music Exchange in Leningrad and Moscow. When he left the London Symphony in 1968 to free-lance he did not make a complete break with orchestral playing. He was hired that year by Sir Georg Solti to play first horn in two complete cycles of Wagner's *Ring of the Nibelungs* within a two-week period at the London Royal Opera House at Covent Garden, an assignment he had turned down a few years earlier because of conflicting schedules.

In 1968 he founded the Tuckwell Wind Quintet, consisting of horn, flute, oboe, clarinet, and bassoon and began to tour almost continually. The quintet did not make its London debut until November 12, 1973, when it performed at Queen Elizabeth Hall. "We waited until we felt we were absolutely ready," he has explained. "We didn't want to give just another duty concert." Two days later, in an impressive display of stamina, he performed twice in the same day, with only a fifteen-minute interval, at the Festival Hall and the Queen Elizabeth Hall on London's South Bank. In 1974 the Tuckwell Wind Quintet traveled 30,000 miles in the Orient, performing in Thailand, Hong Kong, Malaysia, the Philippines, and Korea. Tuckwell derives greater enjoyment from playing chamber music than from his solo performances, even though it brings him less money and he can only devote one-tenth of his working time to it.

Tuckwell laments the fact that phonograph records create an expectation of perfection that cannot be satisfied in a live performance. Nevertheless, his playing of Mozart's Concerto for Horn, K.495 at a "Mostly Mozart" concert at New York's Lincoln Center in the summer of 1978 must have come close to the standard he set in his two recordings of the work. Barton Wimble, writing in the New York *Daily News* (August 7, 1978), noted: "The French horn is a naked instrument, especially when it's played solo. Each mistake sounds ten times bigger than, let's say, a violin's or a piano's. So you have to be really good. And Barry Tuckwell was . . . perfection. The 4th Horn Concerto . . . is an exceptionally difficult work and Tuckwell . . . navigated the rapids with supreme ease."

Despite the long periods of intense concentration required for note-perfect renditions, Tuckwell enjoys making recordings. His extensive discography includes, in addition to the well-known concertos of Mozart, the two by Haydn, the two by Richard Strauss, and those of Weber and Telemann. With pianist Vladimir Ashkenazy, Tuckwell has recorded works for horn and piano by Beethoven, Saint-Saëns, and Franz Danzi. He also is fond of contemporary music. Among the works written for him that he has recorded are: *Voyage* by Iain Hamilton, Thea Musgrave's Concerto for Horn and Orchestra and *Night Music,* Don Banks' Horn Concerto, and Humphrey Searle's Aubade for Horn and Orchestra. In 1977 Tuckwell gave the world première performance of *Actaeon,* a concerto written for him by Richard Rodney Bennett, with the BBC Symphony in London's Royal Albert Hall. For Tuckwell, "a lot of the appeal of a vast amount of contemporary music is like that of doing a jigsaw. The satisfaction lies in getting it right." Tuckwell dislikes exhibitionistic music that is, in his opinion, merely a vehicle for showing off, such as the bel canto operas of Bellini and Donizetti. He also is irritated by what he feels is a tendency of some critics to pay automatic homage to new music, a luxury not enjoyed by some great composers of the past.

Aware that after a certain age playing the horn becomes very difficult in the physical sense, Tuckwell has succumbed to what he calls "stick fever" or the "right arm disease," that is, the urge to conduct. In January 1979 he toured as conductor of the Pittsburgh Symphony Chamber Orchestra, an ensemble of some twenty-five musicians. Writing in the San Francisco *Chronicle* (January 22, 1979) about a concert that included Wagner's *Siegfried Idyll,* Mozart's Symphony No. 29 and Horn Concerto, K. 477, and Beethoven's Piano Concerto No. 2, critic Marilyn Tucker noted that "Tuckwell's style was low-key, thorough and precise. The performances rested on a solid rhythmic base, with Tuckwell, in the most unobtrusive fashion, shaping musical phrases of the utmost fluidity. Mellowness, clarity, crispness and dynamics of all shades of light and dark, these are the things to remember. Obviously, conducting is not just another ego trip for Barry Tuckwell." The conductor's role is, in Tuckwell's view, one of "encouraging, bullying, inspiring, coercing" an orchestra into giving performances that are beyond the routine. An artist-member of the Chamber Music Society of Lincoln Center, which usually plays in Alice Tully Hall, Tuckwell performed in February 1979 with the society in a "cushion concert" at its other home, the Paula Cooper Gallery, in New York's SoHo district. There he joined pianist John Browning, oboist Leonard Arner, clarinetist Gervase de Peyer, and bassoonist Loren Glickman in a performance of Beethoven's Quintet for Piano and Winds in E flat.

In 1965 Tuckwell was made an Officer of the Most Excellent Order of the British Empire, and in 1968 he received the Harriet Cohen International Award for Solo Instruments. He is a member of the Athenaeum Club, an honorary member of the Guildhall School of Music and Drama, and a past president of the International Horn Society. The music publishers G. Schirmer, Inc., have engaged him as editor of the entire literature for the horn, and he is the author of *Playing the Horn,* published by Oxford University Press in 1978.

Described by Winthrop Sargeant as "an eminently sane and cheerful man with virtually no eccentricities," Barry Tuckwell is five feet eleven inches tall, weighs 160 pounds, and has brown eyes and graying brown hair. He sports a moustache and small tuft of beard under his lower lip, grown to protect his mouth, that give him a distinctly Mephistophelian appearance. He and his wife, the former Hilary Jane Warburton, a pianist from New Zealand whom he met during a tour of Australia, have one son, Thomas James. From an earlier marriage, he also has two teen-age children, David Michael and Jane Madeleine. Tuckwell considers travel "one of the most overrated experiences in terms of glamor," citing the expense and emotional stress it involves. On his tours he usually takes two horns, an old German Krupse and a modern American Halton instrument. To keep himself in condition for playing, he practises breath control, and although he is something of a gourmet, he has to watch his diet, avoiding tomatoes, citrus fruits, sweets, and spicy foods. When he is able to take time out from his musical activities he enjoys swimming, sailing, photography, and archaeology.

References: Hi Fi 26:MA 6+ F '76 por; *New Yorker* 53:45+ Mr 14 '77; *Washington Post* B p6 Jl 25 '79 por; *Who's Who,* 1979-80; *Who's Who in Music,* 1972

Turbay Ayala, Julio César (tōōr-bī′ ä-yä′lä)

June 18, 1916- President of Colombia.
Address: b. *Oficina del Presidente,*
Bogotá, Colombia

On August 7, 1978 Julio César Turbay Ayala, a career politician and leader of the moderate wing of his country's middle-of-the-road Liberal

Julio César Turbay Ayala

party, was inaugurated to succeed Alfonso López Michelsen for a four-year term as President of Colombia after narrowly defeating his Conservative opponent in national elections. A champion of Western Hemisphere solidarity, Turbay has served as Colombia's Minister of Foreign Affairs and delegate to the United Nations, as Vice-President, and as Ambassador to the United Kingdom and the United States. Colombia's status as one of a handful of surviving democracies in the Western Hemisphere has been jeopardized in recent years by political terrorism, inflation, unemployment, and an illicit international narcotics traffic. Nevertheless, Turbay remains optimistic about his country's political future. "I aim to deliver to my successor a nation subject to the rule of law," he asserted in his inaugural address, "one in which the people and the armed forces willingly uphold the democratic institutions . . . of a representative government."

Unlike most of Colombia's leaders, who tend to be of aristocratic lineage, Julio César Turbay Ayala comes from a middle-class family. He was born in Bogotá on June 18, 1916 to Antonio A. Turbay and the former Rosaura Ayala. Because he is descended from Lebanese immigrants, he is known to his compatriots as "Turco" ("Turk"), denoting his Near Eastern background. Turbay was educated at the Escuela Nacional de Comercio in Bogotá and earned a diploma from the Colegio Universitario de Botero, a preparatory school. Self-educated in the liberal arts, he never graduated from a university but is addressed as "doctor" on the basis of an honorary law degree he received from the University of Cauca in 1957.

Turbay began his career as a public servant in 1938, when he became a member of the village council of Engative, southwest of Bogotá. In the same year he organized a national movement in behalf of public employees. From 1939 to 1943 he exercised his oratorical and debating skills as a deputy in the legislative assembly of the department of Cundinamarca, and for a time served as its president. He entered national politics in 1943, when he was elected a deputy for Cundinamarca in the Chamber of Representatives— the lower house of Colombia's Congress— where he remained until 1953. During the 1946 and 1949 legislative sessions he was president of the Chamber and for five years presided over its commission on military affairs and foreign relations. In 1947 he was a Colombian delegate to the United Nations General Assembly with the rank of ambassador and in 1949 he became presiding officer of the executive board of the Liberal party's Cundinamarca organization. From 1949 to 1957 he was director of the radio news program *Democracia*.

In 1957-58, under the five-man military junta —known as "gobierno de los quintuples"— that followed the overthrow of the dictatorship of General Gustavo Rojas Pinilla, Turbay served in his first Cabinet post, that of Minister of Mines and Energy. Meanwhile, Colombia's two major parties, the Liberals and the Conservatives, took steps to end the decade of bitter civil strife known as "La Violencia." In December 1957 they concluded a "National Front" agreement that provided for the quadrennial alternation of the Presidency between Liberals and Conservatives for sixteen years beginning in 1958 and guaranteed equal representation between them in public offices. In the first National Front administration, headed by Alberto Lleras Camargo, a Liberal, who took office as President in May 1958, Turbay was given the portfolio of Minister of Foreign Affairs and also served as delegate to the U.N.

As Foreign Affairs Minister, Turbay advocated Latin American solidarity and cooperation with the United States. Although he at first sympathized with the aims of the Cuban revolution that brought Fidel Castro to power in 1959, Turbay grew more and more concerned about the growing hostility between Cuba and the United States and the Castro regime's alignment with the Soviet Union. As chairman of an Organization of American States foreign ministers' meeting at San José, Costa Rica in August 1960, he called on Castro to repudiate a recent offer by Soviet Premier Nikita S. Khrushchev to defend Cuba with rockets against possible attack from the United States and urged the Cuban government to accept "the discipline of the inter-American system." Cuba's acceptance of the Soviet offer, he declared, "jeopardizes hemispheric unity, threatens continental peace and security, and affects the inter-American system." His prophetic remarks at San José were later described by United States Undersecretary of State C. Douglas Dillon as "one of the most important declarations of our time."

In September 1960, while presiding over an inter-American conference on economic aid at Bogotá, Turbay told the conferees that swift social and economic reforms were needed to cope with "the social revolution moving in the depths of our political life" and praised what he called the "new interest" on the part of the United States in helping to improve the lot of its southern neighbors. Later that month, in a speech before the U.N. General Assembly, Turbay warned the Soviet Union against political or military interference in American affairs and asserted that to his knowledge there existed "no threat of aggression against Cuba on the part of the United States or any other American country."

Convinced that the inter-American system "must be strengthened in all its dimensions" to counteract Cuba's Communist trend, in July 1961 Turbay called on the United States to collaborate with other members of the forthcoming Alliance for Progress conference at Punta del Este, Uruguay in taking "immediate measures" for the stabilization of the prices of raw materials and the financing of land reform, low-cost housing, public health, and education, which he considered top priorities for hemispheric development. That summer he also visited Brazil and Peru to inform leaders of those countries that Colombia viewed Cuba's continuing ties with the Communist bloc as incompatible with her hemispheric commitments

In August 1961 Turbay was among the passengers on a Pan American World Airways jet airliner that was hijacked over Mexico and diverted to Havana. He had been on a visit to Mexico City, reportedly to garner support among government officials for concerted Latin American pressure against the Castro regime. But the Cuban government, avoiding confrontation, treated the plane's passengers with courtesy, and Cuban Foreign Minister Raúl Roa even came to the airport to greet Turbay. That same evening, according to Havana radio, the plane was released, "in deference to the presence of Señor Turbay."

Late that year Turbay left the Foreign Affairs ministry and became a candidate for a seat in the Senate—the upper house of the national Congress—to which he was elected for two successive four-year terms, from 1962 to 1966, and from 1966 to 1970. Concurrently with his second Senate term, from 1967 to 1969, he served again as Colombia's Ambassador to the U.N. He was also elected Primer Designado, or Vice-President, for a two-year term by a joint session of the Congress in September 1967, and as such, took on Presidential duties during the absence of President Carlos Lleras Restrepo. As a member of the national executive of the Liberal party from 1966 on, Turbay also took part in bipartisan

discussions between Liberals and Conservatives concerning the National Front and the selection of its candidates.

In the U.N. General Assembly debates that followed the Arab-Israeli six-day war of June 1967, Turbay argued that it was impossible for the world organization to ignore Israel, as the Arab nations might wish, since the Jewish state had been the creation of the U.N. He submitted a four-point peace plan calling for Israeli withdrawal from occupied Arab territory and the establishment of demilitarized zones on some border areas. In January 1968 Turbay, in his role as Vice-President, signed an agreement with Soviet Ambassador to the U.N. Nikolai T. Federenko, reestablishing diplomatic relations between Colombia and the U.S.S.R. after a twenty-year lapse. Turbay resigned his U.N. post in 1969 to return to the Senate and was elected its presiding officer. In 1970 he was named Colombia's Ambassador to Great Britain, in June 1973 he was chosen national chairman of the Liberal party, and in September 1974, following the inauguration of President Alfonso López Michelsen, he was once more elected Vice-President by a joint session of the Congress. He became Ambassador to the United States in April 1975 but relinquished that post in August 1976 to concentrate on establishing a political base for his forthcoming Presidential candidacy.

Meanwhile, in 1974, the National Front, of which Turbay had been a vigorous supporter, officially came to an end, although Cabinet posts continued to be apportioned between the two major parties during the four years of the López Michelsen administration. The 1974 elections also sounded the death knell for the National Popular Alliance (ANAPO), a populist coalition led by former dictator Gustavo Rojas Pinilla, which had challenged the National Front four years earlier, and which Turbay had viewed at the time as a major threat to democratic government in Colombia.

Divergences continued to plague factions within the Liberal party, of which the strongest were Turbay's moderate "Grupo de los 90" and former President Lleras Restrepo's more leftist-oriented "Democratización Liberal." The party leadership therefore decided in September 1976, under an accord known as the San Carlos agreement, to ensure the selection of a single Liberal candidate for the 1978 Presidential election. He was to be chosen on the basis of the outcome of Congressional elections to be held in February 1978, which were to be considered an unofficial Presidential primary contest.

General apathy led about three-fourths of Colombia's 12,300,000 eligible voters to abstain from the elections of February 26, 1978, in which the 311 Congressional seats and some 9,000 state and local offices were at stake. To determine who would be the Liberal Presidential candidate in June, Turbay and Lleras Restrepo each submitted a complete slate of

Congressional candidates for the consideration of the voters. During the heated campaign, candidates accused each other of vote-buying and involvement in the drug traffic, and Turbay's opponents called attention to the recent arrest on charges of embezzlement and fraud of his close political associate Alberto Santofimio Botero. Lleras and Conservative and left-wing spokesmen charged that incumbent President López Michelsen, required by law to remain neutral, was openly lending his support to Turbay.

Nevertheless, Turbay emerged triumphant, declaring when informed of the outcome that the victory was that of democracy and not his own. In March he was confirmed as Presidential candidate and party leader at the Liberal convention. Since the Liberals had scored a substantial victory in the February elections, Turbay was considered the favorite to win the June Presidential contest, in which his chief opponent was to be the Conservative candidate, Belisario Betancur, a university professor and former Minister of Labor.

In the tumultuous campaign for the June election, Turbay was somewhat handicapped by his close identification with López Michelsen. Although the incumbent President had started out four years earlier as a zealous reformer, escalation of crime and political violence soon compelled him to institute a state of siege, leaving himself open to charges of political repression. The government's failure to cope with inflation exacerbated industrial strife, culminating in a crippling general strike in the fall of 1977. Charges of corruption included allegations that top government officials were involved in an international trade in cocaine and marijuana that amounted to some $2 billion a year. According to a White House memorandum made public in April 1978, Turbay himself was allegedly involved in the drug trade with the United States, a charge that he denounced. Other sources tried to implicate Betancur in the illegal export of coffee, but both charges remained unsubstantiated.

In his campaign speeches Turbay promised to work for constitutional reforms, and proposed measures to encourage economic growth, improve health, housing, and education, eradicate crime and corruption, promote oil and gas exploration and agricultural development, and establish a sounder basis in trade relations with the United States. Betancur made similar glowing promises to voters but, as James Nelson Goodsell noted in the Christian Science Monitor (June 1, 1978), the national campaign was based less on issues than on "regional rivalries, family feuds, and the internecine vagaries of Colombian politics."

In a final exchange of invective by the two leading candidates, on May 28, 1978, Turbay charged that because Betancur lacked a national political base of his own, he had to rely on the votes of disaffected Liberals. He warned his fellow party members against "betraying"

the Liberal cause by voting Conservative and asserted that such a course would plunge Colombia back into the political violence of the past. Betancur, on the other hand, tried to persuade the voters that a Turbay administration would merely continue the unpopular López Michelsen regime, equally unable to cope with the country's chronic inflation and social turmoil.

The election of June 4, 1978, in which some 38 percent of the eligible voters went to the polls, resulted in a narrow victory for Turbay, who received 2,506,228 votes to Betancur's 2,358,644. The remaining candidates, representing splinter groups of the left and right, received less than 5 percent of the vote between them. Because of the closeness of the election, Betancur refused to concede defeat until June 20, after an official recount of the vote had been made.

Sworn into office on August 7, 1978, Turbay promised in his inaugural address to respect civil liberties, strengthen democratic institutions, promote economic prosperity, combat corruption and violence, support Latin American integration, and encourage an atmosphere of mutual respect between Colombia and the United States, based on the absolute freedom of each. In keeping with a constitutional amendment of 1968, stipulating that the minority party was to have adequate representation in the government after the National Front agreement expired, Turbay appointed five Conservatives, seven Liberals, and one unaffiliated military man to his thirteen-member Cabinet.

In the wake of stepped up student and guerrilla violence during the weeks following his inauguration, Turbay issued a "security statute" in September 1978 to combat crime and subversion. The law permitted military courts to try civilians arrested for terrorist crimes, increased prison terms for acts of violence, forbade radio and television stations to report on illegal strikes and unrest in times of crisis, and provided penalties for "subversive propaganda." Although it was widely denounced as an attempt by Turbay to establish a dictatorship, and there were reports —denied by the government—that detainees were being tortured, the law seemed to enlist public support and was proclaimed constitutional by Colombia's Supreme Court.

Meanwhile, after having concluded an anti-drug pact with the United States, the Turbay government began in the fall of 1978, with the help of the military, to crack down on the illicit narcotics trade. To ease industrial unrest, the government instituted some economic reforms, including a 35 percent increase in the minimum wage for urban and rural workers effective January 1979. Nevertheless, violence continued, and in the early months of 1979 thousands were arrested, giving rise to charges by human rights activists that Colombia under Turbay seemed to be turning into a "repressive democracy."

Continued success of the military in its anti-guerrilla campaigns led some observers to suggest in late 1979 that Colombia might be following the course of Uruguay, where democracy had given way to an army dictatorship. But although Turbay conceded that military coups might be justified "in extreme cases of an obvious vacuum whhich could lead to general anarchy," he denied that such conditions prevailed in Colombia.

Julio César Turbay Ayala was married on May 15, 1948 to Nydia Quintero. They have a son, Julio César, and three daughters, Diana (Turbay's private secretary), Claudia, and Maria Victoria. A burly man, more than six feet tall and weighing over 200 pounds, the Colombian President is said to be "an uncharismatic speaker with a nasal monotone" who is also noted for his "sardonic wit" and "political shrewdness" and inspires "either devotion or antipathy." According to a profile in the New York Times (June 23, 1978), "he is the subject of numerous jokes, few of them complimentary, and he is among the first to ask what the latest is." The Times article also notes that "Turbay . . . smiles sparingly, but he clearly enjoys himself when politicking in the countryside, where he takes off his tie, rolls up his sleeves, and drinks beer with his constituents. His success, he likes to say, is a triumph of the middle class." Turbay is the author of a biography of Simon Bolívar entitled Biografía del Libertador y sus ideas políticas, and he has been active in the Sociedad Bolivariana de Colombia. His favorite recreation is horseback riding. Once asked what he considered his most notable achievement, he answered: "My marriage."

References: N Y Times A p6 Je 23 '78 por; Quién es Quién en Colombia (1970); Who's Who in the World, 1978-79

Turner, Robert Edward, 3d See Turner, Ted

Turner, Ted

Nov. 19, 1938- Business executive; sportsman. Address: b. Office of the President and General Manager, Atlanta Braves, P.O. Box 4064, Atlanta, Ga. 30302; Turner Communications Group, c/o WTCG-TV, W. 1018 Peachtree Rd. NE, Atlanta, Ga. 30309

Ted Turner's acclaiming himself a "Southern folk hero" is no vain boast; the colorful Atlanta millionaire sportsman, known as "the Mouth of the South" because of his loqua- ciousness, has many credentials to back up his claim. Beginning in 1963, when he was twenty-four, Turner rebuilt his family's failing billboard advertising business and parlayed it into a multimillion-dollar conglomerate that includes several radio and television stations. One is Atlanta's WTCG-TV, dubbed by Turner "the Super Station that Serves the Nation," the first independent station to become a virtual network via satellite and cable. Among the programs telecast by WTCG are the games of the Atlanta Braves baseball team and the Atlanta Hawks basketball team, both bought by Turner in 1976, when they were the worst teams in their respective sports. In their first three years under Turner, the Braves continued to finish in last place, but their morale is that of a winner and a* tendance has increased tremendously. The Hawks finally reached the National Basketball Association playoffs in 1978 and almost reached them again in 1979.

In addition to his other achievements, Turner is a champion yachtsman, winner of the 1977 America's Cup. In August 1979 he was the luckiest survivor of the tragic Fastnet Race, named for the Fastnet Rock, off the southern tip of Ireland. Turner won the race, in which a storm took fifteen lives and caused $4.5 million in damages to yachts.

Robert Edward Turner 3d was born in Cincinnati, Ohio on November 19, 1938 to Ed Turner, a Mississippian who had turned salesman after his family lost its cotton farm in the Depression, and Florence Rooney Turner, the granddaughter of the first chain grocer in Cincinnati. The parents (who divorced when Ted was in college) met when the father rented quarters at an apartment hotel in Cincinnati that was run by the mother's family.

"He sure looks good to be so bad," a family cook once said of Ted Turner, a mischievous child despite the corporal punishment often administered by his father. Turner seldom talks about the somber aspects of his childhood, but he has singled out as especially unhappy the time when, at the age of six, he was left behind in a boarding school in Cincinnati while his father went on a World War II Navy assignment to the Gulf of Mexico with his wife and younger child, Mary Jane. (Mary Jane later died, after suffering for years from lupus.)

Dr. Irving Victor of Savannah, Georgia, a close friend of Ed Turner, has commented on the inconsistency of his treatment of his son: "He idolized Teddy. He was his whole life. . . . He bought him guns, boats. Yet he was tremendously difficult with him. I think he took out a lot of hostility on him." Ted Turner's first wife, Judy Nye Hallisey, has given a different explanation of her father-in-law's motivation in disciplining Ted: "He wanted Ted to be insecure, because he felt that insecurity breeds greatness. If Ted was insecure then he would be forced to compete."

Turner attended public school in Cincinnati until, when he was nine, the family moved to Savannah, where Ed Turner had bought the outdoor advertising company that became the Turner Advertising Company. During summers, Ted Turner worked a forty-hour week for his father's company, cutting grass around the billboards and creosoting the poles. "One summer I made fifty dollars a week, and my father charged me twenty-five dollars a week rent," he has recalled. "I asked him if that wasn't a little high. He said that if I could do better than that for food and lodging seven days a week I could move out."

In the South, Ted Turner attended the Georgia Military Academy, outside of Atlanta, and the McCallie School in Chattanooga, Tennessee, which is described in its catalogue as providing "Chattanooga and the South with college preparation for boys in a Christian context." According to his mother, Turner "hated" McCallie, which was then military-oriented, and he is still remembered at the school as "Terrible Ted." Elliot Schmidt, Turner's American history teacher and dormitory proctor at McCallie, has been quoted as recalling Turner as a smart and inquisitive boy who was assigned to a dorm with older boys in the hope that they "would calm him down," but instead "he started leading them." According to Schmidt, Turner manifested an interest in flora and fauna in unusual ways, such as growing grass in his room—"*lawn* grass, which he clipped with manicure scissors"—and trying "to take in dogs, birds with broken wings, gerbils, snakes, anything he found."

Representing McCallie, Turner won the Tennessee state high school debating contest when he was seventeen. The academic subjects that interested him were history and the classics, insofar as they represented "grandeur and tradition, glorious and beautiful things." In an interview with Peter Ross Range for *Playboy* (August 1978), Turner recounted: "As a kid I was a little bit of an artist and a poet. I painted and sculpted a little, but it was too slow-moving for me to really get into. But the whole idea of grand things always turned me on—the grand idea of building the Parthenon [or] the Pyramids."

Ted Turner wanted to try for an appointment to the United States Naval Academy at Annapolis, but Ed Turner wanted his son trained for business and sent him to Brown University in Providence, Rhode Island with that in mind. In a move that typified his developing ambivalent relationship with his father, Ted obediently enrolled at Brown but decided to major in classics, largely because of the influence of one of his teachers at Brown, John Rowe Workman. Roger Vaughan, who was a fellow student at Brown, observed in *Ted Turner: The Man Behind the Mouth* (1978) that Workman is a classicist whose "hobby is disaster," a subject on which he has collected over 400 books.

Vaughan points out that Workman is "not depressed by his thesis that disaster is what usually precedes human progress" and that "it is not surprising that Turner would choose Workman as a mentor, because Turner has always had a similar quality, a comprehensive and underlying sense of the absurd that certain lucky people are born with." Under pressure from his father, Turner finally changed his major to economics. "We lost Ted, in a sense . . . ," Vaughan quotes Workman as saying. "But we didn't really lose him. The real humanist will always go out of his way to be different."

At Brown, Turner excelled at sailing as well as debating. Experienced in piloting small boats from childhood, he won his first nine regattas on the college dinghy circuit. The Noroton (Connecticut) Yacht Club offered him a summer job and, with it, a chance to race in a fleet of Lightning boats, but his father insisted that he continue working summers for the family business, which by then had expanded to several cities in the South. Complying with his father's wish, Turner worked as an account executive with the flagship company in Savannah.

Recounting Turner's "keen disappointment" at being denied the opportunity offered him by the Noroton Yacht Club, Roger Vaughan notes that "that [disappointment] and the divorce brewing at home was enough to make Ted throw away the $5,000 bonus his father had offered him if he didn't have a drink until he was twenty-one." "Figuring the price of the first drink would be reduced proportionately by subsequent drinks, Turner and some friends got rowdy and landed at a nearby women's college. Ted was suspended from Brown for the ensuing fracas. His father's solution to that problem was a tour of duty in the Coast Guard. After spending six months of active duty with the Coast Guard, Ted Turner returned to Brown, but when he was discovered breaking the then existing rule against female guests in rooms, he was asked to leave a second and final time.

Following a summer cruise with the Coast Guard, Turner became general manager of the Turner Advertising Company's branch in Macon, Georgia in 1960. Two years later, Ed Turner overextended himself by buying into the General Outdoor Advertising Company, the biggest in the country, with a base in Atlanta, Georgia long coveted by Turner père. By early 1963 his financial commitments had become so pressing that he initiated plans for selling out. Meanwhile, Ted had developed a zealot's taste for the family enterprise, and that taste was, ironically, whetted rather than diminished by the acquisition of the Atlanta billboard business. Furious when he learned of his father's plans, he stood up to him, in acrimonious argument. "Ed Turner had been determined to raise a competitive son," Roger Vaughan wrote in his biography of Ted Turner. "Now he was suffering the full onslaught of his creation. . . . Suddenly he was staggered by his own surprising limitations in a business venture he thought would rejuvenate him [and] locked in combat with the beloved son he had so carefully programmed for greatness."

On March 5, 1963, six months after he had purchased the business in Atlanta, Ed Turner killed himself with a pistol in the bedroom of his plantation in South Carolina. Immediately after his father's death, Ted Turner halted the sell-out transactions then in progress, proceeded to sell the two plantations in Georgia and South Carolina to help pay real estate taxes, and set about regaining, through complex financing, the parts of the family business already sold.

As president and chief executive officer, Ted Turner built the various Turner companies into a huge success. In 1970, over the protests of his financial advisers, he purchased Channel 17, an independent Atlanta UHF station that was losing money. By merging Turner Communications Corporation with Rice Broadcasting, he gained control of the television outlet, which became WTCG, flagship station of the Turner Communications Group. Sustaining an initial loss of $2,000,000 on the strength of his billboard revenues, he ground down the local competition, cornering the Atlanta sports, movie-rerun, and situation comedy markets, for an extraordinary 16 percent share of the television audience.

From the beginning, Turner's eye was on an audience vaster than that in Atlanta. Six months after buying WTCG, he purchased another independent station, WRET-TV in Charlotte, North Carolina, but that was hardly the limit of his vision. He was acutely aware of the emerging frontier known as cable television, officially designated CATV (for community antenna television), which brings signals into areas where normal television broadcast reception is limited or inferior. Until 1975, all cable signals were transmitted by microwave through a series of amplifying stations to the communities wired to master antennae; in addition, FCC rules severely limited the access of independent broadcasters to the cumbersome common-carrier cable systems.

Two developments in 1975 contributed mightily to the progress of cable television—and to the Turner Communications Group. One was the relaxation of the FCC's restrictions, after hearings in which Turner's testimony brought him charges of traitor from fellow independent broadcasters; the other was the launching of RCA's first Americom satellite, SATCOM I, into a geo-synchronous orbit 22,300 miles above the equator.

The communications satellites were originally planned for telephone purposes, along with selective use by the three major networks. In the fall of 1975 Home Box Office, a subscriber motion picture service, became the first constant user of the RCA satellite; and on December 27, 1976 Channel 17, WTCG-TV Atlanta, began to beam its signal to the satellite full time. By the end of 1978 HBO was reaching more than half a million homes through 576 cable systems in forty-seven states; WTCG was going into two million cable homes, more than double those in the Atlanta market, and it was adding about 50,000 homes a month. Turner's station was worth an estimated $40 million, and the worth was appreciating at the rate of $1 million a month, with a projected gross of $189 million within ten years.

To market his station's cable audience, Turner opened offices in Chicago and New York, where national advertisers vied for the opportunity to sponsor the televised baseball games of the Atlanta Braves, purchased by Turner in January 1976 partly with such sponsorship in mind. Later in the same year he bought the Atlanta Hawks of the National Basketball Association. "By owning the Braves he avoids contract disputes and renegotiations over broadcast schedules," Roger Vaughan wrote in his biography of Turner. "That reassures his cable customers. And if he hadn't bought a piece of the Atlanta Hawks, they might have left Atlanta and cost Channel 17 one of its most marketable quantities." Turner also bought the rights to telecasting the games of the Atlanta Flames, the professional hockey team, and he amassed the rights to many reruns of network shows and built up a library of 2,700 motion pictures, assuring him of enough material for twenty-four-hour-a-day programming. In 1979 the programming was expanded to include news, special events, prime-time adult programs, and children's shows.

In his attempt to give Atlanta and the Southeast a winning baseball club, Turner early in his ownership of the Braves acquired such players as Andy Messersmith and Jeff Burroughs, in addition to implementing an intensified training program in the Braves's farm system by adding high-calibre instructors at each level. At the beginning of the 1976 season, Charles Feeney, president of the National League, reprimanded Turner for over-fraternizing with players, for approaching un-signed players on opposing teams with offers to pick up their options; for promising to pay his players a $500 bonus for each game the team finished over .500; and for nick-naming Andy Messersmith "Channel," so that Messersmith, number seventeen, would be wearing on the back of his uniform what was in effect an ad for station WTCG-TV.

Turner also alienated opposing managers with his on-field antics, such as personally sweeping the bases after the fifth inning, pushing a baseball from first base to home plate with his nose, and arranging for players to be married in ceremonies on the field. He was forced to sit out the 1977 season when Commissioner of Baseball Bowie Kuhn suspended him for initiating the bid for Gary Matthews' contract prematurely, in a casual remark at a cocktail party at a time when Matthews was still the "property" of the San Francisco Giants.

The notoriety of the suspension had at least one advantage, that of drawing the public's attention to Turner not long before he won the 1977 America's Cup and thus enhancing his fame as winner of that event. Turner had been an increasingly dominant figure in yacht racing for over a decade. Three times winner of the United States 5.5 Meter Championship, he was the Y Flyer National Champion in 1963, the North American Champion in the Flying Dutchman Class in 1965, and the first winner of the Southern Ocean Racing Conference in 1966. In his first try for the America's Cup—the world's championship of ocean racing and an event never lost by the United States in the race's 128-year history—Turner lost the 1974 trials, along with his helm, in his experimental twelve-meter yacht Mariner. With many of his crewmen from 1974, he returned in 1977 at the helm of the proven winner the Courageous. During the summer of 1977 he beat two American competitors in the trials, and in September he defended the Cup successfully against Australia in four races. His victory on that occasion brought him the title of Yachtsman of the Year for an unprecedented third time. With his America's Cup tactician, Gary Jobson, he wrote The Racing Edge (Si-

mon and Schuster, 1979), a book on sailing techniques, tactics, and the "philosophy" of the America's Cup.

Turner is a frenetic man of trim good looks and blithe, positive spirit who, from his seat behind the dugout, with a live public-address microphone at the ready and a wad of tobacco in his jaw, dominates Atlantic-Fulton County Stadium during the Braves's home games just as he dominates any venue he enters. He has described himself as a "work-aholic" and a "regular guy" who "believes in freedom," including the freedom of professional athletes to change teams at will. Others have seen him as "an overgrown kid" who "brings a joyful naïveté to any enterprise." On his serious side, Turner is widely read in history, the Bible, and writers like Joseph Conrad, and he can recite from Edward Fitzgerald's The Rubáiyát of Omar Khayyám and Oliver Wendell Holmes's "The Chambered Nautilus." Simple and frugal in his ways, he cuts his own hair, flies coach, and drives an economy car.

Robert Edward Turner 3d married his second wife, Jane Smith, on June 2, 1964. By her he has two sons, Beauregard and Rhett, and one daughter, Jennie, and he has two children, Laura Lee and Robert Edward 4th, by his first marriage. With their children and Jimmy Brown, who has worked for the family since Ted Turner's infancy, Ted and Jane Turner live on a plantation they recently bought in Marietta, Georgia. "I'm going to be self-sufficient down on the plantation—grow all my own stuff, and I won't have to go to anybody when the world falls apart and the dollar won't buy anything anymore," Turner told Christian Williams in an interview for the Washington Post (February 11, 1979). "But, you know, there'll be a revolution and they'll come and take it away from me." Turner said that if there is one word that explains him, it is the name of his latest yacht, Tenacious.

Williams summed up the private Turner as "a dizzying mixture of fierce pride, non-stop high-decibel speechmaking, philosophical gloom, nightmarish evocations of a ruined earth populated by homo sapiens gone to seed, utter candor, and a sense of personal destiny that is virtually overwhelming." "The destiny is easy to recognize, and he makes no attempt to hide it: he will remake the world of commercial television, dominate international yachting, and simultaneously maintain a nine-teenth-century Southern agrarian home life to which he can return periodically for sustenance."

References: N Y Times C p3 Je 5 '78 pors; Newsweek 87:59+ Je 5 '76 pors; Playboy 25:67+ Ag '78 pors; Sports Illus 49:70+ Ag 21 '78 pors; Washington Post 49:70+ Ag 21 '78 pors; Vaughan, Roger. Ted Turner (1978; Who's Who in America, 1978-79

Uris, Leon (Marcus)

Aug. 3, 1924- Writer. Address: b. c/o
Doubleday & Co., Inc., 245 Park Ave., New
York City, N.Y. 10017

NOTE: This biography supersedes the article
that appeared in Current Biography in 1959.

Each of the eight novels that have placed
Leon Uris among today's most popular writers
of fiction builds its narrative tensions on
the conflicts of recent or current history.
From his first best seller, Battle Cry (1953),
a story of the Marines in World War II,
through such blockbusters as Exodus (1958),
the best of his books on a Judaic theme,
and on to his tribute to the sorrowing land
of Ireland, Trinity (1976), he had interwoven
actual events and actual people with plots
of violence, love, and heroism involving fictitious characters.

As Uris himself acknowledges, he is "not
a member of the critically favored establishment." Some book reviewers have dismissed
his writing as more journalistic than literary
and have berated him for his fondness for
clichés, sentence fragments, and short paragraphs and for his sometimes awkward dialogue. But his storytelling ability is undeniable, and his millions of readers devour
each new lengthy book as an absorbing "page-
turner."

Leon Marcus Uris was born on August
3, 1924 in Baltimore, Maryland, the second
child and only son of Wolf William and

Anna (Blumberg) Uris. The name Uris, a
derivative of Yerushalmi, means Man of
Jerusalem. His sister, Mrs. Esther Kofsky,
lives in Norfolk, Virginia. Both his parents
were Jews of Russian-Polish origin: his
mother was a first-generation American, and
his father emigrated from Poland to the
United States after World War I, stopping
off along the way in Palestine for a year's
stay. He made a living as a paperhanger and
in time became a storekeeper. Leon Uris is
said to be unenthusiastic about recalling his
childhood, which he spent in poor Jewish
neighborhoods in Norfolk, Baltimore, and
Philadelphia. Although he came from a broken
home, it was his family background that
aroused in him a love of literature, as well
as a sympathy with left-wing causes.

From grammar school in Norfolk, Uris went
to a secondary school in Baltimore known
as Baltimore City College and then to John
Bartram High School in Philadelphia. One
of his teachers failed him three times in
English, but willing to believe, as he is often
quoted as saying, that "English and writing
have little to do with each other," Uris continued the practice of writing that he had
begun at about the age of seven when he
wrote an operetta on the occasion of the
death of his dog. Among the literary influences of his high school years was the
Nobel Prize-winning American novelist John
Steinbeck.

In early 1942, shortly after the Japanese
attack on Pearl Harbor, Uris quit high school
in the middle of his last year and left home
to join the Marine Corps. He was stationed
in San Diego, New Zealand, and Hawaii before being sent to take part as a radio operator
in the campaigns at Guadalcanal and Tarawa.
When malaria and other illnesses disqualified
him for an overseas post, he applied for
limited duty in the United States so that
he could remain in the Marines as a private
first class until the end of the war. The
vicinity of San Francisco, where he served
until his military discharge in 1946, continued to be his home for some years after
the war. Unable to support himself as a
writer, he took a job with the San Francisco
Call-Bulletin as manager of a home-delivery
district.

Meanwhile, one after another of the articles
that Uris submitted to magazines met with
rejection slips—until 1950, when Esquire accepted a piece about the selection of the
All American football team, "The All American Razzmatazz," for publication in its January 1951 issue. The sale of the article for
$300 encouraged him to work in earnest
on his long-contemplated novel about the
Marine Corps. For two years he wrote evenings and days off from his job to complete
Battle Cry, which was published in 1953
by G.P. Putnam's Sons after being rejected
by a dozen other publishers.

"My guiding thought throughout was that the real Marine story had not been told," Uris said in an interview with Bernard Kalb for the *Saturday Review* (April 25, 1953). In its close survey of Marine training, life in the barracks, and the ordeals of the battlefield, the novel reflects the positive attitude of the author, who believed in what he fought for during World War II and respected the men, including the officers, of his battalion. The difference in tone from other contemporary war novels seemed refreshing to the critics and appealed enormously to readers, who made Uris's book an immediate commercial success. After selling the screen rights of *Battle Cry* to Warner Brothers, he went to Hollywood to write the script for the film, which was released in 1955.

Although Uris had found that directors and others engaged in film making tended to pay only lip service to scriptwriters, he remained in Los Angeles and tried to work with various studios on other screenplays. But his efforts were unrewarding until the producer Hal B. Wallis hired him to write the scenario of a film about Wyatt Earp to be directed by John Sturges for Paramount. *Gunfight at the O.K. Corral* (1957), an "adult western," became a classic of its kind. William K. Zinsser praised it in the New York *Herald Tribune* (May 30, 1957) as "an almost flawless film" and went on to say, "Leon Uris's script, like everything else, is excellent. It is lean, idiomatic and often very funny."

Uris had in the meantime completed his second novel, *The Angry Hills* (Random, 1955), a spy story of intrigue and adventure that he based loosely on the diary of an uncle, his father's brother, who had fought during World War II in Greece as a member of the British Army's Palestine Brigade. A few years later Uris began working on the screenplay of *The Angry Hills*, which became an MGM release of 1959, but the director Robert Aldrich fired him in 1957. The writer recalls, "Aldrich said I didn't understand the characters in the novel."

The importance for Uris of *The Angry Hills* probably was that it opened the way to his exploration of the subject of Palestine. As his involvement in the Israeli theme became obsessive, he conceived an epic tracing the history of European Jewry from the turn of the century to the establishment of the State of Israel in 1948. To finance his research Uris sold the book in advance to a film company, and to prepare himself for the expedition to Israel he read hundreds of books and underwent a physical training program. After his arrival in the spring of 1956, he logged some 12,000 miles of travel up and down the country into Arab and Jewish communities, conducting scores of interviews, taking photos, and taping notes. Caught by the Sinai campaign that autumn, Uris followed the Israeli troops as a war correspondent before he returned to the United States at the end of the year to begin condensing some million and a half words into a 626-page book entitled *Exodus*.

Translated into several dozen languages, *Exodus* sold millions of copies around the world after its publication in 1958 by Doubleday & Company and is counted among the major publishing successes of all time. Most critics agreed that despite its literary shortcomings, such as its stereotyping of characters, *Exodus* tells a sweepingly powerful and gripping story. "The real achievement of *Exodus*," Dan Wakefield summed up in the *Nation* (April 11, 1959), "lies not so much in its virtues as a novel, as in its skillful rendering of the furiously complex history of modern Israel in a palatable, popular form that is usually faithful to the spirit of the complicated realities. That is no small feat."

Exodus claimed a considerable part of Uris's attention for several additional years. He worked on the screen adaptation of the novel, released by United Artists in 1960, until a clash with the producer Otto Preminger brought about his dismissal. With the Greek photographer Dimitrios Harissiadis, he collaborated on *Exodus Revisited* (Doubleday, 1960), a documentary of places mentioned in the novel. Uris wrote the commentary and a biographic sketch of Harissiadis. That book of photographs was a by-product of Uris's third novel, *Mila 18* (Doubleday, 1961), which in turn had grown out of an account of the Warsaw ghetto resistance movement contained in *Exodus*. His research for *Mila 18* required a return to Israel as well as visits to several other countries to interview survivors of the Jewish uprising in Warsaw during the Nazi occupation of Poland. Not all reviewers agreed with Quentin Reynolds, who appraised *Mila 18* in the New York *Times* (June 4, 1961) as "a book fully worthy to a place alongside *The Wall*" (John Hersey's novel about the Warsaw revolt). But with several important exceptions, critical reception was generally favorable.

Another major historical event, the rebuilding of postwar Germany, provided Uris with much of the raw material for *Armageddon* (Doubleday, 1964), in which he maneuvered his characters in and out of the crises of Berlin from the end of World War II through the airlift of 1948. As usual with Uris's novels, it became a book-club selection and climbed the best-seller list, regardless of several critics' disparaging comments on the author's prose and tendency toward excessive documentation.

On a visit to Mexico in the mid-1960's Uris met in Acapulco a former French diplomat, Phillipe de Vosjoli, who had headed his country's intelligence service in the Western Hemisphere for a decade and who provided Uris with information that he ultimately turned into a spy novel under the title of

Topaz. Because of the political sensitivity of the plot, which involved a Russian espionage network operating within the de Gaulle government during the 1962 Cuban missile crisis, Uris could not find a publisher until 1967, when McGraw-Hill brought out the book under reduced contract terms. The following year, as reported in the New York Post (September 6, 1968), de Vosjoli filed suit against Uris for failing to split profits as agreed. Also named in the breach of contract suit was Universal City Studios, which owned the film rights. Uris began work on the screen adaptation, but was fired after a few months apparently because of disagreement with the producer Alfred Hitchcock. Some reviewers of the film *Topaz*, released in 1969, found it to be less fluid and less engrossing than the novel.

More personally involved in his next novel than he had been in *Topaz*, Uris based *QB VII* (Doubleday, 1970) on a trial that came before a London court in the spring of 1964 after a libel suit had been brought against Uris by Dr. Wladislaw Dering, who had been named in *Exodus* among those guilty of atrocities against the Jews at Auschwitz. The court ruled for Dering, but Uris felt himself vindicated because Dering was awarded "contemptuous damages" of a halfpenny and was obliged to pay court costs. A suspenseful courtroom drama, Uris's fictionalized account sold very well. In the popularity of *QB VII* and the commendation of several book reviewers Uris may have found a measure of consolation for the failure of *Ari*, a musical version of the love story in *Exodus*, for which he wrote the lyrics and book and his collaborator, Walt Smith, wrote the music. *Ari* folded after a run of twenty performances on Broadway in early 1971.

QB VII had been dedicated to Uris's young bride, the former Jill Peabody, a photographer whom he had married in February 1970. He had said that he owes to her much of the inspiration for writing a novel about Ireland. In April 1972 they went to Ireland together to spend a year, with some interruptions, traveling 10,000 miles throughout the country, and while his wife made photographs, occasionally under gunfire in Belfast, Uris acted as her assistant and gathered information about people and places. Their collaboration resulted in *Ireland: A Terrible Beauty* (Doubleday, 1975; André Deutsch, 1976), a book of Jill Uris's highly praised photographs for which Leon Uris wrote the text.

In preparing a survey of present-day Ireland, including Ulster, to accompany the photographs, Uris made a crash study of the history, politics, religion, and other aspects of the culture of the people. He felt increasingly attracted to Ireland when he recognized similarities between the Irish and the Israelis in their struggles to achieve what they consider to be justice. His research became the foundation of *Trinity* (Doubleday, 1976), which throws light on the current crisis in Ireland by tracing the interrelated lives of members of three representative families from the 1840's to the Easter Rising of 1916. The quotation from Eugene O'Neill's play *A Moon for the Misbegotten* that Uris placed at the front of his book explains why he did not carry his story beyond that date: "There is no present or future—only the past, happening over and over again—now."

Impressed by "Uris's self-evident devotion to his material," William C. Woods wrote in the Washington Post (April 25, 1976), "He has obviously plunged into this subject for the love of it. The result is his best novel." Pete Hamill, commenting in the New York Times Book Review (March 14, 1976), had some reservations about style and dialogue and "excess baggage of exposition and information," but he concluded, "None of that matters as you are swept along in the narrative. Uris is certainly not as good a writer as Pynchon or Barthelme or Nabokov; but he is a better storyteller." For *Ireland: A Terrible Beauty* and *Trinity*, Jill and Leon Uris received the John F. Kennedy Award of the Irish Institute, an organization that encourages cultural exchanges between the United States and Ireland.

Because of his disappointment with the film versions of his novels, including *QB VII*, which was shown on ABC as a TV movie in 1974, Uris decided to join the producer Fred Brogger in an independent venture to bring *Trinity* and *Mila 18* to the screen. Jerusalem is the subject he is researching for his next novel and perhaps also for another photoessay book in collaboration with his wife.

Jill Uris is the third wife of Leon Uris. On January 5, 1945, while in San Francisco recuperating from malaria, he had married Betty Katherine Beck, a Marine sergeant. Their three children are Karen Lynn, Mark Jay, and Michael Cady. His first marriage ended in divorce in January 1968, and on September 8, 1968 he married Margery Edwards, whose death the following year was an apparent suicide.

Since 1964 Uris has lived in Aspen, Colorado, where Jill Uris, having moved from Boston, was codirector of a photography school before her marriage. When he is at home, Uris spends most of his time working on his manuscripts. He is convinced that a writer owes his success to stamina, along with an unswerving belief in himself. Skiing and trail biking, for which Aspen provides opportunities in abundance, are among his recreations. Uris has blue eyes and gray hair and stands five feet nine inches tall. Observing him at a party in Denver to launch *Trinity*, Stanton Peckham wrote in *Publishers Weekly* (March 29, 1976), "Uris, appearing considerably more mellow than he did back in the days of *Exodus*, charmed his audience with a brief and beautifully handled after-luncheon talk." During the 1976 Presidential primaries he campaigned for Democratic Senator Henry Jackson. He is an ardent Zionist, a liberal in his stand on such current issues as the women's movement and birth control, and an "old Marine" in his patriotism.

References: N Y Post p43 N 2 '67 por; N Y Times Bk R p48 Ap 3 '77 por; Pub W 209:6+ Mr 29 '76 por; Washington Post mag p22+ My 9 '76 por; Contemporary Authors 1st rev vols 1-4 (1967); Contemporary Novelists (1976); Who's Who in America, 1978-79; World Authors: 1950-1970 (1975)

Van Hamel, Martine

Nov. 16, 1945- Dancer. Address: b. c/o American Ballet Theatre, 888 Seventh Ave., New York City, New York 10019

Clive Barnes, the veteran dance and theatre critic who has followed her career since the mid-1960's, has called Martine van Hamel "a unique acrobat of God" and "a dancer with the wind of genius blowing through her." Such accolades are commonplace to Miss van Hamel, a Dutch ballerina who has been dazzling critics and balletomanes alike with her assured technique, regal carriage, and instinctive musical phrasing since she won a gold medal at the International Ballet Competition in Varna in 1966. A leading dancer with the National Ballet of Canada in the 1960's, she joined American Ballet Theatre as a member of the corps de ballet in 1970 and quickly rose

through the ranks to principal dancer. Best known for her primal Myrtha in Giselle, her luminous Aurora in The Sleeping Beauty, and her eloquent Odette in Swan Lake, Martine van Hamel has infused each of those traditional classical roles with her authoritative, highly individual style. In commenting on her unusual blend of cool classicism and emotional warmth, an admiring Russian colleague once observed, "She really has what you cannot learn."

The youngest of the three children of Diederik A. van Hamel, a Dutch career foreign service officer, and his wife, Martine van Hamel was born in Brussels, Belgium on November 16, 1945. As her father accepted different diplomatic postings, she moved with her family from Belgium to Denmark, Indonesia, Venezuela, and, finally, to Canada. It was while the van Hamels were living in Copenhagen that four-year-old Martine began taking ballet lessons as an outlet for her abundant energy. Mrs. van Hamel, who as a pianist recognized Martine's innate musicality, took her ten-year-old daughter to Paris for an evaluation by the legendary Olga Preobrajenska, one of the greatest of the pre-Revolutionary ballerinas at the Maryinsky Theatre in St. Petersburg, Russia.

Miss van Hamel took classes from Madame Preobrajenska for a short time and, while her father was temporarily stationed in The Hague, she studied at its Conservatory of Music. At eleven she entered the National Ballet of Venezuela's school in Caracas, where she took a standard academic curriculum in the mornings and, in the afternoons, worked on her developing ballet technique under the watchful eye of Henry Danton. Within a year, the young ballerina, the bodice of her red tutu stuffed with Kleenex, was dancing a solo in the National Ballet of Venezuela's production of Aurora's Wedding.

In 1959 Miss van Hamel was offered scholarships by the American Ballet Theatre School and by the School of American Ballet solely on the basis of some still photographs that Danton had submitted in her behalf. Preferring to remain with her family, she enrolled instead at the National Ballet of Canada's new school in Toronto. Because she was unaccustomed to the school's precise Cecchetti-based training, Miss van Hamel was, at first, "shocked and miserable." Although she has since realized that she needed that exacting work "for the discipline," at the time she felt "nobody there was dancing," for to her, dancing had always meant "movement." "It's not pictures, it's not making the most beautiful pose," she explained to Tobi Tobias, who interviewed her for a Dance magazine (October 1975) profile. "Those are only places you go through. It is the in between, really, that dancing is. The movement, the going, the way you cover space, the way you think of space, the way you feel it around you. I was stubborn, and I held on to that.

Gradually, with the give and take between teachers and students—after all, they weren't blind to what I could do—it began to work."

Miss van Hamel's principal instructor was Betty Oliphant, now the assistant director of the National Ballet of Canada, but she also took character classes from the Bolshoi Ballet's Eugen Valukin and private lessons from Galina Ulanova, the Bolshoi's prima ballerina assoluta. By 1962 she was dancing as an apprentice with the company during its Toronto engagements and, in 1963, she officially joined the National Ballet as a soloist. Over the next few years, she assumed principal roles in the company's classical repertory—Les Sylphides, Cinderella, The Nutcracker, Giselle, Bayaderka—and in such contemporary works as Sir Frederick Ashton's Les Rendez-vous, George Balanchine's Concerto Barocco, and Zachary Solov's Allégresse.

A hard-working perfectionist, Miss van Hamel polished her technique by spending her vacations in New York City, where she took classes with Igor Youskevitch, the danseur noble known for his superlative partnering, and Bill Griffith, a taskmaster who forced her beyond her limits. With the encouragement of her teachers, she entered the third annual International Ballet Competition in Varna, Bulgaria in July 1966. She selected as her competition pieces solos from the severely classical Bayaderka and Antony Tudor's haunting Dark Elegies and, partnered by a National Ballet colleague, the flashy pas de deux from Le Corsaire and a romantic duet from Kenneth Macmillan's affecting Solitaire. Her performances in those varied roles won her a standing ovation from the knowledgeable Varna audience and, in a unanimous decision, the gold medal in the junior division. The judges also awarded her a special prize for the best artistic interpretation in all categories.

Back in Canada after her triumph, Miss van Hamel annexed to her rapidly expanding repertory the leading roles in Erik Bruhn's versions of Swan Lake and La Sylphide, Balanchine's Serenade and the "Choleric" section of his Four Temperaments, and Tudor's Offenbach in the Underworld and Jardin aux Lilas. As the principal dancers alternated leading roles in the full-length ballets that were gradually taking over the company's repertory in the late 1960's, Miss van Hamel danced less often. Finding it more and more difficult to maintain technical perfection without frequent performances, she made regular guest appearances with such companies as the Royal Swedish Ballet and the Royal Winnepeg Ballet, but she still felt, in her words, "stagnant." "It wasn't enough," she said to explain her sudden resignation from the company in 1970. "I wanted more people to see me. I wanted to get to the big time."

Moving to New York City, Miss van Hamel auditioned for American Ballet Theatre and was offered a corps de ballet contract. Stunned, she turned down the offer and joined the Joffrey Ballet instead. She danced only three times in her six months with that company and the one ballet choreographed especially for her, Todd Bolender's ultramodern Time Cycle, was roundly panned by the critics. Realizing that her individual style was incompatible with the Joffrey's company image, she resigned late in 1970 and once again tried out for American Ballet Theatre. This time she accepted a corps contract and, less than a year later, moved up to soloist rank.

As a soloist, Miss van Hamel danced most of the standard secondary roles in the company's large and varied repertory, but it was as Myrtha, the steely Queen of the Wilis in Giselle, that she first attracted widespread critical attention. Commenting on her auspicious New York City debut in that role for the New York Times (July 5, 1971), Clive Barnes predicted that Martine van Hamel would be "a major ballerina." "She has enormous quality," he wrote, "with a manner, reserved yet womanly, that is unique, and obvious musical sensibility." With her imperial stage presence, large, sweeping movements, and lyrical legato, Miss van Hamel seemed predestined to dance Myrtha. Over the next few years she gradually mastered the dramatic nuances of the role until she became in the opinion of Arlene Croce, the New Yorker's respected dance critic, "the greatest Myrtha" in the company's history.

During American Ballet Theatre's 1973 summer season in New York City, Miss van Hamel appeared in the dual role of Odette/Odile in a sparsely attended matinee performance of Swan Lake. Ably partnered by Jonas Kage, she turned in a technically outstanding performance that amazed the handful of critics in the audience. Among them was the New York Times's Anna Kisselgoff, who was moved by her "very human" interpretation of the melancholy Swan Queen, singling out her touching "wounded wing" exit in Act II for special praise, and her "almost tender" portrayal of the seductress Odile. Other reviewers shared Miss Kisselgoff's enthusiasm and they too were surprised and impressed by Miss van Hamel's mastery of both halves of the schizoid role.

Always in complete command of the technical requirements of the dual role, Miss van Hamel astounded ballet fans with the exquisitely lyrical phrasing, slow, fluid movements, and extraordinary arched arabesques of her "white" acts and, in sharp contrast, the rippling bourrées, savage, plunging arabesques penchés, and sharply executed multiple fouettés of her "black" act. But it was her unusual characterization of Odile that most fascinated the critics, because, more than any of her contemporaries, Miss van Hamel clearly makes her Odile another version of Odette. They become, in Clive Barnes's words, "sisters under the skin and very much two aspects of an elusive woman."

Promoted to principal dancer in 1973 on the strength of her performance in *Swan Lake*, Martine van Hamel added to her repertory over the next few years other classic romantic ballets, including *Les Sylphides*, *The Sleeping Beauty*, *La Sylphide*, and *Giselle*. Appearing as Princess Aurora for the first time in a new production of *The Sleeping Beauty* in June 1976, she "completely transformed the image and feeling" of that Petipa-Tchaikovsky classic with her gracious manner and serenely flowing musicality. "Miss van Hamel danced exquisitely, with a kind of tender, trembling ecstasy which was precisely the right tone for Aurora," an enchanted Clive Barnes wrote in his *New York Times* review of June 19, 1976. "But that was only part of it. The seamless refinement of her movement, and her utter immersion in the role, compelled one's unquestioning belief in the reality of her impersonation. This wasn't a dancer—this was Aurora, a young woman of a distant time on the verge of self-discovery, come to life."

The same majestic bearing that worked to her advantage in *Swan Lake* and *The Sleeping Beauty* was an obvious drawback to a convincing interpretation of the woodland sprite in *La Sylphide*, but Miss van Hamel sidestepped that obstacle with a playful performance that was at once shy and sensuous, delicate and robust. Having learned to "look light" for *La Sylphide*, she decided in 1976 to attempt the title role in *Giselle*, a part she had avoided for years because she was convinced she did not fit the public's conception of the frail peasant girl. Partnered by Clark Tippet, Miss van Hamel made her long-awaited debut as Giselle at New York's City Center on January 29, 1977. Anna Kisselgoff rated her performance, especially in the lyrical Act II pas de deux, "promising," but Frances Herridge complained that Miss van Hamel was too "queenly" for the part. "It was she who seemed to be dissembling as a peasant maid, like one of those ladies in Louis XVI's Versailles who pretended they were country maids," Miss Herridge groused in the *New York Post* (January 31, 1977). "She was commanding even in death."

Miss van Hamel recognized the problem and candidly discussed it with Carol Lawson in an interview for the *New York Times* (January 2, 1977). "I wasn't Ballet Theatre's idea of a classical dancer, or their idea of a dancer, period. I know that I've always been different. But it isn't because I've had bad training or a weird body. It's just that I express myself differently. . . . I work on movement through myself. I use my body like a ball of clay. I sculpt it by working on it and through it." Because of her singular way of "sculpting" movement, she was more at home in Glen Tetley's abstract, angular ballets, such as *Gemini*, *Le Sacre du Printemps*, and *Voluntaries*. Her superbly controlled strength and suppleness, instinctive phrasing, and volup-

tuous movements gave those physically demanding works a new and sensuous dimension. Tetley himself was, in his words, "thrilled" by her "prodigious technique" and her "sensuality and spirituality." He tailored the title role in *Sphinx*, the first ballet he choreographed especially for American Ballet Theatre, specifically for Miss van Hamel and her remarkable portrayal of the Sphinx—part woman, part bird, part god—brought her an ovation at the ballet's New York City premiere in April 1978.

Other congenial parts were the ballerina roles in Balanchine's glittering *Theme and Variations* and in Harald Lander's technically taxing *Etudes*; the "Lake" segment of *The River*, Alvin Ailey's jazz suite; the elegant dancer in Twyla Tharp's witty *Push Comes to Shove*; the female lead in Eliot Feld's chilling *At Midnight*; Nikiya, the Hindu temple dancer, in Natalia Makarova's faithful restaging of the final act of *La Bayadère*; the central character in Tudor's *Dark Elegies* and the Other Woman in his *Jardin aux Lilas*; Terpsichore in a revival of Balanchine's *Apollo*; and the disdainful Miss Julie in Birgit Cullberg's melodramatic ballet of the same name.

As the quintessential Petipa dancer, Miss van Hamel was especially effective in the virtuoso solo variations of that master choreographer's spectacular *Raymonda*, which was sumptuously restaged for American Ballet Theatre by Rudolf Nureyev, and she revealed an unsuspected comic talent as the irrepressible Swanilda in *Coppélia*, and as Kitri, the effervescent coquette, in Mikhail Baryshnikov's flamboyant production of *Don Quixote*, or *Kitri's Wedding*. In a tour-de-force, she danced all four female leads—haughty La Stella, sexy Giulietta, yearningly romantic Antonia, and Olympia, the pathetically endearing mechanical doll—in Peter Darrell's full-length *Tales of Hoffmann*.

Large-boned and nearly six feet in height when she rises on point, Martine van Hamel has yet to find a completely compatible partner, for few premiers danseurs can match her dominating stage presence. As more than one reviewer has noted, she radiates confidence, power, and strength. Even Clive Barnes, probably her most devoted admirer among the critics, once remarked, "If she reminds one of a swan, and she often does, she tends to bring to mind the fact that a swan can break a man's arm with a judicious sweep of its wing."

Four of her erstwhile partners—Jonas Kage, Vladimir Gelvan, Clark Tippet, and Ivan Nagy—have left the company and another, Rudolf Nureyev, is only an infrequent guest artist. In the past two years, however, Miss van Hamel has been happily paired with Patrick Bissell, American Ballet Theatre's youngest premier danseur, in *Don Quixote*, *The Sleeping Beauty*, and *La Bayadère*; Kevin McKenzie, a new company soloist, in *The Sleeping Beauty* and *Pas de Deux Holberg*; and John Meehan, an Australian principal dancer who perhaps best complements her physically and technically, in *Don Quixote, Swan Lake,* and *Miss Julie.* To her delight, she is dancing more often. "To be onstage and to be dancing helps make you a better dancer," she has said. "You learn the craft of being onstage."

Although her crowded performance schedule leaves little time for guest appearances, Martine van Hamel has occasionally performed with the Eglevsky Ballet and with Dennis Wayne's Contemporary Ballet, with whom she danced Jorge Samanelgo's *Solo: van Hamel* and Cliff Keuter's *Of Us Two,* a duet for her and Bonnie Mathis. At the Jacob's Pillow (Massachusetts) Dance Festival in June 1978, she and Clark Tippet performed the Act II pas de deux from *Swan Lake* and her own *Trio à Deux,* a romantic duet reminiscent of Tudor's *The Leaves Are Fading* that critics described as "pleasant" and "workmanlike." Miss van Hamel's choreographic efforts also include a solo to Debussy created for the 1976 gala benefit for the Lincoln Center Library of the Performing Arts and a trio, also to music by Debussy, choreographed in 1977 for the New York Philharmonic Promenade Concerts.

At five feet seven inches, Martine van Hamel is uncommonly tall for a ballerina and, as Clive Barnes observed in the New York *Times* (July 21, 1975), "She looks more like a Rubens than a Fragonard." She has chin-length auburn hair, large brown eyes, and a wistful smile. Although a rather reticent woman offstage, she brightens considerably when discussing her art. "Dancing is an emotional and physical need," she told one interviewer. "If I don't dance, I'm only half a person." In her early twenties she married a musician, from whom she was divorced in 1973. Miss van Hamel lives alone in a sunny, plant-filled apartment near the Lincoln Center for the Performing Arts on Manhattan's Upper West Side. In her leisure hours she enjoys painting and listening to music.

References: Cue 47:18 Ap 29-My 12 '78 por; Dance 43:67 F '69 por, 49:60+ O '75 pors; N Y Daily News p25 Je 21 '76 por; N Y Times Ja 2 '76 por, II p5+ Ja 2 '77 por; Toronto Globe and Mail p11 Jl 27 '66 por; Encyclopedia of Dance and Ballet (1977); Who's Who in America, 1978-79

Wallace, Irving

Mar. 19, 1916- Author. Address:
P.O. Box 49328, Los Angeles,
Calif. 90049

Because he has sold more than 120,000,000 copies of his books and commands an estimated worldwide readership of more than 600,000,000 persons, Irving Wallace may very well be one of the five most widely read contemporary authors. Wallace's enormous popularity is primarily based on his novels, many of which have been adapted into films. Their laconic titles, invariably beginning with the definite article, include *The Chapman Report, The Prize, The Man, The Word,* and *The Fan Club.* Most of them are long works characterized by labyrinthine but absorbing plots, Grand Hotel-type casts of characters, controversial and timely themes, meticulous research, and endings that are decidedly upbeat.

Despite—or perhaps because of—their popularity, Wallace's novels are usually mercilessly attacked by literary critics. But at least one student of popular culture, John Leverence, in his *Irving Wallace: A Writer's Profile* (1974), has suggested that those novels need to be judged by different criteria than those employed by most book reviewers. "You can't understand Irving Wallace's books if you try to relate them to a long tradition of elite, classical American literature," Leverence once told a reporter. "But if you relate them to the traditions of American popular writing, particularly journalism and film writing, then they make sense."

It was in those two disciplines that Wallace served a long apprenticeship. At fifteen he sold his first magazine article, and eventually he marketed more than 500 of his articles and short stories to national magazines. Later he worked as a screenwriter for all the major Hollywood studios and earned screen credits for fifteen films. Wallace, who published three books of biography before his first novel appeared, has continued to interlard his fiction with nonfiction. More kindly received by critics than his novels and almost as popular with his admirers, his best-selling nonfiction includes The Fabulous Showman, The Nympho and Other Maniacs, and The Two, which he wrote with his daughter Amy. With his son, David Wallechinsky, Wallace edited The People's Almanac and The People's Almanac #2, which they call "the first reference book ever prepared to be read for pleasure."

The only son of Jewish parents who emigrated from Russia as teen-agers and who met and married in the United States, Irving Wallace was born on March 19, 1916 in Chicago, Illinois, to Bessie (Liss) and Alexander Wallace. When Irving was about a year old, his parents moved fifty miles north to Kenosha, Wisconsin, where Alex obtained a job as a clerk in a general store. A few years later he opened his own store in partnership with his brother. Wallace has one younger sister, Esther Biederman, who is now a Tarzana, California, housewife and a freelance writer. His father lives in retirement in Los Angeles, where he had previously worked for some years in the auction business. Wallace's mother is no longer living.

"My mother had grown up reading in Russian the great Russian writers," Irving Wallace recalled to Aaron Latham of New West magazine (January 17, 1977). "She had a great, romantic admiration for writers and novels." Even as a small boy, Wallace was determined to become a writer, and by the time he reached Washington Junior High School in Kenosha he was the mainstay of the school newspaper. At Kenosha Central High School he edited the school paper and won two national journalism prizes: the Grand Gold Cup of the Medill School of Journalism in his junior year for feature and news writing, and, in his senior year, first place in the national feature writing contest sponsored by International Quill and Scroll. In high school Wallace also took part in athletics, winning a letter in track, and, as a debater, was named one of the ten leading young public speakers of America by the National Forensic League in 1933.

An avid sports fan, Wallace worked as a sports stringer for the Wisconsin News of Milwaukee during his high school years and wrote a sports column for the weekly Kenosha Bulletin. He began to write for magazines at the age of twelve and at fifteen sold his first article, "The Horse Laugh," to Horse and Jockey magazine for $5.00. Two years later he sold his first short story, "Sacrifice Hit," to Challenge magazine.

After graduating from high school in February 1934, Wallace continued to freelance. That summer he and two other young journalists organized an expedition to Central America, where they hoped to become the first white men to discover a legendary "Fountain of Blood," which was said to be located in the remote jungles of Honduras. Financed by newspapers, the trio set out in the fall of 1934. During the four-month trip Wallace interviewed Huey Long in New Orleans, climbed Mount Ixtaccihuatl in Mexico, and discovered the fountain, whose waters, rather unromantically, ran red because of mineral deposits.

Back in Kenosha early in 1935, Wallace continued to write magazine articles, while applying to several colleges. Offered several scholarships, he chose one from Williams Institute, a small college in Berkeley, California with an exceptionally good writing program. He remained there for only a few months, however, before deciding that he could better learn about writing on his own. In 1936 he moved to Los Angeles, where he scrabbled for a living as a magazine freelancer, and on the side wrote a few plays that were produced in local theatres. During the late 1930's Wallace wrote for such magazines as For Men Only, Ken, Modern Mechanics, Thrilling Sports, Modern Screen, and Coronet. For Liberty magazine he ghostwrote a number of articles by celebrities, including Boris Karloff, Bob Hope, President Avila Camacho of Mexico, and W. C. Fields (who passed out cold during the interview). In 1940 Liberty sent the young journalist on assignment to China and Japan, where he interviewed Mitsuru Toyama, the head of the militant Black Dragon Society, and Foreign Minister Yosuke Matsuoka.

In October 1942 Wallace enlisted in the United States Army. During World War II he served in the Army Air Force Motion Picture Unit in Culver City and later in the Army Signal Corps Photographic Corps in Los Angeles and New York. Assigned to prepare training and orientation films, Wallace worked during the war with John Huston and Frank Capra. Meanwhile, he continued to write in his off-hours, producing articles, short stories, and ideas for screenplays. He made his first sale to Hollywood in 1943, when he earned a screen credit on Jive Junction (PRC Pictures, 1943).

After his discharge from the Army as a staff sergeant in February 1946, Wallace returned to full-time magazine freelancing. Although he was by then writing for such mass-market and well-paying magazines as the Saturday Evening Post, American Mercury, Collier's, Cosmopolitan, Pageant, and Reader's Digest, he found that, burdened with new family responsibilities, he could not make ends meet. He therefore turned to the more lucrative craft of screenwriting, where he could earn $750 a week, and during the 1950's he ended up working for every major film company in Hollywood. Films for which he received screen credit included The West Point Story (Warner Brothers, 1950), with James Cagney and Doris Day; Meet Me At the Fair (Universal, 1952); Gun Fury (Columbia, 1953); Split Second (RKO, 1953); The Gambler from Natchez (Fox, 1954); Bombers B-52 (Warner Brothers, 1957); and The Big Circus (Columbia, 1959).

"It was a plush hell," Wallace was later to recall of Hollywood in *The Sunday Gentleman* (Simon and Schuster, 1965), "an infernal region dominated by double-dealing, politics, feuds, pettiness, thievery, cretinism, where the writer suffered indignity, disrespect, disdain, and where he could make more money than he could possibly make in any other salaried medium of writing." Determined to make a living writing what he wanted, Wallace moonlighted during his movie years by writing three nonfiction books, all of which sold modestly but received excellent reviews. The first was *The Fabulous Originals* (Knopf, 1955), a series of biographies of the real-life prototypes of such fictional characters as Sherlock Holmes and Dr. Jekyll and Mr. Hyde. It was followed by *The Square Pegs* (Knopf, 1957), which collected the biographies of nine little-known American eccentrics. His third volume was a biography of P. T. Barnum entitled *The Fabulous Showman* (Knopf, 1959).

Perhaps because it was published under a relatively obscure imprint, Wallace's first novel, *The Sins of Philip Fleming* (Frederick Fell, 1959), about a young writer struggling to establish a beachhead for his career, passed out of view with barely a notice, but its author soon received the break he needed to get into full-time book writing. New American Library, the pioneering paperback house, offered him a $25,000 advance on two books and, fortified with that money, Wallace quit Hollywood with a vow never to return.

Wallace then proceeded to write *The Chapman Report* (1960), a novel about the impact of a Kinsey-like sex survey on the lives of some Los Angeles suburban women. The first of the nine consecutive best-selling Wallace novels published in hardcover by Simon & Schuster, *The Chapman Report* attracted the first of the series of critical diatribes that were to continue with each of the subsequent novels. Manard Pont of the San Francisco *Chronicle* (June 5, 1960), for example, fumed that its story was "sophomoric," its plot "outrageously contrived," and its characterizations "trite almost beyond belief." Undeterred by such attacks, its readers kept the book on the best-seller lists for thirty weeks in the United States. Abroad the book prospered just as well, although it ran afoul of censorship in several countries. Sold to Darryl F. Zanuck for $175,000 plus a 5 percent share of the take, *The Chapman Report* became a box-office smash starring Jane Fonda, Shelley Winters, and Efrem Zimbalist Jr., when it was released by Warner Brothers in 1962.

Returning to nonfiction, Wallace wrote *The Twenty-Seventh Wife* (Simon & Schuster, 1961), a spirited biography of Ann Eliza Young, who after running away from her polygamous husband Brigham Young, head of the Mormon Church, spearheaded the crusade against plural marriage in the United States. He next plunged into work on a novel he had been gestating ever since he had interviewed Nobel prize judges years before in connection with a magazine assignment. The result was *The Prize* (1962), which offered an inside look at the Nobel prizes and how they are awarded. Although the novel ultimately affirmed the value of the prizes, its candid discussion of the human frailties of both judges and recipients offended the Scandinavian countries, where the book was banned. A best seller elsewhere, *The Prize* was made by MGM into a deft comedy thriller starring Paul Newman in 1963.

In *The Three Sirens* (1963), Wallace wrote about a team of American anthropologists doing field study on a tribe of sexually permissive South Sea islanders. The premise of his next novel, *The Man* (1964), was that a black man had become the President of the United States. It contained a great deal of detailed information on the daily life of a President, much of which the author obtained firsthand during a ten-day visit made to the White House a few months before President John F. Kennedy's assassination. Although the novel received awards for its positive effect on race relations, it unleashed a storm of controversy that held up its filming for several years. It was finally produced by Paramount in 1972 in a film starring James Earl Jones.

In *The Plot* (1967), set mainly in Paris, Wallace created a thriller of behind-the-scenes intrigue and international espionage at a nuclear disarmament summit meeting. With *The Seven Minutes* (1969), the author returned to the theme of sex, this time to incorporate a cogent history of censorship into a tale about the censorship trial of a bookstore owner for selling "the most obscene piece of pornography written since Gutenberg invented moveable type." The fictional piece of pornography itself is a long-banned novel relating the thoughts in a woman's consciousness during the seven minutes she is engaged in sexual intercourse. *The Seven Minutes* was adapted into a movie produced and directed by Russ Meyer for Twentieth Century-Fox in 1971.

From sex, Wallace turned to the consolations of religion in *The Word* (1972), which tells the story of how a varied group of men and women are affected by the discovery of a new gospel written by James, the younger brother of Jesus, which promises to change the course of Christianity and mankind. Adapted into a television miniseries starring David Janssen, it was broadcast over CBS-TV in November 1978. In *The Fan Club* (1974) four men of diverse backgrounds try to make up for the disappointments of their lives by making their fantasies come true. Obsessed by lust for the reigning film sex goddess of their day, they kidnap the actress and hold her in a mountain cabin. In *The R Document* (1976) Wallace chose a timely post-Watergate political theme, building an exciting plot around the attempt of the FBI to suspend the Bill of Rights and seize power over the country. Wallace's most recent novel, "The Pigeon Project," which was published in April 1979, by Simon

& Schuster, is an espionage thriller about gaining control of a secret formula for human longevity.

In between novels, Wallace has continued to write nonfiction. In 1965 he collected his special favorites among the articles he had written during his journalism career in *The Sunday Gentleman*, updating each piece with an addendum. In 1968 he brought out *The Writing of One Novel* (Simon & Schuster), a detailed exposition of the creative process that resulted in *The Prize. The Nympho and Other Maniacs* (Simon & Schuster, 1971) is a lively account of the lives of thirty women of the past two centuries who defied the conventions of their day to live their own lifestyles. Included, for example, is Victoria Woodhull, the former prostitute who ran for President of the United States in 1872 on a platform calling for free love, short skirts, birth control, and world government.

Wallace has collaborated with his children on several successful nonfiction books. With his son David Wallechinsky—who adopted the family's pre-Ellis Island name—he edited *The People's Almanac* (Doubleday, 1975), a 1,500-page reference compendium that a *Booklist* reviewer (July 15, 1976) called "a real treasury of interesting information, some of it practical, most of it unusual." Soon after its publication the book soared to the top of every major national and local best-seller list and had, by 1979, sold 1,200,000 copies in hardcover and paperback editions. A sequel, *The People's Almanac #2* (Morrow), was published in October 1978. With David Wallechinsky and Amy Wallace, the author's daughter, Irving Wallace edited an entertaining spinoff from the Almanac called *The Book of Lists* (Morrow, 1977), a book composed entirely of lists of people, places, happenings, and things. A second edition is now in preparation. Wallace has also collaborated, with Amy, on a biography of Chang and Eng, the original Siamese twins, entitled *The Two* (Simon & Schuster, 1977).

Wallace's books have made him a millionaire many times over. He has sold the film rights for all his novels, except the first, and for a number of his nonfiction works. His last nine novels have all headed national best-seller lists. Book clubs the world over have chosen his books, and his works have been serialized in leading magazines in the United States, Europe, Israel, Mexico, Japan, South Africa, and Australia. All but two of Wallace's twenty-two books are currently in print. He has received many awards, including, for *The Man*, the 1965 paperback of the year trophy awarded by *Bestsellers* magazine "to the paperback that radiated the greatest positive reader influence in America, and ultimately the world"; the 1974 Popular Culture Association award of excellence "for distinguished achievements in the popular arts"; and the 1975 Venice Rosa d'Oro award.

On June 3, 1941 Irving Wallace was married in Santa Barbara, California to Sylvia Kahn, an editor of *Modern Screen* magazine. Mrs. Wallace recently wrote her own best seller, *The Fountains*, which was her first novel. Their son, David, conceived the idea for *The People's Almanac* after publishing several books, including the best-selling *What Really Happened to the Class of '65*. Besides being a writer, Amy Wallace is a psychic healer who graduated from the Berkeley Psychic Institute. The Wallaces have lived for many years in a seventeen-room French country-style house located in the Brentwood section of Los Angeles, a wealthy and stylish suburb that closely resembles the fictional community of The Briars created by Wallace in *The Chapman Report*. They also own a summer farmhouse on the Balearic island of Minorca and a beach house in the Malibu area.

Wallace has filled his home with original oils, pen sketches, and signed lithographs by such artists as Gauguin, Modigliani, Bonnard, Matisse, Picasso, Chagall, Rivera, Miró, Braque, Magritte, and Toulouse-Lautrec. He also collects unusual canes, miniature electronic gadgets, autographed photographs, and autographed letters. Among the 18,000 books ranged on the walls of his huge, beamed study are many inscribed first or limited editions, including an edition of James Joyce's *Ulysses*, illustrated by Henri Matisse and signed by both the artist and the author.

When concentrating on a novel, Wallace works six days a week, writing during the afternoon and evening in his study. He has written all his books on an ancient rebuilt Underwood typewriter that his parents gave him for his thirteenth birthday. Between books, Wallace takes annual jaunts to Europe, although for many years he suffered from a phobia about flying. In 1972 he took his first flight in thirty-two years and has been boarding planes regularly since then.

Besides traveling, Wallace's recreations include watching athletic events, running and walking each morning, playing ping-pong, boule, poker, and snooker pool, and taking his Bentley S3 Continental sports car or his Rolls-Royce Silver Shadow for late night spins. An affable, pipe-smoking man who has described himself as an "ambivert"—part intro- and part extrovert—the stockily built writer is five feet ten inches tall. He has brown eyes and thick, iron-gray hair. A liberal Democrat who has been involved in political action movements, Wallace campaigned for Eugene McCarthy in 1968 and covered the national political conventions in 1972 for the *Chicago Daily News/Sun Times* wire service.

References: N Y Times C p23 O 1 '76 por;
N Y Times mag p32 Mr 23 '69 por;
New West 2:44 Ja 17 '77 pors; Two Hundred
Contemporary Authors (1969); Who's Who in
America, 1978-79

Watson, Tom

Sept. 4, 1949- Golfer. Address: b. 1726
Commerce Tower, Kansas City, Mo. 64105;
c/o Kansas City Country Club, 62 Indian
Lane, Shawnee Mission, Kan. 66208

Reinforcing Tom Watson's reputation as professional golf's "thinker," Jack Nicklaus once called him "the smartest of the lot" of competitors then vying to succeed Nicklaus as the premier figure on the fairways. In 1977, his sixth complete season on the pro tour, Watson not only defeated Nicklaus in the Masters tournament and in the British Open, but also led the tour in money earned and low-stroke average. In 1978 he was again golf's highest moneymaker and lowest stroker, and by the time he won the Byron Nelson Golf Classic in 1979 (for an unprecedented third time) he was yet again the leader in both money-making and shotmaking.

Watson, who is known for his fast, smooth swing, makes golf look easier than it is. Admired by his fellow pros for his concentration and dedication, he has worked hard at his game and left far behind him a grossly exaggerated reputation for "choking" under last-round pressure. But he does not think he is yet ready to accept the designation as heir to Jack Nicklaus. "The difference now," Barry McDermott quoted him as saying in Sports Illustrated (April 30, 1979), "is that I can play badly and have a chance to win, and years ago I couldn't. At times I hit the ball as well as anyone, but there are times that I'm well behind the pack."

Thomas Sturges Watson was born in Kansas City, Missouri on September 4, 1949 to Raymond Etheridge Watson, an insurance execu-

tive, and Sarah Elizabeth (Ridge) Watson. Watson was introduced to golf at the Kansas City Country Club, in Shawnee Mission, Kansas, where he began at age six to caddy for his father and his father's friends, who nicknamed him "Fly," after Flytrap Finnegan, "the world's worst caddy," a comic-strip character.

In an interview with Dave Anderson for Sport (February 1978) Watson recalled how terrified he was when, at fifteen, he played an exhibition match with his idol, Arnold Palmer. As an amateur, he won the Missouri championship four times and finished in a tie for fifth place in the 1969 United States Amateur tournament. Watson credits Stan Thirsk, the pro at the Kansas City Country Club, with having "given" him his basic swing. In addition to golf, Watson played football and basketball, sports in which he earned letters at his prep school, Pembroke Country Day School in Kansas City.

Like his father and his brothers, Ridge and John, Tom Watson attended Stanford University, where he took a B.S. degree in psychology in 1971. It was during his senior year at Stanford that he decided to turn pro. "Up to that time I didn't play as well as I could or make the grades that I could," he told Dick Friedman of People (August 15, 1977). "I would handle college a lot better now, and if I lost the little finger of my left hand I could enroll in medical school."

"When I came on the tour in 1971-72," Watson has recounted, "I wasn't a seasoned golfer. . . . It was tough for me to start winning." In 1973 he earned $75,000 but failed to win a single tournament, and the following year he led most of the way through the United States Open Championship at the Winged Foot Golf Club in Mamaroneck, New York only to collapse in the final round with a disastrous 79.

After the fiasco at Winged Foot, a sad Watson was sitting in the locker room when Byron Nelson, the preeminent American golfer in the 1940's, approached him and asked if he could talk to him for a minute. In the introduction to Nelson's book Shape Your Swing the Modern Way (1979), Watson recounted what followed: "We went off into a corner and Byron told me that almost every golfer he ever knew had, at some time in his career, suffered exactly what I had just experienced. The pressure had gotten to them and they'd started swinging poorly. He went on to explain to me what, from his vantage point, had happened to my game in that last round. My knees were not working through the shot, he told me, so I was coming out of the shot too soon and lifting up. I was also staying on my right side too long and wasn't moving well to the left side with my knees flexed." Writing in the Christian Science Monitor (January 19, 1978), Phil Elderkin observed: "Basically what Nelson did was take a player who was overly committed to his right side and introduce his entire body to the game. It worked because

Watson was able to accept the change mentally, because he worked hard at it, and because the talent was already there."

Watson guessed that Nelson took a special interest in him because of the similarity in their swings. "I have a light dip in my swing and my knees stay flexed throughout the swing," Watson continued. "Anyway, after his talk with me I went out and worked on the practice tee for hours and discovered how right he was. My knees weren't working well through the shot at all. I quickly made an adjustment and two weeks later I won the Western Open."

After the 1975 United States Open, Nelson gave him another tip, Watson wrote. "He told me that I was always going to have a fast swing, but when it got too fast I should slow down the movement of my feet as I took my stance. That would slow everything down, he said, including my swing. And it helped. I kept referring back to it when I got into the heat of the British Open, which I won later that year." He also won the Byron Nelson Classic and the World Series of Golf in 1975.

In 1976 Watson slumped. "I was not hitting the ball very well all year," he told Sarah Pileggi when she was preparing an article on him for Sports Illustrated (April 25, 1977). "I was throwing the club at the ball, releasing too soon, and hitting a variety of bad shots." He finished the year without a tour victory and dropped from seventh to twelfth place in the earnings rankings.

Watson went back to work on his swing, under the guidance of Ken Venturi and Byron Nelson. Both of the older men stressed the need for him to "hold the angle" (the cock of the wrists) longer and to time the release of the wrist with the forward, driving movement of his legs. At first Watson was unable to recognize the occasions he was "choking," that is, when his swing was breaking down under pressure. Then, one day in December 1976, he was hitting a forty-foot wedge shot in a tournament in Australia and the knack for recognizing such occasions suddenly came to him, as he has recalled, "like a revelation."

The change in Watson in 1977 was spectacular. He won five tournaments, including the Bing Crosby Pro-Am at Pebble Beach, California, the Masters at Augusta, Georgia, and the British Open. In twelve more, he finished among the top ten, and he led the tour in earnings, with $310,653. For his performance, he received the Player of the Year title and the Vardon Trophy for lowest stroke average. His success did no damage to his mental equilibrium. "I don't think I'm the best," he told a reporter after the 1977 tour. "I'm far and away from being a shotmaker like Ben Hogan or Sam Snead or Jack Nicklaus or Arnold Palmer, but I'm trying to improve. I don't ever want to lose that feeling of trying to improve."

In 1978 Watson again swept the major statistical categories, winning the Vardon Trophy with a 70.16 scoring average, accumulating a record $362,429 in earnings, and claiming Golf Digest's Byron Nelson Award on the strength of his victories in the Tucson, Crosby, Nelson, Hall of Fame Classic, and Napa tournaments. In fifteen of his twenty-four American tournaments he had top-ten finishes, including three seconds and a third. Again, he was named Player of the Year.

As the 1979 season was about to begin, Watson discussed the previous tour with a reporter: "My play had less quality in 1978 [than in 1977]. I scored better because I managed courses a little better, didn't make the big mistakes and—mainly—putted better. [But] from tee to green I hit the ball better in 1977. My driving wasn't that good last year. I had trouble hitting the ball from left to right."

In January 1979 Watson broke tournament records with his fourteen-under-par winning total in the Bing Crosby Pro-Am tournament and a nineteen-under-par 269 in the Andy Williams San Diego Open. He garnered his tenth PGA tour victory in twenty-six months when he won the Heritage Golf Classic at Hilton Head Island, South Carolina on April 1, 1979, and after a bitterly disappointing playoff loss in the Masters, he scored an impressive six-shot victory in the Tournament of Champions, on April 22, 1979. On May 13, 1979 Watson became the first three-time winner of the Byron Nelson Golf Classic in Dallas, and later in the same month he won the Memorial Golf tournament at Dublin, Ohio. His winner's purse in the Colgate Hall of Fame Classic at Pinehurst, North Carolina on August 26 made him the first PGA player ever to pass the $400,000 mark in earnings in one season.

Watson practises long and hard, with the zeal of a rookie, because otherwise, he says, "there are fifty persons who can pass me." In all of his movements, as in his golf swing, he tends to be quick, and he is inwardly intense. But he maintains an outward placidity as well as a transcendent mental calm, partly by seeing himself on the links not so much as a competitor (although his built-in aggressiveness cannot be denied) as "an entertainer." He told an interviewer for the Sporting News in February 1978: "Sometimes non-golfers don't understand when I say I hit a bad shot but it turned out well. But that's not important. I just know that as an entertainer I've thrust myself into the public light."

Tom Watson and Linda Tova Rubin met as members of the chorus when the private schools they attended in Kansas City put on a joint production of The Pirates of Penzance. They were married on July 8, 1973. When Tom is not on the pro tour, the Watsons live in a rented apartment in Kansas City. Their recreations include hunting, fishing, dancing, and singing—to guitar accompaniment by Watson. In his newspaper and magazine reading, the golfer pays less attention to sports than he does to current events, especially in business and politics. He is difficult to categorize politically, because he tends to be conservative on economic issues and progressive on social issues. Watson is an Episcopalian and his wife is Jewish.

Watson is five feet nine inches tall, weighs 160 pounds, and has green eyes, tousled red hair, and a grin that has been described as "tight." In his article in the *Christian Science Monitor* Phil Elderkin observed that Watson "would look good modeling clothes" and "has the kind of Huckleberry Finn presence that could sell breakfast cereal." Elderkin went on to observe:

"What lets Watson play tournament golf as though it were invented for his benefit is a swing whose trajectory needs no more room than the width of a curb. Add to this confidence, patience, youth, endurance, and the ability to handle pressure, and failure gets shut out."

References: Christian Sci Mon p17 Ja 19 '78 por; People 8:80+ Ag 15 '77 pors; Sport 66:37+ F '78 por; Sporting News p39 F 4 '78 pors; Sports Illus 46:28+ Ap 25 '77 pors, 50:65+ Ap 30 '79; Who's Who in America, 1978-79

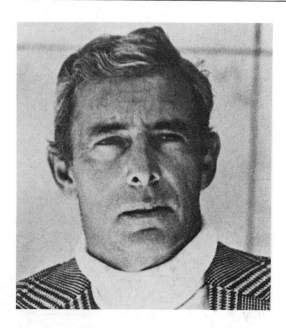

Weitz, John

May 25, 1923- Fashion designer. Address: b. John Weitz Designs, Inc., 600 Madison Ave., New York City, N.Y. 10022

Imagination and utility are the hallmarks of John Weitz, the iconoclastic all-purpose fashion designer. His apparel, accessories, and home products, sold in more than 1,700 department stores and specialty shops in the United States, Europe, and Japan, bring in more than $300,-000,000 in retail sales annually. Weitz first attracted attention in the 1950's for his comfortable, workable women's sportswear. Then, in the mid-1950's, he abruptly switched to men's fashions and, in a few years, revolutionized that staid bastion of conservatism. In his menswear designs, Weitz stressed function over fashion in creating casually elegant clothing that was, at once, contemporary and

classic. "I design clothes for the way people live, not for fantasies that they have to invent for themselves," he said in a recent interview. His designs have won him a handful of Caswell Massy awards, a Harper's Bazaar medallion, a Coty special menswear award and its European equivalent, the Brilliant Pen Award, and earned him an international reputation comparable to that of France's Pierre Cardin, Italy's Brioni, and Britain's Hardy Amies.

John Weitz was born in Berlin, Germany on May 25, 1923, the son of Robert Weitz, a prosperous manufacturer of ready-to-wear clothing, and his wife, Hedy (Jakob) Weitz. In the early 1930's the family immigrated to London, England. There, John Weitz attended Hall School and, from 1936 to 1939, St. Paul's School, where he starred on the varsity rugby team. After leaving St. Paul's, he went to Paris to serve an apprenticeship under Molyneux, a renowned tailor and a master of the figure-flattering bias cut. When World War II broke out, Weitz fled to Shanghai, China. While he waited for a visa to the United States, he played on the rugby team that won the 1941 Chinese championship. Weitz became a naturalized American citizen in 1943 and, later that same year, joined the United States Army. He spent the next three years working as an intelligence operative for the Office of Strategic Services, rising from private to captain.

After the war, Weitz moved to New York City to try his luck as a designer of women's apparel. Noting that many young American women had taken to wearing such masculine garments as blue jeans and Brooks Brothers shirts, he began designing functional styles derived from men's attire. "I saw the things that were American," he explained to Ruth Preston, who interviewed him for the New York Post (October 17, 1975). "The jeans, pea jackets, button-down shirts, fatigues, chinos, shirtdresses. The whole work wear look as Chanel understood it in Europe." Encouraged by Dorothy Shaver, a Lord & Taylor executive interested in promoting a recognizably American style, Weitz turned out casual, sporty clothes designed to meet the needs of active living rather than the arbitrary standards of Parisian couturiers. He based many of his most popular designs on military uniforms or on traditional sportswear. For example, his beach jackets were patterned after the rugby jacket he wore at school; his duffle coats owed their design to the warm, waterproof coats favored by sailors; and his skinny slacks were developed from paratroopers' pants.

Weitz worked for various apparel firms until 1954, when he founded his own company, John Weitz Designs, Inc. By the early 1960's he was annually producing about 1,500 styles —mostly moderately priced sportswear for the kind of family that, in his words, "buys a Jaguar on time"—for a dozen different clothing manufacturers, including Amco of Norvett, Inc., Montgomery Ward, and White Stag. Among his more popular designs were wrap skirts in such durable fabrics as poplin, denim, and suede lined with felt or fleece, quilted cotton shirts that doubled as jackets, pea jackets, jump suits, and car coats. Weitz, who claimed that "a sports car . . . is 'worn,' as well as driven," was closely identified with the so-called "sports car fashions" of the late 1950's and even published a book on the subject, *Sports Clothes For Your Sports Car* (Sports Car Press), in 1958. Those imaginative, yet practical designs earned him the 1959 Designer of the Year Award from *Sports Illustrated* magazine.

Weitz's large and varied line of what he called "not unusual but good and wearable clothes" also included maternity outfits, children's wear, baby garments, uniforms for Longchamps Restaurants waitresses and Cities Service gas station attendants, and two expensive, one-of-a-kind sportswear collections sold exclusively at Henri Bendel, the posh New York City clothing store. The fall collection of "Fred Astaire-inspired" clothes featured open-necked shirts worn with foulard scarves, fleecy pullovers, and slouchy, loose-fitting pants, ultrafeminine lounge wear, a severely cut gray flannel riding habit worn with high black patent leather boots, and white duck plus fours for skiing. A second collection of resort attire "for those who golf, dance, and flirt in a sporting manner" comprised such whimsically named designs as "Antibes '27," a blue, double terry cloth wrap robe, and "Going There Garbo Style," a camel's hair wrap coat over loose gray flannel pants. Those casually elegant clothes won Weitz international recognition as the preeminent designer of the "American look" and an invitation from the Chambre Syndicat, the professional organization representing virtually all the top French couturiers, to present his collections in Paris.

In designing his first boutique sportswear collection, previewed at the Regency Hotel in New York City in June 1963, Weitz used luxurious and exotic fabrics—cashmere, chamois, leather, feathers, English flannel—in bold and innovative ways. Among his most acclaimed creations were a black ostrich feather pullover, saddle leather pants and a matching coat cut like a fisherman's oilskin, a tortoise-shell leather topcoat lined with a bright red horse blanket, a big-sleeved dueling shirt with jeweled buttons, a black moire judo suit, a square-necked cashmere suit blouse, and a hamster hostess skirt. The following year he introduced "On The Fringe," an amusing resort collection for women with "courage but not audacity." Two of the more popular styles from that collection were a blue-and-white striped just-above-the-knee man's shirt to wear poolside and a fanciful lounging costume of silk paisley harem pants and a balloon-sleeved, midriff-baring top.

"Bored to tears," in his words, by the off-the-rack men's clothes he found in department stores and men's specialty shops around the country, Weitz began in 1964 to add menswear to his line. "[The men's clothing industry] creates concepts, not clothing," he complained to Leonard Sloane in an interview for the New York *Times* (November 2, 1965). "I don't think a man should ever have to have courage to fit into something. . . . I decided to go in by designing only clothes I would like to wear. I resent the idea of having my hard-earned shoulders taken away from me. And I don't want my pants to bind. This is a very selfish form of work for me." Weitz himself modeled his first sport coat collection, called "The Brawny Breed," for Lakeland Manufacturing Company in 1965. "It's not that I'm having an attack of egomania," he told reporters. "I swore if I ever designed men's clothes I'd model them myself. . . . I'm a pretty conservative character, and these are all things I'd like to wear."

Most of the coats, from a double-breasted guardsman's coat to a deep-collared all-weather coat, had extra padding for warmth and typified Weitz's "big-chested" masculine look. In all his designs, he stressed the practicality of "working sportswear." Driving jackets, for instance, "should keep you warm," he said. "They should have colors that don't get too filthy and pockets for cigarettes. They shouldn't be so long that you have to sit on them." Most of his coats and jackets had deep, turn-up, pile collars, adjustable neckline zippers or, in the case of his foul-weather sailing coat, a flaring, helmet-like hood for protection against wind and cold and easily accessible, capacious pockets for convenience.

In addition to the completely functional outer wear he created for Lakeland Manufacturing, Weitz redesigned shirts, trousers, jackets, and shoes for middle-aged professionals who needed conservative business attire enlivened with imagination and color. The Weitz wardrobe was built around hip-hugging, contoured trousers without a waistband in solids and checks, fitted Oxford-cloth dress shirts with squared-off shirttails, "noisy" shirts in checks and plaids with built-in permanent collar stays, and unconstructed, soft-as-a-sweater suit coats. Perhaps the most characteristic of Weitz's creations, the comfortable, wide-shouldered, one-button jacket was specifically designed for the corporate traveler. As Weitz delightedly demonstrated to astonished buyers, the jacket was so packable that it could be rolled into a ball without creasing or wrinkling.

Weitz's styles immediately caught on with vertically mobile American business executives. In 1966, to meet that response, Lord & Taylor opened the first John Weitz boutique in their New York store. Within three years there were nearly forty John Weitz Clubs, as the boutiques were called, in department stores and men's shops in the United States, Switzerland, Denmark, Sweden, Austria, Germany, and Italy, selling the whole Weitz line of apparel, accessories, and toiletries. In 1967 domestics sales alone topped the $10,000,000 mark. Under a lucrative licensing arrangement, Weitz also created special American-style sportswear collections for William Hollins & Company, Austin Reed, Ltd., and other American and European chains.

With his reputation firmly established, Weitz added even more imaginative—some said eccentric—designs to his menswear line in the freewheeling late 1960's. Although he estimated that 60 percent of American men had, like himself, gotten "out of the pajama habit," he created an unorthodox sleepwear collection for Host Pajamas that included one-piece sleepers cut like racing-car suits, two-piece sleep suits with middy or "golf-jacket" tops, and Dacron and cotton "hotel pants" borrowed from easy-fitting traditional Mexican farmer pants. Rebelling against the craze for "costumey" evening wear, he designed a functional evening suit with a windbreaker jacket over a collarless shirt accented by a "ranchero" necktie. He devised the ranchero as a more suitable alternative to the traditional necktie—"a man's personal battle flag"—than the then-ubiquitous turtleneck sweater. "The turtleneck for the evening out is wrong," he told Evelyn Portrait in an interview for Cue (January 27, 1968). "A man who makes important decisions all day shouldn't be Errol Flynn at night."

Weitz stretched his "function that forgets about fashion" credo to the limit when he designed several suits for the "typical executive" of 1987. "All I did," he explained to fashion reporters, "was to reasses the value of every single detail in men's clothes and shift things around a bit." For instance, he replaced the single back vent in the suit coat with a single vent to each side, to make it easier for a man to put his hands in his pockets, and paired that jacket with straight, tubular, uncreased trousers, a collarless pullover shirt in Dacron or paper, and a small, silk ascot. "The paper shirt is inevitable," he said. "A man ought to be able to buy seven shirts for about $2.00, and then throw them away at the end of the week." His disposable wardrobe of the future also included paper underwear and paper socks.

Weitz's outspokenness, disregard of the fashion industry's traditions, and undeniable promotional skills offended conservative clothing manufacturers, who disparaged him as a "sissy publicity hound" and "a guy who puts his name in a Grade 2 suit and calls it a Grade 6." Their criticism increased after Weitz wrote The Value of Nothing (Stein & Day, 1970), a graphic, sexually explicit novel exposing the deception and phoniness underneath the superficial glamour of international high fashion. The book's central character is a homosexual couturier who claws and scrambles his way to the top over the bodies of discharged associates and discarded lovers. He is, as Weitz put it, "a man who designed himself." The book was not widely reviewed, but it sold well nonetheless.

Throughout his professional career, Weitz has resisted the industry's annual impulse to create an entirely new style. "I don't feel styles have to change from year to year," he said, as quoted in the Westchester (New York) Herald Statesman (March 4, 1979). "A large crop of the European designers are doing just that and it is only because they are desperately thrashing around for new ideas. Every season doesn't bring a new idea, but the fashion press has forced these designers into thinking it is a necessity." Sympathizing with the bewildered businessmen who have been "basically suckered by fashion magazines" into spending thousands of dollars a year on new clothes, Weitz published Man in Charge; the Executive Guide to Grooming, Manners, and Travel (Macmillan, 1970), which offers a commonsense approach to status dressing.

According to Weitz, a man's basic wardrobe should be built around an impeccably tailored navy blue blazer suit and, for casual wear, a pair of checked trousers and a zippered poplin jacket. As his budget permits, he can add three more suits (in corduroy, gray flannel, and pin-striped navy worsted), a "quiet dinner suit that will last for years," two tweed jackets, and a tan raincoat with a zip-out lining. A few years after the publication of Man in Charge, Weitz revised and expanded that basic wardrobe to comprise two plain, lightweight suits, one in gray and one in navy; a simply cut dinner suit; a navy blazer paired with gray or tan cavalry twill trousers; and, for the summer months, several inexpensive light blue and tan suits in gabardine, seersucker, poplin, or pincord. Once the basic wardrobe was established, Weitz reckoned that a man needed to spend only about $500 a year for replacements or updating. "After that," he said, "you can only try to be pleasant and charming. That is far more important than any clothes."

By 1972 John Weitz's earnings in the United States had risen to $18,000,000, a phenomenal increase largely due to his mushrooming licensing empire, which was second only to those of Pierre Cardin and Christian Dior. The designer received royalties of 3 to 7 percent on such varied items as bed sheets, ice buckets, scarves, handbags, perfume, home sewing patterns, and sunglasses. Among his sixty-odd licensees were such companies as F. Jacobson (shirts) Palm Beach (sport coats and suits), Majer (slacks), Harbor Master (rainwear), Burlington Industries (bedding), and Futorian Corporation (furniture). He has even designed a "boutique specialty car" that sells for about $40,000. "It's stimulating to challenge one's creativeness in areas that may be alien," he told Lammy Johnstone, the syndicated columnist. "If a person has a flair for designing I don't think they should be forced to limit themselves." After a hiatus of more than ten years, he recently resumed designing women's fashions, specializing for the most part in accessories, skirts, and shirts cut without shaping, like a man's shirt.

A handsome man who appears to be years younger than his age, John Weitz is six feet two inches tall and weighs a lean 190 pounds. He keeps himself in athletic trim with vigorous daily exercise. Twenty years ago he was a regular competitor in the annual Grand Prix at Sebring, Florida, but he now restricts himself to less hazardous sports, such as tennis, rugby, swimming, skiing, and sailing on his boat, the *Milagros*. His preferred sedentary recreation is reading. Weitz lives with his wife, the former Susan Kohner, in a sprawling, simply furnished apartment on Park Avenue in Manhattan. He married the actress, who was an Academy Award nominee in 1959 for her performance in *Imitation of Life*, on August 31, 1964. They have two sons, Paul John and Christopher John. Weitz also has two children, Karen and Robert, from an earlier marriage that ended in divorce.

References: N Y Post p45 O 17 '75 por; N Y Times p15 Mr 17 '56 por, III p7 O 29 '72 por; Contemporary Authors 1st rev vols 29-32 (1972); Who's Who in America, 1978-79

Weizman, Ezer (vīts'män ā'zər)

1924- Minister of Defense of Israel. Address: b. Ministry of Defense, Jerusalem, Israel; h. 20 Hageffen St., Ramat Hasheram, Israel

Once considered the "enfant terrible of the Israeli establishment," Ezer Weizman—a maverick nephew of Israel's first President, Dr. Chaim Weizmann—became Minister of Defense following the election victory of Menachem Begin's Likud bloc in May 1977. Trained as one of his country's first fighter pilots, Weizman took part in the struggles of 1948-49 that accompanied the creation of the state of Israel, and after his appointment as commander of the Air Force in 1958, he built it into one of the most effective fighting forces in the world As chief of operations of the General Staff he played a key role in Israel's victory in the Six-Day War of 1967. In 1969-70, as a member of Begin's annexationist Gahal bloc, he served as Minister of Transportation in Prime Minister Golda Meir's national unity government. Formerly known as one of his country's most outspoken hawks, Weizman has emerged since 1977 as a leading moderate in the Israeli Cabinet, advocating a flexible response to Egyptian President Anwar Sadat's peace initiatives, and he is widely regarded as a likely successor to Prime Minister Menachem Begin.

Ezer Weizman—who dropped the second "n" from the family name—was born in Tel Aviv in 1924, the son of Yehiel Weizmann, an immigrant from Eastern Europe and a younger brother of Chaim Weizmann, and Yehudit (Krishevkis) Weizmann, a native of Rishon L'Etzion, one of the first Zionist settlements in Palestine. Soon after his son's birth, Yehiel Weizmann, who worked as director of the British mandatory government's department of agriculture and fisheries, moved his family to Haifa, where he taught at the Technion. Growing up in Haifa with his sister, Yael (now Mrs. Connell Allingham), Ezer was strongly influenced by the Zionist beliefs of his parents. At thirteen he served as a security guard for the family's most prestigious member, Chaim Weizmann, the leader of the London-based World Zionist Organization.

Weizman recalls how his father and uncle used to argue long into the night over Zionist tactics for achieving a Jewish state and protecting Jewish settlements from Arab attack. "Uncle Chaim" favored restraint, but Ezer was more influenced by the activist doctrine espoused by his father. "There are many Weizmanns," he told William Stevenson, the author of *Zanek! A Chronicle of the Israeli Air Force* (Viking, 1971), "and Chaim exercised the least influence over me because he lived abroad."

At sixteen, while undergoing arduous infantry training in the Carmel Mountains as part of a section leaders' course for Haganah, the defensive militia of the Palestinian Jewish community, Weizman looked up, bruised and bleeding, to see three airplanes flying high above. "That moment," he told Mira Avrech of *People* (August 7, 1978), "I decided: 'That is the life for me—no more crawling in the bushes!'" He promptly joined the Haifa Aviation Club and earned his pilot's license in April 1942. When Chaim Weizmann's son, an English pilot, was shot down in combat against Nazi Germany, the young aviator wired his grieving uncle: "I will continue in Michael's place." He signed up with the Royal Air Force at the Jerusalem recruiting station but was at first held back by a British rule prohibiting natives of Palestine from flying in combat.

Eventually allowed to train in Rhodesia, Weizman received his wings in 1945 and served as a fighter pilot in Egypt and India. Mustered out of the RAF in 1946, he was sent by his family to London to study aeronautics. In December 1946 he traveled to Basel, Switzerland to argue before the twenty-second Zionist Congress about the need for developing military and civil aviation for the Jewish community in Palestine. While still in London, he was recruited into the militant Irgun Zvai Leumi and was trained in sabotage. But when approached by the more moderate Haganah to join its nascent air force, he returned to Tel Aviv in 1947, taking charge of a squad of nine Piper Cubs that brought supplies to besieged Jewish settlements in the Negev during the internal strife that preceded the creation of Israel on May 15, 1948. He also assumed responsibility for delivering the Messerschmitts and Spitfires purchased from Czechoslovakia that became the core of Israel's air force, and he took part in the first Israeli air attack on Egypt during the War of Independence. But he was dissatisfied with the cease-fire lines that remained Israel's borders from 1949 until 1967, with East Jerusalem, the Gaza Strip, and Judea and Samaria (the West Bank of the Jordan) remaining in Arab hands. "It was the Land of Israel without the Land of the Bible," he wrote in his autobiography *On Eagles' Wings* (Macmillan, 1976).

Rising rapidly through the ranks as a career military officer, Weizman was promoted from squadron commander to chief of operations of the Air Force, with the rank of lieutenant colonel, in 1950, and he remained in that post until 1953. In 1951 he went to England to study at the RAF Air Command College, and on his return he established the Israeli air force's first officer training course. From 1953 to 1956 he was a base commander and from 1956 to 1958 he served as chief of the Air Force general staff.

As its commander from 1958 to 1966, Weizman persuaded his superiors to upgrade the Air Force from an auxiliary branch of the ground forces into a separate wing of the Israel Defense Forces. As a major step in his modernization, Weizman integrated the French Mirage fighter jet into the Air Force. "It was not until the tenure of Ezer Weizman that the Air Force . . . acquired its final form," Edward Luttwak and Dan Horowitz wrote in *The Israeli Army* (Harper, 1975).

Promoted to chief of operations of the General Staff of the Israel Defense Forces in May 1966, Weizman was the architect of the preemptive strike that decimated the armed forces of Egypt, Jordan, and Syria in the early hours of the Six-Day War of June 1967. But despite his success, he was distrusted by the Labor party establishment because of his annexationist views. "To them I was a wild man, with horrifying opinions," he wrote in his memoirs. Although excluded from the national debate over the future of the territories occupied in the Six-Day War, Weizman let it be known publicly that he supported unilateral annexation of the West Bank and East Jerusalem, a view consistent with that of Menachem Begin, then the leader of the hawkish Gahal bloc. After Weizman was passed over for promotion to chief of staff in favor of General Chaim Bar-Lev in January 1968, he realized that his position in the military was not very secure.

When Gahal party officials offered him the candidacy for a seat in the Knesset for the October 1969 elections, Weizman turned them down. But after Gahal rolled up enough votes in the elections to compel Prime Minister Golda Meir to include the party in her national unity government, he was persuaded to resign his commission as a major general and to accept the post of Minister of Transportation. In so doing, he became the youngest member of the Cabinet. "For the first time," Yuval Elitzur wrote in the Washington *Post* (December 27, 1969), "a popular national figure has reached a prominent position in Israel's power structure without first going through the rough and tumble of machine politics." As Minister of Transportation, Weizman was responsible for Israeli shipping, trucking, railroads, and aviation. On the Cabinet's security committee, he was involved in the formulation of Israel's military and foreign policies.

In January 1970 Israel began to conduct bombing raids deep into Egypt in an effort to persuade the Egyptians to end the "war of attrition" that had been taking its toll in Israeli lives and morale since the Six-Day War. Arguing that the raids were not enough, Weizman proposed that the army seize the western bank of the Suez Canal and intensify the bombings, but his recommendations were rejected. As a result of American intercession, a ceasefire was achieved in August 1970, when the Meir government agreed to take part in negotiations with Egypt and Jordan under the auspices of United Nations special representative Gunnar Jarring. In protest against the ceasefire, the Gahal faction withdrew from the Cabinet.

Although Weizman entertained some misgivings about Begin's decision to take his party out of the government, he resigned his Cabinet post and entered private life, becoming an executive of Mercantile Fruit Carriers, a shipping line, and engaging in other business enterprises. He remained active in politics, however, as the second-ranking leader of Gahal. When Egypt violated the ceasefire in 1971 by mobilizing Soviet-manned aircraft and missiles, Weizman advocated a full-scale war if hostilities resumed and proposed that Israel retain at least part of the Sinai peninsula as well as all of the West Bank. After serving a term as chairman of the executive committee of the Herut faction of Gahal, Weizman was forced out in December 1972 by Begin, who reportedly regarded him as a challenger to his leadership. While affirming his respect for Begin, he later explained their difficulties as "the friction you get between men who lack a 'chemical affinity.'" When the Likud (Unity) bloc, a coalition of Gahal and other factions, was founded in September 1973 under Begin's guidance to challenge the powerful Labor party alignment, Weizman became a member but remained aloof from its leadership.

Weizman staged a political comeback in 1976 as head of the Likud campaign staff and in that post, engineered Begin's campaign for the Prime Ministership in the elections of May 17, 1977. His strategy of playing down the extremist image of Likud and emphasizing the scandal-ridden image of the ailing Labor party, was a key factor in bringing about a narrow victory for the Likud bloc. Prime Minister Begin's new coalition government, consisting of Likud and two Orthodox religious parties, was sworn in on June 21, 1977 following a vote of confidence from the Knesset, with Weizman as Minister of Defense.

Although many observers feared that a Likud government, committed to annexation of Arab territory, would precipitate a new war, Egyptian President Anwar Sadat's journey to Jerusalem and de facto recognition of Israel in November 1977, launched a period of unprecedented face-to-face Arab-Israeli negotia-

tions in which Weizman played a leading role. Following Sadat's speech to the Knesset, Weizman was dispatched to an army base near Alexandria, becoming the first Israeli minister to make an official visit to Egypt. His mission was to help prepare the agenda for Christmas talks at Ismailia between Sadat and Begin. To facilitate the negotiations, two standing committees were created: a military committee headed by Weizman and Egyptian War Minister Abdel Ghany el Gamasy, and a political committee headed by the two foreign ministers.

Substantial progress was made at Ismailia but not enough to bring about a peace settlement. Begin offered gradual withdrawal of Israeli troops from the Sinai and implementation of limited home rule for Palestinians in the West Bank and the Gaza strip for an interim period pending a more permanent arrangement. While accepting some aspects of the plan, Sadat rejected it because it did not go far enough in laying the groundwork for Palestinian self-determination. On January 18, 1978 Sadat broke off negotiations with Israel in protest over continuing Israeli settlement of the disputed lands and Begin's refusal to include removal of Israeli outposts on the Sinai peninsula in the terms of the peace arrangement. Tensions increased in February, when American satellites revealed new Israeli settlements in the West Bank, and when Begin implied that his government did not consider U.N. Resolution 242, which called for Israeli withdrawal to 1967 borders, as applying to the West Bank.

As the minister responsible for the occupied territories, Weizman opposed the creation of any new settlements in those areas for the duration of negotiations. He was furious when he learned, during a visit to the United States in March, that Agricultural Minister Ariel Sharon had authorized two new settlements in the West Bank against his orders, and he telephoned Begin, threatening to resign "if only one tractor moves" to build any further settlements. Although he won that showdown, Weizman failed to secure a Cabinet agreement placing a moratorium on new settlements in Arab territory pending a peace agreement.

Responding to a terrorist raid by the Palestine Liberation Organization in Israel in March 1978, Weizman directed a land, sea, and air invasion of southern Lebanon to eliminate PLO bases. Defending the massive scale of the action, Weizman remarked that Israel was "condemned to fight from time to time." In compliance with a United States-sponsored U.N. Security Council resolution, Israel phased out its troops from Lebanon in early April, allowing a 4,000-member U.N. peace-keeping force to enter the zone.

Attempting to revive the stalled Egyptian-Israeli talks, the United States government tried to persuade Israel to reconsider its refusal to commit itself to discussion of the final status of the West Bank following a five-year interim period of semiautonomy. But the Israeli Cabinet, meeting on June 18, 1978, voted fourteen to five against changing its stance. In favor of greater flexibility on the issue, Weizman stormed out of the meeting, shouting that the Cabinet's decision would "lead us all to another round of wars," and he reportedly ripped a peace poster from the door of a Cabinet meeting room, saying that Begin did not know the meaning of the word peace. But despite a few calls for his resignation, Weizman emerged from the incident secure in his position.

Weizman's popularity with American officials who appreciate his flexibility and his cordial relationship with President Sadat, made him a central figure in the peace negotiations. Several times during 1978, when negotiations faltered, Weizman was chosen to fly to Cairo and present Israel's proposals. In July 1978, when relations between Begin and Sadat appeared to be strained, Sadat stunned Israelis by inviting Weizman and opposition leader Shimon Peres to meet with him in Salzburg, Austria, a few days before he was to confer with Begin at the American-sponsored round-table meeting in Leeds, England. Apparently feeling snubbed, the Israeli Prime Minister gave Weizman permission to accept the invitation, but ruled that subsequent meetings should take place between officials of similar rank.

To expedite Israeli-Egyptian accord, President Jimmy Carter invited Begin and Sadat to confer with him at Camp David, Maryland in September 1978. That summit meeting, in which Weizman was a key participant, laid the groundwork for an Egyptian-Israeli peace treaty and established an open-ended process for final determination of the status of the West Bank and Gaza Strip. After heated debate, the Knesset ratified the Camp David accords. Their first test had come only hours after they were signed in Washington, D.C. on September 17, 1978, when members of Gush Emunim, a religious-nationalist movement, illegally occupied three sites in the West Bank to protest Begin's apparent renunciation of Israel's right to what they considered their Biblical heritage. Weizman, overruling the Chief of Staff of the Army who had tried to compromise with the protesters, ordered their immediate eviction.

Meeting with United States Defense Secretary Harold Brown in Israel in February 1979, Weizman announced plans for a 25 percent cut in the Israeli defense budget over a ten-year period in view of the peace accords. In March and April he met with Egyptian officials in Washington and Cairo to work out details for Israel's phased withdrawal from Sinai. Israeli-Egyptian relations made further progress when the first Israeli ship was permitted to sail through the Suez Canal in late April, and the border between Israel and Egypt was opened a month later. But in June

1979 Weizman was removed, at his own request, from the six-man negotiating team discussing Palestinian autonomy, because he objected to the Begin government's establishment of a new Jewish settlement near Nablus on the West Bank, in the name of security. He was supported in his position by Defense Minister Moshe Dayan and Deputy Prime Minister Yigael Yadin.

According to some critics, Weizman "seemed at times to be conducting his own foreign policy," while others, noting his metamorphosis from hardliner to moderate, call him a "lightweight" who "is trying to please the liberals and the hardliners at the same time." "I haven't changed that much," Weizman told Sally Quinn in an interview in the Washington Post (October 15, 1978). "If there had been a Sadat ten years ago, I would have acted the same. What has changed is Egypt."

Ezer Weizman and Re'uma Shamir Schwartz, the sister of Moshe Dayan's first wife, Ruth, were married on June 6, 1950. They have a son, Shaul, a former paratrooper who was seriously wounded in combat with Egyptian forces in 1970, and a daughter, Michal, who is married to an air force pilot. Six feet two inches tall, the lanky Weizman speaks English with a clipped British accent. He has recently been trying to divest himself of his former public image as a hard-drinking playboy and to emphasize his serious side. As a hobby he likes to fly his red and black Spitfire, but he no longer does stunt flying, asserting that in politics he has "enough close shaves every day" without having to indulge in any acrobatics.

References: N Y Times A p16 Mr 16 '78 por; People 10:24+ Ag 7 '78 por; Time 111:33 Ap 3 '78 por; Washington Post M p1+ O 17 '78 por; Encyclopedia of Zionism and Israel (1971); Weizman, Ezer. On Eagle's Wings (1976); Who's Who in Israel, 1978; Who's Who in World Jewry (1978)

Werblin, David A(braham)

Mar. 17, 1910- Businessman; organization official. Address: b. 880 3d Ave., New York City, N.Y. 10022; Madison Square Garden Corp., 2 Pennsylvania Plaza, New York City, N.Y. 10001

Since late 1977 David A. ("Sonny") Werblin has been applying the expertise acquired during his more than forty-year career in sports and entertainment to upgrading and glamorizing the events that have taken place at Madison Square Garden during his regime as president and chief executive officer of

David A. Werblin

the Madison Square Garden Corporation. In everything he has so far accomplished, whether as theatrical agent, president of MCA-TV, owner of the New York Jets football team, or chairman of the New Jersey Sports and Exposition Authority, Werblin has followed the same guidelines. As listed by Maury Allen in the New York Post (January 14, 1965), those criteria are: "sound business, a willingness to gamble, and a propensity to think big."

David Abraham Werblin was born in the Flatbush section of Brooklyn, New York on March 17, 1910 to Simon Abner and Henrietta (Gross) Werblin. It was his mother who gave him the nickname "Sonny," which has long since replaced David as Werblin's preferred first name. Because their father owned a flourishing paper bag company, Sonny and his two younger brothers grew up in a financially comfortable home. Werblin's dream as a small boy was to become a baseball player for the Brooklyn Dodgers, an idea that eventually gave way to his growing interest in sports writing.

After attending Erasmus Hall High School and James Madison High School, Werblin entered Rutgers University, New Brunswick, New Jersey, in 1927. He had played center on James Madison High's winning football team, and he continued playing football at Rutgers until a shoulder injury he suffered during his freshman year forced him to limit his sports activities to managing the school's swimming team. While an undergraduate, he established Rutgers' Interscholastic Debating League, which not only enabled New Jersey high school students to compete for prizes in rhetoric but also provided him with fees from the schools involved, for finding the judges and the competition sites. In addition, Werblin covered football games as a stringer for seven New York and New Jersey newspapers. All in all, he earned so much money during his collegiate career that, as he quipped to Ray Kennedy who interviewed him for a Sports Illustrated article (September 12, 1977), he eventually had to be broken up "as a monopoly." He earned more in his senior year, he assured Kennedy, than he did for the next five years. In 1931 Werblin graduated with a B.A. degree from Rutgers.

After working briefly as a sportswriter for the now defunct Brooklyn Eagle, and as a copyboy for the New York Times, Werblin joined the Music Corporation of America in 1932 at a starting salary of $21 a week. He started out as a band manager, whose duties included "counting" the house and keeping a watchful eye on the musical instruments for the likes of Guy Lombardo and Eddy Duchin and then advanced to the job of booking agent for bands in some of New York City's major hotels. When Werblin finally became a theatrical agent, he had a hand in promoting the careers of such big-name entertainers as Al Jolson, Frank Sinatra, Jackie Gleason, Abbott and Costello, Rosalind Russell, Joan Crawford, Betty Grable, and Eddie Fisher.

In 1940 Werblin suffered a heart attack and was forced to curtail his activities during a protracted period of recuperation. Turning his attention to the nascent television industry, he became the president of MCA-TV in 1951 and supervised all of that corporation's television operations. In 1964 a writer for Variety summed up Werblin's impact on the television industry when he described him as "the ultimate show business agent, the father of the package deal," and "the masterful practitioner of the time-honored show biz dodge of starting a war and then selling ammunition to both sides." Werblin lured already established stars into television by giving them part-ownership in their programs. That strategy not only ensured success for the show but also proved beneficial for Werblin, who then used his amplified financial resources to recruit more talent for the industry. Sold to the networks as a unit, his so-called "package-deals" included both fully developed programs and casts composed of his own clients. He effectively used the show business ploy known as "walking the talent" a number of times in his career. When, for example, NBC-TV failed to renew its option for Werblin's Wagon Train by the deadline date in 1962, he sold the show to ABC-TV instead and then approached NBC-TV with a new program, The Virginian.

On March 15, 1963 Werblin bought the three-year-old New York Titans football team for $1,000,000 on behalf of a group of five investors known as the Gotham Football Club, Inc. Since MCA-TV held the television contract for the games of the American Football League, the league commissioner, Joe Foss, who knew Werblin personally, thought of him as a possible buyer when the bankrupt team came up for sale. To devote himself full-time to the development of the team, Werblin retired from MCA-TV on New Year's Day of 1965.

As president of the Gotham corporation, Werblin set out to revamp the team, bolster its morale, and refurbish its public image. He rechristened the team the New York Jets; hired Weeb Ewbank, formerly of the Baltimore Colts, as its coach; set up admirable accident and health insurance policies; bought the players some badly needed new equipment; advertised heavily to build up attendance; and moved the team to the new Shea Stadium in 1964. One of the first to perceive sports as entertainment, he paid what were considered at the time to be enormous salaries and bonuses to new players and upped the money paid to those already on the team. Undoubtedly the most spectacular player hired by Werblin, and the one who was to have the most profound effect on the team and the future of pro football in general, was Joe Namath, whom Werblin signed on January 2, 1965, the day after Namath played in the Orange Bowl for the University of Alabama team.

Werblin signed Namath to a three-year contract at a salary of approximately $400,000 and threw in a Lincoln Continental to round out the deal. He was quoted in the New York Times (October 24, 1966) as explaining, "You can't do things cheaply. That's something I learned from my theatrical experiences. A million-dollar set is worthless if you put a $2,000 actor in the main role." The publicity Werblin gained from his press parties and expensive hiring practices began to pay off quickly. Within one month after the signing of Namath, the team sold $654,000 in season tickets, 75 percent of which were new subscriptions.

Criticism came to Werblin from some quarters of the American Football League. Arthur Modell of Cleveland contended, for example, that Namath's inflated salary did "irreparable harm to pro football." A kinder view of his efforts was taken by writer Steve Gelman (New York Herald Tribune magazine, July 15, 1965): "Some promoters, for all their success, are pure con, utterly disliked by men who know the inside operation. Not Werblin. He is shrewd and tough but warm and honest. He hides little. . . . Werblin realizes that part of the pleasure in promoting is letting others in on it. And while promoting, while building up the Jets, he has been dedicated to his fans and his players. Further, he has livened and broadened the world of sports." By October 1966 attendance at Jet games had risen to such an extent that at one game 22,000 more fans were present than had attended all home games in the season before Werblin bought the team.

Werblin not only effected changes in his own team but also became a driving force in the entire AFL. He promoted the expansion of the eight-team league to ten teams in 1965, aware that a large following of loyal fans in two more metropolises would make the AFL more attractive to the television networks, who paid for contract rights according to audience appeal. Knowing that the AFL needed television money to compete more effectively with the older and stronger National Football League, he was instrumental in 1965 in the AFL's signing of a contract with NBC-TV (the former one was with ABC-TV) for $900,000 per team, per season. As if the fierce competition between the two football leagues over the hiring of promising college stars were not enough, the leagues also began competing for cities in which to expand. A frustrated Werblin told a New York Post (November 18, 1965) reporter at the time that the NFL was trying to drive the AFL "out of business" and that "the only way this can end is in a common draft."

His foresight was vindicated on June 8, 1966, when the merger of the two leagues was announced, with a common draft scheduled first, for January 1, 1967, and a complete merger for 1970. The controversial point in the arrangement for Werblin was an $18,000,000 territorial indemnity to be paid by the AFL to the NFL over a twenty-year period. Bitterly opposed to that clause, Werblin voted against the plan and called the arrangement a "Munich."

Almost two years later, in late May 1968, it was revealed that Werblin had sold his 23.4 percent share of the Jets to his four partners for over $1,600,000. Reportedly, the partners were displeased over their exclusion from decision-making, while some players resented the VIP treatment accorded Joe Namath. Werblin explained to newsmen that he had offered to buy the team, but was unable to meet his partners' demand for payment in cash. Convinced that it is impossible to run either a sports or show business enterprise by committee, he told George Vecsey of the New York Times (May 25, 1968): "When it was a failure, nobody else came around. You didn't see them in Kansas City when it was 14 below and your feet stuck to the metal floor. But the moment a profit appeared, we were running things by committee."

After leaving the Jets, Werblin remained in semiretirement in Florida, emerging to form, along with Johnny Carson, Raritan Enterprises, a production and holding company with investments in real estate and the entertainment and leisure industries. Werblin also helped Carson to negotiate his $1,250,000 contract with NBC-TV for his work on The Tonight Show Starring Johnny Carson, which, for a period of time, was produced by Raritan.

In June 1971 Werblin returned to the sports business when he accepted a four-year term as chairman of the New Jersey Sports and Exposition Authority, a public agency created by the state legislature in May 1971. As he explained to Ray Kennedy: "I accepted the position because I feel that if a man can afford to perform a public service in his lifetime, he should, and because it gave me an opportunity to combine the three things I enjoy most—football, horse racing, and entertainment." New Jersey government officials planned to build a sports complex on some 588 acres of marshland in East Rutherford, but before the legislature would agree to float a public, tax-free bond issue to provide funds for the complex, Werblin had to guarantee that a football team would be willing to move to a new stadium when completed. On August 26, 1971 Werblin signed the New York Giants, who played at Yankee Stadium in New York City, to a thirty-year lease. Since racetracks usually earn thirty times as much money as football stadiums, a racetrack was also planned for the sports complex to help cover the costs of building the stadium.

Strong opposition to the project came from environmentalists, from operators of rival New Jersey racetracks, and, most of all, from New York State officials, who lamented the loss of the Giants and feared the further abdication of racetrack patrons. Laws regarding racing in New York State were immediately changed to make its tracks more competitive, plans for a purported sports complex in Queens were announced to discourage Meadowlands' investors, and Governor Nelson A. Rockefeller reportedly used his influence on Wall Street to dissuade firms from buying the New Jersey bonds. After trying time and time again to overcome apparently insuperable obstacles, Werblin became so ill that he was rushed to the hospital. "I was absolutely frustrated...," he told Ray Kennedy. "I still don't know if it was a heart attack or heat exhaustion or both. All I know is that I was damn tense."

Despite his illness and the galling years of frustration, Werblin opened the racetrack on September 1, 1976 and watched the Dallas Cowboys and the New York Giants tangle in the first game in the football stadium on October 10 of that same year. He then went on to entice other teams and events to the New Jersey complex: the Cosmos soccer team, the New York Nets basketball team (for which a new arena was planned for 1980), and the Army-Notre Dame football game. Anecdotes about Werblin's frugal financial management and his obsession with cleanliness and employee courtesy abounded in the press: instead of paying to have the horse manure removed from the racetrack, he arranged to sell it to a local mushroom farmer, and one, journalist saw him picking up a cigarette butt out of a crack somewhere in the complex during one of his endless rounds of inspection.

"My life has been selling tickets," Werblin joked to newspapermen after it was announced on December 16, 1977 that he had been named president and chief executive officer of the Madison Square Garden Corporation in New York City. He went on to explain that he had resigned from the New Jersey sports authority on December 6 because he disapproved of Governor Brendan T. Byrne's decision to make several political appointments to that agency. The $225,000-a-year post placed Werblin in charge of the New York Knicks of the National Basketball Association; the New York Rangers of the National Hockey League; the Washington Diplomats of the North American Soccer League; Roosevelt Raceway on Long Island; the four troupes of the International Holiday on Ice; one racetrack and two hotels in Chicago; real estate; and the Felt Forum.

Among his first moves were the establishment of an open-door policy between Roosevelt Raceway and the Meadowlands track for drivers and horses; the ordering of $2,500,000 worth of improvements at Roosevelt; a May 27, 1978 agreement to copromote boxing matches with Don King; and the takeover of Marketing Concepts, Inc., a producer of industrial shows that was originally an MCA offshoot created by Werblin in 1946. He also signed big-name personnel in 1978 at a total price that involved millions: two Swedish hockey players, Ulf Nilsson and Anders Hedberg; a new Ranger general manager and coach, Fred Shero; a new center for the Knicks, Marvin Webster, known as the "Human Eraser"; and Red Holzman, who replaced Willis Reed as coach of the Knicks.

Werblin credits his one-time theatrical client, Al Jolson, with instilling in him his love for horse racing. "[Jolie] loved horses but he couldn't move anywhere around the racetrack without becoming the center of a mob scene," he told Tommy Holmes for a New York Herald Tribune article (July 29, 1965). "So he liked to take me out with him to make his bets. Usually, he'd go out with a packet of 20 $1,000 bills which he carried in the inside pocket of his coat. When he found something he liked, he'd peel off a couple and hand them to me with instructions." Eventually, Werblin bought stock in the Monmouth Park, New Jersey track and, for a time, served as one of its directors; bought his own stable, Elberon Farms, in Deal, New Jersey; and began racing his own horses in about 1953. Show business inspired the names he chose for his horses, among them From The Top, Road Show, Child Star, One Night Stand, and Silent Screen.

On March 27, 1938 Sonny Werblin married Leah Ray, whom he met while she was a singer with the Phil Harris band. Their three sons are Hubbard Steele, Robert Boomer, and Thomas David. Werblin enjoys listening to pop music and jazz and likes to go bonefishing. Journalists vary in their recorded impressions of the promoter. To some he appears intelligent, unpretentious, gentle-looking, and soft of speech; to others he seems to be driven by a "dynamic push to outwit the next man."

"Everything that I do," Werblin has said, "is a matter of flying by the seat of my pants. If I think it'll work, I'll try it."

References: N Y Herald Tribune mag p10+ Ag 15 '65; N Y Post p25 Ja 14 '65 por, p56 S 3 '76 por; N Y Sunday News II p15 N 8 '64 por; N Y Times p50 O 24 '66 por, p32 D 17 '77 por; N Y World-Telegram and Sun II p13 F 6 '65 pors; Sports Illus 47:75+ S 12 '77 por; Who's Who in America, 1976-77

Werblin, Sonny See Werblin, David A(braham)

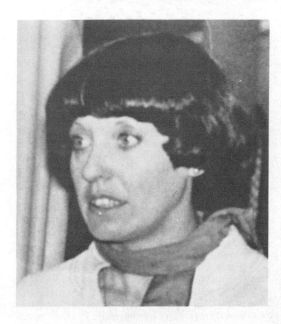

Williams, Betty (Smyth)

May 22, 1943- Northern Irish peace activist. Address: b. c/o Peace House, 224 Lisburn Rd., Belfast 9, Northern Ireland

At the Nobel Prize ceremonies in Oslo, Norway in December 1977, an impassioned Betty Williams recalled in her address the week in mid-August 1976 that began the chain of events that resulted in her selection as co-winner with Mairead Corrigan of the 1976 Nobel Peace Prize: "We are for life and creation and we are against war and destruction, and in our rage in that terrible week, we screamed that the violence had to stop." Shock over the accidental killing of three children in the clash between Provisional IRA and British forces in Northern Ireland drove the two young Irish women, Mrs. Williams and Miss Corrigan, to join Ciaran McKeown, a journalist, in founding the Peace People, or Community of Peace People, a movement that captured world attention.

The Peace People leaders did not expect to solve Northern Ireland's complex political problems but wanted to end the fighting and killing, which had been severe since 1969. After staging a series of peace marches and demonstrations in Northern Irish and English cities in 1976, they focused their efforts on a variety of social projects. Betty Williams has said that perhaps thirty years of change may be required to achieve what she wants for Northern Ireland: a unification of Catholics and Protestants in setting up their own government. On April 15, 1978 Mrs. Williams, Miss Corrigan, and McKeown announced that in order to promote democracy within the Community of Peace People, they were resigning as leaders to give others a chance to run the government, with which they would continue to work.

Betty Smyth Williams was born on May 22, 1943 in Andersonstown, a Catholic section of Belfast, Northern Ireland, the first child of a Catholic mother and a Protestant father, the type of mixed marriage often regarded as akin to treason in Northern Ireland, where Protestants and Roman Catholics have been in conflict for centuries. When Betty was thirteen her mother, who had been a waitress, was paralyzed by a stroke, and Betty assumed much of the responsibility for caring for her sister, Margaret, five years younger, and for running the home. Their father worked in a butcher shop. He tried to raise his daughters to be free of prejudice in a country and city where prejudice was a way of life. Mrs. Williams recalls that her father once scolded her because she identified a little girl she had met as being a Protestant. Another force against bigotry in her early life was her love for her maternal grandfather, a Polish Jew who had lost much of his family in Europe during World War II, but did not show bitterness.

One of the goals that Betty Williams now has for Northern Ireland is the mingling of Catholic and Protestant children in educational and social activities. When she was growing up, few persons ever discussed the possibility of integration of schools in Belfast. The Catholic schools that she attended were St. Teresa's Primary School and St. Dominic's Grammar School. She then took secretarial courses at Orange Academy. On June 14, 1961 she married Ralph Edward Williams, an engineer in the merchant marine, an Englishman, and a Protestant. She traveled for a while with her husband, living in Bermuda in 1964-65 and visiting New York City on several occasions. Because of her lively interest in what was going on in the world and her desire to keep mentally active, Betty Williams wanted to go on working after her marriage. She would move from job to job, enjoying the change, and at the time that she helped to launch the peace movement, she held a clerical post in a firm of technical consultants and moonlighted as a waitress.

In 1968 the Catholic minority in Northern Ireland (about half a million to a million Protestants), inspired in part by the civil rights protesters in the United States, began demonstrating against Protestant discrimination, demanding greater job opportunities, an end to housing restrictions, and electoral reform that would increase their political power. A new militant faction of the Irish Republican Army (IRA), which has always stood for union with the Irish Republic to the south, was organized to help the Catholics in their campaign and to cut the ties between Britain and Northern Ireland. The members of the Provisional IRA, as it was called, resorted to bombings, shooting, and other types of violence to gain its ends, chief of which was the expulsion of the British. Opposing the Provisionals ("Provos" or "Provies") was the pro-British Protestant Ulster Defense League. To maintain control over their respective Catholic and Protestant areas in Belfast and throughout Northern Ireland, those two paramilitary organizations engaged in extensive guerrilla warfare. From 1969 through 1975 the fighting resulted in over 1,400 deaths and injuries, of which more than 1,000 were among the general population.

Like many others in the Andersonstown ghetto, Betty Williams had observed the harrassment of Republican demonstrators by the British troops, and for some years her sympathies lay with the IRA. But she came to realize, she has explained, that violence only generated more violence through vengeance and that brutality and terrorism victimized the innocent. In 1972, when the Reverend Joseph Parker, a Protestant clergyman, organized Witness for Peace in an effort to bring Catholics and Protestants together, she joined his unsuccessful protest against violence. Privately, she urged Provos among her acquaintances to abandon their cause. One day in 1973 when a young British soldier was shot down in a Belfast street almost at her feet, she tried to comfort him as he lay dying on the sidewalk. Other women nearby upbraided her for that gesture of compassion. Recounting the incident to Richard Deutsch, who interviewed her for his book *Mairead Corrigan/Betty Williams* (1977), she said, "I learned that people had obviously lost their sense of value of human life."

During the eighth year of the Catholic-Protestant civil war, on August 10, 1976, an event occurred in Belfast that led to the meeting of Betty Williams, Mairead Corrigan, and Ciaran McKeown and to their resolution to march together for peace. While walking along the sidewalk, a Catholic mother, Anne Maguire, and her three children were struck by a getaway car when the driver, an IRA member, was shot dead at the wheel by British pursuers. Two of the children were killed instantly; the third died the next day; and the mother was seriously injured.

Mairead Corrigan, aunt of the Maguire children, appeared on local television the next day, pleading for an end to violence and slaughter and blaming the IRA for the accident. Betty Williams had seen the accident, and impelled by an anger that overrode her fear, she began canvassing the streets within a few hours with her first peace petition. She herself went on television two days after the children's deaths and called on all women, Protestants and Catholic, to help her bring pressure on the Provisional IRA to end military operations. She also announced plans for a peace march in the Andersonstown area where the children had been killed. Approximately 10,000 women, responding to the call, convened on Saturday August 14, to pray and sing hymns. With Betty Williams and Mairead Corrigan they marched to the Maguires' gravesites, undeterred by the verbal and physical opposition of IRA members and sympathizers, who struck out at the peace demonstrators, singling out the known Protestants and tearing placards from their hands.

Determined to see to it that their movement would endure beyond the emotional climate of the moment, Mrs. Williams and Mairead Corrigan met the next day with Ciaran McKeown, a reporter for the *Irish Press*, who had offered his help to the two women. His newspaper background and his knowledge of politics in Northern Ireland were valuable in helping the organization to get started, and he eventually planned the overall strategy for the movement and formulated its philosophy in the Declaration of Peace, which summed up his own ideas on peace and nonviolence, as did his pamphlet *The Price of Peace*. It was McKeown, also, who suggested the name "Peace People" for the movement.

The Peace People leaders planned a series of marches to be held once a week in different places in Northern Ireland and Great Britain, with either Betty Williams or Mairead Corrigan attending each meeting, until December 4, 1976, a date chosen to be the culmination of the first phase of the peace movement. The August 28, 1976 march from a Catholic area of Belfast into a Protestant sector drew an estimated 35,000 supporters, and, as Deutsch reported in his book, "It demonstrated to those Protestants who were still hanging back that the peace movement was not an exclusively Catholic phenomenon, that it was nonsectarian." Although the Provisional IRA charged that the movement sought "peace at any price" instead of "peace with justice," recruits by the thousands joined the marchers throughout Northern Ireland. "We had tapped into something that must have been there for a long time. Suddenly it broke out in the open," Betty Williams said during an interview for *Family Circle* (March 27, 1978).

By the fall of 1976, as the courageous leadership of Mrs. Williams and Miss Corrigan was stirring worldwide sympathy for their cause, the two women became the popular choice for that year's Nobel Peace Prize. But since their movement had begun six months after the February deadline for acceptance of nominations, the Nobel committee could not consider them as candidates. The sentiment for honoring their work, however, was so strong that the Norwegian press and a group of civic organizations collected private donations of $340,000. In late November 1976 the two women traveled to Oslo, where the money was presented to them as a special Norwegian People's Peace Prize. The following year the 1976 Nobel Peace Prize of $140,000 was awarded to them retroactively. The citation read in part: "Their initiative paved the way for the strong resistance against violence and misuse of power which was present in broad circles of the people." Both award winners have said in interviews that they regretted that Ciaran McKeown had not been named to share in the prize that they accepted on behalf of their movement in Oslo on December 10, 1977, but they insisted that he be given part of the cash award.

Because of having to give up their regular jobs when the campaign against violence demanded their full time, Betty Williams and Mairead Corrigan had received a stipend from the Peace People organization. Money from their prizes enabled them to become volunteers in the movement and to pay their own expenses. The prize money also made possible the purchase of a headquarters building and some small community-center buildings and helped to start up a number of local Peace People chapters. As reported in *Newsweek* (March 27, 1978), within a year and a half after its founding the Peace People had become occupied with projects totaling some $5,000,000. To help fund the projects, the Peace Women, as Betty Williams and Mairead Corrigan had come to be called, often traveled abroad in pursuit of financial aid as well as moral support.

On one such trip, in the fall of 1977, Mrs. Williams met with members of the West German government, industrialists, and financiers, trying to interest them in investing in the economy of Northern Ireland, where there is 40 percent unemployment among the adult population. She is well aware of the link between poverty and the type of discontent that seeks outlets in shootings and bombings, as she had made clear in an interview a few months earlier for *Christian Century* (August 21-September 7, 1977). In that interview she also discussed the shift of the peace movement from its "charismatic phase" of the great rallies to an emphasis on hard work at the grass roots level, getting people involved in their local communities as they bridge their religious and political divisions.

Through the project Lifeline, for example, the Peace People have aided the survivors of those killed in terrorist attacks. They have distributed pamphlets to let Ulstermen know their rights when arrested and to instruct victims of violence in claiming compensation. By March 1978 they had assisted over 150 repentant activists in getting out of the country to avoid retaliation. "People need defending," Mrs. Williams has said, as quoted in *Newsweek* (March 27, 1978). "And if the police or the soldiers are violent, we'll say so. We don't want to be a nice, comfortable peace movement."

Along with threats of physical violence, including the slogan "Shoot Betty" painted on Belfast walls, the movement's leaders have been the targets of continuing criticism. They are often accused of naïveté because of failure to offer political solutions for the troubles of Northern Ireland. Andrew Boyd contended in the *Nation* (April 16, 1977) that the movement began to founder early in 1977 because of Protestant suspicion of its three Catholic leaders. He pessimistically concluded that, like all of the peace groups active in Northern Ireland since 1969, that of Betty Williams and her associates was doomed to fail because an agreement on peace can be reached only by the IRA, the British army, and the other factions that are making war.

Mrs. Williams admits that the movement has not brought peace, but she insists that it has "created a climate for peace to become respectable." Although violence has continued in Northern Ireland, the first eight months of 1977 compared to the same period in 1976 showed a decline in killings from 222 to 96 and in bombings from 464 to 225. Some observers link the decline to United States condemnation of terrorist activities and calls by American political leaders for peace coupled with requests to cease all aid to groups involved in fighting in Northern Ireland. British authorities, however, give the Peace People some credit for the reduction in violence, saying that more people are cooperating with the police and the army.

Rejecting the image of the Community of the Peace People as a "petticoat brigade," Betty Williams emphasizes that the movement is not feminist, despite the preponderance of women active in it. She told Claude Servan-Schreiber in an interview for *Ms.* (December 1976) that men are wanted in the movement because they are the ones who are doing the fighting; hence, they are the ones who must stop. She knows, however, that one reason that men fight is that society makes a "hero of the man who carries a gun." In her Nobel address she acknowledged the importance of women in the peace effort: "The voice of women has a special role and a special soul-force in the struggle for a nonviolent world."

Among the people of courage that Betty Williams admires are the American folk singer and social activist Joan Baez, who aided the Peace People by singing at rallies in Northern Ireland and England, and Martin Luther King, the American civil rights leader and champion of nonviolence. She also paid tribute in her Nobel speech to Egyptian President Anwar Sadat for his initiative in going to Israel to try to make peace. In addition to the Nobel prize and the prize from the Norwegian people, Mrs. Williams received the Carl von Ossietzky Medal for Courage from the Berlin section of the International League of Human Rights in 1976 and an honorary Doctor of Law degree from Yale University in 1977.

Betty Williams is the mother of two children, Deborah and Paul. She enjoys many domestic interests such as cooking, gardening, and dressmaking. Her other recreations include swimming and reading, especially the novels of Dickens and Tolstoy. She is a tall, blue-eyed, black-haired woman whose expansive nature is apparent in her readiness to talk and laugh and even weep. "I'm not a 'holy' person," she told Deutsch. "I smoke, I drink, and I swear, but I have profound faith in God." Interviewed by Paula Bernstein for the New York Daily News (May 25, 1978), she spoke of her reaction to critics who consider her politically naïve: "When they say I haven't a clue to what it's all about, I tell them, 'I love you and I'm the only realist.'"

References: Christian Century 94:746+ Ag 31-S 7 '77; Family Circle 91:38+ Mr 27 '78 por; Ms. 5:62+ D '76; N Y Daily News p80 My 25 '78 por; N Y Times p14 O 11 '77, C p1+ D 8 '77 por; N Y Times Mag p29+ D 19 '76 pors; Deutsch, Richard. Mairead Corrigan/Betty Williams (1977); Les Prix Nobel 1977 (1978)

Williams, Robin

July 21, 1952- Comedian; actor. Address: b. c/o Paramount TV, 5451 Marathon St., Los Angeles, Calif. 90046

Described by critics as "an insanely funny man," a "major comedic talent," and "an astonishing lunar wild man out of Jonathan Winters by way of Lenny Bruce, with a touch of Richard Burton thrown in," Robin Williams attained instant stardom in ABC-TV's Mork and Mindy, the major hit of the 1978-79 season. In the view of a number of critics, the show would have been merely another tired situation comedy if it were not for the wildly exuberant antics of Williams as Mork, an amiable alien visitor from outer space befuddled by the ways of earthmen while exhibiting some strange extraterrestrial habits of his own. A stand-up performer in Los Angeles comedy nightclubs before the series elevated him from obscurity to national popularity, Williams is a remarkable improvisational comic who has been allowed the privilege, unusual for television performers, of ad-libbing much of his material.

But although his show has attracted a dedicated weekly audience of as many as 60,000,000 enthusiastic viewers, and he has earned extravagant praise from television critics for his rapid-fire wit and his vocal, facial, and physical dexterity, Williams is more at home on the nightclub stage, which, he feels, offers him the complete freedom he needs to express his anarchistic zaniness. "Being alone onstage is like legalized insanity," he told Aljean Harmetz of the New York Times (December 28, 1978). "You can become all your fantasies." For Williams comedy is not merely a way of life but an addiction. "I'm a junkie, you see," he told Suzy Kalter of Family Weekly (February 25, 1979). "I just can't stop."

Contrary to the popular image of American comedians, Robin Williams—born in Chicago on July 21, 1952—is of upper-middle-class White Anglo-Saxon Protestant background. His father, Robert Williams, a Ford Motor Company vice-president and Midwestern regional manager of the Lincoln-Mercury division, who was almost fifty at the time of Robin's birth, was a remote figure, addressed as "Sir" by his son. In an interview with Kenneth Turan of Rolling Stone (November 2, 1978) Williams described his father as "a very elegant man, like the Lord Governor General of India" and his mother as "a crazy Southern belle." Since his two half-brothers from his parents' previous marriages were already grown, Robin spent a solitary early childhood in his family's rented thirty-room house, on a twenty-acre estate in Bloomfield Hills, Michigan, an exclusive suburb of Detroit.

To relieve his loneliness Williams invented a group of make-believe characters and acted out all the parts. He spent much of his time in his basement with 2,000 toy soldiers, creating the voices and sound effects for simulated full-scale battles. Williams also tape-recorded and imitated the routines of television comedians, particularly the zany characterizations of Jonathan Winters, his comic idol. Summing up his childhood, he told a reporter for *Time* (October 2, 1978): "My imagination was my friend, my companion."

As Robin Williams was growing up, the Williamses moved frequently, and during an eight-year period he attended as many as six different schools, including the exclusive Detroit Country Day School in Birmingham, Michigan, where he belonged to the *magna cum laude* club. "I was fat and used to get beaten up a lot," he told Sue Ellen Jares of *People* magazine (October 30, 1978). "They called me 'dwarf' and 'leprechaun.' " Always the "new boy," Williams eventually learned that one way to make friends was to make people laugh, and he began to entertain his schoolmates with comedy routines.

When Williams was a high school senior his father retired, and the family moved to affluent Tiburon, California in Marin County just north of San Francisco, an area strongly influenced by the counterculture of the late 1960's. There, he attended Redwood High School, a public school whose relaxed atmosphere and innovative curriculum represented a drastic change from the strict discipline of the private schools to which his parents had previously sent him. "Everyone was on acid, and they had gestalt history classes," he recalled in the *People* interview. Under the liberating influence of his new environment, Williams began to emerge from his private shell. He lost thirty pounds by dieting, played tennis, wrestled, took part in cross-country races, and continued to nurture his comic skills. His classmates voted him "Most Humorous" and "Least Likely to Succeed."

While attending Claremont Men's College in Claremont, California, where he had enrolled to study political science, Williams became so entranced by the theatre that he was unable to concentrate on his studies, and he decided to pursue an acting career, determined to become "another Jason Robards Jr." With the reluctant consent of his father, who would have preferred him to study something practical, like welding, he entered Marin College in Kentfield, California to study Shakespeare. Having won a full scholarship, he then went to the Juilliard School in New York City, where he studied drama and speech for three years

under the noted actor John Houseman and other teachers. On the weekends, he and a partner collected as much as $150 a day performing mime in whiteface in front of the Metropolitan Museum of Art. About that time he began to keep a notebook to jot down his ideas for characters and comedy skits, using "everything in New York as material."

Leaving Juilliard before completion of his studies there, Williams went to San Francisco in pursuit of a girl with whom he had fallen in love, and there he tried in vain to secure dramatic roles. To overcome his depression following the collapse of his love affair, he joined a comedy workshop and began to perform in San Francisco's small nightclubs. His self-confidence received a boost when one of his routines, a "hip version" of *The Lawrence Welk Show*, which he performed at a small club in a church basement, earned him $10. Meanwhile, to make his living, he found a job as a bartender and worked at an organic ice cream parlor in Mill Valley.

While tending bar, Williams met his future wife, Valerie Velardi, a modern dancer and graduate student who was then working as a cocktail waitress. She helped him to organize and catalogue his comedy routines, and at her urging he decided in the summer of 1976 to try his luck in Los Angeles. With other novice performers he appeared at the Comedy Store there on "open mike night," which he described to Don Freeman of *TV Guide* (October 28, 1978) as "a terrorizing combination of the Roman arena and *The Gong Show*." "My stomach was in my shoes, I was so scared," he recalled. "But after less than a minute I felt comfortable. I knew I could make people laugh." Soon, he became a regular performer at the club.

One night, in 1977, Williams was spotted at the Comedy Store by television producer George Schlatter, who was in the process of reviving the kaleidoscopic comedy show *Laugh-In*, which had been immensely popular in the late 1960's and early 1970's. Impressed by what he described as Williams' "fragmented free-association act," Schlatter persuaded the comic to cut his shoulder-length hair and shave off his beard, and hired him as the first member of the new *Laugh-In* troupe. But the program was not destined to last long. During the 1977-78 season Williams appeared, in addition, on the short-lived *Richard Pryor Show* and on *America 2-Night*, a "surreal talk show" with Martin Mull, which also folded after a brief period.

Williams' major break came when Garry Marshall, the producer of ABC-TV's popular situation comedy *Happy Days*, decided on an episode featuring an extraterrestrial alien from the planet Ork, who lands in Milwaukee in the 1950's. After veteran comedians Jonathan Winters and Dom De Luise turned down the role, some fifty actors, including Williams, appeared at an open audition. Recalling his interview with Williams, director Jerry Paris told Aljean Harmetz of the New York *Times* (December 28, 1978): "I asked if he could sit a little differently, the way an alien might. Immediately he sat on his head." Hired on the recommendation of Harvey Lembeck, who considered him the "hottest comic" in the Hollywood comedy workshop that he headed, Williams appeared in the *Happy Days* episode in February 1978 and even upstaged Henry Winkler, who stars in the show as the famous "Fonz." Mail response was so phenomenal that ABC authorized Marshall to create a spinoff series.

The new show, *Mork and Mindy,* which had its première in mid-September 1978, was an instant hit. It features Williams as Mork, a charmingly wacky Orkian visitor to Boulder, Colorado befriended by a twenty-one-year-old girl, played by Pam Dawber, who acts as his foil. Mork, an affable innocent baffled by earth habits, eats plastic, gets drunk on cream soda, ingests water through his index finger, falls in love with department store dummies, talks to eggs and potted plants, and wears his watch on his ankle. He speaks a peculiar English sprinkled with such Orkian expressions as "na-noo, na-noo" (hello), "grebble," "shazbot," and "nimnul." Since reaching seventh place in the Nielsen ratings within two weeks of its première, the show has been consistently among the top ten and was often in the number one spot on the charts. By March 1979 it averaged an estimated 60,000,000 viewers per week. Children throughout the United States were soon mimicking Mork's Orkian gibberish and buying Mork posters and buttons.

Critics credited the program's success almost exclusively to Williams. Reviewing it for *TV Guide* (November 18, 1978), Robert MacKenzie wrote: "If Williams' wild talents are at all repressible, the series would sink like an iron duck." In the *Saturday Review* (March 31, 1978) Karl Meyer said *Mork and Mindy* was based on the same "trash formula" as other mediocre comedy shows, but he praised Williams' performance as a "triumph of Mork over medium." Producer Marshall, while conceding that the show was "silly and crazy," noted that "Robin transcends the premise." According to director Howard Storm, the series "is really 'The Robin Williams Show'" and the other performers were chosen for their ability to respond to Williams. Presented in December 1978 with the Hollywood Women's Press Club's annual Golden Apple award as the "male discovery of the year," Williams has also earned a Golden Globe and a People's Choice Award.

One of the few television actors permitted to ad-lib, Williams presents what the reviewer for *Time* (October 2, 1978) described as a "pastiche of mime, light-speed improvisation and complex clowning." At a breathless pace and with wild unpredictability, he lets the audience in on every thought that races through his mind while offering a rapid-fire repertoire of eerie vocal effects, rubber-faced expressions, and physical routines. Director Howard Storm, as quoted in the New York *Times* (December 28, 1978), said that his main task in dealing with this manic talent is "to make sure Robin doesn't go so far off the wall that only seven people in the audience understand what he's doing."

Despite the unusual freedom granted Williams, he is concerned that the limitations imposed by a television program may erode his creativity. His performances as a stand-up comedian before he became a television star were distinguished by the wide range of characterizations he performed, but on *Mork and Mindy* he is confined to one role. He hopes that his five-year contract to play Mork—at $15,000 per episode, increased to $30,000 for the 1979-80 season—will not be too confining. Chafing at the prospect of becoming merely another "situation comedy comedian," he told Kenneth Turan of *Rolling Stone* (November 2, 1978): "I see me at fifty on the *Hollywood Squares* or some game show, 'Celebrity Underwater Dog.'. . . TV eats you alive."

To avoid getting into a situation comedy rut, Williams treats his television series as only a day job and on Friday and Saturday nights works without remuneration at such Los Angeles nightclubs as the Comedy Store, Off the Wall, and the Improvisation, where he gives live performances to keep his skills well-honed and to develop new material. To satisfy his television fans, Williams usually starts his nightclub act with a two-minute Mork sketch. But soon he proves he can do much more, becoming what Suzy Kalter of *Family Weekly* (February 25, 1979) called "a running, ranting, raving dervish," moving from character to character with appropriate changes in voice and facial expression.

Williams, who never does the same show twice, has been working on some of his characters for a considerable time. The most developed personality is Grandpa Funk, a battered, wizened old geezer based on a real-life San Francisco street character who, Williams explains, "survived because he's so crazy." Other regulars include Andrew, the six-year-old child psychologist, a spastic French waiter at the Chez Chuck, the Reverend Earnest Sincerely, the blues singer Benign Neglect, and the Russian comic Nicky Lenin. Among his favorite impersonations of celebrities are those of actor Peter Lorre and of the ghost of Albert Einstein. In seconds-long bits he gives impressions of Jacques Cousteau speaking for Union Oil, of Laurence Olivier doing a commercial for Ripple wine, of Bette Davis as the Hunchback of Notre Dame, or of Groucho Marx explaining the ideas of Karl Marx. In other routines he does takeoffs on Shakespeare, dances in his ballet "Death of a Sperm," or provides the sound effects for the latest (imaginary) Japanese science fiction movie "Attack of the Killer Vibrators." Toward the end of a performance he sometimes talks seriously about comedy and explains his anarchistic nightclub style. "You're only given a little spark of madness," he is quoted by Bob Abel of *Cue* (February 16, 1979) as advising his audience. "You mustn't lose that madness."

Although he has turned down a bid to appear on the *Tonight Show* and has rejected many game show and other personal appearance requests, Williams is beginning to expand his activities into new areas. His first LP album, *Reality . . . What a Concept* (Casablanca, 1979), has gone "platinum," selling over a million copies. With a friend, Williams has been writing the screenplay for a film in which he is to play several roles and which he likens to one of Woody Allen's "early-early movies." In 1980 he is scheduled to star as the famous cartoon character in the movie *Popeye*, written by Jules Feiffer and to be directed by Robert Altman. One of his nightclub shows has been taped and presented as a special entitled *Robin Williams: Off the Wall* to cable television viewers on Home Box Office. After completing a six-day engagement at the Copacabana in New York City in April 1979, Williams was scheduled to go on a national tour.

Williams has been compared by various critics to Sid Caesar, Danny Kaye, Jonathan Winters, Jerry Lewis, Buster Keaton, Charlie Chaplin, Marcel Marceau, all of the Marx Brothers, and such contemporaries as Steve Martin and John Belushi. According to Bruce Blackwell, writing in the Westchester County *Herald Statesman* (January 14, 1979) he "has the precise comic timing of a Jack Benny, the facial expressions of a Dick Van Dyke, the body control of a Fred Astaire or Ben Vereen, and the vocal dexterity of a Mel Blanc."

As is the case with many comedians, Williams is basically shy in private life in contrast to his extroverted public personality. What distinguishes him, Howard Storm has observed, is that "most comedians protect themselves offstage by brashness. He doesn't." That is probably because his humor does not spring from insecurity or anger. Rather, as Sue Ellen Jares of *People* suggests, it is a product of his "survival mechanism—a reflective, nonneurotic, intelligent calm." Although Williams has a reputation for originality and spontaneity, he has on occasion been accused by fellow comics of "borrowing" material, a tendency that he attributes to his "sponge mind," which enables him to absorb material without always remembering its source. Williams' career is managed by the firm of Rollins and Joffe, which also represents Woody Allen.

Robin Williams, who is lean, sandy-haired, and sharp-featured, stands at five feet eight inches and weighs 135 pounds. A vegetarian and nonsmoker, he keeps trim through dance exercises, roller-skating, practising yoga, and jogging three or four miles a day. He also enjoys chess, backgammon, skiing, surfing, and driving around Los Angeles. Among his favorite authors are J. P. Donleavy and Isaac Bashevis Singer. A science fiction fan, he sometimes amuses himself by playing with Japanese-made toy robots. He has some fluency in French, Spanish and German and has recently been studying Mandarin Chinese. Given to eccentricities, such as buying his clothes at a second-hand store called Aardvark's Odd Ark in West Hollywood, he sometimes wears the same outfit of Chaplinesque baggy pants, loud shirts and rainbow suspenders both in performance and in private. Robin Williams and Valerie Velardi were married in June 1978. They live in an eight-room house in Topanga Canyon, west of Los Angeles, with a parrot, a malamute named Sam, some chickens, and an iguana. They try to continue the casual lifestyle they prefer, even though Williams' stardom makes that increasingly difficult.

References: N Y Times C p13 D 28 '78 por; Newsweek 93:66 My 7 '79 por; People 10:42 + O 30 '78 pors, 12:61+O 29 '79 pors; Rolling Stone p14 N 2 '78 por; Time 112:86 O 2 '78 por; TV Guide 26:12 + O 28 '78 por

---

Wilson, Edward O(sborne)

June 10, 1929- Biologist; educator. Address: b. Museum of Comparative Zoology, Harvard University, Cambridge, Mass. 02138; h. 9 Foster Rd., Lexington, Mass. 02173

With the publication in 1975 of *Sociobiology: The New Synthesis*, the Harvard biologist Edward O. Wilson gave decisive shape to a discipline that by extending population biology and evolutionary theory to the social structure of all organisms, including human beings, he believed would have a significant impact on sociology and psychology. Some members of the academic community resented, and some preferred to belittle or ignore, the intrusion of the world's foremost authority on ants into the social sciences. Others charged him with encouraging racism, and still others opposed him in the perennial nature-nurture, heredity-environment controversy that the book had rekindled with its proposition that human behavior is not the result of cultural influence alone, but rather the product of the interplay between cultural and genetic forces.

The awarding of the Pulitzer Prize in nonfiction in 1979 to *On Human Nature* was therefore for Wilson a vindication and an affirmation of the importance of sociobiology in understanding the character of humanity and in projecting the future of mankind. *On Human Nature* is the third volume of an unintended

Edward O. Wilson

trilogy that began in 1971 with *The Insect Societies*. Far less technical than the two books that preceded it, Wilson's "speculative essay" combines a crusading spirit toward the dissemination of the scientific attitude with an ability to convey ideas through a clear, reasoned, and graceful style of writing. Wilson is the Frank B. Baird Jr. Professor of Science at Harvard and curator of entomology of the university's Museum of Comparative Zoology.

Edward Osborn Wilson was born in Birmingham, Alabama on June 10, 1929, the only child of Inez (Freeman) and Edward Osborne Wilson. On his mother's side he is descended from farmers in northern Alabama and on his father's side, from shipowners and river pilots in Mobile, Alabama. His father's work, as an accountant with the Rural Electrification Administration, made family life somewhat peripatetic, so that Wilson had to acquire his early education in public schools in Washington, D.C., Florida, Georgia, and Alabama.

One of the firmly entrenched biological predispositions that Wilson finds in human beings is biophilia, a love for other forms of life—animals and plants in all their diversity. His own fascination with the natural environment—an interest encouraged by his teachers as well as his parents—emerged in boyhood and was nurtured by reading the *National Geographic Magazine* and by paying regular visits to the National Zoo and Smithsonian Institution during the two years, from the ages of nine to eleven, that he lived in Washington. Having made up his mind to become an entomologist, in adolescence he took advantage of the abundant resources of rural Florida and Alabama to collect and study insects.

During his senior year at Decatur Senior High School, in Alabama in 1946, Wilson decided that the social insect in which he would specialize would be the ant, and during his senior year at the University of Alabama, in 1949, he made his first contribution to science, with a report on the fire ant. His survey, on which he worked as a biology major in college and as an entomologist with the Alabama State Department of Conservation, was the first thorough study ever conducted on the *Solenopeis invicta,* an imported insect that was becoming a pest in the Southeast. After he had obtained his B.S. degree in 1949, he continued his investigation of the fire ant, while earning his M.S. degree in 1950, also from the University of Alabama, and engaging in graduate work in 1950-51 at the University of Tennessee.

Then as a graduate student in biology at Harvard University, Wilson made several contributions to the so-called "new systematics," which combined principles of evolutionary theory and methodology of scientific classification. He collaborated with William L. Brown in 1953 in writing an evaluation of the subspecies concept in animal taxonomy. In 1955, the year in which he was awarded his Ph.D. degree from Harvard, he completed a taxonomic analysis of the ant genus *Lasius,* the most exhaustive study of its kind on social insects that had thus far been undertaken. On completion of a three-year term in 1956 as a junior fellow of Harvard's Society of Fellows, Wilson joined the university's faculty as assistant professor of biology. He advanced to associate professor of zoology in 1958, professor of zoology in 1964, and Frank B. Baird Jr. Professor of Science in 1976. Since 1973 he has also held the position of curator of entomology of Harvard's Museum of Comparative Zoology.

Again in collaboration with W. L. Brown, in 1956 Wilson developed the seminal concept of what he termed "character displacement," an evolutionary process that increases the genetic differences between two closely related species first coming into contact. While involved in theoretical work in classification and speciation, he took part in field expeditions that extended his research to biogeography: in the Windward Islands and Mexico in 1953, New Caledonia in 1954, and Australia and New Guinea in 1955. His efforts in revising the classification of ants on the South Pacific islands led to his discovery and development, from 1959 to 1961, of the taxon cycle: the dispersal of ant species through New Guinea and other islands by adaptation to marginal habitats and the subsequent advance into more favorable habitats where distribution decreases at the same time that splitting results in new species. The taxon cycle was later shown to occur in other organisms.

Another major discovery that Wilson made in the late 1950's was that ants communicate chiefly by means of chemical substances known as pheromones. In later research and analysis he developed, together with William H. Bossert, the first comprehensive theory of pheromone transmission and communication. In his investigation of another aspect of ant phenomena, the caste system, Wilson had devised new techniques in 1953 for analyzing the evolution of castes. Broadening his study to caste systems in social insects generally, in 1968 he published a theoretical paper on ergonomics and in 1978, jointly with George F. Oster, the book *Caste and Ecology in the Social Insects* (Princeton Univ. Press).

Meanwhile, a correspondence that Wilson had perceived in the course of research in the South Pacific archipelago between an island's area and the number of its species encouraged him to develop the first species equilibrium theory. In collaboration with Robert H. MacArthur, he presented that theory in an article in 1963 and in *The Theory of Island Biogeography* (Princeton Univ. Press) in 1967. Linking for the first time population ecology with biogeography, their quantitative theory indicated that species survival is promoted more effectively by a group of interconnected large reserves than by separated small reserves and has had important practical application in conservation planning. To test his proposition that a given area can accommodate only a fixed number of species, in 1969 Wilson took part with D. S. Simberloff in an experiment on small mangrove islands off the coast of Florida. Their demonstration involved methods of removing certain species from the area and studying under controlled conditions the recolonization by other fauna.

Drawing on his own research and that of other biologists, Wilson presented in *The Insect Societies* (Harvard Univ. Press, 1971) a comprehensive survey of information that was endorsed in *Library Journal* (January 15, 1972) as "the most masterful synthesis of knowledge of the social insects to appear in the last half-century." His definitive work, which won much praise from scientists, not only contained detailed descriptions of insect species and their societies, but related its enormous accumulation of factual data to basic concepts in evolution, ecology, and population biology. In a concluding chapter, "The Prospect for a Unified Sociobiology," he suggested, "The principal goal of a general theory of sociobiology should be the ability to predict features of social organization from a knowledge of . . . population parameters combined with information on the behavioral constraints imposed by the genetic constitution of the species. . . . It will apply to both termite colonies and troops of rhesus macaques."

The challenge so greatly intrigued Wilson that extending the approach he had used in studying insects to the social behavior of other organisms, both invertebrates and vertebrates, he completed in 1975 another monumental book, *Sociobiology: The New Synthesis* (Har-

vard Univ. Press). He defined sociobiology as "the systematic study of the biological basis of all social behavior," and he argued that patterns of social behavior are, like physical traits, part of the organism's genetic makeup and evolved in a way to improve chances for preservation of the species. One of Wilson's more startling assertions concerned the evolution through natural selection of the trait of altruism, which has been observed in many animal species. He explained that an individual sacrifices itself for another individual or for a group to increase the chances of survival of genes like its own: "In a Darwinist sense, the organism does not live for itself. Its primary function is not even to reproduce other organisms; it reproduces genes and serves as their temporary carrier."

Sociobiology ignited a blaze of controversy, largely because in a final chapter, "Man: From Sociobiology to Sociology," Wilson ventured the idea that the biological principles underlying the structure of societies in other animals are applicable to the social behavior of human beings. Although the book—an elegant work, splendidly illustrated—was in general exceedingly well reviewed in scientific journals, Wilson drew fire not only from those who attributed all human behavior to free will, but also from scientists like the Columbia anthropologist Marvin Harris and the Harvard biologist Richard Lewontin, who contended that cultural and environmental forces alone shape man's behavior. As reported in *Time* (August 1, 1977), "Edward Wilson has been picketed, and at Harvard, the left-wing Committee Against Racism has called sociobiology 'dangerously racist.' "

Besides endeavoring repeatedly to reassure his critics with the clarification that he saw "maybe 10 percent of human behavior as genetic and 90 percent environmental," Wilson protested the attempted suppression of a scientific theory simply because it could be distorted for political purposes. His insistence upon the freedom to study nature and to confront the implications of scientific findings, however unorthodox, contributed to his decision to write *On Human Nature* (Harvard Univ. Press, 1978), in which he followed through on an idea he had approached in his earlier book: to propose sociobiology as a means of bridging the two cultures, closing the gap so earnestly deplored by C. P. Snow. In the Preface of the third book in his trilogy Wilson told his readers, "*On Human Nature* is not a work of science; it is a work about science. . . . It examines the reciprocal impact that a truly evolutionary explanation of human behavior must have on the social sciences and humanities."

Nearly half of *On Human Nature* is devoted to exploration of genetic behavioral predisposition in the categories of aggression, sex, altruism, and religion. Shaking some of man's most cherished age-old beliefs, Wilson finds, for instance, that theoreticians of Judeo-Christian morality have misunderstood the biological function of sex, which he thinks is primarily to facilitate pair bonding and only secondarily to provide for procreation. He suggests, moreover, that "there is a strong possibility that homosexuality is normal in a biological sense, that it is a distinctive beneficent behavior that evolved as an important element of early human social organization." On another stormy issue he concludes that "modest genetic differences exist between the sexes"—differences increased by cultural forces that are not irreversible.

"The predisposition to religious belief," Wilson acknowledges in *On Human Nature*, "is the most complex and powerful force in the human mind." Of the three present-day contending mythologies, Marxism, traditional religion, and scientific materialism, he opts for scientific materialism, which has as its mythology the epic of "the evolution of the universe from the big bang of fifteen billion years ago through the origin of the elements and celestial bodies to the beginnings of life on earth." Although he accepts evidence that "the genes hold culture on a leash" and that knowledge cannot "change the ground rules of human behavior or alter the main course of history's predictable trajectory," Wilson is by no means despairing. With self-knowledge and the scientific method, he is persuaded, human beings "can hope to decide more judiciously which of the elements of human nature to cultivate and which to subvert, which to take open pleasure in and which to handle with care."

Wilson's other books include *A Primer of Population* (Sinauer, 1971), with W. H. Bossert, and *Life on Earth* (Sinauer, 1973), of which he is one of six authors. He is editor of *Ecology, Evolution, and Population Biology* (1974) and coeditor with T. Eisner of *Animal Behavior* (1975) and *The Insects* (1977), all three of which are of the Scientific American Readings series published by W. H. Freeman. His technical papers for scientific journals number about 180.

On excursions from the Harvard campus Wilson was Hitchcock Visiting Professor at the University of California at Berkeley in 1972 and gave the Messenger lectures at Cornell University in 1976. During 1977 he lectured at the University of Pennsylvania, Johns Hopkins University, Dartmouth College, and McGill University. Currently he is Tarner Lecturer at King's College, Cambridge University (1978-1981) and is serving on the advisory board of the John Simon Guggenheim Foundation (1977-1981).

Among Wilson's awards are the National Medal of Science, given to him by President Jimmy Carter in November 1977, and honorary doctorates conferred by Duke University and Grinnell College in 1978. Other tributes have come from his colleagues in several of the professional societies to which he belongs, including the Entomological Society of America and the American Institute of Biological Sciences. In 1973 he served as president of the Society for the Study of Evolution.

Edward O. Wilson was married on October 30, 1955 to Irene Kelley, a secretary and research assistant. They have one child, Catherine Irene Wilson. Years before jogging became a fad in America, Wilson had made it his favorite form of exercise. He is six feet tall, weighs 160 pounds, and has brown eyes and brown hair. A description of him in *Omni* (February 1979) as "an enthusiastic and unabashed talker" confirmed the impression he gave the large television audience that saw him debate on the *Dick Cavett Show* in 1978. In *Omni*, also, he was quoted as saying that the people he most admires are "the ones who have great goals they persevere toward over long periods of time in a controlled and fully rational way . . . particularly where they involve discipline and endurance." Intellectual courage, Wilson's own admirers might say, would be another attribute of his model.

References: Newsweek 92:118+ O 16 '78 por; Omni 1:96+ F '79 por; Time 110:54+ Ag 1 '77 por; Washington Post B p2+ My 2 '79 por; American Men and Women of Science 13th ed (1976); Calder, Nigel. Spaceships of the Mind (1978); Who's Who in America, 1978-79

Wilson, Lanford (Eugene)

Apr. 13, 1937- Playwright. Address: b. Circle Repertory Company, 186 W. 4th St., New York City, N.Y. 10014; h. Box 891, Sag Harbor, N.Y. 11963

The explorative, venturesome, nonprofit productions of Off Off Broadway have made that arena an important invigorating force in American theatre. One of the first Off-Off-Broadway experimental playwrights to achieve commercial and critical success in Off-Broadway and in American regional and European theatres, Lanford Wilson has adhered to his artistic roots through the Circle Repertory Company, of which he is a founding member and a resident playwright. In plays that he has likened to the post-Warhol New Realism in the art world, Wilson uses fluid scenes that blend monologues, conversations, and direct audience address to probe spiritual and physical decay within individuals, families, segments of society, and whole cultures. His scores of plays, such as *The Rimers of Eldritch*, *The Hot l Baltimore*, and *The Mound Builders*, display "a proliferative sense of peopleness," to use Arthur Sainer's characterization of Wilson's work in *Contemporary Dramatists*, but also

Lanford Wilson

there is abundant evidence that Wilson "loves the theatre, loves the play, and over and over again he veers from the concerns of his people to the attitudes of theatrical frolics."

Lanford Eugene Wilson was born to Ralph Eugene and Violetta Careybelle (Tate) Wilson on April 13, 1937 in Lebanon, Missouri, the locale of his recent *The Fifth of July*. Marital discord, a recurrent theme in his plays, was also part of his early life. When Lanford was five years old, his parents divorced and his mother took him with her to Springfield, Missouri, where she found a job in a garment factory. About six years later she married a farmer and the family went to live in the nearby small town of Ozark, Missouri. After he had graduated from high school in Ozark and had briefly attended Southwest Missouri State College (now University) in Springfield, in 1955-56, Wilson moved to San Diego to be with his father.

The reunion, which eventually inspired an autobiographical play, *Lemon Sky*, was unhappy: Wilson got along well with his stepmother and two young stepbrothers but not with his father, an aircraft worker. Wilson also worked, unenthusiastically, in an aircraft plant and in 1956-57 attended San Diego State College (now University). Joining some friends in a writing course there, he discovered his ability to create strong, naturalistic dialogue through writing short stories. After a year in California, Wilson left for Chicago, where he lived for almost six years. While working as an apprentice artist in an advertising agency and studying in 1957-58 at the University of Chicago's downtown extension, he wrote short stories that were rejected by all the magazines to which he submitted them. In Chicago, also,

his growing excitement over the theatre took the forms of acting in plays, making tentative attempts at playwriting, and building up the courage to try his talent on the New York City stage.

Arriving in Manhattan around the summer of 1962, Wilson saw and disliked every play on Broadway. More to his taste were the non-commercial, experimental works that were then generating the Off-Off-Broadway movement. Areas set aside to serve as small stages in coffeehouses, lofts, storefronts, basements, and church naves all over Manhattan became the workshops and showcases for ensembles of performing artists. "No commercial media could ever hope for OOB's tremendous range: experimental, classical, avant-garde, ethnic, political, musical. Off off is the source—the lifeline—of American theater," Marion Fredi Towbin wrote in an account of the OOB season for *The Best Plays of 1975-1976*.

Wilson's first produced play, *So Long at the Fair*, opened at Off Off Broadway's Caffe Cino in August 1963. A one-act effort about a young man who has come to New York to find his place in the arts and a young woman who has come to his room to seduce him, the play was termed a "tense little comedy" by the *Village Voice*'s Michael Smith, who in his review of August 29 praised the "exactness and inner logic" of Wilson's dialogue, "which at its best springs half-thought-out from the characters' lips."

One of the several jobs that Wilson had during his first years in New York was that of reservations clerk at the Hotel Americana. Between phone calls he wrote a play whose protagonist he modeled largely on the hotel's desk clerk. The title character, Leslie Bright, in *The Madness of Lady Bright*, is a lonely middle-aged homosexual going mad as he contemplates his past with nostalgia and his future with terror. *Lady Bright* was first produced in May 1964 at Caffe Cino, where the following August *Home Free!*, a study of the relationship between a brother and his incestuously impregnated sister, also had its premiere. Other one-act plays opening at Caffe Cino, in 1965 and 1966, included *Ludlow Fair*, about two lonely young women whose dreams of romance are repeatedly unfulfilled; *This Is the Rill Speaking*, in which an impression of life in a small town in the Ozarks is created by six performers playing seventeen characters; *Days Ahead*, a monologue by a middle-aged man who talks to the unseen wife he abandoned twenty years previously for fear that the future would destroy their perfect love; and *Wandering*, in which three characters recite and mime the life history of one of them in a style reminiscent of Ionesco. *Sand Castle*, a one-act play about conflicts within a San Diego family, premiered in August 1965 at another early Off-Off-Broadway landmark, Cafe La Mama, founded by Ellen Stewart three years earlier.

When Wilson was learning his craft, as he told the columnist Sidney Fields, one of the exercises he had set for himself was writing down the speech patterns of five persons talking simultaneously or including in a single scene everything they did in the course of an evening. His technique of layered dialogue and action, which at its best creates a sense of real life unfolding spontaneously on the stage, was developed in his one-act plays and refined in his first two full-length plays, which had their premieres at Cafe La Mama: *Balm in Gilead* in January 1965 and *The Rimers of Eldritch* in July 1966. The former creates an almost documentary-style picture of New York low life: whores, hustlers, and junkies whose lives cross in an all-night cafe. *Rimers*, about a dying Midwestern town, discloses the inhabitants' concerns as the action moves back and forth in time around a murder trial.

In only three years, from 1963 to 1966, the quantity and quality of Lanford Wilson's work brought him recognition as one of America's most promising playwrights. *Balm in Gilead* was the first full-length original play produced Off Off Broadway and was so successful that Ellen Stewart had to stand outside La Mama every night of its run to persuade the fire marshal not to close the overcrowded theatre. *The Madness of Lady Bright, Home Free!, Ludlow Fair, This Is the Rill Speaking*, and *The Rimers of Eldritch* all received Off-Broadway productions between 1965 and 1967, and *Rimers* won the Vernon Rice-Drama Desk Award as Best Off-Broadway Play of 1967.

Further indications of Wilson's widening acclaim were a Rockefeller grant for playwriting in 1967 and an American Broadcasting Company fellowship in motion picture writing at Yale for 1968. His plays, moreover, enjoyed productions in several European countries as well as in American regional theatres. *The Gingham Dog*, a straightforward, four-character drama about the marital breakup of a white lawyer and a black social worker, was first performed in September 1968 at the Washington (D.C.) Theatre Club, which also housed the opening in March 1970 of *Serenading Louie*. In that four-character drama about the collapse of two marriages, Wilson employed simultaneous dialogue and action and shifts between present and past to create a sense of tension mounting to hysteria in the characters' lives. Those techniques also characterize *Lemon Sky*, Wilson's play about his unhappy reunion with his father, which he considers his real "first play" because he had begun writing it ten years earlier. *Lemon Sky* opened at the Buffalo Arena Stage in March 1970 and when it played later in a Los Angeles theatre, won the hearty approval of Wilson's father, with whom he had long since been reconciled.

Wilson had his first Broadway experience when *The Gingham Dog*, starring George Grizzard and Diana Sands, opened to generally unfavorable reviews and closed after only five performances at the John Golden Theatre in April 1969. *Lemon Sky* was similarly received and lasted only sixteen performances in the Off-Broadway Playhouse Theatre in May 1970, although Clive Barnes had concluded his generally approving review in the New York *Times* (May 18, 1970) with the endorsement: "On many levels *Lemon Sky* is a play very well worth seeing. It has the immediacy of the way we live, and something of the smooth-spoken hysteria."

In "the theatre of participation," as Wilson has called the Off-Off-Broadway community, he had been accustomed as a playwright to working closely with actors, directors, and stage designers and technicians. His disappointment in the way his plays were treated in commercial productions contributed at least in part to a writer's block that developed after the completion of *Lemon Sky*. With his Off-Off-Broadway colleagues Marshall W. Mason, Tanya Berezin, and Rob Thirkield, in 1969 Wilson had founded the Circle Repertory Company, whose first stage was in a loft at Eighty-third Street and Broadway.

For a year and a half, however, Wilson, who became the company's resident playwright in 1970, was unable to write plays. When the Circle decided to mount two of his one-act plays not yet produced in New York, Wilson was inspired to round out the bill with a third, *The Family Continues*, an acting improvisation exercise. That play was first performed in May 1972 along with *The Great Nebula in Orion*, about a bittersweet reunion of two Bryn Mawr friends, and *Ikke, Ikke, Nye, Nye, Nye*, a farce about a would-be vamp and a shy man who is secretly a telephone heavy breather.

Full recovery from his writing slump became apparent with a play that Wilson based on his observations of tenants in run-down hotels in Chicago and New York, *The Hot l Baltimore*, which he wrote on a Guggenheim fellowship. That Saroyanesque drama featured a gallery of social outcasts living in a condemned Baltimore hotel and facing their uncertain futures with as much bravado as they can manage. Tailored for the considerable talents of the Circle performers, *The Hot l Baltimore* was staged for its premiere in January 1973 by the company's artistic director, Marshall W. Mason, Wilson's foremost interpreter ever since they had worked together at Cafe La Mama. "Wilson's drama derives its strength from the integrity and compassion invested in its human landscape," Marilyn Stasio wrote in *Cue* (March 3, 1973). "And from the resonance of its purely American voice. This is the most indelible play of the year." *The Hot l Baltimore* won the New York Drama Critics Circle and Obie awards for best play of the 1972-73 season, and Wilson received the Outer Critics Circle John Gassner Award as most promising playwright of the year. The production was transferred in March

1973 to Off-Broadway's Circle in the Square theatre, where it ran for 1,166 performances

Later, for production by the Circle Repertory Company, which moved to a theatre near Sheridan Square in Greenwich Village in 1974, Wilson wrote the Obie-winning *The Mound Builders* (1975), in which archaeologists exploring a vanished Indian culture conflict with a landowner who wants the site commercially developed; *Brontosaurus* (1977), a one-act play about a flamboyant antique dealer's vain efforts to communicate her zest for life and culture to her taciturn young nephew; and *The Fifth of July* (1978), a Chekhovian study in which Berkeley radicals of the 1960's mourn their lost ideals and passions in the post-Vietnam era. The protagonists of *The Fifth of July* appear again, as they were thirty years earlier on the same Missouri farm, in *Talley's Folly*, which closed the Circle Repertory Company's tenth anniversary season in the spring of 1979 and opened the Mark Taper Forum's 1979-80 season in Los Angeles the following August.

Even though Wilson has been criticized for his loose narrative structures, sometimes clichéd characters, and occasionally heavy-handed symbolism, most critics have agreed that he is a master of naturalistic dialogue that attains poetic dimension. Of *The Mound Builders*, Martin Gottfried wrote in the New York Post (February 10, 1975), "The dialogue is so smooth and idiosyncratic it just slips you inside the play's reality like an old sweater." Terry Curtis Fox in the *Village Voice* (November 7, 1977) declared that *Brontosaurus* proved again that Wilson is "a writer with an angelic gift for musical speech," and Michael Billington of the *Guardian* (June 23, 1978) called *The Fifth of July* "a rich example of poetic theatre in full bloom."

Many of Wilson's plays have been published by Hill & Wang. Working occasionally outside of the theatre, he collaborated with Tennessee Williams on a portrait of farm laborers, *The Migrants*, for CBS-TV's *Playhouse 90* in 1974, and contributed a drama about a taxi driver and an elegant jet setter, *Taxi*, to the *Hallmark Hall of Fame* in 1978. *The Sand Castle*, *This Is the Rill Speaking*, *The Rimers of Eldritch*, and *The Mound Builders* have all been given television productions, and *The Hot l Baltimore* was the basis for a short-lived ABC series in 1975. Wilson has also ventured into opera, writing the libretto to Lee Hoiby's music for Tennessee Williams' *Summer and Smoke*, which played at the New York State Theater at Lincoln Center in March 1972. But he remains devoted to the theatre, and particularly to the Circle Repertory Company, whose purpose is "to make the actions of the play become the experience of the audience." Telling Jan Hodenfield of the New York Post (May 6, 1976) that he questioned whether he would ever have an uptown audience in New York, Wilson declared

that he writes "for that decently intellectual, politically aware social realist out there that I think the intelligent half of America is."

Interviewing the slim, brown-haired playwright just after the triumphal Off-Broadway opening of *The Hot l Baltimore*, Guy Flatley wrote in the New York *Times* (April 22, 1973), "His voice is softly Midwestern, his face lean and pale and dominated by crystal blue eyes set beneath thick black brows." Wilson's recreations are gardening and reading, which he can enjoy at his renovated house in Sag Harbor, Long Island, his home away from his Greenwich Village apartment. But he has never written a word in the writing room that he made in his house, because, he has explained, he has "a kind of mild aversion to working alone that everybody at Circle Rep comes by honestly."

References: After Dark 9:43+ Mr '77, 11:38+ Je '78 por; Chicago Tribune p4+ Ag 27 '78 por; N Y Daily News p80 Ap 5 '73 por, leisure p3 Ag 19 '73 por; N Y Post p24 My 6 '76 por; N Y Times II p1+ Ap 22 '73 por, II p5 Ap 23 '78; Newsday B p13+ Ap 23 '78 por; Contemporary Authors 1st rev vols 17-20 (1976); Contemporary Dramatists (1973); Notable Names in the American Theatre (1976); The Best Plays of 1975-1976 (1976); Who's Who in the Theatre (1977)

Wilson, Robert (M.)

Oct. 4, 1941- Playwright; producer. Address: c/o Byrd Hoffman Foundation, 147 Spring St., New York City, N.Y. 10012

In the 1960's and early 1970's several experimental theatre directors won worldwide renown: England's Peter Brook, Poland's Jerzy Grotowski, and America's Judith Malina and Julian Beck, Joseph Chaikin, Richard Schechner, and Robert Wilson. Of that group, only Robert Wilson is still regularly producing works that attract adventurous theatregoers and command critical attention on an international scale. Wilson, who writes and performs in as well as directs his visually stunning, large-scale theatrical creations, rejects traditional theatrical values for a multi-sensual approach. Such works as *The Life and Times of Joseph Stalin*, *A Letter for Queen Victoria*, and *Einstein on the Beach* defy categorization and are more readily experienced than understood, more clearly described than analyzed.

Writing in the New York *Times* John Gruen, the dance and drama critic, observed that Wilson's work is "neither theater, opera nor dance, but partakes of all these arts. It is a visual and aural collage, in which staged events, sometimes employing hundreds of

Robert Wilson

devoted most of his time to teaching, painting, and theatrical activities. Among other things, he built an environmental theatre sculpture of 576 telephone poles in a Loveland, Ohio wheatfield; designed sets and costumes for several Off Off Broadway plays, including the giant puppets for the original production of Jean Claude van Itallie's trilogy, *America Hurrah;* created a dance "event" for the 1964 World's Fair and presented solo and group performances, such as *Byrdwoman* and *Alley Cats,* at his own Byrd Hoffman Studio in the SoHo district of New York City and at other avant-garde theatres.

At about that time, Wilson stopped painting because, as he put it, "the images in my head were so much richer than what I could get on the canvas. . . . What I stopped doing on canvas I started doing on stage." As his visual arts background inspired him to create moving paintings onstage, so his body awareness classes led him to emphasize nonverbal communication. His early works were mostly silent, but he gradually added music, vocal sounds, and snatches of speech. A third characteristic of Wilson's works—their retarded pace—developed partly from his interest in the extreme slow-motion films taken by New York psychiatrist Dan Stern. Those films revealed a world of intimate gestural communication not visible to the naked eye. In his productions, Wilson sought to disclose that world by reversing the practice of playwrights who compress time, and by exploring instead the imperceptible process of change. "Most theatre deals in speeded-up time," he explained to one interviewer. "My plays try to slow it down, to make people more aware of what happens, say, in the moment it takes to blink your eyes."

Wilson described his early theatrical ventures to David Sterritt in an interview for the *Christian Science Monitor* (May 3, 1979): "I started bringing people together from all the different communities I was working in, and started making plays with them. . . . Everyone contributed something. It was like making a dinner together—everyone did what they could do. The plays required no special gifts or talents, but used what people could do naturally. They were architecturally arranged, not literary structures. The main concern was how things were arranged in time and space." To produce the plays, Wilson established in 1969 the non-profitmaking Byrd Hoffman School for Byrds.

The King of Spain, which was given two performances at the Anderson Theatre on New York's lower East Side in January 1969, was Wilson's first large-scale work. The two-hour production, featuring forty apparently unrelated players in a Victorian sitting room, attracted little critical attention, but Molly Haskell of the *Village Voice* was struck by some of Wilson's unusual images: a runner, a black boy lighting candles, four giant furry

people, live animals, endless props and costumes, a plethora of lighting effects and verbal or musical sounds produce a seemingly unrelated series of images—scenes that float before one's eyes like dreams."

Robert M. Wilson was born to D. M. Wilson, a lawyer, and Loree Velma (Hamilton) Wilson on October 4, 1941, in Waco, Texas. (Some sources give 1944 as his year of birth.) A self-described "spaced-out kid," he was obsessed with theatre from his childhood. By the time he was twelve years old, he had written and performed scores of skits and plays in the family garage. While a student at the local public high school, he entered one of his nonverbal plays in amateur drama competition. Wilson's interest in nonverbal communication stemmed partly from his own speech difficulties, chiefly a bad stammer that was finally cured by a therapist when he was seventeen.

In the late 1950's Wilson enrolled at the University of Texas as a business administration major, but he was more interested in his painting and in the body movement classes for brain-damaged children that he taught in his spare time than in his studies. In 1962 he transferred to the Pratt Institute in Brooklyn, New York, where he studied art and architecture. There he continued to teach body awareness and movement to students of all ages and in all states of mental and physical health. Many of his students, including a deaf mute and an autistic boy, eventually became performers in his theatrical productions, which have featured largely amateur casts.

Wilson received an M.F.A. degree from Pratt in 1965. Except for the summer of 1966, which he spent in Arizona as an apprentice to the visionary architect Paolo Soleri, Wilson animal legs suspended from the flies that "walk" across the stage, and a stereotypical black mammy.

Wilson develops his motifs from play to play. Giant animal legs, a runner, and not one, but scores of mammies, plus wild animals and naked children appeared in *The Life and Times of Sigmund Freud,* a three-hour dance-oriented work given two performances at the Brooklyn Academy of Music in 1969. Writing in the *Village Voice* (November 1, 1970), avant-garde director Richard Foreman called *Freud,* which some critics had dismissed as an improvisational "happening," a "masterpiece of 'artist's theatre.' "

Following its premiere at the University of Iowa in December 1970, *Deafman Glance* was twice performed at the Brooklyn Academy of Music in February 1971 and subsequently toured Europe, where it won Wilson international critical acclaim. Developed largely through Wilson's workshop experiments with Raymond Andrews, a young deaf mute, *Deafman* was a surreal fantasy centered around Raymond's life and drawings. In his review of the play for the New York *Times* (March 7, 1971), Clive Barnes warned prospective viewers "to suspend a little disbelief" and "look at Robert Wilson on his own terms." "It is a visual show," Barnes said. "You think of Rousseau and Magritte, you remember the whole Dada ambiance, and yet also the visual primitivism of the piece. And also Mr. Wilson is salutary in pointing out that our minds are a mass of literary litter. The show seems to take Proust . . . as virtually its patron saint." *Deafman* won for Wilson the Vernon Rice Award for best director and an award from Le Syndicat de la Critique Dramatique et Musicale award as the best foreign play of 1970. A three-hour work performed in Paris in 1971 as a companion-piece, *Program Prologue Now, Overture for A Deafman,* was also highly acclaimed.

Invited by the Iranian government to stage a piece for presentation at the annual Shiraz Festival of Arts in September 1972, Wilson created *KA MOUNTAIN AND GUARdenia TERRACE, A Story about A Family and Some People Changing,* a 168-hour extravaganza in which both cast and audience were called upon to wind their way up the slopes of a mountain. Beginning with a six-hour *Overture,* which had as it centerpiece a rambling autobiographical monologue delivered by Wilson's eighty-five-year-old grandmother, *KA MOUNTAIN* touched on such universal themes as the plight of the family, youth and age, and on the peculiarly American myth of the Wild West.

Like his earlier works, *KA MOUNTAIN* featured some spectacular special effects, including a simulated volcanic eruption. Judith Scarle, who reviewed the work for the New York *Times* (November 12, 1972), was one of several perceptive critics who recognized the "thematic" and "rhythmic" connections between the seemingly disparate and disconnected actions. Like her colleague Clive Barnes, she drew parallels with art, in the works of Réné Magritte, and with literature, particularly in the novels of James Joyce.

Recapitulations of his previous works formed the first six of the seven acts of Wilson's *The Life and Times of Joseph Stalin,* a twelve-hour production that was given four all-night performances at the Brooklyn Academy of Music in December 1973. As in most of his plays, the action focuses on what he has called the "single critical moment" in a person's life when "something snapped"—in this case, the death of Stalin's wife in the fourth act. "That moment is slowed to let the audience see a stilled life—almost like a painting, to see time on many levels," he explained to Joyce Wadler in an interview for the New York *Post* (December 14, 1973). "And there are men in history who represent an era. I chose Stalin . . . because he's a man that almost everyone has heard of, so the audience arrives with an idea in common, which is sort of interesting, and because twenty years after his death, we still live in his shadow."

In attempting to analyze the visually abundant production, most critics finally resorted to mentioning a few memorable images—the singing red elephant; the runner who jogs across the stage at irregular intervals; the chorus line of mammies swaying to "The Blue Danube Waltz"; the ballet for thirty-two ostriches. John Rockwell perhaps spoke for them all when he commented on this "painfully personal, exquisitely fashioned exploration of new theatrical ideas" in an article for *High Fidelity* (April 1974): "[Wilson's] work is full of a continual flow of incident. It's just that it's focused differently from the norm. And when Wilson unleashes one of his frequent, overt *coups de théâtre,* the effect is all the more overwhelming for having emerged from the understated backdrop that preceded it. . . . This is a classic instance of a theatre not for everybody." *Stalin* was awarded an Obie special citation in 1974.

In March 1975 Wilson ventured onto Broadway with *A Letter for Queen Victoria,* which had premiered at the 1974 Spoleto Festival and subsequently toured Europe. *Letter,* Wilson's first "literary" script, explored the imperfection of language and the contradictions between conversation and action. It opened with Queen Victoria, played by Wilson's grandmother, reading a letter that one critic called "a larky parody of Victorian verbosity." Another performer, Christopher Knowles, a teenaged autistic boy, recited his own poetry, and in one much-discussed scene, somnambulistic diners, seated before a backdrop covered with the words "chitter" and "chatter," speak endless, disconnected, repetitious sentences while an unseen sniper shoots them, one by one.

Acclaimed as "the most original work in years" by the New York *Daily News*'s Robert Jones, *Letter* was, in the eyes of other reviewers, "inaccessible," less effective theatrically than earlier works, and little more than "an exceedingly private daydream." The most vitriolic notice was turned in by John Simon, the acerbic drama critic for *New York* magazine. In his diatribe for the April 7, 1975 issue, he dismissed the play as "merely tableaux vivants done to monotonous non-music and accompanied by meaningless verbalizing and gyrations." "There is nothing here that hasn't been done already by Surrealism or Dada, *lettrisme* or *spatialisme*, which rules it out as innovation," he concluded. "*Letter* is, moreover, visually barren and aurally empty, which rules it out as theatre and leaves only mindlessness." Apparently, most theatregoers agreed with Simon's assessment. Scheduled for a month's limited run at the ANTA Theater, the play closed after only twenty-two performances.

Wilson's critics have often written of being alternately bored and fascinated by his work and most viewers appear to have had similar reactions. As his reputation grew, performances of his plays often sold out, but particularly in the case of the longer works, only a few diehard members of the audience stayed until the final curtain. Two of his more popular productions—*The $ Value of Man* and *I Was Sitting on My Patio This Guy Appeared I Thought I Was Hallucinating*—were rather short by Wilsonian standards. The two-and-one-half-hour *The $ Value of Man*, a collaborative effort by Wilson and Christopher Knowles, played two weekends at the Brooklyn Academy of Music in 1975. Staged in an arena style to encourage audiences to circulate around the set, *Value* concentrated on images and vignettes parodying modern man's obsession with money and commerce. Although the small-scaled, tightly constructed *Hallucinating*, which consisted of back-to-back recitations of the same forty-five-minute monologue by Wilson and Lucinda Childs, had a very short run at the Cherry Lane Theatre in June 1977, it fared considerably better in Europe.

Wilson calls his creations operas because, as he once put it, "their construction is musical," with certain themes appearing and reappearing "like themes in music." But of all his works, only the ambitious *Einstein on the Beach* came close to being a true opera. Set to an intricate, mixed vocal and instrumental score by Philip Glass, the experimental composer, and featuring the eccentric choreography of Andrew de Groat, the work was built around such spectacular visual motifs as a life-size cardboard train belching smoke and a multicolored spacecraft. The character Einstein, like that of Stalin in Wilson's earlier play, was merely a symbol of the technological age.

After its premiere at the Avignon Festival in France in July 1976 to overwhelmingly enthusiastic critical response, *Einstein on the Beach* completed a successful European tour, then moved to the Metropolitan Opera House in New York City for two sold-out performances in November 1976. Wilson had hoped to take the elaborate production on a national tour, but he could not raise the money. Most of his productions up to that time had been subsidized by grants from foreign governments, from the Guggenheim Foundation, and from the National Endowment for the Arts, but as he explained to John Rockwell of the *New York Times* (November 26, 1978), he had tired of the continual search for patrons and would no longer accept the financial responsibility for his productions. "What we do now is say, 'Here is the script, here is the text, here is the music, here are the designs and the directions—now you do it,' " he said.

Peter Stein, the German avant-garde director, offered his theatre and the services of his company for Wilson's next project, *Death Destruction and Detroit*, which opened at Stein's Schaubühne am Halleschen Ufer theatre complex in West Berlin in February 1979. After seeing the five-and-a-half hour production, John Rockwell told his *New York Times* (March 4, 1979) readers that *Detroit* revealed a wider emotional range than any of Wilson's previous works. Rockwell interpreted the play as an illustration of "man's potential for horrific fantasizing and the countervailing power of love," but most viewers were more interested in the fantastic, otherworldly images and special effects—a smoking crater, Indians disguised as trees, an electrical storm, a fierce battle between a triceratops and a tyrannosaur. Because of financial problems, the American premiere of *Detroit* was postponed until 1980.

Wilson is both bored and annoyed by repeated questions from critics and interviewers about his plays' meanings. At one press conference in Yugoslavia in 1971, rather than submit to the usual interrogation, he repeated the word "dinosaur" over and over for hours. "The fact is, I don't really understand my own stuff," he told John Gruen, who interviewed him for a *New York Times* (March 16, 1975) profile. "Artists very seldom understand what they are doing. My work is a mystery to me, and I feel that words only confuse people about my work. I don't wish to mystify people. It's best not to say anything at all."

Once described as looking "like an Eastern prep school teacher," Robert Wilson stands six feet four inches tall and has close-cropped dark hair and dark eyes. He lives in the SoHo loft that houses the offices of the Byrd Hoffman Foundation. Totally immersed in his work, he has no known hobbies, although he occasionally attends theatre and dance performances, especially the ballets of George Balanchine. "But even there, I just like the architectural arrangement and music," he told one reporter. "I don't like the stories, and I never could get involved in Shakespeare and Tennessee Williams and all that stuff. It requires too much thinking. I just like to see a pretty picture or arrangement."

References: Christian Sci Mon p12 My 3 '79; London Observer p27 Je 4 '78 por; N Y Post p20+ N 27 '76 por; N Y Times II p3 My 8 '77 por; New Yorker 46:29+ Mr 27 '71, 50:38+ Ja 13 '75; Croyden, Margaret. Lunatics, Lovers and Poets (1974); Notable Names in the American Theatre (1976); Who's Who in America, 1978-79

Wright, James C. Jr. See Wright, Jim

Wright, Jim

Dec. 22, 1922- United States Representative from Texas. Address: b. 2459 Rayburn House Office Building, Washington, D.C. 20515

Democrats in the United States House of Representatives caught Washington political pundits off guard in December 1976 when they unexpectedly chose Jim Wright, a twelve-term Congressman from Texas, as their new Majority Leader. Wright, a moderate in a party increasingly dominated by liberals, won the narrow election largely because of his reputation as a skilled mediator and conciliator who excels in finding and guiding the Democratic consensus on national issues. According to Capitol Hill correspondents, Wright has little ambition for higher elective office. Instead, he has set his sights on attaining the House

Speakership when Thomas P. ("Tip") O'Neill Jr. retires. With the exception of Congressman Hale Boggs, who died in a plane crash in 1972, every Majority Leader in the past forty-five years has eventually become Speaker of the House.

James Claud Wright Jr. was born in Fort Worth, Texas on December 22, 1922 to James C. and Marie (Lyster) Wright. His father ran National Trades Day, Inc., a profitable small business that specialized in arranging such sales promotion gimmicks as sack races, pie-eating contests, and softball games for local merchants in the rural areas of northeastern Texas. Educated in the public schools of Dallas and Fort Worth, where he excelled as a Golden Gloves amateur boxer and as a debater, Wright enrolled at the two-year institution of Weatherford College in Weatherford, Texas, a small town west of Fort Worth, in the late 1930's. He then entered the University of Texas, concentrating on politics and economics. When the United States entered World War II in December 1941, he enlisted as a private in the United States Army Air Force. Based in Australia, he piloted a B-24 "Liberator" in dozens of air strikes against Japanese land targets. After completing the required number of missions, Wright returned to the United States and completed the remainder of his enlistment as an Army flight instructor. At the war's end, he was discharged with the rank of captain and awarded the Distinguished Flying Cross.

Returning to civilian life, Jim Wright, as he prefers to be known, worked for a time as a traveling representative for National Trades Day, Inc., and eventually established his own advertising business. Always interested in politics, he joined the local chapter of the Young Democrats and, in 1946, won election to the Texas state legislature. As one of the most liberal members of that body, he supported such then radical proposals as an anti-lynching bill, the abolition of the poll tax, the admission of blacks to the University of Texas Law School, and a lobbyist registration bill. Those positions, which were considerably to the left of those of his constituents, cost him reelection in 1949.

Later that same year, however, Wright was elected to the first of two terms as mayor of Weatherford. During his second, he also served as president of the League of Texas Municipalities, an organization representing about 600 incorporated cities and towns. But his legislative defeat and the realities of managing the affairs of a tightly knit community had a profound effect on Wright's evolving political consciousness. "It was a conservative Bible belt constituency," Texas Representative Bob Eckhardt, who served with Wright in the state legislature, explained to a reporter for the New York Times (May 7, 1977). "They demanded the whole man. The politician had to eat with them, be with them, talk with them.

[Wright] became overly cautious due to his hard fall."

In 1954 Wright decided to challenge incumbent Representative Wingate Lucas in the Democratic primary for the Twelfth Congressional District. Even without the support of the influential Fort Worth *Star-Telegram,* he piled up enough votes to beat Wingate by a comfortable margin and, after winning the November election with similar ease, took his seat in the United States House of Representatives in January 1955. Assigned to the House Public Works Committee just as it embarked on an ambitious legislative agenda of interstate highway construction, Wright repeatedly expressed his displeasure with the imprecise cost estimates of highway lobbyists. "I'm sure we've heard from everybody [on proposed highway construction] except one fellow—the average American who does most of the driving and who will pay the great bulk of the cost," Wright complained, as quoted in the New York *Herald Tribune* (April 14, 1956). A decade later, as a member of a Public Works subcommittee investigating the administration of the Interstate Highway Program, he was appalled by the extent of corruption among officials and contractors involved in the system's vast construction projects. "We have found fraud or carelessness involving right-of-way acquisitions in twenty-four states, shoddy or deliberately dishonest construction practices in twenty-one states, [and] payola accepted by highway department employees in seven states," he wrote in an article for the *Saturday Evening Post* (November 30, 1963). "The Bureau of Public Roads, a tiny agency with an enormous responsibility, has not been able to administer or police the Interstate program effectively."

Because he came from a drought-plagued region of the United States, Congressman Wright took a special interest in water conservation projects. In his book *The Coming Water Famine* (Coward-McCann, 1966), he called attention to the "harsh truth" that the United States was rapidly running out of "usable" water and suggested ways to head off the approaching water famine. Among other things, he recommended the development of an adequate national water policy, an expanded pollution abatement effort, increased research in desalination procedures, upstream land treatment projects, and the construction of long-distance water transport systems. On the House floor, Wright fought an eleven-year battle to win passage of the comprehensive Trinity River development program, which authorized the total development of that east Texas river basin for navigation, flood control, upstream soil conservation, recreation, water quality control, and fish and wildlife preservation. He also acted as floor leader for the omnibus rivers and harbors bill and for water pollution control measures.

After spending six years in the House, Wright decided to run for the United States

Senate seat left vacant by Lyndon B. Johnson's election to the Vice-Presidency in November 1960. One of seventy-three declared candidates for the post, Wright, by his own count, traveled more than 27,000 miles and made 678 speeches in the grueling four-month campaign. "During one week, I averaged eleven speeches a day in as many different localities," he recalled in an article for *Harper's* magazine (April 1967). "But it was like trying to siphon off the Gulf of Mexico with an eyedropper. For there were then 10,000,000 people in Texas; if I had worked sixteen hours a day and wasted no time, it would have taken me some twenty-eight years to talk for one minute with every citizen in the state."

Wright finished third in the special election on April 4, 1961, behind John G. Tower, a Republican, and interim Senator William A. Blakley, a conservative Democrat. According to Wright, who had voluntarily limited individual contributions to $100, both men spent "at least three times" as much as he did. Because he could not bring himself to "initiate alliances with those who could provide the wherewithal in big chunks," Wright pulled out of the Senate race in 1966 after an appeal to the voters failed to generate a sufficient financial response. Convinced that the high price of campaigning imperiled the integrity of American political institutions, he devoted considerable time on the House floor to the passage of election reform legislation and to new standards of Congressional ethics.

During his first decade in the House, Jim Wright proved to be one of the most liberal members of the Texas delegation, particularly on economic issues, but his position on civil rights, perhaps the most important domestic issue of that time, turned out to be less consistent. He was labeled a maverick because he refused to join 101 colleagues from eleven states in signing the so-called "Southern Manifesto" of 1956, a resolution criticizing the Supreme Court's 1954 desegregation decision, but he eventually fell in line with his fellow Southerners in voting against the use of federal monies for integration and against the comprehensive Civil Rights Act of 1964. It was a "nay" vote that he now regrets. He reversed his stand in the mid-1960's, approving both the Voting Rights Act of 1965 and the Civil Rights Act of 1966.

In general, Wright supported both the domestic and the foreign policies of President John F. Kennedy and, as Kennedy's "New Frontier" evolved into the "Great Society" envisioned by President Lyndon B. Johnson, Wright became an integral part of the legislative machinery that churned out laws affecting the widest range of social problems since the 1930's.

In his *You and Your Congressman* (Coward-McCann, 1965), which he himself has described as an "honest" but "not . . . completely objective" book about the United States Congress,

Wright maintains that although national considerations must take paramount priority in legislative decisions, "no member of Congress can ignore the needs, the dreams and aspirations of his own area." Because many of his constituents were employed in the aerospace industry, Representative Wright worked behind the scenes to help General Dynamics, an aircraft manufacturer based in his home district, win the multibillion-dollar contract for the production of the TFX, the experimental swept-wing fighter plane subsequently redesignated the F-111. Moreover, he urged local aerospace firms to diversify their operations so that they would be less dependent on the vagaries of defense contracts, and he promoted other government contracts for non-aerospace companies to provide additional job opportunities. Wright's grateful constituents have regularly returned him to Congress with increasingly impressive majorities. He is so popular that his seat went uncontested in primary and general elections for ten years beginning in 1964, and in recent elections, he has swamped all challengers, receiving as much as 79 percent of the votes cast.

Not surprisingly, Wright turned down all attempts to trim the defense budget and recently voted for a $4 billion increase in defense appropriations. A staunch supporter of the Vietnam war, he introduced a resolution backing President Richard Nixon's conduct of the war in 1969 and was one of only seventy-two House Democrats who voted in favor of using federal troops to evacuate South Vietnamese from Saigon before the city fell to the North Vietnamese in April 1975.

Domestically, Wright has regularly approved federal spending for social programs, particularly in health care, welfare reform, and limited urban renewal, and for education, housing, and consumer protection. A liberal on most labor-related issues, he strongly supports the Humphrey-Hawkins bill, which is designed to reduce the unemployment rate to 4 percent within five years. When that bill passed the House on March 16, 1978, Wright called it the "embodiment" of what America stands for—"not that America owes everybody a living . . . but [that] America owes every American an opportunity to earn a living." As a delegate from the largest oil-producing state, he has voted for the deregulation of natural gas prices and for increased crude oil prices, and he has resisted moves to repeal the oil depletion allowance for the major oil companies. Disagreeing with Gerald R. Ford's concept that "the only way to achieve [energy] conservation is to make the stuff so god-awful expensive that the consumer can't afford it," Wright chaired the first Democratic study group on the growing fuel shortage.

When the House Democratic Caucus convened on December 6, 1976 to choose its leaders for the upcoming Congressional session, Wright was a principal contender for the post of Majority Leader, left vacant by the election by acclamation of Tip O'Neill Jr. as Speaker of the House. His competitors were Representatives Phillip Burton, a liberal and the odds-on favorite, John J. McFall, and Richard Bolling. McFall and Bolling were eliminated on the first two ballots by the "low-man out" rule. On the final ballot Wright edged out Burton by a single vote, 148 to 147.

Describing his new role as that of "part evangelist, part parish priest, and every now and then part Old Testament prophet," Wright promised in his acceptance speech to be a "good listener" and to promote "progressive legislation that will lift this country out of the slough of recession." Wright's election surprised political analysts, many of whom were convinced that he was too conservative for the young, liberal House Democrats. In fact, Congressional Quarterly reported that in 1976, Wright had voted against the consensus of his party 61 percent of the time. (By contrast, Burton voted against the Democratic majority on only 3 percent of the issues.) After taking office as Majority Leader, however, Wright's position moderated considerably and, in the Ninety-fifth Congress, he agreed with his party on 79 percent of the roll call votes. Similarly, his ratings by political interest groups reflected his drift toward the party mainstream. In 1974 the liberal Americans for Democratic Action rated him at 33 percent and the conservative Americans for Constitutional Action at 31 percent. By 1978 his ADA rating had risen to 45 percent while his ACA rating fell to just 4 percent.

Wright's major legislative goal as Majority Leader is the development of a comprehensive energy program, including mandatory gas mileage and speed standards for automobiles and the development of alternative energy sources. Throughout his career he has vigorously fought the encroachment of one branch of government on another. He especially disliked President Jimmy Carter's complaints about the "legislative veto," which gives Congress the right to refuse to approve executive department activities and expenditures and federal regulations. The legislative veto, he said at a White House breakfast on June 21, 1978, serves as "a brake on the overzealous administrator" and on the "nonelected bureaucrats" who write "regulations that have the force and effect of law, without the inconvenience of running for Congress." House Democrats appreciated Wright's articulate and forceful defense of their positions and, in December 1978, reelected him to a second term as Majority Leader.

Jim Wright is a trim, muscular man who stands five feet eleven inches tall and has brown eyes and graying brown hair. His bristling eyebrows—his most distinctive feature—"swoop up and down like seagulls in flight" when he speaks, according to one interviewer. For recreation, he bicycles, swims, plays tennis, and paints in oils and acrylics. An unusually prolific writer for a Congressman, he has contributed articles to *Harper's*, *Coronet*, and the *Saturday Evening Post*, among other publications, and to *Congress and Conscience* (Lippincott, 1970). A third book on government, *Of Swords and Plowshares*, was published by Stafford-Lowdon in 1968. The Congressman and his wife, Betty (Hay) Wright, a former staffer for the House Public Works Committee, were married on November 12, 1972. Wright has four children—Jimmy, Virginia Sue, Patricia Kay, and Alicia Marie—from an earlier marriage to Mary Ethelyn Lemons that ended in divorce.

Reference: N Y Times p8 My 7 '77 por; *Time* 108:23+ D 20 '76; Who's Who in America, 1978-79; Who's Who in American Politics, 1977-78

Wurf, Jerry

May 18, 1919- Labor union official. Address: b. American Federation of State, County and Municipal Employees, 1625 L St. NW, Washington, D.C. 20036; h. 3846 Cathedral Ave. NW, Washington, D.C. 20016

Although he has never been a public employee himself, Jerry Wurf has become the principal spokesman for American civil servants. Since winning the presidency of the American Federation of State, County and Municipal Employees (AFSCME) in 1964, he has raised the union's membership from approximately 200,000 to slightly over 1,000,000, defended his charges against taxpayers' revolts, and withstood competition from rival unions with such skill and determination that his admirers claim he can "walk on water." As AFSCME has grown, Wurf's voice has become increasingly prominent in the AFL-CIO, but he is also a blunt and combative maverick who keeps close ties with such independent labor groups as the National Education Association and the United Automobile Workers.

Jerome Wurf was born in New York City, New York, on May 18, 1919, the son of Sigmund Wurf, a textile jobber, and Lena (Tannenbaum) Wurf. When his mother remarried following his father's death in the early 1930's, Jerry Wurf, as he prefers to be known, moved with her from the Bronx to Brooklyn, where he attended James Madison High School. Challenged by his high school English teacher to avert a failing grade by improving his communication skills, Wurf mounted local political soapboxes to hone his skills as a public speaker. He was especially active in the Young People's Socialist League, which he has since described as "the most important thing in [his] life" at that time. "I was radicalized, but not at the expense of lacking concern for the basic premises of freedom," he explained to Grover Heiman in an interview for *Nation's Business* (March 1975). "That's why Eugene Debs, the socialist leader, was a hero of mine. He never became a zealot and was never taken in by the Communists. He remained a very American man."

In deference to his mother's wish that he remain in the city, Wurf abandoned his dream of attending Tufts University in Massachusetts and enrolled instead at New York University. Forced to transfer to night school by his family's dwindling financial reserves, he received his B.A. degree in 1940 and immediately took a job as a counterman and cashier in a Brooklyn cafeteria. Dissatisfied with the working conditions, he soon organized his fellow employees into Local 448 of the Food Checkers and Cashiers Union of the Hotel and Restaurant Employees. By the mid-1940's he was recruiting members from restaurants, diners, and cafeterias in the surrounding neighborhood, prompting the Yiddish-speaking owners of those businesses to refer to him as "mal'ach hamaves," or "angel of death." When Local 448 was absorbed by a larger union, Wurf opened a restaurant of his own, but the venture failed within a few months.

While working as a labor organizer, Wurf had caught the eye of Arnold S. Zander, the veteran labor leader who had watched his union grow from a single state employees' union in Madison, Wisconsin in 1932 to the national, AFL-chartered American Federation of State, County and Municipal Employees in 1936. Zander hired Wurf in 1947 to organize an AFL union to compete with the CIO's Transport Workers Union—a task Wurf compared to "trying to melt an iceberg with a match."

Unable to make any headway against the powerful Transport Workers Union, Wurf was ready to hand in his resignation, but Zander persuaded him to try his hand at reorganizing AFSCME's troubled New York City affiliate, District Council 37.

Corruption, factionalism, defections to the Teamsters, and poor leadership had reduced District Council 37 to about 700 diehard members at the time Wurf took office. From this core he slowly rebuilt the union, primarily by recruiting laborers and nonprofessional hospital workers. Wurf achieved a major breakthrough in 1954 when Mayor Robert F. Wagner Jr., fulfilling a campaign promise, issued an executive order recognizing the right of union membership for city workers. Fifteen months later, after a one-day strike and a demonstration by 3,000 employees, Parks Commissioner Robert Moses, who had refused to recognize the union, reluctantly agreed to the first representation election. District Council 37 won another victory in 1958 when Mayor Wagner ordered the exclusive recognition in each bargaining unit of the union with majority representation. Having won equality with their organized peers in the private sector, the jubilant members of District Council 37 elected Wurf executive director of their organization in 1959.

At the national level, disapproval of Zander's administration was growing. Under his direction, AFSCME had become heavily involved in several expensive housing projects. Moreover, many rank-and-filers questioned Zander's moderate and increasingly ineffective tactics for obtaining pay raises and benefits. Wurf helped keep the disaffected members in line until a group of insurgents known as the Committee on Union Responsibility asked him to run for president in 1962. Wurf's campaign fell short that year, but two years later, in a bitterly contested election, he dislodged his mentor by a margin of only twenty-one votes. The labor movement had not seen such an upset of an incumbent since Walter Reuther took over the United Automobile Workers in 1946.

In his first few years in office, Wurf revitalized the nearly bankrupt union. To pay its AFL-CIO back dues and to get some badly needed operating money, he sold the housing projects and AFSCME's headquarters in Washington, D.C. He made peace with the Zander faction, fought off raids by competing unions, and rebuilt the organization's internal structure for maximum efficiency and growth. When he discovered that the Central Intelligence Agency routinely used AFSCME's connection with Public Services International, a caucus of public-employee unions, to pass money to anti-Communist union organizers in foreign countries, he immediately terminated the longstanding relationship. More importantly, Wurf adopted a tough negotiating stance and the union began to make rapid gains at the bargaining table. The most notable advance came in

New York, where, in the aftermath of a District Council 37 walkout, the state legislature repealed the Condon-Wadlin Act requiring the dismissal of striking public employees.

AFSCME passed its first major test in 1968. On February 12 of that year, members of the union's Memphis local, most of whom were black sanitation men, walked off their jobs to protest alleged racial discrimination. Earlier that week, supervisors had sent twenty-two black sewer maintenance workers home without pay during a rainstorm, but they had allowed whites to remain on duty. Working closely with the city's black leaders, union members staged marches and mass meetings and set up a boycott of white-owned businesses; they did not picket or interfere with garbage collection by strikebreakers. Wurf himself spent most of that spring in Memphis helping local union officials map strategy. He was eventually convicted of encouraging the stoppage in violation of a back-to-work injunction.

Despite favorable coverage by the national news media, the union gained the upper hand only after the Reverend Martin Luther King Jr., who had come to Memphis to support the strikers, was assassinated on April 4. Twelve days later, the municipal authorities agreed, among other things, to recognize the union, to grant a wage increase, and to make future promotions on the basis of seniority without regard to race. "The business community finally realized that it was paying too high a price to beat these men into the ground," Wurf said afterwards. "They've thrown everything they had at us, and they couldn't break us as long as we could make sure the men and their families would eat." He compared AFSCME's victory to the famous strikes of bygone eras, calling it "our Homestead, our Hart, Schaffner and Marx, our Flint sit-downs."

Disgruntled by the loss of as much as one-third of their purchasing power during the urban fiscal crunch of the 1970's, public employees flocked to AFSCME. Gaining members at an average rate of 1,000 a week, AFSCME was, by mid-decade, the nation's fastest growing union. In April 1978 it became the largest unit in the AFL-CIO when it absorbed a former competitor, the Civil Service Employees Association of New York. (AFSCME has since lost its top ranking to the United Food and Commercial Workers International Union.) Structurally, AFSCME is an industrial union with locals divided along craft lines. In recent years, it has aggressively recruited both women and blacks, two groups often ignored by the labor movement because of their traditional resistance to organization. Most of the rank and file (about 70 percent) are blue collar. Hospital workers compose about 20 percent of the membership, clerks and secretaries 15 percent, equipment operators and craftsmen 15 percent, professional workers and technicians 10 percent, sanitation men and custodians

10 percent, law and correction officers 10 percent, highway laborers 10 percent, food service workers 5 percent, and unclassified employees 5 percent.

Wurf was named a vice-president of the AFL-CIO in 1969, but his influence within the governing body has never been commensurate with AFSCME's numerical strength. One of the organization's sharpest internal critics, he has usually commended AFL-CIO President George Meany, whom he once described as "one of the most misunderstood men in America," although the two have differed on several major issues. In these confrontations Wurf's vote has often stood alone against those of the twenty-five or more other union chiefs on the executive council. Among other things, he opposed United States military involvement in Vietnam, which Meany strongly supported, and he openly endorsed Senator George S. McGovern in 1972 after the parent union, at Meany's instigation, took a neutral stance on the Presidential race.

Once hailed by the Reverend Ralph Abernathy as a man "with a white skin but a black soul," Wurf believes that most of the AFL-CIO's top officials have little understanding of or concern for the ethnic minorities that make up much of its membership. Moreover, he argues, the executive committee is still dominated by building trades and industrial unions while the labor force comprises mostly white collar, professional, and service workers. Too, the AFL-CIO's executives are, on the whole, elderly men—"products of an era and an environment that is no longer," in Wurf's words—who are unable to relate to or communicate with the younger workers.

The executive council of the AFL-CIO has occasionally shown its disapproval of Wurf's associations outside the giant organization and it was particularly displeased by his formation in 1972 of the Coalition of American Political Employees (CAPE). Wurf's chief ally in CAPE is the National Education Association, which competes with the AFL-CIO's American Federation of Teachers, led by Albert Shanker, one of Wurf's avowed foes. To counter CAPE, the AFL-CIO set up in 1974 its own Public Employees Department. Dismayed by the inclusion in the department of unions that do not primarily represent public employees, AFSCME joined reluctantly. When the department failed to support New York City employees during the city's financial emergency in 1975, Wurf unilaterally cut AFSCME's monthly dues from $13,000 to $2,000 and eventually pulled out entirely, saying it was "a waste of time and money."

Notwithstanding these differences, Wurf continues to profess allegiance to the AFL-CIO. "Just because you don't march to the drum doesn't mean you're disloyal, despite what some people might think," he explained to Grover Heiman. "If we disagree we're going to work to change it within the system—so long as we are able to ventilate our views." But he has steadfastly refused to squelch rumors that AFSCME, which has been stung by raids from other AFL-CIO unions, is trying to build a large federation of public employees around CAPE. Since 1975, AFSCME has joined forces with the Communications Workers of America, the Graphic Arts Union, the International Association of Machinists, the International Union of Electrical Workers, the National Education Association, the United Automobile Workers, and the United Mine Workers to form the Labor Coalition Clearing House, which competes with the AFL-CIO for influence in the Democratic party.

Entrusting the tedious details of organizing and negotiating to his aides, Wurf has increasingly devoted his attention to national labor policy. His highest priority is local governmental recognition—by Congressional mandate, if necessary of the right of public employees to bargain collectively. To date, only a handful of states has passed the necessary enabling legislation. Arguing that citizens will ultimately benefit if the union is protected from "backdoor, spoils politics," Wurf envisions bargaining on a regional or cross-jurisdictional basis. "If the clothing workers, the teamsters, restaurant employees and other private sector unions can overcome corporate and geographic barriers to multi-employer bargaining," he insisted in the interview for *Nation's Business*, "so can we."

Finding a way to avoid confrontations between public employees and local governments has been Wurf's second major goal. He holds that the right to strike is a "basic right" that "cannot be denied to a worker" and AFSCME, which brought Baltimore, Maryland to a standstill in 1974 with a widespread, fifteen-day strike, continues to use the walkout as a weapon. But he readily agrees that policemen, firemen, prison guards, and other public safety workers should be willing to submit to compulsory arbitration of disputes. Since 1972 Wurf has frequently spoken in favor of extending mandatory arbitration regulations to other public service employees. "A public employee is very conservative," he told one interviewer. "He doesn't want to strike; doesn't want to lose wages. He doesn't want to mistreat children. He doesn't want to mistreat patients." Public administrators, on the other hand, are often unwilling to accept arbitration as a means to a fair settlement. "It seems to be good politics," Wurf continued, "for inept public managers to provoke strikes that deprive taxpayers of essential services, and then run for Vice-President or something."

Pointing out that the average public employee in New York City in the mid-1970's made under $10,000 a year, Wurf bitterly denounced politicians who blamed government workers for the city's fiscal problems. "The politician who one day is calling us bandits and greedy isn't above calling us two days later and asking us to help in his campaign," he groused during the height of the fiscal crisis. "We've been dealing with this kind of inconsistency and we've been scapegoated to death." In Wurf's opinion, this problem is part of a larger pattern in which workers have been forced to absorb a disproportionately large share of inflation-induced price increases. Warning that this inequity could eventually undermine American labor's longstanding and unique willingness to act as a partner in the free enterprise economic system, he conceded that "a guy who's been collecting garbage for twenty years is no militant." "But," he added, as quoted in the Washington *Post* (September 22, 1973), "when your employer is some elected official who wants to make a show of keeping down taxes, and the worker is the guy who gets it in the neck, you do find him militant."

Wurf understands the widespread concern over the rising cost of government, but he is thankful that voters in several states have turned down what he calls the "Proposition 13 meat-ax approach to cutting taxes." Even before the passage of the California initiative in 1978, Wurf was calling for an overhaul of the tax structure. To ease the tax burden and, at the same time, maintain a high level of public services, he recommends making additional revenue sharing funds available to those localities with equitable tax structures and improving worker productivity. Because increased productivity demands "efficient and creative management" that cannot be obtained under the political patronage system, he suggests recruiting a corps of trained, professional managers who can develop and administer programs designed to boost productivity without resorting to "sweat shops or speed-ups."

Within the past few years, AFSCME has become increasingly visible in its efforts to promote the interests of public employees. The union argues its case in newspaper advertisements and catchy television commercials, and it has recently become more directly involved in political elections. Reputed to have a better political staff than some Presidential aspirants, AFSCME has its own campaigning arm: Public Employees Organized to Promote Legislative Equality (PEOPLE). "Before, we were afraid to politicize the union, and we got nowhere," Wurf has remarked, "so now we are political as hell." Numbered among President Richard Nixon's "enemies," Wurf usually supports Democratic candidates, but he can be critical of the party. For instance, after Senator McGovern's defeat in 1972, he advised Democratic party leaders to recapture those Americans who felt forgotten as the party reached out to various minority groups. And he recently attacked President Jimmy Carter's welfare reform program, charging that the jobs component of the plan is little more than a "forced work" policy that will hurt workers in private industry and especially in the public sector by providing employers with a guaranteed pool of cheap labor.

A craggy-faced man with a thatch of unruly gray hair, Jerry Wurf stands five feet nine inches tall and has a slight build. He walks with a noticeable limp, the result of a childhood bout with polio. With his booming voice and infectious laugh, Wurf is a captivating extemporaneous speaker. He has a reputation as a gruff, hot-tempered boss, but one former employee told Fred Shapiro, "Jerry enjoys having the public think he's a crude labor goon, but a lot of that is for effect. I learned about good wine and good food from Jerry, and a lot about music and literature, too. He's a guy who can be as comfortable with [the American Ambassador] at the Court of St. James's as he can with a garbage collector in Memphis."

For recreation, Wurf likes to go to the ballet, read nonfiction, and listen to classical music and jazz. He lives in a three-story brick house in the Cleveland Park section of Washington, D.C. with his wife, the former Mildred Kiefer, whom he married on November 26, 1960. Mrs. Wurf is a representative and policy coordinator for youth groups. They have two children, Nicholas and Abigail. Wurf has another daughter, Linda Susan, from an earlier marriage that ended in divorce.

References: Fortune 77:104+ Ag '68 por; Nations Bsns 63:38+ Mr '75 pors; N Y Times p33 S 3 '68 por, p7 Jl 3 '78 por; N Y Times Mag p59+ Ap 11 '76 pors; Who's Who in America, 1978-79

OBITUARIES

ALLISON, JOHN M(OORE) Apr. 7, 1905-Oct. 28, 1978 United States diplomat; American consul in Osaka at time of Pearl Harbor attack (1941); Assistant Secretary of State for Far Eastern Affairs (1952-53); Ambassador to Japan (1953-57); helped to draft Japanese peace treaty (1951) and United States-Japanese mutual defense pacts (1954-55); Ambassador to Indonesia (1957-58); later taught at University of Hawaii; died in Honolulu. See *Current Biography* (March) 1956.

Obituary
N Y Times p56 N 6 '78

ALMOND, EDWARD M(ALLORY) Dec. 12, 1892-June 11, 1979 United States Army officer; commanded ground forces in invasion of Inchon in Korean War, in 1950; was awarded Silver Star in World War I and Distinguished Service Medal and First Oak Leaf Cluster in World War II; after World War II, was chief of staff of Far East Command, under General Douglas MacArthur; was commandant of Army War College in Carlisle, Pennsylvania from 1951 to 1953, when he retired, in rank of lieutenant general; in retirement, worked in public relations; died in San Antonio, Texas. See *Current Biography* (March) 1951.

Obituary
N Y Times D p15 Je 14 '79

ANGOFF, CHARLES Apr. 22, 1902-May 3, 1979 Author; editor; joined editorial staff of American Mercury in 1925 as protégé of H. L. Mencken; managing editor (1931-34, 1943-50); taught at Fairleigh Dickinson (from 1954) and other universities; wrote some thirty books, including *H. L. Mencken: A Portrait From Memory* (1956) and series of novels about American Jewish life, beginning with *Journey to the Dawn* (1951), as well as plays, poetry, and literary criticism; died in New York City. See *Current Biography* (Yearbook) 1955.

Obituary
N Y Times A p16 My 4 '79

ARMSTRONG, GEORGE E(LLIS) Aug. 4, 1900-June 19, 1979 Physician; began thirty-year career with U.S. Army Medical Corps as assistant chief surgeon at stateside base hospitals; was chief surgeon for China-Burma-India theatre during World War II; appointed deputy surgeon general (1947) and surgeon general (1951) of U.S. Army; after retirement from military, served as vice-president for medical affairs and director of New York University's Medical Center; died at home in Santa Rosa Beach, Florida. See *Current Biography* (April) 1952.

Obituary
N Y Times B p15 Je 28 '79

BARR, JOHN A(NDREW) Sept. 10, 1908-Jan. 16, 1979 Former corporation executive; educator; served as legal counsel (1938-49) and vice-president and secretary (1949-55) of Montgomery Ward & Co., the mail order and retail house, before assuming its board chairmanship in 1955 and presidency in 1961; as company's top policy maker, rejuvenated management and expanded operations with new catalog outlets and retail stores; was dean of Northwestern University's Graduate School of Management from 1964 until retirement in 1975; died in Evanston, Illinois. See *Current Biography* (January) 1961.

Obituary
N Y Times D p15 Ja 19 '79

BEALS, CARLETON Nov. 13, 1893-June 26, 1979 Journalist; author of more than forty-five books, among them biographies, histories, travel guides, novels, and autobiographical *Glass Houses* (1938) and *The Great Circle* (1940); as crusading free-lance foreign correspondent, covered dozens of guerrilla actions and insurrections in Latin America, including Sandinistas' revolt against American occupation of Nicaragua in 1928, described in *Banana Gold* (1932), and overthrow of Cuban dictator Gerado Machado in 1932; died in Middletown, Connecticut. See *Current Biography* (June) 1941.

Obituary
N Y Times B p15 Je 28 '79

BELTRÁN (Y ESPANTOSO), PEDRO G(E-RARDO) Feb. 17, 1897-Feb. 16, 1979 Former Peruvian statesman; publisher since the 1930's of the independent Lima newspaper *La Prensa*, a civil libertarian and fiscal conservative who became prominent in agriculture, diplomacy, banking, and government; served as Ambassador to the United States (1944-46), chairman of the Central Reserve Bank of Peru (1948-50), and as Prime Minister and Minister of Finance (1959-61); died in Lima, Peru. See *Current Biography* (April) 1967.

Obituary
N Y Times p40 F 18 '79

BENNETT, JAMES V(AN BENSCHOTTEN)
Aug. 28, 1894-Nov. 19, 1978 Penologist; director of United States Justice Department's Federal Bureau of Prisons from 1937 until his retirement in 1964; championed rehabilitation rather than punishment; instituted important reforms in prison system, including job training for inmates, halfway houses, and prisons without bars or armed guards; helped to reduce recidivism rate substantially during his tenure; died in Bethesda, Maryland. See *Current Biography* (April) 1949.

Obituary
Time 112:84 D 4 '78

BENNETT, W(ILLIAM) A(NDREW) C(ECIL)
Sept. 6, 1900-Feb.23, 1979 Canadian statesman; as leader of the economically aggressive Social Credit party served as Premier of British Columbia from 1952 to 1972, setting a new record of prosperity for that province; died in Kelowna, British Columbia. See *Current Biography* (May) 1953.

Obituary
Time 113:45 Mr 12 '79

BERELSON, BERNARD (REUBEN) June 2, 1912-Sept. 25, 1979 Sociologist; educator; dean of graduate library school at University of Chicago (1947); director of behavioral sciences division of Ford Foundation (1951-57); director of Bureau of Applied Social Research at Columbia University (1961-62); director of communications research program (1962-63) and president (1968-74) of Population Council; published *Graduate Education in the United States* (1960), the product of a two-year Carnegie Corporation study; coauthor of *Voting* (1954) and *Human Behavior* (1964); died in North Tarrytown, New York. See *Current Biography* (July) 1961.

Obituary
N Y Times D p15 S 28 '79

BHUTTO, ZULFIKAR ALI Jan. 5, 1928-Apr. 4, 1979 Pakistani statesman; a wealthy landowner and lawyer who, beginning in 1957, held many government and diplomatic posts and as Foreign Minister in the early 1960's framed Pakistan's pro-China policy; heading the Pakistan People's party, assumed the Presidency in late 1971 after a disastrous war with India; later became Prime Minister while retaining ministries of foreign affairs, defense, and interior; a popular leader who built up his nation's prestige and economy; was overthrown by the army in July 1977, was later convicted of having ordered a political assassination, and was executed by hanging in Rawalpindi, Pakistan. See *Current Biography* (April) 1972.

Obituary
N Y Times A p8 Ap 5 '79

BIRNIE, WILLIAM A(LFRED) H(ART) Aug. 4, 1910-Aug. 19, 1979 Journalist, managing editor (1942-43), chief editor (1943-52), and publisher (1952-57) of *Woman's Home Companion;* chief of information for United States Embassy in West Germany (1957-60); senior editor of *Reader's Digest* from 1960 until his retirement in 1967; died at his summer home in Rockport, Massachusetts. See *Current Biography* (September) 1952.

Obituary
N Y Times p12 S 1 '79

BISHOP, ELIZABETH Feb. 8, 1911-Oct. 6, 1979 Poet; was noted for precision, elegance, and imaginative power of her verse, which often evoked images of nature; received 1956 Pulitzer Prize in poetry for her first two volumes of poems, *North & South* (1946) and *Cold Spring* (1955); also published poetry collections *Questions of Travel* (1965), *Complete Poems* (1969), and *Geography III* (1976), as well as travel book *Brazil* (1962), and English translations of Brazilian literature; taught at Harvard University (from 1970) and Massachusetts Institute of Technology (1979); died at her home in Boston. See *Current Biography* (September) 1977.

Obituary
N Y Times B p13 O 8 '79

BONNET, HENRI May 26, 1888-Oct. 25, 1978 French diplomat and scholar; member of League of Nations secretariat (1920-31); director of Institute of Intellectual Cooperation (1931-40); came to United States after fall of France (1940) and joined faculty of l'Ecole Libre des Hautes Etudes; commissioner of information in Free French provisional government (1943-44); French Ambassador to United States (1944-55); died in Paris. See *Current Biography* (February) 1945.

Obituary
Newsweek 92:117 N 6 '78

BOUMEDIENNE, HOUARI Aug. 23, 1927(?)-Dec. 27, 1978 As Algerian chief of state for thirteen years, instituted major economic and social reforms; was a leading spokesman for underdeveloped nations of Third World and for militant Arab states aligned against Israel; took part in struggles that led to Algeria's independence from France (1962), rising to rank of colonel in National Liberation Army; Minister of Defense (1962-65) and Deputy Prime Minister (1963-65) under President Ahmed Ben Bella; led army coup deposing Ben Bella (1965); President of Revolutionary Council and of Council of Ministers (1965-76); President of Algeria (from 1976); died in Algiers. See *Current Biography* (January) 1971.

Obituary
N Y Times A p1+ D 28 '78

BRIGGS, JAMES E(LBERT) May 6, 1906-Feb. 25, 1979 Retired United States Air Force officer; wartime service included tours as senior operations officer in Europe in World War II and as commander of Far East Bomber Command in Korean War; served on planning staff that created CIA in 1940's and as liaison to AEC in 1950's; was second superintendent of United States Air Force Academy (1956-59); from 1959 until retirement with rank of lieutenant-general in 1964; directed Air Training Command at Randolph Air Force Base; died in Albuquerque, New Mexico. See *Current Biography* (June) 1957.

Obituary

Albuquerque Journal A p3 F 28 '79

BROWN, GEORGE S(CRATCHLEY) Aug. 17, 1918-Dec. 5, 1978 Retired four-star United States Air Force general; fought in World War II as a bomber pilot with the Eighth Air Force in Europe; during Vietnam War served as commander of the Seventh Air Force, with jurisdiction over all Air Force operations in Southeast Asia (1968-70); was chairman of the Joint Chiefs of Staff (1974-78) under Presidents Richard Nixon, Gerald R. Ford, and Jimmy Carter; died in Washington, D.C. See *Current Biography* (October) 1975.

Obituary

N Y Times B p6 D 6 '78

BUITONI, GIOVANNI Nov. 6, 1891-Jan. 13, 1979 Italian businessman; fourth-generation head of worldwide family-owned culinary corporation comprising Buitoni pasta, sauces, and canned and frozen Italian specialties and Perugina chocolates and confections; retired from active participation in business in mid-1960's, but remained chairman of Buitoni Foods Corp., the largest of many subsidiaries of Industrie Buitoni Perugina; served as mayor of Perugia, Italy (1930-35); died in Rome, Italy. See *Current Biography* (June) 1962.

Obituary

N Y Times p28 Ja 14 '79

CAIN, HARRY P(ULLIAM) Jan. 10, 1906-Mar. 3, 1979 Former United States government official; conservative Republican Senator from Washington (1947-53); as chairman of the National Security Resources Board (1953-56) won approval of liberals by calling for reform of federal government's personnel security program to weed out subversives and denouncing Senator Joseph McCarthy's disregard for civil liberties; engaged in real estate business in Florida after 1956; died in Miami Lakes, Florida. See *Current Biography* (April) 1949.

Obituary

N Y Times p32 Mr 4 '79

CAPEHART, HOMER E(ARL) June 6, 1897-Sept. 3, 1979 United States Republican Senator from Indiana (1945-63); staunch supporter of private enterprise; a leading critic of the administrations of Presidents Franklin D. Roosevelt, Harry S. Truman, and John F. Kennedy; served as chairman of Senate Banking and Currency Committee; engaged in various business enterprises following his defeat, by Birch Bayh, in bid for fourth Senate term; died in Indianapolis. See *Current Biography* (April) 1947.

Obituary

N Y Times D p21 S 5 '79

CHAIN, ERNEST B(ORIS) June 19, 1906-Aug. 14, 1979 German-born biochemist; shared 1945 Nobel Prize for physiology and medicine with Sir Alexander Fleming and Sir Howard W. Florey, for development of penicillin; lecturer at University of Oxford (1935-48); research director at Istituto Superiore di Sanità, in Rome, Italy (1949-63); head of department of biochemistry at Imperial College of Science and Technology, University of London (from 1963); died in Ireland. See *Current Biography* (November) 1965.

Obituary

Newsweek 94:72 Ag 27 '79

CHAUVEL, JEAN (MICHEL HENRI) Apr. 10, 1897-May 31, 1979 French diplomat; headed Commissariat of Foreign Affairs in General Charles de Gaulle's Free French government at Algiers (1944); secretary general of Ministry of Foreign Affairs (1945-49); head of French delegation to United Nations (1949-52); later served as Ambassador to Switzerland, Austria, and Great Britain, and then as diplomatic adviser to French government, until his retirement in 1963; died in Paris. See *Current Biography* (October) 1950.

Obituary

N Y Times A p11 Je 1 '79

CHILDS, RICHARD (SPENCER) May 24, 1882-Sept. 26, 1978 Civic reformer; founder of "short ballot" movement, which proposed that only the most important public offices be elective; known as "father of city manager government"; author of *Short-Ballot Principles* (1911) and *Civic Victories* (1952); served as general manager of Bon Ami Company (1911-20) and in other business executive posts until his retirement in 1944. See *Current Biography* (September) 1955.

Obituary

Brooklyn Heights (New York) Press p1+ O 5 '78

CHIRICO, GIORGIO DE July 10, 1888-Nov. 20, 1978 Italian artist; exerted influence probably second only to that of Picasso on European avant-garde painting in first half of the twentieth century; over his objections, was widely regarded by art historians as "father of surrealism"; was best known for his enigmatic townscapes and other early metaphysical canvases, including "Melancholy and Mystery of a Street" and "Nostalgia of the Infinite"; died in Rome. See *Current Biography* (June) 1972.

Obituary

N Y Times B p12 N 21 '78

COE, FRED(ERICK) Dec. 23, 1914-Apr. 29, 1979 Producer; director; a major pioneer in translating theatre to the medium of television; was responsible for some 500 hour-long teleplays—including *Marty* and *Peter Pan*—during the golden age of live television drama; in the late 1940's and early 1950's was an executive producer at NBC, in charge of the *Philco-Goodyear Theatre* and the *Mr. Peepers* situation comedy; later headed *Playhouse 90* at CBS; in Hollywood, produced *The Left-Handed Gun*; on Broadway, directed *A Thousand Clowns* and produced, among other plays, *Two for the Seesaw* and *The Miracle Worker*; was filming *The Miracle Worker* for NBC at the time of his death in Los Angeles. See *Current Biography* (January) 1959.

Obituary

N Y Times D p17 My 1 '79

DAVID, DONALD K(IRK) Feb. 15, 1896-Apr. 13, 1979 Retired educator; business and foundation executive; served as head of several large companies before holding the post of dean of the Harvard School of Business Administration (1942-55), of which he had been a faculty member for many years; vice-chairman of the board of the Ford Foundation (1955-66); chairman of the Committee for Economic Development (1957-62), an organization of top businessmen and educators; died in Hyannis, Massachusetts. See *Current Biography* (February) 1948.

Obituary

N Y Times D p13 Ap 16 '79

DE ROCHEMONT, LOUIS (CLARK) Jan. 13, 1899-Dec. 23, 1978 Filmmaker; cofounder and first producer (1934-43) of *The March of Time*, which added editorials on topical issues to newsreels; produced feature film documentaries that based dramatic narrative on factual records, including *The House on 92d Street* (1945), which used FBI files, *Boomerang!* (1946), a reenactment of an actual murder case, and the biography *Martin Luther* (1953); died in Newington, New Hampshire. See *Current Biography* (November) 1949.

Obituary

N Y Times p16 D 25 '78

DÍAZ ORDAZ, GUSTAVO Mar. 12, 1911-July 15, 1979 Former President of Mexico (1964-70); held judicial and administrative posts in native state of Puebla and served in both houses of national legislature before being named Minister of the Interior (1958-63); as President, followed policy of domestic reform, but was best remembered for bloody suppression of student demonstrations in 1968; appointed Ambassador to Spain in 1977, resigned amidst controversy four months later; died at his home in Mexico City. See *Current Biography* (May) 1965.

Obituary

N Y Times D p15 Jl 17 '79

DICKINSON, EDWIN (W.) Oct. 11, 1891-Dec. 2, 1978 American artist in Romantic tradition; inspired by Old Masters as well as by modern schools; drew many of his motifs from atmosphere of Provincetown, Massachusetts; painted the uncompleted *The Fossil Hunters* (1926-28), owned by Whitney Museum, and *Ruin at Daphne* (1943-53), now at Metropolitan Museum of Art, among other distinguished works; taught at Cooper Union, Cornell University, Boston University, and other institutions; died at Cape Cod, Massachusetts. See *Current Biography* (September) 1963.

Obituary

N Y Times p44 D 3 '78

DIEFENBAKER, JOHN G(EORGE) Sept. 18, 1895-Aug. 16, 1979 Prime Minister of Canada (1957-63); lawyer; leader of Progressive Conservative party (1956-67); represented Prince Albert, Saskatchewan in Canadian House of Commons from 1940 until his death; was known as "radical Tory," flamboyant orator, unorthodox administrator, and defender of underdog; as Prime Minister, promoted development of Canada's vast natural resources and Arctic territories, sought greater independence from United States in foreign policy, maintained ties with Cuba, established trade with China, and advocated continued close relations with Great Britain; died at his home in Ottawa. See *Current Biography* (May) 1957.

Obituary

N Y Times A p16 Ag 17 '79

DUNN, JAMES CLEMENT Dec. 27, 1890-Apr. 10, 1979 Retired career diplomat; considered the model of the tactful negotiator excelling in the social graces; served as political adviser on European affairs in the State Department (1937-44); ambassador to Italy (1946-52), to France (1952-53), to Spain (1953-55), and to Brazil (1955-56); represented the United States in many post-World War II conferences; died in West Palm Beach, Florida. See *Current Biography* (May) 1943.

Obituary

N Y Times B p5 Ap 11 '79

DU VIGNEAUD, VINCENT May 18, 1901-Dec. 11, 1978 Biochemist; received 1955 Nobel Prize in chemistry for isolation and synthesis of oxytocin and vasopressin hormones; helped to promote other major developments in biochemistry, including synthesis of penicillin and discovery of structure of vitamin biotin, during tenure as professor and chairman of biochemistry department at Cornell University Medical College in New York City (1938-67); professor of chemistry at Cornell University in Ithaca (1967-75); trustee emeritus of Rockefeller University; received Lasker Award (1948), among other honors; died in White Plains, New York. See *Current Biography* (January) 1956.

Obituary

N Y Times D p23 D 12 '78

EATON, CYRUS S(TEPHEN) Dec. 27, 1883-May 9, 1979 Industrialist; financier; built up multimillion-dollar industrial empire, based in Cleveland, Ohio, including railroads, steel corporations, mining interests, and utilities; while defending capitalism, saw need for peaceful coexistence and normal trade relations between West and Communist bloc; from late 1950's on, met frequently with Communist leaders, including Soviet Premier Nikita S. Khrushchev and sponsored series of Pugwash conferences, bringing together scholars and scientists from both blocs; received Lenin Peace Prize (1960); died at his home on Acadia Farm in Northfield, Ohio. See *Current Biography* (July) 1948.

Obituary

N Y Times A p1 + My 11 '79

FAHY, CHARLES Aug. 27, 1892-Sept. 17, 1979 Jurist; as first general counsel of National Labor Relations Board (1935-40), played a key role in litigation involving New Deal labor legislation; United States Solicitor General (1941-45); alternate United States representative to United Nations General Assembly (1947-49); judge (1949-67), and then senior judge, of United States Court of Appeals for District of Columbia circuit; wrote landmark decision establishing constitutional right to travel (1955); died in Washington, D. C. See *Current Biography* (January) 1942.

Obituary

N Y Times D p23 S 20 '79

FARRELL, JAMES T(HOMAS) Feb. 27, 1904-Aug. 22, 1979 Author; drew on his youthful experience as a cocky, brawling second-generation Irish-American on Chicago's South Side to write his Studs Lonigan trilogy, a classic of the American naturalistic tradition in fiction; later published forty-nine other, much less successful books of fiction and nonfiction, including the Danny O'Neill series of novels; died of a heart attack in his apartment in Manhattan. See *Current Biography* (September) 1942.

Obituary

N Y Times B p15 Ag 23 '79

FIEDLER, ARTHUR Dec. 17, 1894-July 10, 1979 Conductor; one of America's most beloved and colorful musical personalities; as conductor of Boston Pops Orchestra for half a century (1930-79), presented a "middlebrow" repertoire, including popular and show tunes, as well as semiclassical and serious classical music, in concerts, on radio and television, and on recordings, of which some 50,000,000 copies were sold; known as a master showman with a "direct, efficient, no-nonsense" style of conducting, whose aim was "to give audiences a good time"; received Medal of Freedom (1977), among many other honors; died in relapse after recovery from surgery, at his home in Brookline, Massachusetts. See *Current Biography* (May) 1977.

Obituary

N Y Times A p1 + Jl 11 '79

FIELDS, GRACIE Jan. 9, 1898-Sept. 27, 1979 Singer; comedienne; one of Great Britain's most beloved entertainers; typified the "Lancashire Lass," with her broad accent and lively humor; appeared in music halls and revues and in such pictures as *Holy Matrimony* (1943) *Molly and Me* (1945) and was a popular entertainer of troops during World War II; made many recordings of humorous, sometimes slightly risqué songs; gave ten command performances for British royalty, beginning in 1928; was created a Dame Commander of the Order of the British Empire in 1979; died at her home on Capri. See *Current Biography* (April) 1941.

Obituary

N Y Times D p15 S 28 '79

FLANNER, JANET Mar. 13, 1892-Nov. 7, 1978 Journalist; author; as correspondent for *New Yorker* magazine for some fifty years, beginning in 1925, wrote semi-monthly "Letter From Paris" under pen-name "Genêt," vividly describing French social conditions, arts, politics, and people; also wrote profiles of celebrities, compiled in books *An American in Paris* (1940) and *Men and Monuments* (1957); won 1966 National Book Award for first volume of her two-part *Paris Journal* (1965-71); died in New York City. See *Current Biography* (May) 1943.

Obituary

N Y Times B p10 N 8 '78

FORSSMANN, WERNER (THEODOR OTTO)
Aug. 29, 1904-June 1, 1979 German surgeon; at
great personal risk, pioneered the technique
of cardiac catheterization, thus opening vast
new possibilities of heart diagnosis and therapy; in 1929, as intern, succeeded in threading
thin rubber tube through his left elbow vein
and into his heart; along with two American
surgeons who later perfected the technique,
was awarded the Nobel Prize for Medicine
and Physiology in 1956; died in Schopfheim,
West Germany. See *Current Biography* (March)
1957.

Obituary
N r Times D p23 Je 7 '79

FRANKE, WILLIAM B(IRRELL) Apr. 15, 1894-
June 30, 1979 Accountant; former United
States government official; associated with
several accountancy firms before forming own
New York City company, Franke, Hannon &
Withey, in 1929; exercised financial manage-
ment skills as Under Secretary (1954-57),
Assistant Secretary (1957-59), and Secretary
of the Navy (1959-61) in President Dwight D.
Eisenhower's Administration; worked as mem-
ber of Howard National Bank's advisory board
and as investment counselor until retirement
in April 1979; died in Rutland, Vermont. See
Current Biography (September) 1959.

Obituary
N Y Times B p11 Jl 2 '79

FRANKEL, CHARLES Dec. 13, 1917-May 10,
1979 University professor; former United States
government official; faculty member (from
1939) and Old Dominion Professor of Philosophy and Public Affairs (from 1970) at Columbia
University; served as Assistant Secretary of
State for Educational and Cultural Affairs (1965-
67) but resigned in protest against President
Lyndon B. Johnson's Vietnam war policies;
founder (1977) and president of National Humanities Center; author of *The Case for Modern Man* (1956) and other books; was killed
by intruders in his home in Bedford Hills, New
York. See *Current Biography* (April) 1966.

Obituary
N Y Times B p2 My 11 '79

GABOR, DENNIS June 5, 1900-Feb. 8, 1979
Hungarian-born scientist and inventor; had
been associated since 1949 with the Imperial
College of Science and Technology of the University of London in various posts, most recently as professor emeritus of applied physics;
staff scientist at CBS Laboratories in Stamford,
Connecticut since 1967; winner of the 1971

Nobel Prize in Physics for his invention in
1947 of holography, a lenseless technique of
three-dimensional photography, which has had
many applications in industry and science since
the invention of the laser in 1962; died in
London, England. See *Current Biography* (October) 1972.

Obituary
N Y Times p13 F 10 '79

GALLAGHER, BUELL GORDON Feb. 4, 1904-
Aug. 30, 1978 Educator; president of City College of New York (1952-69); president of the
largely black Talladega College in Alabama
(1933-43); professor of Christian ethics at
Pacific School of Religion in Berkeley, California (1944-49); consultant and assistant commissioner in the United States Office of Education (1949-52); championed academic freedom
and civil rights; was confronted by serious
racial tensions towards end of his administration at City College; died in New York City.
See *Current Biography* (May) 1953.

Obituary
N Y Times p56 N 6 '78

GARGAN, WILLIAM July 17, 1905-Feb. 16, 1979
Actor; appeared in Broadway plays for eight
years before beginning, in 1932, a film career
in which he was the leading man in *Rain*
(1932), *They Knew What They Wanted* (1940),
Miracle in the Rain (1956), and scores of other
movies; also performed on television, creating
in 1949 the title role in *Martin Kane, Private
Eye,* TV's first detective; after undergoing surgery for cancer of the larynx in 1960, devoted
himself to volunteer work for the American
Cancer Society; died of a heart attack on a
flight from New York to San Diego, California.
See *Current Biography* (January) 1969.

Obituary
Los Angeles Times I p3 F 19 '79

GOODHART, ARTHUR LEHMAN Mar. 1, 1891-
Nov. 10, 1978 Jurist, university professor;
noted authority on international law; teacher
and fellow of Cambridge University in England
(1919-31); professor of jurisprudence at Oxford University (1931-51); as master of University College (1951-63), was first American
to head a college at Oxford; edited *Law Quarterly Review*; author of *Five Jewish Lawyers
of the Common Law* (1950) and other books;
was named Knight Commander of the Order
of the British Empire (1948); died in London.
See *Current Biography* (July) 1964.

Obituary
N Y Times p38 N 11 '78

GORDON, MAX June 28, 1892-Nov. 2, 1978 Producer or coproducer of some forty-five Broadway shows, including such hits as *The Jazz Singer* (1925), *Roberta* (1933), *The Women* (1936), *My Sister Eileen* (1940), *Junior Miss* (1941), *The Doughgirls* (1942), *Born Yesterday* (1946), and *Solid Gold Cadillac* (1953); helped to pioneer development of American musical revue with such shows as *Three's a Crowd* (1930) and *The Bandwagon* (1931); also produced motion pictures, including *Abe Lincoln in Illinois* (1940), and served as general production director for NBC television; died in New York City. See *Current Biography* (October) 1943.

Obituary

Variety 292:65 + N 8 '78

GOUDSMIT, SAMUEL A(BRAHAM) July 11, 1902-Dec. 4, 1978 Physicist; codiscoverer, with George E. Uhlenbeck, of electron-spin theory (1925), while at University of Leyden in the Netherlands; during World War II, conducted radar research at Massachusetts Institute of Technology, and then headed intelligence effort, known as Alsos, to learn German progress in development of atomic bomb; taught at Michigan, Northwestern, Harvard, and other universities; editor of *Physical Review* (1951-62); senior scientist (1948-70) and physical department head (1952-60) at Brookhaven National Laboratory; died in Reno, Nevada. See *Current Biography* (October) 1954.

Obituary

N Y Times B p6 D 6 '78

GOUIN, FELIX Oct. 4, 1884-Oct. 25, 1977 French statesman; Socialist member of Chamber of Deputies before World War II; one of eighty legislators to refuse to give full powers to Marshal Henri Philippe Pétain after fall of France (1940); member of General Charles de Gaulle's Free French government in London and Algiers (1942-44); president of Consultative Assembly in Paris (1944-45); President, for six months, of provisional government of France after de Gaulle's resignation as Prime Minister (1946); retired from politics in 1958. See *Current Biography* (March) 1946.

Obituary

N Y Times B p2 O 26 '77

GRANAHAN, KATHRYN E(LIZABETH) 1896(?)-July 10, 1979 Former United States government official; was fourth woman to be named United States Treasurer (1963-66); succeeded husband, William T. Granahan, as Representative in Congress from Pennsylvania's Second Congressional District (1956-62); as chairman of postal operations subcommittee, waged war

on unsolicited mail and on sale and distribution of pornography through the mails; died in Norristown, Pennsylvania. See *Current Biography* (October) 1959.

Obituary

N Y Times A p14 Jl 13 '79

GRONCHI, GIOVANNI Sept. 10, 1887-Oct. 17, 1978 Third President of Republic of Italy (1955-62); collaborated with Don Luigi Sturzo in early Christian Democratic movement; served as undersecretary for commerce and industry (1922-23) but resigned in opposition to Fascist regime of Benito Mussolini; held several Cabinet posts after World War II; speaker of Chamber of Deputies (1948-55); died in Rome. See *Current Biography* (October) 1955.

Obituary

Herald-Statesman (Westchester County) A p24 O 18 '78

GUNDERSEN, GUNNAR Apr. 6, 1897-May 22, 1979 Physician; organization official; was president of State Medical Society of Wisconsin (1940), Wisconsin State Board of Health (1943-49), and American Medical Association (1958-59); in 1951 named to President Harry S. Truman's special commission on national health care needs and in 1952, chaired joint commission on hospital accreditation for American College of Surgeons; directed Gundersen Clinic, established by his father, and Adolf Gundersen Medical Foundation; died in LaCrosse, Wisconsin. See *Current Biography* (February) 1959.

Obituary

N Y Times p21 My 24 '79

HALL, LEONARD W(OOD) Oct. 2, 1900-June 2, 1979 Political Party official; lawyer; United States Representative from New York (1939-52); as chairman of Republican National Committee (1953-57), planned and organized President Dwight D. Eisenhower's second campaign (1956) and was key adviser to his administration; also promoted Presidential candidacies of Richard M. Nixon (1960), Barry M. Goldwater (1964), and Nelson A. Rockefeller (1968); died in Glen Cove, New York. See *Current Biography* (July) 1953.

Obituary

N Y Times B p14 Je 4 '79

HALSMAN, PHILIPPE May 2, 1906-June 25, 1979 Photographer; author; internationally known for masterful, insightful camera portraits of such notables as Albert Einstein, Winston Churchill, and Marilyn Monroe; twice elected president of American Society of Magazine Photographers (1945, 1954) and given its

Life Achievement Award in 1975; taught psychological portraiture course at New York City's New School in 1970's; wrote several books, including *Jump Book* (1959) and collaborated with surreal artist Salvador Dali on *Dali's Moustache* (1954); died in New York City. See *Current Biography* (March) 1960.

Obituary

N Y Times C p17 Je 26 '79

HARRIS, ROY Feb. 12, 1898-Oct. 1, 1979 Composer; sometimes called the "Walt Whitman of American music"; was considered one of "big five" American composers, along with Aaron Copland, Samuel Barber, Walter Piston, and William Schuman; composed some sixteen symphonies, including his well-known *Third Symphony* (1938) and his *Folksong Symphony* (1940); also wrote works for chorus, chamber orchestra, solo instruments, and ballet; served as composer in residence at California State University in Los Angeles and at other institutions; died in Santa Monica, California. See *Current Biography* (August) 1940.

Obituary

N Y Times B p19 O 4 '79

HARTNELL, NORMAN (BISHOP) June 12, 1901-June 8, 1979 Fashion designer; official dressmaker to Queen Elizabeth II; known for understated elegance of daytime apparel and distinctive and skillful use of embroidery on elaborate evening clothes; was dressmaker by appointment to royal family since 1938; chaired Incorporated Society of London Fashion Designers (1947-56); recipient of French Legion of Honor (1939) and Neiman-Marcus Award (1947); author of autobiography *Silver and Gold* (1955); knighted in 1977; died in Windsor, England. See *Current Biography* (May) 1953.

Obituary

N Y Times p11 Je 9 '79

HAWORTH, LELAND J(OHN) July 11, 1904-Mar. 5, 1979 Physicist; director of the Brookhaven National Laboratory on Long Island (1948-61), a center for research in nuclear energy for peacetime application; member of the Atomic Energy Commission (1961-63); director of the National Science Foundation (1963-69), a government agency that promotes basic research; special assistant to the president of Associated Universities, Inc. (1969-75), the operating organization for Brookhaven; died in Port Jefferson, New York. See *Current Biography* (December) 1950.

Obituary

N Y Times B p6 Mr 6 '79

HAYA DE LA TORRE, VÍCTOR RAÚL Feb. 22, 1895-Aug. 2, 1979 Peruvian political leader; one of most influential elder statesmen of Latin American democracy; founded (1924) Alianza Popular Revolucionaria Americana (APRA), which advocated overthrow of oligarchy, promoted radical but non-Communist social and economic reforms, championed the cause of Indians, and had the support of labor, peasants, and the middle class; spent years in exile and imprisonment; was candidate for Presidency of Peru in 1931, and again in 1962 and 1963, but never attained political office. See *Current Biography* (June) 1942.

Obituary

N Y Times p24 Ag 4 '79

HILL, ROBERT C(HARLES) Sept. 17, 1917-Nov. 28, 1978 United States diplomat; Ambassador to Costa Rica (1953-54), El Salvador (1954-55), Mexico (1957-61), Spain (1969-72), and Argentina (1973-77); Assistant Secretary of State for Congressional Relations (1956-57); member of New Hampshire state legislature (1961-62); chairman of Republican National Committee foreign policy task force (1965-68); died at his home in Littleton, New Hampshire. See *Current Biography* (June) 1959.

Obituary

N Y Times B p12 N 29 '78

HILTON, CONRAD N(ICHOLSON) Dec. 25, 1887-Jan. 3, 1979 Hotel executive; founder and board chairman of Hilton Hotels Corp. (1946), Hilton International Co. and Hilton-Burns Hotels Co., Inc. (1965); parlayed string of small hotels in Texas into international chain of 260 prestige hotels known for their comfort and service; established Carte Blanche credit card company; author of *Be My Guest* (1957) and *Inspirations of an Innkeeper* (1963); died in Santa Monica, Calif. See *Current Biography* (December) 1949.

Obituary

N Y Times B p5 Ja 5 '79

HITTI, PHILIP K(HURI) June 24, 1886-Dec. 24, 1978 Lebanese-born orientalist; educator; one of foremost authorities on Arab and Islamic culture in United States; professor at American University in Beirut (1919-26); faculty member (from 1926) and professor (1936-54) at Princeton University; first director of its Near Eastern Studies program (1947-54); author of *History of the Arabs* (1937), *A Short History of the Near East* (1966), the standard work in its field, and many other books; died at Princeton, New Jersey. See *Current Biography* (June) 1947.

Obituary

N Y Times D p15 D 28, '78

HOOD, CLIFFORD F(IROVED) Feb. 8, 1894-Nov. 9, 1978 Former corporation executive; was president of United States Steel Corporation from 1953 until his retirement in 1959; had previously served successively and respectively as vice-president and president of the U.S. Steel subsidiaries American Steel and Wire Company and Carnegie-Illinois Steel Corporation; died in Palm Beach, Florida. See Current Biography (April) 1953.

Obituary

N Y Times B p8 N 15 '78

HOVEYDA, AMIR ABBAS Feb. 18, 1919-Apr. 7, 1979 Iranian statesman; after fifteen years in the diplomatic service, held executive positions in the government-controlled National Iranian Oil Company (1958-64); as Prime Minister (1965-77) and Court Minister (1977-78) served as a front man for the government of Mohammed Riza Shah Pahlevi; although out of favor with the Shah at the time of the Iranian revolt that overthrew the Shah, was tried in secret by an Islamic revolutionary court and executed by a firing squad in Teheran. See Current Biography (October) 1971.

Obituary

N Y Times p1+ Ap 8 '79

HOYT, (EDWIN) PALMER Mar. 10, 1897-June 25, 1979 Newspaper publisher; worked way up from copy reader (1926) to publisher (1938-46) of Portland Oregonian; as director of domestic branch of Office of War Information (1943), disdained "pamphleteering" to give country "straight information"; took over as editor and publisher of sensational and largely regional Denver Post in 1946, transforming it into respected newspaper known for objective coverage of national and international affairs; retired in 1971; died in Denver, Colorado. See Current Biography (September) 1943.

Obituary

N Y Times B p6 Je 27 '79

IRVING, JULES Apr. 13, 1924-July 28, 1979 Theatrical producer and director; controversial artistic director of Repertory Theatre of Lincoln Center (1964-72) known for stylish productions of theatre classics as well as experimental new plays; as cofounder and director (1952-64) of San Francisco Actors Workshop, promoted works of Brecht, Beckett, and Pinter in United States; producer-director (1972-79) of television movies and miniseries, including Rich Man, Poor Man and Loose Change; died while vacationing in Reno, Nevada. See Current Biography (July) 1970.

Obituary

N Y Times B p6 Jl 31 '79

JOHN PAUL I, POPE Oct. 17, 1912-Sept. 28, 1978 Supreme Pontiff of the Roman Catholic Church; as Albino Cardinal Luciani, was Patriarch of Venice until his election as successor to Pope Paul VI on August 26, 1978; died of heart attack thirty-three days later, bringing to an end the shortest Papal reign in 375 years. See Current Biography (November) 1978.

Obituary

Newsday p1+ S 29 '78

JONES, PRESTON Apr. 7, 1936-Sept. 19, 1979 Playwright; actor; wrote A Texas Trilogy (1974), a series of three plays about the overlapping lives of ordinary citizens of a fictitious West Texas town, presented at the Dallas Theater Center, at the Kennedy Center for the Performing Arts and, with less success, on Broadway (1976); also wrote A Place on the Magdalena Flats (1976) and Remember (1979); had been working on film adaptation of A Texas Trilogy at time of his death, in Dallas. See Current Biography (February) 1977.

Obituary

N Y Times D p23 S 20 '79

JONES, RUSSELL Jan. 5, 1918-June 9, 1979 Journalist; was combat reporter for Stars and Stripes during World War II; while serving as United Press correspondent in Europe (1949-57), won Pulitzer Prize, Overseas Press Club George Polk Memorial Award, and Sigma Delta Chi Award for his coverage of 1956 Hungarian revolt; in 1960's and 1970's, served as Middle East correspondent for CBS News, then as ABC News bureau chief in Beirut, Tel Aviv, and Moscow; retired in 1977; died at his home in Vienna, Austria. See Current Biography (October) 1957.

Obituary

N Y Times D p15 Je 11 '79

JOOSS, KURT Jan. 12, 1901-May 22, 1979 German choreographer; dance director; taught style combining techniques of classical ballet and modern dance; created internationally acclaimed antiwar ballet The Green Table (1932) and other works; became director of Folkwang school in Essen in 1927 and helped to revive it in 1949, heading its dance company until his retirement in 1968; died in Heilbronn, West Germany, from injuries suffered in automobile accident. See Current Biography (July) 1976.

Obituary

N Y Times B p15 My 31 '79

KARDELJ, EDVARD Jan. 27, 1910-Feb. 10, 1979 Yugoslav statesman; was closely associated with Tito in partisan guerrilla campaign against the Axis invaders during World War II and in the establishment at the end of the war of Tito's Communist government, in which he served as Vice-President and later as Foreign Minister; as Tito's chief theoretician, provided an ideological basis for his country's independence of Soviet influence after Yugoslavia's expulsion from the Cominform and formulated policy on major foreign and domestic issues; died in Ljubljana, Yugoslavia. See *Current Biography* (December) 1949.

Obituary

N Y Times p40 F 11 '79

KELLY, EMMETT Dec. 9, 1898-Mar. 28, 1979 Clown; created Weary Willie, a ragged, sorrowful-eyed, frustrated hobo who often provoked laughter by contending with the spotlight, sometimes trying to sweep it away with a broom; performed with Ringling Bros. and Barnum & Bailey Circus (1942-56) and other circuses; his appearances also in motion pictures, including *The Greatest Show on Earth* (1952), on television shows and commercials, and in nightclub acts made him the country's best-known clown; died in Sarasota, Florida. See *Current Biography* (July) 1954.

Obituary

N Y Times D p34 Mr 29 '79

KENNEDY, STEPHEN P(ATRICK) Oct. 27, 1906-Oct. 17, 1978 Police Commissioner of New York City (1955-61); lawyer; as head of city's 23,000-member police force during administration of Mayor Robert F. Wagner, established reputation as incorruptible, at times controversial, fighter against crime; promoted reforms in crime prevention, traffic control, and conditions for police personnel; died in San Diego, California. See *Current Biography* (June) 1956.

Obituary

N Y Post p88 O 18 '78

KNOWLES, JOHN H(ILTON) May 12, 1926-Mar. 6, 1979 Physician; medical administrator; director of the Massachusetts General Hospital (1962-71); president of the Rockefeller Foundation (since 1972); a controversial figure whose criticism of some policies of the medical establishment led the American Medical Association to block his appointment in 1969 to the post of Assistant Secretary for Health and Scientific Affairs; championed individual effort and professional responsibility in considering social and economic aspects of providing improved health services; died in Boston, Massachusetts. See *Current Biography* (December) 1970.

Obituary

N Y Times A p22 Mr 7 '79

KROSS, ANNA M(OSKOWITZ) July 17, 1891-Aug. 27, 1979 Municipal government official; jurist; first woman to serve as a New York City assistant corporation counsel (1918-23), judge of the Magistrates Court (1934-54), and Commissioner of Correction (1954-66); was noted for her compassionate understanding of offenders' problems and her proposals for prevention of crime and delinquency; died in the Bronx, New York City. See *Current Biography* (November) 1945.

Obituary

N Y Times D p19 Ag 29 '79

LARSEN, ROY E(DWARD) Apr. 20, 1899-Sept. 9, 1979 Publishing executive; associated with Time, Inc., from its founding in 1922 until he retired in April 1979, in various executive posts, including vice-president (1927-39); succeeded Henry R. Luce as president (1939-60); chairman of executive committee (1960-69), and then vice-chairman; had major role in development of *March of Time* radio and news film series; publisher of *Life* magazine (1936-46); as sales chief, helped to expand circulation of *Time* magazine nearly tenfold from 1923 to 1948; died in Fairfield, Connecticut. See *Current Biography* (September) 1950.

Obituary

N Y Times C p20 S 10 '79

LASSWELL, HAROLD D(WIGHT) Feb. 13, 1902-Dec. 18, 1978 Political scientists; one of the country's foremost authorities, noted for pointing out the interrelationship of psychiatry and the social sciences; taught law and political science at the University of Chicago, Yale, City University of New York, and other universities; cochairman of the Policy Sciences Center (since 1975); author of *World Politics and Personal Security* (1935), among other books; died in New York City. See *Current Biography* (July) 1947.

Obituary

N Y Times B p4 D 20 '78

LAWRENCE, MARJORIE 1908-Jan. 13, 1979 Australian-born soprano; from time of Metropolitan Opera debut as Brünnhilde in *Die Walküre* (1935), recognized as one of truest Wagnerian interpreters; stricken with infantile paralysis in 1941, but soon returned to stage singing Venus in *Tannhäuser* and Isolde in *Tristan und Isolde* from specially designed chair; made concert appearances into 1960's while teaching at Tulane University, Southern Illinois University, and University of Arkansas; her autobiography, *Interrupted Melody* (1949), was filmed in 1955; died in Little Rock, Arkansas. See *Current Biography* (April) 1940.

Obituary

N Y Times D p9 Ja 15 '79

LITTLE, LOU(IS) Dec. 6, 1893-May 28, 1979 Football coach; was director of athletics at Georgetown University for five years before becoming head coach at Columbia University, in 1930; guided his Columbia Lions, considered hopeless underdogs, to victory over Stanford in Rose Bowl on January 1, 1934; had an unfanatical, balanced view of sports within context of whole educational process that contributed to deemphasizing of football throughout Ivy League in 1950's; retired in 1956; died in Delray Beach, Florida. See *Current Biography* (November) 1945.

Obituary

N Y Times A p19 My 30 '79

LYNEN, FEODOR (FELIX KONRAD) Apr. 6, 1911-Aug. 8, 1979 German biochemist; shared 1964 Nobel Prize for medicine and physiology with Konrad E. Bloch for research on cholesterol and fatty acid metabolism; joined University of Munich faculty in 1942; director of its Max Planck Institute for Cellular Chemistry (1954-72) and of Max Planck Institute for Biochemistry (from 1972). See *Current Biography* (June) 1967.

Obituary

N Y Times D p17 Ag 9 '79

McCLELLAN, HAROLD C(HADICK) Aug. 20, 1897-Aug. 2, 1979 Business executive; founder, president (1927-62), and board chairman (1962-66) of Old Colony Paint Company; president of National Association of Manufacturers (1953-54); assistant secretary of commerce for international affairs (1955-57); organized United States Exhibition in Moscow (1959); died in Palm Desert, California. See *Current Biography* (October) 1954.

Obituary

N Y Times p24 Ag 4 '79

McDONALD, DAVID J(OHN) Nov. 22, 1902-Aug. 8, 1979 Labor union official; one of pioneering American union leaders who built labor movement into a potent political force; protégé of Philip Murray, whom he succeeded as president of 1,200,000-member United Steelworkers of America in 1952; guided union through major negotiating sessions and 116-day steel strike (1959-60); relinquished post in 1965 after defeat by I. W. Abel; died in Palm Springs, California. See *Current Biography* (June) 1953.

Obituary

N Y Times A p12 Ag 10 '79

McINTYRE, JAMES FRANCIS (ALOYSIUS), CARDINAL June 25, 1886-July 16, 1979 Roman Catholic prelate; leading conservative in church's internal struggle over modernization of secular policies; after twenty-five years as cleric-administrator in New York archdiocese, was appointed Archbishop of Los Angeles by Pope Pius XII; as archbishop (1948-70), supervised ambitious building program to meet demands of rapidly growing congregation; elevated to Sacred College of Cardinals in 1953; died in Los Angeles, California. See *Current Biography* (February) 1953.

Obituary

N Y Times D p15 Jl 17 '79

McKENNA, F(RANCIS) E(UGENE) July 29, 1921-Nov. 10, 1978 Chemist; technical information specialist; librarian; organized (1953) and supervised (1959-67) information center of Air Reduction Company in Murray Hill, New Jersey; president (1966-67) and executive director (from 1970) of Special Libraries Association; headed its publications department and edited *Special Libraries* (from 1967); died in New York City. See *Current Biography* (May) 1966.

Obituary

Wilson Library Bulletin 53:311 D '78

McNEIL, WILFRED J(AMES) Feb. 21, 1901-Aug. 30, 1979 Retired United States Navy officer; rear admiral in Naval Reserve supply corps during World War II; fiscal director of Navy Department (1945-46); as first administrative assistant to Secretary of Defense (1947-49) and then as Assistant Secretary of Defense and comptroller (1949-59), instituted vigorous, sometimes controversial, budget-trimming policies; president of Grace Line from 1959 until his retirement in 1967; died in Bethesda, Maryland. See *Current Biography* (February) 1958.

Obituary

N Y Times B p5 Ag 31 '79

MADARIAGA (Y ROJO), SALVADOR DE July 23, 1886-Dec. 14, 1978 Author; philosopher; diplomat; one of Spain's most distinguished scholars; director of disarmament section of League of Nations (1922-27); professor of Spanish studies at Oxford University (1928-31); Ambassador to United States (1931) and to France (1932-34); Minister of Education and Justice (1934); chief delegate to League of Nations (1931-36); went into exile in England after establishment of Franco dictatorship; author of *The Genius of Spain* (1923), *Christopher Columbus* (1939), *Rise of the Spanish-American Empire* (1947), *Democracy versus Liberty?* (1958), and many other books; died at Locarno, Switzerland. See *Current Biography* (January) 1964.

Obituary

N Y Times B p4 D 15 '78

MARCUSE, HERBERT July 19, 1898-July 29, 1979 Philosopher; university professor; influenced social activists of 1960's with his neo-Marxist, elitist, libertarian, and utopian philosophy; was considered by many as "father of the New Left," a title he rejected; with Max Horkheimer and others, helped to found Institut für Sozialforschung in Frankfurt, West Germany in 1920's; immigrated to United States in 1934; taught at Columbia, Harvard, and University of California at San Diego; professor of politics and philosophy at Brandeis University (1954-65); author of *Reason and Revolution* (1941), *Eros and Civilization (1954), Soviet Marxism* (1958), and *One-Dimensional Man* (1965), among other books; died in Starnberg, West Germany. See *Current Biography* (March) 1969.

Obituary

N Y Times A p1+ Jl 31 '79

MARTIN, FLETCHER Apr. 29, 1904-May 30, 1979 Artist; was noted for realistic, down-to-earth, Depression-era paintings; under sponsorship of WPA Federal Art Project, produced such canvases as *Trouble in Frisco,* acquired by Museum of Modern Art in 1938: later turned to more abstract, decorative style; also executed woodcuts, frescoes, murals, and portraits; artist-correspondent in North Africa and Europe for *Life* magazine (1943-44); taught at University of Iowa (1940) and other institutions; died at his home in Guanajuato, Mexico. See *Current Biography* (February) 1958.

Obituary

N Y Times A p11 Je 1 '79

MASSINE, LEONIDE Aug. 8, 1895-Mar. 16, 1979 Choreographer; dancer; was called "the painter of the ballet" because he approached his work as a synthesis of the visual as well as the musical and performing arts; bridged classical tradition and modern dance in works ranging from the Cubist collaboration *Parade* (1917) to the witty, spirited *Gaieté Parisienne* (1938); was brought from Russia to Paris by impresario Serge Diaghilev in 1913; became a major contributor to modernist phase of Diaghilev's Ballets Russes; later worked in United States with Ballet Russe de Monte Carlo and his own company; died in Cologne, West Germany. See *Current Biography* (April) 1940.

Obituary

N Y Times p24 Mr 17 '79

MAUDLING, REGINALD Mar. 7, 1917-Feb. 14, 1979 British politician; first elected to Parliament in 1950; held important ministerial appointments in Conservative governments, including president of the Board of Trade (1959-61), Chancellor of the Exchequer (1962-64), and Secretary of State for Home Affairs (1970-72); during the 1960's twice narrowly lost contests for Conservative leadership; died in London, England. See *Current Biography* (May) 1960.

Obituary

N Y Times D p19 F 15 '79

MEAD, MARGARET Dec. 16, 1901-Nov. 15, 1978 One of world's foremost anthropologists; pioneered in research methods that helped to turn social anthropology into a major science; curator emeritus (from 1969) of American Museum of Natural History, with which she had been associated since 1926; taught at Fordham, Columbia, and other universities; made many expeditions, to Samoa, New Guinea, Bali, and other parts of South Pacific; author of hundreds of articles and more than a score of books, including all-time best-seller *Coming of Age in Samoa* (1928); commented on American institutions in such books as *And Keep Your Powder Dry* (1942) and *Male and Female* (1949); promoted environmentalism, women's rights, racial harmony, and other causes; died in New York City. See *Current Biography* (May) 1951.

Obituary

N Y Times A p1+ N 16 '78

MEIR, GOLDA May 3, 1898-Dec. 8, 1978 Fourth Prime Minister of Israel (1969-74); pioneer in struggles leading to creation of Jewish state; described as "one of the great women in Jewish and world history" and as a "stalwart lioness"; Israeli Minister to U.S.S.R. (1948-49); Minister of Labor and Social Insurance (1949-56); Minister of Foreign Affairs (1956-66); secretary general of Mapai party (1966-68); as Prime Minister, insisted on "secure, recognized, and agreed boundaries" as part of general peace settlement with Arab nations; resigned in wake of criticism at time of 1973 Yom Kippur war, but continued to be a leading voice in Israeli Labor party; died at Hadassah Hospital in Jerusalem. See *Current Biography* (December) 1970.

Obituary

N Y Times p1+ D 9 '78

MIKOYAN, ANASTAS I(VANOVICH) Nov. 25, 1895-Oct. 22, 1978 Soviet government and Communist party official; one of the last of the Old Bolsheviks; was responsible for Soviet commerce for nearly three decades, as People's Commissar of Trade (1926-30), and in other posts; deputy chairman of Council of People's Commissars (1937-46); first deputy chairman of Council of Ministers (1955-64); Chairman of Presidium of Supreme Soviet of U.S.S.R., or nominal chief of state (1964-65); member of Communist party Central Committee (1923-76) and of its Politburo (1935-66). See *Current Biography* (May) 1955.

Obituary

N Y Times p57 N 6 '78

MINGUS, CHARLES Apr. 22, 1922-Jan. 5, 1979 Jazz musician; composer; bandleader; played several instruments, but was a virtuoso of the bass, which he elevated from humble rhythmic chores to a proud, intricate melodic function; began playing with leading combos in the early 1940's; reached his peak with his own sextet in the mid-1960's; known as "jazz's angry man," because of his rage against dilettantism in jazz; reflected his interest, furious personality in his style, typified by his distinctive method of slightly anticipating the beat rather than playing "on" it; died in Cuernavaca, Mexico. See *Current Biography* (February) 1971.

Obituary

N Y Times B p6 Ja 9 '79

MONNET, JEAN Nov. 9, 1888-Mar. 16, 1979 French economist; international financier; multinational statesman; spiritual father of the European Economic Community (E.E.C.), viewed by him as "a stage on the way to the organized world of tomorrow"; was president of the European Coal and Steel Community, predecessor of the E.E.C., from 1952 to 1955; from World War I on, served with a succession of varied supranational agencies, from the League of Nations to the United Nations; while directing the reconstruction of France after World War II, became convinced of the necessity of unifying fragmented Europe; died at his country home west of Paris. See *Current Biography* (September) 1947.

Obituary

N Y Times p1 + Mr 17 '79

MONSARRAT, NICHOLAS (JOHN TURNEY) Mar. 22, 1910-Aug. 7, 1979 British author; won lasting fame with his World War II fictional epic *The Cruel Sea* (1951), based on his experiences in the British Navy in the North Atlantic; also wrote the novels *Think of Tomorrow* (1934), *The Tribe That Lost Its Head* (1956), and *Master Mariner: Running Proud* (1979), among other works of fiction and nonfiction; for many years was British information officer in South Africa and Canada; in later life lived on Mediterranean island of Gozo, off Malta; died in a London hospital. See *Current Biography* (Yearbook) 1950.

Obituary

N Y Times D p17 Ag 9 '79

MORTIMER, CHARLES G(REENOUGH) July 26, 1900-Dec. 25, 1978 Retired businessman; president (1954-59), chairman (1959-65), and chief executive officer (1954-65) of General Foods Corporation, with which he had begun his association in 1928; helped to develop Maxim freeze-dried coffee, Birdseye frozen vegetables, Gravy Train dog food, and other popular products; died in Orleans, Massachusetts. See *Current Biography* (November) 1955.

Obituary

N Y Times B p5 D 29 '78

MORTON, ROGERS C(LARK) B(ALLARD) Sept. 19, 1914-Apr. 19, 1979 Former government official; businessman; Republican Representative from Maryland (1963-71); Secretary of the Interior (1971-75) and Secretary of Commerce (1975-76); influential in Republican politics as the party's national chairman (1969-71) and as campaign official for Presidents Richard Nixon and Gerald R. Ford; died in Easton, Pennsylvania. See *Current Biography* (November) 1971.

Obituary

N Y Times A p17 Ap 20 '79

MOUNTBATTEN, LOUIS (FRANCIS ALBERT VICTOR NICHOLAS), LORD See Mountbatten of Burma, 1st Earl

MOUNTBATTEN OF BURMA, 1st EARL June 25, 1900-Aug. 27, 1979 British naval officer and public servant; great-grandson of Queen Victoria; as Chief of Combined Operations (1942-43), headed secret task force that planned Allied invasion of Europe, including D-Day campaign; as Supreme Allied Commander for Southeast Asia (1943-46), halted Japanese drive on Indian subcontinent and liberated Burma; last Viceroy (1947) and first Governor-General (1947-48) of India; commander in chief of Allied Forces in Mediterranean (1953-54); First Sea Lord (1955-59); Chief of Defense Staff, from 1959 until his retirement, as admiral of fleet, in 1965; killed on his yacht off Mullaghmore, Ireland, in explosion for which members of Irish Republican Army claimed responsibility. See *Current Biography* (June) 1942.

Obituary

N Y Times A p10 Ag 28 '79

MUIR, MALCOLM July 19, 1885-Jan. 30, 1979 Publisher; rose from file clerk to vice-president (1916-28), then president (1928-37) of McGraw-Hill Publishing Co., where he formulated editorial policies for several technical and business periodicals and, in 1929, founded *Business Week*; as editor in chief and president of *Newsweek* (1937-59), emphasized news analysis; served as chairman (1959-61) and honorary chairman (1961-70) of *Newsweek*'s board of directors; died in New York City. See *Current Biography* (April) 1953.

Obituary

N Y Times A p12 Ja 31 '79

MUNSON, THURMAN (LEE) June 7, 1947-Aug. 2, 1979 Baseball player; considered one of best all-round catchers in American League; joined New York Yankees in 1969 and helped them to win three pennants and two world championships; batted over .300 for five seasons; was named rookie of the year in 1970; won three consecutive Golden Glove awards (1973-75); was designated American League's Most Valuable Player and named captain of the Yankees, in 1976; died in crash of his own private jet plane while trying to land at Akron-Canton Airport in Ohio. See *Current Biography* (November) 1977.

Obituary

N Y Times p1+ Ag 3 '79

MURPHY, GARDNER July 8, 1895-Mar. 19, 1979 Psychologist; pioneer scientist in parapsychology; director of research at the Menninger Foundation (1952-68); believed "radical new kinds of human nature" are possible if there is "a readiness for bold, even extravagant, informed and serious guessing as to potentialities"; taught at several universities, including Columbia (1921-40) and Georgetown (1968-73); among his books is the major systematic work *A Biosocial Approach to Origins and Structure* (1947); died in Washington, D.C. See *Current Biography* (May) 1960.

Obituary

N Y Times D p21 Mr 21 '79

NARAYAN, JAYA PRAKASH Oct. 11, 1902-Oct. 8, 1979 Indian political leader; was closely associated with Mohandas K. Gandhi in Indian National Congress during early 1930's and in Quit India Movement (1942-43); founded Congress Socialist party (1934) and Socialist party (1948); headed Praja Socialist party (1952-57); held several top posts in trade union movement (1946-52); became associated in 1950's with Bhoodan land redistribution movement; was one of organizers and a top leader of Janata Front coalition, with defeated Prime Minister Indira Gandhi in 1977; died at his home in Patna. See *Current Biography* (May) 1958.

Obituary

N Y Times B p17 O 9 '79

NERVI, PIER LUIGI June 21, 1891-Jan. 9, 1979 Italian civil engineer known for simple, economic structures with graceful, curving lines and soaring arches; first to use reinforced concrete—"stone in motion"—to build stadia, theatres, hangars, exhibition halls, and office buildings, most notably UNESCO's Paris headquarters, designed with Marcel Breuer; partner in architectural firms Nervi and Nebbiosi (1923-32) and Nervi and Bartoli (1932-79); taught architecture at University of Rome (1947-61) and Harvard (1961-62); winner of 1964 Gold Medal of American Institute of Architects; died in Rome, Italy. See *Current Biography* (January) 1958.

Obituary

N Y Times B p10 Ja 10 '79

NEWHOUSE, SAMUEL I(RVING) May 24, 1895-Aug. 29, 1979 Publisher; beginning in 1922, built multimillion-dollar communications empire; controlled thirty-one newspapers with total circulation of over 3,000,000, as well as five radio stations, cable television systems with 175,000 subscribers, and Condé Nast Publications, which publishes *Vogue* and other quality magazines; through his Samuel I. Newhouse Foundation, engaged in philanthropic activities, including sponsorship of Mitzi E. Newhouse Theatre in Lincoln Center; died in New York City. See *Current Biography* (March) 1961.

Obituary

N Y Times A p1+ Ag 30 '79

NOVAES (PINTO), GUIOMAR Feb. 28, 1893-Mar. 7, 1979 Brazilian pianist; internationally acclaimed for colorful performances throughout the world of Romantic composers, especially, but also of Bach and Mozart and, among the moderns, Debussy; delighted audiences with her personal charm, individuality of interpretation, and warmth and richness of tone; died in São Paulo, Brazil. See *Current Biography* (June) 1953.

Obituary

N Y Times B p6 Mr 9 '79

O'MALLEY, WALTER F(RANCIS) Oct. 9, 1903-Aug. 9, 1979 Baseball executive; lawyer; board chairman and principal owner of Los Angeles Dodgers, first major-league club on West Coast; acquired controlling interest in Dodgers in 1950, when they were in Brooklyn; enraged New York fans when he moved franchise to California in 1957; lived to see his team set a major-league attendance record of more than 3,000,000 in Los Angeles in 1978; died in Rochester, Minnesota. See *Current Biography* (March) 1954.

Obituary

N Y Times A p13 Ag 10 '79

OTTAVIANI, ALFREDO, CARDINAL Oct. 29, 1890-Aug. 3, 1979 Roman Catholic prelate; was created a Cardinal by Pope Pius XII (1953); became titular archbishop of Berrera in 1962; responsible for defending church and guarding faith and morals as secretary (from 1959) of Sacred Congregation of the Holy Office, known since 1965 as Congregation for the Doctrine of the Faith; leading spokesman of ultra-orthodox wing of church during Vatican Council II (1962-65); died at his Vatican City apartment. See *Current Biography* (December) 1966.

Obituary

N Y Times p24 Ag 4 '79

PARSONS, TALCOTT Dec. 13, 1902-May 8, 1979 Sociologist; university professor; member of Harvard University faculty from 1927 until his retirement in 1973; founder and first chairman (1946-56) of its department of social relations; greatly influenced development of social sciences through his efforts to construct an elaborate, all-embracing theory of human activity incorporating scholarly findings from various disciplines, including Freudian psychology; author of *Structure of Social Action (1937), The Social System* (1951), and many other books; died in Munich, West Germany, where he had gone to lecture. See *Current Biography* (January) 1961.

Obituary
N Y Times D p18 My 9 '79

PARTRIDGE, ERIC (HONEYWOOD) Feb. 6, 1894-June 1, 1979 New Zealand-born English lexicographer; dubbed "word king" by Edmund Wilson; after abandoning budding careers as university professor and publisher, spent half a century compiling sixteen highly readable lexicons and other guides to English and its quirks, including *A Dictionary of Slang and Unconventional English* (1937), *Usage and Abusage* (1942), and *A Dictionary of Catch Phrases* (1977); died at his home in southwest England. See *Current Biography* (January) 1963.

Obituary
N Y Times p1+ Je 2 '79

PICKFORD, MARY April 8, 1893-May 29, 1979 Canadian-born actress; was "America's Sweetheart," dominating screen in silent movie era; as adolescent, acted on Broadway under David Belasco; became first film star to have her name in marquee lights, with *Tess of the Storm Country* in 1914; made 194 motion pictures, including *Coquette* (1929), her first talkie, for which she won an Oscar, and *Secrets* (1933), her last; with Charlie Chaplin and others, owned United Artists; died in Santa Monica, California. See *Current Biography* (April) 1945.

Obituary
N Y Times p1+ My 30 '79

POTOFSKY, JACOB S(AMUEL) Nov. 16, 1894-Aug. 5, 1979 Labor union official; president (1946-72) of Amalgamated Clothing Workers of America, which he had served as an officer since its founding by Sidney Hillman in 1914; also served as vice-president of executive council of AFL-CIO; championed political involvement by labor unions; pioneered in promoting employment of lobbyists in Washington and establishment of union health and recreation centers; noted for his skills as a negotiator and conciliator; died in New York City. See *Current Biography* (October) 1946.

Obituary
N Y Times A p1+ Ag 6 '79

POWER, DONALD C(LINTON) Dec. 25, 1899-Mar. 11, 1979 Former utilities executive; lawyer; as president and chief executive officer of General Telephone Corporation (1951-59), negotiated merger with Sylvania Electric Products to form General Telephone and Electronics Corporation, the largest independent (non-Bell) telephone system in the United States; served as G.T.E.'s chairman and chief executive officer (1959-66) and chairman (1966-71); died in Galloway, Ohio. See *Current Biography* (March) 1960.

Obituary
N Y Times B p12 Mr 12 '79

RANDOLPH, A(SA) PHILIP Apr. 15. 1889-May 16, 1979 Labor union official; respected leader in nonviolent black civil rights movement; as founder and president (1925-68) of Brotherhood of Sleeping Car Porters, headed first black union chartered by AFL and obtained contract for it with Pullman Company (1937); first black vice-president of AFL-CIO (from 1957); founder (1960) and president of Negro-American Labor Council; persuaded President Franklin D. Roosevelt to ban race discrimination in defense industry (1941) and Harry S. Truman to end segregation in armed forces (1948); helped to organize massive March on Washington (1963); died in New York City. See *Current Biography* (October) 1951.

Obituary
N Y Times B p4 My 18 '79

RENOIR, JEAN Sept. 15, 1894-Feb. 12, 1979 French-born filmmaker; directed thirty-six full-length films, for some of which he also wrote the script, including *La Grande Illusion* (1937), considered one of the world's best movies; strongly influenced the New Wave of French directors emerging in the late 1950's; well known in the United States for *The Southerner* (1943) and *The River* (1950), filmed in India; was awarded a special Oscar in 1975; author of several books, including *Renoir, My Father* (1962), about the celebrated Impressionist painter Pierre Auguste Renoir; died in Los Angeles, California. See *Current Biography* (December) 1959.

Obituary
N Y Times D p19 F 14 '79

RHYS, JEAN Aug. 24, 1894-May 14, 1979 British writer; began literary career, as protégée of Ford Madox Ford, with *The Left Bank and Other Stories* (1927); wrote partly autobiographical novels about vulnerable, emotionally homeless women, including *After Leaving Mr. McKenzie* (1931) and *Good Morning, Midnight* (1939); after some years in obscurity, wrote much acclaimed "Caribbean Gothic" novel *Wide Sargasso Sea* (1966), among other works; died near her home in Devonshire, England. See *Current Biography* (December) 1972.

Obituary

N Y Times B p12 My 17 '79

RICHARDS, I(VOR) A(RMSTRONG) Feb. 26, 1893-Sept. 7, 1979 British literary critic; philologist; poet; educator; a leading advocate of "Basic English" as simplest means of international communication; stressed need for coherent feeling and reasoning if Western civilization was to survive; director of Orthological Institute of China (1936-38); director of Harvard Commission on English Language Studies (1939-44); professor (1944-63) and then professor emeritus at Harvard University; author of *Principles of Literary Criticism* (1924), *Practical Criticism* (1929), *Basic English and its Uses* (1943), and other books; died in Cambridge, England. See *Current Biography* (December) 1972.

Obituary

N Y Times p1+ S 8 '79

RICHARDS, JAMES P(RIOLEAU) Aug. 31, 1894-Feb. 21, 1979 Former United States Representative from South Carolina; lawyer; Democratic member of the House (1934-56) and chairman of the Foreign Affairs Committee (1951-56); special ambassador to the Middle East (1957); executive director of the Tobacco Institute, the trade association of the tobacco industry; died in Lancaster, South Carolina. See *Current Biography* (September) 1951.

Obituary

N Y Times p26 F 24 '79

ROBB, INEZ (CALLAWAY) 1901(?)-Apr. 4, 1979 Former journalist; wrote the society column for the New York *Daily News* under the byline Nancy Randolph (1928-38); for International News Service (1938-53) wrote column "Assignment: America," while traveling as correspondent in over forty countries; as widely syndicated columnist for Scripps-Howard Newspapers and United Features Syndicate (1953-69), was noted for lively, provocative, and literate style and content and was honored

for reporting by many news organizations; died in Tucson, Arizona. See *Current Biography* (December) 1958.

Obituary

N Y Times D p13 Ap 6 '79

ROCKEFELLER, NELSON A(LDRICH) July 8, 1908-Jan. 26, 1979 Forty-first Vice-President of the United States (1974-77); during four successive terms (1958-73) as governor, initiated series of innovative and expensive programs that had profound impact on economic, political, and cultural life of New York; in most controversial move of liberal governorship, ordered 1971 Attica prison riot crushed by force; left public life in January 1977, without fulfilling longtime ambition of winning Republican Presidential nomination, to write books and market high-quality reproductions of extensive art collection, and to direct multimillion-dollar Rockefeller Brothers Foundation; died in New York City. See *Current Biography* (March) 1951.

Obituary

N Y Times p27 Ja 26 '79

ROCKWELL, NORMAN Feb. 3, 1894-Nov. 8, 1978 Artist; one of most popular of twentieth-century American painters; evoked idyllic scenes of small-town and rural life in United States; created 317 covers for *Saturday Evening Post* (1916-63), including "Four Freedoms" series, reproduced as posters by Office of War Information during World War II; illustrated official Boy Scout calendar (1926-76), and deluxe editions of *Tom Sawyer* and *Huckleberry Finn*; contributed work to *Boys' Life, Judge, Literary Digest, Look,* and other magazines; received Presidential Medal of Freedom (1977); died at his home in Stockbridge, Massachusetts. See *Current Biography* (January) 1945.

Obituary

N Y Times A p1+ N 10 '78

ROSENWALD, LESSING J(ULIUS) Feb. 10, 1891-June 25, 1979 Businessman; philanthropist; art collector; held various managerial posts at Sears, Roebuck & Company before assuming board chairmanship (1932-39); in 1943 deeded to United States government collection of 25,000 prints and drawings and 7,600 rare books valued at $35,000,000; was president of non-Zionist American Council for Judaism and chairman of Julius Rosenwald Fund set up by his father to further interracial understanding; died at Alverthorpe, his estate at Jenkintown, Pennsylvania. See *Current Biography* (February) 1947.

Obituary

N Y Times C p17 Je 26 '79

SALTONSTALL, LEVERETT Sept. 1, 1892-June 17, 1979 Former United States Senator from Massachusetts (1944-67); began political career in Massachusetts state legislature (1923-36) and served as its speaker from 1929 to 1936; revived state's Republican party in stunning defeat of Boston Mayor James Michael Curley in 1938 gubernatorial contest, ending forty years of Democratic control; as governor (1938-44) and in United States Senate, was staunch supporter of Republican liberal wing, especially on issues of civil liberties and international cooperation; died at his farm in Dover, Massachusetts. See *Current Biography* (April) 1956.

Obituary

N Y Times B p13 Je 18 '79

SAWYER, CHARLES Feb. 10, 1887-Apr. 7, 1979 Former government official; lawyer; a conservative Democrat prominent in Ohio politics; ambassador to Belgium and minister to Luxembourg (1944-45); member of the Loyalty Review Board (1947-48); Secretary of Commerce (1948-53); was involved in many business, publishing, civic, and philanthropic activities; died in Palm Beach, Florida. See *Current Biography* (July) 1948.

Obituary

N Y Times D p11 Ap 9 '79

SCHERMAN, THOMAS (KIELTY) Feb. 12, 1917-May 14, 1979 Orchestra conductor; began career as assistant to Otto Klemperer and then worked on radio stations; founded and conducted (1947-75) Little Orchestra Society, presenting neglected classical works, new contemporary music, and operas in concert form, with unknown artists, at New York City's Town Hall and abroad; later presented children's concerts through New Little Orchestra Society; died in New York City. See *Current Biography* (December) 1954.

Obituary

N Y Times B p10 My 16 '79

SEBERG, JEAN Nov. 13, 1938-Aug. 31(?), 1979 American-born motion-picture actress; as teenager, was discovered by Otto Preminger, who starred her in the mercilessly panned films *Saint Joan* (1957) and *Bonjour Tristesse* (1958); later became international film figure, especially applauded for her performance in the French New Wave picture *Breathless* (1961); her other credits included the female leads in the American film *Lilith* (1964) and the German production *The Wild Duck* (1977); was found dead in her car in Paris on September 8, nine days after she disappeared from her Paris apartment carrying a supply of barbiturates prescribed by her physician. See *Current Biography* (April) 1966.

Obituary

N Y Times p44 S 9 '79

SHUMLIN, HERMAN (ELLIOTT) Dec. 6, 1898-June 14, 1979 Theatrical producer; worked as reporter for theatrical trade papers (1921-25); was producer-director of succession of Broadway hits over three decades, including *Grand Hotel* (1930), *The Children's Hour* (1934) and four other Lillian Hellman dramas, *The Corn Is Green* (1943), *Inherit the Wind* (1955), and *The Deputy* (1964), for which he won Tony award; directed motion pictures *Watch on the Rhine* (1943) and *Confidential Agent* (1945); died in New York City. See *Current Biography* (March) 1941.

Obituary

N Y Times A p18 Je 15 '79

SKINNER, CORNELIA OTIS May 30, 1901-July 9, 1979 Actress; author; daughter of noted actor Otis Skinner, with whom she made her Broadway stage debut in *Blood and Sand* (1921); became popular in 1930's as star of own "monodramas," in which she depicted historic figures; won acclaim as star of *Candida* (1935), *Lady Windermere's Fan* (1946), *Major Barbara* (1956), her own revue *Paris '90* (1952), and *The Pleasure of His Company* (1958), which she wrote with Samuel Taylor; coauthor with Emily Kimbrough of best-selling *Our Hearts Were Young and Gay* (1942), a humorous odyssey of travels through Europe; also wrote biographies, light verse, essays, and anecdotes; died at her home in New York City. See *Current Biography* (December) 1964.

Obituary

N Y Times D p15 Jl 10 '79

STAFFORD JEAN July 1, 1915-Mar. 26, 1979 Writer of traditionally structured and painstakingly crafted novels, including *Boston Adventure* (1944) and *Mountain Lion* (1947), and short stories notable for the sensitivity and subtlety of their psychological probings; winner of Pulitzer Prize in fiction for *Collected Stories* (1969); also contributed literary and other essays to periodicals; died in White Plains, New York. See *Current Biography* (Yearbook) 1951.

Obituary

N Y Times p51 Mr 28 '79

STAKMAN, E(LVIN) C(HARLES) May 17, 1885-Jan. 22, 1979 Educator; plant pathologist; won Emil Christian Hansen gold medal (1928) for devising ways to combat wheat rusts; as University of Minnesota faculty member (1909-53) and adviser to U.S. Department of Agriculture (1919-55), developed high-yielding crop strains resistant to disease and adverse environmental conditions; was president of American Association for the Advancement of Science (1949-51) and special consultant to Rockefeller Foundation from 1953 until death; died in St. Paul, Minn. See *Current Biography* (December) 1949.

Obituary

N Y Times B p8 Ja 24 '79

STILL, WILLIAM GRANT May 11, 1895-Dec. 3, 1978 Composer; after early work as orchestrator and arranger of jazz and popular music, developed symphonic type of black music with his *Afro-American Symphony* (1931) and other works, including songs, symphonic poems, ballets, and such operas as *Troubled Island* (1938); first black conductor of a major American orchestra, the Los Angeles Philharmonic (1936); won Harmon Award (1928), among other honors; died in Los Angeles, California. See *Current Biography* (January) 1941.

Obituary

N Y Times B p6 D 6 '78

STRAUSS, ANNA LORD Sept. 20, 1899-Feb. 23, 1979 Civic leader; president of the New York City branch of the National League of Women Voters (1937-43) and of the national organization (1945-50); member of the United States delegation at the U.N. General Assembly (1951); served with various groups concerned with education, women's rights, civil liberties, and nonpartisan government activities; died in New York City. See *Current Biography* (November) 1945.

Obituary

N Y Times p26 F 24 '79

TATE, ALLEN Nov. 19, 1899-Feb. 9, 1979 Influential man of letters whose work in poetry, biography, fiction, and literary criticism reflects Southern values, such as agrarianism, and a Classical outlook; a member of the Fugitives, who spearheaded the Southern literary renaissance of the 1930's; a founder of the New Criticism, which studies literature apart from its historic and social context; taught at New York University, the University of Chicago, the University of Minnesota, and other universities; died in Nashville, Tennessee. See *Current Biography* (November) 1940.

Obituary

N Y Times p13 F 10 '79

TAWES, J(OHN) MILLARD Apr. 8, 1894-June 25, 1979 Former Governor of Maryland; only man to date to have held all three of Maryland's top posts: governor (1959-67), comptroller (1938-47, 1950-58) and, as interim appointee to complete unexpired term, treasurer (1975); from 1917 to 1945, employed in various capacities in family lumber, canning, baking, and shipbuilding businesses; died at home in Crisfield, Maryland. See *Current Biography* (October) 1960.

Obituary

N Y Times C p17 Je 26 '79

TOLSTOY, ALEXANDRA (LVOVNA) July 1, 1884-Sept. 26, 1979 Social activist; writer; lecturer; youngest daughter of Leo Tolstoy; served as his secretary and, after his death (1910), as executor of his estate; helped to prepare definitive edition of Tolstoy's works (1917-29); after several arrests by Soviet authorities for political reasons, immigrated to United States (1931); helped to establish New York City-based Tolstoy Foundation to aid Russian emigrés (1939) and served as its president; author of *The Tragedy of Tolstoy* (1933), *Tolstoy; A Life of My Father* (1953), and other books; died at Tolstoy Foundation nursing home in Valley Cottage, New York. See *Current Biography* (April) 1953.

Obituary

N Y Times B p4 S 28 '79

TUGWELL, REXFORD G(UY) July 10, 1891-July 21, 1979 Economist; educator; political theorist; one of original members of President Franklin D. Roosevelt's "brains trust"; in long, diverse public career, was under secretary of agriculture (1934-37), chairman of New York City Planning Commission (1938-40), and governor of Puerto Rico (1941-46); as senior fellow at Center for the Study of Democratic Institutions (1966-79), helped draft "for discussion" radically altered United States Constitution; author of more than two dozen books, including The *Brains Trust* (1968), which won Bancroft Prize in history; died in Santa Barbara, California. See *Current Biography* (January) 1963.

Obituary

N Y Times D p15 Jl 24 '79

TUNNARD, CHRISTOPHER July 7, 1910-Feb. 14, 1979 Canadian-born architect; urban and regional planner; was professor of city planning at Yale University, where he joined faculty in 1945; began career as draftsman-designer and housing and town consultant in England; was widely recognized for his concept of the new "linear" or "super" city, a virtually unbroken urban line such as that stretching from Norfolk, Virginia to Portland, Maine; wrote or coauthored several books, including the National Book Award-winning *Man-Made America: Chaos or Control?* (1963); died in New Haven, Connecticut. See *Current Biography* (June) 1959.

Obituary

N Y Times D p19 F 15 '79

TUNNEY, GENE May 25, 1898-Nov. 7, 1978 Boxer; began professional career in 1919; became light-heavyweight champion of United States in 1922; won world heavyweight title from Jack Dempsey (1926) and successfully defended it against him (1927); after retiring as undefeated world champion (1928), held directorships and executive posts with several corporations and banks; directed athletic and physical fitness program for United States Navy during World War II; died at Greenwich, Connecticut. See *Current Biography* (September) 1940.

Obituary

N Y Times D p19 N 9 '78

VELASCO IBARRA, JOSÉ MARIA Mar. 19, 1893-Mar. 30, 1979 Ecuadorean statesman; lawyer; political scholar; a self-described "neoliberal" who stood between capitalism and Communism; became President of Ecuador five times (1934, 1944, 1948, 1952, and 1960), but served only one full term (1952-56) and spent much time in exile, including the past seven years, when he lived in Argentina; died in Quito, Ecuador. See *Current Biography* (November) 1952.

Obituary

N Y Times p26 Mr 31 '79

WALTARI, MIKA (TOIMI) Sept. 18, 1908-Aug. 26, 1979 Finnish author; wrote panoramic historical novel *The Egyptian* (1949), which topped best-seller lists in United States and was made into a successful motion picture (1954); also wrote poems, fairy tales, dramas, and such other novels as *The Wanderer* (1951), *Moonscape* (1954), and *The Etruscan* (1956); died in Helsinki. See *Current Biography* (February) 1950.

Obituary

N Y Times D p15 Ag 28 '79

WAYNE, JOHN May 26, 1907-June 11, 1979 Motion picture actor; biggest box-office attraction in Hollywood history; over span of half century, strode across giant screen in pursuit of villains in more than 200 outdoor action films, most of them westerns, from *The Big Trail* (1930) through *Stagecoach* (1940) and *She Wore a Yellow Ribbon* (1949) to *Rooster*

Cogburn (1975); won best-actor Oscar for *True Grit* (1970), in which he parodied himself; was conservative folk hero, symbolizing rugged, uncomplicated Americanism and anti-Communism; died in Los Angeles. See *Current Biography* (July) 1972.

Obituary

N Y Times A p1 Je 12 '79

WEAVER, WARREN July 17, 1894-Nov. 28, 1978 Educator; organization official; mathematician; director of natural sciences division (1932-55) and vice-president (1955-59) of Rockefeller Foundation; chairman of scientific policy committee (1955-59) and vice-president (1958-59) of Sloan-Kettering Institute for Cancer Research; vice-president of Alfred P. Sloan Foundation (1959-64); board chairman of Salk Institute for Biological Studies (from 1962); author of *Science and Imagination* (1967) and other books; received UNESCO's Kalinga Prize (1965), among many other honors; died in New Milford, Connecticut. See *Current Biography* (April) 1952.

Obituary

N Y Times D p8 N 25 '78

WEBB, AILEEN O(SBORN) June 25, 1892-Aug. 15, 1979 Organization official; a prime mover in the growing American crafts movement since the Depression era; founder (1943) and chairman (1958-76) of 30,000-member American Craftsmen's Council; helped to establish *Craft Horizons* magazine (1941), School for American Craftsmen at Rochester (New York) Institute of Technology (1945), Museum of Contemporary Crafts in New York City (1956), and World Crafts Council (1964); died in her home in Garrison, New York. See *Current Biography* (December) 1958.

Obituary

N Y Times A p16 Ag 17 '79

WELCH, LEO D(EWEY) Apr. 22, 1898-Oct. 21, 1978 Corporation executive; banker; board chairman (1963-65) and a director (until 1977) of Communications Satellite Corporation (Comsat), a government-sponsored private enterprise established during administration of President John F. Kennedy as part of global system of television, radio, and telephone communications; board chairman of Standard Oil Company of New Jersey (1960-63); chairman of National Arbitration Panel (1971-76); died in automobile crash near Cuernavaca, Mexico. See *Current Biography* (December) 1963.

Obituary

Washington Post B p8 O 25 '78

WETMORE, ALEXANDER June 18, 1886-Dec. 7, 1978 Museum official; ornithologist; assistant secretary (1925-44) and secretary (1945-52) of Smithsonian Institution; in course of career collected 26,058 animal and bird skins and over 4,000 skeletal specimens for museum and identified 189 new bird species and subspecies; was trustee of National Geographic Society and acting chairman (1937-74) of its committee for research and exploration; author of dozens of articles and books on ornithology and avian osteology and paleontology; died in Maryland. See *Current Biography* (February) 1948.

Obituary

N Y Times A p25 D 13 '78

WINSTON, HARRY Mar. 1, 1896-Dec. 8, 1978 Gem dealer; in 1932 organized his own firm, Harry Winston Inc., in Manhattan, which he developed into probably the world's largest gem concern; was known as the showman of the diamond industry because of his spectacular purchases and such dramatic gestures as his gift in 1958 of the Hope Diamond to the Smithsonian Institution; died in New York City. See *Current Biography* (April) 1965.

Obituary

N Y Times p28 D 9 '78

WOLCHOK, SAM(UEL) Sept. 20, 1896-Jan. 16, 1979 Businessman; former union official; in succession of top leadership posts, built up membership in New York Clerks Union from fifty in 1922 to 3,000-plus in 1937, then broke with AFL to join new CIO; was president of Retail, Wholesale and Department Store Union, then world's biggest union, from 1937 to 1948; left union during internal squabbles in late 1940's; later served as executive of L. Daitch & Co., the New York supermarket chain, and as account executive for Bear, Stearns & Co.; died in Miami Beach, Florida. See *Current Biography* (October) 1948.

Obituary

N Y Times D p17 Ja 18 '79

WOODWARD, R(OBERT) B(URNS) Apr. 10, 1917-July 8, 1979 Chemist; won 1965 Nobel Prize for chemistry; pioneered in chemical synthesis of complicated organic compounds, including quinine, chlorophyll, cholesterol, lysergic acid, and reserpine and helped determine molecular structure of the antibiotics penicillin and terramycin; on Harvard University faculty since 1941, was named Donner Professor of Science in 1960; at time of death, was working on synthesis of erythromycin; died in Cambridge, Massachusetts. See *Current Biography* (February) 1952.

Obituary

N Y Times D p14 Jl 10 '79

WRIGHT, JOHN J(OSEPH) CARDINAL July 18, 1909-Aug. 10, 1979 Roman Catholic prelate; highest ranking American in the Vatican; as Bishop of Pittsburgh (1958-69), established controversial reputation as an intellectual who was liberal on social issues and conservative in theology; while championing civil rights, peace, ecumenism, and third-world needs, opposed ordination of women and artificial means of birth control; as Cardinal, was assigned to work at stemming the mass defection of priests; died in Cambridge, Massachusetts. See *Current Biography* (February) 1963.

Obituary

N Y Times p32 Ag 12 '79

BIOGRAPHICAL REFERENCES

Almanac of American Politics, 1978

American Architects Directory, 1970

American Bar, 1965

American Catholic Who's Who, 1976-77

American Medical Directory, 1979

American Men and Women of Science 14th ed (1979)

Asia Who's Who (1960)

Baseball Register, 1979

Biographical Directory of Librarians in the United States and Canada (1970)

Biographical Directory of the American Congress, 1774-1971 (1971)

Biographical Encyclopaedia & Who's Who of the American Theatre (1966)

Biographical Encyclopedia of Pakistan, 1971-72

Biographic Directory of the USSR (1958)

Burke's Peerage, Baronetage, and Knightage, 1970

Canadian Who's Who, 1979

Celebrity Register (1973)

Chi è? (1961)

China Yearbook, 1971-72

Chujoy, A., and Manchester, P. W., eds. Dance Encyclopedia (1967)

Concise Biographical Dictionary of Singers (1969)

Congressional Directory, 1979

Congressional Quarterly Almanac, 1978

Contemporary Artists (1977)

Contemporary Authors (1962-79)

Contemporary Dramatists (1973)

Contemporary Novelists (1976)

Contemporary Poets (1975)

Contemporary Poets of the English Language (1970)

Debrett's Peerage, 1974

Department of State Biographic Register, 1972

Dictionary of Contemporary American Artists (1977)

Dictionary of International Biography, 1975

Dictionary of Latin American and Caribbean Biography (1971)

Dictionnaire de biographie française (1964)

Directory of American Judges (1955)

Directory of American Scholars (1974)

Directory of British Scientists, 1966-67

Directory of Medical Specialists, 1972-73

Encyclopedia of Pop, Rock and Soul (1974)

Episcopal Clergy Directory, 1972

Ewen, D., ed. Composers of Today (1936); Living Musicians (1940); First Supplement (1957); Men and Women Who Make Music (1949); American Composers Today (1949); European Composers Today (1954); The New Book of Modern Composers (1961); Popular American Composers (1962; First Supplement, 1972); Composers Since 1900 (1969); Musicians Since 1900 (1978]

Feather, Leonard. Encyclopedio of Jazz (1960); Encyclopedia of Jazz in the Sixties (1966)

Filmgoer's Companion (1977)

Football Register, 1979

Foremost Women in Communications (1970)

Grove's Dictionary of Music and Musicians (1955)

Hindustan Year Book and Who's Who, 1963

Hvem er Hvem? 1973

International Authors and Writers Who's Who, 1978

International Motion Picture Almanac, 1979

International Television Almanac, 1979

International Who's Who, 1978-79

International Who's Who in Art and Antiques, 1976

International Who's Who in Music, 1975

International Who's Who in Poetry (1974-75)

International Who's Who of the Arab World (1978)

International Year Book and Statesmen's Who's Who, 1979

Japan Biographical Encyclopedia & Who's Who, 1964-65

Jews in the World of Science (1956)

Junior Book of Authors (1951)

Kelly's Handbook to the Titled, Landed and Official Classes, 1964

Kleine Slavische Biographie (1958)

Kras Bla Bog, 1964

Kürschners Deutscher Gelehrten-Kalender, 1970

Leaders in Education (1974)

Leaders in Electronics (1979)

Leaders in Profile (1975)

McGraw-Hill Modern Men of Science (1966-68)

Martindale-Hubbell Law Directory, 1979

Middle East and North Africa, 1978-79

More Junior Authors (1963)

Nalanda Year-Book and Who's Who in India and Pakistan, 1958

National Cyclopaedia of American Biography current vols A-M (1926-78)

New Century Cyclopedia of Names (1954)

Nordness, Lee, ed. Art USA Now (1963)

Notable Australians (1978)

Notable Names in the American Theatre (1976)

Nouveau Dictionnaire National des Contemporains (1968)

Official Catholic Directory, 1976

Oxford Companion to Film (1976)

Panorama Biografico degli Italiani d'Oggi (1956)

Political Profiles (1976-77)

Poor's Register of Directors and Executives, 1974

Prominent Personalities in the USSR (1968)

Quién es Quién en la Argentina, 1968-69

Quién es Quién en Venezuela, Panama, Ecuador, Colombia, 1956

Robinson, Donald. 100 Most Important People in the World Today (1972)

Slonimsky, Nicholas. Baker's Biographical Dictionary of Musicians (1958)

Something About the Author (1971-79)

Third Book of Junior Authors (1972)

Thomas, S. Men of Space (1960-68)

Thompson, K. A. Dictionary of Twentieth-Century Composers (1973)

Thompson, O., ed. International Cyclopedia of Music and Musicians, 1964

Turkin, H., and Thompson, S. C. Official Encyclopedia of Baseball (1959)

Twentieth Century Authors (1942; First Supplement, 1955)

Two Hundred Contemporary Authors (1969)

Vem är Det, 1973

Webster's Biographical Dictionary (1971)

Wer ist Wer? (1975)

Who is Who in Music (1951)

Who's Who, 1979-80

Who's Who among Black Americans, 1977-78

Who's Who in Advertising (1963)

Who's Who in Africa, 1973

Who's Who in America, 1978-79

Who's Who in American Art (1978)

Who's Who in American Education, 1967-68

Who's Who in American Politics, 1978-79

Who's Who in Art (1974)

Who's Who in Australia, 1971

Who's Who in Austria, 1971-72

Who's Who in Baseball, 1971

Who's Who in Belgium (1962)

Who's Who in California, 1965

Who's Who in Canada, 1969-70

Who's Who in Chicago and Illinois (1950)

Who's Who in Colored America, 1950

Who's Who in Communist China (1969)

Who's Who in Engineering, 1964

Who's Who in Finance and Industry, 1979-80

Who's Who in France, 1979-80

Who's Who in France (Paris), 1953-54

Who's Who in Germany (1972)

Who's Who in Hollywood, 1900-1976

Who's Who in Israel, 1978

Who's Who in Italy, 1957-58

Who's Who in Labor, 1976

Who's Who in Latin America Pts 1-7 (1945-51)

Who's Who in Library Service (1970)

Who's Who in Malaysia, 1967

Who's Who in Music, 1969

Who's Who in New York, 1960

Who's Who in New Zealand (1968)

Who's Who in Opera, 1976

Who's Who in Philosophy (1969)

Who's Who in Professional Baseball (1973)

Who's Who in Publishing (1971)

Who's Who in Railroading in North America (1959)

Who's Who in Saudi Arabia, 1978-79

Who's Who in Space, 1966-67

Who's Who in Spain, 1965

Who's Who in Switzerland, 1970-71

Who's Who in the Arab World, 1974-75

Who's Who in the East, 1979-80

Who's Who in the Midwest, 1978-79

Who's Who in the Netherlands, 1962-63

Who's Who in the South and Southwest, 1978-79

Who's Who in the Theatre (1977)

Who's Who in the United Nations (1975)

Who's Who in the USSR, 1972

Who's Who in the West, 1978-79

Who's Who in the World, 1974-75

Who's Who in World Aviation and Astronautics (1958)

Who's Who in World Jewry (1972)

Who's Who of American Women, 1979-80

Who's Who of British Engineers, 1970-71

Who's Who of British Scientists, 1971-72

Who's Who of Jazz (1972)

Who's Who of Rhodesia, Mauritius, Central and East Africa, 1965

Who's Who of Southern Africa, 1970

Wie is Dat? (1956)

Women Lawyers in the United States (1957)

World Authors: 1950-1970 (1975)

World Biography (1954)

World Who's Who in Science (1968)

World's Who's Who of Women (1974-75)

PERIODICALS AND NEWSPAPERS CONSULTED

ALA Bul–American Library Association Bulletin
After Dark
Am Artist–American Artist
Am Libs–American Libraries
Am Scholar–American Scholar
Am Sociol R–American Sociological Review
America
Américas
Arch Forum–Architectural forum (disc.)
Arch Rec–Architectural Record
Archaeology
Art N–Art News
Arts
Arts & Arch–Arts & Architecture
Atlan–Atlantic Monthly
Aviation W–Aviation Week and Space Technology

Barron's
Ballet News
Bet Hom & Gard–Better Homes and Gardens
Biog N–Biography News
Book-of-the-Month Club N–Book-of-the-Month Club News
Book W–Book Week (disc.)
Broadcasting
Bsns W–Business Week

Cath World–Catholic World
Chicago Tribune
Christian Sci Mon–Christian Science Monitor
Columbia J R–Columbia Journalism Review
Commonweal
Cong Digest–Congressional Digest
Cong Q–Congressional Quarterly Weekly Report
Cosmop–Cosmopolitan
Crawdaddy
Cue
Cur Hist–Current History
Cur World Leaders–Current World Leaders

Dance Mag–Dance Magazine
Ebony
Ed & Pub–Editor & Publisher
Encounter
Esquire

Facts on File
Family Circle
For Affairs–Foreign Affairs
For Policy Bul–Foreign Policy Bulletin
Forbes
Fortune

Good H–Good Housekeeping
Guardian

Harper's
Hi Fi–High Fidelity
Hi Fi/Stereo R–Hi/Fi Stereo Review
Holiday
House & Gard–House & Garden

Illus Lond N–Illustrated London News
Intellectual Digest (disc.)

Ladies Home J–Ladies' Home Journal
Lib J–Library Journal
Life
London Observer
Look (disc.)
Los Angeles Times

McCall's
Mag Wall St–Magazine of Wall Street
Mlle–Mademoiselle
Modern Maturity
More (disc.)
Ms
Mus Am–Musical America
Mus Courier–Musical Courier (disc.)
Mus Mod Art–Museum of Modern Art Bulletin

N Y Daily News
N Y Tribune (disc.)
N Y Herald Tribune Bk R–New York Herald Tribune Book Review (disc.)
N Y Post
N Y Rev of Books–New York Review of Books
N Y Sunday News
N Y Times
N Y Times Bk R–New York Times Book Review
N Y Times Mag–New York Times Magazine
N Y World-Telegram–New York World-Telegram and Sun (disc.)
N Y World Journal Tribune (disc.)
Nat Geog Mag–National Geographic Magazine
Nat Observer–National Observer (disc.)
Nation
Nations Bsns–Nation's Business
Nature
New Leader
New Repub–New Republic
New Statesm–New Statesman
New Times (disc.)

New York–New York Magazine
New Yorker
Newsday
Newsweek

Omni
Opera N–Opera News

Penthouse
People
Philadelphia Inquirer
Playboy
Pop Sci–Popular Science Monthly
Psych Today–Psychology Today
Pub W–Publishers Weekly

Quest

Read Digest–Reader's Digest
Redbook
Reporter–The Reporter (disc.)
Rolling Stone

Sat Eve Post–Saturday Evening Post
Sat Night–Saturday Night
Sat R–Saturday Review
Sci Am–Scientific American
Sci Mo–Scientific Monthly
Sci N L–Science News Letter
Science
Show Bus Illus–Show Business Illustrated (disc.)
Smithsonian
Spec–Spectator
Sport
Sports Illus–Sports Illustrated
Sr Schol–Senior Scholastic

Theatre Arts (disc.)
This Week–This Week Magazine (disc.)
Time–Time
Times Lit Sup–London Times Literary Supplement
Toronto Globe and Mail
TV Guide

U N Rev–United Nations Review
U S News–U.S. News & World Report

Variety
Village Voice
Viva
Vogue

Wall St J–Wall Street Journal
Washington M–Washington Monthly
Washington Post
Wilson Lib Bul–Wilson Library Bulletin

Yale R–Yale Review

CLASSIFICATION BY PROFESSION—1979

AGRICULTURE
Perdue, Frank

ARCHITECTURE
Pereira, William L.

BUSINESS AND FINANCE
Caddell, Patrick H.
Claytor, W. Graham, Jr.
Della Femina, Jerry
Estes, E. M.
Feld, Irvin
Grade, Lew
Hammond, John
Kirby, Robert E.
Ludwig, Daniel K.
McIntyre, James J., Jr.
McWhirter, Norris
Murphy, Thomas A.
Perdue, Frank
Sawhill, John C.
Steinbrenner, George
  Michael, 3d
Swearingen, John E.
Turner, Ted
Weitz, John
Werblin, David A.

COMMUNICATIONS
Bombeck, Erma
Cowley, Malcolm
Della Femina, Jerry
Drew, Elizabeth
Helms, Jesse A.
McWhirter, Norris
Rafshoon, Gerald (Monroe)
Shannon, William V.
Silberman, Charles E.
Trilling, Diana
Turner, Ted

EDUCATION
Barthes, Roland
Brewster, Kingman, Jr.
Freud, Anna
Gray, Hanna Holborn
Irving, John
Kahn, Alfred E.
Milgram, Stanley
Morrison, Toni
O'Neill, Gerard K.
Rowse, A. L.
Salk, Lee

Sawhill, John C.
Schlesinger, Arthur M., Jr.
Shepard, Sam
Silberman, Charles E.
Simon, Herbert A.
Skinner, B. F.

FASHION
Weitz, John

FILM AND TELEVISION
Allen, Woody
Bakshi, Ralph
Chaplin, Geraldine
Chase, Chevy
Clayburgh, Jill
Drew, Elizabeth
Giannini, Giancarlo
Grade, Lew
Hamilton, Margaret
Howard, Ron
Jewison, Norman
Korman, Harvey
Levine, Joseph E.
Olivier, Laurence
Ritt, Martin
Schuller, Robert H.
Scorsese, Martin
Shepard, Sam
Stigwood, Robert
Summer, Donna
Turner, Ted
Werblin, David A.
Williams, Robin

GOVERNMENT AND
POLITICS
Anderson, John B.
Ashley, Thomas Ludlow
Bilandic, Michael A.
Bolger, William F.
Botha, P. W.
Brewster, Kingman, Jr.
Bumpers, Dale
Caddell, Patrick H.
Claytor, W. Graham, Jr.
Culver, John C.
Eanes, António Ramalho
Ehrlichman, John D.
Fahd, Crown Prince of
  Saudi Arabia
Fauntroy, Walter E.
Feinstein, Dianne
Helms, Jesse A.

Jackson, Henry M.
Jarvis, Howard
Kahn, Alfred E.
Khomeini, Ayatollah
  Ruholla
Kucinich, Dennis J.
Kyprianou, Spyros
Laxalt, Paul
Lougheed, Peter
McIntyre, James T., Jr.
Mihajlov, Mihajlo
Moi, Daniel arap
Mugabe, Robert
Muzorewa, Abel T.
O'Neal, A. Daniel
Rafshoon, Gerald (Monroe)
Sarkis, Elias
Sawhill, John C.
Schlesinger, Arthur M., Jr.
Shannon, William V.
Sullivan, William H.
Thompson, James R.
Turbay Ayala, Julio César
Weizman, Ezer
Wright, Jim

INDUSTRY AND LABOR
Bolger, William F.
Chaikin, Sol C.
Estes, E. M.
Ludwig, Daniel K.
Murphy, Thomas A.
Wurf, Jerry

INTERNATIONAL
RELATIONS
Brewster, Kingman, Jr.
Shannon, William V.
Sullivan, William H.

LAW
Anderson, John B.
Ashley, Thomas Ludlow
Belli, Melvin M.
Bilandic, Michael A.
Bliss, Anthony A.
Claytor, W. Graham, Jr.
Ehrlichman, John D.
Jackson, Henry M.
Kyprianou, Spyros
Laxalt, Paul
McIntyre, James T., Jr.
O'Neal, A. Daniel
Thompson, James R.

LITERATURE
Allen, Woody
Barthes, Roland
Brown, Dee
Cartland, Barbara
Cowley, Malcolm
Donleavy, J. P.
Ehrlichman, John D.
Hughes, Ted
Irving, John
Macdonald, Ross
Morrison, Toni
Rowse, A. L.
Schuller, Robert H.
Shepard, Sam
Trilling, Diana
Uris, Leon
Wallace, Irving
Wilson, Lanford
Wilson, Robert

MILITARY
Claytor, W. Graham, Jr.
Eanes, António Ramalho
Weizman, Ezer

MUSICAL COMPOSITION
Hunter, Alberta
Joel, Billy
Kenton, Stan
Menotti, Gian Carlo
Nelson, Willie
Schickele, Peter
Schwartz, Arthur
Stewart, Rod
Summer, Donna
Swados, Elizabeth

ORGANIZATIONS
Chaikin, Sol C.
Wurf, Jerry

PERFORMING ARTS
Adler, Kurt Herbert
Allen, Woody
Berganza, Teresa

Bliss, Anthony A.
Carreras, José
Chaplin, Geraldine
Chase, Chevy
Clayburgh, Jill
Crespin, Régine
Curry, John
Dale, Clamma
Donleavy, J. P.
Field, Sally
Firkusny, Rudolph
Giannini, Giancarlo
Hamilton, Margaret
Hammond, John
Hunter, Alberta
Joel, Billy
Kenton, Stan
Korman, Harvey
Levine, Joseph E.
Menotti, Gian Carlo
Nelson, Willie
Olivier, Laurence
Rey, Fernando
Ritt, Martin
Schickele, Peter
Seymour, Lynn
Shepard, Sam
Stewart, Rod
Stigwood, Robert
Summer, Donna
Swados, Elizabeth
Troyanos, Tatiana
Tuckwell, Barry
Van Hamel, Martine
Williams, Robin
Wilson, Lanford
Wilson, Robert

PHILOSOPHY AND
RELIGION
Barthes, Roland
Fauntroy, Walter E.
John Paul II, Pope
Khomeini, Ayatollah
Ruholla
Kimball, Spencer W.
Muzorewa, Abel T.
Schuller, Robert H.

SCIENCE AND
MEDICINE
O'Neill, Gerard K.
Steptoe, Patrick C.
Wilson, Edward O.

SOCIAL ACTIVISM
Fauntroy, Walter E.
Hammond, John
Jarvis, Howard
Mihajlov, Mihajlo
Williams, Betty

SOCIAL SCIENCE
Brown, Dee
Caddell, Patrick H.
Freud, Anna
Kahn, Alfred E.
Milgram, Stanley
Rowse, A. L.
Salk, Lee
Schlesinger, Arthur M., Jr.
Silberman, Charles E.
Simon, Herbert A.
Skinner, B. F.

SPORTS
Bradshaw, Terry
Curry, John
Gerulaitis, Vitas
Guidry, Ron
Nyad, Diana
Rice, Jim
Schwarzenegger, Arnold
Stabler, Ken
Steinbrenner, George
Michael, 3d
Turner, Ted
Watson, Tom
Werblin, David D.

VISUAL ARTS
Balthus
Di Suvero, Mark
Kertész, André

CUMULATED INDEX—1971-1979

For the index to 1940-1970 biographies, see
Current Biography Cumulative Index 1940-1970

Aubrey, James T(homas), Jr. Mar 72

Auchincloss, Louis (Stanton) Aug 78

Auden, W(ystan) H(ugh) Sep 71 obit Nov 73

Avedon, Richard Feb 75

Avon, Anthony Eden, 1st Earl of obit Mar 77

Ayub Khan, Mohammad obit Jun 74

Bach, Richard (David) Oct 73

Bachauer, Gina obit Sep 77

Backe, John D(avid) Apr 78

Badillo, Herman May 71

Bailar, Benjamin F(ranklin) Jul 76

Bailey, John M(organ) obit Jun 75

Baker, George obit Aug 75

Baker, Howard (Henry, Jr.) Mar 74

Baker, Janet Jun 71

Baker, Josephine obit Jun 75

Bakke, E(dward) Wight obit Jan 72

Bakshi, Ghulam Mohammad obit Sep 72

Bakshi, Ralph Mar 79

Balaban, Barney obit Apr 71

Balchen, Bernt obit Dec 73

Balenciaga, (Cristóbal) obit May 72

Ball, Lucille Jan 78

Ball, William May 74

Balthus Nov 79

Banfield, Edward C(hristie) May 72

Banzer Suárez, Hugo Sep 73

Banzhaf, John F(rancis), 3d Dec 73

Barber, Anthony (Perrinott Lysberg) Jan 71

Baring, George Rowland Stanley See Cromer, 3d Earl of May 71

Barlow, Howard obit Mar 72

Barnes, Clive (Alexander) Mar 72

Barr, John A(ndrew) obit Mar 79

Barre, Raymond Jul 77

Barry, Rick Mar 71

Barthelme, Donald Mar 76

Barthes, Roland Feb 79

Baryshnikov, Mikhail (Niko-layevich) Feb 75

Barzini, Luigi (Giorgio, Jr.) Jul 72

Bates, H(erbert) E(rnest) obit Mar 74

Bates, Marston obit May 74

Bates, Sanford obit Nov 72

Batista (y Zaldívar), Fulgencio obit Oct 73

Battle, John S(tewart) obit Jun 72

Baum, William (Wakefield) Cardinal Oct 76

Baxter, Anne May 72

Baxter, James P(hinney) 3d obit Aug 75

Bayne, Stephen F(ielding) Jr. obit Mar 74

Bazelon, David L(ionel) Jan 71

Beall, J(ames) Glenn obit Mar 71

Beals, Carleton obit Aug 79

Beame, Abraham D(avid) Jul 74

Bearden, Romare Jan 72

Beauvoir, Simone (Bertrand) de Jan 73

Bech, Joseph obit May 75

Beene, Geoffrey Apr 78

Begin, Menahem Oct 77

Behrman, S(amuel) N(athan-iel) obit Nov 73

Beirne, J(oseph) A(nthony) obit Oct 74

Beitz, Berthold Feb 73

Béjart, Maurice Mar 71

Békésy, George von obit Sep 72

Belkin, Samuel obit Jun 76

Bell, Daniel Dec 73

Bell, Daniel W(afena) obit Nov 71

Bell, Griffin B(oyette) Jun 77

Bell, T(errel) H(oward) May 76

Belli, Melvin M(ouron) Jul 79

Beltrán (Y Espantoso), Pedro G(erardo) obit Apr 79

Bemis, Samuel Flagg obit Nov 73

Ben-Gurion, David obit Jan 74

Bench, Johnny Oct 71

Benchley, Peter (Bradford) Jul 76

Benelli, Giovanni Cardinal Sep 77

Bennett, James V(an Ben-schotten) obit Feb 79

Bennett, W(illiam) A(ndrew) C(ecil) obit May 79

Benny, Jack obit Feb 75

Benson, Sally obit Sep 72

Bentley, Helen Delich Dec 71

Benton, Thomas Hart obit Mar 75

Benton, William (Burnett) obit May 73

Bentsen, Lloyd (Millard, Jr.) Sep 73

Berelson, Bernard (Reuben) obit Nov 79

Berendsen, Sir Carl August obit Dec 73

Berganza, Teresa Jan 79

Bergen, Candice Aug 76

Bergen, Edgar obit Nov 78

Bergland, Bob Sep 77

Berio, Luciano Mar 71

Berkeley, Busby Apr 71 obit May 76

Berle, Adolf A(ugustus) obit Apr 71

Berlinguer, Enrico Jul 76

Berman, Emile Zola Jun 72

Berman, Eugene obit Feb 73

Berman, Lazar Sep 77

Bernstein, Carl Oct 76

Berrigan, Philip (Francis) Feb 76

Berry, Chuck Apr 77

Berryman, James Thomas obit Oct 71

Berryman, John obit Feb 72

Bertolucci, Bernardo Jul 74

Best, Charles H(erbert) obit May 78

Best, Edna obit Nov 74

Betjeman, Sir John Mar 73

Beyen, J(ohan) W(illem) obit Jun 76

Bhutto, Zulfikar Ali Apr 72 obit May 79

Biddle, George obit Jan 74

Biggers, John D(avid) obit Feb 74

Biggs, E(dward George) Power obit May 77

Bilandic, Michael A(nthony) Feb 79

Bird, Caroline (Mahoney) Jul 76

Birdwell, Russell (Juarez) obit Mar 78

Birendra Bir Bikram Shah Dev, King of Nepal Aug 75

Birmingham, Stephen May 74

Birnie, William A(lfred) H(art) obit Oct 79

Bishop, Elizabeth Sep 77 obit Nov 79

Bishop, Isabel Oct 77

Bisset, Jacqueline May 77

Black, Hugo L(a Fayette) obit Nov 71

Black, Karen Mar 76

Blackett, P(atrick) M(aynard) S(tuart), Baron Blackett obit Sep 74

Blagonravov, A(natoli) A(rka-dyevich) obit Apr 75

Blair, David obit May 76

Blake, Eubie Apr 74

Blake, Robert Oct 75

Blanc, Mel(vin Jerome) Jun 76

Blanchfield, Florence A. obit Jun 71

Blanda George (Frederick) Sep 72

Blandford, John B(ennett), Jr. obit Mar 72

Blank, Theodor obit Jul 72

Blatchford, Joseph H(offer) Mar 71

Blattenberger, Raymond obit Jun 71

Blatty, William Peter Jun 74

Blaustein, Jacob obit Jan 71

Blegen, Judith Jun 77

Bliss, Anthony A(ddison) Apr 79

Bliven, Bruce obit Jul 77

Bloomgarden, Kermit obit Nov 76

Blue, Vida Mar 72

Blumberg, Baruch S(amuel) Nov 77

Blumenthal W(erner) Michael Jul 77

Bobst, Elmer H(olmes) Dec 73 obit Sep 78

Boerma, Addeke H(endrik) Dec 74

Boeschenstein, Harold obit Dec 72

Bogdanovich, Peter Jun 72

Boggs, Hale See Boggs, (Thomas) H. obit Mar 73

Boggs, (Thomas) Hale obit Mar 73

Bohlen, Charles E(ustis) obit Feb 74

Bok, Derek C(urtis) Jul 71

Bokassa I, Emperor Apr 78

Bolger, William F(rederick Leonard) Oct 79

Böll, Heinrich (Theodor) Jul 72

Bolotowsky, Ilya Apr 75

Bolton, Frances P(ayne Bingham) obit May 77

Bombeck, Erma Feb 79

Bond, Edward Jun 78

Bonnet, Henri obit Feb 79

Bono, Cher See Cher Jan 74

Bono, Sonny Feb 74

Bontemps, Arna (Wendell) obit Jul 73

Boone, J(oel) T(hompson) obit Jun 74

Borch, Fred J. Oct 71

Bordaberry (Arocena), Juan M(aría) Apr 75

Borg, Björn Dec 74

Borlaug, Norman E(rnest) Jul 71

Botha, P(ieter) W(illem) Sep 79

Boumedienne, Houari Jan 71 obit Feb 79

Bourassa, (Jean) Robert Sep 76

Bourke-White, Margaret obit Oct 71

Bouteflika, Abdelaziz Feb 76

Bouton, Jim Oct 71

Bowen, Catherine (Shober) Drinker obit Dec 73

Bowen, Ira Sprague obit Apr 73

Bowen, William G(ordon) May 73

Bowie, David Oct 76

Boyce, Westray Battle obit Mar 72

Boyd, Bill obit Nov 72

Boyd, Julian P(arks) Jun 76

Boyd, Louise A(rner) obit Nov 72

Boyd Orr, John Boyd Orr, 1st Baron obit Sep 71

Boyd, Stephen obit Aug 77

Boyd, William See Boyd, B. obit Nov 72

Boyer, Charles obit Oct 78

Boyle, Hal obit May 74

Brace, Gerald Warner obit Sep 78

Braddock, Bessie See Braddock E. M. obit Jan 71

Braddock, E(lizabeth) M(argaret Bamber) obit Jan 71

Brademas, John May 77

Braden, Spruille obit Mar 78

Bradlee, Benjamin C(rowninshield) Sep 75

Bradley, Thomas Nov 73

Bradshaw, Terry Apr 79

Brailowsky, Alexander obit Jun 76

Brando, Marlon Mar 74

Brandt, Willy Dec 73

Branzell, Karin obit Feb 75

Braun, (Joachim) Werner obit Jan 73

Bray, Robert S(tuart) obit Feb 75

Breech, Ernest R(obert) obit Aug 78

Brel, Jacques Mar 71 obit Nov 78

Brendel, Alfred Jul 77

Brennan, Peter J(oseph) Apr 73

Brennan, Walter obit Nov 74

Breslin, Jimmy Dec 73

Bresson, Robert Jan 71

Brewster, Kingman, Jr. Sep 79

Brezhnev, Leonid I(lyich) Nov 78

Brick, John obit Dec 73

Briggs, Ellis O(rmsbee) obit Apr 76

Briggs, James E(lbert) obit Aug 79

Britten, (Edward) Benjamin obit Feb 77

Brock, Lou Jun 75

Brock, William Emerson, 3d May 71

Brode, Wallace (Reed) obit Oct 74

Brogan, D(ennis) W(illiam) obit Feb 74

Bronfman, Edgar M(iles) Jul 74

Bronk, Detlev W(ulf) obit Jan 76

Bronowski, J(acob) obit Oct 74

Bronson, Charles Mar 75

Brooke, Sir Basil (Stanlake) See Brookeborough, Lord obit Oct 73

Brookeborough, Lord obit Oct 73

Brooks, Donald (Marc) Mar 72

Brooks, Gwendolyn Jul 77

Brooks, Mel Sep 74

Brothers, Joyce Apr 71

Browder, Earl (Russell) obit Sep 73

Brower, David (Ross) Jun 73

Brown, Dee Aug 79

Brown, Edmund G(erald) Jr. Apr 75

Brown, George H(ay) Jan 71

Brown, George S(cratchley) Oct 75 obit Feb 79

Brown, Harold Oct 77

Brown, J(ohn) Carter Apr 76

Brown, Joe E(van) obit Sep 73

Brown, Larry Mar 73

Brown, Prentiss M(arsh) obit Feb 74

Brownmiller, Susan Jan 78

Broyhill, Joel T(homas) May 74

Bruce, David K(irkpatrick) E(ste) obit Feb 78

Bruce, Louis R(ooks, Jr.) May 72

Brundage, Avery obit Aug 75

Brunner, Edmund de S(chweinitz) obit Feb 74

Brustein, Robert (Sanford) Aug 75

Bryan, Julien (Hequembourg) obit Jan 75

Bryant, Anita Nov 75

Buck, Pearl (Sydenstricker) obit Apr 73

Buckley, James L(ane) Oct 71

Chichester, Sir Francis (Charles) obit Oct 72
Childs, Richard S(pencer) obit Jan 79
Chiles, Lawton (Mainor, Jr.) Sep 71
Chinmoy, Sri Apr 76
Chiperfield, Robert B(ruce) obit May 71
Chirac, Jacques Jun 75
Chirico, Giorgio de Jun 72 obit Jan '79
Chisholm, (George) Brock obit Mar 71
Chou En-lai obit Feb 76
Christenberry, Robert K(eaton) obit Jun 73
Christie, Agatha obit Mar 76
Christo Mar 77
Christofilos, Nicholas C(onstantine) obit Nov 72
Chryssa (Vardea) Nov 78
Chu Teh obit Aug 76
Church, Frank (Forrester) Mar 78
Churchill, Clementine Ogilvy Hozier, Baroness See Spencer-Churchill, C. O. H., Baroness of Chartwell obit Mar 78
Cicognani, Amleto Giovanni, Cardinal obit Feb 74
Clapp, Margaret (Antoinette) obit Jun 74
Clapp, Verner W(arren) obit Sep 72
Clark, Eleanor May 78
Clark, Joe Oct 76
Clark, J(oseph) J(ames) obit Sep 71
Clark, Paul F(oster) obit Mar 73
Clark, Roy Jun 78
Clark, Tom C(ampbell) obit Aug 77
Clarke, Ron May 71
Clay, Cassius (Marcellus Jr.) See Ali, Muhammad Nov 78
Clay, Lucius D(ubignon) obit Jun 78
Clayburgh, Jill Sep 79
Clayton, P(hilip Thomas) B(yard) obit Mar 73
Claytor, W(illiam) Graham, Jr. May 79
Cleland, (Joseph) Max(well) Feb 78
Clemente, Roberto (Walker) Feb 72 obit Feb 73
Clifford, John Nov 72
Clift, David H(orace) obit Dec 73
Cline, John Wesley obit Sep 74

Clyde, George D(ewey) obit May 72
Coanda, Henri (-Marie) obit Feb 73
Cobb, Lee J. obit Apr 76
Cochran, H(orace) Merle obit Nov 73
Coco, James May 74
Coe, Fred(erick) obit Jun 79
Coggan, F(rederick) Donald Jul 74
Cohen, Manuel F(rederick) obit Aug 77
Colby, William E(gan) Jan 75
Coldwell, M(ichael) J. obit Oct 74
Cole, David L(awrence) obit Mar 78
Cole, Edward N(icholas) Jul 72 obit Jul 77
Coleman, John R(oyston) Oct 74
Coleman, William T(haddeus), Jr. Mar 76
Collins, Michael May 75
Colombo, Emilio Apr 71
Comaneci, Nadia Feb 77
Comfort, Alex(ander) Sep 74
Conant, James Bryant obit Apr 78
Condon, Eddie obit Oct 73
Condon, E(dward) U(hler) obit May 74
Cone, Fairfax M(astick) obit Aug 77
Conigliaro, Tony Feb 71
Connors, Jimmy Sep 75
Considine, Bob See Considine, R. B. obit Nov 75
Considine, Robert (Bernard) obit Nov 75
Cook, Marlow W(ebster) Jan 72
Cooke, (Alfred) Alistair May 74
Cooley, Denton A(rthur) Jan 76
Cooley, Harold D(unbar) obit Mar 74
Coolidge, William D(avid) obit Mar 75
Cooper, Dame Gladys obit Jan 72
Cooper, Irving S(pencer) Apr 74
Coppola, Francis Ford May 74
Cordero, Angel Oct 75
Cordier, Andrew W(ellington) obit Sep 75
Cordiner, Ralph J(arron) obit Jan 74
Cornell, Katharine obit Jul 74
Correll, Charles J. obit Nov 72
Corrigan, Mairead Apr 78

Corsaro, Frank (Andrew) Aug 75
Cortázar, Julio Feb 74
Cortney, Philip obit Jul 71
Cosell, Howard Nov 72
Cosgrave, Liam Jun 77
Cost, March obit Apr 73
Costa-Gavras, (Henri) Sep 72
Costa Gomes, Francisco da May 76
Costanza, Margaret Jun 78
Costello, John A(loysius) obit 76
Cot, Pierre obit Oct 77
Coudenhove-Kalergi, Richard N(icolaus), Count obit Oct 72
Coudert, Frederic René, Jr. obit Jul 72
Counts, George S(ylvester) obit Jan 75
Courant, Richard obit Mar 72
Court, Margaret (Smith) Sep 73
Cousins, Norman Aug 77
Cousteau, Jacques (-Yves) Jan 76
Coward, Sir Noel (Pierce) obit May 73
Cowley, Malcolm Jun 79
Cox, Wally obit Apr 73
Cozzens, James Gould obit Oct 78
Craig, Cleo F(rank) obit Jun 78
Craig, Elizabeth May obit Sep 75
Craig, Lyman C(reighton) obit Sep 74
Cranko, John obit Sep 73
Crawford, Joan obit Jul 77
Creasey, John obit Jul 73
Crespin, Régine Sep 79
Crichton, (John) Michael Apr 76
Cromer, 3d Earl of May 71
Cronkite, Walter (Leland, Jr.) Nov 75
Crosby, Bing obit Jan 78
Crosland, (Charles) Anthony (Raven) obit Apr 77
Cross, Milton John obit Feb 75
Crossman, R(ichard) H(oward) S(tafford) obit Jun 74
Crowley, Leo T(homas) obit Jun 72
Crown, Henry Jan 72
Crumb, George (Henry) Dec 74
Csonka, Larry Feb 77
Cullman, Howard S(tix) obit Sep 72
Culver, John C. Nov 79

Cunhal, Alvaro (Barrierinhas) Sep 75

Curry, John Jul 79

Cushman, Robert E(verton), Jr. Nov 72

Dale, Clamma Apr 79

Daley, Arthur (John) obit Feb 74

Daley, Richard J(oseph) Jun 76 (died Dec 76)

Daly, James (Firman) obit Sep 78

Dam, (Carl Peter) Henrik obit Jun 76

Dancer, Stanley Jun 73

Daniels, Farrington obit Sep 72

Däniken, Erich Von See Von Däniken, Erich May 76

D'Arcy, Martin (Cyril) obit Mar 77

Darin, Bobby obit Feb 74

Dark, Alvin (Ralph) Mar 75

Dassin, Jules Mar 71

Daugherty, James Henry obit Apr 74

David, Donald K(irk) obit Jun 79

David, Edward E(mil, Jr.) May 74

Davidson, John Sep 76

Davies, (William) Robertson Jun 75

Davis, Adelle Jan 73 obit Jul 74

Davis, Angela (Yvonne) Nov 72

Davis, Benjamin O(liver), Sr. obit Jan 71

Davis, Chester Charles obit Nov 75

Davis, Edward W(ilson) obit Feb 74

Davis, Joseph S(tancliffe) obit Jun 75

Davis, Meyer obit Jun 76

Davis, Sammy Jr. Jul 78

Davis, William (Grenville) May 73

Davison, Frederic E(llis) Feb 74

Dawson, William obit Sep 72

Day-Lewis, C(ecil) obit Jul 72

Dean, Dizzy obit Sep 74

Dean, Vera Micheles obit Dec 72

Deane, Martha See Young, M. obit Jan 74

Debus, Kurt H(einrich) Nov 73

DeBusschere, Dave Oct 73

DeGaetani, Jan Oct 77

De Kruif, Paul (Henry) obit Apr 71

De Rochemont, Louis (Clark) obit Feb 79

Delaunay, Sonia Aug 77

Delgado, José (Manuel Rodríguez) Feb 76

Della Femina, Jerry Nov 79

Dellinger, David Aug 76

Dellums, Ronald V. Sep 72

DeLorean, John Z(achary) Mar 76

Deloria, Vine (Victor), Jr. Sep 74

Denenberg, Herbert S(idney) Dec 72

Deneuve, Catherine Feb 78

Denfeld, Louis E(mil) obit May 72

De Niro, Robert Aug 76

Dennis, Lawrence obit Oct 77

Dennis, Patrick See Tanner, Edward Everett, 3d obit Feb 77

Dent, Frederick B(aily) Apr 74

Denver, John Jan 75

De Pauw, Gommar A(lbert) May 74

Dern, Bruce Oct 78

Desai, Morarji (Ranchhodji) Jan 78

DeSeversky, Alexander P(rocofieff) obit Oct 74

De Sica, Vittorio obit Jan 75

Deupree, Richard R(edwood) obit May 74

De Valera, Eamon obit Oct 75

Dewey, Thomas E(dmund) obit Apr 71

Dewhurst, Colleen Jul 74

Dexter, John Jul 76

Di Suvero, Mark Nov 79

Díaz Ordaz, Gustavo obit Sep 79

Dickinson, Edwin (W.) obit Feb 79

Didion, Joan Sep 78

Diebenkorn, Richard (Clifford, Jr.) Dec 71

Diefenbaker, John G(eorge) obit Oct 79

Dies, Martin obit Jan 73

Dieterle, William obit Feb 73

Dix, William S(hepherd) obit Apr 78

Dixon, (Charles) Dean obit Jan 77

Dixon, Jeane (L.) Feb 73

Doan, Leland I(ra) obit May 74

Dobzhansky, Theodosius (Grigorievich) obit Feb 76

Doctorow, E(dgar) L(aurence) Jul 76

Dodd, Thomas J(oseph) obit Jul 71

Dodds, Gil(bert Lothair) obit Apr 77

Dodge, Bayard obit Jul 72

Dole, Robert J(oseph) Apr 72

Dollard, Charles obit Apr 77

Domingo, Placido Mar 72

Dominguín, Luis Miguel Mar 72

Doms, Keith Jun 71

Donleavy, J(ames) P(atrick) Jul 79

Donlon, Mary (Honor) obit May 77

Donnelly, Walter J(oseph) obit Jan 71

Donoso, José Feb 78

Douglas, Lewis W(illiams) obit May 74

Douglas, Paul H(oward) obit Nov 76

Dowell, Anthony May 71

Dowling, Eddie obit Apr 76

Dowling, Robert W(hittle) obit Nov 73

Dowling, Walter C(ecil) obit Sep 77

Doxiadis, Constantinos A(postolos) obit Sep 75

Draper, William H(enry) obit Feb 75

Drew, Elizabeth (Brenner) Oct 79

Dreyfuss, Henry obit Dec 72

Dreyfuss, Richard Jan 76

Drinan, Robert F(rederick) Jun 71

Driscoll, Alfred E(astlack) obit May 75

Du Bois, Shirley Graham obit Jun 77

Dubos, René J(ules) Jan 73

Duchin, Peter Jan 77

Duclos, Jacques obit Jun 75

Duerk, Alene (Bertha) Sep 73

Duffey, Joseph D(aniel) Mar 71

Duffy, Bernard C(ornelius) obit Nov 72

Dukakis, Michael S(tanley) Feb 78

Dunaway, Faye Feb 72

Dunn, James Clement obit Jun 79

Dunning, John R(ay) obit Oct 75

Dunninger, Joseph obit May 75

Durham, Carl (Thomas) obit Jun 74

Dutra, Eurico Gaspar obit Sep 74

Duvalier, François obit Jun 71

Duvalier, Jean-Claude Jun 72

Duvall, Robert Jul 77
Du Vigneaud, Vincent obit Feb 79
Dykstra, John obit May 72

Eagleton, Thomas (Francis) Nov 73
Eames, Charles obit Oct 78
Eanes, António (dos Santos) Ramalho Apr 79
Eastwood, Clint Oct 71
Eaton, Cyrus S(tephen) obit Jul 79
Ebsen, Buddy Jan 77
Eccles, Sir John (Carew) Oct 72
Eccles, Marriner S(toddard) obit Feb 78
Ecevit, Bülent Jan 75
Echeverría Álvarez, Luis Nov 72
Edelman, Maurice obit Feb 76
Eden, Anthony, 1st Earl of Avon See Avon, A. E., 1st Earl of obit Mar 77
Edwards, Charles C(ornell) Oct 73
Eghbal, Manouchehr obit Feb 78
Eglevsky, André obit Feb 78
Ehrlichman, John D(aniel) Oct 79
Eiseley, Loren (Corey) obit Sep 77
Eisendrath, Maurice N(athan) obit Jan 74
Eisenstaedt, Alfred Jan 75
Elder, Lee Aug 76
Eliot, George Fielding obit Jun 71
Eliot, Martha May obit Apr 78
Elisofon, Eliot Jan 72 obit May 73
Ellender, Allen J(oseph) obit Oct 72
Ellington, Duke obit Jul 74
Ellington, (E.) Buford obit May 72
Elliott, Osborn Jan 78
Ellsberg, Daniel Dec 73
Ely, Paul (Henri) obit Mar 75
Enrique Tarancón, Vincente Cardinal Oct 72
Entremont, Philippe Mar 77
Erdman, Jean Sep 71
Erhard, Ludwig obit Jul 77
Erhard, Werner (Hans) Apr 77
Erikson, Erik H(omburger) May 71
Ernst, Max obit May 76
Ernst, Morris L(eopold) obit Jul 76

Erskine, G(raves) B(lanchard) obit Jul 73
Ervin, Sam(uel) J(ames), Jr. Oct 73
Erving, Julius May 75
Esposito, Phil May 73
Estes, E(lliott) M(arantette) Jan 79
Ettinger, Richard P(rentice) obit Apr 71
Evans, Alice C(atherine) obit Oct 75
Evans, Bergen obit Apr 78
Evans, Daniel (Jackson) Aug 75
Evans, Dame Edith (Mary) obit Jan 77
Evans, Herbert M(cLean) obit Apr 71
Evans, Walker Sep 71 obit Jun 75
Evergood, Philip (Howard Francis Dixon) obit Apr 73
Evert, Chris(tine Marie) Apr 73
Ewing, (William) Maurice obit Jun 74
Eysenck, Hans J(ürgen) Nov 72

Fabian, Robert (Honey) obit Aug 78
Fahd, Crown Prince of Saudi Arabia May 79
Fahy, Charles obit Nov 79
Fairchild, John B(urr) Jun 71
Faisal, King of Saudi Arabia obit May 75
Falk, Peter Jul 72
Fallaci, Oriana Feb 77
Fälldin, Thorbjörn (Nils Olof) May 78
Farah Diba Pahlevi Mar 76
Farber, Sidney obit May 73
Farley, James A(loysius) obit Aug 76
Farrar, John (Chipman) obit Jan 75
Farrell, James T(homas) obit Oct 79
Fasanella, Ralph Jun 75
Fassbinder, Rainer Werner May 77
Faulkner, (Arthur) Brian (Dean), Baron Feb 72 obit May 77
Fauntroy, Walter E(dward) Feb 79
Faust, Clarence H(enry) obit Aug 75
Fawcett-Majors, Farrah Feb 78
Fawcett, Sherwood L(uther) Dec 72

Feather, Vic(tor Grayson Hardie) Mar 73 obit Sep 76
Feinstein, Dianne Jun 79
Feis, Herbert obit May 72
Feld, Eliot Oct 71
Feld, Irvin Feb 79
Felker, Clay S. Feb 75
Feltin, Maurice Cardinal obit Nov 75
Fenwick, Millicent (Vernon Hammond) Apr 77
Fernandel obit Apr 71
Fidrych, Mark Mar 78
Fiedler, Arthur May 77 obit Sep 79
Field, Betty obit Nov 73
Field, Sally Oct 79
Fields, Dorothy obit May 74
Fields, Gracie obit Nov 79
Finch, Peter Sep 72 obit Mar 77
Fine, John S(ydney) obit Jul 78
Finley, Charles O(scar) Jun 74
Finley, David E(dward) obit Apr 77
Firestone Harvey S(amuel), Jr. obit Jul 73
Firkusny, Rudolf Oct 79
Fischer, John obit Oct 78
Fishbein, Morris obit Nov 76
Fisher of Lambeth, Geoffrey Francis Fisher, Baron obit Nov 72
Fister, George M(organ) obit Jul 76
Fitch, Aubrey (Wray) obit Jul 78
Fitzgerald, Geraldine Oct 76
Fitzgerald, Robert (Stuart) Sep 76
Fitzsimmons, Frank E(dward) May 71
Flack, Roberta Nov 73
Flanders, Michael obit Jun 75
Flanner, Janet obit Jan 79
Fleisher, Leon Jan 71
Fleming, Lady Amalia Nov 72
Fletcher, Arthur A(llen) Nov 71
Fletcher, James C(hipman) May 72
Flood, Daniel J(ohn) Aug 78
Flory, Paul J(ohn) Mar 75
Fodor, Eugene Apr 76
Foley, Martha obit Oct 77
Foley, Raymond M(ichael) obit Apr 75
Folliard, Edward T(homas) obit Feb 77
Folsom, Marion B(ayard) obit Nov 76
Fonda, Henry Nov 74
Fonteyn, Margot Mar 72

Forand, Aime J(oseph) obit Mar 72
Forbes, Malcolm S(tevenson) Feb 75
Ford, Benson obit Sep 78
Ford, Betty See Ford, Elizabeth (Anne Bloomer) Sep 75
Ford, Eileen (Otte) Oct 71
Ford, Elizabeth (Anne Bloomer) Sep 75
Ford, Gerald R(udolph, Jr.) Nov 75
Ford, Henry, II Jun 78
Ford, John obit Nov 73
Foreman, Clark (Howell) obit Aug 77
Foreman, George May 74
Forman, Milos Dec 71
Forrest, Wilbur S(tudley) obit May 77
Forssmann, Werner (Theodor Otto) obit Aug 79
Forsythe, John May 73
Fosdick, Raymond B(laine) obit Sep 72
Fosse, Bob Jun 72
Foster, John S(tuart), Jr. Dec 71
Fowler, William A(lfred) Sep 74
Fowles, John Mar 77
Fox, Carol Jul 78
Fox, Michael (Wilson) Feb 77
Fox, Nellie obit Feb 76
Foxx, Redd Dec 72
Foyle, Gilbert (Samuel) obit Jan 72
Fracci, Carla Feb 76
Frampton, Peter May 78
Francis, Sam(uel Lewis) Oct 73
Franco (y Bahamonde), Francisco obit Jan 76
François-Poncet, André obit Mar 78
Frank, Reuven Jun 73
Franke, William B(irrell) obit Aug 79
Frankel, Charles obit Jul 79
Franklin, John M(erryman) obit Aug 75
Franklin, Walter S(imonds) obit Oct 72
Frasconi, Antonio Mar 72
Fraser, Lady Antonia Oct 74
Fraser, Doug(las Andrew) Oct 77
Fraser, (John) Malcolm Mar 76
Frazer, Joseph W(ashington) obit Sep 71
Frazier, Joe Apr 71
Frazier, Walt Feb 73

Frederik IX, King of Denmark obit Mar 72
Freni, Mirella Apr 77
Fresnay, Pierre obit Feb 75
Freud, Anna Apr 79
Frick, Ford C(hristopher) obit Jun 78
Friedman, Bruce Jay Jun 72
Friel, Brian Jun 74
Frisch, Karl von Feb 74
Frost, Leslie M(iscampbell) obit Jul 73
Frowick, Roy Halston See Halston Dec 72
Frye, David Mar 75
Fuentes, Carlos Oct 72
Fugard, Athol Jun 75
Fukuda, Takeo Jun 74
Fuller, Alfred C(arl) obit Jan 74
Fuller, R(ichard) Buckminster (Jr.) Feb 76
Fürstenberg, Diane von See Von Fürstenberg, Diane Sep 76
Furtseva, Ekaterina A(lexeyevna) obit Dec 74

Gabin, Jean obit Jan 77
Gabo, Naum Apr 72 obit Oct 77
Gabor, Dennis Oct 72 obit Apr 79
Gabriel, Roman Nov 75
Gabrielson, Guy (George) obit Jun 76
Gaddafi, Moamar al- See Qaddafi, M. Sep 73
Gades, Antonio Feb 73
Gainza Paz, Alberto obit Feb 78
Galbraith, John Kenneth May 75
Gallagher, Buell Gordon obit Jan 79
Gallagher, William M. obit Nov 75
Gallery, Daniel V(incent, Jr.) obit Mar 77
Gallico, Paul (William) obit Sep 76
Gambling, John B(radley) obit Jan 75
Gannon, Robert I(gnatius) obit May 78
Garagiola, Joe Jan 76
Garand, John C(antius) obit Apr 74
Garcia, Carlos P. obit 71
García Márquez, Gabriel José Jul 73
Gardiner, Robert K(weku Atta) Jul 75

Gardner, John (Champlin, Jr.) Oct 78
Gardner, John W(illiam) Mar 76
Garfunkel, Art Jun 74
Gargan, William obit Apr 79
Garner, Erroll (Louis) obit Mar 77
Garst, Roswell obit Jan 78
Gaud, William S(teen, Jr.) obit Feb 78
Gebel-Williams, Gunther Dec 71
Geisel, Ernesto Aug 75
Geldzahler, Henry Sep 78
Geller, Uri Sep 78
Geneen, Harold S(ydney) Feb 74
Genet, Jean Apr 74
Genscher, Hans-Dietrich Jun 75
Gentele, Goeran Sep 72 obit Sep 72
Gerard, Ralph W(aldo) obit Apr 74
Geraud, André obit Jan 75
Gerow, Leonard Townsend obit Dec 72
Gerulaitis, Vitas Jun 79
Getz, Stan Apr 71
Giamatti, A(ngelo) Bartlett Apr 78
Giannini, Giancarlo Jun 79
Gibson, Kenneth (Allen) May 71
Giegengack, A(ugustus) E(dward) obit Sep 74
Gierek, Edward May 71
Gilbreth, Lillian (Evelyn) M(oller) obit Feb 72
Gilchrist, Huntington obit Mar 75
Gillette, Guy M(ark) obit Apr 73
Gilligan, John J(oyce) May 72
Ginastera, Alberto (Evaristo) Jan 71
Gingrich, Arnold obit Sep 76
Ginsberg, Mitchell I(rving) Jun 71
Giovanni, Nikki Apr 73
Gipson, Lawrence Henry obit Nov 71
Giroud, Françoise Apr 75
Giscard d'Estaing, Valéry Oct 74
Gish, Lillian Aug 78
Giulini, Carlo Maria Mar 78
Givens, Willard E(arl) obit Jul 71
Glenn, John H(erschel), Jr. Mar 76
Glueck, Eleanor T(ouroff) obit Nov 72

Glueck, Nelson obit Mar 71
Godden, Rumer Aug 76
Goldberg, Rube(n Lucius) obit Jan 71
Goldmark, Peter C(arl) obit Feb 78
Goldwater, Barry M(orris) Jun 78
Goldwyn, Samuel obit Mar 74
Golschmann, Vladimir obit May 72
Gonzalez, Efren W(illiam) Jan 71
González (Márquez), Felipe Jan 78
Good, Robert A(lan) Mar 72
Goodhart, Arthur Lehman obit Feb 79
Goodman, Andrew Apr 75
Goodman, Paul obit Oct 72
Goodson, Mark May 78
Goolagong, Evonne Nov 71
Gorbach, Alfons obit Oct 72
Gordon, Kermit obit Aug 76
Gordon, Max obit Jan 79
Gordon, Ruth Apr 72
Gordy, Berry, Jr. Jul 75
Gorey, Edward (St. John) Nov 76
Gottlieb, Adolph obit Apr 74
Gottlieb, Melvin B(urt) Jan 74
Goudsmit, Samuel A(braham) obit Feb 79
Gouin, Felix obit Oct 79 (died Oct 77)
Goulart, João (Belchior Marques) obit Feb 77
Gould, Chester Sep 71
Gould, Elliott Feb 71
Gould, Laurence M(ckinley) Jan 78
Gove, Philip B(abcock) obit Jan 73
Grace, Princess of Monaco Oct 77
Grace, Alonzo G(askell) obit Dec 71
Grade, Lew Aug 79
Graf, Herbert obit May 73
Graham, Billy Jan 73
Graham, Frank P(orter) obit Apr 72
Graham, Katharine (Meyer) Jan 71
Graham, Shirley See Du Bois, S. G. obit Jun 77
Graham, William Franklin See Graham, B. Jan 73
Gramm, Donald Nov 75
Granahan, Kathryn E(lizabeth) obit Sep 79
Grandjany, Marcel (Georges Lucien) obit Apr 75
Granger, Lester B(lackwell) obit Mar 76

Grant, Lee Mar 74
Grasso, Ella T(ambussi) May 75
Grauer, Ben(jamin Franklin) obit Jul 77
Gravel, Maurice Robert See Gravel, Mike Jan 72
Gravel, Mike Jan 72
Graves, Robert (Ranke) May 78
Gray, Hanna Holborn Mar 79
Gray, L(ouis) Patrick, 3d Sep 72
Grayson, C(harles) Jackson, Jr. Sep 72
Grechko, Andrei A(ntonovich) obit Jun 76
Greeley, Andrew M(oran) Dec 72
Green, Martyn obit Apr 75
Greenspan, Alan Dec 74
Greer, Germaine Nov 71
Gregory, Cynthia May 77
Grey, Joel Jan 73
Grier, Roosevelt Mar 75
Griffies, Ethel obit Nov 75
Griffis, Stanton obit Oct 74
Griffith, Paul H(oward) obit Feb 75
Grigorovich, Yuri (Nikolaevich) Sep 75
Grimes, W(illiam) H(enry) obit Mar 72
Grivas, George (Theodorus) obit Mar 74
Grizzard, George Jun 76
Grofé, Ferde obit May 72
Gronchi, Giovanni obit Jan 79
Grooms, Charles Roger See Grooms, R. Dec 72
Grooms, Red Dec 72
Gropper, William obit Mar 77
Gross, Charles P(hilip) obit Sep 75
Gross, Mason W(elch) obit Jan 78
Grossinger, Jennie obit Jan 73
Gruenberg, Sidonie Matsner obit May 74
Gruening, Ernest (Henry) obit Sep 74
Grzimek, Bernhard Mar 73
Guggenheim, Harry F(rank) obit Mar 71
Guidry, Ron May 79
Guinan, Matthew Sep 74
Gundersen, Gunnar obit Aug 79
Gunter, Ray(mond Jones) obit Jun 77
Gustaf VI, King of Sweden obit Nov 73
Guston, Philip Feb 71
Guthrie, Janet Oct 78

Guthrie, Sir (William) Tyrone obit Jul 71
Guttmacher, Alan F(rank) obit May 74

Haagen-Smit, A(rie) J(an) obit May 77
Habe, Hans obit Nov 77
Hackman, Gene Jul 72
Hackworth, Green H(aywood) obit Sep 73
Haggard, Merle Jan 77
Haig, Alexander Meigs, Jr. Jan 73
Haile Selassie I, Emperor of Ethiopia obit Oct 75
Hailey, Arthur Feb 72
Haitink, Bernard Nov 77
Halberstam, David Apr 73
Haldeman, H(arry) R(obbins) Sep 78
Haley, Alex (Palmer) Jan 77
Hall, Gus May 73
Hall, Leonard W(ood) obit Jul 79
Halsman, Philippe obit Aug 79
Halston Dec 72
Hamill, Dorothy Jun 76
Hamilton, Charles Jul 76
Hamilton, Margaret Apr 79
Hamlisch, Marvin (Frederick) May 76
Hammer, Armand Jun 73
Hammond, John (Henry Jr.) Jul 79
Hampshire, Susan Jan 74
Hampton, Lionel (Leo) Oct 71
Handke, Peter Apr 73
Handley, Harold W(illis) obit Nov 72
Hanks, Nancy Sep 71
Hansen, Alvin H(arvey) obit Aug 75
Hardenbrook, Donald J(ohnson) obit Aug 76
Hardin, Garrett (James) Sep 74
Hargis, Billy James Mar 72
Harkness, Rebekah (West) Apr 74
Harlan, John Marshall obit Feb 72
Harper, Valerie Feb 75
Harridge, Will(iam) obit Jun 71
Harriman, E(dward) Roland (Noel) obit Apr 78
Harrington, Russell C(hase) obit Oct 71
Harris, Bucky obit Jan 78
Harris, Cyril M(anton) Feb 77
Harris, Franco Jun 76
Harris, Julie Aug 77

Harris, Roy obit Nov 79
Harris, Seymour E(dwin) obit Dec 74
Hart, Gary (Warren) May 76
Hart, Philip A(loysius) obit Feb 77
Hart, Thomas C(harles) obit Sep 71
Hartman, Paul (William) obit Dec 73
Hartnell, Norman (Bishop) obit Aug 79
Harvey, Laurence obit Jan 74
Hastie, William H(enry) obit Jun 76
Hatcher, Richard G(ordon) Feb 72
Haughton, Daniel J(eremiah) Sep 74
Hawkins, Erik Jan 74
Hawkins, Jack obit Oct 73
Hawks, Howard May 72
Hawn, Goldie Dec 71
Haworth, Leland J(ohn) obit May 79
Haya de la Torre, Victor Raúl obit Sep 79
Hayakawa, S(amuel) I(chiye) Jan 77
Hayakawa, Sessue obit Jan 74
Haydée, Marcia Oct 77
Hayden, Carl T(rumbull) obit Mar 72
Hayden, Sterling May 78
Hayden, Tom Apr 76
Hayes, Isaac Oct 72
Hayes, Roland obit Mar 77
Hayes, Wayne Woodrow See Hayes, Woody Feb 75
Hayes, Woody Feb 75
Hays, Wayne L(evere) Nov 74
Hayward, Leland obit Apr 71
Hayward, Susan obit May 75
Heald, Henry Townley obit Jan 76
Healey, Denis (Winston) Dec 71
Heatter, Gabriel obit May 72
Heflin, Van obit Sep 71
Heidegger, Martin Jun 72 obit Jul 76
Heiden, Konrad obit Sep 75 (died Jul 66)
Height, Dorothy I(rene) Sep 72
Heilbroner, Robert L(ouis) Jun 75
Heinemann, Gustav (Walter) obit Aug 76
Heisenberg, Werner (Karl) obit Mar 76
Heiser, Victor G(eorge) obit May 72
Heller, Joseph Jan 73

Helms, Jesse A. Jul 79
Helpern, Milton May 73 obit Jun 77
Hemingway, Margaux Mar 78
Henderson, Florence Apr 71
Henning, Doug Aug 76
Henson, Jim Mar 77
Hepworth, Barbara obit Aug 75
Herman, Woody Apr 73
Hernandez, Aileen C(larke) Jul 71
Hernández Colón, Rafael May 73
Herod, William Rogers obit Sep 74
Hershey, Lewis B(laine) obit Jul 77
Hertzberg, Arthur Jun 75
Herzberg, Gerhard Feb 73
Herzog, Werner Aug 78
Heschel, Abraham Joshua obit Mar 73
Hewitt, Henry K(ent) obit Nov 72
Heyerdahl, Thor Sep 72
Hibbs, Ben obit May 75
Hickenlooper, Bourke B(lakemore) obit Oct 71
Hicks, Louise Day Mar 74
Highet, Gilbert (Arthur) obit Mar 78
Hill, Arthur Mar 77
Hill, Arthur M(iddleton) obit Nov 74
Hill, George Roy Apr 77
Hill, Graham Jul 73 obit Jan 76
Hill, Harry W(ilbur) obit Sep 71
Hill, Robert C(harles) obit Feb 79
Hill, William S(ilas) obit Nov 72
Hilleboe, Herman E(rtesvaag) obit Jun 74
Hiller, Stanley, Jr. Nov 74
Hills, Carla Anderson Nov 75
Hilton, Conrad N(icholson) obit Mar 79
Hirohito, Emperor of Japan Mar 76
Hirschfeld, Albert Jan 71
Hitti, Philip K(huri) obit Feb 79
Hobbs, Leonard S(inclair) obit Jan 78
Hochhuth, Rolf Oct 76
Hockney, David Jul 72
Hodges, Gil(bert Ray) obit May 72
Hodges, Luther H(artwell) obit Nov 74
Hoffa, James R(iddle) May 72

Hoffman, Joseph G(ilbert) obit Jan 75
Hoffman, Paul G(ray) obit Nov 74
Hogan, Frank S(mithwick) obit May 74
Holland, (George) Kenneth obit Feb 78
Holland, Spessard L(indsey) obit Dec 71
Holley, Edward G(ailon) Jun 74
Holton, (Abner) Linwood, (Jr.) Feb 71
Holtzman, Elizabeth Nov 73
Homer, Arthur B(artlett) obit Sep 72
Honecker, Erich Apr 72
Hoo (Chi-Tsai), Victor obit Jul 72
Hood, Clifford F(iroved) obit Jan 79
Hooks, Benjamin L(awson) Apr 78
Hoover, J(ohn) Edgar obit Jun 72
Horgan, Paul Feb 71
Horner, Matina Souretis Jul 73
Horsfall, Frank L(appin), Jr. obit Apr 71
Houssay, Bernardo Alberto obit Nov 71
Hoveyda, Amir Abbas Oct 71 obit Jun 79
Howard, Frank (Oliver) Jan 72
Howard, Ron Jan 79
Howe, Helen obit Mar 75
Howe, Irving Apr 78
Howe, James Wong obit Sep 76
Howe, Quincy obit Apr 77
Howell, Charles R(obert) obit Sep 73
Hoyt, (Edwin) Palmer obit Aug 79
Hua Kuo-feng Mar 77
Huck, Arthur obit Mar 73
Huebner, Clarence R(alph) obit Nov 72
Hughes, Howard (Robard) obit May 76
Hughes, Ted Jun 79
Hull, Helen R(ose) obit Sep 71
Humbard, (Alpha) Rex (Emmanuel) Sep 72
Humphrey, Hubert H(oratio, Jr.) obit Mar 78
Hunt, H(aroldson) L(afayette) obit Jan 75
Hunt, Herold C(hristian) obit Jan 77
Hunter, Alberta May 79

Hunter, Jim May 75
Huntington, Anna Hyatt obit Dec 73
Huntley, Chet obit May 74
Hurley, Roy T. obit Dec 71
Hurok, S(olomon) obit Apr 74
Husak, Gustav Oct 71
Hussein, Taha obit Dec 73
Hutchins, Robert Maynard obit Jul 77
Huxley, Sir Julian (Sorell) obit Apr 75
Huxtable, Ada Louise (Landman) Mar 73

Iacocca, Lee A(nthony) Oct 71
Indiana, Robert Mar 73
Inge, William (Motter) obit Jul 73
Ingersoll, Royal E(ason) obit Jul 76
Inönü, Ismet obit Feb 74
Irving, John (Winslow) Oct 79
Irving, Jules obit Sep 79
Iselin, Columbus O'D(onnell) obit Feb 71
Isherwood, Christopher (William) Oct 72
Ishibashi, Tanzan obit Jun 73
Istomin, Eugene (George) Oct 77

Jackson, Glenda Dec 71
Jackson, Henry M(artin) Oct 79
Jackson, Lady See Ward, B. Jan 77
Jackson, Mahalia obit Mar 72
Jackson, Maynard (Holbrook, Jr.) Sep 76
Jackson, Reggie Jan 74
Jackson, William H(arding) obit Nov 71
Jacobs, Jane Mar 77
Jagger, Mick Dec 72
James, Arthur Horace obit Jun 73
James, Daniel, Jr. Mar 76 obit Apr 78
Jamieson, J(ohn) (Kenneth) Jun 74
Jamison, Judith Jan 73
Jarvis, Howard (Arnold) Feb 79
Jarvis, Lucy (Howard) Apr 72
Jastrow, Robert Jan 73
Javacheff, Christo See Christo Mar 77
Jaworski, Leon Jun 74
Jay, Peter Oct 78
Jencks, Christopher (Sandys) Apr 73

Jenner, Bruce Aug 77
Jensen, Arthur R(obert) Jan 73
Jewison, Norman Jun 79
Jhabvala, Ruth Prawer Mar 77
Jobert, Michel Feb 75
Joel, Billy Sep 79
John, Elton Mar 75
John Paul I, Pope Nov 78 obit Jan 79
John Paul II, Pope Nov 79
Johns, Glynis Sep 73
Johnson, Alvin (Saunders) obit Jul 71
Johnson, Frank M(inis) Jr. Aug 78
Johnson, Howard A(lbert) obit Sep 74
Johnson, Lyndon B(aines) obit Mar 73
Johnson, Malcolm (Malone) obit Aug 76
Johnson, Nunnally obit May 77
Johnson, Thor obit Mar 75
Johnson, Virginia E(shelman) Apr 76
Jones, Clara Stanton Jul 76
Jones, E(li) Stanley obit Mar 73
Jones, Howard P(alfrey) obit Nov 73
Jones, Jack May 76
Jones, James Larkin See Jones, Jack May 76
Jones, Preston Feb 77 obit Nov 79
Jones, Quincy (Delight, Jr.) Feb 77
Jones, Russell obit Aug 79
Jong, Erica Jul 75
Jooss, Kurt Jul 76 obit Jul 79
Jordan, Barbara (Charline) Sep 74
Jordan, B(enjamin) Everett obit May 74
Jordan, Vernon E(ulion), Jr. Feb 72
Jordan, (William) Hamilton (McWhorter) Aug 77
Jorgensen, Anker (Henrik) Sep 78
Joseph, Sir Keith (Sinjohn) Feb 75
Josephs, Devereux C(olt) obit Mar 77
Judson, Arthur (Leon) obit Mar 75
Julian, Percy L(avon) obit Jan 75
Jumblatt, Kamal Jan 77 obit May 77
Jurgensen, Sonny Jun 77

Kael, Pauline Mar 74
Kahane, Meir (David) Oct 72
Kahn, Alfred E(dward) Mar 79
Kahn, Ely Jacques obit Nov 72
Kahn, Louis I. obit May 74
Kahn, Madeline May 77
Kallen, Horace M(eyer) obit Apr 74
Kampmann, (Olfert) Viggo (Fischer) obit Jul 76
Kapp, Joe Sep 75
Karamanlis, Constantine Apr 76
Kardelj, Edvard obit Apr 79
Karinska, Barbara Jan 71
Karpov, Anatoly Nov 78
Kästner, Erich obit Oct 74
Katchalski, Ephraim See Katzir, E. Jan 75
Katz, Alex Jul 75
Katz, Label A(braham) obit Jun 75
Katz-Suchy, Juliusz obit Dec 71
Katzir, Ephraim Jan 75
Kawabata, Yasunari obit Jun 72
Kazan, Elia Oct 72
Keach, Stacy Nov 71
Keating, Kenneth B(arnard) obit Jun 75
Keaton, Diane Jun 78
Keeler, Ruby Dec 71
Keita, Mobida obit Jul 77
Keldysh, Mstislav (Vsevolodovich) obit Aug 78
Kellems, Vivien obit Mar 75
Keller, James (Gregory) obit Apr 77
Kelley, Clarence M(arion) May 74
Kelly, Emmett obit May 79
Kelly, Gene Feb 77
Kelly, Grace (Patricia) See Grace, Princess of Monaco
Kelly, John B(renden), Jr. Jun 71
Kelly, Marvin J(oe) obit May 71
Kelly, Walt(er Crawford) obit Dec 73
Kelsen, Hans obit Jun 73
Kemeny, John G(eorge) Feb 71
Kempton, (James) Murray Jun 73
Kendall, Edward C(alvin) obit Jun 72
Kendrick, Baynard (Hardwick) obit May 77
Kennedy, Edward M(oore) Oct 78

Kennedy, Stephen P(atrick)
obit Jan 79
Kenney, George C(hurchill)
obit Oct 77
Kent, Rockwell obit Apr 71
Kenton, Stan Jun 79 obit
Oct 79
Kenyatta, Jomo Apr 74 obit
Oct 78
Kenyon, Dorothy obit Apr 72
Kepes, György Mar 73
Kerkorian, Kirk Mar 75
Kerner, Otto (Jr.) obit Jul 76
Kertész, André Aug 79
Kesey, Ken (Elton) May 76
Khachaturian, Aram (Ilich)
obit Jun 78
Khadafy, Muammar See Qad-
dafi, M. Sep 73
Khalid, King of Saudi Arabia
Jan 76
Khomeini, Ayatollah Ruholla
(Mussavi) Nov 79
Khrushchev, Nikita S(ergeye-
vich) obit Oct 71
Kiley, Richard Apr 73
Killanin, Michael Morris, 3d
Baron Apr 73
Kimball, Spencer W(ooley)
Feb 79
Kimpton, Lawrence A(lpheus)
obit Jan 78
Kincaid, Thomas C(assin)
obit Jan 73
King, Carole Jan 74
King, Cecil R(hodes) obit May
74
King, Muriel obit May 77
Kingdon, Frank obit Apr 72
Kipnis, Alexander obit Jul 78
Kirbo, Charles H(ughes) Sep
77
Kirby, George May 77
Kirby, Robert E(mory) Sep 79
Kirchwey, Freda obit Feb 76
Kirk, William T(albot) obit
May 74
Kirkland, Gelsey Oct 75
Kirkpatrick, Miles W(ells) Feb
72
Kirkpatrick, Ralph Sep 71
Kissinger, Henry A(lfred) Jun
72
Klassen, Elmer T(heodore)
May 73
Klein, Calvin (Richard) Jul 78
Klein, Herbert G(eorge) Feb
71
Klein, Robert Mar 77
Kleindienst, Richard G(ordon)
Oct 72
Klemperer, Otto obit Sep 73
Kleppe, Thomas S(avig) Aug
76

Knatchbull-Hugessen Sir
Hughe (Montgomery) obit
May 71
Knaths, (Otto) Karl obit Apr
71
Knievel, Evel Feb 72
Knipling, E(dward) F(red)
May 75
Knorr, Nathan H(omer) obit
Aug 77
Knowland, William F(ife) obit
Apr 74
Knowles, John H(ilton) obit
May 79
Knudsen, Semon E(mil) Jan
74
Koch, Edward I(rving) Sep
78
Koch, John obit Jun 78
Koch, Kenneth (Jay) Feb 78
Kohl, Helmut (Michael) Aug
77
Kohler, Walter J(odok), Jr.
obit May 76
Kohoutek, Lubos Jun 74
Kollek, Teddy Oct 74
Kollmar, Richard obit Feb 71
Konev, Ivan S(tepanovich)
obit Jul 73
Konstanty, Jim obit Aug 76
Kopit, Arthur L(ee) Dec 72
Korbut, Olga Jul 73
Korman, Harvey Oct 79
Kosinski, Jerry (Nikodem)
Mar 74
Kowalski, Frank, Jr. obit Dec
74
Krag, Jens Otto obit Aug 78
Krasner, Lee Mar 74
Kraus, Lili Oct 75
Kreps, Juanita M(orris) Jun 77
Krips, Josef obit Dec 74
Krishna Menon, V(engalil)
K(rishnan) obit Nov 74
Krishnamurti, Jiddu Oct 74
Kristofferson, Kris Nov 74
Kristol, Irving (William) Sep
74
Kroc, Ray(mond) A. Mar 73
Krock, Arthur obit Jun 74
Kroll, Jack obit Jul 71
Kroll, Leon obit Dec 74
Kross, Anna M(oscowitz) obit
Oct 79
Krupa, Gene obit Dec 73
Krupsak, Mary Anne Jul 75
Kubitschek (de Oliveira), Jus-
celino obit Nov 76
Kucinich, Dennis J(ohn)
Mar 79
Kuhlman, Kathryn Jul 74 obit
Apr 76
Kuhn, Maggie Jul 78
Kuhn, Margaret E. See Kuhn,
Maggie Jul 78

Kuiper, Gerard P(eter) obit
Feb 74
Kunstler, William M(oses)
Apr 71
Kuper, Gerard P(eter) obit
Feb 74
Kusner, Kathy Apr 73
Kuusinen, Hertta (Elina) obit
May 74
Kuznets, Simon May 72
Kuznetsov, Nikolai G(erasi-
movich) obit Jan 75
Kyprianou, Spyros May 79

Lagerkvist, Pär (Fabian) obit
Sep 74
Laich, Katherine (Wilhelmina
Schlegel) Jun 72
Laing, R(onald) D(avid) Mar
73
Laker, Sir Frederick A(lfred)
Jun 78
Lamm, Norman Sep 78
Lance, (Thomas) Bert (ram)
Aug 77
Land, Emory S(cott) obit Jan
72
Landon, Michael Jul 77
Landry, Tom Jun 72
Lang, Fritz obit Sep 76
Langer, William L(eonard)
obit Feb 78
Langlois, Henri Jan 73 obit
Mar 77
Lanusse, Alejandro Augustín
Apr 73
Larkin, Oliver W(aterman)
obit Feb 71
Larsen, Roy E(dward) obit
Oct 79
Larson, Leonard W(infield)
obit Nov 74
Lash, Joseph P. Dec 72
Lasser, Louise Oct 76
Lasswell, Harold D(wight)
obit Feb 79
Latham, Dana obit Apr 74
Laurence, William L(eonard)
obit May 77
Lawrence, David obit Apr 73
Lawrence, Marjorie obit
Mar 79
Laxalt, Paul (Dominique) Jan
79
Layton, Mrs. Roy F(rancis)
obit Jan 76
Lazareff, Pierre obit Jun 72
Lazarsfeld, Paul F(elix) obit
Oct 76
Leachman, Cloris Oct 75
Leahy, Frank (William) obit
Sep 73
Leake, Chauncey D(epew)
obit Mar 78

Leakey, Louis S(eymour) B(azett) obit Dec 72
Leakey, Richard (Erskine Frere) Nov 76
Lear, Evelyn Apr 73
Lear, Norman (Milton) Feb 74
Lear, William P(owell) obit Jul 78
Le Carré, John Dec 74
Le Duc Tho Mar 75
Lee, Christopher Sep 75
Lee, Sherman E(mery) Jun 74
Leech, Margaret obit Apr 74
Lefebvre, Marcel (François) Mar 78
Lefèvre, Théo(dore Joseph Albéric Marie obit Nov 73
Léger, Alexis Saint-Léger obit Nov 75
Léger, Jules Nov 76
Lehmann, Lotte obit Oct 76
Leibowitz, Samuel S(imon) obit Mar 78
Leighton, Margaret obit Mar 76
Leiper, Henry Smith obit Mar 75
Lemass, Seán F(rancis) obit Jun 71
Leone, Giovanni May 72
Leoni, Raúl obit Sep 72
Lercaro, Giacomo Cardinal obit Jan 77
Lescot, Élie obit Dec 74
Lessing, Doris (May) Jan 76
Levant, Oscar obit Oct 72
Lévesque, Réne Jan 75
Levi, Carlo obit Feb 75
Lévi-Strauss, Claude Mar 72
Levin, Yehuda Lieb (Ilyich) obit Jan 72
Levine, David Feb 73
Levine, James Apr 75
Levine, Joseph E(dward) Oct 79
Lewis, David S(loan), Jr. Aug 75
Lewis, Henry Feb 73
Lewis, Oscar obit Feb 71
Lewis, Roger Dec 73
Lewis, Wilmarth Sheldon Jul 73
Lhevinne, Rosina obit Jan 77
Liebermann, Rolf Sep 73
Lieberson, Goddard Mar 76 obit Jul 77
Liebes, Dorothy (Wright) obit Dec 72
Lifton, Robert Jay Nov 73
Lightfoot, Gordon Aug 78
Limón José (Arcadio) obit Jan 73
Lin, Piao obit Oct 72
Lin Yu-t'ang obit May 76

Lindbergh, Anne (Spencer) Morrow Jun 76
Lindbergh, Charles A(ugustus, Jr.) obit Oct 74
Lindsley, Thayer obit Jul 76
Link, Edwin (Albert) Jan 74
Lipchitz Jacques obit Jul 73
Lippincott, Joseph Wharton obit Jan 77
Lippmann, Walter obit Jan 75
Little, Clarence C(ook) obit Feb 72
Little, Lou(is) obit Jul 79
Little, Rich Nov 75
Liu Shao-chi obit Dec 74
Lloyd, Harold (Clayton) obit Apr 71
Lloyd, (John) Selwyn (Brooke), See Selwyn-Lloyd, Baron obit Jul 78
Lloyd, Wesley P(arkinson) obit May 77
Lochner, Louis P(aul) obit Feb 75
Loeb, William Mar 74
Logue, Edward J(oseph) Jun 77
Lombardo, Guy ((Albert) Feb 75 obit Jan 78
Lon Nol Feb 74
Lonergan, Bernard J(oseph) F(rancis) Jan 72
Long, Edward V(aughan) obit Jan 73
Long, Westray See Boyce, W. B. obit Mar 72
Longworth, Alice Roosevelt ᴧug 75
Loos, Anita Feb 74
López Bravo, Gregorio Jul 71
López Michelsen, Alfonso Apr 75
Lopez, Nancy Sep 78
López Portillo (y Pachecho), José Jun 77
López Rodó, Laureano Feb 72
Lopez, Vincent obit Nov 75
Lord, John Wesley May 71
Lord, Walter Oct 72
Lorenz, Konrad Oct 77
Loring, Eugene Mar 72
Losch, Tilly obit Feb 76
Loud, Pat Jul 74
Lougheed, (Edgar) Peter Aug 79
Lowdermilk, W(alter) C(lay) obit Jul 74
Lowell, Robert (Traill Spence Jr.) Jan 72 obit Nov 77
Lowenstein, Allard K(enneth) Sep 71
Lowrie, Jean E(lizabeth) Jun 73
Lozowick, Louis obit Nov 73
Lubin, Isador obit Sep 78

Lübke, Heinrich obit May 72
Lucas, George Apr 78
Lucas, Jerry Jun 72
Ludwig, Christa Mar 71
Ludwig, Daniel K(eith) May 79
Lugar, Richard G(reen) Oct 77
Lukas, Paul obit Oct 71
Lunt, Alfred obit Sep 77
Lupescu, Magda obit Aug 77
Lusk, Georgia, L(ee) obit Feb 71
Lyle, Sparky Jul 78
Lynde, Paul (Edward) Nov 72
Lynen, Feodor (Felix Konrad) obit Oct 79
Lynn, Diana obit Feb 72
Lynn James T(homas) Dec 73
Lynn, Loretta Oct 73
Lysenko, T(rofim) D(enisovich) obit Feb 77
Lyttelton, Oliver See Chandos, O. L., 1st Viscount obit Mar 72

McAuliffe, Anthony C(lement) obit Oct 75
McBride Katharine E(lizabeth) obit Jul 76
McBride, Lloyd Feb 78
McBride, Mary Margaret obit Jun 76
McCall, Tom (Lawson) Jun 74
McCarthy, Joe obit Mar 78
McCarthy, Joseph Vincent See McCarthy, Joe obit Mar 78
McCleery, Albert (Kenny) obit Jul 72
McClellan, Harold C(hadick) obit Sep 79
McClellan, John L(ittle) obit Feb 78
McCloskey, Mark A(lexander) obit Jan 78
McCloskey, Paul N(orton), Jr. Nov 71
McCormick, Edward J(ames) obit Feb 75
McCormick, Fowler obit Feb 73
McCracken, Robert James obit Apr 73
McDonald, David J(ohn) obit Oct 79
Macdonald, Ross Aug 79
McDowell, Malcolm Dec 73
McElroy, Neil H(osler) obit Jan 73
McGannon, Donald H(enry) Feb 71
McGee, (Doctor) Frank obit Jun 74

McGill, Wililam J(ames) Jun 71

McGinley, Phyllis obit Apr 78

McGinnis, Patrick B(enedict) obit Apr 73

McGovern, John W. obit Jun 75

McGregor, G(ordon) R(oy) obit Apr 71

McGuigan, James (Charles), Cardinal obit Jun 74

McIntire, Carl Oct 71

McIntyre, James Francis (Aloysius), Cardinal obit Sep 79

McIntyre, James T(almadge), Jr. Jan 79

McKay, Jim Oct 73

McKayle, Donald (Cohen) Jun 71

McKeen, John E(lmer) obit Apr 70

McKeldin, Theodore R(oosevelt) obit Oct 74

McKelway, B(enjamin) M(osby) obit Oct 76

McKenna, F(rancis) E(ugene) obit Feb 79

McKenney, Ruth obit Oct 72

McKinney, Frank E(dward) obit Mar 74

MacLaine, Shirley Jul 78

McLean, Don May 73

McMahon, Ed Apr 77

McMahon, William Sep 71

MacMillan, Sir Ernest (Campbell) obit Jun 73

McNair, Barbara Nov 71

McNarney, Joseph T(aggart) obit Mar 72

McNeely, Eugene J(ohnson) obit Feb 74

McNeil, Wilfred J(ames) obit Oct 79

MacNeil, Cornell Jan 76

McPartland, Marian Jun 76

MacPhail, Larry obit Nov 75

MacVeagh, Lincoln obit Mar 72

McWhinney, Madeline H(ouston) Jul 76

McWhirter, Norris (Dewar) Nov 79

Mabley Moms Jan 75 obit Aug 75

Mack, Ted obit Sep 76

Madariaga (y Rojo), Salvador de obit Feb 79

Maddox, William P(ercy) obit Dec 72

Madeira, Jean (Browning) obit Sep 72

Magallanes, Nicholas obit Jul 77

Magnani Anna obit Nov 73

Magruder, William M(arshall) Mar 72 obit Nov 77

Maharaj Ji, Guru Dec 74

Mahendra, King of Nepal obit Mar 72

Mahesh Yogi, Maharishi Dec 72

Main, Marjorie obit Jun 75

Mainbocher obit Mar 77

Maiskey, Ivan (Mikhailovich) obit Oct 75

Makarios III, Archbishop obit Sep 77

Makarova, Natalia Feb 72

Malamud, Bernard Jul 78

Malle, Louis Feb 76

Malone, Ross(er) L(ynn, Jr.) obit Oct 74

Malraux, André obit Feb 77

Malvern Godfrey (Martin) Huggins, 1st Viscount obit Jun 71

Mamet, David (Alan) Aug 78

Mangrum, Lloyd obit Jan 74

Manilow, Barry Jul 78

Manley, Michael (Norman) Jan 76

Manna, Charlie obit Dec 71

Manning, Harry obit Oct 74

Mansfield, Michael J(oseph) Jan 78

Mansfield, Mike See Mansfield, M. J. Jan 78

Manstein, Fritz Erich Von obit Sep 73

Mao Tse-tung obit Oct 70

March, Fredric obit Jun 75

Marchais, Georges (René Louis) Jun 76

Marcuse, Herbert obit Sep 79

Marden, Orison S(wett) obit Oct 75

Marek, Kurt W. obit Jun 72

Margrethe II, Queen of Denmark Nov 72

Marías, Julián (Aguilera) Feb 72

Marie, André obit Sep 74

Maritain, Jacques obit Jun 73

Markel, Lester obit Jan 78

Marland, Sidney P(ercy), Jr. Apr 72

Marriner, Neville Aug 78

Marriott, J(ohn) Willard Jun 72

Marsh, Jean Nov 77

Marshak, Robert E(ugene) Jul 73

Marshall, Ray Nov 77

Marshall, S(amuel) L(yman) A(twood) obit Mar 78

Martin, Allie Beth Jun 75 obit Jun 78

Martin, Billy Oct 76

Martin, Fletcher obit Jul 79

Martin, James S(lattin), Jr. Mar 77

Martin, Steve Aug 78

Martin, Thomas E(llsworth) obit Sep 71

Martins, Peter Jun 78

Marx, Groucho Feb 73 obit Oct 77

Massine, Leonide obit May 79

Masson, André Nov 74

Mathews, (Forrest) David Jan 76

Mathias, Charles McC(urdy) Dec 72

Matthews, Herbert L(ionel) obit Sep 77

Matthiessen, Peter Oct 75

Mattson, Henry (Elis) obit Nov 71

Mauch, Gene (William) Dec 74

Maudling, Reginald obit Apr 79

Maurer, Ion Gheorghe Sep 71

Max, Peter May 71

Maxon, Lou R(ussell) obit Jul 71

Maxwell, Vera Jul 77

May, Rollo (Reece) Jun 73

Mayer, Maria Goeppert obit Apr 72

Mayer, René obit Feb 73

Mazzo, Kay Jul 71

Mead, Margaret obit Jan 79

Mead, Sylvia (Alice) Earle May 72

Means, Russell (Charles) Jan 78

Medeiros, Humberto S(ousa) Nov 71

Médici, Emilio Garrastazú 71

Medina-Sidonia, Duchess of Apr 72

Medvedev, Zhores A(leksandrovich) Nov 73

Meerloo, Joost A(braham) M(aurits) obit Feb 77

Mehta, G(aganvihari) L(allubhai) obit Jun 74

Mehta, Ved (Parkash) Sep 75

Meir, Golda obit Feb 79

Melchior, Lauritz (Lebrecht Hommel) obit May 73

Menotti, Gian Carlo Jan 79

Menshikov, Mikhail A(lekseevich) obit Sep 76

Menuhin, Yehudi May 73

Menzel, Donald H(oward) obit Mar 77

Menzies, Sir Robert G(ordon) obit Jul 78

Mercer, Johnny obit Aug 76

Mercer, Mabel Feb 76

Merchant, Livingston T(allmadge) obit Jul 76
Meriwether, W(ilhelm) Delano Jan 78
Merz, Charles obit Nov 77
Meskill, Thomas J. Mar 74
Messerschmitt, Willy obit Nov 78
Messiaen, Oliver (Eugène Prosper Charles) Feb 74
Mesta, Perle obit May 75
Metcalf, Lee obit Mar 78
Meyer, K((arl) F(riedrich) obit Jun 74
Michener, James A(lbert) Aug 75
Michie, Allan A(ndrew) obit Jan 74
Midler, Bette Jun 73
Mielziner, Jo obit May 76
Miers, Earl Schenck obit Jan 73
Mihajlov, Mihajlo Jan 79
Miki, Takeo Apr 75
Mikoyan, Anastas I(vanovich) obit Jan 79
Milgram, Stanley Aug 79
Milhaud, Darius obit Sep 74
Millar, Kenneth See Macdonald, R. Aug 79
Miller, Arnold (Ray) Nov 74
Miller, Arthur Feb 73
Miller, Frieda S(egelke) obit Oct 73
Miller, G(eorge) William Jun 78
Miller, Harry W(illis) obit Mar 77
Miller, Jason Jan 74
Miller, Johnny Sep 74
Miller, Justin obit Mar 73
Miller, Marvin (Julian) May 73
Miller, Neal (Elgar) Jul 74
Millett, Kate Jan 71
Mindszenty, József, Cardinal obit Jun 75
Mingus, Charles Feb 71 obit Mar 79
Minnelli, Vincente May 75
Miró, Joan Nov 73
Miró Cardona, José obit Oct 74
Mitchell, Joni Oct 76
Mitchell, Stephen A(rnold) obit Jun 74
Mitford, Jessica (Lucy) Sep 74
Mohammed Riza Shah Pahlevi Sep 77
Moi, Daniel (Torotich) arap May 79
Moley, Raymond (Charles) obit Apr 75
Mollet, Guy obit Nov 75

Molloy, Robert (William) obit Mar 77
Molyneux, Edward H. obit May 74
Momaday, N(avarre) Scott Apr 75
Mondale, Walter F(rederick) May 78
Monnet, Jean obit May 79
Monod, Jacques (Lucien) Jul 71 obit Jul 76
Monroe, Earl May 78
Monroe, Vaughn (Wilton) obit Jul 73
Monsarrat, Nicholas (John Turney) obit Oct 79
Montale, Eugenio Apr 76
Montgomery of Alamein, Bernard Law Montgomery, 1st Viscount obit May 76
Montini, Giovanni Battista See Paul VI, Pope obit Sep 78
Montoya, Joseph M. Mar 75 obit Jul 78
Moore, Sir Henry R(uthven) obit May 78
Moore, Henry (Spencer) Feb 78
Moore, Marianne (Craig) obit Mar 72
Moore, Mary Tyler Feb 71
Moore, Melba Jan 73
Moore, Roger Feb 75
Moorhead, Agnes obit Jun 74
Moorer, Thomas H(inman) Apr 71
Mora, José A(ntonio) obit Mar 75
Moraes, Frank (Robert) obit Jul 74
Moreell, Ben obit Sep 78
Morgan, Arthur E(rnest) obit Jan 76
Moriarty, Michael Jul 76
Morin, Relman (George) obit Oct 73
Morison, Samuel Eliot obit Jul 76
Morita, Akio Feb 72
Moro, Aldo obit Jun 78
Morón, Alonzo G(raseano) obit Dec 71
Morris, Desmond (John) Nov 74
Morris, Robert Apr 71
Morris, Willie Jan 76
Morrison, Toni May 79
Morsch, Lucile M. obit Nov 72
Morse, (Harold) Marston obit Aug 77
Morse, Wayne (Lyman) obit Sep 74

Mortimer, Charles G(reenough) obit Feb 79
Morton, Craig Jun 78
Morton, Rogers C(lark) B(allard) Nov 71 obit Jun 79
Moss, Frank E(dward) Dec 71
Mostel, Zero obit Nov 77
Mott, C(harles) S(tewart) obit Apr 73
Mott, Stewart R(awlings) Apr 75
Mountbatten, Louis (Francis Albert Victor Nicholas), Lord See Mountbatten of Burma, 1st Earl obit Oct 79
Mountbatten of Burma, 1st Earl obit Oct 79
Mowery, Edward J(oseph) obit Feb 71
Mowrer, Edgar Ansel obit May 77
Moyers, Bill(y Don) Feb 76
Mueller, Frederick H(enry) obit Oct 76
Mugabe, Robert (Gabriel) Apr 79
Muggeridge, Malcolm (Thomas) Jul 75
Muhammad, Elijah Jan 71 obit Apr 75
Muir, Malcolm obit Mar 79
Mujibur Rahman, Sheik See Rahman, Sheik Mujibur Jan 73 obit Oct 75
Muldoon, Robert D(avid) Feb 78
Mundt, Karl E(arl) obit Oct 74
Munro, Leslie Knox obit Apr 74
Munson, Thurman (Lee) Nov 77 obit Sep 79
Murayama, Makio Oct 74
Murdoch, (Keith) Rupert May 77
Murphy, Franklin D(avid) Mar Mar 71
Murphy, Gardner obit May 79
Murphy, Patrick V(incent) Nov 72
Murphy, Robert D(aniel) obit Mar 78
Murphy, Thomas A(quinas) Oct 79
Murray, Dwight H(arrison) obit Nov 74
Murray, T(h)om(as Jefferson) obit Jan 72
Murtaugh, Daniel (Edward) obit Feb 77
Musgrave, Thea May 78

Muzorewa, Abel T(endekai) Mar 79

Myrdal, (Karl) Gunnar Mar 75

Nabarro, Sir Gerald obit Jan 74

Nabokov, Vladimir obit Aug 77

Nagy, Ivan May 77

Naipaul, V(idiadhar) S(uraj-prasad) Jul 77

Naish, J. Carrol obit Mar 73

Nam Il obit Apr 76

Namboodiripad, E. M. S. Nov 76

Narayan, Jaya Prakash obit Nov 79

Nash, Ogden obit Jul 71

Natase, Ilie Oct 74

Navratilova, Martina Sep 77

Nearing, Scott Oct 71

Neel, Alice (Hartley) Aug 76

Neier, Aryeh Nov 78

Neill, A(lexander) S(uther-land) obit Nov 73

Nelson, Ozzie obit Aug 75

Nelson, Willie Feb 79

Neruda, Pablo obit Nov 73

Nervi, Pier Luigi obit Mar 79

Nessen, Ron(ald H.) Jan 76

Nestingen, Ivan A(rnold) obit Jun 78

Nevins, Allan obit Apr 71

Newcombe, John (David) Oct 77

Newhouse, Samuel I(rving) obit Oct 79

Ne Win Apr 71

Newton, Huey P(ercy) Feb 73

Newton-John, Olivia Nov 78

Nguyen Thi Binh Jul 76

Nichols, Roy Franklin obit Mar 73

Nicholson, Jack Oct 74

Nidetch, Jean Dec 73

Niebuhr, Reinhold obit Jul 71

Nimeiry, Gaafar Muhammad al- Nov 77

Nimoy, Leonard Feb 77

Nin, Anaïs Sep 75 obit Mar 77

Nkomo, Joshua (Mqabuko Ny-ongolo) Apr 76

Nkrumah, Kwame obit Jun 72

Noguès, Auguste (Paul) obit Jun 71

Noland, Kenneth (Clifton) Sep 72

Nolde, O(tto) Frederick obit Sep 72

Norell, Norman obit Dec 72

Norman, Jessye Feb 76

North, Sterling obit Feb 75

Norton, Eleanor Holmes Nov 76

Nourse, Edwin G(riswold) obit Jun 74

Novaes (Pinto), Guiomar obit May 79

Novotny, Antonin obit Mar 75

Nyad, Diana Aug 79

Nye, Gerald P(rentice) obit Sep 71

Obolensky, Serge obit Nov 78

O'Boyle, Patrick (Aloysius) Cardinal Jul 73

O'Brien, Lawrence F(rancis, Jr.) Apr 77

O'Connor, Basil obit May 72

O'Connor, Carroll Jul 72

Odishaw, Hugh Feb 71

Odlum, Floyd B(ostwick) obit Aug 76

O'Donnell, Emmett, Jr. obit Feb 71

Odria (Amoretti), Manuel A(polinario) obit Apr 74

Oduber (Quirós), Daniel Jul 77

Oenslager, Donald (Mitchell) obit Aug 75

O'Hair, Madalyn Murray Jan 77

Ohlsson, Garrick (Olof) Jun 75

Oistrakh, David (Fyodoro-vich) obit Dec 74

Oliver, Lyttelton See Chando, O. L., 1st Viscount Mar 72

Olivier, Laurence Jan 79

O'Malley, Walter F(rancis) obit Oct 79

Onassis, Aristotle Socrates obit May 75

Onassis, Christina Feb 76

O'Neal, A(rthur) Daniel, (Jr.) Jun 79

O'Neal, Ryan Feb 73

O'Neill, Gerard K(itchen) Feb 79

O'Neill, Thomas P(hilip), Jr. Apr 74

Ono, Yoko Nov 72

Onsager, Lars obit Jan 77

Ophuls, Marcel Jun 77

Orff, Carl Aug 76

Orr, John Boyd See Boyd Orr, John Boyd Orr, 1st Baron obit Sep 71

Ospina Pérez, Mariano obit Jun 76

Ottaviani, Alfredo, Cardinal obit Sep 79

Otto, Frei (Paul) Oct 71

Owen, David (Anthony Lle-wellyn) Sep 77

Owings, Nathaniel A(lexan-der) May 71

Ozbirn, Mrs. E. Lee obit Mar 74

Pacino, Al(fred) Jul 74

Packard, Eleanor obit Jun 72

Padilla, Ezequial obit Oct 71

Pagnol, Marcel (Paul) obit Jun 74

Pahlevi, Farah Diba See Farah Diba Pahlevi Mar 76

Pahlevi, Mohammed Riza See Mohammed Riza Shah Pah-levi Sep 77

Paisley, Ian (Richard Kyle) Jan 71

Panov, Valery Oct 74

Panyushkin, Alexander S(em-yenovich) obit Jan 75

Papashvily, George obit May 78

Park, Brad Nov 76

Park, Merle Sep 74

Parks, Bert Feb 73

Parsons, Estelle Oct 75

Parsons, Louella obit Oct 73

Parsons, Talcott obit Jul 79

Partch, Harry obit Oct 74

Parton, Dolly Aug 77

Partridge, Eric (Honeywood) obit Jul 79

Pasolini, Pier Paolo obit Jan 76

Pastrana Borrero, Misael Jul 71

Pate, Walter L(acey) obit Jun 74

Patman, (John William) Wright obit Apr 76

Paul VI, Pope obit Sep 78

Paul, Prince of Yugoslavia obit Oct 76

Paul, Alice obit Sep 77

Paul-Boncour, Joseph obit May 72

Pavarotti, Luciano Jun 73

Paxinou, Katina obit Apr 73

Payne, Frederick G. obit Aug 78

Payson, Joan Whitney Jul 72 obit Nov 75

Paz, Octavio Jun 74

Peale, Mundy I(ngalls) obit Jan 73

Peale, Norman Vincent Oct 74

Pearlstein, Philip Feb 73

Pears, Peter Jul 75

Pearson, Lester Bowles obit Feb 73

Peckinpah, Sam May 73

Pei, Mario (Andrew) obit May 78
Pell, Claiborne (deBorda) Mar 72
Penderecki, Krzysztof Jun 71
Penfield, Wilder (Graves) obit Jun 76
Penn, Arthur (Hiller) Jan 72
Penney, J(ames) C(ash) obit Mar 71
Pepitone, Joe Jan 73
Percy, Charles H(arting) Aug 77
Percy, Walker Sep 76
Perdue, Frank(lin Parsons) Jun 79
Pereira, I(rene) Rice obit Feb 71
Pereira, William L(eonard) Jan 79
Perelman, S(idney) J(oseph) Mar 71
Peres, Shimon Jan 76
Pérez (Rodriguez), Carlos Andrés Feb 76
Perlman, Itzhak May 75
Perón, Isabel Jan 75
Perón, María Estele Martínez de See Perón, I. Jan 75
Perón (Sosa), Juan (Domingo) Feb 74 obit Sep 74
Perot, H(enry) Ross Jul 71
Perrine, Valerie Oct 75
Perry, Frank Oct 72
Perse, St.-John See Léger, A. S.-L. obit Nov 75
Persons, Wilton B(urton) obit Nov 77
Pervukhin, Mikhail G(eorgievich) obit Oct 78
Peterson, F(rank) Raymond obit Feb 78
Peterson, Peter G(eorge) Jun 72
Pham Van Dong Feb 75
Phillips, Irna obit Feb 74
Phillips, Wendell obit Feb 76
Piatigorsky, Gregor obit Sep 76
Picasso, Pablo obit May 73
Piccioni, Attilio obit May 76
Pickford, Mary obit Jul 79
Pike, Otis G(rey) Feb 76
Pike, Sumner T(ucker) obit Apr 76
Pinochet Ugarte, Augusto Dec 74
Piston, Walter (Hamor, Jr.) obit Jan 77
Plunkett, Jim Sep 71
Polyansky, Dmitry S(tepanovich) Mar 71
Pomeroy, Wardell B(axter) Jul 74

Pompidou, Georges (Jean Raymond) obit May 74
Pons, Lily obit Apr 76
Poor, Henry Varnum obit Jan 71
Pope, Liston obit Jun 74
Popovic, Vladimir obit May 72
Portal of Hungerford, Charles Frederick Algernon Portal, 1st Viscount obit Jun 71
Porter, Eliot (Furness) Nov 76
Porter, Paul A(ldermandt) obit Jan 76
Porter, William J(ames) Mar 74
Porter, William N(ichols) obit Apr 73
Potofsky, Jacob S(amuel) obit Sep 79
Pound, Ezra (Loomis) obit Dec 72
Pousette-Dart, Richard Mar 76
Poussaint, Alvin F(rancis) Jul 73
Powell, Adam Clayton, Jr. obit May 72
Powell, Anthony (Dymoke) Sep 77
Powell, Jane Dec 74
Powell, Jody Jul 77
Power, Donald C(linton) obit May 79
Power, Thomas S(arsfield) obit Jan 71
Powers, Bertram (Anthony) Jan 74
Powers, John Robert obit Sep 77
Powers, Marie obit Feb 74
Prescott, Robert W(illiam) Jul 71
Presley, Elvis (Aron) obit Oct 77
Preus, Jacob A(all) O(ttesen) May 75
Previn, André (George) May 72
Previn, Dory Sep 75
Prey, Hermann Feb 75
Pribichevich, Stoyan obit Jul 76
Price, Leontyne Oct 78
Pride, Charley Apr 75
Priest, Ivy (Maude) Baker obit Aug 75
Priestley, J(ohn) B(oynton) May 76
Prince, Harold Apr 71
Prinze, Freddie Jun 75 obit Mar 77
Prío Socarrás, Carlos obit Jun 77
Pritchett, V(ictor) S(awdon) Jan 74

Proell, Annemarie Sep 76
Prouty, Winston L(ewis) obit Oct 71
Proxmire, (Edward) William Aug 78
Pryor, Richard Feb 76
Puckett, B(enjamin) Earl obit Apr 76
Puente, Tito Nov 77
Purtell, William A(rthur) obit Jul 78
Puzo, Mario Mar 75

Qabus bin Said Aug 78
Qaddafi, Muammar el- Sep 73
Quayle, Anthony Dec 71
Queler, Eve Jul 72

Rabe, David Jul 73
Rabin, Yitzhak Sep 74
Radcliffe, Cyril John, 1st Viscount Radcliffe obit May 77
Radford, Arthur W(illiam) obit Oct 73
Radhakrishnan, Sir Sarvepalli obit Jun 75
Radziwill, Lee (Bouvier) Apr 77
Rafshoon, Gerald Jul 79
Rahman, Sheik Mujibur Jan 73 obit Oct 75
Rajagopalachari, Chakravarti obit Feb 73
Rakosi, Matyas obit Mar 71
Ram, Jagjivan Oct 78
Raman, Sir (Chandrasekhara) Venkata obit Jan 71
Ramspeck, Robert (C. Word) obit Dec 72
Rance, Sir Hubert Elvin obit Mar 74
Randolph, A(sa) Philip obit Jul 79
Ranganathan, S(hiyali) R(amamrita) obit Dec 72
Rank, Joseph Arthur Rank, 1st Baron obit May 72
Ransom, John Crowe obit Sep 74
Raskin, A(braham) H(enry) May 78
Rathbone, Monroe J(ackson) obit Sep 76
Rather, Dan May 75
Rattigan, Sir Terence (Mervyn) obit Feb 78
Rattner, Abraham obit Apr 78
Ravdin, I(sidor) S(chwaner) obit Oct 72
Ray, Dixy Lee Jun 73
Ray, Man obit Jan 77
Ray, Robert D. Jan 77

Reading, Stella (Charnaud Isaacs), Marchioness of obit Jul 71

Reardon, John (Robert) Nov 74

Reber, Samuel obit Feb 72

Reddy, Helen Apr 75

Redford, Robert Apr 71

Reed, Sir Carol obit Jun 76

Reed, Rex Jan 72

Reed, Willis Jan 73

Reese, Della Sep 71

Rehnquist, William H(ubbs) Apr 72

Reich, Charles A(lan) Jun 72

Reid, Charlotte T(hompson) Jan 75

Reith, John Charles Walsham, 1st Baron obit Jul 71

Rennert, Günther Jun 76 obit Sep 78

Renoir, Jean obit Apr 79

Revel, Jean-François Feb 75

Rey, Fernando Mar 79

Reynolds, Burt Oct 73

Rhodes, James A(llen) Apr 76

Rhodes, John J(acob 2d) Sep 70

Rhys, Jean Dec 72 obit Jul 79

Riad, Mahmoud Nov 71

Rice, Jim Sep 79

Rich, Adrienne (Cecile) Feb 76

Rich, Buddy Jun 73

Rich, Daniel Catton obit Feb 77

Richards, Dickinson W(oodruff) obit Apr 73

Richards, I(vor) A(rmstrong) Dec 72

Richards, James P(rioleau) obit Apr 79

Richardson, Elliot L(ee) Mar 71

Richler, Mordecai May 75

Richter, Burton Sep 77

Richter, Charles Francis May 75

Rickenbacker, Edward Vernon obit Oct 73

Riefenstahl, Leni May 75

Riefler, Winfield W(illiam) obit Jun 74

Rieve, Emil obit Mar 75

Rigg, Diana Oct 74

Righter, Carroll Oct 72

Riklis, Meshulam Dec 71

Riles, Wilson (Camanza) Dec 71

Rinfret, Pierre A(ndré) Jul 72

Ritchard, Cyril obit Feb 78

Ritt, Martin Nov 79

Ritter, Thelma obit Feb 74 (died Feb 69)

Rivera, Geraldo May 75

Rivers, L(ucius) Mendel obit Feb 71

Rizzo, Frank L(azarro) Mar 73

Roa(y García), Raul Nov 73

Robb, Inez (Callaway) obit Jun 79

Robbe-Grillet, Alain Dec. 74

Roberts, C. Wesley obit Jun 75

Robertson, A. Willis obit Dec 71

Robertson, Sir Brian (Hubert) obit Jun 74

Robeson, Paul Mar 76 obit Mar 76

Robey, Ralph W(est) obit Sep 72

Robinson, Brooks Sep 70

Robinson, Edward G. obit Mar 73

Robinson, Frank Jun 71

Robinson, Jackie obit Dec 72

Robsjohn-Gibbings, T(erence) H(arold) obit Feb 77

Roche, Josephine (Aspinwall) obit Sep 76

Rockefeller, John D(avison), 3d obit Sep 78

Rockefeller, John D(avison), 4th Mar 78

Rockefeller, Nelson A(ldrich) obit Mar 79

Rockefeller, Winthrop obit Apr 73

Rockwell, Norman obit Jan 79

Rogers, Fred M(cFeely) Jul 71

Rohatyn, Felix G(eorge) May 78

Rohmer, Eric Apr 77

Rojas Pinilla, Gustavo obit Mar 75

Rollins, Sonny Apr 76

Romero Barceló, Carlos Oct 77

Romnes, H(aakon) I(ngolf) obit Jan 74

Ronstadt, Linda Jan 78

Rooney, John J(oseph) obit Jan 76

Rooth, Ivar obit Apr 72

Roper, Elmo (Burns, Jr.) obit Jun 71

Rose, Alex obit Feb 77

Rose, Leonard Jan 77

Rose, Pete Aug 75

Rosen, Samuel Feb 74

Rosenman, Samuel I(rving) obit Sep 73

Rosenwald, Lessing J(ulius) obit Aug 79

Ross, Diana Mar 73

Ross, Nellie Tayloe obit Feb 78

Rossellini, Roberto obit Aug 77

Rosset, Barnet (Lee, Jr.) Apr 72

Rostand, Jean obit Jan 78

Rothermere, Esmond Cecil Harmsworth, Viscount obit Sep 78

Rothschild, Guy (Edouard Alphonse Paul), Baron de Mar 73

Roudebush, Richard L(owell) Jun 76

Rovere, Richard H(alworth) Apr 77

Rowlands, Gena Nov 75

Rowse, A(lfred) L(eslie) Jul 79

Royall, Kenneth C(laiborne) obit Sep 71

Rubicam, Raymond obit Jul 78

Rubin, Reuven obit Jan 75

Ruckelshaus, William D(oyle) Jul 71

Rudd, Paul Sep 77

Rudolph, Paul (Marvin) Feb 72

Rueff, Jacques (Léon) obit Jun 78

Ruiz Cortines, Adolfo obit Jan 74

Rush, (David) Kenneth May 75

Russell, Bill See Russell, W. F. Jul 75

Russell, Ken Oct 75

Russell, Richard B(revard, Jr.) obit Mar 71

Russell, Rosalind obit Feb 77

Russell, William F(elton) Jul 75

Rutherford, Dame Margaret obit Jul 72

Ryan, Robert (Bushnell) obit Sep 73

Ryan, William F(itts) obit Dec 72

Ryle, Sir Martin Sep 73

Saarinen, Aline B(ernstein Louchheim) obit Sep 72

Sadat, Anwar (el-) Mar 71

Safire, William (L.) Dec 73

Said bin Taimur obit Aug 78 (died Oct 72)

Saillant, Louis obit Jan 75

St. Johns, Adela Rogers Aug 76

St. Laurent, Louis S(tephen) obit Oct 73

Sakharov, Andrei D(mitriyevich) Jul 71
Salisbury, Robert Arthur Cecil, 5th Marquis obit Apr 72
Salk, Lee Sep 79
Saltonstall, Leverett obit Sep 79
Samaras, Lucas Nov 72
Sanders, George obit Jun 72
Sanders, Harland Apr 73
Sanderson, Derek (Michael) Apr 75
Santos, Rufino J(iao), Cardinal obit Nov 73
Sardiña, Adolfo See Adolfo Nov 72
Sargent, Francis W(illiams) Jun 71
Sarkis, Elias Mar 79
Sarnoff, David obit Feb 72
Saroyan, William Nov 72
Sartre, Jean-Paul May 71
Sastroamidjojo, Ali obit May 75
Sato, Elisaku obit Aug 75
Saul, Ralph S(outhy) Feb 71
Saund, Dalip S(ingh) obit Jun 73
Saunders, Carl M(axon) obit Nov 74
Saura (Atarés), Carlos Sep 78
Savalas, Telly Feb 76
Sawhill, John C(rittenden) Apr 79
Sawyer, Charles obit Jun 79
Saxbe, William B(art) Jul 74
Sayre, Francis B(owes) obit May 72
Scali, John (Alfred) Sep 73
Scammon, Richard M(ontgomery) Mar 71
Scheel, Walter Feb 71
Scherman, Thomas (Kielty) obit Jul 79
Schiaparelli, Elsa obit Jan 74
Schickele, Peter May 79
Schiller, Karl (August Fritz) Dec 71
Schiotz, Aksel obit Jun 75
Schiotz, Fredrik A(xel) Apr 72
Schippers, Thomas obit Feb 78
Schlafly, Phyllis Jun 78
Schlesinger, Arthur M(eier), Jr. Jan 79
Schlesinger, James R(odney) Oct 73
Schmidt, Helmut (Heinrich Waldemar) Oct 74
Schmitt, Gladys (Leonore) obit Dec 72

Schmitt, Harrison H(agan) Jul 74
Schneider, Alexander Mar 76
Schneiderman, Rose obit Oct 72
Schorr, Daniel Feb 78
Schranz, Karl Jan 71
Schroeder, Patricia (Scott) Oct 78
Schuller, Robert H(arold) Jun 79
Schuster, M(ax) Lincoln obit Feb 71
Schwartz, Arthur Nov 79
Schwarzenegger, Arnold Apr 79
Schweiker, Richard S(chultz) Feb 77
Scorsese, Martin Feb 79
Scott, David R(andolph) Oct 71
Scott, George C(ampbell) Apr 71
Scott, Sheila Nov 74
Scotto, Renata Sep 78
Scull, Robert C. Apr 74
Seagren, Bob Jun 74
Seaton, Fred(erick) A(ndrew) obit Mar 74
Seberg, Jean obit Oct 79
Secondari, John H(ermes) obit Apr 75
Sedaka, Neil Oct 78
Seferis, George See Sepheriades, G. S. obit Nov 71
Segal, Erich (Wolf) Apr 71
Segal, George Jan 72
Segal, George Nov 75
Segni, Antonio obit Jan 73
Seidman, L(ewis) William Sep 76
Selden, David (Seeley) Jul 74
Selwyn-Lloyd, Baron obit Jul 78
Senanayake, Dudley (Shelton) obit Jun 73
Senior, Clarence (Ollson) obit Nov 74
Sepheriades, Georgios S(tylianou) obit Nov 71
Serban, Andrei Feb 78
Seredy, Kate obit May 75
Serlin, Oscar obit Apr 71
Serling, Rod obit Aug 75
Sert, José Luis Apr 75
Sessions, Roger (Huntington) Jan 75
Seymour, Lynn Nov 79
Shah, Idries Jun 76
Shange, Ntozake Sep 78
Shannon, William V(incent) Jan 79
Shapiro, Irving S(aul) Nov 76
Shapley, Harlow obit Dec 72
Shapp, Milton J(errold) Jul 73

Shaw, Ralph R(obert) obit Dec 72
Shaw, Robert obit Oct 78
Shawn, Ted obit Feb 72
Shazar, (Shenor) Zalman obit Nov 74
Shea, Andrew B(ernard) obit Jan 73
Sheean, Vincent obit May 75
Sheen, Martin Jun 77
Shelepin, Aleksandr (Nikolaevich) Feb 71
Shelly, Mary Jo(sephine) obit Sep 76
Sherman, Allan obit Jan 74
Shepard, E(rnest) H(oward) obit May 76
Shepard, Sam Apr 79
Shikler, Aaron (A.) Dec 71
Short, Bobby Jul 72
Shostakovich, Dmitri obit Oct 75
Shula, Don Mar 74
Shumlin, Herman (Elliott) obit Aug 79
Shumway, Norman E(dward) Apr 71
Shurlock, Geoffrey M. obit Jun 76
Shuster, George N(auman) obit Mar 77
Shvernik, Nikolai (Mikhailovich) obit Feb 71
Sides, John H(arold) obit Jun 78
Sikorsky, Igor I(van) obit Dec 72
Silberman, Charles E(liot) Jul 79
Silverman, Fred Nov 78
Simms, John F. obit Jun 75
Simon, Carly Aug 76
Simon, Herbert A(lexander) Jun 79
Simon, Paul Mar 75
Simon, William E(dward) Apr 74
Simonds, G(uy) G(ranville) obit Jul 74
Simons, Hans obit May 72
Singh, (Sardar) Swaran Mar 71
Sinyavsky, Andrei D(onatovich) Jul 75
Siqueiros, (José) David Alfaro obit Feb 74
Sirica, John J(oseph) May 74
Siroky, Viliam obit Nov 71
Sisco, Joseph J(ohn) Jan 72
Skinner, B(urrhus) F(rederic) Nov 79
Skinner, Cornelia Otis obit Sep 79
Skouras, Spyros P(anagiotes) obit Nov 71

Slayton, Donald K(ent) Feb 76

Slim, William Joseph Slim, Viscount obit Feb 71

Sloane, Eric Sep 72

Slobodkin, Louis (Julius) obit Aug 75

Smallens, Alexander obit Jan 73

Smallwood, Robert B(artly) obit Sep 74

Smith, Betty obit Mar 72

Smith, Chesterfield H(arvey) Nov 74

Smith, Gerald L(yman) K(enneth) obit Jun 76

Smith, H(arry) Allen obit May 76

Smith, Hazel Brannon Sep 73

Smith, Howard K(ingsbury) Jul 76

Smith, Howard W(orth) obit Nov 76

Smith, Mary Louise Oct 76

Smith, (Oliver) Harrison obit Feb 71

Smith, Paul C(lifford) obit Sep 76

Smith, Robyn (Caroline) Nov 76

Smith, Virginia B(eatrice) Jun 78

Smith, William Jay Mar 74

Snow, Edgar (Parks) obit Apr 72

Snyder, Gary Nov 78

Soares, Mário (Alberto Nobre Lopes) Oct 75

Sobeloff, Simon E(rnest) obit Sep 73

Soglow, Otto obit May 75

Solandt, Omond M(cKillop) Mar 74

Soleri, Paolo Feb 72

Somoza (Debayle), Anastasio Mar 78

Sondheim, Stephen (Joshua) Nov 73

Soong, T. V. obit Jun 71

Sound, Dalip S(ingh) obit Jun 73

Souers, Sidney W(illiam) obit Mar 73

Soyer, Moses obit Oct 74

Soyinka, Wole Dec 74

Spaak, Paul-Henri obit Oct 72

Spaatz, Carl obit Sep 74

Spacek, Sissy Jan 78

Spark, Muriel Nov 75

Spassky, Boris (Vasilyevich) Nov 72

Spectorsky, A(uguste) C(omte) obit Mar 72

Speer, Albert Oct 76

Spencer-Churchill, Clementine Ogilvy Hozier, Baroness of Chartwell obit Mar 78

Spender, Stephen (Harold) Mar 77

Spielberg, Steven Jul 78

Spingarn, Arthur B(arnett) obit Jan 72

Spínola, António (Sebastião) Ribeiro) de Sep 74

Spitz, Mark (Andrew) Oct 72

Spottswood, Stephen Gill obit Jan 75

Springsteen, Bruce Apr 78

Sproul, Allan obit Jun 78

Sproul, Robert Gordon obit Nov 75

Stabler, Ken Oct 79

Stafford, Jean obit May 79

Stafford, Thomas P(atten) Jan 77

Staggers, Harley O(rrin) Mar 71

Stakman, E(mil) C(harles) obit Mar 79

Stallone, Sylvester Oct 77

Stanley, W(endell) M(eredith) obit Sep 71

Stapleton, Jean Dec 72

Stark, Harold Raynsford obit Oct 72

Starkie, Walter (Fitzwilliam) obit Feb 77

Staubach, Roger (Thomas) Apr 72

Steel, David (Martin Scott) Jul 78

Steen, Marguerite obit Sep 75

Stegner, Wallace (Earle) Apr 77

Steichen, Edward obit May 73

Stein, Herbert Mar 73

Steinberg, William obit Jul 78

Steinbrenner, George Michael, 3d Feb 79

Steinem, Gloria Mar 72

Steiner, Max(imilian Raoul) obit Feb 72

Steinfeld, Jesse L(eonard) Apr 74

Steinkraus, Herman W(illiam) obit Jul 74

Stella, Frank (Philip) Apr 71

Stengel, Casey obit Nov 75

Steptoe, Patrick C(hristopher) Mar 79

Stern, Bill obit Jan 72

Stevens, George (Cooper) obit May 75

Stevens, John Paul May 76

Stevenson, Adlai E(wing), 3d Apr 74

Stewart, Ellen Jun 73

Stewart, Rod Aug 79

Stewart, Thomas (James) May 74

Stigwood, Robert (C.) Oct 79

Still, Clyfford Sep 71

Still, William Grant obit Feb 79

Stockhausen, Karlheinz Dec 71

Stoica, Chivu obit Apr 75

Stokowski, Leopold (Anton Stanislaw) obit Nov 77

Stolz, Robert obit Aug 75

Stone, Edward D(urell) obit Sep 78

Stone, I(sidor) F(einstein) Sep 72

Stone, W. Clement Feb 72

Stoppard, Tom Jul 74

Storey, David Sep 73

Stout, Rex (Todhunter) obit Jan 76

Stout, Wesley Winans obit Jan 72

Strand, Paul obit May 76

Strang, Ruth (May) obit Feb 71

Strasser, Otto (Johann Maximilian) obit Oct 74

Strauss, Anna Lord obit Apr 79

Strauss, Lewis L(ichtenstein) obit Mar 74

Strauss, Robert S(chwarz) Mar 74

Stravinsky, Igor (Fëdorovich) obit May 71

Strong, Maurice F(rederick) Dec 73

Struthers, Sally (Ann) Jan 74

Stump, Felix B(udwell) obit Sep 72

Suárez González, Adolfo May 77

Sullivan, Ed(ward Vincent) obit Nov 74

Sullivan, William H(ealy) Aug 79

Summer, Donna Jul 79

Summerfield, Arthur E(llsworth) obit Jun 72

Sun Fo obit Dec 73

Susann, Jacqueline May 72 obit Nov 74

Sutton, Percy (Ellis) Mar 73

Suvero, Mark di See Di Suvero, Mark Nov 79

Suzman, Janet May 76

Swados, Elizabeth Feb 79

Swearingen, John E(ldred) Jan 79

Switzer, Mary E(lizabeth) obit Dec 71

Symes, James M(iller) obit Sep 76
Szasz, Thomas (Stephen) Jan 75
Szigeti, Joseph obit Apr 73

Talal obit Sep 72
Talese, Gay Jul 72
Tamm, Igor (Evgenyevich) obit Jun 71
Tanaka, Kakuei Dec 72
Tanner, Edward Everett, 3d obit Feb 77
Tate, Allen obit Apr 79
Tatum, Edward L(awrie) obit Jan 76
Tawes, J(ohn) Millard obit Aug 79
Taylor, George W(illiam) obit Feb 73
Taylor, James Jun 72
Taylor, Theodore B(rewster) Apr 76
Tead, Ordway obit Jan 74
Te Kanawa, Kiri Nov 78
Tello (Baurraud), Manuel obit Jan 72
Teng Hsiao-ping May 76
Teresa, Mother Sep 73
terHorst, Jerald F(ranklin) Feb 75
Terkel, Studs Nov 74
Tetley, Glen Jun 73
Teyte, Dame Maggie obit Jul 76
Thant, U obit Jan 75
Tharp, Twyla Oct 75
Thatcher, Margaret (Hilda Roberts) Jul 75
Theiler, Max obit Oct 72
Thekaekara, Matthew P(o-then) May 74
Theodorakis, Mikis Jul 73
Theroux, Paul (Edward) Nov 78
Thomas, J(ohn) Parnell obit Jan 71
Thomas, Lewis Jul 75
Thomas, Michael Tilson May 71
Thomas, Richard Nov 75
Thompson, James R(obert) Jan 79
Thompson, Llewellyn E., Jr. obit Mar 72
Thompson, Sada Mar 73
Thomson, Sir George Paget obit Oct 75
Thomson of Fleet, Lord obit Sep 76
Thomson, Meldrim, Jr. Oct 78
Thomson, Roy (Herbert) See Thomson of Fleet, Lord obit Sep 76

Thorndike, Dame Sybil obit Aug 76
Thorpe, (John) Jeremy Oct 74
Tiant, Luis Jun 77
Tijerina, Reies Lopez Jul 71
Tinbergen, Niko(lass) Nov 75
Tindemans, Leo(nard) Mar 78
Tippett, Sir Michael (Kemp) Sep 74
Tiselius, Arne (Wilhelm Kaur-in) obit Dec 71
Tisserant, Eugène Cardinal obit Apr 72
Tobey, Mark obit Jun 76
Toffler, Alvin Apr 75
Tolbert, William R(ichard), Jr. Mar 74
Tolkien, J(ohn) R(onald) R(euel) obit Nov 73
Tolstoy, Alexandra (Lvovna) obit Nov 79
Tomlin, Lily Sep 73
Tong, Hollington K(ong) obit Feb 71
Toon, Malcolm Jul 78
Torn, Rip Apr 77
Torre, Joe May 72
Torres Bodet, Jaime obit Jul 74
Torrijos Herrera, Omar Jul 73
Tourel, Jennie obit Jan 74
Toynbee, Arnold J(oseph) obit Jan 76
Trammell, Niles obit May 73
Trampler, Walter Nov 71
Traubel, Helen obit Oct 72
Travolta, John Oct 78
Trefflich, Henry (Herbert Frederick) obit Sep 78
Tregaskis, Richard obit Oct 73
Trenkler, Freddie Jun 71
Trevino, Lee (Buck) Nov 71
Trilling, Diana May 79
Troyanos, Tatiana Aug 79
Trudeau, Garry Aug 75
Truex, Ernest obit Sep 73
Truman, David B(icknell) Jan 72
Truman, Harry S. obit Feb 73
Trumbo, Dalton obit Oct 76
Trussell, Ray E(lbert) Jan 71
Tryon, Thomas Jan 77
Tsaldaris, Constantin obit Jan 71
Tubman, William V(acanarat) S(hadrach) obit Sep 71
Tucker, Richard obit Feb 75
Tuckwell, Barry (Emmanuel) Jul 79
Tugwell, Rexford G(uy) obit Sep 79
Tunnard, Christopher obit May 79

Tunney, Gene obit Jan 79
Tunney, John V(arick) Jun 71
Turbay Ayala, Julio César Jul 79
Turcotte, Ron Nov 74
Turner, Robert Edward, 3d See Turner, Ted May 79
Turner, Stansfield May 78
Turner, Ted May 79
Tvardovsky, Alexandr (Trif-onovich) May 71 obit Feb 72
Tyson, Cicely Aug 75

Ulbricht, Walter obit Oct 73
Ullman, Al(bert Conrad) Aug 75
Ullman, James R(amsey) obit Sep 71
Ullmann, Liv Dec 73
Unden, Bo Osten obit Apr 74
Untermeyer, Louis obit Feb 78
Uris, Leon (Marcus) Feb 79
Usery, W(illie) J(ulian), Jr. Jun 76
Utley, Freda obit Mar 78

Valentino Nov 73
Vance, Cyrus R(oberts) Nov 77
Vandegrift, Alexander Archer obit Jun 73
Vanderbilt, Amy obit Feb 75
Vanderbilt, Gloria Jul 72
Van Doren, Mark obit Feb 73
Van Dusen, Henry P(itney) obit Apr 75
Van Hamel, Martine Sep 79
Van Slyke, Donald D(exter) obit Jul 71
Van Waters, Miriam obit Apr 74
Vargas Llosa, (Jorge) Mario (Pedro) Feb 76
Vasarely, Victor Feb 71
Vasilevsky, Alexander M(ik-hailovich) obit Mar 78
Velasco Alvarado, Juan obit Mar 78
Velasco Ibarra, José María obit May 79
Venturi, Robert (Charles) Jul 75
Vereen, Ben Apr 78
Victor, Sally (Josephs) obit Jul 77
Videla, Jorge Rafaél Apr 78
Vilar, Jean (Louis Côme) obit Sep 71
Vilas, Guillermo Apr 78
Villemure, Gilles Apr 74
Vinton, Bobby Jul 77

Visconti, Luchino obit May 76
Voight, Jon Apr 74
Volcker, Paul A(dolph) Jul 73
Von Bekesy, George See Bekesy, George von obit Sep 72
Von Braun, Wernher obit Aug 77
Von Däniken, Erich May 76
Von Frisch, Karl See Frisch, Karl von Feb 74
Von Fürstenberg, Diane Sep 76
Von Stade, Frederica Aug 77
Voorhees, Tracy S(tebbins) obit Nov 74
Vreeland, Diana (Dalziell) **Feb 78**

Waddington, C(onrad) H(al) obit Nov 75
Wade, (Sarah) Virginia May 76
Waksman, Selman A(braham) obit Oct 73
Waldheim, Kurt May 72
Walker, Dan(iel) Aug 76
Walker, Ralph (Thomas) obit Mar 73
Wallace, Irving Mar 79
Wallace, Mike Nov 77
Waltari, Mika (Toimi) obit Oct 79
Walters, Barbara Feb 71
Walton, Bill Mar 77
Wangchuk, Jigme Dorji, Druk Gyalpo of Bhutan obit Sep 72
Ward, Barbara (Mary) Jan 77
Ward, Douglas Turner Sep 76
Ward, Maisie obit Mar 75
Warner, Jack L(eonard) obit Nov 78
Warner, John W(illiam) Nov 76
Warnke, Paul C(ulliton) Aug 77
Warren, Earl obit Sep 74
Waters, Ethel obit Oct 77
Watkins, Arthur V(ivian) obit Dec 73
Watson, Arthur K(ittredge) Sep 71 obit Oct 74
Watson, Tom Jul 79
Watson-Watt, Sir Robert (Alexander) obit Jan 74
Watts, Alan obit Jan 74
Wayne, John Jul 72 obit Aug 79
V.'eaver, Dennis Nov 77
Weaver, Warren obit Feb 79
Webb, Aileen O(sborn) obit Oct 79
Webster, Margaret obit Jan 73

Webster, William obit Jul 72
Webster, William H(edgcock) Aug 78
Weede, Robert obit Sep 72
Weeks, Sinclair obit Mar 72
Wegner, Nicholas H. obit May 76
Weicker, Lowell P(almer), Jr. Jan 74
Weidman, Charles obit Sep 75
Weigle, Luther Allan obit Oct 76
Weinberger, Caspar W(illard) Jun 73
Weisgal, Meyer W(olf) Oct 72 obit Nov 77
Weiskopf Tom Nov 73
Weissenberg, Alexis (Sigismund) Jun 78
Weisskopf, Victor F(rederick) Nov 76
Weitz, John Sep 79
Weizman, Ezer Sep 79
Welch, Leo D(ewey) obit Jan **79**
Welch, Raquel May 71
Welch, Robert H(enry) W(inborne) Jr. Nov 76
Weld, Tuesday Jul 74
Wellman, William A(ugustus) obit Feb 76
Welty, Eudora Oct 75
Wendt, Gerald Louis obit Feb 74
Werblin, David A(braham) Apr 79
Werblin, Sonny See Werblin, David A. Apr 79
Wertmuller, Lina Sep 76
West, Jessamyn Aug 77
Westin, Av(ram Robert) Aug 75
Wetmore, Alexander obit Mar 79
Weyerhaeuser, George H(unt) Jul 77
Wheaton, Anne (Williams) obit May 77
Wheeler, Burton K(endall) obit Feb 75
Wheeler, Earle G. obit Feb 76
Wheeler, Raymond A(lbert) obit Apr 74
Wheeler, Sir (Robert Eric) Mortimer obit Sep 76
Whitaker, Douglas (Merritt) obit Dec 73
White, Charles M(cElroy) obit Mar 77
White, Kevin H(agan) Dec 74
White, Margaret Bourke See Bourke-White, M. obit Oct 71

White, Patrick (Victor Martindale) Jun 74
White, Paul Dudley obit Dec 73
White, Theodore H(arold) Apr 76
White, William L(indsay) obit Oct 73
Whitehead, (Walter) Edward obit Jun 78
Whitehill, Walter Muir obit May 78
Whitelaw, William (Stephen Ian) Mar 75
Whitlam, (Edward) Gough Jan 74
Whitman, Marina von Neumann Oct 73
Whitman, Walter G(ordon) obit Jun 74
Whitmore, James Sep 76
Whittaker, Charles Evans obit Jan 74
Whitton, Charlotte (Elizabeth) obit Mar 75
Whitworth, Kathy Apr 76
Wicker, Tom Nov 73
Wiener, Alexander S(olomon) obit Feb 77
Wiesenthal, Simon Jan 75
Wigman, Mary obit Nov 73
Wilcox, Herbert obit Jul 77
Wilder, Gene Apr 78
Wilder, Thornton (Niven) Nov 71 obit Feb 76
Wiley, Richard E(merson) Mar 77
Wilhelm, (James) Hoyt Jul 71
Williams, Betty (Smyth) Mar 79
Williams, Dick Dec 73
Williams, Jay obit Sep 78
Williams, Robin Jun 79
Williams, Shirley Oct 76
Williams, Tennessee Apr 72
Wilson, Charles E(dward) obit Feb 72
Wilson, (Charles) Kemmons Sep 73
Wilson, (Charles) Malcolm May 74
Wilson, Edmund obit Jul 72
Wilson, Edward O(sborne) Oct 79
Wilson, I(rving) W(hite) obit Jan 78
Wilson, J(ohn) Tuzo Apr 72
Wilson, Joseph C(hamberlain) obit Jan 72
Wilson, Lanford (Eugene) Mar 79
Wilson, Margaret (Berenice) Bush Oct 75
Wilson, O(rlando) W(infield) obit Dec 72

Wilson, Robert (M.) Aug 79
Winchell, Walter obit Apr 72
Windsor, Duke of obit Jul 72
Winkler, Henry Sep 76
Winston, Harry obit Feb 79
Wiseman, Frederick Dec 74
Wodehouse, P(elham) G(renville) Nov 71 obit Apr 75
Wojciechowska, Maia (Teresa) Sep 76
Wolchok, Sam(uel) obit Mar 79
Wolfe, Tom Jan 71
Wonder, Stevie Mar 75
Wood, Peggy obit May 78
Wood, Robert D(ennis) Dec 74
Wooden, John (Robert) Jan 76
Woodham-Smith, Cecil obit Mar 77
Woods, Bill M(ilton) obit Sep 74
Woods, Tighe E(dward) obit Sep 74
Woodward, Bob Nov 76
Woodward, R(obert) B(urns) obit Sep 79
Wright, Benjamin F(letcher) obit Mar 77
Wright, James Claud, Jr. See Wright, Jim Apr 79
Wright, Jim Apr 79
Wright, John J(oseph) Cardinal obit Oct 79

Wright, Loyd (Earl) obit Jan 75
Wright, Russel obit Mar 77
Wrigley, Philip K(night) Apr 75 obit Jun 77
Wriston, Henry M(erritt) obit May 78
Wriston, Walter B(igelow) Nov 77
Wuorinen, Charles (Peter) Apr 72
Wurf, Jerry Jun 79
Wurster, William Wilson obit Nov 73
Wyeth, James (Browning) Jan 77
Wylie, Max obit Nov 75
Wynder, Ernest L(udwig) Nov 74

Yahya Khan, A(gha) M(uhammad) Jan 71
Yalow, Rosalyn S(ussman) Jul 78
Yamani, Sheik Ahmed Zaki Sep 75
Yergan, Max obit Jun 75
Yim, Louise obit Apr 77
York, Michael Apr 76
Youlou, Fulbert obit Jun 72
Young, Andrew (Jackson, Jr.) Apr 77

Young, Coleman (Alexander) Sep 77
Young, Marian obit Jan 74
Young, Sheila Jan 77
Young, Stanley obit May 75
Young, Whitney M(oore), Jr. obit Apr 71
Youngdahl, Luther W(allace) obit Aug 78

Zabaleta, Nicanor Jun 71
Zander, Arnold S(cheuer) obit Sep 75
Zarb, Frank G(ustav) Sep 75
Zeckendorf, William obit Nov 76
Zerbe, Karl obit Jan 73
Zhivkov, Todor Jan 76
Zhukov, Georgi K(onstantinovich) obit Sep 74
Ziegler, Ronald L(ewis) Nov 71
Zindel, Paul Jun 73
Zirato, Bruno obit Jan 73
Zuckerman, Lord Jul 72
Zuckerman, Sir Solly See Zuckerman, Lord Jul 72
Zukerman, Pinchas Nov 78
Zukor, Adolph obit Aug 76
Zumwalt, E(lmo) R(ussell), Jr. Jun 71
Zwicky, Fritz obit Apr 74